Ships of the World: An Historical Encyclopedia
Ships of Discovery and Exploration
Warships of the World to 1900
Down East: A Maritime History of Maine

THE SEA AND CIVILIZATION

The Sea and Civilization

A MARITIME HISTORY OF THE WORLD

Lincoln Paine

ALFRED A. KNOPF · NEW YORK · 2013

THIS IS A BORZOI BOOK
PUBLISHED BY ALFRED A. KNOPF

Copyright © 2013 by Lincoln Paine

Library of Congress Cataloging-in-Publication Data
Paine, Lincoln P.
The sea and civilization : a maritime history of the world /
by Lincoln Paine. —First Edition.
pages cm
ISBN 978-1-4000-4409-2 (hardback)
1. Ocean and civilization. 2. Naval history. 3. Naval art and science—
History. 4. Navigation—History. 5. Sea-power—History. I. Title.
CB465.P34 2013
910.4'5—dc23
2013015436

Jacket image: *Official Visit of Franz Joseph and Empress Elisabeth of
Austria, Arriving at Miramare Castle in Trieste*, De Agostini
Picture Library / G. Dagli Orti / The Bridgeman Art Library
Jacket design by Jason Booher

Manufactured in the United States of America
First Edition

FOR ALLISON

Now one day, as I was sitting with Abu 'Ali bin Hazim and looking at the sea—we were on the shore at 'Adan—said he to me: "What is it with which you seem to me to be so preoccupied?"

Said I: "God support the Shaykh! My mind is perplexed concerning the sea, so great is the number of conflicting accounts of it. The Shaykh now is the most knowledgeable of men about it, because he is chief of the merchants, and his ships are continually traveling to the furthermost parts of it. Should he be willing to give me a description of it I can rely on, and relieve me of doubt about it, perhaps he will do so."

Said he: "You have encountered an expert in the matter!" He smoothed the sand with the palm of his hand and drew a figure of the sea on it.

—al-Muqaddasi, *The Best Divisions for Knowledge of the World* (375 AH / 985 CE)

Contents

Illustrations

Insert

Maps

20°N 10°N 0° 10°S 20°S 30°S 40°S

100°W

Easter Island
(Rapa Nui)

Pitcairn Island

1000 Kilometers
1000 Miles
500
500
500
0
0

120°W

O c e a n

Marquesas Islands

P a c i f i c

Hawaiian Islands

140°W

P O L Y N E S I A

Society Islands Tahiti

Cook
Islands

Samoa

160°W

Marshall Islands

Tonga

Fiji

Chatham Islands

180°

MICRONESIA

M E L A N E S I A

Santa Cruz Islands

New Caledonia

New
Zealand

160°E

Mariana Islands

Bismarck
Archipelago

Vanuatu

Caroline Islands

Admiralty
Islands

New Guinea

Solomon Islands

140°E

Australia

Philippines

120°E

Oceania

Florida

Bahamas

Cuba

Atlantic Ocean

Yucatán

Hispaniola

Caribbean   Sea

Antilles

20°N

Guatemala

Venezuela

Orinoco

Gulf of Panama

Andes

Marajó Island

0°

Ecuador

Amazon

Galápagos
Islands

Mountains

South America

Aspero

Peru

San Francisco

Lake
Titicaca

Bolivia

Paraná

Pacific   Ocean

Chile

20°S

Paraguay

Andes Mountains

Atlantic   Ocean

40°S

Taitao
Peninsula

Tierra
del Fuego

| 0 | 500 | 1000 Kilometers |
| 0 | 500 | 1000 Miles |

100°W   80°W   60°W   40°W   20°W

Pre-Columbian South America and the Caribbean

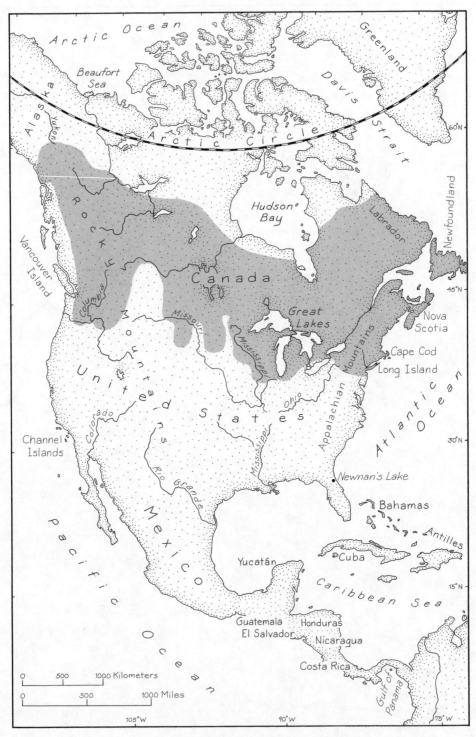

Pre-Columbian North and Central America
The shaded area indicates the range of the paper birch (*Betula papyrifera*),
or canoe birch, and thus of the birchbark canoe.

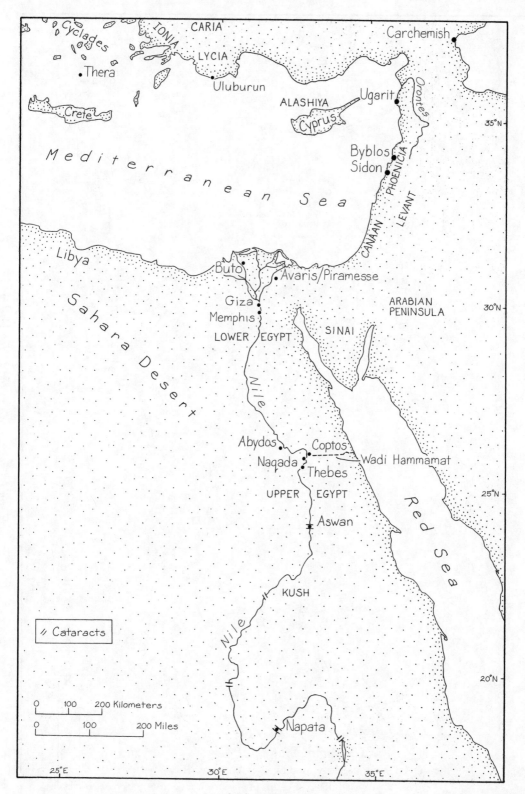

Ancient Egypt

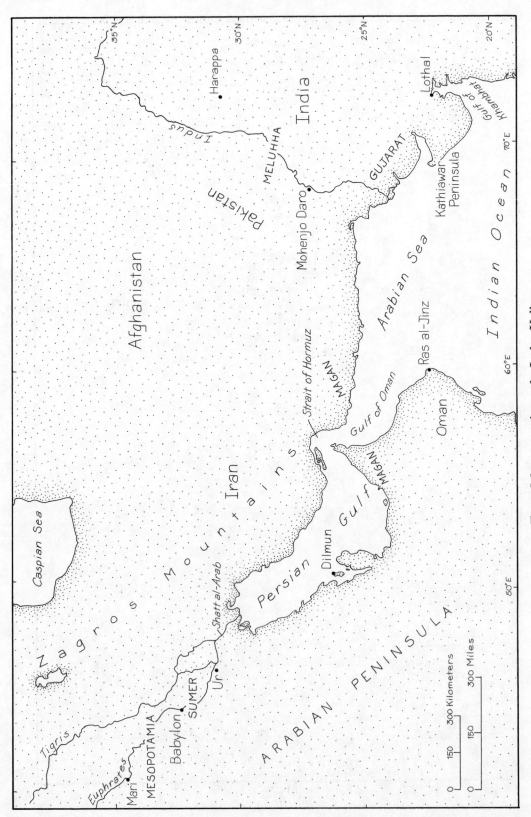

From Mesopotamia to the Indus Valley

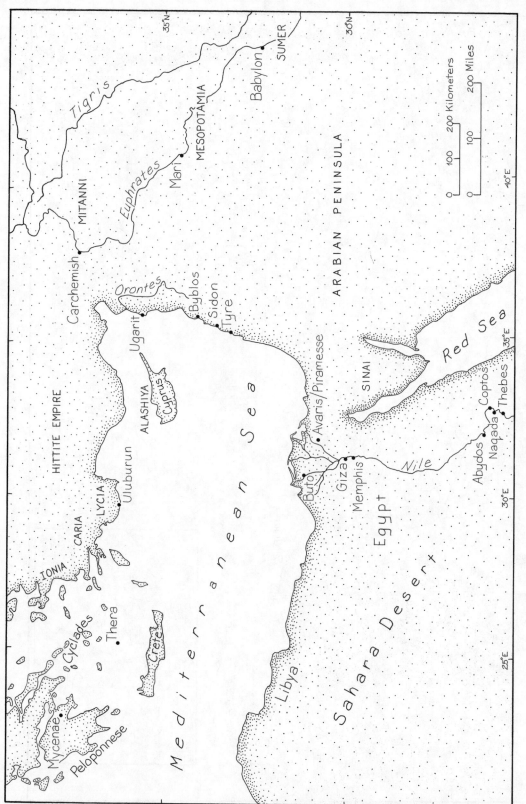

The Bronze Age Near East

The Classical Mediterranean

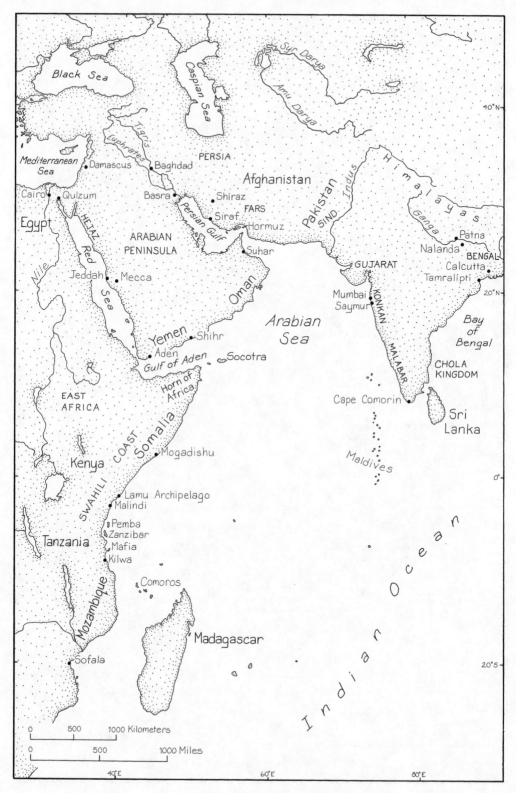

The Muslim Indian Ocean

East and Southeast Asia

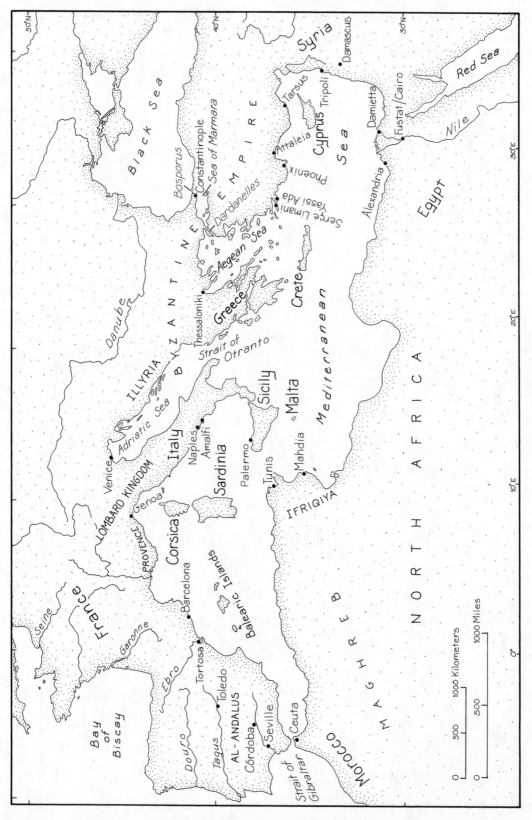

The Medieval Mediterranean

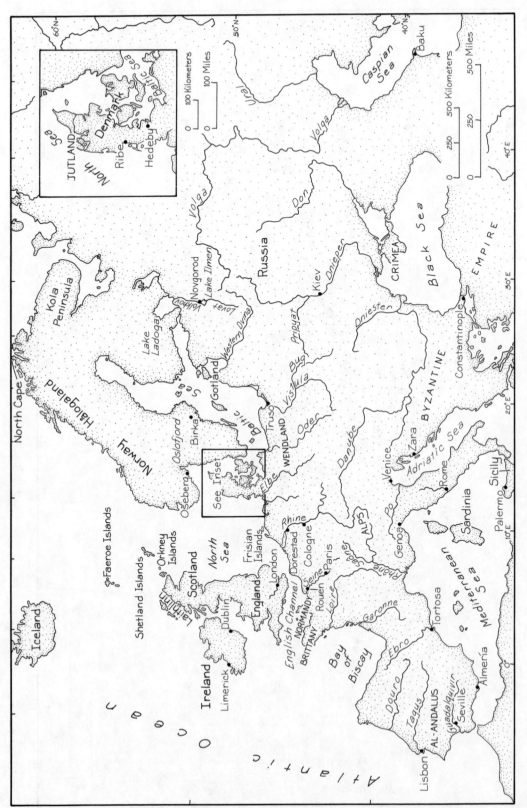

Europe Through the Viking Age

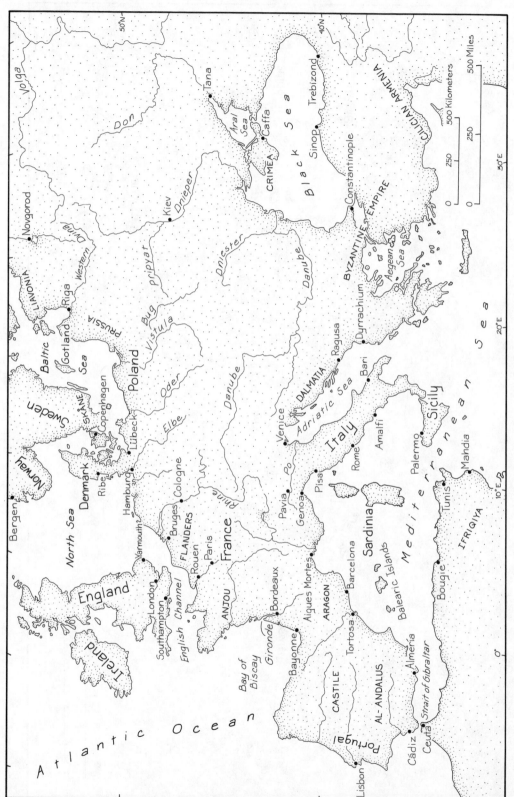

Late Medieval Europe

The Monsoon Seas

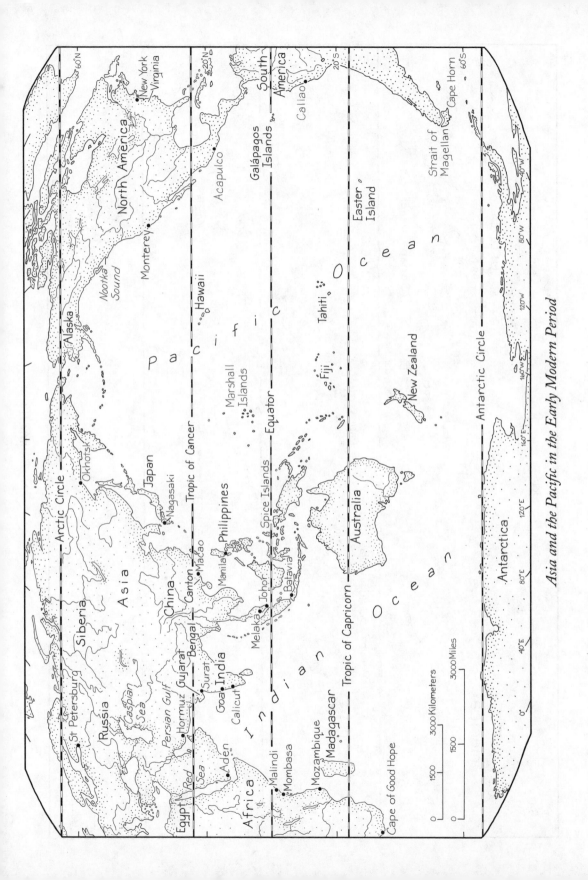

Asia and the Pacific in the Early Modern Period

The Atlantic World

Places and features labeled on the map:

Europe
- Brest
- La Rochelle
- Lisbon
- Seville
- Mediterranean Sea

Africa
- Sahara Desert
- Niger
- Senegal
- São Jorge da Mina
- Arguin
- Cape Bojador
- Cape Verde
- Cape Verde Islands
- Gulf of Guinea
- CONGO KINGDOM
- Congo
- Angola
- Walvis Bay
- Cape Town
- Malindi
- Mombasa
- Madagascar
- Canary Islands
- Madeira
- Azores

North America
- Labrador
- Quebec
- Montreal
- Halifax
- Boston
- New York
- Philadelphia
- Virginia
- Charleston
- Savannah
- Ohio
- Mississippi
- New Orleans
- Rio Grande
- Gulf of Mexico
- Veracruz
- Acapulco
- Havana
- Cuba
- Bahamas
- Hispaniola
- Port Royal
- Caribbean Sea
- Dominica
- Curaçao
- Cartagena
- Corinto
- Venezuela
- Orinoco

South America
- Brazil
- Guiana
- WILD COAST
- Amazon
- Salvador da Bahia
- Rio de Janeiro
- Potosí
- Lima
- Valparaíso
- Buenos Aires
- Río de la Plata

Oceans and lines
- Atlantic Ocean
- Pacific Ocean
- Equator
- Tropic of Cancer
- Tropic of Capricorn

Scale bars
- 2000 Kilometers: 0, 1000, 2000
- 2000 Miles: 0, 1000, 2000

Latitude/longitude: 60°N, 30°N, 0°, 30°S, 60°S; 120°W, 90°W, 60°W, 30°W, 0°, 30°E, 60°E

Early Modern Europe

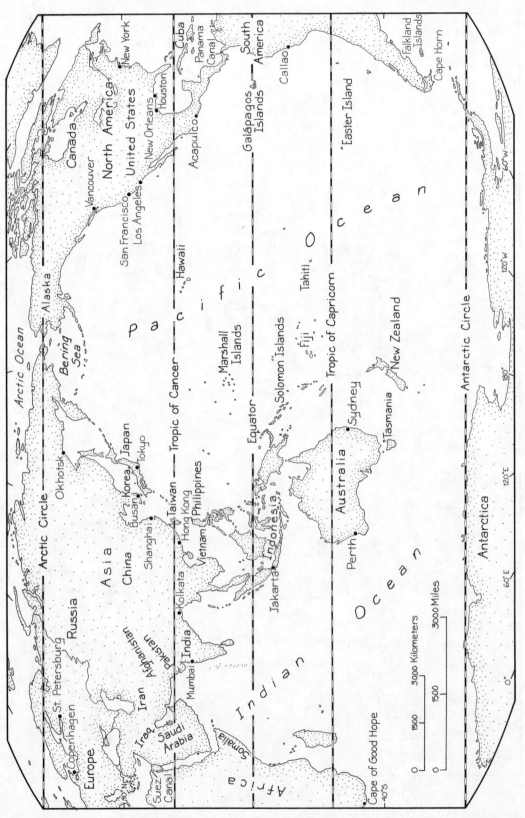

Asia and the Pacific at the Turn of the Millennium

Acknowledgments

No one can write a world history without support and advice from a diverse crew of colleagues, friends, and relatives. Foremost among my creditors is John Wright, friend, colleague, horseplayer, opera buff(a), and literary agent, without whom this book would have remained nothing more than an interesting idea. Once this project was launched, he kept at the pumps to make sure it—and I—stayed afloat. He has my deepest thanks.

Many people generously made time in their own schedules to read and comment on large portions of the manuscript at various stages in its development: Al Andrea of the World History Association; my doctoral advisors, Leonard Blussé and Femme Gaastra, Leiden University; Kelly Chavez, at the University of Tulsa; Martina Duncan, of the Southern Maine Community College; the peripatetic Felipe Fernández-Armesto, now of the University of Notre Dame; John Hattendorf, Naval War College; Joshua Smith, United States Merchant Marine Academy; and Jim Terry, Stephens College.

Others who have offered advice on individual chapters or sections include Nick Burningham; Arthur Donovan, United States Merchant Marine Academy; Matthew Edney, Osher Map Library, University of Southern Maine; David Kalivas and his fellow editors of and subscribers to H-World; Kris Lane, Tulane University; the late Ken McPherson; Nathan Lipfert, Maine Maritime Museum; John C. Perry, Tufts University; Louis Sicking, Leiden University; Tom Vosmer; Lodewijk Wagenaar, Amsterdam Museum; Cheryl Ward, Coastal Carolina University; and the subscribers to MARHST-L, among many others.

I first tried out many of the ideas developed in this book at conferences and in articles, and for the opportunity to do so I thank the organizers of the International Maritime Economic History Association conferences (Fremantle and Greenwich), the World History Association (London), the North American Society for Oceanic History (Manitowoc and Norfolk), and the Maine Maritime Museum in Bath, as well as Lewis R. "Skip" Fischer, of the *International Journal of Maritime History*, and Faye Kert, with *The Northern Mariner/Le Marin du Nord*.

Librarians are indispensable in more ways than they know, and I am privileged to have had the help particularly of Phyllis McQuaide, Hawthorne-Longfellow Library, Bowdoin College; Loraine Lowell, John Plante, Matt Lajoie and Noah Burch of the Glickman Library, University of Southern Maine; Yolanda Theunisssen of the Osher Map Library, University of Southern Maine; Norman Fiering at the John Carter Brown Library, Providence; Kathryn Wellen, of the KITLV in Leiden; and the staff at the libraries of Columbia University and Leiden University.

Picture research is a distinct enterprise altogether, and I have been helped by many individuals and institutions, especially David Neikirk, Adinah Barnett, and Ron Levere, Osher Map Library; Paul Adamthwaite, Naval Marine Archive, the Canadian Collection; Chip Angell; Jennifer Belt and Peter Rohowsky, Art Resource, New York; Anandajoti Bhikkhu; Joe Bonney and Barbara Wyker, *Journal of Commerce;* Sue Hao, US-China Business Council; John Harland; Murari Jha; Zip Kellogg, University of Southern Maine; Betsy Kohut, Freer Gallery of Art and Arthur M. Sackler Gallery; Pamela Long; Anthony Nahas; Kim Goulet Norton and Alex Agnew, Navigator Publishing; Des Pawson, MBE, Museum of Knots and Sailors Ropework; Bob Poole; Pamela Quick, MIT Press; Ulrich Rudofsky; Sila Tripati, Marine Archaeology Centre, National Institute of Oceanography, Goa; Andreas Weber; Zhang Ying, Palace Museum, Beijing; and Herwig Zahorka.

The Bibliography offers a more complete record of my academic indebtedness, although I must and do take full responsibility for the errors of fact and interpretation that have undoubtedly bored their way into the hull of this fragile vessel.

Laboring on this book has made me keenly aware of the enormous debt I owe to teachers from grade school through college. I have forgotten more of them than I remember, but three may stand for the others: John Pariseau, Allen-Stevenson School; Allan Wooley, Phillips Exeter Academy; and the late Steele Commager, Columbia University.

Research on this project took me repeatedly to New York, where I freely availed myself of the hospitality of Georgina Walker and Hal Fessenden, and Madeleine Tramm and Philip Newell, and I am grateful for Caroline and Jim Clark's bed and board in London, and the redoubtable Hôtel Garni Blussé in Amsterdam.

I have been sustained by great friendships in addition to those I have mentioned already, especially Wendell and Soozie Large, Nathan and Eleanor Smith, and Elizabeth Mitchell and Alex Krieckhaus. I applaud Valentina von Klencke for surviving her brief abduction from Köln to the Museum für Antike Schiffahrt in Mainz, and thank Nicole von Klencke for driving the getaway car.

The late Ashbel Green took a great leap of faith in signing this book, and I am indebted not only to him but also to his successor, Andrew Miller, and especially Andrew Carlson, a fair and forthright editor of enormous patience, tact, and goodwill. Nicole Pedersen has also pointed out countless errors great and small and added immeasurably to the quality of the finished work. And it was a great pleasure to entrust the drawing and lettering of the beautiful maps to Rosemary Mosher in this, our fourth cartographic collaboration.

My parents were kind enough to read and comment on early drafts of the manuscript. My daughters, Kai and Madeleine, will have my gratitude if they never write a world history of their own and ask the same of me, but I thank them for their long-suffering good humor and support as I made my way through this project.

Allison has supported this undertaking in every conceivable way since before its inception. She shares no blame for its faults, but all credit for its achievement.

LINCOLN PAINE
Portland, Maine
July–October 2012

A Note on Measures

For distances at sea, I have used nautical miles.
For land measures, I have used the metric system.
By convention, distances on rivers in the United States are given in statute
   miles.

Nautical mile	Kilometers	Statute miles
1	1.85	1.15
0.54	1	0.62
0.87	1.61	1

Meter	Foot
1	3.28
0.3	1

Centimeter	Inch
1	0.39
2.54	1

THE SEA AND CIVILIZATION

Introduction

I want to change the way you see the world. Specifically, I want to change the way you see the world map by focusing your attention on the blues that shade 70 percent of the image before you, and letting the earth tones fade. This shift in emphasis from land to water makes many trends and patterns of world history stand out in ways they simply cannot otherwise. Before the development of the locomotive in the nineteenth century, culture, commerce, contagion, and conflict generally moved faster by sea than by land. The opening of sea routes sometimes resulted in immediate transformation, but more often it laid the groundwork for what was later mistaken for sudden change. The best example of this is the trade networks of the Indian Ocean, the oldest of which were pioneered at least four thousand years ago by navigators sailing between Mesopotamia and the mouths of the Indus River. By the start of the common era two thousand years ago, the Indian subcontinent was a point of departure and destination for merchants and mendicants from across the Arabian Sea and the Bay of Bengal. This is all but unnoticed in the written record, which boasts of no figure comparable to a Gilgamesh or Odysseus, and despite a growing body of archaeological evidence, these undertakings remain largely unrecognized. As a result, the later arrival in Southeast Asia of Muslim traders from the Indian subcontinent and Southwest Asia, of Chinese merchants of various faiths, and of Portuguese Christians seem like so many historical surprises. Only the last were absolute newcomers to the Monsoon Seas that stretch from the shores of East Africa to the coasts of Korea and Japan. The others were heirs to ancient, interlinked traditions of seafaring and trade that long ago connected the shores of East Africa with those of Northeast Asia. This book shows many similar examples of maritime regions that were quietly exploited before events conspired to thrust them into the historical limelight.

Two questions merit consideration before taking on a maritime history of the world as either writer or reader: What is maritime history? and What is world history? The answers to both have as much to do with perspective as with subject matter. World history involves the synthetic investigation of complex interactions between people of distinct backgrounds and orientations. It therefore transcends historians' more traditional focus on politically, religiously, or culturally distinct communities seen primarily in their own terms at a local, national, or regional level. As a subject of interdisciplinary and interregional inquiry, maritime history is a branch of world history that covers obvious topics like shipbuilding, maritime trade, oceanic exploration, human migration, and naval history. Considered as a perspective, however, the premise of maritime history is that the study of events that take place on or in relation to the water offers unique insights into human affairs. The maritime historian therefore draws on such disciplines as the arts, religion, language, the law, and political economy.

An alternative and perhaps simpler way to approach the question, What is maritime history? is to tackle its unasked twin: What is terrestrial history?— the view from the land being our default perspective. Imagine a world of people bound to the land. The ancient Greek diaspora would have taken a different character and been forced in different directions without ships to carry Euboeans, Milesians, and Athenians to new markets and to sustain contacts between colonies and homelands. Without maritime commerce, neither Indians nor Chinese would have exerted the substantial influence they did in Southeast Asia, and that region would have been spared the cultural sobriquets of Indo-China and Indonesia (literally, "Indian islands")—in fact, the latter would have remained unpeopled altogether. The Vikings of medieval Scandinavia could never have spread as quickly or widely as they did and thereby altered the political landscape of medieval Europe. And without mariners, the history of the past five centuries would have to be reimagined in its entirety. The age of western European expansion was a result of maritime enterprise without which Europe might well have remained a marginalized corner of the Eurasian landmass with its back to what Latinate Europe called *Mare Tenebrosum* and Arabic speakers *Bahr al-Zulamat*, "the sea of darkness." The Mughals, Chinese, and Ottomans would have overshadowed the divisive and sectarian polities of Europe, which would have been unable to settle or conquer the Americas, to develop the transatlantic slave trade, or to have gained an imperial foothold in Asia.

The past century has witnessed a sea change in how we approach maritime history. Formerly a preserve of antiquarian interest whose practitioners lavished their efforts on "ancient ships and boats, ship models, images, ethnography, lexicographical and bibliographical matters and flags," maritime history once focused chiefly on preserving and interpreting material that was readily available. This directed historians' attention to European, Mediterranean, and modern North American maritime and naval history. Maritime accomplishment was almost always viewed as a peculiarly European phenomenon that only attained real importance with Columbus's epochal voyage to the Americas in 1492. In this telling, the story proceeded directly and exclusively to an explanation of how Europeans used their superior maritime and naval technology to impose themselves upon the rest of the world.

Taking Europe's "classic age of sail" from the sixteenth to eighteenth centuries as a model for the rest of maritime history is seductive but inadvisable. While the global change wrought by mariners and the dynamics of maritime Europe are of unquestionable importance to a proper understanding of the world since 1500, maritime achievement is more broadly spread and its effects more complicated than such a narrative suggests. European supremacy was far from inevitable. More important, the concentration on Europe's past five centuries has distorted our interpretation of the maritime record of other periods and places and our appreciation of its relevance to human progress. No parallels exist for the almost symbiotic relationship between commercial and naval policy—what we might call a "naval-commercial complex"—characteristic of Europe's maritime expansion. There is nothing like it in classical antiquity, in Asia, or in Europe before the Renaissance, and by the twenty-first century the close ties between national naval strategy and maritime commerce so prevalent in this age had all but vanished. The period of western Europe's maritime dominance was critical, but it is a misleading standard against which to measure other eras.

This Eurocentric worldview was reinforced by the widespread belief among western historians that race was a sufficient explanation for "the inequality of various extant human societies." In the nineteenth and early twentieth centuries, the clearest material manifestation of racial superiority writ large was maritime power and Europeans' ability to extend their hegemony overseas to create and sustain colonial empires half a world away. This gave rise to the ahistorical generalization that there are maritime people like the Greeks and British and nonmaritime people like the Romans and Chinese. Such assumptions mask complex realities. Put another way, the extent to which different nations rely on cars or planes depends on economics, industrialization, geography, and other considerations, and no one would think of ascribing car or plane use to racial or ethnic tendencies. In reaction to this assumption of an innate European and North American superiority at sea, a number of writers

attempted to redress the balance by writing explicitly ethnocentric or nationalist maritime histories about non-Europeans. While these valuable correc-
tives exposed previously untapped indigenous writings and other evidence of
seafaring by people otherwise considered to have had little or no maritime
heritage, they tended to create their own versions of maritime exceptionalism.

Even as this tendency was running its course, Fernand Braudel's magis-
terial *The Mediterranean and the Mediterranean World in the Age of Philip II*
(1949) ushered in a new approach to maritime history. Inspired by his brilliant
analysis of the interplay between geography, economics, politics, military, and
cultural history, maritime historians looking past nationalist paradigms have
embraced the validity of treating seas and ocean basins as coherent units of
study and the past half century has seen a surfeit of works examining individual oceans and seas. This is an enlightening exercise that enables us to consider cross-cultural and transnational connections without constant reference
to the mutable fiction of political borders. At the same time, we run the risk
of replacing a set of arbitrary terrestrial boundaries with an equally arbitrary
division of the world ocean. There is little agreement about how to parcel the
waters of the world into discrete, named bodies of bays, gulfs, straits, channels, seas, and oceans, and in practice sailors rarely recognize such distinctions
drafted from afar. An ancient Greek epigram acknowledges the unity of the
world ocean with stark simplicity:

All sea is sea. . . .
Pray if you like for a good voyage home,
But Aristagoras, buried here, has found
The ocean has the manners of an ocean.

This book is an attempt to examine how people came into contact with one
another by sea and river, and so spread their crops, their manufactures, and
their social systems—from language to economics to religion—from one place
to another. While I have not ignored the climactic moments of maritime history, I have attempted to put them in a broader context to show how shifting
approaches to maritime systems can be read as indicators of broader change
beyond the sea. I have concentrated on a few themes: how maritime enterprise
enlarges trading realms that share certain kinds of knowledge—of markets and
commercial practice, or navigation and shipbuilding; how the overseas spread
of language, religion, and law facilitates interregional connections; and how
rulers and governments exploit maritime enterprise through taxation, trade
protection, and other mechanisms to consolidate and augment their power.

I have sketched this history as a narrative to show region by region the
deliberate process by which maritime regions of the world were knit together.

But this is not a story of saltwater alone. Maritime activity includes not only high seas and coastal voyaging, but also inland navigation.* Islanders may have obvious reasons to put to sea, but the exploitation of freshwater rivers, lakes, and canals has been critical to the growth of countries with large continental territories. The center of North America became economically productive thanks to its accessibility via the St. Lawrence and Welland Rivers and the Great Lakes, and by the Mississippi River and its tributaries. Neither corridor could have reached its potential without the development of maritime technologies—steam power in the case of the Mississippi, and locks and dams in the case of the Great Lakes.

If the geography of water, wind, and land shapes the maritime world in obvious ways, maritime endeavor becomes a determining force in history only when the right combination of economic, demographic, and technological conditions is met. Few fifteenth-century observers could have imagined the prosperity that would accrue to Spain and Portugal as a result of their navigators' peregrinations in the eastern Atlantic. While they sailed in search of a route to the spices of Asia, they also came upon the Americas, a source of untold wealth in the form of silver and gold; of raw materials for European markets and new markets for European manufacturers; and territory—"virgin" in Europeans' eyes—for the cultivation of recently discovered or transplanted crops like tobacco and sugar. Papal intervention in disputes over which lands would be Portuguese and which Spanish resulted in a series of bulls and treaties that partitioned the navigation of the non-Christian Atlantic and Indian Oceans between Portugal and Spain, and helps explain why the majority of people in South and Central America are Spanish- or Portuguese-speaking Catholics.

A maritime perspective complicates our understanding of the "westward" expansion of the United States. California achieved statehood in 1851, two years after the discovery of gold at Sutter's Mill, when the territory was virtually unknown to Americans back east and the number of United States citizens on the Pacific coast numbered only a few thousand. Thanks to the extraordinary capacity of the American merchant marine of the day, tens of thousands of people reached San Francisco by ship, a mode of transportation that was faster, cheaper, and safer than the transcontinental journey, although the distance covered was more than four times longer. The United States conquered

---

* Some may question whether the use of "maritime," from the Latin word for "sea," is appropriate to freshwater shipping. It is worth noting that the Association for Great Lakes Maritime History has seventy-five institutional members in the United States and Canada. The names of ten include "maritime," another thirteen use "marine," and Suttons Bay, Michigan, is home to the Inland Seas Education Association.

the interior of the continent—what are today known as the fly-over states, but at the time could aptly have been called the sail-around territories—in a pincer movement from both coasts, rather than by a one-way overland movement from the east.

Yet for the most part, if ships, sailors, ports, and trades exist, the default tendency among most writers is either to celebrate them in isolation from the world ashore, or to acknowledge them only to explain particular events such as the arrival of the Black Death in northern Italy; the voyages of the Vikings to the Caspian and Black Seas (by river) and to western Europe and North America (by sea); the Mongol invasions of Japan and Java in the thirteenth century; or various other diasporas of people, flora, and fauna. But by situating our collective relationship to oceans, seas, lakes, rivers, and canals at the center of the historical narrative, we can see that much of human history has been shaped by people's access, or lack of it, to navigable water. For example, given non-Muslim westerners' ingrained impression of Islam as a religion of desert nomads, it seems remarkable that the country with the largest Muslim population is actually spread across the world's biggest archipelago. There are no camels in Indonesia, but there are Muslims, and also Hindus—especially on the island of Bali—which is especially curious when one considers Hindu prohibitions against going to sea. If these two religions are so tightly bound to the land, how did they manage to cross the ocean? Have the religions changed over time? Or are our impressions about the nature of these religions wrong? As is written in the Quran, "Do you not see how the ships speed upon the ocean by God's grace, so that He may reveal to you His wonders? Surely there are signs in this for every steadfast, thankful man."

These "signs" indicate that mankind's technological and social adaptation to life on the water—whether for commerce, warfare, exploration, or migration—has been a driving force in human history. Yet many mainstream histories are reluctant to embrace this. Jared Diamond's *Guns, Germs, and Steel: The Fates of Human Societies* gives barely a page to "maritime technology," by which he means watercraft and not the ability to navigate or any associated abilities. What is curious about this is that maritime traffic was central to the diffusion of many of the technologies, ideas, plants, and animals that Diamond discusses in such illuminating detail, not only between continents but also within and around them. In all but ignoring the maritime aspect of his story, he essentially overlooks both the means of transmission and, in the cases of some very important inventions, the things transmitted as well.

To take another example, J. M. Roberts's *History of the World* is, according to the author, "the story of the processes which have brought mankind from the uncertainties and perils of primitive life and precivilized life to the much more complex and very different uncertainties and perils of today. . . . The criterion for the inclusion of factual data has therefore been their historical importance—that is, their effective importance to the major processes of history rather than intrinsic interest or any sort of merit." Roberts acknowledges inland and saltwater navigation, stressing the importance of the former, for instance, in Russia's eastward colonization of Siberia in the seventeenth century. However, he jumps to the ends without reference to the means, or the processes. He notes that from Tobolsk to the Pacific port of Okhotsk three thousand miles away there were only three portages; there is no discussion of the vessels used, the foundation of intermediate settlements, or the impact of river trade on the development of Siberia. He does not even name the rivers, which is rather like talking about the water route from Pittsburgh to New Orleans without mentioning the Ohio or Mississippi.

Had Diamond or Roberts written a century ago, their works likely would have incorporated considerably more maritime content. That they do not reflects changes in the public perception of the maritime world, for the merchant marine and naval services no longer hold the attraction for people that they once did, when ocean liners and freighters crowded the piers of Manhattan, Hamburg, Sydney, and Hong Kong. At the start of the twenty-first century, ships and shipping lines are the warp and woof of globalization. Ships carry about 90 percent of world trade and the number of oceangoing ships has grown threefold in the past half century. But the nature of shipping has led to the relocation of cargo-handling facilities to places remote from traditional port cities, while a growing proportion of the world's merchant fleets has been put under so-called flags of convenience—that is, owners in search of less regulation and lower taxes have registered their ships in countries not their own. As a result, ships no longer stand as emblems of national progress and prestige as they did in the nineteenth and early twentieth centuries.

Although airplanes have replaced ships in most long-distance passenger trades—transatlantic, between Europe and ports "east of Suez," or transpacific—more than fourteen million people annually embark on a sea cruise. This is far more than ocean liners carried before the passenger jet rendered them obsolete in the 1950s, when the names of shipping companies were as familiar as (and far more respected than) the names of airlines today. The idea that people would go to sea for pleasure was almost unthinkable even 150 years ago. The cruise ship industry, to say nothing of yachting and recreational boating, owe their growth to changes in economics and technology, social reform movements that ameliorated the often wretched conditions of sea travel for passengers and crew alike, and shifts in attitudes toward the natural environment of the sea. These also gave rise to the emergence of a

conscious appreciation for the sea and seafaring in painting, music, and literature, and set the conditions for people's interest in the sea as an historical space
interpreted through museums, film, and books.

In fact we live in an age deeply influenced by maritime enterprise, but our
perceptions of its importance have shifted almost 180 degrees in only two or
three generations. Today we see pleasure where our forebears saw peril, and
we can savor the fruits of maritime commerce without being remotely aware
of its existence, even when we live in cities that originally grew rich from sea
trade. In considering the course of maritime history, we must account for this
change and remember that our collective relationship with maritime enterprise has undergone a profound metamorphosis in only half a century.

The idea for this book began to take shape while I was writing *Ships of the
World: An Historical Encyclopedia*—in essence, a collection of vessel biographies
that sought to explore the reasons for certain ships' fame or infamy and to sit-
uate them in a broader historical context. Some of these stories have obviously
found their way into this work. But while ships are integral to the narrative
that unfolds here, this book is less about ships per se than about the things that
they carried—people and their culture, their material creations, their crops
and flocks, their conflicts and prejudices, their expectations for the future, and
their memories of the past. In considering the prospects for this undertaking,
I have been guided by the words of the naval historian Nicholas Rodger, who
has written: "A general naval history would be a prize of great value, and if the
first person to attempt it should fail altogether, he may still have the merit of
stimulating other and better scholars to achieve it." The scope of this work
goes well beyond naval history and entails correspondingly greater risks, but if
nothing else I hope this book will inspire further exploration of this fascinating dimension of our common past.

Chapter 1

Taking to the Water

Reindeer are powerful swimmers, but water is not their natural environment and they are at their most vulnerable when crossing rivers, lakes, or estuaries. People recognized this at an early date, and while humans are no more at home on the water than reindeer, we have an insuperable technological advantage: the arts of boatbuilding and navigation. Hunting quadrupeds is not an activity most people associate with watercraft, but people have myriad reasons for pushing off from land. This much is illustrated in six-thousand-year-old Norwegian rock carvings depicting reindeer hunters in boats. These are the oldest known pictorial representations of watercraft, but the distribution of human communities around the world proves that our ancestors launched themselves on the water tens of thousands of years before that.

It is impossible to know who first set themselves adrift in saltwater or fresh and for what reason, but once launched our ancestors never looked back. The advantages of watercraft for hunting, fishing, or simple transport were too great to be ignored. Travel by water was often faster, smoother, more efficient, and in many circumstances safer and more convenient than overland travel, which presents obstacles and threats from animals, people, terrain, and even the conventions and institutions of shoreside society. This is not to minimize the dangers of life afloat. Even a subtle shift in wind or current can make it impossible to return to one's point of origin and force one ashore among implacable hosts. Still worse, one might be swept away from land altogether. Such misadventures are an inevitable part of seafaring, and developing the means to overcome them is a necessary prerequisite to long-distance voyaging. Part of the solution lies in building maneuverable watercraft, but much depends on gaining an appreciation for how the sea works—its currents, tides,

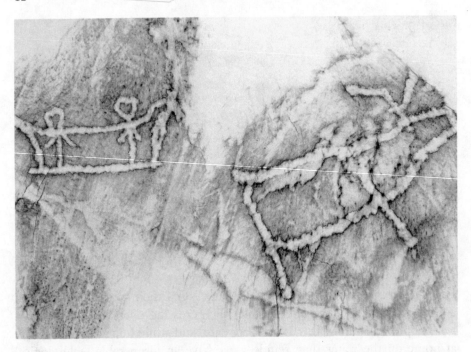

A Bronze Age rock carving from Kvalsund in northern Norway showing two reindeer hunters in a boat (left) and their prey. This is one of thousands of such rock carvings found in the Finnmark region, the oldest of which date to 4200 BCE. Many depict boats of various kinds, most of them longer vessels with many paddlers quite unlike the boxier form shown here, which might represent a skin boat. Courtesy of the Deutsches Schiffahrtsmuseum, Bremen.

and winds, of course, but also its look and feel, the interplay of land and sea, and the way birds, mammals, and fish relate to the marine environment. Only by imagining this complex of interrelationships can we begin to appreciate the magnitude of the earliest seafarers' accomplishments fifty thousand years ago, or about forty thousand years before our ancestors began domesticating dogs or planting crops.

This history begins with Oceania and the Americas, whose inhabitants had completely distinct relationships to the sea and maritime enterprise but whose approaches to inland, coastal, and deep-sea undertakings are echoed in myriad other cultures. The Pacific offers unrivaled examples of long-distance voyaging alongside unexplained instances of withdrawal from the sea. Similarly, while most people in the Americas experienced or were influenced by only freshwater navigation on rivers, lakes, and inland seas, there were voyagers not only on the Pacific, Atlantic, and Caribbean coasts, but also in the

unimaginably harsh environment of the Arctic. No two peoples' approaches
to navigation are alike, even if their environmental circumstances have more
in common than those of northern Canada and Tahiti. But starting with an
overview of the different approaches to seafaring in Oceania and the Americas
allows us to imagine the maritime prehistory of Eurasians whose vessels ultimately attained far greater size and complexity than those found elsewhere,
and who are the primary subject of this book.

Oceania

The islands of Oceania form the locus of the oldest, most sustained, and perhaps most enigmatic effort of maritime exploration and migration in the history of the world. They are sprinkled across some thirty-nine million square
kilometers of the Pacific—an area larger than the continent of Africa—from
the Solomon Islands just east of New Guinea to Easter Island (Rapa Nui) five
thousand nautical miles to the east, and from Hawaii in the north to New Zealand in the south. In the 1820s the French explorer Jules S. Dumont d'Urville
divided the islands into three main groups according to geographic and ethnographic characteristics. Farthest to the west, and the first settled, are the
islands of Melanesia, which lie within a broad band more or less south of the
equator between New Guinea and Fiji. To the east is Polynesia, a huge triangle whose sides are described by a line drawn between Easter Island, New
Zealand, and Hawaii. Micronesia lies north of Melanesia and spans the Pacific
from Palau to Kiribati and encompasses the Marshall, Caroline, and Mariana island groups.* Although many specifics remain unknown and alternative
scenarios have been proposed, it is generally accepted that the distant ancestors of the Pacific islanders first encountered by Europeans originated in the
Solomons, that the pattern of settlement across Melanesia and Polynesia was
generally from west to east, and that the process began about 1500 BCE.

When European sailors crossed the Pacific in the sixteenth century, they
were astonished not only at its extent—nearly ten thousand miles from Ecuador to the Philippines—but by the number of small islands, and the fact that
the vast majority of these were inhabited. The ability of Pacific sailors to conquer enormous distances and to maintain contact between such small and
remote islands has remained a subject of fascination ever since. Marveling at

---

* The suffix *-nesia* comes from the Greek word for island, *neisos*. Melanesia means black islands
(for the relative color of the inhabitants' skin); Micronesia, small islands; and Polynesia, many
islands.

the inhabitants of the Tuamotus in 1768, an officer sailing in the expedition of French explorer Louis Antoine de Bougainville wondered "Who the devil went and placed them on a small sandbank like this one and as far from the continent as they are." A couple of years later, Britain's Captain James Cook suggested that ancestors of the people he encountered in the Society Islands (Tahiti) originated in the western Pacific and that it should be possible to trace their progress all the way from the East Indies. This straightforward conception of Pacific voyaging, articulated by experienced navigators with an appreciation for their fellow sailors, was superseded in the nineteenth century when it was believed that such voyages by non-Europeans could only have been the result of "accidental drift" rather than intentional navigation. One theory held that sailors originating in South America populated the islands of the South Pacific as far west as New Zealand. And yet archaeological, linguistic, and navigational research of the past century demonstrates that the settlement of Oceania occurred as a result of intentional voyaging, and that thirty-five hundred years ago Pacific navigators were the most advanced in the world. Both their vessels and the techniques they devised for crossing thousands of miles of open ocean were unique to them.

The peopling of Oceania represents one of the last stages of mankind's spread across the globe. About ninety thousand years ago, our ancestors left Africa by either walking overland across the Sinai Peninsula, which separates the Mediterranean from the Red Sea, or crossing the Bab al-Mandeb, the thirteen-mile-wide strait at the mouth of the Red Sea between Eritrea and Yemen. From Southwest Asia some followed the coast of the Indian Ocean and by about 25,000 years ago people had reached the southern coast of China. During the last great ice age, which lasted from about 100,000 to 9,500 years ago, so much water was locked up in ice and glaciers that sea levels in Southeast Asia were about 120 meters lower than today and vast expanses of today's relatively shallow seabed were dry land. The islands of the western Indonesian archipelago were part of a continental extension of Southeast Asia known as Sundaland, while Australia, New Guinea, and the island of Tasmania formed a single landmass called Sahul, or Greater Australia. Between them lay stretches of open water and the islands of a biogeographical region known as Wallacea. Rising sea levels only created the configuration of islands and archipelagoes that we know today starting about 5000 BCE.

Archaeological finds show that people had crossed from Sundaland to Sahul by about fifty thousand years ago. The oldest stone tools of the sort necessary for making dugout logboats are only twenty thousand years old, so these trips would have to have been made on rafts of lashed logs. The oldest evidence for sails anywhere in the world is no more than seven thousand years old and comes from Mesopotamia, and Pleistocene seafarers almost certainly propelled their rafts with poles and paddles. Although they crossed considerable distances of open water, they did not necessarily have to sail out of sight of land. The strategy that the earliest long-distance mariners seem to have devised was to go between islands that were visible from one another. A chain of intervisible islands ran between Sunda and Sahul, and east of New Guinea through the Bismarck Archipelago. Then twenty-nine thousand years ago sailors crossed from New Ireland in the Bismarcks to Buka, the westernmost of the Solomon Islands. This introduced a new degree of difficulty. New Ireland and Buka are not visible from each other, but there is an area between the two islands from which it is possible to see both at the same time. More daring still was the occupation of Manus, in the Admiralty Islands north of New Guinea, which could only be reached by sailing completely out of sight of land for at least thirty miles. This occurred no later than thirteen thousand years ago.

The Bismarcks and Solomons remained the limit of eastward expansion for another ten thousand years. Little is known of how society or technology evolved here, though there was clearly interisland exchange in such rarities as obsidian, a sharp volcanic glass frequently traded among ancient people. Still, the region's hallmark is not homogeneity but diversity. Over these ten millennia the people of New Guinea and the surrounding islands came to speak hundreds of languages divided among a dozen language families, a linguistic stew found in no other region of comparable size. Life in the area was interrupted by the cataclysmic explosion of New Britain's Mount Witori around 3600 BCE, an event followed by widespread changes in social organization and technological innovation across Melanesia. People began to live in larger settlements, to produce ceramics, to domesticate dogs, pigs, and chickens, and to develop more advanced fishing gear to catch offshore species. This period lasted for about two thousand years before a new wave of seafaring migrants swept through from Southeast Asia.

These newcomers were part of a movement of Austronesian-speaking people whose ancestors are thought to have originated in southern China, from where they moved east to Taiwan, the Philippines, and Borneo, before doubling back to mainland Southeast Asia.* In the east, these people are distinguished by their ceramics, called Lapita ware, found from the Philippines and northeastern Indonesia to the Bismarck Archipelago. Having merged relatively briefly

---

* Austronesian (literally, "southern islands") is a language family whose speakers are found across the islands of, and parts of mainland, Southeast Asia, in Oceania, and, to the west, on the island of Madagascar.

with the people of Melanesia they encountered along the way, the bearers of
Lapita culture plunged southeast from the Solomon Islands into Melanesia to
reach the Santa Cruz Islands, Vanuatu (New Hebrides), the Loyalty Islands,
and New Caledonia in the twelfth century BCE. One offshoot turned east from
the Santa Cruz Islands or Vanuatu to Fiji, an open-water distance of about 450
nautical miles. Their descendants pushed on to reach Tonga and Samoa by
about 950 BCE, the date of the earliest human habitation in Western Polynesia.
Although kinship ties and trade between colonies and home islands may have
sustained two-way communication between them following their initial settlement, interisland ties gradually loosened. Nonetheless, Polynesians generally
regard Tonga and Samoa as Hawaiki, their ancestral homeland.

After about seven centuries of settlement, there was a resurgence of exploratory seafaring during which Western Polynesians began to venture east and
south. A number of sequences have been suggested. A recent theory holds
that around 200 BCE Samoans and Tongans reached the Society Islands, while
settlers of the Marquesas Islands farther east and north came from Samoa.
Five hundred years later, voyagers from the Societies and Marquesas reached
Easter Island, which is less than a third the size of Manhattan and the most
remote island on earth, more than a thousand miles from its nearest neighbor,
Pitcairn, and nearly two thousand miles from South America. Around 400 CE,
voyagers from the Societies and Marquesas reached Hawaii. The last major
wave of Polynesian settlement spread from the Society Islands southwest to
New Zealand around a thousand years ago.

The chronology of Micronesia's settlement is not as clear, but the small,
widely dispersed islands appear to have been reached variously by people from
island Southeast Asia, by a northern offshoot of the Lapita people from Polynesia, and by Melanesians from the Bismarck Archipelago. (A less likely scenario involves settlers coming directly from Taiwan.) Guam is the largest and
one of the westernmost islands in Micronesia and the earliest material finds
of human habitation date from 1500 BCE. The sketchy archaeological record
suggests that people began arriving in the Marshall Islands, about a thousand
miles east of Guam, by the first century BCE and in the Carolines, which are
closer to Guam, shortly thereafter, but further research may reveal a different
sequence of events.

What prompted the Lapita people to work their way into the open waters of
the Pacific is unknown. Population pressures were probably not a factor, and
the distances involved were too great and the volume and value of goods too
modest to make trade worthwhile, at least on a scale we can comprehend from
this vantage. A more likely possibility depends on the nature of Lapita society,
in which birth order and rules of inheritance may have forced or prompted

generations of the disinherited to make their way in the world on their own. It may have been mere curiosity, but if the Polynesian voyages were a case of discovery for its own sake, they would have no real parallel—at least on a sustained level—until the polar explorations of the nineteenth century. Whatever their rationale may have been, as in any exploration the crucial underlying factor was the confidence that they could return to their point of origin. By and large, the human settlement of the Pacific was the result of deliberate calculation and not of accident or "splendid recklessness," a fact borne out in the oral traditions of Oceania.

Fishing is a major leitmotif in Polynesian mythology, one that accounts for the very existence of the islands and for humans' discovery of places from Hawaii to New Zealand. According to one tradition, the first expedition to New Zealand was led by a fisherman named Kupe from Hawaiki, which in this instance probably refers to the Society Islands. The story relates that the fishermen of Hawaiki kept losing their bait to a school of octopi until their leader, Kupe, decided to give chase—all the way to New Zealand. Kupe evidently anticipated a long voyage and his canoe, *Matahorua*, carried sixty-seven people, including his wife and their five children. After killing the octopus in Cook Strait, Kupe named several islands in the strait for his daughters, visited South Island, and then returned to Hawaiki from a peninsula near modern Auckland called Hokianga nui a Kupe, "Great returning place of Kupe."

Kupe reported the islands as uninhabited, but other traditions and archaeological evidence suggest that when the first Polynesians arrived, the islands had already been settled, possibly by Melanesians from Fiji. Although New Zealand is closer to the Solomon Islands than the Society Islands or Hawaii, they were more difficult to reach, and over time both the Melanesian and Polynesian settlers lost touch with their homelands. That the most extensive, visible, and fertile islands in the South Pacific did not attract a constant flow of sailors from a much earlier date can best be explained by the patterns of navigation imposed by the Polynesians' environment.

Wayfinding and Boatbuilding in Oceania

Sailing the Pacific with any expectation of being able to return to one's point of departure or making remote landfalls requires navigational ability of a high order. The combined landmass of the islands east of New Guinea amounts to less than one percent of the area of the Pacific—and this is divided among about twenty-one thousand islands and atolls the average size of which is less than sixty square kilometers (about twenty-three square miles), although most are much smaller. Just as the exploration and settlement of Oceania were unique accomplishments in world history, so were the navigational practices employed. At the most basic level, the essential elements are shared by navigators everywhere: observation of heavenly bodies (celestial navigation), reading the wind and water, and tracing the behavior of birds, fish, and whales. What distinguishes the Pacific argonauts is the relative importance they attached to these phenomena, and the degree to which they consolidated their observations in a coherent body of knowledge without recourse to writing.

Between the equator and 15°S to 25°S, depending on the season, the prevailing winds are the southeast trade winds, so called not because they were used by trading ships—so were all winds—but from an archaic use of "trade" meaning steadily and regularly. Sailors setting out from the Solomon Islands exploited periodic wind shifts to sail downwind fully confident that if they did not find new land, the trade winds would eventually return and enable them to run home to the west. (Europeans employed a comparable strategy in their exploration of the Atlantic in the fourteenth and fifteenth centuries.) Thus exploration was for the most part the product of two-way intentional voyaging; only occasionally were new islands discovered as a result of being lost at sea. The initial expansion from the Solomon Islands toward the Santa Cruz Islands and New Caledonia, which lie east-southeast, conforms to this model, as does the pattern of settlement for the rest of Polynesia between the equator and about 20°S.

The settlement of New Zealand is an exception that proves the rule. Although the top of North Island lies at 35°S, about two thousand miles from the Solomons, it is on the far side of a belt of variable winds that is difficult to probe from central Polynesia with any reliable expectation of safe return. Thus it was relatively less accessible than the Marquesas, which lie about twice as far to the east of the Solomons but which were reached several centuries earlier. New Zealand also lies in a higher (and colder) latitude, nine hundred miles farther from the equator than Hawaii, in an area more subject to inclement weather. These conditions are thought to explain why the original settlers eventually abandoned the sea road, or *ara moana*, back to Polynesia. Even so, the Maori did not turn their backs to the sea altogether: around 1500 they reached Chatham Island, 430 miles east of New Zealand and probably the last island settled by Polynesian sailors.

That people were able to make so many minute landfalls again and again was due to their outstanding familiarity with the ocean environment and their ability to "expand" the size of their intended landfalls by relying on phenomena other than direct visual contact with their destination. This esoteric knowledge was transmitted orally to a select few from one generation to the next. Some of these techniques are common to other maritime traditions—

following birds that feed at sea but nest on land, noting where different species of fish or sea mammals are found, looking for smoke generated by natural fires, or discerning changes in water color over reefs. In the Pacific, sailors developed the ability to read the patterns of ocean swells and how these change as they are deflected when passing islands. Clouds can announce the presence of islands lying below the horizon by shifts in color, speed, and shape. Finally, there is the "loom" of an island, a faint but telltale column of light above islands, especially atolls with lagoons. Taken together, these phenomena widen the range at which sailors can sense the presence of land by as much as thirty miles, which increases dramatically the likelihood of finding even the smallest speck in the sea.

But locating land at a distance is not the same as purposefully navigating from one island to another, which the sailors of Oceania accomplished by observation of both the environment and the heavens. Their approach to celestial navigation requires memorizing "the direction of every known island from every other one." An island's bearing relative to another is determined by the rising or setting star under which the island lies relative to the observer. When sailing between two islands, a third is chosen as the *etak*, or reference island. The navigator knows the stars under which the *etak* lies in relation to the islands of departure and destination, as well as the stars under which the *etak* lies at various stages of the passage between them. Thus a passage is broken into a series of *etak* stages. Using *etak* depends on knowing how all known islands are related to one another with respect to different stars, so a navigator sailing between, for example, the Caroline Islands of Woleai and Olimarao (117 miles apart) would use Faraulep (70 miles to the north) as the *etak;* but when sailing from Olimarao to Faraulep, Woleai would be the *etak*.

Sailors in different areas of the Pacific tended to apply different methods of traditional navigation. Among the few remaining practitioners today, Marshall Islanders pay most attention to ocean swells, while sailors in the Federated States of Micronesia rely more on the rising and setting of stars. Starting in the 1970s, researchers began interviewing and sailing with the last adepts of traditional navigation to learn their secrets and determine whether these were reliable enough for the sorts of voyages necessary to maintain contact between islands separated by many hundreds of miles of open water. In 1976, the Polynesian Voyaging Society built the *Hokule'a*, a double canoe rigged with claw sails, which sailed from Hawaii via the Tuamotus to Tahiti, about twenty-four hundred miles. Mau Piailug, a wayfinder from Satawal (an island of about four square kilometers) in the Carolines, navigated the *Hokule'a* across the northeast trade winds, the equator, and then into the southeast trades before they made Tahiti, thirty-four days out from Maui. In 1985, a Hawaiian student of

Piailug's named Nainoa Thompson navigated the *Hokule'a* on an expedition that covered many of the old routes within Polynesia—sixteen thousand miles' worth—between the Cook Islands, New Zealand, Tonga, Samoa, Tahiti, and the Tuamotus. In 1999, the Polynesian triangle was closed with a voyage from Hawaii to Easter Island via the Marquesas. The successful completion of these voyages, among others, proved that early sailors relying on an orally transmitted body of navigational knowledge were able to explore the far-flung islands of the Pacific methodically and deliberately, and that given vessels of adequate size and speed they could easily transport the people and goods necessary to populate these islands and maintain communications between them.

By the time of her passage to Easter Island in 1999, the *Hokule'a* was the oldest of a fleet of at least six traditional deepwater craft that had been built in Hawaii, the Cook Islands, and New Zealand. Archaeological remains of ancient vessels in the Pacific are few and the people of Oceania had no written language, so our understanding of ancient boatbuilding practice depends on interpreting written descriptions and illustrations by European voyagers of the sixteenth century and later, in light of surviving practices. Vessels tended to be built of planks lashed together to achieve the desired hull shape after which frames or ribs were inserted to strengthen the hull, a process called shell-first construction. Single-hull vessels were used for fishing in Tonga, Tuamotu, and the Society Islands, and in New Zealand to carry warriors into battle, but these were not stable enough for ocean passages. Shipwrights compensated for this either by adding outriggers or by yoking two hulls with transverse beams on which they could erect a sheltered platform. Outriggers consist of two or more poles laid between the hull and a small piece of wood called a float on the outboard end, and they are found not only in Oceania but throughout Southeast Asia—where they were probably developed—as well as in the Indian Ocean.

Double canoes were the largest and most important vessels used in the colonization of the Pacific. In addition to being more stable, the deck spanning the hulls created more space and protection from the elements for crew, passengers, and cargo. Captain Cook observed double canoes carrying between 50 and 120 people and measuring up to twenty-one meters long and nearly four meters across. In settling the Pacific, Polynesians likely sailed double canoes of between fifteen and twenty-seven meters in length and capable of carrying the people, supplies, and material goods necessary for establishing sustainable communities on uninhabited islands after voyages lasting as long as six weeks. These included edible plants for crops (yams, taro, coconut, banana, and nut-bearing trees); domesticated dogs, pigs, and chickens; and tools and ceramics.

The chronology of Oceanian settlement shows that long-distance voyaging and migration expanded and contracted in centuries-long cycles. When

Boats of the Friendly Islands [Tonga] *by John Webber, an artist who accompanied Captain James Cook's third expedition to the Pacific (1776–80). In the foreground is a small sailing canoe with an outrigger and a platform for passengers. Farther off is a larger double canoe for long-distance passages. "There cannot be a doubt," wrote a nineteenth-century observer, "that the peculiar shape of the Tongan* kalia, *or double canoe, and the arrangement of its large and single [wishbone] sail, are conducive to the attainment of great speed in ordinary weather." (Quoted in Paul Johnstone,* The Sea-Craft of Prehistory, *205.) Courtesy of the British Museum, London.*

Europeans began mapping the Pacific in the eighteenth century, the forces of expansion had been spent for some time, but Polynesians had not abandoned the sea or lost the ability to navigate long distances. During Cook's first voyage, Joseph Banks recorded that the Tahitian Tupia could locate scores of remote islands and that journeys of twenty days were not uncommon. But communication between the Polynesian heartland of Hawaiki and the extremes of Easter Island, Hawaii, and New Zealand had stopped. At some point people would have taken to their boats again to strike out for far horizons, and in so doing they likely would have initiated a demonstrable and sustained interaction with the continents to their east and introduced the people of the Americas to their innovative forms of seafaring. As it happened, the people of the

Americas developed a variety of discrete maritime traditions in isolation from one another, although they never exploited the sea to the same degree that people in many other parts of the world did.

Maritime Trade in South America and the Caribbean

When Christopher Columbus crossed the Atlantic in 1492, he landed in the Bahamas archipelago southeast of Florida. On the advice of Taíno Indians he kidnapped there, he sailed 130 miles across the Bahama Bank to Cuba. From Arawaks he later met on Hispaniola (the island of the Dominican Republic and Haiti) he learned of other people to the south, whom the Spanish called the Cariba or Caniba, from which we get the words "Caribbean" and "cannibal." The usual focus on Columbus tends to leave basic questions unasked: Who were the Taíno, Arawak, and Carib people? Where did they come from, and when? How did they travel? Columbus and his contemporaries had their own answers, some steeped in theological and even mystical belief about the nature of the origin of man. Thanks to the dearth of written histories by indigenous Americans, the first European visitors' preoccupation with ensuring their own prosperity, and the catastrophic loss of population to Eurasian disease throughout the Americas—and with it the oral traditions that might have shed light on these questions—the work of tracing the origins and migration patterns of humans in the Americas has fallen to specialists in disciplines from paleontology and archaeology to linguistics and genetics.

Particularly difficult to tease out is the role played by seafaring and inland navigation in the initial settlement and subsequent dispersal of people and cultures from Alaska and northern Canada, east to Greenland and south to Tierra del Fuego at the tip of South America. Four scenarios for the peopling of the Americas have been posited, none of which can be proven conclusively. Three argue for an arrival by sea—two via the Pacific and one via the Atlantic; the fourth depends on an overland migration from Northeast Asia to Canada. Looked at another way, three favor a Southeast or East Asian origin, while one believes that people arrived from Europe. Of the two maritime Asian routes, one posits a transpacific migration, which was surely impossible more than fifteen thousand years ago, and the other favors a coastal migration from Siberia to Alaska and western Canada. This last theory has achieved wide currency but is not necessarily the last word on the subject.

During the last ice age—when Australia, New Guinea, and Tasmania comprised the landmass of Sahul—the Bering Strait was also dry land and with contiguous areas of Siberia and Alaska formed an Asian-American land bridge known as Beringia. According to the Pacific Rim or coastal route theory of migration, people from Asia reached the Americas in boats by hugging the coast of Beringia. Despite the widespread presence of ice, the warm waters of the eastward-flowing North Pacific current would have ameliorated the conditions on the coasts—just as the Gulf Stream moderates the climate of Iceland and northwest Europe today—and created intermittent ice-free peninsulas and islands where people could replenish their water and food. These coastal migrants would have skirted Beringia as far as the Queen Charlotte Islands off British Columbia, near the southern limit of the ice sheet, before they had the opportunity to turn inland. About eleven thousand years ago, rising sea levels began flooding the land that lies beneath the Bering Strait, which is now forty-five nautical miles wide.

The southerly California current would have hastened migrants' progress as far as Baja California, but the west coast of the United States is notorious for its dearth of harbors, islands, or major rivers south of the Columbia River, on the border between Washington and Oregon. No people on the coast between Oregon and southern California are known to have developed watercraft for exploiting marine resources to any substantial degree. Nonetheless, by thirteen thousand years ago, people had settled in the Channel Islands, an archipelago of eight islands extending 140 miles between the Santa Barbara Channel and Gulf of Santa Catalina off southern California. Similar dates are ascribed to the settlement of coastal Peru and Chile and the center of South America, where a dense network of eastward-flowing rivers rising in the Andes would have fostered very fast migrations; when the Amazon is in flood, it takes little effort to cover 120 kilometers a day going downstream.

The exact sequence and dating of these events is still a matter of vigorous, sometimes rancorous, debate, but the earliest widely accepted archaeological evidence for human settlement throughout the Americas dates from about fifteen thousand years ago. Regardless of how and when people reached the Americas, it was not until about five thousand years ago, roughly contemporary with the rise of literacy in Mesopotamia and Egypt, that the first states emerged there. The climax cultures of pre-Columbian America are those of the Andes and of Mesoamerica, but there were independent flowerings in North America, among the Moundbuilders of the Eastern Woodlands, many of whose sites were located on rivers, and in the desert southwest. Some of these developed autonomously, while others show the imprint of neighboring or ancestral civilizations.

A theory of particular interest to maritime historians is the possibility that Andean civilization emerged from maritime-oriented communities on the coast of Peru and that later Andean culture was carried north by sea to Mesoamerica. This hypothesis maintains that the first people in Peru to coalesce into societies larger than a handful of families were predominantly fishermen living at the mouths of rivers. The arid coast of Peru is home to one of the planet's driest deserts; there is scant rainfall on the coastal plain and 80 percent of runoff from the Andean highlands flows east toward the Atlantic Ocean—yet one of the world's most productive fisheries lies just offshore. The west coast of South America is washed by the cold-water Humboldt current, which sweeps north from Antarctica. As warm air from the Pacific passes over the cold coastal waters, it loses its ability to retain water and generate rain, which accounts for Chile's and Peru's coastal deserts. At the same time, cold water tends to be richer in nutrients than warm water, and the upwelling of the Humboldt current accounts for the bounty of the adjacent fisheries. A similar climatological process occurs in the Atlantic, where the fish-rich, cold-water Benguela current washes the desert coasts of Angola, Namibia, and South Africa.

The first builders of South American monumental architecture lived along the more than fifty parallel river valleys that inscribe the coast of Peru. Excavations at Aspero, on the Supe River north of Lima, show that people derived most of their sustenance from the sea in the form of seabirds, shellfish, pelagic fish, and sea mammals. To the extent that they relied on the land, it was for freshwater and the cultivation of reeds, cotton, and gourds, which could be used for fishing line, nets and floats, and food crops. In the third millennium BCE, the people of Aspero began to erect pyramids—eighteen have been identified—the largest of which covered 1,500 square meters. Farther up the Supe valley, and farther removed from the marine resources that sustained Aspero, is the later site of Caral, with an area more than three times that of Aspero and pyramids as tall as twenty-five meters. A third site known as El Paraíso and begun about 2000 BCE lies to the south, about two kilometers from the sea. Andean sites contemporary with these and of comparable sophistication in terms of architecture were clearly linked to the coast and all have yielded seashells and fish bones.

The coastal polities declined at the start of the first millennium BCE. The reasons are obscure, but one suggestion is that the region was devastated by a severe El Niño event in which warm surface waters prevented the normal upwelling of cold waters on the coast. This would have resulted in a depletion of fish stocks and caused torrential rains and flooding that drove people inland. Whatever the explanation, between 900 and 200 BCE the highlands prospered, especially at the site in west-central Peru known as Chavín de Huantar, which gives its name to a pan-Andean culture that was a forerunner of the Incas. Chavín culture had little immediate connection with the ocean or inland waters per se, but it is of interest to maritime historians. Not only does it seem to have evolved from or been significantly influenced by the marine-oriented society of the Peruvian coast, but Chavín also linked disparate regions that relied to a considerable degree on water transport and associated technologies from Ecuador to Amazonia, a massive region of rain forest and savanna bounded by the Andes, the Guiana Highlands, and the Brazilian Highlands. One of Chavín's earliest long-distance trades was with the southern coast of Ecuador, a source of shells from the thorny oyster, a major prestige gift of the time, and conch. These were being traded south by sea perhaps as early as the third millennium BCE. At their source, oyster and conch shells were used for tools and ornaments, but in Andean and coastal Peru they had a symbolic importance in rituals and were fashioned into beads, pendants, and figurines. Initially they may have been traded for perishable goods that have not survived in the archaeological record, but by the first millennium CE they were probably being exchanged for copper and obsidian.

Research over the past few decades has overturned long-held views that Amazonia was inhabited by primitive forest tribes content to subsist on the jungle's low-lying fruit. The people who lived along the major river systems of tropical South America, notably the Amazon, Orinoco, and their tributaries, are now seen as masters of their environment who planted tropical orchards, built curbed roads up to fifty meters wide as well as causeways, bridges, dikes, reservoirs, and raised agricultural fields. These structures have been found across a vast swath of the continent from eastern Bolivia to Manaus, where the Río Negro meets the Amazon, along the upper Xingu River in Mato Grosso state, and the huge equatorial island of Marajó at the mouth of the Amazon near Belém. While many of these finds date from the first millennium CE, Marajó is home to the oldest known pottery in the Americas, dating from 6000 BCE.

The earliest written account of a journey down the Amazon, by Gaspar de Carvajal, offers vivid descriptions of a number of extensive and highly developed riverside societies. Carvajal was one of fifty-seven men under Francisco de Orellana who in 1542 spent eight months on the Napo, Maraño, and Amazon Rivers. According to Carvajal, the people of "the great dominion of Machiparo" above Manaus had fifty thousand men at arms and occupied territories that "extended for more than eighty leagues" (about 470 kilometers). The Spaniard marveled at the size and quality of the pottery, including jars with a capacity of nearly four hundred liters and smaller pieces the equal of any he had seen in Spain. He wrote of running battles with tribes led by women— the Amazons—while farther east the Spanish encountered "two hundred pirogues, [so large] that each one carries twenty or thirty Indians and some forty," the warriors accompanied by musicians who "came on with so much noise and shouting and in such good order that we were astonished." The people of the Amazon were obliterated by diseases introduced from Europe and Africa, and the survivors were so reduced in numbers that they could not maintain the quality of life of their forebears. As a result, subsequent inter-pretations of pre-Columbian South America were based on observations of a culture in crisis rather than on interaction with vibrant communities linked by extensive river-based networks of trade and transportation.

At the time of European contact there were few long-range saltwater trad-ing regimes anywhere in the Americas, and only two or three intermediate networks in what is now Latin America—one on the Pacific between Ecua-dor and Guatemala and Mexico, and the others on the Caribbean. Researchers began investigating the former after noting similarities in a variety of cultural traits found in the two regions—more than eighteen hundred nautical miles apart—but nowhere in between, thus ruling out an overland route. Affinities in burial practices, ceramic styles, metallurgy, and decorative motifs, among other things, indicate that this maritime exchange could have begun as early as the mid-second millennium BCE. More certain, intermittent trade began in the late first millennium BCE and continued until the arrival of Europeans in the Ameri-cas. The exploitation of marine resources would have prepared fishermen for long-distance trade and might have inspired it in the first place: the opening of the sea route to Mesoamerica may have been related to the need to get shells for trade to the Andes when native stocks declined due to El Niño events or overfishing. In addition to being an exclusive source of a valued commodity and having direct access to inland trading partners, Ecuador has other advantages that favor its being a birthplace of long-distance sea trade in the Americas. Its equatorial location puts it at the meeting point of wind and current systems in the northern and southern hemispheres, and it has an abundance of wood and other materials for constructing oceangoing log rafts called *balsas*.

Sixteenth-century Spanish observers identified a variety of South Ameri-can craft that differed in size and function as well as in materials, construc-tion techniques, and means of propulsion. Floats made of bundled reeds were found in all countries bordering the Pacific, both along the coast and in the mountain lakes—including Lake Titicaca, at an elevation of 3,800 meters, the highest lake in the world—as well as in western Argentina and Bolivia. Log-boat canoes were found as far south as northern Ecuador. Natives of the desert coast of Chile had boats made from the inflated hides of seals and sea lions. The only vessels of complex construction were the *dalca*, a sewn-plank boat found in Chile between the Gulf of Coronado and Taitao Peninsula, and the sewn-bark canoes found from the Taitao Peninsula to the tip of the continent.

The vessels of greatest interest to conquistadors and modern historians alike are the *balsas*, rafts fashioned from an odd number of balsa wood logs—seven, nine, or eleven—tied together and arranged so that the shortest were on the sides and the longest in the middle. According to a sixteenth-century Spanish official, "They are level with the water, which sometimes washes over them, so that passengers of importance cause planks to be installed over crosspieces, and thus they stay dry. At times they also have stakes and crossbeams set up like the sides of a cart, to keep children from falling overboard. . . . To keep the sun off they make a little hut of straw." *Balsas* were propelled by paddles and one or two triangular fore-and-aft or, more rarely, square sails. By far the most novel detail noted by the Spanish was the steering mechanism, which was unlike anything ever devised in Eurasian waters. *Balsas* were steered not with an oar or rudder but by raising and lowering a series of dagger boards called *guares* set between the logs at intervals from stern to bow so that "By sinking some in the water, and raising others somewhat, they succeed in hauling the wind, falling off, and tacking, either coming about or jibing, and lying to, with appropriate maneuvers [of the *guares*] for these purposes." The simplicity of this "centerboard steering" so impressed the author of this description, a Spanish naval officer, that he recommended that *guares* be incorporated into life rafts carried aboard European ships, though without success.

Climatic factors favor a northbound voyage from Ecuador to Mexico or Guatemala over the return trip. Computer models indicate that the fastest northbound passages (mostly in sight of the coast) would have taken forty-six days, compared with ninety-three days southbound. Although the seasonal difference between the longest and shortest voyages from Ecuador was negligible, the best time of year to sail was around April. The best time to start the southward trip was between February and April, but contrary currents and winds required two lengthy offshore passages. Off Guatemala, the *balsa* would sail 200 nautical miles due south before turning east for the coast of El Salvador. The second offshore leg was from the northern end of the Gulf of Panama to the coast of Ecuador, a distance of about 400 miles.

Although there was a fair amount of inland navigation within Mesoamerica, Ecuadorian navigators excited no imitation on the part of the Olmecs (1200–300 BCE), Mayas (300–1000 CE), or Aztecs (1200–1519), none of whom seem to have engaged in anything more than short-range coastal navigation or to have used sails. The only instance of long-range maritime trade known from the east coast of Mesoamerica was maintained by the Putun Maya between the thirteenth and fifteenth centuries. This was well after the height of the Classic Maya period (ca. 430–830), but their diverse trade, which included salt, obsidian, jade and copper, quetzal feathers, cacao beans, cotton, slaves, and pottery, linked coastal trading centers from north of the Yucatán Peninsula to Honduras. Ferdinand Columbus described an encounter that his father had off the latter on his fourth voyage in 1502 when

> by good fortune there arrived at that time a canoe long as a galley and eight feet wide, made of a single tree trunk like the other Indian canoes; it was freighted with merchandise from the western regions around New Spain [Mexico]. Amidships it had a palm-leaf awning like that which Venetian gondolas carry; this gave complete protection against the rain and waves. Underneath this awning were the children and women and all the baggage and merchandise. There were twenty-five paddlers aboard.

Putun Mayan mariners may have raided coastal settlements in Guatemala and Honduras; but neither they nor anyone else from Mexico or Central America seem to have sailed east to the Greater and Lesser Antilles of the Caribbean.*

Although these were settled from South America, the earliest archaeological sites in the Caribbean islands, from the mid-fourth millennium BCE, are found not in the southern part of the chain, as one might expect, but on the islands of Hispaniola and Cuba. Apart from a few archaeological finds in the highlands of Martinique, there is no evidence of human occupation in the Windward Islands until the late 1000s BCE, when a large-scale migration from around the Orinoco delta of Venezuela swept through the Lesser Antilles and Puerto Rico, and subsequently onto Hispaniola and Cuba, where the new arrivals introduced pottery making. While population pressures may account for this emigration from South America, environmental factors seem to have been responsible for the later seventh- or eighth-century colonization of the Bahamas, which was a valuable source of salt. The end of the first millennium also saw the rise of the Taíno culture, which yielded to the native chiefdoms that dominated the Greater Antilles when the Spanish arrived at the end of the fifteenth century. These were among the first Native Americans wiped out by disease and warfare as the islands were overrun by European settlers and African slaves. Their history was quickly lost and most evidence for the patterns and tools of migration in the pre-Columbian Caribbean has been lost permanently.

---

* The Greater Antilles include the large islands of Jamaica, Cuba, Hispaniola, and Puerto Rico. The southward arc of the Lesser Antilles is divided into the northerly Leeward Islands, from the Virgin Islands to Dominica, and the southerly Windward Islands, from Martinique to Grenada.

North America

Curiously, there is little indication of contact between the North American mainland and either the Antilles, ninety miles south of Florida, or the Bahamas, fifty miles to the east. Yet five thousand years ago the people of the Archaic period in Florida had a robust nautical tradition, and among the oldest log canoes found anywhere is a veritable fleet of more than a hundred discovered at Newnan's Lake, near Gainesville, in 2000. More than forty of these date from between 3000 and 1000 BCE, and of the twenty-two whose length can be estimated with any confidence, twenty are between six and nine meters long. Often referred to as dugouts, the oldest log canoes generally antedate the development of metal tools, and they were actually hollowed out by the application of fire and stone scrapers used to remove the charred interior. When the hull was finished, frames could be inserted to keep the sides from deforming, while continuous lines of planks called strakes could be attached to the sides to raise the freeboard, for which reason logboats are often seen as forerunners of planked boats. The Newnan's Lake vessels were clearly intended for sheltered waters, and many of them appear to have been poled rather than paddled. Despite signs of early promise, sailors of the Florida peninsula did not make the transition to open-water navigation.

Logboats of the Pacific Northwest

One of the few places in the Americas where logboats were used extensively for saltwater navigation was on the Pacific coast between the Strait of Juan de Fuca and southeastern Alaska. Coastal people traded diverse goods including furs and hides, candlefish oil, slaves, and dentalium shells harvested off the coast of British Columbia and widely used as a form of currency. By the time of European contact, boat ownership in some places on the coast was all but universal, and when in 1805 the Lewis and Clark expedition descended the Columbia River to the Pacific, William Clark remarked on a village of "about 200 Men of the Skilloot nation[.] I counted 52 canoes on the bank in front of this village manney of them very large and raised in bow." The Nootka (Nuu-chah-nulth) of Vancouver Island, and the Haida of the Queen Charlotte Islands to the north were especially celebrated for the quality of their logboats, which they traded to neighboring tribes.

While logboats can be made from many kinds of straight timber, the cedar of the Pacific Northwest is one of the few species that produces logs wide enough to make the stable and deep hull forms necessary for sea travel. Large dugouts used for long-distance trade, hunting whales, and warfare were about twelve meters long and two meters across and could carry twenty to thirty people and their cargoes or gear. Others reached eighteen meters, and one of twenty-five meters was recorded in the nineteenth century; Meriwether Lewis marveled at canoes with a capacity he estimated at three to four tons. Somewhat smaller "family canoes" carried ten to fifteen people. More common still were the four-meter boats designed for one or two people. Typically they were "ornimented with Images carved in wood the figures of a Bear in front & a man in Stern, Painted & fixed very netely on the canoes, rising to near the hight of a man." Remarking on the construction techniques employed at the start of the nineteenth century, well after European traders had introduced metal tools to the region, Lewis noted that "the only tool usually imployed in felling the trees or forming the canoe &c is a chisel formed of an old file about an Inch and a half broad . . . a person would suppose that the forming of a large canoe with an instrument was the work of several years; but these people make them in a few weeks. They prize their canoes very highly."

Kayaks, Umiaks, and Baidarkas

Renowned though the Nootka and Haida are for their logboats, the two indigenous North American vessels par excellence are the birchbark canoe and the skin boat. Unlike the dugout, which was shaped by removing material from a tree to reveal a boat, both skin boats and birchbark canoes are composite craft. Each is the product of a particular environment, the temperate forest zone of North America in the case of the canoe, and the Arctic zone for the skin boat, three distinct types of which are found from northeastern Siberia across the top of North America to Greenland. In addition to the kayak, designed to carry one person, there were the umiak, a large open boat between five and eighteen meters in length and used for carrying passengers and cargo and for hunting walrus and sea lions; and the baidarka, similar to a kayak but with two and sometimes three cockpits. Kayaks and baidarkas were used chiefly for hunting.

All three types are built around a flexible wooden frame generally constructed from driftwood. Seal, walrus, or polar bear skin attached to the frame by sinew, whalebone, or hide lacing had an elasticity and toughness that made the hulls resilient to shocks from hitting the ice. The light construction and a generally flat bottom allowed umiaks to carry large loads while making it easy to drag them across the ice when necessary. Kayaks and baidarkas were constructed in a similar fashion, but the skin covered the deck apart from the cockpit or manhole in which the paddler sat with his legs outstretched.

Umiak on Whale Patrol *off the coast of northwest Alaska in May 1905(?). The umiak is made by stretching a depilated animal skin over a wooden frame. This vessel seems typical of the type, about ten meters by three meters and with places for five or six paddlers per side and a steersman in the stern at left. Courtesy of the Archives, University of Alaska Fairbanks, S. R. Bernardi Collection, UAF–1959–875–13.*

Despite their broadly similar appearance, there was great variety in kayak design according to the conditions that prevailed in different places.

The inhabitants of Arctic and subarctic North America had a marine orientation as early as 6000 BCE, the date of the earliest archaeological finds in the Aleutians. The later history of the maritime Arctic is characterized by the emergence of cultural traditions in Alaska followed by their eastward spread as far as Greenland. The people of the so-called Arctic Small Tool Tradition hunted marine animals like seals and polar bears from about 2500 BCE, but they depended on the wood of the subarctic forests for heat and light. A defining invention of the Dorset culture that emerged around 500 BCE was the stone lamp fueled by walrus or seal oil, which increased the importance of hunting from kayaks. Weapons included darts and harpoons, frequently thrown with atlatls or throwing sticks, and leather bladders were attached to the harpoon line to keep it afloat and tire the prey. Given the size of the animals hunted, expeditions involved many kayaks, and in rough weather kayakers often lashed their boats together in pairs to increase stability.

Dorset culture was replaced by the bearers of the Thule tradition—the immediate ancestors of the modern Inuit—who appeared in Alaska about a thousand years ago, during the same medieval warm period that facilitated the Norse transatlantic migrations to Iceland, Greenland, and North America. The Thule culture's eastward expansion was so swift and thorough that the people from northern Alaska to Greenland speak one language, albeit in different dialects, whereas Alaska and neighboring Siberia are home to five distinct languages. Thule kayaks were larger than the Dorset, and the Thule also used umiaks for hunting beluga whales. Well equipped to take advantage of the Little Ice Age that began around 1300, they became more seasonal hunters than their predecessors had been, migrating between summer camps for fishing and hunting caribou and winter camps for hunting seals, but always within Arctic or subarctic regions.

The Birchbark Canoe

Boatbuilders living below the tree line have considerably more materials from which to fashion watercraft than do their Arctic counterparts. Most woodland Indian sites from 1000 BCE to the centuries before the arrival of the Europeans were clustered around major rivers—notably the Mississippi, Missouri, Ohio, Illinois, and Tennessee—which were valuable for their fertile bottom grounds and fish resources and as avenues of communication. Tracing the evolution of woodland Indian watercraft over their long history is impossible, but we know that the art of building birchbark canoes was perfected well before the sixteenth century. These were used extensively from the coasts of Newfoundland, the Canadian Maritimes, and New England, westward up the St. Lawrence valley and into central Canada, and across the Appalachian Mountains into the Midwest. Although canoes today are identified almost exclusively with inland waters, the Mi'kmaq are known to have used them to carry copper ingots from Nova Scotia across the Gulf of Maine as far as Cape Cod.

The earliest descriptions of canoes are short on details but uniform in amazement at their capacity, lightness, and speed—factors that evidently impressed their makers, too: the Penobscot word for canoe was *agwiden*, meaning "floats lightly." Following his exploration of the coast of Massachusetts in 1603, the English explorer Martin Pring, awestruck by the canoes he encountered, brought one back to England.

> [I]t was sowed together with strong and tough Oziers or twigs, and the seames couered ouer with Rozen or Turpentine . . . it was also open like a Wherrie, and sharpe at both ends, sauing that the beake was a little bending roundly

vpward.* And though it carried nine men standing vpright, yet it weighed not at the most aboue sixtie pounds in weight, a thing almost incredible in regard of the largenesse and capacitie thereof. Their Oares [paddles] were flat at the end . . . made of Ash or Maple very light and strong, abot two yards long, wherewith they row very swiftly.

The preferred bark for building canoes comes from the paper birch (sometimes called canoe birch) which grows across North America in a wide band, the northern limit of which extends from Labrador to the Yukon River and the coast of Alaska, and the southern boundary of which runs from Long Island to the Pacific coast in northern Washington State. Bark at least one-eighth of an inch thick was peeled from the tree and the sheets sewn together with, preferably, the root of the black spruce, and made watertight with spruce gum, to form the outer shell of the canoe. The variety of such canoes was enormous and depended as much on the use and waters for which they were intended— cargo, passengers, or warfare; lakes, streams, or rapids—as on their makers. Whereas the frame of a kayak was assembled first and the skin wrapped around it, the bark canoe was a "skin first" construction. "The Indian," writes John McPhee in his classic work *The Survival of the Bark Canoe*, "began the assembly with bark. He rolled it right out on the building bed, white side up, and built the canoe from there. Lashing the bark to the gunwale frame, he made—in effect—a birchbark bag. Then he lined the bag with planking. Then—one by one—he forced in the ribs. The resulting canoe was lithe, supple, resilient, strong." To show McPhee just how strong, a canoe builder "cocked his arm and drove his fist into the bottom of one of the canoes with a punch that could have damaged a prizefighter. . . . The bottom of the canoe was unaffected. He remarked that the bark of the white birch was amazing stuff—strong, resinous, and waterproof."

The bark canoe was a vehicle of primary importance after the arrival of Europeans in North America, especially the *canots de maître* or *maîtres canots* built for French *voyageurs* and their Indian partners in the fur trade of central Canada. As one historian has written, these "must be looked upon as the national watercraft type, historically, of Canada and far more representative of the great years of national expansion than the wagon, truck, locomotive or steamship." Canoes and kayaks are rarely built in the traditional manner today, but fiberglass, canvas, and aluminum versions modeled on Native American originals are among the most popular recreational craft in the world, and canoeing and kayaking are Olympic sports, ample testimony to

* A wherry is a light rowing boat for carrying passengers and freight.

the inherent simplicity of their form and function and to the skill required to master their use.

Planked Boats

Sophisticated though the process of making birchbark canoes is, there is a limit to the size they can achieve, and they do not lend themselves readily to other than manual propulsion. The same is true of the kayak and other skin boats. Larger vessels require more rigid construction such as is found in planked boats; the logboat builders of the Pacific Northwest and Newnan's Lake did not take this step. Apart from the *dalca* of southern Chile, the only pre-Columbian planked boat in the Americas is the *tomol*, built by the Chumash Indians, who lived in the Channel Islands and along the coast between Los Angeles and Point Conception, west of Santa Barbara. Southern California is not rich in native maritime tradition, and the Channel Islands seem an unlikely place for such a sophisticated approach to hull construction to have arisen. The first people to reach the islands around 11000 BCE probably did so in reed rafts rather than logboats. The wood and other materials needed for building *tomols* had to be scavenged or acquired through trade: planks were cut from driftwood, the most prized being redwood logs borne south on the California current from the central coast 250 miles away; the cordage used to sew the planks together was made from red milkwood imported from the mainland, as was the tar used to caulk and preserve the hull. Not surprisingly, such boats represented an enormous investment in resources, time, and skill. According to a Chumash who was the source for much of what is known about the *tomol*, "The board canoe was the house of the sea. It was more valuable than a land house and was worth more money." The complexity of the vessel's construction and the high status of the people associated with them have led some to trace the *tomol*'s origins to the mid-first millennium CE, a period when there is evidence of the first stratification of Chumash society.

While plank boats proved a major stepping-stone in the development of deep-water vessels across Eurasia, the Californian *tomol* and the Chilean *dalca* proved technological dead ends. Why the tradition of composite joinery for hull construction did not spread, why sails were not used (or at least not widely), and why long-distance maritime networks did not develop more fully in the Americas are difficult questions to answer. It is tempting to cite environmental constraints, such as the fact that the waters of the Americas lack the enclosed seas that fostered sophisticated developments around the Mediterranean or Baltic, the predictable monsoon systems of the Indian Ocean, or the scattered archipelagoes of Southeast Asia that fostered island hopping. Yet the

Great Lakes comprise an enclosed sea, while the islands of the Caribbean create an almost unbroken chain of intervisible islands from Venezuela to Florida and the Yucatán. Nor was the availability of natural resources a problem; from the sixteenth century onward, Europeans eagerly exploited the New World for its nearly endless variety and supply of timber and naval stores.

The same questions can be asked of maritime communities in Eurasia, where despite the existence of dense networks of cross-cultural contact and exchange, relatively sophisticated construction techniques and means of propulsion developed in some places but not in others. The people of the Baltic did not use sails until the 600s, although they used boats for hunting, fishing, and transportation, and interacted with people in the Mediterranean, where the sail was known by at least the third millennium BCE. Cultural or sociopolitical explanations are likewise inadequate. Mesoamerica produced an unbroken succession of refined states from the Olmecs to the Aztecs, none of which exploited its proximity to the sea to any significant degree. As the example of Oceania shows, populous, centralized states endowed with abundant resources for shipbuilding and trade are not prerequisites for putting to sea. Pacific islanders were never as numerous as their contemporaries in Eurasia or the Americas, yet they ranged farther across the sea than anyone else. But maritime history is seldom susceptible to overarching theories. No less puzzling is the fact that the most comprehensive body of archaeological, written, and artistic evidence for the development of maritime enterprise in the ancient world comes from Egypt, a land associated more with sand than seafaring.

Chapter 2

The River and Seas of Ancient Egypt

Ancient Egypt emerged as a regional power of enormous vigor five thousand years ago. Written, artistic, and archaeological finds make it clear that waterborne transportation was its people's lifeline, and their intimate association with boats and ships permeated every aspect of their lives, from their conception of the afterlife and the voyage of the sun across the sky, to the ways they organized themselves for work and how they envisioned the state. The region's arid climate should not blind us to the Egyptians' profound reliance on river and sea trade for political stability, domestic tranquility, and intercourse with distant people via the Mediterranean and the Red Seas. The last thousand kilometers of the Nile between Aswan and the Mediterranean were a cradle of maritime enterprise on which innumerable vessels moved people and goods, including thousand-ton stone blocks shipped hundreds of kilometers from quarries to the sites of pyramids and other monuments. By 2600 BCE, mariners routinely sailed to the Levant for bulk cargoes of cedar and other goods, and Egyptians also took to the Red Sea in search of incense, precious metals, exotic animals, and other marvels from the land of Punt. In the twelfth century BCE, the sea-lanes of the Mediterranean proved for the first time a double-edged sword as stateless raiders swept across the ancient Near East and precipitated the end of the New Kingdom. In the meantime, the Egyptians' embrace of sea trade had brought them into sustained communication with the leading powers of Mesopotamia and Asia Minor, and helped initiate sustained long-distance voyaging in the eastern Mediterranean.

A Ship in the Desert, 2500 BCE

In the spring of 1954, employees of the Egyptian Antiquities Service were removing debris from around the base of the Great Pyramid at Giza. The effort was a routine bit of housekeeping and there was little expectation of uncovering anything of significance in a place that had been worked over by tomb robbers, treasure seekers, and archaeologists for forty-five hundred years. As they cleared the rubble, workers came across the remains of the southern boundary wall. This was hardly extraordinary; boundary walls had been identified on the north and west sides of the pyramid as well. What was unusual was that this one was closer to the pyramid than the others. Because the archaeological record had long since revealed the Egyptians' fastidious attention to precise measurements and symmetries, archaeologist Kamal el-Mallakh suspected that the wall covered a pit holding a boat connected with the funeral rites of the pharaoh Khufu—or Cheops, as he was known to ancient Greek writers living about midway between his time and ours. Archaeologists had found such pits around various pyramid complexes, including that of Khufu, although all were empty at the time of their modern discovery. Further excavation revealed a row of forty-one limestone blocks with mortared seams. El-Mallakh chiseled a test hole in one of the stones and peered into the impenetrable darkness of a rectangular pit hewn from the bedrock. As he could not see, he closed his eyes. "And then with my eyes closed, I smelt incense, a very holy, holy, holy smell. I smelt time . . . I smelt centuries. . . . I smelt history. And then I was sure that the boat was there." Such was the discovery of the royal ship of Khufu.

The forty-four-meter-long disassembled vessel had been superbly preserved in its airtight tomb for approximately four and a half thousand years. According to one investigator, the boat's timbers "looked as hard and as new as if they had been placed there but a year ago." The boat was almost certainly built for Khufu, the second pharaoh of the Fourth Dynasty. The Great Pyramid was his tomb, and the cartouche of his son, Khafre, was found on several of the blocks sealing the pit. More than twelve hundred pieces of wood were recovered, ranging in size from pegs a few centimeters long to timbers of more than twenty meters. About 95 percent of the material was cedar, imported by sea from Lebanon; the remainder included domestic acacia, sidder, and sycamore. After the pieces had been documented and conserved, the complex work of reconstruction began. The pieces had been arranged logically in the pit: prow at the west end, stern to the east, starboard timbers on the north side, port timbers on the south, hull pieces at the bottom and sides of the pit, and superstructure elements on top of the pile. Carpenters' marks in the form of symbols in the ancient hieratic Egyptian script gave additional clues about how the pieces fit together. Even so, it took thirteen years before the reconstruction was complete; and it was not until 1982, almost three decades after its discovery, that the Khufu ship was opened to the public in a specially built museum alongside the pyramid.

By any measure, the Khufu ship was an astonishing discovery. The largest and best-preserved ship from antiquity or any other period for the next four thousand years, it reveals the technological sophistication of the ancient Egyptians on a far more intimate and accessible scale than do the pyramids or the more arcane arts of embalming and mummification. Like these practices, the burial of the Khufu ship was clearly linked to death rituals in some way, and there is no clearer indication of the central place of boats and ships in Egypt of the third millennium BCE than their honored place in the sacraments of the afterlife. Together with the other twenty-one Egyptian vessels thus far discovered by archaeologists, to say nothing of the hundreds of models, tomb paintings, and written descriptions of ships and boats, as well as records of river and sea transport, the Khufu ship forcefully highlights the importance of watercraft to a civilization that flourished along a fertile ribbon drawn through an African desert.

The Nile: Cradle of Navigation

The dynastic period of ancient Egypt began around 3000 BCE. The Old Kingdom (Third through Sixth Dynasties), during which the pyramids of Giza were built, lasted from about 2700 to 2200 BCE. The Twelfth and Thirteenth Dynasties of the Middle Kingdom lasted about two centuries, ending in about 1700 BCE. The New Kingdom, the period of pharaonic Egypt's greatest prosperity and most active foreign relations, began about 1550 BCE and lasted five hundred years. Thereafter the land came under increasing domination by foreigners from the south and east. In the meantime, Egyptian culture attained a degree of sophistication unmatched anywhere in the world. The Egyptians were literate masters of engineering, the visual arts, medicine, and religious, political, and social organization whose work is characterized by an almost obsessive attention to detail. Their culture thrived for more than two thousand years, their peace and prosperity interrupted only occasionally, and in the great scheme of things briefly. The pyramids at Giza and elsewhere date from relatively early in the history of unified Egypt, but the society that produced these monuments neither appeared nor ended abruptly. Although the conquest of Alexander the Great brought the dynastic age to a close in the fourth century BCE, Egypt has throughout its history been a center of commercial and cultural exchange thanks to its position astride the Nile, the longest river in Africa, and at the intersection of the land crossings between Africa and Asia, and between the Mediterranean and Red Sea and Indian Ocean.

The Nile rises in the mountains of east-central Africa and flows northward into Sudan. In the sixteen hundred kilometers below Khartoum, the river's course is broken by six major cataracts, or sets of rapids. In antiquity the northernmost of these, the First Cataract at Aswan, represented a natural barrier between Egypt and Nubia (northern Sudan), and the early pharaohs' fortification of the island of Elephantine made it a gateway to the south. This was by no means an absolute boundary, and New Kingdom pharaohs pushed as far south as Napata in Kush, between the Third and Fourth Cataracts. North of Aswan, the Nile valley widens slightly for its last thousand kilometers, hemmed in on either side by the Sahara. Egyptian civilization arose within this slip of land, no more than twenty kilometers wide in Upper Egypt but annually inundated by the sediment-rich floodwaters of the Nile until the construction of the Aswan Dams in the twentieth century.

To the west are a few remote oases linked to one another and the Nile by desert tracks, but these were not large enough to support populations capable of threatening the stability of the valley and they offered little to attract any but the most hardened traders. The landscape to the east is bleak but the mountains are rich in deposits of quartzite, alabaster, and gold, which have been mined since pre-dynastic times. Beyond the mountains lies the Red Sea, which was reached via arid, narrow valleys cut by seasonal streams, called wadis. The most important Egyptian towns were generally located near where these wadis reached the Nile, strategic sites that afforded their inhabitants an easy command of north–south and the more limited east–west trade. In the early period these included Elephantine, Hierakonpolis (Kom el-Ahmar), Naqada, Coptos (Deir el-Bahri), and the important royal burial site at Abydos. The majority of these towns were located on the west bank of the river, although Coptos was near Wadi Hammamat and the point on the Nile closest to the Red Sea. At the head of the delta near modern Cairo, Memphis straddled the boundary between the rich agricultural lands of the delta and the traditional centers of power to the south. Memphis was also the city through which Mediterranean commerce funneled into or out of Egypt via the many branches of the Nile and the delta ports, of which Buto was probably the most important from pre-dynastic times. The capital was also near the terminus of the major overland trade routes to Sinai (a major source of copper and turquoise), Canaan (Palestine), and beyond. Thebes (Luxor) later emerged as an important capital near Coptos, with a corresponding mortuary site on the west bank of the Nile.

Upper and Lower Egypt constituted distinct cultural regions and of the towns noted above all but Memphis and Buto were located in the former. By about 3000 BCE, Upper Egypt appears to have been technologically superior, and the ruling elites at Hierakonpolis, Naqada, and Abydos showed the traits of divine kingship and centralized control that would characterize pharaonic rule in a united Egypt. Administrative authority was necessary to guarantee the stability of a society dependent entirely on the Nile for its existence. Although the river's annual inundations followed predictable patterns and in normal times nourished farmers' croplands, the flood was sometimes insufficient and stockpiling grain in times of plenty was a hedge against years of drought and famine. Communication within Egypt depended mostly on the river, too, in part because lands adjacent to the river were either underwater or otherwise impassable for several months each year. Likewise, crossing the innumerable irrigation canals radiating out from the Nile would have entailed the use of endless ferries or bridges. Not until the period of Roman rule in the first century BCE were substantial road-building projects undertaken.

Below Elephantine the Nile is an almost ideal cradle of navigation. On its predictable, northward-flowing current, paddling or rowing toward the Mediterranean is easy. Although the gradient of the river between the First Cataract and the sea is only about 1:13,000—that is, it drops only one meter in every thirteen kilometers—paddling or rowing against the current was challenging, especially when the river was in flood between June and September. However, the prevailing wind is northerly, blowing from the Mediterranean against the current, so that voyagers returning upstream could do so with a following wind. This advantage was amplified after the invention of the sail, and it is hardly surprising that the Egyptian word "to sail" also means "to sail southwards, go upstream." When it first occurred to Nile boatmen to harness the wind cannot be determined, but the oldest known picture of a sail anywhere in the world is found on a vase of the Late Gerzean Culture at Naqada, dated to about 3300–3100 BCE.

Shortly after this, early in the First Dynasty, the rulers of Upper Egypt moved their capital north to Memphis, which became known by the epithet "Balance of the Two Lands," namely Upper and Lower Egypt. So the invention of the sail and the emergence of a unified Egyptian state seem to have been nearly contemporary events, and it is reasonable to speculate that the development of the sail gave the people of Upper Egypt a technological edge that enabled them to bring Lower Egypt within their political and economic sphere. Were this the case, it would not be the last time that nautical advantage had such decisive results. A centralized government requires above all a means of connecting the outer limits of its dominion to itself. Without the development of river craft capable of traveling back and forth reliably and economically, commerce between Upper and Lower Egypt would have been intermittent and probably limited to small quantities of high-value prestige goods, as was the case in the pre-dynastic period. The development of vessels that could head north on the current propelled by paddles (or oars, after about 3000 BCE) and return south under sail removed a major barrier to unifying the Nile valley between the First Cataract and the Mediterranean. Adoption of the sail ensured ease of communication throughout the land, the mobility of government officials and military forces, and the movement of raw materials from agricultural produce to wood and stone, as well as manufactured goods. Reliable transportation, in turn, ensured the well-being of the people subject to the pharaoh's rule—that is, everyone.

Ships and Shipbuilding

The great diversity of Egyptian vessel types is evident from writings, renderings in tomb paintings, sculptural reliefs or models, and archaeological finds of ships and ship remains. While watercraft played a role in political and religious ceremonies, most vessels in daily use were employed for fishing, hunting, and carrying passengers and cargo. The Pyramid Texts written on the walls of Old Kingdom tombs about a century after Khufu include descriptions of more than thirty types of vessels, built from papyrus or wood, and all told, ancient Egyptian sources document about a hundred different kinds. The score of wooden hulls discovered in whole or part represent five different ship types, and all but two sets of fragments are associated with funerary rites or pleasure craft.

The earliest watercraft on the Nile were floats or rafts made from bundles of papyrus. Such rudimentary vessels are common to temperate regions worldwide, and they are found today in such widely dispersed locations as Mesopotamia, Lake Chad in central Africa, and Lake Titicaca in South America. Their use in Egypt can be traced in the pictorial record from pre-dynastic times. Even after the development of wooden boats and ships, Egyptians continued to build papyrus craft, especially for short-distance pursuits such as fishing, hunting, or navigating canals. Larger reed rafts used for hunting were about eight to ten meters long, although if an image showing sixteen paddlers on a side is to be believed they could be longer still. Clay models show that planks were sometimes fitted in the center of the raft to provide a more comfortable and stable platform and to distribute the weight of the passengers and crew more evenly. Because reed rafts tend to sag at the ends, builders turned the ends upward and secured them by running one or more stays to a pole or some other part of the vessel. (Throughout history shipwrights have often resorted to such a solution—commonly called a hogging truss, whether rope or erected as a wood or steel frame—to provide longitudinal support for hulls.) Egyptian builders eventually stiffened their rafts by securing a taut railing rope along the upper edge of the outer bundles of reeds and the upturned ends became less exaggerated. While papyrus is relatively inexpensive and requires little technological sophistication to work, it has a number of drawbacks. Papyrus craft are rafts that rely more on the inherent buoyancy of the papyrus than on the shape and structure of the hull. Moreover, as they become saturated with water, they lose their shape and gradually sink or fall apart, and their working life seldom lasts more than a year.

Wood, on the other hand, is a far stronger and more versatile material with which it is possible to fashion a true displacement hull—a built form that floats thanks to the equilibrium between the downward pull of gravity and the upward thrust of buoyancy. When wooden boats were first built in Egypt is unknown, but it is unlikely to have preceded the development of copper tools, toward the middle of the fourth millennium, a few centuries before the Gerzean jar depicting a sail. Because wood has greater longitudinal strength than papyrus or reeds, on the sheltered waters of the Nile there was little structural need for turned-up ends. Nonetheless, builders of wooden boats retained the papyrus-raft shape—at first, perhaps, because of inexperience with the new material, but later in conscious imitation of the earlier reed forms, especially for ritualistic vessels like the Khufu ship associated with funerals and the afterlife. To achieve the papyriform effect, such watercraft were adorned with extravagant stem and stern pieces, including stylized finials carved in the shape of a cluster of papyrus leaves.

Apart from the sail, the most noticeable thing about the vessel on the Gerzean jar is the highly stylized hull form, but whether the artist was depicting a hull of reed or of wood is impossible to say. The body of the hull has a pronounced sheer to it, with the mast and sail placed well forward, and a small cabinlike structure aft. One reason to suppose that the Gerzean jar shows a wooden-hulled vessel is that the sail is set from a single pole mast. A bipod mast—one with two legs erected like a narrow A-frame—would seem more appropriate to a reed hull because the downward pressure exerted by a mast on a single point would easily work through the hull. The oldest rendering of a ship with a mast, found in Kuwait on a ceramic disc of the sixth millennium BCE, apparently shows such a configuration, and bipod masts are found in various parts of the world where reed boat construction is still practiced today. This does not necessarily reflect the practice in ancient Egypt, and there is no evidence of bipod or tripod masts before the Old Kingdom, when they were stepped in wooden seagoing ships.

The oldest known image of a sail is seen on this ceramic jar of the Naqada/Gerzean II period, named for Gerzeh, Egypt, the site of a cemetery on the west bank of the Nile about eighty kilometers south of Cairo. Dating from the late fourth millennium BCE, just before the start of the dynastic period, this vessel sets a single square sail well forward, and small structures of unknown function are located fore and aft. Courtesy of the British Museum, London.

If wooden hulls were first built toward the end of the fourth millennium, as evidence suggests, progress thereafter was quick. Between 1991 and 2000, archaeologists working at the royal mortuary in Abydos, about fifteen kilometers west of the Nile in Upper Egypt, discovered burial pits containing the remains of fourteen vessels measuring from fifteen to perhaps twenty-four meters in length—six meters longer than the longest of the three ships that sailed on Columbus's first transatlantic voyage more than four thousand years later. These hulls date to the First Dynasty, about midway between the Gerzean jar and the Khufu ship. Although not nearly so well buried as the latter, they were in a remarkable state of preservation thanks to the arid climate. Study of these finds is far from complete, but the presence of the vessels within the most important burial precinct of the early dynastic period testifies to the importance Egyptians attached to watercraft at this critical juncture in their history.

Other vessels may come to light, but it is unlikely that any will rival the Khufu ship for size, completeness, or beauty. Although its exact use is unknown, the Khufu ship was clearly a ship of state rather than a workboat. It repays careful study especially because it was built "shell-first," a technique of hull construction that was typical of ship design across Eurasia and North and East Africa until at least 1000 CE. In shell-first construction, builders fashion the hull by attaching planking edge-to-edge. When the resulting external shell is complete, they stiffen it by adding ribs or frames running perpendicular to the centerline of the hull. The Khufu hull has a flat bottom flanked by two nearly symmetrical sets of planking that form the sides. The planks are joined by a combination of cordage and tenons inserted into hundreds of mortises cut into the edges of the planks, and the hull is reinforced with floor timbers, large, curved pieces of cedar lashed to the strakes.

The use of cordage to fasten planks is common worldwide, and it has a number of advantages over more permanent forms of fastening. The inherent flexibility of sewn boats makes them less liable to damage in a collision or when intentionally run ashore for loading or discharging goods and passengers, a major concern where piers, wharves, or comparable docking facilities do not exist. Evidence of fixed structures to which vessels could tie up in Egypt is slight before the classical period, and vessels either anchored or were beached when not under way. Another advantage is that sewn boats can be put together and taken apart relatively easily. This facilitates making repairs to damaged planks or disassembling a hull to transport it overland in pieces, a common practice for both trade and military campaigns throughout history.

In other boatbuilding traditions, sewn boats are fastened by stitching adjacent planks to one another along the length of the seam between them, as one might sew two pieces of cloth. However, Egyptian shipwrights used transverse lashings that ran perpendicular to the centerline from gunwale to gunwale and the cordage passed through shallow channels drilled into the planks at an angle so that they did not penetrate the hull. Were planks with straight edges attached by perpendicular lashings, the seams would open up easily as the planks slid against each other. The Egyptians overcame this problem by making the planks irregular in shape, so that they nested against one another somewhat like puzzle pieces. Whether transverse lashing was deliberately chosen to conserve material or for some other reason, it is a vastly more efficient use of cordage than seam sewing. The Khufu ship used about five thousand meters of cordage, about one-fifth the amount that would have been necessary to fasten the planks edge-to-edge. This passes through 276 lashing channels, none of which penetrates the hull below the waterline, and there was no caulking of any kind. Nor was any needed, because when exposed to water the wood would swell, and the rope lashings would shrink, resulting in a strong, watertight fit. The vessels are not strictly comparable, but the sewn hull of the *Sohar*, a twenty-six-meter-long dhow built in the 1980s, required roughly 650,000 meters of coconut cord that passed through some twenty thousand holes, which were then plugged with coconut husks and a mixture of lime and tree gum.

The deck of the Khufu ship supports three structures. The deckhouse, consisting of an anteroom and main cabin, is aft of amidships. Forward of that is the open deck, with a light frame for an awning, while toward the bow is a small canopy formed by ten slim poles supporting a plank roof. The graceful forms of the high prow and steeply raked stern pieces give the royal ship its papyrus-raft profile. Although Egyptian vessels were often richly painted—"I conducted the work on the sacred barque, I fashioned its colors," boasts one Twelfth Dynasty official's inscription—there is no evidence that the Khufu ship was so decorated.

What role Egyptians thought burial ships played in the afterlife is a subject of considerable debate. The Nubians may have originated the idea of boats as symbols of royalty, and the practice of burying boats and boat models (less expensive alternatives to real ships) continued for thousands of years. One theory about the Khufu ship is that it was intended to carry the resurrected pharaoh with the sun god Re in an eternal circuit of the heavens. According to Egyptian cosmography, Re had two boats in which he crossed the sky by day and by night, respectively. It is possible that the Khufu ship was first used as a funerary barge to convey the king's embalmed body to Giza, about twenty-five kilometers north of Memphis, or that during his lifetime Khufu himself used it as a pilgrimage boat to visit holy places and thereby assert or renew his authority.

Whether the Egyptians drew a sharp distinction between ritual and recreational travel is difficult to determine. Certainly they knew both kinds. Hunting from papyrus rafts is the subject of a number of narrative illustrations. The social status of the hunter, who is often shown standing, can be determined from his size relative to the raft and the crew. The latter were not necessarily men. In a story about an excursion by Sneferu, Khufu's father, the pharaoh is said to have spent the day being rowed by a crew of twenty naked women, "the most beautiful in form." According to one interpretation, this outing was an imitation of the passage across the sky by Re, who is sometimes depicted as being rowed by the goddess Hathor. Yet the tone of the text suggests a more carefree day on the water and this might well be the first recorded instance of pleasure boating, an activity that remained beyond the reach of all but the most powerful and wealthy until the nineteenth century.

At the other end of the spectrum from royal yachts and funerary ships were the massive, utilitarian barges required to haul the stone used for the pyramids and monuments for which the ancient Egyptians are best known. Because stone was not readily available at the most important burial sites, the Egyptians moved the thousands upon thousands of tons of building materials required for pyramids, temples, statues, and stelae hundreds of kilometers from quarries to the major burial complexes near Memphis and Thebes. Granite came from near Aswan; limestone was available farther north; and quartzite was quarried near both Memphis and Aswan. Quarrying expeditions required sophisticated logistics and were considered worthy of commemoration. It is thanks to records carved in many of the granite stones themselves that we have a glimpse of how they were moved.

On the causeway of the pyramid of Unas (2300s BCE), there is a rendering of three barges, on one of which can be seen two columns laid end-to-end; it is captioned: "Bringing from the workshops of Elephantine, granite columns for the Pyramid Complex called: 'The-Places-of-Unas-are-Beautiful.'" Yet the most vivid illustration of moving stone comes from the New Kingdom temple of Queen Hatshepsut (1400s BCE), which shows how two granite obelisks were carried from quarries near Aswan to the temple complex at Thebes. Calculating the dimensions of Hatshepsut's barges is difficult because there is some uncertainty about the size of the obelisks and how they were carried. It was long thought that each of the obelisks was thirty meters long and weighed about 330 tons. A vessel that carried these end-to-end, as apparently shown, would measure about eighty-four by twenty-eight meters, with a loaded draft of two meters. But the obelisks may have been carried side-by-side and rendered as lying end-to-end due to the Egyptian artistic convention of multiple perspective. The shorter vessel needed in this case would have measured about sixty-three by twenty-five meters, about the size of a barge mentioned in an inscription relating to a contemporary official.

Neither building such large vessels nor loading such enormous cargoes posed any special difficulties. Rather than attempt to lift the stone off the ground and lower it onto the ship, the Egyptians brought the stone to the water's edge via rollers. They then dug a channel under the stone and after loading the barge with smaller stones, the total weight of which was twice that of the obelisk, "the ships were able to come beneath the obelisk, which was suspended by its ends from both banks of the canal. Then the blocks were unloaded and the ships, riding high, took the weight of the obelisk." Such is the explanation given by the Roman geographer Pliny the Elder, writing in the first century BCE, but there is no reason to think that the pyramid builders did not do the same nearly three millennia before his time.

Moving these heavily laden vessels posed more serious challenges. Hatshepsut's barge is shown being steered by four enormous side rudders and towed by a fleet of thirty boats each rowed by twenty-four oarsmen. Computer analyses to determine the characteristics of the vessels that carried to Thebes the two 720-ton Colossi of Memnon about a century after Hatshepsut confirm the accuracy of these images. The quartzite from which the Colossi are carved could have come either from a quarry near Memphis about 675 kilometers downstream from Thebes and on the opposite side of the Nile, or from a quarry near Aswan, on the same side of the Nile, but about 220 kilometers upstream from Thebes. The analysis suggests that a self-propelled barge seventy meters long and twenty-four across could have been rowed upstream from Memphis toward Thebes by a crew of between thirty-six and forty-eight oarsmen. Towing the barge—as shown in the Hatshepsut obelisk relief—would have required a fleet of thirty-two boats, each crewed by thirty rowers.

If the Colossi of Memnon were transported downstream from Aswan, the problem was not one of generating enough power to move the barge against the current, but of controlling the vessel so that it would not outrun the towing boats or careen into the riverbank. To prevent either sort of incident, a wooden raft was attached to the forward (downstream) part of a barge by a hawser, while a heavy stone anchor was dragged astern. According to Herodotus, writing in the 400s BCE, the result was that "the raft is carried rapidly forward by the current and pulls the *baris* (as these boats are called) after it, while the stone, dragging along the bottom astern, acts as a check and gives her steerage way." In all likelihood, what Herodotus describes is a refinement of the procedures developed by the earliest pyramid builders.

While royal vessels incorporated planks of imported cedar, which is long, straight, aromatic, and resistant to rot, domestic wood used for ordinary boats was available only in short lengths. The sycamore fig grows only to ten or twelve meters, and six meters was exceptional for acacia. Neither tree grows especially straight. The reliance on planks from such stock led Herodotus to write that "the method of construction is to lay them together like bricks." He does not indicate the size of the boats in question, but a Sixth Dynasty inscription tells of "a cargo-boat of acacia wood of sixty cubits [thirty-one meters] in its length and thirty cubits in its breadth, built in only seventeen days." Faced with a scarcity of longer planking for ships, traditional Egyptian shipwrights employ similar "brick-work" construction techniques to this day.

Navigation in Daily Life

Although no remains of ships engaged in ordinary trades have come to light, the importance of boats in daily life, as distinct from large-scale expeditions and courtly functions, can be seen in a number of illustrations from the Old Kingdom onward. Such images reflect life on the Nile as it was played out over millennia. Many scenes show men carrying clay jars or sacks of grain and barley along planks laid between ship and shore. In some cases, storage jars are piled high on deck, while in others they are emptied into larger containers and carried in bulk. These images are a sort of propaganda that helped justify the state's highly centralized and almost exclusive control of local, interregional, and foreign trade. Livestock was also carried by boat: a Fifth Dynasty tomb picture shows a vessel with a crew of seven and four cattle. One of the most vibrant descriptions of waterfront bustle comes from an account of the delta city of Piramesse, the New Kingdom capital built in the 1200s BCE. After praising the abundance and variety of food available in the city—barley, emmer wheat, onions, leeks, lettuce, pomegranates, apples, olives, figs, wine, honey, fish, and salt—the author writes that Piramesse's "ships go out and come back to mooring, so that supplies and food are in it every day. One rejoices to dwell within it." Such a proud sentiment could have been heard in almost any of dynastic Egypt's busy river ports.

The degree to which river shipping permeated all aspects of Egyptian life is evident in other ways. Construction of the pyramids and countless other undertakings large and small required the careful organization of labor. Workers of all kinds were grouped in gangs, the names of which were borrowed from shipboard practice, in order of seniority: "forward-starboard, forward-port, aft-starboard, aft-port, and steerage or rudder gangs." Egyptian literature is also rich with metaphorical allusions to ships that suggest an intimate knowledge of how vessels were sailed even among people who did not live by the river. In "The Tale of the Eloquent Peasant" (ca. 2100 BCE), the peasant Khunanup is en route "down to Egypt" from his home in Wadi al-Natrun, about a hundred kilometers northwest of Memphis, when a tenant of the pharaoh's high steward, Rensi, accuses him of trespassing and seizes his two mules. Khunanup appeals to Rensi, and draws a parallel between the justice of his plea, the stability of a ship, and, by extension, the integrity of the kingdom itself:

If you descend to the Lake of Ma'at,
You will sail thereon in the breeze.
The bunt [midsection] of your sail will not be torn,
Nor will your boat be driven ashore.
There will be no damage to your mast,
Nor will your yards be broken.
You will not founder when you come to land,
Nor will the waves bear you away.
You shall not taste the perils of the river.

The Egyptian concept of order in the state and the universe, or Ma'at, depended on ethical personal conduct by everyone from farmer to pharaoh. In this appeal, Khunanup is telling the pharaoh's steward that it is only by seeing the justice of his cause and ruling accordingly that order in Egypt can be maintained. Delighted with Khunanup's speech, the pharaoh tells Rensi to pretend to ignore him so that he can continue enjoying the peasant's eloquence. Over the course of nine meetings, Khunanup repeatedly resorts to the imagery of the ship: "Behold, I am on a voyage without a boat," he tells Rensi. "You who are safe harbor for all who are drowning, / Rescue one who has been shipwrecked." And later he chastises Rensi for being "Like a city without a governor, Like a people without a ruler, / Like a ship on which there is no captain." In a similar vein, five centuries later, the biographical inscription of a New Kingdom official compares Queen Hatshepsut to the mooring lines securing the ship of state against the swift current of the Nile: "The bow-rope of the South, the mooring-stake of the Southerners; the excellent stern rope of the Northland is she."

The eloquent peasant's identification of the kingdom with a ship is the oldest surviving example of the nearly universal metaphor of the ship of state.[*] The analogy is easily grasped because both the ship and the state can be considered self-contained entities governed by a central authority, and the figure of speech has been extended to other institutions and the planet itself.

"Upon the Sea of God's Land"

For all the natural resources they commanded at home, the Egyptians were not aloof from foreign trade. Attractive though the region above Aswan was for its quarries, security south of the First Cataract was a perennial concern. An

---

[*] The verb "to govern" derives from the Greek word meaning "to steer" by way of the Latin *gubernare*, which means "to steer" and "to govern."

inscription on the life of Uni, a Sixth Dynasty official, records two trips there to get granite for the pyramid of Merenre. On his first, his convoy included six barges, three towboats, three auxiliaries, and "only one warship. Never had Ibhet and Elephantine been visited in the time of any kings with only one warship." Uni capitalized on the peaceful relations on his second expedition during which he undertook significant improvements to navigation by digging artificial channels through or around the First Cataract.

Egyptians sailed beyond Aswan not just for stone, but also for precious goods available only from Nubia or via Nubian intermediaries. Around 2300 BCE, a trader named Harkhuf made four trading expeditions south of Aswan, the last during the reign of Pepy II, who was then seven years old. Harkhuf's usual stock-in-trade included incense, ebony, leopards, grain, "ivory, throw sticks and every good product." His last trip is memorable for his acquisition of a "dancing dwarf," almost certainly a pygmy, about which he sent a letter from the field. We can still sense the pharaoh's childish anticipation in his reply. Commanding Harkhuf to come immediately to court, Pepy orders every precaution to ensure the pygmy's safe delivery: "take care that he doesn't fall into the water. When he sleeps at night appoint excellent people, who shall sleep beside him in his tent; inspect ten times a night. My majesty desires to see this dwarf more than the gifts of Sinai and of Punt," both of which were associated with rarities of inestimable worth.

At the northern end of the Red Sea, the Sinai Peninsula forms both a natural barrier between Africa and Asia and a thoroughfare along which goods and cultural influences were traded between Egypt and the Arabian Peninsula, Asia Minor, Mesopotamia, and Iran. It was also a source of mineral wealth in its own right. The distribution of archaeological finds between Mesopotamia and Egypt suggests that in the Late Gerzean period, the land route via Canaan and Syria was superseded by a sea route between Buto and Byblos (Jubayl, Lebanon). One of the most valuable imports from the Levant was cedar, which could be economically transported only by ship. This trade began in the early third millennium BCE, and according to the Palermo Stone, Sneferu ordered "forty ships filled with cedar logs," some of which were used to build a fifty-three-meter-long vessel, eleven meters longer than the Khufu ship.

The oldest written references to Mediterranean trade come from the Palermo Stone, a fragment of a stele incised with the royal annals as of the Fifth Dynasty and the earliest images of Egyptian seagoing ships are found in two nearly contemporary Fifth Dynasty reliefs, from the temple of Pharaoh Sahure at Abusir and the causeway of Pharaoh Unas at Saqqara. One scene in Sahure's temple shows the departure for the Levant of six Egyptian ships with Egyptian crews, while another shows eight ships returning with Egyptian crews and foreigners sporting Syro-Canaanite dress and hairstyles. Egyptians and Syro-Canaanites also appear aboard the two ships in the Unas relief. While the merchants are from the Levant, the goods they carried were not necessarily limited to what was made or grown in their homelands. Goods of Cretan provenance have been found at Egyptian sites associated with Sneferu, while there are bowls of apparently Egyptian origin in Crete from the same period. At this early date, it seems that these were traded via Levantine intermediaries. Yet direct sea trade may have opened between Minoan Crete and Egypt by the end of the third millennium BCE, when Egyptian sources refer to Crete as a western country. At the time, geographical knowledge was such that people were known by the direction from which they appeared to come. The prevailing winds and currents of the eastern Mediterranean flow counterclockwise, so the easiest way to reach Egypt from Crete was to sail due south to the coast of what is now Libya—an open-water passage of perhaps three or four days—and then eastward to the Nile delta. Returning home they sailed east with the winds and currents along the Levant and the southern coast of Asia Minor before turning south again for Crete.

The other channel of Egypt's overseas trade was the Red Sea, which gave access to the mysterious land of Punt, the second place mentioned by the anxious Pepy. Pharaohs had reveled in the gifts of Punt since well before his time, but the question of its exact location has vexed historians and geographers since antiquity. There is general agreement that it lies to the south along the Red Sea, the most likely places being Eritrea in Africa or Yemen on the Arabian Peninsula, or perhaps south of the Red Sea and across the Gulf of Aden on the Horn of Africa, which is today the autonomous Puntland state of Somalia. The Red Sea lies 150 kilometers east of the Nile via the Wadi Hammamat. The arid shores have few trees, and ships had to be carried in pieces to the coast for reassembly and launching. This process is alluded to in an Eleventh Dynasty (2100 BCE) inscription recording an expedition to Punt under Henu, who "went forth from Coptos upon the road . . . with an army of 3,000 men. I made the road a river, and the Red Land (desert) a stretch of field, for I gave each a leathern bottle, a carrying pole, 2 jars of water and 20 loaves to each one among them every day." Clearly Henu "made the road a river" by virtue of the fact that the ship traveled along it, albeit in pieces.

Physically and logistically demanding though they were, expeditions to Punt date from at least the Fifth Dynasty. "The Shipwrecked Sailor," the oldest surviving shipwreck narrative, contemporary with Henu's expedition, gives a sense of the riches to be gained in the trade. In the story, the sole survivor of a crew of 120 lands on an apparently uninhabited island where a serpent befriends him. In gratitude for the serpent's help, the sailor offers to send him ships "laden with all the products of Egypt." The serpent laughs and says, "You do not have much myrrh / I am, sir, the Prince of Punt. / Myrrh belongs to me." After assuring the sailor that he will be rescued and see his home and family again, the serpent presents him with a cargo of "myrrh, oil, ladanum, spice, / Cinnamon, aromatics, eye-paint, giraffe tails, / Large cakes of incense, ivory tusks, / Hounds, apes, baboons, and all fine products." As the serpent predicts, the sailor is rescued and returns home with gifts for the pharaoh.

The fullest account of any Egyptian trading mission on the Red Sea dates from the reign of the New Kingdom's pharaoh Hatshepsut, who ruled as coregent with her short-lived brother, Thutmose II, and as regent for her nephew and son-in-law, Thutmose III. During his minority she assumed fully the role of a pharaoh—including the pharaonic regalia of a false beard—the only woman in Egypt's long history known to have done so. Recorded in magnificent detail on three walls of Hatshepsut's mortuary temple at Thebes, this voyage to Punt took place around 1470 BCE. Artistic representations of ships can be problematic sources for the study of naval architecture because they are often rendered by people who lack technical ability as illustrators, are unfamiliar with the vessels they are showing, or are uninterested in material accuracy. In the case of the Punt expedition artists, however, we have independent verification of their reliability thanks to their carvings of fish, which are so detailed that modern ichthyologists can identify them by species.

The first five scenes show the departure of the fleet, its welcome in Punt, the exchange of wares, the loading of the ships, and the return voyage. The next two show the presentation of tribute to Hatshepsut and her presentation, in turn, of offerings to the god Amon. The eighth panel shows the goods being measured and weighed, while the ninth and tenth show Hatshepsut announcing the success of the expedition to her court and Amon. If the illustrations are correct, the expedition included five ships. Based on the number of rowers shown—fifteen per side—the ships were about twenty-three meters long. Arriving at Punt, a land where the houses were built on stilts, the Egyptians set up shop—literally, "the tent of the king's-messenger"—and laid out their wares, including necklaces, hatchets, and daggers in addition to offerings of "bread, beer, wine, meat, fruit, everything found in Egypt according to that which was commanded in the court." In the Egyptian view there is no doubt as to the status of the Puntites, who are shown giving obeisance and bearing tribute to the Egyptians and who ask, "as they pray for peace . . . 'Did you come down upon the ways of heaven, or did ye sail upon the waters, upon the sea of God's Land? . . . Lo, as for the King of Egypt, is there no way to his majesty, that we may live by the breath which he gives?'"

The fourth scene depicts the true object of the voyage, the return cargo.

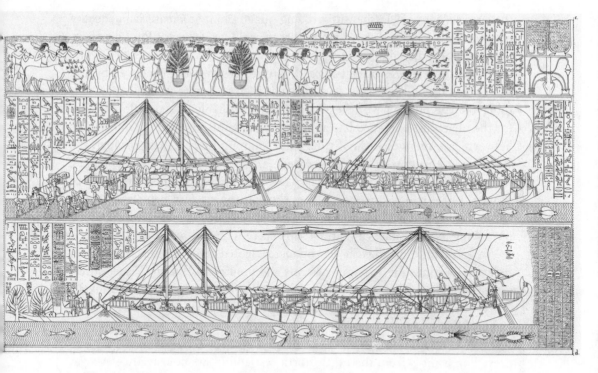

The return of Hatshepsut's ships from Punt on the Red Sea, as shown in the pharaoh's temple at Thebes (Deir el-Bahri), Egypt. The most important goods are the myrrh trees slung from poles carried on the shoulders of the ship's crew. The wooden ships were powered by oars and a single square sail and steered by side steering oars. From Auguste Mari-ette's Deir-el-Bahari: documents topographiques, historiques et ethnographiques recueillis dans ce temple *(Leipzig, 1877).*

Two ships are shown, their crews carrying large sacks of cargo and "fresh myrrh trees" in baskets; these were the most highly valued acquisitions, and in announcing the success of the mission to the court, Hatshepsut says that she has obeyed the command of her father (the god Amon) "to establish for him a Punt in his house, to plant the trees of God's-Land beside his temple, in his garden." Frankincense and myrrh were important for the performance of sacred rituals, but an enumeration of Puntite exports that runs across several scenes includes "ebony and pure ivory, with green gold . . . with cinnamon wood" and, echoing the serpent-prince in the story of the shipwrecked sailor, "incense, eye-cosmetic, with apes, monkeys, dogs, and with skins of the south-ern panther, with natives and their children" (presumably slaves) as well as throwing sticks, cattle, silver, lapis lazuli, and malachite.

Both the exchange between the shipwrecked sailor and the serpent and the later account of Hatshepsut's trading mission hint at a material inequality between Egypt and the exotic lands to the east. The Prince of Punt dismisses as insignificant the sailor's offer to bestow upon him the "specialties of Egypt," and while the Puntites of Hatshepsut's day are described as overawed by and subservient to the Egyptians, their produce is clearly more valuable than anything the Egyptians have to exchange. This probably posed little problem for the pharaohs, but since late antiquity, complaints about trade imbalances between east and west—the dividing line running more or less through the Red Sea and Southwest Asia—have been a recurrent theme among writers, as are politicians' calls for sumptuary laws to restrict the import of "precious things." Older still, as these narratives show, is the western habit of orientalizing, simultaneously investing the east with an aura of exotic mystery and portraying its inhabitants as natural subjects of western authority.

We know little of how the Egyptians navigated the Red Sea, which even today is notorious for its tricky currents and innumerable reefs. Visual observation would have been essential and navigation at night seems unlikely. Northerly winds prevail year-round in the Red Sea as far south as 19°N, well south of Egypt's modern border with Sudan, but the best season for a voyage beyond that point would have been between June and September when the prevailing wind is from the north-northwest and blows at a steady eleven to sixteen knots. With favorable winds, a fast passage to Eritrea might take two weeks or more, and considerably longer northbound, with deeply laden hulls straining against wind and current. Given the dryness of the environment, the ships would have to have carried ample supplies of water, beer, and wine, all of which would quickly go bad in the heat. In addition, food, cargoes, and the ships themselves had to be carried to the port of embarkation, which suggests a highly sophisticated and experienced organization. If Henu needed three thousand men to launch one ship on the Red Sea, Hatshepsut's expedition probably required at least five times as many.

New Kingdom Recovery and Expansion

Unique though Hatshepsut was as a woman pharaoh, her dynamism was characteristic of the New Kingdom in general and especially the Eighteenth Dynasty (1570–1315 BCE). Although Egypt had periodically extended its political influence east and west from the Nile delta and south of Aswan, prior to the start of the New Kingdom the pharaohs generally refrained from overtly expansionist policies. The reasons for the demise of the Middle Kingdom are not known, but by the 1600s BCE most of Middle and Lower Egypt was under the rule of the Hyksos, foreigners likely of Syro-Canaanite origin. Murals at Avaris, the Hyksos capital in the northwest delta, are stylistically similar to those found on Crete and Thera and hint at the possibility of a Cretan expatriate community there, too.

The Hyksos seem to have adapted rather than uprooted Egyptian conventions, but they remained an alien elite distinct from native rulers who continued to control Upper Egypt from Thebes. In the 1560s BCE, King Kamose mounted a riverine campaign to wrest Avaris from the Hyksos. His soldiers used their vessels as mobile bases from which they conducted operations ashore rather than for ship-to-ship operations. One incentive for overthrowing the Hyksos was to eliminate them as middlemen in Upper Egypt's trade with the Levant. In an account of his victorious campaign, Kamose boasts "I have not left a plank under the hundreds of ships of new cedar, filled with gold, lapis lazuli, silver, turquoise, and countless battle-axes of metal. . . . I seized them all. I did not leave a thing of Avaris, because it is empty, with the Asiatic vanished." The narrative suggests a complete rout of the enemy, but credit for the final ouster of the Hyksos goes to Kamose's successor, Ahmose, the first king of the Eighteenth Dynasty and the New Kingdom.

Following the sack of Avaris, the Egyptians pursued the Hyksos into Canaan, a move that signaled a deeper engagement in the region than they had attempted previously. The Near East was undergoing political upheaval thanks also to the westward expansion of the Mitanni kingdom from their homeland in northern Mesopotamia. Ahmose and his successors remained committed to the region, and in the course of seventeen campaigns Thutmose III extended Egyptian control as far as southern Syria. The military expeditions to and administration of this territory depended on Egypt's control of Levantine ports including Byblos, Ulazza, and Ardata (just south of Tripoli, Lebanon), where Thutmose stockpiled matériel for his Syrian campaign. According to the Barkal Stela, "Now every harbor His Majesty came to was supplied with fine bread, various breads, oil, incense, wine, honey, fr[uit] . . . more numerous than anything, beyond the comprehension of His Majesty's army—and that's no exaggeration!" On his eighth campaign, Thutmose sailed his army to Byblos, whose stocks of shipbuilding timber would prove invaluable to the next phase of his expedition against the Mitanni. The invasion was largely unopposed until it approached the Euphrates, where the Egyptians bested the Mitanni in several engagements. When the Mitanni withdrew east of the river, Thutmose launched his prefabricated vessels into the river and proceeded downstream, destroying towns and villages as he went and driving the Mitanni to seek refuge in caves. In bringing the ships up from the coast, the Egyptians drew on their long experience of transporting ships from the

Nile to the Red Sea, a significantly longer distance across far more inhospitable terrain.

At the same time that the Thebans were advancing against the Hyksos in the north, they were also campaigning against the kingdom of Kush, which had expanded northward from Nubia. Egypt's southern boundary had moved back and forth between the First and Second Cataracts since the Old Kingdom, but the New Kingdom pharaohs' conquest of Kush was remarkable for its extent and duration. The Barkal Stela recounting Thutmose III's exploits in Syria was erected at Napata, twenty kilometers downstream from the Fourth Cataract, which remained Egypt's southern boundary for four hundred years. The kingdom was now at the height of its imperial reach, which extended 2,200 kilometers from Napata to Ugarit (Ras Shamra, Syria). The Egyptians concluded alliances with the Hittites of Anatolia, and the Assyrians, Babylonians, and Mitanni of Mesopotamia. In the eastern Mediterranean, the consolidation of Egyptian authority led to increased trade not only with Levantine ports but with Crete, and images of traders in Minoan dress first appear in a tomb painted for Thutmose III's high steward, Rekhmire, in which they are identified as "The People of the Isles in the midst of the Sea." Interest in the Levant waned under Thutmose's successors but revived in the Nineteenth Dynasty. At the end of the thirteenth century BCE, however, mass migrations swept southward by land and sea and destroyed the established order of the Bronze Age Near East and threatened the integrity of Egypt itself.

The birth, expansion, and longevity of pharaonic Egypt depended on harnessing the Nile as a highway of internal communication, while the seas were a filter through which its people absorbed foreign goods and influences, a buffer against invasion, and a thoroughfare for projecting political and military power. Overland communication with Mesopotamia was possible, but saltwater and freshwater navigation facilitated communication between Egypt and the region's leading powers, most of the distance being covered on the Mediterranean and, after a portage of less than a hundred miles, the Euphrates River. What is most striking about the varied maritime endeavors of ancient Egypt is the impetus they gave to the development of maritime communities across the Levant and the eastern Mediterranean, which remained a preeminent center of maritime culture and commerce for nearly four thousand years.

Chapter 3

Bronze Age Seafaring

Southwest Asia constitutes one of the most vibrant cultural and commercial crossroads in the world. Overland routes converge there from Anatolia and the Caucasus, Central and South Asia, and the Arabian Peninsula and the Levant. Lying at the head of the Persian Gulf, Mesopotamia is connected by sea to the lands that ring the Indian Ocean and its subsidiary seas from the Red Sea to the Bay of Bengal. The Tigris and Euphrates also provide a direct connection from the gulf to the heart of Southwest Asia. While these rivers are more erratic than the stately Nile, they were vital arteries of communication by which the trade of the Indian Ocean reached Asia Minor in the north and the Mediterranean in the west. Astride these roads and rivers, the people of Mesopotamia developed some of the refinements of civilization such as writing and city dwelling in the late 3000s BCE, several centuries before the start of dynastic Egypt. The Sumerians and their successor states never achieved the political continuity characteristic of the Egyptians, but the people of Mesopotamia were pioneers in maritime and commercial law, and their oldest literature, including the story of King Sargon's origins and the Epic of Gilgamesh, has echoes in later Greek myth, Judeo-Christian and Muslim scripture, and Persian and Arabic folktales. These stories were carried via the Euphrates to the Levantine coast and from there by ship to the rest of the Mediterranean. Older still were Mesopotamia's maritime links to the east, via the Persian Gulf to the lands of Bahrain, Oman, and southern Iran, and the maritime frontier of the Harappan (Indus Valley) civilization of Pakistan and India, which reached its height in the late third millennium BCE. Traces of this long-range traffic, carried out in sailing vessels built of wood or bound reeds, are faint but unmistakable.

Merchants dealt chiefly in precious and exotic goods, however, and such long-distance trade for elite customers could not survive the unexplained downturn in Harappa's fortunes in the first centuries of the second millennium BCE. Little wonder that Mesopotamian merchants and rulers turned their attention to the Mediterranean, which may help account for Minoan Crete's great prosperity at about the same time, when the island's merchants were trading with Greece, the Levant, and Egypt. The Cretans in turn left their mark on the mainland Greek culture of Mycenae, which emulated and eventually succeeded them as the dominant culture of the Aegean world. The Mycenaean Age lasted until the Sea People—the name given to northern migrants of obscure origin—swept through their territories en route to the Near East and Egypt. The next two centuries evince little of the cultural vitality of the Bronze Age, but the maritime connections endured and it is along these that we can trace the Phoenician and Greek revival that began in the tenth century.

Between the Rivers and the Seas in the Third Millennium BCE

Situated at the head of the 550-mile-long Persian Gulf, Mesopotamia was the home of the world's first literate people, the Sumerians, who settled in the region by about 3200 BCE. Living in small cities, by the end of the fourth millennium BCE the Sumerians were probably more technologically advanced than the Egyptians in many respects. If the Nile is a river between two deserts, Mesopotamia is, according to its Greek name, a land "between the rivers." The Euphrates and Tigris are turbulent streams fed by the snowmelt from the Taurus Mountains of Asia Minor and the Zagros Mountains of western Iran, and prone to chaotic flooding in their lower reaches. About 160 kilometers from the Persian Gulf the rivers merge to form the Shatt al-Arab, a marshland that separated the southernmost cities of ancient Mesopotamia from saltwater. Dramatic changes in water levels and currents caused the rivers to meander; some cities once situated on the banks of the rivers are now far from them, while other sites have been wiped out as watercourses twitched across them like a garden hose in geologic time. Early efforts to harness the rivers for agriculture and transportation led to extensive canalization, a development that both required and nurtured sophisticated patterns of social organization. This is reflected in everything from the laws governing the control, use, and navigation of canals to the Mesopotamian pantheon. Enki, one of the Sumerians' most important deities, is portrayed as flooding the rivers with his life-giving semen and using the canals for transportation, while Ennugi, one of the gods who conspired to send the flood against mankind, was inspector of canals.

The oldest evidence for ships with masts comes from southern Mesopotamia and Kuwait and dates from the sixth millennium. Nonetheless, whereas environmental conditions in Egypt encouraged the use of sails, those in Mesopotamia did not. Not only do the Tigris and Euphrates flow faster than the Nile, over numerous rapids and shallows, but both their currents and the prevailing winds go from north to south making upstream travel very difficult. Consequently, the Mesopotamians developed vessels they could use to best effect on a river system that favored downstream navigation. Boats were an essential means of transportation, but they never achieved the status that they did among the Egyptians. The Mesopotamian boat was a thing of this life, never exalted enough to serve as a vehicle of the gods.

The earliest vessels for which any evidence survives were lightweight boats made of reeds or skins that ran less risk of hitting bottom in the shallows than would a heavier wooden boat and were less susceptible to damage if they did, and which could be easily towed upriver once their cargoes had been off-loaded. The Mesopotamians also made use of disposable rafts supported by either inflated animal skins or airtight ceramic pots. When vessels reached their destination, they could be unloaded, their timber decking sold with the cargo, and the floats either sold or carried upstream to be used again. Watercraft of such simple design were employed well into the twentieth century, when one of the most common vessels found on the Tigris and among the Marsh Arabs of the Shatt al-Arab was still the *quffa*, a circular boat of coiled reeds, like an enormous basket reinforced with wooden ribs and waterproofed with a coat of bitumen, or asphalt pitch. These materials may suggest fragility, but a *quffa* could carry as much as three horses and their handlers, or five tons of cargo.

The record of Mesopotamian maritime accomplishment also differs significantly from that of Egypt. Although there is an abundant supply of economic texts such as contracts and orders or receipts for goods, merchant seals, and illustrations, the only boat remains are fragments of bitumen used to waterproof hulls. Models and pictures of vessels are scarce, and there are few sustained narratives describing the role of ships and navigation. Among the sources that do open a window on the maritime life of ancient Mesopotamia are the legends associated with the birth of Sargon in the 2300s BCE and the Epic of Gilgamesh, a quasi-historical hero of the third millennium whose exploits remained popular in the Near East for more than two thousand years, and echoes of which can be found in the stories of Moses, Noah, and the flood in the Hebrew Bible; Homer's *Odyssey*; and *The Arabian Nights*.

Sumerian king lists include a Gilgamesh who ruled sometime between 2800 and 2500 BCE, but the oldest extant versions of the Gilgamesh epic date from

A Mesopotamian cylinder seal (2.7 centimeters high), and the sealing it makes when impressed into wet clay. Found at Tello, Iraq (the ancient Girsu), on the Euphrates River about 250 kilometers southeast of modern Baghdad and 80 kilometers north of Nasiriyah, the third millennium BCE seal shows the god Ea, identified by his goat head, and two other figures on a riverboat. Courtesy of the Louvre Museum, France/Art Resource, New York.

the early second millennium. The story has two main parts, the first telling of the friendship and adventures of Gilgamesh and Enkidu, and the second relating the story of the flood. Versions of the story survive in the Sumerian, Akkadian, Hurrian, and Hittite languages, and details changed over time to suit the expectations and experience of the audience. Gilgamesh and Enkidu's first adventure is to slay Humbaba, keeper of the forest. According to the Sumerian version of the story, Humbaba lived in the Zagros Mountains to the east. In Akkadian retellings from about a thousand years later, the pair headed west for the cedar forests of Lebanon and the Mediterranean coast, a change consistent with the different geographic orientations of the two cultures. In both versions, when Enkidu dies, Gilgamesh, fearful for his own mortality, sets out to consult Utnapishtim, a man who survived a flood sent by the gods to destroy mankind and was rewarded with the gift of immortality.

To reach Utnapishtim on the island of Dilmun, Gilgamesh has to ride with the ferryman, for whom he cuts 120 poles preserved with a coating of bitumen. (Canal vessels were propelled by poling, and orders for wooden poles up to six meters long survive.) They travel for three days until they reach the waters of death and in crossing the shallows Gilgamesh breaks all the punting poles. "Then Gilgamesh stripped himself and as a sail / held up the animal skin he had been wearing, / and so the little boat sailed on the waters"—a means of propulsion not unlike windsurfing, a sport invented four thousand years later. Learning that Gilgamesh seeks to know whether he, like Enkidu, must die, Utnapishtim offers an explanation of human mortality that reads like an accountant's take on Ecclesiastes: "How long does a building stand before it falls? / How long does a contract last? How long will brothers / share the inheritance before they quarrel? . . . / From the very beginning nothing at all has lasted." He then tells Gilgamesh how he achieved immortality in a story that anticipates that of Noah and the ark.

One day, the gods decided to destroy the city of Shurrupak on the Euphrates, one of the five cities that ancient Mesopotamians believed antedated the flood. Ea (the Akkadian Enki), a god of wisdom well disposed toward mankind, told Utnapishtim to build a boat big enough to take a sample of every living thing. The vessel was huge, its width equal to its length (not unlike an enormous *quffa*) with six or seven decks. Utnapishtim waterproofed the hull inside and out with a mixture of oil, pitch, and asphalt. Because of its inordinate size, the vessel had to be launched with the help of rollers, a method that suggests a flat-bottomed hull. After a storm that lasted seven days, the waters covered the earth, but the boat came to rest on Mount Nimush. A week later, Utnapishtim sent forth in turn a dove, a swallow, and a raven to look for land. The first two birds returned to the ship, but the last did not, signifying it had found dry ground where the flood was receding. After offering sacrifices, Utnapishtim and his wife left the ship and were granted immortality on Dilmun, which probably refers to the island of Bahrain.

Dilmun also figures in the economic records of early Mesopotamia. The Persian Gulf had been a conduit for trade in metals, wood, stone, and other commodities from lands bordering the Indian Ocean as early as the fifth millennium BCE, but until about 2900 BCE the Sumerians seem to have had more contact with and influence on Anatolia, the Levant, and Egypt. Thus their identification of an abode of immortality somewhere in the Persian Gulf may reflect the Mesopotamians' shifting gaze in the third millennium BCE. Lying midway between the head of the Persian Gulf and the Strait of Hormuz and peppered with approximately one hundred thousand burial mounds, as well as the ruins of a substantial city, Bahrain had abundant stocks of fish, dates, and freshwater. On the arid Persian Gulf, the last would have been as much a lubricant of long-distance trade in antiquity as oil is today. Dilmun's natural resources were not insignificant, but its prominence at the time depended on the ability of its merchants to capitalize on their geographic position and to make themselves indispensable middlemen in the trade between two richer regions. The merchants of Dilmun acted as intermediaries in Mesopotamia's overseas trade. One king "had ships of Dilmun transport timber from foreign lands" for building temples; there are numerous receipts for copper carried by Dilmunite traders; and votive models of ships on the Dilmun run have been found in temples in Ur.

The best known reference to Mesopotamia's overseas trade describes how the founder of the Akkadian Dynasty, Sargon, triumphed over his neighbors to make his city a center of interregional commerce around 2300 BCE: "Ships from Meluhha, Magan, and Dilmun made fast at the dock of Akkad." Sargon's capital has not been located, but Akkad was probably in the vicinity of modern Baghdad, about five hundred kilometers from the Persian Gulf. Magan refers to the lands of the lower Persian Gulf, and Meluhha the Indus Valley civilization. According to tradition, Sargon was born in the highlands of the upper Euphrates, of humble origins but with a miraculous infancy not unlike that of Moses about eight hundred years later: "My mother, the *entum*, conceived me, in secret she bore me; / She placed me in a basket of rushes, she sealed 'my door' [the lid] with bitumen; she cast me into the river which did not rise over me; / The river bore me up and carried me to Aqqi, the water-drawer." During his half-century reign, Sargon continued a policy of expansion that began with the defeat of his predecessor, who had unified southern Mesopotamia and expanded Sumer's traditional worldview by "opening the way" for merchants to travel in safety from the Persian Gulf to the Mediterranean, or "from the Lower Sea by the Tigris and Euphrates unto the Upper Sea." For the time being, however, the Akkadians' faced firmly eastward.

East of Hormuz: The Eastern Trade, 2500–1700 BCE

Sargon's reign opened a vibrant period in the history of Mesopotamia's overseas relations. Meluhha, the first place mentioned in Sargon's inscription, lay at the farthest limit of Mesopotamia's overseas contacts and encompassed the coasts of modern Pakistan and northwest India. (The distance from the head of the Persian Gulf to the mouth of the Indus River is 1,150 nautical miles.) It thus included the seaports of the Indus Valley or Harappan civilization, the primary centers of which were Mohenjo Daro, about 225 kilometers up the Indus, and Harappa, about 640 kilometers northeast of Mohenjo Daro. The Indus civilization flourished between 2500 and 1700 BCE and spread across parts of modern Pakistan, Iran, Afghanistan, and northwest India as far south as Gujarat, a much greater area than any of the early Mesopotamian states or Egypt before the Eighteenth Dynasty. The ruins of Harappan society show a high degree of sophistication and organization, with large urban areas divided into neighborhoods apparently distinguished by occupation. Harappan trading networks reached overland into Central Asia and west across Persia and by sea to the Persian Gulf.

Although the Indus civilization was technically literate, the script employed by its people has not been deciphered, and no personal names have survived. "Meluhha" is an Old Akkadian word that was used as a personal name and a place name, and a late-third-millennium BCE inscription mentions a village of Meluhhans at the Mesopotamian city of Lagash. Other texts refer to imported Harappan wood, but the most abundant evidence for trade contact between the regions comes from archaeological finds. Harappan merchants' seals have been found around the Persian Gulf, while the Indus Valley has likewise yielded seals of Mesopotamian origin. Harappan trade routes to the Persian Gulf have also been traced through the distribution of lapis lazuli and carnelian; finished goods fashioned from tin, copper, and marine shells; and arrowheads and jewelry of chalcedony, jasper, and flint.

The coast between the Indus and the Persian Gulf is for the most part arid and inhospitable, but archaeologists have identified a number of Harappan ports including Sutkagen Dor, about 270 miles west of the Indus delta. Others have been found around the Kathiawar Peninsula in Gujarat, where extensive research has been done at the ancient port of Lothal, about five hundred miles southeast from the Indus, and the dates of which mirror those of the Indus civilization as a whole. Lothal is about eighty kilometers southwest of Ahmedabad and about ten kilometers from the Gulf of Khambhat (Cambay), although the sea was probably closer in antiquity. Archaeological finds here include the largest collection of Indus Valley seals and sealings outside of Mohenjo Daro and Harappa, the majority of them found among the ruins of a building thought to have been a warehouse.*

This is one of several structures that have helped identify Lothal as an ancient seaport. The most controversial is a trapezoidal basin lined with burnt brick and measuring 214 by 36 meters, with a depth of 3.1 meters and a sluice gate at one end to prevent it from overflowing. According to one theory, the basin served as a sheltered dock fed by a channel from two nearby rivers. Some have maintained that the ancient rivers could not have filled it. Others argue that while such a basin would have provided shelter from the southwest monsoon, the cost of such an elaborate structure would have been difficult to justify on the basis of trade revenues. Moreover, it would be inconsistent with

---

* A seal is a stamp (such as a signet ring) inscribed with letters or a device indicating its owner; common images on seals include people, animals, boats, and geometric patterns. A sealing is the impression made by such a seal.

what is known of the region's seafaring traditions, and even today many fishermen and sailors in India and Pakistan beach their vessels on the shore without
benefit of piers, wharves, or other man-made structures. Mesopotamian writings frequently refer to docks, starting with Sargon's "dock of Akkad," but the
oldest known structure positively identified as such dates from a millennium
after that. Nonetheless, Lothal was clearly a hub of intraregional trade, and
whatever their true function, the structures there represent a major investment in time and resources that testifies to the region's prosperity.

Persian Gulf Shipbuilding: The "Magan Boat"

Magan, the second place mentioned in Sargon's inscription, refers to the lands
on either side of the Strait of Hormuz—southern Iran and eastern Oman—at
the mouth of the Persian Gulf, which Mesopotamian sources occasionally
refer to as the "Sea of Magan." The region was a source of timber, diorite, and
copper. Some texts refer to "Dilmun-copper," but since there is no copper in
Bahrain or northeast Arabia the attribution probably came about because ships
from Dilmun, or ships that called there, carried copper from Oman. Magan's
strategic significance for the rulers of Mesopotamia is borne out by references
to two military campaigns conducted by Sargon's immediate successors, one
of whom built a fleet to sail against a coalition of thirty-two Magan cities. This
is one of the earliest mentions of a fleet built for purely military purposes.

The full significance of the Magan/Oman connection was not realized until
a series of archaeological discoveries in the 1980s and 1990s at Ras al-Jinz, the
easternmost point in Oman, more than three hundred miles southeast of the
Strait of Hormuz. A site identified as a shipyard yielded the remains of more
than three hundred fragments from ancient vessels dating from 2500–2200
BCE. These consist for the most part of slabs of bitumen impressed with the
remains of reeds, reed bundles, lashings, and mats, and lashed wooden planks
to which the bitumen had been applied. Barnacles are found on the smooth
outer face of many of the slabs, which proves they were exposed to saltwater,
and some of the recycled bitumen has barnacles embedded in it. In addition to
confirming part of the written record about ancient shipbuilding in the region,
the Ras al-Jinz finds revealed details of ship construction preserved in neither
written nor pictorial records. Of particular interest is the ways in which reed
bundles were built up and assembled to form vessels capable of supporting
a sailing rig and carrying cargoes. The Ras al-Jinz hulls were constructed of
lashed reed bundles four to twelve centimeters in diameter. Once assembled,
these were covered with either woven reed mats or animal skins coated with a
bitumen amalgam. This waterproof sheathing transformed the reed float into

a displacement hull, faired the rough surface of the reed bundles, and allowed the hull to move through the water with less resistance. Bitumen also extended the life of the reeds and protected them from barnacles, teredo worms, and seaweeds that could impair the hull's efficiency or actively destroy the hull. A natural indicator of subsurface oil, bitumen is readily available in surface seeps around the Persian Gulf, and it was a standard ingredient in Mesopotamian shipbuilding. Preparation of the bitumen amalgam poses formidable technical challenges and its application is not simply a matter of smearing liquid tar over the hull. The bitumen has to adhere to the hull when wet; it must be pliant enough to maintain its integrity as the hull flexes in a seaway, but strong enough to withstand the impact of being beached repeatedly; and it has to be relatively lightweight. That the Ras al-Jinz slabs were found where they were suggests that they were being stored to be melted down and reapplied to a new vessel, a less complicated process than preparing new amalgam from scratch.

A cuneiform list from the twenty-first century BCE describes large-scale operations dedicated to the construction of both reed and wooden hulls, including more than fifteen hundred pine, palm, and tamarisk trees, eight tons of palm fiber rope, twelve thousand bundles of reeds, fish oil, "asphalt for the coating of Magan type boats," and other materials. These figures give no indication of what was needed for a single vessel, but a replica built at Sur, Oman, in 2005 provides some answers. Working from construction details provided by the bitumen slabs and a study of the 217 surviving boat models and 186 illustrations from seals or sealings of the third millennium BCE, experimental archaeologists built a succession of reed boats, starting with a 1-to-20 scale model, a five-meter-long prototype, and the twelve-meter "Magan Boat." This had a capacity of about thirty *gur* (a standard unit of measure for Mesopotamian vessels), or 7.5 tons, probably an average size for wood vessels, though near the upper limit for reed hulls. The most commonly mentioned large vessels ran about sixty *gur*, and the most capacious ships at the end of the third millennium measured three hundred *gur*, or about ninety tons.

The materials list for the modern "Magan Boat" included almost three tons of reeds, thirty kilometers of fiber rope made from date palm or goat hair (the latter is immensely strong and much easier to handle), more than a ton of timber, and two tons of bitumen mixed with chopped reeds. Wood was used for the keelson, frames, and horizontal beams that spanned the gunwales, but the hull was further strengthened by pairs of reed bundles set like frames. A woven mat lay between the bitumen and the reed bundles. The vessel was rigged with a bipod mast setting a square sail hung from a single yard, and steered with a pair of quarter rudders. The bitumen waterproof seal worked as intended, but it was virtually impossible to keep water from sloshing over the sides and

The Magan Boat, a modern interpretation of an Omani ocean carrier of the late third millennium BCE built in 2005. The A-frame mast distributes the downward pressure across the reed bundles that form the hull. The reeds are made waterproof by the application of a bitumen amalgam, the recipe for which was derived from fragments of ancient sheathing found near Ras al-Jinz, the easternmost point of Oman on the Arabian Sea. Courtesy Tom Vosmer.

as much as three tons of water was absorbed by the reeds, thereby reducing the amount of cargo and stores that could be carried. Nonetheless, sea trials proved the boat a capable sailer, easily handled and relatively fast, attaining speeds of five knots or more in a moderate breeze. With favorable winds one might make the passage from the head of the Persian Gulf to Magan in about a week, depending on the number of stops, while returning against the prevailing northwesterlies would be slower. The duration of the passage to Harappa would depend on the strength of the monsoon winds.

Maritime Trade to the End of the Babylonian Empire

The degree to which the uncertainties of long-distance sea trade affected relations between merchants and the political and religious establishment—

which were often one and the same—is difficult to gauge. Much of Mesopotamia's trade was in the hands of individual merchants, although the temples
were heavily involved and temple complexes could double as warehouses. A
collection of documents from the end of the third millennium BCE describes
the transactions of one merchant, Lu-Enlilla, who withdrew from a temple
thousands of kilograms of wood, timber, and fish, more than fifteen hundred
liters of sesame oil, garments, and hides to trade for copper in Magan. Private
investors could lend money either at a fixed rate, thereby minimizing both
their risk and their reward, or with the intent of sharing in the profits, thereby
assuming more risk if the merchant suffered losses. Mesopotamians did not
have the severe restrictions on interest later dictated by Jewish, Christian, and
Muslim law, and temples and individuals routinely charged interest rates of
20 to 33□ percent. The role of traders not dependent on the temple and state
helps explain why, when the Ur Dynasty collapsed within a quarter century
of Lu-Enlilla's time, Persian Gulf commerce continued, although Mesopotamian merchants seem to have lost much of their trade to Dilmun.

Mesopotamia regained its political cohesion during the First Dynasty of
Babylon, which spanned the nineteenth to seventeenth centuries BCE. In the
1700s BCE, Hammurabi ruled much of lower Mesopotamia and as far west
as the Amorite trading city of Mari on the upper Euphrates. (The Amorites
were a Semitic-speaking people whose spread from Arabia into Syria and
Mesopotamia around the turn of the millennium probably stimulated, or was
stimulated by, a new emphasis on east–west trade both overland and via the
Euphrates.) Hammurabi is best known for his Code of Laws, the most complete to survive from ancient Mesopotamia. Promulgated toward the end of
his reign, many of the laws have a direct bearing on merchants' relations and
interest rates, and seven touch directly on shipping. Three specify the rates
to be charged for hiring vessels of up to sixty *gur*. Others dictate the cost of
building a sixty-*gur* ship—two shekels—and guarantee boats for a year.* The
pay of sailors was fixed at six *gur* of grain per year, but sailors were liable for
any damages arising from their negligence. The law also includes a rare early
example of a "rule of the road," which in this case mandates that the master of
a vessel proceeding downstream has to steer clear of a vessel heading against
the current, and making him liable for any damages resulting from his care-
lessness.[†] One can trace the evolution of commercial law and the rights and
responsibilities of ships' officers and crew from this point forward, but few

---

* A shekel was a silver coin weighing between nine and seventeen grams. Two shekels were the
equivalent of twelve days' rent.
† Rules of the road—that is, a roadstead or narrow stretch of open water where ships ride at
anchor—were so called before the development of the automobile.

navigation rules had the force of law before the advent of steam navigation in the nineteenth century.

Sumero-Akkadian culture spread fairly evenly across Mesopotamia but political unification was difficult to achieve and harder to maintain, and even Hammurabi's success was short-lived. Babylon's imperial demise began in the reign of his son and successor, when the southern Sumerian cities began to reassert their independence. The political situation continued to deteriorate for a century (coinciding with the period of Hyksos rule in Egypt) and in 1595 BCE an invasion by the Hittites of central Anatolia overwhelmed the Babylonians. The north was absorbed into the Mitanni kingdom, which originated in Iran, while southern Mesopotamia fell to the obscure Sealand Dynasty. There was a simultaneous decline in the cohesion of the Indus civilization and the disruptions at both ends of the route led to a thousand-year hiatus in long-distance sea trade between Pakistan and India and the Persian Gulf.

From Minos to Mycenae, 2000–1100 BCE

As if to announce the reorientation of Mesopotamian trade toward the Mediterranean, the last surviving text to mention "Dilmun copper," from 1745 BCE, is also the first to mention Cypriot copper: "12 minas [360 kilograms] of refined copper of Alashiya [Cyprus] and of Dilmun." Throughout antiquity, the island of Cyprus was a major producer of copper (its modern name comes from the Greek word for copper), which is one of the two primary elements, with tin, of bronze, the most durable alloy available in the ancient Near East, where the Bronze Age lasted roughly from 3000 to 1000 BCE. Most Cypriot copper probably entered the Levant through the ports of Byblos or Ugarit, from where merchants carried it overland to the Euphrates and downstream to Mesopotamia.

One of the oldest inhabited cities in the world and the foremost Levantine port of the early Bronze Age, Byblos lies about forty kilometers north of Beirut. It has yielded more Egyptian stone work, including statuary, reliefs, and other pieces than anywhere else in the Near East. The disproportionate number of letters from Byblos found in the Egyptian diplomatic archive at Amarna sheds considerable light on the close and enduring ties between Egypt and this maritime gateway to the Near East, especially in the 1300s BCE. Yet archaeological evidence shows that by then Byblite mariners had been trading to Egypt for two thousand years. Byblos's prosperity long depended on that of Egypt, and when Mesopotamian or Egyptian pioneers developed an overland route through Canaan, the port may have been abandoned briefly. Thanks to the abundant forests in its hinterland, and Egypt's need for wood, Byblos

An oared ship and fish—perhaps intended as a figurehead—on a roiling sea decorate this Early Minoan (2700–2300 BCE) terra-cotta "pan" buried in a tomb on the Cycladic island of Syros. Though highly stylized, the elongated prow anticipates the more realistically rendered bows seen in the Thera murals 1,500 years later. Photograph by Hermann Wagner, D-DAI-ATH-NM #3701. Courtesy of the Deutsche Archäologische Institut, Athens.

reemerged as an important trading center in the early third millennium BCE, and it was likely the port through which the first recorded shipment of cedar passed en route to Egypt during the reign of Sneferu in the 2600s BCE. Five centuries later the port was hard hit by the end of Egypt's Old Kingdom, but it recovered in the second millennium. It was later a major importer of Egyptian papyrus, and the Greeks took the name of the port of Byblos for "papyrus," "book," and, ultimately, the Bible.

In about 1600 BCE, Byblos started trading to the west, especially to Cyprus and Crete, the largest Mediterranean islands east of Sicily. The cultural and material exchanges between the Levant and Crete helped shape the Minoan culture that flourished from the late third millennium through the fifteenth century BCE and left its imprint on the Mycenaeans of mainland Greece. Named for the mythical King Minos, the civilization of ancient Crete has enjoyed good press since the fifth century BCE, when both Herodotus and Thucydides depicted Minos as a conqueror of the southern Aegean. Thucydides notes that "Minos, according to tradition, was the first person to organize a navy. He controlled the greater part of what is now called the Hellenic [Aegean] Sea; he ruled over the Cyclades [Islands]. . . . And it is reasonable to suppose that he did his best to put down piracy in order to secure his own revenues."

This theory of a Minoan thalassocracy—literally, "empire of the sea"—has proved remarkably resilient, especially considering that Minos is a mythical rather than an historical character, that the period of the Minoans' greatest influence ended more than a thousand years before Herodotus and Thucydides, and that the traditions these historians preserve are oral rather than written. There is no doubt that Cretans were sailing to the shores of the eastern Mediterranean as early as the third millennium BCE. But images of a Cretan colonization of the Aegean and as high seas enforcer owe much to Thucydides' interpretation, which reflects his fellow Athenians' concerns about suppressing piracy and other threats to their trade by building the most powerful fleet in the eastern Mediterranean. The reception of his ideas today follows from modern notions of sea power and maritime hegemony as articulated by such strategists as Alfred Thayer Mahan, who promoted the development of fleets in the mold of the ubiquitous and omnipotent Royal Navy at the end of the nineteenth century, when the British Empire was at its height. Archaeology has shown Thucydides' claim of a Cretan colonization of the Cyclades to be overstated at best. The prevailing view is that Neolithic migrants moving west from Anatolia settled the islands and the Peloponnese, to which they introduced new farming techniques and crops, including olives and wine. While contact between Crete and the Cyclades is easy to see, there is little evidence of direct Minoan rule in the archipelago.

Nor did the Cretans exercise hegemony anywhere else in the Mediterranean, where their sailors constituted just one of many groups of traders. At the height of their power and influence, the Minoans traded north to the Aegean islands, west to the Greek mainland, Sicily, and Sardinia, east to Cyprus, Asia Minor, and the Levant, and south to Libya and Egypt. Egyptians of Sneferu's time acquired Cretan pottery through trade with Minoan merchants, through middlemen, or both. Tablets in the eighteenth-century BCE archives at Mari refer to merchants from Crete and Caria (in western Asia Minor) receiving a shipment of tin with the help of an interpreter from Ugarit, and Babylonian cylinder seals of the same period have been found in Crete, which they probably reached by way of Mari, Ugarit, and Cyprus. By this time, Minoan material culture was reaching its climax, with beautiful and complex palaces, villas, and towns at Knossos, Phaistos, and more than twenty other sites. Whether these were all subject to a single Cretan overlord is difficult to say. For some, the absence of city walls suggests that the people of Minoan Crete relied on their fleets for security from foreign invaders. Yet in a period when there is no evidence of any seafaring power capable of launching an overseas invasion against such a remote target as Crete, the sea would have been barrier enough even without a fleet.

Archaeological remains and written evidence of Minoan civilization reveal little about Minoan-era ships. The best source of information is a set of wall paintings excavated in the town of Akrotiri on the Cycladic island of Thera, about seventy miles north of Crete. In 1628 BCE, the island was destroyed by a volcanic eruption that seismologists estimate to be one of the largest of the past ten thousand years, and much of Akrotiri was preserved beneath layers of pumice and ash up to twenty-five meters deep. Unlike the citizens of the better known Pompeii, in southern Italy, who were smothered in the ash of Mount Vesuvius in 79 CE, the people of Akrotiri had ample warning of volcanic activity and the thirty buildings excavated thus far have yielded no human remains and very few personal belongings, indicating that the inhabitants fled the island before the eruption.

A second-story room in a building known as the West House includes two beautifully executed wall paintings. One shows a procession of seven large and four smaller vessels apparently involved in a cult festival sailing from one town to another where crowds of people are assembled. The ships have long, graceful hulls with elongated bows that rise from the water at almost a forty-five-degree angle and terminate at a point higher than the ships' masts. The sailing ships carry a single mast amidships, and one is shown with a square sail set between a yard and a boom; all are steered by a pair of quarter rudders attached to the stern quarters of the hull. In the most lavishly decorated processional ship, eight people sit beneath a canopy and garlands run from the bow and over the masthead to the stern. This and a number of the other vessels have lowered sails. The second painting, poorly preserved, shows similar vessels under oars and with a spearman standing forward, coursing through a sea surrounded by naked corpses. Not surprisingly, some have interpreted this as a battle scene, perhaps showing the repulse of an attack on the otherwise unsuspecting islanders, many of whom are shown going about their normal pursuits in the background. Others see here a fertility rite involving human sacrifice as part of a reenactment of the death by drowning of an agricultural deity performed to ensure the growing season, a reading supported by comparisons with other aspects of Minoan life.

The decline of Minoan civilization was once linked directly to the explosion of Thera, but Minoan society survived another two centuries. When the end came, it was at the hands of the Mycenaeans, to whom the Minoans had introduced writing and a host of other cultural refinements. The Mycenaeans take their name from the Peloponnesian city of Mycenae, celebrated by Homer as the home of Agamemnon, leader of the Greek armies that invested Troy in northwest Turkey for ten years. Both Mycenae and Troy were long thought to be products of the Homeric imagination until Heinrich Schliemann excavated the sites in the nineteenth century. Although he identified the rich cache of ornaments and weapons he found at Mycenae as belonging to Agamemnon, these date to the fifteenth century BCE, around the start of the Mycenaeans' occupation of Minoan Knossos but three centuries before the date traditionally assigned to the Trojan War (1183 BCE). The Mycenaeans established a trading network that encompassed the Aegean, coastal Asia Minor, Cyprus, the Levant, and Egypt and that would survive until the period of destruction and decline associated with the Sea People in the twelfth century BCE. Regional trade and exchange declined precipitously in the ensuing dark age, but the long-distance connections established and maintained by the Minoans and Mycenaeans, among others, survived in an attenuated form until their revival in the eighth century BCE.

Although Mycenaean images are often crude compared with those of their Minoan predecessors, the pictorial record of their ships is extensive. Confirming the Mycenaeans' reputation for belligerence, many decorated vases depict oared galleys with armed soldiers on an upper deck. These galleys are also rigged with a single mast setting a square sail, but rowers and sails are not generally shown in the same illustration, because the two means of propulsion were rarely used at the same time. Mycenaean hulls are generally more elongated than crescent-shaped, and their sails are loose-footed, unlike those depicted at Akrotiri. Despite the Mycenaeans' preference for celebrating their martial prowess, the archaeological record draws our attention to more peaceful pursuits at sea.

Two impressive underwater wrecks reveal a great deal about the richness and variety of the sea trade of the Mycenaeans and their Levantine contemporaries. Dated to about 1315 BCE, the Uluburun site is the most spectacular Bronze Age shipwreck found thus far—though more celebrated for the cargo rather than for the light it sheds on ancient shipbuilding. A portion of the vessel was preserved beneath the cargo—part of the keel, edge-joined planking, and fragments of a wicker bulwark—but not enough to determine the ship's dimensions. The site was identified in the 1980s by a Turkish sponge diver who came across a heap of copper ingots lying at a depth of more than forty meters off the promontory of Uluburun, near the town of Kaş. The ship probably carried around fifteen tons of freight, along with stone ballast and twenty-four stone anchors weighing a total of four tons. The bulk of the surviving cargo consisted of about ten tons of Cypriot copper ingots and a ton of tin. This discovery more than doubled the number of Bronze Age copper ingots previously found in the Near East, and it is about thirty times the quantity of copper mentioned in the earliest known order for Cypriot copper from four centuries before the ship sank. Other items include objects of Mycenaean and Cypriot manufacture, but most were of Near Eastern origin: an ivory writing tablet, a gold chalice, a faience drinking cup in the shape of a ram's head, and many pieces of jewelry. Unfinished goods included glass ingots (most of them cobalt-colored and probably from the Levant), ebony and cedar logs, unfinished hippopotamus horn and elephant ivory, ostrich eggs, amber from the Baltic, and amphorae containing the ingredients for incense and pigments. The provenance of the ship's equipment and the personal possessions of the sailors and merchants—tools, weapons, balance-pan weights, and cylinder seals—suggests that the ship was bound from the Levant for Crete or the Greek mainland.

About a century later, another small merchantman sank east of Uluburun off Cape Gelidonya, a place of strong, unpredictable currents that swirl through jagged, half-submerged rocks and that was described in antiquity as "fraught with disaster for passing vessels." Discovered in the 1950s, the Cape Gelidonya ship was the first excavated by adapting land-based archaeological techniques to an underwater site, a major advance in the investigation of submerged sites. Without a disciplined and orderly approach to the identification and removal of the remains of ships and their cargoes, divers inevitably overlook, lose, or destroy outright clues vital to a more complete understanding of the nature and conduct of maritime culture, trade, and warfare. Little of the Cape Gelidonya hull survived, but the ship likely measured between eight and ten meters long. The cargo consisted of at least a ton of unworked bronze and tin, along with bronze farm tools, weapons, and household objects. Most of these were broken and may have been scrap pieces en route to being recycled—the site also yielded a variety of metalworking tools. Amulets, balance-pan weights, and a finely carved hematite cylinder seal are among the items that likely belonged to the ship's merchant-owner. Like the Uluburun ship, the vessel was most likely sailing along the Anatolian coast en route to the Aegean. Its last port of call may have been on Cyprus, about 150 miles southeast, a major center for ancient bronze production and distribution.

The volume and diversity of the goods associated with the Uluburun and Cape Gelidonya ships make it unlikely that either was destined for one particular port or merchant, although it is possible that at least some of the prestige goods in the Uluburun ship were en route from one ruler to another, either as tribute or as part of a commercial venture. While there are many ancient references to shipments made and received on the basis of firm orders, as in the case of the cedar for Egyptian pharaohs, these ships should probably be seen as floating markets, tramping from port to port.

The Sea People and Warfare at Sea, 1200–1100 BCE

The loss of the Cape Gelidonya ships took place around the start of the Greek Dark Ages, a period of wrenching transformation throughout the eastern Mediterranean. The Egyptians blamed this upheaval on invaders they called the Sea People, a mix of tribes and other groups of uncertain origin who swept across the region in the thirteenth and twelfth centuries BCE fleeing before an overland migration of people equipped with iron tools and weapons moving southward from the Balkans and Black Sea region. By the time their force was spent, the political landscape of the eastern Mediterranean world had changed irrevocably. In Greece, Pylos and Mycenae were sacked and the ranks of the Sea People may have been swelled by Mycenaeans fleeing before them or following in their wake. The landlocked Hittite Empire of Anatolia was overthrown and countless smaller states were crippled by famine or civil war. Of the region's major powers, only Egypt remained, although the pharaoh's power no longer reached into Canaan and Syria, and his influence over Levantine ports was dramatically less than it had been.

The only contemporary sources of information about the origins of the Sea People are Egyptian, which name a total of nine distinct "countries" or groups of people. The first record of them appears in an account of an Egyptian defeat, around 1218 BCE, of a Libyan invasion supported by "northerners coming from all lands" and "the countries of the sea," five of which have been identified with areas in southwest Anatolia, the Aegean, and mainland Greece. Forty years later, Ramesses III stopped an invasion from the northeast involving some of the same people. Thanks to an account of the latter contest from a temple in Medinet Habu (Thebes), the Sea People have received the lion's share of the credit for the onset of the dark age that engulfed the region until the eighth century, but their migration was likely a symptom as much as a cause of the period's widespread economic, political, and demographic disorder.

The broader regional consequences of this upheaval are easy to gauge from the record of imperial survival and collapse, but a more intimate picture of the anxious final days of a smaller coastal state survives in a cache of letters written on clay tablets hardened in the flames of the burning city of Ugarit. Situated in the contested frontier between rival empires about ninety miles north of Byblos, Ugarit was politically subject to the Hittites in the fourteenth century BCE, but her prosperity depended largely on her role as an intermediary in the trade between Egypt, Cyprus, and the Aegean. As the dangers mounted at the start of the twelfth century BCE, Ugarit was called upon to supply troops for the defense of the Hittites fighting in western Anatolia, and of Carchemish, a Hittite stronghold on the Euphrates about two hundred kilometers from the Mediterranean. With a population of perhaps thirty-five thousand people and an economy geared to agriculture and trade rather than combat, any levy of troops was bound to be costly in terms of manpower and morale. Whether keeping these soldiers at home would have enabled Ugarit to defend itself is moot, but the surviving correspondence between the last king, Ammurapi, and the unnamed ruler of Alashiya hints at the invaders' hit-and-run tactics and the desperation of the besieged.

Writing to Ammurapi about the situation on Cyprus, the chief prefect of Alashiya reports that "twenty enemy ships even before they would reach the mountain shore have not stayed around but have quickly moved on, and where they have pitched camp we do not know. I am writing to inform and protect you." Another letter from the king of Alashiya advises Ammurapi to "make yourself as strong as possible" by mustering troops and chariots and reinforcing the city walls. Almost as an afterthought, he asks, "Now, where are your own troops and chariotry stationed? Are they not stationed with you? If not, who will deliver you from the enemy forces?" More than three millennia later, Ammurapi's reply still reeks of fear:

> My father, now enemy ships are coming and they burn down my towns with fire. They have done unseemly things in the land! My father is not aware of the fact that all the troops of my father's overlord are stationed in Hatti [central Anatolia] and that all my ships are stationed in Lukka [Lycia?]. They still have not arrived, and the country is lying [open] like that! . . . Now, the seven enemy ships that are approaching have done evil things to us. Now then, if there are any other enemy ships send me a report somehow, so that I will know.

These letters were among dozens found in the ruins of the city, which the invaders pillaged and abandoned. Many city-states suffered a similar fate, yet despite the widespread destruction survivors of the turmoil managed to maintain at least some maritime connections between the Levant and other shores of the eastern and central Mediterranean. In the first three centuries of the Iron Age that followed, these were far less robust than they had been, but they formed the basis for the Phoenician and Greek overseas expansion in the ninth and eighth centuries BCE.

Inscriptions at Medinet Habu describing Ramesses III's repulse of the Sea People present the most complete pictorial record of a Bronze Age naval engagement. The earliest reference to such a sea battle is on a stele erected at Tanis, in the Nile delta, and refers to Ramesses II's victory over a fleet of "Shardana, rebellious of heart . . . and their battle-ships in the midst of the sea," around 1280 BCE. The Shardana are depicted subsequently as fighting both for and against the Egyptians, and they were among the "northern" allies of the Libyans defeated by the Egyptians in 1218 BCE. The next naval battle in the historical record is described in slightly more detail in a letter from the last Hittite king, Suppiluliumas II, around 1210 BCE. "Against me the ships from Cyprus drew up in line three times for battle in the midst of the sea. I destroyed them, I seized the ships and in the midst of the sea I set them on fire." Whoever these Cyprus-based sailors were, their momentum was little disturbed by this setback, and Suppiluliumas goes on to write that they later landed "in multitudes." Shortly thereafter, the Hittite empire collapsed.

The record of Ramesses III's victory over the Sea People in around 1176 BCE is more substantial, although where the battle took place is a mystery. The traditional view is that it was fought somewhere in or near the Nile delta, but the Egyptians may have intercepted the enemy somewhere on the coast of Canaan, perhaps near Ashkelon. As for the enemy ships that survived the initial battle, "Those who came upon the sea, the consuming flame faced them at the Nile mouths . . . they were dragged up, surrounded and cast down upon the shore, slaughtered in heaps from head to tail." The Sea People may have had the advantage of iron weapons in land fighting, but in this battle their weapon of choice was the spear, while the Egyptians had long-range composite bows and grapnels for use at close range. This meant that the Egyptians could open fire on the enemy ships at a distance and so reduce their fighting effectiveness while remaining relatively unscathed. When the ships closed with one another, the Egyptians threw their grapnels into the enemy's masts and rigging and then backed their vessels away to capsize the Sea People's ships.

Taken together, the accounts of Suppiluliumas II and Ramesses III reveal a good deal about ship-to-ship fighting at the time. Three sorts of weapons are indicated: fire, in the accounts of Suppiluliumas and Ramesses; spears belonging to the Shardana; and bows, slings, and grapnels in the hands of the Egyptians. A fire out of control is one of the most feared and deadly calamities that can befall a ship. If one has the wind at one's back, it can be an effective means of terrifying the enemy and destroying ships, but fire is notoriously indiscriminate and despite scrupulous handling the smallest mistake or the slightest wind shift can turn it back on its user. For this reason, fire is best used at the longest possible range. There is no indication of how either the Hittites or the Egyptians employed fire, but it may have been delivered via flaming arrows. Until the end of the age of sail in the nineteenth century, most naval engagements were decided in boarding actions in which ships served as little more than floating battlefields. Before the development of the ship's gun, bows and arrows and spears could be employed when the ships were still some distance apart, but sea fights generally involved closing the range between vessels so that they lay together hull-to-hull. The use of grapnels to capsize enemy ships as shown at Medinet Habu is rare. More commonly they were employed to lash ships together so that crew sweeping onto the enemy's decks would not fall between the ships and be crushed or drowned.

Throughout the New Kingdom, the Egyptians exploited their shiphandling ability and their dominance on the coastal sea-lanes to establish an effective naval force capable of providing logistical support for long-distance campaigns both at home and abroad. They also used their maritime forces for amphibious operations, as seen in the campaigns against the Hyksos in Avaris and the Mitanni along the Euphrates. Against the Sea People they had the advantage of organization, hierarchical command, and military discipline. The enemy was probably little more than an improvised fleet cobbled together from disparate groups of raiders, well suited for attacking smaller ports and groups of merchantmen in piratical raids, but less capable of seizing larger objectives. Naval warfare between centralized states with comparable fleets, strategies, and tactics would not appear until the next millennium.

Although Ramesses III defeated the Sea People, Egypt's influence over its Asian territories eroded over the course of the twelfth century BCE. This is nowhere better illustrated than in "The Report of Wenamun," the long-suffering agent of the temple of Amon at Thebes dispatched to purchase cedar for "the great and noble riverine barge of Amon-Re" in about 1050 BCE. Wenamun's account demonstrates both the loss of Egypt's prestige and the importance of strong political and military power to safe trade. Sailing from the delta port of Tanis, Wenamun stopped at Dor, where one of his crew absconded with half a kilogram of gold and more than two kilograms of silver. When the local ruler refused to compensate him, Wenamun sailed for Tyre, where he took about three kilograms of silver from a merchant ship that probably hailed from Dor, before continuing to Byblos. Prince Tjekerbaal ordered him repeatedly to leave, but Wenamun refused. A month later, the two entered into negotiations during which Tjekerbaal reminded Wenamun that when the pharaohs of old approached his ancestors for wood, they sent gifts and payment.

Times had changed. Tjekerbaal was no longer subject to the pharaoh, as his ancestors had been, and he was under no obligation to cut wood for Wenamun. He pointed out that Egypt's trade was not even carried in Egyptian ships, as before, but in Levantine vessels. Despite Wenamun's protestations that his ship and crew were Egyptian, Tjekerbaal suggested that this was the exception rather than the rule. Most of the ships carrying Egypt's trade came from her trading partners, including twenty from Byblos and fifty from neighboring Sidon. This may have always been the case, but in the eleventh century BCE the inferiority of Egypt's fleet seemed emblematic of the pharaoh's waning prestige. Eventually, Tjekerbaal allowed Wenamun to send seven finished ship's timbers to Egypt to secure an advance with which to pay for the remainder of the wood. Shortly after Wenamun sailed for home, a storm blew his ship off course to Cyprus where, mistaken for a pirate, he was brought before the queen and pleaded his case through an interpreter. Here the manuscript stops, and of his subsequent travails we know only that he lived to tell the tale. Wenamun's misadventures reflect the growing weakness of Egyptian authority beyond its traditional borders. Yet the distress suffered by the larger states of the Near East was offset by the comparative health of the Levantine ports. Having survived the upheaval associated with the Sea People, local rulers boasted fleets considerably larger than those available in Egypt where during the reign of Ramesses III, for instance, the temple of Amon-Re had had a fleet of eighty-eight ships.

Egyptians would continue to play a role in the maritime realm of the eastern Mediterranean and the Red Sea, but the initiative passed to the Phoenicians and Greeks, who fanned out across the Mediterranean in the first episode of sustained maritime colonization of which a clear record survives, and who would also attempt to discover for themselves the secrets of the Atlantic and the Indian Oceans.

Chapter 4

Phoenicians, Greeks,
and the Mediterranean

The destruction that engulfed the Bronze Age Near East at the hands of the Sea People and other invaders was followed by a centuries-long dark age, the end of which is signaled by the rise of the Phoenician city-states of the Levant in the ninth century BCE and of Greek city-states shortly thereafter. The pace of maritime activity on the Mediterranean then quickly surpassed that of the most prosperous centuries of the previous millennium. Operating from small autonomous port cities with little or no hinterland or river networks, merchants plied ever longer sea routes and wove increasingly complex trade networks across the length and breadth of the Mediterranean. These maritime movements led to sustained two-way traffic in commodities, people, and culture, as distinct from one-way migrations or trade in prestige goods intended principally for elite consumers.

The Phoenicians and Greeks were the first people to create sea-based colonial empires, the implications of which have inspired imitators and fascinated observers down to the present. Over the course of five hundred years, Phoenician and Greek mariners founded or nurtured ports many of which still pulse with trade almost three thousand years later: Tyre and Sidon; Carthage (now a suburb of Tunis), Cádiz, and Cartagena; Piraeus, Corinth, and Byzantium (now Istanbul); and Marseille. They were the first people to build ships specifically for war and develop strategies for their use; to erect port complexes dedicated to facilitating commerce; and to systematically explore the waters beyond the Mediterranean. Our debt to the Phoenicians is immeasurable, but while they invented the alphabet upon which the Greek and Latin alphabets are based, they left virtually no writings of their own. That the Greeks had a more pronounced impact on the historical development of the ancient world arises partly from the fact that they wrote about everything; but they also expanded from a more centrally located and larger demographic base than that of the Phoenicians. In purely maritime terms, they were also the first people to articulate social distinctions between mariners and landsmen, and to perceive rigid distinctions between seafaring and continental states.

The Phoenician Mediterranean: Tyre, Carthage, and Gadir

The invasion by the Sea People brought the prosperous interregional trade of the eastern Mediterranean Bronze Age to a near standstill for about two centuries. By the start of the tenth century BCE, the territory of the Canaanites—the name by which the Phoenicians called themselves—had been reduced to an area roughly the shape of modern Lebanon. To the south lay the Israelites and Philistines in mountain and coastal Palestine, respectively, while Aramaeans occupied the region of modern Syria. Confined to a narrow stretch between the Mediterranean and the Lebanon Mountains, between Acre (Akko, Israel) in the south and the island of Aradus (Arvad, Syria), Phoenicia included some of the best natural harbors on the coast. During the crisis of the twelfth and eleventh centuries BCE, Byblos and Sidon had retained their identity, while Tyre all but vanished from the historical record. In the following century, however, their fortunes reversed as Byblos and Sidon entered a period of decline and Tyre prospered under Hiram I.

Situated on an island half a mile offshore—"at the entrance to the sea," as the prophet Ezekiel later wrote—Tyre comprised two harbors, south and north, and an agrarian settlement on the mainland. This arrangement, in which the port was the dominant town, was unusual. In Judah and Israel, most ports were considered "daughter cities," established to serve towns located a few kilometers inland, either because the coastal lands were inadequate for agriculture or because they were too exposed to raids from the sea. Thucydides describes a similar phenomenon in Greece where "Because of the wide prevalence of piracy, the ancient cities . . . were built at some distance from the sea." Despite its small size and reliance on trade, Tyre had a wealth of valuable resources and specialized manufactures at its disposal: pine and cedar for shipbuilding and export, a metalworking industry, and murex, a shellfish that produced a much prized reddish dye. As important was her strategic location near the boundaries between several wealthy states whose interests her merchants served.

For all their advantages, the Tyrians depended on imported grain, and it was with this in mind that Hiram negotiated to furnish the materials for the

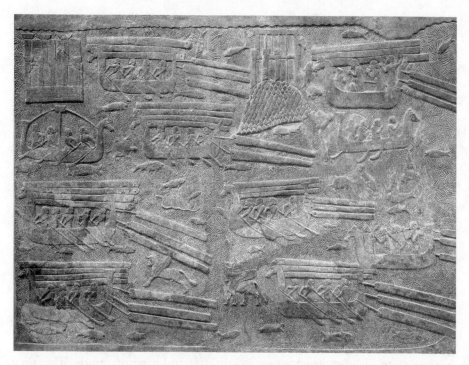

An alabaster relief from a frieze in the palace of the Assyrian king Sargon II (reigned 722–705 BCE) in Khorsabad, Iraq, showing the transportation of cedar logs on the Phoenician coast. The scene recalls descriptions from the Hebrew Bible of Hiram of Tyre's shipments of wood to Solomon for the construction of the temple at Jerusalem in the tenth century BCE. The horse-head bow design is presumably the same as that of the hippoi that Eudoxus found on his attempted circumnavigation of Africa in the fifth century BCE. Photograph by Hervé Lewandowski; courtesy of the Louvre Museum, Paris/Art Resource, New York.

construction of the house of David and the temple of Solomon in Jerusalem. Details of Hiram's work for David are scant, but the Book of Kings reveals what Tyre had to offer in the way of cedar and cypress timber, which was made up into rafts and ferried down the coast. The volume of wood and wheat exchanged was considerable. Hiram allowed Solomon to send ten thousand people a month to the Lebanon Mountains to cut and haul wood down to the sea, and in exchange received 4,500 tons of wheat and 4,600 liters of fine oil "year by year."

Twenty years later, Solomon and Hiram collaborated on a project to send a fleet to Ophir and Sheba for frankincense and myrrh, essentials in the religious rites of the day. Like the Egyptians' Punt, neither Ophir nor Sheba has been positively located, and scholarly guesses range from Sudan and Yemen to the Indus Valley. The Phoenicians supplied the ships, which were carried overland in pieces to the Gulf of Aqaba, and the fleet returned from Ophir with gold, spices, ivory, and precious stones—which recall the cargoes of the ships of Dilmun, Magan, and Meluhha—and sandalwood, which is native to southern India. In later centuries, the Yemeni ports of Aden and Mocha would be celebrated entrepôts of east–west trade, and the identification of Ophir and Sheba with Yemen is credible. These expeditions probably stopped after Solomon's death and the division of the monarchy between Israel and Judah. Jehoshaphat, king of Judah, attempted to revive the Ophir trade in the mid-800s BCE, but, according to the Hebrew Bible, God condemned his collaboration with Israel and destroyed the fleet at Aqaba. Little is heard about shipping on the Red Sea for centuries thereafter, but the Egyptians doubtless benefited from, if they did not control, such trade as there was. Although Phoenician seafarers were always in demand in foreign fleets, Levantine city-states were too small and far removed from the Red Sea to capture its trade directly.

Tyrian prosperity owed much to the rise of the Neo-Assyrian Empire (935–612 BCE). Centered on the upper Tigris city of Assur, a major crossroads of north–south and east–west traffic, Assyria was for a time the only major Near Eastern state without direct access to saltwater and maritime trade. This they remedied by conquering Babylon and opening the way to the Persian Gulf and, in the 870s BCE, by forcing the Phoenician cities of Tyre, Sidon, Byblos, and Arvad to pay tribute. Toward the end of the eighth century BCE, the Assyrians moved to control Syria and the Levant directly and they appear to have encircled but not annexed Sidon and Tyre. The price of independence was high—in 732 BCE the Tyrians paid 4,500 kilograms of gold in tribute. In exchange, however, they retained a virtual monopoly of Assyria's western trade and maintained commercial agents in Ur, Uruk, and Babylon. At the end of the century, the Levantine city-states became pawns in the struggle between Egypt and Assyria. The pharaoh encouraged an uprising by Luli of Tyre, which ended with the city's fall and Luli's flight to Cyprus in 707 BCE. Although Tyre remained nominally independent for another two hundred years, the Phoenicians continued to chafe under Assyrian domination.

The threat of conquest and demands of traders both shaped Tyre's destiny. In his oracle concerning Tyre, the prophet Isaiah refers to the "exultant city . . . whose feet carried her to settle far away." Archaeological and written evidence bears out that the Phoenicians were the first Iron Age traders to cast their commercial net across the Mediterranean. In large part this was a continuation of a Levantine seafaring tradition dating from the third millennium. The coming of the Sea People had disrupted Mediterranean trade,

A bas-relief believed to show the flight of Luli from Tyre to Cyprus in the eighth century BCE. *All the galleys are biremes (with two banks of oars) with side steering oars. Those fitted with rams and masts are warships. The presence of warriors and women (who appear larger) supports the theory that this represents a mass exodus from Tyre before the armies of the Assyrian king Sennacherib (reigned 705–681* BCE*), from whose palace at Nineveh, Iraq, this comes. From Austen Henry Layard,* The Monuments of Nineveh: From Drawings Made on the Spot . . . During a Second Expedition to Assyria *(London: Murray, 1849), plate 81.*

and long-distance routes were broken into shorter segments plied by seafarers sailing within networks of diminished scope, between Phoenicia and Cyprus, and from Cyprus to the Aegean islands, for example. However, legend holds that around 1000 BCE Phoenician voyagers established colonies at Utica in Tunisia, Gadir (Cádiz, Spain), and Lixus, on the Atlantic coast of Morocco about ninety kilometers south of Tangier. While no hard evidence of such early settlement has come to light, the speed of Tyrian westward expansion in the late ninth and eighth centuries BCE suggests a more than passing familiarity with the sea routes and marts of the central and western Mediterranean as well as Atlantic Africa and Europe, where a Phoenician presence can be firmly dated to at least the 700s BCE.

Much of Tyre's westward enterprise can be attributed to trade and commercial interests, but the first colonies of which we have any firm knowledge were founded in the wake of a struggle between sibling heirs to the throne, Elissa and Pygmalion. Following the death of her husband, Elissa (or Dido, as the Romans knew her) fled to Kition, on Cyprus, in about 820 BCE. Six or seven years later, she established Carthage—Qart-hadesht, or "new city"—on the Gulf of Tunis. Unlike other Phoenician settlements, Carthage seems to have been a colony formally modeled on the home city and, apart from Kition, the only overseas settlement in which members of the ruling family and priesthood had a direct hand. The port is strategically located on the southern shore of the seventy-mile-wide Strait of Sicily through which most east–west shipping must pass. As a result, some historians believe that from its inception Carthage was intended as a bulwark against threats to Phoenician aspirations in the central and western Mediterranean. It is difficult to ascribe the fugitive Elissa's choice of such a strategic location to simple luck, and the city's founding reinforces the idea that an older Phoenician settlement existed at nearby Utica. The story of Elissa's flight may be apocryphal, but whether Carthage was founded in response to domestic tensions in Tyre or to oversee her western trade, the colony's bonds with the home country remained strong through the middle of the sixth century BCE.

The Phoenicians' drive to the west was doubtless fueled by a search for metals, particularly Sardinian iron and Spanish tin and silver. Tyrian traders established themselves on a group of islands on the Atlantic coast of southern Spain by the 760s BCE. The archaeology of the area is complicated by the fact that the site has been occupied continuously since before the Phoenicians arrived, and silt deposits long ago joined the islands to the mainland. Called simply Gadir—the Phoenician word for fortress or citadel—it was known to the Romans as Gades, and eventually Cádiz. Gadir's primary attraction was its proximity to the Guadalquivir River and the Río Tinto, which offered access to the silver mines of the Sierra Morena and Huelva. Silver, gold, and tin had been mined in the region since the Bronze Age, but smelting operations in Huelva intensified around the seventh century BCE, probably in response to Phoenician demand for silver. As one historian has put it, "only high economic returns can explain the eccentric location of Gadir"—that is, more than two thousand miles from Tyre, beyond the Strait of Gibraltar on the shores of the

Atlantic, and without another major trading partner in the region. Certainly it is a long way to ship olive oil, perfumes and scented oils, textiles, jewelry, and the other Phoenician and Greek exports for which evidence survives, and it was not until the later eighth and early seventh centuries BCE that Phoenicians began settling along the Andalusian coast of southeast Spain, the Balearic island of Ibiza, and Malta. Phoenician shipping also reached the Portuguese coast, while Gaditeans sailed south to the rich fishing banks between Mauritania and the Canary Islands, about four days from Gadir. The most substantial of the settlements on the African coast was at Lixus, at the mouth of the Loukkos River in northern Morocco, which flowed from the western Atlas Mountains with their wealth of gold, ivory, salt, copper, and lead. Farther south, the Phoenicians reached the island of Mogador (near Essaouira, Morocco) about 380 miles from Gibraltar, where the primary activities seem to have been fishing and whaling.

Even after the bitter fighting that accompanied the fall of the Neo-Assyrians and the rise of the Neo-Babylonian Empire at the end of the seventh century, the Tyrians remained important players in the far-flung network of Near Eastern trade. Writing during his captivity in Babylon, the prophet Ezekiel described Tyre's imports at considerable length. As it had in the days of Hiram four centuries before, Israel supplied "wheat, millet, honey, oil, and balm," but virtually all the other goods he mentions are high-value or luxury items: silver, iron, tin, and lead from Tarshish (perhaps one of Tyre's overseas colonies); slaves and bronze statues from Ionia and central Anatolia; horses from Armenia; ivory and ebony brought by merchants of Rhodes; turquoise, linen, embroidered cloths, coral, and rubies from the Negev Desert; wine and wool from Syria; cassia, iron, saddlecloths, lambs, and goats from Arabia; spices, gold, and precious stones from Yemen and Africa; and so on. Ezekiel also describes the diverse sources on which the Tyrians drew to build and man their fleets, gathering cedar, fir, and oak from the Lebanon and Anti-Lebanon Mountains, Cyprus pine, and linen sailcloth from Egypt, while her crews and shipwrights came from Sidon, Arvad, and Byblos. In short, the web of Tyrian enterprise embraced nearly the entire Near East and Mediterranean.

For all their enterprise, Phoenicians did not have a monopoly of Mediterranean trade. The most important evidence of other merchants, including Greeks and possibly Cypriots, comes from Al-Mina, a neutral trading center at the mouth of the Orontes River just north of the modern Syro-Turkish border. The port, which may have been little more than a landing beach, had been overrun in the twelfth century BCE but was revived later by Phoenicians. Many believe that Al-Mina was the first Levantine port frequented by Greeks and thus the point from which a range of oriental influences such as metalworking techniques, religious ideas, literature, and writing infiltrated the Greek world. By 800 BCE, the date of the earliest Greek pottery found there, it seems to have been a rendezvous for Greek merchants, many of them from the island of Euboea, "famed for its ships" and the launching pad of the first wave of overseas expansion from Iron Age Greece.

Homer and Greek Maritime Expansion, Eighth Century BCE

The oldest image of a ship from post-Mycenaean Greece is on a late-ninth-century BCE jar found on Euboea. While the Phoenicians were the preeminent seafarers of the time, such evidence suggests the involvement of sailors from Euboea in Mediterranean trade. Perhaps more convincing is the sudden diffusion of a Greek alphabet modeled on a Phoenician original. Just as some of the earliest Phoenician writings outside the Levant have been found along their trade routes—in Cyprus and Crete from the tenth century, and Sicily and Sardinia from the ninth—two of the oldest known specimens of Greek writing come not from the Greek mainland or islands but from areas visited by Euboean merchants in southern Italy. Thus the distribution of the alphabet—the last word in low-volume, high-value cargo and the most transformative agent of change in the ancient Greek world—must be credited to ninth-century Euboean merchants frequenting ports across the eastern Mediterranean.

The inscription on a drinking cup found at a Euboean entrepôt on the island of Pithecoussae (Ischia) in the Bay of Naples and dated to about 775 BCE has been translated: "Nestor had a fine drinking cup, but anyone who drinks from this cup will soon be seized with desire for fair-crowned Aphrodite." This is of interest not only because of its antiquity, but because it parallels or alludes to Homer's description of Nestor's drinking cup in the *Iliad*. Several Greek cities claimed Homer for their own, most of them in Ionia in Asia Minor, yet textual and linguistic analysis of the *Iliad* and *Odyssey* suggests that he was from Euboea and that he lived in the early 700s BCE. The background to his epics is the Trojan War fought at Troy (Ilium) in modern Turkey in the mid-twelfth century BCE during the period of widespread upheaval that convulsed the palace economies of the Mycenaeans, the Hittites, and the Levant. As a result, the poems combine anachronistic survivals from the more prosperous Mycenaean age with details of daily life that reflect the reality of Homer's eighth-century audience, one just emerging from several centuries of declining population, technological regression, and relative insularity.

Homer's depiction of Phoenicians, whom the Greeks view with a mixture of envy and mistrust, is especially relevant for understanding the maritime dynamic of the age. While the Euboeans may have been striking out on their own at this point, the Phoenicians had been responsible for maintaining and renewing the post-Mycenaean trade between the Levant and Greece, and for introducing Greek traders to lands farther west. Homer's portrayals of Phoenicians could reflect resentment of their success or a nascent struggle to wrest control of local trade from non-Greeks. The prophet Isaiah, Homer's near contemporary, may have written of Tyre, "whose merchants were princes, whose traders were the honoured ones of the earth," but on the Aegean frontier the Phoenicians could be pretty tough customers not above raiding for slaves. When Odysseus returns to Ithaca and swaps stories with his old retainer Eumaeus, he tells how he spent seven years in Egypt, "amassing a fortune" before a Phoenician—"a scoundrel, swindler, an old hand at lies / who'd already done the world a lot of damage"—enlisted his help to "ship a cargo there for sale / but in fact he'd sell *me* there and make a killing!" Eumaeus counters with a story of how as a child he was kidnapped by Phoenicians and escaped from them while anchored off Ithaca. Such piratical raiding for slaves was not limited to the Phoenicians, and even Eumaeus, poor swineherd that he is, owns a slave whom he "purchased for himself . . . bought him from Taphians, bartered his own goods." Indeed, according to Thucydides, piracy, "so far from being regarded as disgraceful, was considered quite honorable" in archaic Greece.

Although the *Iliad* focuses chiefly on the land campaign at Troy, the poem reveals a considerable amount about ships and shiphandling in Homer's day. Large ships were often rowed, the crews sitting on benches that spanned the open hulls—hollow ships, Homer calls them—and in general ships were distinguished only by the number of rowers they carried. Homer writes of twenty-, fifty- and hundred-oared ships, and images on vases of the twelfth to eighth centuries BCE depict vessels that fit his descriptions. The number of oars corresponds roughly to the number of total crew, although additional hands could also be carried; the Boeotian contingent included fifty ships with 120 men each. This we know from Homer's "catalogue of ships," which enumerates the captains and crew (by town or region) of the 1,186 Greek ships at Troy. Yet the epics include neither ship-to-ship encounters nor fleet engagements, because the vessels at Troy were essentially troop transports propelled alternately by sails and oars. Homer describes the actions of a crew as their ship enters a harbor:

> they furled and stowed the sail in the black ship,
> they lowered the mast by the forestays smoothly,

> quickly let it down on the forked mast-crutch
> and rowed her into a mooring under oars.
> Out went the bow-stones [anchors]—cables fast astern—
> and the crew themselves climbed out in the breaking surf.

The landing here is a brief one in a sheltered bay, but when weather threatened or for longer stays ships were drawn onto the beach and shored up with timbers or stones.

Despite the great number of large ships at Troy, most vessels of the age were small, required only a handful of crew, and depended more on sails (most carried only one) than oars for propulsion, not unlike one that features in the earliest account of shipbuilding in Greek literature. When the *Odyssey* begins, Homer's hero is a virtual prisoner on Calypso's isle and everyone in his crew is dead. With Athena's help, Odysseus builds himself a small ship, felling and squaring the trees for planking, then boring holes through the planks before "knocking them home together, locked with pegs and joints"—that is, mortise-and-tenon joinery characteristic of ancient Mediterranean practice. Whether the planks would have been fastened with mortise-and-tenon joinery, sewn, or both, is unverifiable. With the outer shell of the hull complete, Odysseus inserts close-set frames to stiffen the hull and rigs a mast supported by forestays and a backstay, with a single yard fixed at the top from which is set a single square sail. The ship is turned by a steering oar or quarter rudder.

Homer's account of how Odysseus sailed from Calypso's isle for seventeen days and nights offers a brief but telling glimpse of the sort of celestial observation required of navigators in this early period. Racing across the night sea, Odysseus maintains his course by reference to the Pleiades, Boötes, and especially Ursa Major: "Hers were the stars the lustrous goddess told him / to keep hard to port as he cut across the sea." With their low freeboard and lack of decking, Greek vessels of this period were exposed to the elements and sailors preferred to land at night if they could. But days-long offshore voyages were by no means exceptional.

Since antiquity, commentators have made valiant efforts to match Odysseus's itinerary with real landmarks in the Mediterranean. One difficulty is Homer's seductive if indiscriminate mixing of real places and place names—Troy, Athens, and Sidon—with places invented, otherwise unknown, or identified only by their monstrous inhabitants—the Lotus Eaters, Cyclops, or Scylla and Charybdis. The matter is further complicated because Homer draws on the geography of earlier stories such as Jason and the Argo (which he describes as "sung by the world," that is, already well known), the action of which takes place in the Black Sea, and on Near Eastern antecedents such as the Epic of Gilgamesh, but transposes them to the west. This reorientation makes sense from an Odyssean perspective because Ithaca is off the west coast of Greece. It is also consistent with the new orientation of Homer's Euboean audience, which included sea traders who had been out west and returned with their appraisals, frank or embellished, of the new lands seen and people encountered.

Among the first places settled by the Euboean pioneers of westward expansion was Pithecoussae, where colonists from the town of Chalcis focused on the iron trade, importing ore from the Etruscan island of Elba. Pithecoussae was not an exclusively Greek enclave, and Phoenicians comprised roughly 15 percent of the population. By about 740 BCE, relations between the colonists and the Etruscans were friendly enough for the Greeks to settle on the mainland at Cumae (near Naples). Other settlements soon followed, notably at Rhegium (Reggio Calabria) and Taras (Taranto) in southern Italy, and on Sicily. These colonies, whose founders hailed from different cities, lay along the sea road between Greece and Etruria rather than in the western Mediterranean, which was within the Phoenician sphere of influence. (Greeks and Phoenicians occupied Sicily's eastern and southern coasts, respectively.)

At the end of the eighth century BCE, decades of war had exhausted the Euboean cities of Chalcis and Eretria and the mantle of Greek expansion passed to a new generation of city-states, notably Corinth, on the isthmus that joins the Peloponnese to northern Greece. To avoid sailing around the Peloponnese, many traders frequently used the isthmus as a shortcut, moving their cargoes and often their ships overland from the Saronic Gulf (or Gulf of Aegina) to the Gulf of Corinth. To facilitate this, the Corinthian tyrant Periander built a six-kilometer-long ship track, or *diolkos*, across the isthmus. This was probably an improvement on a preexisting path, and it remained in use for more than a millennium; a ninth-century CE Byzantine admiral hauled a hundred war galleys over it en route to lift a Muslim siege of Ragusa. The *diolkos* was, in effect, an alternative to a canal that Periander had contemplated, the Roman emperor Nero attempted in the first century CE, and which was finally cut in 1893.

Beyond the Mediterranean, Seventh–Fifth Centuries BCE

Seafarers of the ancient Mediterranean were by no means confined to that sea. The Phoenicians had long since exited the Strait of Gibraltar to settle Atlantic ports from Lisbon to Lixus, and there are several credible if distorted reports of voyages and attempted voyages around Africa and to northwest

Europe. Unlike the Phoenicians, who expanded only to the west, the Greeks also turned north into the Black Sea, possibly as a last resort; they initially knew the Black Sea as the Pontos Axeinos ("Unfriendly" or "Inhospitable" Sea), but later dubbed it Euxeinos ("Friendly"). The Black Sea extends about 290 nautical miles from north to south and 540 miles from east to west. To the south and east, the coast rises quickly into the mountains of northern Greece, Turkey, and Georgia, while the north and west are bounded by the flat steppe and broad river plains of Russia, Ukraine, Romania, and Bulgaria, and the Volga, Don, Dnieper, and Danube Rivers provide channels of communication with northern and eastern Europe.

At some point around 700 BCE, Anatolia was thrown into turmoil by tribes native to the shores of the Black Sea who sacked the Lydian capital of Sardis in 652 BCE and attacked a number of Ionian Greek cities. Hard-pressed as they were, Ionian Greeks looked abroad for secure places to resettle. Various Ionian cities had long been interested in the northern Aegean, the Hellespont, and the Sea of Marmara, but the people of Miletus were the first to establish a permanent settlement on the Black Sea in the seventh century BCE, on the island of Berezan in the Dnieper-Bug estuary in what is now Ukraine. Since antiquity, the assumption has been that the impetus for this wave of colonization was a quest for grain and metals, including gold. According to the first-century CE geographer Strabo, there was gold in Colchis (modern Georgia), and the story of Jason and the Golden Fleece was based on the Colchians' practice of using sheep's wool to strain gold from the waters of the Phasis River, a view repeated by many scholars and an aspect of Georgian popular culture today. In fact, gold is not found in Colchis. Greek goldsmiths did not reach there until three centuries after the Milesians established themselves in Berezan. When they did they worked with imported gold, and their handiwork was intended probably as tribute to local rulers in exchange for the right to settle on the coast. The Milesians established seventeen Black Sea colonies that became important centers of trade in their own right. Olbia, on the mainland near Berezan, was close to central Europe; the harbor at Theodosia (Feodosiya, Ukraine) was said to have room for a hundred ships; and Panticapaeum (Kerch) was on the Sea of Azov near the Crimean granaries that accounted for the bulk of Milesian trade with Greece, especially Athens, for three hundred years. In exchange for Black Sea goods, the Aegean cities exported finished bronze goods, pottery, wine, and olive oil.

Greeks also migrated to North Africa, though in modest numbers. Population pressures compelled colonists from Thera to establish Cyrene, near Benghazi, Libya, around 630 BCE. Cyrene grew so strong that it was invaded by the Egyptians, whose defeat led to a civil war that the pharaoh lost, despite having at his command thirty thousand Carian and Ionian Greek mercenaries. These had been recruited first during the seventh century, and in 620 BCE the pharaoh Psammetichus settled them at Naukratis near his capital, Saïs, in the Nile delta. Naukratis became a major grain port, but as always intangibles were also in circulation. The most distinctive of these were Egyptian notions of religious architecture, temple complexes, and statuary, the influence of which animated Greek practice starting in the early 500s BCE.

The Egyptians remained as dependent on the sea as ever, and Herodotus gives accounts of three maritime initiatives undertaken by Psammetichus's successor, Necho II: the digging of a canal between the Nile and the Red Sea, the establishment of a fleet on the Red Sea, and an effort to circumnavigate Africa. The canal was intended to facilitate trade between the Red Sea and the Nile (not the Mediterranean), but it was only completed during the reign of the Persian Darius I a century later. Necho halted the project because of "an oracle which warned him that his labour was all for the advantage of the 'barbarian' "—that is, non-Egyptians—and by that point the project had cost the lives of 120,000 laborers. Herodotus continues: "He then turned his attention to war; he had triremes built, some on the Mediterranean coast, others on the Arabian gulf [Red Sea], where the docks are still to be seen, and made use of his new fleets as occasion arose." Necho probably sought to defend Red Sea shipping against attacks by pirates. Whether the vessels were built and manned by Greeks, Phoenicians, or Egyptians is unknown, but Greek crews and shipwrights were doubtless available at Naukratis. There was ample precedent for Tyrian collaboration in Red Sea ventures, and the antipathy of Phoenician merchants to their Assyrian and Babylonian neighbors may have convinced many to seek their fortunes there, as their ancestors had.

Herodotus has been accused of gullibility and worse, especially with respect to his account of the circumnavigation of Africa ordered by Necho. But he was a keen observer and faithful recorder who logged thousands of miles traveling around the Black Sea and Aegean, in Mesopotamia, the Levant and Egypt, mainland Greece and Italy. A native of the bustling Carian seaport of Halicarnassus (Bodrum, Turkey) in southwest Anatolia, he spent considerable time at sea and was fully aware of what ships and seamen of his day could do. According to Herodotus, the voyage around Africa took three years during which the sailors stopped each fall to plant crops for the following year. He also tells, in some disbelief, how in the course of their voyage from east to west, the sailors had the sun on their right.

The Phoenicians sailed from the Red Sea into the Southern [Indian] Ocean, and every autumn put in where they were on the Libyan [African] coast, sowed a patch of ground, and waited for next year's harvest. Then, having got in their grain, they put to sea again, and after two full years rounded the Pillars of Hercules [Strait of Gibraltar] in the course of the third, and returned to Egypt. These men made a statement which I do not myself believe, though others may, to the effect that as they sailed on a westerly course round the southern end of Libya, they had the sun on their right—to northward of them.

This last detail lends credence to the story, for when sailing east to west along the southern coast of Africa, the sun is to the right—that is, the north. Although many have considered Herodotus's account to be the product of a fecund imagination, the fact that it would take more than two thousand years for another such passage to be completed does not put it beyond the realm of possibility in antiquity. Even allowing for two harvest seasons of four months each, a three-year voyage around Africa—about sixteen thousand nautical miles—required an advance of no more than twenty miles per day. Herodotus follows this story with one about a failed circumnavigation of Africa in the fifth century BCE. Sentenced to death for rape, a cousin of Persia's king Xerxes named Sataspes was offered a reprieve if he would sail counterclockwise around Africa—from Egypt, through the Pillars of Hercules, and then south. Sataspes sailed along Africa's Atlantic coast for several months but was forced to turn back because "his ship was brought to a standstill and was unable to make headway." On such scant details, it is impossible to know how far he might have sailed, but contrary currents and winds in the Gulf of Guinea would have impeded the square-sailed vessels of antiquity. As a Persian noble, Sataspes almost certainly lacked the requisite experience to contemplate, much less complete, such a voyage. Whatever excuses Sataspes may have offered for his failure, Xerxes was unmoved and had his cousin impaled.

Other sources report similar undertakings. Shortly before the time of Sataspes, a Carthaginian merchant named Hanno sailed south of Mogador perhaps as far as Cape Juby, Mauritania (27°58′N), possibly to Cerne Island (16°45′N), off the coast of Senegal, or maybe even to the equatorial coast of Cameroon in the Gulf of Guinea. A sixth-century BCE *periplus* (mariner's guide) from Massilia (Marseille) suggests that some sailors reached Finisterre in northwest Spain, and it refers also to Albion, or England. The fifth-century BCE sailor Himilco took four months on a voyage north of Gibraltar that may have taken him as far as Brittany or southern England, and in the fourth century BCE a Massilian Greek named Pytheas explored the Bay of Biscay, the British Isles, and perhaps unidentified lands farther north, a voyage discussed below in Chapter 9. Most Mediterranean sailors, however, remained in their home sea—"like frogs round a pond," in Plato's phrase—perfecting their trades, their navigational skills, and, above all, their ships.

The Trireme

Archaeological finds of merchant ships from 1000 to 400 BCE are rare, and while the remains of their cargoes have yielded valuable clues about trade and traders, most of the hulls have disappeared and what survives adds little to our understanding of shipbuilding techniques. Although no warships have survived, these were the largest and most complex—and are today the most intensely studied—vessels of the early first millennium BCE. The Phoenicians and Greeks were the first people to make a hard distinction between vessels intended for trade and those built for combat. The idea of using ships to disable other ships rather than as simple troop carriers to be turned into floating platforms for hand-to-hand combat came to the fore around the ninth century BCE, the date of the earliest pictorial evidence of the ship's ram. This may have originated as a forward extension of the keel. In its more developed form it was capped with a heavy bronze fitting, thereby creating what was in essence a massive torpedo of great strength, speed, and hitting power, and designed to punch holes in enemy ships. The only surviving example of a ram itself, found on the Israeli coast near Athlit and dating from the second century BCE, measures 2.25 meters long and was fitted to an armature of cedar, elm, and pine. To support the ram—the one from Athlit weighs 465 kilograms—and prevent the ramming ship from being shattered by the impact of driving into other vessels, ships' hulls had to be heavily constructed.

The largest ships of this early period were penteconters, so called because they carried fifty oarsmen. A penteconter with one bank of rowers would measure twenty meters or longer, which would make for a vessel that was heavy, difficult to maneuver or defend, and an unnecessarily large target. So it is not surprising that the same period saw the development of the first two-banked ships—biremes—which carried the same number of oarsmen seated on two levels in a hull little more than half as long. These stronger, more compact ships could support a raised deck for infantry, archers, and spearmen, which gave them a further offensive capability while keeping the rowers protected and out of the way. For ordinary cruising, oarsmen probably rowed from the upper deck, while the lower position was used only in battle. Eighth-century BCE illustrations show ships with rowers on two levels, but the first true biremes are depicted on reliefs from Nineveh showing Luli of Tyre's flight to Cyprus. These show two banks of rowers; the lower oars protrude through ports cut in the hull (leather sleeves keep out the water), while the upper oars are on the gunwale level. Rather than seating the oarsmen directly on top of each other, the benches are staggered, to keep the ship's center of gravity low.

A natural extension of the bireme, the trireme evolved over the course of the seventh century BCE and was created by the addition of a third bank of oarsmen. (The word "trireme" comes from the Late Latin, meaning "three-oared." Both Greek and Roman sailors used the Greek term *trieres*, meaning "three-fitted.") The most common warships of this period were triaconters, "thirty-oared," and penteconters, or fifties; sixth-century BCE illustrations show both single- and double-banked triaconters and penteconters. Triremes, on the other hand, were vessels with a more or less standard number of oarsmen who sat in a fixed configuration: twenty-seven oarsmen per side on the lowest and middle banks (thalamians and zygians, respectively) and thirty-one thranites per side on the upper bank, for a total of 170. As in biremes, the rowers were staggered, the zygians just above and forward of the thalamians, the thranites just above and forward of the zygians. To compensate for their height above the water—about 1.5 meters as opposed to half a meter for the thalamians—the thranite oars rested on an outrigger that gave the rowers greater leverage.

At Athens, the wealthiest citizens served as trierarchs, responsible for fit-ting out triremes and paying their crew on behalf of the state. While the title means "trireme captain," if the trierarch lacked naval experience, operational control was left to a professional. In addition to the rowers, triremes carried people to keep time with flutes and drums, lookouts, boatswains, and helms-men, and a contingent of infantry, archers, and spearmen. The number of the latter differed depending on the manpower available and the preferred tactics. At the battle of Salamis in 480 BCE, Athenian ships carried about ten marines, while the Persians carried thirty. The low number of Athenian marines may reflect the enormous drain on manpower required to provide thirty-four thousand oarsmen for the fleet, many of them recruited from their allies. The Athenians later widened the upper decks of their triremes to accommodate more marines, a development that also allowed for protective screens to be fitted around the thalamians.

Trireme fleets sailed either in line-ahead formation (that is, aligned bow to stern), or line-abreast (side-by-side), the former being standard for cruising, the latter for going into battle under oars. Although triremes carried a sailing rig (two masts by the fifth century BCE), sails were probably not used when the vessel was being rowed because if the wind was coming from anywhere but dead astern, the vessel would heel too much for effective rowing. Ships could reach impressive speeds under oars alone. Thucydides records one non-stop passage from Piraeus to Mytilene that a trireme made in little more than twenty-four hours, about 7.5 knots, and Xenophon describes the 129-mile run from Byzantium to Heraclea on the Black Sea being covered at an average speed of about seven knots. A replica trireme called the *Olympias* attained sprint speeds of seven knots in its first season. (Triremes were as much as 30 percent faster than penteconters, which remained the standard warship for smaller city-states lacking the resources to build or man larger vessels.)

Practice was essential to perfect the highly refined tactics of trireme warfare, which required coordinating the actions of not only the oarsmen within each ship, but also the actions of different ships. As a defensive measure, ships could maneuver themselves into a circle with their rams pointing outward, against which the best offense would be to circle around the group—a maneuver called a *periplous*—before turning into the enemy ships. Another form of *periplous* involved a ship's wheeling around on a pursuing attacker to strike it from astern or abeam. A distinct maneuver was the *diekplous*, "sailing through and out," in which ships in a line-abreast formation rowed through the enemy line before coming about to strike the ships from astern, the most vulnerable part of a trireme.

As in any age, naval power in classical antiquity depended on vast reserves of natural and human resources as well as a rationale for deploying these at sea. Maintaining a navy required an enormous civic commitment and the statesman Pericles exaggerated only slightly when, at the outset of the Peloponnesian War in 460 BCE, he reminded the Athenians that "Seamanship, just like anything else, is an art. It is not something that can be picked up and studied in one's spare time; indeed, it allows one no spare time for anything else." This the Athenians well knew. On the eve of the second Persian invasion of Greece twenty years before, they had the money, matériel, and motive to build the most powerful and best trained fleet in the eastern Mediterranean. The navies of Syracuse and Carthage were possibly equal to or even larger than theirs, and while the Persian Empire might dwarf Athens and its allies, its ships were drafted from the ranks of disparate subjects commanded by alien officers. This is not to suggest that the outcome of the Persian invasion was never in doubt, for it certainly was, and the Greek victory was due to a combination of scrappy politicking, strategic overreach by the Persians, and a tactical gambit that could have as easily ended in failure as in success.

The Greco-Persian Wars

In 559 BCE, the Neo-Babylonian Empire was laid low by Cyrus the Great, founder of the Achaemenid Dynasty (550–330 BCE), which had arisen among the Persis, a tribe of southwest Iran and from which Persia took its name. Ten years later Cyrus was king of the Medes of northern Iran and by 525 BCE he had conquered Egypt and Lydia with its Ionian Greek city-states. The Ionians accepted Persian rule until 499 BCE, when Cyrus's successor, Darius, mounted an expedition to take Naxos, largest of the Cycladic Islands, about halfway between Ionia and the Peloponnese. Miletus rallied the other Ionian city-states to revolt against Persian rule, but appeals to mainland Greeks garnered a less than enthusiastic response. Sparta, most powerful of the city-states, sent a single trireme to investigate. Athens and Eretria were the only cities to offer substantive help, sending twenty and five ships, respectively, the sailing of which was, in Herodotus's pithy summation, "the beginning of evils for Greeks and barbarians."

After crossing the Aegean, the Athenians marched to Sardis, which they burned before beating a hasty retreat. With only 353 triremes between them, the Ionians were no match for Persia's fleet of 600 Phoenician, Egyptian, and Cappadocian triremes that attacked Miletus in 494 BCE. The few Ionian ships that had not abandoned the cause were destroyed or captured in a battle at the nearby island of Lade that effectively ended the Ionian Revolt. The Persians continued mopping-up operations around the Hellespont and captured a number of Greek cities on either side of the strait. Despite this success, Darius swore to punish the Athenians for the destruction of Sardis and "commanded one of his servants to repeat to him the words, 'Master, remember the Athenians,' three times, whenever he sat down to dinner." In 491 BCE, the Persians launched their first invasion of Greece under Darius's son-in-law, Mardonius. Ferrying his troops across the Hellespont, Mardonius turned south intent on taking Eretria and Athens. After landing the army in Europe, the Persian fleet sailed south along the coast as far as the forbidding promontory of the Athos (Acte) peninsula where a gale sank three hundred ships and drowned twenty thousand sailors. The Persians also suffered military setbacks in Thrace, and while they eventually got the upper hand, Mardonius elected to return home.

Had they pursued their original objective, the Persians would have found little in the way of organized resistance. Athens and Aegina, perennial rivals, had been at war for fifteen years and the Aeginetans had recently defeated a fleet of Athenian and Corinthian ships. It was against this backdrop that Darius mounted a second expedition. Herodotus offers somewhat more detail about the composition of the Persians' "naval contingent," which included "all the ships and men which the various subject communities had been ordered to supply—including the horse-transports which Darius had requisitioned from his tributary states the year before. The horses were embarked in the transports, the troops in the ships of war, and, six hundred triremes strong, they sailed to Ionia." This time, the Persians sailed straight across the Aegean, "presumably because the commanders dreaded the passage around Athos." But there were military and political advantages, too. After subjugating Naxos, the Persians landed on Euboea in preparation for an attack on Attica. There, on the plain of Marathon forty-two kilometers from Athens, the Athenians and Plataeans threw back the invaders and seized seven of their ships. The Persians regrouped and attempted to attack Athens by sea, but by the time their ships stood off the beaches of Phaleron, which served as Athens's port, the Athenian army had returned overland to oppose them and the Persians departed.

Darius plotted a new invasion of Greece, but a revolt in Egypt and a dispute over the order of succession (settled in favor of his son Xerxes) forced its postponement. After Xerxes quelled the Egyptian revolt, his advisors—including Athenian exiles living in the imperial capital at Susa—urged him to renew the war with Athens. Ignoring his uncle, Artabanus, who argued that the war faction was intentionally underestimating the Greeks' ability and resolve, Xerxes prepared an invasion force of 1,207 triremes and 1,800 transports. As before, the Persians left most of the naval operations to the Phoenicians, Egyptians, and Ionian and mainland Greeks who preferred an alliance with the most powerful empire in the world to fighting alongside a handful of their squabbling cousins. It is estimated that as many Greeks fought for as against the Persians.

The size of the fleet alone easily justified Artabanus's concern that Persia's most powerful enemies were not the Greeks but the sea and the land: "So far as I know there is not a harbour anywhere big enough to receive this fleet of ours and give it protection in the event of storms: and indeed there would have to be not merely one such harbour, but many—all along the coast by which you will sail. But there is not a single one." Artabanus must have been well versed in the extensive logistical preparations then under way, which included the forward deployment of provisions, warhorses, and pack animals, and two remarkable feats of engineering. The first was spanning the Hellespont with two bridges of ships (completed in May 480 BCE) so that the army could walk from Asia to Europe. Because the current can run at four knots or more, throwing a bridge of ships across the Hellespont is a considerable undertaking, but there was nothing novel in the idea. Darius had bridged both the Hellespont and the Danube during a campaign against the Scythians in 512 BCE. Xerxes' bridges consisted of triremes and penteconters anchored in the Hellespont— according to Herodotus, the northern, upstream span comprised 360 and the southern span 314 penteconters and triremes—and joined by two flax and four papyrus cables that ran from shore to shore. When this framework was ready, planks were laid from ship to ship and the sides were built up to keep the horses and pack animals from panicking at the sight of the water.

Equally ambitious was digging a canal across the Athos peninsula to avoid a repeat of the disaster of 491 BCE. Although there were doubts about the accuracy of Herodotus's account even in antiquity, excavations in the 1990s revealed a trench 2.5 kilometers long and about 30 meters wide, "broad enough for two triremes to be rowed abreast." Herodotus disdained the project, not because the Persians were seeking to avoid the perils of the sea, but because it was a demonstration of Xerxes' ostentation: "he wanted to show his power and to leave something to be remembered by. There would have been no difficulty at all," Herodotus continues, "in getting the ships hauled across the isthmus on land," as was done on the Isthmus of Corinth.

In the meantime, the Athenians had not been idle. Following Marathon, there had been a stark division between the hoplites (soldiers of the landed class), who took credit, justly, for the victory, and those who favored a naval solution. The staunchest advocate of the latter was Themistocles, a veteran of Marathon who nonetheless argued that the best defense would be to abandon Athens and seek refuge in the newly developed harbor of Piraeus and a powerful navy. Preparation for the defense of Piraeus proceeded, but there were no surplus funds for a fleet until a rich vein of silver was discovered at the nearby Laurion mines. Although the Greeks were aware of Xerxes' preparations for a new invasion, Themistocles argued for a fleet as a defense against not Persia but Aegina, with which Athens was again at war. As Herodotus put it, "The outbreak of this war [with Aegina] at that moment saved Greece by forcing Athens to become a maritime power." Under the program pushed through by Themistocles and the navalists, the Athenians launched six to eight triremes per month over the next three years.

Salamis, 480 BCE

By coincidence, the year before the second Persian invasion, the oracle of Delphi pronounced that Athens's best hope of defense lay in her "wooden walls," and that "Divine Salamis . . . will bring death to women's sons." When the meaning of these utterances was debated at Athens, Themistocles insisted that the "wooden walls" referred not to the wooden palisade around the Acropolis (the most obvious interpretation), but to Athens's triremes, and that the reference to "divine" Salamis, the large island just south of Attica, was auspicious for the Greeks. Themistocles' argument won the day and the Athenians evacuated their women and children to the Peloponnese and the older men and movable property to Salamis. The men of Athens and their allies, including Sparta, Corinth, and even Aegina, were assigned to ships, half of which sailed to Cape Artemisium at the northern end of Euboea. Themistocles argued for this forward deployment to forestall the Persian fleet's passage down the coast and prevent its linking up with the army, which he hoped the Spartans could stall at the pass of Thermopylae about sixty-five kilometers west of Artemisium. A pair of mid-August storms sank about a third of Xerxes' fleet. Two battles were fought, a skirmish initiated by Themistocles to gauge the Persians' ability and resolve, and a Persian attack at Artemisium. The latter engagement was violent—half the Athenian ships sustained damage—though inconclusive, but when Themistocles learned that the three hundred Spartans had been annihilated at Thermopylae, he ordered the Greeks back to Salamis. As the Persians moved south, the Spartans voted to abandon Attica and Salamis in order to concentrate their defense of the Peloponnese on the Isthmus of Corinth. Themistocles pointed out that in the open waters of the Saronic Gulf, the larger Persian fleet's freedom of maneuver would give the enemy a pronounced advantage. He also announced that if the Peloponnesians refused to fight at Salamis, the Athenians would take their two hundred ships, embark their families, and sail to a colony in Italy, leaving the others to fend for themselves.

The Strait of Salamis is a long irregular channel, the eastern approaches to which are guarded by the island of Psyttaleia. The strait narrows quickly to about half a mile before opening into the Bay of Eleusis between Salamis and the mainland. The S-shaped Megarian Channel to the west is narrower still. It was to the Persians' advantage to draw the Greeks into open water, but it was not in Xerxes' interest to prolong his expedition any longer than necessary and all but one of his advisors argued for an immediate attack. The dissenter was the tyrant of Halicarnassus, Artemisia, whose blunt advice was to exercise patience. She reasoned that, lacking supplies and fearing an attack on the Peloponnese, the Greek coalition would dissolve quickly. She also noted the Persian army's logistical reliance on the navy and with considerable prescience counseled that "If . . . you rush into a naval action, my fear is that the defeat of your fleet may involve the army too." Xerxes esteemed Artemisia's candor, but ignored her advice.

According to Herodotus and Aeschylus—a veteran of the battle, which is the subject of his oldest extant play, *The Persians*—the night before the battle a Greek messenger told the Persians that some of the Greeks were planning to escape via the Megarian Channel. The bulk of the Persian fleet was positioned in the eastern approaches around Psyttaleia, and to prevent a breakout a squadron was sent to guard the channel. As the sun rose on the morning of September 25, Xerxes and his retinue overlooked the Strait of Salamis from the mainland. When a Greek squadron turned into the Bay of Eleusis, he ordered his ships to advance into the funnel of the strait on the assumption that the Greeks were fleeing toward the blockaded Megarian Channel, but when the Phoenicians advanced, other Greek ships were launched from Salamis.

As successive ranks of Persian ships rowed into the constricted strait, the battle became general. The lead ships tried to back out of the narrows even as their comrades continued coming up from Psyttaleia and "The Grecian warships, calculating, dashed / Round, and encircled us." The battle seems to have been decided early, but the fighting went on all day and thousands died with their ships, the sailors all but entombed on their benches below, the soldiers thrown from the upper decks and drowned by the weight of their weapons and armor. Those in the water were not spared, "Like mackerel or some catch of fish, / Were stunned and slaughtered, boned with broken oars and splintered wrecks. . . . / The sum / Of troubles, even if I could rehearse them / for ten days, I could not exhaust." The Persians took the measure of their defeat more rapidly than did the Greeks, who anxiously prepared for a new attack but awoke two days after the battle to learn the Persian fleet had quit Phaleron during the night. The battle had probably cost the Greeks 40 triremes, leaving them with about 270, while the Persians had lost around 200 ships, bringing their strength down to 250—a fraction of their number at the start of the campaign. As Artemisia had warned, no fleet meant no supply line and Xerxes evacuated the bulk of his troops from Attica as quickly as possible.

In addition to vindicating Themistocles' strategic vision, Salamis forced the Persians onto the defensive and won for the Greeks unassailable control of the Aegean. The end of the war also ushered in the era of Classical Greece, a period at once profoundly different from and remarkably similar to the Archaic Age that preceded it. People of a common language, religion, and general cultural outlook still inhabited much of what comprises modern Greece, as well as the Hellespont and Ionia, parts of the Black Sea coast, and much of Sicily and southern Italy. Politically the Greek world was rent with ancient rivalries. Yet the differences between the Archaic and Classical periods were of greater moment. If Athens had not eclipsed Sparta as the most powerful city-state in Greece, the two were at least equals. Moreover, Athens's newfound authority derived from a navy that for size, organization, and proven ability was unlike any that preceded it, anywhere in the world. Themistocles' interpretation of the Delphic oracle had had profound consequences not only for Athens and the Greek world, but for the subsequent course of maritime history down to the present. In Thucydides' words, Themistocles believed that "if the Athenians became a seafaring people they would have every advantage in adding to their power. Indeed it was he who first ventured to tell the Athenians that their future was on the sea. Thus he at once began laying the foundation for empire." For the first time it was possible to imagine a far-flung imperial power that derived its wealth from long-distance maritime trade without middlemen and whose prerogatives were enforced by naval superiority.

The Peloponnesian Wars, 460–404 BCE

Athens's opportunity came shortly after the Persian withdrawal, when a joint Greek naval force was sent to root out the last of the Persian threat between Crete and the Hellespont. Relations between Sparta and Athens were good, and when the Spartans were forced to recall their disgraced general, they ceded responsibility for patrolling the Aegean to the Athenians. In 478 BCE, the Athenians formed the Delian League, an alliance intended for the common defense against Persian aggression, with Athens as first among equals. The Athenians appointed the "Hellenic treasurers" to receive tribute at the island of Delos (hence the league's modern name) in the form of silver and ships. The wealth generated by these contributions and from the commercial prosperity that made Piraeus a center of Aegean trade was not used simply for the league's defensive needs. It also helped fund the extravagant building projects such as the Parthenon that are the enduring landmarks of Classical Athens. Because the league's 170 cities were encouraged to contribute silver in lieu of ships, the Athenians shouldered the burden of the league's fighting and consequently developed a navy that could beat all comers. In time the league was transformed from a free association of Athens and her independent allies to a coercive Athenian empire. In 465 BCE, the Athenians suppressed an attempt by the silver-rich island of Thasos to secede, and fifteen years later all pretense of a cooperative alliance was abandoned when the treasury was transferred from Delos to Athens.

The maritime city-state also cast its eye beyond the Aegean. A memorial stone of 460 BCE inscribed with the names of 177 soldiers testifies to the reach of Athenian power in this period: "These died in war in Cyprus, in Egypt, in Phoenicia, in Halieis, in Aegina, in the Megarid, in the same year." Cyprus was a perennial battleground between Greeks and Persians, its chief attractions being copper, grain, and wood, while Egypt offered the prospect of a rich grain trade as well as an opportunity to support resistance to Persian rule. In 450 BCE the Greeks beat the Persians in a battle fought at the Cypriot port of Salamis. After this, Persia's Artaxerxes decided to negotiate the Peace of Callias, a supreme triumph for Athenian naval power: the Persians were prohibited from sending warships west of Lycia in southwest Anatolia or south of the Black Sea, and they could not bring their armies within three days' march of the coast of Ionia, to which they renounced all claims.

The Athenian memorial of 460 BCE also refers to hostilities with Corinth at the start of a fifteen-year conflict known as the First Peloponnesian War. When Athens later intervened in a three-way conflict between Corinth and two of its colonies, the Corinthians urged their Spartan allies to invade Attica to free Greece from the Athenians' overweening power. Destined to last more than a quarter century, the Peloponnesian War is divided into four phases: the Archidamean War (431–421 BCE), the Peace of Nicias (421–415), the Sicilian expedition (415–413), and the Decelean War (413–404). At the outset, the Athenian leader was Pericles, an aristocrat by birth and demeanor but a populist and, in his advocacy of naval power, Themistocles' political heir, which almost guaranteed that the Peloponnesian War would depend more on fleet actions than any fought previously. As reported by Thucydides, Pericles enunciated a comprehensive vision of sea power:

> The whole world before our eyes can be divided into two parts, the land and the sea, each of which is valuable and useful to man. Of the whole of one of these parts you are in control—not only of the area at present in your power, but elsewhere too, if you want to go further. With your navy as it is today there is no power on earth—not the King of Persia nor any people under the sun—which can stop you from sailing where you wish.

In the first six years of the war, the Spartans confined the Athenians to Athens, Piraeus, and the corridor between the long walls that joined them. Yet the Athenians were in no imminent danger so long as they controlled the sea and could import what they needed. Their chief strategic aim was to maintain the free flow of grain from the Black Sea, for which they enlisted the support of Thracian and Macedonian rulers, and which enabled the city to survive a plague that killed a quarter of the population, including Pericles. The conflict widened in 427 BCE when the Athenians sent a fleet to support their Sicilian allies against Syracuse and to interrupt grain shipments from Sicily to the Peloponnese. The first Sicilian campaign ended inconclusively after three years. Of greater consequence was the loss of Athens's naval base at Amphipolis, strategically located near supplies of shipbuilding timber on the border between Macedonia and Thrace. Marching northward, the Spartans seized the town before the Athenian general (and historian) Thucydides could reach it.

This paved the way for a peace that lasted until the citizens of Segesta, in western Sicily, appealed to Athens for help against Syracuse. Leadership of the Sicilian expedition was ill-fated. The opportunistic Alcibiades sailed under suspicion of impiety and was later exiled, and Nicias proved indecisive until a fellow general argued that a withdrawal would be better than a defeat, when

Nicias overruled him. Shortly thereafter, in September 413 BCE, the Syracusan fleet attacked the Athenians in the confines of the harbor. Crushed in battle, forty thousand Athenians and their allies attempted to flee on foot, but most were killed or died while imprisoned in nearby stone quarries. Summarizing the campaign, Thucydides declared it "to the victors, the most brilliant of successes, to the vanquished the most calamitous of defeats . . . their losses were, as they say, total; army, navy, everything was destroyed, and out of many, only few returned."

Thucydides' account of the war ends the same year and his verdict belies the Athenians' resolve. Although their fleet numbered barely a hundred ships and the Spartans had invaded Attica and again confined them within the long walls, they resumed campaigning in the Aegean in 411 BCE. The Athenians sought to protect the Black Sea grain ships, receive tribute from members of the Delian League, and engage the Peloponnesian fleet. Stretched to the limit, they kept the Spartans and their allies on the defensive, but the odds were against them. By 405 BCE, the Athenian fleet was crewed by "all men of military age, slave or free," and a Spartan admiral promised that he would "put a stop to your fornication with the sea. She belongs to me." The following year, the Athenians and Spartans met for the last time in the confines of the Hellespont where in the course of a few hours Athens lost her navy, and with it control of the strait, the grain trade, and her empire. Faced with starvation, the Athenians accepted Spartan peace terms: their navy was reduced to twelve ships, they were forced to join the Spartan-led Peloponnesian League, and the Spartans imposed an oligarchic form of government.

Seafaring and Society in Classical Greece

Peace proved elusive and in the early fourth century BCE, Sparta and Persia were frequently at war, with Athens and other Greek cities often siding with the Persians. Amid this tumult, the Athenians recovered from their humiliating defeat in the Peloponnesian Wars and in the 370s BCE they concluded a number of alliances that in many respects revived their fifth-century empire. Protecting markets and sources of supply remained foremost of their aims. The Black Sea grain trade was the most important and heavily regulated, but fourth-century documents reveal a robust and diverse commerce. Of particular significance was the development of the bottomry loan—"the only form of genuinely productive investment known at the time"—in which a merchant pledged his ships, or its cargo, or both, in exchange for a loan payable at the conclusion of a voyage. Interest rates were variable, but generally high—as much as 22.5 percent in one instance—and they were subject to tight restrictions: loans to shippers resident at Athens could only be made for grain cargoes bound for that city. Such protectionist measures were not unique to Athens. Wine from Thasos could be exported only in Thasian ships, and although Athenian coinage was the most widespread in the Greek world, the Black Sea port of Olbia refused to honor any currency but its own.

The busiest Greek port of the fourth century BCE remained Piraeus, where building had been vigorous after the Persian Wars. Laid out in the previous century by a Milesian architect named Hippodamus, whose rectilinear street schemes were widely imitated, Piraeus was divided into a naval port, a market, and a residential area and had three distinct harbors: Kantharos on the west side of the peninsula, and Zea and Munichia to the east. In 331 BCE, Piraeus had sheds for 372 triremes, and the ships' equipment was stored in the Arsenal of Philon, which measured 120 by 16.5 meters and stood 8 meters high. Kantharos was the site of the grain market and the general trading area where merchants brought samples of their wares, the bulk of which remained in their ships until they were sold. The entrance to Kantharos was guarded by two artificial quays between the ends of which was strung a chain that could be raised to the surface to keep raiders out, a typical form of harbor defense down to the twentieth century. Aristophanes' comedy *The Acharnians* captures the vitality of the harbor, its whiff of sea wrack and odors of goods and ships, the percussion of heavy cargoes, oars, and rigging all in movement, and the accompanying chorus of human voices: "shouting crows around ships' captains, pay being distributed, figureheads of Athena being gilded, the Piraeus corn market groaning as rations were measured out, people buying leathers and rowlock thongs and jars, or garlic and olives and nets of onions, garlands and anchovies and flute girls and black eyes; and down at the docks, the sound of planing spars for oars, hammering in dowels, boring oar-holes, of reed-pipes and pan-pipes and boatswains and warblings." Though not unique, this brief portrait of the Piraeus waterfront is among the most sensuous and densely populated from the hand of an ancient writer.

Despite their dependence on ships and their crews for everything from their daily bread and defense to their extraordinary wealth, the Athenians and most of their contemporaries disparaged merchant mariners and their world. It is difficult to appreciate the hostility that sailors faced in Classical Greece. Starting in the late sixth century BCE, the Athenians' increased reliance on sailors, shipbuilders, shipowners, and investors fostered an increasingly heterogeneous and cosmopolitan society, a natural and potentially revolutionary consequence of expanded maritime trade throughout history. Despite the crucial importance of commerce, neither sailors nor merchants—most of whom were foreigners—were held in high regard. While the battle of Salamis ensured the Persians' withdrawal from Greece, it also brought the tensions between merchant-sailors and the landed aristocracy into high relief. For the latter, the acme of Greek resistance to the Persians was not Salamis but Marathon. Despite his having fought in the naval battles at Artemisium and Salamis, and written about the latter in *The Persians,* Aeschylus wanted to be remembered solely for his part in the battle of Marathon. But Salamis helped validate the notion of democracy in Athens (where the last tyranny had been overthrown only thirty years before), because the defense of the city involved citizens of humble birth, and not just contingents of wealthier hoplite soldiers. The role of the former became permanent in the fifth century BCE as Athens nurtured an ever-expanding empire bound to the home city by its merchant and naval fleets. Not surprisingly, when the Peloponnesian War ended, aristocrats blamed Athens's defeat on its democratic political system.

In the fourth century BCE, Plato and Aristotle were among the most virulent critics of the "naval mob" unleashed by Themistocles. Plato argued that death was preferable to adopting the ways of sailors and "their plausible and ready excuses for throwing down their arms and betaking themselves to 'flight without dishonor,' as it is called. Phrases like this are the normal consequences of employing men-at-arms on shipboard, and what they call for is not infinite commendation, but the very reverse." He also recommended that to avoid the corruption that inevitably arises from sea trade a city should be situated at least eighty stades (fifteen kilometers) from the sea. Aristotle was hardly more generous, allowing that "There can be no doubt that the possession of a moderate naval force is advantageous to a city," but insisting that "The population of the state need not be much increased, since there is no necessity that the sailors should be citizens." Given such disdain, it is hardly surprising that only two shipowners of Classical Greece are known to have owned more than one ship, Phormio and Lampis, "the largest shipowner in Hellas."

Biases against mariners and merchants were by no means limited to the Greeks, and Herodotus noted, "I have observed that Thracians, Scythians, Persians, Lydians—indeed, almost all foreigners—reckon craftsmen [including traders] and their descendants as lower in the social scale than people who have no connexion with manual work." Despite their conspicuous and measurable contributions, seafarers remained suspect and marginalized in many societies, even as merchants and others both relied upon and profited from their labor, not just in the Greek world but elsewhere. There were of course exceptions, and conspicuously absent from the list of "almost all foreigners" are the

Phoenicians and Carthaginians, whose embrace of maritime commerce can be seen in their commercial diaspora and the fact that the most important of the three gods they recognized, Melqart, was a patron of trade and overseas colonies. Largely unaffected by the Greeks' incessant wars, by the start of the fourth century BCE Carthage was among the Mediterranean's strongest powers, and territorially the most extensive. Stranger still, the greatest challenge to its maritime preeminence would come not from Greece, but from a most unlikely quarter, the republic of Rome, which would make the sea its own.

Chapter 5

Carthage, Rome, and the Mediterranean

Despite a shared history, language, and religion, the city-states of Greece were too fractious to remain at peace with each other for long. Two centuries of almost uninterrupted warfare had left them exhausted and power in the Greek heartland ebbed following the meteoric rise of Macedonia's Alexander the Great. His premature death in 323 BCE left the eastern Mediterranean in the hands of powerful warlords who carved huge states from the corpse of the Persian Empire. At the same time, maritime-oriented states in the central Mediterranean were tilting the balance of power away from the east. Phoenician Carthage controlled much of the trade of the western Mediterranean, while the Greek cities of southern Italy kept a watchful eye on each other, Carthage, and the rising power of Rome. The latter emerged as the dominant city of the Latin League by the end of the fifth century BCE, but the Romans did not take to the seas until the First Punic War (264–241 BCE). For the next five centuries Rome's growth and prosperity was inextricably tied to its control of the Mediterranean sea-lanes.

The ascendancy of republican Rome would have been impossible without its citizens' willingness to use the sea for war and trade. So long as they were ignorant of seafaring, the Romans were a threat only to their immediate neighbors on the Italian Peninsula. As they adapted their military abilities to naval warfare they became indomitable. Cultivating their own sea power and that of their allies, they were able to extend their rule to Ionia; to have a say in the foreign affairs of Syria, Palestine, and Egypt long before they formally annexed these countries; to move their armies; and to feed their citizens from the rich granaries of Sicily and Africa. By the start of the common era, Rome was a Mediterranean and Black Sea empire. Although the next few centuries are known as the Pax Romana, the Roman peace, it would be more accurate to call the period the *Pax Mediterraneana*, for it was only here, on what the Romans called *Mare Nostrum*, "our sea," that they were undisputed masters.

The Hellenistic Mediterranean

The triumph of Thebes over Sparta in 371 BCE heralded a shift in the center of political power from southern to northern Greece. A dozen years later, Philip II came to the throne in Macedonia, whose people contemporary Greeks regarded as barbarians, and in 357 BCE he precipitated a decade-long war with Athens by seizing the port of Amphipolis. After taking Byzantium and defeating Athens and Thebes, Philip formed the League of Corinth and committed the Greeks to war with Persia. Assassinated before he could embark on this venture, he was succeeded by his son Alexander in 337 BCE. In a decade of military campaigns, the young Alexander the Great trailed a thin veneer of Greek military might and culture across a large swath of Southwest Asia as far as the Indus River. His strategy reveals his strong sense of the uses and limitations of naval power. Although the Persians had more than three times as many ships, Alexander seized the ports of Ionia to deny them the ability to operate in the Aegean and threaten his rear in either Asia or Greece. In accordance with his interpretation of a prediction that he would "overcome the ships from dry land," he captured Miletus from the landward side while 160 ships blockaded the harbor. Marching east, Alexander defeated Darius at the battle of Issus and turned south toward Egypt, besieging Tyre for six months en route. Egypt offered little resistance and after being enthroned as pharaoh at Memphis, Alexander sailed down a western branch of the Nile until he "went ashore where the city of Alexandria, named after him, is now situated. It struck him that the position was admirable for founding a city there and that it would prosper."

The establishment of Alexandria must count as the most beneficial and enduring of its namesake's achievements. Laid out by the engineer Deinocrates, the city is situated on a bay enclosed by the island of Pharos, to which it was connected by a man-made mole that created a double harbor. To the east lay the protected anchorage of the Portus Magnus of Roman antiquity, the primary port for overseas shipping. To the west was the larger but more exposed Eunostos (literally "good yield," and the god of grain mills), which was the primary outlet for goods from the interior, especially grain, which reached Alexandria via a canal leading from Lake Mareotis to the south. The island of Pharos later gave its name to a 140-meter-high lighthouse designed around 280 BCE by the engineer Sostratus. Said to have been visible for thirty-five miles, the Pharos was considered one of the wonders of the ancient world. As well as a major port, Alexandria was the capital of Egypt, a major seat of learning, and home to one of the greatest libraries in antiquity. After Egypt's annexation by Rome in 31 BCE, it continued to flourish because of the state-sponsored grain trade, which continued until the seventh century CE. Although many of its ancient structures have been submerged or pillaged, Alexandria remains a leading Mediterranean seaport and a lasting testament to Alexander's strategic appreciation of the sea.

The Macedonian's subsequent campaigns across Mesopotamia and Persia were bound to the land until he reached the Indus, where he built a fleet to transport his army to the Indian Ocean. There he divided his forces, part of which returned to the Persian Gulf by sea while he led a smaller group overland to Mesopotamia. When Alexander died at Babylon in 323 BCE at the age of thirty-two, he had no designated successor, and it was not until the start of the third century that the principal centers of power, each ruled by one of Alexander's generals or their descendants, were more or less fixed. Chief among these were Egypt, ruled by the Ptolemies from 304 to 30 BCE, Mesopotamia and Persia by the Seleucids (304–64 BCE), and Asia Minor and the Levant by the Antigonids (279–168 BCE).

According to some accounts, at the time of his death Alexander was considering a Mediterranean campaign against Carthage. Given his relatively limited experience of naval warfare—as distinct from his grasp of the essential strategic considerations—it is difficult to imagine the results of a full-fledged naval contest. The year after his death, a Macedonian fleet crushed an Athenian effort to overthrow Macedonian rule at Amorgos, in the Cyclades, a battle that signaled the end of Athenian power as decisively as Salamis had heralded its beginning 250 years before. Yet Alexander would have met considerable opposition not only from the Carthaginians, then at the height of their power and influence, but also from the Greeks of Magna Graecia and Sicily. The latter had not played a major role in the Persian Wars of the preceding century, and to the Athenians and others they were conspicuous by their absence. Even as Themistocles was arguing for a two-hundred-ship navy for Athens, Gelon, tyrant of the Sicilian city-state of Syracuse, already had one. When a mainland embassy requested his help, he agreed with the proviso that he be given overall command of the Greek forces. He may have attached this unrealistic condition to ensure that he would be refused, thus giving him an honorable way out and allowing him to concentrate on a looming threat from Carthage, which was attempting to enlarge its presence in Sicily.

The Assyrian encroachment on Phoenicia in the seventh century BCE had

Made around 675 BCE by a potter who signed this work, the Aristonothos krater was found in the ancient Etruscan city of Caere (Cerveteri, Italy). This scene seems to show a Greek ship with a ram and raised deck for fighters (left) overtaking an Etruscan sailing ship. It is the oldest depiction of a ship fitted with a ram from the western Mediterranean. While this scene has no immediate literary counterparts, on the opposite side of the krater the artist has shown Odysseus blinding the cyclops Polyphemus—son of Poseidon, god of the sea—from Book Nine of the Odyssey. *Photograph by Faraglia, D-DAI-ROM 8208. Courtesy of the Deutsche Archäologische Institut, Rome.*

left the Carthaginians free to pursue their own destiny. After defeating a fleet from the Greek colony of Massilia (Marseille) at the battle of Alalia, off Corsica, in 535 BCE, the Carthaginians and their Etruscan allies effectively closed the western Mediterranean to Greek shipping. The Etruscans had been the dominant force in central Italy since the end of the ninth century BCE and reached their apogee around the time of Alalia. Their territories extended across the peninsula from the Tyrrhenian Sea (so-called from the Greek name for the Etruscans) to the Adriatic (named for the Etruscan town of Adria).

Numerous models, carved images, and graffiti of boats and ships attest to their involvement in seafaring, as do the proximity of their towns to the sea, manifestations of Phoenician, Greek, and Carthaginian influences on Etruscan culture, and the evidence of an Etruscan presence in Sardinia, Corsica, and other western islands. Etruscan shipwrights are the first known to have rigged ships with two masts, the earliest representation of which, dated to the 450s BCE, is on a painted wall in the Tomb of the Ship at Tarquinia, near the Tyrrhenian coast north of Civitavecchia. They also employed rams, and the oldest written (as distinct from pictorial) reference to a ram is in Herodotus's account of the battle of Alalia.

The fifth century BCE was a period of substantial change in Italy and Sicily. Most notable was the waning power of the Etruscans, whom the Romans bested for the first time in 510 BCE, and whom a Cumaean-Syracusan fleet defeated at the naval battle of Cumae in 474, when they were still regarded as "masters of the sea." Even before this, the Syracusans entered a period of rapid expansion under Gelon. When other Sicilian cities appealed for help, the Carthaginians sent two hundred ships and two hundred thousand crew, infantry, and cavalry from North Africa, Iberia, Italy, Sardinia, and Corsica "under the command of Hamilcar . . . king of Carthage."* In 480 BCE, the year that Xerxes invaded Greece, Hamilcar sailed for Sicily only to be defeated by Gelon at the Himera River. Nonetheless, the Carthaginians continued to expand their presence in Sicily, although the Syracusans remained indomitable foes, especially under Dionysius I, who was tyrant from 405 to 367 BCE. Among the most ambitious, multifaceted, and long-lived rulers in ancient Sicily, he checked the Carthaginian advance in Sicily and extended his rule over much of southern Italy.

Polyremes and Catamarans

Dionysus is credited with being one of the first people to experiment with polyremes, galleys with more than one rower to an oar. Less is known about the manning of polyremes, which were designated by the number of oarsmen in a single vertical file of rowers, than about triremes. But galleys probably never had more than three banks of oars, and polyremes could have only one or two. Later European practice indicates that the maximum number of

---

* This Hamilcar should not be confused with Hamilcar Barca, who fought in the First Punic War and fathered Hannibal Barca, who fought in the Second. The Greek historian Polybius mentions five Hannibals, two Hamilcars, four Hannos, and four Hasdrubals.

rowers per oar was eight, so the largest polyreme would have been designated a "twenty-four." A four (quadrireme in Latin, or *tetrereis* in Greek) could
have one thalamian, one zeugite, and two thranite rowers, while a five (quinquereme, or *pentereis*) might have three rowers per oar on one level and two
per oar on another. The flagship of the Carthaginian commander at the battle
of Mylae in the First Punic War "was a single-banked vessel with seven men
to each oar" and designated a "seven." Aristotle attributed the invention of the
quadrireme to the Carthaginians, and Dionysus is credited with the invention
of the quinquereme, but whether they originated with Syracusan or Carthaginian shipwrights, polyremes were a central Mediterranean innovation.

Why polyremes were developed in the first place is unclear, but the stability provided by a wider ship would have been one advantage. Larger ships
could mount catapults, the oldest form of long-range shipboard artillery. Alexander used shipborne catapults during the siege of Tyre, but the seagoing
catapult did not come into its own until the development of "super-galleys"
by the Antigonid king, Demetrius the Besieger. Catapults were specialized
affairs; a fourth-century BCE inventory of the naval warehouse at Piraeus lists
both arrow-shooting and grapnel-hurling catapults. More creative tacticians
recommended hurling pots of vipers, scorpions, and other natural-born kill-
ers, while improvements in fire weapons were sought constantly. Ramming
continued to be an important aspect of naval warfare in the Hellenistic and
Roman periods, but taking enemy ships by boarding remained a preferred
tactic, and Roman quinqueremes of the mid-third century BCE carried 300
rowers and 120 marines.

The development of polyremes led to the building of ever more extravagant ships and made control of the timber supplies in Macedonia, Cilicia,
Cyprus, and Lebanon a primary objective of Alexander's Hellenistic successors. Because access to tall trees was essential for the shipbuilding industries
that sustained maritime trade, and for the naval forces required to protect that
trade from rivals and to secure access to the wood, the naval struggle in the
Hellenistic period fed on itself. The appetite for wood was further whetted
by the development of ever-larger ships, including leviathans believed to have
been massive twin-hulled vessels. In the mid-third century BCE, the Egyptian
fleet of Ptolemy II Philadelphus boasted two "thirtys" and that of his grandson Ptolemy IV Philopator included a "forty." The dimensions of the latter,
given by the historian Athenaeus, are fantastic, but credible: 15 meters wide,
122 meters long, with room for 4,000 oarsmen, 2,850 marines, and 400 officers and other crew. Theoretically no galley could be larger than a "twenty-
four"—a vessel with three banks of oars, with eight men pulling on each oar.
It is thought that Ptolemy IV's "forty" comprised two "twentys"—that is, with

twenty oarsmen in a single file distributed in some combination among the upper, middle, and lower banks—with a raised platform deck that spanned the two hulls to accommodate the marines and others. The only catamaran galley known by name is Demetrius the Besieger's *Leontophoros*, with 1,600 rowers distributed between two "eights." While larger ships had definite tactical advantages—those of Demetrius "had a speed and effectiveness which was more remarkable than their great size"—the most extreme of these vessels were intended to magnify the power of the rulers who built them rather than for any practical purpose. Plutarch notes that Ptolemy IV's "forty" was "only for show. Hardly differing from buildings that are fixed in the ground, it moved unsteadily and with difficulty, to make appearance for display, not use."

Such showboating reflects the increased importance of navies and naval power in the Hellenistic period, but it was not confined to warships. Athenaeus also describes the *Syracusia*, a huge three-masted grain ship built for Hiero II of Syracuse by the engineer and mathematician Archimedes. Pine and fir were obtained from the forests of nearby Mount Etna and southern Italy, cordage from Spain, and hemp and pitch for caulking from the Rhône valley in France. The hull was fastened with copper spikes weighing up to seven kilograms, and the planks were sheathed in a tarred fabric covered by lead sheets, an inexpensive form of surface caulking. Anticipating the grandest twentieth-century transatlantic liners in opulence, the middle deck featured cabins for 142 first-class passengers—"All had floors done in multi-colored mosaic; in these was worked, in amazing fashion, the whole story of the *Iliad*"—in addition to accommodations for "bilge-watchers," or steerage passengers. The lower deck was reserved for cargo. First-class passengers could use a library, a gymnasium, promenades lined with flower beds, a chapel dedicated to Aphrodite, and a bath. Twenty horses could be carried in separate stalls, and there was ample provision for freshwater and a saltwater fish tank for the cook's use. The ship was defended by four hundred marines who could fight the ship from the bronze tops of the three masts or from a raised fighting deck, the latter fitted with a catapult of Archimedes' design. The number of crew is not specified, but Athenaeus says that "although the bilge was extraordinarily deep, it was bailed by only one man using a screw pump, one of Archimedes' inventions." No linear dimensions survive, but the cargo on the ship's maiden voyage to Alexandria included 60,000 measures of grain, 10,000 jars of pickled fish, 20,000 talents of wool, and 20,000 talents of miscellaneous cargo, about 1,900 tons burden, not including provisions for the ship's complement. The ship proved too large for most ports, and Hiero decided to rename his ship for Egypt's main port and to give the *Alexandria* to his ally Ptolemy III.

Rhodes and Piracy in the Hellenistic Age

Their alliance with Syracuse, the dominant power to their west, ensured that the Ptolemies could focus their attention on their primary rivals, the Antigonids and the Seleucids. The first major sea battle of the Hellenistic age was fought off Salamis, Cyprus, in 306 BCE. Demetrius the Besieger set more than a hundred ships against an even larger fleet belonging to Ptolemy I in an effort to help his father, Antigonus, establish himself as sole successor to Alexander. Though outnumbered, Demetrius is said to have captured forty warships and one hundred transports before besieging Rhodes. The port held out for a year in part because of the Rhodians' ability to run the blockade with grain from Alexandria. By a subsequent treaty, Rhodes aligned itself with Antigonus with the proviso that she never be obliged to wage war against the Ptolemies. To celebrate the lifting of Demetrius's siege, the Rhodians erected an enormous statue to the sun god, Helios. Acclaimed as one of the wonders of the ancient world, the Colossus of Rhodes stood in the port until an earthquake struck the city in 227/226 BCE. The Rhodians' reputation as honest brokers enabled them to make "such sound practical use of the incident that the disaster was a cause for improvement to them rather than of damage." Gifts poured in from around the Mediterranean: silver, catapults, and exemption from duties from Syracuse; silver, timber for twenty ships, bronze to repair the Colossus, the loan of 450 masons and builders, and a shipment of more than thirty thousand tons of grain from Egypt; and comparable gifts from other Hellenistic states.

Rhodes's success owed much to its favorable geographical position, in the southeast Aegean about ten miles off the southwest corner of Asia Minor. At the northern end of the island, the town of Rhodes boasted a complex of five harbors lined with dockyards, ship sheds, and facilities for merchants. The Rhodians fostered alliances with a variety of competing powers—its balancing act between the Antigonids and the Ptolemies being the earliest example— and wielded diplomacy and naval power to achieve hegemony over lesser powers in and around the Aegean. They are also credited with developing the rules that later formed the basis of commercial maritime law in Rome and the so-called Rhodian Sea Law of the Byzantine Empire, although the actual content of their own laws can only be inferred from later writings. The Rhodians also offered protection against pirates and others who tried to inhibit trade, and they were viewed as "the constant protectors not only of their own liberty, but of that of the rest of Greece." Unlike the Athenians, who had discouraged allies from making nonmonetary contributions to the Delian League to limit the growth of rivals, the Rhodians supplied the ships, which they distributed among relatively small squadrons based at different islands and harbors, while the allies contributed crews. The importance they attached to their antipiracy patrols is reflected in their development of a variety of smaller patrol vessels. The most common was probably the *triemiolia*, which is thought to have resembled a trireme, but with only 120 rowers rather than 170. These were not unlike large coast guard vessels of today, imposing in their own right against pirates and smugglers but not fit to face off against full-fledged warships.

While merchants could sail the open sea-lanes to Egypt or from the Bosporus to the Crimea in relative security, piracy was endemic in the island-studded Aegean, in the Adriatic and Ionian Seas between Italy and Greece, and in the heavily trafficked approaches to the Dardanelles and the Bosporus. The Black Sea, whose commerce funneled into the Bosporus, comprised an extremely important source of "necessities" and luxury goods: "the most plentiful supplies and best qualities of cattle and slaves reach us from the countries lying round the Pontus [northern Asia Minor], while among luxuries the same countries furnish us with abundance of honey, wax and preserved fish, while of the superfluous produce of our countries they take olive-oil and every kind of wine. As for corn [grain] there is a give-and-take." The key to this treasure was held by the people of Byzantium, whom the Greek historian Polybius describes as "of great service to other people" and deserving of "general support when they are exposed to peril from the barbarians." This praise notwithstanding, in 220 BCE the Byzantines imposed a toll on ships passing through the strait—possibly to finance their own antipirate activities—and a coalition of states appealed to Rhodes to help have it rescinded. This the Rhodians did through a deft mixture of diplomacy and, as a last resort, war.

By coincidence, one of the best preserved ancient Mediterranean merchant ships excavated to date was probably the victim of piracy. The fourth-century BCE vessel was discovered off Kyrenia in northern Cyprus. Built mostly of Aleppo pine with lead sheathing below the waterline, the fourteen-meter-long hull was found with twenty tons of cargo, including some four hundred amphorae, most of Rhodian origin, and ten thousand almonds. Twenty-nine millstones of volcanic stone from an island northwest of Rhodes were carried as ballast. Personal belongings included enough ceramic plates, bowls and cups, and wooden spoons for a crew of four. Finds of lead net-weights suggest that the sailors fished to supplement a diet of olives, pistachios, almonds, hazelnuts, lentils, garlic, herbs, grapes, and figs. Coins depicting Antigonus and Demetrius date the wreck to about 310–300 BCE, but by then she was an old and often repaired vessel. The evidence that the ship had been attacked by pirates is in the form of eight iron spearheads recovered from the site, some embedded in the outer surface of the planking. Enough of the hull remained for a full-scale replica of the one-masted ship to be built. In 1986, the *Kyrenia II* made a passage from Piraeus to Cyprus, sailing more than four hundred miles at nearly three knots, and in one twenty-four-hour period she averaged almost twice that. Though adequate for trade, such speeds would have made the Kyrenia ship and others like her easy prey for pirate galleys.

Rhodes's antipiracy campaigns were complicated by the fact that pirates operated both on their own account and as mercenaries for foreign rulers. At the end of the third century BCE, for example, the island of Crete was a collection of cities joined in a loose commonwealth presided over by Philip V of Macedonia. So Cretans engaged in seizing merchantmen may have been in Philip's pay and therefore not, strictly speaking, pirates. During the Cretan War of 206–203 BCE, Rhodians faced pirates from at least half a dozen cities, some of which they managed to neutralize and bring into formal alliances. By this time, legitimate maritime commerce was vital to the well-being of individual city-states and kingdoms. No longer an honorable way to make a living, as Thucydides claims it was in Homer's day, piracy was something to which all those with a stake in sea trade paid close attention. Nonetheless, if the testimony of St. Augustine is to be believed, the question of what differentiated pirates from recognized rulers was already current: "It was a witty and a truthful rejoinder which was given by a captured pirate to Alexander the Great. The king asked the fellow, 'What is your idea, in infesting the sea?' And the pirate answered with uninhibited insolence. 'The same as yours, in infesting the world! But because I do this with my tiny craft, I am called a pirate; because you have a mighty navy, you are called an emperor.'"

Rome Before the Punic Wars, 500–275 BCE

By the time of the Cretan War, the focus of naval activity was shifting to the western Mediterranean, where Rome predominated. The Romans were relative latecomers to maritime concerns, and although Roman authors maintained a pretentious abhorrence of seafaring, exploitation of the sea played a critical role in the creation and maintenance of the empire in both its republican and its post-Augustan phases, a fact of which its politicians and generals were acutely aware. The Romans were one of a number of tribes that inhabited the plain of Latium south of Etruria, but Rome was favored thanks to its position near an important crossing on the Tiber River, its proximity to the sea, its central position on the Italian Peninsula, and its easily defended seven hills. In about 510 BCE, the Romans overthrew the last of a succession of Etruscan kings to rule them and established a republic. Despite occasional setbacks, by the end of the fourth century Rome was the leading city of the Latin League, and by the 280s BCE the Romans dominated Etruria, Umbria, and Campania and were setting their sights farther afield on the Italian Peninsula. Up to this point, however, they had shown no interest in maritime pursuits, a fact reflected in their long-term relationship with Carthage, the dominant sea power of the western Mediterranean.

Despite later propaganda intended to demonstrate an ancient animosity, notably Virgil's account of the relationship between Dido (the Phoenician Elissa) and Aeneas, relations between Rome and Carthage were not always hostile. Although they lived only fifteen kilometers from the mouth of the Tiber, the early Romans all but ignored the sea and could easily afford amicable relations with the Carthaginians, with whom they signed their earliest known treaty in 509/508 BCE. This agreement stipulated that the Romans and their allies were not allowed to sail to Carthaginian Africa except to trade, and Carthage was to have hegemony in Sicily and not build forts in Latin Italy. A subsequent treaty of 348 BCE barred Roman traders from the western Mediterranean (though there is little indication of Roman sea trade and none of naval ships for another half century) and protected coastal cities under Roman control from the Carthaginians.

The preferred Roman defense against raiders from the sea, whether state enemies or pirates, was the establishment of *coloniae maritimae* (maritime colonies)—ten in all, including Ostia and Antium (Anzio), among others on the Tyrrhenian Sea, and Sena Gallica (Senigallia), on the Adriatic north of Ancona. The date of Ostia's founding is uncertain, but Antium was colonized after its capture in 338 BCE, when the Romans confiscated some of its warships "while the rest were burnt, and it was decided to use their prows or beaks to decorate a platform set up in the Forum; this sacred place was named the Rostra, or The Beaks." (The word "rostrum," for a speaker's podium, comes from the fact that orators stood by these monuments to address their audience.) The *coloniae maritimae* were small settlements of three hundred families. For the men, the only specific benefit of being a colonist was exemption from service in the legions. In return, they were expected to destroy the ships of anyone who came ashore with hostile intent and to slow the advance of any armies marching up the coast. While their settlements were described as "maritime," the colonists did not necessarily have either ships or maritime experience; they served in a capacity roughly analogous to that of the Minutemen of the American Revolution or Britain's Home Army in World War II. Although officially Roman citizens, their condition was considered "more dangerous and less free," they were far removed from the civic life of the capital, and on balance they were probably no better off than those serving in the legions.

Rome's reliance on *coloniae maritimae* rather than a navy was not entirely successful. During their siege of Naples in 327/326 BCE, the Romans had no vessels with which to attack the Campanian port, while the Neapolitans ranged freely against Roman coastal settlements. Still, it was not until 311 BCE that the Romans built a fleet—two squadrons of ten ships stationed at Rome. These saw little action until 282 BCE, when a squadron was sent "on a voyage of inspection along the coast of Magna Graecia," in violation of a treaty with Tarentum "by which the Romans had bound themselves not to sail past the promontory" at the southern end of the Gulf of Taranto. The Tarentines were suspicious of the Romans, who supported their rivals, Naples and Rhodes, and they responded by sinking or capturing five Roman ships. The ensuing war pitted the Roman armies against the sea-based Tarentines, who widened the conflict by soliciting help from Pyrrhus, king of Epirus, across the Adriatic in northwest Greece. Related by marriage to both Demetrius the Besieger and Ptolemy I and author of a book on military tactics, Pyrrhus was an expansionist in the Alexandrian mold. After several victories over the Romans, he accepted an offer to defend Syracuse from the Carthaginians. Between 278 and 276 BCE, he conquered most of Sicily, but his heavy-handed approach to the Greek cities turned many against him. This combined with reverses in southern Italy and domestic political problems forced him to return to Epirus.

One reason for Pyrrhus's Sicilian campaign had been to forestall an alliance between Rome and Carthage. In 279 BCE the Carthaginian admiral Mago had sailed to Ostia with about 120 ships and an offer of a treaty of mutual assistance against Pyrrhus. The war had already stretched the Romans to the limit, while the Carthaginians feared that a Roman peace with Pyrrhus would give him free rein against them in Sicily. The terms of their treaty reflected Rome's weakness at sea. Whether Carthage provided troops to Rome or vice versa, Carthaginian ships would carry them, and the Carthaginians were bound to provide naval assistance to Rome, although there was no reciprocal requirement. This naval component was especially important given Pyrrhus's dependence on the sea-lanes between Epirus, Tarentum, and Sicily, and while the most decisive engagements of the Pyrrhic Wars were fought on land, naval and maritime concerns were at the forefront of the various combatants' strategic considerations.

The end of the war brought with it a radically changed political landscape. Rome's hegemony now extended throughout all of southern Italy, and Tarentum became one of Rome's naval allies (*socii navales*), from whose lower classes it recruited a majority of its crews. While they had embarked on their war with Pyrrhus in a state of national exhaustion in the wake of their wars with more immediate neighbors, the Romans' success against overseas aggressors left them at once invigorated and wary. The unexpected appearance of Mago's fleet at Ostia doubtless heightened their appreciation for the potential of naval power and forced them to reassess their position vis-à-vis Carthage once peace was restored.

The First and Second Punic Wars, 264–202 BCE

Within a decade of Pyrrhus's withdrawal from Italy, Rome and Carthage were at war. The casus belli was a dispute between the people of Carthage and Messina, Sicily, but it quickly became a struggle for control of Sicily and the western Mediterranean, and it launched Rome on a path to mastery over all of the Mediterranean and Black Seas. The first of the three Punic Wars between Rome and Carthage took place chiefly in Sicily, where the land war simmered for twenty-three years. But it was the naval war that proved decisive in ending Carthage's centuries-long primacy in the western Mediterranean and catapulted Rome into the front rank of military, and naval, powers. As Polybius notes, "those who are impressed by the great sea-battles of an Antigonus, a Ptolemy or a Demetrius would doubtless be amazed . . . at the vast scale of the [naval] operations" in the First Punic War.

By the mid-third century BCE, Carthage ruled the most extensive empire west of Asia Minor or Egypt, including vast tracts of North Africa, southern Spain, the Balearics, Sardinia, Corsica, and western Sicily. The city itself was on a peninsula about five kilometers wide in the Gulf of Tunis. On the seaward side, it was protected by a single wall, while from the land it was protected by three fifteen-meter-high walls with towers every sixty meters. The walls had two levels of stables—the lower could house three hundred elephants, the upper four thousand horses—and the barracks could accommodate twenty-four thousand soldiers. By the second century BCE, at least, the double harbor complex was probably the most sophisticated in the world:

> The harbours had communication with each other, and a common entrance from the sea seventy feet wide, which could be closed with iron chains. The first port was for merchant vessels. . . . Within the second port was an island, and great quays were set at intervals round both the harbour and the island. These embankments were full of shipyards which had capacity for 220 vessels. . . . Two Ionic columns stood in front of each dock, giving the appearance of a continuous portico to both the harbour and the island . . . from which . . . the admiral could observe what was going on at sea, while those who were approaching by water could not get any clear view of what took place within. Not even incoming merchants could see the docks at once, for

a double wall enclosed them, and there were gates by which merchant ships could pass from the first port to the city without traversing the dockyards.

The Carthaginians posed a constant threat to the Romans, who according to Polybius "were handling the operations in Sicily capably enough. But so long as the Carthaginians held unchallenged control of the sea, the issue of the war still hung in the balance." After a three-year stalemate, during which they depended on their allies' ships to reach Sicily, the Romans decided to build "100 quinqueremes and twenty triremes. They faced great difficulties because their shipwrights were completely inexperienced in the building of a quinquereme, since these vessels had never before been employed in Italy." The initial difficulty was overcome when they seized a Carthaginian patrol vessel that had run aground: "It was this ship which they proceeded to use as a model, and they built their whole fleet according to its specifications."

Reverse engineering is notoriously difficult under the best of circumstances, but according to Pliny the Elder, from a standing start with virtually no shipbuilding industry of their own, the Roman fleet "was on the water within 60 days after the timber left the tree." This is all the more astonishing when compared with the three years that experienced Athenian shipwrights had taken to build two hundred ships under Themistocles. Archaeological finds suggest that the Romans may have benefited from Carthaginian construction techniques. Examination of the so-called Punic Ship, a third-century BCE liburnian found off Marsala, Sicily, showed that the Carthaginian shipbuilders had written on the various hull pieces to mark their placement in relation to one another, not unlike the system employed in the Khufu ship twenty-two hundred years before. (A liburnian was an oared vessel—this one had seventeen sweeps on either side—with two men per oar and employed for carrying dispatches and for scouting.) If the ship the Romans used as their template included such builders' marks, it would have made the job of creating a fleet of ships from scratch far easier than it might otherwise have been.

Because the Carthaginian ships were better built and more capably manned, consul Gaius Duilius determined to offset the Carthaginians' superior seamanship by replicating the conditions in which the Romans were unrivaled in battle, and to beat the Carthaginians in boarding actions. Central to the Romans' tactics was the *corvus* (literally, raven), a boarding ramp 11 meters long by 1.5 meters wide with rails along the sides. One end of the *corvus* was hinged at the base of an eight-meter-high mast mounted forward in the ship. When dropped on the deck of an enemy ship, an iron spike at the outer end held the *corvus* fast and the Roman soldiers swept aboard the enemy ship. When Duilius caught a Carthaginian fleet off the northeastern coast of Sicily near Mylae in 260 BCE, the effectiveness of the *corvi* told early. As the Roman marines swarmed the enemy ships, "the fighting seemed to have been transformed into a battle on dry land." Carthaginian attempts to round on the Roman ships from astern were ineffective because the *corvus* could be dropped across a broad arc from port to starboard, thus ensuring that the Romans never lost their advantage. By the battle's end, the Carthaginians had lost 50 of their 130 ships.

Dissatisfied with the lack of progress in Sicily, four years later the Romans took the war to North Africa and came close to forcing an onerous peace on the Carthaginians before their army was soundly defeated. A relief expedition captured more than 100 Carthaginian ships, but en route home the Romans lost more than 280 ships and thirty-five thousand soldiers and crew to storms. Polybius blames the disaster on the commanders' utter disregard for their pilots' advice about the weather and their destination, "the southern coast of Sicily . . . a rocky shore which possesses few safe anchorages." He goes on to draw some general observations about Roman character, their reliance on brute strength, and their stubbornness, and why these are incompatible with success at sea. On land, the Romans frequently prevailed against other men and their machines because they could apply "one kind of force against another which is essentially similar. . . . But when they are contending with the sea and the atmosphere and try to overcome these by force, they meet with crushing defeats. So it turned out on this occasion, and the process will no doubt continue until they correct these preconceptions about daring and force." One theory attributes the heavy losses to the *corvus*, which in an elevated position would have made the ships top-heavy and prone to capsize. If the Romans realized this, they may have decided that the *corvus* was more dangerous than it was worth, which would explain why it is not mentioned after the start of the North African campaign.

The war dragged on another fourteen years punctuated by triumphant successes and epic failures, none of them conclusive. The keystone of Carthaginian strategy was the security of Lilybaeum (Marsala, Sicily), which the Romans blockaded off and on for nearly a decade, though they lost more than a thousand ships in storms. The Carthaginians were able to slip the blockade at crucial junctures until 241 BCE when a fleet laden with grain and manned by relatively unseasoned seamen and marines was intercepted in the battle of the Aegates Islands north of the port. The Carthaginians lost 120 ships and the Romans took ten thousand prisoners. With no possibility of support from home, Lilybaeum's position was untenable and the Carthaginians surrendered.

Despite their longer tradition of seafaring, the Carthaginians never came close to victory in the First Punic War. In some respects this is understandable. Carthaginian sea power depended on its people's role as merchant-sailors. They had never fought a major naval war, and while they were not ignorant of warfare—they frequently fought their Numidian neighbors, even during the war with Rome—it was not a hallmark of their civic life. The Romans' martial spirit and relentless military ambition enabled them to adapt readily to ships and naval warfare, and once they learned to respect the sea, they mastered it.

Trade between Rome and Carthage revived after the war, but despite an avowed policy of nonintervention in Carthaginian affairs, in 238 BCE Rome seized Sardinia; nine years later, this and western Sicily became the first two Roman provinces. Meanwhile, the Carthaginians began enlarging their territory in southern Spain. They certainly needed to increase their revenues from Spanish silver mines to pay Rome; they may have wanted to make up for the loss of Sardinia and Sicily; and it may have been a way to employ disgruntled soldiers who had been forced to abandon the field without themselves suffering a defeat. Chief among these was Hamilcar Barca, who conquered new lands around the Guadalquivir River and founded Carthago Nova (Cartagena) on the southwest coast. Roman interest in the Iberian Peninsula was limited to alliances with individual towns, notably the port of Saguntum. Nonetheless, a treaty of 226 BCE made the Ebro River (which enters the sea about seventy-five miles southwest from Barcelona) the border between the Carthaginian and Roman spheres of influence.

Five years later, Hamilcar's son Hannibal became the supreme leader in Carthaginian Spain and in 219 BCE he seized Saguntum to start the Second Punic War. Marching on Italy via southern France and the Alps, Hannibal defeated the Romans repeatedly between 218 and 216 BCE; at Cannae, on the Adriatic coast east of Naples, fewer than fifteen thousand of eighty thousand Roman soldiers escaped death or capture. Yet Carthage never challenged Rome at sea, and although Hannibal remained at large in Italy for fifteen years, only one fleet reached him there, while Rome received steady supplies of grain from Sicily, Sardinia, and possibly Egypt. Hannibal finally left the peninsula in 203 BCE, when he was recalled to lead the defense of Carthage against the armies of Publius Cornelius Scipio. Although there were no major naval battles, maritime strategy was as important to the outcome of the Second Punic War as it had been in the first, a fact that Scipio appreciated better than anyone.

Scipio's fortunes were inextricably linked to the war in Spain, where he led the capture of Saguntum in 212 BCE and of Carthago Nova three years later. Polybius credits Scipio with perceiving the latter's strategic value. "He discovered first of all," writes Scipio's friend, "that it was virtually unique among the cities of Spain in possessing a harbor which could accommodate a fleet and naval forces, and that it was also conveniently situated for the Carthaginians to make the direct sea crossing from Africa." Scipio further reckoned that if his attempt to take the port failed, "he could still ensure the safety of his men because of his command of the sea." The loss of Carthago Nova left the Carthaginians with only one major overseas port, at Gadir. Returning to Rome, Scipio began planning an invasion of North Africa. Hannibal was recalled to Carthage, where in 202 BCE Scipio defeated him at the battle of Zama, thus earning the honorific Africanus. Hannibal urged the Carthaginians to accept the Roman peace terms before fleeing to the Seleucid court of Antiochus III, "the Great."

Rome Masters the Mediterranean

It has been said that the Romans did not display a "naval mentality" during the Second Punic War, but in fact their naval strategy was tailored precisely to the Carthaginian threat. The Romans had not abandoned their fleet after the First Punic War, but there were excellent reasons for them to avoid the expense of building and manning more ships than they did. With Hannibal's army ravaging Italy, there was little manpower available for a larger fleet, especially considering that most naval losses in the first war had been to the elements and there was no Carthaginian naval threat to speak of. More to the point, the Romans were fighting simultaneously the First Macedonian War (215–197 BCE), in which their fleet played a critical role in the Adriatic and Aegean. Their involvement in the Adriatic began in 229 BCE, in response to pleas from Italian merchants who had been harassed by ships from Illyria, on the Balkan shore. The Romans launched a two-hundred-ship expedition and pressured the Illyrians to guarantee that they would never sail south of Lissus (Lezhe, in northwest Albania) with more than two lightly armed *lembi*, a type of single- or double-banked galley they had developed. (Ideally suited for fast scouting and raiding expeditions, the *lembus* was later adopted by other maritime powers.)

Fighting resumed on the eve of Hannibal's invasion of Italy, when Demetrius of Pharos (the island of Hvar, Croatia) took a fleet of *lembi* for a raiding expedition in the Aegean. Defeated by the Romans, he fled to Philip V of Macedonia, whose anti-Roman tendencies he encouraged. Rome did not commit many resources to the Adriatic, but a lot could be done with relatively few. Ten ships drove off a fleet of a hundred Macedonian *lembi* in 216 BCE, after which the Romans assigned up to fifty ships to the coast between Tarentum and Brundisium. They also forged an alliance with the Aetolian League under which the Romans provided a fleet and were entitled to any movable property in places it seized, terms appropriate to a maritime-based strategy, while the Greek city-states of the league fought the land war and received any captured territories. The war ended in 205 BCE, but five years later the Romans renewed the fight because of Philip's threats to their Greek allies, including Athens and Rhodes, and for fear that he would soon be in a position to attack Italy. "It took Hannibal four months to reach Italy from Saguntum," declared one consul, "but Philip, if we let him, will arrive four days after he sets sail from Corinth." Titus Quinctius Flamininus took his legions to Illyria and in 197 BCE smashed the Macedonian army. Philip surrendered all but five of his regular warships and a "sixteen," and withdrew his garrisons from around Greece. Flamininus grandly proclaimed the Greeks a free people, a contention they would soon dispute.

In the interim, the Seleucid Antiochus the Great had crossed the Hellespont to exercise his dynastic claims to Thrace, which trumped any interest the newly arrived Romans could assert in Greece or the Balkans. In 192 BCE, he landed at the city of Demetrias (north of Euboea) whose citizens believed that they were "free in appearance only, while in reality everything was done at the Roman's nod." The Romans shattered Antiochus's army at Thermopylae, but the experience forced them to reevaluate their view of the Aegean world and their relationship to it. As a modern historian has put it, "The essential unity of the Aegean basin, of the Greek world of Asia and of Europe as a geopolitical system, had been revealed with dazzling clarity." The late date at which the Romans received this epiphany attests to just how removed politically and culturally they had been from the Hellenistic world of the eastern Mediterranean.

Armed with this new awareness, Scipio Africanus and his brother took up the challenge of asserting Roman hegemony in the Aegean. Antiochus's fleet posed a real threat, so rather than cross the Aegean they marched their armies north to the Hellespont. The Roman fleet was under command of Marcus Livius, who drew his crews from the *coloniae maritimae* despite their previous exemption from conscription. Notwithstanding its small size and the crews' reluctance to serve, the value of the Roman navy was acknowledged by no less an authority than Hannibal, who advised Antiochus that "Roman arms were quite as powerful at sea as on land." As if to prove the point, the Romans and their Rhodian allies bested a succession of Seleucid fleets, including one under Hannibal. These defeats rattled Antiochus, as the Roman historian Livy explains, "because with the loss of his command of the sea he was doubtful of his ability to defend his distant possessions." He withdrew his army from the Hellespont, and Scipio's legions crossed into Asia unopposed. After a final battle on land, the Romans dictated a peace that eliminated Seleucid influence from Ionia. Rome now exercised its hegemony over the entire Aegean and after centuries of fending off an eastern despotism, the Greeks had succumbed to a western one.

To preserve their dominance, the Romans embarked on a campaign of divide and rule, one of the first victims being its faithful ally Rhodes, which it repeatedly undermined. After the Third Macedonian War (172–167 BCE), Rome transferred the island of Delos to Athens with the stipulation that Delos be made a duty-free port, which cost Rhodes an estimated 140 talents (about 3,500 kilograms of silver) in income per year in harbor dues alone. A further blow came at the conclusion of the Third Punic War (149–146 BCE) and the destruction of Carthage, which had been an important trading partner. This war had been preceded by Rome's refusing the Carthaginians permission to defend themselves against attacks from neighboring Numidia; forcing it to surrender its arms to Rome; and insisting that the city itself be destroyed and its inhabitants moved eighty stades inland—coincidentally, the same distance that Plato recommended to preserve a city from the corrupting influences of maritime trade. The Carthaginians declined these outrageous demands, but half a century of subservience to Rome in foreign and military affairs had left their navy undermanned, ill-equipped, and poorly trained. Yet even with their overwhelming advantages in preparation, weapons, and experience, it took the Romans three years to win the last of the Punic Wars. When the city finally fell to the army of Scipio Aemilianus, he heeded the war cry of Cato, the Roman senator who with puritanical zeal had long urged his fellow citizens to war by closing his speeches with the words "Carthage must be destroyed." So it was, and with it a maritime power that had flourished for more than seven centuries.[*]

With Carthage defeated and Rhodes marginalized, by the end of the second century BCE there were few external threats to Rome's Mediterranean trade, the commercial center of which was the free port of Delos. The island's prosperity was shattered in 88 BCE, when Mithridates VI of Pontus ordered the murder of a hundred thousand Romans and Italians in Asia Minor and on Delos. The culmination of decades of tension and intermittent hostilities over Roman rule in Greece and Asia Minor precipitated the first of the three Mithridatic Wars fought between 88 and 63 BCE. These involved extensive naval campaigning, and it could be argued that they were not brought to a faster conclusion because the Roman commander, Sulla, advanced into Greece without a supporting fleet. As a result, when Sulla besieged Athens and Piraeus, Mithridates could replenish his forces by sea just as the Athenians had in the

---

[*] Scipio Aemilianus was the adopted son of Publius Scipio, whose father was Scipio Africanus.

Peloponnesian War. When the port fell in 86 BCE, "Sulla burned the Piraeus, which had given him more trouble than the city of Athens, not sparing the Arsenal, or the navy yard, or any other of its famous buildings" that had graced the port for four centuries. Detailed descriptions of the naval campaigns are lacking, although we get glimpses of the magnitude of the effort. In his summary of the wars, Appian notes that "Many times [Mithridates] had over 400 ships of his own," a numerical advantage that enabled him to land an army in Greece but was insufficient for taking Rhodes, still a Roman ally. Mithridates drew support not only from his own territories and immediate neighbors, but from the Roman general Sertorius, who was leading the opposition to Sulla in the civil war in Spain, from which he sent forces to Mithridates by sea. The celebrated general Licinius Lucullus learned from Sulla's error—from which he had in fact rescued Sulla—and although he spent much of his time on the march in the heart of Asia Minor during the second war, his success so depended on the capture of the Black Sea ports of Sinop and Amasus that when he celebrated his triumph at Rome, his procession included "a hundred and ten bronze-beaked ships."

Pompey the Great's Campaign Against the Pirates, 69 BCE

The widespread fighting in the Aegean since the second half of the second century BCE, together with the Roman practice of divesting potential rivals of their fleets, had led to a resurgence in piracy. This did not attract official Roman notice until the turn of the century, and even then the problem was addressed haphazardly. A succession of campaigns against individual pirate bands failed because of their mobility and networks of mutual assistance. Although concentrated in Cilicia in Asia Minor, pirates threatened maritime commerce throughout the Mediterranean. No one and no place was safe. In a speech given in 66 BCE, after piracy had been eradicated, the Roman orator Cicero reminded his audience how dire the situation had been:

> Need I lament the capture of envoys on their way to Rome from foreign countries, when ransom has been paid for the ambassadors of Rome? Need I mention that the sea was unsafe for merchantmen, when twelve lictors [official bodyguards] have fallen into the hands of the pirates? Need I record the capture of the noble cities of Cnidus and Colophon and Samos and of countless others, when you well know that your own harbours and those, too, through which you draw the very breath of your life, have been in the hands of the pirates? . . . Why should I lament the reverse at Ostia, that shameful

blot upon our commonwealth, when almost before your own eyes the very fleet which had been entrusted to the command of a Roman consul was captured and destroyed by the pirates?

The most famous victim of piracy was a young Julius Caesar, who on a winter crossing to Rhodes in 75 BCE was captured and held for nearly forty days. Ransomed for twelve thousand gold pieces, Caesar returned to hunt down and crucify his erstwhile captors. Six years later, the senate assigned Pompey the Great to lead a new effort against the pirates. Despite its importance, his campaign is known only from brief descriptions that focus on his overall strategy. Entrusted with extraordinary powers for three years, Pompey raised a force of 500 ships, 120,000 soldiers, and 5,000 cavalry. Dividing the Mediterranean into thirteen naval districts, he ordered his captains to flush out any pirate bands they might find, but not to leave the zones to which they had been assigned. The one area left unguarded was the coast of Cilicia, which quickly became the last refuge of those pirates who could reach it. The Romans eradicated piracy in the western Mediterranean within forty days, and seven weeks later Pompey received the surrender of the last of the pirates in Cilicia. Sources say that ten thousand pirates died during the campaign, and between four hundred and eight hundred ships were seized. Most unusual is the clemency Pompey showed his prisoners, many of whom he transplanted to the nearby port of Soli, which was renamed Pompeiopolis. His leniency paid off and Pompey had their allegiance when he commanded the Roman armies in the Third Mithridatic War.

The long preoccupation with piracy impressed itself deeply on the Roman psyche. For Cicero especially, pirates and piracy were all that true Romans were not: barbarous, ignoble, perfidious. It was a theme to which he returned repeatedly over a quarter century. In a celebrated letter to his son, Cicero asserts that a pledge made to a pirate is not binding, "for a pirate is not included in the category of public enemies [of the state], but is the common enemy of everyone." This concept was honed to a fine point by the seventeenth-century English jurist Sir Edward Coke: *Pirata est hostis humanis generis,* "the pirate is the enemy of mankind," a phrase still used in reference to people engaged in terrorism, torture, and genocide.

From Caesar to Augustus: The Roman Civil Wars, 49–31 BCE

Rome's overseas success in the east and against the pirates contributed to the erosion of its republican institutions, which were inadequate for running such vast and far-flung provinces and colonies. Reforms proposed in the 130s BCE were rebuffed by a senate protective of its privileges and as tensions mounted, the senate increasingly resorted to martial law, and strongmen began levying large armies by recruiting soldiers with promises of land and booty. Empowered and enriched by his campaign against the pirates, in 60 BCE Pompey formed a secret triumvirate with Crassus and Caesar, who agreed to support each other "to oppose all legislation of which any one of them might disapprove." Two years later Caesar began his conquest of Gaul and over the next nine years annexed Gaul to Rome, invaded Germany, and twice landed in Britain.

Caesar's victories increased his popularity with the people and the resentment of old-line republicans, and it put him at odds with Pompey, who in 52 BCE was appointed sole consul, a first in republican history. In 49 BCE, Caesar precipitated a civil war by leading his army across the Rubicon River into Italy proper, an action punishable by death. Pompey's hastily recruited forces were no match for Caesar's veterans, and Pompey crossed the Adriatic to gather an army. Caesar entered Rome and then sailed to Spain, where he overcame Pompey's supporters there. Returning to Greece, he defeated Pompey at the battle of Pharsalus in central Greece. Pompey fled to Egypt in a merchant ship and blamed himself "for having been forced to do battle with his land forces, while he made no use of his navy, which was indisputably superior. . . . And, in truth," continues his biographer, "Pompey made no greater mistake, and Caesar showed no abler generalship, than in removing the battle so far from naval assistance." The mistake was irreversible, and as he landed on the coast of Egypt, Pompey was murdered by order of the Ptolemaic court. When Caesar reached Egypt, he killed Pompey's murderers and installed Cleopatra, sister and wife of Ptolemy XIII, as queen.

In 44 BCE, upholders of the old republican order assassinated Caesar, only to witness the rise of a new triumvirate: Caesar's ally and general, Marc Antony; his eighteen-year-old nephew and designated heir, Octavian (the future emperor Augustus); and the general Lepidus. At the battle of Philippi, Greece, in 42 BCE, Antony and Octavian defeated their opponents, but part of the republican fleet escaped and joined the renegade Sextus Pompey in Sicily. Designated by the senate as prefect of the fleet and the coastlines (*praefectus classis et orae maritimae*) the previous year, the son of Pompey the Great was keen to avenge his father's death on Caesar's heir. Though outnumbered, he defeated Octavian in the Strait of Messina in 38 BCE but was unable to press his advantage. Two years later, Octavian's trusted general Marcus Vipsanius Agrippa took command of the fleet and developed a naval training station called Portus Julius near Puteoli on the Bay of Naples. After a summer of strenuous

Roman ships carrying Emperor Trajan and his army across the Danube during the first campaign against the Dacians in what is now Romania. This reproduction from a section of Trajan's Column (ca. 113 CE) in Rome, which is attributed to the sculptor Apollodorus of Damascus, is in the Museum of Ancient Shipping, Mainz, Germany. Photograph by the author.

campaigning in the waters around Sicily, in September 36 BCE Agrippa won a momentous victory at the battle of Naulochus, which cost Pompey all but seventeen of perhaps two hundred ships. With Pompey in flight, when Lepidus quit the triumvirate, the contest for absolute supremacy was now between Antony and Octavian.

Relations between the two had soured when Antony, already married to Octavian's sister, married Cleopatra. In 33 BCE, Antony and Cleopatra—as a queen in her own right rather than the mere bride of a Roman general— assembled eight squadrons of sixty-five warships (up to "nines" and "tens"), and three hundred transports. By the spring of 31 BCE, most of this fleet was on the Actium peninsula on the Gulf of Ambracia, north of the Gulf of Corinth, where Agrippa and Octavian caught up with them. With an army hungry, diseased, and dispirited by widespread defections of commanding officers to Octavian, Antony had to force the issue with his fleet. On the morning of September 2, he put to sea with six squadrons facing Agrippa, and Cleopatra's squadron in the rear guard. Shortly after battle was joined, three squadrons withdrew, two surrendered, and Cleopatra's ships turned south. Antony joined her with forty ships and sailed for Egypt. (Sails were usually left ashore when battle was imminent, and the fact that their ships had them suggests that this retreat was premeditated.) Pursued there by Octavian the next year, Antony made a feeble last stand before falling on his sword. When Cleopatra killed herself to avoid the humiliation of becoming Octavian's prisoner, Egypt became a province of the Roman Empire, which it would help feed for the next six centuries.

Mare Nostrum

Octavian's victory in Egypt brought the entire Mediterranean basin under the command of a single imperial rule. To guarantee the safety of the empire and its sea trade, Augustus (as Octavian styled himself) established Rome's first standing navy, with bases at Misenum just south of Portus Julius, and at Ravenna in the northern Adriatic. These fleets comprised a variety of ships from liburnians to triremes, "fours," and "fives." As the empire expanded, provincial fleets were established in Egypt, Syria, and North Africa; on the Black Sea; on the Danube and Rhine Rivers, which more or less defined the northern border of the empire; and on the English Channel. Over the next two centuries there was nearly constant fighting on the empire's northern and eastern borders, but the Mediterranean experienced a period of unprecedented peace and prosperity during which Greco-Roman culture circulated easily around what everyone was entitled to call *Mare Nostrum*—Our Sea. It was the only time that the Mediterranean has ever been under the aegis of a single power, with profound results for all the cultures that subsequently emerged on its shores.

As trade within the Mediterranean basin flourished, the Romans set about improving old and building new ports at an unprecedented rate. Augustus's choice of Misenum for a naval base owed much to its proximity to Puteoli. The most important commercial port of republican Rome, Puteoli thronged with craftsmen and traders, especially from Alexandria and the Levant, whose prosperity depended on Rome's voracious appetite for Egyptian grain and eastern luxuries. A major spectacle at Puteoli was the arrival of the Alexandrian grain fleets. On his last journey away from Rome, Augustus took a ship down the coast of Campania and across the Bay of Puteoli, where he was saluted by the crew and passengers of a ship from Alexandria who "put on white robes and garlands, burned incense, and wished him the greatest good fortune—which, they said, he certainly deserved, because they owed their lives to him and their liberty to sail the seas: in a word, their entire freedom and prosperity." Puteoli underwent numerous improvements at the hands of local entrepreneurs and at the direction of various emperors well into the first century CE. By coincidence, the region was an abundant source of one of the materials best suited for work in harbor construction, pozzolana, a volcanic ash that when mixed with water and lime forms hydraulic cement, which can set and cure underwater.

As well as a commercial and naval center, the Bay of Naples was a resort for Rome's richest and most influential citizens. A list of people with seaside villas and estates there in the first century BCE reads like a who's who of Rome's elite. At Puteoli itself were Caesar's father-in-law and Cicero, who also had estates at Pompeii and Cumae. After leaving public life, the general Lucullus divided his time in ostentatious refinement between his estates at Misenum and Naples, while Pompey the Great had a villa at Cumae, Caesar himself an estate at Baiae, and Augustus a villa on the island of Capri. Emperors continued to frequent the Bay of Naples for centuries, and in the late 400s the last emperor in the west was exiled to Lucullus's villa. Although the villas were off-limits to the general population, the cultivated fish ponds of the larger estates around Baiae were widely known attractions (Cicero scorned several of his political opponents as "fish-pond fanciers"), as were the region's fish farms. According to one theory, Augustus's decision to move Agrippa's naval base from Portus Julius to Misenum was to preserve the local oyster beds. If so, this is one of the earliest known examples of environmental considerations influencing waterfront development.

The popularity of the Bay of Naples belies any suggestion that the Romans viewed sea travel as anything unusual. Boats were the preferred means of transport for visitors from Rome, and there was even a night service from Ostia to Puteoli. So routine was the practice of sailing from the capital that Nero's elaborate conspiracy to kill his mother, Agrippina, was predicated on her traveling by boat between her villa at Bauli and his at Baiae. While she was dining with her estranged son, her ship was rammed "accidentally," and when she left Nero offered her "a collapsible cabin-boat" specially designed to "either sink or fall in on top of her." The ship foundered as intended, but Agrippina was rescued by a passing vessel. Nothing daunted, Nero had her murdered by less contrived means.

Puteoli's successor as Rome's premier port was Ostia. Although its location at the mouth of the Tiber had long made it strategically important, Ostia was not integral to the city's prosperity until the first century BCE. The dictator Sulla authorized some improvements, partly in appreciation for Ostia's loyalty during the civil war, when opposing troops sacked the port, and partly in acknowledgment of its growing commercial significance. In the middle of the first century CE, silting at the mouth of the Tiber forced Claudius to build a large harbor at Portus, just north of Ostia proper. This was enclosed by two breakwaters more than eight hundred meters long, "massive / Piers that reach out to embrace the deep, and leave Italy far behind—a man-made breakwater / that no natural harbor could equal." A mole was erected across the entrance by sinking a ship in which an obelisk had been brought from Heliopolis, in Egypt: "it was first sunk, then secured with piles, and finally crowned with a very tall lighthouse—like the Pharos at Alexandria—that guided ships into the harbour at night by the beams of a lamp." Half a century later, Trajan ordered the excavation of a large hexagonal basin with numbered slips and he established a new port up the coast at Centumcellae, the modern Civitavecchia.

Even after the construction of Portus, Ostia remained the seat of the area's commercial and cultural life. The remains of the city, which rival those of Pompeii, reveal a town of ordinary citizens rather than wealthy estate owners and their retinues. The essentially rectilinear streets were lined with three- and four-story apartment houses, many with street-level stores and offices. The main avenue extends from the Porta Marina, near the ancient shorefront, to the Porta Romana on the road to the capital. In addition to houses, offices, workshops, and laundries, the city boasted an astonishing array of religious buildings that reflect the inhabitants' strong ties to the Roman east. Side-by-side with temples to the gods of the Greco-Roman pantheon and the imperial cults stand Christian baptisteries, a Jewish synagogue, and a host of temples to Near Eastern deities, including a dozen dedicated to the Zoroastrian divinity Mithras, the god of contracts and thus revered by merchants. For rest and relaxation Ostians could visit a number of bathhouses decorated with maritime scenes, while the theater seated between three and four thousand people. Behind the theater is the so-called Piazzale of the Corporations, a pillar-lined square onto which open rooms decorated with floor mosaics advertising shipwrights, stevedores, caulkers, rope dealers, chandlers, and merchants, and their destinations or specialties: grain traders from Narbo (in Gaul), Caesarea in Mauritania (Cherchel, Algeria), Alexandria, or Carthage; importers of wild animals for the Colosseum; grain measurers; tanners; and so on. Long thought to have been business offices, these rooms may have been gathering places for people attending the theater while the insignia advertised groups that contributed in some way to the theater or the cultural life of the city in general.

A sculptural relief of the early second century CE showing the arrival of a ship at Ostia as it passes the Pharos (lighthouse) with its flame blazing in the distance. Among the other figures on board, two men and a woman are offering thanks for a safe passage on a portable altar abaft the sail. The port of Rome teems with life as a man in a small boat works his way under the stern while in the lower right a man is carrying an amphora off a docked ship. The large figure gripping a trident in the center of the scene is Neptune, god of the sea. Photograph by Faraglia, D-DAI-Rom 7898. Courtesy of the Museo Torlonia/ Deutsche Archäologische Institut, Rome.

Although the average freighter of antiquity carried about 120 tons of cargo, the scale of the grain trade to Rome required larger ships with a capacity of well over 1,000 tons. The description of one such vessel survives in a second-century work entitled "The Ship or the Wishes," by Lucian of Samosata, which tells of a grain freighter called the *Isis* that is blown off course en route from Alexandria to Rome and forced to put in at Piraeus. Though the passage occurs in a work of fiction, the *Isis* was likely modeled on a real ship. The appearance of the huge grain carrier apparently created a minor sensation in Piraeus, where such large vessels were now a rarity.

Incidentally, what a huge ship! A hundred and twenty cubits long, the shipwright said, and well over a quarter as wide, and from deck to bottom, where it is deepest, in the bilge, twenty-nine. Then, what a tall mast, what a yard to carry! What a forestay to hold it up! How gently the poop curves up, with a little golden goose below! And correspondingly at the opposite end, the prow juts right out in front, with figures of the goddess, Isis, after whom the ship is named, on either side. And the other decorations, the paintings and the top-sail blazing like fire, anchors in front of them, and capstans, and windlasses, and the cabins on the poop—all very wonderful to me. You could put the number of sailors at an army of soldiers. She was said to carry enough [grain] to feed all Attica for a year.

On the basis of the linear measurements given by Lucian the capacity of the *Isis* has been estimated at 1,200 to 1,300 tons. The captain tells how the ship ended up at Piraeus after seventy days of foul winds and storms in a passage that provides important information on the route normally taken by the grain fleet: north-northeast from Alexandria, passing to the west of Cyprus, then westward along the south coast of Asia Minor as far as Rhodes or Cnidus. From there, the captain explains, "They should have kept Crete to starboard, and sailed beyond Malea," the peninsula at the southern end of the Peloponnese, "so as to be in Italy by now." In a similar incident, the apostle Paul was aboard another Alexandrian grain carrier that was driven south and wrecked on Malta, although all of her complement of 276 people survived.

To avoid food shortages the government made strenuous efforts to guarantee the shipment of between 150,000 and 300,000 tons of grain annually to Rome. An estimated 15 to 30 percent of this was grain paid as taxes and freighted in government ships for free distribution to the masses—the *annona*—but most grain and other cargoes were handled by merchants whose cargoes went in smaller, privately owned ships. Investing in trade was common, commercial loans being capped at one percent per month or 12 percent per year. However, repayment of the loan depended on the safe completion of the transaction, and as a result it was a given that "Money lent on maritime loans can bear interest at any rate because it is at risk of the lender as long as the voyage lasts." Shippers may have had recourse to some form of insurance. According to a biography of Claudius, "he held out the certainty of profit by assuming the expense of any loss that they [the merchants] might suffer from storms." Yet this measure seems to have been intended specifically for grain traders, for whose benefit Claudius also made improvements to Ostia, offered bounties for new ship construction, and exempted shippers from a variety of laws.

Second only to the grain trade was the wine trade. According to one estimate, during the first century BCE between 50,000 and 100,000 hectoliters

(1.3–2.6 million gallons) of wine were shipped annually from Italy to Gaul, carried in upward of 350,000 amphorae. Because wooden hulls are biodegradable and ceramic amphorae are not (although their contents leak out over time), the remains of sunken wine ships are often identified by mounds of amphorae lying on the seabed nested as they were stowed. The waters of western Italy and southern France have yielded an impressive number of finds. One of the largest is that of a forty-meter-long ship found off La Madrague de Giens, France, where it sank in the first century BCE with seven or eight thousand amphorae and a secondary cargo of black-gloss tableware and coarseware pottery, a cargo of more than three hundred tons. The wreck site was littered with large stones from the nearby Giens peninsula left by divers who recovered a significant part of the sunken cargo shortly after it sank. As sponge and pearl divers have done for centuries, the ancient salvors used the stones to speed their twenty-meter descent to the seabed. They managed to recover all but one layer of amphorae on the starboard side, while three layers were still in place to port.

Modern appreciation of Roman seafaring has been shaped by the Romans' own ambivalence about the sea. Maritime trade and naval power were vital to their prosperity, and according to their own foundation stories, they owed their very existence to Aeneas's successful flight by sea from Troy. The maritime milieu of the first half of Virgil's *Aeneid* consciously echoes that of Homer's *Odyssey*, and when Virgil has Aeneas burn his ships upon reaching Italy it does not signify that the future rulers of Rome must abandon the sea, but that they had to fight for their land. Yet in the early imperial period, when Virgil wrote, there was a tendency to revile maritime trade, and by extension the sea itself, because commerce was at odds with the elite's martial values. Yet there is no better indication of the importance the Romans attached to seafaring than a saying attributed to Pompey the Great, who in 56 BCE led a fleet to Africa for grain to ease a shortage at Rome. "When he was about to set sail with it," writes Plutarch, "there was a violent storm at sea, and the ship-captains hesitated to put out; but he led the way on board and ordered them to weigh anchor, crying with a loud voice: 'To sail is necessary; to live is not.'" Although Pompey's biographer wrote in Greek, many medieval European merchant communities later adopted the Latin motto "*Navigare necesse est, vivere non necesse.*"

It would be excessive to claim that the Roman Empire was a product of sea power and sea trade alone, but these were as central to its creation as the Mediterranean was to the empire itself. The empire could not have survived had Roman institutions or sensibilities been in any practical way hostile to maritime enterprise. Perhaps the last word belongs to Seneca, who wrote in the first century of "god, our author . . . [who] gave us winds that we might get to know distant lands. . . . He gave us winds in order that the advantages of each region might become known to all; but not in order to carry legions and cavalry or to transport weapons to destroy mankind." While the Romans never beat their swords into plowshares, they did contribute to the economic integration of the world they occupied, and both shaped and were shaped by the wealth of lands well beyond the Mediterranean, including those bordering the Indian Ocean.

Chapter 6

Chasing the Monsoons

The maritime history of the Indian Ocean unfolded in ways completely different from that of the confined seas of the Mediterranean world. The great distances, the lack of enclosure by opposing shores, and the paucity of island chains linking landmasses ensured that the interactions of Indian Ocean mariners and their respective societies were less intense and immediate than those of the Mediterranean. Seafaring allowed for the transmission of goods and ideas, but without generating the violent rivalries and naval clashes that accompanied such exchanges in the Mediterranean. At the same time, long-distance maritime trade had less impact on political developments, and seafaring never attained the cultural significance it did for people of the Mediterranean. Yet if maritime-driven change was more subtle here than elsewhere, it proved no less durable.

Mediterranean traders became directly involved in the Red Sea and Indian Ocean in the fourth century BCE and their contacts intensified following Rome's annexation of Egypt three hundred years later. The vitality of Mediterranean engagement is borne out by Roman complaints about the drain of precious metals to pay for eastern luxuries, by hoards of Roman coins found in India and Southeast Asia, and even by a Chinese account of a Roman merchant at the Han court in the second century CE. Despite outsiders' interest and participation in the Indian Ocean trade, sailors native to its shores were the primary agents of exchange. Indian investors guaranteed the loans of Mediterranean merchants, and Indian merchants traded in Egyptian Red Sea ports. Early Hindu and Buddhist scriptures and secular laws offer glimpses of the maritime world from the perspective of the Indian Ocean; and Tamil epics from the second century CE on paint a dazzling portrait of a maritime commerce that southern Indians have engaged in, and often dominated, ever since. Connecting the Red Sea and Persian Gulf to the Bay of Bengal and Southeast Asia, and intersecting with coastal and land routes of the subcontinent, these trading networks became the thoroughfares along which successive waves of long-distance navigators penetrated the Indian Ocean world from the birth of Islam in the seventh century to the arrival of European traders at the end of the fifteenth.

Seafaring in Ancient India

Although the name India today identifies a single nation-state, before 1947 it referred to the entire subcontinent south of the Hindu Kush, Karakoram, and Himalaya Mountains and east of the Indus River from which it takes its name. It thus comprised not only India, but Bangladesh and part of Pakistan. Geographically the subcontinent can be divided into three primary regions: the Indo-Gangetic floodplains of the north, which form a broad arc from the Arabian Sea to the Bay of Bengal; the Deccan, a tableland between the Narmada and Krishna Rivers; and the Nigiri Hills at the southern end of the peninsula. The chief ethnic division is between the Aryan population of the north and the Dravidian speakers of the south, whose major languages correspond to the southernmost states of modern India: Kannada in Karnataka, Malayalam in Kerala, Tamil in Tamil Nadu, and Telugu in Andhra Pradesh. The west coast of India is divided between the marshes of the Rann of Kachchh (which spread south from the Indus delta), the Kathiawar Peninsula of Gujarat, the Konkan Coast of Maharashtra state, and the Malabar Coast (Goa, Karnataka, and Kerala). In the east, the Bay of Bengal washes the Coromandel Coast of Tamil Nadu and Andhra Pradesh, Kalinga (northern Andhra Pradesh and Orissa), and the mouths of the Ganga (Ganges) River. The southern end of the peninsula is bordered by two chains of mountains, the Western Ghats, separated from the Arabian Sea by a narrow coastal plain, and the lower Eastern Ghats. India has few major navigable rivers. Those of the west coast are the Indus and, in Gujarat, the Narmada and Tapti. In what is now Bengal, the Ganga delta merges with that of the Brahmaputra, while to the south the Godavari, Krishna, and Kaveri Rivers also empty into the Bay of Bengal.

The millennium following the end of the Harappan civilization around 1700 BCE was characterized by the rise of relatively small chiefdoms and clans along the Indo-Gangetic plain. This is the period in which the Vedas, the foundation texts of Hinduism, were composed. The product of a people bound to the land, the Vedas seldom refer to maritime activities, but they and other sacred and secular South Asian writings contain enough incidental references to sea trade to demonstrate that even if long-distance contacts with the Persian Gulf were interrupted after the demise of the Indus Valley civilization, people continued to go to sea for their livelihoods. One of the oldest references, from the Rig Veda, recounts how the Asvins (gods of healing) came to the help of their friend's son, Bhujyu, while he was on campaign against a neighboring island: "you brought him back in vessels of your own, floating over the ocean, and keeping out the waters. . . . This exploit you achieved, Asvins, in the ocean, where there is nothing to give support, nothing to rest upon, nothing to cling to." The practice of deep-sea navigation is confirmed by an earlier passage that describes Varuna (the Vedic equivalent of Poseidon or Neptune) "who knows the path of the birds flying through the air; he, abiding in the ocean, knows the course of ships." This image suggests the practice of Indian sailors finding their way at sea by following the flight paths of birds, as did their counterparts in Oceania, the Mediterranean, and elsewhere.

That merchants were expected to venture overseas is confirmed by two of the oldest and most comprehensive texts on the legal aspects of seafaring, the *Arthasastra* and the *Laws of Manu*, or *Manusmrti*. The *Arthasastra* is a detailed handbook of governance commonly thought to date from the reign of the first Mauryan king, Chandragupta, in the late fourth century BCE. After coming to the throne of the lower Ganga kingdom of Magadha, Chandragupta extended his authority across the Indo-Gangetic plain. In the northwest he pushed his borders west from the Punjab across Pakistan and into Afghanistan and fought the Hellenistic king Seleucus I. As part of the peace, Seleucus gave his daughter in marriage to Chandragupta's son, Bindusara, and appointed Megasthenes as ambassador to the Mauryan court at Pataliputra (Patna) on the Ganga. In return, Chandragupta gave Seleucus five hundred war elephants, which the latter used to good effect in his wars with Ptolemaic Egypt, a move that would prove a catalyst for the Ptolemies' development of Red Sea trade and the penetration of the Indian Ocean from the west. Chandragupta also expanded south to the Narmada River, the northern border of the Deccan, which Bindusara subsequently conquered along with Kerala and Karnataka to the southwest.

Chandragupta's most important advisor was Kautilya, the putative author of the *Arthasastra*. In his detailed instructions for the role and conduct of the controller of shipping (*navadhyaksa*), a civil office whose functions are comparable to that of a modern coast guard and revenue marine, Kautilya noted that he "should look after activities concerning sea voyages and ferries at the mouths of rivers, as well as ferries over natural lakes, artificial lakes and rivers." The controller collected taxes and duties payable by riverbank villages and towns, fishermen, traders, and divers for conch shell and pearls, as well as port dues from foreign ships and fines for people using river ferries at times or places not prescribed by law. He could confiscate goods being shipped without an official seal, and when fishermen or traders used boats owned by the state or king he collected the appropriate fees. The controller of shipping also had a humanitarian function: "He should rescue boats that have gone out of their course or are tossed about by a gale, like a father. He should make goods that have fallen in water either duty-free or pay half the duty." This rescue work was likely carried out by the ferries he maintained, "big boats in [the] charge of a captain, a pilot, a manipulator of the cutter and ropes and a bailer of water, on big rivers that have to be ferried on [even] in winter and summer, [and] small ones on small rivers flowing [only] in the rainy season."

The controller of shipping may have had an additional military function. According to Megasthenes, Chandragupta's advisors included an admiral, who, like Kautilya's controller of shipping, rented ships to sailors and merchants. Megasthenes observes that whereas artisans, tradesmen, and day-laborers "render services prescribed by the state" as tribute, "shipbuilders receive wages and provisions, at a published scale, for these work for him [the king] alone." The controller of shipping was subordinate to the director of trade, who determined the rates for leasing vessels and encouraged foreign trade by granting exemptions from duties and fees. He was also responsible for deciding when to sail, provisioning ships for their voyages, the prices at which goods should be bought and sold, and the regulations in force at, and dangers peculiar to, various ports of call.

Perhaps revealing an ignorance of practical seafaring, Kautilya broke with prevailing opinion on the benefits of sea trade and how best to conduct it. Whereas most people viewed sea trade as more efficient—"involving little expenditure and exertion and yielding plenty of goods," as Kautilya puts it— he maintained that land transport was safer and less subject to seasonal variation. He further argued that "as between a route along the shore and one on the high sea, the route along the coast is preferable because of the large number of ports, [as is] a river-route, because of perennial use and because the dangers in it can be withstood." Yet rivers can be impassable in the dry season, and most marine casualties take place near coasts, not only because the highest concentration of vessels is there, but because shallow waters and lee shores pose more dangers to seagoing ships than does the open ocean.

It is often claimed that Hindu scripture forbids seafaring, yet the evidence is ambiguous at best. One ancient text cautions that one can lose caste for "making voyages by sea" and "trading with merchandise of any description," while another takes voyages as a given and advises, sensibly enough, "Let him who teaches . . . avoid ships of doubtful solidity." Although a Brahman of the highest caste, Kautilya expresses no reservations about seafaring or overseas trade, and it was not until the fifteenth and sixteenth centuries that some observant Hindus began avoiding overseas travel for purely religious reasons. Even then it was not proscriptions on seafaring that proved prohibitive, but the complexity and cost of the ritual purification required after mingling with non-Hindus. Even if high-caste Hindus declined to go to sea, they had no qualms about investing in, and profiting from, overseas trade.

The *Laws of Manu* offer a fuller exposition of Hindu attitudes toward seafaring than does Kautilya's *Arthasastra*. Probably written around the start of the common era, but reflecting a much older tradition, the *Laws* codify the "social and religious duties tied to class and stage of life" that are an essential feature of Hinduism. They identify the four main castes of priests (Brahmans), rulers, commoners, and servants, and make trade and moneylending the responsibility of commoners. There are no injunctions against overseas commerce, and maritime merchants are given a free hand to conduct their trade as they think best. While the king sets prices for most goods, those carried in long-distance sea trade are subject to a more laissez-faire approach: "When men who are expert in ocean transportation, and can calculate the time, place, and goods, establish an interest rate, that is the rate for the payment of that particular transaction." Moreover, the *Laws of Manu* show that the king owned vessels which traders could rent, and they specify how fees were to be calculated for leasing riverboats. At the same time, "there is no definite rule for (journeys) on the ocean." With respect to accidents, the *Laws* distinguish between a crew's negligence and acts of God: "If anything is broken in a boat through the fault of the boatmen, it should be paid for by the boatmen collectively, (each paying) his own share. This is the decision . . . when the boatmen are at fault on the water; there is no fine for (an accident that is) an act of the gods." While acts of God are not unknown on rivers, this provision apparently applied to accidents at sea.

The *Arthasastra* and *Laws of Manu* presumably synthesize a body of customs and laws of navigation from various parts of Chandragupta's realm, and they survived in some form the breakup of the Mauryan Empire in the 180s BCE. That they were compiled when they were reflects the growth of urban settlements and the expansion of trade in northern India, a process that began in the sixth century BCE. This period likewise saw the development of Jainism and Buddhism, religions derived but distinct from Hinduism and whose spread both encouraged and was encouraged by trade. Because of the extreme doctrine of *ahimsa* (noninjury to living things), Jains were restricted in their occupations: raising animals for slaughter was obviously forbidden, but so was farming because it required pest control. Jains turned increasingly to commerce for their livelihood, and Jainism became especially strong in Gujarat and the southern Indian kingdoms of Pandya, Chola, and Chera—all regions that have played a formative role in India's long-distance sea trade. Reliant as they were on alms for funding their temples, Buddhists were sympathetic to merchants and moneylenders, but in addition they developed a pronounced missionary posture that carried them into Central Asia and China via the Hindu Kush and Karakoram Mountains and east along the silk road, or by ship across the Bay of Bengal to Southeast Asia and onward to China. Although it did not penetrate southern India as thoroughly as Jainism, Buddhism reached Sri Lanka (Ceylon) in 247 BCE, when the third Mauryan king, Ashoka, sent an embassy to the king. Sri Lanka subsequently became the preserve of Theravada Buddhism and a place of pilgrimage and study for priests from throughout Asia.

Ashoka is the best documented Mauryan king thanks to the numerous inscriptions found throughout his domains—pillar edicts clustered in the Gangetic plain, and rock edicts on the subcontinent as far south as Tamil Nadu, along the coasts, and as far west as Kandahar, Afghanistan. Despite, or perhaps because of, his extensive military campaigns, Ashoka is remembered as a model of the repentant, ethical ruler. This transformation came about after he embraced Buddhism in the wake of the horrors of his subjugation of Kalinga, when "A hundred fifty thousand people were deported, a hundred thousand were killed and many times that number perished. Afterwards, now that Kalinga was annexed, the Beloved of the Gods [Ashoka] very earnestly practiced *Dhamma* [ethical behavior], desired *Dhamma* and taught *Dhamma*." The people of Kalinga were renowned for their seamanship; one text refers to the king of Kalinga as the "Lord of the Ocean," while another speaks of the "islands of the Kalinga Sea"—the Bay of Bengal. Although the conquest of the kingdom and its port at Samapa (Ganjam) opened the eastern trading world to the Mauryans, their main port remained Tamralipti (Tamluk), north of Kalinga, which was connected to the capital at Pataliputra via the Ganga and a royal road, a western branch of which led to the Arabian Sea port of Bharuch in Gujarat.

Unlike Hinduism, Buddhism paid little attention to issues of caste and birthright, and merchants could achieve a higher position in society than they theoretically could in Hinduism, and many donated the profits of agriculture and trade to the construction and maintenance of Buddhist sanghas (monasteries). The earliest such religious institutions in India, these initially catered to itinerant missionaries, but they later became permanent monasteries and as such both repositories for trade goods and centers of learning and literacy. As it had been for the Egyptians, the Phoenicians, and the Greeks, literacy was a catalyst for the expansion of trade in India, facilitating the transmission of knowledge about everything from writing itself, which developed in India from about the fourth century BCE, to trade goods and their uses. The Buddhist healing arts, for example, relied in large part on imported spices and herbs, especially from Southeast Asia, and thus stimulated demand for these lucrative items of trade.

The earliest sustained narratives about Indian seafaring are found in the *Jatakas,* a collection of some 550 stories about the Buddha's past lives as a Bodhisattva (enlightened being) first written down in the third century BCE. The stories' antagonists come from various places around the subcontinent, but their overseas journeys invariably take them to Southeast Asia. The "Suparaga Jataka" describes the Bodhisattva as the renowned scion of a family of shipmasters from the west coast port of Bharuch who eventually settled elsewhere. Despite his age and infirmities (in one version of the story, he went blind from exposure to saltwater), a group of merchants beseeches him to sail with them on a voyage to Suvarnabhumi, "the land of gold," in Southeast Asia. Describing the Bodhisattva's qualifications as a mariner, the "Suparaga Jataka" notes that "he recognized all the tell tale signs around him . . . such clues as the fish, the color of the water, the type of [underwater?] terrain, the birds, and the rocks," the same sort of skills one finds in descriptions of wayfinding in Oceania. In the course of their voyage, storms drive the ship well off course, and when the merchants and crew entreat him for their help, he brushes aside their concerns by saying "If you venture out into the middle of the ocean, you must not be surprised to face a cataclysmic storm." The Bodhisattva's virtue ensures their safety and after a succession of narrow escapes they return to Bharuch with a hold filled with jewels and gems. Although the "Suparaga Jataka" says that these were hauled up from the seabed, such mineral treasures are associated with Sri Lanka and the Malay Peninsula.

In the "Samkha Jataka" and "Mahajana Jataka," the Bodhisattva is portrayed variously as a wealthy man esteemed for his generosity in endowing almshouses, and as the rightful heir to a throne usurped by an uncle. Concerned that he may run out of money to give away, Samkha decides to "go in a boat to the Land of Gold and bring wealth" from it. Mahajanaka's intent is to raise funds to pay for his uncle's ouster, also by going to the Land of Gold, against his mother's wishes: "My child, a voyage does not always succeed, there are many obstacles, better not go." Both Samkha's and Mahajanaka's ships sink, but they are rescued by the goddess of the sea, Manimekalai, who returns them home together with the riches they had sought in the first place.

Common to both Samkha's and Mahajanaka's stories are the nearly identical accounts of how the protagonists prepare to survive shipwreck. The "Samkha Jataka" relates that the prince "never wept nor lamented nor invoked any deities, but knowing that the vessel was doomed he rubbed some sugar and ghee, and, having eaten his belly full, he smeared his two clean garments with oil and put them tightly around him and stood leaning against the mast. When the vessel sank the mast stood upright. The crowd on board became food for the fishes and tortoises, and the water all around assumed the colour of blood." Samkha is also said to have taken "precaution against the dangers caused by the fishes and tortoises," though what these might have been is not revealed. These preparations against hypothermia by smearing oneself and one's clothes with oil are realistic. So, too, is the account of what happens to the unprepared Mahajanaka, who "had his whole body burnt while remaining in sea water for seven days," an accurate summary of the gruesome effects of dehydration and a week's exposure to sun and saltwater. While the ventures described in the *Jatakas* are fundamentally successful, the focus on the perils of seafaring is in stark contrast to the emphasis on heroic exploits lavished on western heroes like Gilgamesh and Odysseus.

Persian Trade in the Indian Ocean from the Sixth Century BCE

While ancient Indian texts with maritime content describe voyages across the Bay of Bengal to Suvarnabhumi and Suvarnadvipa, "the island of gold," in Southeast Asia, there was a lively western trade on the Arabian Sea. Greek and Latin texts mention Bharuch (also called Barygaza and Broach) as an important port of call. Located at the mouth of the Narmada River on the Gulf of Khambhat—near the ancient Harappan port of Lothal—Bharuch had ready access to the wealth of the Indo-Gangetic plain and the Deccan. The port's founding in the mid-first millennium BCE followed the revival of sea trade between India and the Persian Gulf and the growth of the trans-Arabian caravan trade that carried Indian goods from the gulf to the Mediterranean ports of Phoenicia and Syria, where they were shipped to Egypt, Greece, and beyond. Whatever the causes for its renaissance, this seaborne trade was significant enough for Neo-Babylonian, Achaemenid, and Hellenistic rulers in turn to take an active interest in the Persian Gulf.

In the early sixth century BCE, a Neo-Babylonian king established the port of Teredon near Basra, Iraq. Within twenty years of his death, Cyrus the Great conquered Babylon and thereby acquired an empire that stretched from eastern Iran to the Mediterranean seaboard. Cyrus came from the province of Fars (also called Pars or Persis) in the tableland of southern Iran, a region separated from the Persian Gulf and the Arabian Sea by the Zagros Mountains. The coast is inhospitable and freshwater often has to be brought in by canals and aqueducts. As a result, coastal rulers often operated independently of states in the interior, and ties between people living on opposite shores of the Persian Gulf could be as strong as, or stronger than, those between coastal communities and their respective hinterlands. Cyrus was a lenient ruler celebrated for proclaiming freedom of religion for all the people within his domains, which he describes as "the entire world from the Upper to the Lower Sea," an echo of the language used in Sargon's day 1,800 years before.

Between about 525 and 510 BCE, the Persian Empire expanded to encompass a broad swath of Anatolia and the Near East from Ionia and Egypt in the west to the Indus Valley. Before his preoccupation with punishing the Greeks for the Ionian Revolt, which precipitated the Persian Wars, Darius took an interest in the maritime borders of his empire, and he established Aginis (Ampe) on the site of Teredon. The extent of Achaemenid involvement in Persian Gulf navigation in the early centuries of the empire is difficult to judge. However in the late fourth century BCE Alexander the Great's admiral Nearchus recorded the names of sixteen Persian river and coastal ports, and described navigational aids near an island about 150 miles from the Shatt al-Arab, where "the shallows . . . were marked on either side by poles driven down, just as in the strait between the islands of Leucas and Acarnania [in the Ionian Sea just north of Ithaca] signposts have been set up for navigators to prevent the ships grounding in the shallows."

Navigation on the Persian Gulf was not as vital to the Achaemenids in the sixth century BCE as it would become, perhaps because it was overshadowed by the commerce of the Mediterranean and Red Seas. In Egypt, Darius may have completed the canal between the Nile and the Red Sea first attempted by Necho II in the previous century, and he commissioned Scylax of Caryanda (in Asia Minor) to sail from the Indus to the Red Sea. Scylax hugged the coast of Pakistan and Iran, crossed the Gulf of Oman to the Arabian Peninsula, and, according to Herodotus, "after a voyage of some thirty months reached the place from which [Necho II] had sent out the Phoenicians" to circumnavigate Africa. Scylax wrote an account of his voyage, but this earliest known description of these waters has not survived.

Darius died before his apparent ambition to initiate sea trade between the Red Sea and the Persian Gulf bore fruit, and his successors had little interest in following his lead. The next comparable effort was the initiative of Alexander, Darius's heir in spirit if not in fact. After heeding the wishes of his troops to halt his eastward march at the Indus River in 325 BCE, Alexander divided his force in three. Two armies returned to the former Persian capital of Susa overland, while Nearchus was commissioned to sail from the Indus to the Persian Gulf. According to Nearchus, "Alexander had a vehement desire to

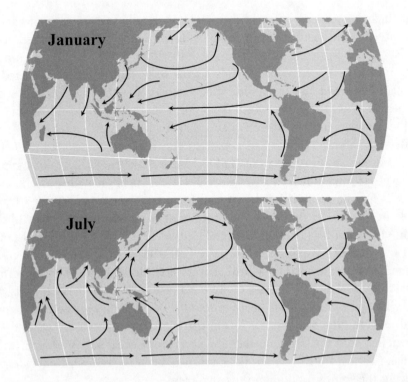

The prevailing winds change around the world between winter and summer, but nowhere is this more apparent than in the Monsoon Seas of the Indian Ocean and East and Southeast Asia, where the prevailing winds shift from northeast to southwest.

sail the sea . . . from India to Persia; but feared lest . . . his whole fleet might be destroyed; and this, being no small blot on his great achievements, might wreck all his happiness." After building a fleet of triremes and other craft, the Greeks waited at the city Alexander founded at Patala (or Potana, near Hyderabad, Pakistan) until "the trade winds had sunk to rest, which continue blowing from the Ocean to the land all the summer season, and hence render the voyage impossible."

This is actually a description of the southwest monsoon, the stronger of two seasonal winds—"monsoon" comes from the Arabic, *mawsim*, meaning "season"—that dictated sailing schedules across the Indian Ocean and the waters of Southeast and East Asia until the development of the steam engine. The monsoons are determined by the relative temperatures of the Asian landmass and the Indian Ocean. In summer, warm air rising over the land creates a high-pressure system that draws strong winds and often torrential rains from the southwest. High winds batter the coasts of the Indian subcontinent and inhibit even coastal navigation, and several times a decade tropical cyclones with winds in excess of 150 kilometers per hour devastate the northern end of the Bay of Bengal. In winter, when the land is colder than the water, a low-pressure system over the Indian Ocean draws the northeast monsoon winds from China and Japan toward the Strait of Malacca, and from South Asia toward Africa. The seasonal variation in wind direction and intensity had a far greater impact on navigation than did the distances involved. Sailors did not hesitate to sail across two thousand miles of open ocean between Aden and southern India or Sri Lanka, but they did so only when the winds were in their favor.*

Nearchus's fleet of eight hundred "ships of war, merchantmen and horse transports" sailed in stages along the coast of Pakistan and Iran, before turning into the Persian Gulf. Hugging the eastern shore, they reached the head of the gulf and proceeded up the Pasitigris River to rendezvous with Alexander at Susa. Shortly before his death the next year, Alexander dispatched three other expeditions with a view to establishing a connection between the gulf and the Red Sea. Two explored the Persian Gulf, but no farther, while a third, under Anaxicrates, sailed down the Red Sea to the south coast of Yemen, the source of most of the aromatic gums, resins, frankincense, and myrrh so important in religious rituals. Red Sea trade would grow rapidly in the following century, but for the moment the long south coast of the Arabian Peninsula between the Red Sea and Persian Gulf remained all but unknown to outsiders.

Following Alexander's death, the territory of the erstwhile Persian Empire was divided ultimately among the Seleucids and the Indo-Greek kingdoms of Bactria (in Afghanistan) and Gandhara (Pakistan). The Seleucids controlled the Persian Gulf and as we have seen maintained diplomatic relations with the Mauryan court of Chandragupta and Bindusara, their best known ambassador being Megasthenes. The importance of the Persian Gulf to the Seleucids is seen in their establishment of garrisons on the islands of Failaka (off Kuwait) and Bahrain. Given the lack of a military threat to their power from anywhere around the gulf, their motive may have been to protect trade from pirates and other hazards, as did the controller of shipping mentioned in the *Arthasastra*. A letter of 288/287 BCE detailing a donation by Seleucus to a temple in Ionia hints at the enormous revenues generated from the empire's foreign trade:

* The northeast monsoon rarely exceeds Force 4 (11–16 knots) in the Indian Ocean, and between the equator and 5°N and north of 20°N the winds are variable. The southwest monsoon averages Force 6 (22–27 knots) in the western Arabian Sea and Force 4–5 in the northern and eastern Arabian Sea and Bay of Bengal, but reaches Force 7 (28–33 knots) across all regions in July and August.

"ten talents [300 kilograms] of frankincense, one talent of myrrh, two minae [1.8 kg] of cassia, two minae of cinnamon, two minae of costus [a flowering plant related to ginger]."

These amounts pale in comparison with the ransom paid to save the prosperous northern Arabian trading city of Gerrha. When Antiochus the Great threatened to attack from the sea in 205 BCE, the Gerrhaeans purchased peace for "five hundred talents of silver, a thousand talents of frankincense, and two hundred talents of the so-called 'stacte' [oil of myrrh or cinnamon]." The only other Seleucid naval campaign on the Persian Gulf took place when "The governor of Mesene appointed by King Antiochus, Numenius, here won a battle against the Persians with his fleet" on the Musandam peninsula. (Which of the ten Seleucid kings named Antiochus Numenius served is unknown, although most opinion favors Antiochus IV [175–164 BCE].) Despite their victory, the balance of power soon shifted to the Parthians of northeast Persia, who achieved independence from the Seleucids in 247 BCE, and about a century later established an empire that would endure in Persia and Mesopotamia into the third century CE.

Neither Seleucid nor Parthian influence in the Persian Gulf seems to have translated into firm political control. In 141 BCE, a Seleucid satrap asserted the independence of a Shatt al-Arab port he named for himself Charax Spasinou, "the palisade of Hyspaosines." He extended his rule as far north as Babylonia, but after his death the Characene kingdom was reduced to the extreme south of Mesopotamia before being drawn into the orbit of the Parthians. Charax Spasinou's subsequent political status is uncertain, but it seems to have survived as a semiautonomous kingdom known not only to traders of the Indian Ocean and Mediterranean, but even to the Chinese, who called it Tiaozhi. Its fame depended on its merchants' role as middlemen in the Indian Ocean, alongside merchants of Gerrha and Sabae, in Yemen. An inland capital near the modern city of Marib, Sabae was said to be so heavily perfumed with the fragrance of incense-bearing trees that "the people are made torpid by the aromatic plants [and] they cure their sluggishness by means of a fumigation of resin and goat's beard." The source of these scents was the forests of myrrh, frankincense, balsam, cinnamon, and cassia trees of the southern Arabian Peninsula. In addition to sailing east, the Sabaeans traded with the coast of Africa "using large rafts. . . . Not a few of the Sabaeans also employ boats made of skins."

Sabae's commercial longevity was astonishing. While it is sometimes equated with the biblical Sheba, the oldest account of its legendary wealth is found in *On the Erythraean Sea*, a second-century BCE geographical treatise by Agatharchides of Cnidus, one of the earliest extant sources of information about Indian Ocean commerce in antiquity. Written around 140 BCE, but based largely on older sources, it offers a valuable summary of exploration in the reigns of Ptolemy II and Ptolemy III. (Erythraean, meaning "red," was the name given by the Greeks to the Indian Ocean, the Persian Gulf, and the Red Sea, which they also called the Arabian Gulf.) Agatharchides wrote "This tribe surpasses in wealth and all the various forms of extravagance not only the nearby Arabs but also the rest of mankind." They were still at it seven centuries later, when a Buddhist monk named Faxian visited Sri Lanka and reported, "The houses of the Sa-poh [Sabaean] merchants are very beautifully adorned." In the meantime, their long-distance trade catered to the wants of Ptolemaic Egypt and their prosperity was not remotely threatened until the Romans attempted to invade southern Arabia in the first century CE.

Ptolemaic Egypt and the Indian Ocean

If the Persian Gulf was a natural conduit for commerce between Mesopotamia and India, the Red Sea held less promise for long-distance trade. Apart from frankincense and myrrh in Yemen, the products of its shores were few, and it was far removed from the abundant commodities and luxuries of South Asia and the Persian Gulf. The difficulties of bucking the sea's northerly winds, navigating its numerous shoals and reefs, and surviving the harsh environment ashore hindered the development of any but the most extraordinary trade. With an average annual rainfall of only four millimeters in the north, water and vegetation were scarce, and most provisions had to be imported from the Nile valley or from abroad. In the pharaonic period, the costs involved were too great to be borne by private merchants, and even pharaohs attempted to reach the riches of Punt, Ophir, and Sheba via sea only occasionally. The Red Sea boasted no equivalent to Charax Spasinou; indeed, in the words of a modern archaeologist, "The Red Sea ports were surprisingly squalid places," and their remains are difficult to discern in the barren landscape.

The Ptolemaic kings who ruled Egypt for the three centuries after the death of Alexander were the first to take a sustained interest in the Red Sea trade. How much shipping there was when Alexander ordered Anaxicrates to sail there is unknown, but in 287 BCE a Ptolemaic squadron defeated Nabataean pirates in the Gulf of Aqaba, so by that time the volume was sufficient to attract predators and merit protection. Egyptian interest in the region grew considerably under Ptolemy II Philadelphus, who hoped to replenish his dwindling supply of war elephants, which the Greeks first encountered during Alexander's eastern campaigns. At the battle of Gaza in 312 BCE, Ptolemy

I captured some of the elephants that Chandragupta had given to Seleucus, but these failed to breed. Although Ashoka exchanged ambassadors with Ptolemy II and may have discussed gifts of war elephants, shipping them across the Indian Ocean to circumvent the Seleucids was probably judged impractical, though not necessarily impossible. As an alternative, Ptolemy II began to import elephants from East Africa. Even this comparatively short-haul trade required significant improvements to navigation, including, perhaps, reopening the canal between the Nile and the Gulf of Suez, and establishing ports on the Red Sea. In the 260s BCE the first load of elephants was shipped 300 nautical miles from Ptolemaïs of the Hunts (about 50 miles south of modern Port Sudan) to Berenike, a port sheltered from the north winds by the Ras Banas peninsula. Other early Ptolemaic ports included Arsinöe (named for Ptolemy's wife) in the vicinity of modern Port Suez, and Myos Hormos (Quseir al-Qadim), due east of Coptos and about 160 miles north of Berenike and 270 south of Suez. From Berenike, the elephants were led through the wadis of the Eastern Desert to Aswan, a twelve-day journey, and then shipped downriver to Memphis. Although there are references to "elephant carriers" (*elephantegos*) in classical sources, how these vessels differed in design from other merchant ships and where they were built are unknown.

The elephant trade was a dangerous business on an unforgiving sea. In a grim account reminiscent of the Old Kingdom story "The Shipwrecked Sailor," Agatharchides describes the loss of an elephant ship south of Port Sudan, where

> the sea, being all shoals, is found to be not more than three fathoms [5.5 meters] in depth and extremely green in color. . . . The region presents no problems for oared ships as waves do not come in from afar, and it furnishes abundant fishing. But the elephant transports, which ride deep in the water because of their weight and are burdened with their gear, encounter great and terrible dangers in these areas. For running with sails set and often continuing through the night, because of strong winds, they are wrecked when they run aground on the rocks and submerged bars. The sailors are unable to disembark because generally the water is deeper than the height of a man. When they do not succeed in saving their ship with their poles, they throw overboard everything except the food. If they do not escape in this way, they fall into great despair because there is neither island nor headland nor another ship to be seen in the vicinity. For these places are completely inhospitable and rarely do people sail through them in ships.

The great dangers notwithstanding, the Ptolemies pursued elephants for their ivory as well as for warfare, and as herds were killed off hunters moved ever southward, establishing new ports at Adulis (Massawa, Eritrea), and south of the Bab al-Mandeb. By the 240s BCE, Ptolemy III had a force of some three hundred war elephants, but the African breed proved no match for the Seleucid animals and the hunt for war elephants was abandoned by the end of the century.

Even more important as a source of revenue for the imperial coffers was the luxury trade with southern Arabia and India, over which the Ptolemies exercised a tight monopoly. The nature of this trade is laid out by Agatharchides, who describes a mature network of trade down the Red Sea and across the western Indian Ocean. Once through the Bab al-Mandeb, ships may have called at the island of Socotra, about five hundred miles east of Aden, and the name of which comes from the Sanskrit Sukhataradvipa, meaning "fortunate" or "most pleasant" island. Agatharchides describes the bustle of Socotra where "one can see riding at anchor merchant vessels from neighboring countries. Most of those encountered there are from the port [Patala] Alexander built by the Indus River. Not a few, however, come from Persia and Carmania [southern Iran] and the whole nearby region." Later, the western terminus of this Indian Ocean trade was on the African mainland, at Malaô (Berbera, Somalia) or farther east on the Horn of Africa at a place called Mosyllon.

The period in which Agatharchides wrote was a turning point in the development of Indian Ocean trade. One theory holds that this is when a Ptolemaic sailor named Hippalus "discovered" the monsoon winds, although for indigenous sailors the monsoons were a fact of life and Nearchus had ascribed his delay in sailing from the Indus to seasonal winds almost two hundred years before. Government-sponsored trade between Egypt and India seems to have begun in the closing decades of the third century BCE, after a shipwrecked Indian merchant was rescued on the Red Sea and brought to Alexandria. Restored to health, "he promised to act as guide on the trip to India for the men who had been previously selected by the king." Eudoxus of Cyzicus was probably the captain chosen for this expedition. He is said to have returned from India with perfumes and precious stones only to have them confiscated by Ptolemy VII. Eudoxus made a second voyage under the auspices of Ptolemy's widow. "But on his return voyage he was driven south of his course by the winds to the south of Ethiopia, and being driven to certain places he conciliated the people by sharing with them bread, wine, and dried figs (for they had no share of such things), and in return therefore he received a supply of freshwater and the guidance of pilots, and he also made a list of some of their words."

If on this second voyage Eudoxus sailed from India on the northeast monsoon and without an experienced navigator, he could easily have been driven south of his intended destination. At the same time, the fact that he could hire pilots on the African coast shows that he was still within the orbit of an active maritime trading world. Upon reaching Egypt, his goods were again confiscated. He managed to keep the stempost of a vessel he had found on the African coast and that sailors in Alexandria told him was from a *hippoi*, a vessel peculiar to Carthaginian Gadir in Spain. On the strength of this, Eudoxus concluded that Carthaginians must have sailed around Africa from west to east, so he fitted out an expedition at his own expense and sailed for the Atlantic via Puteoli and Gadir. Frustrated by contrary winds in the Atlantic, he returned to Spain. Around 100 BCE, he outfitted a second expedition and sailed into oblivion.

The difficulties Eudoxus faced with his royal patrons notwithstanding, Egypt was now open to the Indian Ocean trade, which flourished to such an extent that special officials were appointed to guard against piracy on the Red Sea. Apart from this, we know little of how the trade was conducted. Whether the majority of the traders at this time were from Egypt and the Mediterranean or from the Indian Ocean; whether Egyptian and Hellenistic merchants sailed in their own ships, in those of Indian or Arabian traders, or both; the volume of the trade; or the profits either to individuals or, in the form of taxes and duties, to the government—all these questions remain for the most part unanswered.

Western Indian Ocean Trade in the Early First Millennium

Even after the opening of the Nile–Red Sea canal under Ptolemy II, traders bound for Egypt usually sailed only as far as Berenike, and sometimes Myos Hormos, but rarely up the Gulf of Suez to Arsinöe. Thus neglected, by the middle of the first century BCE the Ptolemaic canal was impassable. Had it been maintained, the course of Egyptian and Roman history might well have followed a different trajectory. Following the battle of Actium, Cleopatra hoped to elude capture by crossing the Isthmus of Suez and establishing Ptolemaic rule somewhere on the Red Sea. When Marc Antony caught up with her in Alexandria, "he found Cleopatra venturing upon a hazardous and great undertaking . . . to raise her fleet out of water and drag the ships across [the Isthmus of Suez], and after launching them in the Arabian Gulf with much money and a large force, to settle in parts outside of Egypt, thus escaping war and servitude." Rome's Nabataean allies burned several of her ships and, succumbing to Antony's assurances that all was not lost, she abandoned the effort. Events proved Antony wrong. Within the year both he and Cleopatra were dead, and Rome annexed Egypt.

The Romans took an immediate interest in the Red Sea trade, and in 26

BCE Aelius Gallus was appointed to lead an expedition of ten thousand soldiers to Yemen. Having moved to Arsinöe all the necessary supplies, from building material and weapons to food and water, the Romans built a fleet of 80 warships (biremes, triremes, and lighter vessels) and 130 transports. Gallus lost a number of ships off the Sinai Peninsula, "on account of difficult sailing, but not on account of any enemy." His expedition to Yemen ended in defeat, but having learned his lesson on returning from Yemen, Gallus had his men disembark at Myos Hormos to march overland to the Nile at Coptos. The kingdoms of southern Arabia—Main, Sabae, Qataban, and Hadramawt—remained independent until the advent of Islam in the seventh century, but Gallus's expedition in no way inhibited the Roman appetite for oriental luxuries. While land caravans played an important part in the carriage of goods from east to west, the geographer Strabo recorded a dramatic expansion in Red Sea trade. Accompanying Aelius Gallus on a visit to Egypt, he "learned that as many as one hundred twenty vessels were sailing from Myos Hormos to India, whereas formerly, under the Ptolemies, only a very few [not so many as twenty] ventured to undertake the voyage and to carry on traffic in Indian merchandise." Myrrh and frankincense came from southern Arabia and Somalia, many spices (above all pepper) and precious stones were Indian, while some exotics—Chinese silks, for instance—reached the west by way of India. There was also a reciprocal slave trade. Eudoxus took "music girls . . . physicians and other artisans" with him to India, and Asian slaves were not uncommon in Rome, but for the time being this was a relatively low-volume trade in people with special talents.

The most exhaustive description of the Indian Ocean trade is the first-century CE *Periplus of the Erythraean Sea*, written in a plain Greek by a native or resident of Egypt. Apart from this, we know nothing about the author—his (presumably) name, background, experience, or age, or what place he occupied in the hierarchy of the merchant community. Unlike the bookish Agatharchides, the anonymous author was not a compiler of other people's information. His enumeration of which goods moved between which ports, his emphasis on certain Indian ports, his relative silence on the trade of the Persian Gulf, and the speculative nature of his descriptions of the Bay of Bengal are indicative of firsthand experience trading between Egypt and India. While he refers to some aspects of shiphandling, he focuses on goods and the ports where they could be traded. The surviving text is short—about twenty printed pages—and traces two primary itineraries, one from the northern Red Sea down the coast of Africa as far as Rhapta (near Dar es-Salaam, Tanzania), and another along the coast of Yemen and then across open water to Indian ports between Barbarikon, on the Indus River, and Muziris (Cranganur) on the Malabar Coast.

The author of the *Periplus* distinguishes five primary trading areas: the Red Sea, East Africa and southern Arabia in the west, and the Persian Gulf (which he all but ignores) and India in the east. The goods can be grouped into nine categories: food and drink; textiles and clothing; household items; raw materials; precious stones; spices and aromatics; drugs and dyes; animals; and slaves. Egypt's most important exports were utilitarian objects such as metals, tools, blankets, and clothing—goods not unlike those itemized in the description of Queen Hatshepsut's expedition to Punt fifteen centuries earlier—and horses and mules. The most valuable imports were myrrh, frankincense, Indian pepper, and other luxuries such as tortoiseshell, ivory, rhinoceros horn, and nautilus shell from Africa and Arabia; turquoise, lapis lazuli, onyx, agate, pearls, diamonds, and sapphires from South Asia; and Chinese silks. The author refers to the Indian port of Bharuch more than any other, but he enumerates seventeen ports between there and Cape Comorin, the southern tip of India, which indicates the Romans' increasing familiarity with the Konkan and Malabar Coasts.

The *Periplus* mentions a number of foods that may have been intended for elite customers overseas—wine, for example—but which may have been carried simply to satisfy the wants of expatriate merchants, as would likely be the case for olive oil and garum, the Mediterranean fish sauce. Excavations at Berenike have revealed a similar impulse on the part of Indian merchants sailing to Egypt. The remains of coconut, rice, amla, mung bean, and Job's tears—all staples of Indian cuisine—have been found at the Red Sea port, although no ancient source mentions any of these as a commodity. Expatriate trading colonies would not have depended entirely on goods imported from home, but whether of Mediterranean or Indian Ocean origin, familiar foods would be a comfort to expatriate traders just as they are today. There is other scattered evidence of Indian Ocean travelers even in the Mediterranean, from an early-second-century BCE inscription at Delos by someone from Hadramawt in southern Arabia; to a statuette of Manimekhala, heroine of the Tamil epic *Manimekhalai*, recovered from the ashes of Pompeii; and notices of Indian embassies to Augustus and of one sent by the Sri Lankan king Bhatikabhaya to the court of either Augustus or Claudius, presumably in response to the needs of the merchant community.

The western port with the strongest ties to the Indian Ocean was Alexandria, whose primacy in the Mediterranean trade was assured by the empire's need for Egyptian grain, but which was also celebrated for its contacts with trade zones beyond the Greco-Roman world. The first-century orator Dio Chrysostom praised the Alexandrians' preeminence in the commerce of the Red Sea and the Indian Ocean and noted that "the trade, not merely of islands, ports, a few straits and isthmuses, but of practically the whole world is yours. For Alexandria is situated, as it were, at the crossroads of the whole world, of even the most remote nations." It was, moreover, "a market which brings together into one place all manner of men, displaying them to one another and, as far as possible, making them a kindred people."

That this was not just rhetorical gilding of Alexandria's reputation is borne out by a singular document (in Greek) of the second century detailing the substance of a loan arrangement between a lender in Muziris, India, and a borrower in need of funds to pay for a shipment to Alexandria. As was likely typical, the goods—in this case nard, ivory, and fabric—were pledged as security for the loan, which the borrower promised to repay to the lender or his agents at Alexandria. In the meantime, the shipper-borrower was responsible for all costs associated with getting the goods from Muziris to either Berenike or Myos Hormos, from there overland to Coptos, and then down the Nile to Alexandria, where all goods were subject to a 25 percent duty. The contract does not give the name or nationality of the borrower, lender, or agents, but the lender was probably a member of a "Roman" (but certainly Greek-speaking) expatriate community in Muziris, and his agents were probably colleagues from Egypt or elsewhere in the eastern Mediterranean. This agreement, along with Dio's description of Alexandria's cosmopolitanism and what we know of Indian Ocean trade generally, indicates the likelihood of other arrangements involving lenders and borrowers from India and elsewhere. Just as trade was not limited to citizens of the Roman Empire, it was not the exclusive preserve of men, either. A second- or third-century inscription tells of "Aelia Isidora and Aelia Olympias, distinguished matrons, *naukleroi* [shipowners or charterers] and merchants of the Red Sea." Unfortunately, we know nothing else of their business, except that they were rich enough to make a dedication in an Egyptian temple and that they employed a captain or business agent named Apollinarios, whose name appears after theirs.

From the start of Rome's Indian Ocean trade, citizens of a certain stripe warned against the constant export of gold to pay for eastern goods. Pliny the Elder complained that Romans squandered their wealth on oriental luxuries, exporting fifty million sesterces per year to Asia (half this amount to India alone) for the purchase of beryl, pearls, ivory, silks, and pepper.* Pliny's

---

* In the imperial period, a sesterce was a bronze coin weighing about twenty-five grams. One hundred million sesterces was a considerable amount, but the wealth of many Romans has been calculated at many times that. The philosopher Seneca was worth three hundred million sesterces and Pliny the Elder at least four hundred thousand; imperial grants of half a million sesterces to impoverished senators were not uncommon. By way of comparison, slaves were reckoned at about two thousand sesterces per head, and needy children received monthly subsidies of twelve to sixteen sesterces in the early second century.

sentiment was widespread, especially among conservatives who worried that Romans were becoming decadent. Augustus's successor, Tiberius, sought to curb the extravagance of the wealthiest and most ostentatious senators, whom he criticized for their "vast mansions . . . cosmopolitan hordes of slaves . . . ponderous gold and silver plate," and above all, "the feminine specialty—the export of our currency to foreign or enemy countries for precious stones." He considered imposing new sumptuary laws but succumbed to political pressure and in the end did nothing.

Southern Indian Maritime Trade in the Early First Millennium

The testimony of Mediterranean merchants, geographers, and politicians about Rome's eastern trade is corroborated by the archaeological record and contemporary writings from southern India, some of which tell of people called Yavanas. At the time of Alexander, this referred to Ionian Greeks but Yavana eventually came to be used for westerners generally—Greeks, Romans, Arabs, and Persians—who traded to and resided in southern India. Roman and imitation-Roman pottery has been found at sites on the Bay of Bengal, notably the Chola town of Arikamedu, near modern Puducherry (formerly Pondicherry), which was a center of local, regional, and international trade for a thousand years from about the third century BCE. These finds are too few and widespread to indicate the existence of a permanent foreign population; they may be the remains of amphorae that made their way via either a coastal route dominated by indigenous traders or by overland and riverine trade from west coast ports such as Bharuch. In addition, archaeologists have recovered hoards of silver *denarii* bearing the images of Augustus and Tiberius, and gold *aurii* of the first, second, and fifth centuries. These would have been valued as bullion in the Deccan, where copper and lead coins circulated, and in southern India, where there was no local currency.

This was a period of formative change in southern India, the economy of which depended on agriculture, crafts, and the mining of iron and semiprecious stones. But the growth of the southern kingdoms was tied to their pepper crops and their location at the intersection of the sea-lanes between Africa and the Near East and Southeast Asia, and the coastal routes around India and Sri Lanka. The Tamil-speaking Chola, Pandya, and Chera people coalesced into independent kingdoms in the early centuries of the common era. Frequently at war with each other and states to the north, they demonstrated their own expansionist tendencies by their forays into Sri Lanka. The Coromandel Coast of southeast India was the meeting ground of a far more varied mix of ethnicities, religions, and languages than the somewhat homogeneous Mediter-ranean, or indeed anywhere else except Sri Lanka. The people and products of Southeast Asia, fifteen hundred miles across the Bay of Bengal, had little in common with those of the Ganga-Brahmaputra delta, about twelve hundred miles to the northeast, who differed in their turn from those of the Persian Gulf or the Red Sea, about two thousand miles northwest and twenty-five hundred miles west, respectively. Catering to these visitors involved a broad cross section of the community who supplied merchants with trade goods, food, gear for their vessels, and protection from theft. Tamil poets of the early first millennium revel in their bustling ports and the networks of trade that connected them to distant shores. Far from inhabiting a subcontinent back-water, they live in cities that do not sleep, whose people not only embrace but exalt the cosmopolitan opportunities of trade. What it lacks in the catalogues of goods and destinations found in contemporary Latin, Greek, or Chinese sources, Tamil literature more than makes up for in its shimmering descrip-tions of the vitality of sea trade and the wealth it brings, and by extension it helps to animate our impressions of other ports of the period.

Ilanko Atikal's second-century *Cilappatikaram,* or *The Tale of an Anklet,* is a love story about Kannaki and Kovalan, both children of prosperous merchants from Puhar (also called Kaveripattinam), the seaport capital of the early Chola kingdom on the Bay of Bengal. Kannaki is a "Noble daughter of a prince among merchants"—a characterization reminiscent of Isaiah's description of the Tyrians, "whose merchants were princes." Puhar is "the city/that pros-pered from the wealth of the ocean," where "lofty banners seemed to pro-claim: /'In this expanse of white sand is the wealth/Brought in ships by men who have voyaged/From their native lands to live here.'" Ilanko Atikal writes how at night the port glows with the lights of artisans, jewelers, fishmongers, peddlers from the interior, and "with the undying lamps of foreigners/Speak-ing strange tongues; and with the lamps/Of guards watching over piles of merchandise." Along the shore of her sheltered coves, "with the beacons lit up to guide ships/. . . were row/Upon row of boats overburdened with a profu-sion/Of fresh produce from the hills and seas."

Kaveripattinam and its merchants are equally celebrated in Uruthirankan-nanar's fourth-century *Pattinappalai,* which presents a livelier accounting of trade than is found in most other sources. In addition to the fish, grain, pepper, and precious stones of southern India, Uruthirankannanar writes of "Swift, prancing steeds [brought] by sea in ships"—horses were a staple export from Persia and Arabia for hundreds of years—gold and gems from the Himalayas, sandalwood, pearls, and red coral from Southeast Asia, manufactured goods from Myanmar, and food from Sri Lanka. Uruthirankannanar is at pains to stress the ethical conduct of Kaveripattinam's seafarers and notes that "For others' goods they have/The same regard as for their own/In trade. Nor do they try to get/Too much in selling their own goods,/Nor give too little when they buy./They set a fair price on all things." A passage in a sequel to the *Cilappatikaram* suggests that the people of Kaveripattinam were relative new-comers to fair dealing and that their initial prosperity may have grown from more rough-and-tumble pursuits. "In the past, we have made feast, devouring the bodies of the survivors of the very many ships that have been wrecked in the sea not far from our shores. We have plundered all the goods they carried, their cargoes of precious aloes and sweet-scented sandalwood, their bales of cloth, their precious objects—gold, diamonds, and rubies—and other booty of shipwreck." The metamorphosis from plunder to productive trade seems to have been made within living memory, but it recalls a comparable transformation in attitudes toward piracy noted by Thucydides in the ancient Mediterranean and notable elsewhere throughout history. The existence of piracy presumes the presence of a lucrative trade, but it only flourishes in the absence of legitimate state power with the means to contain it and redirect pirates' entrepreneurship. The eradication of piracy therefore depends on the ability of states not just to overpower pirates, but to create lawful alternatives for gain. By this time, trade in southern India had passed a critical threshold that facilitated the growth of maritime commerce to the benefit of merchants and kings.

Sasanian-Byzantine Rivalry in the Indian Ocean

The *Pattinappalai*'s mention of food from Sri Lanka is one of the few references to exports from that island, which was best known to Greek and Chinese authors for its transit trade, although these rarely differentiate between products native to Sri Lanka and those that came to the island from elsewhere. A sixth-century Egyptian merchant-turned-monk named Cosmas Indicopleustes (literally, "sailor to India") wrote about Sri Lanka and its trade from personal experience and was particularly impressed by its wealth of goods "from the remotest countries, I mean Tzinitsa [China] and other trading places," including "silks, aloes, cloves, sandalwood, and other products." The silk was Chinese, the aloes and sandalwood Indonesian, and the cloves came from the Spice Islands.

Among the traders in Sri Lanka who caught Cosmas's attention were Nestorian Christians (Cosmas may have been one himself), many of whom had migrated down the coast of India from Persia. (Saint Thomas the Apos-

tle reputedly preached in southern India.) Commerce in the Persian Gulf
had grown markedly following the rise of Ardashir, founder of the Sasanian
Dynasty (224–651). A native of Fars, Ardashir paid special attention to the
provinces bordering the Persian Gulf and he founded or revived several river
and coastal ports, including Astarabad-Ardashir (the old Charax Spasinou) and
Rev-Ardashir (Rishahr). Now part of Bushehr, one of modern Iran's foremost
ports, and about 150 miles from the Shatt al-Arab, Rev-Ardashir has been
occupied off and on since the fifth millennium BCE. Although water had to be
brought in via a forty-kilometer-long canal built in the Achaemenid period,
by Sasanian times it was a sprawling metropolis of 450 hectares (1,100 acres),
one of the largest cities on the Persian Gulf before the twentieth century. The
peninsula sheltered two harbors, one of which boasted a fort overlooking a
hundred-meter-long jetty, and seems to have had a combined commercial and
naval orientation. Ardashir's son Shapur I extended Persian rule across the
gulf to the region of al-Bahrayn, the Arabian coast from present-day Qatar
to Kuwait. Taking advantage of internal discord in the Sasanian Empire in
the early fourth century, Arab tribes crossed the gulf and seized a number of
ports on the Persian coast, but despite occasional setbacks over the course of
the next three centuries, Sasanian control gradually spread along the shores
of the Indian Ocean east to the Indus and west to the Red Sea by both conquest and diplomacy. A fourth-century Chinese source mentions the Persian
king's wooing of a Sri Lankan princess, and in the 400s a successor acquired
the port of Daybul (Banbhore, Pakistan) as part of a dowry.

Although their presence in Sri Lanka was never seriously threatened, Persian merchants were not without rivals, among them traders from the Byzantine Mediterranean. Cosmas relates a possibly apocryphal story about a Sri
Lankan king curious to know whether the Persian or Byzantine emperor was
"the greater and the more powerful." The Greek merchant Sopatrus settled
the matter by producing a gold Greek coin, which the king deemed superior
to the Persian's silver one. The Greeks did mint gold coins and the Persians
did not, but this fact of sixth-century numismatic life had little bearing on the
Persians' superior position in the trade of the western Indian Ocean. Within
a few years of Sopatrus's demonstration, the Byzantines and Sasanians fought
their last campaign of note in the region, over the territory of Yemen. Anxious
to undercut Sasanian dominance in eastern trade with the east, the Byzantine
emperor Justin appealed to the *negus* (king) of Aksum, in what is now Eritrea.
Sea traders had introduced Christianity to Aksum in the fourth century and
the religious bonds between Aksumites and the Byzantine Empire were so
strong that the former were known as "black Byzantines." The persecution
of Aksumite Christian traders at the ports of Mocha and Zafar gave the *negus*

his own reasons to intervene in Yemen. Supported by a Byzantine fleet from Clysma, around 525 the Aksumites overthrew the ruling dynasty and installed a puppet government that ruled Yemen for half a century.

This modest territorial gain was not enough to break the Sasanian hold on trade, and Justin's successor, Justinian, demanded that the kings of Aksum and Yemen, in the name of their shared faith, undermine the Sasanian middlemen by purchasing silk in Sri Lanka and selling it directly to Byzantine traders. The Aksumites lacked the wherewithal to do this because the Sasanian merchants "always locate themselves at the very harbours where the Indian ships first put in (since they inhabit the adjoining country), and are accustomed to buy the whole cargoes." Justinian's plans unraveled completely when Yemeni discontent with Aksumite rule coupled with Persian interest in installing an ally led the Sasanian king Khusrau I to support an invasion by sea. With minimal effort—Khusrau sent eight hundred men in eight ships, two of which sank—the Aksumite rulers of Yemen were overthrown, and a pro-Sasanian ruler ascended the throne. By the start of the seventh century, Persian merchants dominated traffic between the Mediterranean and the Indian Ocean via both the Red Sea and the Persian Gulf.

Though contemporaries could not have anticipated it, the story of Sopatrus and the coins and the campaigns for Yemen are episodes from an age on the threshold of oblivion, between the degraded end of classical antiquity and a period of religious, cultural, and imperial renewal under the banner of Islam. Within barely a century of the events described by Cosmas, Muslim armies had captured Egypt, severed the Byzantine Empire's connection with the Indian Ocean and Christian Ethiopia, and absorbed the Sasanian Empire. By the end of the seventh century, the caliph Abd al-Malik ibn Marwan had broken the Byzantine monopoly on gold coinage and introduced a trimetallic currency standard of gold, silver, and copper into the *Dar al-Islam*, or House of Islam—a trading sphere that by the 700s encompassed a region from Spain to Central Asia, Pakistan, and East Africa. Seafaring merchants were animated by new faiths, bound by new loyalties, and channeled to new ports. Despite the revolutionary changes that swept through these regions, however, the trade routes described by Cosmas not only endured but entered a new phase of unparalleled growth.

Ships of the Indian Ocean

The ships that carried goods and people to Indian shores are the aspect of ancient Indian Ocean seafaring about which we are least informed. Textual and pictorial depictions are few, and virtually no remains of ancient ships have been recovered from anywhere between the Red Sea and the Strait of Malacca. Regardless of their provenance, ancient writings refer to ships of the Indian Ocean only in the most cursory way. The Rig Veda's account of the rescue of Bhujyu claims that he was returned to his father "in a hundred-oared ship." The descriptions of the vessels in the *Jatakas* are vague or highly stylized, but a few points stand out. Samkha tells Manimekalai that he wants "a boat with strong planks through which water cannot pass and which the wind carries," and she fashions a ship with oars and three masts, albeit made of sapphire with gold rigging and sails of silver. The "Mahajana Jataka" says only that the ship carried seven hundred passengers.

Whether this figure should be taken literally is debatable, but such a complement is not completely implausible, especially given what is known about crowding people aboard ship on the Indian Ocean in more recent periods. In 1938–39, the master mariner veteran of commercial sail Alan Villiers joined a crew of 30 aboard a *boom* (a type of dhow) of about 150 tons on a passage from Aden to Zanzibar by way of Shihr where "we embarked 200 passengers, a feat I would have believed impossible if I had not seen it done." There was only one deck, and to ensure that they would not interfere with the handling of the ship, the passengers were obliged to stay out of the way. According to Villiers, "if they could not all fit inboard, they could hang on along the rails. This many of them did, and they hung their gear outboard because there was not room enough for it inside the bulwarks." Such accommodations were probably no different in the mid-twentieth century than they were twenty-three hundred years before. Regardless of the specifics, however, these few details teased from ancient sources leave us with the impression of large, seagoing merchant ships powered by a combination of sails and oars, vessels whose capacity is comparable to those found in the better documented Mediterranean of the same period.

Unlike shipwrights in either the Mediterranean or East Asia, who employed mortise-and-tenon joinery, wooden treenails, or metal fasteners, those in the Indian Ocean seem to have favored sewn fastenings and bound their hull planking with rope made from coir (coconut husks), palm fibers, or grasses. Apart from this apparent similarity, shipbuilders otherwise took many approaches to the design of their craft, and there were local and regional differences in the building of sewn boats. In the western Indian Ocean, shipwrights stitched along the seam between the planks with rope that passed through holes bored into the planks so that the stitching was visible from within and outside of the hull. This gave ships a ramshackle appearance that led western observers to take a dim view of them. In the fourth century BCE, Alexander's helmsman

A lead coin of the Satavahana Dynasty (first and second century) decorated with a two-masted ship with a single side steering oar. The first Indian state to strike coins, the Satavahanas lay at a crossroads between the Indo-Gangetic plain in the north and the Dravidian kingdoms of the south, and their merchants were active in the trade of the Bay of Bengal.

remarked on "the wretched quality of their sails and the peculiarity of their construction." This was a view shared by Pliny the Elder nearly four centuries later, although the Roman admiral had never actually seen the ships he criticized. This lack of direct observation leads him to give a garbled description of an East African vessel that may have been fitted with an outrigger, not unlike those found in Oceania. Indeed, it seems likely that the outriggers of the Indian Ocean and the Pacific share a common ancestor in the Indonesian archipelago. A somewhat more detailed description comes from the *Periplus of the Erythraean Sea*, which mentions "*sangara*, that are very big dugout canoes held together by a yoke" and which have been identified with a double canoe known in Tamil as a *sangadam*. Regardless of their appearance, the ships engaged in long-distance trade on the Indian Ocean and its marginal seas were robust freighters capable of carrying large and diverse payloads from merchants and bulk goods to horses and elephants.

References to ships and other watercraft in the *Periplus* run from general formulations (cargo ships, small and large boats) and generic types (sewn boats, "rafts of a local type made of leathern bags," dugout canoes) to native names for different kinds of vessels. The anonymous author also mentions "long ships . . . called *trappaga* and *kotymba*" and "the very big *kolandiophonta* that sail across to Chryse [Southeast Asia] and the Ganga region." The former two are probably the same as the *tappaka* and *kottimba* mentioned in a Jain work of the early first millennium CE but about which nothing else is known. A third-century sealing from the ancient port of Chandraketugarh, near modern Kolkata, includes the image of a ship and a horse, with an inscription that identifies the former as a *trapyaka*. *Kolandiophonta* were larger vessels used for the voyage between India and Southeast Asia, where they may have originated, and they may be the same type of ship that Chinese sources call a *kunlun bo*.

The earliest written description of an Indian Ocean ship from an Asian perspective comes from the account of a third-century Chinese envoy named Kang Dai. Although he seems to have traveled no farther than the northern Malay Peninsula, Kang Dai heard about seafaring of the western Indian Ocean and relates that from an area possibly near the Indus delta, "one boards a great merchant ship. Seven sails are unfurled. With the seasonal wind [that is, the monsoon] one enters Da Qin [the Roman Empire] in a month and some days." This corresponds to the amount of time required to sail between Aden and southern India, and Indian Ocean traders may have identified Aden with the beginning of the Roman world. So far as is known, the rig of seven sails mentioned by Kang Dai is unique in antiquity. Images of ships are even rarer than written descriptions. Among the oldest are those found on coins issued by the Satavahana (or Andhra) Dynasty, which arose in the western Deccan and whose rule eventually encompassed Bharuch in the west and much of the east coast of India. Dating from the second century CE, many of these coins show a hull with a high bow and stern and carrying two bipod masts and two quarter rudders.

The most compelling pictorial representation of an Indian Ocean ship is a seventh-century wall painting at Ajanta, about 350 kilometers northeast of Mumbai (Bombay). The Ajanta ship seems to correspond broadly to the vessels described in the *Jatakas*, with details not revealed in the stories. The principal sails, one on each of three masts, are oriented like square sails, but they are considerably taller than they are wide, and there is a single headsail set out over the bowsprit. (The "Suparaga Jataka" describes the Bodhisattva's ship running before a following wind with "Her white sails outspread like beautiful wings," which seems to describe square sails that are wider than they are tall.) The bow of the Ajanta ship incorporates an *oculus*, an eye intended to help a vessel see approaching dangers and an ancestor of the more elaborate figurehead. A helmsman works a quarter rudder and there is a structure aft with wide-mouthed jars stowed beneath it. The hull appears relatively deep, but the sheer of the gunwale is flatter than that on the ships shown in the Satavahana coins of the second century.

The lack of discernible Mediterranean influence on Indian Ocean ship design is a helpful reminder that while most written testimony about the commerce and naval history of the period comes from Greek and Roman sources, and people of the eastern Mediterranean were actively engaged in trade on the Red Sea and Indian Ocean as shipowners, charterers, crew, and carpenters, their overall influence on maritime trade and technology was slight. Strabo writes that Aelius Gallus built 80 triremes and other Mediterranean types to carry his ten thousand men to Yemen, but he does not mention the origin of the 120 ships (or their crews) he says sailed between Egypt and India in his day, and today no trace of design elements characteristic of Mediterranean ships can be found in the traditionally built vessels of the Indian Ocean. Of demonstrably far greater and longer-lasting influence were elements of ship design introduced by mariners from island Southeast Asia.

Indian trade and traders had reached Indonesia by at least the early first millennium and first- and second-century finds from northwest Java and northern Bali are identical to those recovered at Arikamedu. Indian goods in Southeast Asia are not limited to Java and Bali, but these have the only concentrations of material that suggest the presence of South Asian traders rather than just their goods. While there is no evidence of Indian penetration farther east, it is likely that the chain of trade extended from the Spice Islands (Maluku and the Bandas) of eastern Indonesia to the Indian Ocean and the Mediterranean. In the coming centuries, the urge to tap the flow of these spices at their source would become a primary driver of state formation, navigational ambition, and even international law across Eurasia. These contacts were not exclusively from west to east, however, and vessel types found throughout the Indian Ocean, including outrigger and double-hulled vessels, probably reflect Indonesian origin or influence. On the coast of India, single outriggers sailed along the coast on alternate monsoons. Double outriggers with floats set equidistant from the hull from either side of the hull are also found in Indonesia and as far west as Madagascar, where they were introduced by Indonesian navigators.

Although Madagascar is only 250 miles from southern Africa, analysis of the Malagasy language indicates that the world's fourth largest island was first settled by natives of Borneo, four thousand miles to the east. When exactly these Austronesian-speaking navigators reached Madagascar, or why they came, is unknown, but it is unlikely to have been earlier than the late first millennium BCE, and probably somewhat later. One theory favors a first migration between the second and fourth centuries CE, followed by the arrival of Bantu-speaking people from Africa, and a later wave of Indonesian settlers in the tenth century. It is likely that Austronesians reached Africa, too, although there is neither archaeological nor linguistic evidence that they did so. The absence of material finds has been attributed to changes in the geomorphology of the coast and the prevalence of perishable goods such as spices, fabrics, or slaves, rather than pottery and iron, which entered the mix in the Islamic era. Had Austronesians reached the coast, their numbers would have been too small to resist absorption by the larger African population, which would account for the lack of linguistic evidence comparable to that found in Madagascar.

If durable goods and language left few traces, studies in ethnobotany, ethnomusicology, and genetics demonstrate the indelible impact of Austronesian migration to Africa. Taro, banana, and the water yam were introduced from

Southeast Asia about two thousand years ago and all three are staple foods in sub-Saharan Africa as far west as the Atlantic coast of Senegambia. Austronesian sailors also seem to have introduced to Africa a variety of musical instruments, including the leaf-funnel clarinet and the stick zither. Affinities between Indonesian and continental African zithers are so strong that some believe that stick zithers may have been introduced first to East Africa and from there to Madagascar. On the other hand, Africans sailing to Southeast Asia, whether voluntarily or as slaves, may have brought the xylophone with them as early as the sixth century.

Southeast Asian navigators also introduced a number of boat construction techniques to East Africa. The *ngalawa*, a type of outrigger canoe found between the Lamu archipelago and Mozambique and on Madagascar and the Comoro Islands well into the twentieth century, resembles prototypes from Java in significant details. The *mtepe*, a nimble sewn boat used in coastal trade along the Swahili coast, is considered "a relic of an Indonesian type bereft of its outriggers," and "the lineal descendant of the large sailing vessels used by Indonesians in their ancient traffic" on the coast of East Africa. The most obvious clue to the *mtepe*'s Indonesian origins is the design of circle-and-dot (rather than naturally rendered) *oculi*. Indonesian craft traditionally have *oculi* painted not only on the bows but at the stern, as does the *mtepe*. A further parallel is the use of woven matting rather than cloth for sails. "The only cargo-carrying vessel on the Swahili coast that is not obviously of Persian or Arab origin," *mtepes* with a capacity of twenty tons were recorded in the nineteenth century. The similarity of East African and Indonesian vessels points to a channel of cultural transmission across the Indian Ocean free of influence from mainland Asia. In the second half of the first millennium, this divided into shorter segments oriented to the rejuvenated trading centers of Southwest Asia and the Indian subcontinent.

After a long period of decline following the fall of the Indus Valley civilization and the withdrawal of Mesopotamian merchants from trade beyond the Persian Gulf, navigation on the Indian Ocean revived in the first millennium BCE and quickly came to encompass some of the longest uninterrupted sea routes in the world, across the Arabian Sea and the Bay of Bengal, with southern India and Sri Lanka lying at the crossroads of east–west exchange. While Mediterranean sailors tended to think in terms of new frontiers lying to the west, in the Indian Ocean the east was more alluring. Greco-Roman sailors from the Ptolemaic period to the Roman Empire were attracted to the point of decadence by the exotica and spices of India and beyond, while

Indian merchants in story and in fact were lured east by the land and islands of gold—Suvarnabhumi and Suvarnadvipa—in Southeast Asia, to which they incidentally transplanted their religions, language, and other cultural phenomena, as well as new goods and crafts. In so doing they laid the foundation for the prosperous trade that followed the rise of Islam and the consequent prosperity of the Near East in the seventh century and after. They also had a demonstrable impact on the political landscape of Southeast Asia and to a lesser extent, chiefly through the reinforcement of Buddhist ties, on China, Korea, and Japan.

Chapter 7

Continent and Archipelagoes in the East

That China should have exercised an attraction on the maritime merchants of the Indian Ocean is not surprising, for it was home to one of the world's oldest and richest cultures. Traders from India to Rome knew of and traded with China (at least indirectly) in antiquity via the silk roads of Central Asia. With their continental origins, the Chinese approached the maritime world more circumspectly than did their contemporaries, but approach it they did. First they harnessed their webs of elaborately branching rivers through feats of hydraulic engineering that protected the land from flooding, improved agricultural capacity, and facilitated inland communication. They then began their annexation of southern China, the Land of the Hundred Yue whose Austronesian-speaking ancestors had launched themselves into Southeast Asia in the second millennium BCE. As a result of these efforts, before the start of the common era it was possible to travel via river and canal from Guangzhou in the southeast to the ancient capital of Chang'an in the northwest.

Although the exploitation and development of reliable water routes through the interior was crucial to the formation and maintenance of the Chinese state, the cultivation of domestic and foreign sea trade helped assure China's primacy among its maritime neighbors. If, as some claim, the catalyst for sea trade was the desire to circumvent the Parthian Empire, centered in modern Iran, and trade directly with Rome, it fell far short of expectations. But the effort brought riches to China and effected cultural and political change in Southeast Asia. Merchant mariners chasing the monsoons helped spur the development of agriculture—to generate food surpluses adequate to attract and feed these sojourners—and gave rise to the earliest recognizable states in Vietnam, Cambodia, Thailand, the Malay Peninsula, Sumatra, and Java. Foreign sailors and their ships dominated long-distance trade, but China was the unmoved mover of maritime commerce and contributed directly to the diffusion of tangible and intangible goods. Buddhism first reached China overland from India, but seafaring monks reinforced it there and established it from Sumatra and Vietnam to Korea and Japan.

The Maritime Geography of East and Southeast Asia

The geography of the contiguous waters of the South China and East China Seas; the continental landmass from the Malay Peninsula to Korea; and the Indonesian, Philippine, and Japanese archipelagoes is far more complex than that of either the Mediterranean or Indian Ocean. The Indonesian archipelago extends about two thousand miles from east to west, about the length of the Mediterranean; but the contiguous seas of East and Southeast Asia extend over two thousand miles from south to north, across fifty degrees of latitude from Java to Korea (roughly 10°S to 40°N)—the same span of latitude as from Tanzania to Turkey, Angola to Portugal, or Peru to New York. The region's physical environments range from the equatorial rain forests of coastal Indonesia to the cooler and drier continental climates of northern China, Korea, and Japan. This geographical diversity had enormous implications for the types of commodities and manufactured goods found there. The rhythm of trade was dictated by the monsoons, the seasons and severity of which differ slightly from those of the Indian Ocean, although the general pattern is similar. In the words of a thirteenth-century Chinese authority, seagoing ships "take advantage of the reliability of the seasonal winds. They go south in the winter and come north in the summer, never the other way around."[*]

The Japanese archipelago consists of four main islands—Kyushu, Shikoku, Honshu, and Hokkaido—and nearly four thousand smaller ones, including offshore chains like the Ryukyus. Japan's mountainous terrain makes overland transportation and agriculture difficult, and the Japanese have always relied on coastwise navigation for transportation. A hundred miles across the Korea Strait from Kyushu lies the mountainous Korean Peninsula, the ragged coasts of which are fringed with hundreds of islands, especially on the Korea Strait and Yellow Sea. China's coast wends more than 7,500 miles from the Yalu

---

[*] The northeast monsoon (September–November to April) averages about Force 4 (11–16 knots) south of 10°N, Force 6 (22–27 knots) in the Luzon Strait between the Philippines and Taiwan, and Force 5 in the north; in December and January, Force 7 (28–33 knots) conditions are common from Vietnam to Japan. The southwest monsoon (May–June to August–September) averages Force 3 or 4 (7–16 knots) throughout the region, although squalls are not uncommon.

River to the Gulf of Tonkin. North of Hangzhou Bay and the mouth of the Yangzi River, the coast is generally low-lying and sandy, while the rockier southern coast is more heavily islanded and indented. The coast of Vietnam is divided into three topographically distinct regions. The Red (Hong) River of the north flows off the Yunnan Plateau to create a broad alluvial flood-plain flanked by mountains. To the north of the delta is Halong Bay, which is distinguished by thousands of limestone islets that thrust up from the sea and are capped by lush, junglelike vegetation. To the south, the Truong Son Mountains spill down to the coast as far as Hue, where forest gives way to long beaches and a broader coastal plain that abuts the dense swamps and mangrove jungle of the Mekong delta.

Farther west mountains hug the coast of western Cambodia and eastern Thailand, while the head of the Bight of Bangkok is dominated by the swamps of the Chao Phraya delta. The Malay Peninsula is about 1,500 kilometers from north to south, is nowhere wider than 300 kilometers, and narrows to only 40 kilometers at the Kra Isthmus. However, apart from an account of Chinese merchants crossing the upper peninsula during the first century BCE, there is virtually no written or archaeological evidence of traffic across the peninsula's heavily forested and all but uninhabited mountains. With its broader alluvial plains, the east coast was home to relatively sophisticated states, while the western coast, though protected from the southwest monsoon by the mass of Sumatra as far north as 5°N, is fringed with dense mangrove swamps some of which extend inland as much as twenty kilometers, and the mountains come much closer to the sea.

Between the Malay Peninsula and Sumatra lies the 500-mile-long Strait of Malacca, the most important thoroughfare between the Indian Ocean and the South China Sea. The northwest opening to the strait is about 175 miles across, but its southeast end is a complicated maze of channels—some less than 2 miles wide—through the Riau Archipelago and Singapore islands. As on the peninsula, the mountainous terrain of the islands of Sumatra and coastal Java to the east makes agriculture and territorial consolidation difficult, and rival states tended to emerge along compact river valleys. Communication between these realms was relatively easy by sea, but the topography made it difficult to unify or exert direct control over terrestrial neighbors. Ruling authority depended largely on treaties and threats rather than territorial control and military force, and was made manifest by the flow of tribute from the periphery to the center of the kingdom.

The waters of Southeast Asia are sometimes referred to as an Asian Mediterranean, a shorthand that implies a degree of regional coherence misleading on both geographic and cultural grounds. The people of the archipelagoes that comprise modern Indonesia, East Timor, the Philippines, and Malaysia have a common ancestry and speak related languages; yet while the Mediterranean is a virtually enclosed sea, only the northwest part of the South China Sea faces a continental shore, including the Malay Peninsula, Thailand, Cambodia, Vietnam, and China. The South China Sea and the smaller seas of eastern Indonesia open to the Pacific and are separated from the Indian Ocean to the south and west by straits that perforate Indonesia's southern islands at intervals of scores to hundreds of miles. The islands of the Mediterranean number in the hundreds, but there are more than twenty-six thousand in Southeast Asia, from Sumatra in the southwest to New Guinea in the east and Taiwan and the Philippines in the north. This diffusion inhibited the development of political units on a par with those of China, South Asia, the Near East, or the Mediterranean basin. Island empires only became possible after farmers and sailors had achieved significant improvements in agriculture and nautical technology starting in the seventh century CE.

Another way to consider the complexity of this region is by reference to its linguistic diversity. The maritime realm between Indonesia and Japan is home to five language families, linguistic divisions on a genealogical par with Indo-European, which is found (interspersed with Afro-Asiatic and Altaic) from India to Ireland. Austronesian languages—twelve hundred of them—are found throughout island Southeast Asia from the Philippines to Indonesia, on the southern Malay Peninsula, and in central Vietnam. Tai languages are spoken on the northern Malay Peninsula and in Thailand, and Austro-Asiatic in Vietnam and Cambodia. Sino-Tibetan includes the Chinese languages and Korean, while Japanese is a language unto itself. This translates into a multiplicity of individual languages, which resulted in predictable problems, as explained by a third-century Chinese prefect stationed in Jiaozhi (northern Vietnam). "Customs are not uniform," he wrote of this commercial hub between China and Southeast Asia, "and languages are mutually unintelligible so that several interpreters are needed to communicate." Equally important, the region has never known a lingua franca comparable to Latin or Arabic, which were shared by the educated and merchant coreligionists of the west.

Tracing the distribution of these languages is one way of determining patterns of early migration through the region. Ancestors of the Austronesian speakers originated in southern China and spread east and south via Taiwan and the Philippines through island Southeast Asia over the course of tens of thousands of years. The first Austronesian settlers in mainland Southeast Asia were probably islanders who migrated via the Philippines and Borneo at the end of the second millennium BCE. Their descendants' Sa Huynh culture (named for a coastal village in central Vietnam) emerged around 600 BCE and spun webs of trade across island and mainland Southeast Asia, with links even to India. Judging from the distribution of artifacts found in modern times, Sa Huyhn trade reached no farther north than central Vietnam, beyond which lay the Dong-Son culture area. Centered on the Red River valley near Hanoi from the seventh century BCE to the first century CE, the Dong-Son culture was that of an Austro-Asiatic-speaking people who had migrated overland from southern China. According to a local tradition that reflects their melding with Austronesian seafarers, the inhabitants of northern Vietnam were descendants of Lac Long Quan, a lord from the sea, and Au Co, the wife of a Chinese invader he kidnapped as insurance against attack from the north.

The Dong-Son are perhaps best known for their massive cast bronze drums. Weighing up to one hundred kilograms and standing one meter high, more than two hundred drums have been found across Southeast Asia as far east as the spiceries of the Banda Islands. The seaward orientation of Dong-Son culture is apparent from the maritime subjects depicted on them as well as in the drums' widespread distribution. Only two drums are known from southern Vietnam and none has been found in Borneo, the Philippines, or northeast Indonesia, which reinforces the idea of a firm demarcation between Austro-Asiatic- and Austronesian-speaking people. Whether the Sa Huynh simply chose not to trade with the Dong-Son or actively blocked their way to the south is difficult to say. Drums have been excavated from burial sites in western Indonesia and mainland Southeast Asia, but they may have been carried out of northern Vietnam by river trade to the Gulf of Thailand before being transported via short-range networks to the south and east.

The Chinese State from the Eighth to Third Centuries BCE

While the seafaring Austronesian-speakers of Southeast Asia originated in what is now southern China, the maritime ambitions of the Chinese of the northern plains were primarily riverine. The ancient heartland of Chinese culture centered on the great bend of the flood-prone Yellow River in the modern provinces of Shanxi, Shaanxi, and Henan, southwest of Beijing and a thousand kilometers from the sea. The proximity of this region to the nomadic tribes of Central and northern Asia made maintaining the integrity of continental borders a primary concern. Inhabited mostly by agrarian or maritime-oriented Yue people, the mountainous coastal provinces of southern China—Zhejiang, Fujian, and Guangdong—were comparatively quiet: northern Chinese expansion into these regions was a gradual and opportunistic process geared as much to securing the trade in exotic tropical goods as to territorial aggrandizement.

The tension between the need for security and the quest for novelties complicated China's evolving relationship to maritime trade. While most dynastic governments sought to insulate the country against invasion from the north and west through such projects as the construction of the Great Wall, the Chinese simultaneously perceived themselves as the kingdom at the middle of the world. The maritime frontier to the east and south was at once a porous border through which alien ideas might flow, and a gateway through which foreigners could send trade goods in the form of tribute. The gist of tribute trade was that as China theoretically produced or grew everything it needed, it had no need of foreign trade. Goods acquired were taken as a material symbol of the giver's acknowledgment of Chinese supremacy, while gifts bestowed by the Chinese were a manifestation of the emperor's benevolence. By and large, "tribute" was an elaborate fiction designed to inflate the Chinese court's sense of its own importance and the Chinese were as often as not purchasing peace or, especially in the case of overseas countries, recognition. Historically the coasts of China were seldom regarded as an avenue of attack.

In China, there has been at different times considerable official opposition to overseas ventures and its by-product, the wanton consumption of luxury goods, the pursuit of which was considered detrimental to the empire's security, economic stability, and morals, as it was in Rome. This was particularly true when Confucian traditionalists had the emperor's ear. With their emphasis on filial obligation and belief in virtuous, paternalistic government, Confucianists tended to scorn commerce. Their essential view is found in two aphorisms in *The Analects of Confucius* compiled in the century of the master's death in 479 BCE: "The gentleman is conversant with righteousness; the small man is conversant with profit" and "When your parents are alive, do not travel far. If you do travel, be sure to have a regular destination." A standard interpretation of the latter injunction is that one must always be available to help, or in the worst case to bury appropriately, one's parents. To be absent in pursuit of trade and unable to fulfill one's obligations was ignoble in the extreme.

Representative of the Confucianists' arguments were those of minister Chao Cuo, who in the 170s BCE urged the emperor to focus his subjects' attention on agriculture and silk cultivation, activities that would tie people to the land and their families. Chao Cuo regarded merchants as guilty of hoarding, profiteering, ostentation, and rising above their station. He maintained that "an enlightened ruler esteems the 'five grains' and despises gold and jade," the stock-in-trade of merchants who "travel all around within the sea without the hardships of hunger or cold." Such disdain for merchants was not unique to China—one imagines Chao Cuo would have gotten a good hearing from a Tiberius or Pliny, or from antiglobalization activists today—but as elsewhere it reflected an ideal rather than reality. Moreover, to the extent that official policy has rejected or embraced interaction with the world beyond the borders of the Middle Kingdom, China's actions have been determined more by strategic imperatives rather than by cultural predilections.

Confucius flourished around the start of the sixth century BCE, when a number of states occupied the area of what is now north-central and eastern China. The earliest recorded sea trade between north and south China dates from the sixth and fifth centuries BCE, when the state of Qi (in Hebei and Shandong Provinces) traded bronze, iron, and silk with the more southerly states of Wu and Yue. In addition to trade, there was a considerable amount of sea-based military activity. Nearly twenty-five naval or amphibious operations are known to have taken place between 549 and 476 BCE, the most important of which, in 482 BCE, was a Yue invasion of Wu that foreshadowed the latter's fall a decade later. The Yue fell to the Chu (centered in Hebei Province) in 334 BCE, who were in turn absorbed by the short-lived but enormously influential Qin Dynasty, the first Chinese empire (221–206 BCE).

The ultimate victory of Qin over its rival states and its subsequent expansion to the south gave it a territory with a coastline longer than that of modern China, from central Korea to northern Vietnam. Nonetheless, overseas enterprise during the Qin focused officially on the singular Daoist quest for the elixir of immortality. Shihuangdi, the first Qin emperor, dispatched two expeditions to search for the immortals, whom Daoists believed to inhabit an island in the Bo Hai (Gulf of Chilhi) enclosed by the Shandong and Liaodong Peninsulas. Just as Nearchus noted that Alexander the Great was apprehensive about sailing from India to the Persian Gulf, the Chinese annals relate, "As the emperor considered that if he himself went to sea he would probably not be successful, he ordered a certain person to embark with a crew of young boys and girls, and to search for [the immortals]." Although they claimed to have seen the islands, contrary winds kept them from reaching their intended destination and they returned to China. A second expedition of several thousand people is said to have reached the Japanese island of Kyushu, a story that may have some truth to it, as we shall see. But during the Qin and Han Dynasties, and even later, the primary orientation of Chinese sea trade was on the Nanhai, or South China Sea.

The Conquest of the Hundred Yue, 221–219 BCE

In the third century BCE, this traffic was in the hands of the Yue, or Hundred Yue, in Chinese eyes an uncivilized people who occupied the coastal region between the lower Yangzi and northern Vietnam. The Qin Dynasty's turn to the south was motivated by a drive for territorial expansion and trade, especially in luxury goods and exotics. In 221 BCE, Shihuangdi sent five armies totaling half a million men to seize the coasts of modern Fujian, Guangdong, and Guangxi Provinces, and northern Vietnam. Formidable as this force was, it bogged down in difficult terrain where it was harassed by an elusive foe and suffered from inadequate supply lines. Success was assured only by the construction of the five-kilometer-long Lingqu Canal, an artificial waterway the importance of which is far greater than its length would imply.

As elsewhere in the ancient world, Chinese canals served for irrigation, transportation, and perhaps above all, flood control. Yet owing to the number, size, and strength of the main rivers, canal building and inland navigation have played a more conspicuous role in the development and sustenance of the Chinese state than elsewhere. The Yangzi (Changjiang) and Yellow Rivers (Huang He) both rise in the Kunlun Mountains of the Tibetan Plateau at altitudes of around 6,100 meters, but they follow very different courses to the sea.* Paralleling the Mekong in its upper reaches, the Yangzi swings south onto the Yunnan Plateau before turning northeast. Below Chongqing it plunges through mountain gorges where before the completion of the Three Gorges Dam in 2006 the difference between high water in the flood season and low water could be as much as sixty meters. Once free of the mountains, the Yangzi winds more sedately through a broad floodplain and passes Nanjing en route to Shanghai where it enters the East China Sea. The Yellow River follows a more northerly course describing a long S shape that brings it into the Ordos Desert near the Mongolian border before it bends south. About 150 kilometers east of the Qin capital at Chang'an, it heads sharply east to Kaifeng where it turns northeast to enter the Bo Hai between the Shandong Peninsula and Tianjin, today the port of Beijing. Though it is shorter than the Yangzi and drains an area only a quarter as large, the Yellow River is vastly more unpredictable in its lower reaches. For much of the last seven hundred kilometers the river is higher than the surrounding land—like the Mississippi as it passes New Orleans—which makes flooding a perennial concern. Between the thirteenth and nineteenth centuries, and again between 1930 and 1947, the Yellow River leaped its banks to carve out new channels that flowed into the Yellow Sea south of the Shandong Peninsula. Since 1947 its mouth has opened to the Bo Hai 250 miles to the northeast.

Taming these turbulent streams (the third and fourth longest rivers in the world, respectively) among myriad others has been a major preoccupation throughout their history, and the Chinese became the most accomplished canal builders in the world. Expertise in canal building for flood control and irrigation led to the development of purpose-built navigation canals, the most impor-

* The Chinese apply the name Yangzi only to the lower reaches of the river they call Changjiang, meaning "long river."

tant of which linked the Yellow River floodplain, which grew chiefly grain and millet, and that of the Yangzi, which was near the northern limit of wet-rice cultivation. The oldest such canals date to no later than the fourth century BCE. The combination of irrigation and transportation canals helped stabilize and integrate the empire by providing reliable harvests and, as crops were the principal form of taxes, a means of transporting them to the capital. In addition, canals eased the way for imperial expansion by facilitating the transportation of armies, a function evident in the Qin's conquest of the Hundred Yue.

In 219 BCE, two years after the start of his invasion of the south, Shihuangdi sent "a force of men in towered ships [*louchuan*] to sail south and attack the hundred tribes of Yue, and ordered the supervisor [Shi] Lu to dig a canal to transport supplies for the men so they could penetrate deep into the region of Yue." Located in Guangxi Province, the Lingqu (Magic, or Miracle) Canal connects the Xiang River, which flows north to the Yangzi, with the Gui River, a tributary of the Pearl River system, which enters the South China Sea near Guangzhou.[*] In addition to digging the Lingqu Canal, Shi Lu made improvements to about twenty-five kilometers of the upper Gui. These relatively modest changes made it possible to go via inland waterway from Guangzhou to Chang'an, a distance of more than two thousand kilometers as the crow flies, "a chain of communication altogether extraordinary" for the third century BCE, or any other time, anywhere in the world.

The Yue campaign lasted ten years, and the fighting and privation proved almost unendurable for the Chinese, many of whom "hanged themselves from the roadside trees in such numbers that one corpse dangled within sight of another." One cannot ignore the individual sacrifices, but the canal testifies to the ability and farsightedness of the Qin engineers, who with a minimum of collective effort created a network of inland waterways that joined the most southerly and northerly of their country's major river systems. A twelfth-century author offers a fair assessment of the project and those responsible for it: "The cruelty and suspicion of Shihuangdi I venture to deplore," he wrote. "But his despotic authority had power to trap the waters permanently, so that vessels could travel overland. For ten thousand generations people have relied upon his canal. But the merit belongs not only to Shihuangdi—[Shi] Lu was also a hero—and on account of all these things it is called the 'Magic Canal.'" Thanks to the subjugation of the Yue facilitated by the Lingqu Canal (still in use after twenty-two hundred years), the Chinese were now said to include a

---

* The Pearl River (Zhu Jiang) refers both to the short, wide river that passes the port of Guangzhou, as well as a larger network of the Zhu Jiang's tributaries including the Xi (West), Bei (North), and Dong (East) Rivers.

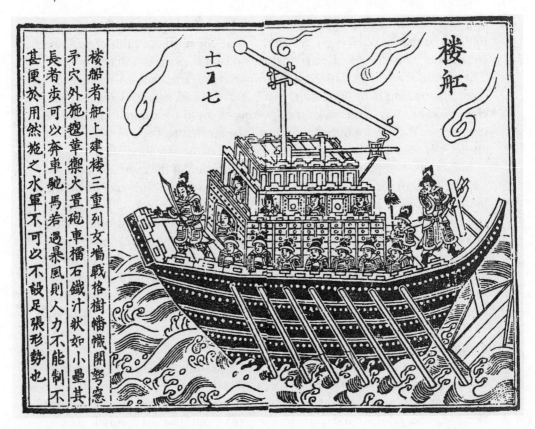

The towered warship (louchuan) *is attested in Chinese sources as early as the third century* BCE. *This woodcut is from a sixteenth-century edition of the* Collection of the Most Important Military Techniques (Wu Ching Tsung Yao) *written in 1044, but it is probably based on earlier drawings and certainly fits written descriptions that are far older than that.*

people who "used boats as their carriages and oars as their horses," a necessity for trade to the south. From this time forward, the southern coastal provinces would remain China's primary outlet to Southeast Asia and the world beyond.

Shihuangdi died in 210 BCE, and although his empire did not long survive him, the basic institutions and organization of the Qin Dynasty were adopted by the Han Dynasty, which emerged victorious from the ensuing upheaval and governed China for four centuries, from 202 BCE to 220 CE.* The Han initially

---

* The Han Dynasty is divided into the Former Han, 202 BCE to 2 CE, and the Latter Han, 25 to 220 CE. A cousin of one of the last Former Han emperors ruled in the interval.

occupied more or less the same territory as the Qin, except for the territory of the Yue, where the Nanyue Kingdom established by a renegade general eventually accepted a status subsidiary to the Han. This mutually beneficial arrangement ensured the Han a stable southern frontier under Chinese rule, while guaranteeing a steady supply of such exotics as "a pair of white jades, 1,000 kingfishers' feathers, ten rhinoceros horns [an esteemed aphrodisiac], 500 purple-striped cowries, a vessel of cinnamon-insects [a delicacy when soaked in honey], forty pairs of live kingfishers and two pairs of peacocks" in exchange for iron and silk from the north. The market for these southern rarities, some native to Nanyue, others acquired from farther afield, grew under the Han's prosperous rule.

The most important of the southern ports was the capital, Guangzhou (then called Panyu), "the center for trade in pearls, round and otherwise, rhinoceros horns, tortoise shells, fruits . . . and textiles." To the west was Hepu, an important pearl fishery on the Gulf of Tonkin. However, the richest of these southern domains were the prefectures of Jiaozhi, along the Red River, and Jiuzhen, whose conquest brought the Dong-Son culture of northern Vietnam within China's orbit for the first time. The Nanyue court grew increasingly pro-Han, but in 112 BCE the young king and a number of Chinese envoys were massacred. In preparation for a retaliatory invasion, Emperor Han Wudi issued a general amnesty throughout the empire and ordered that convicts so freed "as well as 100,000 sailors of the towered ships who are stationed south of the Huai and [Yangzi] rivers, be sent to attack" the Yue. After the fall of Guangzhou, the Han divided Nanyue lands into prefectures including Nanhai and Hepu in modern Guangdong and Guangxi Provinces, respectively, and Jiaozhi, Jiuzhen, and Rinan in northern Vietnam. As the primary purpose of the last three prefectures was to maintain the southern trade, the Vietnamese were allowed considerable autonomy.

Jiaozhi and Funan, First Century BCE–Third Century CE

No contemporary records shed light on Jiaozhi's trade in the first century BCE, but later works indicate that traders were in regular communication with other kingdoms in Southeast Asia and India by no later than the death of Han Wudi in 87 BCE. The *History of the Former Han* includes information on the trading states, routes followed and goods traded, notably "lustrous pearls, glass, rare stones and strange products," which were exchanged for "gold and various silks." Ships setting out from Hepu or Rinan hugged the mainland past the mouth of the Chao Phraya River below modern Bangkok to the upper

Malay Peninsula. There, according to this source, merchants disembarked to cross the forty-kilometer-wide Kra Isthmus "rather more than ten days' journey on foot." When the Chinese reached the shores of the Bay of Bengal, "the trading ships of the barbarians" carried them to Huangzhi, widely believed to be Kanchipuram, capital of the Pallava kingdom in Tamil Nadu. All told, such a venture could take "several years," provided of course one was spared "the hazards of wind and wave to be encountered and death by drowning" or being looted and killed by the "barbarians" encountered en route. The *Annals* include a description of another voyage to Huangzhi made around 2 CE, during the interregnum between the Former and Latter Han Dynasties. Accompanied by a live rhinoceros, the envoys returned from Huangzhi to Rinan via Pizong in only ten months. If the identification of Pizong as an island off the southern Malay Peninsula is correct, the faster time may have been due to the merchants' sailing diagonally across the South China Sea, a more direct route than along the coast although such passages are not otherwise attested until the fifth century.

In the late 30s CE Jiaozhi was consumed by a revolt led by the sisters Trung Trac and Trung Nhi. After a three-year campaign, the Chinese divided Vietnam into commanderies, provincial units subject to civil and military authority. While the Vietnamese sought independence, the Han resolve to subjugate northern Vietnam was dictated by the need to protect the southern trade and not by concerns over territorial security. In fact, Jiaozhi remained fairly calm for about a century after the Trung sisters' defeat, but corruption by Chinese officials and their associates was chronic. Matters came to a head in 136 when ethnic Chams from central Vietnam fomented a rebellion in Rinan that quickly spread to Jiaohzi. Domestic problems made it impossible for the government to divert resources to the south and the Han court negotiated away the rebel-held lands. Despite these problems, as Han authority declined at home Jiaozhi was relatively unscathed and it eventually emerged as a place of refuge for many northerners and one with lucrative commercial opportunities for indigenous and foreign merchants alike.

The state that benefited most from the expansion of trade during the Han was Funan, which flourished between the second and sixth centuries in the lower Mekong basin of what is now southeastern Vietnam and Cambodia. Funan's success depended on a combination of its location at the junction of the monsoons, where the Gulf of Thailand meets the South China Sea, and its productive agricultural sector. Northbound merchants could reach the port of Oc Eo from the west on one monsoon, and sail from there to China on the next. The Mekong delta port could accommodate these traders for several months at a time because Funan produced enough surplus rice and other food to sustain both its own population and communities of foreign merchants. The timing of the monsoons also meant that Indian and Chinese merchants were rarely at Oc Eo at the same time, for the same wind that brought one group to Funan sent the other home. The name of Funan is known only from Chinese writings, but these show that the strongest foreign influence in the region emanated from South Asia. A foundation story tells how a native princess called Lin-ye led an attack on a passing ship that was repulsed by the passengers and crew. She subsequently married one of the passengers, an Indian Brahman named Kaundinya, and together they inherited the rule of Funan. Whatever the truth of this story, Funan's subsequent territorial expansion was oriented toward preserving and dominating trade to the west. In the early third century, General Fan Shiman "attacked and conquered the neighboring kingdoms. All recognized themselves [as] his vassals . . . he took the title of 'Great King of Funan.' Then he had great ships built and crossing the immense sea he attacked more than ten kingdoms . . . including Dunsun," a small trading state at the top of the Malay Peninsula.

Around the year 250, the king of Wu, one of several kingdoms that rose from the ashes of the Han Dynasty, dispatched the envoys Zhu Ying and Kang Dai to learn what they could of Funan and the western trade. Their memoirs offer a mixed portrait of a vibrant Funanese culture. The envoys were offended by the nakedness and tattoos of the people but noted appreciatively that they "live in walled cities, palaces, and houses." Funan's bureaucracy and economy were robust: "Taxes are paid in gold, silver, pearls, and perfumes. . . . There are books and depositories of archives and other things. Their characters for writing resemble those of the Hu," a people whose alphabet was of Indian origin. Indian influence was prominent, and they met a representative from a kingdom on the subcontinent. Kang Dai notes the availability of goods from Da Qin (the Roman Empire), which came via Indian ports, and he describes aspects of the trade between the Malay Peninsula and India and between India and the Roman Empire. A lost work by Kang Dai reportedly tells of a Chinese merchant who sailed between India and China by way of Southeast Asia.

Funan's pivotal role in the chain of east–west exchange can be seen in the diversity of goods found throughout its territories. Archaeologists have identified more than 350 riverine and coastal sites associated with the port of Oc Eo, and excavations have yielded artifacts from around Southeast Asia, China, India, Persia, and the Mediterranean. The finds of westernmost origin include a coin and two medallions bearing the images of the second-century Roman emperors Antoninus Pius and Marcus Aurelius. A third-century Chinese work entitled *The Peoples of the West* devotes considerable attention to Da Qin, which can mean either Rome proper, the Roman Empire in general, or the empire's Asian provinces. This early account of the silk road lists sixty-three products of Da Qin, from gold, silver, and gems to frankincense, myrrh, and "twelve types of aromatic plants." A section entitled "The Sea Route to Da Qin" explains that "In early times only the maritime routes [to Da Qin] were discussed because they didn't know there were overland routes." This is perfectly consonant with the emphasis on sea routes to the east in contemporary western sources. Furthermore, finds in central Thailand, Vietnam, and around the Java Sea show that Funan's absorption of foreign religions, principles of statecraft, and material artifacts spurred parallel developments throughout Southeast Asia. Despite the greater distances involved, the sea route was probably no more hazardous than the silk road across Central Asia, and it was faster and almost certainly subject to fewer duties because shipboard goods passed through the hands of fewer taxing authorities.

Four centuries before the Byzantine emperors Justin and Justinian urged the kingdom of Axum to break the Sasanian monopoly on Indian Ocean trade, the Chinese attempted to bypass the Parthian middlemen to open direct trade with Rome. Between 97 and 101 CE, an envoy named Gan Ying crossed Asia to the Persian Gulf port of Charax Spasinou (the Chinese Tiaozhi) in hopes of joining a ship bound for a Roman port on the Red Sea. Possibly alert to his intentions, the Parthians discouraged Gan Ying by telling him that the three-month voyage could take two years and that "all the men who go by sea take stores for three years. The vast ocean urges men to think of their country, and get homesick, and some of them die." For whatever reason, Gan Ying abandoned his plan. Even had he completed his journey, it is unlikely that the new route would have altered significantly the existing patterns of trade, for similar initiatives undertaken from the west met with comparably lackluster results.

Among the best known of these took place in 166 when, according to the *History of the Later Han*, a merchant (or merchants) claiming to represent the Roman emperor reached the Han court. Elaborating on the relationship between the three major Eurasian powers of the third century, the official history notes that the Romans

> traffic by sea with Anxi [Parthia] and Tian-zhu [India], the profit of which trade is tenfold. . . . Their kings always desired to send embassies to China, but the Anxi wished to carry on trade with them in Chinese silks, and it is for this reason that they were cut off from communication. This lasted until [166 CE] when the king of Da Qin, An-tun [Marcus Aurelius Antoninus], sent an embassy which, from the frontier of Rinan, offered ivory, rhinoceros horns, and tortoiseshell.

In fact, the "embassy" may have been something of a fraud. Elephant tusks, rhinoceros horn, and tortoiseshell were not of western provenance but were routinely available in Southeast Asia. In all likelihood, as even the author of the annals hints, these were simply traders passing themselves off as representatives of imperial Rome to improve their standing. There is no hint that their deception was uncovered at the time, but even an imposter's knowledge of the west would have been of more than passing interest to Chinese officials.

China and Southeast Asia from the Third to Sixth Centuries

The Han Dynasty came to an end at the start of the third century under pressure from the Xiongnu, a nomadic people whom the Han had fought since the first century, and China entered a 370-year-long period characterized by militarism and short-lived petty states. In its final decades the Han Dynasty was under the effective control of General Cao Cao, who tried but failed to maintain the integrity of the empire. The deciding moment was at the battle of the Red Cliffs, one of the most romanticized in Chinese history. Fought on the middle Yangzi near modern Wulin in December 208, the battle pit Cao Cao with a fleet of river ships and about two hundred thousand soldiers against the combined forces of Sun Quan and Liu Bei, the future rulers of the kingdoms of Wu and Shu Han, respectively. Cao Cao was defeated, and a dozen years later China was divided among the kingdoms of Wei, founded by Cao Cao's son, with its capital at Luoyang on the Yellow River; Liu Bei's Shu Han Dynasty (superseded by the Western Jin in 265) in the upper Yangzi valley to the southwest; and Sun Quan's Wu Dynasty in the east, with its capital at Jiangkang (Nanjing) on the lower Yangzi. Because the states of Wei and Shu Han blocked Wu's access to Central Asia, an invaluable source of horses, the kings of Wu turned to maritime trade to circumvent their territories. The Wu invaded Jiaozhi to secure the traditional trade in tropical exotics, and because the Red River valley provided access to the horse pastures of the Yunnan Plateau. Wu rulers sought trade with and recognition from more distant rulers as a means of confirming their legitimacy as Sons of Heaven. Linyi, a kingdom founded in 192 on Jiaozhi's southern border, Funan, and Tang-Ming, in Cambodia, all sent envoys in return. Of more immediate importance to the future of Chinese maritime trade, Wu encouragement of sinicization south of the Yangzi, a region previously outside the mainstream of Chinese culture, initiated a centuries-long process that paved the way for the massive influx of northern Chinese forced south during the tumult of the fifth and sixth centuries.

The kingdom of Wu's position was always precarious, and by the 250s it was almost constantly at war in defense of its inland borders. Availing themselves of their overlords' northern preoccupations, Jiaozhi rebelled, abetted by the kings of Linyi, Funan, and, eventually, the Western Jin. To avoid the disturbances in Jiaozhi, trading ships from the Nanhai began bypassing northern Vietnam to sail directly for Guangzhou. Although this was firmly under Chinese rule, it was remote from the capital and a place "where only the poor officials, who cannot otherwise be independent, seek to be appointed." The advantage of a posting to a port dependent on exotic goods and beyond the prying eyes of imperial bureaucrats was that corruption was easy and enormously lucrative. By the end of the fourth century, Guangzhou was infamous as "the place of strange and precious things, one bag of which can provide for several generations" if one was willing to accept merchants' bribes to expedite the handling of their goods, as most governors seem to have been. Jiaozhi eventually recovered its trade, but Guangzhou's emergence as one of China's premier ports dates from this period.

The defeat of the Wu and consolidation of Jin rule in 280 created a boom in the southern trade as buyers and sellers hastened to make up for the long years that northern China had gone without access to southern luxuries. But while the century ended with great promise for the expansion of the Nanhai trade, between 304 and 316 the Xiongnu seized most of northern China, and the Jin court relocated from Luoyang to Nanjing. The rise of non-Han Chinese rulers sparked the flight of perhaps a million northerners that resulted in the first wholesale penetration of the Yue south by ethnic Chinese, who brought with them their core cultural and political institutions, including language and modes of governance. Now, for the first time, the preponderance of China's foreign trade seems to have been conducted by sea.

These newcomers vied with each other for supremacy and in Jiaozhi they antagonized the indigenous people and foreign merchants. In the near term, instability led to high tolls and rampant corruption among officials whose avarice had only grown in the hundred years since Guangzhou was described as a plum assignment for impoverished administrators. At the start of the fourth century customs officers in Jiaozhi and Rinan routinely levied taxes of 20 to 30 percent on imports, and one prefect became notorious for undervaluing goods by more than half, and then intimidating the offended merchants "with his ships and war-drums. Because of this, the various countries [from which the traders had come] were furious." Later still, a popular saying held that "The governor of Guangzhou need only pass through the city gates just once, and he will be enriched by thirty million strings of cash."* The Jin government exerted no meaningful control over its representatives in Guangzhou,

---

* *Cash* were copper coins minted with a hole in the center; a string of a thousand *cash* was a standard unit of currency.

yet while corruption cost the imperial coffers dearly, the merchants of Linyi endured the most immediate losses. After diplomatic overtures to the Jin court failed, Linyi invaded Jiaozhi. Over the next seventy years, the Chinese came to regard the people of Linyi as nothing more than pirates, which in the absence of more legitimate opportunities for trade they may have become. Between 421 and 446, however, they sent six missions to the Liu Song Dynasty (successor to the Eastern Jin), and they are said to have offered tribute of ten thousand catties (six thousand kilograms) of gold, one hundred thousand of silver, and three hundred thousand of copper in 445. Nonetheless, the Liu Song launched a brutal campaign during which the Chinese reportedly executed everyone in Linyi's port of Khu-tuc before looting the capital's palaces and Buddhist temples of untold quantities of gold.

The political situation in and around southern China remained chaotic, but there were periods of stability and even prosperity, which is reflected in the intensification of overseas trade. During the fourth century, the Jin court had received only three missions from the south, all from Linyi, but between 421 and the start of the Sui Dynasty in 589, sixty-four trade missions arrived from various kingdoms across Southeast Asia—as many as would come in the three centuries of the prosperous Tang Dynasty. Yet Linyi never recovered from the sack of 446, and Funan also began an inexorable decline. These changes had less to do with Chinese policy or corruption than with a redirection in the long-distance trade of Southeast Asia: the abandonment of the coastal route between the Malay Peninsula and Funan in favor of an open-water passage across the South China Sea between the Strait of Malacca and southern Vietnam or China.

Faxian and the Strait of Malacca Route in the Fifth Century

Although it is possible that some ships had taken this direct route across the South China Sea as early as the first century, if not earlier, it was not the norm for long-distance traders. The first person to write about a direct sea route clearly identifiable as such was Faxian, a Buddhist monk who after a long sojourn in India (which he had reached overland from China) and Sri Lanka, returned home by sea in 413–14. His misadventures on the journey take up much of the last book of his journal, which provides information about the route he followed, navigational practice, how mariners addressed the dangers of seafaring, and travelers' superstitions. Faxian's journey was made in two stages interrupted by a five-month stay on an island in Southeast Asia. Both of the ships in which he sailed carried more than two hundred people, but beyond that he does not describe the vessels except to note that en route from Sri Lanka to Yepodi (possibly Borneo or Java) his ship sailed with a smaller vessel in tow, "in case of accidents at sea and destruction of the big vessel." This was scant provision for the number of lives at stake, and when danger struck the crew seems to have felt that their safety took precedence over that of their passengers. (The idea that the officers and crew of a ship should sacrifice themselves for their passengers in the case of shipwreck is of recent vintage.) During a gale, "The merchants wished to get aboard the smaller vessel; but the men on the latter, fearing that they would be swamped by numbers, quickly cut the tow-rope in two." Those remaining on the larger vessel began to lighten ship by jettisoning their goods, although Faxian held on to his books and religious articles. The fate of the smaller boat is unknown, but after thirteen days Faxian's battered ship reached an island, possibly one of the Andamans or Nicobars, in the eastern Bay of Bengal, where the crew fixed the leak before putting back to sea. Normally the captain would have navigated by "observation of the sun, moon, and constellations," but overcast skies forced him to hug the coast of the Malay Peninsula despite the slower progress and greater risk of encountering pirates. After three months, "they reached a country named [Yepodi] where heresies and Brahmanism were flourishing, while the Faith of Buddha was in a very unsatisfactory condition." In May 414, Faxian joined another ship bound for Guangzhou at the start of the southwest monsoon. The passage should have taken "exactly fifty days," but a month out they ran into storms that blew for several weeks during which "the sky was constantly darkened and the captain lost his reckoning" and was unable to find a familiar coast. The ship was driven off course and may have passed through the Luzon Strait between Taiwan and the Philippines and into the Philippine Sea before the captain turned northwest and brought the ship to land finally on the Shandong Peninsula, thirteen hundred miles north of the intended destination.

If Faxian's Buddhism went unnoticed in the Bay of Bengal, his shipmates from Yepodi blamed his faith for their troubles: "Having this Buddhist monk on board has been our undoing, causing us to get into this trouble," they claimed. "We ought to land the religious mendicant on some island; it is not right to endanger all our lives for one man." He was only spared becoming a castaway when one of the ship's company threatened to report his defamers to the emperor, "who is," he reminded his fellow travelers, "a reverent believer in the Buddhist faith and honors the religious mendicants." It is likely that the merchants who blamed Faxian's religion for their problems were from Southeast Asia, for Faxian mentions Chinese merchants only obliquely, when he notes that some of his shipmates were returning home to Guangzhou. His silence on this subject, and that of other contemporary sources, suggests that there was little immediate Chinese involvement in the Nanhai trade, or at least that the majority of shipowners were Malays, Indians, Chams, or Funanese. If this was the case, it may have been because the Chinese considered the trade too risky, or because this direct crossing of the South China Sea was relatively new, although the fact that Faxian reports that the passage should have taken "exactly fifty days" implies that the route was well established.

One reason for the opening of the more direct sea route via the Strait of Malacca may have had to do with the rise of Buddhism in Southeast Asia and China, and the increasing importance that the Chinese attached to maintaining communication with the great centers of Buddhist teaching in Sri Lanka and northern India. Missionaries had introduced Buddhism to China via the silk road in the first century BCE, but the religion did not begin to take root until three hundred years after that, around the same time that Buddhist teachers began reaching Jiaozhi. Merchants and missionaries opened the sea route for the transmission of Buddhism into China in the third century. One of the most prominent was Kang Senghui, son of a merchant of Sogdiana (now Uzbekistan) who reached China by way of India and Jiaozhi, and converted the king of Wu to Buddhism.

China's embrace of the new religion led to changes in both the nature and the scope of long-distance sea trade. While merchants continued to traffic in luxuries, there was a new emphasis on religious artifacts from relics to incense and, sailing in Faxian's wake, scholars and translators. Missions from Sri Lanka began reaching China in 405. On the east coast of the Malay Peninsula south of the Kra Isthmus, Panpan became known especially for its store of religious artifacts and ritual materials. In Southeast and East Asia, as in India, the ecumenical qualities of Buddhism made it accessible for all, not just wealthy elites. This gave merchants a broader consumer base to satisfy, which in turn contributed to their profits and the desirability of engaging in trade. The official history of the Liu Song Dynasty describes the material and spiritual role of the sea-lanes to India, Persia, and the Byzantine Empire when it notes that ships bring "valuable products of the sea and mountains. And also the doctrine of devotion to the lord of the world [i.e., the Buddha]. Thus there is a chain of great and small ships on the route, and the merchants and envoys gather to exchange." Nor were the only beneficiaries of the growing traffic those at either end of the east–west trade. While the opening of the route across the South China Sea helped doom Funan and other coastal polities unable to compensate for the loss of commerce, it created new opportunities for others. So a king of Kantoli (on either the Malay Peninsula or Sumatra) dreamed that his people "would become rich and happy and merchants and travelers would multiply a hundredfold" were he to engage in trade with China.

The Sui Dynasty

Buddhism received its highest official sanction in China during the reign of Emperor Sui Gaozu, founder of the Sui Dynasty (589–618), whose genius lay in his appreciation of the fact that national unification was a function not just of military might but also of cultural cohesion and internal communication, although the latter could serve military ambition, too. Practical as well as devout, Gaozu employed Buddhism to unify China—for the first time in nearly four centuries—by building temples, subsidizing monasteries, and mining its teachings for affirmation of the legitimacy of his own rule. By the end of the century, Buddhism was to all intents and purposes the state religion, although Daoists received a measure of government support and Gaozu's advisors included many strict Confucianists. While encouraging this spiritual renaissance, Gaozu sought to renew the nation's infrastructure, and in 584 he ordered his chief engineer, Yuwen Kai, to build a new capital at Chang'an and to refashion the seven-hundred-year-old canal linking the capital, on the shallow and fickle Wei River, with the Yellow River. The new waterway was called the Guangdong Qu, the Canal for Expanded Communication. Even as this work was under way, Gaozu was developing his plans for the conquest of Chen, last of the independent southern dynasties, which fell in 589 in a carefully orchestrated campaign along the Yangzi, its northern border. Gaozu's forces included two fleets built in the Yangzi and Han River valleys and on the coast south of the Shandong Peninsula. Arrayed against these were the five-decked "Azure" and "Yellow Dragon" ships of Chen, each of which carried eight hundred men, many armed with crossbows. In the event, the Sui commander prudently avoided a fight in the Yangzi gorges, where his men would have been at a disadvantage, and overran the Chen defenses from the land.

Gaozu's son and successor, Sui Yangdi, was, like his father, a devout Buddhist, energetic, and harsh. To his Confucianist critics he was extravagant in his construction of a second capital at Luoyang and an extensive network of canals. The latter required the corvée labor of millions of men and women, but it had the undeniable effect of strengthening the internal ties of the newly reunited country. The Sui canals linked Chang'an to the area around modern Beijing in the north and to Hangzhou in the south. The northerly stretch was the longest, covering about 1,350 kilometers. To the south the most heavily trafficked canals during the Sui and Tang Dynasties were the Bian Canal, which ran from the Yellow River near Kaifeng southeast toward the Huai River and the Grand Canal; and the Grand Canal itself, which continued south to Yangzhou, crossed the Yangzi, and then wound its way south for another 435 kilometers to Hangzhou.

To commemorate the opening of the improved waterway between Luoyang and Yangzhou, Yangdi led a lavish procession of "dragon boats, phoenix vessels, war boats of the 'Yellow Dragon' style, red battle cruisers, multi-decked transports, lesser vessels of bamboo slats. Boatmen hired from all the waterways . . . pulled the vessels by ropes of green silk on the imperial progress to Yangzhou. . . . The boats followed one another poop to prow for more than 200 leagues [100 kilometers]." The Sui sovereigns proved better canal builders than rulers. Their dynasty lasted less than forty years, but more than five hundred years after Yangdi, when the Song court was forced to relocate to Hangzhou (which they renamed Lin'an), the poet-statesman Lu You wrote "The only reason that our Imperial Court can now stay at [Lin'an] is because we have this canal. Both the Bian [Canal] and this one were made by the Sui dynasty and benefit our Song. Is this predestination?"

The Sui emperors sought to re-create the China of the Han era by consolidating control over the empire's territory while defining the Middle Kingdom's relations with lesser states on the periphery of Chinese culture and beyond. Although both Jiaozhi and Linyi initially recognized Sui suzerainty and sent envoys to the new emperor, in 601 Jiaozhi declared independence. The Chinese responded decisively, but rather than invade by the time-honored route through Guangdong and Guangxi Provinces, the Sui armies marched onto the Yunnan Plateau and attacked from the west down the Red River. Following Jiaozhi's surrender, the dynasty charged a provincial governor with overseeing the seaborne trade and controlling "the barbarians of all the kingdoms south of the sea . . . arriving in boats after traveling unknown distances . . . bringing goods by the Jiaozhi route." Farther afield, in 607 the Sui exchanged embassies with states in Southeast Asia. Yet the Sui dynasts would not benefit from these productive initiatives thanks in part to their disastrous military campaigns on the Korean Peninsula.

Northeast Asia

China and the Chinese have had a long and complex history with the people of Northeast Asia and although the region had only indirect contact with areas west and south of China, the Middle Kingdom proved less a buffer than a filter through which alien ideas and institutions flowed from more remote corners of Eurasia. The Japanese archipelago was first inhabited about thirty thousand years ago, and while some people reached the northern island of Hokkaido by way of the Kamchatka Peninsula and the Kurile Islands, the more important route was across the Korea Strait to the islands of Kyushu and Honshu. Continental influences became especially pronounced from the fourth century BCE, when Chinese states took an increasingly active interest in the Korean Peninsula. At this time, the northern state of Yan (whose capital lies beneath modern Beijing) invaded the peninsular state of Gojoseon (Old Choson), which occupied the area between Pyeongyang and Seoul. Refugees from this attack moved down the peninsula and across the Korea Strait in a migration that seems to have been the catalyst for Japan's transition from the hunter-gatherer Jomon culture to the more sedentary and technologically advanced Yayoi. The ancient story that members of an expedition sent by the Qin emperor to find the Daoist elixir of immortality settled on Kyushu may recall this exodus from the Korean Peninsula to Japan. At this point, Yayoi culture seems to have absorbed a host of Chinese practices already present in Korea, including metallurgy and paddy rice cultivation. And unlike China or Korea, Japan essentially skipped from the Neolithic to the Iron Age and adopted simultaneously bronze- and ironworking technologies imported in the third century BCE.

In the 180s BCE, a Yan renegade named Wiman seized the throne of Gojoseon and barred trade between the smaller states in southern Korea and China. The Han emperors tolerated this arrangement until 109 BCE, when they conquered Gojoseon and divided the peninsula into three commanderies, the only time the Chinese succeeded in establishing a full colonial presence in Korea. These eventually evolved into the kingdoms of Goguryeo (Koguryo), Baekje (Paekche), and Silla. Baekje occupied the southwest part of the Korean Peninsula, and acted as an intermediary between China and Japan. Silla, in the southeast, also traded with Japan. The heart of Goguryeo was astride the Yalu River, but despite its proximity to the Middle Kingdom it was not until the fourth century that Goguryeo began to emulate Chinese forms of governance, law, writing, and Buddhism. In the fifth century, Goguryeo annexed the Liaodong Peninsula and eastern Manchuria and became the dominant power on the Korean Peninsula, with Silla as a junior partner. Fearful of Goguryeo expansion, Baekje recruited soldiers from the Yamato state in Japan, which had emerged in the plains of Honshu Island a century before, possibly under Baekje influence.

Chinese references to Japan are few until well into the common era, but it is known that a Japanese mission reached a Chinese commandery in northern Korea in the first century BCE, and that when a Japanese mission arrived at the Han court in 57 CE, the emperor sent the king of Wa (as the Japanese were called) an inscribed gold seal. By the third century, the Chinese appear to have formed a clear picture of the people, government, and customs of "the mountainous islands located in the middle of the ocean to the southeast" of the Korean Peninsula. Among the more bizarre observances recorded was the

Japanese practice of employing ritual abstainers to ensure the safety of difficult enterprises like seafaring.

> When they travel across the sea to come to China, they always select a man who does not comb his hair, does not rid himself of fleas, keeps his clothes soiled with dirt, does not eat meat, and does not lie with women. He behaves like a mourner, and is called a "keeper of taboos" [literally, "man with mourning death"]. If the voyage is concluded with good fortune, every one lavishes on him slaves and treasures. If someone gets ill, or if there is a mishap, they kill him immediately, saying that he was not conscientious enough in observing the taboos.

People can be quick to blame problems aboard ship on outsiders—foreigners or the religiously compromised like Faxian or the biblical Jonah—but if this account is accurate, the practice of embarking a ritual scapegoat to ensure safe passage at sea is apparently unique to the Japanese tradition.

Direct contact between China and Japan was infrequent in the Yamato period, but there was considerable movement of people, commodities, culture, and religion by way of Korea, which bore a strong imprint of Chinese culture. Relations between Yamato and the Korean kingdoms were more intense. After Sillan envoys accidentally destroyed a Japanese fleet in 300, the kingdom sent shipwrights to Yamato to build replacement ships. A century later, Goguryeo defeated a Yamato invasion of the peninsula where the Japanese probably intended to frustrate Silla's expansion at the expense of their ally Baekje, where Japanese merchants congregated in Mimana, near modern Busan (Pusan). The Chinese declined the Japanese king's request to be made supreme commander of an invasion against Goguryeo, and in 512 the Yamato court ceded control of Mimana to Baekje.

Fifteen years later, the Yamato raised a force of sixty thousand troops against Silla, but despite this support for Baekje, Goguryeo's advance against Baekje continued. By the end of the century it was the most threatening of China's northern neighbors and frequent raids finally provoked retaliation by Emperor Sui Gaozu in 598. The land and sea campaign ended with Goguryeo's perfunctory acknowledgment of Chinese supremacy, but in 612 Sui Yangdi launched a second invasion that included three hundred ships that crossed from the Shandong Peninsula to Korea for an attack on Pyeongyang. This and two subsequent expeditions failed thanks to the defenses erected against a seaborne attack. Although the presence of Korean ships can be assumed, there is no mention of a sea battle. Yangdi only refrained from a fourth invasion because, thanks to his preference for lavish construction projects and foreign adventures over addressing domestic crises like a disastrous flood of the Yellow River, China was on the verge of civil war. In 616, he moved his capital to Yangzhou, where he was murdered two years later. But rough-hewn though its end may have been, the Sui Dynasty laid the foundation from which sprang the unrivaled prosperity of the Tang Dynasty, the brilliance of which would shimmer across Asia.

The Ships of East Asia

Detailed study of shipbuilding in East Asia is hampered by a dearth of archae-ological finds and written descriptions. The remains of Dong-Son logboats in northern Vietnam have transverse bulkheads and sides raised by the addition of planks fastened by lashings and mortise-and-tenon joinery similar to that found in western Eurasia. Many Dong-Son drums are decorated with bands of paddled warships carrying archers, spearmen, and drums, the latter presum-ably struck to help the paddlers keep time (as in Greek triremes), for signaling, or for encouragement in battle. In these scenes, the drum is in a deckhouse aft, just forward of where the helmsman stands by a quarter rudder. The hulls are crescent-shaped, although no hogging trusses to support the ends are vis-ible. On some, the paddlers appear to sit on the deck, which suggests that the vessels might be rafts—perhaps of bamboo, with turned-up ends achieved by steaming, as was the practice in China. Others interpret the vessels as log-boats, a view supported by the fact that some of the images appear to show elevated platforms where archers are stationed.

These images bear comparison with a bronze ship model on the island of Flores in south-central Indonesia, but believed to have been cast in northern Vietnam or southern China around the first century CE. The model measures 56 centimeters long, 19.5 centimeters high, and 8.5 centimeters broad and there is an upper deck surmounted by three platforms of uncertain purpose. Those at the bow and stern are taller, supported by four uprights, while the platform amidships is longer and erected on eight posts. Below the deck are a dozen paddlers, six on either side of the hull, sitting with their feet forward. The vessel also seems to have a keel, with a pronounced overhang forward. While the Dong-Son boats are generally shown with one quarter rudder, no steering mechanism survives on the Flores boat, and the figure of the helms-man (if there ever was one) is missing. Study of the ancient model is compli-cated by the fact that it remains a venerated object that can be accessed for study only after the performance of appropriate rituals, a difficulty that attests to the remarkable durability of maritime traditions in parts of island Southeast Asia.

The first-century bronze ship model from Kampong Dobo on the island of Flores in eastern Indonesia seems to represent a seagoing warship. It measures 56 centimeters long by 8.5 centimeters broad at the stern, and has an overall height of 19.5 centimeters. The twelve paddlers portrayed may be stock figures, and the vessel on which this is based surely carried more than the three warriors and a helmsman (much of which is missing) in the model. Photograph by Herwig Zahorka, Wiesbaden, Germany.

Later Chinese sources offer some information about foreign ships, both those that came to China from Linyi, Funan, or Posse (the latter thought to refer either to a place on the Malay Peninsula, or to Persia), and those engaged in trade between foreign ports. The envoy Kang Dai, who wrote of a ship with seven sails in the western Indian Ocean, sketches the salient features of a large Funanese vessel of the third century:

> In the kingdom of Fu-nan they cut down trees for the making of boats. The long ones measure 22 meters and their breadth is 2 meters. The stem and the stern resemble the head and tail of a fish, and they are decorated all over with ornaments of iron. The large boats can carry a hundred men. Each man has a long oar, a short oar [a paddle], and a pole for quanting [pushing a pole against the streambed]. From stem to stern there are 50 men, or more than 40, according to the boat's size. In full motion they use the long oars; when they sit down they use the paddles; and when the water is shallow they quant with the poles. They all raise their oars and respond to the shouts in perfect unison.

Kang Dai does not elaborate on this vessel's purpose, but given its extreme length-to-breadth ratio it was probably intended for ceremonial occasions in relatively sheltered waters rather than for trade or warfare. Another third-century text entitled *Strange Things of the South* describes a vessel called a *kun-lun bo*, which may correspond with "the very big *kolandiophonta* that sail across to Chryse [Southeast Asia] and the Ganges region" mentioned in the *Periplus of the Erythraean Sea*. Kunlun is the Chinese name of an otherwise unidentified country in Southeast Asia, while *bo* is a word of unknown origin. According to *Strange Things of the South*, "The people of foreign parts call ships *bo*. The large ones are more than fifty meters in length and stand out of the water four to five meters. . . . They carry from six to seven hundred persons, with 10,000 bushels of cargo"—according to various interpretations, 250–1,000 tons. These ships carried as many as four fore-and-aft sails of woven leaves. Unlike in Chinese and Indian Ocean ships, "The four sails do not face directly forwards, but are set obliquely and so arranged that they can all be fixed in the same direction, to receive the wind and to spill it." Similar details are found in the seventh-century Ajanta ship, and in descriptions of ships with seven hundred passengers from the *Jatakas*. This adjustable rig was probably similar to that illustrated in bas-reliefs of ships on the ninth-century Javanese temple complex at Borobudur. These show quadrilateral sails that were canted forward when set fore and aft, or swung perpendicular to the centerline of the hull when running downwind. *Strange Things of the South* explains that ships with this rig were more stable than those with taller, fixed masts and that they could use high winds to their advantage when other vessels would be forced to ride out gales under bare poles.

Southeast Asian shipbuilders used cordage to fasten their vessels, but their method of sewing hulls differed from that employed in the Indian Ocean. Rather than bore holes straight through the planks so that the stitching could be seen on the outside of the hull, shipwrights achieved a more finished look with a technique known as "lashed-lug and stitched-plank" fastening. The planks were stitched to one another through holes bored diagonally from the inside face to the edge of the plank so that the stitching was visible only from within the hull, as in the Egyptian Khufu ship. The inside face of the plank also had raised lugs carved out of them through which holes were bored so that frames could be lashed to them. At some point, shipwrights began inserting dowels in the edges of the planks to prevent the planks from slipping against each other, and in time builders of larger ships abandoned stitching altogether. Sewn-plank fastening was common throughout Southeast Asia and as far north as Jiaozhi, Hainan Island, and Guangdong.

In maritime matters, people of the ancient Yue culture area of southern China demonstrated greater affinities with the Austronesian-speaking people of Southeast Asia than with their Han overlords, but in most respects the

Chinese approach to hull form, propulsion, and steering differed significantly from that of virtually every other maritime community in Eurasia. In this regard, the Chinese were surprisingly resistant to outside influence, while their ideas about ship design were seldom adopted outside Northeast Asia. The distinction between Chinese and others' approaches to the design of seagoing ships may be attributed to the influence of concepts honed in craft intended for freshwater navigation. Thanks to the diverse employments and conditions encountered, from navigating the tumultuous rapids of the Three Gorges or the flat waters of the canals, to fishing, to living aboard boats, there was within this tradition of inland watercraft as much variety in design as could be found in any strictly seagoing culture. While planks tended to be joined edge-to-edge, as in the shell-first tradition, they were fastened to the bulkheads and frames with a care that suggests frame-first development. Unlike vessels in other traditions, in which both bow and stern tend to taper to a fine edge, Chinese vessels have a relatively sharp bow below the waterline though the hull is often squared off above the waterline. However, the stern generally ends in a flat transom below the waterline. This allowed for the adoption of a centerline or axial rudder, the oldest evidence for which is a first-century clay model of a riverboat, a good thousand years before they were used anywhere else. However, it is doubtful that Chinese seagoing ships mounted centerline rudders until considerably later. A fifth- or sixth-century fresco from the Buddhist cave complex at Dunhuang in Central Asia shows a Chinese sailing ship mounting a quarter rudder, and the earliest extant rendering of a Chinese oceangoing ship with a centerline rudder is in a bas-relief from the Bayon temple at Angkor Thom, Cambodia, dated to the twelfth century, contemporary with the earliest evidence for centerline rudders in the Indian Ocean and northern Europe.

The Chinese practice of constructing hulls with two or more layers of planking created what was in effect a laminated hull. This imparted great longitudinal strength to the vessel, while the outer planks also served as a sacrificial layer easily replaced—or overlaid by an additional skin of planks—in the event of damage from collision or degradation. The insertion of frames and especially bulkheads gave hulls enormous lateral support, as well. Despite the prevailing belief that these bulkheads were watertight, this is unlikely if only because a lack of limber holes to allow the water to drain would have led to widespread rot. Archaeological evidence from later thirteenth- and fourteenth-century ships shows that except for the foremost and aftermost bulkheads, all had limber holes that allowed water to run between compartments. It may well be that in the event of the hull's being stove in these could be blocked to confine the inrushing water to one part of the hull, thus protecting the rest of the cargo and decreasing the risk of sinking. The use of bulkheads also allowed for innovative designs. Riverboats built for the rapids of the upper Yangzi often had free-flooding compartments forward of the foremost watertight bulkhead. In these, the hull was pierced with holes. This reduced the hull's resistance to the water and enabled boats to shed water quickly when the bow dipped beneath the waves and so increased the vessel's maneuverability in a highly dangerous environment in which the currents could exceed thirteen knots, and the crew had to add a couple of knots in order to give the helmsman steerage way. Fishermen also used free-flooding compartments between bulkheads in the center of the vessel to keep fish alive until they reached market, a practice not attested in Britain until the eighteenth century.

Inland vessels were propelled by paddling or rowing, poling, towing, and sailing. Although rowing was widespread, the repertoire of Chinese shipping included nothing comparable to the oared galleys of the ancient and medieval Mediterranean. Rather than face backward and pull the oar, as in the west, Chinese oarsmen stood facing forward, and as the motion of the oar was intended to gain much greater purchase on the water—so that rowers could propel their craft "at a moderate speed with a minimum of effort"—usually on the side of the boat opposite to that where the blade entered the water, which it did at angles of up to sixty degrees. In addition to oars carried on an axis perpendicular to the hull, larger junks and sampans were propelled by powerful oars called *yulohs*. These were slightly curved oars usually half as long or more as the hull and balanced on a pivot at the stern (or less often at the bow). A lanyard led from the forward part of the handle to the deck, and the *yuloh* was powered by pushing simultaneously on the lanyard and the handle so that the blade feathered along an axis parallel to the hull. Larger *yulohs* could be handled by up to six men, four to work the handle, and two to work the lanyard.

Towing, or tracking, was a common means of moving vessels throughout China's networks of internal waterways. Animals could be used, but on the upper Yangzi the vessel's crew—up to 80 people on vessels of 120 tons—was so employed, and in the Three Gorges these could be supplemented by gangs of as many as 250 people. Photographs from the early twentieth century illustrate the brute labor required to move these huge vessels against torrential currents. In one, two files of trackers bent double on a muddy riverbank are harnessed to towing lines, their right arms grabbing the hawser behind their backs while they keep their balance by touching the ground with their left hands. In gorges where there was no riverbank, a narrow gallery too low for a man to stand upright was cut into the rock, and tracking teams struggled forward, certain of death from slipping or being yanked from the gallery by their hawsers if the pilot made a wrong move.

Gangs of trackers bending to their work towing a riverboat along the banks of the Yangzi River. Sixteen trackers are seen in the gang in the foreground, which is pulling the second vessel from the left. The photograph was taken in the 1930s, but little had changed in the millennium since Zhang Zeduan painted Along the River During the Qingming Festival *eight centuries before (see insert, figure 11). Photograph by Dmitri Kessel; courtesy of* Life *magazine.*

While the Chinese had sails by at least the end of the first millennium BCE, they were not used extensively on inland waters owing to the prevalence of bridges, at least until the development of a hinged mast (called a tabernacle mast) that could be easily lowered and raised. The earliest sails were square sails, but by the second or third century the balanced lugsail was ubiquitous in river craft. (The balanced lugsail is a quadrilateral fore-and-aft sail set from a boom and yard, with the luff forward of the mast.) The primary materials for the sail were woven mats of bamboo or reed stiffened by bamboo battens. These keep the sail flat, thus allowing the vessel to sail closer to the wind than otherwise, making it easy to douse or reef the sail, and providing a means for the crew to ascend the mast. Because the junk sail is broken into smaller sections, each of these is exposed to less pressure than an unbattened sail of the same overall area and the sail can therefore be made of weaker material. When the junk sail was first taken to sea is not known, but the ship in the Dunhuang fresco is shown running before the wind with a single square sail.

In addition to being employed for peacetime trade and transportation, rivercraft were also used for warfare. The frontline vessel in both Shihuangdi's campaign against the Hundred Yue and Wudi's invasion of Jiaozhi a century later was the *louchuan*, or towered ship. Based on interpretations of the images on Dong-Son drums and Chinese bronzes from the fourth century BCE, these seem to have been decked vessels of twenty to twenty-five meters in length,

The largest of the ships from the Dunhuang cave complex in Gansu Province, central China, about 2,300 kilometers from the nearest saltwater. The Buddhist ship of faith sailing from the shores of illusion to the paradise of Amitabha (Amida) Buddha has the square ends typical of Tang Dynasty ships, but the square sail suggests an Indian or Indian Ocean point of reference. Courtesy of the RMN–Grand Palais, Paris/Art Resource, New York.

propelled by forward-facing rowers stationed below, and fought by archers and soldiers armed with dagger axes and bows stationed above deck and in the towers. The main antiship weapons were fifteen-meter-long beams mounted on pivots, a design not unlike the Roman *corvus* but intended simply to smash enemy ships to pieces rather than to hold them fast for a boarding action.

It is doubtful that such weapons were used in the campaigns against Jiaozhi or the Korean Peninsula, the fleets for which likely comprised only armed troop transports. Whether they would have encountered vessels specifically designed for combat is difficult to know, for while the kingdom of Silla established an office of maritime administration (*Seonbuseo*) responsible for civilian and naval shipping in the sixth century, references to and archaeological finds of individual ships on the Korean Peninsula, as well as in Japan, are few. According to the *Nihongi* (which was compiled in the eighth century and may include anachronisms that reflect the authors' experience), the gods who introduced shipbuilding to Japan specified the use of Japanese cedar and camphorwood. The need for water transport was dictated by Japan's rugged terrain and the availability of coastal routes, but the throne may have had an interest in developing a fleet for trade or warfare early on. Emperor Sujin Tenno (third or fourth century) reportedly mandated that ships be built in all the coastal provinces of his realm, and the ships accidentally burned by the envoys from Silla in 300 CE were said to have been given to the throne as tribute from the provinces in exchange for gifts of salt, while another passage refers to a vessel being "enrolled among the number of Imperial vessels." How big these were or how they were constructed is unknown. One entry in the *Nihongi* mentions a ship built from a large tree, which might suggest a logboat of some sort, but another tells of the construction of a ship of thirty meters, which is indicative of a vessel of more complex design. These are only tantalizing hints of robust maritime cultures whose particulars do not come into sharp relief for several centuries.

The inland origins of the Chinese state did not predispose its people to maritime pursuits, but the exploitation of rivers and canals facilitated territorial expansion and domestic stability, while accumulated wealth enabled members of the elite to import exotic goods, the most extraordinary of which came from Southeast Asia. The exposure to alien ideas that resulted from these exchanges was anathema to Confucianists, but the rise of Buddhism and the resulting demand for religious texts, statuary, incense, and other religious paraphernalia spurred trade not only with Southeast Asia and India but also Korea and Japan, where Buddhism was introduced from China. Initially the sea route between China, Southeast Asia, and the Indian Ocean wound through a series of small, loosely defined coastal and island networks, but when fifth-century mariners began crossing the South China Sea from the Strait of Malacca to Vietnam, they inaugurated the longest sailing routes the world would know for the next millennium and ensured the spectacular growth in long-distance trade that flourished in the early centuries of the Islamic caliphates and China's Tang Dynasty.

Chapter 8

The Christian and Muslim Mediterranean

Maritime life in the medieval Mediterranean was shaped by the collapse of the Western Roman Empire, the rise to power of the Byzantine Empire and the Islamic caliphates, and the emergence of religious ideology in political conflict. Disputes over heresies undermined the cohesion of the Byzantine Empire in the seventh century and the resulting stresses are reflected in diminished activity that led to truncated or abandoned shipping routes, and fewer and smaller ships. In its weakened state, the empire was unable to prevent the expansion of Islam in the Levant, whose seafaring communities helped carry the new faith west. Muslim states' encouragement of industry, trade, and the arts revitalized existing port cities of North Africa and gave rise to new ones, and emirates of the eighth and ninth centuries ruled most of the major islands from Cyprus to the Balearics. In the tenth century, rivalries between Shiites and Sunnis contributed to the loss of Muslim territories to Christian princes. The outstanding long-term change, however, was the gradual decline of the maritime primacy of Egypt, the Levant, and the Aegean, which had constituted the fulcrum of the Mediterranean for millennia. In their place arose commercial and naval powers—Muslim giving way to Christian—that emerged from almost complete obscurity in the central and western Mediterranean.

These developments were accompanied by a major transition in naval architecture as Mediterranean shipwrights abandoned shell-first for frame-first hull construction, a process more economical in material, labor, skill, and time and that ultimately gave rise to the ships that launched European mariners into the Atlantic and beyond. Interfaith conflict posed real obstacles to trade and led to the most intense period of Mediterranean naval warfare since the end of republican Rome. Even so, merchants' efforts to reconcile different religious and legal principles among Jews, Christians, and Muslims fostered the creation of novel forms of financing commerce, the spread of legal practices designed to protect merchant shippers and their investments, and the forging of compromise solutions to which all could subscribe, regardless of faith. Eventually, this nascent international law fostered further commercial expansion within and beyond the Mediterranean.

Through a Glass Darkly: The Serçe Limani Wreck and the Medieval Mediterranean

In 1973, archaeologists discovered the remains of an eleventh-century merchant ship in the Turkish harbor of Serçe Limani about twelve miles north of Rhodes. The ballast of the "glass wreck" included about three tons of cullet—broken and raw glass—along with a striking array of other goods, ship's gear, tools, weapons, and personal possessions. What prompted archaeologists to focus on the Serçe Limani site before turning to other known shipwrecks was the ship's date and the possibility that it might show whether shipwrights had begun to construct ships frame-first rather than in the ancient shell-first sequence, that is, by fastening hull planking to a preerected skeleton of keel and ribs, the method most familiar in western shipbuilding for the past five hundred years. As it happens, the find at Serçe Limani is the latest of three shipwrecks clustered in southwest Turkey through which we can trace the transition from shell-first to frame-first shipbuilding. The two other ships were located off the island of Yassi Ada, about sixty-five miles by sea to the southeast. The older Yassi Ada B wreck dates from the second half of the fourth century. With a length of almost nineteen meters and a beam of less than seven, the ship was of typical shell-first construction, with edge-joined planks fastened to one another by mortise-and-tenon joints and reinforced with frames inserted after the hull was formed. While there is nothing novel in the hull's construction, Yassi Ada B is thus far the oldest known Mediterranean ship likely to have been rigged with a fore-and-aft sail.

From the south side of the island, the seventh-century Yassi Ada A ship (so-called because it was found before the older Yassi Ada B site) belongs to a transitional shipbuilding phase. In the lower part of the hull the shipwrights edge-joined the planks in the shell-first manner, but the mortise-and-tenon joints were unpegged and widely spaced, a less elaborate joinery than that found in older vessels. Above the waterline, they simply nailed the strakes to existing frames, some of which they fastened to the keel with iron bolts before fitting the planks. Quarter rudders were mounted between two beams that ran the width of the hull aft, and the helmsman probably steered from a raised helm-deck. Archaeologists also identified hatches forward and amidships. The hull is surprisingly slender for a cargo vessel, 21 meters long by 5.2 meters. Some believe that this reflects a renewed interest in speed to outrun pirates, although there could have been an economic rationale for faster ships. Nothing of the rig survives, but given the hull shape and the probable placement of the mainmast and quarter rudders the ship would have sailed best with a two-masted, lateen rig rather than a square sail.

The Serçe Limani ship probably measured 16 by 5 meters, with a depth in hold of nearly 2.5 meters—tall enough to stand up in—and a loaded draft of about 1.4 meters. There is no clue as to where the ship originated, but the keel is of elm and the planking of pine. One of the more curious aspects of the ship's overall construction is that the shipwrights shaped the timbers with saws rather than axes and adzes, the shipbuilder's tools of choice worldwide. There were about forty framing stations in the ship, with frames or half frames fastened to the keel with iron nails, and the planks were fastened to the frames with nails and wooden treenails; there is no evidence for any edge-joining of planks. The boxy, thirty-five-ton hull was designed for maximum capacity and the ship apparently carried a two-masted, lateen rig.

When, where, and why shipwrights realized that one could erect a hull's frame around a centerline keel and then attach planks to the frames are questions not answered in any contemporary sources. Most modern discussion attributes this technological change to the wrenching economic transformations that roiled the Mediterranean between the third and eleventh centuries: the barbarian invasions and division of the Roman Empire; decades of plague in the sixth century; the conflict between the Byzantine Empire and the Muslim caliphates; and sectarian violence within Christianity and Islam. This was not an era of uninterrupted decline, and there were periods of dazzling brilliance and prosperity across the Mediterranean. Yet Rome's *Pax Mediterraneana*—an historically anomalous period in which there was almost no conflict at sea—was a thing of the past. With less state support of maritime commerce, the inherent uncertainties of sea trade discouraged investment in large, expensive ships, and it behooved merchant-owners of relatively modest means to run ships that were small and easy to build. These comparatively inexpensive frame-first hulls also gave smaller polities such as the Italian city-states the opportunity to develop niche trades in which they could compete against more established maritime powers.

Whereas the shell-first sequence requires considerable skill at all stages of construction, frame-first lends itself to a more hierarchical workforce; the most skilled shipwrights were responsible for erecting the keel, stem- and sternposts, and frames; fixing the planks to a skeleton frame required less experience; and caulking the seams between planks entailed no knowledge of carpentry at all. Though frame-first hulls require more maintenance, this is offset by the fact that they can be built and repaired faster and at less expense, and hull forms can be duplicated more easily. In addition, plank-on-frame construction requires less wood, which lowered the material cost of shipbuilding. Thus, the shift to frame-first construction was a technological revolution that resulted in a manufacturing one.

How the fore-and-aft lateen sail evolved is likewise unknown. All sails work by exploiting the difference in air pressure from one side to the other. With a square sail, wind blowing from astern creates high pressure behind the sail and low pressure in front; as the sail seeks to go toward the area of lower pressure it moves the hull forward. Whether the physics involved are understood, the basic idea is obvious to anyone who has stood in a strong breeze. The same principle applies to fore-and-aft sails (the lateen is but one of many types), which are cut to belly slightly in the direction away from the wind, thus allowing for an area of low pressure on the leeward side of the sail that exerts pull in that direction. The square sail is most effective when sailing directly downwind, but by swinging the yard forward and down, one can create a triangular shape not unlike a lateen. In its perfected form, a lateen enables a vessel to sail closer to the wind—at an angle of between sixty-six and forty-five degrees to the wind direction—compared to only about ninety degrees with a square sail. The lateen sail is especially well suited to ships of small to medium size— a capacity of thirty to sixty tons burden was typical of the period—because they require smaller crews than does a square sail for a vessel of comparable size. The lateen rig was suited to the times because it offered the mobility and speed necessary to avoid encounters with pirates or hostile states in an era of instability.

The adoption of the lateen occurred between the second century, the date of the oldest pictorial evidence, and the sixth century, after which there is no iconographic evidence of the square sail in the Mediterranean for several hundred years. It is commonly thought that the latter was abandoned completely until northern Europeans reintroduced it in the fourteenth century, but this is probably not the case. When artists began showing ships with square sails in the thirteenth century, they depicted rigging details similar to those employed by sailors of the ancient Mediterranean but unlike those found in northern Europe. This suggests that sailors continued to use the square sail, but only in vessels too small or otherwise insignificant to have attracted the attention of artists.

The Serçe Limani ship is revealing not only for what it shows us about developments in naval architecture and shipboard life; analysis of the associated finds also invites reconsideration of the nature of relations between Christians and Muslims. The glass cullet carried as ballast suggests that the ship was en route from a Syrian port with a local glassblowing industry to Constantinople, probably the foremost glassmaking center in the world. Apart from the cullet, the site yielded eighty pieces of intact cups and other glassware not intended for recycling. By themselves, these intact pieces would have constituted a significant contribution to the study of medieval glass. The painstaking recovery, recording, and categorization of nearly a million glass fragments allowed for the reconstruction of hundreds of beakers, dishes, bowls, ewers, jars, lamps, and other items, and in so doing revolutionized the study of medieval Islamic art.

Much of the rest of the cargo seems to have been perishable goods, although about ninety wine and oil amphorae were carried as ballast. More modest finds include copper pots, padlocks, adzes, drill bits and chisels, combs, chess pieces, and sixty-four spears and javelins. The provenance of the amphorae and weapons show that most of the ship's complement, perhaps eleven people all told, were likely Hellenized Bulgarians from near Constantinople. Other personal effects include forty Byzantine copper coins and three gold Fatimid dinars. One of the nine anchors is stamped with Arabic letters, as is a glass weight (one of sixteen) that dates the wreck to no later than 1025. Another clue to the nature of cross-cultural relations beyond the seas comes from the nearly nine hundred decorated lead sinkers used for weighing down fishing lines or fishing nets. These were manufactured in a Byzantine workshop, probably in Constantinople, from lead mined in Iran.

The surprising variety of material goods in this thousand-year-old time capsule offers us a glimpse of the Mediterranean as an arena of collaborative exchange between Byzantine and Muslim merchants in the century before the Crusades, when the balance of power shifted sharply to the west. The material evidence for peaceful relations among merchants is corroborated by the contemporaneous formulation of maritime and commercial laws that at once respected and transcended the legal norms peculiar to Christianity, Islam, and Judaism, which allowed trade to flourish even where religious politics presented apparently insurmountable obstacles. The glass wreck is thus a multifaceted prism through which we can see the essential political, technological, and commercial developments that marked the progress from late antiquity to the early modern period.

The Eastern Roman Empire

Faced with the growing problems of governing a sprawling empire, in 293 Diocletian divided the rule of the Roman Empire between two co-emperors, a move that ultimately led to the division of the state into eastern (Greek) and western (Latin) halves. The outer limits of the empire were seldom peaceful, and the so-called Pax Romana was a fiction. The Roman peace was enforced by pacification, all but endless warfare against barbarian tribes to the north, west, and south, and against more highly developed states of ancient lineage in the east. Rome's security depended on the strength of the empire's long, heavily fortified borders, especially along the Rhine and Danube Rivers. Ultimately, the armies and bureaucracy upon which the state relied proved unaffordable and unreliable, and probes by Germanic tribes climaxed with the Barbarian Migrations of the fourth and fifth centuries.

For conservative contemporaries, a ready explanation for Rome's problems was the rise of Christianity, which grew despite official persecution and internal schisms. The fates of religion and the empire were joined by Constantine, whose troops proclaimed him emperor of the west in 306. Six years later, he converted to Christianity, and in 324 he defeated his co-emperor, Licinius, at the battle of the Hellespont. This was the first major fleet engagement in the Mediterranean in 350 years. Constantine had 200 triaconters and penteconters against 350 triremes under Licinius. Whether Constantine's victory was due to better commanders, who may have deployed only part of their fleet to ensure freedom of maneuver in the narrows, or to a storm that drove Licinius's ships ashore on the second day of the battle, the defeat broke Licinius, who shortly thereafter was captured and executed.

Constantine established his capital at Byzantium, which was officially renamed Constantinople in 330 and eventually became the sole capital of the empire known as Rum (Rome) to contemporaries, and as the Byzantine Empire by later writers. Situated on a peninsula at the southern end of the Bosporus where it meets the Sea of Marmara, Constantinople (now Istanbul) was at a major crossroads of trade and communication between Asia and Europe and the Black Sea and Mediterranean, and it was the first major European capital founded in a port. A major consideration in the choice of Constantinople was its geographical setting, which offered "the quiet shelter of harbours to navigators," especially along the Golden Horn, a four-mile inlet north of the peninsula that provided "anchorage throughout its whole extent." As important, there was more than enough waterfront to accommodate the merchant and naval shipping of the commercial, political, and economic center of empire. Just as all roads once led to Rome, all sea-lanes now led to the Byzantine capital. Growth was rapid, and by the sixth-century reign of Justinian I greater Constantinople was home to an estimated eight hundred thousand people. Even after the coming of Islam in the seventh century and the rise of the Italian maritime republics in the eleventh, Constantinople's size and strategic location guaranteed its place in the first rank of European and Mediterranean cities.

Within half a century of the founding of the new capital, barbarian tribes were overrunning the empire's Rhine-Danube frontier and setting in train a series of events that would lead to the loss of the western empire and the rise of new states from Britain to North Africa. Visigoths crossed the Danube and sacked Rome in 410. Emperor Honorius was forced to withdraw the last Roman legions from Britain and enlisted Visigothic help in pushing the Vandals into Spain. In 429, Gaeseric led the Vandals across the Strait of Gibraltar into North Africa from where they became the first power to contest Rome's control of the Mediterranean in five hundred years. Settling in rich but weakly defended Carthage, the Vandals took to the sea and established themselves in the Balearics, Corsica, and Sardinia, where they were well positioned to attack the Italian mainland, Illyria, and Greece. In 455, Gaeseric plundered Rome without retribution, and in 476 the last western emperor was banished to the Neapolitan villa built by the Roman general Lucullus after the Mithridatic Wars.

By the start of the sixth century, the north coast of the Mediterranean was divided among the Byzantines, the Ostrogoths of northern Italy, the Visigothic kingdom of Toulouse in southwest France, and Vandal Spain. Byzantine relations with the Ostrogoths were generally good, but just as he sought to undermine Persian supremacy in the trade of the Indian Ocean, Justinian was eager to reassert imperial authority in the west to protect maritime commerce against the Vandals and Visigoths. In 533 Justinian's general Belisarius sailed with ninety-two warships and five hundred transports to seize North Africa and Sardinia and in a single battle brought the Vandal kingdom to an end. Turning next to Ostrogothic Italy, Belisarius captured Sicily, Naples, and Rome before bogging down in the face of stiff resistance and Justinian's refusal to send reinforcements, in part because he feared Belisarius's popularity. By midcentury, however, the Byzantines had regained Italy, Sicily, and the coast of Visigothic Spain, including the Guadalquivir River ports of Seville and Córdoba, and Ceuta, across the Strait of Gibraltar. Apart from western North Africa and the Frankish and Visigothic coast from Saguntum to the Italian border, the Mediterranean littoral was again under a single rule. But the Byzantines' comparatively strong commercial and naval presence in the Mediterranean was scant compensation for its weakness on land and their imperial revival was brief. By the early 600s, the Lombards from central Europe had overrun much of Italy, the Avars were camped at the gates of Constantinople, and in 624 the Visigoths expelled the Byzantines from Spain for the last time. Yet none of the new western powers was inclined to harness the maritime potential of the territories they controlled, which enabled the Byzantines to maintain sea-links to their central Mediterranean territories.

Ideology and Conflict

Maritime commerce carried Judaism, Christianity, and Islam around the Mediterranean, just as sea trade facilitated the spread of Buddhism from India and Sri Lanka to Southeast Asia and China. While religion could unite people across broad regions, sectarianism frequently undermined religious bonds. Christianity was the official religion of the Byzantine state, but highly politicized doctrinal differences led to persecution of Coptic and Nestorian Christians. As a result, when Sasanian Persia invaded the Levant in the 610s, Copts and Nestorians found the more tolerant Persian rule preferable to that of their fellow Christians in Constantinople. The Sasanians captured Damascus, Antioch, Jerusalem, and Alexandria, and in 626 they were encamped at Chalcedon (Kadiköy, Turkey), across the Bosporus from Constantinople. This proved the high-water mark of their advance. Three years later, the Byzantines seized the Persian capital at Ctesiphon on the Tigris, while their fleet reoccupied the ports of Syria and Egypt. With the defeat of the Sasanians, the Byzantines remained the largest and most coherent state in the Mediterranean basin.

All but unnoticed in the struggle between the rival empires was the emergence of the prophet Muhammad, whose followers seized the great inland trading city of Damascus in 635 before overwhelming a Byzantine army at the battle of the Yarmuk River (between Jordan and Syria), thereby releasing the Semitic peoples of the Levant from nearly a thousand years of alien Hellenistic-Roman-Byzantine rule. Turning east, the Arabs captured Ctesiphon and by 642 Arab armies had reached the borders of greater India, a conquest worthy of Alexander and with far more enduring results. To the west, Amr ibn al-As established Fustat (later Cairo) at the head of the Nile delta and took the port of Alexandria.

The capture of Mediterranean ports gave the Arabs access to ships and experienced mariners, which enabled them to attack the Byzantines by sea. Initially, the caliphs focused on conquering Byzantine territories around the eastern Mediterranean basin. Occupying Egypt and Syria, with their ports and naval professionals, made it possible to attack Cyprus and Constantinople itself. At the end of the century, Umayyad armies took the Byzantine province of Africa, which they called Ifriqiya and which became the point of departure for expansion into western North Africa and the Iberian Peninsula. Sicily was conquered in the ninth century, around the same time that exiles from al-Andalus established an independent emirate on Crete. Common to all these developments was the replacement of Christian rulers by Muslim ones; but the Christian and Muslim worlds were both rent by political rivalries and confessional schisms that created ample opportunity for cooperation between Christians, Muslims, and Jews.

Muslim maritime expansion began in 648 when, sailing at the head of a fleet of seventeen hundred ships, the governor of Egypt, Muawiya ibn Abi Sufyan, secured an annual indemnity from the people of Cyprus. When they lent ships to the Byzantines seven years later, he captured the island and in so doing touched off the first naval conflict between the empire and caliphate. Following the loss of Cyprus, Emperor Constans II marshaled a fleet of seven hundred to a thousand ships to seize the port of Phoenix, on the Lycian coast north of Cyprus. Surviving accounts of the engagement are often contradictory, yet on one point all agree: the Muslims scored a stunning victory at the battle of the Masts (Dhat al-Sawari), which Christian authors refer to as the battle of Phoenix. The outcome proved that Muslims could fight at sea; but domestic struggles within the caliphate prevented them from following up until after Muawiya became the first Umayyad caliph.

In 678, the Umayyads initiated a decade-long siege of Constantinople during which they occupied a naval base on the Sea of Marmara but were unable to capture the Byzantine capital. The agreement ending the siege resulted in the demilitarization of Cyprus and obliged the Cypriots to remain neutral in any conflict between empire and caliphate. The island became a way station for merchants, passengers, naval fleets, and spies. Although the Cypriots remained Christian and in theory neutral, the island's ambiguous status gave Muslim commanders a strategic advantage against the Byzantines, as both Muslim and Christian authors alike recognized. In his *Taktika* of around 900 the emperor Leo VI notes that "When the barbarians from Egypt and Syria and Cilicia are gathering for an expedition against the Romans [that is, the Byzantines], the commanders of the naval provinces must proceed with their squadron to Cyprus." A tenth-century Arabic writer concurred, noting that the first stage of any naval expedition against the Byzantines was a rendezvous in Cypriot waters. Cyprus remained subject to condominium rule until the resumption of full Byzantine authority in 965.

Even before the campaigns against Constantinople, Muslim armies had swept across North Africa—*Bilad al-Maghrib*, or Lands of the Sunset—as far as Ifriqiya.* In 695, Carthage fell to an Arab army but the new governor decided that the port was too exposed to attack from the sea and founded a new one in nearby Tunis, an almost impregnable site located on a lake separated from the sea by a narrow isthmus across which the Arabs dug a channel. The Byzantines made no attempt to retake Carthage due to domestic unrest at Constantinople, where seven emperors ruled between 695 and 717, when the Umayyads launched a major invasion. Their progress was unbroken until the ascension of Leo III, "the Isaurian," who raised the walls at Constantinople, laid up supplies, and strung a chain across the mouth of the Golden Horn, the first time such a measure is known to have been taken there. Even with a fleet of eighteen hundred ships and a large army, the Umayyads were unable to block Constantinople's access to the Black Sea granaries and they were forced to abandon the siege.

The failure against Constantinople did not deter the Umayyad advance across North Africa. Following the establishment of Tunis, Musa ibn Nusayr led an Arab-Berber army to Tangier, and in 711 an army of twelve thousand under Tariq ibn Ziyad crossed the Strait of Gibraltar to land near the rock named in his honor, Jabal Tarik, or Gibraltar. Musa and Tarik pushed their armies north to the Tagus River, Toledo, Tarragona, and Barcelona, and established the capital of al-Andalus at Seville, about eighty-five kilometers up the Guadalquivir from the Atlantic. Although Córdoba became the capital forty years later, Seville remained a major commercial port and naval base under Muslim and, from the thirteenth century, Christian rule for nine hundred years. Remote as it was, al-Andalus was one of the first parts of the Muslim world to break decisively with the political authority of the caliphate. When Abu al-'Abbas as-Saffah established the Abbasid Caliphate in 750, he murdered most members of the Umayyad house except for Abd al-Rahman I, who fled west and founded the independent Umayyad Emirate of al-Andalus. Even without this overt split, al-Andalus was destined to follow a distinct historical arc thanks to its being the Muslim state with the most immediate and prolonged contact with Latin Europe, its position astride the Strait of Gibraltar, its encounter with Viking raiders, and its largely hostile relations with Ifriqiya and Muslim Sicily.

Muslim forces first raided Sicily in 652, but the island was not hotly con-

---

* Maghreb, which means "west" or "setting sun," can refer to the lands from western Libya to Morocco, or specifically to Morocco. Ifriqiya comprised western Libya, Tunisia, and eastern Algeria.

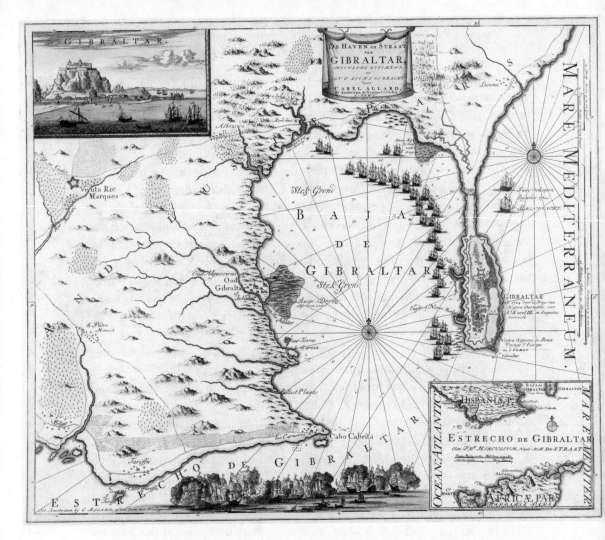

Although drawn ten centuries after Muslim armies under Tariq ibn Ziyad crossed from Ceuta, North Africa, to the rock named for him—Jabal Tarik—Carel Allard's "The Bay and Strait of Gibraltar" clearly shows Gibraltar's commanding position at the Mediterranean's only outlet to the Atlantic Ocean. Allard's map and its inserts illustrate the capture of the port by an Anglo-Dutch fleet in August 1704, during the War of the Spanish Succession. The insets depict a view of the rock of Gibraltar (top left); a map of southern Spain and North Africa (lower right); and a naval battle (below). Courtesy of the Rijksmuseum, Amsterdam.

tested until the first half of the eighth century, when Ifriqiyan ships began raiding Sicily, Sardinia, and the Balearic Islands. At the end of the eighth century, Charlemagne responded to an appeal from the Balearics for help against Moorish attacks and for thirty years the archipelago was a base for Frankish ships patrolling between Italy, Sardinia, Barcelona, and the Frankish coast.

The Franks' interest in northern Italy accelerated following their overthrow of the Lombard kingdom, and Charlemagne's attempt to incorporate Venice into his territories brought them into conflict with the Byzantines in 806. Nominally subject to Constantinople, Venetian merchants were eager to trade with the Franks, and a treaty of 812 confirmed Venice's status as Byzantine territory while allowing its citizens to trade with the Franks and obliging them to support the Franks against pirates in the northern Adriatic. Under the de facto protection of the two great powers, Venetian naval and commercial power grew steadily.

Frankish-Byzantine rivalry and the scaling back of the Byzantine naval presence in the west to deal with a Bulgar threat on the Black Sea opened the way for Ifriqiyan expansion in Sicily. In 800, the Abbasid caliph Harun al-Rashid had appointed Ibrahim I ibn al-Aghlab emir of Ifriqiya, the first of the autonomous Aghlabid emirs who would rule for a century. One of Ibrahim's priorities was creating a fleet to protect Ifriqiya's trade. The year after the resolution of the Venetian crisis, the Byzantine *strategos* of Sicily reached an agreement with Muslim ambassadors to ensure the rights of merchants in each other's ports, and somewhat later the rulers of Christian Naples asked for Aghlabid support against the neighboring duchy of Benevento. The first Muslim forces on the Italian Peninsula raided Naples's enemies on both coasts, gained control of the Strait of Otranto, and sent a fleet as far north as the mouth of the Po River and Istria (modern Slovenia), opposite Venice.

The Aghlabids began raiding Sicily in the 820s but they did not establish a foothold on the island until invited to support a revolt by the Byzantine naval commander. An expeditionary force of seventy to a hundred ships and ten thousand troops sailed from Tunis in the summer of 829 and two years later the Aghlabids captured Palermo, which, renamed al-Madinah, became the capital, primary naval base, and commercial center of the new emirate. The conquest of the island took the rest of the century—Syracuse fell in 878, Taormina in 902—during which the Aghlabids continued their offensive in the Adriatic. Their 866 siege of Ragusa (Dubrovnik, Croatia) was thwarted by the unanticipated arrival of a hundred Byzantine ships that reached the Adriatic via the ancient *diolkos* over the Isthmus of Corinth, presumably to avoid Cretan and Aghlabid fleets in the Aegean and Strait of Otranto. Over the next three decades, Byzantine, Carolingian, and Aghlabid forces vied for control of southern Italy and the Adriatic, but by the early tenth century the Strait of Messina was the effective line of demarcation between Muslim Sicily and Christian Italy. Lying as they did on the front lines between the Aghlabids and Byzantines, Naples, Amalfi, and other southern Italian ports went out of their way to avoid hostilities with Muslim Sicily. With their long-standing trading privileges at Constantinople, between the ninth and eleventh centuries the merchants of Amalfi leveraged their city's neutrality and its central location to become middlemen between the kingdoms of western Europe, Muslim North Africa—especially Egypt—and the Byzantine Empire. Amalfitans were "renowned across nearly the whole world," while the port itself was celebrated as a meeting place of "Arabs, Libyans, Sicilians and Africans" and regarded as "the most prosperous town in Lombardy, the most noble, the most illustrious on account of its conditions, the most affluent and opulent."

In one view, Muslim power in the Mediterranean reached the high-water mark at the start of the tenth century, when one or another emirate or caliphate occupied in whole or part Cyprus, Crete, Sicily, Malta, the Balearics, and, in the Aegean, Paros and Naxos in the Cyclades north of Crete, Aegina near Athens, and Nea off the Dardanelles. Of the major Mediterranean islands, only Corsica remained subject to Christian princes. Yet while the *Dar al-Islam* had grown, Muslims were no more unified than Christians, a point of special relevance with respect to the naval balance of power in the Mediterranean. In the west, the Umayyads ruled in Spain, and augmented their gains by capturing the Balearics, which would remain under Muslim rule for three centuries. Several smaller emirates ruled over Morocco, while the Aghlabid governors of Ifriqiya exercised considerable freedom of action in North Africa and on Malta and Sicily. Farther east, the emirate of Crete was beholden to no one, and Cyprus was held in common with the Byzantines, while on the mainland the Tulunids ruled Egypt from 868 to 905.

Within barely half a century, the picture had changed irrevocably as the Abbasid Caliphate fractured along sectarian lines. Syria was lost to the Shiite Hamdanids of Iraq in 906, Ifriqiya to the Shiite Fatimids three years later, and Egypt, for the second time, to the short-lived Ikhshidids (935–969), who were, like the Abbasids, Sunni. To the west, meanwhile, Abd al-Rahman III made a definitive break with the rest of the Muslim world by styling himself caliph, or successor to Muhammad, rather than emir, a mere commander or prince. The Umayyad Caliphate of Córdoba did not long survive him, and by the end of the century political power in al-Andalus and the Balearics had devolved on some thirty independent statelets called *taifas*. Of all these developments the most consequential was the emergence of the Fatimids, who toppled the Aghlabids in Ifriqiya and Sicily. In 921, they founded a new capital about ninety miles south of Tunis at the port of Mahdia, which became a staging ground for raids on Italy, France, Spain, and islands from Malta to the Balearics. They went on to conquer Egypt and much of the Levant, and their new capital at Cairo (al-Qahira, "the triumphant," established in 969) quickly eclipsed Baghdad as the commercial and political center of the Muslim world, with profound effects for trade in the Mediterranean and on the Monsoon Seas. Despite this reloca-tion of the center of power in the Muslim world from the head of the Persian Gulf and Baghdad to the eastern Mediterranean, and the Fatimids' maritime orientation while in Ifriqiya, on the sea-lanes of the Mediterranean the rise of Fatimid Egypt resulted not in triumph but catastrophe.

The Contest for Crete

The best lens through which to view the failure—or lack—of maritime strat-egy in the Mediterranean in this period is the island of Crete, the history of which reveals many of the socioreligious, political, and military complexi-ties of the age. The conquest of the Maghreb and al-Andalus had eliminated Romano-Byzantine influence from North Africa and the western Mediter-ranean. But in al-Andalus, ethnic and confessional strains between Arabs, Berbers, Syrians, and Romano-Gothic converts to Islam called *muwalladun* impeded unity for much of the Islamic period. Following a series of bloody purges, fifteen thousand *muwalladun* and others fled al-Andalus in about 813. About half the exiles—most of whom were artisans from the inland cities of Toledo and Córdoba—migrated to Morocco. Despite having little or no mari-time background, the remainder seem to have sailed via Sicily or Ifriqiya and the Aegean to Egypt where "people, called Andalusians, entered [Alexandria] having with them much booty taken from the islands of Greece." Expelled by the Abbasid governor of Egypt and discouraged from settling in other Muslim territories, in about 824 the exiles sailed to Crete.

The island was poorly defended and there was little love lost between Cre-tans and the Byzantines, whose rule was marked by onerous taxation and cor-ruption. The Andalusians established their capital at al-Khandak (or Chandax, now Iraklion), which became the vibrant urban center of an autonomous Cretan emirate. Taxation was moderate and the island was transformed from a backwater province on the Byzantine frontier to a prosperous economic power in its own right, exporting wine, honey, cheese, and wood, especially for Egyptian shipyards. As important, Crete became a launching pad for raids on islands in the Ionian and Aegean Seas, the Greek mainland, and Asia Minor. The island's loss can be attributed to the Byzantines' failure to recognize the geopolitical shift in the eastern Mediterranean following the loss of Egypt, the Levant, and North Africa to Muslim armies. No one with a strategic interest in the region could ignore Crete unless they held undisputed control of the sea; once such mastery was lost it was only a matter of time before the island was contested between rival powers.

The emirate of Crete flourished independent of any mainland state. If Muslims had a common enemy in Christian Constantinople (and vice versa), the political divisions among the Abbasids and the new dynasties to the west militated against any meaningful coordination. A glaring example of this occurred in the aftermath of the Muslim Leo of Tripoli's bold raid on Thessaloniki, the second city of the empire, in 905. Given that the Cretans' occupied strategic islands around the Aegean and had considerable experience fighting the Byzantines, soliciting their advice or support would seem to have been a sensible step for any invader. Yet Leo so failed to communicate his intentions that when he approached Crete on his return to Tripoli (in Lebanon), the Cretans mistook his fleet for a Byzantine invasion. The confusion was understandable, for Constantinople had challenged Muslim control of Crete from the outset and made at least four unsuccessful attempts to retake the island.

It would be more than half a century after Leo's humiliating sack of Thessaloniki that the Byzantines conquered Crete. In the end the island's fate was sealed by the lack of coordination among rival Muslim states, including the Fatimids, whose preoccupation with seizing Egypt prevented them from perceiving Crete's strategic significance—not to the *Dar al-Islam* necessarily, but to their own ambitions. Just as the Byzantines had neglected to consider Crete's importance in the Mediterranean of the ninth century, Muslim leaders' collective failure to keep the island from reverting to Byzantine control changed utterly the balance of power in the eastern Mediterranean. Nikephoros Phokas seized the island in 961, and as emperor four years later he ordered an invasion of Cyprus that ended the three-century-old condominium arrangement with the caliphate. This was part of a concerted effort by Nikephoros and his successors, who brought much of Syria and the Levant under Byzantine rule for the first time since the 640s. Efforts to retake Sicily failed, however, and the island prospered under the Kalbid governors, who ruled for a century. The Fatimids maintained an active interest in Italy and they enlisted the Kalbids in their struggle with Umayyad Córdoba. The Kalbids raided al-Andalus in the 950s, but they were no match for the Umayyad fleet and Abd al-Rahman III retaliated with raids on Ifriqiya.

These examples of the lack of coordination and shared purpose on the part of Muslim states underscores the fact that while it is customary to think in terms of a Mediterranean divided between Christian and Muslim spheres of influence, power among the littoral states split along innumerable secular and religious fault lines. This is evident not only from the military record, but from the expansion of eastern Mediterranean trade between Byzantine and Muslim ports in the eleventh century, and the unexpected mix of materials and crew associated with the Serçe Limani ship. International relations of the eleventh century and later would become even more complicated as Christian

Europe was convulsed by the schism of 1054, which saw a hardening of lines between the Greek Orthodox east and the Latin Catholic west, and within the latter the emergence of new maritime powers that would reshape trade in completely new ways.

Naval Power

In the meantime, the proliferation of Muslim states was a mixed blessing for the Byzantines. After the seventh century they never encountered a major fleet such as they had faced at the battle of the Masts or during the sieges of Constantinople, and the Byzantine navy was never in danger of being overwhelmed by an enemy force. Yet because there was no single "Muslim" navy, they could not concentrate their own naval power to achieve a decisive victory at sea. Instead, the Byzantine fleet was often stretched to the limit, as it was during the ultimately fruitless effort to retake Sicily after the loss of Crete. While the Byzantine and Abbasid navies were capable of mounting large-scale offensive operations over long distances, most fleets operated within a fairly small radius from their home port.

So long as there were no rivals with the means or inclination to build a standing fleet, the Byzantine navy was a more or less provisional force of small squadrons to which merchant ships, sailors, and fishermen could be seconded as needed. When the enlarged fleet had accomplished its mission, it was disbanded, the costs of maintenance being too high to sustain in peacetime. Between the founding of Constantinople and the emergence of Islam, the size of naval ships shrank, partly because large ships were not needed and partly because the growing threat posed by barbarian invasions across the northern frontier put greater emphasis on river and lake operations carried out in conjunction with land forces. When necessary, substantial imperial fleets could put to sea, as they did against the Vandals in the fifth and sixth centuries, but even so the ships were considerably smaller than they had been in antiquity.

By the fifth century, the Byzantine warship par excellence was the single-banked *dromon* ("racer"). Initially these were small ships, manned by 20 to 50 crew, but with the rise of the caliphate navies and the resumption of fleet engagements in the seventh century they began to grow rapidly, although they seem never to have had more than two banks of oars. The *dromon* had a single deck that provided protection for the rowers and two or even three lateen-rigged masts. Rowed by between 100 and 120 oarsmen, larger *dromons* carried a total complement of about 160 men, and in exceptional cases upward of 200. Unlike the galleys of antiquity, the *dromon* did not carry an underwater ram.

Instead, it was fitted with a spur, a heavy beam attached to the stempost above the waterline and designed to shatter enemy ships' steering gear and oars. The spur was not an integral part of the hull and its development likely resulted from the transition from shell-first to frame-first construction, because hulls built on the latter principle could not withstand the shock of ramming. (Rams may have been abandoned as naval operations moved from the high seas to shallow inland waters, where they would have been impractical.) Muslim ships apparently differed little from their Byzantine counterparts—their shipwrights came out of the same tradition, after all—except that they are thought to have been larger, heavier, and slower, reflecting a trade-off between speed and size that is a constant in naval architecture.

In addition to carrying rowers, crew, and soldiers, ships were fitted out to carry horses. Several independent accounts describe knights on horseback disembarking from ships via gangplanks, although how they mounted their stiff charges in their low, narrow stalls is unknown. Despite the prolonged period of maritime conflict between the Byzantine and Muslim states and the evolution of new shipbuilding methods and weapons in this period, apart from a few buildups in preparation for specific campaigns, the generally cautious approach to naval power on all sides seems to have prevented the escalation of gratuitous naval arms races and the ensuing fiscal and military crises characteristic of the Hellenistic age or the twentieth century.

Hostilities with Sasanian Persia prompted the Byzantines to establish permanent regiments of locally recruited soldiers and sailors tasked with defending the provinces in which they lived. To counter the threat from the caliphate later in the seventh century, the navy was put on a more permanent footing with the formation of the fleet of the *karabisianoi*, literally "those of the war galleys," under a commander who was in essence the chief of naval operations. The *karabisianoi* became a power unto themselves and were implicated in several coups before Leo the Isaurian disbanded them. In their place there emerged a tripartite naval organization with an imperial fleet based at Constantinople, provincial fleets that operated for the most part locally, and three fleets attached to naval themes (military districts) whose admirals reported directly to the emperor. Dependent on the central government at Constantinople for much of their support, the provincial fleets constituted the naval branch of themal armies and their smaller ships patrolled against pirates and enemy raids. Ships of the naval themes were manned and provisioned from the themes where they were stationed. The Aegean theme protected the Dardanelles, the Samian theme the southern Aegean, and the Kibyrrhaiot theme, based at Attaleia (Antalya) in Asia Minor opposite Cyprus, the eastern Mediterranean. This arrangement of imperial, themal, and provincial fleets survived with little modification until the mid-eleventh century.

These forces were built and stationed at ports of different sizes and orientations found around the empire. A *neorion* was an artificial harbor of any kind, but in naval usage it designated an arsenal where ships could be fitted out and repaired and weapons stored. The main arsenal on Constantinople's Golden Horn was known simply as the Neorion, although there were commercial *neoria*, too, notably Constantinople's Prosphorion on the Golden Horn, and the Harbors of Julian (or Sophia) and of Theodosius on the Sea of Marmara. A shipyard specializing in the construction of warships and stockpiling naval stores and weapons was more commonly called an *exartysis* (from the Greek verb "to rig"), a term that came to be used for the bureaucracy responsible for maintaining the imperial fleet. Each theme had one mainland and one island arsenal: at Abydos and on Lemnos; on Samos and at Smyrna; and at Attaleia and on Rhodes. Important provincial shipyards were found in Sicily and Calabria, at Ravenna and Dyrrachium (Durrës, Albania), on Euboea, and on the Black Sea at Amisos (Samsun, Turkey), Amasra, Trabzon, and Kherson.

Thanks to the empire's long and active seaboard, experienced mariners were readily available to man its ships. Service in the fleet was frequently incumbent on men registered with the state and whose maintenance was paid for out of the revenues from his lands or, if these were insufficient, through other people's taxes. Most crews served in the regions where they lived, but the naval themes occasionally supplied men to other areas. The permanent crews of the naval themes and provincial fleets represented only the nucleus of a force that could be enlarged as circumstances required, through conscription or by hiring domestic or foreign mercenaries, especially Varangians from Kievan Rus, Franks, Venetians, Genoese, and others drawn from the merchant communities settled in Constantinople.

While maritime trade and naval defense were central to the health of the Byzantine Empire, medieval attitudes toward mariners and their business were in constant tension. The Byzantine heirs of Rome's naval tradition made their capital one of the foremost seaports of the age, and occupied an archipelago-studded sea no different in its geography or resources than it was in the time of their Attic and Ionian ancestors. And as in ancient Greece, contempt for those intimately connected with the sea was common. Upon being informed that a ship docked within sight of the palace belonged to the empress, the ninth-century Theophilus ordered the ship destroyed on the grounds that it was beneath the imperial dignity to be involved in trade; or, as he scolded his wife: "God made me an emperor, you would make me a ship captain." In ninth- and tenth-century lists of imperial precedence, admirals of the imperial fleet and the Kibyrrhaiot theme never ranked in the top twenty, and those of the Samian and Aegean themes fell near the bottom.

At the same time, cities like Constantinople depended on overseas trade for

food, ordinary commodities, and luxuries, and the Byzantine state's investment in the navy shows its commitment to securing the sea-lanes. So, too, did
the government's efforts to channel traffic to specific ports, not only to ensure
the collection of duties and taxes but also to monitor the comings and goings
of foreign traders who were issued passports and limited in where they might
trade and how long they might stay. The provisions of a 907 treaty with Kievan Rus are typical: "Such Russes as arrive here shall dwell in the St. Mamas
quarter. Our government will send officers to record their names, and they
shall then receive their monthly allowance, first the natives of Kiev, then those
from . . . the other cities. They shall not enter the city save through one gate,
unarmed and fifty at a time, escorted by an agent of the Emperor. They may
conduct business according to their requirements without payment of taxes."
Despite the suspicion with which alien merchants were viewed, the barriers to
social advancement faced by seafarers led to the Byzantines' increasing dependence on foreigners to carry their trade.

   Relying on foreign recruits to round out ships' crews is a common practice
among navies, although one usually overlooked except when the navy in question is that of a people who, like the Muslim caliphs, are thought to have an
innate fear or abhorrence of the sea. Much has been assumed about the religious context within which Muslims view the sea, and some critics have been
content to conflate the desert origins of Islam with the religion itself and to
conclude that, as one historian recently maintained, "At worst, Islam was hostile to the sea, at best it ignored it." One story that is often cited as evidence
of Muslims' antipathy to maritime pursuits relates how, having been informed
that the " 'The Sea is a great creature upon which weak creatures ride—like
worms upon a piece of wood,' " Umar, the second caliph, "recommended . . .
that the Muslims be kept away from seafaring. No Arab traveled by sea save
those who did so without Umar's knowledge and were punished by him for it."
While the Arabs of Mecca and Medina may have been newcomers to maritime
trade, Arabia is a peninsula and Oman, Yemen, and Nabataea in particular have
ancient traditions of seafaring. Pre-Islamic Arabic poetry preserves examples
of Arabs' awareness of the sea, and the Quran is filled with passages about seafaring and ships guided by Allah's beneficence: "It is God who has subdued the
ocean for you, so that ships may sail upon it at His bidding; so that you may
seek His bounty and render thanks." As traders within or between the Byzantine and Sasanian Empires, Arabs had a more than passing familiarity with
imperial military and fiscal policy, and they quickly adopted the administrative
procedures they found in the lands they conquered. This is especially evident
in the context of the caliphate's naval organization, which reflected Byzantine
practice and was replicated across North Africa and in al-Andalus.

The importance that naval power would have for the security of Egypt was not lost on Muawiya, who in seizing Alexandria was quick to occupy the city's dockyard, which the Arabs called *dar al-sina'a*, literally "place of work," a word that entered Romance languages as "arsenal," probably through Venetian merchants who were trading to Egypt by the early eighth century. In light of the Muslims' reputation for lubberliness, the growth in the number of Egyptian shipyards following the conquest is noteworthy. Whereas the Byzantines had gotten by with one arsenal at Alexandria and another on the Gulf of Suez, the Muslims built others at Rosetta, Damietta, and Tinnis in the Nile delta, and another at Fustat. To help ensure a native supply of wood, the government established and regulated acacia plantations "for the fleet" from at least the eighth century.

The caliphate also maintained an arsenal at Akka (Acre) and a major naval base at Tarsus in Asia Minor. The founders of Tunis relocated a thousand Coptic shipwrights and their families from Alexandria, and it is they who are credited with enabling the Umayyads to establish a fleet that would redefine the balance of naval power in the central Mediterranean. South of Tunis, Susa (Sousse) was the site of an Aghlabid arsenal until it was superseded by the Fatimid capital at Mahdia. Situated on a narrow, kilometer-and-a-half-long peninsula separated from the mainland by a large wall, Mahdia offered excellent protection for the fleet inherited from the Aghlabids. Ports in the western Maghreb and al-Andalus antedated the coming of Muslim rule, but while Ceuta and Algeciras stood watch over the Strait of Gibraltar, it is unlikely that either was home to an arsenal until Abd al-Rahman II's creation of a navy in the ninth century.

By the 700s, governors of the coastal provinces of the caliphate had autonomous fleets of which the Egyptian, the best known, is likely representative. The three primary sources of support were payments in cash for the maintenance of ships and crews, the requisition of goods needed by the fleet, and drafting sailors from a nationwide levy. In the early stages of the Muslim expansion, most ships' crews were Greeks and Egyptian Copts native to coastal areas formerly under Byzantine control. Uthman, the third caliph, is said to have decreed that Muslims could not be drafted to fight at sea against their will, yet the two groups who seem to have supplied most of the marines were descendants of Arab immigrants to Egypt (*Muhajirun*), and non-Arab converts to Islam (*Mawali*). Berber and Visigothic sailors and fishermen, transplanted Arabs, and perhaps Copts made up the crews of North African fleets. Villages, cities, and provinces were expected to provide seamen (and their upkeep) on the basis of the census. To ensure against desertion, elders or officials guaranteed that their sailors would "fulfill their expedition as sailors, without turning

aside," or going absent without leave. Alternatively, villagers could pay someone from another area to represent them, a practice that may have resulted in
a fleet manned chiefly by professional sailors.

Generally speaking, seafaring tended to attract only the poor. (Under the
Umayyads, the Egyptian fleet had a three-part scale for paying sailors, the
crew being the least well paid, followed by marines of non-Arab descent and
then marines of Arab descent. The sailors' bread was also said to be of inferior quality.) Even so, high-caliber crews could only be ensured by offering
adequate compensation, which was generally forthcoming only in response to
a crisis. As a Muslim historian observed after a Byzantine attack on Damietta
in 853, "from this time [the government] began to show serious concern for
the fleet, and this became an affair of the first importance in Egypt. Warships
were built, and the pay for marines was equalized with that of soldiers who
served on land. Only intelligent and experienced men were admitted to the
service." At the other end of the Mediterranean, when the Umayyads established a fleet in the ninth century, Abd al-Rahman II ordered that "men of
the sea be recruited from the coasts of al-Andalus, who got good salaries." In
extreme cases, governments turned to impressment, and in Fatimid Ifriqiya
prospective crew were sometimes jailed to ensure their availability at the start
of the sailing season, a practice even some Fatimid officials criticized. Like
the Byzantines, Muslim rulers also relied on mercenaries to man their ships,
and Aghlabid and Kalbid rulers in Sicily apparently raised crews from among
slaves, freemen, Jews, and Christians, and drew their officers from the ranks
of free and enslaved Slavs.

A striking difference between Muslim and Byzantine fleets was in the division of labor. Muslim crews tended toward greater specialization, whereas
Byzantine sailors "were at the same time rowers as well as fighting men." If
they happened to be skilled in ship repair, for instance, they did this work in
addition to rowing and fighting. Similarly, officers were supposed to be skilled
in reading the weather and celestial navigation and qualified to lead their men
in battle. A Muslim commander had broad responsibility for his ships starting
with their building: "He should check the construction of ships, their com-
ponents, assemblage of parts, and their proper removal and joining. He must
try to find the best oars and select them carefully; he should also make the
best selection of masts and sails." But the crews under his command included
caulkers who apparently had no other function, as well as specialist navigators,
meteorologists, and surgeons, while separate officers commanded the oarsmen, who did not fight, and the marines, who did not row.

Although Andalusian rulers depended on mariners to ensure communication and transportation with the Maghreb, the seafaring communities of the

western Mediterranean do not loom large in the accounts of contemporary writers. This disjunction resulted from the fact that while Muslim and Christian states controlled the lands of the western Mediterranean, they made little effort to exercise dominion at sea. But seafarers were certainly there and by the end of the eighth century, Muslim and Christian authors alike distinguished between "Moors"; Berbers from western Algeria and Morocco; and "Saracens," Arabs from the Umayyad Emirate of Córdoba. Such broad categories mask the fact that there was considerable mixing among these groups, and ignore altogether the survival of Christian Mozarab seafaring communities of whom rulers in both Spain and Morocco were suspicious and who raided and traded to Provence, Corsica, the Balearics, and Sicily on their own account. The emirate's indifference to its maritime communities changed following raids by Danish Vikings in 844, in response to which Abd al-Rahman II devised a comprehensive approach to coastal defense from Lisbon to the Mediterranean and established arsenals at Seville, Almería, and Tortosa.

Strategy, Tactics, and Weapons

Neither the Byzantines nor the Arabs sought pitched engagements at sea unless the outcome was certain, which it rarely was. While some of the fundamentals for the strategic use of offensive sea power were in place, resources, cost, politics, geography, and difficulties of communication made naval operations problematic. Naval tactics were of considerable interest to both Byzantine and Muslim audiences, but surviving manuals were written by authors with little or no practical experience of naval warfare and who plagiarized ancient sources, which with their use of rams, for example, were irrelevant to medieval warfare. In addition to disabling ships with their ships' spurs, fleet commanders had a variety of long-range weapons, including catapults for hurling stones, javelins, ceramic pots filled with poisonous insects and snakes or quicklime, and firepots. The most sophisticated weapon of the age was a kind of flamethrower known today as "Greek fire." The inventor was a Syrian refugee named Kallinikos who "manufactured a naval fire with which he kindled the ships of the Arabs and burnt them with their crews" during the Muslim siege of Constantinople in the 670s. As a weapon system, Greek fire comprised a flammable liquid made from raw or distilled crude oil heated in a pressurized bronze container and sprayed through a nozzle attached to a pumping apparatus. Greek fire gave those deploying it an enormous psychological advantage. In addition to the fire itself, the bellows used to heat the liquid created a terrifying noise, and the nozzles through which the flames shot were fashioned in the shape of wild animals so that "The fire to be hurled at the enemy through tubes was made to issue from the mouths of these figure-heads in such a way that they appeared to be belching out the fire."

Greek fire was one of the Byzantines' most closely guarded secrets, handed down over centuries through the descendants of Kallinikos. In a tenth-century handbook of imperial administration, Constantine VII wrote that anyone who revealed details about the weapon should be stripped of his rank or office and "anathematized and made an example for ever and ever, whether he were emperor, or patriarch, or any other man." Despite these threats and precautions, knowledge of Greek fire was already available to Muslim fleets by 835, when Aghlabid sailors used it in Sicily, and in the following decade Abd al-Rahman II armed his Andalusian ships with it. The Aghlabids bequeathed their expertise to the Fatimids, who brought it with them in their conquest of Egypt and quickly introduced it to the south. The tenth-century geographer al-Muqaddasi claimed it was indispensible for transiting the Bab al-Mandeb where "Every ship . . . needs to carry armed men, and personnel to throw Greek fire." Even before they acquired Greek fire, however, the Muslims developed protection against it. According to an eighth-century account, the head of the Egyptian arsenals invented "something which was never before heard of. He took cotton and some mineral substances; he mixed them all together and smeared the ships of the fleet with the mixture, so that when the fire was thrown by the Greeks upon the ships, they did not burn. And this I saw with my own eyes: the ships were struck by Greek fire and did not burn but the fire was at once extinguished." In addition, there was fireproof clothing. One recipe called for dipping a cloak in a mixture of talc, alum, ammonium, hematite, gypsum, stale urine, and egg whites. Such garments were used to protect both soldiers and horses (Greek fire was also employed on land), though whether these were used at sea is unknown. For protection against traditional weapons, however, sailors did wear protective chain mail, cuirasses, and padded jackets.

Throughout their centuries of conflict with Muslim powers, the Byzantines' great advantage was that they never lacked for essential naval stores like wood, tar, hemp, and sailcloth. Shipbuilding timber was found on the coasts of Asia Minor, the Greek mainland, the Adriatic coast of Illyria, southern Italy and Sicily, and on Cyprus and Crete. The disadvantage of this embarrassment of riches was that regardless of which part of the empire they attacked, invaders were usually able to secure both the materials and expertise necessary to build or repair their own ships, and it was the quest for just these advantages that stimulated some of the earliest Muslim campaigns. Caliphs and emirs were under constant pressure to guarantee supplies of wood for shipbuilding, construction, and fuel for domestic and industrial uses like smelters and kilns, the need for which could not be satisfied by the comparatively meager forests of northern Syria, the Maghreb, or al-Andalus. The battle of the Masts was so named in Arabic chronicles because it was fought to procure mast timber from the wooded slopes above Phoenix, and Cyprus, Crete, and Sicily were as attractive for their forests and other natural resources as for their commanding position along the major east–west axis of Mediterranean trade.

Commerce

Archaeological and written records testify to the diversity of routes and goods in circulation around the Mediterranean, yet in the late Roman period a preponderance of shipping was dedicated to the *annona*, shipments of grain to be made into bread for free distribution to the masses—the bread of "bread and circuses." This practice underwent drastic change in the fourth century when the Alexandrian fleets were redirected to Constantinople and those of Africa declined in significance as the population of Rome dwindled. In the sixth century, an estimated twelve hundred to eighteen hundred ships were involved in the *annona* trade, most of them making two round-trips in a season. In addition to these state-subsidized vessels, another six hundred to nine hundred independent traders were homeported at Constantinople. The *annona* stopped following the Persian capture of Alexandria in 617, and the Byzantines ended the free distribution of grain for good the following year. Any hope for the trade's revival ended with the Arab capture of Egypt and Abd Allah's reopening of the ancient canal between the Nile and the Red Sea to facilitate grain shipments to the ports of Jeddah, established in 646, and Yanbu, which served the holy cities of Mecca and Medina, respectively. This benefited not only the citizens of the Arabian ports, but also the growing numbers of pilgrims who performed the hajj. Improvements to the abandoned canal between the Nile and the Red Sea—the Canal of the Commander of the Faithful—made it navigable only when the Nile was in flood. Nonetheless, Alexandria's loss of her largest Mediterranean trading partner caused the population to fall from an estimated eight hundred thousand people at its imperial peak to perhaps one hundred thousand in 860. Although it hardly compensated for Alexandria's lost opportunities, trade did intensify along the coasts of North Africa, as well as between Ifriqiya, Sicily, and southern Italy, and between and along the coasts of the western Maghreb and al-Andalus. This was due both to the vitality of the Islamic state and also to Carolingian expansion into northern Italy and central Europe, which stimulated transalpine trade to satisfy the demand for Mediterranean goods in the north. The growth in the slave and lumber trades was a boon to Adriatic shippers, especially Venetians and Muslims, who were sometimes rivals but often worked in a symbiotic relationship.

Too few records survive to give us more than the occasional snapshot of trade over the centuries. The most exhaustive single list of goods commonly handled is found in the tenth-century Arabic *Treatise Concerning the Leasing of Ships*, which reels off a series of commodities, essential and luxury foodstuffs, animals, textiles, raw materials, slaves, precious stones, gold, and silver. Essential foods include various grains and beans, oil, honey, vinegar, dates, olives, raisins, and salt. Among the luxuries are rice, edible lupine, "marmalades, concentrated juices, licit drinks, and that which is used for seasoning cheese, dried yogurt, rape, yogurt, butter, dried curd, and cottage cheese" as well as "fruits from trees . . . eaten for pleasure . . . walnuts, hazelnuts, pine nuts, and other dried and fresh fruits . . . fried meats, fish, pepper, vegetables, seeds, and eggs." These lists are complemented by the archaeological manifests from Yassi Ada, Serçe Limani, and other sites that have yielded an eclectic array of goods that reveals a more complex economic life than ordinarily encountered in written texts.

The natural and man-made hazards of medieval seafaring notwithstanding, people from across a broad economic, religious, and geographic spectrum traveled by ship for any number of reasons. Merchants frequently accompanied their goods; ambassadors and other dignitaries shuttled between Constantinople and Venice or the Po valley, Mahdia and Palermo, or Ceuta and Seville; and church officials frequented the route between Rome and Constantinople. A major reason for nonmerchants to travel was to make pilgrimages or collect relics, although this was sometimes incidental to trade in ordinary goods. Venice's Basilica of St. Mark was erected to house his body after merchants stole it from the evangelist's church in Alexandria.

Regardless of one's station, conditions aboard ship were onerous. Under Byzantine regulations, male passengers were allocated a space of 3 cubits by 1 cubit (1.1 square meters), while "Women on board are to have a space allowance of one cubit; and a boy . . . half a cubit." While the ship carried water for the ship's company, passengers were responsible for their own food, which they prepared themselves. Whether women were allowed to commingle with men in Byzantine ships is unknown, but Muslim practice encouraged the strict separation of the sexes by assigning men and women to different decks or at least ensuring that women had segregated toilets, "so that they are not exposed to view when they need to use them." There are also instances of women sailing aboard ships in military operations. When the caliph Uthman gave Muawiya permission to attack Cyprus, he said "If thou sailest with thy wife we allow thee to do so; otherwise not," on the assumption that Muawiya would not risk his wife's life at sea. She and possibly her sister sailed with the fleet, while the wife of another officer is said to have praised the efforts of a subordinate for saving their ship.

Such consideration of course did not apply to slaves, few of whom wrote about their hardships. Nonetheless, there is an abundance of anecdotal evidence preserved by a number of writers from different backgrounds. Taken together these passages describe a floating hell inconceivable to anyone fortunate enough to have been spared the experience. According to John Kaminiates, after sacking Thessaloniki, Leo of Tripoli shipped thousands of enslaved captives to Tarsus in conditions that bear comparison with those of the later Atlantic slave trade:

> [T]he barbarians put leg irons on all of us and stuffed and crammed each and every one into the ships for all the world like some piece of inanimate matter, not even allowing us to breathe the air freely but curtailing its circulation through sheer congestion and over crowding. . . . We were afflicted by many other unpleasant forms of constraint such as hunger and thirst and were black and blue from the overcrowding. . . . But the most painful constraint of all was the belly, which it was impossible to devise any means of dealing with, since the business of nature must needs take its course and swiftly find an outlet. Many people, preferring modesty to motion, tried to hold it in, and in their unavailing efforts to do so frequently put their lives at risk.

While slavery was common within Europe, many European slaves were exported to al-Andalus, Africa, and the Near East. Venetian merchants were at the forefront of the trade, buying slaves at Rome for export to Africa as early as 748, even as the pope was attempting to end the traffic in Christians by purchasing and manumitting them. Efforts to curtail the trade continued but Venetian merchants (among others) continued to flout treaties and papal decrees limiting or banning the sale of Christians to Muslims for centuries.

Contracts and Jettison

At the same time, more scrupulous adherence to religious restrictions on usury led to significant changes in the way maritime trade was financed, not only among Christians but among Muslims and Jews as well. The Byzantine state acknowledged the considerable risks involved in travel by sea and allowed the highest interest rates to be charged on maritime loans, starting at 12 percent per year in the sixth century and rising to 12 percent per voyage—about twice the rate for ordinary loans—by the ninth century. The considerable danger entailed made it difficult to amass capital for large-scale shipping ventures.

As a result, the drafting of ever more sophisticated commercial contracts and insurance was as important to the growth of maritime trade as were developments in politics, weaponry, or shipbuilding. Medieval law was essentially personal and religious rather than territorial and political; that is, people were bound by the law of their community rather than of the state. Muslims and Jews were governed generally by one or another school of law rooted in religious tradition, while Christian merchants operated under codes of laws promulgated by their own states and that owed more to Romano-Byzantine practice. Intracommunal disputes were handled according to the merchants' religio-legal tradition, while intercommunal disputes were adjudicated under the religious laws of the host community. Yet over time, Jewish, Christian, and Muslim commercial contracts developed similar features. This is hardly surprising, for while merchants are competitive, they are also collaborative, sharing information and adapting to different modes of doing business so as not to jeopardize their ability to work at all.

Byzantine maritime law was codified in the so-called Rhodian Sea Law, a name that harks back to the heyday of Rhodes as a maritime power in the third century BCE, although the law as it survives was probably codified between 600 and 800 CE. The underlying principles were shared by Mediterranean maritime merchants throughout this period, and many of the law's tenets are reflected in the Muslim *Treatise Concerning the Leasing of Ships and the Claims Between (Contracting) Parties*, a collection of *responsa* on the subject of maritime law compiled by an Andalusian jurist in the tenth century. Broadly speaking both the Rhodian Sea Law and the *Treatise* treat five aspects of shipping: ships' owners, the crew, and merchants; the carriage of goods; the laws of jettison and general average; the salvage of lost ships and cargoes; and commercial law and contracts.

The few substantive differences between Byzantine and Islamic maritime law chiefly concern how and when people were paid for their services and questions of liability. Whereas Byzantine crews tended to work for a share of the profits of a voyage (a practice that continued in the heyday of the Italian maritime powers), Muslim sailors were paid in accordance with Quranic principles: "Whoever hires an employee, let him do the hire at a fixed wage and for a defined duration." There were benefits and drawbacks to both systems. Sharing in profits gave sailors the incentive to ensure a voyage's success, but offered no security in the event of failure. Fixed wages made life more predictable for the crew (and whoever was responsible for tallying the costs of the voyage), but wage earners had no vested interest in the voyage's outcome, and owners no reason to pay more than absolutely necessary. As the changing nomenclature suggests, owners everywhere gradually prevailed, and sailors went from being part of the ship's "company" who shared in the financial and physical welfare of the ship, to being poorly salaried "crew" exploited chiefly for their physical strength and routinely cheated.

A contract to transport goods via ship generally specified the vessel, including its name, rig, officers, and route. All traditions stressed the importance of checking a ship's seaworthiness, and load lines were marked on ships' hulls to ensure they were not overloaded—a practice abandoned by the early modern period and not revived until the late nineteenth century. Major innovations in Muslim law were linking freight charges to the distance covered and factoring in the difference in prices obtained if goods had to be sold at a port other than that stipulated in the contract. By the eleventh century, Jewish, Christian, and Muslim merchants employed essentially three types of commercial contracts—the sea loan, the *societas maris* (association of the sea), and the *commenda* (something given *in commendam*, in trust)—which spread risk, created larger pools of potential investors while guaranteeing legal remedies for dishonest actions, and enabled people to profit from trade without resorting to usury. Islam, Judaism, and Christianity all proscribed lending money at interest to coreligionists, although there were no prohibitions on charging interest to people of other faiths.

In Byzantine law, a lender extended a sea loan to a merchant who contracted to repay it at a fixed rate of interest. The lender could not recoup his loan if the ship failed to reach its destination, but his profit was not diminished if the borrower had to sell his cargo at a loss. Although the interest charged was payable only upon the successful conclusion of a voyage and not if the capital was lost, in 1236 the pope condemned sea loans on the grounds that such interest was a form of usury. The agreement known as a *societas maris* was a partnership of "capital, labor or anything else: skill, knowledge or connections perhaps" in which the investors, whether of money, work, or goods, shared equally in the profits or loss of the venture. The *societas maris* was regarded as a consensual agreement rather than one in which an investment was handed over to one of the parties. Similar to this was the *isqa* of Jewish law, which envisioned a single lender of capital whose investment was "a semi loan and a semi trust." The loan carried no interest and had to be repaid regardless of the outcome of the voyage. If it was a success, the trust had to be repaid, together with any profits it generated, while if it failed, the trust was lost.

Unlike either the *societas maris* or *isqa* was the Muslim *qirad*, which combined aspects of the partnership with a hiring of labor, but without the taint of usury. In the *qirad*, money was not lent but transferred from a "sedentary" investor to a trading associate, or "labor-investor." Any profit realized through manipulation of the investment was shared, at predetermined rates, between the sedentary investor and the trader. Losses to capital were borne solely by the sedentary investor, the assumption being that if he failed to profit financially, the labor-investor had likewise lost his investment of time and labor. The *qirad* is widely believed to have been the precursor to the quintessential medieval maritime contract, the *commenda*.

Modern historians have described the *commenda* as an "innovation of the highest importance [that] contributed greatly to the faster growth of maritime trade as compared to the slower progress of capitalistic forms in land trade" and "the lynch-pin of the fantastic success of the Commercial Revolution in the Mediterranean from the eleventh to the thirteenth centuries." Broadly speaking there were two types. In a unilateral *commenda*, one or more lenders loaned money to a traveling merchant who used the capital to trade. If the voyage was profitable, lender and merchant would share in the profits at a predetermined rate, usually three-quarters for the lender and one-quarter for the merchant. Bilateral *commendae* involved capital from both a lender and the traveling merchant, in which case the profits were shared evenly. Under a bilateral contract, both parties were liable in proportion to the amount of their respective contributions, but under a unilateral contract the borrower was not liable for any losses due to shipwreck, piracy, or capture by a hostile power. In the words of the Statutes of Marseille of 1253, if "the ship . . . is broken up, wrecked, or captured on that voyage, from then on the said [borrower] or partner who went on the ship . . . or his heirs, may in no wise have action taken against him." The similarities of the *commenda* to the *qirad* are striking and Jewish merchants referred to *commendae* as "partnerships according to Muslim law." Although the mechanisms involved in the transmission of the principles of the *qirad* from Muslim to Christian merchants cannot be divined, the fact that the *qirad* exercised greater influence on the development of commercial contracts in Europe than did agreements previously devised by Christian merchants demonstrates the intensity of cross-cultural contact among Mediterranean men of affairs.

Apart from contracts, one of the most complex issues to be considered in maritime trade was jettison, the deliberate throwing overboard of goods to save a ship, normal practice in the face of storms, when a ship was leaking, or when fleeing a pursuer. In principle, the decision to jettison was a deliberative one involving the captain, crew, and merchants whose cargo was involved. If time allowed, the parties negotiated the compensation due to those whose goods were to be sacrificed. In an emergency, however, a captain could order cargo jettisoned without consultation. If this decision was challenged, the captain and crew had to present evidence to justify their actions. The Rhodian Sea Law addresses jettison in cursory fashion, noting simply that everyone in the ship shared in the risk so that all should lose in proportion to the value of their cargo: "if goods are thrown overboard in order to lighten the ship, what is sacrificed for the common benefit should be made good by a common contribution." The *responsa* in the *Treatise Concerning the Leasing of Ships* go into greater detail, establishing the shares payable by those whose goods were not jettisoned and the basis for determining the value of goods that were, what is now known as general average loss, the principles of which remain essentially unchanged in modern maritime law.*

The Muslim approach gradually spread. According to the *Libro del Consulado del Mar* (Book of the Consulate of the Sea), a digest of maritime law promulgated at Barcelona in the 1300s but the roots of which are much older, the captain had to explain the need for jettisoning cargo and the risks of not doing so. But the larger issue involved general average: whether losses were to be assessed by weight or value, whether values were determined based on prices at the place of purchase or the intended place of sale, whether the ship and its gear were included, whether nonmerchant passengers and the crew were liable because their lives were saved, and how slaves should be considered. The Rhodian Sea Law fixed the value of personal slaves at three minas, but "if any one is being carried for sale, he is to be valued at two minas." Most Muslim jurists deplored the concept of human jettison, but some ruled that slaves could be jettisoned provided that they could swim and were within reach of land, while others considered it permissible to sacrifice non-Muslims to save Muslims. Taking a more equitable view, a twelfth-century jurist maintained that if necessary people could be "chosen by lot [and] indiscriminately subjected to being thrown overboard, regardless of their social status and allegiance, whether they were males or females, slaves or free men, Muslims or *dhimmis* [protected minorities]." In general, however, the issue of human jettison was of secondary concern because the lives of free people had no monetary value and maritime codes were preoccupied with commercial rather than humanitarian concerns.

The codification and refinement of principles of commercial maritime law rationalized the way people conducted business and helped create an enlarged multicultural trading network whose benefits, restrictions, and penalties could be easily understood by all participants. By the time these were committed to writing, the Byzantine Empire and *Dar al-Islam* in the Mediterranean were at or past their mercantile prime. Yet they were not being challenged by anything

---

* "Average"—in Latin, *averia*—comes from the Arabic *awar*, meaning "damage to goods."

so obvious as an empire. Instead, small city-states on the Italian Peninsula were enriching themselves at the expense of their former Byzantine overlords and of their Muslim antagonists and competitors. To a degree not seen since the time of Carthage, the citizens of Venice, Genoa, Amalfi, and Pisa actively embraced maritime trade and forged relationships between merchants and the state that made commerce a civic virtue and led to developments as unexpected as they were unprecedented. These would change the nature and conduct of trade not only in the Mediterranean, but also among the newly minted commercial enclaves of northern Europe.

Chapter 9

Northern Europe Through the Viking Age

As late as the twelfth century, much of northern Europe was a backward and remote corner of Eurasia, far removed from the high civilizations of the Mediterranean and Near East. The earliest historical records—foreign and subject to bias, ignorance, and guesswork—do not flatter, but the nautical dimension of its disparate cultures is evident in the sketch of northern Europe teased from the archaeological record and writers from Herodotus on. To a degree found nowhere else, the people of the European subcontinent are bound equally to salt- and freshwater; but the process of integrating fully the great river networks that today facilitate transcontinental exchange with the coastal and deep-sea shipping lanes of the Baltic, North, Mediterranean, and Black Seas, and the Arctic and Atlantic Oceans, only began in the Middle Ages. While northern Europeans absorbed the sophisticated influences of pagan and Christian Rome, seafaring developed from within, most notably among Angles and Saxons in the third to eighth centuries, Frisians from the fifth to ninth centuries, and Scandinavian Vikings in the ninth to eleventh centuries. Considered by volume, value, or organizational sophistication, this maritime activity was on a far smaller scale than in the Mediterranean or Monsoon Seas. The emergence of ports of trade such as Dorestad in the Netherlands, Birka in Sweden, and Novgorod in Russia reflects the ambition of local sovereigns to capture the benefits of trade in the form of revenues, or exemption from revenues; Frankish kings routinely curried favor by relieving their agents and religious houses from paying duties. The indifferent defense against foreign— especially Viking—attack shows that sea trade was not yet the priority it would become.

The Vikings' infamy is often overstated, for they were no more violent than their contemporaries. In their favor, they helped integrate the extremes of western and eastern Europe and to draw Scandinavia into the mainstream of European political development. Although the first raiders sprang from loosely organized pagan tribes far removed from the influence of imperial or monarchical rule, they were quick to take advantage of the opportunities afforded by adopting Christianity and centralized government. Yet once they had absorbed the religion and principles of governance of their southern neighbors, the people of Scandinavia proved too few and remote from the chief centers of economic and political activity to play more than a supporting role in the development of northern Europe and the British Isles after the eleventh century.

Ninth-Century Travelers in Northern Europe

Toward the end of the ninth century, England's Alfred the Great commissioned a vernacular translation of the *History Against the Pagans*, a work by Paulus Orosius written to debunk claims that Christianity was responsible for the Roman Empire's decline. Written in the fifth century, Orosius's work remained a standard text for a thousand years, until well after the cultural and political integration of northern and Mediterranean Europe was under way. To compensate for its omissions regarding the north, the Old English translation includes additional passages about northern Europe and narratives of three voyages in Scandinavia and the Baltic. The more audacious narrator is Ohthere, a Norse merchant-landowner and whaler from Hålogaland, the narrow coastal plain above the Arctic Circle. Motivated by a basic curiosity "to investigate how far the land extended in a northerly direction, or whether anyone lived north of the waste [or wilderness]," Ohthere decided to sail beyond the North Cape, the limit of the whalers' hunting grounds about three days north of Tromsø. From the North Cape, he sailed east and then south for nine days to the mouth of the Varzuga River on the south side of the Kola Peninsula. Here "the land was all settled" by people whose language was similar to that of "Finnas," whose language he knew from traders who crossed the mountains into Hålogaland. Ohthere's daring paid off, for the Kola Peninsula was rich in walrus, which were valued for their tusks—some of which he presented to Alfred—and for their hide, which was "very good for ship-ropes," especially standing rigging and halyards.

Ohthere's second passage was from Hålogaland south to Kaupang (literally, "trade bay"), an emporium on the shore of the Oslofjord, and from there to Hedeby, an important commercial center on the southern Jutland peninsula.

It is unclear how long it took Ohthere to sail along the "North Way" (that is, Norway) from Hålogaland, but he notes that if one stopped at night it would take about a month. The five-day passage from Kaupang south took him along the Swedish coast, through the Danish archipelago, and twenty-two miles up the Schleifjord to Hedeby. This well-protected port was established by Denmark's King Godfred, who in an effort to deny Charlemagne access to the Baltic trade had relocated the merchant community of Reric, about 120 miles to the southeast, at the turn of the ninth century.

Hedeby also figures in the account of Ohthere's contemporary, Wulfstan, who was probably an Anglo-Saxon with strong ties to the Scandinavian communities in England. According to his account in the *History Against the Pagans*, Wulfstan sailed four hundred miles in seven days, from Hedeby east past Wendland (Germany and Poland) to the mouth of the Vistula River. His actual destination was the port of Truso near the junction of the Elblag and Vistula, just before the latter reaches the Baltic. Wulfstan offers no details about his ship or route and the only commodities he mentions are fish and honey, the latter being the principal sweetener in the centuries before sugar was introduced to Europe.

Taken together, Ohthere's and Wulfstan's spare accounts introduce many places of more than passing interest to their contemporaries. In addition to the four major regions referred to—northern Norway, the southern Scandinavian peninsula, Jutland, and the Vistula estuary—both men knew something of the British Isles. Ohthere also refers to Ireland and the Orkney and Shetland Islands. Wulfstan demonstrates his familiarity with the route to the port of Birka on Lake Mälaren west of modern Stockholm. This was reached by sailing south of the principal islands of the Danish archipelago and Skåne (in southern Sweden and then under Danish rule), by the island of Bornholm ("the land of the Burgendas," who migrated south and gave their name to Burgundy), before turning north past the islands of Øland and Gotland en route to the myriad islands of the Stockholm archipelago, 500 miles from Hedeby and about 350 miles north of Truso.

There is no indication of the routes that Ohthere or Wulfstan took to reach Alfred's court, but three suggest themselves. Ohthere may have sailed from Norway to the Viking kingdom of York (Jorvik), the capital of which was a thriving mercantile and manufacturing center with a population of about ten to fifteen thousand people, enormous for a northern European city of the time. From there it was an easy coastal passage to the Thames estuary. Wulfstan likely followed the twelve-kilometer portage from Hedeby to a landing on the Eider River, which flows to the North Sea. From there he could have hugged the Frisian coast to the mouth of the Rhine before crossing to Britain, the route favored by Frisian middlemen in the trade between the Baltic and North Sea. Alternatively, he might have sailed direct from the mouth of the Eider to York.

What is perhaps most remarkable about these two accounts, one by a Norseman and the other by someone with, at the very least, close ties to the Scandinavian community, is the absence of any reference to plunder, raids, or fighting of any kind. The late ninth century was, after all, the height of Viking expansion. At about the same time that Ohthere and Wulfstan were offering their reports to Alfred, Norse Vikings were settling Iceland; Rollo was besieging Paris (he was later given Normandy); Viking Dublin was a thriving mercantile center; the Varangian Rus were on the verge of moving their capital south from Novgorod to Kiev, closer to the wealth of the Byzantine Empire; and Alfred's great claim to fame was halting the Danish Vikings' advance into Anglo-Saxon Wessex. Yet Ohthere's and Wulfstan's primary concerns seem to be the procurement of highly specialized or prestige goods. Equally striking is that these voyages could take place at all, for prior to the seventh century the sail was unknown to Nordic mariners. Thanks to the insights they provide into these disparate subjects, the stories of Ohthere and Wulfstan make a good point of departure from which to explore the rise of long-distance maritime enterprise in northern Europe.

Maritime Northwest Europe to the End of the Roman Empire

Given their proximity to the long-standing centers of Mediterranean culture, northern Europeans' comparatively late adoption of centralized government and urbanism, to say nothing of the sail, seems remarkable. Yet northern Europe was known to the people of the ancient Near East and Greece chiefly as a source of obscure barbarian invaders like the Sea People, and what little information was available about the north was accepted with reservation. Herodotus was circumspect about the region's geography, "for I cannot accept the story of a river called by non-Greek people the Eridanus, which flows into the northern sea, where amber is supposed to come from; nor do I know anything of the existence of islands called the Tin Islands, whence we get our tin. . . . I have never found anyone who could give me first-hand information of the existence of a sea beyond Europe to the north and west." Evidence of north–south trade antedates Herodotus and Greek colonization on the Black Sea by many centuries, as the presence of Baltic amber in the fourteenth-century BCE Uluburun wreck attests; but how this exchange worked is unknown. The tin of Cornwall in southwest Britain reached the

Mediterranean via the Bay of Biscay and the Loire and Garonne Rivers. Greek and Etruscan trade began reaching northern France and western Germany in the sixth century BCE, as shown by the discovery of a 1,100-liter bronze mixing bowl for wine. Probably made in Sparta, the so-called Vix krater was found in Burgundy, having been brought up the Rhône and Saône Rivers and then a short distance overland to the upper Seine, which flows north past Paris to the English Channel.

This transpeninsular river route is one of many characteristic of the European subcontinent. Rivers facilitate transportation and commerce in many regions of the world, but practicable river routes through continental interiors from one sea or ocean to another are relatively few. The number of European rivers that allow for communication between the Mediterranean, Black, and Caspian Seas, in the south and east, and the Baltic and North Seas, and the Atlantic Ocean, to the north and west, is stunning. The longest of these routes includes the Danube and the Rhine, which rise within a hundred kilometers of each other in the Alps, while their tributaries are even closer, and so provide an almost continuous river route across Europe between the Black and North Seas. Central Europe and European Russia are crisscrossed by innumerable combinations of rivers. The Danube, Dniester, and Dnieper flow east and south to the Black Sea, and their headwaters are within more or less easy reach of the Elbe, which flows north and west to the North Sea, and the Oder, Vistula, and Western Dvina, which flow to the Baltic. The success of the ninth-century trading center of Novgorod and its predecessor, Staraya Ladoga, depended on their location on the Volkhov River, which flows north from Lake Ilmen to Lake Ladoga, from which the Neva drains to the Baltic. Lake Ilmen, in its turn, is fed by the Lovat, which flows from within easy reach of the Dnieper. Novgorod commanded the trade between the Baltic and Byzantium until it was superseded by Kiev, on the Dnieper. A second Dnieper route incorporated its tributary the Pripyat and a short portage to the Bug, a tributary of the Vistula. Farther east, the Volga rises just over three hundred kilometers from the Baltic (and within striking distance of the Western Dvina and Dnieper) and flows to the Caspian Sea. This gave northern European merchants the most direct access to the silk road of Central Asia and the trade of Iran. The lower Volga comes to within a hundred kilometers of the Don, before they diverge, the Don turning west toward the Sea of Azov and Black Sea.

After two centuries of disruptions resulting from Celtic migrations, western Mediterranean merchants resumed their northern trade in the fourth century BCE. Among the busier transpeninsular routes was the Aude-Garonne-Gironde corridor between Narbonne on the Mediterranean and the Bay of

Biscay port of Bordeaux. This route was favored by Greek traders from Massilia (Marseille), one of whom, Pytheas, probably used it to reach the Bay of Biscay in the 320s BCE. His account of his travels, *On the Oceans*, survives only in fragments quoted by later writers, some hostile to his claims, but we can sketch the broad outlines of his itinerary. Once in the Bay of Biscay, he sailed to Brittany. The dramatic tides of the Atlantic coast and English Channel—up to 4.5 meters at Quiberon and 16 meters at Mont St. Michel, compared with maximums of less than 1 meter in the Mediterranean—always impressed Mediterranean sailors, and Pytheas apparently discussed them at length. He crossed from France to Cornwall and continued up the west coast of Great Britain to the Orkney and Shetland Islands north of Scotland, which were first inhabited by the fourth millennium BCE. Most intriguing is his claim of sailing six days to a land he called Ultima Thule, where sunlight lasted nearly twenty-two hours and that has been identified as either Iceland (as medieval writers believed) or Norway. Even if his remarks are based on hearsay rather than firsthand experience, they suggest that western European seafarers (as distinct from the inhabitants of mainland Scandinavia) had reached lands on the edge of the Arctic Circle by this early date.

Turning south, Pytheas likely hugged the east coast of Great Britain, with a possible trip across the North Sea to the Netherlands, another source of amber. If he did cross the North Sea, he evidently returned to complete his tour around Britain, the circumference of which he put at between 6,860 and 7,150 kilometers—within 3 to 7 percent of the actual figure—probably by combining sailing times and latitude calculated by measuring the angle of the sun at noon and other measurements. When the astronomer Hipparchus translated Pytheas's estimates about two centuries later, they came out to a highly accurate 48°42'N in Brittany, 54°14'N (possibly the Isle of Man), 58°13'N (the Isle of Lewis, in the Outer Hebrides), and 61° in the Shetlands, where there were nineteen hours of sunlight, which is consistent with his claim.

The beginnings of sustained Mediterranean interest in northwest Europe dates from Julius Caesar's invasion of northern Gaul—which entailed several sea campaigns against the sailing fleets of the Veneti in western France and the Bay of Biscay—and his two crossings of the English Channel to Britain in the 50s BCE. Although Gaul became a Roman province in 51 BCE, civil war prevented the Romans from capitalizing on Caesar's almost flawless invasion of Britain, and when stability returned, Augustus and his successors focused on pushing Roman authority north of the Rhine by land and sea. An Augustan fleet sailed to Jutland in around 10 BCE, and twenty-five years later another, said to number a thousand vessels, reached the Ems River just north of the border between the Netherlands and Germany. Despite these and other demonstrations of power, Rome's authority on the continent effectively stopped at the Rhine and Danube.* Claudius is credited with establishing standing provincial fleets for service in Germany and Britain, which he invaded in 43 CE. The *Classis Germanica* (German fleet) was responsible for denying use of the river to Germanic tribes as well as for security at the mouth of the Rhine, a major point of departure for traffic to Roman Britain. The German fleet's home port was Cologne (Colonia Claudia) on the Rhine, but subsidiary flotillas were located at provincial capitals and garrison towns like Mainz, about halfway between the North Sea and the Swiss border. Charged with safeguarding the lines of communication between Boulogne and Richborough and later Dover, the *Classis Britannica* was based on the English Channel at Gesoriacum (Boulogne, France) about twenty miles west of the Dover Strait.

Roman Gaul's prosperity continued to attract Germanic tribes from beyond the Rhine. During a revolt in 69–70, Julius Civilis, prince of Batavia (the region at the mouth of the Rhine), mustered a fleet of "all the bireme and single-banked vessels he had, and to these added a larger number of small craft carrying thirty to forty men apiece and fitted out like liburnians. There were captured craft assisted by improvised sails made from coats of many colours." His crews included many Batavians who had served in the *Classis Germanica*. The Romans were outnumbered but had "the advantage of experienced rowers, skilled helmsmen, and ships of greater size." Nonetheless, when the fleets encountered each other off the mouths of the Waal and Meuse Rivers, they gave each other a wide berth. In response to further Germanic incursions through the Dover Strait and across the North Sea to Britain, the Romans built a string of coastal forts on both sides of the English Channel, known as the Saxon Shore. Gaul was less easily defended, and when legions were withdrawn for service elsewhere in the mid-third century, Frankish tribes poured across the Rhine as far south as Spain, where they commandeered a fleet in Tarragona for a raid on North Africa. It was not until the reign of Marcus Aurelius Probus in the 270s that the Rhine frontier stabilized.

This incidentally led to one of the most remarkable feats of seamanship in Europe or the Mediterranean to that point. After pacifying the border, Probus relocated a large number of Frankish tribesmen to the Black Sea coast of Asia Minor. In 279 "some of them revolted and disrupted the whole of Greece with their large navy," which they cobbled together from whatever ships they could

---

* The exceptions that prove the rule are Agri Decumates, a small province that occupied a triangle of land between the upper Danube and upper Rhine, and Dacia, north of the lower Danube. These were the last provinces established, in 106 CE, and the first abandoned, in the next century.

steal locally. The erstwhile prisoners pressed on to Sicily, "where they attacked Syracuse and killed many of its inhabitants. Then they sailed across to Africa, and although beaten off by an army from Carthage, they were still able to return home [to the coast of the North Sea] through the Strait of Gibraltar." The earliest seaborne Saxon raids on Gaul, to which Danes and Frisians also contributed, took place two years later and further eroded the defenses of the beleaguered empire and led to the burning of the *Classis Germanica* at Cologne.

Barbarian tribes continued to cross the Rhine throughout the fourth century, and the end of Roman rule in Britain resulted from an invasion of Gaul by barbarian tribes at the start of the fifth. In 410 the emperor Honorius withdrew his legions and "sent letters to the cities in Britain, urging them to fend for themselves." In the ensuing chaos, native Briton rulers recruited Angle, Saxon, and Jutish mercenaries from the continent for help against invaders and each another. In so doing, they may have sowed the seeds of their own demise, for the Saxons are said to have "sent back news of their success to their homeland, adding that the country was fertile and the Britons cowardly." With guarantees of land and pay for maintaining "the peace and security of the island," the newcomers expanded their authority and by the mid-seventh century the territory of modern England comprised seven kingdoms: Anglian Northumbria, Mercia and East Anglia, Saxon Essex, Sussex and Wessex, and Jutish Kent. Wales and Scotland remained in the hands of Britons. Saxon mariners also established themselves on the Loire from where they and Danish raiders struck the Garonne valley and Iberian Peninsula. Following the collapse of Roman authority in Gaul and Italy, in 476 the western empire expired.

Germanic tribes were attracted by the prosperity of Gaul and Britain, the wealth of which was evident not only in the major cities and garrison towns, but on the sea-lanes that ran along the coasts of Gaul from the Rhine to the Garonne, and between Gaul and the British Isles. Elite Britons and Roman officials and soldiers throughout areas under Roman control sought out wine, olive oil, glassware, jewelry, pottery, and weapons from Gaul, while Britain exported grain, cattle, gold, tin, iron, slaves, hides, and hunting dogs to ports at the mouths of the Rhine, Seine, Loire, and Garonne. A host of more mundane cargoes have turned up in shipwrecks from the period. A second-century barge excavated at Blackfriars in London sank with a cargo of ragstone, a standard building material. Although this came from Kent via the Medway and Thames Rivers, teredo worm holes in the hull prove that the ship had spent considerable time at sea. Finds associated with a third-century wreck from St. Peter Port in the Channel Islands indicate that its crew of three traded from the Iberian Peninsula to the North Sea, and the cargo on its last voyage included barrels of pitch from the Les Landes region of southern France. The Roman-era trade routes were disrupted but not altogether ended by the barbarian invasions. Even as the last legions were leaving Britain, church missionaries were heading north to Ireland and Britain, and prestige goods continued to reach the British Isles from the farthest corners of the Mediterranean. Among the effects of a seventh-century East Anglian chieftain named Raedwald found in a ship burial at Sutton Hoo, England, were an eastern Mediterranean dish, an Egyptian bronze bowl, and two silver spoons inscribed with the names Saul and Paul in Greek letters. From closer by, the site also yielded thirty-seven gold coins from Merovingian Gaul dating from 575 to 625, the year of Raedwald's death and, presumably, the interment of his ship—and coincidentally the year of the latest coin found with the Yassi Ada A ship off Turkey.

Frisians and Franks

The collapse of Roman authority disrupted the balance of power that had prevailed along the Rhine–English Channel frontier since the first century, and the primary sea-lanes of the imperial period declined in importance as trade passed into new hands to be carried in new directions. The Frisians were the first people in northern Europe to be distinguished for their maritime trading networks, which resulted from their adaptability to a treacherous, sea-soaked environment. Around the start of the fifth century, rising sea levels flooded parts of the Netherlands and a lake the Romans had called Lacus Flevo doubled in size to form the Aelmere.* Rather than flee to higher ground, the Frisians capitalized on their aqueous habitat to become the foremost traders in northern seas. By the sixth century, Frisians were in regular contact with the Franks and the Danes, and they were sailing to British ports like York and London. To the north they sailed to Jutland where their trade helped spur the founding of the eighth-century entrepôt at Ribe, on the west coast of the peninsula. This effort was undertaken by an unknown Danish ruler who sought to channel the trading networks of the North Sea through his domains. The choice of Ribe was due to the advantages that came of crossing the Jutland peninsula overland—sixty kilometers to Kolding Fjord—rather than sailing by way of the Skagerrak and Kattegat, or through the sheltered, hundred-mile-long Limfjord that snakes between Jutland and the island of Vendsyssel. Ribe

---

* In the twelfth century, the inundation of the Aelmere formed the Zuider Zee. In the twentieth century, Dutch engineers enclosed and divided this "Southern Sea" into the Ijsselmeer and Markermeer to protect the Netherlands from further flooding.

was frequented primarily by Frisian and Frankish merchants from the North Sea, but the site has yielded goods from Norway, Birka, the Baltic, and even the Black Sea, which attests to the eastward reach of Scandinavian and Slavic trade networks at this early date.

South of Frisia, the Salian Franks had emerged as the most powerful of the Germanic tribes to cross the Rhine. In 486 Clovis defeated the last Roman ruler in Gaul, but with their acceptance of Christianity he and his Merovingian successors secured Romano-Gaulish support against the Visigothic kingdom of Toulouse and other Germanic tribes who followed heretical teachings. By midcentury, the Frankish kingdom encompassed most of modern France, the Low Countries, Switzerland, and southern Germany. For all its size and resources, its long seacoast was exposed to Saxon and Danish raids, the most famous of which is recounted in the Anglo-Saxon epic *Beowulf*, and in Gregory of Tours's *History of the Franks*. According to the latter, at some time between 516 and 534 the Danish king Chlocilaicus (Hygelac in *Beowulf*) raided northern Frisia and sailed into the Aelmere. From there the Danes sailed up the Vecht and Rhine to the junction of the Waal before being caught by the Franks near modern Nijmegen, about a hundred kilometers from the sea. Chlocilaicus was killed and his army crushed, presumably near an intended rendezvous with the fleet.

The Frisians' own expansionist designs resulted in frequent hostilities with the Franks who sought to reclaim ancestral lands north of the Rhine in a process that would climax under Charlemagne. Early in the seventh century, the Merovingians built a church at Utrecht and their most important northern port was at nearby Dorestad. Although its population never exceeded two thousand, Dorestad had a kilometer-long waterfront on the Rhine and was the site of a mint from 630 to 650, when it fell to the Frisians. Although Pepin II restored it to Merovingian rule in 689, it was not until fifty years later that Charles Martel launched a major naval expedition that paved the way for Frisia to become Frankish territory.

Neither Pepin nor Charles Martel was king; rather they served as hereditary mayors of the palace (major-domos) for the moribund Merovingian Dynasty. The mayors shunned the throne until 751, when Pepin III was crowned king of the Franks, the first of the Carolingian Dynasty, which takes its name from his son, Charlemagne (Carolus Magnus, or Charles the Great), who expanded the Frankish kingdom beyond all recognition. A supreme military strategist and tactician, he deployed riverine fleets to brilliant effect in four separate campaigns: in 789 against Slavs living along the Elbe and its tributaries; two years later against the Avars in Hungary, via the Danube; in 797 against the Saxons, by way of the Weser and Elbe; and finally against the Slavs of north-central Germany, again on the Elbe. Of these, the war against the Avars was the most decisive, because it destroyed the last vestiges of their power. Charlemagne's experience of moving his armies on the Danube inspired him to try digging a canal, the *Fossa Carolina* or Karlsgraben, between the Swabian Rezat River, in the Rhine-Main catchment area, and the Altmuhl, a tributary of the Danube. Although the distance was less than two kilometers and the difference in elevation between the Rezat and Altmuhl only ten meters, the local geology presented insurmountable obstacles and the project was abandoned. Such a link between the Rhine and Danube would frustrate engineers until 1992, when the 171-kilometer-long Rhine-Main-Danube Canal opened.

Viking Expansion

Charlemagne's campaigns to push Frankish rule beyond the Rhine coincided with the start of the period of Scandinavian expansion known as the Viking age. The etymology of "Viking" is uncertain. One theory holds that it comes from the Old English *wic*, meaning a temporary encampment such as raiders would have established and cognate with the Latin *vicus*, meaning village. Another explanation is that it comes from Viken, the region around Oslofjord from which the first wave of Norse Vikings in England may have come in order to escape Danish overlordship. This would account for why only the English used the word Viking while others called them Northmen, Danes, Varangians, Rus, pagans, and heathens. Medieval authors did not always specify the origin of different raiders, but the people of Scandinavia were not an undifferentiated mass even though they shared a variety of cultural attributes, including religion and language, and their rulers were often linked by bewilderingly intricate webs of kinship and obligation. Bearing in mind the many exceptions to the rule, Danes tended to go west and south to the Frankish empire, England, and Spain; the Norse west to northern Britain, Ireland, and Iceland; and the Swedes east to Russia and the Black and Caspian Seas.

The first Viking attack as such—seaborne, swift, severe—was the infamous raid by three ships on the Holy Island monastery of Lindisfarne on the North Sea coast of Northumbria in 793. News of the attack spread quickly, and the Northumbrian cleric Alcuin, whom Charlemagne had recruited as his teacher at Aachen, wrote Æthelred I of Wessex:

We and our fathers have now lived in this fair land for nearly three hundred and fifty years, and never before has such an atrocity been seen in Britain as we have now suffered at the hands of a pagan people. Such a voyage was not thought possible. The church of St. Cuthbart is spattered with the blood of the priests of God, stripped of all its furnishings, exposed to the plundering of pagans—a place more sacred than any in Britain.

The claim that "Such a voyage was not thought possible" is difficult to accept; Alcuin certainly knew that Anglo-Saxons had reached England by sea, just as Frisian traders did in his day. But if Anglo-Saxon England had forgotten its origins momentarily, the Viking raids were a sharp reminder that the seas around Britain provided poor insulation against determined invaders.

Some have proposed that Alcuin meant only that such a voyage was not thought possible *in winter*, when the prevailing southwesterly winds blow toward Norway. According to a thirteenth-century text, the ordinary sailing season in Norway was from early April to early October, but the Lindisfarne raid took place at the start of the Medieval Warming Period. This lengthened the sailing season and created conditions favorable for the settlement of Iceland and Greenland and long-distance voyaging as well as, perhaps, for midwinter raiding. Landsmen could always hope for bad weather, and a four-line poem penned in the margins of a ninth-century manuscript reveals a scribe's gratitude for an ill wind that kept marauders from putting to sea or coming safely to shore:

> The wind is fierce to-night
> it tosses the sea's white mane
> I do not fear the coursing of a quiet sea
> by the fierce warriors of Lothlend [Laithlinn].

The Lindisfarne raid was followed by attacks on other Northumbrian monasteries and on Saint Columba's sixth-century abbey on Iona in the Hebrides, but the Norse did not limit themselves to British religious houses. A raid on southwest France six years after the sack of Lindisfarne prompted Charlemagne to erect a chain of coastal guard stations with ships and soldiers at major ports and river mouths. This was widely regarded as a success at the time, and may explain why the first wave of Viking raids on France ended in the early 800s and did not resume in earnest for a generation. The most significant northern threat during Charlemagne's reign came from Denmark's King Godfred, who attacked Frisia in 824, perhaps to preempt Carolingian encroachment on Saxony and southern Denmark. Godfred's most significant action was the sack of the Slav emporium of Reric, which Charlemagne preferred to Saxon or Danish ports, and the relocation of its merchants to Hedeby. The Carolingians nonetheless continued their northward advance and Christianity was pushed beyond the Elbe by Charlemagne's successor, Louis the Pious.

In the 820s, a Danish leader from Hedeby named Harald Klak appealed to Louis for support against his rivals. Louis encouraged Harald to convert, which he did because "a Christian people would more readily come to his aid and to the aid of his friends if both peoples were worshippers of the same God." Harald returned to Hedeby accompanied by a priest named Ansgar on the first of many missions that would earn Ansgar canonization and the cognomen "Apostle of the North." After establishing a school in Hedeby, Ansgar took his missionary work to Birka, in Sweden, where he converted many people and ministered to Christian captives. Ansgar was serving as archbishop of Hamburg when Eirik I of Denmark sacked the port and leveled many churches, but following a change of heart Eirik allowed him to build a church and school at Hedeby, which "was especially suitable for this purpose and was near to the district where merchants from all parts congregated." This willingness to accept Christianity proved profitable and thanks to Ansgar's evangelizing, Frisian, Frankish, and other merchants "made for the place readily and without any fear—something which was not possible previously." Although the Vikings harassed Europe for centuries, in the end their adoption of southern religion and commercial practices transformed them more than they transformed Europe.

Even as Ansgar was evangelizing Scandinavia, Norse and Danish Vikings renewed their raids in the west where they struck Dorestad in 834 and the Thames estuary and the mouth of the Loire the next year. Annual attacks over the next fifteen years targeted strategic trading centers including London and York, and Rouen, at the mouth of the Seine, and Nantes on the Loire. Until the 840s, these raids were seasonal events in which the Vikings generally took advantage of fair weather in the summer to sail across the North Sea before running home on the prevailing autumn winds. The whole dynamic of the Viking age shifted dramatically when Scandinavian sailors began wintering abroad, as they did for the first time on Noirmoutier, a center of the salt and wine trades at the mouth of the Loire. This afforded the northerners a year-round home in a more congenial environment than Denmark or Norway, but it also positioned them to raid southern France and the Iberian Peninsula. Arabic accounts record six Viking expeditions against al-Andalus between 844 and 971, two of which reached the Mediterranean. In the first, a Danish fleet of fifty-four ships attacked Lisbon before sailing up the Guadalquivir to pillage Seville. Ambushed by forces from Córdoba, the Danes lost an estimated two thousand men. Most of the survivors withdrew under an armistice and sailed home with only twenty ships, but some converted to Islam and settled down, many as dairy farmers renowned for their cheese. This expedition follows a recurrent pattern found elsewhere: controlling river mouths, attacking inland river towns and their hinterlands, and relying on speed at sea and ashore. But the numbers involved in such operations were too few for a wholly Scandinavian identity to take root, even when Viking chiefs became local rulers.

A curious upshot of the raid of 844 was Eirik II's request for diplomatic relations with Abd al-Rahman II, emir of Córdoba, who sent to Jutland one of his foremost diplomats, al-Ghazal, a veteran of negotiations with the Byzantine Empire. Al-Ghazal was welcomed warmly and remained in Denmark for more than a year. The terms of the Danish-Andalusian treaty are unknown, but it did not long survive Eirik, and in 859 sixty-two ships under the Danish prince Björn Ironside and a soldier named Hastein attacked al-Andalus. In the meantime, however, Abd al-Rahman had built a fleet that patrolled as far north as the Bay of Biscay. Andalusian forces captured two Danish ships on the south coast of Spain and prevented any from entering the Guadalquivir. East of the Strait of Gibraltar, the Danes sacked Algeciras before being bested by an Umayyad fleet armed with Greek fire. After a small detachment raided the North African coast, the Danes sailed via the Balearics to southern Gaul and raided up the Rhône as far as Valence, unopposed because the Franks had abandoned Charlemagne's Mediterranean fleet. After four years away, Björn and Hastein returned home with a dozen ships and their crews. Although it had virtually no long-term consequences, their undertaking illustrates the Vikings' mobility, hitting power, and sheer bravado in a long-range expedition with a force that never numbered more than four thousand people.

Vikings first wintered in the British Isles in 851, on the Isle of Thanet in the Thames estuary. They soon took Canterbury and London, and in 866 they stormed the Northumbrian city of York, which lies on a spit of land between the Fosse and Ouse Rivers 120 kilometers from the sea. As an ecclesiastical center and port of call for Frisian merchants, York boasted extensive ties to the continent and provided many of the earliest evangelists to northern Europe, including Willibrord, "Apostle to the Frisians" and first bishop of Utrecht in 695. From 875 to 954 it was the center of the Norse kingdom of York. Anglo-Saxon resistance to Scandinavian incursions was feeble until the reign of Alfred the Great, who was crowned in 871, the same year that a Danish army under King Guthrum landed in East Anglia. The Danes marched on Wessex but failed to capture the elusive Alfred, who defeated them at the battle of Edington in 878. According to the terms of their treaty, Guthrum and his leading men received baptism in a ceremony in which Alfred became Guthrum's godfather, an act that made England a second avenue of religious influence into Scandinavia. Their treaty and common religion notwithstanding, Alfred worked tirelessly to assure the defense of Wessex, establishing encampments at the most important crossroads and bridges, organizing a small, mobile army, and launching a fleet of ships to counter the Danes. Seven years after Edington, a second treaty defined the territory under Danish control—the so-called Danelaw, chiefly the kingdoms of Northumbria and East Anglia. This did not result in a complete cessation of hostilities, but it put the rulers of Wessex on an equal footing with the Danes.

Alfred may have prevented the Danish annexation of Wessex, but the Danes would remain a major force in the British Isles for another 150 years. Nor were they the only foreigners to have settled down, for between 790 and 825 Norse Vikings had formed an independent state, known as Laithlinn, in the Orkney and Hebrides Islands and the neighboring coasts of the Scottish mainland. This became the point of departure for seasonal raids on Ireland, where the Vikings imposed tribute and to which they built a (metaphorical) "bridge of ships from the Hebrides." (The Strait of Moyle between Northern Ireland and the Mull of Kintyre is only eleven miles across.) In 837, two fleets of sixty ships sailed into the Boyne and Liffey Rivers. Though the Irish defeated them in battle, four years later the Norse of Laithlinn fortified a landing site at Dublin, the first of many *longphorts* that would ring the coast of Ireland at Waterford, Cork, Limerick, and elsewhere. Dublin, however, remained preeminent, and it became in effect the capital of the Norse British Isles when Ímar, heir to the throne of Laithlinn and "king of the Norwegian Vikings of the whole of Ireland and Britain," settled there. Irish forces ousted the Norse from Dublin in 902, but fifteen years later one of Ímar's grandsons retook it before going on to add York and Northumbria to his dominions.

By far the boldest of the Viking initiatives was their transatlantic venture to Iceland, Greenland, and North America. Although the Norse encounter with Iceland was a natural extension of their westward voyages to the Shetland and Faeroe Islands, which they settled in the eighth century, they may have heard about Irish monks who are believed to have sought solitude there before the ninth century. The Icelandic *Book of Settlements* relates that before the Norse "there were men there whom the Norsemen style 'papar.' These were Christians, and people consider that they must have been from the British Isles, because there were found left behind them Irish books, bells and crosiers, and other things besides." The written sources have not been confirmed by archaeological finds—one suspects the ascetic monks left little to find—but there are no hard grounds for disputing the claim.

Iceland's founding father is generally considered Ingólf Arnarson, who landed in 874 and whose homestead at Reykjavík (Steamy Bay) eventually became the site of Iceland's capital. The sagas ascribe the major impetus for settlement to a reaction to the authoritarian policies of Harald Fairhair, who united much of Norway for the first time and in so doing amassed considerable power for himself. The pace of colonization was swift; in some years as many as two thousand people reached Iceland with their belongings, seeds, and livestock. By the end of the "age of settlement" in 930, Iceland's population numbered more than twenty thousand, and it may have trebled by 1100. This is all the more remarkable considering the size of their ships and the distances involved: nine hundred miles from Norway to Iceland, in good conditions a six-day sail across open ocean with no landmarks.

Varangians, Byzantines, and Arabs

At the same time that Danish adventurers were raiding al-Andalus and Norse dissidents were settling Iceland, Swedish Vikings—known as Varangians—were on the move along the rivers of eastern Europe in pursuit, ultimately, of the Byzantine and Arab riches of the eastern Mediterranean and Asia. This trade seems to have been partly responsible for the growth of Swedish Birka, whose prosperity fostered that of Hedeby and other ports to the west. Wulfstan's report to Alfred only hints at the vitality of Baltic trade in the late ninth century, and while no contemporary writings enlarge on his account, archaeology does. Moreover, this commerce was not a new phenomenon. The emporium of Birka had been preceded by the nearby Helgö, where archaeological finds have included a fifth- or sixth-century statue of the Buddha from South Asia and a bishop's staff from Ireland. Strategically situated between Sweden and the Gulf of Finland, the island of Gotland had been a center of trade with the eastern Baltic since the fifth century. Gotlanders dominated the trade of Grobin, in Latvia, from 650 to 800, and they were heavily involved with that of the Lithuanian river port of Apuolé as well.

By the time Wulfstan sailed for Truso, the increase in trade had sparked the rise of many emporia and port towns along the southern and eastern shores of the Baltic. Some of these grew organically from earlier agrarian settlements to accommodate trade and develop various manufactures, but many bear the mark of outside influence, from Danes, Gotlanders, and Swedes. The densest concentration of ports was west of the Vistula delta, including Starigard (Oldenburg) east of Kiel Bay, Ralswiek, on the island of Rügen, Menzlin and Wolin in the Oder estuary, and Kołobrzeg. Located above the mouth of the Vistula near modern Elblag, Truso was well protected from the sea. Wulfstan says nothing about the local population, but archaeological finds suggest that Danish influence was dominant. Truso seems to have been a center of seasonal trade until it became a permanent settlement around 850. Farther east, at the southern end of the Curonian Lagoon, was the site of Kaup (Mokhovoye, Russia), whose prosperity depended on its trade with Birka.

The real prize in all these ports was their access to trans-European river corridors, and it is not surprising that the most important of these lay not directly on the Baltic but well to the east. In contrast to the litany of Viking raids in the west, accounts of the Scandinavian progress south across Russia, the Baltic states, Belarus, and Ukraine to the Black and Caspian Seas focus not on the plundering of wealthy religious houses—Christianity only took root here later—but on the establishment of trading centers at Staraya Ladoga and Novgorod near Lake Ladoga, and at Kiev on the Dnieper, about nine hundred kilometers south. According to the Russian *Primary Chronicle*, this came about because the Slavs were experiencing a bout of internecine strife. "They said to themselves: 'Let us seek a prince who may rule over us, and judge us according to the Law.' They accordingly went overseas to the Varangian Russes [and said], 'Our whole land is great and rich, but there is no order in it. Come to rule and reign over us.'" Three brothers came, the oldest and longest-lived of whom, Rurik, settled at Novgorod. "On account of these Varangians, the district of Novgorod became known as the land of Rus. The present inhabitants of Novgorod are descended from the Varangian race, but aforetime they were Slavs." The explanation offered in the *Primary Chronicle* does not settle definitively the question of why the Varangians originally came to Staraya Ladoga, but it is conceivable that as in post-Roman Britain, local tribes hired foreign mercenaries only to become subject to them. Rurik's cohorts Askold and Dir continued south from Novgorod and decided to relocate to the Slav settlement of Kiev. Inspired by the site's more central and commanding location on the heights overlooking the Dnieper, Rurik's successor, Oleg, transferred his capital from Novgorod to Kiev.

The Byzantine Empire was the wealthiest and most accessible attraction for the Rus and in 907 Oleg invaded, laying waste the territory outside Constantinople and securing from Leo VI an indemnity of nearly a million silver pieces and a trade agreement giving preferential treatment to Rus merchants. Among its terms was the stipulation that "Whosoever come as merchants shall receive supplies for six months, including bread, wine, meat, fish, and fruit. Baths shall be prepared for them in any volume they require. When the Russians return homeward, they shall receive from your Emperor food, anchors, cordage, and sails, and whatever else is needed for the journey." Relations between Kiev and Constantinople generally improved, although there were occasional setbacks, notably when the Rus invaded Byzantine territory in 941 and 970. Vladimir the Great did the most to align Rus and Byzantine interests. Scandinavian soldiers had previously served in the Byzantine army, but at the request of Basil II, Vladimir sent six thousand soldiers to help in a civil war. This corps became the genesis of the emperor's Varangian Guard, an elite force in which many Scandinavians served and that survived through the twelfth century. Rus-Byzantine ties strengthened further when in 988 Vladimir married Basil's sister (over her strenuous objection) and she convinced him to accept baptism. Given the importance of Byzantium as a political, military, and trading power, this was no hardship for Vladimir (a dubious candidate for the sainthood accorded him by a zealous church in the thirteenth century). Yet his conversion further illustrates the Scandinavians' flexibility in adapting to the particular circumstances of the lands they settled.

Farther east, the Rus were drawn to the trade of the Volga River and Caspian Sea. The Khazars, whose ruling nobility had converted to Judaism in the eighth century, had nominal control over access to the Caspian from their capital in the Volga delta, but the Rus reached the sea in the late ninth century. Around 910 they raided the port of Abaskun on the Iranian shore. Three years later, according to the historian al-Masudi, "there came about 500 ships, manned each by 100 persons," who promised the Khazars "half of what they might take in booty from the peoples of the sea-coast" in exchange for access to the Caspian. This expedition ranged around the coast and as far inland as Ardabil, in northwest Iran, before the Rus established themselves on islands near Baku, in Azerbaijan. The Rus proved invincible, in part because "the nations round the sea . . . had not been accustomed in time past to any enemy making his way to them there, for only merchant-ships and fishing vessels used to pass therein." Thirty years later another large force entered the Caspian, this time ascending the Kura River to capture the city of Barda'a, in Azerbaijan. Presumably under pressure from their Muslim neighbors, in 965 the Khazars denied passage to the Rus, who retaliated by sacking their major cities and so precipitated the end of Jewish rule.

In eastern Europe as elsewhere, Scandinavians were essentially pragmatic traders whose voyages tended to follow the established if lightly used routes of the day. The Baltic's ancient riverine trade with the Mediterranean and Southwest Asia exported furs, wax, honey, and slaves in exchange for gold, silk, and silver from Byzantium. Muslim lands were the source of myriad silver coins that have been found in hoards around the Baltic. Excavations at one of the seventeen farms on the island of Rügen yielded a basket with more than two thousand coins buried sometime after 844. Varangian traders also funneled goods more traditionally associated with the luxurious east, and Chinese silks have been found at Birka, York, and Dublin. We know that the Rus had access to Asian spices, too, for Abraham ben Jacob, a Jewish merchant who visited Mainz in the tenth century, reported finding silver dirhams minted in Samarkand as well as "quantities of such spices as are usually found in the Far East, pepper, imber [ginger], cloves, nard, costus and galingal [blue ginger]." Rus merchants doubtless had a hand in conveying these from east to west.

The Norse Atlantic World

The century and a half after 900 was the climactic period of Scandinavian expansion. By the start of the tenth century, Vikings were part of the political landscape in the places they had settled—the Danelaw and Laithlinn, and in Ireland, Normandy, and Russia. In Scandinavia itself, rulers taxed trade and used their newfound wealth to purchase the support of local chieftains. In this the Danish kings were especially successful, thanks to their command of the trade across Jutland and of the sea routes from the North Sea to the Baltic, which passed through the archipelago between Jutland and Skåne. (The Store Belt, widest of the three passages between the North Sea and Baltic, narrows to five miles; the most direct, the Øresund, is less than two.) Norway had been united under Harald Fairhair at the end of the tenth century, but the emergence of a strong kingship took place more slowly in Sweden.

Harald's success in consolidating the monarchy had sparked the initial settlement of Iceland, which remained a conspicuous exception to the trend toward centralized power then developing in Scandinavia. A more egalitarian *thing* (assembly), such as prevailed in Iceland, however, did not mean an absence of law, and just as the king of Norway could exile someone, the *thing* could do the same. Near the end of the tenth century, Eirik "the Red" Thorvaldsson managed to be banished from Norway for murder, and then from Iceland for the same crime. A century before, a mariner blown off course en route to Iceland had sighted lands to the west, and with few other options the exiled Eirik spent three years exploring the coasts of what he called Greenland before returning to convince several hundred Icelanders to join him. They settled in two groups, Eirik's Eastern Settlement in the south and the Western Settlement about 160 miles up the Davis Strait near Nuuk (formerly Godthab). Greenland in turn became the jumping-off place for what turned out to be the first voyage to North America by Europeans (an event not understood as such at the time) thanks again to a sailor's overshooting his destination.

Navigational error in the North Atlantic was not all that uncommon in this period. Coastal navigation was the norm for most voyages around northern Europe, but sailing between Scandinavia and the British Isles, the Faeroes, Iceland, and Greenland required open-water passages of at least three hundred miles. Navigational instruments were few. The sounding lead (a long line with a weight at one end to determine the depth of water) was standard equipment, and the Norse could measure the angle of the sun to determine latitude, while they shaped their course with the aid of a "sunstone." Working on the same principle as a sundial, a sunstone was a dial with a pointer in the middle that cast its shadow on notches incised around the outer ring, with different sets of markings being used to account for the sun's altitude at different seasons. Mostly, sailors relied on the observation of natural phenomena, including the flight paths of birds, shoals, tidal streams, fog banks, the color of water, and the presence of ice—including the "ice blink," the reflected light of glaciers visible from over the horizon. For long-distance voyages they practiced latitude sailing, running north or south to the parallel on which their destination lay and then following that parallel east or west as closely as possible.

While meteorological conditions during the Medieval Warming Period may have been somewhat more benign than they are now, short days, fog, and overcast skies limited the hours of good visibility, and none of the tools or techniques available to Scandinavian mariners was infallible, especially when sailing to a new destination. Returning to Iceland after a voyage from Norway, Bjarni Herjolfsson learned that his father had joined Eirik in Greenland and decided to follow him there. Bjarni sailed too far south and wound up on a coast that was "well wooded and with low hills," unlike mountainous, treeless Greenland. Bjarni refused to land and subsequent exploration was left to Leif Eirikson, who visited places he called Helluland ("slabland," for its glaciers, probably Baffin Island), Markland ("woodland," southern Newfoundland), and Vinland (for its grapes). Leif's kinsman Thorfinn Karlsefni later spent two or three years at Vinland with a party of sixty men and five women including his wife, Gudríd, who gave birth to the first European in North America.

Eirik's Saga and the *Greenland Saga* agree that the Greenlanders intended to exploit the region—which encompassed the shores of the Gulf of St. Lawrence as far south as New Brunswick—for its wood, furs, grapes, and walnuts. But it was too remote and the Greenlanders' numbers too few—only four or five hundred at this point, and never more than twenty-five hundred—to exploit Vinland fully. The essential accuracy of the sagas is corroborated by archaeological finds at L'Anse aux Meadows in northeast Newfoundland, near the entrance to the Strait of Belle Isle. This was a year-round settlement that could accommodate about one hundred people so that they did not have to make the round-trip from Greenland in one season. L'Anse aux Meadows seems to have been occupied until about 1030, but people continued sailing to Vinland for some time after that. In the 1070s, the chronicler Adam of Bremen wrote of an island called "Vinland because vines producing excellent wine grow wild there. That unsown crops also abound on that island we have ascertained not from fabulous reports but from the trustworthy relations of the Danes." Somewhat closer, Markland remained a source of wood for Greenlanders until at least 1347 when, according to an Icelandic source, "There came also a ship from Greenland, smaller in size than the small Icelandic boats; she was anchorless, and came into the outer Straumfjördur [in western Iceland]. There were seventeen men on board. They had made a voyage to Markland, but were afterwards storm-driven here." Norse Greenland seems to have died out or been abandoned sometime after 1410, when an Icelandic crew returned home after four years in the Eastern Settlement. Sources hint at no difficulties at the time, but the next written reference to Greenland, in a note regarding John Cabot in 1497, mentions no Greenlanders of European descent. Even so, English cod fishermen and traders—especially from the port of Bristol—had begun sailing to Iceland on a regular basis earlier in the fifteenth century, and the odds are good that some reached Greenland and possibly the Newfoundland Banks well before Cabot's time.

From Anglo-Saxon to Norman England

Five hundred years before, however, the English remained minor players in the drama then unfolding in the North Atlantic. Alfred had exercised his prerogatives as king wisely, and his successors built on the foundations he laid. Edward the Elder enlarged his realm and by 918 ruled all England south of the Humber and had won the submission of Northumbria, Strathclyde, Scotland, and Dublin. This rapid expansion set Wessex on a collision course with other aspirants to supremacy in the British Isles, a crisis that came to a head in the battle of Brunanburh in 937. Under Edward's successor, Anglo-Saxon armies sailed north in hundreds of ships and were victorious in a dramatic battle that was, according to a poem in the *Anglo-Saxon Chronicles*, bloodier than any fought "since Angles and Saxons / came here from the east, / sought out Britain over the broad ocean, / . . . seized the country." The Anglo-Saxon resurgence slowed during the long reign of Æthelred II, when disaffected Danes settled in England rather than submit to Denmark's centralizing king, Harald Bluetooth, a convert to Christianity whose evangelization and monarchical policies alienated many of the aristocracy. In the 980s, these old-guard Danes sailed for southern England where they forced Æthelred to pay nearly 150,000 pounds of silver and gold—Danegeld, or "Danish tribute"—over twenty years to prevent further violence.

Among the beneficiaries of this latest wave of Danish incursions into England were the merchants of the Duchy of Normandy across the English Channel. Although the Vikings never threatened the integrity of the Frankish kingdoms as directly as they did those of England, they had occupied the coast around the mouth of the Seine and sailed upriver to attack Paris. At the start of the tenth century, the French king purchased their allegiance in exchange for the land they already inhabited, and the Duchy of Normandy became a buffer between the French heartland and further incursions from the sea. A major commercial and political force in their own right, in Æthelred's time the Normans engaged in coastal fishing, especially for whales, and carried on an active commerce with the British Isles, Scandinavia, the Faeroe Islands, and Iceland. Their chief exports included grain, salt, iron, and lead, while the merchants of Rouen also specialized in wine, sealskins, whale oil, salted whale meat, and blubber, as well as slaves. Slavery was a constant of medieval trade and a striking part of the life stories of even the most prominent figures of the time. A teenaged Saint Patrick was enslaved in Ireland before joining the church in the fourth century, and four hundred years later Bede wrote of a fellow Northumbrian who was taken south to London and sold there to a Frisian merchant. Olaf Tryggvason, a contemporary of Æthelred's who became king of Norway, was traded as a young boy for "a precious garment" before ending up in Kiev. While the northern European slave trade lacked the organization and scale of that of the Mediterranean or Indian Ocean, it was no less savage and degrading. Warner of Rouen's blistering tenth-century satire, *Moriuht*, follows the wanderings of its Irish protagonist in search of his wife, Glicerium, after her abduction. When Moriuht attempts to follow Glicerium's kidnappers,

> He is captured by Vikings and vigorously tied up with chains. . . . As his body, struck powerfully by their whips and hands, is spun from their hands across the deck of the ship, the Vikings stand about and marvel at the active prodigy as they piss on the middle of his bald head. . . . He is subjected to insults and then in place of a wife he is forced by the Vikings to perform the sexual service of a wife.

Sold in Northumbria and again in Saxony, he earns his freedom from a widow by sleeping with her and then makes his way to Rouen. In a nearby port "full to bursting with the merchandise of wealth supplied by Vikings," Moriuht finally redeems Glicerium for "half a penny" and their daughter for "a quarter of a coin with . . . half a cooked loaf of bread." Warner regards his fellow academic as a fool and exaggerates his literary failings and sexual proclivities for comic effect, but his horrific depiction of enslavement rings true. The brutal rape and humiliation of captives regardless of sex or age, the appallingly low value of human life, and the division of families were as typical of medieval slavery as they are today.

Æthelred II was hardly troubled by such run-of-the-mill indignities, but he did object to the Normans' willingness to trade with his enemies. A treaty with Richard, duke of Normandy, officially closed all ports to raiders of the other's territories, but the terms were unenforced. In 1002 Æthelred tried to

1. An Egyptian faience plate decorated with a papyrus raft being poled on the Nile. The longitudinal papyrus bundles are held together by lashings. Dating from 1400–1200 BCE, this plate was found in a tomb at Enkomi, on Famagusta Bay in eastern Cyprus, which testifies to the interconnectedness of the eastern Mediterranean more than three thousand years ago. Courtesy of the British Museum, London.

2. A detail from a Late Minoan (thirteenth-century BCE) mural in the West House at Akrotiri on the island of Thera (Santorini) in the Cyclades. The ships, their crews, and the dolphins cavorting around them are rendered in an animated style quite unlike anything in art of the same period from Egypt or the Near East. Photograph by Erich Lessing; courtesy of the National Archaeological Museum, Athens, Greece/Art Resource, New York.

3. A black-figure *kylix* (wine cup) illustrated with a pirate's bireme bearing down on a sailing merchantman under shortened sail. This was made at Athens in the last quarter of the sixth century BCE, just before the Persian Wars that would catapult Athens to the forefront of the Greek city-states. Courtesy of the Trustees of the British Museum, London.

4. An artist's conception of the port of Carthage showing the outer commercial harbor and the inner naval harbor, within which there was "an island, and great quays were set at intervals round both the harbour and the island. These embankments were full of shipyards which had capacity for 220 vessels." Courtesy of DeA Picture Library/Art Resource, New York.

5. The three-masted merchant ship depicted in the landlocked temple complex of Ajanta, India. In addition to its three tall sails, the ship sets a square spritsail from a yard over the bow, which is adorned with an *oculus*, or eye, to help the ship see danger. A steering oar is clearly visible on the port quarter, while a number of jars, possibly for drinking water, can be seen beneath a shelter on deck. Marine Archaeology Centre, National Institute of Oceanography, Goa.

6. A sixth-century Byzantine mosaic shows a fisherman hauling a net while his mate steers their small boat, probably a reference to the calling of Saint Peter and Saint Andrew (Matthew 4:18). The mosaic is in the Basilica di Sant'Apollinare Nuovo in Ravenna. The Adriatic port was the site of a Roman naval base under Augustus, and capital of the Western Roman Empire (402–476) and of the Ostrogoths (until 554) before it became the capital of Byzantine Italy. Courtesy of Art Resource, New York.

ΠΥΡΡΗΚΩΝ. Ηραιος δε και τοσοκλαγω πρ πολο ωτ πυρι

σολεερω μαψ πυρ πολ ΤΩΝ ΤΩΝ ΗΝΗΑΗΠ σΟΛΟΝ

7. A Byzantine imperial *dromon* fitted with Greek fire, a medieval flamethrower, attacking a ship in the fleet of the rebel Thomas the Slav in 821. Greek fire was developed in the seventh century by a Syrian Byzantine refugee from the Arab conquest. Despite dire threats of eternal damnation and more temporal punishments, knowledge of how to make it soon spread to navies across the Mediterranean. This illustration is from a twelfth-century Sicilian manuscript of John Skylitzes's eleventh-century *Synopsis Historion* (vitr. 26-2, fol. 34v). Courtesy of the Biblioteca Nacional, Madrid/Art Resource, New York.

8. The first-century BCE gold Broighter boat, named for the town in County Derry, northern Ireland, where it was found in 1895. Part of a votive deposit to the sea god Manannán Mac Lir, this is probably a model of an oceangoing vessel, of wood rather than hide-covered, complete with seats, oars, rowlocks, steering oar, and mast. The twenty-centimeter-long model probably represents a vessel twelve to fifteen meters long. Courtesy of the National Museum of Ireland, Dublin.

9. Shipbuilding scene from the Bayeux Tapestry, which recounts the story of William, duke of Normandy's campaign to take the English throne in 1066. To the left, a man is shaping a plank with a side axe. In the center, the master shipwright is checking the lines of the hull of the upper ship by eye while someone else finishes the planks of the completed hull, and a third man bends over a breast augur. Two men are applying the finishing touches to the hull below, one with an axe or adze, and the other with a drill. To the right are five complete hulls being drawn to the water's edge, as we know from the caption in the following panel: *"Hic trahunt naves ad mare"* (Here they drag the ships to the sea). Courtesy of the Musée de la Tapisserie de Bayeux, France.

10. A ship crossing the Persian Gulf, from Yahya Ben Mahmoud al-Wasiti's thirteenth-century manuscript of the *Maqamat* (Assemblies, or Entertaining Dialogues), by al-Hariri of Basra (1054–1122). Although the stylized rig is difficult to interpret, the ship apparently has three decks and a fluked anchor hangs from a projection from the bow. The image is best known for al-Wasiti's depiction of a centerline rudder, the first known from the Indian Ocean region and roughly contemporary with the oldest depiction of a rudder from Europe. Photograph by Gerard Le Gall; courtesy of the Bibliothèque Nationale de France, Paris/Art Resource, New York.

11. A passenger-carrying junk at Kaifeng, China, one of some twenty-eight vessels depicted in Zhang Zheduan's 5.25-meter-long scroll painting *Qingming Shanghe Tu* (Along the River During the Qingming Festival) of about 1125. The boat is being pulled by five trackers (out of frame to the left). The bipod mast is supported by numerous stays, and the massive centerline rudder is readily visible. (Scrollable versions of the *Qingming Shanghe Tu* are available online.) Courtesy of the Palace Museum, Beijing.

12. A Venetian great galley from a fifteenth-century ship-building treatise by Michael of Rhodes. Great galleys helped open regular commercial sea trade between Genoa and Venice and the markets of Flanders in northwest Europe. Although they originated as oared warships, their primary means of propulsion was a massive lateen sail, and oars were reserved for auxiliary propulsion. Courtesy of David McGee, ed., *The Book of Michael of Rhodes.* Vol. 1, *Facsimile: A Fifteenth-Century Maritime Manuscript*, image from page 236. © 2009 Massachusetts Institute of Technology, by permission of MIT Press.

13. *The Doge of Venice Departing for the Lido in the* Bucintoro *on Ascension Day* by Antonio Canaletto (1697–1768). Starting in the year 1000, the doge annually boarded the elaborately carved and gilded state barge to cross the Venetian lagoon to perform the *sposalizia*, a wedding rite that symbolized Venice's dominion over the Adriatic and its trade, and thereby affirmed its exclusive relationship with the sea against other prospective suitors. Courtesy of the British Museum, London.

14. A detail from the scroll commissioned by Takezaki Suenaga to commemorate the repulse of the Yuan (Mongol) Chinese invasion of Japan in 1281. At right, the three Oyano brothers are boarding a Chinese ship under a hail of arrows. To the left, Suenaga is cutting the throat of a Mongol warrior while another lies dead on deck. The Mongols cowering belowdecks are portrayed with distinctly simian faces. Although there is no mast adequate for a sail, it has probably been lowered for battle. Details characteristic of Chinese vessels of the time include the winch for an anchor forward and the heavy centerline rudder. Courtesy of the Imperial Museum, Tokyo.

OPPOSITE: 15. An illustration from a 1341 manuscript of the Iranian national epic, *Shahnamah* (Book of Kings), written by Firdawsi at the start of the eleventh century. Here the legendary king Kay Khusraw is crossing the Sea of Zareh in pursuit of his maternal grandfather, Afrasiyab, who killed his father. The Sea of Zareh is actually a salt lake called the Goud-e Zereh near the border between Afghanistan and Iran and fed in part by the Helmand River, and crossing it would not have taken the seven months described by Firdawsi. Courtesy of the Freer Gallery of Art, Smithsonian Institution, Washington, D.C.: Purchase, F1942.12.

til þe come in to iiij. fadun deep and yf it be stremp
spunde it is betwene sheshant and isle in the entre
of the chanel of ssaundres and soo goo youre cours
til ye stane syyt fadun deep. than goo est nortst est
a longe the see. + c

16. A ship taking soundings, from the *Ordonances of Armoury, Jousting, Sword, and Axe Combat, and Chivalry* (fol. 138v), written in the mid-fifteenth century for Sir John Astley. The ship is a carrack, or galleon, the forerunner of the full-rigged ship with a combination of square sails on the fore and main masts, and a fore-and-aft lateen sail on the mizzen. The bow incorporates a heavy forecastle protected by shields, while two of the crew man the topcastle at the top of the mast. The text explains what course to steer after the water has reached a certain depth. Courtesy of the Pierpont Morgan Library/Art Resource, New York.

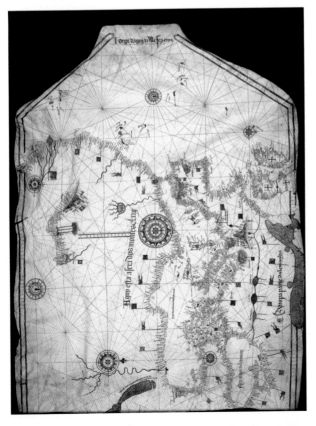

17. Jorge Aguiar's portolan chart of the Mediterranean drafted in 1492, the year of Columbus's epochal discovery, and the oldest extant chart of Portuguese origin. Drawn on a sheepskin, the neck of which is west, the chart shows Madeira, the Azores, the Canaries, and the Cape Verde Islands, and the coast of Africa from Cape Verde to Egypt and the Red Sea. Clearly seen on the Iberian Peninsula are Lisbon and Granada, newly taken from the Moors, while Genoa and Venice dominate the Italian Peninsula. The Rhine and Danube Rivers are treated as one, flowing between the North Sea and Black Sea, and while ports in the British Isles and around the Black Sea are well represented, the coasts of Denmark and the Baltic are blank. Courtesy of the Beinecke Rare Book and Manuscript Library, Yale University, New Haven, Connecticut.

18. Noah's ark as seen by the Mughal illustrator Miskin, who painted this miniature in about 1590. As popular a figure in the Quran as he is in the Hebrew Bible, Noah (in Arabic, Nuh) kneels on the third deck facing aft, his head wreathed in a flaming halo, while the crew—dressed only in loincloths—sail the ship. Others try to maintain order among the castaway menagerie, which includes elephants, tigers, leopards, dromedaries, monkeys, pelicans, and doves, and other passengers, one of whom has fallen over. While the animals are shown in pairs, Miskin's ark apparently carries no women. Courtesy of the Freer Gallery of Art, Smithsonian Institution, Washington, D.C.: Purchase, F1948.8.

19. Johan Bruun's *Kronborg Castle, View from the Øresund*, 1739. The Øresund is the narrow strait between Denmark and what is now Sweden where all ships had to anchor to pay their toll for passage through the sound, under the supervision of the guardship of the Danish crown, shown at center. Courtesy of the Handels- og Søfartsmuseet på Kronborg, Helsingør, Denmark.

OPPOSITE: 20. "John Bull Taking a Luncheon, or British Cooks Cramming Old Grumble-Gizzard with Bonne-Chére." Drawn just after the battle of Aboukir, James Gillray's cartoon shows Admiral Lord Nelson in the forefront of British admirals and naval heroes—including Warren, Howe, Bridport, Duncan, and St. Vincent—offering platters of ships to a gluttonous John Bull, who complains, "What! more Frigasees? why you sons o' bitches you, where do ye think I shall find room to stow all you bring in?" Published October 24, 1798, by H. Humphrey. Courtesy of the National Maritime Museum, Greenwich, England.

21. *Giant Demon Attacks a Ship* from the seventeenth-century *Sripal Ras* (The Annals of Sripal), written by Yasovijayji and Vinayvijayj. The verse epic recounts the story of the lay Jain devotees Sripal Raja and his queen, Mayana, who together and singly endure many tests of faith. Seeking to make a name for himself, Sripal Raja traded on land and sea. This illustration shows his ship as an armed British trader, the most powerful and long-ranging vessels known to the merchant community of Gujarat of the 1770s when this was painted. Courtesy of the Freer Gallery of Art, Smithsonian Institution, Washington, D.C.: Purchase, F1999.22.

JOHN BULL taking a Luncheon: ___ or ___ British Cooks, cramming Old Grumble-Gizzard, with Bonne-Chére.

22. Jean Dupas's gold, silver, and palladium leaf and paint mural *History of Navigation*. Measuring more than six meters high by nearly nine meters long, the mural is an exotic interpretation of its subject designed for the first-class salon of the Compagnie Générale Transatlantique (French Line)'s ocean liner *Normandie* (1935–41). The ship itself exemplified the aesthetic celebrated in the Exposition Internationale des Arts Décoratifs et Industriels Modernes held in Paris in 1925. This was known as "ocean liner style" for decades before the demise of the ocean liner gave rise to the more generic term "art deco." Courtesy of the Metropolitan Museum of Art, New York/Art Resource, New York.

23. Stephen Bone's *On Board an S-Class Submarine: Up the Conning Tower*. An official Royal Navy war artist, during World War II Bone spent time in a variety of warships to capture the realities of the isolated and often claustrophobic conditions of life at sea. Courtesy of the National Maritime Museum, Greenwich, England.

24. The port of Singapore has been one of the world's busiest for the past two decades, thanks in large part to its embrace of containerization. So efficient is this form of cargo transportation that there are no people visible on the ship or the wharf. All the work of transferring containers between ship and shore is done by solitary crane operators fifty meters or more above the pier. Courtesy of the Maritime and Port Authority of Singapore.

25. A huge catch aboard a trawler in the Gulf of Alaska. Judging from the two members of the crew seen toward the bow, the bulging trawl net is at least ten feet across. This picture illustrates the strain that modern industrial fishing with its sophisticated electronic tracking devices, mechanical efficiency, and phenomenally strong gear like nylon netting has put on fish stocks worldwide. Photograph by the Alaska Fisheries Science Center, Marine Observer Program; courtesy of the National Oceanic and Atmospheric Administration, Washington, D.C.

26. The *Nimitz*-class aircraft carrier USS *Dwight D. Eisenhower* being replenished by the fleet oiler USNS *Big Horn*. The *Eisenhower* is nuclear-powered and the hoses leading from the *Big Horn* supply jet fuel for the carrier's air wing, while helicopters transship dry goods, including mail for the crew. The U.S. Navy has long been in the vanguard of underway replenishment, which is essential to long-distance overseas operations such as those shown here in the Arabian Sea. Photograph by Darien G. Kennedy; courtesy of the U.S. Navy.

enhance this ineffectual agreement by marrying Richard's daughter, Emma. This political marriage failed in its chief purpose due to Æthelred's decision the same year to massacre all the Danes in England—men, women, and children—which only invited more Danish pressure and ultimately brought about the end of Anglo-Saxon England. Denmark's Svein Forkbeard was well positioned to avenge the massacre and he led repeated attacks on England from 1002 to 1013, when Æthelred fled to Normandy and Svein ascended his throne. Three years later, Svein's son Knút (or Canute) became king of England; he added Denmark to his crown after his brother's death and Norway after the death of (Saint) Olaf Haraldson. A judicious and able ruler, Knút's deft diplomacy included marrying Æthelred's widow, Emma of Normandy. The exhaustion on all sides after forty years of nearly constant war and the fact that one person ruled Denmark, England, and Norway led to a period of unprecedented peace and prosperity. Knút's creation of a North Sea empire was a remarkable accomplishment, but one that owed as much to timing and luck as anything else. The culmination of Danish rule in England, which lasted a generation, marks the precipitous highpoint of the Viking age. Knút died in 1035, and seven years later England was ruled again by the native Edward the Confessor, while Olaf Haraldson's son, Magnús the Good, was king of Norway and Denmark.

The only significant rival to Magnús's rule was his uncle, Harald Sigurdsson (known as Hardradi, or "the Ruthless"), whose peripatetic career demonstrates the reach of Viking influence across Europe. Following the death of his half brother, Olaf Haraldson, Harald fled to the court of Yaroslav the Wise in Kiev. As a member of the Byzantine emperor's Varangian Guard, he fought for the Byzantines in Bulgaria, Sicily, Asia Minor, and the Holy Land before returning to Norway to claim the crown in 1047. Norway prospered during Harald's nearly two-decade reign, but he waged almost incessant war against Denmark's Svein III until his overwhelming victory at the battle of Nissa in 1062. Although Svein "Leapt from the bloodied gunwales,/Leaving his fallen comrades," he kept his throne, and two years later he and Harald came to terms.

Another outlet for Harald's restless aggression opened with the death of England's Edward the Confessor in 1066. His brother-in-law Harald Godwinson succeeded him, but there were three other pretenders to the throne. William, duke of Normandy and Emma's great-nephew, claimed that Edward had made him his heir—plausible enough considering that Edward had been reared in the Norman court—and that Harald Godwinson had made himself William's vassal. Svein III was theoretically heir to all the territories once ruled by his uncle, Knút. Harald Hardradi's pretensions to the throne were weakest, based as they were on reports that Edward had promised the crown to Harald's predecessor, Magnús the Good. Yet Harald Hardradi was first off the mark, and with a fleet of 250 or more ships and an army of twelve to eighteen thousand men he sailed up the Ouse River and forced York's surrender. His victory was short-lived and five days later, on September 25, Harald Godwinson surprised the Norse at Stamford Bridge in a battle so stunning that the survivors needed only twenty-four ships to return home with their fallen king.

In the meantime, William of Normandy had spent months planning an invasion of England. He finally sailed on September 27, and the next day landed on the Sussex coast. Racing south, Harald reached London a week later and after five days set off to catch William before the Normans became entrenched. On October 22 his weary army assembled atop Senlac Hill, nine miles from Hastings, where it collapsed under repeated assaults by William's cavalry, archers, and infantry. William fought his way to London where he was crowned on Christmas Day. His English domains remained under threat from internal dissent and foreign intervention and he could assert his authority only when he had both ships and armies at his disposal, which according to the *Anglo-Saxon Chronicles* was not very often. When Denmark's Knút II and Robert of Flanders threatened to invade in 1085, William "travelled into England with a greater raiding-army of mounted men and infantry from the kingdom of France and from Brittany as had ever sought out this country before." As additional security he embarked on a scorched-earth policy and had "the land near the sea laid waste, so that if his enemies landed they would have nothing on which to seize so quickly." This desperate policy shows the degree to which the Norman descendants of Viking raiders had abandoned the role of sea hunter to become the hunted. The events of 1066 marked a new epoch for northern Europe, but for the moment Norman England seemed vulnerable.

Sources for the massive naval expeditions of 1066 reveal little about how Harald Hardradi, William the Conqueror, or Harald Godwinson managed to gather the great numbers of ships they required. Generally speaking, northern European fleets were assembled as needed on the basis of obligations owed one's overlord. As far back as the first century, Tacitus referred to Germanic chiefs relying on warrior cohorts of a hundred men selected from each district under their rule, and it is possible that a similar practice applied to maritime communities in Scandinavia and the British Isles. According to the seventh-century *Census* [or *History*] *of the Men of Alba*, every twenty households in the kingdom of Dalriada (northern Ireland and southern Scotland) were required to supply two ships and twenty-eight crew when summoned—all told, 177 ships and 2,478 crew.

Apart from the ad hoc levies of the *Census*, British rulers seem to have been largely indifferent to naval affairs prior to the ninth century, and while Alfred the Great is frequently credited as the founder of the English navy, the only evidence for a fleet is a brief mention of his design for ships to be sailed against the Danes. The number of ships, where they were based, how they were administered, paid for, or manned—all these are unknown, as are details about the hundred-ship fleet deployed by Edward the Elder at Brunanburh. Later in the tenth century Edgar and Æthelred II evidently established, or continued, a system to finance the fleet by mandatory levies of ships and men, called the *ship-soke*, in which administrative divisions equivalent to three hundred households were required to furnish one ship and sixty men. Select crews of sailor-warriors were levied on the basis of one man per five households, each of which contributed 3½ shillings to his maintenance for two months. Æthelred also hired English and Danish mercenaries. The *ship-soke* had parallels in Norway, where Harald Fairhair instituted the first large-scale ship levy in the ninth century, when every three households had to provide one crewman and his maintenance for two and a half months. This evolved into a more sophisticated levy of ships, men, and provisions throughout Scandinavia called a *leidang*.

Under normal circumstances, it seems that almost anyone could be sent up for service with the fleet, for Olaf Tryggvason was obliged to set firm guidelines for the crew of the *Ormr inn Langi* ("long serpent"), his flagship at the battle of Svold: "No man younger than twenty years of age was to serve on this ship, and none older than sixty. No effeminate cowards or beggars were to come aboard, and hardly anyone was allowed aboard unless he was distinguished in some way." Such strict guidelines probably did not apply in 1066, when Harald Hardradi gathered at least 250 ships for his invasion of England, and William's fleet numbered between 700 and 3,000 ships (the sources do not agree) manned by 7,000 crew who ferried another 7,000 soldiers and knights together with their gear and horses.

In their brisk telegraphic style, the captions of the Bayeux Tapestry merely hint at the logistical complexities and organizational sophistication required to coordinate such a formidable undertaking: "Here William orders the ships to be built. Here they pull the ships to the sea. These men carry weapons down to the ships. And here they pull a cart loaded with weapons. Here William crosses in a large ship over the sea and comes to Pevensey. Here the horses disembark. And here the soldiers hurried to Hastings to requisition food." Well aware of the Norman threat, Harald Godwinson had "gathered a greater ship-army and also land-army than any king in the land had ever gathered before," but his experience highlights the drawbacks of the temporary levies. William delayed so long in putting to sea that Harald was forced to relax his watch on the coast because "the men's provisions were gone, and no one could hold them there any longer. Then the men were allowed to go home, and the king rode inland, and the ships were sent to London." Although disbanding the fleet freed Harald to deal with Harald Hardradi, it left his southern flank exposed.

Such a casual system for raising a fleet could work only so long as the weapons involved were what sailors would own anyway. Northern Europeans had no long-range weapons like ballista or catapults and the nature of their ship design precluded ramming, so ships sailed as transports and became platforms for hand-to-hand combat more by accident than design. Oddr Snorrason offers a lengthy depiction of Olaf Tryggvason's last stand in the *Ormr inn Langi* at the battle of Svold (one of the only fleet engagements of the Viking age to have been described in any detail), where Olaf faced the scores of ships marshaled by his enemies with only four of his own. Olaf had his ships chained together, with the *Ormr inn Langi* in the middle because it was "much longer and higher in the gunwales than other ships. That made for a good battle stage as if it were a fort." Against this Eirik Håkonsson had a ship called *Járnbarðinn* ("Ironprow"), which was "extensively reinforced with iron and sharp spikes" at bow and stern as protection against boarders, an unusual configuration for the time. Eirik's victory is attributed to his embracing Christianity and removing the idol of Thor from the bow of his ship, and to his erecting a large tower on the *Járnbarðinn*, from which to drop heavy beams on Olaf's ship. Advantageous conversions were common enough, but the latter tactic seems to have been an improvised stratagem for which Viking ship design was not well suited. Nonetheless, it appears to have worked in this case and Olaf and his eight surviving comrades ended the battle by throwing themselves into the sea. The Swedes and Danes had "posted small boats around the larger ships so that they could fish out those who dove overboard and bring them to the chieftains," and all save Olaf were pulled from the water. Whether he drowned or escaped has been debated ever since.

Ships of Northwest Europe

The Viking ships present at the battle of Svold represent the culmination of a line of development in northern European shipbuilding the origins of which were hundreds if not thousands of years old. The ships of northern Europe were distinct from those of the Mediterranean or the Monsoon Seas in two key respects: the hulls tended to be built with strakes overlapping rather than laid flush and joined to one another by clenched bolts, a style called lapstrake or clinker; and until shortly before the start of the Viking age the sail was apparently unknown on the continent north of the Rhine. When sails were developed in or introduced to Gaul and the British Isles is unknown, but Pytheas's claim that Ultima Thule lay six days from the Shetland Islands or Great Britain assumes the use of a sail by at least the fourth century BCE. The Shetlands are four hundred miles from where the Arctic Circle intersects the coasts of Norway and Iceland, so if Pytheas and his crew sailed from the Shetlands, they would have to have averaged seventy miles per day, about twice the speed possible under oars.

The next positive evidence for sails in the British Isles comes from the Broighter "boat," a twenty-centimeter gold model of a boat from the north of Ireland dated to the first century BCE. Fitted with eighteen oars, a steering oar, and a mast and yard for a square sail, a life-size version of the model would yield a boat of between twelve and fifteen meters long. There is little reason to believe that mariners of Pytheas's day, or even earlier, could not rig their hide boats with a mast and sail, and it seems likely that if he had fallen in with far-ranging mariners who did not use sails, he would have mentioned it. Whether sails were used throughout the British Isles or whether there was a line of demarcation between areas of ships with sails and those without them is hard to know. Regardless, the practice of building large, unrigged vessels continued as late as the seventh century.

The Broighter boat is contemporaneous with the oldest firsthand account of northern European ships, in Caesar's *Conquest of Gaul*. During a naval campaign against the Veneti on the south coast of Brittany in 57 BCE, Caesar was especially impressed with their seamanship and the differences between their ships, designed to weather the rough Atlantic littoral, and those of the Mediterranean. "The Gauls' own ships were built and rigged in a different manner from ours," he wrote.

> They were made with much flatter bottoms, to help them to ride shallow water caused by shoals or ebb-tides. Exceptionally high bows and sterns fitted them for use in heavy seas and violent gales, and the hulls were made entirely of oak, to enable them to stand any amount of shocks and rough usage. . . . They used sails made of raw hides or thin leather, either because they had no flax and were ignorant of its use, or more probably because they thought that ordinary sails would not stand the violent storms and squalls of the Atlantic and were not suitable for such heavy vessels. In meeting them the only advantage our ships possessed was that they were faster and could be propelled by oars.

Caesar had ships built on the Loire, but smaller and fitted with rams, they were no match for those of the Veneti. "Perfectly equipped and ready for immediate action," the Veneti ships rode so high in the water that when the Romans "tried erecting turrets they found that they were still overtopped by the foreigners' lofty sterns and were too low to make their missiles carry properly, while the enemy's fell with great force." The Romans finally gained the advantage by cutting the halyards of the Veneti ships with "pointed hooks fixed into the ends of long poles." Because the Veneti ships carried no oars, the Romans could then pick off the powerless ships one by one.

Caesar gained additional experience on his two crossings to Britain, and for the second he ordered the construction of ships suited to crossing the English Channel. As he writes:

> To enable them to be loaded quickly and beached easily he had them made slightly lower than those which we generally use in the Mediterranean. . . . To enable them, however, to carry a heavy cargo, including a large number of animals, they were made somewhat wider than the ships we use in other waters. They were all to be of a type suitable for both sailing and rowing—an arrangement which was greatly facilitated by their low freeboard.

The largest collection of Roman-era vessels on the Rhine was discovered during the construction of a hotel in the 1980s, when workers uncovered the remains of five fourth-century vessels adjacent to what had been the *Classis Germanica* base at Mainz. Four were slender, open *lusoriae*, general-purpose transports and patrol boats measuring about 21 by 2.5 meters, with a single mast rigged for a square sail, and thirty oars. (The fifth and smallest vessel was an inspection boat with a small cabin for officials.) In building these, shipwrights fastened planks around a temporary frame, which was then removed before permanent frames were inserted into the complete hull, a process that would have facilitated the mass production of these river craft, which made up a growing proportion of the imperial fleet in the post-Augustan era.

This hybrid method of hull construction is similar to the "Romano-Celtic" design associated with vessels found in Roman Gaul and Britain. Described as a "frame-based" shipbuilding technique, this is known from the remains of the second-century Blackfriars barge excavated at London, and from the third-century sailing merchantmen found at St. Peter Port, on the island of Guernsey in the Channel Islands. Neither hull was built using the shell-first method found in the Mediterranean and elsewhere in northern Europe; nor were complete frames erected before planks were fastened to them. Instead, the frame was erected in stages: a section of framing was assembled and after planks were attached to this, the frames were extended beyond the last completed strake. In this way, the framing rather than the planking was the dominant element in determining the shape of the hull. Neither this style, nor that of the Mainz vessels, developed into a fully frame-first sequence, which was only introduced from the Mediterranean, where it evolved, in the later Middle Ages.

The Blackfriars, St. Peter Port, and Mainz vessels all carried sails, but although Roman patrol craft especially would have been well known to people living along the Rhine-Danube corridor, and in fact many of the crews were recruited from the indigenous population, there is little evidence of sails being used north of the Rhine until well after the end of Roman rule in Gaul. One of the best preserved vessels of the period is a fourth-century vessel found in the Nydam bog near Schleswig, about eighty kilometers north of Kiel. The twenty-two-meter-long hull has thole pins for thirty oars and was steered with a quarter rudder, but there is no evidence of either mast or rigging. The layout of the shell-first, lapstrake Nydam boat conforms to a first-century description of Germanic vessels by Tacitus: "The shape of their ships differs from the normal [that is, Roman] in having a prow at each end, so that they are always facing the right way to put into shore. They do not propel them with sails, nor do they fasten a row of oars to the sides. The rowlocks are movable, as one finds them on some river-craft, and can be reversed, as circumstances require, for rowing in either direction."

The Nydam boat may represent the kind of vessel in which the Angles, Saxons, and Jutes crossed the North Sea to Britain in the fourth and fifth centuries. Although such a large-scale, long-distance migration under oars alone would have been challenging, large vessels powered solely by oars were still being used in England in the seventh century as we know from the remains of the Sutton Hoo ship. When excavated in 1939, the twenty-seven-meter-long clinker hull no longer existed, because in reacting with the soil its timbers and iron fastenings had dissolved, leaving clear casts, traces, and impressions of their form and placement, and even evidence of repairs. The ship was manned by twenty-eight rowers but although there is no evidence of a mast or sail, the hull shape and construction details like a keel suggest that it could have been rigged, and a half-scale model built in 1993 demonstrated excellent sailing ability. Regardless of whether the Sutton Hoo ship was rigged, it clearly belongs to the transitional phase in northwest European shipbuilding that led to the ships of the Viking age.

Written and visual depictions of Viking-era ships are no more detailed than Oddr Snorrason's descriptions of the *Ormr inn Langi* and *Járnbarðinn* at the battle of Svold but the rich archaeological record makes up for this: more than twenty ships from the critical ninth and tenth centuries have been excavated across an area running from Oslofjord to the coast of Jutland and eastward to the Vistula. The Vikings had a variety of vessels for both warfare and general use, although merchantmen and warships had several features in common. Like the Nydam and Sutton Hoo vessels, the double-ended hulls were of shell-first, clinker construction and steered with a single quarter rudder, and relatively flat bottoms allowed them to be run up on shore. The incorporation of a keel made it possible to rig a mast and square sail; yet while sailing was useful on long passages, when maneuvering inshore or against fickle winds, or going into battle, rowing was imperative. Unlike warships, which were generally open-hulled throughout, *knarrs* and other merchantmen were decked forward and aft, where the rowers sat, with a break amidships in which were crowded the passengers and cargo, everything from food and tools to trade goods and livestock, including sheep, cattle, and horses, which were routinely carried by ship. The Norse introduced horses to Iceland, and for his invasion of England, William embarked two or three thousand knights who would have traveled with the same number of warhorses in ships of similar design.

Among the earliest and most aesthetically dramatic Viking-era ship finds are the Norwegian Oseberg ship (21.6 meters by 5.1 meters broad), built around 815–20 and excavated in 1904, and the Gokstad ship (23.3 meters by 5.2 meters), unearthed from a burial mound in 1880 and dated to about 890–95. Once considered archetypes of the longship (*langskip*), these are now believed to be *karvi*, a type smaller than either the longship or the merchant's *knarr*. Both ships were rigged, and the Oseberg ship is the oldest northern Scandinavian ship for which there is indisputable evidence of a sail. As was typical of Viking ships, shields could be fastened to racks that ran above the single row of oarports on either side of the Oseberg and Gokstad hulls. That they were found in burial mounds suggests they probably belonged to a chieftain or other important personage, as did the Sutton Hoo ship.

Of slightly later date are five ships scuttled off Skuldelev to block the approaches to Roskilde, Denmark, during the wars between Harald Hardradi and Svein III. The fragmentary remains have been identified as belonging to two *knarrs* (Skuldelev 1 and 3), two warships (Skuldelev 2 and 5), and a fishing boat (Skuldelev 6), which date from between 930 and 1030.[*] The newest and best-preserved vessel, Skuldelev 3, was fourteen meters long and could carry about five tons with a crew of five to nine people. With a capacity of fifteen to twenty tons, the sixteen-meter Skuldelev 1 was probably built in Norway and is the sort of ship that would have been used for overseas trading. Skuldelev 5, "the small warship" (seventeen meters), and Skuldelev 2 are notable for their roughly 7-to-1 length-to-beam ratio, much narrower than the 4-to-1 ratio of

---

[*] The remains originally identified as Wreck 4 turned out to be part of Wreck 2. This was not discovered until later, and the fourth and fifth ships have always been known as Wrecks 5 and 6.

The Gokstad ship of 895 is a large clinker-built karvi *intended for ocean sailing. Built primarily of oak, the hull measures twenty-three meters by five meters and could carry about sixty-five people. The ship was found in a burial mound near Sandefjord, Norway, with three smaller boats, a bed, cooking implements, and twelve horses, six dogs, and other animals. Courtesy of the Vikingskipshuset, Oslo.*

the other ships. Vessels of comparable design seem to have been copied from the Baltic to Normandy and Ireland, where the thirty-meter-long Skuldelev 2 was built. The bottom planks of both warships have been worn thin from being run up on beaches. Skuldelev 2 is the longest Viking ship yet found and although the total number of oars is unknown, its complement has been estimated at between fifty and a hundred men. The Icelandic sagas indicate that ships with between thirteen and twenty-three pairs of oars were considered longships, and the Skuldelev 2 would have been at the bigger end of the spectrum.

Those that carried more than twenty-five pairs were called "great ships," the most celebrated of which is Olaf Tryggvason's *Ormr inn Langi*. As described in Oddr's twelfth-century *Saga of Olaf Tryggvason*, the massive ship was built near

Trondheim and the slip where it was laid down was still visible in Oddr's day: "seventy-four ells [thirty-six meters] long, not counting the raised portions at stem and stern." Ships built for the king were sumptuously decorated, and Olaf "had the ship painted all sorts of colors, then had it gilded and adorned with silver. On the prow of the ship there was a dragon head." The ships in Svein Forkbeard's expedition to England were more lavish still. "On one side lions moulded in gold were seen on the ships, on the other side . . . dragons of various kinds poured fire from their nostrils. Here there were glittering men of solid gold or silver nearly comparable to live ones, there bulls with necks raised high and legs outstretched were fashioned leaping and roaring like live ones." Such embellishment was intended to exalt the king and terrify the enemy. Of greater utility, though still ornamental, were wind vanes and on Svein's ships carvings of "birds on the tops of the masts indicated by their movements the winds as they blew."

Fewer ship remains survive from the east, where there is no indication that the Varangian Rus influenced the construction of native Slav craft, which were built for rivers rather than seas. According to Constantine VII, as part of the tribute due their Kievan overlords, the Slavs built logboats called *monoxylon* ("single wood"), which could be easily portaged around the ten sets of rapids that interrupted a seventy-kilometer stretch of the Dnieper below Dnipropetrovs'k. *Monoxyla* could also be rigged; traders would put in to the river in June and when they reached the Black Sea, fitted "such tackle as is needed, sails and masts and rudders, which they bring with them," before following the coast to the ports of the Bulgar Empire and the Bosporus. *Monoxyla* were adequate for trade, but they were no match for the Byzantine fleet with its larger ships, better organization, and superior weapons. Nor did the Rus ever develop a blue-water naval capability either on the Black Sea, where they exercised little power, or on the Baltic, where their trade was carried by others.

As the eleventh century drew to a close, the unfettered spirit of the Viking age was clearly spent. Except in Iceland, local chieftains were incapable of maintaining their autonomy against increasingly centralized monarchies and urban centers. While the Norman Conquest of 1066 is often taken as the end of the Viking age, that date applies only to England and France. An event of comparable significance in the east would be the death of Yaroslav the Wise in 1054, after which Kievan Rus adopted an increasingly Byzantine orientation. Coincidentally, this is also the date of the east-west schism in the Christian Church. Iceland was independent from 1000 to 1264, when it was brought under the Norse crown, and in the fifteenth century the Orkney and Shetland

Islands passed from Norse to Scottish control and the Greenland settlements died out.

Extensive though the Vikings' trade was, virtually all of it was in prestige, luxury, or highly specialized items and in this respect it was not unlike that of the Frisians and others who preceded them. With few exceptions there was virtually no bulk commerce in northern Europe before the eleventh century. Farmers lacked the surplus capacity for an export trade and the only agricultural products shipped in bulk with any frequency were wine, that of Burgundy and the Seine being shipped via river and coastal waters to the Rhine delta, and wool. The bulk trades characteristic of the maritime commerce of the later Middle Ages—in grain, fish, and wood, as well as wine—were all but unknown. When population and agricultural and artisanal output began to expand, trade was organized around guilds and free associations of merchants whose use of bigger ships of distinctly novel design forced radical changes in the organization of maritime transportation and the conduct of war at sea. Such adaptations were by no means unique to western Eurasia, and similar approaches to long-distance trade could be found in southern India from where they spread across the Monsoon Seas.

Chapter 10

The Silk Road of the Seas

The history of Eurasia in the seventh and subsequent centuries is dominated by the advent of the Muslim caliphates and the resurgence of a unified China, and understandably so. Within little more than a hundred years, Islam was the dominant religion across an arc of Asia and Africa from Portugal to Kazakhstan and the Indus. In Central Asia it butted up against the western border of Tang China, whose armies had simultaneously pushed the Middle Kingdom's borders west across two thousand miles of desert and steppe. Yet at the very moment of immediate contact, upheaval within the *Dar al-Islam* and in China directed merchants' attention away from the silk road across Central Asia to the silk road of the sea. Bustling maritime markets at either end of this maritime trade route from Southwest to Northeast Asia drew merchants and mendicants from around the Monsoon Seas and helped give their respective empires a cosmopolitan flourish. Segments of this commercial network had been in place for hundreds of years, but by the seventh century, mariners on the Monsoon Seas were gaining ever more confidence and expanding the scope of their voyaging, and local rulers in whose territories they stopped, such places as Srivijaya and the Chola kingdom, were able to amass the wealth and prestige necessary to build durable and influential states of their own. So was born a virtuous circle in which the transmission of goods and culture benefited local and regional rulers whose more powerful and stable states in turn drew the attention of merchants from ever greater distances.

Muslim Mariners in the Indian Ocean

At the start of the seventh century, Southwest Asia was divided between the Byzantine and Sasanian Empires. The Byzantines controlled most of Asia Minor, the Levant, and Egypt, while the Sasanians ruled Iran, Iraq, and parts of eastern Asia Minor. On the Arabian Peninsula they controlled the adjacent mainland territory of al-Bahrayn as well as the island of Bahrain and the coast from Kuwait to Qatar; Oman, at the southeast corner of the peninsula; and Yemen, with its port of Aden on the Arabian Sea. Other parts of Arabia lay beyond the reach of imperial rule—the Hejaz, which borders the Red Sea and includes the holy cities of Mecca and Medina; Hadramawt, on the south coast between Yemen and Oman; and Yamana, an inland territory in northern Arabia. Islam's advance in the east mirrored its westward expansion in speed and extent. In 634, Muslim armies took the great Syrian trading city of Damascus, which became the capital of the caliphate for more than a century, and Persia was conquered in 643, a year after the capture of Alexandria. By the start of the Umayyad Caliphate in 661, Islam held sway across the Arabian Peninsula, Mesopotamia, and eastern Asia Minor, and Muslim armies had advanced into the Caucasus Mountains. East of the Caspian Sea, between 694 and 714 al-Hajjaj ibn Yusuf ath-Thaqafi, viceroy of al-Iraq, campaigned into Afghanistan and across the Amu Darya (Oxus River) to the Syr Darya, about 325 kilometers to the north, and many of the Persian and Turkic people of Transoxiana (the heart of modern Uzbekistan) began converting from Zoroastrianism, Buddhism, and Christianity to Islam. Transoxiana was a commercially and strategically important region through which the western approaches to the silk road passed en route to Kashgar and the Taklimakan Desert, where they merged with routes from Afghanistan and India. At midcentury, Muslim expansion into Central Asia slowed. Although Abbasid forces defeated the Chinese at the battle of the Talas River in modern Kazakhstan in 751, Tibetan tribes moving north checked their eastward advance. At the height of their expansionist phase, the Tibetans fought the Chinese and Arabs. Although the Tibetans were eventually contained by Muslim and Chinese armies acting simultaneously, though not in concert, their disruptions forced merchants to exploit more fully the sea routes between the Persian Gulf, India, Southeast Asia, and China.

Muslim armies reached the head of the Persian Gulf in 635, where they established a military encampment at Basra. Within a decade, the Sasanian Empire had fallen, and by the start of the eighth century Islam had spread as far east as the Indus River and its adherents included many Persian and

Omani mariners who carried their new religion with them on trade routes that flourished as the Muslim state consolidated. The increase in trade without an accompanying extension of political authority led to an increase in piracy in the Arabian Sea between the Indus delta and Gujarat. In an effort to restore order, the viceroy al-Hajjaj ordered Muslim armies into the Indian subcontinent in 711, a year before Tariq ibn Ziyad landed at Gibraltar to begin the Muslim conquest of the Iberian Peninsula. Although this could be considered a natural extension of al-Hajjaj's campaign in Transoxiana and Afghanistan, the casus belli was quite specific. According to the ninth-century historian al-Baladhuri,

> the king of the island of Rubies [Sri Lanka] sent to al-Hajjaj some women who were born in his country as Moslems, their fathers, who had been merchants, having died. He wanted to court favour with al-Hajjaj by sending them back. But the ship on which they were sailing was attacked by some of the Meds of ad-Daibul [Banbhore, Pakistan] in barks, and was captured with all that was in it.

Al-Hajjaj authorized a series of punitive expeditions the last of which, led by Muhammad ibn-al-Kasim, was reinforced by "ships laden with men, weapons and supplies." Ibn-al-Kasim conquered the port of Daybul, slew its king, and forced the submission of Sind, an area roughly coterminous with modern Pakistan. Many of the Buddhist inhabitants converted to Islam, and the conquest helped restore order to the shipping routes that skirted northwest India and the coasts of Konkan and Malabar south to Sri Lanka. But Sind would prove the eastern limit of Islam's territorial expansion in South Asia for three hundred years.

Despite their great progress in spreading Islam, the Umayyad caliphs in Damascus suffered the strains of ancient tribal factions overlaid with theological schisms and tensions between Arab Muslims and foreign converts. Tensions were especially acute between Arabs and Persians, whose cultural and imperial identity had far deeper and broader roots than those of anyone else inundated in this first wave of Arab conquest. When a collateral descendant of Muhammad named Abu al-'Abbas as-Saffah rebelled against the Umayyads, troops from northern Persia supported him and he was proclaimed caliph in 749. Abu al-'Abbas established himself at al-Kufah, on the lower Euphrates, but his brother and successor Abu Jafar al-Mansur erected a new Abbasid capital at Baghdad, on the west bank of the Tigris, in 761–62. The transfer of the administrative machinery of state 750 kilometers east of Damascus spelled the end of Syrian predominance in the Muslim world and turned the caliphate's focus from the Mediterranean and North Africa to Central Asia and the Indian Ocean, with enormous repercussions for the trade of the Monsoon Seas.

According to the ninth-century geographer al-Yaqubi, the site of Baghdad had been revealed to al-Mansur, who predicted that it would become "a waterfront for the world. Everything that comes on the Tigris [up] from Wasit, al-Basrah, al-Ahwaz, Faris, Uman, al-Yamanah, al-Bahrayn, and the neighboring places, can go up to it and anchor at it. In the same way whatever is carried on boats on the Tigris [down] from Mosul, Diyar Rabiah, Azerbaijan and Armenia, and whatever is carried on boats on the Euphrates from Diyar Mudar, al-Raqqah, Syria, the Frontier, Egypt and North Africa, can come to this terminus and unload here." A further advantage was that it was easily defended. Two centuries after al-Yaqubi, the geographer al-Muqaddasi recalled the advice given to al-Mansur, which in his rendering noted that Baghdad was "in a place between rivers so that the enemy cannot reach you except by ship, or by bridge, by way of the Tigris or the Euphrates."

Within fifty years of Baghdad's founding the population had swollen to perhaps half a million people, making it the largest city in the world outside China; in the west, its nearest rivals were Constantinople, Alexandria, Damascus, and Basra. The city's swift rise owed much to its location on the Tigris at a point where the river comes to within fifty kilometers of the Euphrates. Here, in central Iraq, it lay astride the continental trade routes between Persia, Central Asia, and India in the east, and Syria, the Mediterranean, and North Africa in the west. The riverbanks were lined with shipping, from round reed *quffas* sent downriver from the hill country around Mosul, to seagoing ships fresh from voyages on the Persian Gulf and the Indian Ocean. Canals provided access to the Euphrates and the western trade, while Baghdad was a terminus of the pilgrim road from Mecca in the southwest. Although the capital was nearly five hundred kilometers upriver from the Persian Gulf, the Tigris did open Baghdad to the trade of the Indian Ocean world. So al-Yaqubi could declare: "This is the Tigris; there is no obstacle between us and China; everything on the sea can come to us on it"—a claim that echoes Sargon's boast about the dock of Akkad, although mariners now sailed farther than Dilmun, Magan, and Meluhha. By the tenth century, Baghdad was possibly the busiest port in the world, while its outports—among which contemporaries counted those of southern Iran and the island of Socotra—were described as "the frontier of India."

Although their prosperity declined in the final decades of the Sasanian Empire, the Persian Gulf ports of Ubulla, Basra, and Siraf remained active in long-distance trade during the transition from Sasanian to Muslim rule. Al-Baladhuri asserts that before the start of the Islamic era Ubulla was preeminent. As one of two capitals of the Umayyad province of Iraq (the other was al-Kufah), Basra quickly eclipsed Ubulla, although its success owed more to politics than geography. The original military camp was on the site of the ancient Charax Spasinou, but it was fifteen kilometers from the Shatt al-Arab and functioned as a port only thanks to a canal that connected it to Ubulla.* Nonetheless, Basra attracted shipping from around the Muslim world and beyond. Well before it became a port of entry for Baghdad, which was founded more than a century later, Basra flourished in its own right and at its peak during the eighth and ninth centuries it was home to more than two hundred thousand people of many faiths and ethnicities, and it was noted for its manufactures, agriculture (dates in particular), and its vibrant literary, artistic, and religious communities.

Basra's primary rival was Siraf, on the Persian shore about 375 miles from the head of the gulf. Founded by the fourth-century Sasanian king Shapur II, Siraf had a spacious roadstead that accommodated deeper-draft ships more easily than the ports of the northern gulf, but it was situated in an otherwise hostile environment subject to extreme heat and lacking sufficient water to sustain a large population, much less agriculture. The latter problem was overcome by the construction of cisterns and freshwater canals that fed luxuriant gardens cultivated by the wealthy merchant elite, which prospered from the trade of Baghdad and of Shiraz, the capital of the Persian province of Fars 225 kilometers to the northeast. The port's praises were sung by geographers and historians throughout the Abbasid era, and with good reason: its merchants could be found sailing as far as China, while they imported teak and other woods from India and East Africa for constructing houses, mosques, ships, and navigation towers called *khashabs*. Comparing Siraf with Shiraz, the tenth-century Persian geographer al-Istakhri noted, "Siraf nearly equaled Shiraz in size and splendour; the houses were built of teakwood brought from the Zanj country [East Africa] and were several stories high, built to overlook the sea."

The Abbasids blazed brilliantly for barely a century before rebels and autonomous governors on the periphery of the caliphate began challenging Baghdad's rule. Closer to home, the caliphate faced dissent across the social spectrum, from merchants to slaves. As in many states with a substantial slave population, the caliphates were plagued by uprisings. The earliest revolts occurred in the 680s, but Zanj unrest culminated in a fourteen-year insurrection (869–883) that began as a revolt rooted in economic grievance but quickly metastasized into an assault on the authority of the caliph in which hundreds of thousands—more than half a million in some estimates—died. The Zanj received support from Persian Gulf merchants who resented the caliphate's interference in their trade. Together they seized Ubulla, Abadan, and, in 871, Basra, the fall of which was the government's biggest defeat. Basra's loss bene-

---

* The modern port of Basra was founded on the site of Ubulla in the 1700s.

fited Siraf, Suhar, and other ports over which the Abbasids exerted only nomi-nal control—and sometimes none at all—and which were quick to capitalize on Baghdad's weakness.

In the tenth century, the Abbasid caliphs were reduced to the status of pup-pets under the political control of Persian Shiite emirs called Buyids who exer-cised almost absolute power at Baghdad and along both shores of the Persian Gulf. The rise of the Buyids coincided with the Fatimids' relocation from Ifriqiya to Cairo and the ensuing revival of the Red Sea trade, which had been secondary to that of the Persian Gulf since the end of Byzantine Egypt. In 976, Siraf was wracked by a weeklong series of earthquakes. This was not a defining event in and of itself, but it was a portent of the gulf's commercial decline. Seljuq Turk invaders from Central Asia captured Shiraz in 1062 but established their capital at Isfahan, 750 kilometers north of Siraf, and took little interest in maritime trade. Unrest in southern Persia, the consequent emergence of a pirate state on the island of Kish in the Strait of Hormuz, and the continued growth of the Red Sea ports under the Fatimids all conspired to make the Persian Gulf less attractive to merchants.

At first blush it seems paradoxical that the Muslim capture of Egypt in the seventh century did not lead to an increase in traffic on the Red Sea, apart from the pilgrim and grain trade to Mecca. The Nile and Red Sea had been vital avenues for exchange between the Mediterranean and the Indian Ocean since antiquity, but the establishment of Baghdad made the Persian Gulf the primary terminus of trade from the western Indian Ocean. Such commerce as flowed through the Red Sea before the Fatimid revival was in the hands of Persian Gulf mariners frequenting Jeddah and Aden where by the ninth century one could find "all the merchandise of Sind, Hind, China, Zanzibar, Abyssinia, Fars [Persia], Basra, Jiddah, and Kulzum." In 646 the Orthodox caliph Uthman had designated Jeddah as the port of Mecca, about seventy-five kilometers to the southeast. Surrounded by salt flats and reefs through which ships can enter only via a narrow entrance, Jeddah was nonetheless one of the most important harbors in the Muslim world, especially during the hajj, when the bulk of grain and other supplies for the pilgrims—and in some periods a majority of the pilgrims themselves—came by sea via Qulzum (the ancient Clysma, now Suez). It was also a major entrepôt for goods bound to or from Egypt because it was more dangerous and less profitable for Indian Ocean ships to sail north of Jeddah. Red Sea traffic increased with the rejuvenation of Egypt's commercial prosperity, and again after the Seljuqs captured the Sinai in the 1060s. With the normal overland route from North Africa to Mecca impassable, prospective hajjis traveling via Egypt embarked on a three-stage journey that took them by boat up the Nile to Qus or Aswan, where they joined a camel caravan that took three weeks to reach the humble port of Aydhab, which had a permanent population of only about five hundred. Aydhab's shipmasters charged extortionate fares for the 150-mile passage to Jeddah as well as for any provisions pilgrims might be forced to buy. But the Aswan–Aydhab–Jeddah route remained practicable until the first Mamluk sultan of Egypt overthrew the crusader states of Palestine and in 1267/68 reopened the Sinai route to Mecca.

East Africa

So long as Baghdad remained the primary market of the western Indian Ocean, the Red Sea functioned as a branch line for Persian Gulf shipping. Even though one could find a wealth of merchandise in Aden, much of this passed through Persian Gulf ports first. This was true even of goods from the nearby coasts of East Africa. Persian Gulf trade with East Africa was not a new endeavor, but starting no later than the eighth century there was a concerted push south of the Horn of Africa, where Islam began to exert a definite though limited influence. After their foray across the Red Sea into Yemen in the sixth century, the kings of Aksum had abandoned their maritime aspirations and Omani traders from Siraf and Suhar gradually assumed their role on the African coast north of the Horn of Africa. By the eighth century they were settled on the island of Socotra, which they used as a staging ground for trading and raiding beyond the Horn. Omanis and their Persian and Arab followers initially confined themselves to the relatively protected archipelagoes and offshore islands scattered along the coasts of Kenya and Tanzania, and even after settling on the mainland they did not penetrate the interior to any significant degree. Many of their ports were temporary in nature, or at least constructed of perishable materials, and most of the permanent towns established after the turn of the millennium were no more than a few kilometers from the sea.

Physical structures from the first three centuries of the Muslim presence in East Africa may have been impermanent, but many sites nonetheless reached impressive size—as much as twenty hectares (fifty acres) in some cases—and formed the basis for cities still thriving today: Mogadishu in Somalia; the ports of Kenya's Lamu archipelago; the Tanzanian islands of Pemba, Zanzibar, and Kilwa; and Sofala, Mozambique, which was the coastal terminus of the gold trade from Zimbabwe and effectively the southwest limit of Indian Ocean shipping until the arrival of the Portuguese at the end of the fifteenth century. While they owed their overseas connections to Muslim merchants, these sites were originally settled and continued to be dominated by African Swahili speakers who by the eighth century had spread south along a two-thousand-kilometer stretch of the coast from Kenya to Mozambique, and who were established in the Comoros archipelago in the ninth and tenth centuries. Despite a long-standing belief that Swahili culture was indelibly marked by Arabic and Islamic influences from an early date, these were absorbed by rather than imposed upon the Swahili, who evolved a complex society that mediated between foreign and local African traditions. Part of the confusion has to do with the very word "Swahili," which comes from the Arabic *sawahil,* meaning "coast." However, Swahili is a Bantu language with a limited Arabic vocabulary—chiefly specialist religious, commercial, and nautical terms— most of which entered the language between the seventeenth and nineteenth centuries, when the Omani Empire included part of coastal East Africa.

Among the earliest Swahili sites thus far excavated is at Shanga, where finds of Persian ceramics show that Muslim sailors were visiting by the end of the eighth century. The town prospered and by the eleventh century it was the site of a Friday mosque and other structures built with coral and stone rather than more perishable wood and thatch. Of slightly later date is the town of Kilwa, on an island that measures four by six kilometers in an enclosed bay on the Tanzanian coast. Kilwa reached its apogee between the late twelfth and sixteenth centuries, but excavations have revealed articles of Arabo-Persian and Chinese provenance (the latter shipped by way of Persian Gulf ports) dating from the ninth century. According to the sixteenth-century *Kilwa Chronicle,* the city was founded by Ali ibn al-Husayn, the son of a sultan of Shiraz. Sailing in seven ships, al-Husayn, his five brothers, and his father established themselves in seven locations in the Comoros and on the mainland opposite the Lamu archipelago, which al-Husayn is said to have bartered from a mainland ruler for some cloth. The story of al-Husayn echoes legends explaining the establishment of Mogadishu and the migration of Persians to India's Konkan Coast in the eighth century. Whatever its veracity, the story was probably half a millennium old when it was written down: finds at Kilwa include eleventh-century coins bearing the name of al-Husayn and his successors. Nor were members of al-Husayn's family the first people to reach the Comoros. Initially settled by Malagasy speakers from Madagascar, the archipelago grew in importance because it lay about midway between northern Mozambique and Madagascar and astride the offshore route between Sofala and Kilwa, the broad eastern arc of which was dictated by the prevailing winds and currents. In addition to the regular traffic between the Persian Gulf and Africa, there was direct trade between Srivijaya and East Africa and possibly Madagascar. Here Srivijayan merchant sailors were said to be "welcomed hospitably and conduct a lucrative trade . . . because each understands the other's language," because Malagasy derives from the Austronesian language of the island's first settlers.

Exports from East Africa were varied but consisted chiefly of natural resources, principally gold, mangrove wood, tortoiseshell, iron for Indian metalsmiths, and ivory. Imports are harder to determine until the ninth century, when Chinese ceramics and glass were added to the manifest of Muslim and Indian merchants. Because these are less perishable than organic materials, it is easier to trace their distribution through time and space, which is one reason the history of East Africa comes into comparatively clear focus at this time. Yet there was another less heralded mainstay of Indian Ocean commerce: the trade in enslaved Africans. There were already enough slaves in Iraq to mount a rebellion in the seventh century, but the traffic in slaves shot up in the ninth century. Between 850 and 1000 CE, slavers shipped an estimated 2.5 million black Africans from south of the Horn of Africa, which in time was called the Cape of Slaves. Another 10 million followed before 1900. The Indian Ocean slave trade has received less scrutiny than its later Atlantic counterpart, partly for want of written records, and partly because of differing attitudes toward slaves and the slave trade in Asia. Unlike in European societies, slaves in the Muslim world had broad legal rights and could hold high office, earn money, and own property, even while being the property of someone else. They could purchase their freedom and marry other slaves or free persons. Initially, at least, the degree of racial prejudice associated with slavery was less in the Islamic world than elsewhere, and Islam forbade the enslavement of Muslims and *dhimmis*— "protected people," as Christians, Jews, Zoroastrians, and other recipients of divine scripture were called. Nevertheless, black Muslims were routinely enslaved, a fact about which African rulers and Muslims jurists complained, just as African Christians would later complain about their treatment at the hands of European Christians.

Hardly any documentation about the medieval East African slave trade exists, but we do know of a few individuals who rose to high rank—one ruled Egypt, first as regent and then in his own right—and writers did record unintended consequences of the trade like the Zanj rebellions. A unique source for the trade per se is the story of an unnamed African ruler and an Omani merchant named Ismail ibn Ibrahim ibn Mirdas. In 922, Ismail was en route to Pemba Island when he was forced south of his destination. Landing near Sofala, he and his crew began bartering with the locals—"a trade that was excellent for us, without any hindrances or customs duties," so common in the rest of the Indian Ocean world. When the trading was completed, the local king boarded the ship to see off the merchants. "When I saw them there," recalled Ismail, "I said to myself: In the market in Oman this young king would certainly fetch thirty dinars, and his seven companions sixty each. Their clothes alone are worth not less than twenty dinars. One way and another this would give us a profit of at least 3,000 dirhams, and without any trouble."* So he bundled the king and his retainers in with the two hundred slaves already aboard his ship and sailed for home. The king was sold at Oman, which would be the end of the story were it not for the fact that several years later Ismail fetched up again near Sofala only to find himself before his erstwhile prisoner.

Recounting his adventures to the justifiably nervous Omani, the unnamed king told how after being sold he lived in Basra and Baghdad, where he converted to Islam. He escaped his owner by joining pilgrims bound for Mecca, from where he continued to Cairo. Determined to return home, he sailed up the Nile and struck out for the coast, where he boarded a vessel that brought him home. Without definite news of his fate, his people had not chosen a successor, so he resumed the throne. "My people listened to the account of my story, and it surprised them, and filled them with joy." More important, he told Ismail, "Like myself, they embraced the religion of Islam. . . . And, if I have forgiven you, it is because you were the first cause of the purity of my religion." Bidding Ismail farewell, the king asked him to "let Muslims know that they may come here to us as to brothers, Muslims like themselves. As for accompanying you to your ship," he observed, "I have reasons for not doing so." The king's refusal to avenge his kidnapping on Ismail testifies to his reverence for his new faith, but as his penultimate remarks reveal, his people's adoption of Islam had a practical side and they could promote their new faith in the same way a business might post a sign saying "Arabic spoken here."

The story of Ismail and the king comes from the *Book of the Wonders of India*, a remarkable collection of 136 stories gathered from friends and acquaintances by a Persian merchant named Buzurg ibn Shahriyar. Buzurg names twenty-five of his informants, who are collectively responsible for half the stories, Ismail being the source of six. Twenty-six of the datable stories take place between 908 and 953, and the oldest dates from the reign of Harun al-Rashid at the turn of the ninth century. Some of them relate fantastic or highly embellished events or miracles similar to those associated with Sinbad the Sailor in *The Arabian Nights*, but many reflect the ordinary interests of merchants everywhere. Most of Buzurg's informants hail from Suhar, Siraf, or Basra, and although they relate adventures and mishaps from East Africa, Jeddah, and Aden to China, the destinations mentioned most often are in India and Sri Lanka. For this reason the compilation is an invaluable mirror of medieval Arab and Persian commerce on the Monsoon Seas. Merchants lucky and hapless, navigators with a sixth sense for the weather, and survivors

---

* The dirham was a silver coin weighing less than 3 grams; the dinar was a gold coin of 4.25 grams.

of shipwreck account for the bulk of the more sober narratives. A brief tale told by Ismail, for instance, recounts how he sailed from the Malay Peninsula to Shihr, on the coast of central Yemen, and after beating off sixty-six pirate boats completed the three-thousand-mile passage in forty-one days. His cargo was worth six hundred thousand dirhams, not including the goods the sultan of Oman exempted from duty or those that "escaped the customs and were not discovered"—in a word, smuggled. Buzurg never moralizes, which imparts a chilling quality to his stories: about a shipwrecked girl raped by a sailor as she clings to flotsam while the narrator looks on; Indian suicides who hire people to drown them; and slaves, who except for Ismail's unnamed king are enumerated with complete indifference, a hundred in this ship, two hundred in that. But it is this matter-of-fact quality that anchors these stories in the experience of their intended audience, deep-sea mariners with little use for nostalgia.

The Way East

Sasanian mariners began making the six-thousand-mile passage to China beginning in the second century, and before the start of the Islamic era Ubulla, at the head of the Persian Gulf, was renowned as "the port to al-Bahrain, Uman, al-Hind [India] and as-Sin [China]." Their role in this long-distance trade is noted in accounts of three Buddhists who traveled no farther west than the east coast of India. In 673, a Chinese monk named Yijing made his way to Guangzhou, where he "fixed the date of meeting with the owner of a Persian ship to embark for the south." Four decades later, the Indian Vajrabodhi sailed for China from the Pallava kingdom in southern India. Stopping in Sri Lanka— doubtless at Mantai, the premier South Asian port of call for traffic between Persia and China—their ship joined a fleet of thirty Persian vessels, each with a complement of five to six hundred people and cargoes of precious stones, among other things. The commercial orientation of Persian seafarers is also the subject of an observation by a Korean Buddhist named Huichau, who after sailing to India in around 725 described the merchants from the Persian Gulf:

> The inhabitants being by nature bent on commerce, they are in the habit of sailing in big craft on the western sea, and they enter the southern sea to the country of the Lions [Sri Lanka], where they get precious stones, for which reason it is said of the country that it produces precious stones. They also go to the Kunlun country [Southeast Asia] to fetch gold. They also sail in big craft to the country of Han, straight to [Guangzhou] for silk piece goods and the like ware.

The oldest secular account of the passage from the Persian Gulf is provided by a Sirafi merchant named Sulayman al-Tajir, who traded in China around 850. Because the largest ships could not reach the head of the Persian Gulf, on the first stage of the journey east, "the goods are carried to Siraf from al-Basra, 'Uman and other [ports], and then they are loaded on the Chinese boats at Siraf. This is because the waves are abundant in this sea and the water is at a low [level] in some places." ("Chinese boats" refers not to ships built in or from China, but to those that traded to China, in the same way that nineteenth-century European and American square-riggers in the tea trade were referred to as China clippers.) The first port of call was at Masqat on the Musandam peninsula, where crews topped up their water before sailing direct to Kulam Malay (Quilon, India), a month away. Here ships bound for China paid duties of a thousand dirhams. After rounding India and Sri Lanka they called in the Nicobar Islands, again for water, although there was also a small-scale trade in ambergris, which the natives exchanged for iron. They next sailed to Kalah (probably Takuapa, on the west coast of the Malay Peninsula below the Kra Isthmus) and then south to Sumatra. Once through the Strait of Malacca, the ships might call at the Buddhist kingdom of "Zabaj" (Srivijaya) or sail directly across the South China Sea to southern Vietnam or Guangzhou. By Sulayman's time, Persian Gulf mariners seem to have stopped trying to make the entire six-thousand-mile passage to China in one ship. Major changes taking place along the length of the sea route made breaking the trip in South Asia more worthwhile than it had been.

One reason that Muslim expansion into India stalled after the capture of Daybul in the eighth century is that the subcontinent was undergoing a major political realignment that saw the rise of a number of powerful kingdoms, some founded on territorial expansion, others on overseas trade. The number of sixth-century Indian dynasties and kingdoms is almost incalculable; the borders of even the most enduring were mutable; and the incomplete historical record shows that many were short-lived. By the start of the seventh century, however, central and southern India were dominated by the dynasties of the Chalukyas, whose origins lay in Karnataka in the southwest, and the Pallavas in the southeast. Under Pulakeshin II, the Chalukyas conquered the Konkan Coast between the Gulf of Khambhat and modern Goa, and sent a fleet of a hundred ships against a place called Puri, possibly Elephanta Island in the harbor of modern Mumbai. Crossing the Narmada River into north India, the Chalukyas marched east to Orissa and Andhra Pradesh, and having spanned the subcontinent, Pulakeshin was known as "lord of both the eastern and the western seas." He next attacked the Pallavas to the south, who were heavily invested in the long-distance trade of the Bay of Bengal and who

A tenth-century stone carving of a boat from the Pala kingdom in northeast India. The upturned stern is an unusual feature in vessels of the Indian Ocean, but the pavilion near the center of the boat probably houses someone of political or ritual importance. Courtesy of the Victoria and Albert Museum, London.

clashed repeatedly with the Chalukyas. The struggle for control of southern India swung back and forth for more than a century and embroiled the smaller southern Indian kingdoms of the Pandyas and Cheras, and the kings of Sri Lanka.

Contemporary with the start of the Abbasid Caliphate in the mid-eighth century, two major powers emerged in northern India, the Rashtrakuta Dynasty founded by a Chalukya general, and the Buddhist Palas of Bengal and the eastern Ganga valley. Pala rule continued until the Muslim conquest in the thirteenth century, when Buddhism was virtually eliminated from the land of its origin, but in the meantime the Palas exerted a pronounced influence on Buddhist practice in Southeast Asia and China, where the religion continued to flourish. To the southwest, the Rashtrakutas forged one of India's most extensive and wealthiest empires, which controlled the western coast of the subcontinent as far south as Kerala. Much of its wealth came from the commerce that flowed through ports in Gujarat and Konkan, which were home to communities of Persian and Arab Muslim traders as well as Jews, Nestorian Christians, Buddhists, and Jains.

Plying the old Sasanian routes to India, Sri Lanka, Southeast Asia, and China, Muslim traders from Arabia and the Persian Gulf planted the faith and customs of their lands and tribes of origin—Persian or Arab, Omani, Hadrami, or Yemeni—and established expatriate communities notable for the accommodations they struck with their host rulers and each other. Muslim trading communities along the Konkan Coast between Khambhat and Saymur (modern Chaul, south of Mumbai) were quite large and had considerable autonomy. Tenth-century Saymur had a population of about ten thousand *bayasira*, people born in India of Muslim parents, as well as first-generation merchants and settlers from Oman, Siraf, Basra, and Baghdad. Their communal leader served at the pleasure of the Rashtrakuta king and was presumably responsible for the appointment of port authorities and other officials who looked after Muslims' affairs. Among them were a number of people identified as *nauvittaka*, "one whose wealth (*vitta*) lies in his (possessing) ships or *nau.*" Some of these officials were specifically exempted from paying the customs dues and tolls normally owed the king.

Islam was also transplanted farther south to the Malabar Coast of Karnataka and Kerala and to Sri Lanka.[*] Caste restrictions prevented intermarriage between Muslim merchants and anyone except low-caste Hindu wives, with whom they often contracted "temporary marriages." The offspring of these unions were known as Mappila, from the Malayalam meaning "big children," and in time this was the name applied to the community of mestizo Muslims as a whole, which survived until well after the arrival of the Portuguese in the sixteenth century. Muslims were by no means the first expatriate communities established in India, where they were preceded by the Greek and Roman Yavanas of antiquity, and subsequently by Jews, Nestorian Christians, and Zoroastrian Persians. A seventeenth-century English merchant preserved a story about how a group of Persian refugees emigrated to India to escape Muslim persecution. As in the foundation narrative preserved in *The Kilwa Chronicle*, the Persians are said to have taken a fleet of seven ships from the Persian Gulf and settled at Swaley, Surat, and Khambhat, in each place making a treaty with the local raja explaining why they had come and begging leave "to be admitted as sojourners with them, using their own law and religion, but yielding themselves in subjection to their government," in other words, to become autonomous subjects of the raja.

---

[*] Malabar is a hybrid of the Dravidian *malai* (mountain) and Persian *bar* (land). Al-Idrisi wrote of "Manibar" in the mid-twelfth century, and the geographer Yakut referred to "Manibar" in 1228. Zhao Rugua called the region "Malimo" (1225), while John of Montecorvino (1293) and Marco Polo (1298) both wrote about "Malabar." The region is known locally as Malayalam or Kerala.

The Chola Kingdom

Muslim influence on the Coromandel Coast was less pronounced. Under Pallava influence, southern India became increasingly Hinduized and there was a steady growth in the number and size of Brahman villages and Hindu temple complexes. This continued under the Chola kingdom of Tamil Nadu, which in the late ninth century became as important to the growth of long-distance trade in the Indian Ocean as the Fatimid Caliphate in Egypt or the Song Dynasty in China. Tamil merchants had a well-articulated approach to commerce and their influence could be found from China to the Red Sea. Traders began their apprenticeship at the age of ten and proceeded by stages to become independent merchants at the age of forty-one. Southern Indian trade was transformed by the simultaneous evolution of town merchant assemblies (*nagarams*), which were involved in regulating trade, and merchant guilds, many of which specialized in specific goods like cloth, oil, or horses. The guilds developed in Karnataka around the turn of the millennium and forged close ties with temples, which were central to the exchange economy. They served as repositories for money in the form of donations that could be lent to guilds (and with greater risk to individuals) at interest, normally 12.5 to 15 percent per year but twice that in some instances. The spread of Hindu institutions led to a decrease in the number of Buddhists and Jains, whose adherents had long been prominent in maritime trade. Nonetheless, the Cholas continued a strategic patronage of Buddhism in deference to traders from Southeast Asia, whose ties with India intensified in the same period. Southeast Asian rulers similarly endowed Hindu temples in southern India, as well as Buddhist monasteries and temples both at home and in India, probably with a view to commercial and political influence as much as for spiritual benefit.

The existence of foreign trading communities became especially important for southern India's overseas trade as an increasingly conservative strain of Hinduism took hold. After the eighth century, the increased attention to the observance of purity rites led to a diminished involvement in overseas trade by Hindus relative to other communities. The difficulties of maintaining caste are evident in Abu Zayd's tenth-century description of the complex, to say nothing of expensive, rituals associated with eating: "There are certain Indians, who never eat two out of the same dish, or upon the same table, and would deem it a very great sin if they should. When they come to Siraf, and are invited by the considerable merchants, [whether they are] a hundred in number, or more or less, they must each have a separate dish, with the least communication with the rest." This is not to say that Hindus forsook the sea entirely or were completely absent from overseas trade. Indian merchants sailed between India and Southeast Asia, and in later centuries *banias*—Hindu merchants—also called at Aden. When the Portuguese reached Malabar in the fifteenth century, they found its foreign trade in the hands of Hindu Chetties from the Coromandel Coast and *banias* from Gujarat, in addition to Malabari and Arab Muslims.

Southern India was famed for its pepper, which had markets both east and west, and was known as a transshipment point for spices from Indonesia. Indian sources are a poor guide to the activities of maritime merchants, but Abu Zayd includes a revealing description of a highly disciplined approach to long-distance seafaring that must have facilitated the expansion of trade along the routes favored by Indian navigators. "There are, among the Indians," he writes, "certain men . . . whose devotion consists in seeking after unknown islands, or such as are newly discovered, there to plant coco-nut trees, and to sink wells of water for the use of ships that sail to those parts." The deliberate establishment of a network of such basic facilities—the versatile coconut tree provided food, wood for ships, leaves for sails, and coir for rope—can only be explained by a need for them and an ability to share accurate navigational instructions with fellow sailors.

Despite the prosperous trade and great distances involved, relations between South and Southeast Asia were not always peaceful. Abu Zayd tells the curious story of a young king of Comorin—the southernmost part of India—who one day announced to his chief advisor: "I am taken with a desire . . . to see before me, in a dish, the head of the mehrage [maharaja] King of Zapage." Word of his intentions reached the king of Zabaj (Srivijaya on Sumatra or Sailendra Java), who decided to punish "this giddy prince" and commanded his ministers "to prepare a thousand ships of middling burthen, and to equip them with all things necessary, arms and ammunition, and to man them with as many of his best forces as they could carry." To conceal his true purpose, the king announced that he intended to call on his tributary subjects. The fleet reached India after "a passage of ten, or twenty days sail, with a very easy gale," and because the king of Comorin and his courtiers "were effeminate creatures who all the day long, did nothing but consult their faces and rub their teeth, eternally with mirrors and tooth-picks in their hands, or carried after them by slaves," they were taken completely by surprise. The giddy prince was captured and executed, and the king of Zabaj "departed for his own territories, and neither did he, or any of his [men], lay hands on the least thing in the kingdom of Komar [Comorin]." But he did send back the king's head as a reminder to his successor. "The news of this action being conveyed to the kings of the Indies and of China, it added to the respect they before had for the mehrage." Even if this story is not strictly true, it was certainly plausible to contemporary audiences and demonstrates the expanding reach of the Malay maritime states of Southeast Asia.

Srivijaya, the Malay Peninsula, and Java

The longest-lived and most influential power in Southeast Asia seems to have been Srivijaya, the name given to a succession of trading states between the seventh and fourteenth centuries, whose core lay in southeastern Sumatra and whose influence expanded from time to time to include parts of the Malay Peninsula and Java. Srivijaya's raison d'être was the gathering flood of traffic that flowed via the Strait of Malacca between the Indian Ocean and Southeast Asia and China. As had been the case in Funan before ships began sailing direct from the Strait of Malacca and across the South China Sea in the fifth century, Srivijaya's prosperity depended on its ability to generate the surplus food, mostly rice, to sustain large communities, especially during the interlude between the monsoons. Reliant though it was on seafarers for its wealth, because of their mobility and frequent contact with potential or actual enemies, native and foreign merchants alike were highly suspect. In a seventh-century curse, the king singles out shippers and traders as "most likely to rebel" and warns that "if you go over [to the enemy], you will be killed by the curse."

By the seventh century, and for several hundred years thereafter, the seat of Srivijayan power seems to have been in the vicinity of modern Palembang, about eighty kilometers up the Musi River from the eastern approaches to the Strait of Malacca. Palembang figures prominently in the accounts of the Chinese Buddhist monk Yijing, who recorded the peregrinations of more than thirty-seven monks, himself included, who had sailed for or from India. His ship left at the start of the winter monsoon and after weathering storms in which "the pair of sails, each in five lengths [of material], flew away, leaving the somber north behind," made its first port of call in Sumatra. Yijing subsequently made his way to Kedah, on the east coast of the Malay Peninsula, before crossing the Bay of Bengal to the mouth of the Ganga via the Andaman Islands, "the land of the Naked People" who "eagerly embarked in little boats, their number being fully a hundred. They all brought cocoa-nuts, bananas, and things made of rattan-cane and bamboos and wished to exchange them. What they are anxious to get is iron only." Yijing does not say whether he was still aboard a Persian ship at this point, and he may well have boarded a Malay or Indian vessel to reach Tamralipti on the Hugli River, a major port of entry into northern India since Mauryan times. Earlier in the century, another

Chinese monk named Xuanzang had described Tamralipti as a flourishing, protected port in "a recess of the sea; the water and the land embracing each other. Wonderful articles of value and gems are collected here in abundance, and therefore the people of the country are in general very rich." From Tamralipti Yijing made his way up the Ganga to the Buddhist monastery complex at Nalanda, which was then home to more than thirty-five hundred monks. He also visited other monasteries, narrowly escaping death from disease and robbers in the process. While the dangers encountered by Yijing and his fellow monks were considerable, they were hardly worse than those encountered by overland travelers, and as his experiences beyond the confines of Nalanda show, peregrinations ashore were neither safer nor more comfortable than travel by sea. Whether merchant or monk, no matter how one traveled to India the journey was arduous.

As important to the east–west trade as Srivijaya were various city-states and stopping places on the Malay Peninsula, notably the east coast states of Panpan and Langkasuka, from the fifth to eighth centuries, and Tambralinga, from the end of the tenth century. These may have been tributary to Palembang from time to time, but for the most part they were autonomous if not fully independent entities. To the west, the mountains come much closer to the sea, which makes agriculture and territorial consolidation more difficult, and alien influence—from India, Srivijaya, or elsewhere—was far less pronounced. Yet it is the west coast that figures most prominently in Arabic sources, which refer repeatedly to places called Kalah, which may have been a generic term for a stopping place where sailors could await a favorable wind, acquire tin (the primary mineral export from the "land of gold"), and make repairs.*

Ambiguity similarly revolves around the name Zabaj, which Arabic authors used for Srivijaya or the Sailendra kingdom on neighboring Java, or both. Separated from Sumatra by the twelve-mile-wide Sunda Strait, Java became a destination for Indian merchants early in the first millennium, and the Javanese state of Heluodan (Ho-lo-tan) sent tribute to China in the fifth century. However, the political history of Java is known only from the establishment of the Hindu Mataram kingdom (732–928) on the Kedu plain of south-central Java. The Kedu plain was the richest center of rice agriculture in the Indonesian archipelago, and its prosperity drew foreign merchants, scholars, and religious figures, especially from India. The people of Mataram adopted many aspects of Indian culture, especially Hinduism and, during the brief eighth-century rule of the Sailendras, Buddhism. During the ninth century, Sailendra

---

* Kalah probably referred to the region of Kedah, Malaysia, except in the ninth century when the name also referred to an island in the vicinity of Takuapa, Thailand, to the north.

authority shifted to Sumatra. On Java, the seat of power moved eastward to
the valley of the Brantas River, a region that combined agricultural productivity with a strategic location astride the principal trade route to the Spice
Islands, nine hundred miles to the east. The Brantas is the only major river of
central Java that flows into the Java Sea, near the modern city of Surabaya, and
it connected the trade of the Indonesian archipelago with Java's agricultural
hinterland. The rise of the lower Brantas region was due to its importance as
an international port of call, and ninth- and tenth-century inscriptions record
the presence of foreigners from Malabar, Sri Lanka, Kalinga, and Bengal in
South Asia, and Angkor, Champa, and what is now Myanmar in mainland
Southeast Asia. Java's growth encouraged expansion and excited envy.

An inscription of the period notes the presence of 135 vessels at a port
in East Java, but the nature of the monsoon meant that buyers and sellers
of spices rarely encountered one another. The winter monsoon that brought
western traders to East Java to purchase spices and exotic woods sent the
purveyors of those goods homeward to the east. Merchants from the Indian
Ocean and China returned home on the summer monsoon, when traders from
eastern Indonesia shipped their goods to East Java to be laid up for the next
season. As a result, foreign writers thought that the spices themselves originated in East Java. Although this was not true, the impression that it was one
of the richest emporia in the world was close to the mark. As a Chinese report
of the late twelfth century puts it, "Of all the wealthy foreign lands which
have great store of precious and varied goods, none surpasses the realm of
the Arabs. Next to them comes Java, while Srivijaya is third. . . . Srivijaya is
an important thoroughfare on the sea routes of the foreigners on their way to
and from [China]."

The wealth that underlay the political power of Srivijayan and Javanese rulers derived from their access to the world's most sought-after spices—cloves,
nutmeg, and mace—from the Spice Islands (Maluku) of eastern Indonesia.
The Spice Islands have had a far greater role in shaping world trade than
their minute size, remote location, small population, and modest selection of
exports would ever suggest. While there is a tendency to think of them as an
influence in world history only as a result of European interest in the fifteenth
century and later, the scent and profit of spices were no less alluring to Asian
merchants for centuries before that. Cloves are the dried buds of the clove
tree, a tropical evergreen native to a handful of volcanic islands in Indonesia's North Maluku Province, the most important being Ternate and Tidore,
which have a combined area of about 220 square kilometers—about a quarter
the size of New York City. Three hundred miles to the south are the ten volcanic Banda Islands, with a combined area of roughly fifty square kilometers,

mere pinpricks in a sea ten thousand times as big. These are home to the nutmeg tree, sought after for its seed, the nutmeg, and the seed's dried husk, mace. Both clove and nutmeg trees are particular about their environment— a traditional saying has it that "nutmegs must be able to smell the sea, and cloves to see it"—and they require careful cultivation. Their spices were sought as much for medicinal as for culinary uses; nutmeg was valued for providing gastrointestinal relief, and perhaps as a mild hallucinogen, while cloves have anesthetic and, purportedly, aphrodisiac properties. The overlords of the islands on which they grew prevented their successful transplantation elsewhere until the sixteenth century, and it was this limited availability that gave Javanese merchants their advantage and in time would lure Europeans to the farthest reaches of Asia. Such were the stakes in the conflicts that engaged kingdoms and lesser states from southern India and Sri Lanka to Sumatra and Java, the Malay Peninsula and mainland Southeast Asia, all of which were also rivals for the profits and prestige that came from trading with China.

While merchants from Java, Srivijaya, and the Malay Peninsula competed for the portion of this trade that passed through the Strait of Malacca, a new contender for supremacy in the region emerged in southern India, where the Cholas embarked on a period of imperial expansion under Rajaraja I. This began with the conquest of the Maldives in 1007, followed by the capture of Sri Lanka, with its all-important port of Mantai. Rajendra I continued his father's policy with a campaign into Bengal, which was known especially for its cotton, "the like of which is not found in any other" kingdom, according to Sulayman al-Tajir. "A piece of this cloth can be passed through the circle of a ring as it is so fine and beautiful." Finished cotton was a staple of the maritime trade to Southeast Asia, where cotton manufacturing became an important craft in its own right, as well as to China. Rajendra next set his sights east and launched a massive raid on Srivijaya and its tributaries in 1025. Sailing from the port of Nagapattinam, more than fifteen hundred miles across the Bay of Bengal, the Cholas attacked a number of places on Sumatra and the Malay Peninsula. According to an inscription from the Chola capital at Thanjavur (Tanjore), Rajendra "dispatched many ships in the midst of the rolling sea and having caught . . . the king of Kadaram" (Srivijaya and its peninsular tributaries) went on to capture or plunder a total of fourteen places. Eleven have been identified with a fair degree of certainty, including Palembang "with the jeweled wicket-gate adorned with the great splendor and the gate of large jewels," Langkasuka "undaunted in fierce battles," Tambralinga "[capable of] strong action in dangerous battles," and Kedah "of fierce strength, which was protected by the deep sea."

Medieval South Asian literature offers few clues about the size or logistics of such long-range operations. The fullest extant account of a naval campaign comes from Dhanapala's tenth-century prose romance, the *Tilakamanjari*, which recounts the story of a Sri Lankan expedition to punish feudatories who withheld taxes and did not come to court when summoned, among other affronts. After extensive military and ritual preparations—offering "oblations to the sea with curd, milk, rice, food, ointment, garlands and ornaments"—the ships were loaded with supplies: water, of course, and "ghee, oil, blankets and medicines and articles which are not available in the Eastern Archipelago." The voyage across the Bay of Bengal was uneventful, but the shouts and murmurs of the landing are recounted in boisterous detail:

> There was noise all around. People began talking. "Sir, give us a little way." "Anga, don't push me." "Mangalaka, pushing others with the elbow does not show your bravery." . . . "Tarangika, run away. Your fat thighs are impeding the entire army." . . . "Brother, while falling down you have unnecessarily broken your thigh bone dashing against the ship. Now you will have to be guided by your servant." . . . The soldiers were talking among themselves. . . . In this way, after everyone had assembled on the shore the atmosphere was filled with a fresh wave of courage.

Once the ships were unloaded, and the camp established—"The site was cleared of bushes. The palace attendants put camps for women. The courtesans also got their tents"—the chief pilot of the expedition, Taraka, took five ships to scout the shallow coastal waters. Again Dhanapala's dialogue rings true as Taraka orders his men to avoid low-lying mangrove trees, rebukes others for grounding in the mud, and generally challenges their fitness for the work at hand: "Adhira, do not be diverted by my talk, proceed steadfastly. Wash your drowsy eyes with salt water. Rajilaka, regardless of my instructions the ship is sailing to the south. It seems that you have forgotten the direction. You do not follow the northern direction even when told." Such literary treatment of maritime expeditions lacks the numerical specificity often found in western or Chinese accounts of comparable undertakings, which in their turn generally omit such intimate, nonheroic perspectives on military campaigns; but the distinct approaches are complementary. Taraka's exasperation is certainly not unique to his command or this campaign, and though left unrecorded, similar expressions of encouragement and frustration were doubtless barked during the Andalusian invasion of Crete, the Norman landings in England, and countless similar missions. Like this one, the few extant accounts of naval activity in the Indian Ocean focus almost exclusively on amphibious operations. While ship-to-ship and fleet engagements were not unknown—especially between pirates and merchants—reports of them are few and imprecise.

The Chola report of the destruction of fourteen Srivijayan cities is admittedly one-sided, but the raids so disrupted normal patterns of trade that the Chinese launched an inquiry into why so few ships from the Nanhai were calling at Guangzhou. Yet the effects were short-lived. Srivijayan envoys returned to China in 1028, and over the rest of the century trade missions from Srivijaya outnumbered those from Java and southern India combined; only Champa (southern Vietnam) and Dashi, "the land of the Arabs," accounted for more. The Cholas were unable to capitalize on Srivijaya's weakness as much as they might have liked, but their attacks did loosen Palembang's hold on more remote ports on the Strait of Malacca and the Malay Peninsula. The Cholas continued to intervene in the affairs of Southeast Asia until the 1060s, when they launched their last military venture across the Bay of Bengal. Shortly after this the emerging Burmese kingdom of Pagan helped Sri Lanka's Vijayabahu I end the Chola occupation of their island. The Burmese may have offered no more than token support, but the Cholas withdrew shortly thereafter, and in 1075 Vijayabahu invited Buddhist monks from Pagan to reconsecrate the temples in his kingdom.

Indian Ocean Ships

The nature of Indian shipbuilding in the medieval period is difficult to assess. Our assumptions about how ships of the Indian Ocean were built are based on a handful of visual representations of negligible precision, a few quotations from written sources, and two archaeological sites. Given that the subcontinent was home to myriad states of great cultural, linguistic, and technological diversity, what is known from one isolated text or archaeological find may have no broader application. Sri Lanka seems to have had the reputation for building the largest ships. According to an early-ninth-century Chinese source, the biggest vessels calling at Annam and Guangzhou were from Sri Lanka and had "stairways for loading and unloading which are several tens of feet in height." The only seagoing vessel of Indian Ocean origin known from the archaeological record, a ship of the same period found off Belitung Island in the Java Sea, was probably of more modest size. Believed to have sunk around 826, it was likely built in the Persian Gulf region using mostly imported African mahogany, with a keelson of *Afzelia bipindensis* (which had to be imported from the region of Zaire, in the interior of Africa) and beams of Indian teak. The Belitung ship probably measured between twenty and twenty-two meters long, with a beam of about eight meters, and a depth of hull of more than three meters. The hull was fastened by discontinuous stitching that passed over the seams between the planks, and it was stiffened by frames stitched directly to the planks, again with the lashings passing through and visible from outside the hull. The woods found in the Belitung ship were of high quality—teak was especially prized for its durability—but other woods were perfectly acceptable in shipbuilding. Abu Zayd describes the coconut tree as the almost perfect commodity for shipwrights and traders alike:

> There are people, at Oman, who cross over to the islands [probably the Maldives] that produce the coco-nut, carrying with them carpenters' and all such like tools; and having felled as much wood as they want, they let it dry, then strip off the leaves, and with the bark of the tree they spin a yarn, wherewith they sew the planks together, and so build a ship. Of the same wood they cut and round away a mast; of the leaves they weave their sails, and the bark they work into cordage. Having thus completed their vessel, they load her with coco-nuts, which they bring and sell at Oman. Thus is it that, from this tree alone, so many articles are convertible to use, as suffice not only to build and rig out a vessel, but to load her when she is completed, and in a trim to sail.

Abu Zayd notes that shipwrights in the Persian Gulf applied a whale-oil preservative to their hulls. Despite the value of whale oil, whaling was a cautious enterprise, probably limited to harpooning already dead whales and towing them to shore where "This oil, mixed up with another kind of stuff, in use with seamen, serves for [preserving] of ships, to secure the seams of the planking, and to stop up leaks." Whale oil was probably the substance of choice, but it was not the only one, and a later visitor to Aden noted that shipwrights there coated their hulls with a compound of lime and animal fat called *nura*.

The primary fastener employed by shipwrights around the Indian Ocean was cordage. According to a passage on ships and shipbuilding in the eleventh-century *Yuktikalpataru*, "iron should not be tied to a sea-going vessel by means of a string because that iron may be attracted with magnetic iron in the sea and may cause danger." A widely accepted interpretation of this passage is that "no iron [should be] used in holding or joining together the plank of bottoms intended to be sea-going vessels, for the iron will inevitably expose them to the influence of magnetic rocks in the sea, or bring them within a magnetic field and so lead them to risks." But magnetic attraction was probably not regarded as a significant problem, for a later passage in the *Yuktikalpataru* refers to "special vessels, made of the foil of iron and copper etc. or of lodestone." Certainly a hull sheathed in "the foil of iron" would be at as much risk from "magnetic iron in the sea" as a hull merely fastened with iron fittings. An injunction against iron also makes little sense given the importance of iron as a cargo in Indian Ocean trade; it was routinely carried between the subcontinent, Arabia, and East Africa, the last of which was the source of most of the iron used in Southwest Asia by the twelfth century.

Only one medieval hull has been found in all of India and it does little to clarify our understanding of shipbuilding traditions on the subcontinent, and especially injunctions against the use of iron. Excavated on the Kerala coast about thirty kilometers south of Cochin in 2002–2003, the Thaikkal-Kadakkarappally boat was a two-masted vessel about twenty-one meters long and four meters in beam. Most unexpected, the planks, which have been dated to between the eleventh and fifteenth centuries, were fastened with clenched nails. The vessel has many other features not normally attributed to Indian Ocean shipbuilding traditions, including a double thickness of planking, and bulkheads inserted into the frames to divide the hull into eleven compartments. Although these features are common to Chinese vessels, the wood is native to Kerala, where the vessel likely spent its working life. If these attributes are not characteristic of indigenous practice in medieval Kerala, they may have been introduced by Chinese sailors who began frequenting southern India during the Song Dynasty (960–1279).

Probably the most significant development traceable to this period is the adoption of a centerline rudder in place of steering oars or quarter rudders mounted on the sides of the hull. Al-Muqaddasi alludes to such a steering system in his account of the tricky navigation in the northern Red Sea, where captains served as their own lookouts. "If a rock should be sighted he cries out: 'To the right!' or, 'To the left!' Two cabin boys are so stationed to repeat the cry. The helmsman has two ropes in hand which he pulls right or left, according to the directions. If they are negligent about this, the ship may strike the rocks, and be wrecked." Much has been made of the development of centerline rudders and the singular problems associated with mounting them to sewn hulls on vessels with tapered sterns, as shown on ships depicted in four eleventh-century hero stones found near Mumbai. Unfortunately, how these rudders are mounted is unclear from the illustrations. The hero stones show one-masted, sewn-plank warships going into battle under oars with archers and spearmen fighting from platforms erected amidships. These do not show any sails, but so far as is known, Indian Ocean ships were rigged with square sails, and there is no evidence of fore-and-aft sails in the western Indian Ocean until the coming of the Portuguese in the sixteenth century.

The best source of information about ships built and sailed in Southeast Asia are the bas-reliefs on the ninth-century Buddhist temple of Borobudur. Built near modern Yogyakarta between 760 and 830, the stupa rises through nine terraces of diminishing perimeter from a base 160 meters square. Borobudur is not only "the largest and most elaborate Buddhist monument" in

One of only a handful of vessels depicted in the nearly five linear kilometers of ninth-century bas-reliefs carved into the walls of Borobudur, the largest Buddhist temple in the world, in central Java. The most distinctive features of the Borobudur ships are the outriggers, which might have been used as platforms for paddlers and barriers against attack rather than for stability. The bipod main- and mizzenmasts set a distinctive type of sail called a layar tanja, *a sort of oblique square sail or lugsail. Quarter rudders are mounted on a large beam that projects from either side of the hull. Courtesy of Ananda-joti Bhikkhu, www.photodharma.net.*

the world, but a unique source of information about Southeast Asian ships: seven are depicted, five ships with outriggers and two smaller vessels without. While the carvings are not overly detailed, they give a good overall impression of how the ships were built and rigged. The five largest carry two bipod masts, each setting a canted rectangular sail. When set in the fore-and-aft position (parallel to the hull) as they are shown at Borobudur, about a third of the boom and yard extended forward of the mast. When running before the wind, the sails could be let out so that they lie forward of the mast perpendicular to the hull, as in a square-rigged ship. In addition, the ships all have bowsprits, and three are shown setting a quadrilateral headsail, one of which may have been canted like the main and foresails. The ships' most distinctive features are the outriggers, which are apparently set on both sides of the hull of the larger ships. Unlike outriggers found on most vessels around the world,

The Samudra Raksa *(Defender of the Seas) was built by traditional shipwrights from the Tanjean Islands north of Bali from a model based on interpretations of five bas-reliefs of ships from the temple at Borobudur on the island of Java. Between August 30, 2003, and February 23, 2004, the ship sailed from Jakarta, Indonesia, to Accra, Ghana. It is now housed in its own museum in the Borobudur Archaeological Park. Courtesy of Nick Burningham.*

these are relatively short, from slightly more than half to three-quarters the length of the hull. Judging from their size, they may have been intended not as stabilizers but as obstacles against enemy boarders. This defensive aspect is confirmed by the hull superstructure, which includes deckhouses amidships with pitched roofs, but the details of which are hidden behind what appear to be protective screens running the length of the ship and intended to shield the crew from attackers.

Improvements to Navigation

This is the first period in which writers began to record the sorts of navigational practices and aids to navigation employed around the Indian Ocean and its subsidiary seas. The best documented were found in the lower reaches of the Tigris and Euphrates, the Shatt al-Arab, and the headwaters of the Persian

Gulf, which were notoriously difficult to navigate, as a succession of writers attest. Two of the most ambitious improvements to navigation dating from the caliphate were the stemming of a whirlpool in the lower Tigris and the erection of light towers. According to Nasir-i Khusraw, who sailed down the Euphrates in a vessel called a *busi* in 1052, the former project was undertaken by a local woman who presumably had a vested interest in safe navigation, perhaps as a shipowner: "They say that once, at the mouth of the Ubulla channel, there was a huge whirlpool that prevented boats from passing but a wealthy lady of Basrah had four hundred boats [perhaps small *quffas*] constructed and filled with date pits. The boats were then tightly sealed and sunk in the whirlpool, and now ships can sail through." Less easily remedied were the shifting sandbars and flats formed by silt deposited by the Tigris and Euphrates, which could only be avoided by prudent seamanship and local knowledge. As the tenth-century geographer al-Istakhri wrote, "In this sea there are many marshes, and difficult narrows, the worst of which is between Jannaba [on the coast of Persia] and Basra at a place called Haur Jannaba, which is a place to be feared and through which scarcely a ship comes unscathed in rough seas."

At some point after this, the route was marked by massive, manned light towers. About a day after passing Abadan, which was effectively an island in the middle of a marsh, Nasir-i Khusraw described how "At dawn something like a small bird could be seen on the sea. [The] closer we approached the larger it appeared." The ship was forced to anchor when the wind changed, and he learned that the structure was an elaborately wrought and finished lighted navigational mark called a *khashab*.

> It consisted of four enormous wooden posts made of teak and was shaped something like a war machine, squarish, wide at the base and narrow at the top. It was about forty ells above the surface of the water and had tile and stone on top held together by wood so as to form a kind of ceiling. On top of that were four arched openings where a sentinel could be stationed. Some said this *khashab* had been constructed by a rich merchant, others that a king had it made. It served two functions: first, that area was being silted in and the sea consequently [was] becoming shallow so that if a large ship chanced to pass, it would strike bottom. At night lamps encased in glass so that the wind would not blow them out were lit for people to see from afar and take precaution, since there was no possibility of rescue. Second, one could know the extent of the land and, if there were pirates, steer the ship away.

These light towers were intervisible, so that the one ahead would come into view as the other was receding astern, and the obvious expense—teak was imported from India—and care that went into their construction testifies to the importance that merchants and local authorities attached to the maintenance of safe navigation.

Although Jeddah, Qulzum, and Aydhab remained regionally important ports in this period, improvements to navigation on the Red Sea were few. Local knowledge was a prerequisite, and at Jeddah goods bound from the Indian Ocean to Egypt were generally put aboard ships from Qulzum, not only because they were smaller and safer than the larger Sirafi ships, but because their captains were better acquainted with the natural and man-made hazards. "Upon the whole coast there are no kings," reports Abu Zayd, "or scarce any inhabited place; and, in fine, because ships are every night obliged to put into some place of safety, for fear of striking upon the rocks; they sail in the day time only, and all the night ride at anchor. This sea, moreover, is subject to very thick fogs, and to violent gales of wind, and so has nothing to recommend it."

The evidence for navigational practice per se comes from scattered references to individuals and their training rather than to the theories and instruments actually employed. Dhanapala's tenth-century *Tilakamanjari* refers to the accomplishments of the expedition's lead pilot, Taraka, whose father was a pilot and who thanks to his own mastery of the nautical sciences became head of the sailors' guild. His first job as an independent shipmaster came only "after studying all technical texts" and he is also described as "well versed in nautical science." Indians were not alone in producing guides to navigation, and the earliest pilot books known by name were written by Persians who sailed in Indian ships around the year 1010. Their works, called *rahmanis* in Arabic—a corruption of the Persian *rah nama* (book of the road)—and their accompanying maps are also mentioned by al-Muqaddasi when he describes researching his treatise, *The Best Divisions for Knowledge of the World* (985). In the course of visiting ports on the Arabian Peninsula from the Red Sea to the Persian Gulf, al-Muqaddasi interviewed countless "shipmasters, cargo masters, coastguards, commercial agents, and merchants—and I considered them among the most discerning of people. . . . I noticed, too, in their possession navigation instructions which they study carefully together and on which they rely completely, proceeding according to what is in them" regarding anchorages, winds, soundings, and courses between ports.

In his fifteenth-century *Book of Profitable Things in the Principles of Navigation*, the Omani navigator Ahmad ibn Majid explains that navigators should be able to track the courses of the sun and moon, determine "the risings and settings of the stars," know distances and routes between ports, and how to use various navigational instruments to determine latitude. "It is also desirable that you should know all the coasts and their landfalls and the various guides such as mud, or grass, animals or fish, sea-snakes and winds. You should consider the tides, and the sea currents and the islands on every route, make sure all the instruments are in order, and inspect the protection afforded the ship and its instruments and its men." Although Ibn Majid's epitome of navigational practice dates from the fifteenth century, he refers to a number of antecedent navigational manuals, the oldest of which are Persian works from the twelfth century, and his recommendations bear comparison with the advice given in the "Suparaga Jataka," as well as late-first-millennium practice in the Mediterranean and northern Europe.

Between the seventh and eleventh centuries, Indian Ocean mariners led the process of integrating the disparate regional markets of the Monsoon Seas between East Africa and the Red Sea in the west, and Southeast Asia and China in the east. In so doing, they laid the foundations for the all but uninterrupted maritime growth of this region that has lasted to the present day. The maritime trade of Monsoon Asia shows many of the hallmarks of what we now call globalization, a process that creates networks of interdependence in which changes in one place can have ripple effects that spread from region to region. The clearest manifestations of this are seen in the rise and shifting fortunes of the Islamic caliphates and the Tang and Song Dynasties, whose wealth exerted powerful forces on the maritime endeavor of the two realms, as well as on other regions from East Africa and India to Southeast Asia and Japan. The resulting interdependency had many positive benefits, facilitating the growth of commerce and its underlying enterprises from agriculture to crafts, and encouraging the spread of religion and technology. At the same time, technological and political change in one place could have a negative impact on another thousands of miles away. Overall, however, the period was one of growth in maritime trade and political consolidation. While much of this resulted from local initiative, these were spurred by the unification and intensifying sea-mindedness of China in the Tang and Song Dynasties.

Chapter 11

China Looks Seaward

The founding of the Tang Dynasty (618–907) ushered in a golden age of Chinese civilization, when an ecumenical and broad-minded spirit infused the visual, written, and performing arts, gave new life to religious, philosophical, and political discourse, and made China an object of wonder and renown across Asia. The Tang emperors pushed Chinese influence farther west than ever before or since, but by the middle of the ninth century the borders of the Celestial Kingdom had contracted so far that the venerable capital of Chang'an was closer to barbarian lands than to the center of Han China. Between the later Tang and the Song (960–1279) Dynasties, the Chinese capital was displaced ever eastward, to Luoyang, Kaifeng, and ultimately Hangzhou (Lin'an).* The former two are on the Yellow River and closer to the heart of the canal system that knit the empire together while Hangzhou lay on the sea itself.

These moves by the court bureaucracy were accompanied by a dramatic demographic shift as hundreds of thousands of Chinese fled the western and northern provinces for the relative security found south of the Yellow River and later of the Yangzi. Faced with dramatic reversals on their continental borders and insecurity on the silk road, the government adopted a more flexible approach to overseas trade and traders as it sought to increase its revenue from customs duties and other taxes. Dependent on Korean intermediaries for trade with Korea and Japan in the early Tang, by the tenth century Chinese merchants were plying the sea-lanes of Asia, and their influence was felt from

---

* The Song Dynasty is traditionally divided into the Northern Song (960–1127) and, after the Jurchen Jin invasions, the Southern Song (1127–1279).

southern India to Japan. While China's near neighbors adopted policies similar to those of the Middle Kingdom, the states of Southeast Asia tended to be more laissez-faire, largely because they were subject to a far greater number of influences: Chinese, of course; Arabs and Persians (mostly Muslim, but also Zoroastrian, Nestorian Christian, and Jewish); Hindus and Buddhists from India and Sri Lanka; and above all indigenous Malays, Javanese, Burmese, Khmers, and others.

The Belitung Wreck's Tang Cargo

As important as the Belitung wreck is for what it reveals about shipbuilding techniques in the Indian Ocean region, it is equally so for the evidence its so-called Tang cargo yields about the nature of east–west sea trade. Apart from about ten tons of lead ingots that served as ballast, and which could be sold or traded at the ship's final destination, the overwhelming bulk of the ship's cargo consisted of Chinese ceramics, sixty thousand pieces in all, many of them still intact. Most were bowls turned out by kilns in Changsha, now the capital of landlocked Hunan Province, south of the Yangzi; but there were also hundreds of mass-produced inkpots, spice jars, and ewers. One of the bowls bears a Chinese date that corresponds to the year 826, which falls squarely within the date ranges suggested by Chinese coins and radiocarbon dating of the ship's timbers and of a sample of star anise, a spice native to China and Vietnam. When shipped, the Changsha bowls were nested and wrapped in straw or packed in large storage jars from Vietnam. In addition to this mass-market cargo, the Belitung ship also included numerous pieces of silverware, some etched in gold, and the largest gold cup of Tang origin in existence, as well as more refined ceramics with cobalt blue decorations from Zhejiang Province.

The discovery of a Chinese cargo in a ship almost certainly built in, and manned by sailors from, Southwest Asia and sunk in Southeast Asian waters is in itself indicative of the international nature of trade thirteen hundred years ago. More striking still is the choice of decorative motifs applied by the Chinese potters, which testifies to a keen understanding of their intended markets. Most of the bowls bear geometric designs or inscriptions from the Quran rendered in red and green and were obviously destined for markets in the Abbasid Caliphate. Green-splashed bowls were popular in Persia, while those adorned with lotus symbols were intended for Buddhist customers. The symbiotic relationship between maker and market is obvious from the potters' design choices, but the striking blue employed in the Zhejiang ware required cobalt, which in the ninth century had to be imported from Persia. While it is not difficult to envision the circumstances under which pieces of exceptional quality would have appealed to elite customers, the Near East did not want for potters of its own. One is forced therefore to wonder about the social dynamic that made a small, inland city in south-central China a producer of everyday goods that would grace the tables of people thousands of miles away by sea. Even if we take this initiative to be a form of early globalization resulting from cheaper labor and other inputs—some of which had to be imported— these would have to have been inexpensive enough to offset the relatively high cost of transportation, the cheapness of which is a defining characteristic of globalization today. Finally, we have to consider the interrelationships among manufacturers, maritime merchants, and an ubiquitous Chinese officialdom, and how these affected long-range trade, and people's attitudes toward it, during and after the Tang Dynasty.

China in the Sui and Tang

Just as the short-lived Qin Dynasty of the third century BCE laid the groundwork for the prosperity of the Han Dynasty, so the Sui Dynasty anticipated the flowering of Chinese culture under the Tang. In both cases, the earlier dynasty brought a variety of disparate power centers under the rule of a single emperor who imposed order on a diverse population spread across a vast territory. The transitions from one ruling house to the other were not seamless, but the continuities were strong, and the Tang debt to Sui initiatives was considerable, especially for their massive investment in the canal system and their embellishment of Luoyang, at the junction of the Grand Canal and the Yellow River. Despite their conspicuous failures against the kingdom of Goguryeo on the Korean Peninsula, the sheer size of the Sui armies attested to China's military might, which, coupled with a vigorous diplomacy, ensured a period of unrivaled prosperity and expansion during the Tang's first century, not only in Central Asia but also on the Korean Peninsula and in northern Vietnam.

In 618, Li Yuan, duke of Tang, captured the Sui capital of Yangzhou on the Grand Canal near its junction with the Yangzi, and soon thereafter he became the first Tang emperor, known to history as Tang Gaozu. A soldier by profession, Gaozu had a keen administrative sense and he restored political and economic stability to the empire by improving education, reinstating the examination system for government officials, minting a uniform coinage, and enacting new, less punitive laws. By the end of the seventh century Chinese arms had restored peace to China proper, defeated the Eastern and Western Turks to extend Chinese rule from Mongolia to the Amu Darya in

Turkmenistan, and made the revived capital at Chang'an probably the most cosmopolitan city in the world. With a population of perhaps one million, Chang'an attracted merchants, envoys, and monks from Japan and Korea, Southeast Asia, Central Asia, India, the caliphates, and the Byzantine Empire. Surrounded by tributaries of the Wei River, itself a tributary of the Yellow River, Chang'an was served by five canals on which came bulk shipments of silk and rice from the Yangzi-Huai area and, from closer by, timber for the city's prodigious construction needs. Chang'an's situation was complicated by the canals' tendency to flood, low water in the Wei River, and the Sanmen Rapids, a treacherous bottleneck on the Yellow River that could be circumvented only by portaging grain and other cargoes overland from Luoyang for about 130 kilometers before loading it back on boats for the final push up the Yellow and Wei Rivers. Chang'an's closest rivals in size were Luoyang, which served as the dynasty's eastern capital from the middle of the seventh century, and Yangzhou, which became a major port for ships from the south.

The Korean Campaigns

Toward the end of his reign, Gaozu's successor Tang Taizong resumed the Sui emperors' efforts to extend Chinese influence onto the Korean Peninsula. Goguryeo had erected massive fortifications along the western bank of the Liao River against a possible Tang attack, but Taizong became increasingly preoccupied with the prospect of bringing the peninsula under his control. His opportunity came when a coup deposed the king of Goguryeo, nominally a Chinese vassal, and the usurper severed the overland route from China to its ally, the kingdom of Silla. In 644, Taizong dispatched more than forty thousand troops to the mouth of the Daedong (Taedong) River below Pyeongyang. The sources reveal little about the outcome of this amphibious expedition, which was supposed to act in concert with an army marching overland from the north, but the invasion as a whole failed and Taizong canceled plans for a new campaign shortly before his death. In 655, his successor, Tang Gaozong, attacked Goguryeo again, this time to avenge an attack on the Khitan, a Mongol-speaking Manchurian tribe that had submitted to the Tang. As before, the conflict involved the three Korean kingdoms, with Silla seeking the Chinese as allies against Baekje, who were supported by the Japanese.

In assessing their prospects for a Korean campaign, the Chinese had probably not considered the possibility of intervention by the Japanese, who viewed the proceedings on the Korean Peninsula with mixed feelings. Chinese mores had begun to permeate Japanese court society at the end of the sixth century, when they were introduced by Korean traders and migrants. Buddhism was officially recognized in Japan in 587, but at the same time the court embraced Confucian ethical and legal teachings and the promotion of government officials on the basis of merit. The Japanese also absorbed Chinese literary tastes and artistic styles, and Chinese city and temple layouts became models for their own. Emulous though it was of the Middle Kingdom, the Yamato court had a formal alliance with Baekje, whose Prince Pung had lived in Japan for two decades. In 663, a Japanese fleet sailed in support of Prince Pung's claim to the throne, only to be destroyed by a Tang force at the battle of the Geum River. They lost four hundred ships and "King Pungjang of Baekje with a number of others embarked in a ship and fled to [Goguryeo]." Three years later, Goguryeo was weakened by a succession crisis and, seizing the initiative, the Chinese defeated the kingdom in a land campaign two years after that. At a tactical level, China's Korean campaign of the 660s succeeded when previous efforts had failed because their alliance with Silla enabled the Chinese to launch an amphibious campaign across the Yellow Sea, and once established on the lower peninsula they were able to fight Goguryeo on two fronts. The southern front was probably easier and less costly to maintain by sea than were the forward bases in Liaodong and northern Goguryeo, which could be reached only by long overland marches.

Flush with victory, the Chinese divided the entire peninsula into commanderies, effectively reducing their ally, Silla, to the same status as Goguryeo and Baekje. But they failed to keep a grip on the peninsula due to the Koreans' collective resistance coupled with severe problems at home. Within a decade, Silla quickly gobbled up Baekje and Goguryeo and forced the Chinese to withdraw to Liaodong. Survivors of Goguryeo's ruling dynasty established the state of Balhae (Parhae in Chinese), which straddled the Yalu River and served as a buffer between Silla, China, and the Khitan from 710 to 934. On the domestic front, Gaozong's campaigns had been costly and the end of hostilities coincided with droughts and famines that led to massive internal migration to avoid taxation and seek out better land. Further straining the imperial treasury were the swelling bureaucracy and lavish building programs, especially in Luoyang, which Gaozong had formally designated as a second capital, a move that foreshadowed the decline of Chang'an and the northwest provinces. The Chinese were simultaneously engaged in a prolonged struggle with the kingdom of Tibet and tribes of both the Eastern and Western Turks. In the 690s, the Tibetans defeated a Tang army only three hundred kilometers from Chang'an, the Eastern Turks descended on Gansu Province, and Hebei Province was invaded by the same Khitan whose invasion by Goguryeo had prompted the Tang intervention on the Korean Peninsula.

These varied threats were contained by the start of the new century, and in

712 China enthroned one of its greatest monarchs, Tang Xuanzong. Although his half-century reign ended in calamity, it was under the "Brilliant Monarch" that Tang China reached the apogee of its imperial reach. With China at peace with her continental neighbors, one of Xuanzong's first priorities was to restore the primacy of Chang'an over Luoyang, where the court had relocated for a total of twenty-three years between 657 and 705. Integral to this project was the renewal of the canal system and improvements to navigation on the Yellow River—most notably by reducing the portage around the Sanmen Rapids to only eight kilometers—to ensure that tax rice originating in the lower Yangzi valley could reach the capital efficiently and reliably. In the seventh century Taizong had allowed tax grain to be converted to silk and copper cash to reduce the cost of transporting imperial taxes to Chang'an (which was borne by the prefectural governments), but rice remained the principal form of payment, and stockpiles provided the court with a hedge against famine in the event of drought, flood, or war.

China was also resurgent in Central Asia where rulers from Tashkent, Samarkand, and Bukhara requested help against Muslim armies encroaching from the south. Emperor Tang Xuanzong granted honorific titles of nobility to rulers in the Pamirs, Kashmir, and the Kabul River valley. In connection with this, the Pallava king Narasimhavarman II sent an envoy to China with the monk Vajrabodhi in acknowledgment of which the Tang emperor recognized him as leader of the "Southern Army Which Cherishes Virtue." The Tang Dynasty was at its peak when it suffered defeats on its western, northern, and southern borders. In 751, Gao Xianzhi, architect of much of China's success in Central Asia, executed the king of Tashkent for failing to defer to the imperial throne. To avenge his father, the late king's son enlisted the help of Turks and an army from the newly declared Abbasid Caliphate and in July their combined forces routed Gao at the Talas River near the border between Kazakhstan and Kyrgyzstan. The same year an army from the newly emerged kingdom of Nanzhao destroyed a Tang army of eighty thousand. This was especially galling because Nanzhao, which occupied the strategic region where the Red River flows closest to the Yangzi, was a creation of the Tang. Humiliating as the losses in Central Asia and Nanzhao were, most decisive was that of a Tang army under An Lushan, a military governor in eastern Manchuria who launched an unprovoked attack on the Khitan.

Though badly defeated and widely suspected of treasonous intentions, An Lushan was promoted by the emperor. Proving his detractors right in 755, he seized Hebei and Henan Provinces and drove south to the Yellow River where he took Kaifeng and seized control of the Grand Canal. He went on to capture Luoyang and Chang'an and forced Xuanzong to flee before internecine strife took its toll on the rebels and imperial forces finally defeated the last of them in 763. Almost immediately, however, Tibetan forces seized Chang'an, and although they withdrew the following year, they raided the capital almost annually for more than a decade. It would be a thousand years before the Qing Dynasty restored Chinese authority to the region that now comprises China's westernmost Xinjiang Uygur Autonomous Region.

The contraction of China's western borders, the disruption to the overland silk road, and the rise of Baghdad led to an unprecedented flowering of trade on the Monsoon Seas, with profound consequences for the traders and states of South and Southeast Asia, as well as for China itself. In the short term, however, such outcomes were far from apparent. Although An Lushan's rebellion had its greatest impact on northern and northwest China, unrest spread to Guangzhou, where in 758 Persian and Arab merchants unaccountably rioted and decided to "destroy the warehouses and burn down the dwellings." The motive for a Tang army's massacre of "several thousand Persian merchants" at Yangzhou two years later is likewise unknown, but the upshot was the withdrawal of Persian and Arab merchants from China to Annamese ports. Nonetheless, within a decade Guangzhou had recovered and the number of ships calling from overseas rose from only five a year to about forty.

Although the seat of government was restored to Chang'an, the capital was now closer to China's troubled western borders than to its geographic center. The An Lushan rebellion had permanently weakened the centralized dynastic authority and a combination of the loss of tax records, widespread redistribution of land, and southward migration to the more tranquil provinces between the Huai and Yangzi Rivers destroyed the old financial structures. The government attempted to introduce reforms and promoted the payment of taxes in cash as well as crops and other goods, but it could not administer the system effectively. This led to widespread corruption, and a growing gap between rich and poor as many people abandoned their land to work as tenant farmers on larger estates and others flocked to Buddhist monasteries.

Since early in the Tang, Confucianists had viewed Buddhism as a twofold threat to the state. It violated Confucian principles of governance by ignoring the precedence of rulers over subjects, and it undermined the state's economic stability because Buddhist lands, temples, nuns, and monks were exempt from taxation. Tang Taizong and Tang Xuanzong had both banned illegal ordinations, but by the mid-ninth century conditions were ripe for another government campaign against Buddhist holdings under Tang Wuzong. This crackdown laicized and returned to secular tax-paying status a quarter million monks and nuns—who had continued to work as farmers, artisans, merchants, investors, and moneylenders—and closed thousands of Buddhist monasteries and shrines whose statues, ornaments, and other decorations of gold, iron, and copper were melted down and returned to circulation.

The Japanese Monk and the Korean Merchant

These events are known from official histories as well as the more personal eyewitness account of Ennin, a Buddhist monk "in search of the Law" who in 838 attached himself to a Japanese embassy to the Tang court. Renowned as the greatest teacher of Tendai Buddhism, Ennin authored a fascinating diary of his nearly decadelong sojourn in China, a work celebrated for its vivid portrait of the Chinese Buddhist community at a crucial point in its history but that also offers an intimate view of China's inland shipping, the maritime trading networks of Northeast Asia, and Tang officialdom. Unfortunately, Ennin writes little about the vessels in which he sailed except to note that the mission was announced with the appointment of an ambassador and subordinate officials including "ship construction officers" who oversaw the building of four ships that together carried about 650 people. After two false starts, the expedition sailed the 475 miles between Hakata Bay, on northwest Kyushu, and the China coast north of the Yangzi, where two of the ships grounded in the mudflats and were destroyed by the sea, though not before the crew and tribute goods were rescued and brought to the mainland.

Ennin intended to visit China for a year but wound up staying nine. Some delays were due to the imperfect state of ninth-century communication, but this was a minor inconvenience compared with the highly ritualized and inscrutable demands of the Tang bureaucracy. At Yangzhou, the authorities refused Ennin permission to visit a Buddhist monastery in Zhejiang Province on the grounds that it was too far to go in the time the Japanese emissaries would take to conduct their business at Chang'an. Ennin was forced to wait until the official party returned from the capital en route home; but rather than return to Japan he ingratiated himself with the Korean merchant community on the Shandong Peninsula and remained in China. He eventually made his way to Chang'an, but afraid to leave the capital without proper papers, between 841 and 845 he petitioned the court for a passport a hundred times. He was only allowed to go when all unregistered foreign monks were deported during Tang Wuzong's campaign against Buddhism.

That Ennin was able to stay in China, visit Buddhist monasteries in Shanxi Province, and sojourn in Chang'an was due in part to the support he received from the large community of expatriate Koreans. At this time, Sillan merchants dominated the maritime trade of the Bo Hai, Yellow Sea, and East

China Sea at least as far south as Mingzhou (now Ningbo), and they forwarded many of the exotics imported into China's southern ports to Korea and Japan. Because of their familiarity with both China and Japan they served as intermediaries in commercial and diplomatic transactions between the two countries. The Koreans in China were concentrated along the coast between the Shandong Peninsula and Chuzhou (now Huai'an), a major port of entry for ships from Korea and Japan where goods were transshipped to smaller craft for distribution along the Grand Canal, Huai River, and other inland waters. The Korean quarter at Chuzhou was administered by a Korean general manager and an official interpreter, and there were comparable officials on the Shandong Peninsula where Ennin spent much of his time as a guest of the Mount Chi Monastery, which overlooks one of the easternmost anchorages in China. These quasi-administrators did not represent the kingdom of Silla but rather Sillan merchant interests.

The most prominent trader during Ennin's time in China was Jang Bogo (Chang Pogo), whose history is known from Korean, Chinese, and Japanese sources. Of humble origins, Jang made his mark as a soldier in the Chinese army before returning to Korea around 828. Appalled by the piracy and slave trading endemic on the Yellow Sea, he persuaded the king of Silla to name him commissioner of a garrison on Wando Island, on the southwest coast. He was successful in reducing if not eliminating piracy, and he capitalized on the resulting stability by developing a prosperous trading network that radiated to Japan and the China coast. He was well known as the founder and patron of the Buddhist monastery at Mount Chi, and Ennin records a letter he wrote Jang thanking him for his hospitality and his gracious offers of assistance. Around the time that Ennin arrived in China, Silla was embroiled in a succession dispute. Jang had helped enthrone the short-lived Sinmu Wang, who promised to take Jang's daughter for a consort should he become king. When Jang proposed that Sinmu's heir accept his daughter as a consort, royal advisors pleaded that an islander would not dignify the royal bedchamber. Jang was murdered to prevent his avenging this insult, and by the time Ennin returned to the Shandong Peninsula en route home in 845 Jang's trading empire was a fading memory.

The Silla government also closed Jang Bogo's garrison on Wando Island, and toward the end of the century sea trade fell off due to political instability in China and Korea. Peasant revolts on the peninsula in the 890s quickly coalesced around two leaders who established the kingdoms of Later Goguryeo and Later Baekje. With Silla no more than a rump state, the principal contest for Korea's future lay between these two kingdoms, and key to the outcome was mastery of the coast and sea-lanes. Wang Geon parlayed the maritime expertise gained in his family's business (his grandfather was a leading merchant in Jang Bogo's day) to become an accomplished naval commander during the war. As King Taejo he proclaimed the Goryeo state (918–1392), with its capital at Gaeseong (Kaesong), and he accepted the submission of the kingdoms of Silla (after an independent existence of 993 years) and Later Baekje, thereby uniting the Korean Peninsula under a single throne.

Goryeo's relations with the Northern Song were tested in the eleventh century as both realms came under pressure from the Khitan Liao and Jurchen nomads of Manchuria. When the land routes were blocked by the Khitan, Korean and Chinese merchants trading across the Yellow Sea maintained informal contacts between the two courts. Most foreign trade entered Goryeo through Yesong, the port of entry for Gaeseong. As the official *Song History* relates, "There are several hundred Chinese in the capital, most of them [Fujianese] who have come by junk for the purposes of trade." Merchants from more distant lands reached Goryeo by sea, too, and according to the official Korean history, in 1037 Muslims, Indians, and others arrived from the south having come via Chinese ports.

From the Late Tang to the Northern Song

Buddhists were not the only community to suffer from Tang Wuzong's attentions. Forced to limp by with less revenue than it required either for its military security or for the maintenance of the canals and other infrastructure, the government harassed Muslims, Manicheans, Nestorian Christians, and Zoroastrians, too. Difficult as things were for minorities around Chang'an, however, Chinese citizens in the traditionally prosperous regions between the Yellow and Yangzi Rivers experienced even greater hardships. Despite the fiscal benefits of closing the monasteries and returning people to tax-paying status, pirates in gangs of a hundred or more were at large, operating in concert with corrupt officials of the state markets in the formerly secure Yangzi plain. A decade later disaffection was widespread among both the peasantry and the army, and a yearlong uprising in what is now eastern Zhejiang, including the ports of Hangzhou and Mingzhou, combined elements of both.

The unrest of the 850s was a mere prelude to the devastation unleashed by the rebel Huang Chao, who came to the fore two decades later. After seizing most of Fujian Province, Huang Chao petitioned the court to be made protector general of Annam. Officials opposed this on the grounds "that the markets and shipping of the South Seas constituted immeasurable wealth, and that if the bandits acquired them they would become increasingly prosperous," at the expense of the imperial treasury. After this rebuke, Huang Chao marched south to Guangzhou, China's principal port for overseas trade. As related by the Persian Abu Zayd, the city capitulated after a nearly yearlong siege, whereupon Huang Chao's forces killed 120,000 Muslim, Jewish, Christian, and Persian merchants.* Huang Chao subsequently captured Luoyang and Chang'an and forced Emperor Tang Xizong to flee, just as Xuanzong had during An Lushan's rebellion 120 years before. But control of supplies from the south was no less important to rebels than to emperors, and because the capital was unable to feed itself, Huang Chao's occupation was brief and brutal. With canal transportation at a standstill and food unavailable, the inhabitants of Chang'an were reduced to cannibalism, as "Communication with the southeast is cut: no way for grain supplies to be brought in," in the words of a contemporary lament. Xizong eventually regained the upper hand, but despite the government's ultimate victory, the dynasty never recovered from the damage to its finances, prestige, and administration.

Insofar as foreign trade was concerned, the picture could not have been bleaker. According to reports from Indian Ocean traders, Chinese officials began

> tyrannizing those of the merchants who journeyed to them. And when this happened, it combined in it the appearance of tyranny and aggression towards Arab ship captains and boat owners. Then they . . . forcibly deprived [the merchants] of their properties. They legalized that which custom had not hitherto allowed as a part of their activities. Then God, great be His name, completely stripped them of blessings. And the sea forbade its side [to passengers], and, by the decree emanating from the Almighty, blessed be His name, desolation befell the ship captains and guides [as far as] Siraf and Uman.

In effect, the government officials' criminality created precisely the conditions the court had sought to avoid when it denied Huang Chao's request to become protector general of Annam. Following the rebellion, power devolved on a number of military commanders, one of whom forced the last Tang emperor to abdicate in 907. China thereafter lapsed into an interregnum during which the empire was divided into three distinct regions: the Sixteen Prefectures around modern Beijing and the passes between Manchuria and China; the territory between there and the Yangzi, which was ruled by a succession of five short-lived "dynasties"; and the area south of the Yangzi, which was divided among ten longer-lived kingdoms.

Compared with the last decades of the Tang, the half-century interregnum

---

* Abu Zayd claims that the number of victims was known thanks to the Chinese penchant for record keeping.

of the Five Dynasties and Ten Kingdoms was relatively calm. When the last emperor of the Fifth Dynasty unexpectedly died leaving a seven-year-old heir, his generals chose one of their own to assume the throne. Emperor Song Taizu managed to bring most of the remaining splinter states under the rule of the new dynasty, which had its capital at Kaifeng. The most important transportation hub in China, Kaifeng lies on the Yellow River at the intersection of four canals, including the Grand Canal, and canal boats and other inland vessels moored in a vast lake within the city walls. It is also closer than either Chang'an or Luoyang to the major sources of rice, wheat, and other commodities essential for the sustenance of a large imperial metropolis. The city already had a prosperous foreign quarter during the Tang and served as the capital for all but one of the Five Dynasties, but under the Song its population quickly grew to about a million people. Although far more people lived here than in any other single city in China, it is indicative of the importance of urbanization in Song China that an estimated six million people—about half the world's urban population at the time—lived in cities, and increased urbanization was a major catalyst for encouraging new attitudes toward and improvements in transportation and commerce.

The Song purchased peace from the neighboring Khitan Liao and Xi Xia tribes of the northwest, but while their inland borders were no longer threatened, transcontinental trade had fallen off. Dependent as it was on revenues from trade to cover its payments to the Liao and Xia, the Northern Song could not afford to ignore the potential of sea trade, which it encouraged to a greater degree than any previous dynasty. Developments during the Tang had laid the groundwork for this new openness to overseas commerce. The vulnerability of Chang'an to invasion from the steppes had been revealed repeatedly and deficiencies in the transport system had forced the court to move to Luoyang in times of stress, most drastically in the 690s when about 100,000 families—perhaps half a million people—were forcibly relocated from Chang'an. In the eighth century, the permanent loss of the empire's western territories exposed the ancient capital to attack by Tibetan and Central Asian armies, and this in turn led to a decline in the authority and influence of the northwest clans that had formed the core of China's leadership since the Qin Dynasty. Coupled with the widespread flight of northerners toward the Huai and Yangzi valleys, which were less susceptible to invasion, the periodic relocation of the national capital inclined the Chinese to look south and seaward. These changes would have profound implications for the development of China's maritime trade, from the numbers of ships and ports to the direct participation of Chinese in overseas ventures, as well as for China's trading partners in Southeast Asia from Vietnam to Sumatra, Java, and beyond.

China and Southeast Asia

One reason for the increase in the number of Chinese seaports in the Northern Song was that after a thousand years of more or less constant occupation by their more powerful neighbors, the people of Jiaozhi in northern Vietnam had finally achieved independence as the kingdom of Dai Viet. While the Chinese allowed this to happen in part because they needed to concentrate government resources on the more pressing threats from Inner Asia and Manchuria, Jiaozhi had also become a liability. During the Sui and early Tang Dynasties, Jiaozhi was ably administered by Chinese authorities, although finding qualified officials willing to serve there was a perennial difficulty. An infamous illustration of the government's problem dates from the reign of Tang Taizong, who appointed Lu Zushang to the post of governor-general in Jiaozhou, a region that encompassed parts of northern Vietnam and southern China. "Giao [Jiaozhou] is a large frontier region," noted the emperor, "and it is necessary to have good officials to look after it; up to now, none of the governor generals has been equal to his responsibilities. You have the ability to pacify this frontier; go and defend it for me, and do not refuse on account of its being far away." Doubtless flattered by the appointment, Lu had the temerity to decline the posting on the grounds that "In the south there is much malaria; if I go there I shall never return," a reaction that reflected not simply a concern for his health, but a Confucian anxiety about being buried far from his ancestral home. To spare Lu such an unsettling destiny, the magnanimous Taizong had him beheaded.

As part of a raft of administrative changes, in 679 Jiaozhi and adjacent provinces in northern Vietnam became the protectorate of Annam, meaning "pacified south." Only five years later, however, Kunlun merchants at Guangzhou murdered a corrupt governor who "tried to cheat them of their goods." Long-distance retaliation by the Tang was impossible. Faced with a shortage of men to deal with threats from Inner Asia, Gaozong was forced to withdraw the bulk of the Chinese armies stationed there. But the authorities who remained took the lesson to heart and for the next sixty years there are few reports of routine corruption in China's busiest international port. Sanskrit inscriptions from about a century later record two raids on Annam's southern neighbor, the Cham state of Huanwang, as the kingdom of Linyi was now called, in which "ferocious, pitiless, dark-skinned men born in other countries, whose food was more horrible than corpses, and who were vicious and furious, came in ships . . . took away the [Hindu temple linga], and set fire to the temple" near Panduranga (Phan Rang), south of Cam Ranh Bay. Where these raiders originated is unknown, but they knew that Panduranga, Kauthara (Nha

Trang), and Hoi An (near modern Da Nang) were centers of a substantial trade. Although the people of Huanwang had access to a few choice products of their own for foreign markets, notably ivory, rhinoceros horn, and aromatic woods, their prosperity derived from their active engagement in coastal and long-distance trade, as well as the services they provided foreign sailors.

Following the merchants' revolt during the An Lushan rebellion at mid-century, foreigners banned from trading at Guangzhou moved to Annam, the favored entrepôt of traders sailing between Southeast Asia and China. To counter its success the governor of Guangzhou requested an imperial decree depriving Annam of the right to admit traders in 792. This was denied on the grounds that Guangzhou's problem was, as it had been a century before, corrupt officials:

> The merchants of distant kingdoms only seek profit. If they are treated fairly they will come; if they are troubled, they will go. Formerly, [Guangzhou] was a gathering place for merchant vessels; now, suddenly they have changed to Annam. If there has been oppressive misappropriation over a long period of time, then those who have gone elsewhere must be persuaded to return; this is not a matter of litigation, but of changing the attitudes of officials.

Content that the Annamese would remain faithful subjects of the empire, in the 780s Tang authorities put Annam under the rule of a local leader named Phung Hung, a move that marked the start of northern Vietnamese control of their own affairs. When the Chinese subsequently attempted to reassert their authority over Annam, a native anti-Tang faction enlisted the support of the kingdom of Nanzhao. Setting their sights down the Red River, Nanzhao armies scored dramatic victories over the Chinese and their Annamese allies. The Chinese withdrew from Annam to Guangdong to await reinforcements, which were supplied by ships from Fujian. Officials requisitioned many of the ships from merchants, whose cargoes they plundered or destroyed to make room for the armies' supplies, and to add insult to injury they held shipowners liable for any losses resulting from shipwreck. Brutal though these measures were, the armies of Nanzhao were routed in 865 by an army under Gao Pian, who reestablished nominal control over Annam and proved one of the most evenhanded Chinese officials to serve there.

Well respected even by the Vietnamese, Gao built a new capital in the vicinity of Hanoi, the traditional seat of power in the region, and took other measures to restore Annam's prosperity. He went to great lengths to promote safe navigation between the capital and the sea as well as in the Gulf of Tonkin, which he regarded as so dangerous that, he claimed, "You must give up hope of coming back alive, as soon as you board a ship [in this area]." According to a stele enumerating his accomplishments in Annam, Gao sought to

Banish distress by bringing food;
Prosperity comes riding in boats.
I devised plans against civil disorder . . .
Causing the sea to form a channel,
Where boats can pass in safety,
With the deep sea stretching out peacefully,
A highway of supply for our city.

For the first thirty years after the end of the Tang, Annam remained an autonomous province under the nominal control of one or another of the kingdoms of China's tenth-century interregnum. The Vietnamese finally shucked off more than a thousand years of Chinese rule in 939. Unification under a single king took several decades, but later in the century Dinh Bo Linh overcame his rivals through military savvy, diplomacy, and sheer audacity. (When his enemies threatened to execute his child, he asked, "How can a great man compromise a great affair simply because of his son?") Foreign traders acknowledged the stability achieved during his reign and in 976, according to a Vietnamese history, "merchant boats from different nations beyond the sea arrived and presented the goods of their countries." Nonetheless, for the first century or more of independence, the rulers of the kingdom of Dai Viet focused on consolidating their authority in the middle and upper reaches of the Red River and they remained somewhat aloof from the deltaic lands of the coast, a region even the Chinese had not bothered to name. There was a modest degree of riverine trade between the coast and the upper Red River, but it was not until the revival of China's maritime trade under the Southern Song Dynasty (1127–1279) that the delta port of Van Don became a major destination for Chinese, Javanese, Malay, Khmer, and other merchants. Van Don had ready access to Nanzhao and Yunnan, Cambodian Angkor (which lay across the Annamite Mountains and down the Mekong River), and the local and long-distance trade that skirted the coast of Vietnam from China to the Strait of Malacca. Although Dai Viet bore the unmistakable imprint of Chinese influence in terms of governance and culture, apart from a brief occupation during the fifteenth century Vietnam was never again ruled from China.

Conducting Maritime Trade

The kingdoms of Dai Viet, Champa, Java, and Srivijaya owed their prosperity to their participation in an increasingly vibrant and profitable international trade centered on China where their resources were in high demand. The focus of the Sui and Tang emperors was on securing the internal integrity of the empire, but China's territorial expansion increased the number of tribes and states sending embassies laden with exotic flora, fauna, textiles, slaves, and performing artists. Even from beyond the reach of direct imperial control, tropical rarities excited the senses of the Celestial Kingdom's elite, whose appetite for the novel and curious animated merchants the length and breadth of the Monsoon Seas. Emperors welcomed exotic gifts while new foods transformed a rather bland Chinese cuisine that previously consisted for the most part of "fish and vegetables mostly uncooked," as Yijing observed, comparing it to the more lavish culinary arts of India where "All vegetables are to be well cooked and to be eaten after mixing with the asafoetida, clarified butter, oil, or any spice." Emperor Tang Xuanzong's taste for exotics from distant lands attracted the censure of a traditionalist advisor who counseled the emperor against accepting gifts from abroad: "His Majesty, having newly ascended the throne, should show the world how he behaves himself abstemiously, by showing examples of frugality to the people, and not indulging in the weakness of being fond of rare and curious foreign trash." But pious thrift was not a hallmark of the Tang, and disregarding his advisor's admonition Xuanzong received many gifts from southern emissaries, everything from a troupe of musicians and elephants from Srivijaya and Champa to rare birds from eastern Indonesia.

Apart from animals, which were incidental to the main cargoes delivered by foreign ships, China's bulkiest imports were exotic woods, especially sandalwood and aloeswood. Native to India and eastern Indonesia, sandalwood came in the form of finished goods such as carvings, boxes, and furniture, and as raw material for carpentry, sculpture, and incense intended for Buddhist settings. Aloeswood from Champa and Sumatran camphorwood were treasured for their medicinal qualities and burned as incense, and the insect-repellent qualities of camphorwood made it an excellent material for chests. The demand for Buddhist texts and objects of veneration was essential to the revival of China's southern trade during the Tang, but to a greater degree than in the west, people developed a secular appreciation for scented woods and oils, which were used as perfumes, air fresheners, and aphrodisiacs, and the trade in exotic woods continued even after Buddhism's decline in China. For the wealthy, woods from overseas undoubtedly had cachet simply by virtue of being foreign, and rosewood from Java and India was used for furniture, including—thanks to a belief in its efficacy in relieving headaches—wooden pillows. China was not merely a consumer of goods and it exported a variety of goods from silks and ceramics to bronze bells and paper. However, it also exercised a powerful political and economic influence on the Asian seaboard from Korea and Japan to Srivijaya.

During the late Tang and Five Dynasties periods the easing of official attitudes toward private property and commerce was reflected in the gradual relaxation of government control of merchant activity. Increased agricultural output freed farmers to grow more lucrative cash crops, especially in the marginal lands of Zhejiang, or to abandon farming altogether to take up work as artisans or merchants. The expansion of trade also led to China's experiments with paper currency. In the eighth century, tea merchants faced the prospect of transferring ever greater quantities of copper cash from the capital—where they had to sell the tea—back to their home provinces. At the same time, provincial governments were required to make monetary gifts to the throne. Rather than absorb the cost and risk of transferring large quantities of copper cash from and to Chang'an, merchants began to deposit their cash with provincial "memorial-presenting courts" in the capital who issued them a letter of credit called "flying money." These could then be redeemed at the provincial capital, while the provincial gift could be paid from the funds deposited at the memorial-presenting court in Chang'an. In 812, the central government adopted this practice to facilitate the payment of provincial taxes. The system was retained by the Northern Song authorities, and in the eleventh century these transactions amounted to three million strings of cash annually. Although it was technically a government monopoly, merchants used flying money in private trade, and they began printing an early form of paper money called an "exchange medium," in essence a promissory note backed by a deposit of cash held by an exchange medium shop. The government followed suit and began to issue its own paper currency, but inadequate reserves led to inflation and notes fell to a quarter of their face value.

Sometime before 715, the Tang court established the first office of maritime affairs—*shibosi*—to oversee the commerce of Guangzhou and collect the duties on imported goods. Visiting in midcentury, the Buddhist priest Jianzhen found there "argosies of the Brahmans, the Persians and the Malays, their numbers beyond reckoning, all laden with aromatics, drugs, and rare and precious things, their cargoes heaped like hills." Other *shibosi* followed at Hangzhou and Mingzhou, near the mouth of the Yangzi. Overseas trade opened up considerably in the tenth century as the coastal kingdoms and dynasties of the Tang-Song interregnum lured merchants to their ports to profit from their commerce and gain the respect of foreign rulers. As the Song consolidated their power, they reinstituted the *shibosi*, whose officers had a variety of responsibilities: inspecting foreign ships to ensure that the government got to bid first on all imports (which could be purchased only at approved government stores); collecting duties and taxes; welcoming emissaries; and accommodating victims of shipwreck or other misfortunes. Before sailing abroad, Chinese traders had to sail to a port with a *shibosi*, which upon receipt of an itinerary, crew list, and cargo manifest could issue a pass that would allow them back into the country. Foreigners and Chinese alike were subject to strict export controls on horses and ironware among other things, above all copper, the drain of which was a perpetual concern from the Tang onward.

Such administrative oversight was not unique to the Chinese, and maritime trade from the Indonesian archipelago and the Korean Peninsula and Japan could not have grown without a corresponding increase in commercial sophistication and government oversight. Rulers capitalized on foreign trade by subjecting imports to duties and taxes, the collection of which required the creation of ever-larger bureaucracies. How such officials operated, and how successfully, varied widely, and while little information about authorized ports survives, even less is known about the innumerable landing places used by local traders, smugglers, and pirates who stalked both coastal and inland waters. As the careers of Jang Bogo, Wang Geon, and others attest, Korean merchants were the leading long-distance carriers of Northeast Asia in the ninth century, and they conducted much of the commerce between Japan and China. To facilitate this trade, the Japanese assigned special interpreters to Tsushima Island, but from the seventh century all foreign trade funneled through the Kyushu Headquarters (*Dazaifu*) on Hakata Bay, near modern Fukuoka. At first this agency was charged with overseeing official embassies, but starting in the 800s it was responsible for inspecting imports, although no duties were assessed, and for housing and feeding visiting merchants, who were not charged. The Yamato government maintained a strict monopoly of trade, determining not only where foreigners could visit and for how long but also regulating exports and reserving rights of preemption on all imports. The decline in Korean sea trade in the later ninth century was partly responsible for the lack of trade missions from Japan to China between 853 and 926, but the Japanese probably exacerbated the problem by limiting the time that Korean merchants could stay at Hakata for fear they were spies.

Well into the Tang, most goods reaching the port of Guangzhou were carried to the capital and other northern markets not by sea but either overland or via the network of rivers and canals opened by the construction of the Lingqu Canal in the third century BCE. This situation changed dramatically during the Song, when the ports of Fujian underwent the most spectacular growth of any in China. Located at the mouth of the Min River on the mainland opposite northern Taiwan, Fuzhou flourished and the ninth-century Arab geographer Ibn Khurdadhbih mentioned it as one of the four principal ports visited by Muslim sailors, together with Jiaozhi in Annam, Guangzhou, and Yangzhou. Before this, southern Fujian had been beyond the pale of Chinese settlement, suitable for exiles such as the scholar-official Han Yu, who in 819 was banished to southern Fujian, a region with

> Typhoons for winds, crocodiles for fish—
> Afflictions and misfortunes not to be plumbed! . . .
> Poisonous fogs and malarial miasmas
> Day and evening flare and form.

Later in the century, northerners fleeing the collapse of law and order sought refuge in Fujian, and after the Huang Chao rebels sacked Guangzhou, the expatriate community there dispersed, some to the south but a substantial number to the previously insignificant port of Quanzhou in Fujian.

At the end of the Tang Dynasty, Quanzhou was ruled by Wang Yenpin, of whom it was said that "Whenever the barbarian trading ships were dispatched, there had never been a loss either due to shipwreck or deficit in trade. For this, people called him 'the secretary who summons Treasures.'" Whether Wang was all that successful (or autonomous) is debatable, and Quanzhou's spectacular growth would have to wait until the Song court lifted restrictions on maritime trade. But when it did so, in the middle of the eleventh century, the results were dramatic, and a government agent could report that "the port was clogged with foreign ships, and their goods were piled like mountains." Part of Quanzhou's allure was that while local officials engaged in illicit trade, they charged only 10 percent for the right to trade—a form of private tax that was only two-thirds the official amount levied at Guangzhou. The government eventually recognized Quanzhou's indisputable primacy as a clearinghouse for foreign trade, and in 1087 established there the site of the fourth *shibosi* after Guangzhou, Hangzhou, and Mingzhou. The older Fujianese port of Fuzhou had declined in the early Song when there was an exodus of commercial capital and expertise north to Lin'an and south to Quanzhou, and it never received comparable recognition.

All the coastal kingdoms that emerged from the collapse of the Tang pursued trade with the south, and the rulers of the Song Dynasty made no effort to reverse the trend. Capitalizing on the expertise of the Muslim maritime communities in Yangzhou, which had developed as a result of the trade via Guangzhou, Quanzhou, and elsewhere, by the eleventh century Chinese shippers were carrying their own trade as far as Java. Many of these were Hokkiens, inhabitants of Fujian descended from Arab and Persian Muslims whose farflung connections were so valuable that foreign traders at Guangzhou preferred to deal with Hokkien middlemen rather than Chinese natives of Guangzhou. A product of the Song's liberalized approach to foreign trade, the Hokkien would become a lasting force in the commercial world of Southeast Asia.

Ships of East Asia

Tang authors divulge little on the subject of ship design or shipbuilding; the oldest detailed illustrations of ships date from after the Tang Dynasty; and archaeological finds are few. Even so, shipping of all kinds was essential to the Chinese way of life, for as one observer noted at the prosperous start of the eighth century, "Great ships in thousands and tens of thousands carry goods back and forth. If they once lay unused it would spell ruin for ten thousand merchants. If these were ruined, then others would have no one on whom to depend for their livelihood." The number of vessels required to keep the empire afloat, as it were, was astonishing. When the An Lushan rebellion ended, among the more urgent needs was to rebuild the devastated canal fleet, and the government established at least ten shipyards on the banks of the Yangzi for the purpose.

Shipping on inland waterways was generally in the hands of extended families whose lives and livelihoods centered figuratively and literally on their vessels, many of which served as floating homes and workplaces. The author of an eighth-century history recorded that "There is a saying among those who live among the rivers and lakes that 'water won't carry ten thousand,' by which they mean that large vessels do not exceed 8,000 or 9,000 piculs capacity"— between 550 and 650 tons, not including people and their household goods.* Yet a woman known as Aunt Yu had "a huge boat on board of which people were born, married and died. . . . There was a crew of several hundred." Every year they made a round trip along the Gan, Yangzi, and Huai Rivers within the modern landlocked provinces of Jiangxi and Anhui, "reaping enormous profits. This was nothing other than 'carrying ten thousand.'" The number of people who lived on boats in the Tang is unknown, but tenth-century Quanzhou was home to "floating boat people" who made their living as fishermen and traders, while in other inland areas as much as half the population was waterbound. The practice of living on houseboats has never died out, and while there are far fewer today, an estimated forty million Chinese lived on the water "in some shape or form" in the mid-twentieth century.

As was true in antiquity, sails were used on inland waterways, but the primary means of propulsion remained rowing with oars or *yulohs*, while moving against stronger currents or in narrow canals required towing. The monk Ennin describes how when he traveled from the coast to Yangzhou via canal, "Two water buffalo were tied to over forty boats, with either two or three of the latter joined to form a single craft and with these connected in a line by

---

* A picul was a unit of weight equivalent to what one man could carry, about sixty kilograms.

hawsers." With this configuration, the Japanese embassy covered about thirty kilometers per day. The canal was busy around the clock, and writing of a night passage Ennin describes with wonder how "Boats of the salt bureau laden with salt, with three or four, or again, four or five boats bound side by side, followed one after another without a break for several tens of *li*," their progress illuminated by blazing torches. (One *li* is about half a kilometer.) On tamer stretches of canal or river, a boat's crew hauled their own vessel, but haulers with local knowledge were hired for treacherous stretches such as the Yangzi's Three Gorges and the Sanmen Rapids on the Yellow River.

The major development in construction technique of this period across China was the introduction of iron fastenings (nails and clamps) no later than the eighth century. Nonetheless, on the coast of China, the mouth of the Yangzi was the effective dividing line between the shallow waters of the keel-less, shallow-draft, flat-bottomed "sand ships" (*shachuan*) of the north, which are thought to date from the Tang Dynasty, and the *fuchuan*, with its deep, V-shaped hull intended for blue-water navigation and built along the rockbound and embayed southern coast between Fujian and Guangzhou. Ships typically had no cabins, the passengers being allotted space on deck for their goods and themselves; they carried companies of archers for protection against pirates; and they usually towed a smaller dispatch boat. Even less is known about the ships of Korea and Japan, although there is a tendency to see echoes of Chinese tradition in the vessels of the Korean and Japanese kingdoms.

Chinese sources reveal more detail about Southeast Asian ships, which, according to an eighth-century source, were called *kunlun bo*: "With the fibrous bark of the coconut tree, they make cords which bind the parts of the ship together. . . . Nails and clamps are not used, for fear that the heating of the iron would give rise to fire. [The ships] are constructed by assembling [several] thicknesses of side planks, for the boards are thin and they fear they would break." This explanation for why shipwrights did not employ iron is not unlike the *Yuktikalpataru*'s explanation for why Indian shipwrights did not use iron. Yet Southeast Asian sailors frequented Chinese ports at this time—which is how the author knew about their ships—and they were aware that Chinese hulls were fastened with iron without fear of fire. As Chinese merchant ships began sailing overseas from the tenth century, even sedentary shipwrights in Southeast Asia would have seen for themselves how they were built. Nonetheless, there is no evidence for iron fittings in Southeast Asian ships before the sixteenth century. Instead, they were fastened with a combination of lashings and dowels inserted into holes drilled into the edges of planks, a method of joinery that allowed for the construction of ships much larger than those in which the Portuguese first reached Southeast Asia in the early 1500s. Sewn-

One of several vessels carved in the bas-reliefs representing scenes of daily life among the Khmers on the Bayon temple at Angkor Thom, Cambodia, around 1185. With its mast-and-batten sails, axial rudder, and anchor winch forward, the ship has been identified as a Chinese merchant junk. But the features of the passengers and crew—including two men playing a board game forward—seem Southeast Asian rather than Chinese. Detail of a photograph by l'Ecole Française d'Extréme-Orient in Jean Yves Claeys, Angkor *(Saigon: Editions Boy-Landry, 1948).*

plank fastening was common throughout all of Southeast Asia and as far north as Hainan Island and Guangdong Province in southern China. Although the land of the Hundred Yue had been governed from the north since before the start of the common era, its people had greater cultural affinities with their Southeast Asian neighbors in northern Vietnam than with their Han over-lords. We can perhaps discern a northern influence in the multiple thicknesses of planking in *kunlun bo* of the eighth century, but four hundred years later the seagoing vessels of southern China were still being built with the sewn-plank techniques familiar elsewhere in Southeast Asia.

This period also saw the adoption of fore-and-aft sails in Chinese ships. All sailing traditions seem to have started with a square sail from which a variety of different fore-and-aft configurations derived. In Southeast Asia, "fore-and-aft

A Southeast Asian paddled vessel from a bas-relief in the Bayon temple at Angkor Thom, Cambodia. Carved directly below the junk, this seems to show a riverboat of a type once ubiquitous on the lower reaches of the Mekong River. Above the boat, fishermen can be seen hauling their bulging nets while helmsmen steer their boats and a third member of the crew sorts the fish. Below are scenes from the market ashore. From a photograph in Jean Yves Claeys, Angkor *(Saigon: Editions Boy-Landry, 1948).*

sails of unspecified form set from two or more masts" were in use by the third century CE, and the canted, quadrilateral sails of the eighth-century Borobudur ships are clearly set fore-and-aft. Assuming a degree of cross-fertilization between Southeast and East Asian maritime traditions, the former was the source of the Chinese lugsail, a four-sided, battened sail set from a boom and yard that extend forward of the mast. The earliest representation of such a Chinese lugsail on a seagoing ship is on a frieze of the twelfth-century Bayon temple at Angkor Thom in Cambodia.

Naval Warfare

Given the number of rivals for the control of sea trade the potential for naval warfare was considerable, yet written notices are few, brief, and, apart from the battle of the Geum River between Chinese and Japanese fleets, refer almost exclusively to amphibious operations. Long distances presented no obstacle to determined campaigners. Srivijayan raiders sailed twelve hundred miles across the South China Sea to attack Kauthara, and even the Chinese campaigns against the Korean kingdoms—one per decade from 644 to 663—involved passages of at least three hundred miles across the Yellow Sea. The sources give few clues about the size or rig of the ships involved in any of these expeditions, but all references suggest that fighting, and even transport, was done in relatively small vessels.

When Huanwang threatened Annam in the tenth century, the Chinese governor built a fleet of thirty-five fast boats carrying only fifty men each—twenty-three oarsmen, twenty-five warriors, and two crossbowmen. The Southern Han kingdom may have employed similar vessels when they invaded Annam in the 930s. Rather than risk an encounter with them on the water, the Annamese planted massive stakes tipped with iron points in a northern branch of the Red River so that the sharpened ends were covered at high tide. As the Southern Han sailed into the estuary, Vietnamese in smaller craft harassed the invaders in a feint, and when they retreated upstream, the Southern Han followed. As the tide fell, their ships were stuck on the stakes and about half the force was slaughtered in a battle that proved a turning point in Vietnamese history.

Stray remarks in the Chinese annals suggest that the vessels employed on the Korean campaigns were not terribly large, either. The first involved nine hundred ships and forty thousand troops, an average of forty-four people per vessel. Even accounting for a number of these vessels being intended exclusively for carrying grain and other supplies, the largest ships probably had a total complement of no more than two hundred people, including crew. At the Geum River in 663, the Japanese lost 400 ships to a Chinese fleet of only 170. Whether this can be attributed to a difference in size between individual units, or to the Chinese securing a tactical advantage in the confined waters, is impossible to say. According to the Japanese chronicle, "The Japanese warships which first arrived engaged the Tang fleet, but had not the advantage, and therefore retired. Great Tang stood on its guard in strict order of battle." Such deliberation in deciding when and how to deploy their forces suggests that commanders on both sides had at least some experience of fleet engagements, but how such battles were fought remains unknown.

Because the high civilization of China was the cultural cynosure of all Northeast Asia, the Yellow Sea figures prominently in the written accounts of trade and warfare from the earliest times. The Sea of Japan (in Korean, Tonghae, or Eastern Sea) played a far less obvious role in the relations between the underdeveloped east coast of Korea, western Japan, and the territory of the Jurchen. Apart from those on either side of the Korea Strait, the principal ports of Korea and Japan all had a southerly orientation, and there were no major ports on the eastern shore of the Korean Peninsula, or the western side of Honshu. Yet even the Jurchen in the vicinity of northeast Korea and modern Vladivostok had seafaring experience, and in 1019 fifty Jurchen ships raided along the east coast of Korea, the islands of Ise and Tsushima, and the Japanese port at Hakata Bay on Kyushu. Yet the Jurchen never fully exploited this maritime capability and the focus of their southward expansion was always on the more direct overland routes toward northern China.

China's embrace of sea trade under the Northern Song was due to a combination of misfortune and opportunity. The collapse of its western frontier forced the emperor and many of his subjects to relocate to the east, closer to the center of the empire's elaborate canal system and to the seaports upon whose business the treasury increasingly relied for revenues. Through all these vicissitudes, the Chinese economy continued to grow, however. Imports once considered exotic and rare came to be seen as commodities, while mass-produced ceramics and other goods fed a growing export market that spanned the Monsoon Seas. At the same time that China's sea trade was expanding, that of the Korean kingdoms was in decline, opening the way for Chinese merchants to dominate the traffic of Northeast Asia. China's receptivity to trade had profound consequences for the states of Southeast Asia, not just in neighboring Vietnam, which achieved its independence from China, but also more southerly realms. From Champa to Srivijaya and Java, new, increasingly centralized states developed their own institutions to profit from and maintain trade. In the coming centuries, their prosperity would attract attention not only from their traditional trading partners in China and the Indian Ocean, but also from the Mediterranean world to the west.

Chapter 12

The Medieval Mediterranean and Europe

The establishment of the Fatimid Caliphate in Egypt in the tenth century signaled the start of a major realignment of Mediterranean and European commerce. The Red Sea became the destination of choice for Indian Ocean trade, which had spillover effects across the Levant. Yet the rise of the only major Muslim state with maritime roots also led to a decline of Muslim fortunes in the central Mediterranean. The Fatimids possessed considerable naval experience, but they established their new capital up the Nile at Cairo and political realities directed their energies to threats from Southwest Asia, so that by the start of the Crusades at the end of the eleventh century they had lost their initiative on the Mediterranean. Political and religious factionalism likewise rendered the North African emirates incapable of effectively resisting the incipient commercial and military strength of Genoa, Pisa, Amalfi, and Venice. The Italian city-states hardly presented a united front, but a host of religious, political, economic, and commercial changes in Latin (Catholic) Europe facilitated their takeover of Muslim-dominated trade routes and territories.

The wealth of the Byzantine Empire, the caliphates, and Levantine ports continued to attract western traders and rulers, but the expansion of east–west trade across the Mediterranean was especially beneficial to merchants from western and northwest Europe and contributed incidentally to the establishment of wholly distinct and vibrant trading regimes on the Baltic and North Seas. And as the volume and value of trade between south and north grew, so did the impetus for mastering the Atlantic sea-lanes between the Mediterranean and northwest Europe. The consequent merging of northern and southern Europe's distinct approaches to shipbuilding and navigation resulted in the development of many of the tools European sailors would employ to illuminate the sea of darkness and discover for themselves new worlds.

The Mediterranean

The rise of the Italian port cities and the ascendancy of the merchant class to a place of privilege and authority are hallmarks of the earliest stages of Europe's medieval commercial revolution. In no Mediterranean society since Phoenicia and Carthage did merchants enjoy such respect or influence as they did in the great emporia of Venice on the Adriatic, Genoa on the Ligurian, and Pisa and Amalfi on the Tyrrhenian Sea. Though few in number, the Venetians and Genoese extended their commercial and political influence throughout the Mediterranean, to the Black Sea, and, most influentially, to northern Europe, which they first reached via Alpine routes to the fairs of Champagne and the centers of German trade, and after the thirteenth century by sea through the Strait of Gibraltar to Flanders and England.

Situated in the midst of an extensive lagoon that runs about fifty kilometers from the Po estuary in the south to the mouth of the Piave River in the north and with an average width of about eleven kilometers between the *lidi* and the mainland, the islands of Venice were home to an amphibious people who congregated in island parishes characteristically dominated by a church overlooking a wharf or boatyard. The Venetians depended on wheat purchased in the Italian interior since they could grow none themselves, and Venetian barges routinely ascended the Po the more than three hundred kilometers to Pavia—capital of the kingdom of Italy—and Milan as early as the sixth century. It was in the river trades that the Venetians honed the commercial, martial, and diplomatic skills that served them in their expansion down the Adriatic and into the eastern Mediterranean. Aghlabid raids rendered the Adriatic an anarchic sea in the tenth century, but the Venetians grew increasingly assertive. In the year 1000, Pietro II Orseolo defeated Dalmatian pirates in a series of battles that established Venice's primacy in the northern Adriatic. Diplomatically, Orseolo secured the backing of both the Byzantines and what would be known as the Holy Roman Empire by arranging marriages between Venetians and the ruling families of each. In later centuries, Orseolo's rule came to be seen as the commencement of the Most Serene Republic's rise, and the anniversary of his departure on the Dalmatian campaign was celebrated in an ever more elaborate ceremony by which Venice was spiritually joined to the Adriatic. The *sposalizio* ("wedding") took place annually on Ascension Day when the doge, his retainers, members of the clergy, and ambassadors to Venice put out in the splendid state barge *Bucintoro*. Declaring "We wed thee, Adriatic, as a sign of our true and perpetual dominion," the doge dropped into the sea a gold ring blessed by the Patriarch of Grado. In this act, Venice proclaimed its mastery over the sea and affirmed its exclusive relationship against other prospective suitors.

Naval power in the Italian maritime cities evolved in completely different ways from that of the Byzantine Empire and the caliphates. Lacking a vast territory, Venice's fleet was concentrated in one place, and when the city did acquire colonies, these were astride shipping lanes with which the Venetians were already intimately familiar; thus the exercise of naval power evolved organically from merchants' priorities. The organization of Venice's naval forces likewise reflected the city's commercial foundations. Merchants sailed in armed ships as a matter of course—the difference between "armed" and "unarmed" vessels was usually determined by the size of the crew—and regulations specifying the type and quantity of weapons carried by both crew and merchants merely codified standing practice. Ships on long voyages routinely sailed together for safety, but in 1308 the Signoria required that ships bound for Cyprus and Cilician Armenia or for the Black Sea port of Tana sail in convoy.

The majority of ships in Venice were privately built and owned, although the government regulated their size and rig so that in the event of war it would have access to the sorts of vessels it needed. Shipbuilders were originally concentrated on the Rialto, but by the twelfth century they had moved to the area of the Arsenale, which combined the functions of government shipyard, chandlery, and weapons depot. In wartime, the state purchased or hired ships from private owners, and if additional vessels were needed, these could be ordered from private yards or shipwrights could be seconded to the Arsenale. By the 1200s, Venice had the industrial capacity to provide the Fourth Crusade with about three hundred ships including horse transports, round ships, and fifty galleys. A century later, Dante drew on his memory of the government shipyard to describe the eighth circle of hell where,

> As in the Venetians' arsenal in winter the
> tenacious pitch boils to recaulk their worn ships,
>   for they cannot sail; instead this man works on a
> new ship, that one plugs the ribs of a craft that has
> made many voyages,
>   this one repairs at the prow, this one at the stern
> another makes oars, another twists shrouds, another patches
> foresail and mainsail.

In anticipation of wartime emergencies, the state required that all able-bodied men between the ages of twenty and sixty be registered in their home parish. All eligible parishioners were divided into groups of a dozen, one of whom, chosen by lot, joined a ship while the others contributed one lira per month toward his maintenance. (In extraordinary circumstances, the number drafted was much higher.) The state provided five lira per month per sailor, who could get out of service by paying the government six lira for someone to go in his stead.

Around the same time that Venice was asserting its dominion of the Adriatic, and half a century before William the Conqueror invaded England, Norman knights began appearing in Italy where they hired themselves out to one or another rival Christian noble. The most infamous of these mercenaries was Robert Hauteville, called Guiscard ("cunning"). In 1059, the pope named him duke of Apulia, Calabria, and Sicily, provided he could wrest these territories from Byzantine and Kalbid control. Two years later, he and his brother Roger defeated a Byzantine army sent to enforce Constantinople's claim to Apulia and Calabria. When the port of Reggio fell, the way was open for the Hautevilles' invasion of Sicily. In 1060, the Normans landed virtually unopposed and made an alliance of convenience with one of several rival emirs. Palermo fell in 1072 followed shortly by the rest of Sicily, thus ending 250 years of Muslim rule on the island. The year before capturing Palermo, Guiscard seized the Adriatic port of Bari, the last Byzantine stronghold in Italy. A decade later, he crossed to Dyrrachium with about 150 ships intending to march on Constantinople, but he postponed his plan when the pope enlisted his help against the Holy Roman Empire. The Byzantines recouped their losses with Venetian help, and in 1085 Guiscard crossed the Adriatic a second time, but his sudden death eliminated the Norman threat to the Byzantines, and Emperor Alexius I was able to turn his attention to the threat posed by the Seljuq Turks.

Even though Norman control of the Strait of Otranto posed a direct threat to Venetian interests, Alexius could only enlist Venetian support "with promises and bribes." Laid out in a chrysobull (imperial decree) in 1082, these included acknowledging the Venetian doge and his successors as lords of Venice, Dalmatia, and Croatia, and granting them additional commercial advantages at the empire's principal ports as far east as Antioch. This was the Byzantines' first major concession to Venice as a commercial carrier and a significant step in the Venetians' evolution from regional purveyors of salt, fish, and grain to a major Mediterranean power. Alexius has been criticized for selling out the empire, but the long years of warfare had forced the Byzantines to extreme measures and his immediate aim was to arrest the economy's downward spiral. In this he seems to have been successful.

In addition to opening Byzantine ports to Venetian traders, the chrysobull of 1082 set aside a quarter for them in Constantinople,

> from the ancient quay of the Hebrews as far as the Vigla, including the anchorages between these two points, not to mention the gift of much real property both in the capital and in the city of Dyrrachium and wherever else the Venetians demanded it. But the main reward was the free market [Alexius] afforded them in all provinces under Roman [Byzantine] control, so that they were enabled to trade without interference as they wished; not a single obol was to be exacted by way of customs duties or any other tax levied by the treasury. They were completely free of Roman authority.

While these free trade provisions gave the Venetians a pronounced advantage in the commerce of the eastern Mediterranean, they were unable to carry all the empire's trade. Genoese and Pisan merchants based in Constantinople took up the slack, although they had to pay tariffs of between 4 and 10 percent.

Less than four hundred kilometers to the west of Venice, Genoa lies on the Ligurian Sea where the coast turns west toward France and the Iberian Peninsula. The hardscrabble Genoese faced the sea with their backs to the steep hills of the Apennines. They had few opportunities for agriculture, mining, or lumbering and limited access to the interior. To seaward, Genoa fronted on a narrow continental shelf where fish were scarce. Such success as the Genoese had at sea derived from their ability to exploit what is probably the best natural harbor between Barcelona and La Spezia. The fact that it is the northernmost harbor in the western Mediterranean gave them a favorable position for trade with central and northern Europe via the Po valley and the Alpine passes. (Pavia is 115 kilometers north of Genoa, much of the way through the mountains, and Milan is on the other side of the Po 35 kilometers beyond Pavia.) About seventy-five miles down the coast at the mouth of the Arno River, Pisa had better access to the markets and manufactures of Florence, but at the same time was more easily embroiled in the politics of Tuscany and the Italian interior.

Genoese and Pisan merchants competed fiercely for the growing trade of the western Mediterranean, but although they spent much of the eleventh century at war with each other, they put aside their differences to evict the Muslim emir of Sardinia in 1015, and more memorably to attack Mahdia. When the Zirids broke with the Fatimids in midcentury, Ifriqiya had been plunged into a period of incessant warfare that severely disrupted Mahdia's trade, which was taken up by Pisan and Genoese merchants, among others. For African gold, the Italians traded European slaves, furs, and tin, as well as wood and grain when these were in short supply. They used the gold, in turn, to buy silks, spices, medicinals, and other luxuries in Byzantine and Muslim markets to the east. Taking advantage of the Zirids' weakness, in 1087 Pisa and Genoa joined forces to attack Mahdia. The most substantive account of the undertaking comes from a Pisan victory song that includes few details of the actual fighting, but whose religious overtones anticipate the more explicitly pious nature of the First Crusade. Just as the Venetians could not take full advantage of the privileges granted by the chrysobull of 1082, the outcome of the Mahdia campaign proved indecisive because neither Pisa nor Genoa had the wherewithal to seize the territory for themselves.

The Crusades

A decade after the Mahdia campaign, Alexius summoned western Christian rulers for military help against the Seljuqs. An earlier appeal had borne no fruit, but in 1095 he sent an embassy to Pope Urban II, whose response was to preach the First Crusade. The Crusades were holy wars sanctioned by the pope and undertaken by individuals "for the salvation of their souls and the liberation of the Church" in Jerusalem, and whom the pope promised to "relieve . . . of all penance imposed for their sins, of which they have made a genuine and full confession." Acknowledging that some might take the cross for other reasons, Urban specified that absolution applied only to those who fought "for devotion alone, not to gain honour or money." For the mass of crusaders, the prospect of attaining anything more than spiritual benefit was remote: most probably joined for religious reasons, or at least "In the name of God and profit." If the Crusades were not undertaken for material gain, commercial shipping would prove the crusader states' lifeline, to the great profit of Venice, Genoa, and Pisa. The armies of the First Crusade converged on Constantinople in 1097 before marching southwest across Anatolia. One contingent crossed the upper Euphrates to take Edessa (Urfa, Turkey), while the remainder took Jerusalem and, thanks to the timely arrival of twelve Genoese galleys at Port Saint Symeon (the ancient al-Mina), Antioch. The Genoese had taken the cross and came as crusaders, but for their services they received commercial privileges in the port, as did the Pisans who followed in 1099. Although last off the mark, by 1100 the Venetians had a fleet of some two hundred ships en route to the Levant, and over the long term they profited more from the crusader states than any of their maritime rivals.

The relative ease with which the Italians were able to supply the Crusaders was due partly to the century-long decline of Muslim naval power in the Mediterranean. By the eleventh century, the Fatimid fleet theoretically numbered between seventy-five and ninety galleys, five of them assigned to the Red Sea. More than half were stationed at Cairo and ports in the Nile delta, while perhaps twenty-five were distributed among Ashkelon, Acre, Sidon, and Tyre. Fleet administration was overseen by the emir of the sea (*emir al-bahr*, a title that entered European languages as "admiral") and there was a standing force of about five thousand sailors and marines. In addition to being over-stretched, the Fatimid forces were handicapped by the maritime geography of the eastern Mediterranean, where sources of freshwater were in short supply, especially as Levantine ports fell to the crusaders, and neither the place nor time of the Christian fleets' coming were predictable. The loss of Cyprus and Crete to the Byzantines in the 960s all but ensured Egyptian naval forces had to fight defensively.

The Fatimids also suffered from having the only standing navy in the eastern Mediterranean. The crusader states had neither ships nor the manpower to crew them, but an endless stream of armed shipping brought merchants, pilgrims, and crusaders to the Holy Land for two centuries. The fleets seldom coordinated with each other, so the Fatimids faced not a unitary navy that it might destroy root and branch in a single campaign, but a kaleidoscope of fleets from not only Venice, Genoa, and Pisa, but also the Byzantine Empire, Spain, France, Sicily, and even England and Scandinavia. Given these geographic, strategic, and logistical disadvantages, that the Fatimid fleet remained remotely effective for as long as it did is remarkable.

As if to accentuate the importance of maritime power to the crusader states, the first to fall to a resurgent Islam was the landlocked county of Edessa, the loss of which prompted the Second Crusade (1147–49). This was not limited to the Holy Land, but included campaigns on the Iberian Peninsula and against the pagan Wends, Slavs living in what is now northern Germany. The eastern crusade was a fiasco, and the Baltic campaign fared little better although it did initiate a century-long period of eastward expansion. But the pressure on al-Andalus was considerable. At its greatest extent, the Umayyad Caliphate of Córdoba reached as far north as the mountains of Asturias and León, and it was here that the Iberian *Reconquista* took shape under Alfonso VI, king of León and Castile and self-styled emperor of all Spain. The caliphate had lost its monopoly on power in al-Andalus at the beginning of the eleventh century, and Christian kings took advantage of divisions among the roughly thirty or so Muslim *taifas* that had sprung up in its place. The starting point of the *Reconquista* is generally taken to be Alfonso's capture of Toledo in 1085, news of which helped fuel the drive to reclaim the Holy Land from Muslim rule prior to the First Crusade. This also led the *taifas* to seek help from the North African Almoravids who defeated Alfonso in 1086 and consolidated their authority over al-Andalus, including the major ports from Cádiz to Almería and the Balearics. They were succeeded by a rival Berber dynasty, the Almohads, who had been active in the Atlantic Moroccan port of Salé and "who organized their fleet in the most perfect manner ever known and on the largest scale ever observed." By midcentury, the Almohads had advanced into al-Andalus, where they made their capital at Seville, and after consolidating their control of Almoravid North Africa they ousted the Normans from Mahdia, Sfax, and Tripoli (in Libya), which they had controlled for less than a decade.

The rulers of Norman Sicily had been conspicuous by their absence from the First Crusade. This was not due to a desire to placate Sicilian Muslims, although they comprised a significant proportion of the population. Muslims continued to raid Sicily into the 1120s, and the Norman kings of Sicily attempted to extend their control over parts of North Africa and fought the Almohads. However, the Normans had an emphatically pragmatic approach in their overseas relations, and as early as the raid on Mahdia they had declined to occupy the port on behalf of the Pisans and Genoese because they had come to an accommodation with the Zirid emir. At the same time, Genoese and Pisans were welcome as traders and furnished with letters of protection. As a result in part of this policy of forbearance, Norman Sicily was one of the most cosmopolitan and prosperous kingdoms in western Eurasia, with a cultural brilliance that reflected and harmonized the diverse origins and faiths of its Muslim, Orthodox, Latin Christian, and Jewish inhabitants.

Following the pope's call for an Iberian crusade, the Genoese negotiated with the king of Castile to support a campaign against Almería, in exchange for which they were promised one-third of the city. They received comparable concessions from the count of Catalonia for the capture of the Ebro River port of Tortosa. The campaign was an enormous undertaking for Genoa, which fielded more than 225 galleys and other vessels and twelve thousand men in addition to the ships' crews. After taking Almería in October 1147, the bulk of the Genoese forces wintered at Barcelona before going on to take Tortosa. Unable to shoulder the expense of occupying such distant territories as a communal project, the city sold its interest in Tortosa to the count of Barcelona and leased its holdings in Almería to a wealthy Genoese merchant before Almohad forces recaptured the port, which remained an integral part of Muslim Spain for another three centuries.

Inconclusive though its overseas campaigns were, involvement in the Second Crusade helped consolidate Genoa's political position with respect to the Holy Roman Empire. When Frederick I, "Barbarossa," marched into northern Italy in 1158 and demanded that the cities pledge fealty and pay tribute to him as emperor, the Genoese successfully pleaded for special consideration because they had brought an end to "the attacks and damages of the barbarians that used to vex the coastline from Barcelona to Rome every day," and every Christian could "now sleep and rest securely under his fig tree and arbor." Rhetorical flourishes aside, Genoese aspirations were not defined by religious politics, and in 1152 and 1160 the Genoese negotiated treaties with the North African ports of Bougie (Béjaïa, Algeria) and Ceuta, and began trading with Atlantic Moroccan ports to which gold caravans from West Africa had been diverted to avoid Bedouins blocking the way between sub-Saharan Africa and the Mediterranean.

The Second Crusade in Iberia was not confined to Spain or the Mediterranean. Only a week after the fall of Almería, Portugal's first king, Afonso I, captured Almoravid Lisbon with the support of about thirteen thousand northern European crusaders—from Flanders, Normandy, Scotland, England, and the Rhineland—who had sailed from England in a fleet of about 165 ships. Afonso urged them to join his assault on Lisbon, one of the most populous cities on the peninsula and "the richest in trade of all Africa and a good part of Europe." Following prolonged negotiations over compensation, Afonso agreed that neither he nor his men would have any share in the booty that came from the sack of the city, and he exempted his allies and their heirs from paying duties on their goods and ships "from now henceforth in perpetuity throughout all my lands." After a four-month siege, Lisbon fell in what contemporaries considered one of the few successes of the Second Crusade and what is now taken as a pivotal moment in the *Reconquista*.

The main reason for the failure of the Second Crusade in the east was a poorly conceived decision to attack Damascus, the state least hostile to the crusader kingdoms and the defense of which united a host of otherwise fractious Muslim rulers. Nur al-Din emerged as the preeminent leader in Syria, and after routing the crusaders at Damascus in 1154 he rallied his coreligionists to oppose the crusaders elsewhere. He was succeeded by his deputy in Cairo, Saladin (Salah al-Din Yusuf), who founded the Ayyubid Dynasty (1169–1254) and became one of the crusaders' most capable adversaries. But by this time the Egyptian navy had been weakened beyond repair. Saladin made recovery of the Levantine ports a priority, but this was accomplished from the land rather than the sea, and thanks to the fleet's considerable shortcomings they were ceded again during the Third Crusade. Despairing over the loss of ten ships blockading Tyre, Saladin's biographer wrote: "It became clear from this disaster . . . that the rulers of Egypt had not attended to the needs of the navy nor recruited suitable men for its service; instead they had collected obscure, ignorant, weak and untried men on a random basis. It was therefore no surprise that when confronted with danger they were gripped with fear, and when ordered to obey they were unable to do so." Saladin appealed to the Almohads of Iberia for naval support, but sources differ about whether they replied favorably. Even if 190 ships were sent, as a later author reports, they were of little help.

During this period, the Byzantine Empire had been plunged into turmoil by a combination of military setbacks at the hands of the Seljuqs, conflict between the eastern and western Churches, and a succession crisis. In 1182, the future emperor Andronicus ordered the massacre of the Latin population at Constantinople. A contemporary estimate of sixty thousand dead seems high but testifies to the great number of foreign traders in the city and the violence unleashed by Andronicus. Revenge for the slaughter was swift, as Latin refugees fleeing Constantinople pillaged Byzantine ports throughout the Aegean, but it would reach its devastating climax two decades later.

In 1198, Innocent III called the Fourth Crusade. Rather than attempt a direct assault on the Holy Land, the crusaders planned to invade by way of Alexandria—an objective that could be justified in the name of liberating its large Christian population—or Cairo, "because they could better destroy the [Ayyubid] Turks by way of Babylon [Cairo]." There was, however, a powerful commercial incentive for attacking Egypt, which was the chief terminus for the Indian Ocean trade and the richest state in the Muslim Mediterranean. Organizers planned to recruit thirty-five thousand soldiers, including forty-five hundred knights and their horses, to be carried in some three hundred ships supplied by Venice at a cost of eighty-five thousand marks—about twenty thousand kilograms of silver, or twice the yearly revenues of the kings of either France or England—payable in the spring of 1202. By the fall of that year, only a third of the crusaders' army and funds had reached Venice. Determined to receive payment in full, the Venetians coerced the crusaders into raising the balance through plunder, the first victim being Zara (Zadar, Croatia). An attack on a Latin Christian city was anathema to many, but two hundred ships joined Doge Enrico Dandolo to take the port, and the stage was set for the next diversion of the Fourth Crusade from its original goal.

The following year, the crusaders sailed to Constantinople to help restore the beleaguered Isaac II, who resumed the throne with his son Alexius as co-emperor. The two prevailed upon the Franks to remain at Constantinople, but when they reneged on their debt to the crusaders, including "200,000 silver marks, and provisions for every man in your army," the Franks declared war.*

---

* Orthodox authors generally referred to Catholics, and Muslim authors to Christians generally, as Franks, regardless of their place of origin.

Isaac and Alexius were murdered by their own subjects, and the Franks looted the city of "so much, indeed, that no one could estimate its amount or its value. It included gold and silver, table-services and precious stones, satin and silk, mantles of squirrel, fur, ermine and miniver. And every choicest thing to be found on this earth," including the four gilded bronze horses of the Basilica of St. Mark in Venice. The value of the crusaders' spoils was put at a staggering four hundred thousand marks.

Baldwin of Flanders was elected emperor of what is known as the Latin Empire of Constantinople (1204–61), which comprised about a quarter of the late Byzantine Empire. The doge of Venice became "lord of a quarter and of a half [of a quarter; that is, three-eighths] of the Roman Empire," including the ports of Dyrrachium, Ragusa, and Corfu on the Adriatic; Corone and Modone in the Peloponnese; Rhodes and Negroponte (Euboea); Gallipoli; and Rhaedestus and Heraclea on the Sea of Marmara—all important links in the Venetians' lengthening chain of trade. Venice also claimed three-eighths of Constantinople itself, and unlike any of the other participants in the campaign, she did not have to pledge fealty to Baldwin. The remainder of the old empire was divided between the empire of Nicaea under Theodore Lascaris, which ran from the Black Sea to the Aegean; the Seljuqs; and, on a narrow strip of eastern Asia Minor bordering the Black Sea, the Orthodox empire of Trebizond (Trabzon).

To all intents and purposes, the Most Serene Republic monopolized Byzantine trade and dominated the sea route to the Levant, but the Venetians were not without competitors. Although the Latin Empire effectively excluded Genoese merchants from their traditional trading quarter in Constantinople and banned them from the most profitable Aegean trade, Genoa was experiencing an economic boom: Genoese bankers were lending money to the crusader states, the pope, and individual crusaders; their trade in the western Mediterranean was expanding; and in 1252 Genoese and Florentine bankers began minting gold coins. Outside of the Byzantine Empire, Sicily, or Iberia, the latter two having inherited the practice from their Muslim predecessors, these were the first gold coins issued in Europe since the early eighth century. More than a symbol of Latin Europe's economic rejuvenation, gold coins were also essential for its future prosperity.

Their mutual expansion put the rival cities on a collision course and open warfare between Genoa and Venice erupted in 1257. Hostilities were limited initially to the waters around Acre and Tyre, but the calculus changed with the Treaty of Nymphaeum (1261) between Genoa and the empire of Nicaea. For the right of passage into the Black Sea and other considerations, the Genoese agreed to provide Michael VIII Palaiologos with fifty armed ships for his campaign against the Latin empire of Constantinople. This naval force tipped the balance in Michael's favor and he entered Constantinople the same year. The treaty notwithstanding, the Venetians remained the most important carriers in the Aegean, but as such they were a favorite target for pirates. Theodore Lascaris had sponsored pirates to harass Venetian and Latin shipping, and conditions worsened after Michael's capture of Constantinople. A Venetian-Byzantine treaty addressed the problem of Venetian pirates operating against imperial interests, and vice versa, as well as abuses by Byzantine customs officials. But the fatal flaw of Byzantine policy was that with no fleet of its own, the empire had to leave the suppression of piracy to foreign powers—essentially asking the foxes to guard the henhouse. This weakness was exacerbated by the threat of attack from the ousted Franks, whose machinations led to the War of the Sicilian Vespers, the longest and best documented naval conflict of the period, although in the end it hardly involved the Byzantines at all.

The Norman kingdom of Sicily had come to an end at the close of the twelfth century, when control of the island passed ultimately to Charles I, duke of Anjou (in France), who hoped to use Sicily as a springboard for a campaign against Constantinople. The Byzantine emperor Michael enlisted the help of Peter III of Aragon, who drove Charles out of Sicily. (In so doing Peter laid the groundwork for a Spanish Mediterranean empire encompassing the Balearics, Corsica, Sardinia, and, for more than four centuries, Sicily. The crowns of Sicily and Aragon remained joined until the end of the War of the Spanish Succession in 1712.) Chief architect of the Aragonese naval success was the Calabrian admiral, Roger of Lauria, "a man of inestimable worth" in Boccaccio's words, who between 1283 and 1305 won six major naval engagements in which he displayed a strategic and tactical ability apparently unique in the age of medieval galley warfare. Lauria's approach to manning his ships was distinct from that of contemporary naval powers, for he commanded a polyglot collection of warriors and crews without regard to nationality or religion. People from different regions specialized in different types of warfare. Lauria's oarsmen were generally Sicilian; the crossbowmen Catalan (their reputation second only to that of the Genoese); and the corps of *almugavars* ("footsoldiers skilled in the use of lances, missiles, and shields, and who range far and wide by day and night," not unlike modern special forces), as well as heavy and light cavalry, were Aragonese. Initially Roger relied on the compulsory service required of the subjects of the crown of Aragon, but as the size of the fleet and duration of the war increased, so did resistance to the crown's prerogatives. Conscription was tried, but the better solution was to offer incentives in the form of pay competitive with wages in the merchant fleet, a share of booty from raids and warfare, and forgiveness of debts. The conflict spread to the western Mediterranean and in 1285 naval power proved decisive against a Franco-Angevin invasion of Aragon, when Philip III led eight thousand knights across the Pyrenees. These could only be supported by sea, and when Lauria defeated a French fleet in a night battle off the Spanish coast and then took the port of Rosas, the French withdrew. But it was the deaths of Charles, Peter, and Philip in 1285–86 that brought the war to a close.

The Mediterranean Breakout

Only a decade before, the Genoese had opened a new epoch in the history of the Mediterranean and Europe, if not the world, with the establishment of regular sea trade between the Mediterranean and the North Sea. The earliest record of a direct voyage from Genoa to Flanders is that of Nicolozzo Spinola in 1277. It is hardly surprising that the Genoese initiated this route: they had been active on the Atlantic coast of North Africa as far south as Salé and Safi for a century; they were employed as shipwrights and sailors in Galician ports on the Bay of Biscay; and they were past masters in the overland trade to northern Europe. Much has been made of the obstacles presented by the winds and currents that flow through the Strait of Gibraltar from west to east, but these are overblown. Ships have routinely sailed through the Strait of Gibraltar since before Cádiz was Gadir. Although it is on balance easier to enter the Mediterranean than to leave it, easterly winds prevail five months of the year—in March, July to September, and December—and coastal currents flow toward the Atlantic.

Shortly after its conquest by Ferdinand III of Castile in 1248, Seville was awash in shipping from around the Mediterranean and northern Europe. According to the *Estoria de España,*

> ships come up the [Guadalquivir] river every day from the sea, including *naves* [ships], galleys, and many other sea-going vessels. They stop under the [city] walls, and bring in all kinds of merchandise from all over the world: from Tangiers, Ceuta, Tunis, Bougie, Alexandria, Genoa, Portugal, England, Pisa, Lombardy, Bordeaux, Bayonne, Sicily, Gascony, Catalonia, Aragon, other parts of France, and many other regions of the sea, both Christian and Muslim.

That is to say, medieval mariners perceived the Strait of Gibraltar as neither barrier nor boundary. The chief obstacle to regular navigation between the Mediterranean and northern European ports was a lack of commercial incentive, not inadequate ships. However, the growth of the Iberian and northern

European economies helped make the sea route competitive with the trans-alpine routes between Venice and Genoa and northern France, while the decline of trading opportunities in the Levant compelled merchants to seek out alternative outlets for their energy and capital.

The search for new business ventures received additional impetus in 1291 when the Mamluk sultanate that ruled Egypt and Syria completed the Muslim *Reconquista* of the Levant with the capture of Tyre and Acre. In response, some Genoese wanted to invade Egypt in alliance with the Mongols, who since 1259 had controlled the continental silk road all the way to the Black Sea. That the Genoese sought commercial advantage from a campaign in Egypt is seen from two other efforts made in 1291. The first was their negotiation with the Ilkhans of Persia to build a fleet to divert Indian Ocean trade from the Red Sea to the Persian Gulf, a plan that fell victim to civil unrest in Genoa. Better known was the attempt by Ugolino and Vadino Vivaldi to reach the Indian Ocean by sailing around Africa, an undertaking that if successful would have enabled the Genoese to bypass Egypt altogether, much as Eudoxus had sought to circumvent the Ptolemies 1,500 years before. The Vivaldis fared no better than Eudoxus, and after passing through the Strait of Gibraltar they were last reported somewhere on the coast of West Africa roughly opposite the Canary Islands before they sailed into history, two centuries before Portugal's Vasco da Gama rounded the Cape of Good Hope from the Atlantic to the Indian Ocean.

Any prospect for a revival of the Italians' Levantine trade disappeared when the Mamluks decided that the only way to safeguard the coast against attack from the sea was to raze virtually every port from the Sinai to the Gulf of Alexandretta (or Iskanderun). The Levant's maritime vitality was eliminated as thoroughly as it had been by the Sea People at the end of the Bronze Age. The destruction was not accompanied by the same violence, but the consequences were far more enduring. Beirut and Tyre eventually recovered, but most Levantine ports remained dormant until the twentieth century, and the heirs to millennia of maritime commercial expertise simply sat out the most dynamic centuries of oceanic trade.

As the Levantine ports atrophied, Indian Ocean merchants began avoiding the Red Sea, sailing instead to Hormuz at the mouth of the Persian Gulf. From there, caravan routes ran west and north, with one branch leading to the Mediterranean port of Ayas, in Cilician Armenia, and the other to Trabzon, on the Black Sea. The Venetians had had access to the Black Sea since the Fourth Crusade, but the Genoese were the first to really profit from the trade, and their merchant colonies ringed the coast from Constantinople to the Crimea and around to Sinop. The Crimea was among the most polyglot places in the world, where Turks, Mongols, Catalans, Venetians, Genoese, Syrians, Jews, Armenians, Arabs, and traders from central Europe came together to trade everything from grain, hides, and slaves to silks and spices. Caffa (Feodosiya, Ukraine) was as impressive an entrepôt as Theodosia had been in antiquity, and the fourteenth-century traveler Ibn Battuta commended the "wonderful harbor with about two hundred ships in it, both ships of war and trading vessels, small and large, for it is one of the world's celebrated ports." But the best situated port was Tana (Azov, Russia), only a short portage from the Volga River and the trade of the Caspian Sea, Persia, and the silk road.

Black Sea merchants profited not only from the decline of the Levantine ports but from the prosperity and stability of the Pax Mongolica that descended on Central Asia in the mid-1200s. Trade was generally beneficial for all concerned, but there were hidden hazards. At some point in about the 1330s, a plague had erupted in China, from where it spread westward across the Eurasian steppes. In 1347 a Genoese ship carried the disease from Caffa to Europe. So long as it had remained land-bound, the disease made its way slowly, but once injected into the arteries of western maritime trade, the Black Death moved with horrific speed. In the words of a Byzantine chronicler: "A plague attacked almost all the sea coasts of the world and killed most of the people. For it swept not only through Pontus, Thrace and Macedonia, but even Greece, Italy and all the islands, Egypt, Libya, Judea and Syria." After incubating over the winter, the disease continued on to other centers of maritime trade: Genoa itself, Pisa, Venice, Marseille, Bordeaux, and Bayonne; from the south of France to England, Calais, Cologne, Copenhagen, Bergen, Lübeck, Novgorod; and from these ports via river into the heart of Europe. Had it not been for the Genoese initiative in beginning regular galley trade between the Mediterranean and Flanders in the 1200s, the plague's effects on Europe would have been dramatically different. Maritime trade was not the only vector of the disease, but it was the most efficient.

The Black Death had mortality rates as high as 90 percent in some parts of northern China, and killed perhaps twenty-five million people in Europe alone—between a third and a half of the total population—although local losses could be far worse: the population of Venice fell by 60 percent. Despite the agonizing and terrifying personal losses throughout Eurasia and North Africa, Europe's economy recovered quickly. Labor shortages led to higher wages for workers, whose numbers were increased by peasants leaving the land in search of work in cities, and higher wages led to an increase in consumption and improved living standards, which in turn stimulated trade. Industry also advanced as people developed new devices to compensate for the sudden shortage in manpower. Venetian and Genoese commerce recovered, too, even on the Black Sea.

The Hanseatic League and the Trade of Northern Europe

Even without the convenience of Genoese shipping, the plague would have found its way into Europe from the east. Yet its spread along a clockwise circuit from the Mediterranean to the ports of Europe's Atlantic, North Sea, and Baltic coasts testifies to the rapid expansion of northern European trade following the Italians' opening of the sea route from the Mediterranean to Flanders. Here, trade was dominated by German merchants of what came to be known as the Hanseatic League. Prior to this, northern European trade had been in essence a regional commerce. Compared with the exotic trades and interplay of mature and mutually emulous cultures in and around the Mediterranean, northern Europe's economic strength rose from a dull base. Traffic in high-value, low-volume goods represented only a fraction of total commerce on the Mediterranean, but it had even less of a role in the North and Baltic Seas. Nonetheless, Danes, Germans, Flemings, English, and others enriched from the carriage of bulk commodities were gradually narrowing the gap between the relatively impoverished north and the prosperous south, and more immediate exposure to southern trade hastened the process.

The initiative for this came not from France and the British Isles, the kingdoms closest to the Mediterranean, but from Flanders and the Baltic. Following the dynastic struggle for the English throne in 1066, the North Sea became a relatively peaceable arena of long-distance trade as merchants sailed between Bergen, Ribe, Hamburg, Bremen, Utrecht, and Flanders; up the Rhine to Cologne; along the coast of France; and to a variety of Scottish and English ports from Berwick in the north to Bristol on the Irish Sea. By the twelfth century the most active merchants hailed from Scandinavia and Flanders, but German merchants from the Rhine valley, especially Cologne, and Bremen began to join their numbers. At the same time, German merchants grew increasingly involved in the trade of the Baltic. This new orientation was linked directly to Germanic migration across the Elbe into central and eastern Europe. This accelerated in the tenth century but it was not until the twelfth century that growing population coupled with economic opportunity and crusader zeal propelled the Saxons into Mecklenburg and Pomerania (western Poland). In 1143 Henry III, "the Lion," duke of Saxony, founded the city of Lübeck on an island between the Trave and Wakenitz Rivers. This location, about twenty kilometers from the Baltic and sixty-five kilometers east of Hamburg, on the Elbe, gave its merchants easy access to the North Sea, the Rhineland, and central Germany.

As was true in the Mediterranean, the line between commerce and crusade was frequently indistinct. A contemporary of Henry the Lion wrote that "dur-

*Seal of the city of Lübeck from 1280. The Hanse-
atic merchants of Lübeck sought explicitly to marry
"across sand and sea" the distinctive expertise of
seafaring and overland merchants, identified here
by their characteristic dress. While the hull has the
double-ended form and quarter rudder typical of the
Vikings' ships, the lack of oarports identifies this as
a cog dependent entirely on sails for power, although
one steered with a* firrer *rather than a centerline
rudder. From Ernst Wallis's* Illustrerad Verldshis-
toria *(Chicago, 1894).*

ing all the campaigns which he undertook as a young man into the land of the
Slavs"—probably a reference to the disastrous Baltic theater of the Second
Crusade—"there was never a mention of Christianity, but only of money."
More successful spiritually and otherwise was the Livonian Crusade preached
at the time of the Fourth Crusade in support of a church founded on the
Western Dvina. In 1201, the capital of the see was moved to the new city of
Riga at the mouth of the Dvina, which opened the Christian east to military
support and trade from Lübeck. German crusading and colonization of coastal
Prussia began in the 1230s and despite many setbacks it was complete half
a century later. The relationship between trade and crusade found succinct
expression in the letter of a Reval merchant who in 1274 wrote a colleague in
Lübeck: "Our two towns belong together like the arms of Christ crucified."

More important, the establishment of Lübeck signaled a new development
in the conduct of trade in northern Europe, one that sought explicitly to marry
"across sand and sea" the distinctive expertise of seafaring and overland merchants in partnerships that furthered their mutual interests. Maritime trade
always depends to a greater or lesser degree on a combination of inland and
sea routes, but the Lübeckers were apparently the first to recognize the benefits that would accrue from an exploitation of the local knowledge unique to
each. The oldest extant Lübeck city seal, of 1224, shows a cog—the principal
cargo ship of the day—carrying two men, one dressed in a landsman's traveling coat, the other, at the helm, in seaman's attire. This simple illustration
identified Lübeck as the meeting place of seafaring merchants of the Baltic
and beyond and overland merchants from the Rhineland. Mariners benefited
from their inland counterparts' familiarity with markets in the interior, while
the Westphalian merchants profited from the sailors' knowledge of the Baltic
and North Seas. Because they could coordinate their purchases on the basis
of what would be most profitable, they were able to maximize their earnings.

Like many innovative forms of business enterprise, this partnership proved extremely attractive. In 1241, Hamburg and Lübeck concluded a treaty granting each other's merchants reciprocal privileges. Similar agreements were concluded with other coastal and inland towns, and Lübeckers easily convinced their fellow Germans to trade exclusively with them, thus extending the reach of the *hanse*—in effect a merchant guild—via a network that crossed Germany and, as merchants and settlers branched out, Prussia (northeast Poland), Lithuania, Livonia (roughly Latvia and Estonia), and Novgorod. Hanse merchants established *kontors* (trading centers) where they tended to congregate or be confined to special quarters depending on local circumstances. There were gated Hanse establishments in Novgorod (founded around 1200) and at the Steelyard in London (1281), but there were fewer restrictions at the *kontors* in Bruges (1252) and Bergen (1343). By the mid-1300s, the Hanse had evolved from "a community of German merchants" who traveled together both for safety and to increase their leverage in securing privileges in foreign lands to "an association of Hanseatic towns" in which the needs of individual traders were superseded by those of the city from which they came. The "Hanse of the Towns" originated in an assembly of merchants' representatives held in 1356 to address agreements made by merchants in the *kontor* of Bruges with the count of Flanders and the king of England. Trading privileges had always been negotiated by merchants on the spot, but by 1374 representatives of the Hanse towns had established the principle that all decisions made by individual *kontors* were subject to approval by a general diet of the Hanseatic towns.

As in the Varangian period, there was a lively trade between the Baltic and the Black Seas, although as a consequence of the Mongols' destruction of Kiev in 1240, the preferred route had shifted to the west and now went by way of the Oder or Vistula Rivers to Kraków and the Prut, a tributary of the Danube, or the Dniester. Farther west, the primary arteries of trade in Germany flowed north through Wendish territories to the Baltic: the Trave near Lübeck and Starigard, the Peene and Oder near Wolin and Szczecin, respectively, and the Vistula at Gdansk. Lübeck was the primary seat of trade to which other Hanse towns (about eighty-five in all) generally looked for guidance, and the Low German spoken by the majority of Lübeckers became the lingua franca of commerce in the Baltic. At the same time, the Hanse's monopolistic power effectively barred competitors—Gotlanders, Wends, Prussians, Estonians, and Russians—from the most lucrative trades.

Among the Hanseatic merchants' most determined competitors were the Danes, who were also trying to establish themselves in the eastern Baltic. Henry the Lion's pressure on the Wends had driven many of them to piracy and their raids on the Danish coast as far north as Jutland compelled Denmark's Valdemar I, "the Great," into an alliance with Henry. In 1169, the Danes destroyed a Wendish fortress on the island of Rügen at the mouth of the Oder River and took advantage of Frederick Barbarossa's preoccupation with Italy and crusading to extend their rule in the east. In the second half of the thirteenth century, Denmark relapsed into civil war and much of their trade fell into German hands. Yet the Danes had laid the foundation for a prosperous trade. Many towns had been established in Denmark, notably Copenhagen (København, or "merchants' harbor") on the Øresund near the rich herring fisheries off Skåne, then Danish territory in what is now southern Sweden. The productivity of these fishing grounds, which remained a primary engine of economic growth in the Baltic for centuries, can be glimpsed in the exuberant description of the thirteenth-century *History of the Danes:* "The east side of Zealand [Sjælland] is separated from Scania by a strait which annually brings a rich booty to the fishermen's nets. The entire sea is generally so full of fish that often the vessels are stopped and can hardly be rowed clear through great exertion and the booty can no longer be caught by artificial means but can without difficulty be caught by hand." Many of the merchants who purchased fish at Skåne were Germans bearing silver from the newly opened mines of the Harz Mountains, and salt—an essential commodity in the fish trade—from Lüneberg, south of Hamburg.

Although Hanse traders never dominated Denmark the way they did Norway, where the Bergen *kontor* was established in 1343, many German merchants settled in Denmark. Rising tensions led to war between the Hanse of the Towns and Denmark in the 1360s. The Treaty of Stralsund (1370) confirmed Hanse control of Skåne, restored their trading privileges in Denmark, lowered customs dues, and gained the Hanse towns a voice in the election of the Danish king. This was the high point of Hanse political power in the Baltic. Twenty years later, the crowns of Denmark and Norway were brought together in a personal union under Margaret of Denmark, who envisioned a confederation of the three Scandinavian kingdoms with Denmark supreme. To that end she supported a revolt against the king of Sweden, whose father was the duke of Mecklenburg. In retaliation, the duke's subjects, including citizens of the Hanse towns of Wismar and Rostock, waged a pirate war against Margaret and her allies. These pirates were known as Vitalienbrüder, or "victual brothers"—victual referring to the fact that they were self-sufficient in food, brothers attesting to their essentially egalitarian organization. (This and similar names were also used for outlaw gangs on land.) That they lived beyond the law and knew it is obvious from their motto, "God's friends and the foe of all the world," a sentiment reminiscent of Cicero's condemnation of piracy. The Vitalienbrüder were active across the Baltic; an estimated fifteen hundred pirates were reported along the Livonian coast in 1392, and two years later as many as three hundred ships were at large in and around the Danish archipelago. When the pirate wars ended in 1395, the Vitalienbrüder retained a base on the island of Gotland from which they continued to plunder merchant shipping and hired themselves out to princes from Calais to Finland and Russia. Their reign of terror lasted until 1401, when the Teutonic Knights of Prussia rounded up and executed hundreds of them and occupied Visby.

Four years earlier, Margaret's nephew, Eric of Norway, had been acknowledged as king of Denmark and Sweden. The Kalmar Union over which he ruled was a federation of three countries with a common king but it especially helped establish Danish merchants in the Baltic on a par with those of the Hanse. The weakening of the union at midcentury reflected both the growing sense of national identity within the three kingdoms and the diminished threat posed by German traders. The political power of the Hanse was likewise undermined by the rise of nation-states elsewhere in Europe, while Dutch competitors threatened their commercial supremacy. The Danes preferred dealing with the Dutch because they posed no threat of cultural dominance like that exercised by the Germans. Moreover, because they sailed between the Baltic and North Seas, they diminished the importance of the Hanse's Lübeck-Hamburg axis. The Dutch also became a source of revenue for the Danish kingdom when in 1429 the crown began forcing ships to pay tolls before transiting the Øresund.

For all the commercial, cultural, and political power Lübeck and Hamburg wielded, from the twelfth to the fifteenth centuries the most important port in northern Europe was Bruges, the center of administrative and political power in the county of Flanders and home to a great number of foreign communities. Bruges owed its identity as a port to a storm in 1134 that scoured the Zwin River and opened the city to the North Sea, about fifteen kilometers away. This allowed shippers to off-load in the center of town, where there were markets, a weigh house, and a fixed crane for shifting goods. Yet dredging equipment of the time was inadequate to maintain the channel in the heavily silted river, and eventually none but the smallest vessels could reach the city, and downstream ports opened at Damme and Sluys.

Part of Bruges's appeal lay in its accessibility to merchants from southern Europe, the Baltic, and the British Isles, but it was also at the center of a vibrant industrial economy in its own right. In the twelfth century, Flanders, Hainault, and Brabant produced the best luxury textiles in northern Europe, which is what attracted Genoese and Venetian merchants to sail there directly. In addition, Bruges manufactured armor, illuminated manuscripts, and, later, printed books. Thanks to its commercial networks, by the fourteenth century almost any product available in Europe could be found in Bruges. A list of unknown authorship enumerates the scores of products imported directly from more than thirty places in northern and southern Europe, North Africa, the Levant, Asia Minor, and the Black Sea. These include foodstuffs like herring, grain, cheese, bacon, honey, wine, spices, dates, almonds, and sugar; textiles such as wool, cotton, and silk; animal by-products from furs, skins, and leather to tallow, grease, and beeswax; metals and minerals both precious and base (copper, iron, tin, lead, pewter, coal, and alum); and hunting birds. Bruges remained the center of northern Europe's international commerce until the end of the fifteenth century when ships outgrew the shallow waters of the Zwin altogether and the focus of trade shifted due east to the Scheldt River port of Antwerp.

Hanseatic and Flemish mariners were well placed to dominate the trade of England, which produced few exports apart from wool, tin, coal, and lead, and which relied on continental sources for iron, salt, naval stores, and wine. The Anglo-Norman aristocracy had turned their backs on the sea to concentrate on consolidating political power in England, but a more intractable problem was the legacy of cross-Channel dynastic politics, under which English kings ruled substantial French territories. When Henry II ascended the English throne in 1154, he brought with him the French counties of Anjou and Maine (his birthplace), and the duchies of Aquitaine and Gascony. At the nadir of their fortunes the French kings had only limited access to the English Channel, but between 1203 and 1259 they retook Rouen and Normandy, as well as La Rochelle on the Bay of Biscay; built a port at Aigues-Mortes on the Mediterranean; and compelled England's Henry III to renounce his claims to all his continental holdings save Aquitaine. With its rich vineyards around Bordeaux and the Gironde estuary, this was an especially lush prize and such a mainstay of England's overseas trade that the tun—a barrel with a capacity of 252 gallons (1,270 bottles) of wine—became the standard by which a ship's capacity was determined. (Though the unit of measure has changed, ships' sizes are still given in terms of their tonnage.) This had both commercial and military applications, and in the early 1200s ships with a capacity of eighty tuns were considered suitable for naval operations and had to be registered with the crown.

This made sense in the context of medieval naval warfare because fleet encounters were rare in northern European waters and there was a far greater need for ordinary merchant ships to serve as auxiliaries and transports, notably in the English campaigns against the Welsh and Scots, as well as during the Hundred Years' War with France (1337–1453). Influenced by the Angevin experience in the War of the Sicilian Vespers, the French had taken a theoretically more aggressive approach to naval warfare. In 1293, Philip IV employed Genoese advisors for the construction of the Clos des Galées at

Rouen, the first such arsenal in northern Europe, and Philip hired Genoese squadrons and their crews to supplement and even lead his forces against the English. The French were not always willing followers, notably at the battle of Sluys in 1340, where they lost 200 of 230 ships and seventeen thousand men, partly because French commanders ignored their Genoese advisors. But naval engagements were rare—there were only four in the Hundred Years' War— and even when losses were considerable they were decisive only to the extent that they hindered or facilitated the transportation of men and matériel.

Edward I's immediate response to the establishment of the Clos des Galées was to order twenty-six English towns to contribute twenty galleys to the defense of the realm; but impressed ships made up the bulk of the English fleet, with the balance comprised of vessels contributed by the Cinque Ports and foreign hires. Established sometime between the eleventh and thirteenth centuries, the Cinque Ports—Hastings, New Romney, Hythe, Dover, and Sandwich—originally regulated the annual herring fair at Yarmouth, but their strategic location by the Dover Strait made them the ports to which the crown turned to defend the shipping lanes to the continent. The exercise of royal prerogative should not be mistaken for royal authority. The crown depended heavily on the expertise of the Cinque Ports shipowners, but the royal charters that stipulated how many ships they were required to loan the king gave the Cinque Ports extraordinary privileges, including the right of wreck and freedom from taxes, which they routinely abused.[*] For much of the medieval period English merchant shippers were a law unto themselves. When Edward I sailed to Sluys in 1297, more than 165 men died in a riot between crews from the Cinque Ports and their rival, Yarmouth. Eight years later, the king commissioned a Cinque Ports ship called *Le Snak* to patrol the English Channel against pirates, only to have *Le Snak*'s crew steal £300 from ships belonging to London merchants. By the same token, the crown was frequently in arrears for crews' wages and offered shipowners nothing for the use of their vessels until parliamentary pressure in 1380 required payment of a modest sum for wear and tear on ships' gear.

Privateering and Letters of Marque

The English did not establish a naval base and shipyard until 1420 at Southampton. But this was a tentative effort and soon abandoned. Rather than

---

[*] Traditionally, sovereigns were entitled to any wrecked ship or cargo cast up on their shores. Abolition of the right of wreck made it possible for goods recovered from a wreck to revert to their original owners.

attempt to develop a formal naval establishment, Henry VI began issuing letters of marque to captains of armed merchant ships. Technically, a shipowner who had been robbed on the high seas by the subject of another ruler could seek compensation by taking his case to court in the country of his robber. If this was not possible, or the verdict's partiality was suspect, the victim could appeal to his own sovereign for a letter of marque entitling him to seize property from the compatriots of the original robber, up to the value of what he had lost, although such niceties were readily ignored. Yet privateering, as sailing with letters of marque came to be known, was not simply a peacetime system of alternative justice; kings and princes also used privateers to augment their fleets in time of war. To fund his campaigns against the Angevins, Roger of Lauria issued letters of marque for a 20 percent cut of the prizes taken, and in 1292 revenue from raiding accounted for half his fleet's budget. An English letter of marque issued in 1400 spells out what the bearer could and could not do—or at least to whom he could and could not do it:

> Commission to William Prince, master of a barge called *le Cristofre* of Arundell, to take mariners for the same, to go to sea on the king's service; provided that neither he nor any liege of the king in his company on the barge take any ships, barges, or other vessels, merchandise, goods or chattels of any of the realms of France, Spain, Portugal or other parts except only of the realm of Scotland.

In other words, William Prince was an agent of the crown with the authority to seize Scottish vessels and their cargoes, but not those of any other country. Whether Prince respected the limits suggested by the king is unknown, but many commissioned privateers exceeded their writ and plundered allies and even their fellow countrymen. This lack of discipline was a major flaw in the privateering system. Another was that even if commissioned privateers were scrupulous about targeting only specified enemies, they were under no obligation to serve the king. So although letters of marque did disrupt enemy trade and provided some income to merchants whose opportunities for normal trade were limited by hostilities, as naval auxiliaries privateers were of negligible strategic benefit to the crown.

The Ship

Ordinary merchants were willing to seek such commissions in part because medieval sea trade was a rough-and-tumble business to begin with, and partly because their ships required little or no modification to ready them for more belligerent pursuits. Even as ship design, rigging, and construction techniques evolved, the distinction between warships and merchantmen remained slight. Outwardly, the most pronounced transformation in ship design was in the north, where the sleek lines characteristic of the Viking-influenced double-ended ships gave way to the cog, a relatively squat, boxlike vessel of heavy shell-first construction reinforced by frames and transverse crossbeams that protruded from either side of the hull. Cogs were characterized by a relatively flat bottom with high sides and straight rather than curved stem- and sternposts. The sternpost probably assumed this form first in order to accommodate the centerline rudder, which dates to about 1200 in Europe. Despite its long pedigree in China, and tenth-century allusions to them in the Indian Ocean, the centerline rudder developed independently in northern Europe, where it was mounted with a hinged "pintle-and-gudgeon" system rather than lashings.*

Cogs were powered by a single square sail on a mast stepped amidships and many were fitted with elevated castles fore and aft, and a topcastle fitted to the mast. The stern- and forecastles were initially independent structures mounted on deck but eventually became fully integrated into the hull. As the name suggests, castles offered protection against attack and an advantage in height when attacking, and they were not limited to cogs. A survey of sealings depicting ships from 1150 to 1300 shows that nearly half carried a castle of one sort or another, and the unfinished Bremen cog of 1380, which was excavated in the Weser River in the 1960s, had a complete sterncastle and the structural members for a forecastle. In addition to providing cover in combat, the sterncastle offered shelter for the helmsman, who manned the tiller on the main deck, and the one on the Bremen cog enclosed a windlass and capstan for weighing anchor, stepping the mast, loading heavy cargo, and trimming the sail.[†]

Although the commercial and technological initiative for regular trade between the Mediterranean and the ports of France, England, and Flanders lay with the Italians at the end of the thirteenth century, cogs first appeared in the Mediterranean as early as the Fifth Crusade (1217–21). Mediterranean shipwrights began to adopt the cog as a model for their own designs in the early 1300s. Giovanni Villani, a Florentine chronicler, attributes the change to the economic advantage they offered:

* The pintle and gudgeon are pieces of hardware—the pintle with a pin, the gudgeon with a socket for the pin. Two or more gudgeons are attached to the sternpost (or transom), and a corresponding number of pintles to the leading edge of the rudder. These keep the rudder fastened to the hull while allowing the helmsman to maneuver it to turn the ship.

† The windlass and capstan are mechanical devices for lifting heavy weights, the salient difference being that the barrel of the capstan around which the rope is wound is vertical and that of the windlass is horizontal.

At this time, certain people of Bayonne in Gascony passed through the straits of Sevilla (Gibraltar) with their ships, called *Bayonnese cogs* [*coche Baonesi*], with which they pirated on this sea and caused much harm. Since then the Genoese, the Venetians and the Catalans have begun to employ cogs for their seafaring, and have abandoned the use of their larger ships [*navi grosse*] in order to secure the seaworthiness and lower costs of the cogs. This circumstance has constituted a substantial change in our concept of sailing.

Villani's *navi grosse* were wide, high-sided vessels with ample room for low-value bulk goods like grain and wine. Built for capacity and economy, those of ordinary size were easy prey for galleys, although the larger ones were built with high castles. The relative advantages of the galley and *navi*, or round ships (as medieval sailing vessels are known), can be seen in the report of a battle fought between Venetian and Genoese ships in 1264. Ordinarily, Venetian convoys bound for the Levant were escorted by galleys, but that year a convoy of round ships consisting of the *Roccaforte*, a large state-owned *buss* built for combat and commerce, and a number of smaller hundred-ton round ships called *tarettes* sailed for Syria unescorted. The *Roccaforte* was an exceptional vessel for her time, thirty-eight meters long, fourteen meters across, and more than nine meters from the keel to the top of the stern- and forecastles, and likely rigged with three masts. Her capacity of perhaps five hundred tons was more than twice that of the average large merchantman such as the *tarettes* in her convoy. A Genoese fleet of sixteen galleys under Simone Grillo ambushed the *Roccaforte* and her consorts off the island of Saseno (Sazanit, Albania). Although they could do little against the towering *buss*, the galleys were more than a match for the *tarettes*. The Venetians transferred the more valuable goods from the *tarettes* to the *Roccaforte* before scuttling three of the smaller vessels and setting the rest adrift to be plundered of their oil, honey, and other cargo.

After looting the *tarettes*, Grillo offered the Venetians in the *Roccaforte* safe quarter, but the Venetian ship was all but impregnable to an assault from the low-slung Genoese galleys, and her commander offered the taunting reply "that if they [the Genoese] were stout fellows, let them come on, and that the ship was all loaded both with gold and the richest merchandise in the world." Leaving the unscathed *Roccaforte* to proceed to Ragusa, Grillo's galleys sailed off with the captured *tarettes*. There may have been no more than half a dozen ships as large as the *Roccaforte* in the Mediterranean at any point in the thirteenth century. Consequently, the ordinary merchantman was at the mercy of galleys, which could be even longer than the *Roccaforte*. One of the earliest and most complete specifications for war galleys comes from the chancery records of Charles I, the Angevin king of Naples ousted in the War of the Sicilian Vespers in 1282. These vessels were forty meters long and nearly four meters in beam and carried 108 oars. Unlike in antiquity or the early medieval period, when rowers were aligned in vertical files or more than one man was assigned to an oar, rowers now sat on benches angled toward the stern—a seating configuration called *alla sensile* (from the Spanish *sencillo*, meaning simple)—with one oar for each rower. In addition to the oarsmen, these Angevin galleys carried two masters, four helmsman, two ship's boys, and thirty-six marines; a total complement of 152 people.

By the end of the century, the Venetians had developed the "great galley," the design of which was tailored to the routes for which they were intended—whether Trabzon, Alexandria, or, the largest, Flanders. The galley of Flanders was a response to the need for a large, stable merchant ship capable of withstanding the long oceanic passage to England and Flanders, a distance of about 2,500 miles. Longer, broader, and deeper than ordinary galleys, the earliest great galleys measured about forty meters on deck by five meters in beam, with a capacity of about 140 tons, but by the mid-fifteenth century the standard length was about forty-six meters, with a capacity of 250 tons. They had twenty-five to thirty rowing benches that sat up to three oarsmen, each of whom pulled a single ten-meter-long oar balanced with a lead weight. Yet great galleys were essentially sailing ships rowed only when the ship was in danger and when entering or leaving port, and captains frequently left most of the oars ashore, although the crews were kept to defend the ship.

Although shipwrights steeped in the distinct traditions of northern and southern Europe now had direct exposure to one another's designs and techniques, there was as yet relatively little exchange in terms of shipbuilding technology. Mediterranean shipwrights adopted the centerline rudder and some essential elements of the cog, and northern Europeans built galleys on Mediterranean lines. But northern ships were still built shell-first and set a single square sail while southern ships were built frame-first and were lateen-rigged, often on two or more masts. Another distinction was that Mediterranean merchant galleys dwarfed their northern competitors. Although the Bremen cog was small, with a capacity of about fifty tons, the largest cogs carried only three times as much, barely half as much as a *tarette*. Looked at another way, in 1439 a Venetian great galley sailing from Southampton carried 2,783 cloths and more than fourteen thousand tons of tin whereas a typical northern cog carried only 752 cloths.[*]

For the moment, relatively slight changes to northern and southern ship-

---

[*] A "cloth" measured two yards by twenty-four yards, about forty square meters.

ping were sufficient to transform regional and interregional maritime commerce. Enlarged capacity, smaller crews, and the ability to sail long distances without stopping for provisions led to dramatic falls in shipping costs, which were already significantly lower than transport costs for goods moved by land. According to the Florentine merchant Francesco Balducci Pegolotti, in 1336 the cost of shipping a sack of wool seven hundred miles from London to the Gironde estuary was one-eighth that of taking the same sack of wool four hundred miles by road from the Gironde to the port of Aigues-Mortes. In this instance, transportation by land was fourteen times more expensive than by sea. Freight rates fell by about a quarter in the fourteenth century, and further still in the fifteenth. Pegolotti calculated that transportation accounted for nearly a quarter of the price paid for alum (a fixative for dyes), and 30 percent for woad (a blue dye), but less than a century later transport costs for the same goods represented only 8 percent of the price.

In terms of shipboard comfort, there were no improvements. If anything, the increase in ships' size and capacity probably led to worse conditions. Galley crews slept on their benches, while pilgrims and merchants slept below deck in unenviable discomfort. The thirteenth-century Statutes of Marseille required shippers to set aside a minimum of less than one square meter per passenger on pilgrim ships, and this remained the norm for hundreds of years. "The berths of the pilgrims are so arranged," wrote Brother Felix Fabri in a 1483 account that could probably stand for most ships of the age, "that, for the length of the ship, or rather of the hold, one berth is alongside the next without any space in between, and one pilgrim lies by the side of the other, along both sides of the ship, having their heads towards the sides of the ship and their feet stretching out towards each other. Since the hold is wide, there stand along the middle of it, between the berths, chests and pilgrims' trunks." In Fabri's ship, the only light below decks came through four hatches in the main deck, which were also the only source of fresh air. This did not provide much relief because "The whole galley, within and without, is covered with the blackest pitch, as are even the ropes, planks, and everything else, that they may not easily be rotted by the water." Exacerbating the claustrophobic conditions was the stench of the bilgewater, which collected in a well around the mainmast. According to Fabri, "this well does not contain human filth, but all the water which visibly and invisibly enters the galley filters through and collects in that well, and a most loathsome smell arises from it, a worse smell than that from any latrine for human excrement." Such conditions were no worse than those found aboard round ships, and the speed and safety of the great galleys made them the preferred means of transportation for those who could afford them. Given the dismal conditions described by Brother Felix, it seems strange to modern sensibilities that not more people remarked on them. Yet accounts of shipboard life are rare, even in the correspondence of merchants whose occupations kept them at sea for long periods.

Conducting Trade

In the eleventh century, the merchant's profession frequently passed from father to son, but partnerships with nonfamily members were common. Both formal and informal mechanisms were devised to ensure honest dealings among unrelated merchants. Although cooperation between merchants of different faiths was not unknown, especially in the Mediterranean, most partnerships were formed on the basis of a shared religion, each governed by its own laws. Regardless of their faith, however, merchants worked cooperatively as well as competitively, sharing information and looking after each other's business when circumstances warranted. In the *Dar al-Islam*, the leader of the merchant community was known as the representative of merchants (*wakil al-tujjar* in Arabic), whose primary though by no means sole function was to represent his fellow traders in legal disputes. In addition, the representative of merchants acted as a banker, forwarded correspondence, and maintained a warehouse for his clients. These storage facilities, called *fonduks* in Arabic, were found in cities across North Africa and the Near East and served the same purpose as the quarters reserved for foreign merchants in Constantinople.

All shippers arriving at Muslim ports were required to pay duties, but the amount varied according to one's status: 1.5 to 2 percent of annual earnings for Muslims, 5 percent for non-Muslims living within the *Dar al-Islam*, and 10 percent for non-Muslims living outside the *Dar al-Islam*. The latter could trade in Muslim ports provided they had a written certificate of safe passage called an *aman*, which was valid in all ports within the *Dar al-Islam*. These passports guaranteed freedom of worship, testamentary rights, the right to provision and repair ships, abolition of the right of wreck, extraterritoriality, and permission to address the head of the Muslim community, among other things, and were the result of negotiations or a treaty between an imam and a Christian state. Armed with an *aman*, merchants could trade during periods of warfare between Christian and Muslim states, and Christian merchant ships were found in Alexandria and Damietta even at the height of Saladin's naval operations against the crusader states between 1179 and 1187.

Such guarantees helped ensure Christian access to Muslim markets, and while the extension of trade privileges between Christian states reflects a similar effort to open markets, no reciprocal policies evolved on the Christian side with respect to Muslims. Latin Europeans were generally hostile to people of other faiths, and Muslim jurists discouraged trade outside the *Dar al-Islam* on the grounds that exposure to alien laws and religion would result in spiritual corruption, at least in the Mediterranean. This prohibition was not absolute and there was a Muslim trading community in Constantinople from at least the late tenth century, and a treaty between Basil II and the Fatimid caliph Abu al-'Aziz Mansur stipulated that prayers would be said for the latter in the mosque at Constantinople. In 1189, Isaac II negotiated a treaty that allowed for the establishment of a second mosque. An ambassador, an imam, muezzins, and readers of the Quran sailed for the Byzantine capital and, according to Saladin's biographer, "The day they entered Constantinople was a great day among the days of Islam; great numbers of merchants and travelers were present." Western Europeans were appalled, but the Byzantines' accommodation of Muslims was due in part to their shared resentment of western crusaders.

As the numbers of individuals with an interest in maritime commerce increased, and as ships and their cargoes grew ever larger, investors developed new ways to safeguard their investments. Spreading risk through webs of *commendae* and other contracts offered people a hedge against the inherently insecure business of sea trade, and the great advance of the late medieval period was the development of insurance. Although some forms of primitive insurance existed—the sea loan is considered one—it was not until the fourteenth century that Italian merchants began issuing premium insurance. From the start, insurers assumed broad risks: "of God, of the sea, of men of war, of fire, of jettison, of detainment by princes, by cities, or by any other person, of reprisals, of arrest, of whatever loss, peril, misfortune, impediment or sinister that might occur with the exception of packing and customs," according to a Florentine contract of 1397. Theft by officers or crew was not covered. As is true today, premiums varied according to the season and other considerations such as the length of the voyage, whether the ship had to sail through a region known for piracy, and the type of ship employed. (Galleys customarily paid lower premiums than round ships.) The premium on a policy written in 1350 for a ship sailing from Palermo to Tunis and back was 14 percent, and three other policies drafted at Palermo the same year insured cargoes at rates of between 15 and 20 percent. Rates trended downward over time—8 percent for a passage on the Atlantic from Cádiz to Sluys in 1384, and 6 percent for a run from Constantinople to Venice in the 1430s, between 12 and 15 percent for the long passage between London and Pisa in 1442, but only 5 percent for the comparable trip from Sluys to Pisa in the quarter century after 1450. Despite these exorbitant rates—ordinary premiums today are about one percent—

insurers could lose considerable sums. By and large, however, commercial shipping in the late Middle Ages was increasingly productive and profitable, and merchants eagerly sought out new markets and opportunities for gain in an effort that would soon transform the world.

Between the twelfth and fifteenth centuries, Europe underwent a metamorphosis. For thousands of years, the subcontinent had divided the Mediterranean from the North Sea and Baltic, but by the fourteenth century a combination of sea and river routes connected all shores of Europe and made it one of the most vibrant, if not yet the richest, trading networks in the world. The Varangian opening of the rivers of eastern Europe to continuous trade between the Mediterranean and Black Seas and the Baltic in the late first millennium was mirrored in the thirteenth by Genoese and Venetian merchants who pioneered the western sea route from the Mediterranean to the North Sea. This facilitated the transmission of goods, ideas, and, less desirable, disease. By the fifteenth century, the commerce of Europe was so interconnected that one could purchase Russian furs at Bruges from either Hanseatic merchants from the Baltic or Venetians fresh from Tana on the Black Sea.

Although the commerce of the age was transformative, the total volume of trade carried to Venice during an entire year of the fifteenth century could probably fit in a single twenty-first-century cargo ship. Yet modern cargo ships are routinely run by crews of fewer than thirty and use facilities far removed from the center of the ports they serve. In medieval Europe, maritime commerce engaged huge amounts of capital and manpower and lay at the heart of civic identity for many cities. What ultimately made the commercial revolution of the European Middle Ages revolutionary was the quickening pace of interregional exchange and the allocation of resources and talent to the constant search for new markets, whether within the familiar realms of the Mediterranean and Europe, or in the fabulous lands of the Orient.

Chapter 13

The Golden Age of Maritime Asia

By the eleventh century a steady stream of trade flowed along interlinked routes between the western and eastern extremes of Eurasia by sea and land. There are no reports at this time of individual goods, or even people, traveling from the Atlantic coasts of Morocco or Spain and the Pacific shores of China or Japan, or vice versa; but the possibility that this did happen is quite good and it was certainly happening by the fourteenth century. While the rise of Fatimid Egypt attracted trade to the Red Sea, Christian merchants and naval powers were in the ascendant on the Mediterranean. Jewish and Muslim merchants were driven into more marginal trades or abandoned the Mediterranean for the Indian Ocean, where they capitalized on the commercial relationships elaborated in the preceding centuries. In so doing, they helped sate Mediterranean and northern European appetites for spices and other eastern luxuries and thus complemented the efforts of Venetian, Genoese, and other western Christian merchants. By this time, long-distance seafaring and trade on the Monsoon Seas had entered a settled, mature phase. But this should not be equated with stagnation. The expansion of sea trade led to growth in the size and numbers of ships, attempts to exercise naval power over ever greater distances, and advances in navigational aids, including printed sea charts and the magnetic compass.

Maritime Aspirations in Southern Song and Yuan China

At the start of the twelfth century, the principal states in Northeast Asia were those of the Khitan Liao, which occupied northern China and eastern Mongolia, the Xi Xia of north-central China, and the Northern Song. After a century and a half, the balance of power was abruptly overturned by the Jurchen, subjects of the Khitan Liao. After declaring the Jin Dynasty, they seized the Khitan capital of Dadu (Beijing) and in 1127 the Northern Song capital of Kaifeng.* Song Gaozong, brother of the captured emperor, established the capital of what is known as the Southern Song Dynasty at Lin'an (Hangzhou), the first and only seaport capital of a united China. While China's maritime trade had been growing for centuries, the Southern Song rulers' embrace of overseas ventures constituted a deliberate effort to compensate for the lack of favorable trading opportunities to the north and west. This openness to the sea had been foreshadowed by the gradual migration of China's political center to the southeast, but it became imperative following the establishment of the Jurchen Jin Dynasty. Four hundred thousand Chinese fled southward, many of them to the mountainous coastal provinces of Jiangsu and Fujian, where agriculture was difficult—a fact that had accounted for their slow development in the first place. This demographic redistribution fostered continued urbanization and a corresponding growth in manufacturing, especially of ceramics, and trade.

The decision to make Lin'an the capital reflected the ruling elite's recognition of the importance of maritime trade to both ordinary citizens and the government, whose predicament can be summarized succinctly. Prior to the fall of Kaifeng, two-thirds of the tribute missions to China arrived by sea. This was already considerably more than in previous centuries, but with the move to Lin'an all tribute came by sea, and in the opening years of the Southern Song Dynasty, maritime trade accounted for up to 20 percent of the government's revenues. This could never have happened without official sanction at the highest levels, and in a sharp departure from the throne's traditional posture on overseas commerce, Gaozong observed that "The profit derived from foreign trade is most great. When the management was proper, the income was sometimes counted by millions [of *cash*]. Is this not far better than taxing the people? It is why we pay much attention to it. We could thus be lenient to the people, and let them be a little more prosperous."

This shift in attitude was especially beneficial to the merchants of southern Fujian, many of whom were ethnic Hokkiens who had turned to overseas trade during the tenth-century interregnum. With the Song restoration, they began to attract growing numbers of Muslim and Tamil merchants to Quanzhou, which became China's leading international port. Of far greater long-term import was the direct participation of Hokkien merchants in the trade with

---

* The word Khitan is the origin of the word Cathay, as medieval Europeans called China.

Southeast Asia. Initially they worked under the tutelage of more experienced and well-connected foreigners, but as they honed their navigational skills and knowledge of markets, the Hokkiens became their own masters and for the first time significant numbers of private Chinese traders began venturing overseas on their own account and in their own ships. Although they could be found trading as far as southern India, most Hokkiens generally sailed no farther than the emporia of Java, Sumatra, and the Malay Peninsula, where western goods brought by Indian Ocean merchants were readily available. Focused as they were on relatively nearby markets—it is less than two thousand miles from Quanzhou to the Strait of Malacca—the Chinese came to dominate the routes between Southeast Asia and China, and in the process they established overseas communities that in some cases have endured to this day.

Western mariners still accounted for a sizable share of China's foreign trade, however, and Quanzhou was home to a sizable expatriate community. An early-thirteenth-century author writes of "two types of foreigners—one has fair skin and the other dark—living in Quanzhou in the lane for foreigners." The broad distinction here is probably between Arabs and Persians from Southwest Asia and Indians and Malays from South and Southeast Asia. The modern city boasts numerous remains of Muslim mosques, Hindu temples, and Tamil and Arabic inscriptions. Bilingual Tamil and Chinese inscriptions point to a southern Indian community originating in the Chola port of Nagapattinam, while Zhao Rugua's thirteenth-century work, *On the Chinese and Arab Trade*, confirms a direct trade between Quanzhou and Malabar and Gujarat.

As Chinese merchants gained a greater share of the goods destined for China's burgeoning consumer market, the old tributary system withered. Southeast Asian rulers no longer had to promote the sale of their goods in China, and with ample revenues from duties and the right to purchase and resell goods at favorable prices the Chinese government had no need to lavish money and effort on visiting dignitaries. Yet open trade was not without negative consequences for China, which experienced such a severe drain on precious metals and copper *cash* that between 1160 and 1265 a succession of emperors banned their export, "ordered the officers-in-charge to use only silk, rough sewn silk, brocade, patterned silk, porcelain and lacquerware to trade" in their place, and enacted sumptuary laws to curb the import of exotic finery like pearls and feathers. Ceramics remained a staple of China's export trade, their production being concentrated around the ports of Mingzhou, Wenzhou, Quanzhou, and Guangzhou. Whether they comprised a greater or lesser share of China's exports by volume or value than silks and other perishables, they have been found in far greater abundance at terrestrial and underwater archaeological sites from Korea and Japan to East Africa and the Levant. Their distribution corroborates the written record. Sulayman the merchant had praised Chinese glazed ceramics in the ninth century, but they are not mentioned as a significant export in Chinese sources until the eleventh century, and two hundred years later Zhao Rugua was able to specify which types of ceramics were exported to which countries, from the Philippines to Zanzibar.

The Rise of Yuan China

As much as they opened themselves to the world overseas, many Chinese during the Southern Song hoped to regain the territory lost to the Jurchen Jin and Xi Xia. Eager to support any potential allies, in 1196 the court appointed a Mongol tribal leader named Temüjin "bandit suppression commissioner." A decade later, Temüjin's fellow Mongols elected him emperor with the title Chinggis (Genghis) Khan. After consolidating the tribes of the Mongolian plateau, he embarked on a campaign against the Jurchen Jin, the Mongols' traditional enemies. By 1217, the Mongols had eliminated Jin authority north of the Yellow River, but Jin forces in Henan Province were in an almost impregnable position. Chinggis's son and successor Ogedei negotiated with the Song for permission to march through their territory to attack the Jin from the south. The Song reluctantly agreed, but when the Jin were defeated they attempted to occupy the land seized by the Mongols, which gave Ogedei ample excuse to strike south of the Yangzi. The Mongol army was probably the best in the world, but the Song withstood them for more than half a century thanks to their greater numbers and the fact that they were defending a territory interlaced with rivers and canals and ill-suited for cavalry, the mainstay of the Mongol military.

This environmental advantage was enhanced by the fact that since the eleventh century the Song had maintained a standing river fleet whose ships and weaponry were more advanced than those found anywhere else. The principal warship was a human-powered paddleboat, some extreme models of which mounted more than twenty paddle wheels and had complements of two to three hundred men. In time, however, the maximum number of wheels was fixed at seven, the odd wheel being mounted on the centerline of the hull, either amidships or astern. By the 1200s, the Chinese were also manufacturing true explosive bombs, the most lethal of which were called "thunder-crash bombs." To fight the Song on their own terms, the Mongols built their own paddleboat fleet, with which they opened the way from the Han River to the Yangzi and Lin'an, which Qubilai Khan's forces took in March 1276. Although the emperor surrendered, Song loyalists spirited two of his young sons to safety first in Fuzhou and then in Guangzhou. The arrival of a Yuan fleet at the Pearl River in 1279 forced the Song diehards to sea yet again; and to avoid the boy emperor's capture, it is said, his tutor took him in his arms and leaped into the sea.

The vigorous pursuit of the last remnants of Song resistance was a foretaste of Qubilai's increasingly bold maritime aspirations. Although he was a native of Central Asia and established his capital at Dadu to be nearer the Mongol heartland, no Chinese ruler has ever promoted maritime activity—canal building, coastal trade, and four major overseas expeditions—with the enthusiasm shown by the grandson of Chinggis Khan and founder of the Yuan Dynasty. If the Southern Song had taken to the sea out of necessity, Qubilai seems to have viewed the ocean as an extension of the steppe. The Mongols provided the initiative for these expansionist campaigns, but these were feasible thanks to the Song legacy of shipbuilding, navigation, and commercial organization. The sheer number of vessels available to the Yuan was staggering. In 1257, more than nineteen thousand ships were registered in the prefectures of Mingzhou, Wenzhou, and Taizhou alone, and a fifth of them had a beam of more than three meters. When the Yuan captured Fujian, an estimated seven thousand vessels were operating on the coast and nearly twice that number on the rivers. The defeat of the Song freed huge numbers of these for a variety of uses, but the Yuan embarked on an ambitious construction program of their own and in 1273 ordered two thousand ships from yards around the country. A decade later, the strain on timber resources moved the Buddhist monk Duanhong to despair: "Tens of thousand trees were chopped down [for shipbuilding]; sorrow stroke green mountains." While the problem of deforestation antedated the Yuan, it has never been reversed in the eight centuries since. By the late fourteenth century, timber shortages made it difficult to sustain domestic shipbuilding operations and during the Ming and Qing Dynasties many merchants contracted for vessels in Siam (Thailand) and on Borneo, where the cost of building ships could be 40 to 70 percent less than in China.

Yuan officials continued Song efforts to improve navigation through dredging channels, building warehouses, docks, and anchorages, erecting lighthouses and beacons, and developing safer shipping routes. The division of China between the Jurchen Jin and Southern Song had been accompanied by a rise in domestic grain smuggling along the coast between the Yangzi delta and the Shandong Peninsula. With the coming of the new dynasty, the smugglers—many of whom backed the Yuan from the start—began working for the state transporting grain around the Shandong Peninsula and across the Bo Hai to Dadu's port at Tianjin (then called Zhigu). The time-honored practice of hugging the treacherous sand-banked coast proved costly in ships, time, lives, and money until 1293, when the former pirates Zhu Jing and Zhang Xuan pioneered a deep-sea route that gave a wide berth to the peninsula, and they began to sail earlier in the season. What had been a journey of a month or more with horrendous losses became a journey of about ten days with overall losses of a sustainable one percent. At its height in the early fourteenth century, the sea transportation service regularly carried more than two million piculs of rice a year, the record being three and a half million piculs in 1329, the last year for which records survive.

Development of this route was necessitated by Qubilai's establishment of his capital at Dadu, which for the time being was beyond the reach of the Grand Canal. In 1194, the Yellow River had jumped its banks west of Kaifeng to flow into the Huai River and, ultimately, the Yangzi. The main branch of the Yellow River would not reach the sea north of the Shandong Peninsula again until 1855. The redirection of the river's main channel led to delays in completing the canals that make up the northern end of the Grand Canal. The final section, the Huitong Canal, opened in the 1320s, but the sea route remained the preferred way of shipping grain until 1417, when the Huitong was widened enough that all grain bound for the northern capital could be transported efficiently via inland waters.

The rapid expansion of long-distance sea trade led to corresponding advances in navigational practice, including the development of an early form of the compass. The Chinese had long known about the properties of a magnetized needle, but their use of the "south pointer" was for centuries limited to geomancy and feng shui. The first accounts of the compass being used for shipboard navigation comes from a work written in 1117 by Zhu Yu, the son of a port official and governor of Guangzhou, a connection that gave the author entrée into the seamen's world. In the course of describing overseas shipping, Zhu touches briefly on navigational practice: "The ship's pilots are acquainted with the configuration of the coasts; at night they steer by the stars, and in the day-time by the sun." Like mariners in the shoal waters of northwest Europe, they used a sounding lead, which they employed in the same way: "They also use a line a hundred feet long with a hook at the end, which they let down to take samples of mud from the sea-bottom; by its [appearance and] smell they can determine their whereabouts." Zhu also remarks that "In dark weather they look at the south-pointing needle."

The Chinese compass consisted of a needle pierced through the stem of a rush so that it would float in a bowl of water. In the "dry compass" devised in the Mediterranean and Europe in the thirteenth century, and introduced into Asia by European mariners in the 1500s, the needle is mounted on a pivot and calibrated to a compass card. The earliest reference to a compass in the

Indian Ocean dates to 1232, but compasses east of Suez were of the Chinese wet compass type. Common to both eastern and western traditions, however, is the fact that the compass was used as a substitute for celestial navigation in inclement weather, and that it allowed for a longer sailing season. "During the night it is often not possible to stop [because of wind or current drift], so the pilot has to steer by the stars and the Great Bear. If the night is overcast then he uses the south-pointing needle to determine the south and north." So wrote the author of an *Illustrated Record of an Embassy to Korea* in 1124. When published thirty years later, this work included what is believed to be the world's first printed map. By the fourteenth century, the Chinese were producing "seaway compass charts" showing compass courses and distances. The question of whether knowledge of the compass spread from China to the Mediterranean and Europe has generated more heat than light, but even if the rudiments of the compass originated elsewhere, the refinements that led to the practical dry-card compass developed independently in the west.

The Yuan Dynasty made few changes to their predecessors' maritime revenue-collection system. They increased the number of ports with a *shibosi* to seven and officials went into business themselves by lending ships and capital to foreign merchants and splitting the profits with them seventy-thirty, the government taking the larger share. This practice was implemented during a brief ban on private overseas trade in the 1280s (there was another in the 1310s), but it continued even after the ban's repeal. In the 1290s, the emperor issued twenty-one edicts governing the conduct of foreign trade. Most dealt with the duties on imports (one-fifteenth on coarse goods, 10 percent on fine), penalties for evading taxes, and smuggling, particularly by Buddhist, Daoist, Nestorian, and Muslim clergy who "in many cases were smuggling commoners who went abroad to trade and secretly sought to avoid the percentage levies." There were regulations about the arming of merchants, the specific forms that captains needed for their ships and their crew, and which foreign ports ships could visit. The edicts also prohibited trafficking in certain cargoes, partly out of concern for the stability of the economy and partly for strategic considerations: "No gold, silver, copper, iron, men, or women were to be sold to foreign countries."

None of these restrictions had a deleterious effect on China's maritime sector or the imperial purse. The Venetian merchant-author Marco Polo visited Quanzhou in the 1270s and noted "The splendid city of Zaiton [Quanzhou] is the port for all the ships that arrive from India laden with costly wares and precious stones of great price and big pearls of fine quality." Comparing Quanzhou with the largest port most of his audience would have known, he continued, "And I assure you that for one spice ship that goes to Alexandria or elsewhere to pick up pepper for export to Christendom, Zaiton is visited by a hundred. For you must know that it is one of the two ports in the world with the biggest flow of merchandise." The cost of freight and duties came to half the value of what merchants imported, "yet from the half that falls to their share they make such a profit that they ask nothing better than to return with another cargo. So you may readily believe that [Quanzhou's] contribution to Qubilai Khan's treasury is no small one." Given the profits of sea trade, it is no wonder that the Great Khan encouraged it.

Yuan Campaigns Against Japan and Java

As always, China's maritime trade was oriented primarily to the south, but the Yuan took a renewed interest in Japan. Korea's withdrawal from the sea had resulted in limited exchanges between southern Korea and Japan from the early eleventh century, and it fell to Song merchants to revive Japan's foreign trade. At the end of the twelfth century Japan underwent a major transformation that resulted in the ascendancy of the warrior class that would dominate Japanese society until the Meiji Restoration in the 1860s. Warfare had been endemic for much of the century, but the final showdown came in the Genpei War (1180–85), a succession struggle that pitted the Taira (Heike) clan of central Honshu against the Minamoto (Genji), whose capital was to the east at Kamakura, near modern Tokyo.

The conflict ended at the naval battle of Dan-no-ura, fought in the Strait of Shimonoseki between Kyushu and Honshu at the western end of the Inland Sea. According to *The Tales of the Heike*, a fourteenth-century compilation of stories about the war, "The Genji had more than three thousand boats; the Heike, only a few more than a thousand, including a few large Chinese-type vessels." The remainder were small craft and a local official is said to have switched sides "with all the men under his command—a total of more than two thousand—and had them board around two hundred boats." The battle ended with the Genji warriors "boarding the Heike boats, shooting dead the sailors and helmsmen with their arrows or cutting them down with their swords." The eight-year-old emperor is said to have drowned when his grandmother "took him in her arms. Comforting him, she said, 'There's another capital down there beneath the waves!' So they plunged to the bottom of the thousand-fathom sea." The rout of the Taira clan was absolute, but according to one conjecture, some survivors—including perhaps the emperor last seen leaping into the sea—may have fled overseas to the Ryukyu Islands. This theory is suggested by the abundance of Taira names and Heian court idioms in the Ryukyuan language and the sudden growth of Ryukyuan sea trade in this period, two primary exports being sulfur for China's fledgling gunpowder industry and horses.

Following the battle of Dan-no-ura, power devolved on the Minamoto clan. Although the Minamoto shoguns gradually usurped many of the emperor's prerogatives and wielded the real power in the land, the emperor and shogun remained distinct sources of influence, the former based in the capital at Kyoto, the latter in Kamakura. These multiple centers of authority fostered trade within Japan as well as with Korea and China. So great was the latter that a local Chinese history of 1259 made the exaggerated claim that "Lined up stern to bow, the Japanese cross the stormy sea and come to sell their merchandise" at Mingzhou. This commercial revival was fueled in part by the start of a money economy, the medium of which was copper *cash* imported from China; the Japanese did not begin to distribute their own coinage until the late 1500s. The development of financial instruments facilitated the transfer of funds between merchants, while artisans' guilds—for sake brewers, cotton weavers, and moneylenders, among others—gave tradesmen and merchants a standing previously denied them. By the end of the fifteenth century, it is estimated that the volume of trade on Japan's Inland Sea was equal to that of the Baltic in the same period, although the Baltic is forty times larger.

The Mongols began seeking Japanese acknowledgment of their hegemony before the final elimination of Song resistance but without success. In 1266, Qubilai Khan sent an emissary to ensure Japan's recognition of his supreme authority, only to be rebuffed. The obvious springboard for a punitive invasion was the Korean Peninsula, which the Mongols had conquered in the course of six campaigns between 1231 and 1270. Against the advice of the Koreans, who had no interest in fighting the Japanese, Qubilai ordered the construction of an invasion fleet. Korean resisters appealed for support to the Japanese, who dithered, and the invasion sailed in November 1274. In the traditional telling, the Mongol invasion included thirty to forty thousand soldiers and sailors; a more conservative estimate is that the Mongol host numbered only two or three thousand, and that they were met by a comparable force of Japanese warriors. The Mongols landed near Hakata on Kyushu, but after several battles they decided to return home. Their withdrawal coincided with a storm, although Chinese and Japanese sources differ as to its significance. The Mongols emphasized the power of the typhoon, thereby shifting the blame for their defeat to divine intervention, but Japanese writers mention the storm only in passing and none attributes it to the gods.

While alarming, the Mongol invasion did not overawe the Japanese, who simultaneously began planning for a retaliatory invasion of Korea and erecting a coastal wall to forestall any future landings. They abandoned the Korean adventure, but the wall proved its worth when the Mongols invaded a second time in 1281. Again, tradition tells of an armada that embarked a hundred thousand or more soldiers and sailors, although a force of only ten thousand has also been suggested. Sailing from Korea, the Yuan force quickly overran the islands of Tsushima and Ike but could find no suitable landing place near Hakata because of the wall. A second fleet arrived from China about two months after the advance force, but the invaders were restricted in their movements and under constant harassment from the Japanese, who attacked them in their ships and on the islands. According to both Japanese and Mongol accounts, the Mongol fleet was partially destroyed by a typhoon as it prepared to sail away. However, the only writers to describe this phenomenon as a *kamikaze*, or "divine wind," are Japanese courtiers and the term does not appear in accounts by participants in the actual fighting.

Japanese vessels were probably much smaller than their Chinese counterparts and played a commensurately minor role in forestalling the Yuan fleet. At the battle of Dan-no-ura during the Genpei War, the Heike were said to have had "a few large Chinese-type vessels," but there is no indication of what that means, and most of their vessels were likely small boats with as few as ten crew. Illustrations in the narrative scrolls of Takezaki Suenaga, a Japanese veteran of the Yuan invasions, show obvious differences between Chinese and Japanese vessels, as well as between the Korean oarsmen and Mongol warriors. The foreign vessels are decked, with oarports below, while the Japanese have open boats paddled or poled by crew in a standing position. None of the Chinese or Japanese vessels is depicted with masts or sails, but all have squared ends fore and aft, and centerline rudders. There is no way to judge the actual size of the vessels shown in the Takezaki scrolls, but it is unlikely that Japanese ships had a capacity of more than thirty tons (about fifteen meters long) before the mid-1300s. According to records of the port of Hyogo, only six of the sixteen hundred ships that called there a century on were greater than a hundred tons, perhaps a third the capacity of thirteenth-century Chinese merchantmen.

Qubilai continued to press for the subjugation of Japan, but his attention soon turned to Southeast Asia, the scene of the Yuan's most audacious maritime undertaking: an invasion of Java, twenty-five hundred miles from China. As was the case with Japan, Dai Viet, and other continental neighbors, Qubilai's intent was to be recognized as overlord. That Java should be singled out for such consideration was an acknowledgment of its having become the primary carrier of the spice trade of the eastern Indonesian archipelago and its potential to threaten ships transiting the Strait of Malacca. In 1222, a local chief named Ken Angrok had usurped the throne of the Javanese kingdom of Kadiri (1045–1222) and founded the East Java kingdom of Singhasari. Ambitious successors capitalized on his consolidation of power and began an aggressive policy of overseas expansion, a process that would reach its apogee with the kingdom of Majapahit (1293–1528).

Java was ideally situated to dominate the trade of island Southeast Asia. Its large rice surpluses gave it a valuable crop to trade with the Spice Islands, which were isolated from foreign traders by the Javanese fleet and commercial policies and by the monsoons. Java did not exercise effective control over the Strait of Malacca, which was exposed to attack by raiders from the region between Pagan and the Khmer Empire. Yet, Yuan officials considered Singhasari's ambitious King Kertanagara a grave threat to the free transit of the strait. The Chinese belief that Java had a commanding hold on the trade of Southeast Asia is borne out by Marco Polo's description, based on hearsay rather than firsthand observation: "The treasure in the island is beyond all computation. It is from this island that the merchants of Zaiton [Quanzhou] and Manzi [southern China] in general have derived and continue to derive a great part of their wealth, and this is the source of most of the spice that comes into the world's markets." Although it is unlikely that he sought to govern neighboring Sumatra, Kertanagara was probably just as eager as the Chinese to prevent the rise of rivals.

In 1289, Yuan envoys sent to Java to discuss these matters returned from Kertanagara's court with their faces disfigured and tattooed. In retaliation, Qubilai dispatched an expedition said to number twenty thousand soldiers. Anticipating this, Kertanagara ordered his fleet to intercept the Mongols, which they failed to do. In the meantime, Kertanagara was killed by Kadiri rivals, and when the Yuan forces reached Java, his son-in-law and heir, Raden Vijaya, promised to make himself a vassal of the Khan in exchange for their help avenging Kertanagara's death. The combined Mongol-Javanese force conquered Kadiri, whereupon Raden Vijaya turned on his erstwhile allies and expelled them. Raden Vijaya founded the kingdom of Majapahit with his capital at Trowulan, on the Brantas River about fifty-five kilometers southeast of modern Surabaya. For the next two and a half centuries, Majapahit remained the dominant maritime trading power in Indonesian waters and exerted some degree of hegemony over much of the archipelago. According to the fourteenth-century *History of the Kings of Pasai*, written in northern Sumatra, "People in vast numbers thronged [Majapahit]. . . . There was a ceaseless coming and going of people from the territories overseas which had submitted to the king. From the east they came from the Banda Islands, from Seram . . . bringing their offerings of beeswax, sandalwood, massoia bark, cinnamon, cloves and nutmeg piled in heaps."* With almost exclusive access to the Spice

---

* Seram is a large island on the northern edge of the Banda Sea. Massoia is a flavoring from the bark of the massoia tree (*Cryptocaria massoia*), which is native to New Guinea.

Islands, Majapahit prospered on the strength of expanding demand for spices in East Asia, the Near East, and Europe.

The Yuan may have lost, but the twenty thousand Chinese—a substantial number of whom may have remained in Southeast Asia as prisoners or deserters—introduced copper *cash* into the Javanese economy. Although the Javanese had struck gold and silver coins as early as the eighth century, in the years following the Yuan expedition the use of *cash* spread across the archipelago as far as the Philippines. China exercised considerable influence on political and commercial developments elsewhere in Southeast Asia as well. Yuan campaigns in northern Myanmar and Vietnam weakened the kingdoms of Pagan, Angkor, and Dai Viet and facilitated the growth of the Tai states. These in turn attracted the interest of Chinese merchants who became instrumental in the founding of the kingdom of Ayutthaya (1351–1767) on an island in the Chao Phraya River above modern Bangkok. Ayutthaya's prosperity depended on a combination of Tai military ability, the appropriation of Angkorean administrative techniques, control of extensive agricultural and resources from the north, and the commercial advantages that came from easy access to maritime trade.

The Yuan campaigns are notable for their aggressive ambition, and as is the case with naval campaigns generally, the logistical challenge of sending so many men and ships such great distances cannot fail to impress, even if the outcome fell short of the mark. These amphibious operations are not the only manifestation of the Yuan Dynasty's exploitation of the sea, however. More notable in many respects was Qubilai Khan's decision, in 1292, to send a Yuan princess betrothed to the Ilkhan of Persia not by land, as one would expect of heirs to the steppes at the height of the Pax Mongolica, but by sea. Fourteen ships were required for her entourage, which included the Venetian Marco Polo, who was returning home with his father and uncle after a quarter century in China. The prosperity and security of the Monsoon Seas at the end of the thirteenth century is obvious not only from the fact that Qubilai Khan entrusted the agent of an important matrimonial alliance to a fleet of ships. Equally telling, Marco Polo's account of his passage home, which lasted twenty-one months, takes up about a quarter of *The Travels*. This was one of the most popular books in Europe in the fourteenth and fifteenth centuries and because its account of the ports of the Indian Ocean and China Seas was the most detailed guide available, it served as a vade mecum for the pioneers of Europe's age of expansion.

The Written Sea

Polo's account was one of the first descriptions of Asia or the Indian Ocean to appear in any European language in the eight hundred years since Cosmas Indicopleustes visited Sri Lanka a century before the rise of Islam, and it ignited an inextinguishable curiosity about the east. Europeans' collective ignorance of places remote from their immediate experience—essentially anything east or south of the Black and Mediterranean Seas—was greater than that of other people with whom they shared the Eurasian landmass. Yet Polo's curiosity was characteristic of the spirit of the age, and around this time there was an outpouring of descriptive writing about the wider world by peripatetic authors from places as far-flung as Christian Europe, Moorish Spain, Morocco, Persia, and China.

During the four centuries of the Song and Yuan Dynasties, Chinese knowledge about maritime Asia grew faster than at any time before or since. There is a venerable tradition of Chinese writing about the Nanhai, but the growth in sea trade with the south during the Song was a catalyst for the systematic acquisition and description of geographic and economic knowledge, as exemplified in such works as Zhao Rugua's *Description of Barbarous Peoples* (or *Records of Foreign Nations*), written around 1225. The head of the *shibosi* at Quanzhou, Zhao Rugua had access to earlier geographical texts and dynastic histories, but thanks to his official position in what was probably the busiest port in the world, he was uniquely situated to report on China's imports and exports, and the places her trade originated, and he is the first Chinese author to describe various parts of Africa, Southwest Asia, and the Mediterranean. Zhao's work consists of a gazetteer of places and a glossary of goods. The latter details forty-three types of commodities, most of them raw materials, from camphor and frankincense to precious woods, spices, and animal products such as ivory, rhinoceros horn, and beeswax. The remainder are manufactured goods such as glass from India and "several of the countries of the Dashi [Arabs]," rattan mats from the Philippines, and both raw and finished cotton. Originally cultivated in India, by the late twelfth century cotton was grown in Hainan, Indo-China, the Philippines, and Indonesia. The gazetteer describes forty-six places with which China traded, either directly or indirectly, or otherwise known to Zhao Rugua. These range from the "Countries in the Sea" such as Japan, the Philippines, and Borneo, to the more distant countries of Southeast Asia, the Indian Ocean, and its tributary seas from Baghdad to the Somali coast, and a number of Mediterranean ports and regions including Alexandria, Sicily, and Andalusia.

Although a handful of Christian emissaries and Italian merchants traded along the silk road across Mongol-dominated Asia, for most European Christians traveling east posed insurmountable problems. Not the least of these were the expense and difficulty of navigating the alien religion and languages of the *Dar al-Islam*, which stretched from the shores of the Atlantic to India, and beyond which there were Muslim communities on all the major land and sea routes to China. The most intrepid author to have taken advantage of this was the peripatetic Moroccan Ibn Battuta, who between 1325 and 1354 traveled from Tangier to China. Along the way he took side trips from the Red Sea to Mombasa, toured the most important western Indian ports, and served as a *qadi* (judge) in the Maldives, whose people had recently converted from Buddhism to Islam. From there he continued east to China via Sri Lanka and the Strait of Malacca. In an astonishing "small world" moment, Ibn Battuta writes that his host in Fuzhou asked him to receive a fellow merchant and

> when we conversed after our formal greetings it occurred to me that I knew him. I looked at him for a long time. He said: "I see you looking at me as though you knew me." I said: "Which country are you from?" He said: "From Ceuta." I said: "I am from Tangier." He greeted me again and wept and I wept too. I said: "Have you been to India?" He said: "Yes, I have been to the capital Dihli." When he said that to me I remembered him and said: "Are you al-Bushri!" He said: "Yes."

This chance meeting of compatriots from the Atlantic coast of Morocco in a port city on the Pacific coast of China nearly nine thousand sea miles away testifies to the scale and scope of the maritime networks that already bridged the seas of Africa and Eurasia centuries before the age of European expansion.

Ibn Battuta, Marco Polo, and other travelers and geographers were no less conscious observers and recorders of the world than al-Masudi, Buzurg ibn Shahriyar, or Herodotus. They are well attuned to different cultures and cultural differences, but their works offer little insight into the day-to-day life of the merchant seafarers whose enterprise maintained the lines of communication strung the length of Eurasia in the thirteenth and fourteenth centuries. The closest we can come to looking into the mind and business practices of the medieval seafaring merchant in the Indian Ocean, and the Mediterranean, is through the letters of the Cairo Geniza.

Because Jewish tradition forbids the destruction of papers containing the name of God, hoards of documents and letters written by members of the Jewish commercial network centered on Cairo in the eleventh and twelfth centuries were secreted in the *geniza* (storeroom) of a synagogue. This correspondence occasionally alludes to storms and problems obtaining food for a passage—seafaring passengers were usually responsible for their own food, utensils, and bedding until the late nineteenth century—but little beyond that. To the extent that such letters color our fragmented picture of the world of the early medieval merchant, it is through their attention to the sorts of generic problems familiar to anyone who travels for a living today: plans fulfilled, last-minute changes to itineraries, unexpected windfalls, and missed opportunities. Many of the letters brim with the timeless and universal concerns about the well-being of family and friends, anxiety about not receiving expected letters, and, occasionally, news of dramatic events ranging from shipwreck to piracy and war. But the authors focus primarily on business: the quantities of goods sold, at what price and to whom, and disputes arising from the complicated webs of consignment and trust upon which all merchants relied. The letters are replete with details about the conduct of trade through intermediaries and relations with foreign rulers.

The majority of these documents pertain to the commercial life of the Mediterranean, but a substantial number were written by merchants who traveled between Egypt and India. Jewish merchants had long been active on the Indian Ocean, but by the turn of the millennium the wealth of the Fatimid Caliphate was drawing trade away from the fading markets of the Persian Gulf to the Red Sea, while Christian merchants were attaining an increasingly dominant position in the trade of the Mediterranean. With this dual motivation, Muslim and Jewish merchants alike turned their attention to the wealth of the Indian Ocean. While most of the Geniza documents were written by merchants active on the Mediterranean, it is on the newly revived but otherwise poorly documented commerce of the Arabian Sea that the Geniza letters cast the strongest light. They also show that two hundred years before Ibn Battuta, such encounters as he experienced in Fuzhou may not have been all that uncommon. The five Indian Ocean trading families most represented in the Geniza letters hailed from or were active in Morocco, Tunis, Cairo, Yemen, and the Malabar Coast of India. The career of Abraham ben Yiju seems not atypical. A native of Mahdia, in Tunisia, he built his business in Aden before sailing to India where he lived mostly in Mangalore as a merchant and proprietor of a bronze foundry. Shortly after arriving in India, he purchased and freed an Indian slave who became his wife. His eighteen-year stay in India—during which he sojourned in a few other Malabari ports and traveled to Aden—ended in 1149, and he eventually settled in Cairo.

One of Abraham's correspondents was Madmun ben Hasan-Japheth, a shipowner of Persian descent whose family had lived in Aden for several generations. Like his father before him, Madmun was head of the Jewish community in Yemen, superintendent of the port of Aden, and a representative of merchants there, a position his descendants held until the 1200s. In a letter to Abraham characteristic of the Geniza correspondence, Madmun explains that he is sending a cargo of mats imported to Aden from the Horn of Africa together with personal gifts including "two [sets] of fine, large paper, government paper, the like of which no one has" in India, as well as sugar and raisins.

He also reports on the safe arrival of a cargo of iron and cardamom and asks Abraham to get in touch with three other merchants—two Indians and a third who could be either Jewish or Muslim. "And if they can they should dispatch a ship from Mangalore, and send in it any available pepper, iron, cubeb, and ginger; it should set out at the beginning of the season for al-Dyyb [the Maldives] taking some coir, fine aloes wood, mango and coconuts, because all these are selling well."* Madmun provides detailed information on the prices these will fetch, and offers to invest in the enterprise: "If they are equipping a ship in Aden, and they want me to take part, I will share [in it] with them. If there were a ship sailing from Mangalore this year, I would send them gold, sugar, raisins and [other] goods."

The Commercial World of the Arabian Sea

The Geniza records are replete with instances of commercial collaboration across religious lines, which include several references to "partnerships according to Muslim law," the *qirad*, or *commenda*. Interfaith borrowings were not limited to Jews and Muslims: on the Monsoon Seas religious and other institutional boundaries between people of different faiths were far more porous than in the Mediterranean world. Another example is found in the institution of the *karim*, "a convoy or group of nakhodas, or shipowners" adopted by Jewish merchants to compensate for the inadequacies of state protection against piracy in the Red Sea. One theory holds that the word comes from the Tamil *karyam*, meaning "business." Initially, the *karim* seems to have been an informal collection of merchants, but by the 1200s it had achieved a prominence in the trade between Egypt, Aden, and India comparable to that of the Hanse in northern Europe at roughly the same time, although *karimi* merchants never exercised the same degree of political autonomy or influence.

On the Red Sea, the chief threat came from pirates who could threaten merchants and pilgrims en route to Jeddah, Aydhab, Quseir-al Qadim, and other Egyptian ports. Rather than dedicate government resources to commerce protection across the entire sea, the Fatimids entrusted local merchants with their own security. Madmun ben Hasan-Japheth was empowered to conclude agreements with "the lords of the seas and deserts"—in effect to pay for protection for both shipping and desert caravans—and to coordinate the activities of the *karim*. This seemingly offhand approach belied the sultan's dual interest in the Red Sea. Revenues from the trade were vital to the state treasury, but

* Cubeb (*Piper cubeba*) is a fruit of the pepper family.

Egyptian rulers were additionally obliged to regulate access to the Red Sea to protect the pilgrimage sites of Mecca and Medina from infidels, and in this they were successful. Although enemies and rivals from around the Mediterranean posed a significant and persistent threat to Egypt, especially after the start of the Crusades, they reached the Red Sea only once. In 1183, the rogue crusader Reynald de Châtillon launched a fleet of ships which he assembled from parts carried overland to the Gulf of Aqaba, perhaps inspired in this effort by the example of Jehoshaphat recorded in the Old Testament. Reynald captured or destroyed about twenty ships before the Fatimid squadron based at Qulzum routed him.

The Fatimid fleet concentrated its efforts in the northern Red Sea; in the Gulf of Aden and Arabian Sea, Yemeni and other merchants were completely on their own. By the same token, they had little to fear from state-sponsored violence, although the Geniza letters do mention an attack on Aden by the emir of Kish and its defeat by ships belonging to a celebrated merchant named Ramisht. Aden did not begin to fulfill its potential as a port until the Zurayid emirs of Yemen (1080–1173) took an interest and import duties quickly became an important source of their revenue. Aden's prosperity under the Zurayids owed much to the broader changes sweeping the Arabian Sea. Trade in the Persian Gulf had begun to tail off due to Baghdad's decline under the Seljuqs. Siraf and other ports were eclipsed by the emirate of Kish (in Arabic, Qais or Kays), an island in the Strait of Hormuz. Benjamin of Tudela reported that Kish was a magnet for merchants from India, Mesopotamia, Yemen, and Persia who came there to trade "all sorts of silk, purple, and flax, cotton, hemp, worked wool, wheat, barley, millet, rye, and all sorts of food, and lentils of every description, and they trade with one another, whilst the men from India bring great quantities of spices thither. The islanders act as middlemen, and earn their livelihood thereby."

Despite Aden's strong fortifications and its distance from the Persian Gulf, its wealth and the lack of a naval presence made the port a tempting target for the emir of Kish, who in 1135 demanded a share of Aden's revenues. When this was denied, he launched an expedition comprising fifteen vessels and about seven hundred men to seize the port. This proved too small to assault Aden itself, but for two months the Kishites intercepted and plundered ships that attempted to enter or pass the port. "We faced each other," according to one of the Geniza letters, "but they did not dare to land, while the people of the town had no vessels for attacking their ships." The stalemate was finally broken when two ships belonging to Ramisht sailed into Aden. "As soon as the ships entered the port, they were manned with a great number of regular troops, whereupon the enemy was chased from the port and began to disperse on the sea."

In the 1930s, Alan Villiers spent a year sailing with Muslim sailors on the Red Sea and western Indian Ocean. The bulk of his time was spent aboard a boom *called* Triumph of Righteousness *in transit from Aden to Mogadishu and Basra by way of Shihr, Mombasa, and the Rufiji delta, among other stops. "With the* Triumph *packed to the gunwales with mangrove poles for the voyage home to the Gulf," he wrote, "her crew had to sleep where they could" in conditions unchanged in a thousand or more years. Courtesy of the National Maritime Museum, Greenwich, England.*

Ramisht was no run-of-the-mill trader and he is renowned for his sumptuous endowments at Mecca: a gold waterspout, a silk covering for the Kaaba, and a hospice for Sufi pilgrims. According to an anonymous contemporary who knew the family, one of Ramisht's employees

> told me that when he came back from China twenty years before, his merchandise was worth half a million dinars; if that is the wealth of his clerk, what will he himself [Ramisht] be worth! It was Ramisht who removed the silver water-spout of the Ka'ba and replaced it with a golden one, and also covered the Ka'ba with Chinese cloth, the value of which cannot be estimated. In short, I have heard of no merchant in our time who has equaled Ramisht in wealth or prestige.

Given the general state of trade in the Persian Gulf, Ramisht's wealth seems extraordinary: the value of the Kaaba covering was recorded as either four thousand or eighteen thousand dinars—at a time when a lower-middle-class family could live in Cairo on twenty-four dinars a year. But if Ramisht was more successful than most, he was not unique. The freedman of a governor of Aden who died in 1152 left an estate valued at 650,000 local dinars, 300,000 Egyptian dinars, seventeen hundred pounds of silver ornaments, and vast quantities of perfumes, spices, weapons, and other merchandise; there is no record of what the governor himself was worth.

Notwithstanding the benefits to the state of a prosperous trade, later Egyptian rulers seem to have viewed successful merchants in the India trade as a threat rather than an asset. The Mamluks were especially quick to undercut anyone they suspected of amassing excessive influence. As a result, the more institutionalized nature of the later *karim* may have evolved to protect merchants not from pirates as much as from the caprice of political rulers. Perhaps the most outrageous of these was al-Malik al-Mansur, the first Rasulid sultan of Yemen, who notoriously cheated merchants by impounding the pepper they imported and then forcing them to repurchase it at a profit of 50 percent for himself. He further decreed that when he made purchases from the merchants, a *buhar* should measure 170 kilograms, but that when he sold, it should be only 100 kilos. Although their actions were no less arbitrary, not all rulers acted against merchants' interests, and some went so far as to exempt a portion of merchants' import duties. The benefits of such largesse to the port, and therefore the sultanate, were obvious. A fourteenth-century Rasulid sultan "dispensed unaccustomed justice" by conferring honors on the maritime merchants of Aden and abolishing many of their taxes, with the result that "the merchants began to tell to every part on land or sea of his good conduct and his great liberality."

Compared with the uncertainties of conducting trade in the lands of their coreligionists, Muslim merchants seem to have had a more stable and satisfying reception on the coasts of the Indian subcontinent. Contrary to a conventional narrative that stresses religious animosity between Hindus and Muslims, maritime enterprise in medieval India often transcended confessional divisions. A number of stories accounting for good intercommunal relations have little to do with business per se. According to one inscription from the turn of the eleventh century, a Muslim merchant saved a Hindu king from shipwreck near Goa. In acknowledgment of this act of charity, his grandson was made a regional administrator and allowed to found a mosque at Goa, the upkeep of which was paid for by duties collected in the port. Other inscriptions reveal that Hindu rulers from the Konkan Coast routinely made the pilgrimage by sea to the Hindu shrine in the predominately Muslim port of Somnath in Gujarat. A later tradition holds that the Chalukya king of Gujarat, Jayasimha Siddharaja, founded Muslim communities there in the twelfth century, and several sects claim to have converted Siddharaja to Islam.

Somnath was not merely a center of religious devotion for Hindus but an integral part of the commercial network of the Monsoon Seas. "The reason why in particular Somnath has become so famous," according to an Arab historian a century before Siddharaja, "is that it was a harbour of sea-faring people, and a station for those who went to and fro between Sofala in Zanj [East Africa] and China." As such, it played an important role in the economy of the Chalukya kingdom, and Jain merchants, who exercised considerable authority, may well have encouraged Siddharaja and other rulers to treat their Muslim counterparts generously. Whatever the case, the Hindu-Muslim accommodation endured and just as Hindu Chola kings endowed temples for the benefit of Buddhist merchants from Southeast Asia, Chalukya rulers did so for Muslims. A bilingual Arabic and Sanskrit inscription of the thirteenth century describes the endowment of a mosque by Nuruddin Firuz, a shipowner from Hormuz. Lauded as a "great and respected chief, prince among seamen, king of kings of merchants," Firuz built the mosque with the help of prominent Hindus, and he and the Hindu ruler of Gujarat were described as "righteous friends."

The thirteenth century represents a watershed in the history of Islam in South and Southeast Asia, thanks in part to the ripple effects from the rise of the Mongol Empire, which led to the final demise of the Abbasid Caliphate, confirmed the Mamluks as the rulers of Egypt, and rejuvenated Muslim interest in South and Southeast Asia. Muslim merchants had established enclaves of varying size in India, East Africa, China, and mainland Southeast Asia in the preceding centuries, but these were essentially merchant communities with limited if any political power. Territorial expansion into northern India had led to the capture of Delhi in 1025, but it took another two centuries for an independent Delhi sultanate to break away and envelop Bengal by 1225, and Gujarat in 1297. By this time, the first Muslim-ruled kingdoms had started to emerge "below the winds" in island Southeast Asia, starting with a handful of port cities like Samudra-Pasai on northwest Sumatra, which became a major supplier of pepper to both China and western markets. Whether the first Muslim rulers here came from Bengal, Gujarat, southern India, or the Arabian Peninsula is unknown, but Samudra-Pasai and its rivals attracted Muslims from across Asia and East Africa, and this period has been described as a "moment of incandescence" when Islam assumed a completely new aspect in the political world of the Indian Ocean. From this point on, the religion flowed easily through the existing networks of trade to the east. For indigenous people, the wealth of Muslim merchants was notable and their practices were worthy of imitation. For traders, profession of a common faith facilitated transactions and increased trust, and many Southeast Asian rulers converted to Islam to attract Muslim traders to their ports.

Samudra-Pasai flourished as an independent sultanate thanks to its strong ties to the Muslim trading networks of the Monsoon Seas and because its nearest large neighbors—Srivijaya, Java, and the emergent state of Ayutthaya in Thailand—were preoccupied with keeping each other in check. Rivalry between Ayutthaya and Java was resolved by the establishment of the new port of Melaka by Paramesvara, who had ties to the Majapahit kingdom on Java, the royal house of Srivijaya, and a noble family of Pasai. Located on the Malay Peninsula near the middle of the Strait of Malacca, the port's strategic position was enhanced by the Melakans' adoption of Islam, under Paramesvara or one of his successors, and the exemplary business practices followed by their rulers. To a greater extent than even Srivijaya had, Melaka depended almost exclusively on its mastery of foreign trade, which provided its primary source of revenue through an elaborate system of taxes. Goods coming from the west were assessed customs duties, while those from the east were subject to a complex arrangement under which the sultan was permitted to buy certain goods below the market price. The sultans of Melaka further profited from direct participation in trade through ship ownership and other investments.

The commercial character of Melaka is attested by the existence of *kampongs* or ethnic communities including Gujarati Muslims (the most influential group before the coming of the Portuguese in the following century), Kelings from the Coromandel Coast, and traders from Fujian, Luzon, and Bengal, among other places, each group being represented by their own *syahbandar,* or harbormaster. Melaka also became the source of the prevailing maritime legal tradition for Southeast Asia, which was codified in the Melaka maritime code, *Undang-undang Laut Melaka,* around the end of the fifteenth century. This is one of the oldest comprehensive sets of Muslim-based maritime law and as such bears closer comparison with the chapters of the Rhodian Sea Law than with the more discursive *Treatise Concerning the Leasing of Ships.* One unusual aspect of the law is the attention it pays to relations between men and women aboard ship, a reflection of the high status and active participation of women in trade and other aspects of public life throughout Southeast Asia, even after the coming of Islam.

Zheng He and the Climax of Chinese Maritime Endeavor

Melaka's initial prosperity was also linked to its close ties with China, whose single greatest burst of maritime commercial expansion coincided with

Paramesvara's rule. Starting in the 1330s, the Yuan Empire sustained a number of violent shocks including famine, plague (which killed tens of millions of Chinese before it reached the greater Mediterranean basin), and repeated flooding of the Yellow River. These calamities emboldened ethnic Chinese opponents to Yuan rule, and in 1356 rebels led by Zhu Yuanzhang captured Nanjing, which became the imperial capital. Having consolidated his power along the middle and lower reaches of the Yangzi, twelve years later Zhu captured Dadu (which he called Beiping, "the north pacified") and established the Ming ("brilliant") Dynasty. Ming Taizu, as he is known, installed reform-minded Confucianist bureaucrats who set China on a sinocentric path from which it would rarely deviate over the next six centuries.

As a native Chinese dynasty, the Ming had to turn their back to the sea in order to focus on the defense of their continental borders. The dynasty's attitude toward maritime affairs is best captured in an edict of 1371 that "not even a little plank is allowed to drift to the sea." That the ban on trade was so absolute was probably due to the Neo-Confucian cast of the bureaucracy, whose priorities for the government were antithetical to the encouragement of those activities that made maritime trade feasible, namely travel, technological advances in shipbuilding and navigation, the encouragement of financial institutions, and the legal protection of private property. Nonetheless, Taizu and his successors recognized the need for coastal defense against pirates and they ordered the construction of thirty-five hundred ships for a variety of missions: four hundred warships based near Nanjing, twenty-seven patrol vessels and combat ships assigned to coast guard stations, and four hundred grain fleet escorts. Nor were their missions limited to coastal waters. Embracing Ming Taizu's dictum that "To repel them at sea is easy, to check them after they are ashore is hard," Chinese ships pursued pirates to the Ryukyu Islands and Korea and fought them in Dai Viet, which the Ming occupied from 1408 to 1428.

The most spectacular reversal to the ban of 1371 took place between 1405 and 1433 when Ming Chengzu, also known as the Yongle emperor, dispatched six enormous fleets, and a successor a seventh, to India, the Red Sea, the Persian Gulf, and East Africa. Led by a Muslim eunuch named Zheng He, these expeditions involved hundreds of ships and tens of thousands of sailors, soldiers, and traders who logged ten to fifteen thousand miles per voyage. Chengzu's motives were apparently threefold: to increase China's international prestige while reaffirming his own legitimacy, through force if necessary; to encourage tribute trade and eliminate threats to that trade by expatriate Chinese; and a desire to find his predecessor, whom he had deposed and probably killed but who was rumored to be living abroad. The first three voyages (1405–11) took the Chinese as far as the southwest Indian city of Calicut (Kozhikode), "the

A Chinese postage stamp commemorating the six hundredth anniversary of the first of seven Ming Dynasty expeditions to the Indian Ocean under Zheng He. The design, size, and rig of the largest "treasure ships" in the fleets are disputed, but the number and variety of ships that sailed is not. Courtesy of China Post.

great country of the Western Ocean." Outward bound, the treasure fleet sailed from the Yangzi, and after stopping in Fujian Province proceeded to ports in Champa, Java, and Sumatra or the Malay Peninsula. Passing through the Strait of Malacca, the fleet headed west across the Bay of Bengal to Sri Lanka before reaching Calicut, about forty-five hundred miles from Nanjing. On the last four voyages (1413–33), the Chinese ventured farther still, to Hormuz, Aden, and other ports on the Arabian Peninsula, and to the East African ports of Mogadishu, Brava, and Malindi. On the final expedition, smaller squadrons were detached to visit Bengal, while some Chinese Muslims, including the author Ma Huan, visited Mecca after sailing from Aden to Jeddah in a local vessel.

If the primary purpose of these voyages was to seek recognition and trade, they were a success. In all, thirty states including Egypt and Mecca sent ambassadors to the Ming emperor. While these are known from Ma Huan's account, the *Chronicle of the Rasulid Dynasty* of Yemen also notes "the arrival of the vessels of the junk at the 'protected port' [of Aden], accompanied by a messenger from the Lord of China with a magnificent gift for our Lord the sultan al-Malik al-Nasir . . . the present of the Lord of China was conducted to him in procession. It was a splendid present consisting of all manner of rarities, splendid Chinese silk cloth woven with gold, top quality musk, storax, and many kinds of china-ware vessels, the present being valued at twenty thousand *mithqals.*" A later Yemeni historian adds that the emissary

> had an audience with al-Malik al-Nasir without kissing the ground in front of him, and said: "Your Master the Lord of China greets you and counsels you to act justly to your subjects." And [the sultan] said to him: "*Marhaban* [welcome], and how nice of you to come!" And he entertained him and settled him in the guesthouse. Then al-Nasir wrote a letter to the Lord of China: "Yours it is to command and [my] country is your country." He dispatched to him wild animals and splendid sultanic robes, an abundant quantity, and ordered [the envoy] to be escorted to the city of Aden.

Such exchanges were probably typical of those conducted in the many ports visited by the Chinese fleet.

While many have accentuated the commercial and generally pacific nature of Zheng He's expeditions, especially in comparison with the blatantly coercive and ideologically driven conduct of the Portuguese in the following century, the military aspect of the expeditions was not insignificant. On his first voyage, Zheng He defeated a band of several thousand pirates led by a Chinese renegade based in Palembang who was tried and executed in Nanjing. Zheng He also defeated the king of the Rayigama kingdom on Sri Lanka, who was pardoned, and a pretender to the throne of Samudra-Pasai. Such military actions helped ensure the free flow of trade, but these expensive, government-sponsored expeditions were not without their critics, and the flowering of China-based maritime commerce shriveled abruptly. The last voyage took place in the reign of Ming Xuanzong, who is said to have resumed them out of nostalgia for the exotics so common in his youth; but the revival did not survive him. The reasons for this renunciation of the sea were many. Domestically, the empire endured a succession of river floods, hundreds of thousands of people died from epidemics (some possibly started by sailors from the returning fleets), the currency depreciated, and the army was preoccupied with resistance to their occupation of Vietnam and Mongol raids in the north. Partly in response to the last, Chengzu had relocated the capital north from Nanjing to Beijing in 1421, a move that all but guaranteed a decline in official interest in maritime affairs even as he promoted Zheng He's voyages.

The renewed preoccupation with China's north and west had a demographic component as well, and between the fourteenth and fifteenth centuries, migration to the north of the Yellow River caused the population of the coastal provinces of Zhejiang, Fujian, and Guangdong to fall by more than half. In time, there was no memory of Zheng He's voyages, although it is unknown whether official documents were simply lost or, as some believe, hidden or burned because they were "deceitful exaggerations of bizarre things far removed from the testimony of people's ears and eyes." The second Ming embargo on maritime trade in the 1430s was vastly more severe than that enacted by Ming Taizu. Chinese ships and sailors were prohibited from going abroad; no ships could be built for overseas voyages; the construction of warships and related armaments was sharply curtailed; and the coastal defense system created by Taizu and Chengzu was abandoned. As drastic, the government prohibited private foreign traders from visiting China. This ban on maritime trade lasted until the mid-1500s, when the Portuguese were allowed to trade at Macau, and in 1567 Chinese merchants were finally allowed to trade overseas. The loss of maritime initiative had far-reaching implications, and certainly the world would be an unimaginably different place today had large numbers of Chinese been actively engaged in the trade of the Indian Ocean when the Portuguese arrived seventy-five years later.

Zheng He's expeditions had an enormous impact on the region's economy, its political alignments, and even its religious development, and the impetus they gave to the region's commercial expansion was partly responsible for the attraction the Monsoon Seas held for European merchants. A major influence on the growth of the Southeast Asian economy was the introduction of coinage. The Chinese facilitated the transition to a more money-oriented economy through the steady infusion of huge amounts of copper *cash*, the impact of which was felt especially in the trading states of the Malay Peninsula, Sumatra, Java, and Sulawesi. After the last of the treasure ship expeditions, local rulers began to mint their own coins, generally from tin rather than copper; but irrespective of medium the increased circulation of a currency that could be used for even small payments helped lubricate the wheels of commerce, facilitated the payment of taxes, and gave rulers more disposable wealth.

Sailors who quit the fleets swelled the population of overseas Chinese traders, whose numbers had already increased as merchants who defied Ming Taizu's ban on overseas shipping were forced to settle abroad. Ma Huan wrote of three distinct communities in northern Java: native Javanese, western Muslims, and Chinese "from Guangdong [Province] and Zhangzhou and Quanzhou and other such places, who fled away and now live in this country . . . many of them follow the Muslim religion doing penance and fasting." The fact that Zheng He and other prominent members of the expeditions were Muslim had an especially profound effect on Melaka, whose formative years coincided with the first two decades of the Zheng He expeditions. Paramesvara welcomed the Chinese enthusiastically and he himself bore tribute to the Ming court in 1411, and the city's tributary relationship with China insulated the city-state from interference by either Ayutthaya or Majapahit. By the time of the renewed ban on overseas Chinese trade in the 1430s, Melaka's population was between one hundred and two hundred thousand and the port's position was assured, at least until the coming of the Portuguese in 1511. Six centuries later, Malayan Chinese still revere Zheng He and incense burns in his memory at the Sam Poh Kong Temple in Melaka to this day. It is a mark of the truly adaptive nature of Southeast Asian culture that a Chinese Muslim admiral should be commemorated in a Buddhist shrine in a city founded by a Hindu-Buddhist prince whose successors embraced Islam and that quickly became a center of Islamic teaching, was subsequently ruled by Portuguese Catholics followed in turn by Dutch and English Protestants, and that is now the fourth largest city in the largest Muslim nation in the world.

Ships and Shipping on the Monsoon Seas

Notwithstanding the importance of spices, aromatics, medicinals, and other high-value, low-volume goods, the focus of the monsoon trades was on bulk goods—the Indian iron, wood, mangoes, and coconuts ordered by Madmun ben Hasan-Japheth; the flax, cotton, hemp, worked wool, wheat, barley, millet, and rye seen by Benjamin of Tudela at Hormuz; Chinese porcelain, lacquerware, and silk; cotton from Bengal and the Coromandel Coast; or from the Maldives, "cowrie shells and *qanbar* . . . [which] is made into cords for sewing ships together. These cords are exported to India, China, and al-Yaman, and are better than hemp." And then there was the horse trade carried in the ships of the Arabian Sea.

Indian rulers began importing horses overland from Central Asia by the sixth century BCE. Inscriptions prove that horses were being imported to Sri Lanka five hundred years later, and in the third century the Chinese envoy Kang Dai learned that merchants from northern India routinely exported horses by sea to the Malay Peninsula or Sumatra where the king paid half price for any that died in transit. Kang Dai's testimony is corroborated by a contemporary sealing showing a ship and a horse, while the fourth-century *Pattinappalai* refers to the "swift, prancing steeds" brought by ship to Kaveripattinam in Tamil Nadu. The Arabian Sea horse trade boomed following the foundation of the Delhi sultanate, whose rulers banned the sale of horses to Hindu kingdoms. Shortly thereafter, Zhao Rugua wrote that "in the mountains [of Oman] horse raising is carried on on a large scale. The other countries which trade here purchase horses, pearls and dates which they get in exchange for cloves, cardamom seeds and camphor." Abdullah Wassaf, a Persian contemporary of Marco Polo's, related the story of a horse trader who contracted to supply the king of Pandya in southern India with fourteen hundred horses every year and reported (secondhand) that "ten thousand horses were annually exported" from the Persian Gulf to the Malabar and Coromandel Coasts of India. According to Marco Polo, "the merchants of Hormuz and Kais, of Dhofar and Shihr and Aden . . . buy up the best horses and load them on ships and export them to this king [of Maabar, on the Coromandel Coast] and his four brother kings. Some of them are sold for . . . more than 100 marks of silver. And I assure you that this king buys 2,000 of them and more every year, and his brothers as many. And by the end of the year not 100 of them survive." These sources attribute the Indians' profligate importation of horse to their mistreatment, but except in the northwest, the subcontinent is a difficult place to raise horses. Pasturage was limited, the grasses unsuitable for horses, and the climate too hot to produce herds adequate for military needs. Even an eighteenth-century attempt by the East India Company to establish a stud farm manned by English experts in the state of Bihar failed.

This testimony about the horse trade is critical to a proper understanding of the nature of Indian Ocean ships, about which there is so little quantifiable information. A succession of thirteenth- and fourteenth-century writers from across Eurasia—Venetian, Persian, Arabic, Turkish, and Chinese—maintain that the sewn boats of the Indian Ocean were poorly built. This bias may be attributed to the fact that the authors were more familiar and comfortable with the rigid construction techniques of their homelands or simply leery of going to sea at all. Yet there is no clearer indication of these vessels' robust construction than the explicit references to horse transports, although how these differed from ordinary ships, if at all, is not known. Describing military operations at Goa in 1342, Ibn Battuta reports that "We had two tarides, open at the stern, carrying horses; they are so constructed that the horseman mounts his horse inside the vessel, puts on his armour and comes out." Wang Dayuan's *Record of Overseas Countries and People* (1349) relates that in India

> They build ships . . . to transport horses. Their sides are of planks, and they use neither nails nor mortar, but coco-nut fibre. Each ship has two or three decks with a board shed [over the upper deck?]. To make head[way] against leaking, the sailors take turns, day and night, without any intermission, at bailing out the water. In the lower hold of the ship they carry a mass of pressed-down frankincense; above this they carry several hundred head of horses.

The claim that these ships carried hundreds of horses is impossible; Mediterranean ships probably carried no more than forty horses, if that. Nonetheless this is a considerable cargo, especially when taking into consideration the enormous requirements for food and water at sea in a hot climate. The water alone for one horse for one month—the normal time for a direct passage from Oman to the Malabar Coast—would weigh more than one metric ton. Where the horses were carried is another question. For the sake of stability and sanitation, it would make sense to carry them lower in the ship; but if horses were stowed belowdecks, it would be imperative to guarantee adequate air circulation. Nor would frankincense benefit much from being stowed beneath a horse, even one on short rations. These disparate sources seem to exaggerate the tendency of these stitched-plank hulls to leak—all ships leak—and apart from Ibn Battuta they ignore entirely the pronounced advantages of sewn-plank construction. Despite the concurrence of opinion, none of these writers was a mariner by trade, and the last word on the sewn ships of the Indian Ocean should go to Vasco da Gama, who pioneered the sea route between Europe and India in 1497–99 and was disinclined to flatter Muslim shipwrights. Yet the stitching of sewn boats at Malindi, he observed, "endures all the strain of sailing" and the coir-stitched planks were "as secure as if they are nailed."

We are considerably better informed about Chinese shipbuilding. Polo's description of the Chinese ships in which he sailed offers familiar details but still manages to impress, just as it did his contemporaries. He does not give linear dimensions, but notes that the largest vessels "carry a much bigger cargo than ours. One ship will take as much as five or six thousand baskets of pepper." Bulkheads divided the hulls into as many as thirteen compartments, and the ships stepped between four and six masts and carried up to "ten smaller boats lashed to their sides outboard." The largest ships were manned by 250 to 300 crew and the accommodations included sixty cabins for merchants. Polo's account is borne out by a number of other sources and the evidence gleaned from the excavation of two ships, the Quanzhou wreck, which sank in the harbor no earlier than 1273, and the Sinan (Shinan) wreck, which sank in the waters of Sinan Province, South Korea, fifty years later.

The "spices and pepper ship" at Quanzhou measured about thirty-five meters long by ten meters in beam, with a loaded draft of three meters. The remains of the cargo included 2,300 kilograms of laka-wood, sandalwood, and black pepper from Java, garu-wood from Cambodia, betel nuts from Indonesia, frankincense from central Arabia, ambergris from Somalia, and tortoiseshell. The Quanzhou ship probably did not sail all the way to Africa, but these finds confirm Marco Polo's description of the port, which he visited within a few years of the ship's sinking. Somewhat smaller (thirty-two meters long by ten meters broad) and of roughly similar construction, the two-masted Sinan wreck was built of red fir and red pine. The cargo included more than twelve thousand pieces of Chinese ceramics—celadon vases, plates, and bowls, stoneware, incense burners, and porcelain pieces—one of China's most important exports, substantial quantities of which have been found around the western Indian Ocean as far away as the Red Sea, the Persian Gulf, and the coast of East Africa. Other objects of trade were twenty thousand Chinese copper *cash* and more than a thousand pieces of red sandalwood up to three meters long. When found, many of these items were still packed in shipping containers marked with the year—1323 in the Gregorian calendar.

By coincidence this is only two years before Ibn Battuta began his travels, and the Sinan ship is likely similar to one of the thirteen Chinese ships he encountered at Calicut:

> The Chinese vessels are of three kinds; large ships called *junks*, middle sized ones called *zaws*, and small ones called *kakams*. The large ships have anything from twelve down to three sails, which are made of bamboo rods plaited like mats. . . . A ship carries a complement of a thousand men, six hundred of whom are sailors and four hundred men-at-arms, including archers, men with shields and arbalests, that is men who throw naphtha. Each large vessel is accompanied by three smaller ones, the "half," the "third," and the "quarter."

Had Ibn Battuta measured the ships he saw at Calicut, it might have helped historians determine the size of the ships in Zheng He's fleets, one of the most contentious issues surrounding the expeditions. Much of the debate turns on how to interpret the units of measurement given in the surviving sources and the theoretical limits on the size of wooden hulls. On the basis of a strict translation of the units of length, the actual size of which differed from place to place around China, the largest ships were between 117 and 135 meters long and 48 to 55 meters broad. Based on what is known of wooden ship construction, however, 60 meters seems a more reasonable if possibly conservative estimate for the largest ships, which carried as many as nine masts setting fore-and-aft sails. Less contested are the numbers of ships and people involved. Zheng He's first expedition comprised 317 ships, including 62 "treasure ships" (*baochuan*) with a total complement of 27,870 people. The second expedition sailed with 249 ships. The third carried 30,000 people in 48 ships, most of which must have been of the largest size. The fourth fleet comprised 63 ships and 28,560 crew; the sixth, 41 ships; and the last expedition sailed with more than 100 ships. (Figures for the fifth fleet do not survive.) All the expeditions sailed with a variety of specialized vessels, the most important of which were the treasure ships, so-called because they carried treasure "of untold quantities." In addition, there were supply ships, water carriers, troop transports, at least three classes of warships, and purpose-built horse carriers.

The trading networks of the Monsoon Seas between the eleventh and fifteenth centuries were the most dynamic of any in the world, with the longest routes, the busiest ports, and the most diverse selection of goods in circulation. As a result, there were many centers of maritime vitality along the southern and eastern littoral of Asia, whose merchants were in regular communication with each other and facilitated the exchange of ideas, manufactures, and raw products over vast distances and incidentally fostered the formation of distinctive hybrid communities whose members mediated between indigenous populations and traveling merchants. In rumor and fact, the vitality of maritime Asia attracted ever more merchants and travelers from the Mediterranean basin and Europe, whose reports added to the region's allure and helped set in train the events that would culminate in the discovery of a direct sea route to Asia and, incidentally, Europe's discovery of the Americas.

Chapter 14

The World Encompassed

Columbus's crossing of the Atlantic; Gama's opening of an all-sea route between Europe and the Indian Ocean; Magellan's circumnavigation of the globe, from east to west; and Urdaneta's first west-to-east crossing of the Pacific—these were the navigational triumphs of the age, indeed of any age. They made possible the forging of new links between formerly unconnected regions of the globe, and laid the foundation of Europe's gradual ascendancy on the world stage. Singular though these accomplishments were they must be seen as the result of deliberate processes of purposeful exploration, as incidents rather than accidents of history. They were the result of long experience through which mariners, shipwrights, and cartographers steadily improved the capabilities of their ships and the art of navigation, expanded their knowledge of oceanic currents and winds, and refined the methods by which to profit from the commercial exploitation of newly encountered lands and people. While we celebrate these milestones, we must bear in mind that such progress was hard won. Hundreds of Spanish sailors died just in the four-decade search for the winds that would carry ships across the Pacific from Asia to the Americas, and the search for the Northwest and Northeast Passages from the Atlantic to the Orient in the sixteenth century were costly failures because these routes were impassable with the technology, experience, and climate of the time. Above all it has to be acknowledged that the introduction of Eurasian and African diseases in susceptible populations of the Americas led to catastrophic and wholly unanticipated loss of life—more than 80 percent (some estimates put the figure at 95 percent) of the population—and the consequent eradication of entire states and cultures.

The Portuguese and Spanish have received the lion's share of credit for inaugurating the age of European expansion, but nationalist assignments of credit obscure a more complex reality. The Genoese and Venetians pioneered the first commercially successful long-distance sea trade between the Mediterranean and Flanders and England toward the end of the thirteenth century, but theirs were not the only long-distance voyages taking place on the Atlantic at that time. Muslim and Christian navigators alike had long been involved in the coastal trade between the Iberian Peninsula and southern Morocco, as far south as Salé, while Iberian and French navigators plied their coastal waters to Flanders and England, and English and Danish fishermen and traders routinely sailed to Iceland. Though largely undocumented, these voyages contributed to the collective knowledge mariners brought to the Atlantic enterprise.

Genoese and Iberians in the Eastern Atlantic

The discovery and occupation of the four major archipelagoes between the latitudes of Lisbon and Cape Verde, the southwestern tip of West Africa, presaged the European advances down the Atlantic to the Indian Ocean and Asia and across the Atlantic to the Americas. In terms of opening new vistas, the seminal discovery of the age was that of the Canary Islands, an archipelago of twelve islands the easternmost of which lies less than fifty miles from Morocco. Some of the islands were settled by Berber-speaking people in antiquity—certainly before Islam reached northwest Africa—and Renaissance Europeans knew that a Numidian king had dispatched an expedition to the islands in the first century BCE. According to Pliny the Elder, the Numidians found no living people, although one island held evidence of human habitation and wild animals including large dogs—in Latin *canes*, hence Canary Islands. Ten centuries later, the Sicilian geographer al-Idrisi hinted at an Almoravid expedition to the islands. Their fourteenth-century rediscovery is attributed to the Genoese Lanzarotto Malocello, sailing in the service of the Portuguese king. The island of Lanzarote appears on a chart drawn by the Majorcan cartographer Angelino Dulcert in 1339. According to Boccaccio, a Portuguese expedition sailed to the Canaries two years later; but in 1344, the pope assigned temporal jurisdiction of the islands to Luis de España, a Spaniard who had sailed as admiral of France. Although the Portuguese objected on the grounds of prior discovery, in a decision with far-reaching consequences they made no effort to pursue their claim. Later in the decade, a Castilian expedition returned to the Canaries with a group of natives who had learned Catalan in an effort to evangelize their fellow islanders. It was not until 1370 that the Portuguese king granted two islands to Lansarote da Framqua—possibly the same person as Lanzarotto de Malocello—who was later ousted by Castilian rivals.

Although the Canaries are farther south than Madeira, they were the first to be reached due to their proximity to Africa and because the prevailing northeast winds gave the Europeans' square-rigged ships an easy run to the southwest. Madeira is favored by the same winds, but because it lies three hundred miles offshore (and nearly five hundred miles southwest of Lisbon), sailors needed great confidence in their ability to return from so far out at sea—or to have been blown off course—before they encountered it. Sailors returning from the Canaries could have encountered Madeira and its smaller neighbor Porto Santo when sailing north in search of favorable westerlies to carry them home to Portugal. Whatever the circumstances of their discovery, Madeira appears in the Medicean Atlas of 1351, where it is identified as Isola de Legname, "island of wood." (The Portuguese name, Madeira, or wood, was current by 1408, when the island is so named on a map.)

That those responsible for the discovery of the Canaries and, perhaps, Madeira were Italians is due to the fact that in the fourteenth century Genoese mariners increasingly found themselves in foreign and especially Portuguese employment. The Portuguese had long encouraged foreign merchants to settle in Portugal, and in 1317 King Dinis appointed the Genoese Manuele Pessagno (or Peçanha) admiral of the fleet and stipulated that Pessagno and his heirs should retain twenty experienced Genoese officers—Malocello may have been one—to command the ships and crews, most of whom were Portuguese. Lanzarote Pessagno, the fourth admiral of the family, is credited with finding the Azores, an archipelago of nine islands between seven and nine hundred miles west, and upwind, of Lisbon. Islands that can be plausibly identified as the Azores first appear in sketchy form on the celebrated Catalan Atlas of 1375 drawn by the Majorcan cartographer Abraham Cresques. An independent maritime power from 1276 to 1343, Majorca was a repository for much of the geographic knowledge amassed by sailors and merchants pushing the boundaries of the known world farther into the Atlantic, and Angelino Dulcert and Abraham Cresques were among the finest mapmakers of the day. The islands were probably first encountered by homeward-bound navigators in search of prevailing westerlies. Uninhabited and therefore difficult to exploit, the islands went unnamed in surviving sources until the fifteenth century. The association of Italian names with the Atlantic islands newly claimed by Portugal and Castile and the flourishing practice of cartography on Majorca testify to the multinational character of exploration in this period.

Navigation

The European exploration and exploitation of the eastern Atlantic was due to any number of causes, and it is impossible to distinguish any one of them as of paramount importance. Newly discovered and translated classical geographies excited people's curiosity about the world. Literacy was expanding beyond the traditional confines of the church and ecclesiastical universities, which led to the growing secularization of vernacular literature like that of Dante, Boccaccio, and Chaucer. The latter two were especially drawn to, and drew from, the commercial life of their times. Boccaccio's father represented the Bardi bank of Florence and merchants throng the stories of the *Decameron;* Chaucer was the son of a wine merchant and his *Canterbury Tales* reveal a more than passing knowledge of business and trade. His description of the Shipman invites us to consider the mental map of the fourteenth-century English mariner, which spanned from North Africa to the Baltic:

> As for his skill in reckoning his tides,
> Currents and many another risk besides,
> Moons, harbours, pilots, he had such dispatch
> That none from Hull to Carthage was his match.
> Hardy he was, prudent in undertaking;
> His beard in many a tempest had its shaking,
> And he knew all the havens as they were
> From Gottland to the Cape of Finisterre,
> And every creek in Brittany and Spain;
> The barge he owned was called *The Maudelayne*.

From a technological standpoint, literacy and improvements to navigation were accelerated by the invention of movable type, and the first printed sailing directions were published in Venice in 1490, only thirty-five years after Gutenberg's Bible. The practice of compiling information about sailing routes was nothing new, but whereas earlier guides tended to emphasize the commercial opportunities in different places, there was now a distinction between merchants' manuals with raw data about various commodities, their prices, and where to purchase them, and navigational instructions. Ancient works such as the *Periplus of the Erythraean Sea* sometimes combined this information in one text, but as new tools and methods for determining direction or fixing one's position developed in the early modern period, navigational information was increasingly differentiated.

As to the actual practice of navigation, we can consider four distinct approaches: coastal piloting, dead reckoning, latitude sailing, and position fixing. Coastal piloting is in principle the easiest but in some respects the most dangerous type of navigation, for inshore hazards are more numerous than those encountered on the open sea. As the term suggests, the essence of coastal piloting is sailing more or less in sight of land and relying on a familiarity with its terrestrial and hydrographic features to get safely from place to place. Sailors everywhere learn from a young age the landmarks and seamarks of their own waters: the location of shoals, rock outcroppings, the best holding ground for anchors, the direction of the prevailing winds, the nature of tidal currents along the shore or in the approaches to a bay, harbor, or river mouth. Similarly, they have a familiarity with terrestrial features: bays, headlands, hills, stands of trees, or man-made structures. Knowing the depth of water is of great importance, but so, too, is a familiarity with the composition of the seabed, which differs from place to place. For this reason, sounding leads attached to long lines marked off at fixed intervals were fashioned with a hollow depression on the underside that could be smeared with tallow or wax; when the lead landed on the bottom, a sample stuck to the tallow. By gauging the depth and composition of the seabed—white sand in one place, crushed shells in another—one could approximate one's location even when well out of sight of land.

Regional differences in geography dictated distinctive approaches to navigation. The rivers that facilitate commerce between inner Europe and the English Channel or North Sea deposit tons of silt into shallow waters where powerful tides constantly reconfigure the seabed, so soundings and a knowledge of tides and tidal currents are crucial for sailing northern European waters. The Mediterranean is generally too deep for taking soundings when out of sight of land; the major river deltas are few, the most important being the Rhône near Marseille, the Po south of Venice, and the Nile; and there is almost no tide to roil the shallows twice a day. The distinct concerns of Mediterranean and northern European sailors are reflected in the written instructions developed for the two regions. Whereas the mid-thirteenth-century *Lo Compasso da Navigare* gives directions by compass bearings and distances within the Mediterranean, northern European instructions give compass directions and information on tides and soundings. Even the earliest written English sailing instructions, which date to the 1460s but may incorporate fourteenth-century material, do not bother with distances:

An [when] ye come out of Spain and ye be at Cape Finisterre, go your course north-north-east. An you guess you 2 parts over the sea and be bound into [the] Severn [River, for Bristol], ye must go north by east till ye come into soundings. . . . An if ye have 100 fathoms deep or else 80, then ye shall go north until ye sound again in 72 fathoms in fair grey sand. And that is the ridge that lieth between Cape Clear [Ireland] and [the] Scilly [Islands].

The spread of literacy and quantitative approaches to navigation made the dissemination of rutters—a guide to sea routes—and *portolani* increasingly common in the Renaissance. Yet some of the finer points of navigation are so changeable and require such an intimate familiarity with specific waterways that recording them is little more than a temporary expedient. This is still true, hence the periodic release of "notices to mariners" giving changes to published charts.

Medieval laws governing pilots included severe penalties for negligence or fraudulent claims of ability. *Il Consolato del Mar* (the customs of the sea), a codification of some five centuries' worth of maritime laws and customs published at Barcelona in the mid-fifteenth century, specifies that

> If it should happen that the pilot would not know the waters in the locality that he had claimed he knew well and will not be able to perform the services that he had agreed to perform, he should be immediately decapitated, and no mercy or leniency should be given him. The patron of the vessel may order that his head be cut off without taking this matter before any tribunal of justice if he does not wish to do this, because the pilot lied to him and exposed him, all those who are in his company aboard the vessel, as well as the vessel and everything aboard it.
>
> It shall not, however, be within the exclusive determination of the master of the vessel whether the pilot is decapitated. Such a decision shall be reached after consultation and examination of the issue by the navigator, the merchants, and the rest of the crew.

Likewise, the fifteenth-century English *Black Book of the Admiralty* stipulates that "if a ship is lost by default of the lodeman [leader, or pilot] the mariners may, if they please . . . cut off his head without the mariners being bound to answer before any judge because the lodeman has committed high treason against his undertaking of the pilotage."

In addition to having a good feel for the features above and below water and the forces acting upon them, sailors had to know how to determine a ship's direction and speed, and how to estimate leeway, a vessel's sideways drift due to the wind or current. Drawing on this information enabled one to estimate one's position by dead reckoning. An observant mariner did not require sophisticated equipment to do this well. For instance, speed could be calculated by throwing a floating chip overboard and counting the seconds it took to pass between two points on the ship's hull. So the data that could be compiled in a portolan or rutter was useful but no substitute for experienced observation, especially when venturing into unknown waters of which no one had any prior knowledge.

Navigational Instruments

One reason navigational guides became more common in this period is that the growing number of ports that mariners might visit made it harder to retain all the information one might need, especially after the compass came into use. The earliest written evidence that Europeans had discovered a navigational application of a magnetized needle comes from a work of about 1180 by the English polymath Alexander Neckham:

> [S]ailors, as they sail over the sea, when in cloudy weather they can no longer profit by the light of the sun, or when the world is wrapped up in the darkness of the shades of night, and they are ignorant to what point of the compass their ship's course is directed, they touch the magnet with a needle, which is whirled round in a circle until, when its motion ceases, its point looks to the north.

There is no evidence of a Chinese origin for the western compass, but this echoes Zhu Yu's description of the south-pointing needle earlier in the century. At first, the "needle and stone" (lodestone, or magnetite) were used to locate Polaris when a visual sighting was impossible.* According to Vincent of Beauvais, writing about 1250, "When clouds prevent sailors from seeing Sun or star, they take a needle and press its point through a straw and place it in a basin of water. The stone is then moved round and round the basin, until the needle, which is following it, is whirling swiftly. At this point the stone is suddenly snatched away, and the needle turns its point to the Stella Maris."

The notion that the needle was attracted to the North Star was soon abandoned, although the magnetic pole was not understood for centuries. Even so, the traditional star shape of the compass rose reflects this original belief that the compass had a celestial orientation. At the same time, sailors' tradition of sailing "by the wind" is reflected in the division of the mariner's compass into points. Although astronomers divided the circle into 360 degrees in antiquity, Mediterranean sailors thought of direction in terms of the eight winds: north, northeast, east, southeast, and so on. With the development of the compass,

---

* Other English names for Polaris—officially called Alpha Ursae Minoris—are the North Star, Pole Star, Stella Maris, Star of the Sea, and Lodestar.

these "winds" were further divided into eight "half winds" (north-northeast, east-northeast, east-southeast . . .) and sixteen "quarter winds" (north-by-east, northeast-by-north, northeast-by-east, east-by-north, and so on), for a total of thirty-two points of 11.25 degrees.

The adoption of the compass for navigation contributed to the development of the medieval portolan, or sea chart, by Mediterranean navigators. The Italian *portolano* originally referred to a collection of written sailing instructions, the oldest surviving of which is *Lo Compasso da Navigare.* In time these were accompanied by maps that showed with remarkable felicity the outline of the Mediterranean coast. This attempt at geographic realism was a sharp departure from the highly stylized—and useless for navigation—medieval T-O maps, the intent of which was to represent an ordered world with Jerusalem at the intersection of the T, the arms of which represent the Danube, the Nile, and the Mediterranean. Between the arms lay Europe, Asia, and Africa, and the whole was encircled by Oceanus, the O. In addition to their realism, portolans are characterized by the liberal incorporation of wind roses each with radiating rhumb lines extending to the edges of the map to create a bewildering tangle of intersecting lines. These were colored according to widely adopted convention: black or brown for the winds, green for the half winds, and red for the quarter winds. Ports were identified by name—always written on the landward side perpendicular to the coast—and occasionally by flags or other insignia. On Angelino Dulcert's map of 1339, for instance, Lanzarotto Malocello's association with Lanzarote is indicated by the cross of Saint George, tutelary saint of his native Genoa.

Compasses provide a sense of direction, but not of place. Being able to fix one's position relative to one's home port or destination, if the latter was known, was essential. The easiest way to do this was by reference to a stationary object on land, but absent landmarks on the horizon, one must look skyward. The relative constancy with which the moon, stars, and planets make their rounds over the course of the year makes it fairly easy to determine latitude—one's position north or south of the equator—by measuring the angle between the horizon and either the sun or, in the northern hemisphere, the North Star. The oldest instrument for measuring altitude was the astrolabe, the origins of which can be traced to classical antiquity. The astronomer's astrolabe was too cumbersome and complex to be useful at sea (Chaucer's unfinished *Treatise on the Astrolabe,* the oldest technical manual in English, runs to fifteen thousand words), but the Portuguese had a mariner's astrolabe by 1481. Use of this simpler instrument was widespread and it is mentioned in the accounts of voyages by Bartolomeu Dias, Vasco da Gama, and Pedro Álvares Cabral. Developed somewhat before the mariners' astrolabe was the mariner's quadrant, which appears in the written record around 1460. Other devices added to the navigator's repertoire included the cross-staff (end of the fifteenth century), Davis's backstaff (end of the sixteenth century), octant (1730), and, ultimately, the sextant (1759), which remained the standard tool for navigators until the development of electronic navigation. A practical method of determining longitude—one's position east or west of a given meridian—at sea would have to await the invention of an accurate timepiece in the eighteenth century.

Of Caravels and Carracks

Improvements in navigational practice were accompanied by advances in shipbuilding. The medieval period had seen the maturing of two distinct traditions, the shell-first cogs of the Atlantic coast and the Baltic and the frame-first round ships of the Mediterranean, which could reach impressive size. A Genoese contract of 1268 called for the construction of ships measuring thirty-seven by nine meters. The major drawback to sailing such large ships, however, was their unwieldy lateen rig. Although lateen-rigged vessels can sail closer to the wind than square-riggers, which work best with a following wind, they are more difficult to handle. It is impossible to shorten sail in a lateener by furling it on a yard or boom. Instead, the yards must be lowered, the larger sails removed, and smaller ones bent on. Even tacking is a laborious process that requires lowering the yard—which could be fifty meters long—from the mast, swinging the yard and sail to the vertical, and repositioning them on the leeward side of the mast, evolutions that required large crews.

Soon after Mediterranean shipwrights began building cogs modeled after northern European prototypes they began experimenting with new sail configurations that incorporated both the fore-and-aft lateen of the Mediterranean and the square sail of the north, a change that yielded ships with three and four masts, square sails set forward and lateen sails aft. Columbus's *Santa María* set five sails: a single square sail on the foremast, a square mainsail and topsail on the main, a lateen sail on the mizzen, and a square sail set below the bowsprit called a spritsail. As time went on, Mediterranean sailors knew these vessels simply as "ships"—*naves* in Italian, *não* in Portuguese, and *nao* in Spanish—while the English used the word "carrack."

At the same time that the *nao* was emerging as the standard cargo carrier of the day, and also a formidable warship, the narrower, more versatile caravel had evolved from the *qarib*, a smaller general-purpose vessel associated especially with North Africa and the Iberian Peninsula. The oldest mention of a *caravela* dates from about the thirteenth century, although there is no clue to its rig or dimensions and the evidence for its subsequent development is sketchy. At the start of the fifteenth century, caravels seem to have been generally two-masted, lateen-rigged vessels (*caravela latina*), but by midcentury, when they were in widespread use in Portugal and southern Spain, they were also being built with three masts. Rigged with square sails on the fore- and mainmasts and a lateen mizzen, the *caravela redonda* was more efficient running before the wind, while its comparatively high length-to-beam ratio made it more maneuverable than the *nao*. Not surprisingly, the heyday of the caravel and *nao* coincides with the period of Atlantic exploration that began under the auspices of Dom Henrique of Portugal and reached its apogee with Columbus, and they were the forerunners of the square-rigged ships of the classic age of European sail that followed.

Dom Henrique and His Time

Dom Henrique—Prince Henry, "the Navigator"—was one of the earliest and most vigorous promoters of the commercial potential of the Atlantic Ocean. The third son of João I and the English Philippa of Lancaster, he is often credited with founding a school of navigation at Sagres in southwest Portugal. In point of fact Henrique was not a mariner—he probably never sailed farther than northern Morocco—and he had no school at Sagres or anywhere else. Henrique was motivated by an abiding belief in the medieval concept of just war, and an obligation to preach the true faith to heathens and crusade against heretics and Muslims. A strong advocate of the Church militant, as a teenager he cajoled his father to embark on a crusade against Morocco, and he took part in the capture of Ceuta in 1415. The victory proved something of a white elephant, for the city was of little economic or strategic significance to Portugal but costly to maintain and impossible to surrender without losing face. A subsequent Portuguese attack on Tangier, thirty miles to the west, failed, and Henrique eventually turned to more commercial pursuits.

Under his sponsorship, Portuguese caravels reached the archipelagoes of the eastern Atlantic and opened the coast of Guinea, as West Africa was called, which was a source of gold, slaves, and malagueta pepper, a spice of the ginger family used as a substitute for black pepper. His interest in the coast of Africa derived partly from his failed efforts to establish Portuguese control of the Canaries, which Castile had claimed in the early fifteenth century. Ever alert to the possibility of commercial advantage, in the 1420s Henrique sponsored a series of voyages down the coast of Africa in the apparent hope of establishing a kingdom of his own, rich in slaves, gold, and the produce of the untapped coastal fisheries. In the 1430s, he organized the colonization and exploitation of the Madeira Islands for lumber, wine, and, from the 1450s, sugar. (Originally cultivated in New Guinea, sugar had been introduced to the Mediterranean by Muslim traders.) By the end of the century, Madeira was the largest exporter of sugar in the world, shipping more than 1,200 tons per year to Europe. Henrique initiated the settlement of the Azores in 1439, and judging from the rapid rise in their population and industrial and agricultural output, navigation between Portugal and the two island groups was considerable from the start.

By 1434, the Portuguese knew the coast of Africa as far as Cape Bojador—the Bulging Cape—south of the Canaries in what is now Western Sahara and until then widely believed to be the southern limit of safe navigation. In that year, Gil Eanes passed the cape. Antão Gonçalves and Nuno Tristão reached Rio de Oro (Dakhla, Western Sahara), the site of a few Moorish villages whose inhabitants were captured and enslaved in 1441, and in that year or the next Tristão reached Cabo Bianco (Nouadhibou, Mauritania). In 1445, an expedition reportedly numbering twenty-six ships sailed for Rio de Oro, and a few vessels continued on to the Senegal River and Cape Verde. Three years later the Portuguese built a trading post near Rio de Oro on the small island of Arguin in the Mauritanian gulf of the same name. Thanks to its supplies of freshwater, this became the center of a lucrative trade in ivory, gold, and slaves, and of a coastal fishery.

In 1454, when the Venetian merchant Alvise da Cadamosto stopped in Portugal en route to Flanders, Henrique offered him three-quarters of the proceeds of any expedition to Guinea he fitted out himself, or half if he used one of Henrique's ships. The following year he sailed south. Cadamosto's account is one of the liveliest of the era to survive, for he has an eye as much for the people and their customs as for their trade. He offers enticing details of the founding and prosperity of the Madeiras, the Canaries, and Arguin, where "Portuguese caravels are coming and going all the year" and where merchants licensed by Henrique traded "cloaks, carpets, and similar articles and above all, corn [grain], for they are always short of food," for the raw wealth of Guinea—"every year . . . a thousand slaves" and gold dust. South of the Senegal River he reached the territory of Lord Budomel, a Wolof king who traded a hundred slaves for seven horses and invited Cadamosto to his house about forty kilometers from the coast. "My journey inland was indeed more to see interesting sights and obtain information, than to receive my dues." After a month as the Budomel's guest, he sailed farther south, to a place where the North Star was visible "only when the weather was very clear . . . about a third of a lance above the horizon. We also had sight of six stars low down over the sea, clear, bright, and large." This was the constellation Crux, or the Southern

Cross, a constellation that would come to serve much the same navigational function in the southern hemisphere that Polaris did in the north. Cadamosto was also one of the first people to sight the Cape Verde Islands, which lie about four hundred miles west of Africa and are first mentioned in official documents in 1460. By this, the year of Henrique's death, the Portuguese had explored about two thousand miles of coastal West Africa, including expeditions up the Senegal, Gambia, and other rivers. Turning the corner into the Gulf of Guinea would take another decade.

Regardless of the geographical achievements, Henrique's sponsorship of these voyages was predicated on financial returns, and he set clear objectives for his captains, regulating the distances to be covered and ensuring that details about the navigation and geography of the coast, trade goods, and prices, and local languages were collected systematically. Once south of the zone of Islamic influence and Arabic speakers, acquisition of this information was hampered not only by the difficulty of the navigation, but by the inability to communicate through interpreters. This would remain a problem until the Portuguese rounded Africa and reached the arabophone coast of East Africa in 1498. The challenges of language and the lack of an indigenous tradition of coastal navigation to draw upon help explain why the pace of Portuguese exploration in the last half of the fifteenth century appears so slow, and why their progress once they reached the Indian Ocean was so swift.

While one result of the Portuguese voyages down the west coast of Africa was the discovery of a route to India, there is no indication that Henrique had any broader program in mind than crusading against heathens and infidels, and his own aggrandizement. At the time, no one considered the possibility of sailing around southern Africa or of finding a shortcut to the Indies, the goal that had animated the Vivaldi brothers 150 years earlier. Government support for further exploration of the African coast died with Henrique, as Afonso V, his nephew, focused on territorial gains in infidel Morocco. These brutal campaigns proved a hard school for Portuguese soldiers, some of whom later took their fight against Muslims to Asia.

Defining Space

European expansion ushered in a new era in world history not simply because it catapulted Eurasia's comparatively backward west-enders from their obscure peninsula onto the world stage, but because the Europeans introduced to the world a variety of cultural and legal novelties that we now take for granted. Two are particularly indelible. One was the evolving symbiosis between rulers and merchants so characteristic of the Italian city-states like Venice, Genoa, and Florence, through whose influence this dynamic spread to Iberia and northern Europe. The other was the notion that political control could be exercised not only over lands across the ocean but over the oceans themselves. While many had used their navies to extend their authority overseas—to seize islands, or to control strategic passages and choke points—no one had ever presumed to divide the sea preemptively and to treat it as a political space analogous to territory on land. The Romans had called the Mediterranean *Mare Nostrum*, "Our Sea," but that was simply a statement of fact, and classical jurisprudence regarded the sea as the property of all people, a global commons. By the thirteenth century, both Venice and Genoa were asserting their jurisdiction over the northern Adriatic and Ligurian Seas, respectively, in an effort to ensure that all goods passed through their ports, where taxes and other fees were collected. According to contemporary legal interpretation, they had earned such jurisdiction by custom, specifically by virtue of having held it for a century or more. Others argued that the city-states could receive a "use" of the sea as a gift from the Holy Roman Emperor, and deny others the freedom of navigation.

All this changed with a series of papal bulls that asserted Portuguese claims to lands not yet ruled by Christian princes. Confirming the advances made under Dom Henrique's sponsorship, the bull *Romanus Pontifex* of 1455 stated that Portugal's Afonso V "justly and lawfully has acquired and possessed . . . these islands, lands, harbors, and seas" in Guinea, and that no one was allowed to interfere with his or his successors' efforts to convert the inhabitants to Christianity. The bull applied not only to Ceuta and Guinea, but "to all those provinces, islands, harbors, and seas whatsoever, which hereafter . . . can be acquired from the hands of infidels or pagans" in the name of Afonso and his heirs. This was hardly the first instance of the Church's intervention in secular affairs, but Pope Callixtus III was anxious to settle disputes among western leaders in order to free them to crusade against the Ottomans, who had just captured Constantinople.

A quarter century later, the Treaty of Alcáçovas between Portugal and Castile included two provisions of especially far-reaching significance. Isabella's right to the throne of Castile was acknowledged, and the dispute over the Canary Islands was resolved in favor of Castile. The Portuguese retained ownership of Madeira, the Azores, and the Cape Verde Islands, and they were given free rein in the exploration of the Atlantic. Moreover, the treaty enjoined Isabella and Ferdinand of Aragon, her husband, to forbid their subjects or anyone "equipped or provisioned in their ports" to sail to the Portuguese islands or the "lands of Guinea discovered or to be discovered." Alcáçovas thus gave

Portugal the lion's share of the territorial gains, and it was clear that should the Spanish seek out new lands via the Atlantic, they would have to go north or west. As it happened, the Canary Islands, which they retained, proved the ideal point of departure for ships sailing westward to the Americas, as Christopher Columbus and his followers would soon learn.

With the threat of Castilian interlopers removed, the Portuguese were free again to pursue their Atlantic trade. The possibility that a round-Africa sea route to the Indies might exist began to take hold after the Portuguese turned into the Gulf of Guinea in 1471. Credit for acting on this possibility goes to Henrique's grand-nephew, João II, who fostered a program of maritime expansion with a view specifically to circumnavigating Africa. He began by sending six hundred soldiers and craftsmen to build a fortress at São Jorge da Mina (Elmina, Ghana), which became the focal point of Portugal's West African trade in slaves and gold and the base of operations for voyages farther south. The Portuguese crossed the equator around 1473, and in 1482 Diogo Cão reached the mouth of the Zaire (Congo) River, "which enters the sea with such a rush that 20 leagues [sixty miles] from the coast its waters are sweet." A few years later Cão got as far as Walvis Bay, Namibia. In addition to extending Portuguese knowledge of the physical geography of Africa, these voyages introduced the Portuguese to the kingdom of Congo, which would become among the largest suppliers of African slaves to the Americas, as the Portuguese would be the most important carriers.

At this point, the possibility that the Portuguese might actually reach the Indian Ocean by sea was so real that João dispatched four expeditions to the east in one year, two by sea, and two overland through the Levant. He had two distinct objects in view: to reach the Christian king of Ethiopia and to ascertain the likelihood of reaching the Indian Ocean by sea and assess the commercial conditions there should that be achieved. The emissary to Ethiopia died, but Pêro da Covilhã spent five years visiting Aden, Cannanore, Calicut, Goa, and the coast of East Africa before returning to Egypt. Learning of his fellow emissary's death, Covilhã may have sent home an account that stressed the trade of Calicut and mentioned that it was possible to reach there from "the Guinea Sea," though it is unlikely that any report reached Portugal before the late 1490s. He then went to Ethiopia, where he remained until his death.

The most fruitful of the four expeditions was that of Bartolomeu Dias, who in 1487 sailed with three ships on a voyage that brought European ships into the Indian Ocean for the first time, to land, on February 3, 1488, at Mossel Bay, 160 miles east of the southern tip of Africa, and 600 miles shy of the southernmost community of Muslim traders in Africa. On his return, Dias saw what he called the Cape of Storms, an apt name given the conditions that prevail at the junction of the Atlantic and Indian Oceans, but when he returned to Portugal in December 1488, João dubbed it the Cape of Good Hope, the hope being that the trade of the Indies was finally within reach.* Domestic problems prevented the Portuguese from following up immediately on Dias's monumental achievement. Moreover, many nobles still tied to the land resisted overseas ventures while even among those who supported commercial undertakings there was considerable debate about the wisdom of actually breaking into the Indian Ocean trade, about which they knew almost nothing. It is against this complex background of intra-Iberian and interfaith rivalry, coupled with the increased opportunities for trade in coastal Africa and the expanding knowledge of the ocean world and the technologies required to work profitably within it, that we must assess the most celebrated accomplishments of the age and the people who brought them to pass.

Christopher Columbus

The exploratory activity on the Atlantic had attracted any number of ambitious mariners, one of whom, the Genoese-born Christopher Columbus, conceived a bold plan "that he would sail south and west, discovering great stretches of highly fertile land, both islands and terra firma, all extremely rich in gold and silver, pearls and precious stones and teeming peoples; and that, sailing in this direction, he would eventually come to the land of India, with the noble island of Cipangu [Japan] and the realms of the Grand Khan." He was not the first to believe such a voyage was possible, and one can say with complete candor that he failed: Columbus underestimated the size of the earth; he did not reach Asia; and he did not tap into the great spiceries of the Orient. None of this diminishes his epochal accomplishment in establishing an unbroken link between Eurasia and Africa in the east and the Americas in the west. If he excelled his contemporaries, it was not necessarily in navigational ability or intuition, but in his persistent vision and relentless pursuit of the financial and political support without which the honor of bridging the Atlantic would have fallen to another.

Born in the mid-fifteenth century, Columbus served his apprenticeship in the Ligurian and Tyrrhenian Seas and seems to have sailed into the Atlantic for the first time in his early twenties. By 1476 he was based in Lisbon, where he married Filipa Moniz, whose father, Bartolomeo Perestrello, was the son

---

* The Cape of Good Hope (34°20'S, 18°25'E) is widely held to be the southernmost cape in Africa; in fact this distinction belongs to Cape Agulhas (34°50'S, 20°E).

of an Italian merchant in Lisbon and had been raised in the household of Dom Henrique. A participant in the expedition sent to claim the Madeiras, Perestrello was rewarded with the governorship of the island of Porto Santo, where he settled in 1446. Although he died twenty years before his daughter's marriage, Filipa's dowry seems to have included his personal papers, including sailing instructions and portolan charts for the Atlantic. According to Columbus's biographer, Bartolomé de Las Casas, in Perestrello's day

> the world was buzzing with all sorts of discoveries that were being made along the Guinea coast and among the islands of the Atlantic, and Bartolomeu Perestrelo hoped to make some discoveries of his own using Porto Santo as his base. Such discoveries were indeed forthcoming . . . and it must therefore have been the case that Bartolomeu Perestrelo had in his possession instruments, documents, and navigation charts and that these were given to Christopher Columbus by his mother-in-law. He took great delight in contemplating these and it is believed that this gift . . . led him to inquire further into the practice and lessons to be drawn from the experience of the Portuguese in making sea-voyages to Mina del Oro [Elmina] and the Guinea coast where the Portuguese were . . . busily employed.

Columbus gained practical experience of sailing between the Canaries, Madeira, and Azores. He made at least two voyages along the Guinea coast and was part of the expedition charged with building the fort at São Jorge da Mina, while northern voyages took him to Galway, Ireland, and possibly Iceland.

In addition to the documented discoveries of the time, there was a growing body of lore about lands to the west of the four archipelagoes. Medieval tradition, some of it embellishing more ancient stories, spoke of various islands to the west, notably St. Brendan's Isle and Antilia, the Island of the Seven Cities supposedly founded by Iberian bishops fleeing the Muslim invasion in the eighth century. Voyages by accident and design also expanded sailors' knowledge of the Atlantic, especially its great size. Shortly before the start of his voyage in 1492, Columbus and his fellow officers met a man who forty years before had sailed west as far as the Sargasso Sea—a vast stretch of ocean strewn with patches of sargassum seaweed, which he told Columbus not to fear—and had seen land birds flying west before fear of winter storms made the crew turn for home. In the Portuguese archipelagoes, reports circulated of flotsam drifting in from the west: unfamiliar trees and plants, canoes and boats, strangely carved pieces of wood, even people and corpses of neither European nor African origin. According to a marginal note written by Columbus in one of his books, "Men of Cathay came to the West. We have seen

Sebastiano del Piombo's portrait of a man thought to be Christopher Columbus was painted in 1519, thirteen years after the navigator's death at the age of about sixty. The inscription above his head reads "the Ligurian Colombo, the first to enter by ship into the world of the Antipodes 1519." Courtesy of the Metropolitan Museum of Art, New York/ Art Resource, New York.

many notable things and especially in Galway, in Ireland, a man and a woman with miraculous form, pushed along by the storm on two logs." His son likewise related how "On the island of Flores, which is one of the Azores, the sea flung ashore two dead bodies with broad faces and different in appearance from the Christians. Off Cape Verga, and elsewhere in that region there once were seen covered boats or canoes [kayaks, perhaps] which were believed to have been crossing from one island to another when a storm drove them off their course."

The possibility of a westward route to Asia also attracted the interest of cosmographers armed with Ptolemy's second-century *Geography*, which circulated widely in a Latin edition of 1476. Among the first to promote the idea was Paolo dal Pozzo Toscanelli, a Florentine banker, geographer, and cartographer who wrote the king of Portugal that China was only five thousand miles west of Portugal and that a voyage there could be broken by stops on the islands of Antilia and Cipangu (Japan). The suggestion was never acted upon, but Columbus seems to have seized upon the theory, and may have corresponded with Toscanelli. A major problem with both Toscanelli and Columbus was that their estimate of the length of a degree (Columbus's is found in another marginal note) was too short by about a third. By his calculation, "the perimeter of the earth on the equinoctial circle is 20,400 millas" of 4,810 to 4,860 feet. In fact a mile is 5,280 feet, and the equator is 24,901 miles (40,075 kilometers) long. This error was compounded by his belief that Asia ended thirty degrees east of where it does and his reliance on Marco Polo's erroneous claim that Japan was fifteen hundred miles east of China. In sum, Columbus thought China lay about thirty-five hundred miles west of the Canary Islands; the actual distance is more than four times that. The possibility of an intervening continent was not even considered.

After nearly a decade in Portuguese shipping, and with allies at court thanks to his wife's family, Columbus approached João II with his proposal for a westward voyage to the Indies. After consulting with his advisors, João declined to sponsor him but suggested that he might reconsider later. He may have withheld his support because his advisors told him Columbus's theories were incorrect, because Columbus sought excessive compensation, or because João did not want to divert resources from the encouraging progress in the newly revived African voyages. Regardless, in 1485, Columbus left Lisbon for Castile, where he hoped to interest Isabella and Ferdinand in the same venture. Although he was ultimately successful, the outcome of his lobbying was by no means a foregone conclusion. The commission convened to examine his calculations judged him overly optimistic; but the Catholic Monarchs held out the possibility of considering his proposal after they had defeated Granada, the last Muslim kingdom on the Iberian Peninsula, and they backed their assurances with the occasional stipend of a few thousand maravedis. (Masters and pilots normally earned two thousand maravedis a month, and seamen half that.)

These gifts notwithstanding, Columbus's first loyalty remained to his dream, and in 1488 he returned to Lisbon at João's invitation. His timing could not have been worse, as his arrival coincided with the return of Dias from his voyage beyond the Cape of Good Hope. With a sea road to the Indies beckoning, João lost interest in Columbus's venture and the Genoese returned to Spain. Isabella and Ferdinand continued to string him along but after a further rebuff in 1492, again on the recommendation of experts, he decided to try his fortune in France. (His brother Bartolomé had already floated the idea to England's Henry VII and the French court.) He had just set out when he was summoned back to court, thanks to Luis de Santángel, who was in effect Ferdinand's business manager. Santángel reasoned that whatever emoluments Columbus sought for his venture, the crown's outlay was modest and the profits that might accrue could be substantial, whereas the potential loss should he make a worthwhile discovery for someone else would be impossible to recoup. In the event, Columbus secured ample guarantees: the hereditary offices of admiral, viceroy, and governor-general in all lands and islands he might discover, with the right to name his own governors, and 10 percent of the profits from trade. While one can see in these demands the vanity of a social climber, whatever his mistakes and faults, Columbus cannot be accused of underachievement. No one ever accomplished more to earn ennoblement and its attendant perquisites. Moreover, it has to be acknowledged that lobbying played a crucial role in his success. Funds, honors, and profits were not low-lying fruit, and as the stories of Henrique, Columbus, and countless others demonstrate, in the history of exploration persistence, flattery, and self-confidence are often as important as—if not more important than—being right.

Funding for Columbus's first expedition, an estimated two million maravedis, came from a variety of sources. Santángel's deft accounting enabled the crown to contribute little more than half the total, while Columbus put up about a quarter, probably borrowed from Giannoto Berardi, a Florentine trader who had moved to Seville in 1485 and was "a central figure in the lobby that promoted Atlantic expansion as an objective of Spanish policy and raised Columbus to eminence" at court. To satisfy a debt owed the crown, the town of Palos de la Frontera paid for the caravels *Niña* and *Pinta* (captained by the brothers Vicente Yáñez and Martín Alonso Pinzón, respectively) and their crews, and Columbus hired the *Santa María*, a Galician-built *nao*, as his *capitana*, or flagship. She was not an especially large vessel for her day, twenty-seven meters long and eight meters in beam at most; with only one deck and a year's provisions, there were few creature comforts, and sleeping arrangements for the forty crew were fairly rude. (Crew accommodations in European ships improved somewhat after Columbus's crew adopted the hammocks used by Caribbean islanders.) The caravels were even smaller, the *Niña* measuring no more than twenty-one by six meters and the *Pinta* twenty-three by seven meters.

Sailing from Palos on August 3, 1492, the ships reached the Canaries nine days later. There the *Pinta*'s rudder was repaired and the rig on the *Niña* was changed from a *caravela latina* to a *caravela redonda*, with square sails on the fore- and mainmasts, and a lateen on the mizzen. This made her much better suited to capturing the northeast trades, and she became Columbus's fastest and favorite ship. (The *Pinta* was rigged as a *caravela redonda* from the start.) The ships sailed again on September 6. They reached the seaweed-thick Sargasso Sea after ten days, and three days later they were out of the trades and into a week of light and variable winds. Conditions improved considerably between October 2 and 6, when they sailed an estimated 710 miles, including their best day's run of 182 miles. By this time they were close enough to land to follow the paths of birds heading southwest, but despite this and other tantalizing indications that land was near, by October 10 the crew of the *Santa María* were near mutiny and Columbus apparently agreed to put about if they did not sight land within a few days.

The next night they were in the Bahamas archipelago and on October 12, after a voyage of about three thousand nautical miles in thirty-three days, they landed on the Taíno island of Guanahaní, which Columbus claimed for Spain and named San Salvador. Sailing through the Bahamas for two weeks, they took aboard seven Taínos, who returned with Columbus to Spain, to be taught Castilian and Christianity so they could help with the work of conversion on their return. The Taínos also directed him to a place called Cuba, "which I believe must be Cipango according to the indications that these people give of its size and wealth." Yet Cipangu and China would remain nothing more than shimmering mirages on an ever-receding horizon, and Columbus's frustrated haste was already obvious in a diary entry (addressed to his king and queen) for October 19:

> I am not taking much pains to see much in detail because I want to see and explore as much as I can so I can return to Your Highnesses in April, Our Lord pleasing. It is true that, finding where there is gold or spices in quantity, I will stay until I get as much of it as I can. And for this reason I do nothing but go forward to see if I come across it.

The Spanish explored the northeast coast of Cuba for six weeks, and at the beginning of November Columbus dispatched an embassy to the inland village of Holguín in the hope that it would prove to be a major Asiatic capital. He was disappointed to learn that his interpreter, whose languages included Hebrew, Aramaic, and Arabic, could make no headway with the local people. Despite being told that it took more than twenty days to circle Cuba in a canoe, Columbus defiantly maintained that it was not a large island but a peninsula of Asia. In late November, Martín Alonso Pinzón in *Pinta* split off from the others without authorization to explore on his own. On December 5, *Santa María* and *Niña* sailed east to Cape St. Nicholas, the northwestern tip of Hispaniola in what is now Haiti, and a week later they took possession of the land in the name of Ferdinand and Isabella. The presence of gold artifacts and the friendliness of the local chief were encouraging, but disaster struck shortly after midnight on Christmas Eve when the *Santa María* grounded on a reef. No one died but the ship was a total loss. It would have been virtually impossible to cross the Atlantic with more than sixty men in *Niña*—Pinzón was still absent with the *Pinta*—so thirty-nine men volunteered to remain in a fort fashioned from the flagship's timbers and named La Navidad. *Niña* sailed on January 4, 1493, and fell in with the *Pinta* at Isla Cabra two days later.

The return to Europe was far more difficult than the voyage out. The ships were poorly provisioned and Columbus insisted that they sail back the way they had come, a curious recommendation given that their westward passage had been abetted by prevailing easterlies. Eventually he turned north and the *Niña* and *Pinta* caught the same band of westerlies that blow past the Azores toward Portugal. The midwinter departure left them so exposed to storms that at one point Columbus sealed a description of his discovery in a barrel and threw it overboard in hopes that it would survive even if he did not. Some idea of the inadequacies of fifteenth-century dead reckoning can be gleaned from the fact that when land was sighted on February 15, it was thought to be variously Madeira, Lisbon, Castile, or one of the Azores. In fact it was Santa Maria, in the Azores, where the *Niña* anchored three days later, having been separated from the *Pinta* shortly before. The Portuguese authorities detained a shore party for violating their territory, but the men were freed and Columbus sailed on. Again beset by vicious storms, a week later the *Niña* was off Lisbon, the last place the architect of an important new discovery for the king of Spain would want to find himself. Summoned to court, Columbus reluctantly presented himself to João II, who, according to a later report, "hearing the news of the location where Columbus said the discovered land was, became very confused and believed really that the discovered land belonged to him" by the Treaty of Alcáçovas. Certainly João would have been piqued to learn that Columbus had found Asia more or less where he said he would, and it would be another five years before the Portuguese followed up on Dias's rounding of southern Africa. In the meantime, it was essential that he clarify Portugal's rights under the Treaty of Alcáçovas.

The Atlantic After 1492

Columbus and his shipmates may have been disappointed with their initial encounters to the west, but so far as they or anyone else was concerned, they had reached the outskirts of Cipangu and China. But the possibility that they were in violation of the terms of the Treaty of Alcáçovas, as João seems to have believed, was quite real. Columbus boldly claimed that the islands were in the same latitude as the Canaries—that they were in effect a remote extension of that archipelago—when patently they were not. Sharing his anxiety, the Spanish monarchs decided on a two-pronged strategy, raising funds for a follow-up expedition and lobbying Pope Alexander VI (one of only two Spaniards ever to be Bishop of Rome) for recognition of their claim. Between May and September 1493, Alexander issued four papal bulls asserting his view—which was that of Ferdinand and Isabella—of the Spanish claim. The *Inter Caetera* drew a north–south line a hundred leagues west of the Azores and Cape Verde, or approximately 31°W. The first three bulls confirmed and clarified the limits of Portuguese and Spanish claims, but the fourth essentially denied Portugal rights to any lands "found or to be found . . . notwithstanding apostolic constitutions and ordinances . . . made by ourselves or our predecessors." Rather than rely on the arbitration of a Spanish pope to reverse this, João negotiated a clarification of their kingdoms' respective claims directly with the Catholic Monarchs. The result was the Treaty of Tordesillas of 1494, which moved the line of demarcation 370 leagues (1,110 nautical miles) west of the Cape Verde Islands. As was soon discovered, the line crossed the eastern bulge of South America near the mouth of the Amazon River—the line is first shown on the celebrated Cantino map of 1502—thus establishing the basis for Portugal's claim to Brazil.

Columbus's first voyage had lasted seven months and was one of exploration. Over the next eleven years he would make three more, each of which lasted longer than two years and combined exploration with the more mundane tasks of colonial administration. Columbus's shortcomings as a leader ashore emerged on the second voyage (1493–96). Departing from the Canaries, his fleet of seventeen ships made landfall on Dominica. Sailing north they had several encounters, some violent, with the Caribs, a cannibal tribe who frequently enslaved Arawaks such as the Spanish had met the year before. Yet Columbus's return to La Navidad left no doubt that the Arawaks were less peaceful and submissive than he had claimed, for not one settler survived, most if not all having been killed, possibly for stealing gold and women although the actual reason remains a mystery.

Chief among Columbus's responsibilities was to establish a viable colony, but from April to September 1494 he explored Cuba and Jamaica and forced his crew to swear that Cuba was part of mainland Asia. Back at Hispaniola he ignored a royal summons to return home, but he managed to remain in the monarchs' good graces and they appointed him to lead a new expedition. The fleet was divided into two groups, Columbus commanding three ships to explore the southern Caribbean and the coast of South America. The conclusions he drew from this voyage reflect an intensifying spirituality more than a maturing sense of geography. Cruising the coast of Venezuela, he came across pearl fisheries in the vicinity of the Orinoco but took the freshwater discharge of the vast river as evidence not of a vast continental watershed but of the "earthly paradise . . . from which flow four of the chief rivers of this world," the Ganga, Tigris, Euphrates, and Nile, as described in Genesis. Returning to Hispaniola, Columbus found that the situation there had turned from bad to worse. Ferdinand and Isabella had received a steady stream of negative reports and had launched an investigation into his and his brother's governance, an uprising against their administration by European settlers on Hispaniola, and their refusal to stop enslaving Indians. An official from court arrived in August 1500 to address these problems and the brothers returned to Spain in chains.

Eventually released, Columbus undertook his fourth voyage in 1502, but not before a fleet of thirty-two ships had sailed with enough of a lead to allow a new administrator to establish his authority. The objects of Columbus's final expedition were to find a strait to the west and to claim and settle territory on the coast of Central America between Honduras and Panama. He achieved neither goal. Two ships had to be abandoned in Panama, and the other two were so heavily damaged in a collision that they had to be run aground on Jamaica. Six of their company eventually reached Hispaniola in Indian canoes and returned to rescue their shipmates eight months later. Columbus returned to Spain in November 1504 and spent the last two years of his life wealthy but resentful of being stripped of some of his honors and grants, and bitter that licenses were now being issued to others to sail to Hispaniola.

Several of these voyages were made by former shipmates of Columbus, to whom probably all explorers of this generation can be related by fewer than six degrees of separation. In 1499, Alonso de Hojeda, a veteran of Columbus's second voyage, returned to the pearl fisheries of Venezuela. Among those sailing with him was the chameleonesque Amerigo Vespucci—banker, ship's chandler, explorer, confidant of Columbus's, and, by accident rather than by design, namesake of the Americas. It is unclear how much expertise Vespucci had before joining Hojeda, but his writings implausibly suggest that he commanded the expedition. He subsequently entered Portuguese service and in 1501 returned to South America in search of a westward passage through the continent. Vespucci's fame stemmed from the attribution to him of several accounts of New World exploration and the false claim that he was the discoverer of South America. Readers of these included the German cartographer Martin Waldseemüller, who applied the name Ameriga to the southern continent in a 1507 edition of Ptolemy's *Geography*. Six years later—when both

Columbus and Vespucci were dead—Waldseemüller labeled South America Terra Nova; but by that time the name America had stuck and was being applied to North America as well.

Vasco da Gama and the First Atlantic–Indian Ocean Voyage

By this time, Spanish claims to the Americas had been eclipsed by the Portuguese opening of an enormously lucrative sea trade between Europe and Asia, just as João II had confidently predicted. A succession crisis had prevented an immediate follow-up to Dias's voyage of 1488, but Manoel I, "the Fortunate," continued his predecessor's drive to the Indies. Opponents of his plan argued that India was too far away, the cost in men and matériel would leave the kingdom exposed to its enemies, and a profitable commerce would excite rivals. Manoel prevailed and in 1497 "named Vasco da Gama, *fidalgo* [nobleman] of his household, as Captain-Major of the sails that he was to send there"—two *nãos*, a caravel, and a storeship. Provisioned for three years, the ships had a total complement of 140 to 170 crew, including pilots, interpreters, and 10 *degredados*, criminal exiles. The latter were convicts who were left in unfamiliar places until their ship returned. In the meantime, they were expected to learn about the region's people and their customs, trade, and language. If they survived, they won their freedom and the opportunity to benefit as a translator and intermediary.

Gama's fleet departed Lisbon in June 1497 and after watering in the Cape Verde Islands sailed in a broad westward arc before turning southeast. They reached the coast of what is now South Africa in early November. After a week of rest and repairs, they sailed again, doubling the Cape of Good Hope on November 18 and, bucking contrary winds, reached Mossel Bay a week later. Their encounters with local inhabitants were characterized by mutual suspicion, but in January 1498 they had better luck at a place they called Terra da Boa-Gente ("land of good people") in southern Mozambique. At the Zambezi delta they met "a youth who . . . was from another land a good distance from there and who said that he had seen ships as large as those that we had brought, at which signs we rejoiced greatly for it really seemed to us that we were coming closer to where we wanted to go." Their next stop was the island of Mozambique where friction with Muslims erupted into violence, as it would again at Mombasa, much of it instigated by the Portuguese. They had more cordial relations with the king of Malindi, a rival to Mombasa, and here they hired a pilot to guide them to Calicut. After four months of almost daily contact with Arab traders in East Africa, the Portuguese departed Malindi on

April 24 and crossed to Calicut in twenty-two days. At long last, the Portuguese had opened the sea route from Europe to the Indies.

The samorin of the largest and most cosmopolitan trading center on the Malabar Coast was initially well disposed toward the Portuguese, but his opinion was tempered by their overbearing manner and the antagonism of the sophisticated Muslim traders who disdained their second-rate offerings of cotton, beads, tin ornaments, trousers, and hats.* Gama attempted to leave in early August, but the samorin insisted that they pay duties for the cinnamon, cloves, and precious stones they had purchased. When the unsold Portuguese goods were seized and members of the crew detained ashore, Gama took eighteen hostages. The crisis was resolved a week later although the Portuguese kept a number of hostages, five of whom returned to India in 1500. Departing before the end of the southwest monsoon, the Portuguese took three months to cross the Arabian Sea and thirty of the crew died before they reached Malindi. Down to two ships, they reached Lisbon in July 1499. Gama's voyage was the culmination of the Portuguese age of discovery, and in one stroke it altered the pattern of Eurasian trade forever.

With the Arab-Venetian monopoly of the spice trade broken, Lisbon became, briefly, the most important entrepôt in Europe, and Manoel styled himself "Lord of the Conquest, Navigation, and Commerce of Ethiopia, Arabia, Persia, and of India." To follow up on Gama's extraordinary achievement, he entrusted a second fleet of thirteen ships to Pedro Álvares Cabral, who landed at Porto Seguro, Brazil, in April 1500 and dispatched one ship home to report on the discovery. (Vicente Yáñez Pinzón, a veteran of Columbus's first voyage, had reached the coast south of Recife three months before, but the Portuguese Cabral is popularly credited as the European discoverer of Brazil.) Cabral's expedition had otherwise mixed results; only six ships reached Calicut, where the Portuguese managed to antagonize the samorin and local traders even more than Gama had. They established a factory (a trading station manned by factors, or commercial agents) in the city, but a riot by Muslim traders left forty Portuguese dead. Thinking that the samorin was behind this, Cabral bombarded the city, killing four or five hundred people and sinking between ten and fifteen trading ships. Although this made it impossible for the Portuguese to trade at Calicut, they were able to establish a factory about a hundred miles south at Cochin (Kochi), whose ruler viewed the Portuguese as an ally against the samorin, his overlord and rival. Moreover, Cochin was found to be the home of a community of Christians whose bishop was appointed in Syria, and Cabral learned that Saint Thomas the Apostle was

---

* Samorin is a corruption of *samudri raja*, meaning "king of the sea."

buried in Mylapore, on the Coromandel Coast. The Portuguese settled in São Thomé de Meliapur in 1523 and it became the headquarters of Portuguese trade in the Bay of Bengal.

Some of these Christians returned to Portugal, together with two Italian merchants who had lived in India for decades. The intelligence gained from these men, together with that gleaned from captured charts and other documents, increased Portuguese knowledge of the Indian Ocean trade tremendously and helped them to identify the most strategic ports. After consolidating their position in India, between 1510 and 1515 they captured and fortified Goa, Melaka, Hormuz, and Colombo. Only Aden and the Red Sea proved impregnable. They also established innumerable factories around the Indian Ocean and farther east.

From Magellan to the Treaty of Zaragoza

Despite the initial lack of commercial promise in the Americas, the Spanish continued to exploit their foothold in this new world while the Portuguese reaped the benefits of their ever-increasing trade in the Indian Ocean and the Spice Islands, which Francisco Serrão reached in 1511. There remained, however, the question of whether the latter lay within the Spanish or Portuguese sphere of influence as defined at Tordesillas, and whether a western route would be shorter than that via the Cape of Good Hope. The first person to attempt to answer these questions was the Portuguese Fernão de Magalhães, or Ferdinand Magellan, who sailed for Spain. A veteran of seven years in the east, including the capture of Melaka, Magellan was encouraged in this plan by his correspondence with Serrão, who was a trusted advisor to the local sultan. Magellan fell out with Manoel I when the king refused to support his proposed itinerary and, like Columbus before him, he submitted his proposal to the king of Spain. Charles I (soon to be Emperor Charles V) offered Magellan a ten-year monopoly on the route and two years later Magellan sailed from Sanlúcar de Barrameda with 237 men in five ships provisioned for two years.

Magellan's position was difficult because the Castilians resented sailing under a Portuguese commander and the Portuguese considered him a traitor. As one of Manoel's agents wrote: "Please God the Almighty, that they may make such a voyage as the Cortereals"—that is, be lost at sea—"and that your Highness may be at rest, and for ever be envied, as you are, by all princes." After reaching the coast of Brazil near Rio de Janeiro, they headed for the Río Plata and then put into Puerto San Julian, Argentina, for the winter. On April 1, 1520, a simmering conspiracy led by two captains and Juan Sebastian de

Elcano, master of the *Concepción*, came to a head. Magellan moved quickly and the mutineers surrendered. One captain was decapitated, drawn, and quartered, and when the fleet sailed the other captain and a priest were marooned. After wintering at Santa Cruz, the ships reached the entrance to the Strait of Magellan between Patagonia and Tierra del Fuego on October 21. Down to three ships (one had wrecked and another turned back to Spain), the Spanish spent five weeks defying the winds and currents of the rockbound strait.

Their route across the Pacific is unknown. Leaving the strait at about 52°S, the Spanish would have been in the teeth of the prevailing westerlies that nineteenth-century sailors called the "Furious Fifties." Given the time of year, the ships probably sailed north across the equator to about 10°N where they picked up the northeast trades for their westward passage. Whatever the case, they saw no land for fourteen weeks, during which twenty-one of the crew died. Antonio Pigafetta's memoir depicts the sufferings of the starving, scurvy-ridden crew and their desperate sorceries to create food—horrific scenes that would be repeated countless times in the age of sail.

> We ate biscuit, which was no longer biscuit, but powder of biscuits swarming with worms, for they had eaten the good. It stank strongly of the urine of rats. We drank yellow water that had been putrid for many days. We also ate some ox hides that covered the top of the mainyard to prevent the yard from chafing the shrouds, and which had become exceedingly hard because of the sun, rain, and wind. We left them in the sea for four or five days, and then placed them for a few moments on top of the embers, and so ate them; and often we ate sawdust from boards. Rats were sold for one-half ducado apiece, and even then we could not get them. But above all the other misfortunes the following was the worst. The gums of both the lower and upper teeth of some of our men swelled, so that they could not eat under any circumstances and therefore died.

This is one of the earliest descriptions of scurvy, a disease that results from a lack of vitamin C. Because it usually manifests after about a month without fresh vegetables, it became a significant problem for sailors only with the long-distance voyages of the age of European expansion. Its cure was not definitively ascertained until the nineteenth century.

On March 6, the three ships reached Guam (about 13°N) in the Mariana Islands, which the Spanish called the Ladrones ("thieves") because the islanders stole from them; in retaliation the Spanish burned forty or fifty houses and killed seven islanders. A week later they reached the island of Samar in the Philippine archipelago. On Limasawa, Magellan's Malay slave, called Enrique, could make himself understood in his native language, and thus was one of the first people to circumnavigate the globe. In April the Spanish reached the island of Cebu where Magellan converted the local rajah and several thousand of his subjects to Christianity. To impress his new ally with the might of Christian arms, Magellan led an expedition against one of the rajah's reluctant vassals on the island of Mactan where on April 27, 1521, he was killed along with a dozen of his men. After the loss of twenty-four more crew, the survivors burned the *Concepción* and distributed the remaining crew and provisions between the *Trinidad* and *Victoria*. After several aimless months in the Philippines, Juan Sebastian de Elcano and Gonzalo Gómez de Espinosa took charge of the expedition.

Upon reaching the Spice Island of Tidore, the Spanish learned that Francisco Serrão had died around the same time as Magellan, but they were warmly received by the local ruler, with whom they traded red cloth, hatchets, cups, linen, and other items for cloves, mace, nutmeg, cinnamon, and sandalwood. On December 21, *Victoria* sailed with forty-seven European and thirteen Malay crew. After stopping on the island of Timor they set out across the Indian Ocean, doubled the Cape of Good Hope twelve weeks out, and reached the Cape Verde Islands on July 8 after twenty-one weeks at sea. Twenty-one of the crew had died and they had lost their foremast. A watering party of thirteen men was arrested by the Portuguese, but Elcano pressed on with his reduced and enfeebled crew. On September 6, 1522, eighteen Europeans and three Malays limped ashore at Sanlúcar. The first circumnavigation of the globe had taken two years, eleven months, and two weeks. The disastrous loss of life notwithstanding, the Magellan expedition was a milestone in the history of navigation. Magellan had proved that the Americas were not attached to Terra Australis—a hypothetical southern continent that explorers would search for until the nineteenth century—and that the Pacific could be crossed, if only by brute determination. Such was Magellan's accomplishment that Luis Vaz de Camões appropriated it for Portugal in the *Lusiads*, his epic about the Portuguese age of exploration, claiming Magellan as "a true Portuguese in the undertaking if not in allegiance."

Awful though their ordeal had been, Elcano's men fared far better than the crew of the *Trinidad*, who had attempted to sail east across the Pacific. Contrary winds forced the *Trinidad* back to Tidore, where the Portuguese arrested the crew, only four of whom would return to Spain. Charles V dispatched two fleets to rescue the *Trinidad*'s men in 1525 and 1526. Only a quarter of the 450 men of the first expedition reached the Spice Islands, where the Portuguese held them until 1536. The second lost its flagship and returned to Spain before it reached the Pacific.

The return of the *Victoria* invested the issue of the line of demarcation between Spanish and Portuguese spheres of influence with new urgency. A panel of Portuguese and Spanish experts convened in 1524, its members including Elcano and Columbus's son Ferdinand for Spain, and Juan Vespucci (Amerigo's nephew) for Portugal. Debates over where to draw the line in the Atlantic and how to determine longitude ensured that little progress was made, and the Pacific boundary was only settled by the Treaty of Zaragoza of 1529, by which Charles paid 350,000 ducats to Portugal in exchange for fixing the line about three hundred leagues (nine hundred miles) east of the Spice Islands. Despite the treaty, thirteen years later a Spanish fleet sailed from Mexico to the Philippines (named for the future Philip II) on a mission for the "discovery, conquest and colonization of the islands and provinces of the South Sea towards the west." The expedition ended badly and again the survivors returned to Europe in Portuguese ships.

The next phase of Spanish interest in the east began with Philip's plan "to establish a route to New Spain [Mexico] from the Islands of the West," that is, an east–west route across the Pacific. Five years later, five ships and 350 men sailed from La Navidad, Mexico. The pilot in fact, though not in name, was Friar Andrés de Urdaneta, a veteran of the 1525 rescue mission who had since become an Augustinian missionary. Ineligible to serve as captain-major, he was asked to name the head of the expedition and chose Miguel López de Legazpi. The fleet sailed west at a latitude of between 9°N and 13°N, stopping at Guam before going on to claim the Philippines and establish Spain's only colony in Asia. Apart from the great distances involved, the westward crossing of the Pacific posed few problems. The puzzle was finding the winds favorable for a west-to-east crossing of the Pacific, which had eluded Spanish mariners for more than forty years. On June 1, 1565, at the start of the southwest monsoon, Urdaneta began the return voyage serving as pilot aboard the galleon *San Pablo*. Sailing via the San Bernardino Strait north of Samar, Urdaneta maintained a northeasterly course until he found westerly winds in about 39°N. The Spanish sailed east for fifteen weeks, dropping south as they approached North America to make their first landfall at San Miguel Island, off Los Angeles. Continuing south they reached Acapulco on October 8.

The success of the Spanish venture in the Philippines depended on their reception by the Chinese, who were well established there. In 1571, Spanish sailors at Manila rescued the crew of a Chinese ship near Mindoro, a gesture that reaped handsome dividends. The next year, Chinese traders returned to Manila, and "With this the foundation of a lucrative commerce was laid." In exchange for American silver, the Chinese brought silk, "fine gilt china and other porcelain wares," benzoin, musk, and spices brought in Portuguese ships from Macau. Trade across "the Spanish Lake," as the Pacific became known, was limited officially to two ships of not more than three hundred tons per year—but such restrictions were routinely flouted and ships of a thousand tons were being built by the early seventeenth century. Almost every year until 1815 at least one "Manila galleon" crossed the Pacific each way. Despite the phenomenal riches carried aboard these ships between 1565 and 1815, only four were seized—all by English raiders.

The Portuguese objected to the Spanish colonization of the Philippines, which were clearly within the Portuguese sphere of influence, but their protests were dampened by the fact that the Philippines had no precious spices. Nonetheless, the debate lingered until 1750, when the two countries agreed to annul the boundaries stipulated by the bull *Inter Caetera* and the Treaties of Tordesillas and Zaragoza. By the eighteenth century French, English, and Dutch mariners had long since developed the financial wherewithal, navigational acumen, and military strength to challenge the Iberian overseas empires and stripped these documents of their force, a process that took the better part of the sixteenth and seventeenth centuries.

Chapter 15

The Birth of Global Trade

With the voyages of Columbus to the Americas and Gama around the Cape of Good Hope to Asia, Europe was fully embarked on what is aptly called the age of expansion. This era was unprecedented not only because extraordinary floods of people, ideas, and material wealth, as well as flora, fauna, and pathogens, were unleashed around the world, but because Europeans were for the first time in the vanguard of world change. This is not to say that they effected great and recognizable transformations wherever they went. Certainly they did in the Americas; elsewhere "they crawled like lice on the hide of Asia" and Africa, and made little dent in ancient patterns of trade and institutions of government. It would not be until the eighteenth and nineteenth centuries that Europeans would exercise extensive control over the Indian subcontinent, Southeast Asia, China, and Africa. Yet none of these later efforts would be possible were it not for the maritime superiority achieved by the Portuguese, the commercial and financial acumen perfected by the merchants of Italy, the Low Countries, and England, or the legal doctrines articulated by canon and civil lawyers from the Mediterranean to the Baltic. While maritime initiative shifted among various European powers, supremacy at sea would remain a European monopoly until the end of the nineteenth century.

Spain, Portugal, and the Atlantic

Despite the overt similarities between Spain and Portugal—staunch crusader Christianity forged in the crucible of the anti-Muslim *Reconquista*, their location at the turning point between Mediterranean and Atlantic Europe, and their shared experience in the discovery and exploitation of the Atlantic archipelagoes—the two kingdoms embarked on their imperial projects from completely different angles and so launched themselves on distinct historical trajectories. The Portuguese found themselves in a dynamic, multilateral, and geographically vast Asian commercial network of great antiquity and complexity. As the Spanish quickly realized, in terms of sea trade the Americas constituted a blank slate. When Columbus crossed the Atlantic he encountered no preexisting maritime commercial system, ports did not exist, and the arts of boatbuilding and navigation were nowhere near as sophisticated as those of coastal Eurasia. The Spanish could maintain their transatlantic links unimpeded by European rivals, who lacked the wherewithal or incentive to compete on a transatlantic stage. Only the Portuguese had the shipping or experience to contest Spanish claims, but they had no reason to violate the Treaty of Tordesillas, especially since for fifty years after Columbus's first voyage, Spain's overseas territories produced little of value. These factors help explain the explosive if haphazard way in which Spain's sprawling American empire grew.

The nerve center of Spain's overseas empire was the Casa de la Contratación, "house of trade," which Isabella of Castile established at Seville in 1503. The Casa was charged with diverse functions regarding the trade and settlement of the Americas: regulating the flow of emigrants, collecting taxes and duties, licensing pilots, administering commercial law in the colonies, and keeping up-to-date information about new discoveries, especially on the *padrón real*, or master chart. The last was the responsibility of the *piloto mayor*, whose function was to "make a royal model map of the navigation of all the regions that have so far been discovered that belong to the royal crown" and copies of which were to be issued "only to such persons as the monarch or the Casa de la Contratación may order." Among those not so favored were the English, Dutch, French, and Portuguese, as well as Spanish Jews and unconverted Muslims, who had been expelled from Spain in 1492 and 1502, respectively.

Striking out from Hispaniola and Cuba, Spanish explorers made increasingly bold forays along the coasts of and into North and South America, the most spectacular achievements being Hernando Cortés's toppling of the Aztec Empire with its capital at Tenochtitlán (Mexico City), and Francisco Pizarro's overthrow of the Inca Empire, which stretched along a thousand miles of the Andes from Ecuador to Chile. These defunct states were superseded by the viceroyalties of, respectively, New Spain (from modern Mexico to the border of Panama) and Peru. After silver mining began in the 1540s at Potosí, Bolivia, and Zacatecas, Mexico, the spectacular cargoes carried by Spanish ships attracted the attention of French, English, and Dutch corsairs.

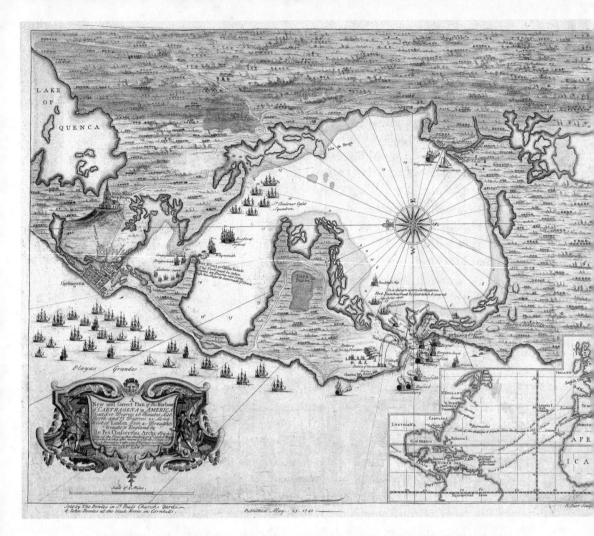

Pierre Chassereau's "A New and Correct Plan of the Harbour of Carthagena [Colombia] in America," the best natural harbor on the Caribbean. This hand-colored copper engraving was published at London in 1741. Courtesy of the Smith Collection, Osher Map Library and Smith Center for Cartographic Education, University of Southern Maine, Portland.

To improve security, in 1564 the Casa de la Contratación ordered all transatlantic ships to sail in one of two convoys. The New Spain fleet sailed for San Juan de Ulúa, an island opposite Veracruz, Mexico, usually in July, while the Tierra Firme fleet served Cartagena, Colombia, and Nombre de Dios, Panama, between March and May. Both fleets sailed via the Canaries and the Caribbean islands, usually Dominica, a crossing of about a month. The Tierra Firme ships reached Cartagena about two weeks later, while those bound for New Spain took another month or more, including a stop in Puerto Rico for provisions. The returning fleets sometimes rendezvoused in Havana, but in any case they aimed to be in the Bahama Channel by August, before the height of the hurricane season.

The Spanish had to found their own ports in the New World, but because of the seasonal nature of the transatlantic and transpacific trades and the conquistadors' preoccupation with exploring, consolidating, and exploiting the interior, these tended to be haphazard affairs with small year-round populations and little if any infrastructure. On the Atlantic side, the most important were Havana and Veracruz. Strategically situated on the north coast of Cuba, Havana became one of the most important Spanish strongholds in the Americas and the principal rendezvous for convoys returning to Spain. Veracruz was said to have been "founded" in 1519, but a merchant described it the next year as having "neither house, hut, water nor firewood: only sandy beaches," and eighty years later it boasted only four hundred Spanish households. With its ancient Phoenician name transplanted to a new world, Cartagena was situated on a large bay and protected from seaward by the island of Tierrabomba. This combined with its relatively salubrious environment and its proximity to the Isthmus of Panama made it an ideal homeport for the Tierra Firme fleet.

Spain's connection to Peru and its silver hinged on the pestilential Isthmus of Panama, and the ports of Nombre de Dios (replaced by Portobelo in 1597) on the Caribbean coast and Panama on the Pacific. Their names notwithstanding, these godforsaken places were little more than graveyards that sprang to life only to load and off-load the fleets' invaluable cargoes—silver eastbound, European goods westbound. In 1546, a visitor wrote "These two towns are so infested, that of one hundred men who enter, if they remain in it for a month, there aren't twenty who are spared from sickness, and the majority of those who fall sick die." En route back to Havana, twenty-six of the author's shipmates were buried at sea. Panama's main trading counterpart was Callao, the port of the viceregal capital at Lima, which was also served by Valparaíso. The principal shipyard on the Pacific coast was at Guayaquil, Ecuador, with its easy access to wood and pitch, while south of Callao, Arica (founded in 1545) served the highland mines of Potosí. The decision to ship silver via the Pacific and Panama was based more on political than logistical considerations. It was vastly cheaper and faster to carry Potosí silver to Buenos Aires and from there across the Atlantic, but pressure from the viceroyalty of Peru led to the Río Plata port's official closure in 1594. Trading at Buenos Aires was not legalized until 1776, and port improvements did not begin until the nineteenth century.

Lobbying by the merchants of Seville likewise prevented the development of a robust Pacific coast trade between Mexico and Peru, and north of Panama there was only a handful of ports. The most important were Realejo (Corinto,

Nicaragua), which boasted a shipyard and easy access to the Caribbean via Lakes Manaus and Nicaragua and the San Juan River; Huatulco, until its sack by Thomas Cavendish in 1597; and after Huatulco's abandonment, Acapulco, the eastern terminus of the Manila galleon. (Thanks to the Treaty of Tordesillas, Spanish ships could not sail between Spain and the Philippines via the Indian Ocean.) Like Nombre de Dios and Portobelo, Acapulco was a fine harbor on a fetid shore and came alive only when the galleons called. After five or six months at sea, the crews were invariably weakened by malnutrition or disease and had to recuperate in the town's rude huts and tents before starting the 450-kilometer trek to Mexico City. (The westward voyage to the Philippines took only three months.) Apart from the Manila galleon, Acapulco had little purpose. As was true of all Spanish-American ports, it existed for the maintenance of ties between the home country and the viceroyalties; although separated by eight thousand miles of the Pacific, the Philippines were administratively part of New Spain. Centuries passed before any of these American ports developed the cosmopolitan or commercial identities so striking in the dynamic trading environments of their Eurasian and African counterparts.

Slaves, Spices, and Portugal's *Estado da India*

Spanish America relied heavily on imported slave labor thanks to royal prohibitions on enslaving indigenous people, the devastation of native populations by Old World diseases, and the survivors' lack of familiarity with even the rudiments of newly introduced crops (such as wheat and sugarcane), livestock (cattle, pigs, and sheep), and industries (mining and sugar mills). The Treaty of Tordesillas guaranteed the Portuguese exclusive rights to trade in Africa, where they negotiated for a steady supply of slaves with various kingdoms. Among their earliest partners was Congo, whose King Nzinga embraced Christianity in 1491 (taking the Portuguese name João in the process) and whose Christian successors continued to sell slaves to the Portuguese. In 1540, Congo's King Afonso proudly wrote to Portugal's João III, "Put all the Guinea countries [to the north] on one side and only Congo on the other, and you will find that Congo renders more than all the others put together. . . . No king in all these parts esteems Portuguese goods as much as we do. We favor the trade, sustain it, open markets, roads, and markets [*sic*] where the pieces [prime male slaves] are traded."

The pace of the slave trade escalated through the sixteenth century. While they sanitize a vicious human experience, the raw numbers are revealing: twelve thousand slaves were shipped in the first quarter of the century, forty thousand in the second, and a further sixty thousand between 1550 and 1575. Together with the transoceanic migration of an estimated 240,000 white Europeans over the same period, this was an unprecedented feat of demographic relocation. The first slaves taken directly from Africa to the Americas arrived in 1530, but the sharp increase thereafter was due to the development of sugar plantations in Brazil. Portuguese settlement there began with the establishment of São Vicente, near Santos, in 1532; Salvador da Bahia, colonial Brazil's first capital and its primary port, was founded in 1549. At least fifty thousand more Africans were shipped to Brazil in the last quarter of the century, but the deadly conditions of servitude and the environment were such that by 1600 the number of living slaves was no more than fifteen thousand. Nonetheless, the sugar industry boomed and the number of ships sailing annually between Recife and Lisbon grew from 40 in 1584 to 130 in 1618, and the sugar of Brazil was held to be worth more than all the pepper, spices, and other specialties shipped from the *Estado da India*—"the state of India," as the Portuguese called their far-flung holdings in the Indian Ocean and beyond.

The absence of any high-seas maritime tradition on the west coast of Africa or in the Americas enabled the Portuguese and Spanish to spin their own maritime webs, from which they excluded virtually everyone else. The situation in the Monsoon Seas was a different matter altogether, crisscrossed as they were by a fully functioning trading network with myriad participants of far greater linguistic, religious, cultural, and political diversity than anything Europeans had previously encountered. The Portuguese worked with stunning speed to channel the trade in pepper and spices to their advantage, but they quickly grasped that this was not a static system easily susceptible to their designs. The opening of the direct sea route from Europe was new, but Asia's regional trades were more extensive and the opportunities for profit more diverse than the Portuguese had anticipated, and their presence in the Indian Ocean did not permanently disrupt or distort the traditional patterns and cycles of Asian trade. Within Asia they constituted only one group in a crowded field, but because they worked their way into virtually every major corner of the region, their experience is the most convenient lens through which to view sixteenth-century maritime Asia in a global context.

Once in the Indian Ocean, the Portuguese might have adapted themselves to the generally laissez-faire patterns they found there. Lacking the capital, ships, or manpower to monopolize the spice trade themselves, they relied on a combination of diplomacy and aggression to demand protection money from Muslim, Hindu, and other maritime merchants and to channel trade through Portuguese-held ports. Ships' guns were critical to their success in staking claims in often hostile territories, and as rudimentary as shipboard ordnance was, for most of the 1500s only Europeans had it. The mariners of the Indian Ocean were not acquiescent to Portuguese demands, but they lacked practical experience of naval gunnery, and the Portuguese established their mastery over the key strongholds of the Indian Ocean with only a few heavily armed ships. The establishment of a Portuguese presence in Monsoon Asia began with Dom Francisco de Almeida, first viceroy and governor of Portuguese India. With a fleet of twenty-two ships in 1505 he captured Kilwa and Mombasa in East Africa, seized a small island as a forward base against Goa in India, and built a fort at Cannanore (Kannur, Kerala); additional fortresses on Sri Lanka and Socotra and near Melaka followed.

Opinion about which policies would best serve Portugal's interests was divided. Almeida viewed fortresses as a potential drain on Portuguese resources. As he wrote to Manoel I, "the more fortresses Your Highness possesses, the weaker your power will be. All your forces should be on the sea, because if we are not strong there, which the Lord forbid, everything will go against us. . . . There is no doubt that, so long as you are powerful at sea, India will be yours and that, if you are not, fortresses on land will be of little use to you." This was not a winning argument and the chief architect of the *Estado da India* was Almeida's successor, Afonso de Albuquerque. Possessed of an uncanny strategic sense, a precocious ability to husband meager resources with a ruthless efficiency honed in a decade of fighting in Morocco, and considerable luck, Albuquerque laid the cornerstones of the *Estado*. A critical advantage was that despite the obvious benefits of maritime commerce in the form of revenues and the accessibility of foreign goods, the petty rulers of the Indian Ocean littoral were too weak at sea and preoccupied with internal politics to mount an effectively coordinated resistance to the Portuguese. Despite their meager numbers and distance from home, the Portuguese had several advantages: the full backing of the crown, a singleness of purpose that enabled them to defeat or exploit rivalries among their potential adversaries, and ships with cannon. Such organized resistance as they faced at sea tended to be orchestrated from afar, by states with the clearest understanding of the threat the Portuguese posed to their trade, especially the Ottoman Empire and Mamluk Egypt.

While no friend of the Mamluks, the Ottoman sultan offered to help protect Mecca and Medina, and in 1507 he sent workmen and artillery to fortify Jeddah, where an attack was believed imminent, and to arm a fleet to take the war to the Portuguese in India. Victorious at the battle of Chaul, near Mumbai, in 1508, the next year this fleet was annihilated at the battle of Diu in Gujarat. It was to counter this Mamluk-Ottoman coalition that Albuquerque determined to capture Goa the next year. As he later reported to Manoel,

I have taken Goa because Your Highness ordered me to, and because it was part of the marshal's instructions. I have also done so because it was the head of the league that had been formed to throw us out of India. If the fleet which the [Ottoman] Turks had assembled in the river of Goa (well-manned and with other weapons for the purpose) had sailed, and if the Mamluk fleet had arrived as they hoped it would, all would have been lost for a certainty.

Albuquerque favored Goa as his headquarters because ships based there could patrol the sea-lanes between India and Arabia, it was easily defended, and it controlled the trade (especially in horses) to the Deccan and the Hindu empire of Vijayanagar. So decisive was his victory that the sultan of Gujarat and the samorin of Calicut both offered, so he claimed, to let him build forts in their territories. "And this is the result of our holding Goa, without my waging war upon any of these princes." Many Portuguese opposed the capture of Goa, despite its strategic location, on the grounds that the area was unhealthy and expensive to maintain, and that it would encourage further opposition to the Portuguese. Albuquerque persuaded the king that Goa should be held (as it was until 1961), for which reason he "often used to say that he deserved more thanks from the King D. Manuel for defending Goa for him against the Portuguese, than he did for capturing it on two occasions from the Turks."

The second key to Portuguese success in Asia was Melaka, which Albuquerque captured in 1511, ostensibly to avenge the arrest of sailors seized at the instigation of Gujarati and Coromandel merchants who had warned the sultan of Portuguese brutality in India. By his own admission, Albuquerque had attacked Goa with a crusader's zeal: "Then I burned the city and put everyone to the sword and for four days your men shed blood continuously. No matter where we found them, we did not spare the life of a single Moslem; we filled the mosques with them and then set them on fire. The peasants and the Hindu priests I ordered to be spared. . . . It was a very great deed, Sire, well fought and well accomplished." By his own estimate, it cost the lives of six thousand Goans. While reports that the sultan of Melaka had arrested Portuguese sailors may have been true, Albuquerque already had the city in his sights: "I am very sure that if this Malacca trade is taken out of their hands," he wrote to Manoel, referring to the Muslim merchants who supplied Venetian middlemen at Alexandria, "Cairo and Mecca will be completely lost and no spices will go to the Venetians except those that they go to Portugal to buy." Or as the apothecary-turned-writer Tomé Pires put it: "Whoever is lord of Malacca has his hand on the throat of Venice." After the capture of Melaka, two Portuguese ships sailed for the Spice Islands. One returned to Goa with cloves, mace, and nutmeg, while the other was lost and its crew, under Magellan's friend Francisco Serrão, wound up on Ternate, whose sultan hired them as mercenaries against his rival on neighboring Tidore. Serrão spent the rest of his life there, but he continued to correspond with friends and encouraged Magellan's plans for a circumnavigation. The Portuguese in Goa sent an annual ship to Ternate starting in 1523 but, well beyond the reach of the Estado's authority, the Spice Islands became a sump of corruption, and it was one of the few places in Asia from which the Portuguese were expelled due to local opposition.

The involvement of the Ottomans and Mamluks in opposing the Portuguese on the Indian Ocean cannot be fully appreciated without reference to the fluid political situation in the Mediterranean. Although the Portuguese failed to conquer Aden until 1513, their interruption of the trade to the Red Sea devastated the Mamluk sultan's finances, and by 1508 spice cargoes at Alexandria were only a quarter of what they had been a decade before, which dealt a severe blow to Venetian trade as well. Despite a host of confessional, political, and other disagreements, Mamluk Egypt, Venice, the Ottoman Empire, and, to a lesser extent, Safavid Persia found common cause in countering the commercial threat posed by the Portuguese. The Venetians attempted to curry favor with all three Muslim powers, seeking an alliance with Persia against the Ottomans, encouraging the Ottomans to support the Mamluks, and leveraging Mamluk anxiety to wrest favorable trading privileges for themselves at Alexandria, where traffic soon revived. While Mamluk and Safavid sea power was negligible, the Ottomans had adopted a sophisticated approach to maritime trade and naval affairs even before their overthrow of the Byzantine Empire.

An offshoot of the Seljuq Turks who had poured into Byzantine Anatolia starting in the eleventh century, the Ottomans first crossed the Dardanelles in 1352 and two years later seized Gallipoli where they established a shipyard. A century later, Mehmed II realized the importance of having at his disposal a wholly Ottoman fleet, and after erecting forts on either side of the Bosporus to control the comings and goings of Italian ships, "the Sultan gave orders that triremes [galleys] should be built everywhere along his shores, knowing that the domination of the sea was essential to him and his rule. . . . For this reason he decided to secure control of the sea for himself." After his conquest of Constantinople in 1453, Mehmed seized the Black Sea ports of Amasra, held by the Genoese, and Sinop, part of the empire of Trebizond, and by 1484 the Ottomans had "won the key of the door to all Moldavia and Hungary, the whole region of the Danube, Poland, Russia and Tatary and the entire coast of the Black Sea." Control of the major river mouths earned the Ottomans the bulk of revenues from trade that had formerly flowed to treasuries in eastern Europe, and by the start of the sixteenth century the Black Sea was an Ottoman lake in all but name and one from which foreigners were excluded for 250 years.

In 1510, the year of the sack of Goa, the Knights of Rhodes destroyed an Ottoman fleet carrying matériel to Mamluk Egypt. The Venetians were blamed for their coreligionists' actions, but relations were restored and a Venetian emissary was instructed to "Urge the Mamluk sultan to get from the Turk artillery, lumber, ships and all the things necessary to pursue the effort" against the Portuguese. Appeals for Mamluk help from Calicut, Cambay, and Melaka added urgency to the sultan's plight, as did reports of an impending Portuguese-Safavid alliance. Albuquerque assured Shah Ismail that "if you desire to destroy the [Mamluk] Sultan by land, you can reckon upon great assistance from the Armada of the King my Lord by sea." Ottoman supplies eventually reached Egypt, but a second Red Sea fleet was not launched until 1515, the year Albuquerque took Hormuz, and just two years before the Ottomans overthrew the Mamluks. Assuming direct responsibility for safeguarding the holy places, the Turks were now face-to-face with the Portuguese.

For the time being, though, the Portuguese held the upper hand and it would take the better part of two decades for the Ottomans to put them on the defensive in the northern Indian Ocean or keep them from sailing into the Red Sea with impunity. The principal architect of the Ottomans' seaward-looking strategy was Ibrahim Pasha, Suleiman the Magnificent's vizier, who was inspired by a chance encounter with the ship captain and cartographer Piri Reis en route to Egypt. Piri Reis is best known for his delineation of a world map of extraordinary finesse and incorporating details from "new charts of the Chinese and Indian Seas" as well as information about the newly discovered Americas. He was also the author of *Book of the Sea*, an atlas and navigational guide to the Mediterranean to which, at Ibrahim Pasha's request, he added an introductory text about the Indian Ocean based on secondhand sources. By 1536, the Ottomans had established or refortified naval bases at Suez, Jeddah, and the island of Kamaran near the Bab al-Mandeb, and they had taken Baghdad from the Safavids and secured access to the Persian Gulf trade via Basra, thus becoming the first state since the Abbasid Caliphate with ports on both the Persian Gulf and the Mediterranean. Of more enduring significance, they had revamped the Mamluks' corrupt and onerous customs regime, which led to a forceful revival of trade from India and Southeast Asia to the Red Sea, despite a continued Portuguese blockade of the sea and occasional incursions into it. Ottoman success compelled the Portuguese to consider a rapprochement, but they could not accept the sultan's demand for "freedom for the Muslims of India to trade in . . . merchandise of that land," even though they were willing to allow Portuguese ships at Ottoman ports. Despite the failures of these negotiations, with Basra in Ottoman hands, Turkish and Portuguese officials did not hesitate to embrace free trade with each other, usually on their own initiative and for their own profit, and by midcentury trade accounted for two-thirds of Basra's revenues.

In the following decade the Ottomans studiously cultivated diplomatic relations with Muslim states from the Horn of Africa to Aden and the south coast of Arabia, the coast of India, and Sumatra. This was accompanied by a concerted military commitment, and between 1536 and 1546 the Ottomans and Portuguese fought nineteen battles over Indian Ocean ports—all but four of them in waters beyond the Red Sea and Persian Gulf—including Suez, Mocha, Basra, Diu, and Melaka. Despite a lack of success on the subcontinent and in Southeast Asia, the Ottomans secured control of Yemen and the Hadramawt, although the Portuguese were not finally ousted from Aden until 1548, by a fleet under Piri Reis. Four years later, the now octogenarian admiral of the Indian Ocean fleet left Suez with twenty-four galleys for an attack on Hormuz. This effort failed and Piri Reis took his fleet to Basra before deciding to return to Suez with only three ships, a decision for which he was executed. In 1554, the remainder of Piri Reis's fleet was ordered to sail from Basra to Suez, but the Portuguese captured six of the galleys and the remainder fled for Gujarat.

At the same time, an enterprising captain named Sefer Reis had been given command of four galiots with orders to rendezvous with the Basra fleet. Possibly the scion of a Jewish trading family, Sefer Reis spent his entire career in the Indian Ocean, which gave him a distinct advantage over his predecessors, who were chosen on the strength of their experience in the wholly different naval environment of the Mediterranean. Rather than fight the Portuguese on their terms, Sefer used the monsoon winds to keep the Portuguese downwind of his galleys to prevent their square-rigged *naos* from attacking him. After learning of the Portuguese victory over the Basra fleet, Sefer blockaded Diu with his four galiots and returned to Mocha with five Portuguese prizes. The Portuguese diverted substantial resources to combat Sefer in the Red Sea, but he used his superior local knowledge and a variety of ruses to ambush or evade them. In 1565, he embarked on a campaign to oust the Portuguese from East Africa but became ill and died in Aden, whereupon the project was abandoned.

Sefer's success was such that in 1560 the Portuguese ambassador at Rome had urged his superiors to come to terms with the Ottomans on the grounds that "the volume of spices which passes through the Red Sea to Cairo and from Hormuz to Basra is enormous," and because "Your Majesty's expenses in India are very great, and will grow even greater if some solution is not found." The Ottomans proposed to the Portuguese that their commercial agents be allowed "in Sind, Cambay, Dabul, Calecut, and any other ports [the Ottomans] desired," with reciprocal privileges for the Portuguese at Basra,

Cairo, and Alexandria. They also held out the prospect of dismantling the Ottoman fleet at Basra. The Portuguese rejected this overture because such an arrangement would have made any trade via the Cape of Good Hope hopelessly uncompetitive.

Nonetheless great quantities of pepper and other spices continued to reach Alexandria, from where the Venetians and others distributed them around the Mediterranean. The Ottomans maintained an active interest in the trade, and by the end of the century Mocha's revenues had grown tenfold under Ottoman administration and it was one of the most important ports in the greater Indian Ocean, its chief export being coffee, which had been introduced from Ethiopia in the first millennium. Aden, on the other hand, was ruined, and it was said that "When anger is felt against a certain person, they post him here." The Ottoman government placed virtually no restrictions on the Persian Gulf trade, "such that all things that are traded from anywhere in India go through Hormuz, even pepper, despite being strictly forbidden." One reason for the different approaches to the commerce of the Persian Gulf and the Red Sea was that the latter was the entryway for pilgrims bound for Mecca. The timing of the hajj was dictated by the lunar calendar and changed from year to year, but seafaring hajjis depended on the seasonal monsoon and had to bring goods they could sell to pay for their stays in Mecca, which could last months. Far fewer hajjis sailed via the Persian Gulf.

The failure of negotiations with the Portuguese provided an opening for the Ottomans to pursue a more vigorous foreign policy articulated by the grand vizier Sokullu Mehmed Pasha. His most ambitious proposal was to dig canals across the Isthmus of Suez and between the Don and Volga Rivers to create an all-water route from the Caspian Sea to the Red Sea, but the plans were shelved following a rebellion in Yemen and the renewal of hostilities with Venice. Sokullu also encouraged support for opponents of the Portuguese in Asia. In 1562, the sultan of Aceh sought to purchase cannon and siege guns for a campaign against Melaka. The huge distances involved (more than five thousand miles from Istanbul to Aceh via Egypt) and the fear that the guns might be captured tempered the Ottomans' enthusiasm for this project, but Suleiman sent an emissary, known only as "His Majesty's Servant Lutfi," and eight gun founders. Aceh had long traded with the Ottomans, but the city-state also paid tribute to Melaka and it was at least as interested in expanding its control over Muslim rivals as it was in fighting the Portuguese. En route to the east, Lutfi enlisted the support of Muslim merchant communities in India and Sri Lanka, which brought hostility against the Portuguese and their allies to an unprecedented high. A coalition of Deccan sultanates severely weakened the Hindu empire of Vijayanagar, a Portuguese ally, and a Christian king installed by the Portuguese in the Maldives was deposed. The Acehnese ambassadors who accompanied Lutfi to Istanbul subsequently returned home with "500 Turks, many large bombards, abundant ammunition, many engineers and masters of artillery," who besieged Melaka. This operation was unsuccessful but it did prevent the Portuguese from sending reinforcements to the Spice Islands, which contributed to the Portuguese ouster from Ternate. The official Ottoman campaign against the Portuguese ended with Sokullu's assassination in 1579, but a decade later a fleet of five ships was sent to seize Mombasa. The initial landing was successful, but the Ottomans found themselves under siege by an army of twenty thousand Zimba, as a Portuguese chronicle calls an otherwise unidentified African army. Rather than submit to the Zimba, the Ottomans surrendered to the Portuguese, thus ending Ottoman efforts to influence events in the Indian Ocean.

The *Estado da India* and the Trade of Asia

Their overbearing reputation notwithstanding, the Portuguese of the *Estado da India* routinely collaborated with local merchants. They were often in the minority of the trades they claimed to monopolize and many sailed on routes they never attempted to dominate. Indian merchants often chartered Portuguese ships to carry their cargoes, and many ships under Portuguese officers were otherwise manned by Asians. The simple reason for this was that Portugal's population was no more than 1.4 million in 1525, most of whom were in fact contemptuous of seafaring. Few with alternative prospects willingly embarked on a six- or seven-month voyage that one passenger described as "without any doubt the greatest and most arduous of any that are known in the world," especially when the odds of returning were so slim. Between twenty-four hundred and four thousand people, most of them young men, sailed annually for Africa, Brazil, and Asia, yet by 1600 there were only around two thousand Portuguese in "Golden Goa," and probably never more than ten thousand between Mozambique and Japan at any one time. Of these, fewer than one in ten returned to Portugal, "some dying there in the countrie, others beeing cast away [and slayne by divers occasions,] and the rest by povertie not able to returne againe: and so against their willes . . . forced to stay in the Countrie." Portuguese women were generally forbidden to emigrate, and those Portuguese men who stayed in Asia were encouraged to marry natives, their preference being for Muslims or high-caste Hindus.

The stereotype of Asians uninterested in maritime commerce is as at variance with the facts as the image of Portuguese as inveterate seafarers. During the Mughal Empire (1526–1764), Bania (Hindu) shipowners had a commanding presence in both Bengal and at Surat. They also functioned as agents for other people's ships and worked for two groups of clients in particular, Mughal officials with an interest in shipping, and Europeans—whether private country traders or, in the seventeenth and eighteenth centuries, the various East India Companies—engaged in either intra-Asian trade or trade between Europe and Asia. Hindu merchants were noted for their frugality and lack of ostentation, but highly respected for their commercial acumen and disciplined approach. "When they are still very young and in the laps of their parents and hardly able to walk," according to an employee of the Dutch East India Company writing in the 1680s, "they already begin to be trained as merchants. They are made to pretend to engage in trade while playing, first buying [cowries], followed by silver and gold."* In addition to commerce and moneylending, many were *sarrafs*, money changers who specialized in collecting taxes; some were also responsible for transferring government funds around the subcontinent. Foreign coins were not legal tender in the Mughal Empire, but one could take these, or bullion, to the mint and turn them into Mughal coins. This took time, however, and an alternative was to obtain the equivalent in rupees from a *sarraf*.

The subcontinent consumed vast quantities of eastern spices, precious and semiprecious stones, tin from Malaya, and silver from southwest Asia, especially Mocha, the "treasure chest" of the Mughal Empire. And as in the past, Arabia and Persia provided horses. Indian, Arab, and Persian merchants shared the traffic of the Arabian Sea and the Bay of Bengal. As many as a thousand Gujaratis may have lived at Melaka in 1500, and perhaps twice as many were trading across the Bay of Bengal at any given time. In addition to Melaka, their primary destinations included Pegu, in Myanmar; the peninsular ports of Tenasserim/Mergui and Kedah; and, on Sumatra, Samudra-Pasai and Aceh. Cambay was superseded as Gujarat's premier port by Surat, which already had a thriving pilgrim trade to Jeddah, the most profitable in the Indian Ocean and one that attracted investment from the royal household, government officials, and major merchants. With the incorporation of Gujarat into the Mughal Empire in 1573, Surat was connected to the Indian heartland and it grew further still. To the south, Dhabol and Chaul traded to western Asia as well as Bengal and Melaka. In the Malabar ports of Calicut, Cannanore, and Cochin, *pardesi* (foreign) merchants—Arabs, Persians, Jews, and Africans—focused on the western trade, while Mappila merchants sailed mainly to Bay of Bengal ports and Southeast Asia.

The idea of the Portuguese and the Ottomans (by proxy) going to war in

* A cowrie is the shell of a marine snail used for money (hence its Linnaean designation, *Cypraea moneta*) in various places around the Indian Ocean, Southeast Asia, and Africa.

Southeast Asia would have been unthinkable had the Ming Dynasty not abandoned the sea after the last of Zheng He's voyages in 1433. As it is, though, the Portuguese helped revive trades left moribund by a shrunken Chinese market and a dearth of Chinese shipping. If the initial rationale for discovering the sea route to the Indian Ocean was to acquire spices, the realities of Asian trade encouraged the Portuguese to diversify. At the siege of Melaka, a group of Chinese merchants approached Albuquerque to announce their intention to sail with the start of the monsoon. Eager to establish cordial relations with potential trading partners, he granted them safe passage and gave them letters of introduction to the king of Ayutthaya saying that "King Manuel of Portugal had been informed that he was a heathen and not a Moslem and so he had a great affection for him and desired to have peace and friendship with him" and promising merchants of his kingdom "all the protection they might need."

This offer was disingenuous. The greatest threat to peaceful trade was the Portuguese, and at this point their greatest export to Asia may well have been guns and mercenaries to control trade or as commodities for sale to the highest bidder. Assuming a role previously unheard of in the Indian Ocean, the Portuguese instituted a system of passes—*cartazes*—which all non-Portuguese merchant ships had to carry. The fee for the pass—essentially protection money—was nominal, but the *cartaz* obligated the holder to sail via Portuguese-controlled ports and to pay duties amounting to about 5 percent. Nor did possession of a valid *cartaz* guarantee freedom from harassment by the Portuguese, who plundered many ships with valid passes.

In 1513, Portuguese ships arrived at Macau, a peninsula in the Pearl River delta and gateway to Guangzhou and southern China, where they hoped to establish themselves and capitalize on the official Chinese withdrawal from overseas trade. They were refused and when they tried again in 1521–22 the emperor responded by banning all maritime trade in Guangdong Province. In barring Chinese ships from going abroad, the Ming government's intent was to funnel tribute trade exclusively through imperial ports. Among China's most important trading partners at this time was Japan, a major source of the silver that was the preferred medium for paying taxes. A riot between rival Japanese merchants at Mingzhou (Ningbo) in 1523 led to a suspension of Japanese trade there, but China's demand for silver and Japan's appetite for silk led to an increase in smuggling and piracy in the coastal provinces. This was exacerbated by the lack of profitable employment among Chinese traders, many of whom relocated to Japan, Southeast Asia, and the Ryukyu Islands, from where they engaged in illicit commerce with their homeland. In Japan, they were joined by similarly disenfranchised local sailors with whom they plundered coastal shipping and the Chinese mainland. Rather than acknowledge the fault of their own policies in nurturing this outlawry, the Chinese officials labeled these recreants *wokou,* "Japanese pirates."

Denied the opportunity for legitimate trade, the Portuguese simply joined smugglers active in Fujian and Zhejiang where corruption among the Chinese officials was rife and they could sail with impunity. According to a complaint filed by the commander of coastal defense, Zhu Wan, in 1548, "the Portuguese sailed their ships one after another into the interior. After unloading the goods, they publicly hauled up two ships at Duan-yu-zhou for repair. In the eyes of those pirates and barbarians, do they know that the authorities are still there? They are not to blame though," because the government was not prepared to enforce its own laws. While acknowledging that the Portuguese were smugglers, an opponent of Zhu Wan's policies argued that the local economy benefited because as commercial intermediaries they paid well for trade goods and double the market price for food and provisions. Persisting in their efforts to establish themselves in China officially, within a decade they had secured extraterritorial rights at Macau, which remained Portuguese territory until 1999. Confined to this enclave, westerners were not allowed to enter China proper until 1583 when the Jesuit missionary Matteo Ricci settled at Guangdong, where he embarked on a deep study of Chinese culture and religion and undertook to introduce Catholicism and the fruits of western learning and technology, including especially clocks and other mechanical devices. This effort ultimately took him to Beijing, where he died in 1610.

Having reached China, it was only a matter of time before the Portuguese ventured to Japan, where they established themselves at Nagasaki and served as middlemen between Japan and China. Their timing was impeccable, for in an effort to curtail the depredations of the *wokou* the Chinese had severed relations with Japan in 1548, nine years before the founding of Macau. Civil war had engulfed Japan for almost a century, and the revenues that accrued to the shogunate from the revived commerce helped tip the balance toward stability and unification. The Portuguese traded silk, gold, and silver but virtually no western goods except the harquebus, a cumbersome but lethal gun that the Japanese quickly learned to manufacture and deploy for themselves. (Cannon were introduced in 1551, but these proved harder to manufacture and their use spread more slowly.) In 1549, a mission led by (Saint) Francis Xavier introduced Christianity. Whereas Ricci converted only two thousand Chinese before his death, by the end of the sixteenth century there were an estimated three hundred thousand Japanese Christians. This success excited the hostility of Buddhist clergy whose intrigues convinced the government that the Christians constituted a threat to the country's hard-won political stability. The shogun began restricting their activities in 1565; Christianity was outlawed completely in 1614; and the Portuguese were expelled brutally in 1639. Their only real legacy was a minute community of Dutch traders who had followed them to Japan but whose religious modesty made them acceptable to the authorities.

The Japanese Invasion of Korea, 1592–98

The shoguns not only limited the activities of foreign traders, they also imposed tight restrictions on Japanese merchants, who were all but barred from sailing abroad. At the end of the sixteenth century, however, the likelihood of Japan's withdrawing from active participation in the affairs of Northeast Asia and beyond would have seemed remote, for no sooner had the regent, Toyotomi Hideyoshi, ended the Japanese civil wars and brought Japan under unified rule than he invaded the Korean Peninsula. In so doing, he certainly sought to reopen trade with China, for although the Ming eased their ban on Chinese traveling overseas in 1567, Japan remained off-limits. Hideyoshi also seems to have viewed an invasion of Goryeo and China as a natural extension of the unification of Japan as well as a convenient outlet for soldiers and mariners idled by the peace. An edict of 1588 ordered "sea captains and fishermen of the provinces and seashores, and all those who go in ships to the sea [to] subscribe to written oaths that henceforth they shall not engage in the slightest piratical activity." Japan's soldiers were probably as well armed and seasoned as any in the world, and lacking either recent experience of large-scale warfare or firearms, Goryeo was ill-prepared for an unprovoked invasion. About 140,000 Japanese landed near Busan in May 1592 and within ten weeks Seoul and Pyeongyang had fallen.

Goryeo's salvation depended on an unlikely combination of the Chinese army, Korean guerrillas, and Admiral Yi Sun-sin. Goryeo was divided into sixteen naval districts, two for each of the kingdom's eight provinces. An admiral of Jeolla (Cholla) Province, Yi combined a sophisticated and aggressive strategy with the severe tactical discipline necessary for converting apparently certain defeat into a series of paralyzing victories. Among the tools at his disposal was the heavily armed and protected *geobukseon*, or turtle ship, a two-masted, covered galley. According to a contemporary description

On its upper deck were driven iron spikes to pierce the feet of any enemy fighters jumping on it. The only opening was a narrow passage in the shape of a cross on the surface for its own crew to traverse freely. At the bow was a Dragon-head in whose mouth were the muzzles of guns [cannon] and another gun was at the stern. There were six gun ports each, port and starboard, on the lower decks. Since it was built in the shape of a big sea-turtle, it was called *Kobuk-son*. When engaging the enemy wooden vessels in a battle, the upper deck was covered with straw mats to conceal the spikes. It rode the waves swiftly in all winds and its cannon balls and fire arrows sent destruction to the enemy targets as it darted at the front, leading our fleet in all battles.

Turtle ships constituted something of a dead end in warship development and no more than five were probably available to Yi at any one time. All the same, they were critical to the Koreans' success. In the summer of 1592, Yi forced ten engagements, the most decisive of which came in June at the battle of Hansan Island. Feigning retreat before superior numbers, Yi lured eighty Japanese ships out of harbor and then enveloped them in what he called the "crane wing" formation. With the loss of sixty ships, the Japanese were unable to open the passage around the Korean Peninsula to the Yellow Sea and thus move supplies or troops to the front lines by ship. The resulting delays combined with China's entry into the war forced the Japanese to evacuate Pyeong-yang and Seoul and to open peace negotiations. These drawn-out discussions eventually collapsed and Hideyoshi renewed the invasion in 1597. The Japanese had absorbed the naval lessons of the earlier campaign, and Yi Sun-sin had been sacked as a result of court intrigues. His incompetent successor lost more than 150 ships at the battle of Chilcheonryang and the Japanese were poised to sail into the Yellow Sea. Hastily reinstated, Yi rallied a dozen ships and on September 16 fought the Japanese to a standstill at the battle of Myeongryang, a strait that narrows to only three hundred meters and through which the tide can race at more than ten knots. Prevented from deploying logistical support by sea, Japanese ground forces were again put on the defensive.

The Japanese began their withdrawal late the next year but the Koreans and Chinese pressed their attack on both land and sea. On the night of November 19, 1598, a week before the last Japanese forces left Korea, Yi attacked at the battle of Noryang. The Koreans inflicted great losses on the Japanese, but Yi was killed at the height of the battle—"a fitting end to such a career," in the words of a twentieth-century British admiral and historian who declared Yi "equal in his profession" to the Royal Navy's celebrated Lord Nelson. Yet the subsequent absence of naval warfare in Northeast Asia was due not to the overwhelming might of one power, but to the lack of interest in naval affairs on the part of China and a withdrawal from overseas ventures by Japan and Korea for more than 250 years.

The Changing Mediterranean

The Portuguese held their own against Ottoman intrigues in the Indian Ocean, and they commanded strategic strongholds from East Africa to China. Even so, while they dominated the Asian trade to Europe in the first half of the century they could not shut down trade to the Persian Gulf and Red Sea. In 1560 nearly 4.5 million pounds of spices reached Venetian, Ragusan, Genoese, and French ships in Alexandria, and five years later, twenty-three ships from India and Aceh were reported at Jeddah. The Portuguese share of the overall trade may have risen again after 1570, when small quantities of spices began reaching the Americas via Macau and Manila, but surviving statistics suggest a decline in Europeans' per capita consumption of pepper over the century, and a modest rise in that of other spices. Yet Europe was only one market among many and in this period the size of the Malabar pepper crop probably doubled, while the production of cloves, nutmeg, and mace grew fivefold, outcomes that cannot be attributed to the Portuguese and European demand alone.

Similarly, Venetian and other merchants had not been driven off the Mediterranean for want of spices at the start of the century because in spite of the attraction of exotics, as alluring for historians as for consumers, most Mediterranean shippers dealt in more mundane, high-volume commodities like cereals, livestock, wine, fish, metals, leather, and manufactures. Unreliable crops made grain "responsible for more espionage . . . than the affairs of the Inquisition itself," and merchants were well attuned to the vagaries of the harvest: scarcity in one place might be met by surplus from another, but profits could only be made by those fortunate enough to arrive before prices began to fall or to escape the ravages of piracy, which in the eastern Mediterranean was most often directed against grain ships. The center of the grain trade was Sicily, as it had been intermittently since antiquity, but it did not always dominate the market. Levantine grain could cost less in Spain, and a sharp rise in Turkish production in the mid-sixteenth century led to surpluses, although grain could only be exported to Christian countries through an elaborate black market.

Despite the continued growth of Mediterranean trade, the start of transatlantic, transpacific, and Atlantic–Indian Ocean shipping meant that the Mediterranean was no longer the primary arena of western sea trade, but only one region among many. Nonetheless, its shipping remained a cornerstone of the European economy: Venetian tonnage doubled between 1498 and 1567, and from 1540 to 1570 that of Ragusa grew by 75 percent. Yet changing political and economic fortunes saw the rise of vigorous commercial enterprises in French and Ottoman territories. In 1568, the Ottomans opened their trade to Christian Europeans by issuing "capitulations" to French merchants.* The equivalent of the medieval *aman* (safe-conduct pass), these proved invaluable in the mid-seventeenth century, when European merchants could trade legally in Ottoman ports only under the protection of the French flag. Christians were not the only ones to seek protection from the French. Attacks by the Knights of Malta and other corsairs—sailors who plundered ships without the official sanction of a privateer's commission but with greater national allegiance than a pirate—compelled many Muslim merchants to put their cargoes under the French flag and many Mediterranean hajjis opted to sail for Egypt in French ships.†

English commercial efforts in the eastern Mediterranean were put on a rational footing with an Ottoman grant of capitulations in 1580 and the formation of the Levant Company the next year. The English advantages were pronounced. They produced woolens more cheaply than their rivals; the Ottomans charged them only 3 percent customs duties (compared with 5 percent paid by the French and Venetians); they sailed large, heavily armed ships that could sweep aside Spanish opposition in the Strait of Gibraltar; and as Protestants they had no qualms about ignoring papal interdicts against supplying war matériel to the Ottomans, including iron guns and gunpowder. Ironically, the greatest threat to the company was other Englishmen—corsairs who preyed indiscriminately on the shipping of all nations and sold their prizes in the North African regencies. English merchants may have suffered less direct harm than did those of other nationalities, but the burden of reprisals for their countrymen's actions fell on the lawful traders of the Levant Company. The Dutch followed the English into the Mediterranean, where the Italians hired them for their expertise in the grain trade, and they negotiated for Ottoman capitulations of their own in 1612.

The Rise of the Dutch

While Iberian mariners were weaving a worldwide web of trade around Africa and across the Atlantic, Pacific, and Indian Oceans, the Dutch were busily engrossing the bulk trades of Europe from the Baltic to the Mediterranean. They also benefited from the Portuguese decision to market their pepper at

---

* "Capitulations" refers to the chapters (*capitula*) in the agreement and has nothing to do with surrender.
† The Knights of Malta originated in the early eleventh century as the Hospitallers of St. John of Jerusalem, a religious order that cared for pilgrims in the Holy Land. After the fall of Acre in 1291 they moved to Rhodes, where they became corsairs. Expelled by the Ottomans in 1522, they relocated to Malta, where they remained until ousted by Napoleon in 1798.

Antwerp, which had superseded Bruges as northern Europe's premier port in the 1400s. Lacking reserves to fund their Asian expansion, the Portuguese could only keep their ships running if they had access to ready cash from merchants who dealt with the problems of retail sale. This was most easily done at Antwerp, to which German merchant families like the Fuggers and Welsers diverted huge quantities of copper and silver to pay for Asian spices. The Portuguese also benefited from this arrangement, and by the 1520s Manoel I derived half his income from spice exports to northern Europe. Antwerp's connection to the Iberian world strengthened in 1516 when Charles, duke of Burgundy, who possessed the Netherlands, became Charles I of Spain. The city's fortunes were subsequently tied to the tensions between Spain and her fellow Netherlanders to the north.

The Dutch predisposition to maritime trade was a consequence of the paucity of natural resources at home. Living in the delta of some of northwest Europe's largest rivers, the Dutch were surrounded on three sides by salt- and freshwater from which they had to protect themselves by "a heavy yearly expenditure for dykes, sluices, mill-races, windmills and polders." Farming was possible, but in itself could not pay for these improvements. "Wherefore the inhabitants," in the words of a 1543 petition from the Dutch provinces to Charles, "must maintain themselves by handicrafts and trades, in such wise that they fetch raw materials from foreign lands and re-export the finished products, including diverse sorts of cloth and draperies, to many places, such as the kingdoms of Spain, Portugal, Germany, Scotland and especially to Denmark, the Baltic, Norway, and other like regions, whence they return with goods and merchandise from those parts, notably wheat and other grains." The Hanseatic merchants had guarded their control of the Baltic jealously, but by the end of the fifteenth century a majority of ships sailing through the Øresund were Dutch. Even though ice closed the Baltic to navigation for five months of the year, a thousand grain ships sailed from Gdansk to the Netherlands in 1471, and twice that number left the port a century later. By then, most Dutch ships still sailed north in ballast or with cargoes of low-value Iberian salt for the fisheries, the backbone of the Dutch domestic economy.

The Baltic trade provided not only for foodstuffs and luxuries like Russian furs, it was also vital for the Dutch shipbuilding industry, which imported virtually all its naval stores: wood, tar, iron for fastenings, hemp for rigging, and flax for sails. Reliant as they were on maritime trade, the Dutch developed highly sophisticated commercial and shipbuilding practices. They adopted wind-powered sawmills, compensated for the use of inferior wood with superior fabrication, and built ships of distinct design for different trades. Until the Dutch Revolt against Spanish rule (1568–1648), few individuals in the

Netherlands could afford to build ships on their own. As a result, the Dutch developed the practice of dividing the investment in ships into as many as sixty-four shares. This meant that many more people from all walks of life were invested in maritime commerce than elsewhere. To this system of apportioning risk and spreading wealth the Dutch married the development of the *fluit*, the most efficient merchantman of the day. Measuring four to five hundred gross tons with a length-to-beam ratio of about five or six to one, *fluits* are often described as floating boxes, with a sharp turn of the bilge, sharp stem and sternposts, and sterns that tapered sharply upward. They carried more sails of smaller size—usually square sails on the fore and main and a lateen mizzen—and because fewer hands were needed to take in sail, they had smaller crews. Although *fluits* were generally slow, most carried no armament, and for protection they sailed in convoys guarded by purpose-built warships.

Unlike his Burgundian father, Charles I, the Spanish-born Philip II tried to curb the privileges long enjoyed by the Dutch; to root out Calvinists, whose numbers were growing especially in the northern provinces; and to impose stiff taxes on merchants. The final breach came in 1568, the start of the Eighty Years' War, which ended with the independence of the Republic of the Seven United Provinces—the modern Netherlands. Antwerp was an early casualty in the struggle, and after its capture by the Spanish the population fell by more than half. Amsterdam welcomed the exodus of southern commercial expertise and capital and quickly became a warehouse for an almost infinite variety of products: wine, fruit, and sugar from southern Europe; Asian pepper, spices, and silks; American silver; and, encroaching on the English and Hanse trade in northern luxuries, Russian furs, leather, wax, and caviar, the last of which moved north via river from the Caspian to the White Sea.

Penetration and Expansion in Russia

In June 1553, three English ships sailed for the White Sea. Despite an underlying desire to find a Northeast Passage to China, their primary interest was to find new markets for English woolens. The crews of two ships froze to death on the coast of Lapland, but Richard Chancellor reached the Northern Dvina River and from there traveled to the court of Ivan IV, "the Terrible," at Moscow, more than a thousand kilometers to the south. Though "robbed homewards by Flemings," he gave a favorable report of his mission, which established cordial relations between the czar and Mary I and promised to give the English a firm hold on the Russian fur trade. In the sixteenth century, Russia referred chiefly to the Grand Duchy of Muscovy, centered on Moscow, about 750 kilometers northeast of Kiev. Although situated in "the Rus-

Seal die of the English Muscovy Company, 1555. The world's first joint-stock company was estab- lished with the aim of opening trade to northern Russia, which at the time had no other outlet to the sea. The English exported textiles in exchange principally for fur. Courtesy of the British Museum.

sian Mesopotamia" from which flowed the Volga, Western Dvina, Dnieper, Don, and Northern Dvina Rivers, Russia had only one saltwater outlet, on the White Sea. This remote, subarctic coast was not obviously conducive to long-distance trade, but its commercial potential was recognized by London merchants of the Muscovy Company and later still by the Dutch.

Chartered with a monopoly of the Russian trade and all lands "northwards, north-eastwards or north-westwards" not previously known to or visited by English traders, the Muscovy (or Russia) Company was the world's first joint- stock company in which people could freely buy and sell shares and receive dividends on their investments while leaving the direction of the company's day-to-day affairs in the hands of management. As in a partnership, sharehold- ers were liable for all company debts, but this was limited to the size of an individual's investment, a fundamental principle for all publicly traded compa- nies. This structure became the model for the Levant Company (1581), East India Company (1600), and the Dutch East India Company (1602). Muscovy Company merchants led the way north for forty years before Dutch traders eased the English off their perch in the early 1600s thanks to their access to a more diverse selection of goods. Although Russian merchants did not enter the sea trade in any numbers, Ivan established a port at Archangel, Russia's only saltwater port from 1584 until the founding of St. Petersburg in 1703.

Hemmed in on the west by the Grand Duchy of Lithuania and Poland, and to the south by Cossacks and the khanate of Crimea, Muscovy turned to the east. Ivan the Terrible, who assumed the title "Ruler of all Russia," defeated the Kazan and Astrakhan khanates to gain access to the lower Volga and Cas- pian. Ivan also oversaw Russia's advance across the Ural Mountains into Sibe- ria, an effort that would push the empire's eastern border to the Pacific by the 1630s. This expansion was initiated by a renegade Cossack named Yer- mak who, "being famed for attacking ships on the Caspian sea and on the

Volga together with many free warriors, even plundering the royal treasure," invaded the Sibir khanate via river and portage from the Volga to the Irtysh and ultimately the Ob River between 1579 and 1584. Yermak's men used flat-bottomed riverboats called *doshchaniks*, powered by a single square sail and up to twenty oars. These had a capacity of 35 to 150 tons and a maximum length of about thirty-eight meters. The double-ended *strug* measured between six and eighteen meters long.

Progress across Siberia continued at a brisk pace as merchants searched for furs, and tsars issued charters for rights to territories from which, as a deed of 1558 puts it, "no kind of dues have come . . . to my [Ivan's] royal treasury, and this land has not been given to anyone and has not been entered in anyone's name in registers, deeds of sale or legal documents." This was nothing more than a Russian rendering of the doctrine later known as *terra nullius*, literally "no one's land," the conceit being that land not in productive use—that is, untaxed—did not belong to its inhabitants, and that nation-states were free to take title and impose their laws on its people. Walter Raleigh invoked the same imagery in giving the name Virginia (which also honored Elizabeth, the Virgin Queen) to the undefined territory of North America to which he sent an expedition in 1584. He was more explicit still in his promotion of the settlement of Guiana, which he described as "a Countrey that hath yet her Mayden-head, never sackt, turned, nor wrought, the face of the earth hath not been torne, nor the vertue and salt of the soyle spent by manurance." This constituted a more sophisticated rationale for colonization than the simple claim of discovery and symbolic taking of possession of land, but it only became a matter of diplomatic importance in the late eighteenth and nineteenth centuries, when the Russians, Spanish, English, and Americans staked competing claims in the Nootka Sound area of North America.

European Naval Administration and State Formation

Western Europeans were able to consolidate and build on the pioneering accomplishments of Columbus, Gama, and others of their generation thanks to advances in naval organization, shipbuilding, and gunnery. But the transformation was slow and uneven. Until well into the 1500s, and later still in some countries, the primary purpose of maritime conflict was not to advance a nationalist agenda. Most violence at sea was essentially commercial, carried out by private individuals to further their own interests, and even the Venetian convoy system was organized with a view to protecting merchants against pirates as much as for protection against hostile actions by other states. Few people expected to conduct a voyage of any length without having to defend themselves against an aggressor. As one historian has put it, "For those who used the sea lines of communication in order to explore economic opportunities, efficient use of violence was one of several entrepreneurial skills which were necessary for profit."

Most rulers lacked the wherewithal to build or maintain standing navies. When monarchs ordered fleets to sea, they were generally made up of vessels and crews acquired on a temporary basis by ship musters, requisitioning, or chartering to supplement small warship squadrons built and maintained for the purpose. A hallmark of naval affairs in the sixteenth century was the development of state navies under central control and a gradual shift from private, commercial warfare to public, political warfare that presupposes conflict between two or more states with the material support of their respective citizens. States came to monopolize the use of violence at sea in what was to some degree a mutually reinforcing system: as states generated the revenues to build and manage standing fleets and the apparatus for efficient revenue collection, they increased their capacity to protect their citizens' trade and to channel commerce in ways beneficial to themselves.

At its most basic, naval administration is concerned with military operations and logistics—acquiring, repairing, and provisioning ships and crews—and sound finances and physical infrastructure are essential to the development of a permanent navy. (In this period and for several more centuries, prize courts for the adjudication of ships and cargos lawfully captured and the distribution of prize money raised from their sale were also integral to naval administration.) The most sophisticated European fleets of the time were those of the Venetians, the organization of which was substantially the same as in previous centuries, and the Ottomans, whose navy reached its peak during the reign of Suleiman the Magnificent. In the 1550s, there were more than 120 double slipways at the Imperial Arsenal in Pera on the Golden Horn, another thirty at Gallipoli, and a shipyard at Sinop on the Black Sea. Subsidiary fleets were stationed in the Aegean at Kavala, Lesbos, and Rhodes and at Alexandria and Suez in Egypt, while a smaller squadron at Mocha guarded the entrance to the Red Sea. There were also river squadrons on the Danube and Sava in the Balkans. Independent of this structure was the corsairing fleet at Algiers, which was not under obligation to fight for the Ottomans but which produced a number of the Ottomans' best known officers, starting with Hayreddin "Barbarossa," a native of Lesbos who with his older brother ruled Tunis and Algiers.

Shipyard workers were grouped into various occupational corps: carpenters, oar makers, caulkers, ironsmiths, pulley makers, and so on. Galleys, which comprised the bulk of the fleet until the seventeenth century, were for the most part manned by crews levied in the provinces and who were, in the view of a Venetian diplomat at Istanbul, "very well treated and paid." Although captives tended to form a high proportion of the crews in corsair fleets, including the Algerines and the Christian Knights of Malta, galley slaves and convicts comprised a smaller percentage of Ottoman than of Christian crews. In 1562, a Venetian official estimated that only thirty Ottoman galleys had any slaves in their crews. Nine years later, the year of the battle of Lepanto, convicts comprised 47 percent and slaves 10 percent of the crews of thirty Neapolitan galleys, and in 1584 convicts comprised 60 percent and slaves nearly 20 percent. One reason for the reliance on unfree crews was the adoption of a new style of rowing called *a scaloccio*. Instead of having one man per oar with three to five oars per bench in the *alla sensile* manner, *a scaloccio* put three to five rowers on each oar. A primary benefit of this arrangement was that skill counted for less than brute strength, and it was possible to have only one or two experienced rowers per oar, the others being employed solely for their muscle. A further benefit of relying on convicts was that their maintenance cost half that of free sailors.

The only two western European states with standing navies were Portugal and England, and only Portuguese ships were deployed beyond European waters. Little is known of the administrative structure of the fleet, but the Portuguese were able to operate throughout the eastern hemisphere thanks to their access to bases of operation from Brazil to Africa, India, Southeast Asia, and Macau, some three hundred in all at one time or another, including Melaka, Hormuz, Mozambique Island, and especially Goa, and, in Brazil, Bahia. The latter two developed renowned shipyards whose vessels were fully the equal of those built in Portugal. Of course ships were fundamental to success, and Portuguese vessels tended to be bigger and more heavily armed than their contemporaries. As important, Portuguese shipwrights tailored the design of their ships to the work for which they were intended.

The most important Portuguese ship types for the *Carreira da India* (the India run) were the merchant *nau* or carrack, the galleon, and the fleet caravel (*caravela de armada*). The last was an enlarged version of the *caravela redonda* used in the Portuguese exploration of Africa and Columbus's transatlantic voyages. Of between 150 and 180 tons with two covered decks, fleet caravels were too small to carry cargo on long voyages, but they were well suited for service as escorts for the Indies voyage or for coast guard functions. Generally four-masted, they were square-rigged on the foremast and lateen-rigged on the other three and set a square spritsail forward. Beamier than its predecessors, to make it a steadier gun platform, the fleet caravel is regarded as "the first ocean-going sailing ship developed exclusively for war at sea by any European navy." (Although some Venetian shipwrights were committing design concepts to paper by the fifteenth century, the first printed shipbuilding manual did not appear until 1587—published in Mexico City of all places—by which time the caravel was well past its heyday.) More than twice as big as fleet caravels, galleons developed around the middle of the century. The word "galleon" was applied to a variety of broadly similar vessels found from Venice to the Netherlands, but the Portuguese galleon was designed chiefly for naval duties. They were generally longer but narrower than *naus* and had lower forecastles, and they carried four masts with square sails on the fore and main and lateens on the mizzen and bonaventure mizzen, all of which made them faster and more maneuverable than *naus*.

In northern Europe, the first country to attempt the creation of a state navy was England. Although Henry VII is notable for ordering the construction of a dry dock at Portsmouth, his successor, Henry VIII, was the first king in nearly a century to promote English naval ambition. Early on he ordered construction of the *Mary Rose*—launched in 1510, accidentally sunk in battle against the French in 1545, and raised from the seabed in 1982—and the monumental *Henri Grace à Dieu* of 1514. With its echoes of competition between the Hellenistic kings of antiquity, this early-sixteenth-century trend toward gigantism—shared by Denmark, France, and under James IV, Scotland—quickly gave way to smaller, more compact galleons with better sailing qualities, stouter construction, and greater operational versatility. Yet the stability of the English naval establishment had its roots not in the ships per se, but in setting up facilities for naval stores and ship maintenance and the infrastructure to oversee them. The clerk of the king's ships was an ancient office supported by the clerk controller and the keeper of the storehouses, most of which were on the Thames. Henry enlarged the naval bureaucracy in the 1540s with the appointment of a lieutenant of the admiralty, treasurer, surveyor and rigger of ships, and master of the naval ordnance, and an administrative and advisory body collectively known as the Navy Board. In 1557, the navy was given a fixed budget and the following year, when Elizabeth came to the throne, "the Queen's Majesty's Navy" was found to have twenty-three serviceable ships maintained in the Medway, which enters the Thames estuary below Chatham.

Denmark followed England in attempting the creation of a state navy, thanks to Hans of Denmark's determination to maintain Sweden as part of the Kalmar Union and to counter the commercial and military pretensions of the Hanse cities. Around the turn of the century Hans began to develop a navy of heavily armed ships paid for from the Sound tolls levied on ships passing through the Øresund. These were not duties so much as protection money, justified on the grounds that the Danes provided security in the Skagerrak, Kattegat, and Baltic, over which they claimed dominion. This was particularly resented by the Hanse merchants, who were likewise troubled by the favor shown the Dutch. The Baltic fault lines were confirmed in 1522 when the future Gustav I Vasa jump-started the formation of a Swedish navy by purchasing about a dozen armed merchant ships from the Hanse cities of Lübeck and Stralsund. Five years later, Gustav took the bold step of dissolving the monasteries (a year before his Danish counterpart did so, and nearly a decade before England's Henry VIII) and used the proceeds to build Sweden's first permanent fleet, the flagship being the *Stora Kravelen* of 1,700 tons.

The expanded use of ships' guns was as important to the naval revolution of the sixteenth century as improved administration. Rudimentary cannon were developed in the thirteenth century but were not practically employed at sea until the 1470s, when the Venetians began mounting large centerline guns in their galleys, which had long been overshadowed, literally, by the high free-board of carracks and cogs. Mounting a single large gun in the bow, galleys became the offensive naval weapon par excellence. The largest class, the galleass, was a Venetian invention based on the three-masted great galley, whose large hull made an excellent gun platform and which the Venetians fitted with the heaviest guns they could. An accounting of four Neapolitan galleasses that sailed with the Spanish Armada is probably typical: each carried five cannon (which fired stone or metal shot weighing about twenty-five kilograms) and forty-five smaller guns designed to fire shot ranging in weight from twelve kilograms down to antipersonnel grapeshot. In all, this was enough guns to arm five ordinary galleys. Upward of fifty meters long, these galleasses were powered by oars and sails. With twenty-one to thirty oars per side and three to seven rowers per oar, galleasses were too expensive to supersede the ordinary galley as the standard warship. Somewhat smaller were the galiot (sixteen to twenty oars per side) and the bergantin (as few as eight oars per side), both of which were favored by Mediterranean corsairs.

At first, sailing warships had no way to counter armed galleys. Mounting heavy guns high on the main deck made ships unstable and ineffective against low-slung galleys, and so long as ships were clinker-built, as was normal in northern Europe until the sixteenth century, it was impossible to cut watertight gun-ports in the hull. When sailing ships did start carrying heavy guns, they were mounted aft, as close to the waterline as possible, and aimed through gun-ports pierced in the flush planking of the transom stern. This was not an ideal platform for offensive operations, as tactics of the day demonstrate. Ships attacked first with their bow chasers, came up into the wind to fire their lighter broadside guns, turned into the wind to bring the heavy stern guns to bear, and then fell off to fire the opposite broadside. The importance of stern-mounted guns is reflected in the fact that well into the seventeenth century paintings of warships generally featured the stern with its heavy guns (and lavish ornamentation) rather than a broadside profile. By the 1570s, English shipwrights began launching sailing galleys and galleons, the latter characterized by carvel (flush) planking with high sterns and cutaway forecastles—"crudely . . . the forepart of a galley with the afterpart of a ship"—which allowed heavy guns to be mounted forward. Only later did the heavy guns spread fore-and-aft to create the broadside battery standard between the seventeenth and nineteenth centuries.

In terms of armament, the English had a pronounced advantage over other countries thanks to the availability of iron. While technically inferior, harder to cast, and heavier than bronze guns, cast-iron guns had the virtue of costing only a fifth as much, which led to their widespread adoption in the Navy Royal (as it was called until 1707) and created a brisk export market. Among the most willing buyers were the Danes during the Scandinavian Seven Years' War (1563–70), the first to involve repeated battles between armed sailing war fleets. The Swedes appear to have relied more on state-owned, purpose-built warships but the greatest inequity between the fleets came from the Swedes' access to high-quality, long-range bronze guns, while the Danes initially relied on wrought-iron guns before they began purchasing more advanced English cast-iron guns. No detailed accounts of the fleet engagements fought between 1563 and 1566 survive, but superior gunnery and greater maneuverability seem to have enabled the often outnumbered Swedes to keep the Danish-Lübecker fleet from forcing a boarding action until the battle of Bornholm. Here, on July 7, 1565, the evenly matched fleets of about twenty-seven ships each fought a pitched battle at close range from which the Danish-Lübecker fleet withdrew after the loss of the flagship. The utility of shipboard gunnery was still uncertain, however. Ships' guns usually fired one shot per hour on average, and most guns of the day fired only twenty-five to thirty rounds in a *season*. Although ships' guns could prevent the enemy from closing, they had not proven their worth as antiship weapons.

Naval Warfare from Lepanto to the Armada

The English, Danes, and Swedes had demonstrated the value of rationalized approaches to naval administration and the destructive potential of modern armaments, but until the 1570s the epicenter of naval power remained firmly in the Mediterranean. In the course of barely a quarter century, however, the focus shifted dramatically to northwest Europe. The outlines of this transformation can be traced through three naval campaigns (all involving Spain): the battle of Lepanto (1571), the battle of São Miguel in the Azores (1582), and the Spanish Armada (1588).

In 1570, the Ottomans besieged the port of Nicosia on Venetian-occupied Cyprus. Desperate for allies, Venice secured help from Pius V, who set aside the Papal States' traditional rivalry with the Most Serene Republic, and from Spain's Philip II, who was indifferent to Venetian troubles but eager to reverse the Ottomans' capture of Tunis, Tripoli, and Djerba (1551–60). Prospects for joint action were dim, but Venice, Spain, and the Papal States hammered out a Treaty of Alliance in May 1571. Don Juan of Austria, Philip II's half brother, was designated commander-in-chief over Sebastiano Venier, Venice's general-at-sea, and Marcantonio Colonna, the pope's commander-in-chief. On October 7, the fleets met off the Curzolari Islands, forty miles west of Lepanto (Naupaktos, Greece), at the mouth of the Gulf of Corinth. To ensure that the Christian fleet would fight as one, ships of all flags were mixed through the different squadrons, with Don Juan, Venier, and Colonna sailing side-by-side in the center squadron of a combined fleet of 207 galleys and 6 galleasses. Commanded by Müezzinzâde Ali Pasha, with Uluç Ali Pasha and Şuluç Mehmed Pasha, the Ottomans had 213 galleys and 33 galiots.

Despite the Ottomans' numerical superiority in ships, their galleys tended to be more lightly built, and with nothing comparable to the heavy firepower of the six Venetian galleasses, they were probably outgunned by a ratio of two to one. The allies also had better protection in the form of pavisades, screens of shields that protected the crews against Turkish arrows and small arms, and they carried a greater number of harquebuses, which though cumbersome were more effective at close range than arrows. The power of the galleasses told early, and they disrupted the Turkish line as it passed and veered toward the shore. By early afternoon Ali Pasha was dead, the Turkish standard captured, and the Turkish fleet in disarray. The Ottomans lost 210 ships, including 117 galleys and 13 galiots captured, and about thirty thousand casualties, three times that of the allies. The celebrated victory demonstrated to Christian Europe that the Turks were not invincible, but in the short run the Ottomans proved more resilient than the coalition. As one official told the Venetians, "You have shaved our beard, but it will soon grow again; but we have severed your arm, and you will never find another." Uluç Ali oversaw the construction of a new fleet the next year, but the Venetians built hardly any new galleys, and while Venetian merchants were allowed to resume their trade to Alexandria, the Ottomans completed their capture of Cyprus in 1573.

Lepanto proved the last major Ottoman-Habsburg confrontation at sea. The Christian alliance did not long survive the battle, and the Ottomans concluded truces with Venice in 1573 and the Habsburgs four years later. This

freed the two imperial powers to concentrate on other crises: for the Ottomans, Safavid Persia; for the Spanish Habsburgs, the Dutch Revolt and the
Portuguese succession. Spain's lack of a standing Atlantic fleet was put to the
test in 1580, when Portugal's King Sebastian died without an heir and Philip
II claimed his throne. The Azores refused to accept Philip as king and sided
with the pretender, Dom Antonio, who was also supported by European rulers who felt threatened by the expansionist Habsburg Empire and eyed the
Azores as a strategic prize from which they could harry Spain's transatlantic
treasure fleets. In 1582, the French decided to support Dom Antonio's aspirations with an expedition of about sixty ships led by Philippe Strozzi. A Spanish
fleet under the Marquis of Santa Cruz brought the French to battle off the
island of São Miguel. Descriptions of the battle suggest that it opened with
ships firing their broadside guns before closing for a boarding action. Though
outnumbered two to one, Santa Cruz smashed Strozzi's force and with it the
Azorean threat to Spanish rule in Portugal.

Strozzi's force included a contingent of English ships, volunteers with no
official sanction from Elizabeth I, one of whose diplomatic preoccupations was
dealing with Philip II, her former brother-in-law and suitor. While inclined to
support her fellow Protestants in the Netherlands—which took two-thirds of
English wool exports—Elizabeth was at pains to check the more belligerent
of her Protestant subjects who sought to despoil the despised Catholic monarch. England's navy was not yet an effective instrument of state policy and
as in Spain royal ships comprised only a fraction of what might be needed in
wartime. At the same time, the line between personal prerogative and affairs
of state was poorly defined, and Elizabeth had no compunction about lending
her ships for private commercial ventures by which she could both profit and
covertly challenge her enemies.

Elizabeth's greatest provocation came in 1585 when she secretly approved
a mission by Francis Drake to circumnavigate the globe. The voyage had
several aims: to reconnoiter the Pacific coast of Spanish America and, if it
could be found, return via a Northwest Passage; to establish relations with
people not yet subject to European princes; and to plunder Spanish shipping.
In December 1577, Drake sailed with five ships and 180 men. They captured
half a dozen Spanish ships and a Portuguese pilot near the Cape Verde Islands
before pressing on to South America. Drake executed a mutineer at Puerto
San Julian, the same place Magellan had executed a mutineer on his circumnavigation in 1520, and he renamed his ship the *Golden Hind*. Down to three
vessels, Drake transited the Strait of Magellan and the English flag first flew in
the Pacific on September 6, 1578. A severe storm sank one ship, while another,
under John Winter, returned to England. Driven south, Drake established
that the Strait of Magellan did not separate South America from a southern

continent, Terra Australis, as previously believed, but that its southern shore was made up of islands to the south of which lay open ocean, now known as the Drake Passage.

Working their way north, the English looted Valparaíso, Arica, and Callao, and on March 1, 1579, captured *Nuestra Señora de la Concepción* off Colombia with a cargo that reportedly included eighty pounds of gold and twenty-six tons of silver. Drake followed the west coast of North America perhaps as far as the Strait of Juan de Fuca before abandoning his search for the Northwest Passage. After anchoring in a "convenient and fit harbor" generally believed to be Drake's Bay, about twenty-five miles north of San Francisco Bay, he named the coast Nova Albion and claimed it for England. After a twelve-week passage to the Philippines, the English refit the *Golden Hind* and then purchased spices in the Spice Islands. Their last stop in Asia was on Java, from where they embarked on a nonstop passage of nearly ten thousand miles—remarkable for its lack of incident—before anchoring off Sierra Leone. The first English circumnavigation of the globe ended on September 26, 1580. After lying low while the consequences of his voyage were considered at London, Drake was knighted by Elizabeth aboard the *Golden Hind*. She also "ordered the ship itself to be brought ashore and placed in her arsenal near Greenwich as a curiosity," one of the earliest museum ships on record.

The diplomatic contortions over Drake's expedition reveal something of the complexities of sixteenth-century diplomacy. England and Spain were not at war, but the Spanish considered the Strait of Magellan and the Pacific coast of South America Spanish territory to which foreigners could not sail without permission. Elizabeth could have issued a letter of marque, though not without risking war with Philip. At the same time, Drake was not a common criminal or pirate seizing property indiscriminately, and he had Elizabeth's tacit support. News of Drake's exploits inflamed Spanish opinion and elicited a variety of reactions in England. Even before Drake's return, Portuguese protests forced John Winter to surrender his share of the spoils—goods, in the words of the lord admiral (and one of Drake's chief investors), "piratically taken on the seas by Francis Drake and his accomplices." Elizabeth's eventual embrace of Drake was due largely to the phenomenal success of the voyage. The accounting is murky, but £264,000 (equal to about half the English crown's annual revenues) was officially deposited in the Tower of London; Drake's crew divided £14,000; and Drake himself was allowed to keep £10,000. Yet some Iberian merchants claimed the value of *Nuestra Señora de la Concepción*'s cargo alone to be £330,000, and a published estimate of 1581 put the total value of Drake's booty at £600,000, twice the amount officially accounted for.

Tensions between England and Spain were further strained by Elizabeth's

execution of her Catholic cousin, Mary Queen of Scots, and by her increasingly open support of the Dutch Revolt. In 1585, Philip began formulating
plans for an invasion of England using troops gathered under the duke of
Parma in the Spanish Netherlands supported by a powerful fleet from Spain.
To accomplish this, Philip authorized a force of twenty-eight thousand crew
and soldiers and 130 ships, 27 of which belonged to the crown: 19 galleons of
the Castilian and Portuguese squadrons, 4 Neapolitan galleasses, and 4 Portuguese galleys. The balance was a mix of armed merchantmen and unarmed
storeships requisitioned or leased from their owners. Ranged against this formidable assemblage, the English had nearly 200 ships, 34 belonging to the
crown, 105 armed merchantmen, and victuallers and coasters, with a combined complement of just under sixteen thousand men.

When the Armada finally sailed in June 1588, it was under the reluctant
duke of Medina Sidonia, who had assumed command following the death of
Santa Cruz, hero of São Miguel. The loss of Santa Cruz was regrettable, but
it only compounded the deficiencies of the fleet's inadequate administration,
corrupt provisioning, and poor strategic planning by the autocratic Philip,
who had no naval experience. The ships sailed from La Coruña on July 22
and a week later were off Plymouth. The Spanish knew that their only hope
of beating the English was in boarding actions, which they could not force.

> But unless God helps us by a miracle the English, who have faster and hand-
> ier ships than ours, and many more long-range guns, and who know their
> advantage as well as we do, will never close with us at all, but stand aloof and
> knock us to pieces with their culverins, without our being able to do them
> any serious harm. So we are sailing against England in the confident hope of
> a miracle.

No miracle was forthcoming, but the English guns were not as effective as
either they hoped or the Spanish feared. The fleets skirmished up the English
Channel for eight days until the Spanish anchored off Calais in anticipation of
rendezvousing with Parma's transports, which were not ready. Forced out of
their anchorage by English fireships, the Spanish lost four ships at the battle
of Gravelines, bringing their total losses over eleven days to only eight vessels.* Forced northward by wind and tide, by August 9 the Spanish commanders had little choice but to make for home by sailing around Scotland and
Ireland. Little did anyone imagine that only sixty-seven of their storm-tossed
ships would return to Spanish ports, nearly fifty having been lost at sea or
wrecked on the rocky coasts that ring the British Isles.

---

* Fireships were usually worn-out vessels loaded with combustibles, set alight, and steered,
towed, or allowed to drift down on enemy ships to set them on fire.

The story of the Armada has almost as many interpretations as interpreters. Some Englishmen were disappointed that they had not accomplished more, but the loss of the Armada demonstrated that Catholic Spain was not invincible and thus had much the same effect on Dutch and English Protestants that the victory over the Ottomans at Lepanto had had on Christian Europe as a whole. Yet as happened after Lepanto, the victors were unable to capitalize on their success. The next year Drake led the so-called counter-armada to destroy the remnants of the Spanish fleet, establish Don Antonio on the Portuguese throne, and seize the Azores. The ill-conceived expedition failed and the English fleet returned with only about two thousand of the ten thousand men embarked fit for duty. Far from destroying the Spanish Armada, the "irretrievable miscarriage, that condemned the war to an inefficient conclusion" sixteen years later, was one of the factors that led to the creation of Spain's permanent Atlantic fleet, the Armada del Mar Océano.

Ships big enough to make the long passages across the Atlantic, around Africa to the Indian Ocean, and across the Pacific were essential to European expansion. For much of the sixteenth century Spain and Portugal faced virtually no competition in the Americas or Asia from other Europeans, apart from a handful of freebooters and pirates who nibbled at the flanks of their Atlantic empires. In the more distant waters of the Monsoon Seas, Portugal managed a commercial network at the absolute limit of what its resources would allow; yet it was not until the end of the century that its exclusive control of seaborne trade between Asia and Europe was effectively challenged, not by Asians resentful of Portuguese arrogance but by Dutch merchants envious of their success and eager to strike a blow against their Spanish overlord.

The losses sustained by the Armada and Philip's determination to focus his efforts on backing the Catholic faction in the French wars of religion gave the Dutch rebels a much needed respite, as did his decision to lift an embargo on Dutch shipping so that Spain could continue to receive the goods it needed from northern Europe. Blockading the Flemish coast around Antwerp, the Dutch channeled still more commerce to Amsterdam, where many Antwerp merchants had taken refuge. The combination of their commercial expertise and international connections with Amsterdam's concentration of shipping and industry ignited the port's meteoric rise, and in so doing helped assure the Dutch Republic's eventual independence from Spain in 1648. By that time, the Dutch were the world's foremost traders, and the torch of ocean trade had passed for the first time to northern Europe, where it would blaze without rival for nearly two hundred years.

Chapter 16

State and Sea in the Age of European Expansion

The seventeenth century represents the coming of age of the maritime powers of Atlantic Europe. Apart from the Iberian kingdoms, no one had been satisfied with the church-sanctioned division of the non-Christian world between Spain and Portugal, but it was not until the 1600s that Hugo Grotius articulated cogent and accessible arguments in favor of "the free sea." People and governments deployed this thesis in opportunistic and sometimes contradictory ways, but support for the doctrine encouraged broader participation in intercontinental trade. For the most part these were private initiatives, typically undertaken by joint-stock companies endowed with considerable latitude of action to defend their business and their flag. The Dutch in particular exercised armed force with the blessing of their home government to create an empire of "ledger and sword" that overlay far older networks of trade in which Asian merchants continued to predominate.

Companies took on such sweeping responsibilities because, notwithstanding the baroque grandeur of their courts and their ships, European monarchs lacked navies capable of executing their will overseas. Even so, rivalries between England, the Dutch Republic, France, and Spain turned the English Channel and adjacent waters into the dark alley of seventeenth-century trade, where corsairs and privateers threatened all comers, and tricked-out ships of state occasionally swaggered out with their gilded entourages as a reminder of who was in charge. But the ineffectiveness of naval power is obvious from the staggering numbers of merchant ships captured in the course of five major conflicts in less than half a century. Between the first Anglo-Dutch War and the Nine Years' War (1652–97), the English are thought to have seized between 3,600 and 4,300 enemy merchantmen, while in the same period they lost between 5,500 and 6,300 of their own. Many of these vessels were ransomed back to their owners or recaptured.

Northern European warships rarely operated beyond European waters. Over the course of the seventeenth century, ships, fleets, and infrastructure grew in size and complexity, and innovative approaches to financing and administration were adopted. Combined with legal and diplomatic remedies, these gradually exerted a stabilizing influence on maritime trade, and smugglers and pirates working without political sanction found themselves increasingly marginalized. The apparent free-for-alls in the Caribbean and the Indian Ocean at the end of the century were less a sign of widening chaos than a demonstration of more effective navies, especially on the part of the English, who in the following century would become the world's preeminent naval power.

The Capture of the *Santa Catarina*

Northern European states lacked the means and motive to mount effective naval campaigns against the Iberian powers overseas, but their governments condoned the activities of merchants willing to challenge Spanish and Portuguese dominance of trade in Asia, Africa, and the Americas. Hoping to put a stranglehold on the Dutch rebels, in 1598 Spain's Philip III banned Dutch shipping from Iberian ports as well as Portuguese holdings in Africa, the Americas, and Asia. The embargo hobbled Dutch trade in the Mediterranean and between Iberia and the Baltic, but it spurred Dutch interest in oceanic shipping. The number of vessels sailing to West Africa for gold, gums, ivory, and São Thomé sugar rose from three or four per year to an average of twenty in the decade after 1599. Even before Philip's embargo, Dutch merchants began to consider ways to reach Asia via either a Northeast Passage or by following the Portuguese into the Indian Ocean. The Portuguese held close the secrets of navigation to the east: in 1504 Manoel I issued a royal decree calling for the routine destruction of logbooks and charts describing Asian waters. Northern Europeans gained some familiarity with the Monsoon Seas as crew, merchants, and adventurers in Portuguese pay, and in 1591–94, James Lancaster commanded three English ships as far as the Malay Peninsula. Yet information about the Indian Ocean and beyond remained sparse and anecdotal until the publication of Jan Huyghen van Linschoten's *Itinerario* in 1595. The Dutch Linschoten had spent several years as a merchant with his brothers in Seville and Lisbon before becoming secretary to the archbishop of Goa in 1583. After a decade in India he returned home and wrote his *Itinerario* of

Goa, and the Indies, concerning their manners, traffiques, fruites, wares, and other things, the better to understand the situation of the Countrey, and of the coasts lying on the East side, to the last and highest part of the borders of China, which the Portingales have travelled and discovered, together with their Ilandes . . . [and] a briefe note of the Orientall coastes, beginning at the redde, or the Arabian sea, from the towne of Aden to China: and then the description of the coastes before named.

Based largely on secondhand information, Linschoten's "briefe note" presented detailed descriptions of major ports, their inhabitants, forms of government, and chief trading goods. The *Itinerario* became a Baedeker for merchants aspiring to capture the riches of Asia, and Cornelis de Houtman took a copy on the first Dutch expedition to the Indies in 1595–97. This voyage barely broke even and only a third of his 240 crew survived, but Houtman won permission from the sultan of Banten, in western Java, for Dutch ships to trade there. Between 1598 and 1601 fifteen provincial merchant companies sent a total of sixty-five ships to trade in the Spice Islands and make commercial treaties with local rulers. Indicative as it was of the Dutch entrepreneurial spirit, this competition drove up the cost of pepper and other spices in Asia while depressing the prices at which they could be sold at home. To counter the decline in profits, in 1602 the various companies came together as the Verenigde Oostindische Compagnie (United East India Company, or VOC). Whereas the earlier companies had been "established . . . solely for the purpose of doing honest business and trading in peace and not from hostility or maliciousness," the VOC was both a trading entity and an instrument of the state chartered by the States-General (the Dutch parliament) and invested with the powers to wage war, contract treaties, establish forts, administer the law, and in most respects act as an arm of the Dutch government, which in effect it was. The state's view was epitomized in a comment by Johan van Oldenbarnevelt, the leading politician of the day: "The great East India Company, with four years of hard work, public and private, I have helped establish in order to inflict damage on the Spanish and Portuguese." In effect, the VOC went on to create its own version of the *Estado da India*. The main difference was that its ruling body, the Heren XVII (seventeen gentlemen) in the Netherlands, and the governor-general and council of the Indies in Batavia (now Jakarta), had greater freedom from political control, demonstrated vastly more commercial acumen, and drew on infinitely greater financial resources, distribution networks, and industrial capacity, especially shipbuilding, than the *Estado* ever mustered.

Two years earlier, an Amsterdam fleet had sailed under Admiral Jacob van

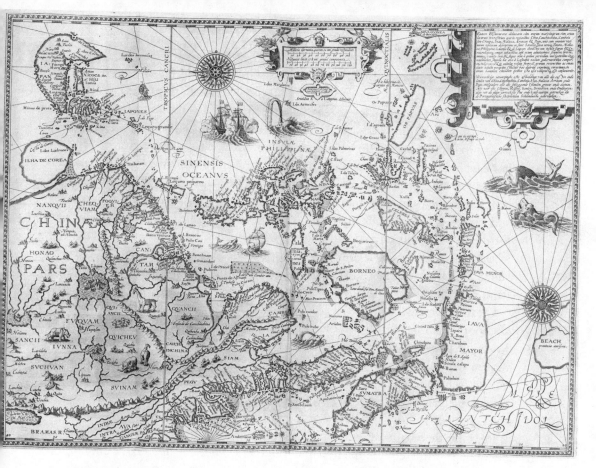

Map of the coasts of Southeast Asia and China—east is at top—published with the Itinerario: Voyage ofte schipvaert van Jan Huyghen van Linschoten naer Oost ofte Portugaels Indien, 1579–1592 *(Travel account: Voyage of the sailor Jan Huyghen van Linschoten to the Portuguese East Indies) in 1596. Linschoten presented detailed descriptions of major ports, their inhabitants, forms of government, and commodities and rarities—trade secrets the Portuguese had jealously guarded throughout the sixteenth century. The* Itinerario *became the standard guidebook for merchants aspiring to capture the riches of Asia, and Cornelis de Houtman took a copy on the first Dutch expedition to the Indies in 1595–97. Courtesy of the Osher Map Library and Smith Center for Cartographic Education, University of Southern Maine, Portland.*

Neck, who took two ships to investigate the possibility of establishing a Dutch presence in China. Sailing into the Pearl River delta, the Dutch anchored before "a great town spread out before us, all built in the Spanish style, on the hill a Portuguese church and on top of it a large blue cross. . . . According to Huygen [van Linschoten]'s notebook this had to be Macao." Van Neck sent twenty men to negotiate with the Portuguese, who, determined to prevent their meeting with local officials and securing the right to trade in China, executed all but three of them. In the meantime, Admiral Jacob van Heemskerck had reached Banten, where he found six rival Dutch ships and countless other merchants from around Asia. With pepper prices too high for his liking, he took the *Witte Leeuw* and *Alkmaar* to the northern Java port of Japara, where the sultan arrested twelve of his crew and forbade him to trade. Sailing east he established a factory at Gresik and seized a Portuguese ship and letters recounting the fate of Van Neck's men at Macau. Unable to avenge his countrymen's judicial murder out of concern for the men held at Japara and others he planned to leave as agents at Gresik, Van Heemskerck sailed for the Malay Peninsula port of Pattani, whose queen had allowed the Dutch to establish a factory as a counterweight to the Portuguese. While there, the sultan of Johor's brother encouraged him to wait for the Portuguese ship due from Macau.

On the morning of February 25, 1603, the *Witte Leeuw* and *Alkmaar* were at anchor in the Singapore Strait off Johor when first light revealed a richly laden Portuguese *nao* at anchor before them. The *Santa Catarina* was en route from Macau to Melaka, just as the Dutch had hoped. With the help of Johorese galleys, the Dutch battered the Portuguese ship for ten hours before she surrendered. In acknowledgment of his assistance, Van Heemskerck presented the sultan of Johor with gifts worth ten thousand guilders and reimbursed a Johorese merchant whose ship he had despoiled the previous year. When auctioned at Amsterdam, the remainder of the *Santa Catarina*'s silks, camphor, sugar, aloes, and porcelain netted three hundred thousand guilders, enough to build fifty or sixty merchants' houses in Amsterdam. The fantastic wealth of the *Santa Catarina*'s booty notwithstanding, the outstanding importance of this incident derives from the long-term legal consequences of Van Heemskerck's actions.

Hugo Grotius and The Free Sea

The Portuguese vigorously protested the capture of the *Santa Catarina*, but Van Heemskerck claimed that he was entitled to avenge the crimes against his countrymen at Macau because Prince Maurits of Orange had commissioned him to use force. A Dutch court concurred in judging the capture a lawful prize, but to bolster their claim the directors of the VOC asked the precocious Hugo Grotius, then twenty-one, to draft a justification of their decision. His complete work, *De Jure Praedae* (The Law on Prize and Booty), remained unpublished until the nineteenth century. One chapter, however, appeared anonymously as *Mare Liberum* (The Free Sea) in 1609. The essence of Grotius's thesis is that "it is lawful for any nation to go to any other and to

Portrait of Hugo Grotius (1583–1645) by Jansz. van Mierevelt. Grotius sat for this portrait at the age of twenty-eight, seven years after writing his seminal Mare Liberum *(The Free Sea), the legal justification for his countrymen's attack on a Portuguese merchant ship in Southeast Asia and, more broadly, on the right of Dutch merchants to sail to and trade in a region over which Portugal claimed a monopoly. His arguments for "the right of navigation and the liberty of traffic" earned him the appellation "father of international law." Courtesy of the Museum Rotterdam.*

trade with it," and that Portuguese claims to a monopoly of trade on the basis of a papal grant, territorial possessions in the Indies, or custom were groundless. Furthermore, in the absence of a competent legal authority to which to appeal, Van Heemskerck was entitled to avenge any wrongs committed by the Portuguese to hinder Dutch trade. Support for this argument, and for the practice of using a business to achieve political ends, was far from universal even within the Netherlands where many merchants believed that their interests were best served by peaceful trade.

The *Santa Catarina* affair and publication of *Mare Liberum* did not initiate the examination and refinement of legal norms governing trade, the right to possession of unoccupied territory, privateering, freedom of the sea, and other matters pertaining to maritime expansion. Few of Grotius's legal theories were new, and several of his arguments regarding the laws of nature and of nations derived from classical antecedents. The need to rearticulate them sprang from the determination of northern European states to counter Iberian pretensions in Asia and the Americas, an effort already evident in the sixteenth century. Although Spain demonstrated almost no interest in North America, Giovanni da Verrazano's exploration of the coast from North Carolina to Newfoundland in 1524 and Jacques Cartier's three voyages up the St. Lawrence River between 1534 and 1542 (both men sailed for France) had to be legitimated in the face of Spain's monopolistic claims under the Treaty of Tordesillas. Francis I argued that neither Spain nor Portugal had any right to land they did not effectively occupy, and Pope Clement VII reinterpreted the bull *Inter Caetera* to apply to "known continents, not to territories subsequently discovered by other powers," which freed the French, among others, to launch their own voyages of discovery. Planning for Cartier's third voyage alarmed the Spanish court, although the French king was reported to have said "that he did not send these ships to make war nor to contravene the peace and friendship with your Majesty [Charles V]." Rather, he blithely insisted that "the sun gave warmth to him as well as to others, and he much desired . . . to learn how [Adam] had partitioned the world." Francis furthermore drew sharp distinctions between discovery and occupation, and between the spiritual and temporal power of the popes, who, he claimed, had no business apportioning land among secular sovereigns.

The English made similar arguments to justify Francis Drake's forays into the West Indies in the 1580s, and in the next decade the evangelist of English expansion Richard Hakluyt observed that because "the sea & trade are common by the lawe of nature and of nations, it was not lawfull for the Pope, nor is it lawfull for the Spaniard, to prohibit other nations from the communication & participation of this lawe." English support for the doctrine of the free sea was reversed under James I, who was also James VI of Scotland. More dependent than the English on fish for food and with a relatively modest overseas trade, oriented toward the Baltic, the Scots had long claimed an exclusive right to waters out to twenty-eight miles from shore. After ascending the English throne, James began applying this Scottish notion of a closed sea to keep the Dutch from fishing in English waters, and many assumed that Grotius wrote *Mare Liberum* with a view to preserving Dutch rights to the Dogger Bank fishing grounds of the North Sea as much as to justify Dutch actions in Southeast Asia.*

Indeed, John Selden's *Of the Dominion, or, Ownership of the Sea* (also known as *Mare Clausum*, "the Closed Sea") was drafted in 1619 as a justification of James I's requirement that foreigners purchase a royal license to fish. The most famous rebuttal to Grotius, Selden's work was not released at the time for fear of offending the king of Denmark, whose fishermen also frequented British waters. Selden justified his interpretation of the law by pointing to the "Customs of so many Nations both ancient and modern." While his chief focus

---

* The Dogger Bank is a large (17,600 square kilometers), shallow area of the North Sea renowned for its fishing. It lies about sixty miles from the English coast, but the name comes from that of a Dutch fishing vessel.

was the fisheries, he delineated an absurdly expansive conception of England's territorial sea. The "sea-territory of the British Empire" to the south and east ended at the continent, but "in the open and vast ocean of the north and west they are to be placed at the utmost extent of those most spacious seas which are possessed by the English, Scots, and Irish." In other words, Britain's territorial sea included the North Atlantic all the way to North America, where the French, Dutch, and the English had been making fitful attempts to establish colonies of their own.

The Dutch in Asia: Batavia, Taiwan, and Nagasaki

Tightly argued and influential as his work is, Grotius was writing at the behest of political masters who changed course as conditions warranted. The Dutch vigorously advocated free trade in European waters, where their shippers were dominant and any restrictions on their movements threatened their profits. Yet once they had removed the Portuguese from Southeast Asia, they abandoned the notion of the free sea to preserve their own monopoly against the English and even restricted where and what indigenous mariners could trade. The VOC expelled the Portuguese from the Spice Islands in 1605 and signed treaties with local rulers to fortify the islands. Soon their greatest competition was from their anti-Catholic allies, the English. The Twelve Years' Truce ended hostilities with Spain in 1609, but by 1618 war was again on the horizon, and rather than risk a confrontation with England, the States-General allowed the English a fixed share of the spice trade in exchange for help in paying for the Dutch garrisons. The VOC's governor-general, Jan Pieterszoon Coen, grudgingly followed his superiors' lead, and a combined Anglo-Dutch squadron besieged the Spanish colony at Manila and captured many Chinese junks in an effort to divert the silk trade to Batavia. An empire builder in the mold of Afonso d'Albuquerque, Coen became governor-general of the VOC in 1618. Over the objections of the local ruler of what is now Jakarta, the next year he founded the castle of Batavia, which became the administrative capital of an informal yet growing Dutch empire in Asia and a major emporium of the East Indies. Celebrated through the early 1700s as the "Queen of the Orient" and "Holland in the Tropics," Batavia was a city of brick town houses, government buildings, hospitals and churches, and canals. Within the city walls lived the ruling Dutch minority alongside the prosperous and numerically larger Chinese community, while discrete communities of Bugis from south Sulawesi and colonies of Madurese, Balinese, and Ambonese lived beyond the city limits.

The Chinese government had accepted the Portuguese version of the *Santa Catarina* affair and, viewing the Dutch as pirates, refused to allow them to trade. In 1624, the Dutch built Zeelandia Castle on Taiwan. Less than a hundred miles from the Chinese mainland, Taiwan was home to an indigenous population of Austronesian-speaking people whose predilection for headhunting had dampened Chinese interest in the island before the sixteenth century, when it became a haven for pirates. By 1603, there was a small Chinese presence lured by the abundance of deer, whose skins were coveted by the Japanese. The island's strategic location made it attractive to Iberian and Japanese merchants who made halfhearted efforts to settle there, but the real pioneers were the Dutch, who made Zeelandia an entrepôt for merchants from China, Japan, the Philippines, Southeast Asia, and Batavia. Like Batavia and Spanish Manila, Dutch Taiwan was predominantly Chinese and, in the words of a Dutch official, "The Chinese are the only bees on Formosa [Taiwan] that give honey." By 1645 the island's Chinese population numbered fifteen thousand, many of them engaged in the island's sugar industry, which the Dutch had introduced from Southeast Asia.

On the mainland, the Ming government's position had become increasingly parlous. In 1610, the Mongolian Manchus had severed ties with the Ming Dynasty and over the next quarter century they consolidated their hold over Mongolia and founded the Qing Dynasty. When a rebel army took Beijing and the Ming emperor hanged himself in 1644, many Chinese appealed to the Manchus to intervene. As so often before, imperial loyalists retreated to the south and southeast coasts, where resistance to the Qing was strongest, although it depended on unreliable warlords and adventurers. Among the more notable of these was Zheng Zhilong, whose family controlled much of the sea trade between Hangzhou and Guangzhou. Zheng defected to the Qing following their capture of Hangzhou in 1646, but his son Zheng Chenggong, known as Koxinga, proved intensely loyal.* Born to a Japanese mother in the port of Hirado, north of Nagasaki, the younger Zheng rose in the service of the Southern Ming. In 1659 he attacked Nanjing, but Ming loyalists failed to rise in support and his forces—between fifty and one hundred thousand men in a thousand vessels—retreated down the Yangzi to Jinmen (Quemoy Island), off Xiamen. He then decided to relocate his followers to Taiwan and in 1662 forced the Dutch off the island.

Zheng died within the year, but his followers constituted a clear and present threat to the mainland. To avoid attacks from Zheng's successors, the

---

* Honored by the Longwu emperor, Zheng was known as "the gentleman of the imperial surname," or *kokseng ya* in Fujianese.

Manchus ordered the entire population of Zhejiang, Fujian, Guangdong, and Guangxi Provinces to relocate at least thirty kilometers from the coast. The displacement of millions of people ruined China's overseas trade for the next two decades. In 1683, the Kangxi emperor ordered one of Zheng Chenggong's former captains to invade Taiwan. A force of three hundred ships and twenty thousand troops easily took the island and, to prevent foreign traders from establishing themselves there, the government annexed Taiwan, lifted the prohibition on China's overseas trade, and allowed people to move back to the coasts. With its dearth of desirable commodities, however, Taiwan was again relegated to the margins of Asian trade, although it later became Fujian's rice basket and, in the late twentieth century, a major center of shipbuilding and global trade in its own right.

The Dutch expulsion from Taiwan was partly offset by their privileged position as the only Europeans allowed in Japan. Under Hideyoshi's successor, Tokugawa Ieyasu, Japanese merchants had begun trading with Southeast Asia. Ieyasu supported foreign trade but subjected it to tight regulation, and ships could not sail from Japan without a government-issued vermilion seal, called a *shuin*. Between 1604 and 1635, 370 ships sailed with vermilion seals, and "Japan towns" could be found in the Philippines, Vietnam, Thailand, Myanmar, Sumatra, and Java. But the fate of Japan's maritime expansion was linked ultimately to that of Japanese Christians. In the 1630s, Ieyasu's grandson Tokugawa Iemitsu issued a series of maritime prohibitions (*kaikin*) with a view to stemming Christian influence. These kept Japanese from sailing overseas and prevented anyone who had lived abroad for more than five years from returning home. Following the Shimabara rebellion involving mostly Christian peasants, the Portuguese (long suspected of smuggling priests into the country) were barred from Japan in 1639. From this point, Japan's connections to the outside world were channeled through the "four gates": Tsushima, for trade with Korea; Satsuma, for trade with the island kingdom of Ryukyu; Matsumae, in southwest Hokkaido, for relations with the Ainu; and Nagasaki, for merchants from China, Taiwan, and Batavia.

The first Dutch to visit Japan were survivors of a Pacific crossing in a Dutch privateer four decades before. Three of the crew, including the English sailor William Adams, obtained passes to trade abroad and were allowed to operate from Hirado. The Dutch hoped to trade with Chinese merchants who called there, and to use the port as a base from which to raid Portuguese and Chinese shipping bound for Macau, Manila, and Nagasaki. The seizure of ships trading to Nagasaki cut into the shogun's profits, and he ordered the VOC merchants to desist. Realizing that the only way to maintain profitable relations with Japan was to guarantee peaceful trade, the Dutch refrained from attacking Iberian shipping even when the Dutch Republic was at war with Spain. The VOC went to almost any lengths to guarantee access to Japan, and the Heren XVII's prescription for the conduct of Dutch merchants signals a definitive break between the medieval crusader ideals still discernible in the Iberian consciousness of the sixteenth century and the modern age of commercial capitalism:

> Company officials . . . should above all be provided with modesty, humility, politeness, and friendship, being always very obliging in regard to the Japanese, so that their hearts shall in the end be won over to us. *Modesty* consists of prudent behavior and circumspection in all transactions; *Humility* means that one shall never raise jealousy with haughty actions towards this easily offended nation, but will always behave oneself as the lower one in rank; *Obedience* means that we should not resist their laws, without being too timid, or too indulgent, always trying to maintain the Company's rights in a discreet manner.

So agreeable were the Dutch that when the shogun ordered them to tear down their warehouse at Hirado—because the lintel bore the Christian date *Anno Domini 1639*—the Dutch promptly complied. Satisfied with this show of respect, the Japanese allowed them to stay, moving them to the artificial island of Deshima in Nagasaki Bay, which served as the VOC headquarters for more than two centuries. The company remained Japan's only window on the world beyond East Asia until the arrival of an American fleet effected the next sea change in Japanese history in 1853.

Asian Trade in the Age of Partnership

Limited though the Dutch trade with Japan was, it provided them with a competitive advantage in intra-Asian trade because apart from the Chinese they were the only carriers of Japanese silver, gold, and copper, which they could sell in India, thereby reducing the amount of specie they had to export from Europe to pay for Asian goods. Because Europe produced little of interest to Asian markets, most Asian goods had to be purchased with bullion. Between 1600 and 1623, the English East India Company alone shipped £1.1 million worth of bullion and goods to Asia, more than two-thirds of it silver. This deficit drove the European search for lucrative intra-Asian "country" trades because the prevailing mercantilist doctrine of the time maintained that states needed to hold gold and silver to pay for wars, and if these were not available domestically, they had to be acquired from trade or colonies. To this end, the government promoted commerce, often through protectionist policies that encouraged domestic manufacturing; imposed high tariffs on or banned the import of foreign goods; and developed colonies that provided both raw materials and markets for domestic manufacturers. But the Dutch learned early on that they would not have to rely entirely on precious metals to finance their purchases. Van Heemskerck was assured that the most sought-after commodity in Southeast Asia was not silver but cloth from the Coromandel Coast. Nor was pepper all that was on offer for the Dutch. "Bring us textiles," urged the port master of Pattani, "and we will all declare war on the Portuguese."

Similar recommendations were forthcoming from Gujarati merchants the Dutch met at Aceh and Banten. The VOC did not take an especially active interest in India until their position in Southeast Asia was assured, but when they began setting up factories, on the Coromandel Coast as well as at Cambay, Broach, and Surat, they focused on textiles. Between 1620 and 1700, the value of the VOC's trade increased from three million to fifteen million florins, yet the share of pepper and spices declined from about three-quarters to a quarter. The share of textiles and silk, however, rose from 16 percent to more than half. While the value of English imports from Asia nearly equaled that of the Dutch, the East India Company took little interest in the country trade, which was left to private English traders, or interlopers.

At the end of the sixteenth century, English merchants active in the eastern Mediterranean viewed the success of the Dutch and English voyages to the Indies with concern. To capitalize on the burgeoning trade with Asia, a group including members of the Levant Company applied to the crown for a charter for the East India Company, which they received in 1600. Further removed from the corridors of political power than its Dutch counterpart, the East India Company never enjoyed comparable latitude of action. Lacking the resources or commercial sophistication of their Dutch rivals, the English abandoned their factories in the Indonesian archipelago by the end of the seventeenth century, but they more than made up for these losses by focusing on Indian textiles. Their reliance on low-value, high-volume goods within the framework of traditional intra-Asian trade—in Indian cotton, lead, silver, and pepper, and Chinese silk, porcelain, and lacquerware—yielded significant profits that were not diverted to maintaining monopolies on high-value goods like those that burdened the *Estado da India* and the VOC.

Breaking into the Indian market required a combination of diplomacy and naval superiority. The English and Dutch demonstrated the latter by seizing Mughal merchantmen, which the Portuguese were supposed to protect, and by besting the Portuguese in a series of battles off Surat and Bombay (modern Mumbai). These actions convinced Emperor Jahangir to allow the establishment of English and Dutch factories at Surat and elsewhere. This apparent concession brought more trade to Surat and gave the Mughals the upper hand in negotiating with the English and Dutch. The Mughals were no match for Europeans at sea, but the Europeans were impotent on land, as James I's ambassador, Sir Thomas Roe, found when he spent three years in Agra vainly trying to negotiate a commercial treaty with Jahangir. In 1634, the English built a fort at the village of Madraspatnam in Coromandel, just north of the Portuguese factory at São Thomé. The ports most clearly identified with English rule in India were not established until midcentury. About 150 miles south of Surat, Portuguese Bombay was given to Charles II as part of his Portuguese bride's dowry in 1661. Charles leased the unprepossessing port to the East India Company, which later transferred its headquarters there from Surat.

The high profile of Europeans in the country trades should not obscure the dominant role of Asian merchants in the Monsoon Seas. The Mughal ruling elite was deeply invested in overseas commerce in the seventeenth century. At first their involvement was limited to support of the hajj, but they soon developed a taste for trade for its own sake. From the 1640s to 1660s, members of the Mughal royal family, nobles, and high-ranking officials were financing trade and building merchant ships of up to one thousand tons. Most Indian merchants were not nobles or politically well connected, but their profits could be considerable nonetheless. Records are scanty, but in 1654–55 twelve Indian-owned ships (five belonging to Emperor Shah Jahan) returned to Surat from the Red Sea and seventeen from the Persian Gulf; the value of the nineteen cargoes whose manifests survive totaled more than three million rupees.[*]

The Mughals were also involved in Bengal's maritime trade. The Portuguese had become active in Bengal at the end of the previous century, at Chittagong, Satgaon, and later Hugli, in the Ganga estuary upstream from the future site of Calcutta. So many Portuguese were engaged in piracy, however, that in 1632 Shah Jahan expelled them from Hugli and invited the Dutch and English to trade there. Bengal fed off Surat's growing trade with Southwest Asia, but Bengal merchants preferred to let merchants at Masulipatnam and Surat serve as intermediaries in the trade of the western Indian Ocean. The bulk of their own trade was directed toward eastern markets from Myanmar to Manila, to which they exported textiles, silk, sugar, and opium. Imports of tin, precious stones, gold, and elephants came from South and Southeast Asia, while Sri Lanka, southern India, and the Maldives sent cinnamon, areca nuts, cowries, pepper, coconut oil, and coir.

---

[*] The rupee was a silver coin weighing about ten grams. Servants earned the equivalent of three to four rupees per month.

Despite their engagement in these overseas networks, the Mughals made little commitment to protect their trade and they had no navy. The closest they came was an alliance of convenience with the Siddis of Janjira. Descended from East African slaves who had settled on the island of Janjira about forty miles south of Bombay, the Siddis constituted the principal non-European naval force in western India. They were in the vanguard of the Mughal wars with the Hindu Maratha state, which brought them into frequent conflict with the English. Although the Marathas had virtually no maritime trade, the Maratha leader Shivaji created a fleet and articulated a coherent naval strategy for dealing with the Siddis, but he was unable to put it into effect for want of experienced officers and crews. He was also unsuccessful in wooing the English, who struggled for decades to remain neutral in the conflict between the Siddis and Marathas around Bombay.

For all the wealth and the commercial acumen available at Surat—an estimated thirty thousand merchants were based there—the port was riven by divisions of caste and occupation, ethnicity, religion, and language. Nonetheless, it was a vibrant emporium with strong ties to the Indian hinterland and a full range of services from sailors and porters to commercial agents and moneylenders. It was also a place where a man could rise from rags to riches. The wealthiest Surati merchant of the late seventeenth and early eighteenth centuries was Mulla Abdul Ghafur. A Shiite Gujarati merchant (*bohra*), Ghafur started life at the bottom of the economic ladder but made a fortune in the Red Sea trade. At a time when the entire seagoing merchant fleet of Surat numbered about a hundred ships, he owned seventeen with a total capacity of five thousand tons, and at his death his estate was estimated at 8.5 million rupees. Nonetheless, whether because of the fractious social climate or because the nouveaux riches tend to be shunned no matter what their background or language, his Arab, Persian, and Turkish counterparts seem to have spurned him.

The closest Ghafur came to leading his fellow merchants was when he rallied them to demand that the Mughal government win compensation from the East India Company and the VOC for the depredations of European pirates. Most of the offenders were English who had been driven out of the Caribbean. Many had taken refuge on the island of Madagascar, from where they could attack shipping around the Indian Ocean, especially in the lucrative trades of the Arabian Sea. The first attack on Surat ships in the Red Sea, in 1686, led to mutual reprisals between the Mughals and English before the two sides came to terms. Piracy intensified in the 1690s, among the worst offenders being Henry Avery (possibly one of several aliases). In February 1695 he left a proclamation in the Comoros—a customary port of call for English ships—

announcing his intention to seize any ship not flying the English flag. This infuriated East India Company officials, who had long been at pains to assure other traders that not all English were pirates, and that not all pirates were English. It was an understandable assumption; while Avery's two ships lay in wait for pilgrim ships returning from the Red Sea, they were in company with five vessels from English colonies in North America. Avery seized a ship belonging to Ghafur with a cargo of silver valued at £50,000–60,000, as well as the largest of the Mughal ships, the cargo of which was valued at half a million rials. Many of his crew eventually returned to the Americas and England, but the authorities never caught up with Avery.

The only state in the western Indian Ocean to offer sustained resistance to a European power on the high seas in the seventeenth and eighteenth centuries was Oman. For most of the 1500s, the Portuguese had held undisputed sway over Muscat, Suhar, and Hormuz. Concerted opposition began at the end of the century when Omanis took Suhar, but the Portuguese were not thrown on the defensive until the early 1620s when the Omanis expelled them and the Persian Safavids took Hormuz with English help. The Omani reconquest of the coast began in earnest with the rise of the Yarubid imamate in 1625. Diverted by their contests with the English and Dutch in India, Portuguese authority in the Persian Gulf region steadily eroded until Sultan ibn Saif I expelled them from Muscat a quarter century later.

Between 1652 and 1665, the Omanis took the fight to the Portuguese in India and in East Africa, where they captured the port of Mombasa. The Omani fleet consisted of captured Portuguese ships and purchases from the English and the Dutch, who willingly accommodated anyone undermining European rivals. From the early years of the *Estado da India*, a majority of the crews on European ships in the Indian Ocean were non-Europeans, so manning their fleet was not a challenge for the Omanis, although they also employed Europeans. The Portuguese regained the upper hand in the 1660s, but the Omanis remained active antagonists into the next century. As the scope of Omani influence widened—the East African island of Zanzibar was ruled by Oman from 1698 to 1890—the imam's ability to control his subjects diminished, and in the eighteenth century the Omanis became known for outright piracy against Europeans, Persians, Indians, and Arabs.

Europeans in South America and the Caribbean

The Dutch effort to undermine Portugal's monopolistic claims in Asia had a parallel in their infiltration of Spanish and Portuguese America, especially the underdeveloped islands of the Caribbean and the Wild Coast of South America, between the Orinoco and Amazon deltas—Guyana, Suriname, and French Guiana. In defiance of Philip III's embargo of 1598, more than a hundred Dutch ships annually sailed to the salt lagoons of Venezuela, which provided a springboard for further ventures in the Caribbean, Guiana, and Brazil. Spanish authorities ruthlessly executed unauthorized traders, destroyed crops, and forcibly relocated settlements away from the coasts to remove any incentive or potential source of supply for interlopers. But the Dutch ignored these penalties and became major carriers of sugar from Brazil (where they often sailed under the Portuguese flag) and Venezuelan salt and tobacco. Just as independent merchants trading in Asia came together as the VOC, in 1621 the Geoctroyeerde Westindische Compagnie (Chartered West India Company, or WIC) amalgamated competing interests in the Netherlands and three years later its fleet captured Bahia, Brazil. A Spanish force retook the city, but in 1626 Piet Heyn sank twenty-six Iberian ships, "by which happy result [the WIC]—by so many preceding disasters and damages so much weakened—began to recover her breath and bounded back on her feet." Heyn returned to the northern Caribbean, and in early September 1628 his thirty-one ships chased the Spanish *flota* under Don Juan de Benavides into the Bay of Matanzas, fifty miles east of Havana. The Dutch looted the twenty-two ships of forty-six tons of silver, gold, and merchandise valued at more than eleven million guilders, a net profit of some seven million guilders for the WIC. Imprisoned in Spain, Benavides was tried and executed "for his lack of care in the loss of the New Spain fleet." That Heyn predeceased him in action against the armada of Flanders was probably small consolation.

Although the Dutch occupied coastal Brazil only from 1630 to 1654, the consequences were significant. Introduced from Madeira, sugar was more valuable to Portugal than its Asian trade, and the profits now accrued to the Dutch. Failing to attract sufficient numbers of Dutch and German settlers to work the land, the West India Company began importing slaves—twenty-four thousand by 1654, and another hundred thousand in the next seventy-five years—not only for themselves but for the new colonies that had been planted in the Caribbean since the 1620s, English on St. Christopher (St. Kitts), Nevis, Antigua, Montserrat, and the previously uninhabited Barbados; French also on St. Christopher, as well as Martinique, Guadeloupe, and St. Barthélemy. The first settlers' cultivation of diverse crops for subsistence and trade soon gave way to a plantation-based sugar monoculture worked by slaves. Ousted from Brazil, the Dutch settled six islands in the Lesser Antilles. Of these, Curaçao, off the coast of Venezuela, would become one of the busiest—and most corrupt—trading centers in the Caribbean.

Even as the Dutch were being forced out of Brazil, England's Oliver Cromwell was endorsing an ambitious plan to sweep the Spanish from the Caribbean. The Spanish repulsed two assaults on Santo Domingo in early 1655, but rather than return with nothing to show for their efforts, General Robert Venables and Admiral William Penn pressed on to Santiago de la Vela in Kingston Harbor, Jamaica. Significantly outnumbered in a place of almost no consequence, the Spanish formally ceded Jamaica to England. The renamed Port Royal became the fastest-growing English settlement in the Americas, rivaling Boston in size (about six thousand people) though with a vastly more diverse population of Europeans, Africans, and Native Americans. A major redistribution center for slaves and goods, for about two decades Port Royal was also the undisputed center of English piracy in the Caribbean, much of it endorsed by colonial governors eager for a share of the takings and heedless of the consequences for Anglo-Spanish diplomacy.

On June 7, 1692, a massive earthquake submerged two-thirds of the town and killed an estimated five thousand people. Even before this, increasingly vested as they were in the fruits of legitimate trade, European governments, supported by the growing class of Caribbean plantation owners, had begun to clamp down on piracy. The Treaty of Madrid (1670) between England and Spain outlawed privateering: "No private offense shall in any way weaken this friendship and alliance, nor stir up ill-will or dissensions . . . not by reprisals or other such odious proceedings shall one man compensate for the transgression of another, unless justice be denied or unjustly delayed." An English law of 1677 made it a felony for a ship to sail under a flag not its own, and Parliament passed An Act for the Restraining and Punishing of Privateers and Pirates in 1683. The Anglo-French Treaty of Whitehall (1686) similarly outlawed privateering, and the Treaty of Ryswyck (1697) rendered letters of marque and reprisal null and void. It was against this background of law and order that more enterprising pirates like Henry Avery began turning to the low-lying fruit of the Indian Ocean and the Pacific coast of Spanish America. North America, though closer, held little interest for most self-respecting outlaws.

The Scramble for North America

The French and English had tested Spanish claims in North America in the sixteenth century, but there was little incentive for governments or others to underwrite more than the occasional exploratory expedition. The real trailblazers on the North Atlantic were fishermen, for the simple reason that so far as anyone knew the only reason to sail for North America was to fish.

The first documented crossing of the North Atlantic other than by Scandinavian Vikings was by John Cabot in 1497. A Venetian veteran of the Mediterranean spice trade, Cabot sought sponsors for his undertaking within a few years of Columbus's first voyage. Rebuffed by Spain and Portugal, he turned to England's Henry VII, who granted him letters patent "to seeke out, discover, and finde, whatsoever iles, countreyes, regions or provinces of the heathen and infidelis, whatsoever they bee, and in what part of the world soever they be, whiche before this time have beene unbeknowen to all Christians." Cabot sailed from Bristol, then one of England's premier ports. His course is unknown, but one theory holds that his *navicula* (little ship) *Mathew* sailed due west from Ireland to a landfall in northern Newfoundland. From there he turned south and followed the coast possibly as far as Placentia Bay. Cabot returned to Bristol the same summer with no trade goods, but Henry VII granted him additional patents and he sailed the next year with five ships. One put back to Bristol; the other four disappeared without trace.

Though Cabot left little to show for his efforts, reports of rich fishing grounds spread quickly among the fishermen of Bristol, who already were sailing at least as far as Iceland and who would play a leading role in the development of Europe's North American colonies for at least a century. According to a dispatch filed by Milan's ambassador to England shortly after Cabot's return in 1497, his crew claimed

> that the sea is covered with fish which are caught not merely with nets but with baskets, a stone being attached to make the basket sink in the water, and this I heard the said Master [Cabot] relate. And said Englishmen, his companions, say that they will fetch so many fish that this kingdom will have no more need of Iceland, from which country there comes a very great store of fish.

The attraction of the long-distance fisheries was due to the importance of fish in the European diet. Dried, salted, or pickled fish was a less expensive source of protein than meat, and Church prohibitions against eating meat on fast days—including Fridays and during Lent—increased demand across Christian Europe. The most important food fish in northern Europe was herring (also called pilchards or sardines), which by the eleventh century were being netted in enormous quantities in the Baltic and North Seas. Because of their high oil content, herring spoil quickly unless they are brined or pickled in a salt solution; in optimal conditions they can be kept in pickling barrels for up to ten months. The Hanse's monopolistic control coupled with a partial collapse of the herring fishery in the early fourteenth century drove English fishermen to seek cod around Iceland. Large, cold-water bottom feeders, cod were traditionally caught by jigging with a hook and line. Although more labor intensive to fish, a good-sized cod weighs about thirty kilograms and they can grow to three times that. Unlike herring, cod have almost no fat and in a dry, cool climate can be air-dried without salt, which made them an ideal food source in northern latitudes where the weather is favorable and salt relatively scarce.

Exploitation of the North American fisheries from the sixteenth century was by no means limited to the English. In 1500, the brothers Gaspar and Miguel Corte-Real sailed from Lisbon to Greenland, Labrador, and Newfoundland, and they reached Nova Scotia on a second voyage. Unnamed fishermen from Portugal, France, and England also made their way west, and a report of 1527 noted fourteen fishing ships at St. John's, Newfoundland, from Brittany, Normandy, and Portugal, and it was against this backdrop that Francis I sponsored Cartier's voyages of the 1530s and 1540s. The tensions that arose from such crowding led to a steady search for new fishing grounds that drew Europeans westward from the Grand Banks south of Newfoundland to Nova Scotia and the Gulf of Maine. By the early 1600s, there were an estimated four hundred fishing vessels of various nationalities on the coast of northern New England.

Sailing for a French royal monopoly, in 1605 Samuel de Champlain established a colony at Port Royal (now Annapolis Royal, Nova Scotia), from which he led the settlement of the St. Lawrence River valley, where the land was fertile, the Gulf of St. Lawrence fishing grounds were accessible, and the potential for fur trading was apparently limitless. New France was plagued by a chronic lack of settlers, partly due to the climate and scarce opportunities but also because the Company of New France charter (1627) prohibited Huguenots, who were persecuted at home, from sailing to Canada. As a result, it took half a century for the population to reach ten thousand. New France also failed to secure the fur trade of Hudson Bay, which Pierre-Esprit Radisson and Médard des Groseilliers were the first Europeans to exploit directly. Finding their own government unresponsive, the brothers-in-law appealed to England's Charles II, who chartered the Hudson's Bay Company with rights to the watershed of Hudson Bay—an area of nearly four million square kilometers comprising parts of Quebec, Ontario, Nunavut, and Alberta, and all of Manitoba.

Perhaps chastened by this reverse, the French turned their sights to the south. In 1679, René-Robert Cavalier, Sieur de La Salle, determined to find a water route to Asia through the middle of the continent. Having sailed in the first ship built on the Great Lakes to Green Bay, on Lake Michigan, La Salle, the Jesuit diarist Father Louis Hennepin, and a few others proceeded down the Illinois and Mississippi Rivers. Reaching the delta in 1682, La Salle claimed for France "the land of Louisiana, near the three mouths of the Colbert [Mississippi] river, in the Gulf of Mexico." Jean-Baptiste Le Moyne, Sieur de Bienville, founded Biloxi, Mississippi, and Mobile, Alabama, before moving the capital of the Louisiana territory to New Orleans, about ninety miles up the Mississippi from the gulf. Trade between the new port and the Illinois territory was arduous. Initially the French depended on native craft like birch-bark canoes, dugouts, and buffalo-hide skin boats known as "bullboats," but they soon developed *bateaux plats*, flatboats with a tapered bow and stern, and *radeaux*, flatboats with squared ends, propelled by paddling, rowing, poling (when the river was low), and towing. A northbound flatboat took three or four months to go the twelve hundred miles from New Orleans to Illinois, depending on the size of the crew; a vessel of forty to fifty tons generally required about two dozen men. Downstream the same distance could be covered in two or three weeks. These passage times remained the norm until the steam age in the nineteenth century.

Transportation between the watersheds of the upper Mississippi and the St. Lawrence was relatively easy, and France's North American colonies could be reached by way of either Montreal or New Orleans. Unfortunately, these two access points were three thousand miles apart. Between them lay Spanish Florida and England's rapidly growing North American colonies. The English view of the function of overseas colonies differed markedly from that of the French. Far from prohibiting the departure of undesirables, the English encouraged the migration of religious dissidents, the poor, malcontents, and criminals. Speculating on the opportunities afforded by the colonies in 1576, Sir Humphrey Gilbert wrote that "Also we might inhabite some parte of those Countreys, and settle there suche needie people of our Countrie, which now trouble the common welth, and through want here at home, are inforced to commit outragious offences, whereby they are dayly consumed with the Gallowes." In short North America would make an excellent penal colony.

Gilbert's half brother Sir Walter Raleigh made two attempts to establish colonies in North Carolina, but both failed. Twenty years later, in 1607, the Virginia Company sent two groups of colonists west. One wintered on the Kennebec River in Maine but abandoned their settlement because there were "no mynes discouered, nor hope thereof" and for "feare that all other winters would proue like this first." A few months earlier, three ships of colonists had founded the first permanent English settlement in North America, at Jamestown on the James River above Chesapeake Bay. The colony's early years were plagued by disorganization and disease as the dismal Chesapeake climate devoured settlers faster than they could be landed. Between 1618 and 1622, more than thirty-five hundred colonists reached Jamestown, but in the latter year the population was barely half that. Jamestown's survival was due only to the desperate persistence of the company's investors and the willingness of young men (mostly) to indent themselves in exchange for such opportunities as America might afford. The first slaves were landed in 1619 by an English ship that had seized them from a Portuguese slaver. Virginia's population finally began to grow in the 1620s, and the settlers developed a brisk coastal trade with Dutch Nieuw Amsterdam, and English Plymouth and Boston.

The most immediately promising exploration of what is now the northeastern United States was that of Henry Hudson, an Englishman whom the VOC contracted to search for a Northeast Passage to the Orient in 1609. An amendment to his contract enjoined Hudson "To think of discovering no other route or passage, except the route around the north or northeast, above Nova Zembla." But two weeks after entering the Barents Sea—named for Willem Barentsz, a Dutch explorer who had sailed there in search of a Northeast Passage in the 1590s—in May 1609, Hudson put about and sailed west across the Atlantic. After coasting between Maine and the Chesapeake, he entered New York Harbor and sailed 125 miles up the river that bears his name to what is now Albany. En route back to the Netherlands, Hudson landed at Dartmouth, England, leading some to speculate that he was in English pay. (His next and last expedition, in search of a North*west* Passage, was in an English ship. After a bitter winter in Hudson Bay, his rebellious crew set him and eight shipmates adrift in the ship's boat; they were never seen again.) Reports of Hudson's voyage spurred the Dutch to establish trading posts along the Hudson at Albany (1614) and on Manhattan Island, which became the colony of Nieuw Amsterdam (1624).

The English never lost interest in northern Virginia, as they called it, especially after John Smith published *A Description of New England* (1614) to entice prospective settlers. "And of all the foure parts of the world that I haue yet seene not inhabited," wrote the veteran of European wars, Mediterranean trade, enslavement in Turkey, and Jamestown, "could I have but meanes to transport a Colonie, I would rather liue here then any where." This was one of several English works extolling the virtues of transatlantic settlement and it became a key reference for the Separatists, or Pilgrims, New England's first permanent English colonists, who settled on Massachusetts Bay at Plymouth. The Pilgrims' lone ship, the *Mayflower,* sailed from Plymouth, England, with 102 men, women, and children on a passage that was uneventful by the standards of the time. In almost ten weeks at sea, a child was born and only one of their number died. But once ashore they were inadequately prepared for the brutal winter, which killed half of them. Their prospects would have been worse were it not for the intervention of Tisquantum (or Squanto), whose résumé offers a New World perspective on the intensifying transatlantic links of the early seventeenth century. Captured by English explorers in 1614, Tisquantum was taken to Spain from which he escaped to England. He sailed on a voyage to Newfoundland and in 1619 made his way back to Cape Cod, only to find that disease had wiped out his village. This was a northern version of the pathogenic ravages that afflicted the native populations of Spanish America, and it created a wilderness along the coast that English colonists eagerly exploited. Tisquantum was kept under guard by the leader of a neighboring tribe who sent him to live with the Pilgrims because he spoke English. Even with his help, a decade on the Plymouth Colony had only about three hundred inhabitants.

Privation and hardships notwithstanding, the early North American settlements attracted immigrants from England, France, the Netherlands, and Sweden. Puritan Boston was founded in 1629, and twenty-three thousand people reached New England before the English Civil War (1642–46) ended the first wave of settlement. Although this is referred to as the Great Migration, over the course of the century New England attracted fewer immigrants than the Chesapeake and vastly more people migrated to the Caribbean islands than to all of mainland North America. Yet New England's population grew steadily thanks to natural increase and an astonishing safety record. In the 1630s, none of the 198 ships that made the ten-and-a-half-week crossing was lost at sea. The Puritans attributed their good fortune to divine providence, but it probably owed more to a sense of shared purpose and deliberate organization, and the relatively low incidence of the sorts of disease that plagued the majority of transatlantic immigrants afloat and ashore, especially in the tropics. New England colonists tended to travel as families, shared strong religious bonds, and worked for themselves rather than as indentured servants for exploitive masters.

The founders of Massachusetts sought to create a Calvinist sanctuary for landed gentry and their servants, but New England's rocky soil forced them to take to the sea as fishermen and traders. The disruptions caused by the English Civil War "set our people on work to provide fish, clapboards, plank, etc., and to sow hemp and flax . . . and to look out to the West Indies for a trade," exporting wood and fish to the Caribbean sugar plantations. Bostonians captured a considerable share of the intercolonial and transatlantic trades. To England itself, North America supplied naval stores and shipbuilding timber. Although wood was plentiful in England, the cost of transporting it to the coast was prohibitive, and England's access to naval stores from the Baltic was at the mercy of European politics. A late-sixteenth-century treatise "containing important inducements" for settlement in North America stressed that "It may also be a matter of great consequence for the good and securitie of England; that out of these Northerly regions we shall be able to furnish this realme of all manner of prouisions for our nauies; namely, Pitch, Rosen, Cables, Ropes, Masts and such like." A cargo of masts reached England in the 1630s, but the trade got its real start during the First Anglo-Dutch War, when the Danes, who were allied with the Dutch, closed the Baltic to English shipping.

The importance of New England masts, the tallest of which measured thirty-five meters, has been likened to that of oil today, an apt comparison as is suggested in the relieved diary entry of naval administrator Samuel Pepys during the Second Anglo-Dutch War:

> There is also the very good news come, of seven New-England ships come home safe to Falmouth with masts for the King; which is a blessing mighty unexpected, and without which (if for nothing else) we must have failed the next year. But God be praised for thus much good fortune, and send us the continuance of his favour in other things. So to bed.

New England was not the only source of naval stores, but for most of the seventeenth century, southern oak, pine, pitch, and tar from the Carolinas were invariably carried by New Englanders.

New merchant centers arose after the Restoration. Located at the junction of the Ashley and Cooper Rivers, Charleston, South Carolina, was established in 1670 and attracted settlers from the northern colonies as well as Scotch-Irish Presbyterians, German Lutherans, and, especially during the 1680s, French Huguenots fleeing the persecution unleashed by Louis XIV. Shortly thereafter, the Carolinas became a place of refuge for Caribbean pirates and buccaneers whom the great powers had run out of the Caribbean. Charleston was the most important city in British North America south of Philadelphia, which William Penn (whose father had taken Jamaica) founded in 1691 on a spit of land between the Delaware and Schuylkill Rivers. The Quaker proprietor of Pennsylvania welcomed the thousand Scandinavian and Dutch immigrants who had settled around the mouth of the Delaware River over the previous forty years, as well as German Mennonites and other immigrants. Within five years the population of Pennsylvania stood at five thousand.[*] Though its merchant fleet was somewhat smaller than those of either Boston or New York, Philadelphia rivaled—if it did not exceed—those cities thanks to its promise of religious tolerance, its agricultural productivity and manufacturing, and its more central location on the colonial seaboard.

European Navies

The lack of more hands-on involvement in the Americas by European governments was not entirely due to apathy about the fate of their colonies. They lacked the wherewithal to exercise their will across the ocean. In spite of care-

---

[*] Swedish colonists settled New Sweden (Wilmington, Delaware) between 1637 and 1655.

ful attention to the minutiae of administration and vast expenditures on ships, weaponry, and ports, European navies rarely operated far from home, and almost never beyond European waters; until the eighteenth century, most battles were identified by a coastal place name, within a day's sail of where the engagement took place. The exceptions were the Spanish, whose ships escorted the treasure fleets to and from the Americas, and the Portuguese, who maintained units in Brazilian and Asian waters. Armed merchantmen of the Dutch East India and West India Companies also sailed overseas, but these were not naval squadrons operating on state business. More than half a century of warfare among the maritime states of Atlantic Europe had forced them all to adopt more sophisticated approaches to naval affairs, but long-distance operations were few.

For the first two decades of the seventeenth century, there was little for navies to do. Spain concluded a peace with England's James I in 1604 and hammered out a truce with the Dutch five years later. This period of relative peace was interrupted by the Thirty Years' War, which began as a contest between the Holy Roman Emperor and the Protestant king of Bohemia in 1618, and three years later by the renewal of hostilities between Spain and the Dutch Republic. The resumption of war signaled the start of a European naval competition that would continue almost unchecked in peace and war into the twentieth century. Although the Thirty Years' War and the Dutch rebellion were distinct conflicts, Philip IV's chief minister, Count-Duke Olivares, sought to link them, chiefly to wrest Spain's Baltic trade back from the Dutch. Maintaining access to the region's naval stores and grain was crucial to the Spanish war effort generally, while usurping the trade was intended to deny its profits to the Dutch.

In Olivares's calculation, a united front of Habsburg Spain and Austria, and Poland-Lithuania (an enemy of Sweden, which backed the Dutch), would envelop France, which though Catholic had allied with the Dutch Republic. Olivares was encouraged by the success of Spain's armada of Flanders, which in 1621 included a dozen frigates stationed at Dunkirk and could call upon privateers who preyed on French, Dutch, and English shipping. Developed by shipwrights in the Spanish Netherlands, these frigates were relatively small and fast three-masted warships ideally suited to commerce raiding, convoy protection, and scouting. The Spanish navy achieved an impressive record in the first half of the decade and in 1625 Philip IV wrote the governor of the Spanish Netherlands "from now on the land-war will be reduced to the purely defensive. . . . In Mardyck [by Dunkirk], we will build up a fleet of fifty warships." This proved impossible, but royal frigates and privateers sank scores of Dutch fishing vessels and their escorts as far afield as the Shetlands and

Iceland. On the administrative side, in 1623 the Spanish created the Admiralty of the North to control trade between Spain and Flanders; forced neutral ships into Dunkirk to be inspected for contraband; and imposed a host of sweeping protectionist measures, including charging duties of 40 percent on French trade with Spain. (Spaniards trading in France paid 2.5 percent.) In the end, however, Olivares had to abandon his Baltic ambitions to focus on hostilities with France and the fallout from Piet Heyn's capture of the silver fleet in Cuba.

Olivares's French counterpart and rival, Cardinal Richelieu, chief minister to Louis XIII, was likewise concerned about Dutch and English dominance of the French carrying trades, as well as Muslim and Christian corsairs in the Mediterranean, Spain's great and growing naval ambition, and the naval threat posed by the Huguenot rebels of La Rochelle, one of the country's most flourishing ports. These problems came to the fore with the renewal of hostilities between Spain and the Netherlands—which threatened French commerce even as it offered French merchants the opportunity to capitalize on the Spanish embargo on Dutch shipping—and the threat of a naval war with the Huguenots and England. In 1621, the Huguenots established their own admiralty and over the next four years attacked a number of French ports. Hoping to diminish English support for the Huguenots, Louis XIII arranged the marriage of his daughter Henriette Marie to Charles I. Yet the English feared the prospect of a French naval revival, and despite the personal alliance of Stuarts and Bourbons they occupied the Ile de Ré off La Rochelle in 1627. The French repelled them and though they returned the following year, their appearance was inconsequential and La Rochelle fell after a fourteen-month siege that effectively ended the French Wars of Religion.

Huguenot resistance was facilitated by the fact that although reforms had been under way since the sixteenth century, France had no national navy. Rather, the grand admiral of France had authority in Picardy and Normandy on the English Channel and Poitou and Saintonge on the Bay of Biscay; but Brittany, Provence, and Guyenne each had its own navy and distinct approaches to maritime law. This made it impossible for the French crown to raise revenues adequate for the creation of a state fleet or even to move fleets between provinces. A year before the siege of La Rochelle, Richelieu abolished the office of the grand admiral of France and called for the construction of a navy virtually from scratch: forty warships, thirty galleys, and ten galleons, "true citadels of the sea." He also attempted to improve French seaports for the benefit of the navy, but his efforts were thwarted by nature, indifference, and outright opposition. Nonetheless, the navy was ready when France formally allied with the Dutch against Spain in 1635, and at the battle of Guetaría in the Bay of Biscay the next year divested the Spanish of seventeen galleys and ships, and four thousand sailors.

Peter Pett and the *Sovereign of the Seas*, by Sir Peter Lely, circa 1645–50. Pett holds *a pair of dividers, symbols of his expertise as a ship designer and builder. At left is a stern view of his heavily decorated* Sovereign of the Seas *(1637). Like the Hellenistic super-galleys of antiquity, the* Sovereign of the Seas *was intended partly "to make appearance for display." Such pretension is a nearly universal tendency. An early Chinese work recommended ships so large that they were unmanageable in bad weather—"But the fleet cannot fail to be furnished with such ships, in order that its overawing might may be perfected." Courtesy of the National Maritime Museum, Greenwich, England.*

Richelieu was certainly justified in complaining of "the ignominy of seeing our king, the foremost of Christian rulers, weaker than the pettiest princes of Christendom in terms of naval power." Yet many English were equally contemptuous of the Navy Royal. "Such a rotten, miserable fleet, set out to sea, no man ever saw," wrote one contemporary. "Our enemies seeing it may scoff at our nation." Eager to restore the navy's prestige, which had fallen since the days of Elizabeth and Drake, Charles I determined to reassert England's ancient if fanciful title to the waters around the British Isles by building a navy equal to the claim and securing publication, at long last, of John Selden's *Of the Dominion; or, Ownership of the Sea*. Having dissolved Parliament in 1629, Charles raised money for the fleet not through direct taxation payable to the Exchequer, the prerogative of Parliament, but by issuing writs for "ship money" payable to the navy in kind or cash. This scheme generated more than £800,000 over six years and, money in hand, Charles informed the shipbuilder Phineas Pett of "his princely resolution for the building of a great new ship." Critics warned that "the art or wit of man cannot build a ship fit for service with three tier of ordnance," but they dissuaded neither Charles nor Pett's son, Peter, who built the ship. Built at a cost of £65,586—the equivalent of about ten 40-gun ships—as her name advertised, the *Sovereign of the Seas* was as much an instrument of propaganda as of war. In a pamphlet otherwise devoted to interpreting the "Decorements whiche beautify and adorne her . . . the carving worke, the figures, and mottoes upon them," playwright and essayist Thomas Heywood managed a brief account of the ship's armament:

> She hath three flush Deckes, and a Fore-Castle, an halfe Decke, a quarter Decke, and a round-house. Her lower Tyre [tier] hath thirty ports, which are to be furnished with Demy-Cannon [firing thirty-pound shot] and whole Cannon through out, (being able to beare them). Her middle Tyre hath also thirty ports for Demi-Culverin [ten-pounders], and whole Culverin: Her third Tyre hath Twentie sixe Ports for other Ordnance, her fore-Castle hath twelve ports, and her halfe Decke hath foureteene ports. . . . She carrieth moreover ten peeces of chase Ordnance in her, right forward; and ten right aff.

Heywood further notes that Charles's responsibility for national honor and security "should bee a great spur and incouragement to all his faithful and loving Subjects to bee liberall and willing Contributaries towards the Ship-money." In fact, the attention Charles lavished on his naval program was much resented by his faithful and loving subjects, and in the *Sovereign of the Seas* can be seen some of the excess and arrogance that contributed to his eventual overthrow.

Such ostentation might have been tolerated had the fleet proved equal to policing English coastal waters, but during a more than monthlong standoff between a Spanish fleet under Antonio de Oquendo and the Dutch admiral Maarten Harpertszoon Tromp in 1639 it proved completely ineffective. The year before, Olivares noted that Spain had won eighty-two victories at sea in seventeen years. But the tide was turning. The destruction of the squadron at Guetaria took place the same year and the following spring Dutch ships had captured seven hundred soldiers being convoyed to Flanders. In September, Oquendo was sent north with more troops, but harried by Tromp, he anchored in the Downs north of Dover. This was obviously England's territorial waters, but the English fleet was powerless to enforce a peace and after a long standoff, on October 21 the Dutch took or sank thirty-two Spanish warships and transports. Dunkirk privateers had ferried five thousand of the soldiers to Flanders and Oquendo himself managed to reach Dunkirk and return to Spain, but the battle of the Downs was a blow both to Spain and to Charles's claim to sovereignty of the seas.

As important, it signaled the definitive arrival of the Dutch Republic in the top rank of European naval powers, one whose management was a cross between that of the French and the English. The Dutch navy, the organization of which remained essentially unchanged from 1597 to 1785, included five admiralties in the maritime provinces of Friesland, Holland, and Zeeland. The fleets were paid for by taxes on merchants collected by the admiralties, and supplemented in wartime by extraordinary revenues voted by the States-General. Each admiralty was responsible for levying its own crews, maintaining and building its own ships and warehouses, and organizing convoys, and they could issue privateers' commissions and adjudicate prizes and other matters of maritime law. This organization worked well against the Spanish and English fleets of the seventeenth century, but was outmoded in the subsequent age of highly centralized state violence calling for ever larger and more heavily gunned ships.

The Dutch at War, 1652–80

Three years after the humiliation of the Downs, Charles's increasingly contentious relations with Parliament and Puritan leaders erupted into civil war. Defeated by Oliver Cromwell, Charles was tried for treason and executed. The substitution of the Commonwealth (1649–60) for the monarchy did little to alter the direction of English foreign policy, however, and in 1651 Parliament passed the Navigation Act. Under this protectionist legislation, the first of several such measures that came into force over the next two centuries, goods could be imported into England and its overseas territories "only in such [ships] as do truly and without fraud belong only to the people of this Commonwealth, or the plantations thereof . . . and whereof the master and mariners are also for the most part . . . people of this Commonwealth." The only exception was for ships carrying the trade of their own country. So, for instance, a French ship could carry French wine to England or New England, but it could not carry New England wood to England. The law's intent was to bolster English shipping and to undercut the Dutch. The government further insisted that all ships, foreign and domestic, dip their flags to English warships as a mark of respect for England and its navy. In a reprise of Charles's showboating, Cromwell authorized the construction of three "great ships," including the eighty-gun *Naseby*. Nicknamed the "Great Oliver," *Naseby*'s original adornments included: "In the *Prow* . . . Oliver on horseback trampling 6 nations under foote, a *Scott, Irishman, Dutch, French, Spaniard* & English as was easily made out by their several habits: A *Fame* held a laurell over his insulting head, & the word *God with us*."

On May 8, 1652, Tromp's fleet was protecting Dutch convoys when it sought shelter in the Downs—the site of his triumph over Oquendo thirteen years before. Ordered to leave, Tromp sailed for France, but was followed by the English, whom he engaged in what became known as the battle of Dover (or the Downs), the casus belli for the English declaration of war, the most decisive engagement of which came at the battle of the Gabbard Shoal (also known as North Foreland and Nieupoort) on June 2–3. Each fleet had more than a hundred ships, although the English vessels were generally larger and much of the Dutch fleet comprised hired or converted merchantmen.

The two-day battle is significant as one of the first fought between two fleets drawn up in line of battle, the classic formation that endured into the twentieth century. By this time, the ships of the major navies mounted their heaviest guns amidships rather than forward or aft. Once it was determined that ships could be maneuvered to bring a heavy concentration of broadside fire on a specific part of the enemy fleet, the line of battle became the tactic of choice for fleet engagements. The preferred maneuver was "crossing the T," so that one's broadsides raked the enemy ships from stem to stern while the enemy could respond with only a handful of guns mounted in the bows. The Dutch lost nineteen ships at the Gabbard, and the English blockaded the Dutch coast. Two months later, Tromp was killed at the battle of Scheveningen (or Texel, within sight of The Hague) but both fleets suffered heavily in what proved to be the last major engagement of the war.

Anglo-Dutch commercial rivalry reemerged in the early 1660s, when the English began raiding Dutch settlements in West Africa under the guise of protecting slave traders of the newly chartered Royal African Company. In retaliation, Michiel De Ruyter, whom James, Duke of York, would later call "the greatest [admiral] that ever to that time was in the world," sailed to Africa, where he retook all but one of the captured outposts before crossing the Atlantic to raid English Caribbean islands and returning home via the Newfoundland fishing grounds. When war officially began in January 1665, the two fleets were roughly comparable in numbers, but the English ships tended to be larger, their guns heavier, and their fleet better organized. In the Four Days' Battle of June 1666 English losses were double those of the Dutch, but the English prevented a junction of De Ruyter with the French, who had declared war on England. Hastening to sea again, the English bested the Dutch in the St. James's Day battle off North Foreland and went on to burn 160 merchant ships off the island of Vlieland.

The costs of the war, the Great Plague of 1665, and the London fire of September 1666 exhausted the English treasury and forced Charles II to order the fleet laid up and to open talks with the Dutch in 1667. While these were under way, De Ruyter crossed to England and in the most bold and daring action of the wars sailed up the Medway to the Chatham dockyard and relieved the English of twenty-three ships. Orders had been given to burn the *Royal Charles* (the old *Naseby*) to prevent her capture, but as Pepys relates, "the Dutch did take her with a boat of nine Men, who found not a man on board her. . . . They did carry her down at a time, both for tides and wind, when the best pilot in Chatham would not have undertaken it, they heeling her on one side to make her draw little water; and so carried her away safe." Incompatible with Dutch needs, the English flagship was displayed as a trophy at Rotterdam, and her counter decoration is still on display at the Rijksmuseum in Amsterdam.

The peace of Breda confirmed the Dutch possession of what is now Suriname and the diminutive Banda island of Pulo Run, while the English acquired title to the North American colony of Nieuw Amsterdam. Early in the war Charles had written his sister that this was "A very good town, but we have got the better of it and 'tis now called New York"—in honor of his brother, the Duke of York, later James II. The acquisition of New York removed an adversary from the middle of the English North American colonies, but the spices of the Banda Islands were vastly more valuable at the time, and the financial power of the Dutch Republic remained the envy of all Europe. "In this city of Amsterdam," wrote Sir William Temple shortly after the Second Anglo-Dutch War, "is the famous Bank, which is the greatest Treasure either real or imaginary, that is known any where in the World. [The] security of the Bank lies not only in the effects that are in it, but in the Credit of the whole Town or State of Amsterdam, whose Stock and Revenue is equal to that of some Kingdoms."

Early in the war the prospect of conquering the Spanish Netherlands had led France to side with the Dutch, but their relations deteriorated when the French doubled customs tariffs on Dutch imports. This was one of many mercantilist initiatives implemented by Jean-Baptiste Colbert, Louis XIV's minister of finance from 1665, and of the navy from 1669, until 1683. Others included subsidizing French industry, luring foreign manufacturers to France, establishing or bolstering overseas colonies, and building up the French merchant marine and navy, which had fared poorly since the modest improvements of Richelieu's day. Colbert also embarked on an ambitious program of internal improvements: repairing roads, digging canals, abolishing or consolidating the kingdom's innumerable internal river and road tolls, and managing the forests with a view to ensuring supplies of ship timber.

Although the English and Dutch people would have preferred peace, Louis XIV subsidized Charles II to gain his help against the Dutch Republic. With war imminent, the Dutch had seventy-five ships of the line against which the French could field only twenty-two; the English contributed another sixty-five. Nevertheless, De Ruyter held the upper hand over the allies throughout 1672 and 1673. Tired of war with the Dutch and their alliance with the French, the English concluded a peace with the Dutch Republic, thus leaving the French to face the combined naval power of the Dutch and its ally, Spain. Focus of the conflict switched to the Mediterranean where the French defeated the Spanish and Dutch fleets and killed De Ruyter in the process, in 1676. The Franco-Dutch War dragged on for two more years by which time the share of European trade carried by the merchants of neutral England had grown considerably.

The ensuing peace did not lead to disarmament, and the expansion of the English and French navies mirrored the growth of their merchant fleets and foreign trade. Between 1661 and Colbert's death in 1683, the French navy grew from 18 warships and a handful of auxiliary units to 276 warships, while England's Navy Royal had 173 warships. Such increases would not have been possible without a concomitant improvement in fleet administration, which became more bureaucratized and systematic. This is most evident in Pepys's establishment of a standard system for rating warships on the basis of the number and size of guns carried, "the final administrative recognition that the age of the line of battle had arrived." This establishment determined officers' pay, overall manning requirements (a fixed number of men being required for each gun), and provisioning. Small changes were made from time to time, but the rating system was remarkably static. In 1779 the establishment was:

Rate	Guns	Men
First	100–120	850–875
Second	90–98	700–750
Third	64–80	500–650
Fourth	50–60	320–420
Fifth	32–44	200–300
Sixth	20–28	140–200

A warship of sixty guns and above was considered fit to lie in the battle line and referred to simply as a line-of-battle ship (later battleship) or ship of the line. First-rates had three full gun decks, but the backbone of the battle fleet was the two-decker of sixty to ninety guns. In the age of sail, the standard ship's gun fired an iron ball. The largest caliber was nearly seven inches and weighed forty-two pounds. A first-rate ship like Lord Nelson's HMS *Victory*, launched in 1765, carried thirty 32-pounders, twenty-eight 24-pounders, forty-four 12-pounders, and two carronades. Developed at the Carron iron works in Scotland in the 1770s and known as ship smashers or devil guns, carronades fired sixty-eight-pound shot at a range of no more than 375 meters, a quarter that of ordinary guns. They were designed specifically to cause as much damage as possible to the hull and crew, who were killed or severely wounded by the massive splinters created on impact. (Sepsis from resulting infections was a leading cause of death.) Gunners also devised a variety of specialty ammunition designed to destroy masts and rigging (chain shot) and sails (bar shot). Antipersonnel ordnance included grapeshot, canister (musket balls packed in a cylindrical canister), and langrage (canisters filled with metal scraps). The biggest change, however, was that ships' guns were fired much more frequently. English ships normally carried forty rounds per gun during the Anglo-Dutch Wars, and in the eighteenth century French gunners were firing five or six rounds per hour and British crews could attain much higher rates of fire for short periods.

Tactics remained relatively unchanged after the seventeenth century, but strategy became ever more complex, involving not just fleet actions but convoy protection and extended blockades. Frigates (fifth- or sixth-rates in the English system) cruised against enemy shipping, carried dispatches and diplomatic missions, scouted, and performed other assignments, while smaller types were used for various specialized activities such as bomb-ketches designed for shore bombardment. Taking a theoretical approach to the problem of naval warfare, Colbert established schools of gunnery and navigation. The English adopted the more empirical practice of issuing *Fighting Instructions* that built upon the experience of actual battle and transmitted lessons learned to be used in future actions. On balance, the English approach produced better results as would become abundantly clear in the eighteenth century.

Whatever their religious, commercial, or political differences, the leading powers of Atlantic Europe shared at the highest levels a commitment to maritime commerce. Because of this, they all wrestled with the question of whether to embrace the doctrine of the free sea, and to what degree. By the end of the seventeenth century, the proliferation of overseas settlements and commercial enclaves in the Americas and Asia forced European powers to recognize that the sea was less a private fiefdom than a commons held by all. The cases of

Jacob Van Heemskerck and Henry Avery at either end of the century illustrate the shift. In taking the *Santa Catarina*, Van Heemskerck operated with the sanction of the government-sponsored VOC. Less than a century later, pirates of Avery's ilk were falling victim to a collective quest for a more stable and secure trade. In the 1500s, he might have ranked among the Elizabethan sea dogs who opened the way for English ships and trade in hostile seas. But Avery was born after his time, and his rogue behavior threatened profits that his countrymen (and others) nurtured with diplomacy and political tact rather than indiscriminate force. Violence at sea was not a thing of the past: naval warfare in the eighteenth century would encircle the globe. Yet the conflicts to come were affairs of state administered by ever more centralized bureaucracies in the furtherance of more explicitly national interests.

Chapter 17

Northern Europe Ascendant

The eighteenth century is the last in which sail-powered ships predominated worldwide. Sailing warships continued to be built well into the nineteenth century, and merchant ships into the twentieth, but it was in the eighteenth century that the full potential of the sailing ship was unleashed and the world first made whole. The 1700s also saw an unprecedented rise in the number of people who put to sea—merchant crews, naval sailors, voluntary and involuntary migrants, and explorers—as a result of European initiative. Large-scale migration by both free people and slaves began in the sixteenth century, and more people migrated in the nineteenth; but the 1700s are significant because this is when the commercial acumen that had been perfected in the carriage of cargo was adapted to that of people, who proved ill-suited to such treatment.

Though not necessarily the most arduous, the longest voyages were those of exploration, whether driven by merchants seeking new markets and sources of raw materials or governments intent on annexing new lands. Mariners of all stripes had an abiding interest in improvements to navigation, from greater accuracy on charts to easier and more reliable methods for determining course and position. These entailed a more nuanced understanding of the physical sciences and more precise instruments for measuring angular distance, compass direction, and time, and explorers were in the forefront of testing and refining these. The age was also characterized by a new interest in zoology, botany, and ethnography. The results of late-eighteenth-century explorations were widely disseminated and resulted in unprecedented efforts at cross-cultural comparisons articulated in an ever-expanding body of written and visual representation that transformed people's awareness of the physical world and each other.

Life and Death Afloat

At the start of the War of the Austrian Succession (1740–48), the Royal Navy's Commodore George Anson sailed from England with six ships. He was charged with harassing Spanish shipping on the Pacific coast of the Americas and capturing the Manila galleon, an apparently straightforward mission that took four torturous years. The story of the planning and execution of this voyage is one of almost unrelieved misery and reveals many of the logistical challenges faced by naval administrators in the half century after European fleets began oceanic operations. These sufferings were not unique to naval crews, however, and although civilians and slaves ordinarily spent less time at sea, the ships that carried them were subject to less official oversight and many endured conditions worse than those faced by Anson's crews.

Soon after his assignment, Anson discovered that he was short three hundred sailors. He collected 170, thirty-two of them from the naval hospital at Chatham. He was also assigned five hundred invalid "soldiers, who from their age, wounds, or other infirmities, are incapable of service in marching regiments," and more than half of whom deserted before embarkation. The crews began to suffer from scurvy and other ailments after a withering autumn rounding of Cape Horn in 1741. The lieutenant of Anson's flagship, the *Centurion*, reported that he could "muster no more than two Quarter-masters, and six Fore-mast men capable of working; so that without assistance of the officers, servants and the boys, it might have proved impossible for us to have reached [Juan Fernández] Island, after we had got sight of it." They were there joined by three other ships, one of which had "already thrown over-board two thirds of their complement." The English burned Paita, Peru, before sailing north to cruise off Acapulco. After repairs on the coast, the *Centurion* and *Gloucester* (which was later scuttled) sailed for Macau. While cruising off the Philippines seven months later, Anson captured the Manila galleon *Nuestra Señora de la Covadonga* with a cargo worth about £250,000. Despite the loss of three ships (two others had turned back from South America) and more than thirteen hundred crew—just four of them to enemy action—Anson's capture of the Manila galleon outshone any other achievement of the war. Under the prize system of the day, members of the ship's company were entitled to a share, proportionate to one's rank, of the value of captured enemy ships. As head of the expedition and captain of the *Centurion*, Anson made about £91,000, while a surviving seaman's share was worth £300—the equivalent of about twenty years' pay. Spectacular though the results were for these men, the four-year voyage did nothing to alter the outcome of the war, and the appalling cost in men and matériel underlined the enormous difficulties of conducting long-range naval operations.

As ordeals like the Anson voyage show, European navies would never have been able to operate effectively beyond home waters if they did not attend to their crews. Larger ships on longer voyages put ever more sailors at risk of previously rare or unknown ailments whose virulence was exacerbated by an inadequate knowledge of communicable disease, a poor understanding of hygiene and nutrition, and primitive means of food preservation. French and British crews suffered the most from these deployments thanks to their governments' commitment to controlling trade from North America to Southeast Asia. Yet following the War of the Austrian Succession, progress was remarkably swift. Barely a decade after the *Centurion*'s circumnavigation, the Seven Years' War (1757–63) was the first in which European fleets deployed around the world, in the Americas, the Pacific, and the Indian Ocean, and while tropical disease continued to ravage fleets, malnutrition became less of a problem. Closer to home, it was by ensuring a constant supply of fresh food to ships on station that Admiral Edward Hawke was able to maintain a close blockade of the port of Brest. "It is an observation, I think, worthy of record," wrote naval surgeon James Lind, "that fourteen thousand persons, pent up in ships, should continue for six or seven months, to enjoy a better state of health upon the watery element, than it can well be imagined so great a number of people would enjoy, on the most healthful spot of ground in the world." Attention to his crew's diet paid handsome dividends and enabled Hawke to stifle French merchant trade and to contain the demoralized Brest squadron and prevent its resupply by sea. When the French broke out with twenty-one ships in November 1759, they lost seven of them and twenty-five hundred men fighting or fleeing from the British in the rocky confines of Quiberon Bay.

Not all illnesses were peculiar to tropical climates, and ships were natural incubators of contagious ailments the causes of and cures for which were unknown. Called generically ship fever, these included typhus, typhoid, yellow fever, dysentery, and other afflictions. The names of these usually fatal diseases are familiar, but their symptoms are not. Dysentery is characterized by diarrhea mixed with mucus and blood. Typhoid is caused by *Salmonella* bacteria and results in high fever, headache, intestinal disorders including diarrhea, and physical and mental collapse. Never in short supply in eighteenth-century Europe or aboard ship, lice spread typhus, a near relative to typhoid that generates high fever, delirium, and rashes. Carried by mosquitoes and therefore more prevalent in the tropics, yellow fever comes on suddenly and often fatally, though not before its dying victims are rendered prostrate from fever, headache, hemorrhaging, jaundice, and other symptoms. Also borne by mosquitoes, malaria induces fever, chills, nausea, and anemia; left untreated it is fatal.

Malnutrition was another leading cause of death at sea. Scurvy was commonplace among crews forced to subsist for long stretches on salted meat or fish and grains, chiefly in the form of hardtack, or ship's biscuit. In the late 1700s, sailors in the Royal Navy were issued weekly four pounds of salt beef, two pounds of pork, two pints of peas, three pints of oatmeal, eight ounces of often rancid butter, and twelve ounces of cheese. Some sailors realized that fresh vegetables and especially lemons were invaluable in preventing scurvy as early as the sixteenth century, and in 1615 the East India Company's Captain William Keeling noted when "I began to allow each messe a pottle [half gallon] of water to drinke by night ordering allso the due expence of our lemon water to prevent scurvvie." James Lind is frequently credited with having proved the efficacy of lemons in preventing scurvy following Anson's voyage, but his own writings suggest an uncertainty about both its cause and its cure. The Royal Navy did not mandate that ships carry antiscorbutics until 1796, and similar provisions in the merchant marine were not adopted for another fifty years.

Drink was of equal importance to food. Clean water was hard to find and more difficult to preserve. Most water was drawn from rivers just upstream from the ports through which they flow, the Thames above London, for instance. Even if the source of the water was relatively clean, its quality on long voyages could hardly be maintained. Writing on his passage to Southeast Asia in 1614, VOC governor-general Gerard Reynst observed that, "The water and the wine which are daily taken from the hold are about as hot as if they were boiling, and this is the reason why much of the victuals go bad." Apart from being vile, the usual allowance of water—one liter per day per man in Spanish ships of the 1600s—was inadequate for the maintenance of good health. A 150-pound man consuming thirty-five hundred calories per day normally needs about two to three liters of water, and in hot climates the requirement is about ten liters. A method for distilling freshwater from salt was known within a decade of Reynst's complaint but improvements were slow. In 1762, Lind demonstrated a distillation process and recommended that stills be put aboard Royal Navy ships. Eight years later, Parliament awarded Charles Irving £5,000 for a device that could render almost one hundred liters of freshwater from three hundred liters of saltwater in an hour. In the 1780s, the still carried by HMS Bounty distilled only about twelve gallons of water per day—not so much for the ship's complement of 117 men as for the cargo of breadfruit trees they were trying to get to the West Indies. Finally, in 1772 the Royal Navy required that all warships carry a still. Merchant crews and passengers were again less fortunate. British regulations did not require government-run emigrant ships to carry distillers until 1864, and even then the law did not apply to privately run ships.

In northern Europe, the usual substitute for water was beer. English records from the Armada campaign show that seamen received one gallon of beer per day, the standard allowance for more than two centuries. On his first voyage to the Indies in 1598, Jacob van Neck had written that "we dranke the last Beere, and we began our first allowance to drinke water, foure mutskins [of about eight ounces] or measures everie day, and three of wine." Yet beer could only be brewed and carried in the winter months; in warmer climes it soured quickly. The challenge was to develop a brew that could survive a long voyage without going flat or sour, a process that seems to have taken until the mid-eighteenth century, when brewers began increasing the amount of hops to create a more stable and alcoholic beer. This improvement notwithstanding, when the Royal Navy began operating regularly in the West Indies in the mid-1600s, rum, a by-product of sugarcane, became the beverage of choice. A century later, Admiral Edward Vernon fixed the rum ration: "every day mixed with the proportion of a quart of water to every half pint of rum . . . served . . . in two servings in the day, the one between the hours of 10 and 12 in the morning, and the other between 4 and 6 in the afternoon." The revolutionary aspect of Vernon's diktat was that the rum could no longer be drunk neat. In addition to water, the rum could also be fortified with a helping of lime juice and sugar to make a crude ancestor of the daiquiri known as grog, in honor of Vernon, who was dubbed "Old Grogram" for his signature grogram cape. In 1789, the *Bounty* mutineers set their former messmates adrift with, among other provisions, a gallon of rum, which Lieutenant William Bligh issued in daily rations of one teaspoonful per man. It is this, some believe, that enabled the nineteen castaways to sail thirty-six hundred miles in a seven-meter-long boat without losing one of their number.

Life and Death in the Slave Trade

Naval crews were not the only people afflicted by disease or malnutrition at sea, but they received legislative protection from the worst features of shipboard life earlier than either slaves or free passengers. Depending on their ports of origin and destination, transatlantic travelers spent between five and ten weeks at sea in conditions almost none could have imagined or anticipated. The fate of slaves was unfathomably worse than that of anyone else, and it was in part due to reports of the abject brutality involved that abolitionists in Britain, France, and the United States began to sever the debate on the slave trade from that on the institution of slavery itself. Life as a working slave was appalling, but as an appeal to public emotion accounts of the horrific conditions aboard slave ships had no equal. Addressing Parliament in 1806, Foreign Secretary Charles James Fox observed that "Slavery itself, odious as it is, is not nearly [so] bad as the slave trade."

Only fifteen autobiographical accounts by African-born slaves transported to the British colonies of the Caribbean and North America survive, and of these only one, by Olaudah Equiano, treats the transatlantic passage in any detail. Equiano wrote his account three decades after his passage, at the age of about ten, and however impressionable his experience was, his narrative is doubtless colored by that of others he heard from fellow slaves. More immediate and graphic is the published testimony of such witnesses as Alexander Falconbridge, a "surgeon in the African trade" in the 1780s, and author of one of many indictments of the trade by people with firsthand experience of it. "During the voyages I made," wrote Falconbridge, describing the virtual entombment of slaves belowdecks,

> I was frequently a witness to the fatal effects of this exclusion of the fresh air. I will give one instance, as it serves to convey some idea, though a very faint one of the sufferings of those unhappy beings. . . . Some wet and blowing weather having occasioned the port-holes to be shut and the gratings to be covered, fluxes [that is, dysentery] and fevers among the negroes ensued. While they were in this situation, my profession requiring it, I frequently went down among them, till at length their apartments became so extremely hot, as to be only sufferable for a very short time. But the excessive heat was not the only thing that rendered their situation intolerable. The deck, that is, the floor of their rooms, was so covered with the blood and mucus which had proceeded from them in consequence of the flux, that it resembled a slaughter-house. It is not in the power of the human imagination, to picture to itself a situation more dreadful or disgusting. Numbers of the slaves having fainted, they were carried upon deck, where several of them died, and the rest were, with great difficulty, restored.

DESCRIPTION OF A SLAVE SHIP.

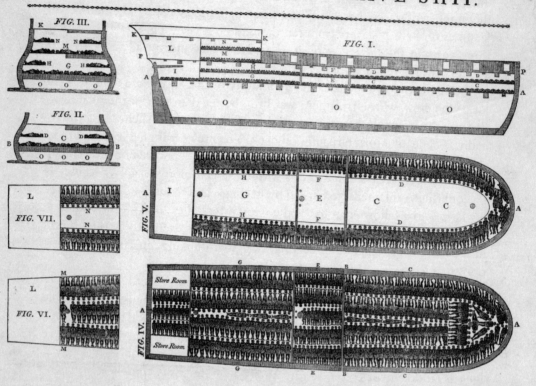

FIG. III.

FIG. II.

FIG. VII.

FIG. VI.

FIG. I.

FIG. V.

FIG. IV.

Store Room

Store Room

DIMENSIONS OF THE SHIP

	Feet	Inches
Length of the Lower Deck, gratings and bulk-heads included at AA	100	0
Breadth of Beam on the Lower Deck inside, BB	25	4
Depth of Hold, OOO from cieling to cieling	10	0
Height between decks from deck to deck	5	8
Length of the Mens Room, CC on the lower deck	46	0
Breadth of the Mens Room, CC on the lower deck	25	4
Length of the Platforms, DD in the mens room	46	0
Breadth of the Platforms in mens rooms on each side	6	0
Length of the Boys Room, EE	13	9
Breadth of the Boys Room, EE	25	0
Breadth of Platform, FF in boys room	6	0
Length of Womens Room, GG	28	6
Breadth of Womens Room	23	6
Length of Platforms, HH in womens room	28	6
Breadth of Platforms in womens room	6	0
Length of the Gun Room, II on the lower deck	10	6
Breadth of the Gun Room on the lower deck	12	0
Length of the Quarter Deck, KK	33	6
Breadth of Quarter Deck	19	6
Length of the Cabin, LL	10	6
Height of the Cabin	6	0
Length of the Half Deck, MM	16	6
Height of the Half Deck	6	2
Length of the Platforms, NN on the half deck	16	6
Breadth of the Platforms on the half deck	6	0
Upper deck, PP		

Nominal tonnage — 297
Supposed tonnage by measurement — 320
Number of seamen — 45

It may be expected, from this mode of packing a number of our fellow-creatures, that there was great mortality among them...

LONDON: PRINTED BY JAMES PHILLIPS, GEORGE-YARD, LOMBARD-STREET. M.DCC.LXXXIX.

The amount of space allotted to each slave was only about 5 to 6 square feet (0.5 to 0.6 square meters), and the height between decks usually made it impossible to stand upright. In 1788, Sir William Dolben proposed regulating the number of slaves that could be carried per ship to reduce the number of fatalities on British slavers from ten thousand per year. This law lapsed after three years in the face of opposition from traders and the identification of abolition with French revolutionaries.

Abolitionists also sought to tie the iniquity of the slave trade to the dismal lot of the crew, whose treatment was little better than that of their captives. Because the tween decks were reserved for the slaves, such shelter as the crew had was beneath a torn tarpaulin on deck. The crews were fed less than their counterparts in other merchant or navy ships and they were not allowed any spirits. Officers treated their crews with an uncommon savagery because, as Falconbridge explained, "to harden the feelings, and to inspire a *delight in giving torture* to a fellow creature, is the natural tendency of this unwarrantable traffick." Falconbridge recounts endless "barbarities exercised by the officers in the slave trade" including beating, flogging, dunking, and other humiliations that led to desertion and suicide.

The movement to ban the slave trade spanned the Atlantic, but to secure passage of the U.S. Constitution in 1787, American abolitionists had to table the issue and settle for the prospect of revisiting the question in 1808, when the government banned it, one year after Great Britain, but seven years before any other European government. Although the importation of slaves was illegal, enforcement of the law in American waters was complicated by the fact that interstate trade in slaves by sea—from Charleston to New Orleans, for instance—remained legal, and the government made no serious effort to interdict slave traders until the 1820s.

The Colonial Passenger Trade

While survival rates were worse for slaves than for free passengers, the difference is less dramatic than one might suppose—a fact that does not reflect well on the carriage of slaves, but indicates the deplorable circumstances of life afloat for most people. Although there are examples of colonial legislation in North America aimed at mitigating the conditions to which free passengers were subject earlier in the century, the first national laws to lessen the physical horrors of the slave trade preceded those intended to guarantee minimum standards for nonslaves. As British North America began to prosper in the eighteenth century, it attracted immigrants from beyond Great Britain, including French Huguenots and Germans from the Rhineland. The French tended to migrate to the Southern colonies, to which some of them had been introduced through their involvement in the slave trade, while Germans tended to sail for Philadelphia. A German immigrant wrote of his experience in 1725: "The ship voyage is as one takes it. For my part, I maintain that it is a comfortable trip if one carries along victuals to which one is accustomed and controls one's imagination." But the halcyon days of the Great Migration to New England were long past and such sanguine views of an Atlantic crossing were probably rare in the eighteenth century. More people would seem to have concurred with Gottlieb Mittelberger, who left Germany in 1750 to take up a four-year post as organist in Pennsylvania. Mittelberger originally had no intention of writing about his experiences and did so solely to warn innocent travelers of "the sad and miserable condition of those traveling from Germany to the New World, and the irresponsible and merciless proceedings of the Dutch traders in human beings and their man-stealing emissaries—I mean the so-called Newlanders. For these at one and the same time steal German people under all sorts of fine pretexts, and deliver them into the hands of the great Dutch traffickers in human souls. From this business the latter make a huge profit." His description of shipboard life is a litany of agonies almost indistinguishable from Falconbridge's account of a slave ship:

> During the journey the ship is full of pitiful signs of distress—smells, fumes, horrors, vomiting, various kinds of sea sickness, fever, dysentery, headaches, heat, constipation, boils, scurvy, cancer, mouth rot, and similar inflictions [*sic*], all of them caused by the age and the highly salted state of the food, especially the meat, as well as the very bad and filthy water, which brings about the miserable destruction and death of many. Add to all that shortage of food, hunger, thirst, frost, heat, dampness, fear, misery, vexation, and lamentation, as well as other troubles.

With such apotropaic testimony in circulation, it is remarkable that anyone would consider the prospect of leaving Europe for America, but leave they did. Of the 11.4 million people who sailed to the Americas between 1500 and 1820, 2.7 million were Europeans; the remainder—more than three-quarters of the total—were African slaves.

The Balance of Power in Eighteenth-Century Europe

Religious conflict, warfare, land hunger, the apparent abundance of opportunity, and the diminished threat of pirates and privateers were all inducements for crossing the Atlantic. By the eighteenth century, the security of overseas territories was increasingly assured by the naval power of their home countries, and the governments of England, France, and the Dutch Republic were assuming a role in transoceanic affairs that had previously been delegated to private interests. But there was no direct correspondence between a strong navy and a large merchant marine. The Dutch Republic maintained a vigorous carrying trade even as its navy declined; the French built a huge navy and had a prosperous merchant marine, although merchants wielded comparatively little influence in naval circles; and Russia's navy antedated the creation of its commercial fleet altogether. England was the country in which naval and foreign policy objectives tallied most closely with the aims of merchants.

State fleets did not fight each other regularly beyond the Mediterranean or European Atlantic until the "second hundred years' war" (1689–1815) between England and France. Whereas all the major fleet actions of the Dutch Wars were fought in the English Channel or southern North Sea, between England's Glorious Revolution of 1688 and the end of the Napoleonic Wars, England and France and their respective allies were at war for sixty-three years and fought about forty major fleet engagements, only two of which took place in northern Europe. The proximate causes of the individual conflicts differed, but common to all was the aim of preventing any one power—Britain, France, or Spain—from dominating European affairs, which accounts for the shifts in alliances at the margins. The wars had enormous consequences beyond Europe, chief among them being the emergence of Great Britain as the first truly global power, a result that could hardly have been anticipated: there was no Great Britain until the Act of Union in 1707, and seventy years later the American Revolution cost Britain dear in territory and prestige.

Conducting prolonged campaigns in distant seas depended on healthy crews, adequate funds for sustained operations, and overseas bases, problems first solved during the Nine Years' War, or War of the English Succession.[*] When the Dutch Protestant William III of Orange and his wife, Mary, overthrew England's James II, Mary's Catholic father, in 1688, France was at war with both the Netherlands and England. While the two states over which William ruled had a naval agreement, the English and Dutch had different motives for fighting France and seamless coordination was not assured. Many English understandably regarded William as a usurper, and William's supporters suspected the navy of Jacobite sympathies. To the extent that this was true, it may have reflected a professional respect for James's seamanship. As lord high admiral, he had distinguished himself in the Anglo-Dutch Wars,

* This conflict is also known as the War of the Grand Alliance, the War of the Palatine Succession, and, in North America, King William's War.

when one officer described him as "better acquainted in these seas than many masters which are now in his fleet; he is general, soldier, pilot, master, seaman; to say all, he is everything that man can be." Regardless, given that William had managed to elude the English fleet, and that the navy's record following his landing was undistinguished, there were grounds for concern, especially after the French defeated an Anglo-Dutch fleet at the battle of Beachy Head (or Bévéziers).

The English fleet could not be written off thanks to the government's increased attention to naval affairs and because France's naval administration and strategic vision were inadequate for a prolonged naval war. For all their scrupulous care, the preparations laid down by the naval ministers Colbert and his son and successor, Seignelay, proved unequal to the exigencies of actual hostilities. When war came, there were deficiencies in implementation across the board: manning requirements could not be fulfilled, ships were in disrepair, promised armaments were delayed, and fetid provisions sickened the crews. The English were not without their problems, and they resorted to impressment to fill their ships' rosters. One ship had a complement of more than 600 men, nearly two-thirds of whom were ordinary seamen ("inferior sailors" as distinct from "the more expert and diligent . . . rated *able* on the navy-books"), and of these, 120 had never been to sea. As Admiral Edward Russell complained, "The fighting part is by much the least trouble that an Admiral of the English Fleet meets with."

Another preoccupation was how to finance the navy's operations and infrastructure. In the seventeenth century, England and France had constructed or renewed naval bases, shipyards, and port facilities, and attended to their sailors' welfare by building hospitals for the wounded and ensuring funds for veterans and widows. Warships in the age of sail were extremely labor-intensive machines and keeping crews at full strength would remain a major problem through the nineteenth century. Financing naval operations and infrastructure proved more susceptible to improvement. The inadequate budgeting that had long hampered England's naval establishment was alleviated somewhat in 1694 when the Scottish merchant and entrepreneur William Paterson raised a loan of £1.2 million, the subscribers to which became the Governor and Company of the Bank of England. This institution became the government's banker and debt manager, and increased the flexibility with which the state addressed its financial obligations in war and peace. By managing the national debt and guaranteeing the availability of loans, the bank ensured that the government could prosecute wars, either directly or through subsidies to continental allies. The Bank of England was far in advance of any comparable institution in Europe, except the Netherlands—the bank's policies were known as "Dutch finance"—and gave the island nation unprecedented diplomatic and military leverage.

A steady stream of revenue and advances in administration enabled the British to maintain a brisker, more sustained operational tempo than any navy had demonstrated previously, and to do so increasingly beyond home waters. The shape of things to come was heralded in the campaign of 1694–95 when rather than return from the Mediterranean to England for layup and repairs, Admiral Edward Russell put into Cádiz, the first time a British squadron wintered on foreign station. Such long-range, long-term operations became the norm in the eighteenth century. Other indications of the new orientation of England's naval ambitions were the completion of the new royal dockyard at Plymouth, on the western English Channel north of Brest, and the conclusion of an alliance with Portugal that allowed English ships to reprovision at Lisbon.

Four years after the end of the Nine Years' War, Charles II of Spain died leaving his throne to Philip of Anjou—his grandnephew and Louis XIV's grandson. The specter of the House of Bourbon ruling France and Spain prompted England and the Dutch Republic to declare war. Apart from the political calculus, Dutch and English merchants saw an opportunity to increase their trade to the West Indies at Spain's expense. In the first engagement of the War of the Spanish Succession, in July 1702, an Anglo-Dutch force under George Rooke destroyed a Spanish treasure fleet and its French escorts in the Spanish port of Vigo. The attack came after most of the cargo had been taken ashore, but the loss of ships hobbled Spain's transatlantic trade, the lion's share of which fell to French merchants, and opened the West Indies to further encroachment by English and Dutch interlopers. Of greater strategic consequence was the British capture of Gibraltar and of Port Mahon, on Minorca. An attack on Toulon ultimately failed, but not before the French scuttled fifty ships to prevent their capture. With two bases in the western Mediterranean and the French fleet sunk at Toulon, the Royal Navy, as it was now called, could guarantee British merchants access to the lucrative trades of the Mediterranean, harass France's commerce with the Levant, and keep an eye on North African corsairs. Although Minorca was lost in the Seven Years' War, Gibraltar would prove a springboard for the extension of British power into the eastern Mediterranean, especially Egypt, and until the 1950s it was a vital link in the chain of British ports that led via Malta and Suez to the Red Sea, India, Hong Kong, and Australia.

By the 1730s, Britain possessed the most powerful navy in the world, and it was possibly the equal of those of France and Spain combined. In addition to its English bases it had Mediterranean outposts at Gibraltar and Minorca, and Antigua and Jamaica in the Caribbean, as well as ships stationed from

Barbados to Boston, and access to the facilities of the Bombay Marine, the East India Company's naval arm since the early seventeenth century. Even so, apart from the capture of Portobelo, on the Caribbean coast of Panama, by a force of only five ships, decisive naval operations in the War of the Austrian Succession were limited to European waters. But the experience of long-range campaigns would prove invaluable for the British, who put the naval conflict's hard-won lessons to work in the campaigns of the Seven Years' War. The scale and scope of naval warfare was completely different, and the stunning block- ade and eventual destruction of the Brest fleet was one of only three battles fought in European waters. Between 1757 and 1759, British and French naval squadrons of up to eleven ships of the line fought in the Indian Ocean in support of their respective East India companies and their allies, and after Spain joined the war Royal Navy ships sailed from India to the Philippines to capture Manila. However, the most widely dispersed operations were in the Americas. In 1758, twenty ships took part in the capture of the French for- tress of Louisbourg in eastern Nova Scotia. From there the fleet advanced up the St. Lawrence and managed to land troops upstream from Quebec, which enabled them to take the city from the rear, and set the stage for the capture of Montreal and all Canada. Extensive though this territory was, its popula- tion was a fraction of that of the thirteen colonies to the south; and in com- mercial terms, Britain's North American holdings paled in comparison with its Caribbean plantations. George III made the case in a letter to the first sea lord at the height of the American Revolution: "If we lose our sugar islands, it will be impossible to raise money to continue the war; the islands must be defended, even at the risk of an invasion of this island." Great Britain was never at risk during the American Revolution, and Britain's Caribbean islands were maintained. But against all odds the thirteen rebellious colonies won their independence.

The American Revolution

The proximate causes of the American Revolution can be traced to crown policies implemented in the wake of the Seven Years' War, but the roots of the colonists' self-confidence can be traced to the previous century. All but ignored by king and Parliament during the English Civil War of the 1640s, merchants and cod fishermen in British North America had carved out a place for themselves in the trade with the West Indies, which, stripped of their for- ests to make way for sugarcane, depended on North America for much of their food and virtually all of their wood. As a result, the eighteenth century saw an explosive growth in shipbuilding in British North America, which accounted for about one-third of the ships in the British merchant marine. American shipwrights launched about a thousand vessels in the 1600s, the majority of them relatively small by the standards of the day and not competitive with larger, English-built vessels but more than adequate for the trade of the western Atlantic and Caribbean. Colonial seamen and shipwrights benefited from the Navigation Acts because they were allowed to serve under the British flag and to build ships for British owners. On the whole, however, the colonists deeply resented the prohibitions in the Navigation Acts, the expectations of which were unrealistic for the simple reason that there were not enough ships to serve all of Britain's far-flung colonies. Moreover, by law European goods imported into the colonies had first to be unloaded and reloaded in England. This re-exportation caused unnecessary delays, drove up handling costs, and resulted in the imposition of double duties on some goods—for import to and export from England. The number of enumerated goods that could be exported only to England and not to other British colonies, much less to foreign ports, increased steadily. By the 1750s, these included sugar, molasses and rice, copper and iron ore, tobacco and cotton, and naval stores like tar, lumber, pitch, and hemp, and as a result, smuggling was rampant.

Although Britain's financial system gave it the flexibility to prosecute wars more easily than its enemies, the conflicts of the eighteenth century were enormously expensive. To allay the cost of servicing the debt, and to pay for the continued defense of the North American colonies—including those won from France in the Seven Years' War—the government imposed taxes designed to raise revenues and regulate trade; enforced the Navigation Acts more stringently to prevent illicit trade with non-British colonies in the West Indies; and transferred jurisdiction over smuggling cases from the provincial courts, where it was virtually impossible for the government to win a case, to vice admiralty courts. Resistance to these policies took many forms and reached a theatrical climax in the Boston Tea Party of 1773. That spring, the East India Company had received permission from Parliament to get a tax drawback on tea exported to Ireland and North America. This allowed them to set prices that undercut smugglers, but at a cost to the treasury of about £60,000 per year. The focus of the ensuing debate turned on the principle of taxing the colonies. Despite dire predictions from such parliamentarians as William Dowdeswell—"I tell the Noble Lord now, if he don't take off the duty they won't take the tea"—Prime Minister Lord North refused to reconsider.

When three East India Company ships reached Boston, citizens demanded that their tea be returned to England. A standoff was resolved when thirty to sixty colonists boarded the ships and dumped their cargoes into the harbor.

In retaliation, Parliament passed the Intolerable (or Coercive) Acts, which annulled the Massachusetts Bay Colony charter, closed the port of Boston, allowed legal cases against agents of the crown to be heard in England, and required private citizens to quarter soldiers in their homes. All but the last applied to Massachusetts alone, but in solidarity many of the colonies closed their ports to ships from England, and in the fall of 1774 the First Continental Congress convened in Philadelphia. In February 1775, Parliament tightened the noose with the passage of the Restraining Act, which prohibited New England fishermen from "carrying on any Fishery . . . upon the banks of Newfoundland . . . or any other part of the Coast of North America." Two months later a British regiment sent to round up rebel leaders in Lexington, Massachusetts, fought the local militia in the opening skirmish of the American Revolution.

The patriots' prospects were dim. The Royal Navy maintained more than two dozen ships of the line in North American waters; the colonies had none. While the colonies had laid down thousands of merchantmen in the seventeenth and eighteenth centuries, they had virtually no experience of building warships and they had limited access to ships' guns, ammunition, or powder. Few colonists had any naval experience and most coordinated efforts failed, notably two attempts to seize gunpowder on Bermuda and in the Bahamas, and a catastrophic expedition to Penobscot Bay in which all of thirty-nine ships were lost in a bungled effort to seize a small British fort at Castine, Maine. What few successes there were at sea invariably resulted from individual initiative, almost always by privateers bearing commissions issued by either the Continental Congress or individual states. American privateers also played a vital role freighting war matériel from sympathetic French and Dutch suppliers, mostly via the Caribbean, though such support was not without risk for all involved. In retaliation, British privateers and warships seized Dutch shipping and trading stations in the Caribbean, West Africa, and South Asia.

The French were happy to support an enemy of Britain without actually going to war, but American diplomats lobbied persistently for a more decisive relationship and in February 1778 France signed the Treaty of Amity and Commerce. This would not have happened without a less heralded success for the Americans' freshwater fleet at the battle of Valcour Island in Lake Champlain. The British had hoped to sever New England from the rest of the colonies by driving down Lake Champlain between New York and Vermont and into the Hudson River valley. To counter this threat, Benedict Arnold assembled a small force of soldiers and shipwrights at Skenesborough, New York, and built a fleet of three galleys, one cutter, and eight flat-bottomed gunboats called gundalows. In October 1776, Arnold's fleet fought a four-day battle against Captain Thomas Pringle's five warships, twenty gunboats, and twenty-eight longboats. The battle was a tactical defeat but a strategic victory for Arnold because Pringle was forced to postpone his southward advance until the following spring. In the meantime, the Continental Army reinforced its position in the Hudson valley and when fighting resumed, the Americans forced the surrender of a British army at Saratoga, New York. It was this success in turn that persuaded the French that the rebels might win the war.

In 1780, a French fleet brought the Comte de Rochambeau with an army of six thousand soldiers to support General George Washington. The following March, the Comte de Grasse sailed for North America via the West Indies. On August 30, 1781, his fleet of twenty-eight ships of the line reached Chesapeake Bay where another thirty-three hundred French troops disembarked to join Washington and Rochambeau's siege of General Charles Cornwallis, then dug in on the Yorktown peninsula. A few days later the Royal Navy's Rear Admiral Thomas Graves sailed from New York to the Chesapeake, arriving on September 5. Rather than attack while de Grasse's ships were at anchor, Graves formed up in line of battle. The French fleet stood out of the bay in some disorder and Graves attacked, but as a result of mixed signals the rear division barely took part in the battle of the Virginia Capes. The French lost about two hundred men, double the British casualties, but they drew the British away from the Chesapeake and prevented a junction of Graves and Cornwallis. Light winds over the next few days prevented a renewal of the battle but by September 10 de Grasse was back in the Chesapeake. Caught between the French fleet and the Continental Army, Cornwallis surrendered on October 19, and the independence declared by the United States five years before was secure.

War between France and Britain continued in the Caribbean and Indian Ocean, where Vice Admiral Pierre André, Bailli de Suffren, led an especially impressive campaign. Suffren had left France at the same time as de Grasse, and after preventing a British takeover of the Dutch Cape Colony in southern Africa, in February 1782 he succeeded to command of the French naval forces in the Indian Ocean: three 74-gun ships, seven 64s, and two 40s. The British had taken the Sri Lankan port of Trincomalee from the Dutch and were fighting Hyder Ali, sultan of Mysore and a French ally in southern India. Despite being outnumbered and having no local base—he was forced to winter in Dutch-held Aceh on Sumatra—Suffren captured Trincomalee in August 1782 and the following year prevented the British from taking Cuddalore four days before news of the peace negotiations arrived. En route home, Suffren returned to Cape Town where the British officers he had just finished fighting readily acknowledged his brilliant conduct of the Indian campaign. "The good Dutchmen have received me as their savior," Suffren wrote, "but among the tributes which have most flattered me, none has given me more pleasure than the esteem and consideration testified by the English who are here." His success did nothing to alter the balance of power on the subcontinent, and whatever tactical and strategic lessons he imparted to his subordinates would be swept away in the French Revolution a decade later.

The French Revolutionary and Napoleonic Wars

Just as animosity between England and the Dutch Republic survived England's transition from monarchy to commonwealth and back to monarchy in the seventeenth century, French hatred of perfidious Albion endured the revolution from monarchy to republic to empire from 1789 to 1815. Eight months after France declared war on Britain in 1793, Vice Admiral Samuel Hood accepted the surrender of Toulon by French royalists, but in so doing he had diverted resources from the more urgent campaign to seize France's Caribbean colonies, which accounted for 40 percent of her foreign trade and two-thirds of her blue-water merchant marine. The British took a number of islands, but their initial success was undermined by a combination of presumption toward the French colonists and the loss of about sixty-five thousand men, including roughly twenty thousand sailors, to tropical disease between 1793 and 1801. Even the tactical victory in the battle of the Glorious First of June 1794—fought so far out to sea that it could not be associated with a landmark—was a strategic failure because the British failed to prevent a desperately needed grain convoy from reaching France.

Attention turned again to the Mediterranean in 1798, when Admiral Horatio Nelson was assigned to watch a French fleet mustering at Toulon under François-Paul Brueys d'Aigalliers. "Exceeding hard Gales" forced Nelson off station just as Brueys sailed for Egypt with an armada of twenty warships, three hundred transports, and more than thirty thousand soldiers under Napoleon Bonaparte. Initially ignorant of Brueys's intended destination and lacking ships suitable for scouting the enemy—"Was I to die this moment, *want of frigates* would be found stamped on my heart!"—Nelson caught up with the French in Egypt just after Napoleon's army landed. Brueys had anchored his thirteen ships and four frigates off Aboukir east of Alexandria, but he made two crucial miscalculations: that Nelson would not attack until morning, and that his own ships did not need to clear for action their shoreward-facing guns because Nelson would be unable to attack from that side. He was disappointed on both counts. Nelson attacked at once and sent five ships between the French line and the shore to achieve an overwhelming tactical and strategic victory that cost the French eleven ships of the line and two frigates, and stranded their army in Egypt for two years.

In the meantime, Napoleon had returned to France and as first consul scored a series of stunning victories over continental armies. Britain subsidized a number of countries to keep them in the war, but they were antagonized by the Royal Navy's insistence on the right to search their vessels for contraband. At the end of 1800 Russia, Prussia, Sweden, and Denmark declared a policy of armed neutrality, embargoing British shipping in their ports and denying the Royal Navy the right to search neutral ships. Diplomatic efforts to change Danish policy failed, and in March 1801 Admiral Sir Hyde Parker and Nelson sailed for the Baltic with thirty-nine ships. A preemptive attack on Copenhagen to prevent Denmark from going over to the French compelled the Danes to lift their embargo (Russia and Sweden soon followed suit), and netted the British fifteen Danish ships of the line and as many frigates.

Exhausted by war, Britain and France concluded the Treaty of Amiens in 1802, but hostilities resumed the next year. When the British got wind of Napoleon's plans for an invasion of England, Nelson was ordered to contain Vice Admiral Pierre Villeneuve's fleet at Toulon. In the spring of 1805, Villeneuve slipped Nelson's blockade, rendezvoused with the Spanish fleet at Cádiz, and crossed the Atlantic to Martinique, all in an effort to keep the British from massing their ships for the defense of England. Nelson set off in hot pursuit, and when Villeneuve learned that Nelson had reached the Caribbean, he returned to Cádiz almost immediately with Nelson again on his heels. Daunted by the prospect of an engagement with the British fleet, Villeneuve stayed put until he learned that Napoleon was relieving him of command. Early on the morning of October 19, eighteen French and fifteen Spanish ships of the line weighed anchor; within two and a half hours, signal flags had passed the news to Nelson along a chain of frigates stretching fifty miles to the southwest. The Combined Fleet took two days to straggle out of Cádiz, and at first it seemed as though Villeneuve would make a run for the Mediterranean, but on October 21 he turned back to face the enemy off Cape Trafalgar.

Eleven days before, Nelson had outlined his plan of attack in a memorandum to his officers:

The whole impression of the British Fleet must be to overpower from two or three ships ahead of their Commander-in-Chief, supposed to be in the Centre, to the Rear of their fleet . . . something must be left to chance; nothing is sure in a Sea Fight, beyond all others. Shot will carry away the masts and yards of friends as well as foes. I look with confidence to a Victory before the

Van of the Enemy could succour their Rear. . . . [I]n case Signals can neither be seen or perfectly understood, no Captain can do very wrong if he places his ship alongside that of an enemy.

Nelson divided his fleet into two divisions and as the fleets closed he ordered his most famous signal run up: "England expects that every man will do his duty." The battle was hard fought from the outset, and Nelson's *Victory* was in the thick of it, at one point being enfiladed by three French ships. In the early afternoon Nelson was shot as he paced the quarterdeck and three hours later—having been informed of the capture of fifteen of the enemy ships—the hero of Aboukir, Copenhagen, and now Trafalgar died. His death was not in vain, for with Trafalgar he had destroyed the French battle fleet and the Royal Navy would have no serious rivals for a century.

A total of 43,000 men fought at Trafalgar, and combined casualties totaled 17 percent; more than 3,100 sailors killed and 4,100 injured, with the Franco-Spanish fleet suffering more than three times as many casualties as the British overall, and ten times as many killed. This disproportion was hardly unusual, and the British usually fared even better against their opponents. By one estimate, in six major fleet engagements between the Glorious First of June and Trafalgar, British fatalities were only one-sixth that of their enemies, and in the course of ten single-ship actions during the Seven Years' War the French suffered 855 dead, thirteen times more than the British. There are many reasons for these asymmetrical outcomes, but the English had cultivated a psychological advantage based on a belief that the point of battle was to attack. After the loss of Minorca during the Seven Years' War, Admiral John Byng had been executed not for giving up the island or for cowardice, but "for failing to do his utmost to take or destroy the enemy's ships," a capital crime in the Articles of War.

Peter the Great and Russian Maritime Ambition

Even as western European powers vied for dominance in the Atlantic and Mediterranean at the end of the seventeenth century, Russia was fitfully emerging as a maritime power of sorts under Peter the Great. The tsar's achievement was not the construction of a big fleet or the development of a naval bureaucracy—he managed these, although neither proved especially durable—but securing for Russia saltwater ports on the Baltic and Black Seas and pressing his country's eastward expansion across Siberia toward the Pacific and North America. In 1683, Peter became the first tsar to visit the White Sea port of

Archangel and ordered the establishment of its first shipyard. Thirteen years later, and more than two thousand kilometers to the south, he invaded the Ottomans' Black Sea stronghold of Azov in a campaign that failed because the Russians could not prevent the fort's replenishment by sea. Peter ordered the construction of twenty-five galleys and fourteen hundred river barges on the Voronezh River, a tributary of the Don, and captured Azov the next year. With the Black Sea proper now in reach, he embarked on a massive shipbuilding campaign, but most of the vessels launched ultimately rotted or were handed over to the Turks (as was Azov) by treaty in 1713. In the meantime, Peter had made a yearlong tour of western Europe where he spent considerable time in the Netherlands and England working in shipyards to learn shipbuilding and gaining a mastery of navigation and naval organization. The tsar also recruited shipwrights and faculty for the Moscow School of Mathematics and Navigation, established in 1700 (the St. Petersburg Naval Academy followed fifteen years later); he prepared the way for Russian shipwrights, seamen, navigators, and engineers to apprentice in the west; and he modeled Russia's highly detailed Naval Statute of 1720 on antecedents from France, Britain, the Netherlands, Denmark, and Sweden.

As much as Russia's fledgling navy drew on the experience of other maritime powers, it gained practical experience of its own in the Great Northern War (1700–21) against Sweden and her allies. Progress in the first decade went slowly, except for the capture of a Neva River fort near where Peter founded St. Petersburg in 1703. Eight years later the Russians captured Swedish-held cities from the Vistula to the Finnish border, and in 1714 a fleet of galleys ferried sixteen thousand troops to take Helsingfors (Helsinki), which was then Swedish territory. The Swedish fleet of twenty-eight ships (including sixteen of the line) withdrew to the entrance to the Gulf of Finland, where the Russians defeated them at the battle of Hangö. Peter's fleet included eleven ships of the line, four frigates, and ninety-nine galleys modeled on a Venetian prototype, some Russian-built and others ordered from the Netherlands and England. The latter development alarmed the Swedes, who complained that the sales contravened Anglo-Swedish treaties. In an anonymous pamphlet entitled "The Northern Crisis or Impartial Reflections on the Policies of the Tsar" (1716), Sweden's very partial Ambassador Count Carl Gyllenborg wrote, "This savage, cruel, and barbarous people design to become masters of the Baltic. The Tsar's fleet will soon outnumber the Swedish and the Danish put together . . . and will be the master of the Baltick. We shall wonder then at our blindness that we did not suspect his great designs." In London, concern about the tsar's "seducing artificers in the manufacturers of Great Britain into foreign parts" led to an act of Parliament intended to curb the recruitment of skilled craftsman by Russia. Yet Peter's strategy succeeded brilliantly, and by the Treaty of Nystad, Sweden ceded Livonia, Estonia, Ingermanland, and part of Karelia (near St. Petersburg), thereby reversing several centuries of Russian isolation from the Baltic and establishing it firmly as a major force in European affairs.

Although Russian foreign policy veered sharply under Peter's successors, hostility to the Ottomans remained a constant. Azov fell again in 1736, but it was not until the reign of Catherine the Great that the Ottoman monopoly over the Black Sea was finally shattered. At the start of the Russo-Turkish War of 1768–74, Catherine dispatched fourteen ships of the line and seven frigates from the Baltic to the Mediterranean. Concerned about a Franco-Ottoman rapprochement, the British refurbished the Russian fleet and offered the services of experienced officers. The Ottomans had more ships of the line than the Russians, but on June 25, 1770, their fleet was almost completely destroyed in a fireship attack in the Bay of Chesma, on the Aegean coast of Turkey, an epochal event that finally fulfilled Peter's hopes for the Russian navy. The Treaty of Küçük Kaynarca gave Russia a number of fortresses on the Sea of Azov and at the mouth of the Dnieper and opened the Black Sea, the Bosporus, and the Dardanelles to Russian and other shipping for the first time in two centuries.

In theory, only Russian merchant ships were allowed to sail through the straits, but others, the French especially, circumvented this restriction by putting their ships under the Russian flag. This fledgling commerce was disrupted by the Russo-Turkish War of 1787–92, which erupted over Russia's annexation of the Crimea and construction of a naval base at Sevastopol. By war's end, Russia's commercial and political activity on the Black Sea centered on Odessa, in what is now Ukraine. Under a succession of able administrators—two of them French—the port grew from a hamlet of two thousand people in 1794 to a bustling city of seventy-five thousand half a century later. Before the coming of the railroad in the mid-nineteenth century, Russia's Black Sea ports depended less on trade with northern Russia than on the sea trade with ports in the Ottoman Empire, the Aegean, and beyond. Although many Russians immigrated to Odessa in this period, the merchant community was more cosmopolitan than any in the empire, comprising Armenians, Jews, Greeks, Tatars, and German Mennonites, as well as traders from France and other western European countries. Turks came, too, though it was not until the Treaty of Adrianople (Edirne) in 1829 that Turkish ports—as distinct from the straits—were opened to Russian shipping.

The Trade of Asia

Russian access to the Black Sea endowed the tsar with unprecedented influence over the Orthodox populations of the Ottoman Empire from the Balkans to the Middle East, and alarmed the British, who feared that Russia might succeed France as the main threat—albeit not a naval one per se—to their Indian trade. During the Seven Years' War, the East India Company's armies (manned almost exclusively by Indian soldiers) had defeated the governor of Bengal, an autonomous province of the Mughal Empire that became the cornerstone of British India. The Mughal governor was replaced by a company puppet, and a few years later the enfeebled Mughal emperor was convinced to appoint the East India Company itself as *diwan* (treasurer) of Bengal, Bihar, and Orissa. From its base at the Hugli River port of Calcutta, the company moved swiftly to maximize its profits from Bengal, one of the richest areas in India. Thanks to its control of Bengal's invaluable silk and cotton manufactures, the amount of silver the company had to export to India to pay for imports to Europe fell more than 90 percent, from almost 5 million guilders in 1751–52 to less than 400,000 twenty years later. Yet between 1760 and 1780 the value of exports from Bengal grew nearly threefold, to 12.5 million guilders per year. The total value of the Dutch and English companies' imports to Europe grew fourfold in the eighteenth century, but the composition of the trade changed markedly. In the late 1630s, spices (including pepper) accounted for more than two-thirds of the VOC's shipments and textiles less than 15 percent. A century later the share of spices had fallen to 14 percent, and that of textiles had grown threefold. The English were never as dependent on spices, which represented only 4 percent of their exports in 1731–40, when textiles accounted for more than three-quarters.

The greatest stimulant to Europe's Asian trade was Chinese tea, which had been introduced to Europe in limited amounts from the 1660s. The Dutch were the first to pursue the trade regularly, and by 1715 the VOC was purchasing about sixty or seventy thousand pounds per year for the Netherlands, a figure that rose to four or five million pounds by the end of the century. More remarkable was the success of their English rivals, whose purchases grew from twenty thousand pounds per year in 1700 to one hundred thousand pounds in 1706, and six million pounds sixty years later. Until the British government lowered its extortionate import duties on tea (between 79 and 127 percent) in 1784, it is estimated that more than seven million pounds of tea—about half the total imported into continental Europe by the VOC and other trading companies—were smuggled into Britain annually. Reduction of tariffs to 12.5 percent had the combined effect of lowering the retail price of tea, eliminating smuggling, and increasing Britain's share of tea imports to Europe from 36 to 84 percent.

In keeping with China's long tradition of limiting the pernicious influence of foreigners, the Qing Dynasty (1644–1912) implemented what came to be

The British artist Thomas Daniell's aquatint Calcutta from the River Hoogly *shows the seat of British power in India in 1788, nearly a century after the East India Company established Fort William. The river teems with a variety of different watercraft, from the Bengal* dingi *at left, a private pleasure barge propelled by sixteen rowers, and two* badgras, *houseboats with enormous triangular rudders and lowered masts, at right. The scene is dominated by the company's single-masted, square-rigged "pinnace-budgerow"—in essence a Europeanized* badgra *with long galleries of windows used by company officials on the rivers of India. Courtesy of the Arthur M. Sackler Gallery, Smithsonian Institution, Washington, D.C.: Gift of Lee and Roy Galloway, S1999.8.8.*

known as the Canton system of trade to maintain a safe distance between their subjects and Europeans. The principles were laid out in the Five Regulations of 1759, which limited where and when ships and people could go (European women, including servants, were confined to Macau); required that all trade be conducted only through the government-sanctioned Cohong (*gonghang*) merchants; limited contacts between Europeans and Chinese; and prevented foreigners from learning Chinese. Only a few hundred Europeans were present in Canton (as the English called Guangzhou) at any time in the eighteenth century, a negligible number in comparison with the thousands of Fujianese and Cantonese who emigrated to or traded with Southeast Asia after the Qing government eased restrictions on Chinese maritime trade in 1683.

This vast increase in Chinese participation in the commercial and political world of Southeast Asia was a function of private enterprise without government support, but on such a large scale that the overseas Chinese became "merchants without empire," not unlike the Muslim traders on the coast of India in earlier centuries. Chinatowns had long anchored the colonial cities of Macau, Manila, Batavia, and Melaka, in all of which Chinese merchants and artisans far outnumbered European settlers. Junks of five or six hundred tons from Amoy (Xiamen) frequented Brunei, on Borneo, which was outside the European sphere of influence, and in 1776 an East India Company visitor wrote that "the commerce between China and Borneo [is] somewhat like the trade from Europe to America" in scale. By the end of the century it is estimated that Amoy was the home port of a thousand seagoing junks.

The Chinese also insinuated themselves into the administrative structures of indigenous states like Mataram Java and Ayutthaya in Thailand, where rulers appointed them tax farmers to keep such lucrative sinecures away from indigenous rivals. In some places the Chinese formed their own fledgling polities under the auspices of local overlords. As their numbers grew, Chinese settlers turned increasingly to agriculture, cultivating food crops and pepper. Other attractions included mining for tin on the Malay Peninsula and gold on Borneo, where there was a gold rush at the end of the century. While the Portuguese, Dutch, and later the British gravitated toward places where Chinese merchants were already active, the overseas Chinese and Southeast Asians were less dependent on Europeans. Bugis merchants from Sulawesi eventually wrested control over several Malay states from the Dutch, and their settlement in the southern Malay Peninsula attracted Stamford Raffles to the island of Singapore, at the eastern end of the Strait of Malacca. In 1819, he leased the island from the sultan of Johor and founded a trading settlement with a view to fostering Chinese trade and undermining the VOC. His choice was exemplary. When the island formally became a British crown colony in 1867 the population had reached 100,000, and today the independent city-state of Singapore is home to five million people and ranks as one of the five busiest ports in the world.

By the time Raffles settled on Singapore, American merchants had entered the trade of the Monsoon Seas, where they hoped to find profitable trading opportunities in a world dominated by the British, who after the American Revolution did all in their power to choke the trade of their former colonists. In 1783, the *Empress of China* sailed from New York with a cargo of ginseng, wine, and brandy, miscellaneous wares, and twenty thousand dollars in silver. One of thirty-four western ships at Canton that year, the *Empress of China* realized a profit of more than 25 percent and loaded tea, gold, silk, and porcelain for the return passage. But like their European counterparts, the Americans produced little that the Chinese wanted or needed. John Ledyard, a Connecticut-born veteran of James Cook's third voyage of exploration, promoted the idea of harvesting furs in the Pacific Northwest for sale in Canton as a way of breaking into the lucrative China trade without running a deficit. In September 1787, a consortium of Boston merchants, shipowners, and captains sent out the *Columbia Rediviva*, under John Kendrick, and *Lady Washington*, commanded by Robert Gray. Sailing by way of Cape Horn, they reached the Spanish settlement at Nootka Sound on the west coast of Vancouver Island off British Columbia, where they found three English ships engaged in the same trade. After swapping ships with Kendrick, Gray sailed for Canton, traded the skins for tea, and returned home via the Cape of Good Hope, thus completing the first circumnavigation of the globe under the American flag.

Merchants from Salem, Massachusetts, were in the vanguard of the China trade, and having helped establish an American presence at Canton they turned to pepper from Sumatra and coffee from Mocha. Imports of the former rose at a great rate, reaching one million pounds in 1802 and more than seven times that two years later. Americans also began trading in Japan after the French invasion of the Netherlands in 1795. Because no VOC ships were available to sail from Batavia to their factory in Japan, the Dutch hired ships from neutral countries like Denmark and the United States. By 1807, eleven U.S. ships had reached Deshima under the Dutch flag. This was a humble start, but four decades later the United States would take the lead in ending Japan's self-imposed isolation from western powers.

Maritime Exploration in the Eighteenth Century

Americans were among the pioneers of transpacific trade and were preceded there only by the Spanish Manila galleon and Russian fur traders. Other Europeans' engagement with the Pacific had been sporadic and limited to the occasional exploratory voyage, and a few attempts to catch the Manila galleon and harass Spanish coastal trade between Peru and Mexico. But the ocean itself was vast, the technology of the time so inadequate, and the measures of success so particular that the Pacific remained out of bounds. As a result, by the eighteenth century much of the world map still remained a blank.

Although British and French navigators would reap most of the credit for opening the Pacific, Russians were taking an interest in the North Pacific even before Peter the Great put Russia on the road to naval power. By 1619, Russia had pushed its eastern border to the Pacific, establishing river ports along the way including Yakutsk on the Lena. In 1649, a decade after the first Russians reached the Pacific, Semyon Dezhnev led a hundred men in seven *koches* (a type of one- or two-masted, square-sailed vessel) down the Kolyma River to the Arctic, around the Chukotski Peninsula, and south through the Bering Strait to the Anadyr River, a distance of roughly fifteen hundred miles. Only about a dozen men survived this first European transit of the strait and Dezhnev's expedition was all but forgotten. However, the proximity or contiguity of northeast Siberia and northwest America was widely suspected, and shortly before his death Peter the Great appointed the Danish navigator Vitus Bering to explore eastward of the Chukotski Peninsula. After a three-year trek across Siberia, in 1728 Bering sailed the *Sviatoi Gavril* (Saint Gabriel) from Kamchatka as far as the Arctic Circle, and the next year he sighted Alaska. A decade later, Bering took two brigs from Okhotsk along the Aleutian Islands as far as the Alaska Peninsula. En route back, the expedition reached the Komandorsky Islands, 175 miles shy of the Kamchatka peninsula, where Bering and a number of his crew died on the island that now bears his name. The survivors reached Kamchatka in 1742 with thirty thousand dollars' worth of sea otter skins, and there followed an island-hopping fur rush through the Aleutians to Alaska. In 1799 the Russian government chartered the Russian-American Fur Company with a monopoly on trade north of Vancouver Island.

By this time, English, French, and Spanish explorers had been busily sketching in the map of the Pacific for more than three decades. The wealth generated from international trade helped finance a wave of government-backed expeditions animated by a spirit of inquiry into natural phenomena and human society. Central to their mission was the resolution of two outstanding mysteries of the Pacific: whether the vast and assuredly rich southern continent, Terra Australis, existed in temperate latitudes of the southern hemisphere and whether there was a western outlet for a Northwest Passage. Our retrospective admiration for the cultural and scientific outcomes should not obscure the commercial and diplomatic imperatives that underlay them. As much as they owed to Enlightenment sensibilities, these voyages were motivated by imperial rivalry and a desire to expand trade. The potential of commercial advantage was essential to the success of exploration. In 1642, the VOC had commissioned Abel Jansen Tasman "to discover the partly known and still unreached South and Easternland [Australia] for the improvement, and increase of the Comp[an]y's general welfare." Sailing from Batavia, Tasman reached Tasmania, New Zealand, Tonga, and northern Australia, but "no riches or things of profit but only the said lands and apparently good passage [toward South America] were discovered." When a second voyage proved even less rewarding, the VOC summarily abandoned the effort.

In 1764–66, John Byron, a veteran of Anson's agonizing circumnavigation in the *Centurion*, was ordered to search for the western outlet of the Northwest Passage, the expectation being that such a discovery worked toward "the advancement of the Trade and Navigation" of Great Britain. Insisting that his ships were not up to the task, he opted to cross the Pacific. Keeping between 20°S and the equator, Byron believed that a continental landmass lay somewhere over the horizon, and his report forced the Admiralty to turn its exploratory focus to the South Pacific. Shortly after his return, Samuel Wallis was sent out in HMS *Dolphin* to find "Land or Islands of Great extent . . . in the Southern Hemisphere between Cape Horn and New Zeeland . . . in Climates adapted to the produce of Commodities useful in Commerce." The great accomplishment of this expedition was the European discovery of Tahiti, where the English spent six idyllic weeks recovering from scurvy and marveling at the people and climate.

By coincidence, two ships under Louis Antoine de Bougainville arrived at Tahiti a few months after the *Dolphin*'s departure. Bougainville's expedition is notable for including the naturalist Philibert Commerson and his helpmate, Jeanne Baret, who disguised herself as a manservant. In addition to finding and taking possession of any places useful to trade and navigation, Bougainville was instructed to "examine the soils, trees and main productions [and] bring back samples and drawings of everything he may consider worthy of attention. He will note as far as is possible all the places that could serve as ports of call for ships and everything related to navigation." Reports about the island paradise of Tahiti from participants in the two expeditions had a profound effect on the European imagination. Here was a society, in Commerson's words, in "the state of natural man, born essentially good, free from all preconceptions, and following, without suspicion and without remorse, the gentle impulse of an instinct that is always sure because it has not yet degenerated into reason"—a manifestation of the concept of the "noble savage" then in vogue. As a greater familiarity with the realities of life in Oceania would show, these assumptions owed more to a loss of reason on the part of Europeans than to a lack of it among Polynesians.

Cook's Voyages

The primary motive for Captain James Cook's first voyage in *Endeavour* in 1768–71 was to observe the transit of Venus across the sun for "the improvement of astronomy on which navigation so much depends." Edmond Halley had suggested the idea of measuring the transit of Venus from places remote from one another in 1716, and on Wallis's recommendation Tahiti was chosen as Cook's destination. Sailing with Cook were eight naturalists including Joseph Banks, aged twenty-five but already an advisor to George III and a member of the Royal Society, the expedition's sponsor. As one colleague wrote to the Swedish naturalist Carl Linnaeus, originator of the binomial system of biological classification, "No people ever went to sea better fitted out for the purpose of Natural History, nor more elegantly. They have got a fine library of Natural History; they have all sorts of machines for catching and preserving insects; all kinds of nets, trawls, drags and hooks for coral fishing. . . . All this is owing to you and your writings." During the expedition, they collected thousands of specimens of clothing, ornaments, weapons, fauna, and flora, including more than eight hundred species of plants previously unknown to science.

The *Endeavour* spent three months at Tahiti, where the transit of Venus was successfully observed. After six months in New Zealand, Cook abandoned his secondary objective, the search for Terra Australis, and sailed west hoping to reach the Indian Ocean via Tasmania. The onset of winter drove *Endeavour* north, and Cook put into Botany Bay, south of modern Sydney, so named for "the great quantity of New Plants" collected there over the next week. Skirting the Australian coast, the *Endeavour* was holed on the Great Barrier Reef and after six weeks of repairs sailed through the Torres Strait between Australia and New Guinea en route for Batavia.* Infestation by malaria-bearing mosquitoes that spawned in the heavily silted river and stagnating fish ponds had earned the Queen of the Orient a new nickname: Cemetery of the East. Shortly after reaching the port in robust health, seven of Cook's company died and another twenty-three succumbed to diseases contracted in the Indies before the ship reached England in July 1771.

A year later, Cook sailed again with HMS *Resolution* and *Adventure*. Investigating the possibility of a Terra Australis lying south of Africa, the *Resolution* crossed the Antarctic Circle and Cook explored the fringes of the southern ice pack before rendezvousing with the *Adventure* in New Zealand. After cruising the South Pacific from Vanuatu to Easter Island, Cook discovered the uninhabited South Georgia and South Sandwich Islands southeast of Cape Horn. No less remarkable than this expedition's extraordinary contribution to geographic knowledge is that thanks to Cook's strict regimen for cleaning and airing the ship, only one of *Resolution*'s crew died from illness in the course of the three-year, seventy-thousand-mile voyage.

---

* The strait is named for the Spanish explorer Luis Baéz de Torres, who sailed through it in 1606.

In July 1776, Cook was off again with the *Resolution* and *Discovery*, this time to find the Northwest Passage, for the discovery of which Parliament had pledged £20,000. After stops in Tasmania, Tonga, and Tahiti, in January 1778 Cook's crews reached the Hawaiian Islands, probably the first Europeans to do so. After a brief stay, they sailed for Nootka Sound, the choice of which reflects the intensifying European interest in the Pacific Northwest. Published reports of Bering's expeditions prompted Spanish authorities to establish missions in southern California in 1769 and to counter Russian and British designs on the region by dispatching expeditions of their own. Advised that Catherine the Great was planning to expand Russian claims in North America, in 1775 the viceroy of New Spain dispatched an expedition to Alaska, although it got no farther than Vancouver Island. Bruno de Hezeta passed the mouth of the Columbia River (later named for Robert Gray's *Columbia Rediviva*), and the area was further explored by Spanish expeditions under Don Alejandro Malaspina and Dionisio Alcalá Galiano, and by the British under George Vancouver, who encountered both Galiano and Gray in Puget Sound and the San Juan Islands.

Cook continued along the coast to the Alaska Peninsula, crossed the Bering Sea and through the Bering Strait as far as Icy Cape, Alaska. Cook had covered a lot of new ground but, he wrote, "In justice to Behrings Memory, I must say he has deleneated this Coast very well and fixed the latitude and longitude of the points better than could be expected from the Methods he had to go by." The British then spent six months in Hawaii, but a week after sailing a sprung foremast in the *Resolution* forced them to return. An argument between a group of Hawaiians and a shore party led to a skirmish in which four marines and Cook were killed. Command of the expedition fell ultimately to John Gore, who returned to Icy Cape before abandoning the search for a Northwest Passage.

The Second Settling of Australia

When Cook embarked on his third voyage, Australia had barely begun to take shape on the world map and no one could suspect the profound consequences that his discoveries would have on the continent's future. In 1781, James Mario Matra, a dispossessed loyalist, veteran of the *Endeavour* expedition, and correspondent of Joseph Banks's, proposed the settlement of the area around Botany Bay as "an asylum to those unfortunate American loyalists to whom Great Britain is bound by every tie of honour and gratitude to protect and support," and one that would be well positioned to threaten the Asian and transpacific interests of the Netherlands and Spain in the event of war. The idea of gaining a foothold in Australia was appealing, but Home Secretary Lord Sydney had other ideas about who should people it. The English had acted boldly on Sir Humphrey Gilbert's idea of using North America as a dumping ground for convicts, which was enshrined as policy in the Transportation Act of 1717. Colonial legislatures attempted to prevent the landing of criminals in North America—about a thousand a year in the eighteenth century—but the practice continued until the Revolution, whereupon the British government began housing them in pestilential hulks in the Thames. In Sydney's view, Australia was the solution to the convict problem.

In January 1788, eleven ships carrying 780 convicts sailed into Botany Bay after nearly thirty-six weeks at sea. Governor Arthur Phillip soon shifted his settlement about ten miles north to the future site of Sydney. "We got into Port Jackson early in the afternoon, and had the satisfaction of finding the finest harbor in the world, in which a thousand sail of the line may ride in the most perfect security," and where the land was also better. Given the rough material with which he had to work, Phillip was inordinately optimistic about the fledgling colony's potential. "We have come today to take possession of this fifth great continental division of the earth, on behalf of the British people, and have founded here a State which we hope will not only occupy and rule this great country, but also will become a shining light among all the nations of the Southern Hemisphere. How grand is the prospect which lies before this youthful nation." The first free settlers other than marines and their families did not reach Australia until 1793, yet the practice of transportation continued until 1868, by which time more than 160,000 convicts had landed in Australia.

Ships and Navigation

Exploration was now understood as a distinct discipline rather than an incidental benefit of commerce or hostilities, but there was as yet no such thing as a ship designed for the purpose. Most vessels so employed were warships of modest size—frigates or smaller—good for cruising close inshore, but big enough to carry naturalists, their libraries and equipment, supplies for the ship, and the specimens collected on the voyage. This lack of occupational specialization was typical of the age. While local traditions yielded vessels with distinct characteristics reflective of their environment and occupation— colliers, fishing smacks, mast ships—in fact many seagoing ships could be used in any number of trades. Because there were no passenger ships per se, passenger overcrowding and its associated ills remained a serious problem. A very few well-off people could pay for some privacy in a tiny cabin, but most people were carried belowdecks like so much live cargo.

External factors had an effect on the economic efficiency of the shipping industry, but until the advent of theoretically sound refinements to hull design and route selection, passage times between many ports remained almost unchanged; between the 1710s and 1780s, ships took about thirty-five or forty days to sail between New England or New York and the West Indies—an average speed of less than two knots. Mathematicians, physicists, and others began to weigh in on the issue of hull design in the seventeenth century, but their work was not widely embraced outside of France, and the education of ship constructors—the people charged with actually building ships—remained practical and informal until the spread of formal education and literacy toward the end of the century. Nonetheless, shipwrights were neither fearful nor incapable of innovation.

New rigs like the two-masted brigantine—square-rigged on the foremast and fore-and-aft-rigged on the main—required smaller crews than vessels of comparable size and as a result soon dominated the routes between Europe, Africa, the Caribbean, and North America.* About twenty-five meters in length, and with a capacity of about 160 to 170 tons, these were less expensive to build and man than three-masted, full-rigged ships and had a greater carrying capacity for a given length than schooners, the North American ship par excellence. Apparently developed in the southern colonies in the early part of the century, when they were known as "Virginia-built," with small crews and high speed, fore-and-aft-rigged schooners were favored by merchants, smugglers, privateers, slave traders, pilots, and fishermen, and used as naval dispatch boats and to patrol against other schooners, which in most cases were faster than square-rigged warships. Initially no more than twenty to twenty-five meters long and rigged with two masts, by the end of the 1800s schooners with between three and six masts were commonplace in the lumber and coal trades on both coasts of North America, and the design was widely copied in Europe, Africa, and Asia.†

Average ship sizes in the Americas changed little in the eighteenth century, but the eradication of piracy meant that extra crew to man the guns were no longer needed, which left more space available for paying cargo and increased the tonnage-to-crew ratio, a standard measure of economic efficiency. A fifty-ton Boston ship typically carried a crew of seven in 1716; half a century later, the number was five. Comparable figures for New York vessels were eleven and seven. Jamaica ships carried one gun per 18 tons in 1730, and one gun per 162 tons forty years later; for Virginia vessels, the ratio rose from one gun per 29

---

* Originally "brigantine" and "brig" were used interchangeably; in current usage, a brig is square-rigged on both masts.
† Two- and three-masted schooners sometimes set square sails on the foremast. There was one seven-masted schooner, built in 1902.

tons to less than one gun per 1,000 tons. Falling insurance rates were another indicator of the decline in violence against ships; on most routes in peacetime rates were about 2 percent. Further economies were realized by faster turn-around times in port, which resulted from the construction of facilities for warehousing, chandlery, banking and insurance, and provisioning, especially in colonial North America. Centralized warehouses saved merchant-captains the trouble of sailing port-to-port in search of cargo. This was a vast improvement over the seventeenth-century Chesapeake, for instance, where collecting a cargo of tobacco usually entailed sailing from wharf-to-wharf along a river and haggling at each stop.

The art of navigation improved even faster than ship design in the centuries of European expansion thanks to scientific advances, the construction of more sophisticated and finely tuned instruments, and the spread of literacy and book learning. In many respects, seamen were already well equipped with instruments to determine vessel speed, latitude, depth of water, and direction. The most significant breakthrough with respect to the last was Edmond Halley's solution to the problem of correcting for magnetic variation in compasses, which he solved in the course of two voyages to the South Atlantic in the 1690s. (A third cruise, in the English Channel, resulted in publication of the first chart of tidal currents.) Establishing latitude remained a function of measuring the altitude of various celestial bodies against the horizon, although the instruments became simpler, lighter, and more accurate as manufacturing techniques improved.

Determining longitude was considerably more problematic. Using dead reckoning over weeks or months at sea could give only a rough approximation of longitude—one's position east or west of a prime meridian running between the poles—and miscalculations led to the loss of countless ships. An early method of fixing longitude based on celestial observation required precise timekeeping and could not be adopted until the development of an accurate timepiece. The quest for a more reliable technique began in earnest following the loss of three ships of the line and their 1,400 crew on the Scilly Islands in October 1707. Seven years later, Parliament enacted a £20,000 reward "for such Person or Persons as shall discover the Longitude at Sea." This was hardly the first offer of financial incentive, which had been proposed by Spanish, Venetian, and Dutch authorities as early as the sixteenth century. Moreover, the French Academy also provided an award for scientific advances beneficial to navigation and commerce, and there was considerable collaboration among French and English theoreticians and instrument makers. Initially the focus was on calculating time by lunar distances—determining the time at a prime meridian by measuring the angular distance between the moon and a star or planet and checking the result against tables in a nautical almanac. The real breakthrough, however, was the work of a clockmaker named John Harrison whose first marine chronometer (or clock), known as H1, was tested at sea in 1736. This and two successors were too big to be practical—H1 weighed about thirty-two kilos—and in 1761 he completed work on H4, which measured twelve centimeters in diameter and weighed just over a kilogram. Another clockmaker named Larcum Kendall was commissioned to make a facsimile of the H4, which James Cook took with him on his second circumnavigation. Cook was unstinting in his praise and assured the Admiralty that "Mr Kendal's Watch has exceeded the expectations of its most Zealous advocate and by being now and then corrected by Lunar observations has been our faithfull guide through all the vicissitudes of climates." Lunar distances were widely used to determine longitude until the price of chronometers came within reach of the average navigator in the 1800s.

A separate problem from determining one's place on the globe was how to represent it on a chart. The second-century Ptolemaic concepts of latitude and longitude were understood by a few European mathematicians, but they were not reintroduced to European cartographers until 1450, when Ptolemy's work was translated into Latin. A little more than a century later, Gerard Mercator published a world map entitled a "New and More Complete Representation of the Terrestrial Globe Properly Adapted for Use in Navigation." Mercator's breakthrough was to devise a projection in which meridians and parallels intersect at right angles, and a straight line drawn between two points represents a line of constant bearing, called a rhumb line or loxodrome, and intersects all meridians at the same angle. Although the shortest route between two points on the globe is a great circle, this requires constant course corrections, which was virtually impossible prior to the development of electronic aids to navigation in the twentieth century. While somewhat longer than a great circle, the virtue of the rhumb line was the ease with which it could be followed by a navigator. On long courses where the difference between a great circle and a rhumb line was significant, the course could be divided into a series of shorter rhumb lines entailing occasional changes in compass heading. How Mercator came up with his projection is not entirely understood, and although Edward Wright devised a mathematical explanation that could be easily followed by other cartographers and navigators in 1599, the Mercator projection was not widely used until the 1700s, when it was embraced especially by marine surveyors.

Even without maps based on scientific projections, great progress was made in charting coastal waters by cartographers centered in Antwerp and Amsterdam. In 1584, Lucas Janszoon Waghenaer published his *Spieghel der Zeevaerdt*

(Mirror of navigation, or Mariner's mirror), a collection of forty-four charts of northern European waters that focused on the contours of the coast (often out of scale to provide details of harbors), landmarks, profiles of the coast as seen from seaward, and depth of water. Waghenaer's compilations were so popular that the English adopted the term "waggoner" to describe any collection of charts with accompanying descriptions of the coasts. Waghenaer's methods were refined by Willem Blaeu, whose *Het Licht der Zeevaerdt* (The light of navigation, 1608) rendered coasts and harbors more accurately, among other improvements. In acknowledgment of his accomplishments, the VOC named Blaeu their chief examiner of pilots and chartmaker. Cartographers in other nations expanded the scope of waggoners and other pilot books to incorporate as much information as they could about all the major sea routes of the world, but institutionalization of the discipline proceeded fitfully. France established its Dépôt des Cartes et Plans in 1720; the English East India Company appointed Alexander Dalrymple their hydrographer in 1769, and he held the same position concurrently with the Royal Navy from 1795. Charting by navies, merchants, and explorers progressed in spite of this haphazard approach. Among the more notable accomplishments beyond European waters was the British charting of the St. Lawrence River during the Seven Years' War by a team of surveyors including James Cook and Joseph F. W. Des Barres. Between 1774 and 1780, Des Barres published the *Atlantic Neptune*, the first comprehensive compilation of charts of the east coast of North America. In the next century, improvements in navigational instruments would be dwarfed by the invention of wholly new technologies for propulsion but there would be no comparable advances in navigation until the invention of sonar and radar, the gyroscopic compass, and global positioning systems in the 1900s.

The scope of maritime trade and naval operations expanded dramatically in the eighteenth century. Voyages considered exotic or possibly fatal at the beginning of the century became commonplace and explorers opened previously remote lands and people to interaction with the rest of the world. New combinations of commercial and state power were in evidence, while countries with previously untapped or underdeveloped maritime resources like Russia and the United States were launching themselves on the world stage. Among the most far-reaching developments occurred in Asia, where Europeans had at long last succeeded in reshaping the ancient patterns and composition of trade. This was most evident in the English East India Company's takeover of Bengal, which prefigured the British Raj in India, but also in the

United States' engagement in the fur trade between the Pacific Northwest and Canton, and the rapid growth of the China tea trade. In some respects, these were merely variations on trends one can trace from the end of the fifteenth century, and few if any people foresaw the enormous changes in the balance, reach, and pace of global power that would result from the technological and economic revolutions already under way on both sides of the Atlantic.

Chapter 18

"Annihilation of Space and Time"

"Annihilation of Space and Time." So trumpeted a newspaper headline announcing the arrival of the first commercially viable transatlantic steamship in New York on April 22, 1838, barely three decades after the inauguration of regular steamship service on the Hudson River. In an age of the jumbo jet and Internet, it is difficult to appreciate the staggering advance represented by the arrival of the *Sirius* and, the following day, the *Great Western*, after transatlantic crossings of eighteen and fifteen days, respectively. The best times under sail were three weeks eastbound and twice that westbound. Soon, steamships would routinely make the crossing in less than two weeks, and by the turn of the century the fastest ships easily crossed in fewer than six days. Yet the invention of the marine engine had global implications far beyond what its sea-minded developers could have imagined. Initially, the greatest impact was on coastal and short sea trades, but steam technology did as much to open continents as to connect them: steam shipping gave rise to an era of canal digging and other improvements to inland navigation that transformed landscapes, created opportunities for industrial and economic development in continental interiors, facilitated the movement of goods and people across the land, and thereby changed the tempo of life for people worldwide.

The development of steam navigation cannot be separated from the rise of industrialization generally. This led to realignments in trade that favored states with flexible financial markets upon which to draw for investment in capital-intensive machinery. It also produced tensions between industrialists, merchants, and shippers, at one end of a widening economic spectrum, and laborers and seamen at the other. The financial division between rich and poor was not absolute and industrialism fostered the growth of a professional middle class whose bourgeois values gave rise to a humanitarian impulse characterized by a belief in fairness and social welfare. In Great Britain, the superpower of the nineteenth century, the same merchant marine that facilitated the growth of British economic and industrial power was at once an emblem of much that was wrong with unfettered capitalism and a vector for the reforms that mitigated its worst excesses.

The Advent of Steam

Inventors in England and France began experimenting with the application of steam power to mechanical ends in the seventeenth century. The most significant practical developments occurred at the end of the 1700s in England, at the hands of engine designer James Watt and his partner, Matthew Boulton. Steam held obvious attractions for shippers, who had always depended entirely on expensive human energy or the fickle wind and tide. Mechanical power would liberate them from these physical constraints, open up new vistas, and create a wealth of new opportunities. But the obstacles to the adoption of steam were not only technological but also financial and political, and the first person to build a practical steamboat was a resounding commercial failure. In 1785, the hapless American inventor John Fitch petitioned the fledgling United States Congress for support of his "attempt to facilitate the internal navigation of the United States." Propelled by a device that mimicked the action of canoe paddles, Fitch's *Steamboat* logged two thousand miles in and around Philadelphia with paying passengers.* Although the New Jersey and Virginia legislatures gave him exclusive rights to all "water craft, which might be urged or impelled by the force of fire or steam" in their states, he was unable to fund his work and he died penniless and forlorn in 1798.

It was not until the merging of Robert Fulton's technological and entrepreneurial genius with the wealth and political connections of Robert Livingston that steam propulsion succeeded. The inaugural run of Fulton's forty-five-meter-long side-wheel steamer, the *North River Steam Boat*, took place on the Hudson River between New York and Albany in 1807; after that there was no looking back. In less than a century, steam power would dominate global maritime commerce and naval warfare, although sail remained competitive in at least some markets into the 1900s. In the three decades between the *North River Steam Boat*'s debut and the arrival of the *Sirius* at New York, steam

---

* Distances for inland waterways in the United States are conventionally given in statute rather than nautical miles.

navigation had a tremendous impact on continental developments, especially in the United States. In 1809, Livingston and Fulton secured a monopoly over steam navigation on the Ohio and Mississippi Rivers and engaged fellow inventor Nicholas Roosevelt to determine the feasibility of running steamboats the nineteen hundred miles between Pittsburgh and New Orleans. Two years later, Roosevelt's side-wheeler *New Orleans* began service. As Fulton confided to a friend, "The Mississippi, as I before wrote you, is conquered; the steam boat which I have sent to trade between New Orleans and Natchez [Mississippi], carried 1500 barrels = 150 tons, from New Orleans to Natchez, against the current 313 miles, in 7 days, working in that time 84 hours." By 1814, when the *New Orleans* sank, there were three more steamboats operating on the river—two in defiance of the Livingston-Fulton monopoly—and twenty-one arrivals were recorded at New Orleans. An early challenger was Henry Shreve, whose two-decked, shallow-draft stern-wheeler *Washington* proved the forerunner of the classic Mississippi River steamboat, although stern wheels were not widely adopted until the 1860s. Twenty years later there were more than twelve hundred arrivals, and in 1840 New Orleans was the fourth busiest port in the world, thanks to its enormous cotton exports. By the end of the century more than four thousand steamboats would be built to ply the "Father of Waters."

As impressive as the growth in the sheer number of vessels were increases in speed and the length of the sailing season. The busiest route on the Mississippi-Ohio system was between New Orleans and Louisville, Kentucky, 1,332 miles. Between 1815 and the 1850s, the average time for the northbound passage fell from twenty days to under seven, while the southbound passage was halved, to just over five days. Clearing rivers of tree trunks and other obstacles expanded the scope of operations. In the 1830s, Shreve designed a twin-hulled snag-boat fitted with steam pulleys, cables, chains, and other devices to remove the "great raft," a thicket of trees, mud, and other growth that choked two hundred miles of the Red River, a tributary of the Mississippi that rises in the Texas panhandle. The Army Corps of Engineers took six years to clear the raft, and in 1839—two years after the Republic of Texas won its independence from Mexico, and six years before its annexation by the United States—the Red River was navigable for twelve hundred miles from the Mississippi to Fort Towson on the Oklahoma-Texas border.

To the north, steam similarly expanded opportunities for Canadians and Americans living around the Great Lakes, yet the steamship's utility and the profitability of western settlement were limited by the impossibility of reaching the upper lakes from the sea. Proposals for a canal between Lakes Ontario and Erie dated from the early eighteenth century but, as with steam power, overcoming the technological, geographical, and political obstacles required people of vision and connections. One such was Gouverneur Morris, who first imagined a canal—if later claims are credible—while stationed near Lake Champlain during the American Revolution. He did not actually set eyes on Lake Erie until 1800, whereupon he wrote a friend,

> At this point commences a navigation of more than a thousand miles. . . . [K]now then, that one-tenth of the expense borne by the British in the last campaign, would enable ships to sail from London through Hudson's River into Lake Erie. As yet, my friend, we only crawl along the outer shell of our country. The interior excels the part we inhabit in soil, in climate, in everything. The proudest empire in Europe is but a bubble compared to what America *will* be, *must* be, in the course of two centuries.

The federal government abandoned financial support for a westward canal and it fell to New York state to build, between 1817 and 1825, the Erie Canal between the Hudson and Lake Erie, a difference in elevation of 165 meters. As with the coming of the steamboat to the Mississippi, the benefits were immediately evident. The time needed for the 363-mile trip from Albany to Buffalo fell from thirty-two days to no more than six for a flatboat freighted with fifty tons of cargo. Shipping costs plummeted by as much as 95 percent—from 120 dollars to 6 dollars for a ton of grain carried from Buffalo to New York City. By seizing the initiative when the federal government balked, the state had earned for itself the first place in the competition for overseas trade, and New York became the primary port of entry for immigrants to the United States, taking the lead that Philadelphia had held throughout the eighteenth century. At the same time, Canada embarked on a parallel set of improvements. The fifteen-kilometer-long Lachine Canal, which bypasses the thirteen-meter drop of the Lachine Rapids on the St. Lawrence above Montreal, opened in 1825, and four years later, the forty-two-kilometer Welland Canal, parallel to the Niagara River, made it possible for ships to sail between the St. Lawrence River and Lake Ontario south to Lake Erie, a difference in elevation of a hundred meters.

While few improvements to inland navigation had such immediate and dramatic effects as those in the Mississippi drainage or on the Great Lakes, similar efforts were by no means confined to the United States. Britain had more than 4,700 miles of canals by 1875, and the floating population was estimated at between eighty and a hundred thousand people, widely regarded as outcasts, living aboard twenty-five thousand barges. In the Netherlands, France, and Germany, the science of hydrology was usually directed at flood control and reclamation, and in some instances navigation was almost inciden-

tal to the main object. Such was the case with Johann Gottfried Tulla's ambitious program to straighten the upper Rhine, which, he proposed, should be
"directed into a single bed with gentle curves adapted to nature . . . or where it
is practicable, a straight line." Work on the Rhine started in the same year as
the digging of the Erie Canal, and over the next six decades Tulla's program of
dike building, channel cutting, and removing islands shortened the distance of
the Rhine between Basel and Worms from 200 to 160 miles—and pushed the
problems of flooding downstream. More than a century and a half later, cities
built on the once stable banks of the middle Rhine like Cologne are subject
to periodic flooding as a result of the increased velocity of the upper river.
Although the Rhine is now a major shipping corridor all the way to Switzerland and a crucial component of a trans-European system of rivers and canals
that links the North Sea to the Main and Danube Rivers and the Black Sea,
navigation was not part of Tulla's plan and steamers did not reach the upper
Rhine until 1831.

"The Beginning of the New Age in Steam Power"

Even as ground was being broken on the Erie Canal in 1817, a group of New
York investors announced the establishment of the first regular transatlantic sailing ship service: "It is our intention that these Ships shall leave New
York, full or not full on the 5th, and Liverpool on the 1st, of every Month
throughout the year—and if it be necessary to employ a Steam Boat to tow
them out of the River we wish it to be done." The Black Ball Line's offer of
regularly scheduled sailings was a bold initiative and because of a shipping glut
that depressed prices on the North Atlantic, a hangover from the end of the
Napoleonic Wars and the War of 1812, it was not until 1821 that a competi-
tor service was established. A more intractable problem faced by the sailing
packets was the great difference in sailing times between passages to and from
Europe, which in the Black Ball Line's first year averaged about twenty-five
days eastbound and forty-three days westbound. Steam power held the promise of equalizing the time at sea, but although a handful of ships crossed the
Atlantic more or less under steam starting in 1819, it was not until the 1830s
that the idea of building a steamship specifically for the purpose became practical. American entrepreneurs were especially eager to take the plunge, but
credit for the first purpose-built transatlantic steamer ultimately fell to British
engineer Isambard Kingdom Brunel. When his company, the Great Western
Railway, built a train line from London to Bristol, he is said to have suggested
that the company extend the service to New York via a "steamboat." Considerably larger than any vessel of its day, Brunel's seventy-two-meter-long

wooden-hulled *Great Western* was trussed with diagonals of wood and iron, the latter a relatively new material in shipbuilding. This internal strength helped accommodate the ship's hundred-ton boilers and engine, which were supplemented by a four-masted rig. For her 150 passengers the *Great Western* also boasted a vast passenger saloon measuring twenty-three by thirty-four meters.

In the meantime, firms in Liverpool, Britain's second largest port and Bristol's main rival, had entered the race to be first to offer transatlantic steamship service. Realizing that they could not build a new ship before the *Great Western* sailed, the British & American Steam Navigation Company chartered and modified the Irish Sea steamer *Sirius* for the passage. Departing Cork, Ireland, on April 4, 1838, the *Sirius* entered New York Harbor on April 22 to garner the exultant headline from the *New York Herald*:

> Arrival of the *Sirius* Steamer in Seventeen Days from Cork.
> The Beginning of the New Age in Steam Power.
> The Broad Atlantic bridged at last.
> Annihilation of Space and Time.

The *Great Western* reached New York the next day, her departure having been delayed by a fire that ignited the deck beams around the funnel. Damage was minimal, and after repairs she sailed from Bristol on April 8 to cross the Atlantic at an average speed of 8.8 knots, 2 knots faster than the *Sirius*. More important for establishing the feasibility of transatlantic steamer service, she had used barely half of her eight hundred tons of coal.

The race between the *Sirius* and *Great Western* took place one year after the British government had decided to overhaul its cumbersome and expensive postal service, an effort that dovetailed neatly with the Admiralty's need to ensure access to oceangoing steam shipping in wartime and steamship companies' need for outside investment. This confluence of interests led to the disbursement of government subsidies for carrying the mails. In 1837, the Peninsular & Oriental Steam Navigation Company (P&O) received the Admiralty's first contract for subsidized mail service from Falmouth to Spain, Portugal, and Gibraltar. Three years later P&O extended this route to Alexandria, where passengers took the "overland route" to Port Suez to join another ship for the passage onward to Calcutta, by way of Galle, Sri Lanka. Four years after that, P&O service was extended to Singapore and China, and in 1852, via a feeder line from Singapore, to Australia.

Acknowledging the success of the *Sirius* and *Great Western*, in 1838 the Admiralty let a subsidy for transatlantic service to Samuel Cunard of Halifax, Nova Scotia. His rivals protested the award, but Cunard's prudence made him an outstanding choice. Not all were favorably disposed to his ships' meager comforts, however. In January 1842, Charles Dickens and his wife took the line's flagship, *Britannia*, on the author's first visit to the United States. Singularly unimpressed, in a blizzard of letters before sailing Dickens panned his accommodations with gusto. "Our cabin is something immensely smaller than you can possibly picture to yourself," he wrote his brother. "Neither of the portmanteaus could by any mechanical contrivance be got into it. When the door is open, you can't turn around. When it's shut, you can't put on a clean shirt, or take off a dirty one. When its [*sic*] day, it's dark. When it's night, it's cold." Dickens grudgingly acknowledged that the adjacent lady's cabin was "really a comfortable room . . . well-lighted, sofa'd, mirrored and so forth." But if Cunard harbored spartan tendencies, no one could fault the line for the care of its managers and masters, who gave it an exemplary safety record. In its first three decades Cunard lost only two ships, and no one died in either accident.

The same could not be said of other companies, the most infamous being the New York and Liverpool United States Mail Steamship Company, known as the Collins Line, founded specifically to compete with Cunard. Throughout the 1840s, the United States Congress debated the wisdom of relying on subsidized British ships to carry the mail between the United States and Europe. For more than one senator, the only reasonable response was an American subsidy for American ships: "I suggest cost not be considered. . . . I suggest, too, that Congress grant a carefully selected American shipping expert a completely free hand to proceed with the absolute conquest of this man Cunard." An obvious choice was Edward Knight Collins. Having cut his teeth in the packet trade between New York, Mexico, and New Orleans, Collins entered transatlantic service with the sailing packet *Shakespeare* in 1837. His Dramatic Line of square-riggers was a great success, and in 1846 he submitted a bid for a congressional subsidy of $385,000 to run steamers on twenty round-trips per year between New York and Liverpool. As in England, the enabling legislation provided that the ships could serve as naval auxiliaries, and the ships were to be "under the inspection of a naval constructor in the employ of the Navy Department . . . and so constructed as to render them convertible at the least possible cost, into war steamers of the first class." With funds in hand, Collins ordered four wooden, bark-rigged, side-wheel steamships. Measuring just over eighty-five meters in length, the *Atlantic*, *Arctic*, *Pacific*, and *Baltic* were pacesetters on the North Atlantic, nearly 50 percent faster than the *Britannia*'s 8.5 knots. However, their enormous fuel and maintenance costs forced Collins to request a new subsidy of $858,000, which a profligate Congress duly approved.

Their potential as auxiliaries notwithstanding, the Collins Line ships were renowned for their sumptuous appointments, which the navy's overseer, Matthew Calbraith Perry, decried as "extravagantly showy." Writing in *Harper's New Monthly Magazine*, John Abbott reported that the *Arctic*'s main cabin had "an air of almost Oriental magnificence. . . . When this saloon is brilliantly lighted in the evening it is gorgeous in the extreme." The "large, airy" dining room "with windows opening upon the ocean as pleasantly as those of any parlor" seated two hundred and the "state-rooms are really *rooms*, provided with every comfort which can be desired. . . . Some of these rooms have large double beds with French bedsteads and rich curtains." This may have been journalistic puffery, for a passenger on the *Arctic*'s running mate, *Atlantic*, enjoined prospective travelers "*to take a whole state-room to one's self . . .* rather than have a fellow-citizen so near you as to breathe half your air, and make you breathe all his." Regardless, to many both in and out of Congress, the ships were a manifestation of America's "national glory," and thirty thousand people turned out to watch the *Arctic*'s launch in 1850. As Abbott proclaimed, "The United States have never yet done any thing which has contributed so much to their honor in Europe, as the construction of this Collins line of steamers. We have made a step in advance of the whole world. Nothing ever before floated equal to these ships. . . . No one thinks of questioning their superiority."

This proved a lamentable oversight and although other shipwrecks would cost more lives, the loss of the *Arctic* in 1854 became for more than half a century the benchmark against which all shipwrecks were measured. When the *Titanic* sank in 1912, the *New York Post* observed that "Ocean tragedies have been numerous and sensational in the intervening decades but . . . to parallel the present week's story . . . one would have to go back to the story of the ill-fated *Arctic*." Steaming westbound about fifty miles south of Newfoundland in patchy fog, the *Arctic* had collided with the *Vesta*, a French iron-hulled auxiliary steamer en route from St. Pierre to France. The immediate assumption aboard both ships was that the smaller *Vesta* was doomed, and the *Arctic*'s captain, James C. Luce, sent his first mate to offer assistance. When informed that water was pouring into his ship's uncompartmentalized hull, however, he abandoned the French steamer and his lifeboat to race for Newfoundland, but the rising water extinguished the boiler fires and the engines and pumps fell silent.

The *Arctic* exceeded the requirements of the safety regulations set forth in the Steamboat Law of 1852, which stipulated that vessels over 1,500 tons carry six lifeboats, including at least one of metal construction. All six of the *Arctic*'s were Francis Metallic Lifeboats fitted with watertight compartments. As would prove the case with the *Titanic*, what was wanted was quantity not quality. The mate's lifeboat having been abandoned, there were only five boats

for the ship's company, more than three hundred of whom died. In the meantime, after watching in horror as the American superliner paddled into the
fog, taking with it some ten feet of his ship's bow, the *Vesta*'s captain found
that the remainder of the iron hull had withstood the collision relatively well.
Shoring up the foremost of the ship's three watertight bulkheads, he reached
Newfoundland, and after extensive repairs the *Vesta* returned to France.

The loss of life aboard the *Arctic* was horrendous by any standard. That she
was the pride of the American merchant marine heightened the tragedy. But
what fixed the infamy of the *Arctic* in the public imagination were reports of
the crew's appalling behavior: sixty-one of the eighty-six survivors were members of the ship's company. The *New York Daily Times* observed, "One in view
of their conduct, can scarcely help deploring their escape as much as the loss
of the dead." More shocking still, the survivors included not one woman or
child—not even Collins's wife and two children (Collins himself was not on
board)—a fact memorialized by editorialists, ministers, and others of the day,
most hauntingly Walt Whitman, who wrote

> Of the flower of the marine science of fifty generations . . . Of the steam-
>   ship *Arctic* going down,
> Of the veil'd tableau—Women gather'd together on deck, pale, heroic,
>   waiting the moment that draws so close—O the moment!
> A huge sob—A few bubbles—the white foam spirting up—and then the
>   women gone,
> Sinking there, while the passionless wet flows on—

Despite ample precedent, no charges seem to have been filed against the *Arctic*'s crew, but public indignation animated congressional opponents of the mail
subsidy, who could now point to the fatal extravagance of its beneficiaries. As
one congressman asserted, "If [the Collins Line] had spent in lifeboats for that
vessel the money which they spent in gingerbread ornaments and decorations,
there might have been hundreds of valuable lives saved."

The tragedy was followed by widespread calls for reform. The fate of the
sturdy *Vesta* (aptly named for the virgin goddess of hearth and home) made it
clear that iron hulls with watertight compartments were more likely to survive
a collision than uncompartmentalized wooden hulls. That western shipwrights
did not incorporate compartmentalization into their construction principles
prior to this seems inexplicable. The concept was known and employed in
Chinese ships from a very early date, and in the eighteenth century Benjamin Franklin, among others, proposed building hulls in emulation of "the
well known practice of the Chinese, to divide the hold of a great ship into a
number of separate chambers by partitions tight caulked . . . so that, if a leak

should spring in one of them, the others are not affected by it; and, though that chamber should fill to a level with the sea, it would not be sufficient to sink the vessel." Franklin believed that whatever additional cost this might entail would be offset by reduced insurance rates "and by a higher price taken of passengers, who would rather prefer going in such a vessel." In a pamphlet called *Steam-Lanes Across the Atlantic* (1855), superintendent of the U.S. Naval Observatory Lieutenant Matthew Fontaine Maury included these among a number of improvements suggested in the wake of the disaster:

> Life-boats and life-preservers, water-tight compartments, station-bills for passengers and crew to "save ship" were among the remedial plans, and among those preventive were fog signals, true compasses, rate of sailing, lookout, and lanes, or a double track for the steamers crossing this part of the Atlantic, viz, a lane for them to go in and another for them to come in.[*]

The last recommendation fit Maury's interests well. An analysis of Cunard and Collins Line logbooks showed that their ships sailed within a band about three hundred miles wide. After consulting the extensive oceanographic data held by his office, Maury recommended that westbound steamers keep to a northerly lane twenty to twenty-five miles wide, and that eastbound steamers use a more southerly lane of fifteen to twenty miles in width. These lanes would reduce the likelihood of steamers colliding with one another and lessen the likelihood of collision between steamers and sailing ships, whose "public-spirited ship-masters" were enjoined to avoid the steamer lanes to the extent possible. The New York Board of Underwriters published Maury's recommendations and he mapped the steam lanes in that year's edition of his *Explanations and Sailing Directions to Accompany the Wind and Current Charts.* Although the U.S. Navy and many shipping lines required that their captains follow these lanes, compliance was voluntary. The benefits, however, could not be ignored and several subsequent accidents were attributed to ships not being in their proper lane. In 1889, the steam lane issue was debated at a conference in Washington convened "to decide the momentous question of fixed routes for steamers crossing the Atlantic," but Maury's plan was not adopted until a meeting of the International Maritime Conference in 1900, forty-six years after the *Arctic*'s loss.

Serving as they did the elite markets of northwest Europe and the eastern United States, the transatlantic subsidies are the best known, but subsidies supported other shipping routes, too. The United States used them to encour-

---

[*] A station bill is a posted document indicating the duties of the crew and where passengers should gather in an emergency.

age trade to the Caribbean and on the west coast of North America. At the same time the Collins Line subsidy was let, the Sloo Line received one for service to the east coast of Panama via Charleston and Savannah, and W. H. Aspinwall's Pacific Mail Steamship Company received one for its service from the west coast of Panama to San Diego, Monterey, San Francisco, and Astoria. Aspinwall's timing was exceptional, for the discovery of gold in California the following year ignited a mass migration to the west coast. While steamship operators benefited enormously from the unexpected windfall, the majority of the seventy-five thousand "forty-niners" who embarked for California did so in more than 750 sailing ships that sailed from east coast ports to San Francisco via Cape Horn, most of them nonstop. Although the distance from New York or Boston to the Golden Gate is more than thirteen thousand miles via the Horn (and some ships actually covered more than twenty thousand miles in search of favorable winds) compared with less than three thousand miles overland, an ordinary sailing ship could cover the longer distance in less than six months, and clippers could make the passage in four months or less. By comparison, the transcontinental journey along the Oregon Trail from Independence, Missouri, to Portland, Oregon, took six months, and that was in addition to the time, effort, and expense required to reach Missouri. These factors had kept the numbers of westward migrants small, and in the years 1843–45 only four or five thousand settlers had set out for the Pacific Northwest. The explosive growth of the American population in California, which had seceded from Mexico in 1846, led to its admission as a state in 1850. Thanks to its strong maritime connections with the east coast, California is the only one of the lower forty-eight states apart from Louisiana that did not initially border another of the United States.

Paths of the Seas and the Heyday of Commercial Sail

Maury's recommendation that steamships follow prescribed shipping lanes across several thousand miles of open ocean was a natural extension of his earlier research into how to plot faster sailing times across the world's oceans, which in turn drew on advances in the study of the oceans that began making real headway in the late 1700s. In the early centuries of European overseas expansion, a nation's knowledge of safe and efficient routes comprised a jealously guarded body of trade secrets. The institutionalization of state-sponsored surveys intended for the broad dissemination of hydrographic knowledge proceeded slowly in the eighteenth century, but even without formal organization, substantial advances were made. In 1768 Benjamin Franklin was asked, in his capacity as deputy postmaster of the American colonies, to

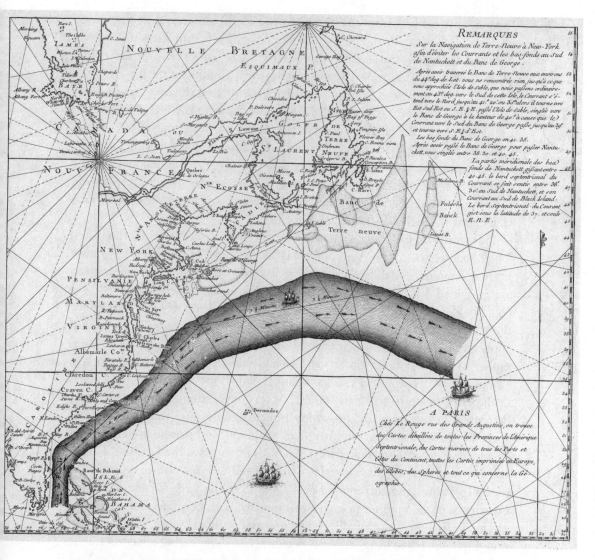

Benjamin Franklin's Gulf Stream map, which shows the width, strength, and course of the warm-water current as it flows between the truncated Florida peninsula and the Bahamas, along the coast of the United States to the vicinity of Cape Hatteras and Chesapeake Bay, where it branches off in a more easterly direction south of the major fishing banks below Nova Scotia and Newfoundland. This French copy of an original by Franklin's cousin Timothy Folger was drawn and published by George Louis Le Rouge circa 1780–83. Franklin intended for copies to be given to all French ships supplying arms to the Americans during the Revolution. Courtesy of the Osher Map Library and Smith Center for Cartographic Education, University of Southern Maine, Portland.

explain why passages from the colonies to England took less time than those to North America. With the help of his cousin, a Nantucket ship captain, Franklin described "the *Gulph Stream*, a strong Current so called which comes out of the Gulph of Florida, passing northeasterly running at the rate of 4, 3½, 3 and 2½ Miles an Hour," and which retards westbound ships and speeds eastbound ones. The post office published a chart showing the Gulf Stream, and Franklin refined the chart by observations made on three transatlantic crossings between 1775 and 1785. A decade after Franklin's initial research into the Gulf Stream, the East India Company surveyor George Rennell mapped the Agulhas current along the southern coast of East Africa, and after the turn of the century Alexander von Humboldt measured the northward-flowing Peruvian current, which was soon named for him.

This search for order in the chaos of the deep manifested itself in other ways. The first director of the Admiralty's Hydrographical Office (1795), Admiral Francis Beaufort, established a table that categorized winds by their speed and provided descriptions of the wind's effects on the water so that its force could be determined without an anemometer. The Beaufort scale allowed for the transmissibility of reliable information about wind speeds. The practical application for this was anticipated by Alexander Dalrymple, who as hydrographer of the East India Company had undertaken "the very useful work of examining the Journals of the [company's] Ships, for improving the Charts in the Navigation of the East Indies." Maury revolutionized this process by designing an "abstract log" in which captains could note the direction and speed of the wind and current, magnetic variation, and ocean temperature on a daily basis. Compiling data from thousands of voyages, the Depot of Charts and Instruments produced a series of *Wind and Current Charts* showing the prevailing winds and currents for every month of the year, "to generalize the experience of the mariner in such a manner that each may have before him, at a glance, the experience of all" and so plot the optimal course to his destination. First published in 1848, Maury's charts had a staggering effect on sailing times and shipping costs. The average time for the passage from New York to San Francisco fell from 188 days to 145 days in 1851 and 136 days four years later. The release of Maury's charts coincided with the development of the clipper ship, but a report in 1854 estimated that use of the charts worldwide was saving the British merchant marine ten million dollars per year, and Maury deserves most of the credit.

Although the early nineteenth century had seen the development of a variety of fast ship types, it was not until the California gold rush that "the search for speed under sail" became an imperative. The early 1850s saw the full flower of the clipper age, when speed generated higher profits than sheer volume. The first extreme clipper, the *Stag Hound* of 1850, was the creation of the Boston naval architect Donald McKay, who subsequently launched such renowned and evocatively named vessels as the *Flying Cloud, Sovereign of the Seas*, and *Great Republic*. The *Stag Hound*'s launch excited great interest and the *Boston Atlas* was effusive in its praise of McKay's accomplishment:

> This magnificent ship has been the wonder of all who have seen her. Not only is she the largest of her class afloat, but her model may be said to be the original of a new idea in naval architecture. She is longer and sharper than any other vessel of the merchant service in the world, while her breadth of beam and depth of hold are designed with special reference to stability. Every element in her has been made subservient to speed; she is therefore her builder's *beau ideal* of swiftness; for in designing her, he was not interfered with by her owners. . . . Her model must be criticized as an original production, and not as a copy from any class of ships or steamers.

Stag Hound's route was typical of many ships in the California trade. American merchants had been trading to China since just after the Revolution, and the trade expanded following Britain's victory in the First Opium War of 1839–42. Rather than sail out and back to Asia, ships generally circumnavigated the globe from east to west, sailing via Cape Horn to California, China, and, frequently, London. The average clipper could sail from New York to San Francisco in about 120 days, the fastest could make the passage in under 100, and the record was shared by the *Flying Cloud* and *Andrew Jackson*, both of which completed the run in 89 days—the *Flying Cloud* twice. No sailing vessel of any kind bettered this time until 1989 when the high-tech racing yacht *Thursday's Child* covered the distance in under eighty-one days and in 2008 the *Gitana 13* made the passage in forty-three. However, these carried no cargo. That it took 130 years to register a 10 percent gain in speed testifies to the genius of the clipper builders.

Like any thoroughbred, clippers were too refined for more ordinary pursuits, and after the initial excitement of the gold rush passed a new breed of American square-rigger emerged, known as the medium clipper or Down Easter, the latter name deriving from the fact that many were built in Maine, downwind and east of Boston. Although Down Easters were built for capacity, the spirit of experiment and improvement that informed the clipper age was not forgotten and they had relatively fine lines. Such changes in ship design were not unique to the United States, and they enabled square-riggers of wood and later iron and steel construction to compete in a number of long-distance trades into the twentieth century. California grain, Chinese tea, Australian grain and wool, British coal, jute from India, and guano from Peru's

Chincha Islands were among the cargoes carried in square-rigged ships and barks worldwide.

The deepwater sailing ship more than held its own until the 1880s. Many of the period's technological advances benefited both sail- and steam-powered ships, and sail gained a few advantages of its own. In Britain a great hurdle was overcome when the Merchant Shipping Act of 1836 revised the tonnage measurement rules in force since 1773. Because tonnage is the basis on which port dues are charged, measurement rules tend to produce vessels of similar design as people seek to take advantage of them. The crude, earlier formula used as its only variables a ship's length and beam, and as a result British shipbuilders produced "the most unsightly and unmanageable ships in Europe"— short, deep in proportion to beam, with flat sides and bottoms, and said to be "built by the mile and served out by the yard." The new rules were not made mandatory until 1855, and progress was slow in the intervening years, but British sailing ships tended to develop finer lines, which made them faster and handier. Shipbuilders also took advantage of the increasingly widespread use of iron and steel for hulls. Because these required less material for a given size, an iron or steel ship had more cargo space than a wooden ship of the same dimensions. At the same time, steel rigging, chain, and labor-saving winches and capstans reduced the number of crew needed. By the 1870s, the better sailing ships had twice the capacity of older, wooden ships of comparable tonnage and carried crews one-third the size. Sail had three further economic advantages: steamships needed more engineers and stokers than sailing ships needed sailors, which made their manning costs higher; sailing ships had no fuel costs; and steamers cost more to build. Overall, the registered tonnage of the British merchant marine grew more than 80 percent between 1850 and 1880. Sailing ship tonnage increased through the 1860s and although it declined in the next decade, sailing ships still accounted for more than 60 percent of Britain's merchant tonnage in 1880.

The Opening of China and Japan

The end of the Napoleonic Wars freed European powers to leverage their naval and commercial superiority in ways that represented a fundamental break with the accommodations reached by the majority of European and Asian merchants since the sixteenth century. This shift began in India in the 1750s and around the turn of the century in China. Two factors drove the British, the need to diminish their silver exports to pay for tea, and a desire to displace the Chinese as the dominant commercial carriers in East and Southeast Asia. Between 1805 and 1820, there were an estimated eighty-five thousand tons of Chinese shipping (about three hundred junks) operating in East and Southeast Asia, and nearly three times that under the flag of the East India Company.

By the 1820s, virtually the only product the East India Company imported from China was tea, and duties amounted to nearly 10 percent of the British government's total revenue. As British and other foreigners had little the Chinese wanted in exchange, they were forced to pay silver for tea. The pressing need for bullion to pay for the Napoleonic Wars and for the pacification and administration of India had forced the East India Company to search for an alternative to silver, which took the form of Bengal opium. So successful was the company's cultivation of China's appetite for opium that it was able to stop carrying silver to China in 1805, and two years later it was actually importing Chinese silver. The problem with this trade was that it was illegal in China, where the first laws proscribing opium for nonmedicinal purposes were enacted in 1729. Opium consumption had moral and economic consequences the Chinese could ill afford. Trade in daily goods declined as addicts devoted more and more of their income to the drug, and bullion outflows from China had a direct impact on the imperial treasury.

In 1839, the emperor's imperial commissioner at Canton, Lin Zexu, destroyed about twenty-one thousand chests of opium.[*] In response, the East India Company dispatched a force of four thousand soldiers and sixteen ships to demand satisfaction. At the outset of the conflict, the British blockaded Canton and a number of ports as far as the Yangzi. The emperor lost faith in Lin Zexu, but his replacement proved little better and was likewise cashiered for apparently ceding Hong Kong to the British. Yet there was little anyone could do in the face of Britain's technological advantage. The Treaty of Nanking forced China to pay twenty-one million dollars in restitution, opened the "treaty ports" of Canton, Amoy, Fuzhou, Ningbo, and Shanghai to British traders, abolished the Canton system, and allowed the British to trade wherever they wanted and to occupy Hong Kong. The French and the Americans obtained comparable concessions in 1844, and they were followed by the Germans, Russians, and Italians. The First Opium War may have illustrated China's technological and cultural decline under the Qing Dynasty, but the "unequal treaties" undermined any prospect that China would attain its former stature as a regional hegemon or that it would be viewed as an equal partner on the world stage. The drug-induced malaise fueled by opium contributed to the collapse of the Celestial Kingdom and the turbulent decades of

---

[*] A chest of Malwa (western Indian) opium weighed sixty kilograms, a chest of Patna (Bengal) opium seventy-three kilograms.

civil war and oppressive communist rule that ensued; China only began to find its way again at the end of the twentieth century.

Having prised open the trade of China, westerners next looked to Japan, where restrictions on the movements of official emissaries, shipwrecked foreigners, and even repatriated Japanese castaways were severe. American whalers marooned in Japan were typically rounded up and mistreated, and Japanese blown offshore and returned by foreign ships could be imprisoned for their misfortune. Calling at the island of Kunashir in 1811, the Russian surveyor Vasilii M. Golovnin and six of his crew were imprisoned for two years, while the Japanese rebuffed the attempts of Stamford Raffles to send ships to Japan from British-occupied Java during the Napoleonic Wars. But it was concern for the safety of their whalers and their interest in Pacific trade generally that prompted the United States to take the lead in opening Japan. On the third visit of an American naval squadron, in 1854, Matthew Calbraith Perry convinced the shogun to sign the Treaty of Kanagawa, which opened the ports of Shimoda (southwest of Tokyo) and Hakodate (near the southern tip of Hokkaido) to American ships. By the next year, Britain, Russia, and the Netherlands had obtained trading privileges along the same lines.

Despite some resistance by traditionalists, Japan quickly shucked off two centuries of Tokugawa isolationist policy. Reformers may have feared that if they did not learn from China's lesson the Japanese might suffer a similar humiliation at the hands of westerners. Following the shogun's ouster, the emperor took the reign name Meiji, meaning "enlightened ruler," and the Charter Oath drafted in 1868 by leaders of the restoration included as its fifth and final point, "Knowledge shall be sought throughout the world so as to strengthen the foundations of imperial rule." Although the United States had initiated contact, it was soon preoccupied with civil war and Japan turned to Britain and France for help in modernizing its economy and navy. The country's transformation was astonishing. The value of its foreign trade rose from less than two million dollars in 1859, when the Peninsular and Orient Line established bimonthly steamer service between Yokohama and Shanghai, to more than twenty-eight million dollars seven years later. The western expatriate community grew to several thousand, although the Chinese outnumbered Europeans, just as they had at Manila, Batavia, and other Asian entrepôts. In 1875, Yataro Iwasaki founded the Mitsubishi Mail Steamship Company (forerunner of the modern Mitsubishi companies and now part of the NYK Line) and introduced a Japanese-run service to Shanghai. Iwasaki also took over the government shipyard at Nagasaki—later the Mitsubishi Shipbuilding Company—founded with Dutch help in the 1850s, and started turning out steamships, thus setting the country on the path to becoming one of the premier shipbuilders in the world.

Suez, Compound Engines, and the Telegraph

Contact between Europe and maritime Asia was made immeasurably easier following the opening of the Suez Canal in 1869. With their dominance of major Mediterranean trade routes and proximity to Egypt, the French not unreasonably believed that they would profit most from a shortcut to the Indian Ocean, and eagerly subscribed to the Suez Canal Company (Compagnie Universelle du Canal Maritime de Suez), founded by Ferdinand de Lesseps with the support of his friend and patron, Said Pasha, Ottoman viceroy of Egypt. The canal was 192 kilometers long from Port Said (named for the viceroy) to Port Suez (the ancient Clysma) and, as built, 22 meters wide on the bottom, between 60 and 90 meters across on the surface, and 8 meters deep.[*] While the French viewed the canal as a means to counter British dominance of ocean trade, and the British government resolutely defied British shipowners to oppose any efforts to plan or construct a canal, the canal confounded virtually all expectations. Mediterranean countries did not reap a windfall from the canal's opening; rather, as *The Economist* presciently observed in 1869, the canal was "cut by French energy and Egyptian money for British advantage." (In fact the engineering was French, but the energy was provided by Egyptians, 120,000 of whom died in the eleven years it took to dig the canal—"all for the advantage of the 'barbarian,'" as an oracle had warned Necho II in the sixth century BCE.) Among Britain's considerable advantages were strong capital markets to draw on for shipbuilding, longer experience of building iron steamships, and the best engines and steamship coal in the world. British tonnage comprised 60 percent of the total transiting the canal in its first year, three times that of French ships; twenty years later Britain's share was three-quarters of the total and France's was only 8 percent. In 1910, British tonnage still made up more than 60 percent and the German merchant marine accounted for 16 percent.

By 1875, the government of Said Pasha's successor had rung up a massive debt and, now convinced of the canal's importance to Britain, Prime Minister Benjamin Disraeli arranged to buy out his share in the Suez Canal Company for £4 million in return for a controlling interest. The next year, Egyptian finances were put under Anglo-French control, and in 1882 the British bombarded Alexandria and seized the canal to begin a forty-year occupation of Egypt. To preserve appearances, the Suez Canal Convention of 1888 guaranteed that "The Suez Maritime Canal shall be always free and open, in time

---

[*] As of 2010, the canal had been lengthened to 193 kilometers and it is now 24 meters deep, with a width on the bottom of 123 meters and 313 meters at the surface.

of war as in time of peace, to every vessel of commerce or of war, without distinction of flag.... The canal shall never be subjected to the exercise of the right of blockade." Needless to say, these principled sentiments were inevitable casualties of war.

The canal was first and foremost a steamship thoroughfare and it might have failed were it not for the development of the high-pressure compound marine engine by the Liverpool shipowner and engineer Alfred Holt, founder of the Ocean Steam Ship Company, better known as the Blue Funnel Line. Holt's shipping career began when he inaugurated steam service from Liverpool to the West Indies, and to Brazil and the river Plate, and a monthly service between Jamaica and New York. In 1863, he and his brother decided that there was too much competition in the Atlantic trades and launched a steamer service to China. Holt claimed that the switch was prompted by a colleague's remark that "'Steamers may occupy the Mediterranean, may tentatively go to Brazil and the River Plate, but China is at least safe for sailing vessels.' I suppose the fiend made me say, 'Is it?'" In the 1850s, John Elder had developed a high-pressure, compound engine that reduced coal consumption by more than half, and in 1866 Holt fitted three Blue Funnel ships with compound engines for service to the Orient. Thanks to their dramatically greater efficiency, these could steam eighty-five hundred miles nonstop before taking on coal at Mauritius and continuing onward to Penang, Singapore, and China.* The opening of the Suez Canal made uninterrupted passages of eight thousand miles unnecessary, but without the efficiencies realized by the compound engine it is thought that no steamship could have afforded to reach India, much less China, even via Suez.

The gains realized by Elder's compound engine were eclipsed in the 1880s by the invention of the triple-expansion engine, which uses steam at high, intermediate, and low pressure, and is about a third more efficient than a compound engine. More efficient still was the steam turbine, perfected for use in ships by Charles A. Parsons, who built a six-horsepower steam turbine in 1884 and quickly realized that it would be well suited to driving ships. One problem to overcome was the phenomenon of cavitation, the result of a vacuum forming around a propeller screw turning at high speed. When Parsons finally hit on the correct configuration of screws and shafts, in trials his 31.5-meter *Turbinia* attained speeds of thirty-four knots.

Parsons labored in relative obscurity until the international naval review

---

* A simple reciprocating engine has a single cylinder in which the piston is moved by steam. A compound steam engine adds a second lower-pressure cylinder, which recycles steam from the first cylinder to do additional work.

held to celebrate Queen Victoria's diamond jubilee in June 1897. *Turbinia* romped through the anchored fleet with breathtaking agility and easily out-ran her pursuers in a dramatic demonstration of the new technology. Shortly thereafter he founded the Parsons Marine Steam Turbine Company, the prospectus of which clearly enunciated the benefits of his engine: "Increased speed, increased carrying power of vessel, increased economy in steam con-sumption, reduced initial cost, reduced weight of machinery, reduced cost of attendance on machinery, diminished cost of upkeep of machinery, largely reduced vibration, and reduced size and weight of screw propeller and shaft-ing." The Admiralty ordered turbine engines for a torpedo-boat destroyer in 1899 and a light cruiser in 1903, but the technology received its greatest boost in 1905 when First Lord of the Admiralty John A. "Jackie" Fisher decided to install them in HMS *Dreadnought*. Commercial interests were somewhat slower to embrace the new technology, but in the same year Cunard chose tur-bines for the *Mauretania* and *Lusitania*, whose seventy-thousand-horsepower engines were three times more powerful than those of the *Dreadnought*.

Just as the compound engine helped ensure the success of the Suez Canal, the submarine telegraph contributed significantly to the expansion of mer-chant shipping in the age of the steamship. The overland telegraph had achieved commercial practicality by the end of the 1830s, and within twenty years insulated submarine cables had been laid across the Irish Sea and the English Channel. In 1866, the *Great Eastern* ran a cable from Ireland to New-foundland. The third of Isambard Kingdom Brunel's innovative ships, the iron-hulled *Great Eastern* measured more than 211 meters long and nearly nineteen thousand gross tons, and no vessel of greater length or tonnage would be built for forty years. Propelled by paddle wheels and a single screw, with five funnels and six masts, the *Great Eastern* never entered the Australia trade for which she was originally intended. Proving too big for economical transatlantic service, the ship went on to lay five transatlantic cables, as well as one between Suez, Aden (which Britain occupied as a coaling station in 1839), and Bombay. Just as telegraph lines on land tended to follow railway lines, submarine cables followed shipping lines, and by the 1870s Bombay was connected to Australia and there were direct links from continental Europe to the United States and Brazil. Transpacific lines were not laid until the early twentieth century, from the United States to the Philippines via Hawaii and from Canada to New Zealand and Australia.

The telegraph contributed to the growth of British ports, but the real win-ners were the burgeoning industries of continental Europe, whose buyers, no longer reliant on ships to convey their wishes, could now order raw materials directly from their overseas suppliers. British ships captured an increasingly

large share of the trade even to continental ports, and in 1870 the British merchant marine comprised 43 percent of the world's total tonnage (as indicated
in ship registers); thirty years later this figure was 51 percent. Overall, the
annual value of international trade grew an estimated 30 percent in the first
three decades of the nineteenth century, to about £400 million. By 1870, it was
worth £2 billion, and by the eve of World War I it had reached £6 billion—
a twentyfold increase in just over a century. Part of this growth was related
directly to the overseas migration of millions of Europeans, among others,
and the increasingly strong ties between the resulting expatriate communities
and their homelands.

Mass Migration and Safety at Sea

The greatest episode in human migration took place between 1815 and 1930,
when 56 million Europeans emigrated overseas. The countries with the highest emigration were Great Britain (11.4 million), Italy (9.9 million), Ireland
(7.3 million), Austria-Hungary (5 million), Germany (4.8 million), and Spain
(4.4 million). English-speaking countries received the lion's share—32.6 million went to the United States, 5 million to Canada, and 3.4 million to Australia. Less well known is the story of immigration to South America. Brazil
took in 4.4 million Europeans and 6.5 million sailed for Argentina, where it
was said that "Mexicans descend from the Aztecs, Peruvians from the Incas,
and Argentines from the ships." Cuba's population also exploded in the nineteenth century, leaping from 150,000 in 1763 to 1.3 million in 1860. The
main sources of this growth were slaves, Chinese laborers, loyalists fleeing
independence movements elsewhere in the Spanish Americas, and Spaniards.
In addition to Europeans, who were by and large voluntary emigrants, about a
million East Indian coolies were shipped to the Caribbean, South Africa, Fiji,
and elsewhere in the British Empire; a quarter million Chinese reached Cuba
and Peru; and the Japanese government helped arrange the transportation of
about 165,000 laborers to Brazil, which was home to the second largest population of overseas Japanese after Manchuria.

Despite minor improvements, such as limiting the number of people that
could be carried per registered ton, shipboard conditions for most passengers
on most routes worsened through the first half of the nineteenth century, and
reached their nadir during the mass exodus from Ireland during the Great
Hunger. In the 1840s, about 1.3 million Irish emigrated to the United States,
most in what were grimly dubbed "coffin ships." In 1846 alone, more than 20
percent of all passengers died before reaching North America. A New York

doctor who visited the sailing ship *Ceylon* the next year testified to a Senate committee on the conditions he found:

> We passed through the steerage . . . but the indescribable filth, the emaciated, half-nude figures, many with the eruption [of boils or rashes] disfiguring their faces, crouching in the bunks or strewed over the decks and cumbering the gangways, broken utensils and debris of food spread recklessly about, presented a picture of which neither pen nor pencil can convey a full idea. . . . Some were just rising from their berths for the first time since leaving Liverpool, having been suffered to lie there during the entire voyage wallowing in their own filth.

The rate of illness aboard British ships was more than three times that on American or German ones. Following American precedent, British legislation of 1849 set minimum space requirements at 14 to 30 square feet (1.3 to 2.8 square meters) per passenger depending on the height of the deck, those on the orlop (lowest) deck being entitled to more space. Passenger berths could be no smaller than six feet by eighteen inches, and there could be no more than two tiers of bunks per deck. The practice of requiring passengers to supply their food for a six-week voyage began to change in 1830 when the city of Bremen legislated that ships provide passengers with cooked food. The British law of 1849 required that passengers be provided with three quarts of water daily as well as a weekly allowance of "2½ [pounds] of bread or biscuit (not inferior to navy biscuit), 1 lb. wheaten flour, 5 lbs. oatmeal, 2 lbs. rice, 2 ozs. tea, ½ lb. sugar, ½ lb. molasses." By 1872 death rates fell to less than twelve per thousand aboard sailing ships, and to only one in a thousand on steamers, and these figures were halved again in the next five years. At this point, when virtually all transatlantic passengers traveled via steamship, all ship fares included food, although many passengers were still required to provide their own utensils and bedding.

Keeping order among passengers was a major problem aboard immigrant ships. Testifying before a legislative inquiry in New South Wales about whether the failure to segregate passengers by sex was "very injurious to the moral condition of the emigrants," the second mate of a German ship reported: "There were about forty girls on board, some of them not more than from ten to twelve years old, and I am sure, and can lay an oath upon it, that I know for certain that every one left the ship as a prostitute. . . . All the sailors, every one, had their girls in the forecastle." The most common approach to prevent such extremes of perversion was to separate passengers according to familial status—families in one part of the ship, single people in another—and by sex. Men and women aboard British ships on the three-month passage to

Australia were segregated as early as 1834, but no similar restriction applied on the North Atlantic until 1852.

Such reforms as were undertaken tended to benefit European emigrants, but others were less fortunate. When the slave trade was abolished new opportunities for exploited labor opened in the coolie trade, the shipment of unskilled Indian and Chinese laborers, which lasted until after World War I. Britain was initially the leading carrier of coolies, but was superseded by France and Spain, while the United States was fourth. Technically indentured servants, coolies were slaves in all but name, kidnapped or duped into leaving China, and, like the indentured English before them, often worked to death by their masters. (Fifty percent of the coolies in Cuba did not survive their term of indenture.) Conditions endured by coolies were even worse than those encountered by impoverished European immigrants. The mortality rate was about 12 percent, but individual ships could lose 40 to 50 percent, and the trade was repeatedly compared with that in slaves, most eloquently by Frederick Douglass, a former slave himself, who described it as

> almost as heart-rending as any that attended the African slave trade. For the manner of procuring Coolies, for the inhumanity to which they are subjected, and of all that appertains to one feature of this new effort to supply certain parts of the world with cheap labor, we cannot do better than to refer our readers to the quiet and evidently truthful statement . . . of one of the Coolies rescued from the ship *Dolores Ugarte*, on board which ship six hundred Coolies perished by fire, deserted and left to their fate by captain and crew.

Mutinies aboard coolie ships were not uncommon, especially if the coolies believed they were bound for the guano-covered Chincha Islands off Peru. Battened belowdecks, mutineers often resorted to setting fires and, when allowed on deck, attacking the crew. In the case of the *Dolores Ugarte*, it was reported that after an ineffectual attempt to douse a mutineers' fire the captain abandoned ship. One hatch was opened but no more than sixty people survived.

Such callous behavior aligned perfectly with Alexander Falconbridge's observation that "a delight in giving torture to a fellow creature is the natural tendency" of the slave trade. This also helps explain the indifference and depravity evident in contemporary testimony about the passenger trades of the nineteenth century. The contempt shown by crews for the people in their charge, whether aboard the *Arctic* or the *Ceylon*, can be attributed to the fact that no one cared very much for sailors. In 1854, an American newspaper estimated that in the course of eighteen months, losses occurred at the rate of "one vessel lost every eleven hours; one stranded every forty-four hours; one abandoned every seventy-five hours, and one sailing and never afterwards heard from, every ten days." Between 1830 and 1900, 20 percent of British mariners perished at sea, and under a law passed in 1870, sailors who signed on for a voyage and then sought to break their contract for fear the ship was unseaworthy could be jailed for three months, as more than sixteen hundred were in the next two years. Even after the peak of the desperate, famine-fueled migration to North America, an estimated one in six sailing ships in the passenger trades sank en route, and in 1873–74 more than four hundred ships and five hundred lives were lost just on the coast of the United Kingdom.

In thirty years, ship losses in Britain had doubled, driving up insurance rates and leading to hideous loss of life, and Parliament at long last legislated minimum standards for the safe operation of ships. One of the most far-reaching developments was the adoption of load lines showing the depth to which a ship could be loaded safely. In the 1830s Lloyd's Register had recommended that ships have a freeboard of three inches for every foot of depth of hold. (The earliest ship classification society, Lloyd's was formed in 1760 as the Register Society at the coffee shop of Edward Lloyd; it published the first register of ships four years later.) By the mid-nineteenth century, the optional "Lloyd's rule" was inadequate to stem the losses due to overloading. Parliamentarian

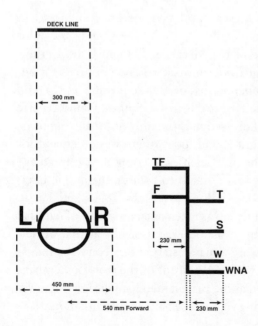

Plimsoll Mark, or Load Line. The distance between the deck line and the mark to which a ship can be loaded safely is called freeboard, which varies according to when and where the vessel is sailing. Tropical (T), summer (S), and winter (W) are the marks that must not be submerged when the vessel is trading in a designated tropical, summer, or winter zone. Additional consideration is given to vessels sailing in freshwater (F) or carrying lumber (L). Winter, North Atlantic (WNA) designates the most dangerous waters—yet among the busiest—routinely used by commercial shipping. The initials on either side of the circle at the center of the mark indicate the classification society under whose rules the ship was designed and built. Here, LR stands for Lloyd's Register.

Samuel Plimsoll maintained that because the value of a ship and its cargo for insurance purposes was whatever the owner said it was, insurance encouraged shipowners to send worn-out and overloaded ships to sea without regard to the safety of either passengers or crews, much less cargoes. Shipowners framed their opposition to reform in terms of the new mantra of free trade, the triumph of which was the repeal of the seventeenth-century Navigation Acts in 1850. Greed had replaced disease as the greatest threat to passengers and crews. As a supporter of shipowners who rejected regulation and oversight of their management put it, "They do not want a fussy, meddlesome, crochetty interference with their business, [nor] an artificial stimulus given to foreign trade by the imposition of needless, frivolous and embarrassing restrictions upon their trade." Nonetheless, Plimsoll and others persevered and after two decades of lobbying passed the Merchant Shipping Act of 1876, the first modern load line legislation. Where the line should be fixed was not determined until 1894, and other countries were slow to follow Britain's lead; Germany passed legislation in 1903 and the United States not until 1924. Six years later the international Load Line Convention of 1930 established uniform regulations governing how deeply ships could be loaded depending on where they were sailing and the season.

Competition on the North Atlantic

Regardless of the dangers attendant on sea travel, people were going to sea in ever greater numbers and not just to emigrate or for business but to travel for travel's sake. The year after passage of the Merchant Shipping Act, Katherine Ledoux published *Ocean Notes for Ladies*, a work best remembered for her macabre observation, "Accidents, too, and loss of life are possible at sea, and I have always felt that a body washed ashore in good clothes, would receive more respect and kinder care than if dressed in those only fit for the rag bag." Off-putting though such advice might sound today, there was a demand for guides to shipboard etiquette and the practicalities of going to sea. In an age of congested and soulless air travel, it is difficult to conjure the public fascination generated by ocean liners, especially between the 1890s and 1950s, when the size of a nation's merchant fleet was taken as a barometer of national greatness and the launch of new ships was followed as avidly as that of new consumer electronics today. Ships were a manifestation of a country's industrial and engineering prowess, and while 51 percent of the world's merchant tonnage sailed under the Red Duster, as the British merchant ensign is known, other countries competed for bragging rights especially in the elite transatlantic passenger trade.

The British-built, three-masted ship Tusitala *of 1883 and the German-built Cunard Line passenger ship* Berengaria, *commissioned in 1913, outward bound from New York around 1930. The last generation of deep-water working sail and the heyday of the ocean liner—which provided regularly scheduled trips across all the major oceans, especially the North Atlantic—all but coincided. Square-riggers remained commercially competitive in some trades through the 1930s, while the engine-only steamship dominated long-distance routes from the 1890s until the coming of the passenger jet in the 1960s. From a Cunard Line brochure for the* Berengaria *in the Norman H. Morse Ocean Liner Collection; courtesy of the Osher Map Library and Smith Center for Cartographic Education, University of Southern Maine, Portland.*

By the turn of the century, British primacy on the North Atlantic was under threat from both Germany and the United States. Foremost of the German shipping executives of the time was Albert Ballin, who eventually became general director of the Hamburg-America Line (Hapag). Although a Jew of modest origins, Ballin had a steadfast belief in Germany's maritime potential that earned him the friendship of the maritime-minded Kaiser Wilhelm II. By 1900 he had helped make Hapag the largest shipping line in the world, with ninety-five oceangoing ships serving a diversified portfolio of routes around the world, and by 1914 twice as many ships served 350 regular ports of call. As remarkable, the world's second largest company was the Bremen-based Norddeutscher Lloyd. Although its operations were global, by the 1880s the company was supreme on the North Atlantic, where it carried 816,000 passengers between 1881 and 1891, 50 percent more than Hapag, and more than Britain's White Star and Cunard combined. In 1897 it ushered in a new generation of superliners with the *Kaiser Wilhelm der Grosse*. The first of only fourteen ships ever built with four funnels, this was the first non-British ship to set a transatlantic speed record since the Collins Line's *Baltic* in 1854, winning the "blue riband" with an average speed of more than twenty-two knots.*

In 1902, American financier J. P. Morgan mounted a more complex challenge to Britain's merchant marine with the founding of the International Mercantile Marine, a conglomerate that acquired a controlling interest in five major shipping companies and forged revenue-sharing agreements with Hapag and Norddeutscher Lloyd. In response to Morgan's acquisition of the White Star Line, the British government offered Cunard a loan of £2.6 million for the construction of two passenger liners, with an annual subsidy for each, on condition that the company remain wholly British for twenty years and that the ships could be requisitioned in wartime. The result was construction of the *Lusitania* and *Mauretania*, the largest and most luxurious liners of their day. The sister ships traded honors for the fastest transatlantic ship until 1909, when the *Mauretania* set a westbound record that stood for twenty years; eastbound, she beat her own record seven times. A U-boat sank the *Lusitania* in 1915 but the *Mauretania* remained in service until 1935.

By this time, the opulence of the gilded-age ocean liner had given way to a sleeker aesthetic. The first vessel to employ on a grand scale the ocean liner style (later known as art deco) characteristic of the interwar transatlantic fleet was the French Line's *Ile de France* of 1927. Her spacious public rooms included a three-deck-high restaurant, a four-deck-high grand foyer, and a Gothic chapel adorned with fourteen pillars. And for the benefit of her Prohibition-weary American passengers she sported what was thought to be the longest bar in any passenger ship. By the end of the decade, the prewar rivalry on the North Atlantic was in full swing. In 1929, Norddeutscher Lloyd's *Bremen* and *Europa* captured the blue riband, an achievement especially notable because they were the first major civilian ships built with bulbous bows, originally developed by the American naval architect David Taylor in 1912. Although such a rounded appendage below the waterline looks ungainly, the bulbous bow deflects water and thereby reduces resistance and improves speed, fuel efficiency, and stability. The bulbous bow remained something of a novelty

---

* From the late 1800s, ships setting record speeds on the transatlantic run were said to have won the blue riband (ribbon), although there was no tangible prize of any kind until 1935, when Robert K. Hales, MP, ordered a silver trophy to be awarded the shipping company with the current record.

until after the *Bremen's* launch, but it did not become a standard feature in hull design until after World War II.

Following the success of the *Ile de France*, the French Line determined to build the largest and most beautiful ship in the world, the design of which fell to naval architect Vladimir Yourkevitch, then an émigré laboring in obscurity in an automobile factory, but who had been responsible for the hull form of the Russian navy's innovative *Borodino*-class battlecruisers of 1912. Yourkevitch's design resulted in the *Normandie*. German engineers overseeing trials of the Russian-designed French ship pronounced it "unimprovable." In addition to a bulbous bow, *Normandie's* hull had an "unmistakably and distressingly pear-shaped" sectional profile amidships. Above the waterline, to heighten the ship's streamlined appearance, Yourkevitch enclosed all the deck machinery and designed the three ovoid funnels with a slight rake and in diminishing size. Ignoring the economic devastation of the Great Depression, the *Normandie* was intended for a deluxe trade, and no two of the four hundred first-class rooms were decorated alike. As Ballin had done with the *Vaterland* (later the United States Line's *Leviathan*) in 1913, rather than allow the funnels to interrupt the ship's grand public spaces—the air-conditioned dining room was longer than the Hall of Mirrors at Versailles—Yourkevitch used split uptakes to create massive open areas, and from center stage of the ship's theater, the first on a ship, one could see daylight beyond the open promenade of the first-class grill room 150 meters aft. The *Normandie* was being converted to a troopship in 1942 when she caught fire and capsized at her berth in New York. She is survived by her great rival, Cunard's faster but somewhat dowdier *Queen Mary*, which entered service a year after the *Normandie* and is today a floating hotel in Long Beach, California.

The North Atlantic "ferry" was far from the only passenger route but for opulence, strength, and speed its ships were the gold standard of the merchant marine. Catering to the world's financial and political elite, they also had to withstand the demands of the most treacherous seas routinely served by commercial shipping—"Winter, North Atlantic" in the formulation of the Load Line Convention. Though more benign, the vast distances of the Pacific made that ocean the final frontier of the passenger liner. Completion of the transcontinental railways across the United States (the first in 1869) and Canada (1885) accelerated the growth of transpacific shipping. For Australians laboring under "the tyranny of distance" from Britain and the rest of the world, this opened an alternative route to England, via the Pacific, North America, and the Atlantic, while Japan and the Orient generally were now accessible to gilded-age American globe-trotters.

Tourists were as easy a mark for satirists as for pickpockets and scam artists (shipping company brochures routinely warned prospective passengers to be wary of "professional gamblers"), and the English translator Osman Edwards revised the lyrics to "Yankee Doodle" to mock the acquisitiveness of Americans he encountered in Japan at the turn of the century:

> Doodle *San* will leave Japan
> With several tons of cargo;
> Folk will stare, when all his ware
> Is poured into Chicago,
> There's silk, cut velvet, old brocade,
> And everything that's *joto*
> And ancient bronzes newly made
> By dealers in Kyoto.

Edwards's portrayal of Yanks as gauche arrivistes conforms to a standard stereotype of the tourist, and Americans were no worse than any of their contemporaries. But while travelers may well have been gulled by artistic forgeries, the new aesthetic sensibilities awakened in travelers of all kinds had a transformative effect on art and literature. Modernism made its American debut with the Armory Show of 1913, which was exhibited in New York, Boston, and (Edwards's gibe notwithstanding) the Art Institute of Chicago, and the western avant-garde of the early twentieth century owes an enormous debt to the lines of communication laid down by practical shippers in the nineteenth.

Cruising and Yachting

In 1876–77, Anna Brassey and her railroad magnate husband circumnavigated the world in their yacht, *Sunbeam*, with calls at Brazil, Chile, Tahiti, Hawaii, and Japan, before returning home via Hong Kong, Macau, Singapore, Penang, Ceylon, the Suez Canal, and Portugal. Built for long-distance cruising on a grand scale, the three-masted topsail schooner carried nine guests and a crew of thirty-two, and Brassey's book, *A Voyage in the* Sunbeam; *Our Home on the Ocean for Eleven Months*, popularized the idea of the world tour. Two years later, a company advertised a round-the-world cruise aboard the former Peninsular and Orient steamer *Ceylon*, "a yacht in every sense, carrying no cargo, and . . . replete with every luxury and comfort . . . an excellent band on board also a steam launch for landing passengers." Despite the attractions of the ship, the itinerary, and the company's promise to preserve "the character of a private yachting party of friends, as distinguished from a compliment [*sic*] of ordinary passengers," the ship was not full when it sailed. But thanks to the telegraph, the company could advertise the possibility of joining the ship at one of its many ports of call.

Soon, transatlantic companies faced with excess capacity in the off-season began to experiment with using their ships for cruising. In 1891, Albert Ballin sent the *Augusta Victoria* on a winter tour of the Mediterranean. This proved a great success, but the battened-down ships designed for the North Atlantic lacked the amenities required of more indolent vacationers in warmer climes, and ten years later Hapag commissioned the first purpose-built cruise ship, the *Prinzessin Victoria Luise*, with accommodations for two hundred first-class passengers on pleasure trips to the Mediterranean, Scandinavia, and the Caribbean. Other ships followed and opened new routes to destinations as varied as continental interiors via the world's major rivers and the icy wastes of the Arctic and Antarctica. Long-distance passenger liners are a thing of the past; their death knell was sounded by the commercial success of the passenger jet, which made its first commercial transatlantic flight in 1958. Nonetheless, the number of people who take sea cruises every year—between fourteen and twenty million passengers worldwide in 2010—far exceeds the number of passengers ever carried by ship at the height of the passenger trades. This figure includes passengers on sea voyages of more than sixty hours with at least two ports of call and does not count "cruises to nowhere"—"nowhere" being international waters where duty-free shopping and gambling are allowed—which had their origins during Prohibition.

As nineteenth-century industrialization and commercial expansion drew huge numbers of people into cities, steamboats created opportunities for city dwellers with limited funds to escape the squalor and enjoy a few hours on the water. By the 1860s, enterprising steamboat operators were building excursion steamers "designed especially to secure elegance, speed, comfort, ample accommodation, and even luxuriousness of interior appointments," as well as a reasonable measure of safety. For the first time, people had the opportunity of a benign on-the-water experience free of backbreaking work, imminent danger, or indefinite separation. For many such day trips were "the only airings, away from the din and sweltering confusion" of the city. So wrote the *New York Times* in an 1880 report on "a vast and growing trade" that in a quarter century had sprung from nothing to transport as many as twenty-five million people every summer on excursions around New York Bay, the Hudson River, Long Island Sound, and the nearby Atlantic beaches. Many companies purchased land within ten to thirty miles of their respective cities where they built picnic gardens and miniature resorts for day-trippers and weekenders. In time many of these places grew into suburban villages and towns in their own right, served by year-round ferry service.

Proximity to land was no guarantee of safe passage, however, and the industry lurched from improvement to improvement in the wake of horrific accidents. More than six hundred passengers drowned when a collier sank the *Princess Alice* on the Thames near London in 1878, and the burning of the *General Slocum* in New York's East River in 1904 left around a thousand people dead, mostly women and children on a church-sponsored excursion. Most disquieting was the flooding and capsize of the Great Lakes excursion vessel *Eastland* in the Chicago River in 1915. Though she was only half submerged and less than twenty feet from shore with three bow lines still fast to the pier, 841 people died. The *Princess Alice* disaster led to the implementation of rules of the road for inland waters, while the *General Slocum* incident sparked an overhaul of the negligent U.S. Steamboat Inspection Service.

Notwithstanding such tragedies, for the better off and more adventurous in spirit, yachting was growing in popularity. Cruising and racing for pleasure is generally thought to have had its origins in the Netherlands in the seventeenth century, from where Charles II introduced the sport to England after being presented with the ninety-two-ton yacht *Mary* by the city of Amsterdam. More than twenty yachts were commissioned over the next two decades and the weakness for ridiculous and diminutive yacht names was apparent from the start: Charles's *The Folly*, Prince Rupert's *Fanfan*, and the *Jamie*, named for the future James II. The Royal Cork Yacht Club, the world's oldest, traces its origins to 1710, and the Royal Yacht Squadron at Cowes and the New York Yacht Club followed in 1815 and 1844, respectively. Although yachting was the preserve of the very wealthy on a par with the Brasseys—Morgans and Vanderbilts in the United States, the British tea baron Sir Thomas Lipton, and Germany's Kaiser Wilhelm II—races generated as much popular enthusiasm as thoroughbred horse racing does today.

Gradually, however, yachting spread to the members of the growing middle class. Extolled as "the most difficult, complicated, and comprehensive" of all sports, as Edwin Brett wrote in 1869, it was followed "by men of adventurous temperament; by men who like life in the open air, particularly in wild weather . . . who delight in testing their skill, daring, and perseverance against those of their brother sportsmen in the most refined and scientific of all forms of racing." Brett believed "the number of born yachtsmen . . . very considerable," and his survey offered something for a range of tastes and pockets, from five-ton, single-handed yachts to three-hundred-ton steamers. The popularity of ocean cruising was excited by the exploits of such sailors as Joshua Slocum, who sailed around the world single-handed between 1895 and 1898, and whose account of his travels has never gone out of print. Many have followed in his wake, but a new era dawned in 1969, when six men set out to compete in the first nonstop solo circumnavigation under sail. Only Robin Knox-Johnston finished within the rules, sailing 30,123 miles in 313 days; after rounding Cape Horn, challenger Bernard Moitessier decided to keep sailing east and after 37,455 miles in 301 days put into Tahiti. The solo, nonstop circumnavigation remains the highest accomplishment of the ocean sailor, men and women alike. In 2005, Ellen MacArthur held the world record for sailing a trimaran around the world in under 72 days; the youngest person to achieve the feat, Jessica Watson, sailed a ten-meter sloop nearly twenty thousand miles in 210 days before she was seventeen.

Exploration

Extreme cruising, whether alone around the world or aboard ship in polar seas, takes its inspiration from sentiments like Brett's summons to people "of adventurous temperament," but polar destinations were only opened by explorers of the nineteenth century. The Pacific remained the region of greatest interest to the British, French, Russians, and, from the 1830s, Americans, but after 1815 there was a burst of comparatively quixotic Arctic and Antarctic ventures motivated as much by national pride and personal vanity as by rational economic or political calculation. If the benefits were not immediately apparent, however, these voyages helped lay the foundations for the sorts of oceanographic research that remain the primary focus of maritime exploration today. The English had abandoned the search for a Northwest Passage after a 1616 expedition by William Baffin and Robert Bylot (one of Henry Hudson's mutineers) to Lancaster Sound, north of Baffin Island, and Hudson Bay. Inspired by favorable reports from whalers operating west of Greenland, in 1818 John Ross renewed the quest from the Atlantic in the first of a series of expeditions that gradually penetrated the Canadian Arctic. Seven years later, Frederick William Beechey sailed through the Bering Strait to attempt the passage from west to east. But Arctic exploration reached its greatest intensity in the decade after the disappearance of Sir John Franklin's *Erebus* and *Terror*, when more than a dozen British and American ships searched for signs of the expedition, remains of which were found in 1854. The Northwest Passage remained impassable by boat until the Norwegian Roald Amundsen pioneered the route in the twenty-one-meter sloop *Gjøa* in 1903–1906, a quarter century after Adolf Nordenskiöld, a Swede, made the first transit of the Northeast Passage from the Barents Sea to the North Pacific.

The Antarctic continent was first spotted in 1820 by the Russian explorer Fabian Gottlieb von Bellingshausen, followed the same year by the British sealer William Smith, sailing as pilot of a Royal Navy ship, and the Connecticut sealer Nathaniel Palmer. Sealers and whalers continued to visit Antarctica through the century, but no one stepped foot on the continent until 1895, when the Sixth International Geographical Congress pronounced Antarctica "the greatest piece of geographical exploration still to be undertaken." Unlike the Arctic, which is an ice-covered sea, Antarctica is an icebound continent, but navigating the coast required seamanship of an extraordinarily high caliber, epitomized in the unexampled small boat passages of Sir Ernest Henry Shackleton after his ship, *Endurance*, was crushed by ice in the Weddell Sea in 1915.

Navigation around Antarctica and other newly discovered coasts proceeded hand-in-hand with painstaking and time-consuming coastal surveys. During his quarter century as hydrographer of the navy (1826–51), Admiral Beaufort oversaw a complete resurvey of the British Isles, as well as partial surveys of the Mediterranean and Arctic. Observations were not limited to oceanographic matters, and since the time of Cook and Bougainville, ethnography and the investigation of terrestrial flora and fauna had been routine if ancillary features of expeditions engaged in maritime exploration and coastal surveys. It was for just such work that the twenty-one-year-old botanist Charles Darwin joined HMS *Beagle* on the ship's five-year survey of South American waters in the 1830s. Darwin's close friend Joseph D. Hooker, later director of the Royal Botanical Gardens at Kew, accompanied an expedition commanded by James Clark Ross, John Ross's nephew, to locate the South Magnetic Pole and undertake oceanographic, botanical, and zoological observations in and around Tasmania, New Zealand, and Antarctica.

In the early 1870s, the Royal Society began pushing for a large-scale expedition to combine the various lines of inquiry that were coming to define the discipline of oceanography, a term coined by Maury in 1859. Commanded by Captain George Strong Nares, the Royal Navy screw corvette *Challenger* was fitted with a wide array of equipment for measuring currents and the temperature of air and water, collecting bottom samples from depths of up to thirty-seven hundred meters, and taking soundings in depths up to eleven thousand meters. Over the course of three and a half years, the *Challenger*'s team of six civilian scientists discovered more than four thousand previously unknown specimens of marine animals and plants. In the twentieth century, the horizons of maritime exploration widened to embrace disciplines as diverse as physical, chemical, and biological oceanography, climatology, fisheries science, and commercial endeavors from oil exploration to undersea mining.

Oil: From Whaleship to Tanker

Although governments had stopped sponsoring voyages to the Arctic in the seventeenth century, Basque, Dutch, and English whalers had long been active in the waters of Newfoundland and the Arctic. Originally whaling was tied closely to shore stations where whale blubber was rendered into oil. Around 1750, the adoption of tryworks—iron cauldrons erected over fire pits for boiling blubber aboard ship—enabled whalers to remain at sea for months. This coincided with the start of the hunt for sperm whales, whose spermaceti produced a superior candle, and had considerable repercussions for the growth of the Nantucket whaling industry, which by 1775 boasted about three hundred ships that sailed as far as Brazil and the Falkland Islands.

The Nantucket whale fishery contracted severely during and after the American Revolution, while the British government began subsidizing whalers venturing to the South Atlantic, the Indian Ocean, and the Pacific. The start of the Pacific whale fishery started in 1787 when a British ship under a Nantucket captain began catching sperm whales off the coast of Chile. Lacking opportunities at home, American captains commanded two-thirds of the British whalers in the southern fishery between 1788 and 1812, but the unsubsidized American whaling industry languished until after 1815. Within six years there were 120 U.S.-flag whaleships in the Pacific, most hailing from Nantucket, New Bedford, and other ports from southern New England and Long Island. At the industry's peak in the 1840s, the American whaling fleet numbered more than six hundred ships that routinely spent up to four years away from home, though they made periodic stops at Hawaii, Tahiti, and other ports to off-load their oil and obtain fresh provisions. By the 1840s, sperm whales were overfished but there was a flourishing market for the pliant whalebone—as a stiffener for corsets, in umbrellas, and for industrial brushes—from baleen whales, which filter food from the water with baleen plates, and the industry was rejuvenated by Thomas Roys's 1848 report of bowhead and right whales (both of which are baleen whales) in the Bering Strait. Up to this point, whale oil had been widely used for lighting, although there were many cheaper fuels available, especially kerosene, which became widespread in the United States and Europe in the 1850s. But whale oil remained a constituent in lubricants, soaps, perfumes, and margarine, and by the twentieth century whales were threatened with extinction thanks to the development of ever more efficient means of hunting them. In 1937 nine nations "desiring to secure the prosperity of the whaling industry and, for that purpose, to maintain the stock of whales" signed the International Agreement for the Regulation of Whaling

This whale's tooth incised with the picture of a ship of the line is typical of the sailor's art of scrimshaw—engravings, scrollwork, and carvings in bone or ivory. In the nineteenth century, when an anonymous Dutch or German sailor carved this, European whalers frequently concentrated their efforts in the North Atlantic and Arctic Oceans and their tributary seas like the Davis Strait and the Barents Sea. Courtesy of the Zuiderzeemuseum, Enkhuizen, The Netherlands.

and established an Antarctic whale sanctuary. Four decades later the International Whaling Commission imposed a ban on commercial whaling, and vast whale sanctuaries now encompass the entire Indian Ocean and the waters surrounding Antarctica.

The mass production of kerosene had begun with the discovery of oil in Pennsylvania in 1859, and until the end of the century it was the most important product refined from oil. In addition to lighting, it was used in early internal combustion engines, although the preferred fuel was gasoline, a by-product of kerosene cracking. The birth of the oil age can be dated to 1885, when Karl Benz registered a patent for his Motorwagen. Within decades, the automobile had changed human society beyond all recognition, with enormous implications for the history of maritime trade, naval warfare, and geopolitics. Given the great distances between industrialized Europe and North America and the world's major petroleum reserves—at the time found only in the Caspian Sea and the continental United States—the personal car could hardly have succeeded without the development of the oceangoing oil tanker, the prototype of which, the *Glückauf*, was coincidentally launched the year Benz received his patent.

The United States had been a major exporter of kerosene, which was known as case oil because it was usually shipped in five-gallon cans carried two to a case. This was costly and inefficient, but carrying oil in bulk was problematic. Wooden barrels weighed too much, and explosive fumes gathered in the spaces between the barrels. One solution was to pump oil directly into a ship's hull, an approach pioneered by Caspian Sea oilman Ludwig Nobel, brother of Alfred Nobel of prize fame. In 1878, Nobel built the tanker *Zoroaster* to carry oil from Baku to Astrakhan and up the Volga River for distribution into Europe. (Zoroaster, or Zarathustra, was the prophet of the ancient Persian religion whose cult was associated with fire altars built around natural petroleum seeps.) In 1885 Wilhelm A. Riedemann contracted the British firm of Armstrong, Mitchell & Co. to build the *Glückauf*, a hundred-meter auxiliary barkentine whose hull was divided into eight tanks separated by bulkheads. On her maiden voyage she carried "910,221 gallons petroleum in bulk," or 21,672 barrels, a measure held over from the whaling trade. Resistance to the new tankers came mostly from longshoremen concerned for their safety— German dockworkers nicknamed the *Glückauf* (good luck), the *Fliegauf* (blow up)—and worried that the less labor-intensive method of loading the ships threatened their livelihood. Nonetheless the design was technically sound and enormously profitable and by 1906, 99 percent of the world's oil was carried in tankers.

As a fuel, oil had enormous advantages over coal: it burned more efficiently and therefore took up less space, and it was easier and cleaner to handle. In 1912, newly appointed First Lord of the Admiralty Winston Churchill ordered the construction of five oil-fueled *Queen Elizabeth*–class battleships. To ensure that the navy not be caught short during the pending conflict with Germany, in June 1914 Churchill negotiated for the Admiralty a 51 percent share in the Anglo-Persian Oil Company (the forerunner of BP), which had begun exporting oil through Abadan three years before. Many questioned the wisdom of abandoning one of Britain's great industrial advantages, namely its native coal, the best in the world for powering marine engines, but the switch to oil was based entirely on military considerations and during World War I oil-burning British ships had significantly better operational endurance than their coal-fired counterparts in the German fleet. But there was no shortage of British coal, which accounted for three-quarters of the eighty million tons of marine coal consumed annually—the bulk of it by British ships—and by the end of World War I, Britain maintained 181 overseas coaling stations.

The availability of petroleum-based fuels also facilitated the adoption of diesel engines for ships, which began in the early 1900s. Although diesel-powered motorships developed in the 1920s had better fuel economy, smaller propulsion plants, greater carrying capacity, and smaller crews than steam-

*Built for transpacific service between Seattle and Shanghai, the Great Northern Steam-
ship Company's passenger freighter* Minnesota *was driven by a pair of triple-expansion
steam engines whose insatiable demand for coal made for unrelenting toil by the ship's
stokers. This photograph was taken while the ship was under charter to the U.S. Navy
as the troopship USS* Troy *(there was already a battleship USS* Minnesota*) during
World War I. But the conditions in the inferno belowdecks in steamships remained the
same regardless of the ship's mission. Courtesy of the U.S. Naval History and Heritage
Command, Washington, D.C.*

ships, the only countries to really embrace the new technology were Norway, Denmark, and Sweden. From Great Britain and Germany to Japan, most
shippers preferred to pay the lower initial cost of steamships rather than order
more expensive, but in the long run more economical, diesel engines, and in
1935 more than 80 percent of the world fleet was still powered by coal- or
oil-fired steam engines. What no one could foresee at the time is that while
Churchill's decision would shape the course and conduct of international relations into the twenty-first century, in the same period the British merchant
marine and Royal Navy would all but vanish from the world stage.

The transatlantic crossings of the *Sirius* and *Great Western* represent a watershed in the history of human transportation and communication. But as events
would show, underlying the developments that brought about increased speed

and reliability at sea was an even more dramatic acceleration in the pace of change itself. As a result, the steam age at sea lasted barely a century before a raft of new technologies swept it aside, and the decades since the 1950s have been in some respects even more revolutionary than the preceding century and a half. In the meantime, where commercial interests led, navies followed. Despite a drastic fall in naval budgets through the 1850s, naval planners followed developments in marine engineering and readily adopted them when they seemed suitable for military applications and fiscal prudence allowed. Yet these and other advances upset the global balance of power and ushered in a half century of warfare whose naval tactics and weaponry were unprecedentedly lethal.

Chapter 19

Naval Power in Steam and Steel

Between the mid-nineteenth and mid-twentieth centuries, the technology of naval ships and weapons, the analysis of naval doctrine and strategic thought, and the tactical application of naval power underwent more extensive and profound change than in the previous twenty-five hundred years. Transformed from the "wooden walls" of Themistocles to what Winston Churchill called "castles of steel," the navies of the world grew to unprecedented size in numbers of ships and personnel. Their guns were capable of hitting moving targets at distances of up to twenty miles and they operated in three dimensions: on the surface, beneath the surface, and in the air. While improvements in hygiene, food preservation, and the fleet train made sailors less likely to die of disease, infection, or malnutrition, the leading causes of death in the age of sail, naval combat grew increasingly deadly. In the course of ten major wars fought between 1652 and 1815, the Royal Navy lost 1,452 ships. Only 204 (14 percent) were lost in action; more than half the losses were the result of accidents, mainly shipwreck and foundering; and captures accounted for a third. Of the 1,694 surface warships lost by all combatants in World War II, 81 percent sank as the result of enemy action, 9 percent were scuttled, 5 percent were lost in accidents, and 5 percent were captured. Navies' embrace of technological change to improve their ability to attack and to defend themselves required, in turn, a growing dependence on industrial output to ensure the reliable flow of replacement vessels.

As technology changed so, too, did the rationale for and doctrines of naval warfare. By the end of the nineteenth century, European maritime powers had embarked on their last burst of overseas expansion, an effort driven in part by mercantilist ambition to acquire raw materials and open new markets for domestic industry. Inextricably related to this was the need to acquire overseas coaling stations and bases for the navies required to protect outposts of empire and the sea routes to them. Increasingly complex ship and weapons technology, together with more intricate approaches to diplomacy and statecraft, gave rise to more scientific approaches to the application of naval power. Training became an academic discipline and prospective naval officers received their education in naval academies while national staff and war colleges became incubators of naval doctrine. By the 1950s, the age of the battleship was over, and the world was on the cusp of yet another metamorphosis in sea power that would see the rise of nuclear-armed and nuclear-powered navies, as well as sporadic efforts by nonstate actors to engage in asymmetric warfare.

Navies Enter the Machine Age

For the first half of the nineteenth century, the initiative for adopting steam, iron, and steel remained squarely with merchant shippers. Although institutional lethargy can be blamed for some naval officials' resistance, there were practical reasons to proceed cautiously and not jettison several thousand years of experience in sail-powered, wooden fighting ships. Steam technology was so unreliable that even commercial steamships intended for high-seas service carried auxiliary sailing rigs until late in the century. Before the invention of the high-pressure compound engine, the notion of leading fleets of ships dependent on fuel-hungry engines of questionable reliability back and forth across the Atlantic as Villeneuve and Nelson had done under sail was out of the question. Nor were the economics of steam technology any more favorable to navies than to merchants. According to an 1852 study, a ninety-gun screw steamship with a five-hundred-horsepower engine cost 40 percent more than an otherwise identical sail-powered ship, and until 1861 the British and French were more inclined to retrofit sailing ships with engines than to build new steam warships.

The value of the new technologies began to tell during the First Opium War. Although iron hulls and fittings had tremendous advantages over wood, they wrought havoc on magnetic compass readings, a problem solved by Sir George Airey in the 1840s. This was just in time for the East India Company to order the iron-hulled side-wheeler *Nemesis*, which epitomized Britain's military and technological advantage over China. In battles at the Bogue Forts, Amoy, and Ningbo, the hull of the *Nemesis* suffered much less damage from enemy guns than British or Chinese wooden ships. The experience of the Mexican navy's British-built *Guadeloupe* in contending with secessionist movements in the Yucatán and Texas was similar, and her British captain was particularly impressed by the fact that when penetrated by enemy fire, the hull did not splinter. At the same time, the effort to discover vulnerabilities in the new technology was relentless. Iron construction was reasonably impervious to shot from smoothbore, muzzle-loading cannon but not to breech-loading guns with rifled barrels and explosive shells. Improved armament also exacerbated the most glaring weakness of the paddle wheel, the machinery of which is above the waterline and vulnerable to enemy fire. First-rate steam-powered warships were not a realistic option until after the development of the screw propeller whose engines could be placed below the waterline.

Engineering difficulties notwithstanding, the British and French remained locked in a naval arms race and by midcentury they had a hundred steam warships between them; the rest of the world's navies had a total of eighteen. The rivals set aside their differences to support the Ottoman Empire against encroaching Russian influence in the Caucasus, Persia, and the Near East, the gateways to British India, and to keep Russian warships out of the Mediterranean. Non-Turkish warships had been prohibited from transiting the Bosporus and Dardanelles until 1833, when the Ottomans secretly granted the Russian fleet freedom of passage. Citing the "ancient rule of the Sultan," which had closed the straits in 1475, the London Straits Convention of 1841 revived the prohibition, thus corralling Russia's Black Sea fleet. When war began in October 1853, a Russian battleship fleet sailed to Sinop—twice as far from Istanbul as from Sevastopol—and using the new explosive shells developed by France's Admiral Henri-Joseph Paixhans destroyed an Ottoman frigate squadron. The Ottomans welcomed the British and French fleets into the Black Sea, and while Russian and Turkish armies battled in the Balkans and Caucasus, French and English ships bombarded the forts at Sevastopol, in the Crimea, and Kinburn, in the Dnieper estuary. Although the steamships could enter and withdraw from action at will, their wooden hulls were vulnerable to Russian shell fire, and the French built a collection of floating batteries sheathed in four-inch iron plate that withstood shelling even when well within range of the forts. After the war, the Treaty of Paris opened the Black Sea to the merchant shipping of all nations, but the sea was "perpetually interdicted to the Flag of War, either of Powers possessing its coasts, or of any other power," a condition that Russia repudiated in 1870 when it began building a new Black Sea fleet.

Impressed with the destruction of the Ottoman fleet at Sinop by exploding shells and the resilience of the French ironclads in the Crimea, France's surveyor of the navy, Stanislas Dupuy de Lôme, designed *La Gloire*, whose wooden hull was clad with iron plate and reinforced with iron fastenings. With a single iron deck, the single-screw, three-masted ship mounted thirty-six 6.4-inch (16.2 cm) muzzle-loading, rifled guns. Far from helping the French achieve naval superiority over the British, however, *La Gloire* prompted the Royal Navy to develop plans for what became the most powerful and heavily armored ship afloat. Launched in 1860, at 128 meters HMS *Warrior* was half again as long as the 120-gun first-rate HMS *Howe*. *Warrior's* primary armament consisted of thirty 68-pounder and ten 110-pounder breech-loading guns, twenty-six of which were mounted on the main deck within a central citadel, essentially an armor-protected box. Her superior speed enabled her to outdistance and outmaneuver any battleship then afloat, and although designed to fight under steam, she was rigged as a three-masted ship and her ten-ton, two-bladed propeller could be hoisted free of the water to reduce drag when under sail. Classified as a forty-gun frigate, during her trials she received the accolade that defined her challenge to the existing naval order: "She looks like a black snake among the rabbits"—the rabbits being the stubbier, high-sided ships of the line like the *Howe*.

The American Civil War

By the 1870s, all the world's major navies had converted to iron-hulled, steam-powered ships armed with exploding-shell guns and armor protection for their vital spaces, including engines, primary batteries, and magazines, a wholesale transformation that resulted from the experience gained in the American Civil War. Commerce raiding and naval warfare on the coasts and rivers of the United States played critical roles in the conflict, but these are regarded as something of an aside because the war's most obviously decisive battles took place on land and there were no fleet actions to speak of. When hostilities began, the U.S. Navy had about nine thousand men and forty-two ships, a dozen of the Home Squadron, and the rest dispersed among the Mediterranean, Brazilian, Pacific, and East Indies Squadrons to protect American commercial interests, and the African Squadron, which patrolled against slave traders. With fifty-three hundred ships, the United States merchant marine was second only to that of Great Britain, with fifty-eight hundred; together the two nations accounted for 82 percent of the world's registered ships. Yet with no imminent threats to its commercial or territorial security, the U.S. Navy was under no compulsion to keep pace with the latest developments in the European navies. John Ericsson's sloop of war USS *Princeton* (1843) was among the first screw-propelled warships ever built, and the navy adopted ordnance officer John A. Dahlgren's shell gun in the 1850s, but the navy's technological innovations were otherwise few. The Civil War changed everything. Whereas the prewar fleet consisted mostly of sail-powered ships with a handful of side-wheelers, about 10 percent of the seven hundred ships commissioned during the war were iron or ironclad vessels, many of them monitors and gunboats without sailing rigs of any kind and most of them propelled by screws rather than paddles. While the Confederacy produced far fewer ships, unrigged armored vessels, including primitive submarines, made up an even higher proportion of the Southern fleet.

Blockade and Blockade-Running

The Union and Confederacy approached the naval war from distinct positions. Small though the U.S. Navy was—and about 10 percent of the officer corps resigned their commissions to serve the South—the North had the shipbuilding expertise, industrial infrastructure, and manpower to expand its fleet with relative ease. The South had no warships and limited shipbuilding capacity because it had traditionally depended on the Northern states for most of its industrial manufactures and foreign trade. That the naval conflict would be an instance of what is now called asymmetric warfare was clear from the outset, when Confederate president Jefferson Davis issued letters of marque to anyone who sought to capture Northern shipping. President Abraham Lincoln responded by warning that "If any person, under the pretended authority of said [Confederate] States . . . shall molest a vessel of the United States or the persons or cargo on board of her, such person Will be held amenable to the laws of the United States for the prevention and punishment of piracy." In a word, death.

British reaction was swift and negative; one parliamentarian declared that "Anybody dealing with a man under those circumstances as a pirate and putting him to death would . . . be guilty of murder" and another insisted that the Northern states "must not be allowed . . . so to strain the law as to convert privateering into piracy, and visit it with death." Five years before, Great Britain had helped draft the Declaration of Paris ending privateering and clarifying the rights of belligerents and neutrals. The four points of the declaration were short and to the point:

1. Privateering is, and remains abolished.
2. The neutral flag covers enemy's goods, with the exception of contraband of war.
3. Neutral goods, with the exception of contraband of war, are not liable to capture under the enemy's flag.

4. Blockades, in order to be binding, must be effective, that is to say, maintained by a force sufficient really to prevent access to the coast of the
enemy.

Fearful that in a war against a European power the government might need
to issue letters of marque to augment its inferior forces, the United States had
declined to ratify the agreement. As the superior power against the South,
the Lincoln administration now sought to sign the Declaration of Paris, but
the British and French demurred until the conclusion of hostilities. Lincoln's
resolve was tested when Confederate privateer William W. Smith was captured, tried for piracy, found guilty, and sentenced to die. President Davis
asserted that Smith was not a common criminal and that his government
would execute one high-ranking Union prisoner of war for every Southerner
executed for piracy. The U.S. court's ruling was overturned, and Smith and
other Confederate privateers were thereafter treated as prisoners of war.

At the same time, Lincoln declared a blockade to prevent the Confederacy
from trading cotton for munitions and other necessities. Stopping trade at
Southern ports without involving foreign powers posed a different problem for
Lincoln. Issuing an executive order to close ports and arresting ships for violating municipal law would uphold the government's position that the United
States faced nothing more than a domestic insurrection and that the Confederacy had no standing as a sovereign state. However, the detention of foreign
ships for smuggling would antagonize Britain and France, which were already
suspected of Southern sympathies. The alternative was to blockade the South,
an act of war that gave the Confederacy the status of an independent belligerent and required the deployment of massive numbers of blockading ships. Lincoln chose the latter option and by July there were squadrons off most major
ports along the twenty-five-hundred-mile coast from Virginia to Texas. The
dramatic escapades of blockade-runners give the impression that the blockade was ineffective, yet more than two-thirds of the three hundred blockade-
runners were eventually captured or destroyed. Moreover, there were only
thirteen hundred attempts to slip the blockade. Before the war, the country's
largest export ports after New York were New Orleans, Mobile, Charleston,
and Savannah, and more than three thousand ships cleared the port of New
Orleans alone. The blockade drove up the cost of imports, reduced the government's revenues from trade, and hobbled the South's ability to pay for or
import war matériel from abroad.

The Confederate States Navy's offensive capability depended on nine commerce raiders, five built in Great Britain, which between them captured more
than 250 merchantmen. After the war the United States argued that in letting

the Confederacy acquire ships from English and Scottish yards, Great Britain had violated its neutrality and was therefore liable for the destruction wrought by the British-built raiders. The *Alabama* claims (so-called because the CSS *Alabama* alone accounted for five million dollars in losses) were resolved under the Treaty of Washington (1871), by which an international tribunal found that Britain had not exercised "due diligence" and awarded the United States $15.5 million in damages. The outright loss of merchant ships was aggravated by the tenfold increase in the cost of insurance on American ships and the consequent transfer of more than a thousand vessels—more than eight hundred thousand tons of shipping—to foreign, mostly British, registry to give them the protection of a neutral flag. The American merchant marine never recovered, thanks to a combination of protectionist legislation that prevented the purchase of foreign-built ships or the return to American registry of any ship sold foreign; prohibitive tariffs that inhibited the growth of iron shipbuilding; and a redirection of national investment toward inland development.

Ironclads and the River War

Lacking the wherewithal to build a fleet comparable to the Union's, Confederate navy secretary Stephen Mallory determined to shift the terms of the contest. "I regard the possession of an iron-armored ship as a matter of the first necessity," he wrote in May 1861; "inequality of numbers may be compensated for by invulnerability; and thus not only does economy but naval success dictate the wisdom and expediency of fighting with iron against wood." The South embarked on a campaign to convert existing vessels into ironclads that could operate with impunity against wooden ships. The first was built around the hull of the screw frigate USS *Merrimack*, which was captured with the Gosport Navy Yard in Norfolk, Virginia. The result was the central battery frigate CSS *Virginia*, with a forty-three-meter-long casemate consisting of a sixty-one-centimeter-thick shell of oak and pine sheathed with ten centimeters of rolled iron and armed with twelve guns.

To counter the threat posed by the *Virginia*, the U.S. Navy ordered prototypes of armored steamships of distinct design: two broadside ironclads, and one with a revolving turret, John Ericsson's *Monitor*. Revolutionary in the extreme, the *Monitor* was the first practical warship built without a sailing rig or oars. The vessel consisted of a hull fifty-five meters long by nearly thirteen meters in beam upon which rested an iron "raft," the dual function of which was to protect the hull from ramming and to provide the vessel with stability in a seaway. Driven by a single propeller, she could steam at six knots. Visually and technologically, the *Monitor*'s most distinguishing feature was its rotating turret. Measuring six meters in diameter and nearly three meters high and mounted on a steam-powered spindle, it incorporated two seven-ton Dahlgren smoothbore shell guns. The resulting profile earned the *Monitor* the epithet "cheesebox on a raft."

The *Virginia* handily sank two wooden steam frigates and damaged a third off Norfolk before being brought to battle by the *Monitor* on March 8, 1862. The ships fought at close range for four hours, but neither was able to inflict decisive damage on the other. Injuries were few: the *Monitor* had 1 wounded, and the *Virginia* 2 dead and 19 wounded. (By way of comparison, in 1812 a fifteen-minute engagement between the evenly matched wooden frigates USS *Chesapeake* and HMS *Shannon* killed 78 and wounded more than 150.) The Confederates were eventually forced to destroy the *Virginia* on their retreat from Norfolk, and the *Monitor* sank at the end of the year while under tow to Wilmington, North Carolina. Their premature ends notwithstanding, it was clear that though the two ships had failed to destroy each other, they had rung the death knell of the wooden warship.

This was most evident in the river war, a cornerstone of Union general Winfield Scott's strategy of drawing a noose around the Confederacy by sea and river, a program dubbed the Anaconda Plan. Scott felt that victory over the Confederate states could be achieved most quickly and economically by "enveloping them all (nearly) at once by a cordon of posts on the Mississippi to its mouth from its junction with the Ohio, and blockading ships of war on the sea-board," and on tributaries of the Mississippi and Ohio as well. He further noted that "the transportation of men and all supplies by water is about a fifth of the land cost, besides the immense saving in time." Scott's plan was adopted piecemeal, but the strategic mind-set that underlay his idea is clear from the fact that virtually all Union armies were named for rivers; the Southern preference was to name armies for states and military districts. The most important of the river campaigns was fought for control of the Mississippi. In April 1862, Flag Officer David G. Farragut sailed up the Mississippi to capture New Orleans, Baton Rouge, and Natchez, while to the north gunboats helped secure the Tennessee and Cumberland Rivers. With its sixty-meter-high bluffs, Vicksburg, Mississippi, held out until July 4, 1863. Fort Hudson, Louisiana, soon followed, and the heart of the Confederacy was encircled.

Naval Doctrine and Three Short Wars

The technological novelties displayed in the Civil War and refined thereafter had profound consequences for the function, composition, and strategy of naval forces as well as for seemingly unrelated issues such as colonial expansion. Well into the twentieth century, naval strategists tended to draw on traditional rivalries of the age of sail, with the actions and composition of the Royal Navy taken as the benchmark against which to measure success or failure. Warfare under steam required new theoretical assessments, but the empirical evidence for combat under steam derived from naval operations that were brief in duration or limited in scope, did not involve the Royal Navy, and were uncharacteristically decisive in their effects. By far the most forcefully articulated, patriotically satisfying, and enduring of these naval doctrines was that espoused by Alfred Thayer Mahan. A veteran of the Civil War and a vigorous advocate of American expansion, in 1886 Mahan joined the newly established U.S. Naval War College to develop principles of naval strategy drawn from history. Four years later he published a collection of his lectures as *The Influence of Sea Power upon History*. Mahan argued that the chronicle of naval operations offered teachings of universal applicability that "can be elevated to the rank of general principles . . . notwithstanding the great changes that have been brought about in naval weapons . . . and by the introduction of steam as the motive power."

Focusing on fleet engagements between European powers from the Second Anglo-Dutch War to the American Revolution, Mahan viewed sea power as the ability to strike at an enemy's economic well-being, and he maintained that navies were essential to protect a nation's overseas commerce and its colonies, and to interdict enemy trade through blockade: "It is not the taking of individual ships or convoys, be they few or many, that strike down the money power of a nation; it is the possession of that overbearing power on the sea which drives the enemy's flag from it, or allows it to appear only as a fugitive; and which, by controlling the great commons, closes the highways by which commerce moves to and from the enemy's shores." Although *The Influence of Sea Power upon History* is couched in appropriately objective terms, Mahan's larger aim was to encourage the revitalization of the U.S. Navy. In an article published the same year, he inveighed against American apathy toward the development of a fleet adequate to containing and profiting from the "unsettled political conditions, such as exist in Haiti, Central America, and many of the Pacific islands, especially the Hawaiian group." Foremost in his mind regarding the Americas was the prospect of opening a canal across the Isthmus of Panama (which Ferdinand de Lesseps had attempted in the 1880s), and the fear that European powers already present in or with designs on the Caribbean would be able to build fortresses "which will make them practically inexpugnable," at a time when "we have not on the Gulf of Mexico even the beginning of a navy yard which could serve as the base of our operations." He was likewise concerned that the kingdom of Hawaii could fall into European or Japanese hands.

In sharp contrast to Mahan's views were those of the Jeune Ecole, a school of thought developed in France that focused primarily on *guerre de course*, or commerce warfare. Whereas Mahan advocated a strategy that took the almighty Royal Navy as its ideal, the Jeune Ecole is generally dismissed as the "strategy of the weak." While this is not an inapt description, it was by no means a strategy of the meek. In its original formulation, the Jeune Ecole anticipated total war against all of a nation's economic and military resources—including its "overbearing power on the sea"—as well as the abrogation of international law regarding neutral shipping, contraband, and civilians. Inspired partly by the success of Confederate raiders during the Civil War and by the potential of the torpedo and submarine, advocates of the Jeune Ecole eschewed engagements between fleets of capital ships—that is, warships of the largest class. They reasoned that a large number of torpedo boats offered the prospect of breaking blockades by targeting enemy warships and of bringing the war to the enemy by sinking its commerce. Moreover, many torpedo boats could be built for the cost of one battleship and they could be dispersed among a number of smaller ports. Advocates of the Jeune Ecole were a minority even within the French naval establishment, and they never advocated the wholesale abandonment of capital ships. They viewed these as an appropriate weapon against Italy, whose navy was smaller and whose modest foreign trade made the country less susceptible to commerce warfare than Britain. The outcome of three relatively unheralded naval conflicts—the Sino-Japanese War of 1894–95, Spanish-American War (1898), and Russo-Japanese War (1904–1905)—seemed to vindicate Mahan's advocacy of capital ships as a way of keeping the enemy not only "out of our ports, but far away from our coasts." These conflicts had several features in common: they were brief; they were the first to involve flotillas of modern seagoing warships; the victories were one-sided; and, more important for the fate of the Jeune Ecole, they entailed virtually no commerce warfare. They consequently had a disproportionate impact on the evolution of naval strategy and the conduct of the two great naval wars of the twentieth century.

The Chinese defeat in the First Opium War had been emblematic of a general decline in the authority of the Qing Dynasty, and between 1850 and 1873 China endured four overlapping internal rebellions in the midst of which they had to fight the British and French in a Second Opium War (1856–60) and make further concessions to western powers. One was the establishment by the British, French, and American consuls of the Maritime Customs Service to collect duties from foreign traders. Considered the most scrupulous branch of the Chinese government, under the leadership of Robert Hart from 1864

The submarine tender USS Bushnell *raising the bow of the submarine AL-3 to inspect its torpedo tubes. This World War I–era photograph was taken off Queenstown (Cobh), Ireland, where the U.S. Navy maintained a significant presence designed to counter the German U-boat threat to convoys. Photograph by Burnell Poole; courtesy of the family of Burnell Poole.*

to 1907 the service accounted for a quarter of the government's income and instituted innumerable improvements to navigation at the treaty ports (more than forty by the 1900s) and on major rivers. Following the suppression of the Taiping Rebellion in 1864, the Chinese undertook to modernize its industry and military through the "self-strengthening movement." Included among the reforms was the creation of four regional navies, the most important being the Beiyang Navy at Weihai, on the Shandong Peninsula. Yet improvements were sporadic and even the most promising efforts were marred by a degree of corruption that confounded foreign observers.

Japan's engagement with western powers had proceeded far more smoothly. In 1869, the Japanese founded a naval academy and with British and French help expanded its indigenous shipbuilding capacity. They also began to expand overseas, briefly occupying Taiwan and formally annexing the Ryukyus in 1879. More significant still was Japan's interest in Korea, where the tectonic plates of Chinese, Japanese, and Russian ambition grind together. The "hermit kingdom" of Korea had been a tributary of China since 1637 and its trading relations with Japan were governed by a treaty of 1609. In 1875, Japan forced the government to agree to the "unequal" Treaty of Kanghwa granting Japan trading privileges and specifying that Korea was a sovereign nation, a blatant effort to remove Chinese influence from Korean affairs. Nevertheless, Chinese advisors persuaded Korea to accept treaties with the United States and the leading European powers, partly to counter Japanese influence.

In 1894, a peasant rebellion led to Chinese and Japanese intervention in Korea. Japanese cruisers sank two Chinese vessels and captured a third near Incheon and a week later Japan declared war on China. The Chinese fleet thereafter sailed no farther east than the mouth of the Yalu River and thousands of Japanese troops landed unopposed at Wonsan and Busan. On September 17, a Japanese cruiser squadron overwhelmed a Chinese flotilla plagued by weak leadership, inadequate training, and useless ordnance. Two months after the battle of the Yalu, the Japanese took the undefended ports of Dalian (then called Dairen) and Port Arthur (Lüshunkou), and they later captured Weihai and with it the Beiyang Navy's battleship. Under the terms of the Treaty of Shimonoseki, Japan acquired Taiwan (which it held until the end of World War II) and the Liaodong Peninsula, while Europeans took advantage of China's unexpected defeat to wring further territorial concessions for themselves.

The origins of the Sino-Japanese War had as much to do with relations between Japan and Russia as between Japan and China. While western European states had nibbled at China's seaward flanks in the wake of the Opium Wars, Russian diplomatic successes proved more enriching, enduring, and destabilizing. Russia had been humiliated in the Crimean War and it failed to modernize at a rate comparable to that of the leading European nations, but between 1858 and 1864 the empire permanently acquired by treaty 1.7 million square kilometers of Chinese territory—an area the size of Alaska (which it sold to the United States in 1867). This included part of the Pacific coast north of the Korean Peninsula, where the Russians established a naval base at Vladivostok in 1871. The potential for conflict between Russia and Japan was widely acknowledged, and in the spring of 1895 the Russian minister responsible for the Trans-Siberian Railway observed that "The hostile actions of Japan [against China] are directed mainly against us," while just after ratification of the Treaty of Shimonoseki the Japanese minister to Russia noted that "Russia does hope ultimately to bring the entire area from northeastern Manchuria down to Manchuria's southern coast under her influence." Eager to acquire a warm-water port on the Pacific (Vladivostok was icebound several months a year), Russia convinced Japan to cede the Liaodong Peninsula back to China in exchange for additional reparations payments. Three years later, the Russians obtained a twenty-five-year lease on the peninsula and the right to extend the Trans-Siberian Railway to Dalian and Port Arthur. Hostilities with Russia were now imminent, and Japan dedicated its reparations revenue from China to quadrupling the size of its navy. The czar responded in kind by calling for a Pacific fleet 30 percent larger than Japan's.

Biding their time, the Japanese remained reliable allies of the western powers. During the Boxer Rebellion in 1900–1901 they helped lift the siege of the western enclave at Tianjin, and in 1902 they signed the Anglo-Japanese Alliance, which recognized that Japan was "interested in a peculiar degree, politically as well as commercially and industrially in Korea," and that it would be admissible for the Japanese "to take such measures as may be indispensable in order to safeguard those interests if threatened either by the aggressive action of any other Power, or by disturbances arising in China or Korea." The Russians had taken advantage of the Boxer Rebellion to send a hundred thousand troops into Manchuria, where they remained, and in 1903 they occupied the Korean port of Yongamp'o just south of the Yalu. The Japanese called for negotiations, and when these collapsed, Admiral Heihachiro Togo launched a destroyer attack against Port Arthur on February 8, 1904—two days before a formal declaration of war. Only three of twenty Japanese torpedoes hit their targets, but the Russians never gained the initiative. Seven months later, the Japanese intercepted the Russian fleet as it tried to run for Vladivostok and forced it back to Port Arthur where it remained until the Japanese army overran the base in January 1905.

Three months before, the Second Pacific Squadron (formerly the Baltic Fleet) had sailed for the Far East under Vice Admiral Zinovi Petrovich Rozhestvensky. This was a motley flotilla of four new and three old battleships, six cruisers, an armored cruiser, four destroyers, and more than a dozen auxiliaries. Their eighteen-thousand-mile passage was complicated by poor intelligence, which led to the fleet's firing on English fishing trawlers in the belief that they were Japanese destroyers; having to sail around the Cape of Good Hope to avoid detention by the British in the Suez Canal; and the reluctance of European powers to risk losing their neutral status by offering coaling facilities to the Russians. After seven months in transit (including surreptitious stays in French Madagascar and Indo-China), Rozhestvensky reached the Strait of Tsushima on May 27, 1905, where Togo's fleet of four battleships, eight armored cruisers, twenty-one destroyers, and forty-four torpedo boats intercepted him. Operating in home waters with better speed, training, and morale, the Japanese sank, scuttled, captured, or interned thirty-four Russian ships, with nearly five thousand dead, and took six thousand prisoners. Japanese losses at the battle of Tsushima amounted to just over a hundred sailors dead and three torpedo boats. Under the terms of the Treaty of Portsmouth, mediated by the United States, Russia and Japan evacuated their forces from Manchuria, but Japan was allowed to lease the Liaodong Peninsula and it gained control of Korea, which it formally annexed in 1910. In the meantime Japan strengthened its 1902 alliance with Britain and recognized United States hegemony in the Philippines, which it had won in the Spanish-American War in 1898.

At the end of the nineteenth century, Spain's overseas empire was in eclipse and unrest in Cuba and its other Caribbean colonies prompted American policy makers to plan for a possible war with Spain in the Caribbean and the Philippines. In January 1898, President William McKinley dispatched the battleship USS *Maine* to Havana out of concern for U.S. interests. Two weeks later, an explosion sank the ship and killed 252 of the crew. The ship's captain cautioned his superiors that "public opinion should be suspended until further report," but a naval court of inquiry determined that the explosion was the result of a mine, although it was "unable to obtain evidence fixing responsibility for the destruction of the *Maine* upon any person or persons." A Spanish investigation suggested that an internal explosion destroyed the ship, a view supported by the chief of the U.S. Navy's Bureau of Steam Engineering. Such findings were beside the point. Fired by a jingoist press in the full bloom of yellow journalism, Congress acceded to popular opinion and declared war on April 25. The Americans blockaded Cuba, and in July four Spanish cruisers and two torpedo boats were sunk attempting to reach Santiago.

Despite Cuba's proximity to the United States, the Pacific loomed larger in American strategic considerations and, as Mahan wrote to Assistant Secretary of the Navy Theodore Roosevelt, "we have much more likelihood of trouble on that side than the Atlantic"—that is, not from Spain, but from Japan, whose interest in Hawaii rivaled that of the United States. Six days after the declaration of war with Spain, Commodore George Dewey led four steel-hulled cruisers and two gunboats of the China-based Asiatic Fleet into Manila Bay. The poorly maintained Spanish squadron of wooden gunboats and a small cruiser was no match for the newer American fleet. The gunnery was appalling on both sides—less than 3 percent of the nearly six thousand shells fired by Dewey's ships hit their targets—but after two hours, the Spanish fleet was destroyed. Dewey proceeded to blockade Manila, which fell in August. The outcome of the Spanish-American War made the United States a major Pacific power. Spain ceded the Philippines, Guam, and Wake Island, and the United States annexed the kingdom of Hawaii. Such clear-cut success only increased apprehension about the navy's ability to fight a two-ocean war. The two-month passage of the battleship USS *Oregon* from San Francisco to Florida via the Strait of Magellan highlighted this problem and spurred renewed interest in a canal across Central America, work on which began in 1904.

The Naval Arms Race to World War I

Even as the United States and Japan were announcing their arrival on the world stage, the established order of the Pax Britannica was being challenged in Europe. The passenger ship companies' jockeying for position on the North Atlantic starting in the 1890s mirrored a more serious rivalry between Germany and Great Britain that developed in the wake of German unification in 1871. Shortly after the Napoleonic Wars, Foreign Secretary Viscount Castlereagh had propounded a policy by which Britain's naval strength should be equal to that of the next two largest navies combined, and for the rest of the century no one nation had either the ambition or the wherewithal to unbalance this equation. The pace of British naval building declined markedly following the Franco-Prussian War of 1870, though, in part because no one could decide which of the new technologies and designs on offer to adopt. As Prime Minister William Gladstone remarked, "The fashion in building ships of war is as fickle as that of ladies' hats." Indecision gave way to a robust rearmament with passage of the Naval Defence Act of 1889, which called for the construction over five years of ten battleships, thirty-four cruisers, and eighteen torpedo gunboats. Moreover, the bill institutionalized "a definite standard," that the Royal Navy be equal in strength to "the fleets of two powers combined, one of which should be France."

The other was Russia, initially; but Germany soon emerged as a more potent threat. This manifested itself in the rapid increase of its international trade, and the concomitant quest for overseas colonies and a world-class fleet. The German naval shipbuilding program concentrated first on torpedo boats and gunboats. During an international naval review in 1887, Germany was represented by its torpedo boat squadron, commanded by Captain Alfred von Tirpitz. After a tour as chief of the Eastern Asiatic Cruiser Division, when he established the German naval base at Qingdao (Tsingtao), China, Tirpitz returned to Germany as secretary of state of the Imperial Navy Office. In 1898 he secured passage of a navy law with funds for nineteen battleships, eight coastal defense ships, forty-two large and small cruisers, and a host of other vessels. Capitalizing on the American victory over Spain and the possible repercussions for German interests in China, two years later he urged passage of a bill doubling the number of battleships. Although the official line was intended to relieve tensions with Britain, and Germany was leery of conflict with France and Russia, Tirpitz believed that "For Germany, the most dangerous enemy at the present time is England. It is also the enemy against which we most urgently require a certain measure of naval force as a political power factor. . . . Our fleet must be constructed so that it can unfold its greatest military potential between Helgoland and the Thames. . . . The military situation against England demands battleships in as great a number as possible." Tirpitz did not believe that Germany could build a navy large enough to defeat the Royal Navy, but because much of the British fleet was dispersed around the world, Germany could build a "risk fleet"—that is, one large enough to challenge the British in their home waters. Overseas commitments like protection of the Suez Canal, which Italy and Austria-Hungary might threaten in a hypothetical Anglo-German conflict, would compel Britain to equivocate in her negotiations with Germany. The only alternative, which neither Tirpitz nor anyone else foresaw, was that the British would either forge unimaginable alliances or continue building to the two-power standard. They did both, reevaluating their suspicions of France and Russia, with whom they signed diplomatic accords in 1904 and 1907, respectively, and embarking on a massive shipbuilding campaign that led with a revolutionary new battleship.

By the turn of the century, the world's capital ships bristled with a variety of large-caliber guns. The *King Edward VII*–class battleships (1901) mounted four 12-inch (30.5 cm), four 9.2-inch (23.4 cm), and ten 6-inch (15.2 cm) guns, and the *Lord Nelson*s (1904) carried four 12-inch and ten 9.2-inch guns. At this point, naval architects began thinking in terms of an all-big-gun ship— powerfully armed, heavily armored, and fast. With such a ship, the captain could choose when to fight and at what range, the gunnery officer could more easily judge the gunners' accuracy (because all the shell splashes would be from guns of the same caliber), and the arsenal of shells carried would be more uniform. The Italian designer Vittorio Cuniberti published a plan for such a vessel in 1903, and the United States designed the USS *Michigan* and *South Carolina*, which mounted eight 12-inch guns in four centerline turrets. Yet the lead in actual development was taken by the Royal Navy under First Lord of the Admiralty Jackie Fisher, who oversaw plans for a ship mounting ten 12-inch guns in five turrets, driven by steam turbines, with watertight bulkheads and 11-inch (27.9 cm) belt armor for protection against torpedoes. The aptly named *Dreadnought* also mounted a light armament of eighteen 12-pounder guns specifically for use against torpedo boats. Fisher wanted fast, hard-hitting ships for his navy, and he led by example. The usual building time for a capital ship was thirty-three months, but HMS *Dreadnought* was laid down on October 2, 1905, launched on February 9, 1906, and went to sea on October 3, 1906.

If proponents of the all-big-gun ship were optimistic to believe that the *Dreadnought* would give Britain an insuperable lead in naval construction and design, others were wrong to think that Britain could have avoided an arms race by not building an all-big-gun ship. Both groups ignored the general trend toward the development of such vessels. Germany responded to the British challenge with orders for four *Nassau*-class ships mounting twelve 11.3-inch (28.7 cm) guns, and in 1907 Italy laid down Cuniberti's *Dante Alighieri*, the first ship to mount triple-gun turrets. Nor can the element of populist support be overlooked. A year after its founding in 1898 (with strong backing from the Reichsmarine), the German Navy League had 240,000 members, vastly more than its counterparts in other countries, who provided ample support for Tirpitz's naval budgets. The Royal Navy had far deeper roots in Britain, but the public only became alarmed by the potential threat of German naval power with the publication of Erskine Childers's espionage novel, *The Riddle of the Sands* (1903), which posited a German amphibious invasion from the Frisian Islands and the realism of which was based on the author's firsthand knowledge of sailing a small boat on the coast of Germany. Nor was Childers wide of the mark, for the German general staff had entertained plans for just such an invasion as early as 1897.

Across the Atlantic, the U.S. Navy was preoccupied by the twin threats of Germany and Japan, and the difficulty of coordinating fleets in two oceans. The Germans had made no effort to disguise their interest in South America and the Caribbean, and a Naval War College study warned that when "Germany's accelerated [shipbuilding] program is completed, she . . . will surpass us in naval strength. Germany will then be ready to take issue with us over the Monroe Doctrine" under which the United States opposed European influence in the Americas. One solution was to increase the United States' presence in the Caribbean, to which end President Theodore Roosevelt supported a Panamanian revolt against Colombia, recognized Panamanian independence, and negotiated with the new government to build a canal from Colón to Panama. Ten years in the making, when it opened in August 1914 the eighty-kilometer-long Panama Canal cut the distance from San Francisco to New York from more than thirteen thousand to less than fifty-three hundred miles.

While the American estimate of the German threat was based on projected fleet strengths, the Japanese posed a more immediate problem. The Anglo-Japanese Alliance had allowed the British to pull warships out of East Asia on the understanding that the Japanese would protect their interests. In their wars with China and Russia, Japan had demonstrated their naval capabilities in ways Americans never had, and Roosevelt hosted the Russo-Japanese treaty negotiations at Portsmouth partly to get a measure of the Japanese. His decision to send the Great White Fleet of sixteen battleships on a round-the-world cruise in 1907 was intended as a demonstration of American resolve and naval capability. Relations with Japan were also tainted by an undisguised racial animosity, and anti-Japanese riots in California led to the Gentlemen's Agreement of 1907, which limited Japanese immigration to the United States.

While the naval arms race contributed to the climate of mistrust that led to the start of World War I in July 1914, naval operations took a far different turn than anyone expected. In creating a powerful battle fleet, Germany was able to force the British to concentrate their forces in their home waters, as planned, but Germany likewise had to recall its own Far East Squadron from Qingdao. After defeating a squadron of older British ships off Coronel, Chile, this force was all but annihilated in the battle of the Falklands. If Germany's High Seas Fleet was too powerful for the Royal Navy to ignore, it was too weak for the German high command to risk in battle. Apart from a few "tip-and-run" raids against British North Sea ports in 1914 and 1915, the only major fleet action, involving about 150 British and 100 German ships, was the battle of Jutland, fought on May 31, 1916, the conduct and results of which have been debated ever since the smoke cleared. Although the British lost six battlecruisers and armored cruisers to only two German, the British maintained their numerical advantage, and apart from a few minor sorties, the High Seas Fleet remained confined to port for the duration of the war.

Emphatically more lethal was the war against Allied shipping by German submarines and surface raiders. Five German navy cruisers and a handful of armed merchant cruisers—passenger liners and freighters fitted with guns and carrying false papers—collectively captured or sank 620,000 tons of Allied shipping while diverting Allied naval assets from other assignments. Seventy-five ships were involved in the hunt for the German cruiser *Emden* before she was sunk in November 1914, and in the spring of 1917, fifty-four vessels were assigned to search for the freighter *Wolf,* which nonetheless managed to reach Germany after a fifteen-month cruise. Yet even in Allied countries commanders of the German surface raiders were often regarded as gallant. After the war, Felix Graf von Luckner became an international celebrity for his exploits as commander of the three-masted ship *Seeadler*—the only sailing ship so employed—in which he captured sixteen ships without loss of life on either side.

The Development of the Submarine

The gravest threat to Great Britain was unrestricted submarine warfare against merchant shipping bound for England. The idea for an underwater vessel had been around for hundreds of years—Leonardo da Vinci drew a rough sketch of one in 1500. A primitive submarine called the *Turtle* had been deployed in New York Harbor during the American Revolution, though to little effect; in 1801 Robert Fulton built one that he tried to sell to the French and British governments; and during the American Civil War, the *H. L. Hunley* sank the screw sloop USS *Housatonic* in Charleston Harbor. Driven by a hand-cranked screw propeller, the *Hunley*'s weapon was a spar torpedo, an explosive charge carried on the end of a long spar and detonated when placed against a ship's hull. That the *Hunley* and other submersibles had to make physical contact with their target in order to place their torpedoes (what are now called mines) limited their utility. The success of submersible boats had to await the invention of both a more practical and reliable submarine and a self-propelled torpedo.

The latter was achieved first, by Robert Whitehead, a British engineer living in Trieste whose "locomotive torpedo" of 1866 had a range of 185 meters at a speed of seven knots. The potential of torpedoes as an inexpensive means of sinking even ironclad battleships was obvious, and most of the world's navies purchased the right to manufacture them from Whitehead. The torpedo quickly gave rise to the torpedo boat and the torpedo boat destroyer. The former were smaller and faster than the battleships and cruisers that were their preferred prey, and difficult to hit with guns designed for use against big surface ships. Torpedo boat destroyers were designed to protect the larger ships against the new threat. In time, ships of all sizes would be armed with torpedoes, and in the twentieth century destroyers would be the primary defense against the ultimate torpedo boat, the submarine.

In the nineteenth century, most work on practical submarines was carried out by a handful of private inventors, notably the Irish-American schoolteacher John P. Holland, and in England the Reverend George Garrett, who later collaborated with Swedish weapons maker Thorsten Nordenfelt. The French navy demonstrated official if limited interest in submarines and ordered the experimental *Plongeur* in 1863. Two decades later, Dupuy de Lôme noted that "we are going to recommence the study of the submarine and we will end the conflict of the torpedo boats and the battleships by suppressing both of them." The French launched several more submarines before 1900, the most promising of which used batteries for underwater propulsion and a steam engine when surfaced, the same configuration hit on by Holland for his eponymous sixth and last creation.

"The forerunner of all modern submarines," in the opinion of British submariner and historian Richard Compton-Hall, the *Holland* was designed "entirely along the lines of submarines today [the 1980s] with frames, plating and general arrangements which . . . would not be out of place in any submarine drawing-office today." Her primary armament consisted of three 18-inch (45.7 cm) torpedoes fired from a single torpedo tube in the bow. As assistant secretary of the navy, Theodore Roosevelt urged that the navy purchase the vessel, and in 1900 she was commissioned as USS *Holland*. The navy ordered six more submarines on the same model and in 1905 President Roosevelt joined the crew of the USS *Plunger* for a dive in Long Island Sound. "I went down in it," he wrote, "chiefly because I did not like to have the officers and enlisted men think I wanted them to try things I was reluctant to try myself. I believe a good deal can be done with these submarines, although there is always the danger of people getting carried away with the idea and thinking that they can be of more use than they possibly could be." Dupuy de Lôme's view proved more prescient, but Roosevelt's was more influential.

During World War I, torpedoes, submarines, and mines made the close blockade of the German coast envisioned by prewar British planners untenable, so the Admiralty opted for a distant blockade. The Grand Fleet kept watch on the northern approaches to the North Sea between the Orkneys and Norway while other units patrolled the English Channel. In November 1914, Britain declared the North Sea a war area. Three months later Germany adopted a strategy of unrestricted submarine warfare in the waters around Great Britain, where all French and British vessels were deemed fair game and neutral ships might also be attacked. Among the converts to this strategy was the apostle of the decisive fleet action himself, Tirpitz, who the month before wrote "In view of the extraordinary importance of trade disruption, namely in supplying the west of England with food, I can promise an unqualified success from a cruiser war." The irony was twofold. The naval arms race that had poisoned relations among the great powers was an expensive and ineffective means of actually prosecuting a naval war, the burden for which fell increasingly on smaller, less glamorous vessels including converted merchantmen, trawlers (used as minelayers and minesweepers), and submarines. But in September 1914, Germany had only thirty-seven submarines, less than half as many as the Royal Navy.

With the adoption of unrestricted submarine warfare, Allied merchant ship losses doubled from a monthly average of sixty-one thousand tons between the first six months of the war and the middle of 1915. Neither Britain's "war area" nor Germany's "military area" was legal in terms of international law regarding blockade. The first two articles of the Declaration of London (1909) specified that "A blockade must not extend beyond the ports and coasts belonging to or occupied by the enemy"; and "In accordance with the Declaration of Paris of 1856, a blockade, in order to be binding, must be . . . maintained by a force sufficient really to prevent access to the enemy coastline." Yet the German strategy met with vigorous opposition because it depended on the use of submarines, which lacked the manpower to send prize crews aboard enemy ships; which stood little chance of surviving an engagement with an armed merchantman while surfaced; and whose commanders therefore had little recourse but to sink their prey and, increasingly, to do so without warning. The May 1915 sinking of the passenger liner *Lusitania* with the loss of 128 American citizens threatened to drag the United States into the war, and after considerable debate Germany suspended the practice of unrestricted submarine warfare in September.

The end of the submarine campaign around the British Isles freed U-boats for service in the Mediterranean, where British, Australian, and New Zealand troops were pinned down at Gallipoli. While Turkey would likely have allied with Germany anyway, it became a certainty when the Royal Navy requisitioned two Ottoman battleships under construction in British yards; Turkey concluded a secret treaty with Germany the same day. Promoted by Winston Churchill, the Gallipoli campaign was intended to divert Turkish forces away from the oil fields of Mesopotamia and the Suez Canal, open a second front to alleviate pressure on Russia in the Caucasus, signal Allied support for Serbia, and prepare for an attack on Istanbul. Churchill initially believed the Dardanelles could be forced by the navy alone, but when three battleships were sunk and three heavily damaged in March 1915, it was decided to land troops on the west side of the Gallipoli Peninsula. This was accomplished with heavy losses, and after almost nine months more or less pinned down on the beaches, the troops were withdrawn. In the meantime, the expedition's utter failure had forced Jackie Fisher's resignation as first sea lord and Churchill's ouster as first lord of the admiralty.

By the end of 1916, many Germans believed that a resumption of unrestricted commerce warfare could force a British surrender by the fall of 1917. Included in this calculus was the likelihood that the United States would join the Allies, but that its contribution would come too late to make a difference. Unrestricted warfare resumed February 1, when there were 120 U-boats operational between the Mediterranean and Baltic. In the first three months, German submarines sank more than two million tons of shipping, nearly two-thirds of it British, for the loss of only nine U-boats. Part of the problem was

the Royal Navy's preference for hunting submarines over protecting merchantmen by implementing a convoy system. Although the British had more than
three hundred destroyers, this was inadequate for an effective convoy system,
and the only source of support was the United States. Assigned as liaison to
London immediately after the United States declared war in April 1917, Rear
Admiral William S. Sims was a forceful advocate for convoys. When a mere
six destroyers arrived at Queenstown (Cobh, Ireland), he urged Washington
"we can not send too soon or too many." A week after the Americans reached
Queenstown, the first British convoy sailed from Gibraltar and, according to a
Royal Navy study after the war, was "an entire success, and from that moment
it may be said that the submarine menace was conquered." With a naval staff
still rooted in Mahanian concepts of sea power, the U.S. Navy was initially
as resistant to convoys as the British, but new capital ship construction was
dropped in favor of antisubmarine vessels, and more than four hundred submarine chasers of all kinds were commissioned by war's end. Together these
provided adequate coverage for the transatlantic supply convoys vital to the
British war effort.

The Interwar Treaties

Under the terms of the armistice signed November 11, 1918, a majority of the
German fleet was interned pending a permanent disposition to be worked out
at Versailles. Ten days later, seventy ships, including nine dreadnoughts and
five battlecruisers, sailed into the Grand Fleet's Orkney Islands anchorage at
Scapa Flow. Weighed down by the humiliation of this surrender, and loath
to see the fleet dispersed to Germany's erstwhile enemies, Admiral Ludwig
von Reuter ordered his men to scuttle their ships on June 21, 1919. Fifty-two
ships sank, including ten battleships and ten battlecruisers. But embarrassing
to the Allies though the scuttling of the German fleet was, many greeted the
action with relief, for at a stroke it removed the issue of whether and how the
ships should be apportioned among the victors. The United States viewed any
distribution of the Central Powers' ships as inherently destabilizing, particularly because the Royal Navy already possessed forty-three capital ships, one
more than the United States, Japan, France, and Italy combined. Moreover,
President Woodrow Wilson's call for a reduction in national armaments "to
the lowest point consistent with domestic safety" became the basis for Article
8 of the Covenant of the League of Nations.

The United States failed to ratify the Treaty of Versailles or join the League
of Nations, but it did convene the first of three naval arms limitation con-

The battleship USS Arizona *passing through the Panama Canal in the 1930s. Launched in 1918, four years after the opening of the canal, the* Arizona *was one of the "all-big-gun" battleships pioneered in 1905 by the Royal Navy's HMS* Dreadnought. *Impressive though these powerful battlewagons were, their heyday was short, coinciding as it did with the rise of the submarine and the aircraft carrier. Dispatched to the Pacific in 1939 as tensions with Japan were rising, in December 1941 the* Arizona *was sunk at its berth in the Japanese air raid on Pearl Harbor, where it remains as a war memorial. Courtesy of the Library of Congress, Washington, D.C.*

ferences intended to rein in the world's leading naval powers. Many in the U.S. Navy still viewed Britain as a potential threat to American interests and world stability and the Americans sought to at least equal the British as the world's premier navy, while the British remained suspicious of French determination to maintain its submarine and cruiser forces. The Americans and Japanese were mutually suspicious, as they had been since the end of the Russo-Japanese War. Even before World War I the Japanese had begun considering how to take on the American fleet, while the Americans developed War Plan Orange as a response to a hypothetical takeover of the Philippines, the route to which ran through the Marshalls, Micronesia, and the Carolines, where Japan now held formerly German islands as mandated territories. In a 1919 memorandum to President Wilson, Rear Admiral William S. Benson stated flatly "Japan has no rival in the Pacific except America. Every ship built or acquired by Japan can have in mind only opposition to American naval strength in the Pacific."

The Washington Naval Treaty of 1922 fixed the ratio of capital ship tonnage for Britain, the United States, Japan, France, and Italy in the proportion of 5:5:3:1:1, with Britain and the United States each allowed 525,000 tons in capital ships. The United States and Japan each were entitled to convert two battlecruisers already under construction to aircraft carriers, and the treaty limited the size of new carriers. Inequities in the distribution of power excited nationalist indignation, especially in Japan, which had declared war on Germany in August 1914, nearly three years before the United States. The Americans also made repudiation of the Anglo-Japanese alliance of 1902 a condition for their acceptance of the treaty, for as the author of the memorandum that guided American negotiators wrote, they wanted to place the "wise administration of sea power in the hands of an undivided Anglo-Saxon race." Neither Germany nor Russia (then embroiled in a civil war) was represented at the conference.

The London Naval Conference of 1930 confirmed the 5:5:3 ratio in battleship construction (Italy and France refused to sign) and came up with fixed definitions and tonnage limits for cruisers, destroyers, and submarines, which the Washington Treaty had ignored. Japan was limited to about two-thirds the cruiser and destroyer tonnage of either the United States or Britain. Only in submarines was there parity. Four years later, Japan repudiated the terms of the Washington and London treaties. As ominous, the London Naval Treaty (1935) between Britain and Germany allowed the latter to build a fleet, although the aggregate tonnage could not exceed 35 percent that of the naval forces of the British Commonwealth.

Perhaps the most remarkable aspect of these negotiations and the formulation of naval strategy in the interwar period was the refusal to acknowledge the realities of World War I. In his memo to Wilson, Benson had recommended that German and Austrian submarines be scrapped:

> Not only should these submarines be destroyed, but all submarines in the world should be destroyed, and their future possession by any Power forbidden. They serve no useful purpose in time of peace. They are inferior to surface craft in time of war except in ability to treacherously attack merchant ships. In the present war, 99 per cent of submarine attacks were illegal attacks on merchant ships. Civilization demands that naval war be placed on a higher plane and confined to combatant vessels.

This was wishful thinking of the worst kind, but it reflected not only revulsion from Germany's unrestricted submarine campaign but also the abiding influence of Mahan, who had died in 1914. In *The Influence of Sea Power*, Mahan conceded that "steam navies have as yet made no history which can be quoted as decisive in its teaching," but the obvious lessons of the submarine campaigns were lost on his acolytes. However unsettling the consequences, the Jeune Ecole's assumption of an abrogation of international law in the case of total war had been correct. Yet as before the war, most navy officers worldwide considered capital ships the gold standard against which naval power should be measured and they tailored their strategies accordingly. American war gamers relegated submarines to the role of scouts for the U.S. fleet, and if submariners assigned to the "enemy" fleet actually dared to attack, they were chastised. Reflecting on the thinking of interwar strategists, submarine commander and naval historian Edward L. Beach later wrote, "The minds of the men in control were not attuned to the changes being wrought by advancing technology. Mahan's nearly mystical pronouncements had taken the place of reality for men who truly did not understand but were comfortable in not understanding."

In addition to their counterparts in other navies and submariners in their own, the "gun club" had to contend with an even newer and less understood phenomenon, naval aviation. In 1910, only seven years after the Wright brothers' demonstration of manned flight, a pilot flew a plane off the deck of the anchored cruiser USS *Birmingham*. In August 1917 a pilot landed a plane on the deck of the battlecruiser–cum–aircraft carrier HMS *Furious* while that ship was under way, and the next year *Furious* launched seven planes in a successful raid on a German Zeppelin base. The Japanese commissioned the world's first purpose-built aircraft carrier, the *Hosho*, in 1921, and by 1930 there were eleven aircraft carriers in commission worldwide. As with submarines, strategists initially thought of aircraft carriers as support vessels. Their potential came to be realized with improvements to radio communications and as the operational radius and payload capacity of carrier aircraft increased.

World War II

When World War II began in 1939, flag officers worldwide shared a common anxiety: the number of battleships available to them was inadequate. The lack of ships was real, but the war would require fleets of a completely different composition than strategists envisioned even as late as 1941. Going into the war, battleships dominated doctrine, but the outcome of World War II depended on aircraft carriers, submarines, destroyers, convoy escorts, cargo ships, and landing craft, all in far greater numbers than were available or than anyone imagined could be built. The fate of the world's biggest battleships, the *Yamato* and *Musashi*, offers one example of the vast gulf between expectation and experience. Advocates of carrier aviation greeted these ships with skepticism in the late 1930s, and Admiral Isoroku Yamamoto told one of the ships' designers, "I'm afraid you'll be out of work before long. From now on, aircraft are going to be the most important thing in the navy; big ships and big guns will become obsolete." As they prepared for her last mission in April 1945, the *Yamato*'s junior officers are said to have gibed that "the world's three great follies, prize examples of uselessness are the Great Wall of China, the pyramids and the *Yamato*." The battleship saw little action before the battle of Leyte Gulf in October 1944, but changes in her armament reflected the shifting balance of power in naval warfare. Commissioned with 24 antiaircraft guns, by 1945 she carried 152 of them, and her 46-centimeter (18.1-inch) main guns, the largest ever mounted in a ship, fired antiaircraft "incendiary shotgun" projectiles. Even these were not enough to save her. While en route to Okinawa on April 7, she was attacked by nearly three hundred carrier planes and sunk with the loss of 2,500 lives.

The promise of carrier aviation in offensive operations against capital ships was first revealed in the November 1940 British attack on Taranto, when British carrier planes from HMS *Furious* permanently disabled one Italian battleship and put two others out of service for nearly six months. Close study of the Taranto action may have convinced Yamamoto to attempt a preemptive Japanese strike on the American base in Hawaii. Even before Taranto demonstrated the feasibility of such an attack in wartime, a U.S. fleet exercise had yielded the same conclusion in 1938, and a report of the following year warned that the Japanese would likely "damage Major Fleet Units without warning, or possibly . . . block the Fleet in Pearl Harbor." President Franklin D. Roosevelt made this the home port of the U.S. Navy's Pacific Fleet in 1940, in a modest effort to counter Japanese aggression in the Pacific. Relations reached the breaking point when the United States banned oil exports to Japan the following summer. Yet despite official warnings, the experience of war games, worsening diplomatic relations, and the knowledge that Japan had begun the Sino-Japanese and the Russo-Japanese Wars with surprise attacks, preparations at Hawaii for a preemptive strike were inexcusably lax.

The Carrier War

On December 7, 1941, a Japanese fleet of thirty ships under Admiral Chuichi Nagumo launched two strikes of high-level bombers, dive-bombers, torpedo planes, and fighter planes from a point about 220 miles north of Oahu. The primary target was Pearl Harbor's "Battleship Row," where two of seven battleships were permanently destroyed. As luck would have it, none of the U.S. Navy's carriers was in Pearl Harbor at the time. The USS *Enterprise* and *Lexington* were delivering planes to Wake Island, twenty-three hundred miles southwest of Pearl Harbor, and Midway Island at the end of the Hawaiian chain thirteen hundred miles to the northwest. The attack on Pearl Harbor was carried out in conjunction with surprise attacks on American bases in the Philippines, as well as British Hong Kong and Singapore, and on December 10 bombers and torpedo planes based in Indo-China sank the Royal Navy's capital ships *Prince of Wales* and *Repulse* off the Malay Peninsula.

Although Japanese and American admirals alike often used battleships as their flagships, carrier task groups were at the heart of the most important naval operations of the Pacific War. At the battle of the Philippine Sea in June 1944, for instance, Task Force 58 was made up of four carrier groups about fifteen miles apart. Each comprised three or four carriers surrounded by between three and five cruisers and between twelve and fourteen destroyers that provided early warning of and protection against enemy submarines and aircraft. Carrier aircraft were designed for distinct missions. Fighter aircraft were intended to fight other aircraft and were the core of the combat air patrols launched against incoming planes. Dive-bombers attacked ships from a high altitude by diving at a ship and releasing their bombs at as low an altitude as possible before leveling out. Before the development of effective bombsights, this was the most accurate means of delivering a bomb to a relatively small target like a ship. Ships' decks tended to be unarmored and bombs could easily penetrate them, although sinking a ship in this way was difficult. Most lethal to ships was the torpedo bomber, which flew directly toward its target before releasing the torpedo at an altitude of less than thirty meters. But this angle of attack left planes vulnerable to antiaircraft fire and combat air patrols.

In addition to large fleet carriers, the United States, Great Britain, and Japan built a limited number of light carriers, most on narrow hulls originally intended for cruisers. Of more utility and built in far greater numbers, especially by the United States, were escort carriers. Known as jeep carriers and baby flattops, these were crucial for ferrying replacement aircraft to distant theaters of operation, and they were deployed in support of amphibious landings in the Pacific. In the Atlantic, escort carriers also provided air cover for convoys and sailed as part of detached hunter-killer groups, usually one escort carrier and four or five destroyer escorts fitted with radar and sonar and armed with ever more effective depth charges, hedgehogs, and other antisubmarine weapons.

The Submarine War

The battle of the Atlantic, the titanic struggle to defeat Germany's unrestricted submarine war against Allied shipping, overshadows all other submarine efforts of the war in terms both of ships sunk and losses to submarines and their crews. Collectively U-boats sank well over two thousand Allied and neutral ships, most of them in the North Atlantic and, after the United States entered the war, the Caribbean and Gulf of Mexico. Grim as this figure is, it represents only a fraction of the successful merchant ship passages made carrying food, war matériel, and other supplies to Great Britain and, after 1941, the Soviet Union. More impressive, fewer than ten thousand Allied soldiers were lost in troop transports. On the German side, the casualties were appalling. Of the 863 U-boats that put to sea, 754 were lost—a staggering 87 percent—together with 27,491 officers and crew, about three-quarters of the personnel of the U-boat arm. Yet despite the experience of World War I, submarine warfare was an insignificant component of Germany's prewar planning. In September 1939, Germany had only twenty-two seagoing U-boats in operation, and a handful of submarines designed for coastal operations. In the first year of the war only three U-boats were launched, and for the first eighteen months there were seldom more than six to eight boats on patrol at any one time. This paucity of numbers was compounded by the unreliability of German torpedoes—a problem that bedeviled the Americans, too—probably a quarter of which detonated prematurely or not at all, or were unable to maintain the proper depth.

When France surrendered on June 22, 1940, Admiral Karl Dönitz moved his submarine operations to Brest, Lorient (which he chose as his headquarters), Saint-Nazaire, La Pallice (La Rochelle), and Bordeaux. All had excellent dockyard facilities, to which Dönitz added bombproof submarine pens that still exist. More important, they were hundreds of miles closer to the Atlantic shipping lanes than Germany's North Sea bases. In May 1940, U-boats had sunk nine ships in the North Atlantic, and in June fifty-three; the numbers thereafter rose steadily. U-boats collectively sank more than eleven hundred ships (over five million tons of shipping) before the United States entered the war. In 1942, more than a thousand ships were sunk in the North Atlantic, many of them by submarines ganged in "wolf packs" whose activities were coordinated via radio transmissions between the U-boats and headquarters in Germany or France.

One reason for the sharp increase in sinkings that year was the failure of the Americans to institute coastal convoys or impose a blackout along the east coast of the United States, so that individual ships were clearly silhouetted against the illuminated backdrops at night. In what the Germans called the "Happy Time," from January to July U-boats sank nearly four hundred ships between the Gulf of St. Lawrence and the Caribbean. The Americans' refusal to attempt the most rudimentary precautions against the U-boat threat is baffling, especially because the United States had been involved in the battle of the Atlantic since early in the war. Circumventing domestic isolationists, Roosevelt had engineered a number of pro-Britain policies. The neutrality patrol of September 1939 kept warships of any nation at least two hundred miles from the coasts of North and South America. Under the destroyers-for-bases deal, the United States transferred fifty old destroyers to Britain in exchange for naval bases in Newfoundland, Bermuda, and the Caribbean. The Lend-Lease Act of 1941 allowed the United States to sell weapons, munitions, aircraft, and ships to "any country whose defense the President deems vital to the defense of the United States," and that summer the United States assumed the defense of Iceland, an important staging ground for Atlantic convoys. By the fall, the neutrality patrol had expanded to allow U.S. Navy ships to sail in harm's way; two U.S. destroyers exchanged fire with U-boats, and on October 31 the USS *Reuben James* was torpedoed and sunk with the loss of 115 men. Yet Allied countermeasures only became truly effective in 1943, when the Americans were running coastal convoys, Allied intelligence could routinely break encoded radio transmissions (thanks to the seizure of an Enigma encryption machine from the captured *U-110*), and improvements to sonar and radar were making it easier to find and attack submarines.

Moreover, U.S. submarines were conducting precisely the same campaign against Japanese commerce. Within hours of the attack on Pearl Harbor, Chief of Naval Operations Harold N. Stark had issued the order: "Execute unrestricted air and submarine warfare against Japan." This was an abrupt about-face. The United States was a signatory to the London Naval Treaty, which specified that "a warship, whether surface vessel or submarine, may not sink or render incapable of navigation a merchant vessel without having first placed passengers, crew and ship's papers in a place of safety," and less than three months before, Roosevelt had described an attack by a German submarine on an American merchantman as "violating long-established international law and violating every principle of humanity." Although the United States began the war with more than a hundred submarines, twenty-nine of them in the Asiatic Fleet, prewar doctrine had called for them to be used primarily as forward scouts for the battle fleet, and to sink warships. In consequence, submarine commanders tended to be timid, and during the Japanese invasion of the Philippines they sank only three Japanese transports. The reluctance to pursue aggressively enemy shipping was compounded by the failure of American torpedoes, which routinely ran too deep or failed to detonate, problems not solved until September 1943. The Americans also lacked a commerce warfare doctrine and failed to adequately use aerial reconnaissance to direct submarine operations or to concentrate on oil tankers, the Achilles' heel of Japan's overseas trade and the primary reason for its invasion of the Dutch East Indies.

Japan depended vitally on merchant shipping for imports it could not produce at home—especially food and fuel—but it, too, was slow to respond to the submarine threat by forming convoys and it continued to lavish resources on aircraft carriers rather than destroyers and other escort vessels for antisubmarine and convoy work. The Japanese had an estimated six million tons of merchant shipping in 1941, and during the course of the war they built or otherwise acquired more than four million tons, but by August 1945, they had lost nearly nine million tons. Of the thirteen hundred Japanese merchant ships lost or damaged beyond repair, about 55 percent were credited to submarines. Fifty-two of the 288 U.S. submarines that saw service during the war were lost, together with thirty-five hundred officers and crew.

According to a postwar study, American submarines had sunk so many Japanese merchant ships that the country would have been forced into submission for lack of fuel, war matériel, and food. Yet the Pacific campaign of the "Silent Service" is overlooked for several reasons. Instruments of stealth and deceit, submarines are viewed more comfortably from the perspective of the aggrieved victim than from that of the proud victor. For Americans, chalking up success in the Pacific to submariners risked legitimating the U-boat war in the Atlantic or otherwise drawing uncomfortable parallels between German and American strategy, an issue raised at the Nuremberg war crimes trial of Admiral Dönitz.

In September 1942, the *U-156* had sunk a requisitioned British passenger ship carrying among other people 1,800 Italian prisoners of war. Although the Germans radioed their intention to escort the survivors' lifeboats to safety and displayed Red Cross flags, an American plane attacked the flotilla, which by then included three other German and Italian submarines. To ensure that his U-boats were never put needlessly at risk again, Dönitz issued the "*Laconia* order" stating that "All attempts at rescuing members of ships that have sunk . . . are to cease." In his defense, however, Dönitz secured an affidavit from Fleet Admiral Chester W. Nimitz, who swore that "On general principles, the U.S. submarines did not rescue enemy survivors if undue additional hazard to the submarine resulted or the submarine would thereby be prevented from accomplishing its further mission." The submarine had once again proved as insidious as its critics always claimed.

Amphibious Operations

In addition to aircraft carriers and submarines, and the various vessels designed to protect or hunt them, World War II saw the development of a third class of vessels barely imagined before the war: landing craft for amphibious operations. Boarding ramps and gangways have long been used for discharging troops, horses, and equipment, but through the 1930s amphibious landings tended to be cumbersome affairs in which soldiers clambered over the side of the hulls of small craft to wade ashore, and ramps had to be fitted to the top of the bulwarks to land motorized transports. In the 1930s, the Japanese developed a landing craft with an integral bow ramp for personnel and light vehicles, and New Orleans boatbuilder Andrew Higgins adapted this to a boat designed for work in the Louisiana bayous. Formally known as a "landing craft, vehicle, personnel" (LCVP), the eleven-meter-long Higgins boat could carry a platoon of thirty-six soldiers, or a dozen troops and a jeep, and had a draft of only three feet aft and two feet forward. The propeller was protected so that it could easily back off the beach, and it was designed to turn around without broaching in the surf. More than twenty-three thousand were built and they were widely viewed as integral to the Allied success. Marine general Holland M. Smith, who commanded amphibious operations in the Pacific, wrote that the Higgins boat "did more to win the war in the Pacific than any other single piece of equipment," and General Dwight Eisenhower, who oversaw Allied landings in North Africa, Sicily, and Normandy, described Higgins as "the man who won the war for us. If Higgins had not designed and built those LCVPs, we never could have landed over an open beach. The whole strategy of the war would have been different."

The Higgins boat was one of more than thirty types of American and British landing and amphibious craft, from amphibious jeeps to 117-meter-long LSTs (landing ship, tank). With massive double doors in the bow, an LST could carry three smaller LCTs (landing craft, tank), each with five medium tanks or 330 infantry and their equipment. Landings on hostile shores were executed with a choreographic precision. Troop transports halted several miles off the coast and the smaller landing craft were lowered and circled near the transport before the troops boarded them via rope net ladders or vehicles were lowered into them by crane. Waves of landing craft would then approach the beach, disgorge their troops, and return to the transports for more men. Once the beachhead was secured, the landing craft were loaded with supplies. Mechanized vehicles drove onto the beach under their own power, while palletized goods were dragged onto the beach by tractors or other vehicles and nonpalletized goods were passed hand-to-hand by gangs of soldiers and sailors. Landing craft also carried the wounded back to transports or hospital ships.

Two Coast Guard–manned Landing Ships, Tank (LSTs) with their bow doors open to the beach on Leyte Island, the Philippines, in 1944. Sailors are laying down a sandbag causeway from the LSTs to the beach to speed up the off-loading operations. Well suited though they were to carrying huge quantities of cargo, their unwieldy form explains why LST was popularly said to stand for "large, slow target." Courtesy of the National Archives, Washington, D.C.

Shipbuilding

As the prodigious output of the Higgins yards suggests, the difference between victory and defeat depended on which side could produce more ships and matériel and get armies and their supplies where they needed to go. Meditating on the battle of the Atlantic, Churchill wrote,

> The only thing that ever really frightened me during the war was the U-boat peril. . . . How much would the U-boat warfare reduce our imports and shipping? Would it ever reach the point where our life would be destroyed? Here was no field for gestures or sensations; only the slow, cold drawing of lines on charts, which showed potential strangulation. . . . Either the food, supplies,

and arms from the New World and from the British Empire arrived across the oceans, or they failed.

In this numbers game, the industrial capacity of the United States gave the Allies an insuperable advantage. Well into the 1930s, the combination of the Great Depression, isolationism, and pacifism had militated against building a fleet up to the limits allowed by the naval treaties. Roosevelt took the first steps toward naval rearmament by directing funds appropriated for the National Industrial Recovery Act of 1933 to build 2 aircraft carriers, 4 cruisers, 20 destroyers, and other ships. The following year Representative Carl Vinson secured passage of the first of four acts to increase the size of the navy. Japan's repudiation of the London Treaty and invasion of China and Adolf Hitler's rise to power in Germany facilitated further increases, culminating in the Two-Ocean Navy (or Vinson-Walsh) Act of July 1940, which called for 13 battleships, 6 aircraft carriers, 32 cruisers, 101 destroyers, and 39 submarines.

With its own shipyards taxed by the need to build and repair warships, and under regular threat from German bombers during the battle of Britain, the British ordered 60 Ocean-class freighters from the United States under the Lend-Lease program. When Britain placed its order, Roosevelt called for more than 300 additional tankers and dry-cargo Liberty ships, a modification of the Ocean class. As of 1941, the U.S. Maritime Commission was on track to build five million deadweight tons of shipping in 1942, and seven million in 1943.* In January 1942, these figures were increased to eight million and ten million tons, respectively. When it was pointed out that this rate would not produce enough ships to transport and provision the soldiers destined for service overseas—1.8 million in 1942 and 3.5 million in 1943—the targets were increased to twenty-four million tons for 1942–43. In the end, American shipyards turned out twenty-seven million tons of shipping over the two years, 125 percent of the original goal. (Munitions manufacturing and war construction attained only 60 percent of their goals.) This output was achieved thanks to unprecedented levels of prefabrication and subassembly, and the introduction of new methods and people—including women and minorities—into the shipbuilding trades. All told more than fifty-five hundred merchant and naval vessels were constructed under Maritime Commission contracts during World War II, including 2,710 Liberty ships and nearly five hundred Victory ships, which were roughly the same size as Libertys but more than a third again as fast.

---

* Unlike gross tonnage, deadweight tonnage is the weight of a vessel's cargo as determined by calculating the volume of water displaced by a vessel when "light" and when full of cargo.

The Korean War

As the Allies and Axis powers battled each other around the world, Soviet-Japanese relations were eerily calm. In 1938, Japan and the Soviet Union had clashed over the border between the Japanese puppet state of Manchukuo (Manchuria) and the Soviet Union. The Russian victory at the battle of Khalkhin Gol (or Nomonhan) forced the Japanese to set their sights on Southeast Asia; but the mutual need for a stable border in Northeast Asia led to the Japanese-Soviet Neutrality Pact of 1941. Under Lend-Lease agreements negotiated after the German invasion of the Soviet Union that June, the United States committed to supply the Soviets via the Arctic, the shortest but most dangerous route; the Persian Gulf, the longest run; and across the Pacific from the United States to Vladivostok. Because of the neutrality pact, the Japanese allowed ships sailing under the Soviet flag safe passage. Technically only goods with civilian applications could be sent via Vladivostok, but these included dual-use cargoes like food, fuel, trucks, locomotives, and engineering equipment. Thus while the Arctic convoys are the best known, more Allied ships sailed to Vladivostok than to all other Soviet and Persian Gulf ports combined, and in far greater security.

Two days after the United States dropped the atomic bomb on Hiroshima, the Soviet Union declared war on Japan. Its armies proceeded to occupy the Liaodong Peninsula where, as Churchill, Roosevelt, and Stalin had agreed at the Yalta Conference, "The former rights of Russia violated by the treacherous attack of Japan in 1904 shall be restored, viz. . . . The commercial port of Dairen [Dalian] shall be internationalized, the pre-eminent interests of the Soviet Union in this port being safeguarded, and the lease of Port Arthur as a naval base of the U.S.S.R. restored." Chinese communists welcomed the Soviets' presence at Port Arthur as a deterrent to American intervention, and they remained until 1955.

After declaring war on Japan, the Russians moved into Korea and on August 10 the United States proposed to divide the peninsula along the 38th parallel, a plan to which the Soviets agreed. The Russians backed the totalitarian communist rule of Kim Il Sung, while the Americans supported the authoritarian right-wing government of Sygnman Rhee. Both the Soviets and the United States withdrew their forces in 1948, but whereas the Russians had left their protégé with planes, tanks, and a cohesive army, the Americans withheld arming Sygnman Rhee's regime. In the summer of 1950, the armies of Kim Il Sung crossed the 38th parallel, and quickly reduced the territory under South Korean control to an area around the port of Busan. The United Nations condemned the invasion and, led by the United States, landed troops at Busan. General Douglas MacArthur, supreme allied commander in Japan, proposed an amphibious landing at Incheon, about twenty-five kilometers from Seoul. With a tidal range of ten meters, treacherous currents, and a granite wall rather than a beach to seaward, this was a risky move. Compounding these problems were a schedule shorter than that for any comparable operation in the Pacific War and the fact that the American forces who would lead the operation were out of training. Nonetheless, on September 15 a flotilla of 260 ships, including old LSTs commandeered from the Japanese fishing fleet, landed thirteen thousand troops at Incheon, followed the next month by landings on the east coast. In the aftermath of the massive Chinese counterattack at the Chosin Reservoir, in December the navy evacuated more than 100,000 troops, 17,500 vehicles, and 350,000 tons of cargo from Hungnam in "an amphibious invasion in reverse" that lasted two weeks. Apart from these operations and providing carrier-based air support for ground troops, naval operations in the Korean War were otherwise limited.

Although usually regarded as an episode of the Cold War between western-style democracies and communist regimes, in its geostrategic background the Korean War had more in common with the conflicts of the first half of the twentieth century than with those of the second. The explicit appeal to the status quo of 1904 at the Yalta Conference and the role of amphibious operations would be forgotten quickly in the rhetoric and nuclear posturing of the Cold War. But as one historian has noted, "what created 'an entirely new strategic situation in the Far East' was not that Russia was interested in Korea—it had been for decades—but that the United States was interested." This was of a piece with America's self-imposed postwar burden, which began with the occupation of Germany and Japan, but grew as the United States anxiously embroiled itself in the assorted conflicts of the Cold War to contain communism and the petro-war to guarantee the flow of Middle East oil.

The technological and tactical metamorphosis of naval warfare in the century between the start of the Crimean War and the end of the Korean War was stunning in speed and scope. In barely three or four generations, the wooden walls that had characterized naval warfare since antiquity vanished utterly. In their place came previously unimaginable propulsion plants, navigation systems, and weaponry wielded with a precision and lethality that redefined the nature of naval combat and extended the range and speed at which fleets could fight. This transformation both required and made possible wholesale changes to the ways in which ships' crews were recruited and prepared for service ashore and afloat, and specialization and professionalization became watchwords of the service. Yet as in the merchant marine, the pace of change accelerated in the 1950s, and by the latter part of the decade the tactics and strategies so highly refined in two world wars were rendered obsolete, replaced by doctrines that addressed new concerns from the power of the atom to asymmetrical warfare.

Chapter 20

The Maritime World Since the 1950s

At the start of the twentieth century, the size of a country's merchant marine and navy served as a barometer of economic and military prestige, but this was no longer the case by the start of the third millennium, when it could be justly said, "The world maritime industry increasingly operates without reference to specific national interests." There are many reasons for this, but the summary explanation is globalization, a process to which the maritime industries have been both midwife and mirror, most obviously in their embrace of containerization and flags of convenience. One aim of this book has been to consider the ways in which mariners have fostered cross-cultural interdependence over five thousand years of literate civilization and for many millennia before that. As in all spheres of life, progress has been fitful, with bursts of creative, expansionist energy punctuated by longer periods of settled routine and at times contraction. At present we are in the midst of an era of sustained and dynamic change. Developments in maritime technology, commerce, warfare, exploration, and exploitation have altered our collective and individual relationships to the sea and maritime enterprise more in two or three generations than at any other time on record. Our interactions have been dictated by a host of new and in many cases previously unimaginable circumstances ranging from technology and legal regimes to international relations and the application of military force.

Shipping, Ships, and Ports in the Age of Containerization

The most obvious reason for the shift in people's appreciation of seafaring and its related disciplines is that maritime industries have largely vanished from public view, thanks to almost incalculable increases in automation and efficiency. Today, there are about 1.2 million seafarers in international trade worldwide, which means that less than half of one percent of the population moves 90 percent of the world's freight over seas that cover 70 percent of the earth's surface. Taken in these terms, shipping is a hyper-efficient industry. The introduction of steam and steel in the nineteenth century led to transformative increases in economic efficiency, reliability, range, speed, and, in the case of warships, killing power. While ships' profiles and crew assignments changed, merchantmen and warships alike still required large companies of men. Instead of fisting canvas high in the rigging, they had descended to the infernos below deck to sweat as trimmers, stokers, and oilers in the bowels of steamships. But ships still called in the same ports, their crews flooded sailor towns as they had for millennia, and denizens of seaports the world over were wreathed in the sights, smells, and sounds of the sea and distant lands. This is no longer the case.

Ships have long been capable of carrying vastly more cargo than unmechanized or low-tech handling systems could effectively absorb, but stevedores in the 1950s performed essentially the same work in much the same way as stevedores in antiquity. Cranes facilitated lifting bundles of various kinds from the wharf into the hold and vice versa, but the real work was trying to arrange goods below deck, a physically demanding, often dangerous, and always time-consuming process that kept most vessels in port for as much time as they spent at sea. The contents of a ship's hold frequently took as long to cross a pier as it did to cross an ocean.

A 1954 study of the freighter *Warrior* revealed that it carried a little more than five thousand tons of goods divided among 194,582 cases, cartons, reels, barrels, drums, and other packages, as well as fifty-three vehicles. These arrived at the Brooklyn pier where the ship berthed in more than eleven hundred shipments. Loading the ship took six days (of one eight-hour shift per day) and more than five thousand dollars in rope and lumber was needed to secure the cargo above and below deck. The ship reached Bremerhaven in ten and a half days, and stevedores working around the clock took four days to off-load the cargo, the last piece of which reached its ultimate destination more than a month later, and more than three months after the first item in the *Warrior*'s cargo had been sent from its point of origin to Brooklyn. The actual sea voyage from Brooklyn to Bremerhaven accounted for less than 12 percent of the cost of shipping and handling the goods; more than half went to loading and unloading the ship.

Into this morass of expense and inefficiency drove American trucking magnate Malcom McLean, who purchased a shipping line so that he could wheel

Stevedores, or longshoremen, off-loading cargo from a ship on the Mississippi River at New Orleans in the 1940s. While deck cranes provided some degree of automation, handling cargo remained a labor-intensive occupation, and a total of thirteen people can be seen in this tight picture of a relatively small ship. Within twenty years, the nature of commercial shipping had changed beyond all recognition, as is easily seen in the aerial photograph of the port of Singapore (see insert, figure 24). Courtesy of the Louisiana Digital Library.

his trucks onto the ship, forward them to a distant port, and drive them off to their ultimate destination. McLean decided that he could achieve even greater savings by removing the trailer bodies—or containers—from their wheelbase and stacking them, so in 1956 he purchased a surplus tanker, which he renamed the *Ideal-X*, and converted it to carry fifty-eight containers from Newark, New Jersey, to Houston, Texas. Loading the containers proceeded at a brisk pace of seven minutes per container, and when the voyage was complete, McLean discovered that the cost of loading the ship came to less than 16 cents per ton, compared with $5.83 per ton for loading the same amount of cargo in break-bulk form. Study after study found comparable results and in the 1960s, before the container revolution was fully realized, Belgian researchers showed that twenty men operating in a container terminal could load five thousand tons of cargo—about 165 containers—in the time it would take a hundred men to handle only twelve hundred tons of break-bulk goods. Even in its infancy, containerized goods required less than one-twentieth the manpower of break-bulk cargo.

Reducing inefficiencies in cargo handling was hardly a new goal. The Dutch had all but standardized the cargo-carrying *fluit* in the seventeenth century, and two hundred years later, short-haul ferries carried fully loaded railroad cars across rivers and lakes. A further step was taken in the 1920s with the Seatrain Lines' launch of two ships capable of carrying nearly a hundred railroad cars, loaded by crane, but this service never expanded beyond the original route between New Orleans and Havana. McLean's innovation stemmed from his ability to think outside the box, as it were, and ignore everything that shippers knew or thought they knew about shipping. This was facilitated by his having virtually no experience of ships or many of the other areas of expertise that would be affected by his ideas. "McLean understood that reducing the cost of shipping goods required not just a metal box but an entire new way of handling freight. Every part of the system—ports, ships, cranes, storage facilities, trucks, trains, and the operations of shippers themselves—would have to change." And, in less than a generation, everything did.

Efficiency required purpose-built "fully cellular container ships," the holds of which comprise a series of deep bays lined with vertical guides that keep stacks of containers aligned. It took several years before there was international agreement on standard sizes for containers, the basic unit being a box twenty feet long, eight feet wide, and eight and a half feet tall. Although the most common unit is twice as long, container ships are customarily measured in terms of twenty-foot equivalent units, or TEUs; a forty-foot container hauled by an eighteen-wheeler counts as two TEUs. The hull of the 9,600 TEU *Xin Los Angeles* (the biggest container ship in the world when launched in 2006; the largest being built as of 2013 are 18,000 TEU) is 337 meters long, 46 meters across, and can carry eighteen rows of containers on deck in stacks of up to eight tiers; below deck, the hold is sixteen containers wide and ten tiers deep. Loading containers is done by huge shoreside gantry cranes that pluck a container from the back of a truck, lower it into the hold, pluck another container from inside the hold and lower it onto the back of another truck. Cranes in a small port like Oranjestad, Aruba, can move twenty to thirty containers per hour. Larger individual cranes move at twice that rate, and in the most efficient ports, several cranes work a ship simultaneously to ensure turnaround times of only eighteen hours for even the largest vessels.

Containerization required completely new approaches to shoreside shiphandling, and effectively spelled the end of the cosmopolitan seaport. Container terminals are situated on large, flat areas with easy access to highways and railways and ample space for storing containers and parking trucks, and they are dominated by massive gantry cranes that run parallel to the water's edge and are capable of hoisting or lowering a thirty-ton container into the lowest tier in the outermost row of a ship nearly fifty meters wide. Ensuring the smooth flow of containers requires the intricate choreography of ships, trucks, and trains so that the right container goes on the right vehicle in the right order. The last is crucial to a ship's stability, and computer-generated loading plans have to take into account a container's weight (the heaviest generally going lower in the hold) and the port where it is to be offloaded. Determining the bay, tier, and row for each container on a ship that may carry upward of four thousand of them requires complex algorithms. This infrastructure makes container ports completely incompatible with traditional working waterfronts, and from the start new ports had to be built, usually on marginal land well away from congested urban areas. But these sprawling centers of material distribution lack the cultural amenities of city life, and with crews given only a few hours for shore leave, if any, they have none of the feel of seaports as they were up until the middle of the twentieth century. Alexandria, Quanzhou, Venice, Batavia, San Francisco, and Rio de Janeiro were centers not just of commerce but of people. Even ports that served as gateways to a more prominent parent city developed complex, cosmopolitan identities in their own right, as was the case with Piraeus and Ostia. Container ports like the Port Newark–Elizabeth Marine Terminal on New York Harbor and the Port of Felixstowe on the North Sea coast of England bear the same relationship to traditional ports that suburban malls have to downtown shopping districts, and even the nomenclature is the same: box ships supply box stores.

Containerization could not reach its potential without a thorough overhaul of rules and regulations governing freight forwarding, customs clearance, and insurance. A container in an intermodal environment might be "stuffed" at a factory in one country, driven or put on a train through one or more countries en route to a port in a third, shipped overseas to a fourth country, and delivered for "unstuffing" in a fifth. Subjecting the cargo to customs inspections at each border would slow the delivery time and thus run counter to the spirit of expediting trade, so new methods of approving cross-border shipments had to be devised. Insuring containerized cargo against loss was also problematic when it became nearly impossible to determine who was at fault for damages in a closed container that passed through five or more hands. And shippers resisted delaying cargoes for inspection by law enforcement officials trying to stop smuggling, human trafficking, and, in recent years, bombs.

Once regarded as insoluble obstacles to the success of containerization, these bureaucratic issues were ultimately solved thanks to computerization and the revision of rules regarding bills of lading and insurance liability.

Even if basic delays were not an issue, the detailed investigation of all cargoes is impossible simply due to the overwhelming volume of trade in the container age. In 2007, the strategically located port of Singapore handled twenty-eight million TEUs, more than any other port, many of them being transshipped between long-haul ships and vessels serving feeder routes from Australia to India to China. This was more than 10 percent of the world's containers, equal to more than 80 percent of the containers handled by the four largest European container ports combined, and a third more than passed through the three largest ports in the United States. By far the busiest long-distance routes are across the Pacific between Asia and North America, between Europe and Asia, and between North America and Europe. Although the linear dimensions of the locks of the Panama Canal (320 meters long by 33.5 meters across, with a depth of 12.6 meters) long dictated the maximum size of most ships, in the late 1990s shipowners realized that larger ships could profitably spend their entire career shuttling across the Atlantic or the Pacific, or between Asia and Europe, and they began ordering "post-Panamax" ships on the theory that they would never have to transit the canal anyway.

Periodically enlarged since its opening, the Suez Canal has always been able to accommodate ships too large to fit through the Panama Canal, but oil tankers began to outgrow the Suez Canal in the 1960s thanks to the growth of the Japanese economy and hostilities in the Middle East, the source of most of the world's oil. Between 1900 and the 1960s, tankers averaged less than 20,000 deadweight tons (dwt), but the first very large crude carrier (VLCC, up to 250,000 dwt) was built for service between the Middle East and Japan. The closure of the Suez Canal for six years after the Arab-Israeli Six-Day War in 1967 forced tankers bound from the Persian Gulf to western Europe or the Americas to sail via the Cape of Good Hope. To offset the cost of the longer distances by improved economies of scale, shippers ordered ever-larger ships and the first ultra-large crude carrier (ULCC, more than 250,000 dwt) slid down the ways in 1968. The largest ship ever built, the Japanese *Seawise Giant* (1979) had a capacity of more than 555,000 dwt, and at 458 meters (1,504 feet) was longer than the Sears Tower is tall. Just as containerization has led to the creation of distinctive new and remote ports, the deep draft of VLCCs and ULCCs—some require up to twenty-six meters of water below the keel—limits the number of ports they can access to off-load their cargoes. In the United States the only facility they can reach is the Louisiana Offshore Oil Port (the Loop), in the Gulf of Mexico eighteen miles south of Grand Isle, the pipeline of entry for about 10 percent of the country's foreign oil imports.

Increased ship size and faster turnaround times are an inevitable result of a broader trend toward designing merchant ships for ever more specialized purposes, which began with the delineation between cargo and passenger ships. Bulk cargoes were more susceptible to innovation than break-bulk, and automation brought huge gains in efficiency in loading commodities like grain, coal, and iron ore even in the nineteenth century. In 1839, the brig *Osceola* delivered the first bulk cargo of grain from Chicago to Buffalo, New York, where it took a week to off-load 1,678 bushels of grain (about fifty-three tons). Today, grain is routinely off-loaded by mechanical crane and bucket systems at rates of a thousand tons per hour. The growth of Europe's population and economy created high demand for agricultural products from around the world. Shipping grain and wool posed no difficulty, but the next breakthrough was the development of shipboard refrigeration, initiated by the French with shipments from Argentina in the 1870s and Australians and New Zealanders in the 1880s. Perfection of cold storage afloat meant that meat and dairy products could be shipped to markets halfway around the world. By the early 1900s, refrigerated ships (or reefers, for short) also carried fruits and flowers from growers in the Caribbean and West Africa to markets in Europe and North America. Following the success of oil tankers, shippers began to experiment with tankers for liquid chemicals (called packet tankers) and, with the perfection of refrigeration, potables and comestibles. In the 1970s, the Guinness brewing company maintained a fleet of tankers to carry stout across the Irish Sea, and following her retirement from that trade the *Miranda Guinness* entered service as a wine and olive oil tanker in the Mediterranean.

The paradox is that despite the wild proliferation of ship types for niche markets, the gigantic size of many ships, and the growth in the sheer numbers of the world fleet—45,000 ships of more than a thousand tons in 2010, half again as many as a century ago—the shipping industry as a whole has largely faded from view. Not only has the supporting infrastructure been moved away from population centers, but the number of people employed at sea and alongshore has actually shrunk. The dockworkers who feared that tankers like the *Glückauf* would lead to a decline in the number of people needed to handle the ship at sea or wharfside were proven correct almost immediately, and break-bulk cargo handlers faced the same fate with containerization. An English study showed that by 1970 productivity per man-hour had risen eighteenfold, from 1.67 tons to 30 tons. Global figures are not available, but despite huge increases in the volume of goods handled, the story was the same everywhere: waterfront employment crashed—on the East Coast of the United States from

51,000 in 1952 to 15,000 twenty years later; from 60,000 in England in the 1960s to 15,000 in 1972; from 30,000 in the 1950s to around 2,000 at the turn of the millennium in Australia. Since the nineteenth century, maritime labor unions had been among the most active, radical, and successful in the call for workers' rights. The rise of containerization coincided with the peak of their power, which all but guaranteed that efforts to resist downsizing the workforce would be fierce. Yet the change was not without positive consequences for dockworkers able to keep their jobs, as wages tended to rise owing to the more technically sophisticated nature of the work, and what had been a largely casual workforce gave rise to one with more permanent employment.

If the *Glückauf*'s dockworkers could have even envisioned a ship the size of the *Seawise Giant*, with a capacity more than two hundred times that of its forerunner, they would never have believed that it could be sailed by a crew of forty—only ten more men than the *Glückauf* itself. Comparable reductions in manning requirements can be found across the board. As automation has taken hold in engine rooms, on deck, in galleys, and on the bridge, the size of crews has fallen sharply. No more than seventeen people are needed for the average modern ship employed in blue-water trades, and some naval architects have been working to develop fully automated vessels requiring no crew at all. At the same time, unions, governments, and other organizations concerned about lost jobs, environmental protection, crew morale, and safety have fought to keep manning requirements at what some shipbuilders and accountants consider artificially high levels. The container ship *President Truman* of 61,875 gross tons was designed to sail with a crew of only eleven, but under United States regulations the ship is required to carry a crew of twenty-one. Such efficiencies have implications for working conditions aboard ship, safety from piracy, and the relationship between seafarers and the shoreside communities they ultimately serve but to whom they are all but invisible and unknown.

Flags of Convenience

The working conditions and wages of shoreside laborers are subject to the law of the land, and so are those of sailors. However, thanks to shipowners' growing reliance on flags of convenience and the emergence of a global labor market for merchant mariners, sailors increasingly work on ships of a different nationality from their own or that of their employers. The national flag has long afforded a ship the protection of the country it represents, and the custom of flying another nation's flag to benefit from diplomatic privileges it offers is an old one. The French allowed foreign vessels to fly the tricolor to trade to Ottoman ports in the Black Sea in the sixteenth century, and by the twentieth it was widely accepted that any country had the right to grant nationality, including its laws and the protection of its flag, to ships. The practice of registering ships began in Britain, where the first registry was published as a way to determine where a vessel was owned to ensure that it was in conformity with the Navigation Acts stipulating which ships could legally land goods in English ports. Other countries followed suit, and in the nineteenth century the intent of registration came to focus on ships' technical details for reasons of safety. Information published in registers now includes when and where a ship was built, particulars about its hull material, dimensions, propulsion, alterations, and inspections. But authorities' interest in such matters varies from country to country, a fact that shippers have eagerly exploited.

Faced with a glut of merchant shipping after World War I, the United States government sought to sell surplus tonnage without disadvantaging American companies in a saturated market. In 1922, six American freighters were transferred to the Panamanian flag. As one of the Americans involved in the transaction explained, "The chief advantage of Panamanian registry is that the owner is relieved of the continual but irregular boiler and hull inspections and the regulations as to crew's quarters and subsistence. We are under absolutely no restrictions. So long as we pay the $1 a net ton registry fee and 10 cents yearly a net ton tax" to the government of Panama. Because the freighters were entering the transpacific trade where the primary competition was from Japanese ships, the American owners crewed their Panamanian-flagged ships with Japanese and Chinese seamen whom they could pay much less than the going rate for American mariners. With "German stewards, Cuban firemen, and West Indian sailors, or crews of any nationality the management may wish," the operating expenses of the passenger ships *Reliance* and *Resolute* under Panamanian registry were lower than what they would have been with American crews protected by union agreements. (A subsidiary incentive for the transfer of passenger ships was that during Prohibition, U.S. courts ruled that American ships could not serve alcohol even when in international waters.) Although these two ships were soon sold to German owners, this was effectively the start of the adoption of flags of convenience for the explicit purpose of avoiding onerous safety regulations, domestic tax obligations, and labor laws.

More ships transferred to Panamanian registry throughout the 1930s, and especially after the start of World War II, when shipowners sought to circumvent restrictions of the Neutrality Act, which barred American ships from entering a war zone and so idled much of the fleet. By war's end, a combination of political instability in Panama, grievances by American labor unions, and opposition from Europe's traditional maritime states began to sour owners on Panamanian registry. To capitalize on this disaffection as well as to promote economic development in Liberia, Edward R. Stettinius, a secretary of state under Franklin Roosevelt and Harry Truman, proposed the creation of a Liberian ship registry to compete with Panama's. Drafted by members of Stettinus's staff with the approval and input by maritime lawyers from Esso, the forerunner of Exxon and operator of one of the world's premier tanker fleets, the new registry was up and running by 1949. Among the other advantages to the foreign "beneficial" owners of Liberian-flagged ships were that they did not need to incorporate in Liberia or hire Liberian seamen, and there was no provision for Liberian inspection or control of any ships registered there. The government also contracted with a U.S. company established by Stettinus and Associates to collect the $1.20 per ton registry fee, of which it retained 27 percent. By 1968 Liberia's was the biggest registry in the world.

The growth of the flag of convenience registries continues to provoke opposition from labor unions and traditional shipowning nations, who argue that ships should be subject to the "legal restraints of the nations of the owners, of the crews, or of the ports at which they [call]." Maintaining that "flag of convenience" is a misnomer, shipowners insist that these registries are really "flags of necessity" and that the law of the country where the ship is registered should prevail. An uneasy compromise has evolved. Flags of convenience provide corporations with tax shelters and allow them to hire crews from an ever-expanding global labor market dominated by sailors from developing nations. As of 2000, Filipinos (230,000 officers and ratings) and Indonesians (83,500) comprised about a quarter of all the seafarers employed worldwide. However, their conditions are often substandard, with poor pay, inadequate training or qualifications, limited time off, and social isolation. Many of the worst problems have been addressed by international treaties, while labor unions, notably the International Transport Workers' Federation, are vigilant in rooting out abuses and advocating for better conditions.

Flags of convenience received little public scrutiny until a series of shipwrecks with devastating commercial and environmental consequences brought them to world attention. In 1967, the supertanker *Torrey Canyon* ran aground and split in two off Cornwall, England, spilling 123,000 tons of oil that spread across 120 miles of the English coast and 55 miles of Brittany. Assigning liability for the disaster was complicated by the fact that the Italian-crewed ship had been chartered to British Petroleum by a Liberian subsidiary of an American company, while the plaintiffs hailed from Great Britain and France. Subsequent accidents also aroused public ire, but the environmental and economic impact of the *Torrey Canyon* was not exceeded until 1978, when the VLCC

Amoco Cadiz grounded a mile off the coast of Brittany about a hundred miles south of where the *Torrey Canyon* came to grief. The wreck devastated one of the most diverse and abundant fisheries in Europe and underscored problems in supertanker design and operations. In the course of twelve hours, three unrelated pieces of equipment critical for steering, towing, and anchoring failed utterly and official inquiries showed that structural and safety standards were inappropriate for the huge vessels then being launched.

To balance the conflicting expectations of owners, sailors, flag states, and ports of call that these and similar disasters revealed, the International Maritime Organization (IMO) has adopted a raft of conventions covering almost every conceivable aspect of shipping from pollution and ship design to labor and personal safety. A direct result of the *Torrey Canyon* disaster, the IMO's convention on pollution from ships (MARPOL) covers problems resulting from catastrophic failures as well as more mundane but incrementally more significant problems like the disposal of sewage and garbage at sea as well as air pollution from ship's engines. The International Convention on Standards of Training, Certification and Watchkeeping for Seafarers established minimum standards for ships' crews from the engine room to the bridge. Still others mandate the establishment and observance of traffic separation schemes in constricted waters not unlike those proposed by Matthew Fontaine Maury in the nineteenth century. The English Channel had been so divided in the 1960s, but among the first reforms following the *Amoco Cadiz* was the creation of a third traffic lane thirty miles west of Ushant for inbound tankers, which forces these leviathans to give the Breton coast a wide berth and affords them more "drift time" in the event of a catastrophic failure.

The most comprehensive and effective regulations are those encompassed in the Safety of Life at Sea (SOLAS) conventions, the first of which was adopted in 1914 in response to the *Titanic* disaster. These now cover all aspects of shipboard operations, occupational safety, medical care and survival functions, ship design, fire detection and protection, life preservers and lifeboats, radio communications and navigational practice, and the carriage of cargoes including dangerous or hazardous goods, as well as special provisions governing the operation of nuclear-powered ships. All told, these highly technical and legalistic regulations run to tens of thousands of pages, but the result has been astonishing. Between 2005 and 2008, ferries, cruise ships, and other commercial vessels over a hundred gross tons carried an average of 1.7 billion people annually, but no more than a thousand people died in any one year, and the odds of dying in a shipboard accident were only 1 in 1.6 million, a record that would stagger late nineteenth-century travel advisors like Katherine Ledoux and maritime industry reformers like Samuel Plimsoll.

The Fisheries and the Global Commons

These statistics on mortality among seagoing people do not include fisher-men, the great majority of whom work on vessels of less than one hundred gross tons in what has always been among the most dangerous industries in the world. As a fisherman's wife remarked to Sir Walter Scott in the early 1800s, "It's no fish ye're buying—it's men's lives." Until the nineteenth century, fishing was a small-scale, domestic venture, as it remains throughout much of the world. This is so even in industrialized countries like the United States, where lobstering, for instance, is the livelihood of sole proprietors who own and operate their own boats through four seasons, sometimes assisted by one or two sternmen, but in many cases alone. The world's fishing indus-try has undergone as much change over the past century and a half as any other maritime enterprise. This began with the introduction of steam engines, the growth of the ice trade (and later the invention of icemakers) to preserve fish, and the proliferation of new and more durable types of fishing gear. The twentieth century saw the deployment of sophisticated targeting apparatus ranging from sonar to spotter planes, and the launching of large factory ships to which smaller vessels can transfer their catch for processing, so enabling them to remain at sea for months at a time. Equally important for the global-ization of the fish market is the jet plane, which allows fish to be sold halfway around the world within twenty-four hours of being landed.

The principal tools of the commercial fisheries are the longline, otter trawls and beam trawls, and seine nets. At an artisanal level, these are labor-intensive technologies that result in fairly limited but sustainable returns. Since World War II, however, they have been employed on an industrial scale that threat-ens the stability of the fish stocks themselves. As a retired English fisherman observed in a 1972 documentary:

> Up to the time [World War II] started, fishing was still prosecuted in the old style. . . . There was some evolution, but the thing had not greatly altered from the days of Galilee, really, because the drift net was more a primi-tive method of fishing. You shot your nets and you waited until the herring caught you. . . . The result was of course we did not catch all the herring. We only caught some of them, and that was quite a good idea because there was always some left for another year. . . . From the end of the war, that's when the depredation took place. That's when the final killing took place.

One innovation was the introduction of nylon fishing gear, which made it possible to make much longer nets and lines than was possible with natural fibers. Today longlines can be up to a hundred kilometers long, with shorter lines and baited hooks placed at regular intervals. Longlines are generally intended to target specific species, whether pelagic fish like tuna and swordfish or demersal species like cod and haddock, but they also catch an enormous quantity of nontargeted fish and other animals, including sharks, sea turtles, and albatrosses. More degrading to the environment are trawls, gaping nets the width of a football field designed to be dragged across the seafloor to catch cod, monkfish, pollock, shrimp, and other species. Universally regarded as the most destructive form of fishing, their impact on the ocean floor has been likened to clear-cutting a forest, and they have been widely implicated in the destruction of coral reefs and other undersea habitats.

While people's growing appetite for fish is the major impetus behind the expansion of the fisheries in recent years, 20 percent of all fish is simply ground into fishmeal, and about 7 percent is unwanted bycatch that is simply dumped back into the sea dead or dying. Scientists have been assessing fish stocks since the nineteenth century and in recent decades the U.N.'s Food and Agriculture Organization has taken a lead in monitoring fisheries worldwide, devising management programs, establishing marine protected areas where no fishing is allowed so that depleted species can revive, and regulating the types of fishing gear that can be employed. An additional mandate is cracking down on illegal, unreported, and unregulated fisheries, which may be the biggest threat to the long-term viability of many species. As with commercial shipping, the best approach to solving the most intractable issues facing the fisheries and the people who work them has proven to be international cooperation as agreed to in various conventions on high-seas fishing. The Agreement on Conservation and Management of Straddling Fish Stocks and Highly Migratory Fish Stocks, for example, specifically addresses fish populations that straddle the boundaries between a nation's exclusive economic zone (EEZ)—an area of the sea out to two hundred miles from shore—and the high seas, as well as fish that routinely migrate between national EEZs and the high seas. The agreement seeks to establish the basis for the conservation of fisheries by improving the measurement of fish stocks and establishing catch quotas, regional fishing organizations, and mechanisms for ensuring compliance, including the right to board and inspect vessels.

The unintended consequences of industrial fishing have not been limited to the environment. The drive for larger boats and tougher, more advanced gear has made fishing an increasingly capital-intensive enterprise that has marginalized many fishermen, in much the same way that medieval seamen went from being members of a ship's company to mere hired crew. Traditionally, fishing was a fundamentally democratic business in which members of the crew divided a fixed portion of the boat's catch and contributed the same share of expenses for running the boat as they received in profits. But many now work for fixed salaries as employees on boats whose owners' only connection to the industry is as investors. The uncertainty of life in the fishing industry is compounded by governments' endless tinkering with requirements for fishing gear (to reduce bycatch, for instance) and catch limits, which can result in entire fishing grounds being put off-limits, thus leaving fishermen without any livelihood. The case of the United States and Canada is instructive. In the 1960s, foreign fleets complete with factory ships descended on the Gulf of Maine, where landings of haddock, herring, and cod collapsed. In the United States, congressional legislation prohibited foreign fishing vessels from operating within the EEZ, but this was a political rather than a scientific solution that did little to ease the strain on fish stocks from domestic fishermen. Likewise, the Canadian cod fishery declined so precipitously that in 1996 the Canadian government banned cod fishing, at the cost of about twenty to thirty thousand jobs, less than five hundred years after Matthew Cabot's reports of the abundance of cod had opened North America to European exploration.

The United States was able to define and enforce its right to its EEZ in part because it is a global superpower. Citizens of countries at the other end of the geopolitical spectrum—failed states like Somalia, where central authority collapsed in 1995—have no such options. Taking advantage of Somalia's lack of a government, foreign fleets descended on the Somali coast, often within the territorial limit, and began overfishing stocks that coastal communities had recently begun to harvest for themselves. With no coast guard to protect their interests and no voice in the international community, local fishermen began seizing and ransoming foreign fishing vessels and their crews. This retributive privateering quickly attracted the interest of local warlords, terrorists, and others who expanded the scope of their operations to seize piratically and indiscriminately anything from container ships and tankers to cruise ships and private yachts regardless of flag. While this has become an obvious criminal problem, the underlying cause, namely illegal fishing, is a more disturbing threat to the global commons.

The World Fleet in the Nuclear Age

The SOLAS provisions on nuclear-powered ships have the narrowest application of any in the convention, but they were drafted in response to one of the most technically sophisticated engineering feats of the postwar era, one achieved almost simultaneously in the United States and the Soviet Union.

The driving force in the United States was Hyman G. Rickover, who first considered nuclear propulsion for ships as a naval officer on assignment to the Atomic Energy Commission's reactor complex at Oak Ridge, Tennessee, in 1946. As head of both the navy's Bureau of Ships' Nuclear Power Division and, concurrently, the Naval Reactors Branch of the Atomic Energy Commission, Rickover went on to develop plans for the world's first nuclear-powered vessel, the submarine USS *Nautilus*, commissioned in 1955.

One advantage of nuclear fuel over fossil fuels is that it produces heat to create steam through fission rather than fire. Without the need for oxygen, a nuclear-powered submarine can stay submerged almost indefinitely, and in 1960 the USS *Triton* completed the first underwater circumnavigation of the globe, covering 27,723 miles in less than sixty-one days. Nuclear power held another attraction for the Soviets, who relied on maritime transportation to reach the resource-rich but almost impassable territories of northern Siberia. Because nuclear fuel can last a decade or more, it obviated the need for regular supplies of fuel to be stockpiled at icebound ports that were nearly as remote by land as they were by sea. Moreover, it allowed for faster, more powerful ships. The first nuclear-powered surface ship, the icebreaker *Lenin*, was launched two years after the *Nautilus*, and in 1960 it opened the way for merchant ships to service the ports of Dikson and Dudinka on a regular basis. In time the sailing season along the northern sea route lengthened from two to ten months, and the *Arktika* became the first surface ship to reach the geographic North Pole in 1977, nineteen years after the *Nautilus* had crossed it, submerged. With the recession of sea ice due to climate change, Russian shippers hope to exploit the shorter Northeast Passage between Europe and Asia, a distance of about 6,750 miles compared with 11,000 miles via the Suez Canal.

The public has always been leery of nuclear-powered surface ships, and apart from the Russian icebreaker fleet, only four have been built for non-military service, and two of them were experimental vessels. But navies and secretive governments are less inhibited by public sensibilities. In 1966–67, a nuclear accident resulted in the death of thirty of the *Lenin*'s crew, a fact covered up for decades, which allowed the Soviet Union to continue building nuclear-powered icebreakers with little scrutiny. Over all, in addition to thirty-five nuclear-powered surface ships—including eleven U.S. aircraft carriers—almost five hundred nuclear-powered submarines have been built, nearly all of them by the former Soviet Union and the United States. Despite the operational benefits associated with nuclear power, these fleets are better known not for their propulsion plants but for their nuclear weapons, which enable them to project overwhelming force, in some cases over thousands of miles.

Nuclear naval strategy represented an almost complete departure from everything that went before. While the United States and NATO were concerned with safeguarding world trade, in oil above all, and deterring a Soviet attack on western Europe or the United States, focus soon shifted to the deployment of conventional ballistic missiles, which by the 1990s had ranges of more than six thousand miles. In essence, submarines had become mobile missile bases.

This was not their only function, and "attack submarines" were designed for operations against other submarines and surface units. But there have been very few fleet engagements on the high seas since World War II, the most significant being the 1982 Anglo-Argentine war for the Falkland Islands, the deadliest encounter of which involved the sinking of the World War II–era light cruiser *General Belgrano* by a conventional torpedo fired from the nuclear-powered submarine HMS *Conqueror*. For the most part, offensive operations at sea have been undertaken in support of land-based operations, notably in the Vietnam War, the United States' invasions of Iraq in 1990 and 2003, and of Afghanistan in 2001. In all of these wars, ship- and submarine-based missiles and carrier aircraft were launched against inland targets—Afghanistan is landlocked—in support of ground forces. In essence, this is a vindication of the strategy advocated by Francisco de Almeida, Portugal's first viceroy in India that "All your forces should be on the sea, because if we are not strong there . . . fortresses on land will be of little use to you."

As was true of Portugal in the sixteenth century, the U.S. fleet exists to project power and safeguard trade, not to fight fleets of comparable capabilities because there are none. With eleven aircraft carriers—as many as the rest of the world's navies combined—and a budget request for 2012 of $176 billion, nearly twice the budget of the world's second largest *military* (navy, army, and air force) establishment—the United States Navy is almost incalculably larger and more powerful than any other in the world. Yet for all its seagoing assets, in recent years it has proven stunningly ineffective in exercising the sort of force historically associated with navies, even something as basic as eradicating piracy. This is due partly to the composition of the United States Navy, which is ill-suited to such assignments, and partly because of changes in international law. The post–Cold War world is not beset by the sort of bilateral military tensions between nation-states with global aspirations like those characteristic of the previous 350 years. Working within a new framework of multilateral maritime agreements respecting the environment, safety, and the rights and responsibilities of sovereign nations—a regime that reflects a growing consensus that the sea is a global commons—even superpowers like the United States cannot preserve security save by shared responsibility.

Collaboration within a framework of international law is actively supported by many countries with navies smaller than that of the United States, but this is not a recasting of the debate between Mahan's "overbearing power on the sea" and the Jeune Ecole's "strategy of the weak," for it goes beyond the use of navies in traditional conflict. One of the clearest affirmations of this view was voiced by then chief of naval operations Admiral Michael Mullen. "As we combine our advantages," he told an International Seapower Symposium in 2005, "I envision a 1,000-ship Navy—a fleet-in-being, if you will, made up of the best capabilities of all freedom-loving navies of the world. . . . This 1,000-ship Navy would integrate the capabilities of the maritime services to create a fully interoperable force—an international city at sea. So this calls for a new—or maybe a not so new but very different—image of sea power." This sentiment found further expression in a joint strategy document by the U.S. Navy, Coast Guard, and Marines, which focuses on the "global system comprised of interdependent networks of trade, finance, information, law, people and governance" that are vital to the national interest.

That the material composition of the United States Navy resembles, and will for some time, the fleets of a previous age reflects in part the simple fact that the lifespan of naval ships—and naval doctrines—runs to decades. Even without the inevitable domestic opposition to letting go of these obvious emblems of military, industrial, and national prowess in favor of a fleet more appropriate to the country's needs, they will be around for a long time. Whether Mullen's is the phrase that will launch a thousand ships remains to be seen. So long as the United States possesses a fleet that can project American military power around the world with impunity, it will be difficult to convince other powers that they should not compete with the U.S. Navy as it is now rather than as it might be in the future. Nor is it obvious that the United States would accept a more level playing field. But it behooves the United States and other nations to consider the political and diplomatic feasibility of a multinational "thousand-ship navy," because the greatest threats at sea—among them smuggling, piracy, and overfishing—are stateless and criminal rather than political. Regardless of their source, as Mullen put it, the "challenges are too diverse to tackle alone and require more capability and resources than any single nation can deliver."

The past half century of world history has been one of incomparable vigor driven by myriad forces, not the least of which has been maritime enterprise in all its forms. If we take economic expansion and mechanical efficiency as the standard, the story offers a straightforward narrative of progress. Over thousands of years, the volume of sea trade grew from nothing to more than 2.6

billion tons per year in 1970. In the four decades since, that figure has more than trebled, to over eight billion tons, while ships became bigger and faster but immeasurably safer than ever. In the process, maritime enterprise has hastened globalization while it has itself been globalized. Most ships and crews have been rendered all but anonymous, stripped of their national identities by flags of convenience and made invisible by their displacement to the industrial wastelands on the margins of the ports they serve.

Some people claim that such changes have robbed the maritime world of its romance and allure, but for many people experience of the sea never held romance—promise, perhaps, of a better life in a new land, good tidings from abroad, or simple profit. Still, the sea held no promise for slaves, coolies, indentured servants, or the dispossessed, and across cultures people have reviled maritime commerce for its noxious cargoes of alien people and ideas, deadly plagues, and ruthless enemies from beyond the sea. At the same time, we have come to know that while the sea is fickle and unforgiving, it is a fragile environment susceptible to human depredation on a scale as unimaginable to our ancestors as the ships and other technologies we have created to make it so.

Seafaring is one of humankind's oldest collective pursuits, the benefits of which are nicely summarized by the Byzantine historian George Pachymeres:

> Sailing is a noble thing, useful beyond all others to mankind. It exports what is superfluous, it provides what is lacking, it makes the impossible possible, it joins together men from different lands, and makes every inhospitable island a part of the mainland, it brings fresh knowledge to those who sail, it refines manners, it brings concord and civilization to men, it consolidates their nature by bringing together all that is most human in them.

The benefits of maritime enterprise are not as evenly distributed as Pachymeres proposes, but the weight of evidence suggests that most people at least tacitly agree with this optimistic assessment. What is new since he wrote eight centuries ago is a global consciousness of the sea and the growing realization that maritime history offers an invaluable perspective on the history of the world and ourselves.

Notes

Introduction

5   "ancient ships and boats": Harding, "Organizational Life Cycles," 7.

5   "classic age of sail": The phrase is from the title of a collection of essays edited by John B. Hattendorf, *Maritime History*, vol. 2, *The Eighteenth Century and the Classic Age of Sail* (Malabar, FL: Krieger, 1997).

5   "the inequality": Toynbee, "My View of History," 10, in Manning, *Navigating World History*, 41. In the same vein, Nicholas Rodger notes that "Naval history is certainly one of the few historical subjects in which there are authors who still think that success or failure can be explained by references, overt or implied, to the innate superiority of national character" ("Considerations," 118).

6   nationalist maritime histories: These include Mookerji, *Indian Shipping* (1912); G. A. Ballard, *Rulers of the Indian Ocean* (London: Duckworth, 1927); Hadi Hasan, *A History of Persian Navigation* (1928); K. M. Panikkar, *India and the Indian Ocean: An Essay on the Influence of Sea Power on Indian History* (London: Allen & Unwin, 1945); Hourani, *Arab Seafaring in the Indian Ocean in Ancient and Early Medieval Times* (1951); and Needham, et al., *Science and Civilisation in China*, vol. 4, pt. 3, *Civil Engineering and Nautics* (1971).

6   works examining individual oceans and seas include Neal Ascherson, *Black Sea* (New York: Hill & Wang, 1995); Braudel, *The Mediterranean*; Paul Butel, *The Atlantic*, trans. Iain Hamilton Grant (London: Routledge, 1999); Nigel Calder, *The English Channel* (New York: Viking, 1986); K. N. Chaudhuri, *Trade and Civilization in the Indian Ocean: An Economic History from the Rise of Islam to 1750* (Cambridge: Cambridge University Press, 1985); Charles H. Cotter, *The Atlantic Ocean* (Glasgow: Brown & Ferguson, 1974); Richard Hall, *Empires of the Monsoon: A History of the Indian Ocean and Its Invaders* (London: HarperCollins, 1996); Peregrine Horden and Nicholas Purcell, *The Corrupting Sea: A Study of Mediterranean History* (London: Blackwell, 2000); Paul Jordan, *North Sea Saga* (New York: Pearson-Longman, 2004); Milo Kearney, *The Indian Ocean in World History* (London: Routledge, 2003); Charles King, *The Black Sea: A History* (New York: Oxford University Press, 2004); Kirby and Hinkkanen, *The Baltic and North Seas*; Matti Klinge, *The Baltic World*, trans. Timothy Binham (Helsinki: Otava, 1995); Predrag Matvejevic, *Mediterranean: A Cultural Landscape* (Berkeley: University of California Press, 1999); Walter A. McDougall, *Let the Sea Make a Noise: A History of the North Pacific from Magellan to MacArthur* (New York: Basic Books, 1993); McPherson, *The Indian Ocean*; Palmer, *The Baltic*; Pearson, *The Indian Ocean*; Pryor, *Geography, Technology and War*; Himanshu Prabha Ray,

Archaeology of Seafaring: The Indian Ocean in the Ancient Period (New Delhi: Pragati, 1999); Auguste Toussaint, *History of the Indian Ocean* (London: Routledge, 1966); and Villiers, *Monsoon Seas.*

6   "All sea is sea": In Jay, *Greek Anthology*, 7.639 (p. 195).

8   "Do you not see": Quran 32:31.

8   "maritime technology": Diamond, *Guns, Germs, and Steel*, 78, and 241, 313, 341–42, 359.

8   "the story of the processes": Roberts, *History of the World*, xiv.

10   "A general naval history": Rodger, "Considerations," 128.

1. Taking to the Water

11   Norwegian rock carvings: Ellmers, "Beginning of Boatbuilding in Central Europe," 11–12.

14   "Who the devil": Jean-Louis Caro, *Journal*, in Bougainville, *Pacific Journal*, 200.

14   from the East Indies: Cook, *Journals*, vol. 1, *Voyage of the Endeavour*, 154; Irwin, *Prehistoric Exploration*, 13–16.

14   "accidental drift": Kirch, *On the Road of the Winds*, 238; Lewis, *We, the Navigators*, 16–17; and Irwin, *Prehistoric Exploration*, 13–16.

14   Sundaland to Sahul: Kirch, *On the Road of the Winds*, 68.

14   oldest stone tools: Horridge, "Story of Pacific Sailing Canoes," 541.

15   intervisible islands: Kirch, *On the Road of the Winds*, 68–69; Irwin, *Prehistoric Exploration*, 18–23.

15   Mount Witori: Kirch, *On the Road of the Winds*, 88.

16   Lapita culture: Ibid., 93–95, 209–10.

16   A number of sequences: Ibid., 231, and an alternative scenario, 245.

16   Micronesia's settlement: Ibid., 170; Irwin, *Prehistoric Exploration*, 126–27.

16   What prompted the Lapita people: Kirch, *On the Road of the Winds*, 97; Irwin, *Prehistoric Exploration*, 42.

17   "splendid recklessness": Hornell, *Water Transport*, 253.

17   fisherman named Kupe: I have followed the outline in Buck's *Coming of the Maori*, 5–7; for another interpretation of this and associated traditions, see Walker, *Ka Whawhai Tonu Matou*, 34–43.

17   Although New Zealand is closer: Irwin, *Prehistoric Exploration*, 104–10.

17   average size: By way of example, the average size of the forty-eight islands in the Federated States of Micronesia is 14.4 square kilometers, but the median size is only 1.5 square kilometers; only six are more than 10 square kilometers and only three more than 100 square kilometers.

18   navigational practices: McGrail, *Boats of the World*, 342–45.

18   trade winds: In *Robinson Crusoe* (1719), Daniel Defoe writes "The winds [in the China Sea] seemed to be more steadily against us, blowing almost Trade, as we call it, from the East, and E.N.E."

18   "expand" the size: Lewis, *We, the Navigators*, 196.

19   ocean swells: Ibid., 224–61; Genz, "Oceania," 146.

19   "the direction of every known island": Lewis, *We, the Navigators*, 174.

19   *etak*, or reference island: Ibid., 173–79

19   *Hokule'a*: Ibid., 312–26. Literally "star of gladness," Hokule'a is otherwise known as Arcturus. The Polynesian Voyaging Society is an excellent resource for information

about traditional Pacific navigation and boatbuilding generally. The most complete introduction to Pacific boatbuilding remains Haddon and Hornell, *Canoes of Oceania*. McGrail, *Boats of the World*, 311–45, is more accessible and up-to-date.

19 Mau Piailug: "Pius Mau Piailug."

20 Double canoes: McGrail, *Boats of the World*, 324–26.

20 capable of carrying: Ibid., 338; Kirch, *On the Road of the Winds*, 109–11.

22 coastal migration: Fladmark, "Routes"; Erlandson et al., "Kelp Highway Hypothesis."

23 dearth of harbors: Arnold and Bernard, "Negotiating the Coasts," 110.

23 120 kilometers a day: Carvajal, *Discovery of the Amazon*, 99.

23 Andean civilization emerged: Moseley, *Maritime Foundations of Andean Civilization*, 7–17.

24 reeds, cotton, and gourds: Moseley, *Incas and Their Ancestors*, 47.

25 Chavín's earliest long-distance trades: Stanish, "Origins of State Societies in Ancient Peru," 45–48.

25 thorny oyster: Zeidler, "Maritime Exchange in the Early Formative Period," 252.

25 views that Amazonia: Mann, *1491*, 280–311.

25 "the great dominion of Machiparo": Carvajal, *Discovery of the Amazon*, 199.

25 four hundred liters: Ibid., 201.

25 "two hundred pirogues": Ibid., 218.

26 more than eighteen hundred nautical miles: Callaghan, "Prehistoric Trade Between Ecuador and West Mexico," 798.

26 Affinities: Coe, "Archaeological Linkages," 364–66; Anawalt, "Ancient Cultural Contacts."

26 intermittent trade: Shimada, "Evolution of Andean Diversity," 430–36.

27 *balsas*: rafts; Edwards, *Aboriginal Watercraft*.

27 "They are level": Salazar de Villasante, in ibid., 62.

27 "By sinking some": Jorge Juan y Santacilia, *Relación Histórica del Viage a la América Meridionel* (1748), in Edwards, *Aboriginal Watercraft*, 73–74, and n. 33. Juan y Santacilia went on to become chief constructor of the Spanish navy, and his two-volume shipbuilding treatise, *Examen marítimo, theórico práctico . . .* (1771), remained in print for fifty years. See Ferreiro, *Ships and Science*, 272–75.

27 fastest northbound passages: Callaghan, "Prehistoric Trade Between Ecuador and West Mexico," 801–3.

27 excited no imitation: Chapman, "Port of Trade Enclaves in Aztec and Maya Civilization," 131–42.

27 none of whom: Epstein, "Sails in Aboriginal Mesoamerica."

27 Putun Maya: Allaire, "Archaeology of the Caribbean Region," 711–12.

28 "by good fortune": Colón, *Life of the Admiral Christopher Columbus*, chap. 89 (pp. 231–32).

29 oldest log canoes: Wheeler et al., "Archaic Period Canoes."

29 forerunners of planked boats: McGrail, *Boats of the World*, 172–80.

29 Coastal people traded: Fisher, "Northwest from the Beginning of Trade," 120–24.

29 "about 200 Men": DeVoto, *Journals of Lewis and Clark*, Nov. 4, 1805 (p. 275).

29 Large dugouts: McGrail, *Boats of the World*, 172.

30 "ornimented with Images": DeVoto, *Journals of Lewis and Clark*, Nov. 4, 1805 (p. 276); Ames, "Going by Boat," 27–28, 31–32.

30 "the only tool": DeVoto, *Journals of Lewis and Clark*, Feb. 1, 1806 (pp. 316–17).

30 Kayaks, Umiaks, and Baidarkas: Chapelle, "Arctic Skin Boats," 174–211.

32   Dorset culture was replaced: Snow, "First Americans," 186–93.
32   "It was sowed together": Martin Pring, "A Voyage . . . for the discouerie of the North part of Virginia," in Quinn and Quinn, *English New England Voyages*, 222.
33   The preferred bark: Adney and Chapelle, *Bark Canoes and Skin Boats*, 14–15, 29.
33   "The Indian": McPhee, *Survival of the Bark Canoe*, 50.
33   "cocked his arm": Ibid., 21.
33   "must be looked upon": Adney and Chapelle, *Bark Canoes and Skin Boats*, 135.
34   "The board canoe": Fernando Librado, in Hudson et al., *Tomol*, 39.

2. The River and Seas of Ancient Egypt

37   "And then with my eyes closed": In Jenkins, *Boat Beneath the Pyramid*, 53.
37   "looked as hard": In Lipke, *Royal Ship of Cheops*, 2.
39   The most important Egyptian towns: Wilkinson, *Early Dynastic Egypt*, 346–60.
40   "to sail southwards": Montet, *Everyday Life in Ancient Egypt*, 173, note.
40   "Balance of the Two Lands": Wilkinson, *Early Dynastic Egypt*, 58.
41   The score of wooden hulls: Ward, *Sacred and Secular*, 12. Egyptian ship remains from antiquity include fourteen hulls from Abydos, two from Giza (one unexcavated), five or six from Dahshur (four on exhibit, in Cairo, Pittsburgh, and Chicago), part of a fifth-century BCE hull from Mataria, near Cairo, and a collection of ship timbers from Lisht.
41   Larger reed rafts: Landström, *Ships of the Pharaohs*, 41, 94–97.
42   A bipod mast: Hornell, *Water Transport*, 46, 49; Johnstone, *Sea-craft of Prehistory*, 10, 70.
42   The oldest rendering: Carter, "Boat-Related Finds," 91. This ceramic disc shows a bipod mast but not a sail.
43   royal mortuary in Abydos: O'Connor, "Boat Graves and Pyramid Origins"; Pierce, "After 5,000-Year Voyage"; Ward, "World's Oldest Planked Boats."
44   The inherent flexibility: In the fourteenth century, Ibn Battuta wrote, "The Indian and Yemenite ships are sewn together with [cords], for that sea [the Red Sea] is full of reefs, and if a ship is nailed with iron nails it breaks up on striking the rocks, whereas if it is sewn together with cords, it is given a certain resilience and does not fall to pieces." *Travels*, 4:827.
45   The Khufu ship used: Ward, *Sacred and Secular*, 140.
45   no caulking: Ibid., 124.
45   sewn hull of the *Sohar*: Severin, *Sinbad Voyage*, 40: "Kunhikoya announced that I would need about fifteen hundred bundles of coconut string to build the ship I needed. I calculated the total length, and it came to four hundred miles! This seemed a colossal amount, but events proved Kunhikoya right."
45   "I conducted the work": In Breasted, *Ancient Records of Egypt*, vol. 1, §746 (p. 326).
45   The Nubians may have originated: Ward, *Sacred and Secular*, 6.
45   One theory: Jenkins, *Boat Beneath the Pyramid*; Landström, *Ships of the Pharaohs*; and Lipke, *Royal Ship of Cheops*.
46   "the most beautiful in form": In Simpson, *Literature of Ancient Egypt*, 17.
46   "Bringing from the workshops": In Landström, *Ships of the Pharaohs*, 62.
46   two granite obelisks: Habachi, "Two Graffiti at Sehel," 99. One inscription refers to "two great obelisks, their height 108 cubits" (57 meters), which would have weighed

2,400 tons each and required a barge 95 meters long by 32 meters wide, with a loaded displacement of 7,300 tons and a draft of 3 meters. For measurements of Hatshepsut's barge, see Landström, *Ships of the Pharaohs*, 129–30.

47   "the ships were able": Pliny, *Natural History*, 36.14 (vol. 10:29).

47   Colossi of Memnon: Wehausen et al., "Colossi of Memnon and Egyptian Barges." The statues depict Amenhotpe III (1410–1372 BCE) but later Greek visitors took them to represent Memnon, an Ethiopian king whom Achilles killed at Troy. See Casson, *Everyday Life in Ancient Egypt*, 141.

47   "the raft is carried": Herodotus, *Histories*, 2.96 (p. 119).

47   "the method of construction": Ibid.

47   "a cargo-boat of acacia": In Landström, *Ships of the Pharaohs*, 62. The Egyptians used two cubit measurements, one equal to 0.45 centimeters and the royal cubit of 0.525 meters; Wachsmann, *Seagoing Ships*, 345n16.

48   "ships go out": In Pritchard, *Ancient Near East*, 1:259.

48   "forward-starboard": Ward, *Sacred and Secular*, 8–9.

48   "down to Egypt": In Breasted, *Ancient Records of Egypt*, vol. 1, §322 (p. 148).

49   "If you descend": "Tale of the Eloquent Peasant," in Simpson, *Literature of Ancient Egypt*, 25–44, esp. 33, 36. Ma'at was both the concept and goddess of universal order and justice.

49   "The bow-rope of the South": In Breasted, *Ancient Records of Egypt*, vol. 2, §341 (p. 143).

49   ship of state: See for instance, Sophocles, *Oedipus the King*, ll.27–30 (420 BCE); Plato, *Republic*, 6.488 (340 BCE); Horace, *Odes*, 1.14 (23 BCE); Sebastian Brant, *Das Narranschiff* (Ship of Fools, 1494); and Whitman, *Leaves of Grass*, 262–63: "O Captain! My Captain!" on the death of Abraham Lincoln (1865). Explaining his purpose in gathering traditional sailing ships for Operation Sail 1976 as a means of building international goodwill, maritime historian Frank O. Braynard wrote, "We are all seamen on the ship Earth."

50   "only one warship": In Breasted, *Ancient Records of Egypt*, vol. 1, §322 (p. 148).

50   "ivory, throw sticks": In ibid., vol. 1, §353 (p. 161).

50   sea route between Buto and Byblos: Redford, *Egypt, Canaan, and Israel*, 22.

50   "forty ships": In Wachsmann, *Seagoing Ships*, 9. The Palermo Stone is a list of pharaohs and their activities from the predynastic period through the middle of the Fifth Dynasty.

50   Fifth Dynasty reliefs: Wachsmann, *Seagoing Ships*, 12–18.

51   Crete and Egypt: Casson, *Ancient Mariners*, 17–18; Wachsmann, *Seagoing Ships*, 298.

51   "went forth from Coptos": In Wachsmann, *Seagoing Ships*, 238.

52   "laden with all the products": "The Shipwrecked Sailor," in Simpson, *Literature of Ancient Egypt*, 52–53.

52   this voyage to Punt: Wachsmann, *Seagoing Ships*, 18–29.

52   carvings of fish: El-Sayed, "Queen Hatshepsut's Expedition."

52   "the tent of the king's-messenger": In Breasted, *Ancient Records of Egypt*, vol. 2, §§260–65 (pp. 108–10).

54   how the Egyptians navigated: Hydrographer of the Navy, *Ocean Passages of the World*, 89.

55   Murals at Avaris: Wachsmann, *Seagoing Ships*, 298; Kuhrt, *Ancient Near East*, 169.

55   "I have not left a plank": In Pritchard, *Ancient Near East*, 2:90–91.

55   the Barkal Stela: Hornung, *History of Ancient Egypt*, 77, 90.

56   "The People of the Isles": Casson, *Ancient Mariners*, 17, 20.

3. Bronze Age Seafaring

58 Enki: Kramer and Maier, *Myths of Enki*, 3.

58 Ennugi: Dalley, *Myths from Mesopotamia: Epic of Gilgamesh*, tablet XI, p. 110.

59 The oldest evidence for ships with masts: Carter, "Boat-Related Finds," 89–91.

59 *quffa*: Agius, *Classic Ships of Islam*, 129–32; Hornell, *Water Transport*, 101–8.

59 fragments of bitumen: Carter, "Boat-Related Finds," 91–99.

59 Epic of Gilgamesh: West, *East Face of Helicon*, 402–17.

60 "Then Gilgamesh stripped": Ferry, *Gilgamesh*, 62.

61 "How long does a building stand": Ibid., 64.

62 "had ships of Dilmun": In Potts, *Arabian Gulf in Antiquity*, 1:88.

62 "Ships from Meluhha": In ibid., 1:183.

62 "My mother, the *entum*": In Kuhrt, *Ancient Near East*, 48.

62 "from the Lower Sea": In Gadd, "Dynasty of Agade," 421.

63 a village of Meluhhans: Potts, *Arabian Gulf in Antiquity*, 1:165–67.

63 ancient port of Lothal: Deloche, "Geographical Considerations," 320; Ghosh, *Encyclopedia of Indian Archaeology*, 1:297, 2:257–60. The prevailing alternative view is that the basin served as a reservoir for potable water or irrigation, a theory more in keeping with historic and current practice, although this identification is also problematic. See Leshnik, "Harappan 'Port' at Lothal," which goes too far in writing that "Lothal's identification as an international emporium" depends on the identification of the basin as a dock.

64 "dock of Akkad": Potts, "Watercraft," 135. The Akkadian word for a quay or wharf, *karum*, eventually referred to the commercial quarter of a town or to any association of merchants seeking collective security in alien lands. See Kuhrt, *Ancient Near East*, 92.

64 the Ras al-Jinz finds: Cleuziou and Tosi, "Black Boats of Magan," 750–52; Vosmer, "Ships in the Ancient Arabian Sea," 236, and personal communication, Sept. 23, 2005.

65 "asphalt for the coating": In Cleuziou and Tosi, "Black Boats of Magan," 747.

65 "Magan Boat": The dimensions are 13 meters length overall, 11.1 meters length at the waterline, 3.9 meters maximum beam, and 10.5 tons displacement. The sail was 45 square meters. Ancient and ethnographic evidence indicate that the ancient shipwrights would have mixed various materials into their bitumen depending on its use. See Vosmer, "Magan Boat Project," 51, 53.

65 capacity of about thirty *gur*: Vosmer, "Building the Reed-Boat Prototype," 235.

67 Lu-Enlilla: Potts, *Arabian Gulf in Antiquity*, 1:145; Oppenheim, "Seafaring Merchants of Ur," 13.

67 interest rates: Van de Mieroop, *Ancient Mesopotamian City*, 197–98.

67 a vessel proceeding downstream: Potts, *Mesopotamian Civilization*, 133.

68 "12 minas of refined copper": In Potts, *Arabian Gulf in Antiquity*, 1:226.

70 "Minos, according to tradition": Thucydides, *Peloponnesian War*, 1.4 (p. 37).

70 Neolithic migrants: Liritzis, "Seafaring, Craft and Cultural Contact in the Aegean," 237–43; but see Wiener, "Isles of Crete? The Minoan Thalassocracy Revisited."

70 archives at Mari: Wachsmann, *Seagoing Ships*, 83.

71 wall paintings: Doumas, *Wall-paintings of Thera*; Sherratt, *Wall Paintings of Thera*. Wachsmann, *Seagoing Ships*, 86–122, interprets all the scenes as ritualistic. On the term "quarter rudder," see Mott, *Development of the Rudder*, 6–7.

72   Uluburun site: Bass, "Bronze Age Shipwreck."

73   "fraught with disaster": Pliny, *Natural History*, 5.35.131 (vol. 2:319).

73   Cape Gelidonya ship: Bass, "Cape Gelidonya"; Bass, "Return to Cape Gelidonya"; and Throckmorton, *The Sea Remembers*, 24–33.

75   "northerners coming from all lands": In Breasted, *Ancient Records of Egypt*, vol. 3, §574 (p. 241).

75   "twenty enemy ships": In Wachsmann, *Seagoing Ships*, 343–44.

75   "My father": In ibid.

76   "Shardana, rebellious of heart": Sandars, *Sea Peoples*, 50.

76   "Against me the ships": In Redford, *Egypt, Canaan, and Israel*, 254.

76   Ramesses III's victory: Kuhrt, *Ancient Near East*, 387; other sources give 1191 or 1186 BCE.

76   "Those who came": In Redford, *Egypt, Canaan, and Israel*, 256.

78   "The Report of Wenamun": In Simpson, *Literature of Ancient Egypt*, 142–55.

4. Phoenicians, Greeks, and the Mediterranean

80   territory of the Canaanites: Aubet, *Phoenicians*, 12–16.

80   Hiram I: Ibid., 35–37.

80   "at the entrance to the sea": Ezekiel 27:3.

80   "daughter cities": Patai, *Children of Noah*, 136.

80   "Because of the wide prevalence": Thucydides, *Peloponnesian War*, 1.7 (p. 39).

81   temple of Solomon: 1 Kings 5.

81   Ophir and Sheba: 1 Kings 9:27, 22:48–49; 2 Chronicles 8:18, 20:34–37.

82   "exultant city": Isaiah 23:7.

84   established Carthage: Aubet, *Phoenicians*, 187–89.

84   Gadir: Ibid., 187–89, 247–49.

84   "only high economic returns": Ibid., 240.

85   "wheat, millet": Ezekiel 27:12–25. See Tandy, *Warriors into Traders*, 66.

85   Al-Mina: Polanyi, "Ports of Trade in Early Societies," 30, 33.

86   "famed for its ships": Evelyn-White, "Homeric Hymns to Pythian Apollo," l.219 (p. 341).

86   "Nestor had a fine drinking cup": I am indebted to Jim Terry for this translation. See Murray, *Early Greece*, 96; Powell, *Homer*, 31–32; and Tandy, *Warriors into Traders*, 203. The Homeric parallel is in the *Iliad*, 11.745–58 (p. 317).

87   "whose merchants were princes": Isaiah 23:8.

87   "amassing a fortune": Homer, *Odyssey*, 14.321–34 (pp. 310–11).

87   "purchased for himself": Ibid., 14.512–14 (p. 316). Taphos is thought to have been an island off the west coast of Greece.

87   "so far from being": Thucydides, *Peloponnesian War*, 1.5 (p. 37).

87   images on vases: Casson, *Ancient Mariners*, 41–42, and figs. 11–12.

87   "catalogue of ships": Homer, *Iliad*, 2.584–862 (pp. 115–24).

87   "they furled and stowed": Ibid., 1.514–22 (p. 92).

88   "knocking them home": Homer, *Odyssey*, 5.273 (p. 160). See Casson, *Ships and Seamanship*, 217–19, and Wachsmann, *Seagoing Ships*, 227, citing Homer, *Odyssey*, 9.382–88.

88   mortise-and-tenon joinery, sewn: McGrail, *Boats of the World*, 126, 134–38.

88   "Hers were the stars": Homer, *Odyssey*, 5.303–4 (p. 161). Pleiades is otherwise known

as the Seven Sisters, Boötes as the Herdsman or Plowman, and Ursa Major as the Great Bear.

88   "sung by the world": Ibid., 12.77 (p. 273). The best known version of the Jason story is the third-century BCE *Argonautica*, composed by Apollonius while living at Rhodes, which was then at its height as a commercial maritime power. Apollonius was subsequently librarian of the library at Alexandria.

89   Ithaca is off the west coast: A persuasive case has been made recently that the ancient island of Ithaca is now, thanks to seismic activity, the Paliki peninsula on the island of Cephalonia, and that the modern Ithaca (Ithaki), to the east, is the ancient Doulichion. See Bittlestone, Diggle, and Underhill, *Odysseus Unbound*.

89   Pithecoussae: Tandy, *Warriors into Traders*, 72.

89   ship track, or *diolkos*: Werner, "Largest Ship Trackway in Ancient Times."

90   Pontos Axeinos: King, *Black Sea*, xi–xii.

90   settlement on the Black Sea: Tsetskhladze, "Did the Greeks Go to Cholcis for Metals?" "Greek Penetration of the Black Sea," and "Trade on the Black Sea."

90   Theodosia: Strabo, *Geography*, 7.4.4 (vol. 3:237).

91   canal between the Nile and the Red Sea: For an overview of the confusion surrounding the existence and date of this canal, see Redmount, "Wadi Tumilat."

91   "an oracle": Herodotus, *Histories*, 2.159 (p. 145).

91   "The Phoenicians sailed": Ibid., 4.42 (p. 229). See Lloyd, "Necho and the Red Sea."

92   "his ship was brought": Herodotus, *Histories*, 4.43 (p. 229).

92   Hanno: Ibid., 4.196 (although he does not mention Hanno by name); Pliny, *Natural History*, 2.67.169 (vol. 1:305); and Arrian, *Indica*, 8.43 (vol. 2:433).

92   Himilco: Pliny, *Natural History*, 2.67.169 (vol. 1:305); Avienus, *Ora Maritima*, 114–29, 380–89, 404–15.

93   "like frogs round a pond": Plato, *Phaedo*, 109b.

93   The Trireme: The most thorough study is Morrison and Coates, *Athenian Trireme*. For an alternative view on the trireme's development, see Wallinga, "Trireme and History."

94   *trieres*: Casson, *Ships and Seamanship*, 77.

94   impressive speeds: Morrison and Coates, *Athenian Trireme*, 94–106; Casson, *Ships and Seamanship*, 281–96.

95   tactics of trireme warfare: Whitehead, "*Periplous*"; Lazenby, "*Diekplous*."

95   "Seamanship, just like anything else": Thucydides, *Peloponnesian War*, 1.142 (p. 121).

96   "the beginning of evils": Herodotus, *Histories*, 5.97 (p. 317).

96   "commanded one of his servants": Ibid., 5.105 (p. 319).

96   "naval contingent": Ibid., 6.95 (pp. 355–56).

97   "So far as I know": Ibid., 7.49 (p. 391).

98   bridges of ships: The number of ships given by Herodotus tallies with what we know about the dimensions of the ships used. The Athenian navy's ship sheds at Zea, near Piraeus, accommodated triremes with a beam of about 5.4 meters. Penteconters are narrower, and a mix of the two types lying side by side would comfortably span the Hellespont at its narrowest. See Morrison and Coates, *Athenian Trireme*, 4–5.

98   "broad enough for two triremes": Herodotus, *Histories*, 7.24 (p. 384). See Isserlin et al., "Canal of Xerxes."

98   "The outbreak of this war": Herodotus, *Histories*, 7.44 (p. 390).

98   "wooden walls": Ibid., 7.141 (p. 416).

99   "If . . . you rush": Ibid., 8.68 (p. 471).

100   "The Grecian warships": Aeschylus, *Persians*, 316–430 (pp. 62–63).

100   The battle had probably cost: Strauss, *Battle of Salamis*, 78–80, 104, 204.

100 "if the Athenians": Thucydides, *Peloponnesian War,* 1.93 (p. 90).
101 "Hellenic treasurers": Ibid., 1.96 (p. 92).
101 "These died in war": In McGregor, *Athenians and Their Empire,* 92.
102 "The whole world": Thucydides, *Peloponnesian War,* 2.62–63 (p. 160).
103 "to the victors": Ibid., 7.87 (p. 537).
103 "all men of military age": Xenophon, *History of My Times,* 1.6.24, 31 (pp. 82–83).
103 "put a stop": Ibid., 1.6.15 (p. 81).
103 "the only form": Austin and Vidal-Naquet, *Economic and Social History,* 148–50, 360.
104 Olbia refused: Ibid., 331.
104 "shouting crows": Aristophanes, *Acharnians,* 547–55 (p. 34).
105 Aeschylus wanted: Pausanias, *Description of Greece,* 1.14.5 (vol. 1:75).
105 "naval mob": Thucydides, *Peloponnesian War,* 8.72 (p. 579), where Warner translates *nautichos ochlos* as "the men serving in the navy." See also Aristotle, *Politics* (4.1291), and Plutarch, "Themistocles" (19.4).
105 "their plausible and ready excuses": Plato, *Laws,* 706c (p. 1298).
105 "There can be no doubt": Aristotle, *Politics,* 7.6.1327b (vol. 2:2106).
105 "the largest shipowner in Hellas": Demosthenes, "Against Aristocrates," 23.211 (vol. 3:361). See Millett, "Maritime Loans," 47. For a discussion of legal and popular attitudes toward maritime traders in Athens, see Reed, *Maritime Traders in the Ancient Greek World,* esp. 43–61.
105 "I have observed": Herodotus, *Histories,* 2.167 (p. 148).

5. Carthage, Rome, and the Mediterranean

108 "overcome the ships": Arrian, *Anabasis of Alexander,* 1.20.1 (p. 85).
108 "went ashore where": Ibid., 3.1.5 (p. 225).
108 The establishment of Alexandria: Fraser, *Ptolemaic Alexandria,* 1:25–27; Strabo, *Geography,* 17.1.6–10 (vol. 8:23–43).
109 Gelon, tyrant: Herodotus, *Histories,* 7.158–61 (pp. 424–25).
111 Tomb of the Ship: Hagy, "800 Years of Etruscan Ships," 242–43, fig. 38; Casson, *Ships and Seamanship,* 70, and fig. 97; and Brendel, *Etruscan Art,* 271–73.
111 They also employed rams: Herodotus, *Histories,* 1.166 (p. 66).
111 "masters of the sea": Diodorus Siculus, *Library of History,* 11.51 (vol. 4:257).
111 "under the command of Hamilcar": Herodotus, *Histories,* 7.165–66 (p. 426). See Green, *Greco-Persian Wars,* 120–22, 148–49.
111 polyremes: Casson, *Ships and Seamanship,* 97–116. For an ancient understanding of the development of galleys, see Pliny the Elder, *Natural History,* 7.56.206–9 (vol. 2:645–47).
112 "was a single-banked vessel": Polybius, *Rise of the Roman Empire,* 1.23 (p. 66).
112 Roman quinqueremes: Ibid., 1.26 (p. 69).
112 timber supplies: Meiggs, *Trees and Timber,* 133–39.
112 Ptolemy IV's "forty": Athenaeus, *Deipnosophists,* 5.203e–204d (vol. 2:421–25), written around 200 CE, four centuries after the fact. Descriptions and diagrams of the "forty" can be found also in Casson, *Ancient Mariners,* 131–33, and *Ships and Seamanship,* 108–12.
113 *Leontophoros:* Casson, *Ships and Seamanship,* 112–14.
113 "had a speed": Plutarch, *Lives,* "Demetrius," 43.5 (vol. 9:109). See Casson, *Ships and Seamanship,* 140n20.
113 lead sheets: Hocker, "Lead Hull Sheathing in Antiquity," 199.

113   "All had floors": Athenaeus, *Deipnosophists*, 5.206d–209b. See Casson, *Ships and Seamanship*, 184–99.

114   "such sound practical use": Polybius, *Histories*, 5.88 (vol. 3:219). See Casson, "Grain Trade," 73.

114   "the constant protectors": Polybius, *Histories*, 27.4 (vol. 6:495).

115   *triemiolia*: Gabrielsen, *Naval Aristocracy of Hellenistic Rhodes*, 86–89.

115   "necessities" and luxury goods: Polybius, *Histories*, 4.38 (vol. 2:395).

115   imposed a toll on ships: Ibid., 4.47–48 (vol. 2:415–27).

116   "It was a witty": Saint Augustine, *City of God*, 4.4, in Pennell, *Bandits at Sea*, 18.

116   pretentious abhorrence of seafaring: Many modern historians affirm this view. Arnold Toynbee is an eloquent exception: "The Roman Empire has made its mark on the mind of posterity as a land power which gave mobility to its invincible infantry by constructing and maintaining a magnificent network of roads. Yet, in truth, sea-power, not land-power, was the instrument with which the Romans extended their empire from Italy to the whole perimeter of the Mediterranean Sea." *Constantine Porphyrogenitus and His World*, 323.

117   "while the rest were burnt": Livy, *Rome and Italy*, 8.14 (p. 179). On the *rostra* in the forum, see Pliny the Elder, *Natural History*, 16.2.8 (vol. 4.391–93).

117   *coloniae maritimae*: Salmon, "Coloniae Maritimae"; Thiel, *History of Roman Sea-power*.

117   "more dangerous and less free": Gellius, *Attic Nights*, 16.13.9.

118   "on a voyage of inspection": Appian, *Roman History (Samnite History)*, 7 (vol. 1:77).

118   Pyrrhus was an expansionist: Franke, "Pyrrhus," 475; Thiel, *History of Roman Sea-power*, 29.

119   "those who are impressed": Polybius, *Rise of the Roman Empire*, 1.63 (p. 109).

119   "The harbours had communication": Appian, *Roman History (Punic Wars)*, 14.96 (vol. 1:567).

120   "were handling the operations": Polybius, *Rise of the Roman Empire*, 1.20 (pp. 62–63).

120   "was on the water": Pliny, *Natural History*, 16.74.192 (vol. 4:513).

120   Punic Ship: Frost, "Marsala Punic Ship"; Frost et al., *Lilybaeum (Marsala)*.

120   *corvus*: Polybius, *Rise of the Roman Empire*, 1.22 (p. 65). *Corvus* is the Latin translation for the Greek *korax* ("crow"), the word by which the device was called by both Romans and Greeks in antiquity. See Wallinga, *Boarding-Bridge of the Romans*.

121   "the fighting seemed": Polybius, *Rise of the Roman Empire*, 1.23 (p. 66).

121   "the southern coast of Sicily": Ibid., 1.37 (p. 82).

121   why it is not mentioned: Goldsworthy, *Punic Wars*, 116.

122   steady supplies of grain: Casson, "Grain Trade," 82.

122   "He discovered": Polybius, *Rise of the Roman Empire*, 10.8 (p. 408).

123   "naval mentality": Briscoe, "Second Punic War," 66.

124   "It took Hannibal": Publius Sulpicius, in Livy, *Rome and the Mediterranean*, 31.7 (p. 28).

124   "free in appearance only": Livy, *Rome and the Mediterranean*, 35.32 (p. 216).

124   "The essential unity": Errington, "Rome Against Philip and Antiochus," 284.

124   "Roman arms": In Livy, *Rome and the Mediterranean*, 36.41 (p. 275).

124   "because with the loss": Ibid., 37.31 (p. 308).

125   harbor dues: Habicht, "Seleucids and Their Rivals," 337.

125   "Carthage must be destroyed": Florus, *Epitome of Roman History*, 1.31 (p. 137).

126   "Sulla burned the Piraeus": Appian, *Roman History (Mithridatic Wars)*, 12.41 (vol. 2:311).

126   "Many times": Ibid., 12.119 (vol. 2:471).

126 "a hundred and ten bronze-beaked ships": Plutarch, *Lives*, "Lucullus," 37.3 (vol. 2:595).

126 "Need I lament": Cicero, *Pro Lege Manilia*, 12 (pp. 45–47).

127 twelve thousand gold pieces: Suetonius, *Twelve Caesars*, "Julius Caesar," 4, 74 (pp. 11, 40).

127 "for a pirate is not included": Cicero, *On Duties* (*De Officiis*, 3.107), in Souza, *Piracy in the Greco-Roman World*, 150; Coke, *Third Part of the Institutes*, 113. For current uses, see for example, U.S. Dept. of State press release, "The Secretary and the Minister Agreed That Terrorism Is a Common Enemy of Mankind." ("U.S., Republic of Korea Hold Security Consultative Meeting," Nov. 15, 2001, http://www.pentagon.gov/releases/2001/b11152001_bt588-01.html.)

128 "to oppose all legislation": Suetonius, *Twelve Caesars*, "Julius Caesar," 19 (p. 16).

128 "for having been forced": Plutarch, *Lives*, "Pompey," 76.3 (vol. 5:313). Pharsalus was twenty-five miles from the nearest inlet of the Aegean.

128 prefect of the fleet: Welch, "Sextus Pompeius and the *Res Publica*," 37–41.

131 "put on white robes": Suetonius, *Twelve Caesars*, "Augustus," 98 (p. 104).

131 pozzolana: Oleson, "Technology of Roman Harbors," 148. The word comes from 13, the modern name for Puteoli. See Vitruvius, *De Architectura*, 5.12 (vol. 1:311–17).

131 Lucullus's villa: D'Arms, *Romans on the Bay of Naples*, 109.

131 "fish-pond fanciers": See Cicero, *Letters to Atticus*, 1.19 (p. 87), 1.20 (p. 95), and 2.9 (p. 137).

131 local oyster beds: Pliny, *Natural History*, 9.79.168–69 (vol. 3:277–79); D'Arms, *Romans on the Bay of Naples*, 136–38.

131 night service from Ostia to Puteoli: D'Arms, *Romans on the Bay of Naples*, 134.

131 "a collapsible cabin-boat": Suetonius, *Twelve Caesars*, "Nero," 34 (p. 227).

132 "massive / Piers": Juvenal, *Satires*, 12:75–79 (p. 243).

132 "it was first sunk": Suetonius, *Twelve Caesars*, "Claudius," 20 (p. 193). The obelisk, which now stands in front of St. Peter's in Rome, weighs 322 tons—not including the pedestal; Casson, *Ships and Seamanship*, 188–89.

132 Piazzale of the Corporations: Scrinari and Lauro, *Ancient Ostia*, 22–24.

133 "Incidentally, what a huge ship!": Lucian, "The Ship or the Wishes," 5–6 (vol. 6:435–37). The dimensions are length, fifty-five meters; beam, fourteen meters; depth of hold, thirteen meters.

134 "They should have kept": Lucian, "The Ship or the Wishes," 9 (vol. 6:441). See Casson, "*Isis* and Her Voyage," 47–48, and *Ancient Mariners*, 208–9.

134 the apostle Paul: Acts 27–28.

134 the *annona*: McCormick, *Origins of the European Economy*, 87, 104–5, 108–10. The populist practice of providing free wheat dates from the second century BCE; the phrase *panem et circenses* (bread and circuses) was coined by Juvenal in the first century CE.

134 "Money lent on maritime loans": Paulus, *Sententiae* II, xiv, 3, in Temin, "Economy of the Early Roman Empire," 144.

134 "he held out the certainty": Suetonius, *Twelve Caesars*, "Claudius," 18 (p. 192). See Longnaker, "History of Insurance Law," 644–46.

134 grain traders: Temin, "Economy of the Early Roman Empire," 137.

134 wine trade: Tchernia, "Italian Wine in Gaul," 92.

135 "When he was about": Plutarch, *Lives*, "Pompey," 50 (vol. 5:247).

136 "god, our author": Seneca, *Natural Questions*, "Winds," 5.18.13–14 (vol. 2:121–23).

6. Chasing the Monsoons

139   "you brought him": Rig Veda, 1.116.5 (p. 287).

139   "who knows the path": Ibid., 1.25.7 (p. 61). See Hornell, "Role of Birds in Early Navigation."

139   "should look after activities": *Kautilya Arthasastra*, 2.28.1 (vol. 2:162). The authorship and date of the *Arthasastra* are controversial; the earliest written version may date to the second century CE but is probably based on a compilation of various documents going back five centuries.

140   "He should rescue": Ibid., 2.28.8–9 (vol. 2:162).

140   "big boats": Ibid., 2.28.13 (vol. 2:163).

140   "render services": Strabo, *Geography*, 15.1.46 (vol. 7:81).

140   director of trade: *Kautilya Arthasastra*, 2.16.1–25 (vol. 2:127–29) and 3:176–79.

140   "involving little expenditure": Ibid., 7.12.18–21 (vol. 2:360).

140   "making voyages": *Baudhayana*, 2.1.2 (Müller, *Sacred Books*, 14:217–18).

140   "Let him who teaches": *Âpastamba Prasna*, 1.11.32.27 (Müller, *Sacred Books*, 2:98).

141   proscriptions on seafaring: Pearson, "Introduction," pp. 17–18; Winius, "Portugal's 'Shadow Empire,'" 255.

141   "social and religious duties": Manu, *Laws of Manu*, xviii.

141   the four main castes: Ibid., 8.410 (p. 195); *"When men who are expert"*: 8.157 (p. 169); *"there is no definite rule"*: 8.406–409 (p. 195). Whether and for whom charging interest is legal is a complicated question in both the Hindu and Buddhist traditions. Some early texts deemed the charging of interest a crime worse than abortion or murdering a Brahman, although it was allowed to commoners, but regulations were relaxed in the medieval period. See Sharma, "Usury in Early Medieval Times."

142   "A hundred fifty thousand people": Major Rock Edict XIII, in Thapar, *Early India*, 181.

142   "Lord of the Ocean": In Tripati, *Maritime Archaeology*, 29.

143   writing itself: Salomon, "On the Origin of the Early Indian Scripts," 278.

143   "he recognized all": Aryasura, *Once the Buddha Was a Monkey*, 96, 98. Aryasura's Sanskrit version, which dates to the early centuries of the common era, is based on the older Pali "Supparaka-Jataka" (Cowell, *Jataka*, vol. 4:86–90).

143   "My child": In Levi, "Manimekhala," 603–5. See "Mahajana-Jataka," in Cowell, *Jataka*, 6:21–22).

143   "never wept nor lamented": In Levi, "Manimekhala," 603.

144   "precaution against the dangers": In ibid., 599.

144   "had his whole body burnt": In ibid., 603–5.

145   "the entire world": In Pritchard, *Ancient Near East*, 1:208.

145   "the shallows": Arrian, *Indica*, 8.41 (vol. 2:427).

145   Darius may have completed: Redmount, "Wadi Tumilat." See above, chap. 4.

145   "after a voyage": Herodotus, *Histories*, 4.44 (p. 230).

145   "Alexander had a vehement desire": Arrian, *Indica*, 8.20–21 (vol. 2:363–67). Arrian (and Strabo) drew on a now lost account of India written by Nearchus.

146   The monsoons are determined: Somerville and Woodhouse, *Ocean Passages for the World*, 82–88, 117–27.

147   "ships of war": Arrian, *Indica*, 19 (p. 363). In antiquity, the Pasitigris River flowed directly into the Persian Gulf. Now called the Karun, it flows into the Shatt al-Arab.

148   "ten talents [300 kilograms] of frankincense": In Salles, "Achaemenid and Hellenistic Trade," 260. The earliest mentions (before the seventh century CE) of cinnamon and

cassia refer not to the cinnamon and cassia of India, Southeast Asia, and China, but to otherwise unidentified wild shrubs or small trees native to southern Arabia and East Africa. See Crone, *Meccan Trade*, 253–64.

148 "five hundred talents": Polybius, *Histories*, 13.9 (vol. 4:427).

148 "The governor of Mesene": Pliny, *Natural History*, 6.152 (vol. 2:453). See Potts, "Parthian Presence," 277.

148 Charax Spasinou: Salles, "Achaemenid and Hellenistic Trade," 256; Casson, *Periplus*, 180.

148 "the people are made torpid": Agatharchides, *On the Erythraean Sea*, 101c (p. 164, note "m").

148 "using large rafts": Ibid., 103a (p. 167).

148 Agatharchides of Cnidus: None of Agatharchides' work is preserved by itself, but portions of books 1 and 5 were transcribed by Diodorus Siculus, Strabo, and Photius. These fragments have been published in Agatharchides of Cnidus, *On the Erythraean Sea*.

149 "This tribe surpasses in wealth": Agatharchides, *On the Erythraean Sea*, 104b (p. 167).

149 "The houses of the Sa-poh": Faxian [Fa-hian], *Travels of Fa-Hian*, chap. 38 (p. lxxiv).

149 "The Red Sea ports": Sidebotham, "Ports of the Red Sea," 27.

150 elephants from East Africa: The Ptolemaic elephant corps employed forest elephants (*Loxodonta africana cyclotis*), which are smaller than Indian elephants and the better known savanna elephant, *Loxodonta africana Africana*. See Agatharchides, *On the Erythraean Sea*, 10n2.

150 Myos Hormos: Peacock and Blue, eds., *Myos Hormos-Quseir al-Qadim*, 1–6.

150 "the sea, being all shoals": Agatharchides, *On the Erythraean Sea*, 85b (pp. 141–42).

151 "one can see": Ibid., 105a (p. 169).

151 "he promised to act": Strabo, *Geography*, 2.3.4 (vol. 1:377–79).

152 "he found Cleopatra": Plutarch, *Lives*, "Antony," 69.3 (vol. 9:295–97). Although Plutarch seems to describe a north–south route from the Mediterranean to the Red Sea, a distance of nearly two hundred kilometers, sixty kilometers is about the length of the ancient east–west canal.

153 "on account of difficult sailing": Strabo, *Geography*, 16.4.23 (vol. 7:357).

153 "learned that as many": Ibid., 2.5.12 (vol. 1:455); *not so many as twenty*: 17.1.13 (8:53); *"music girls"*: 2.3.4 (1:381).

154 The goods can be grouped: Casson, *Periplus*, 39–41.

154 coconut, rice, amla: Wendrich et al., "Berenike Crossroads," 70.

154 inscription at Delos: Sedov, "Qana,'" 26n12.

154 statuette of Manimekhala: Wheeler, *Rome Beyond the Imperial Frontiers*, plate 15 and p. 163.

154 Indian embassies: Weerakkody, *Taprobanê*, 51–63.

154 "the trade, not merely of islands": Dio Chrysostom, *Discourses*, 32.36 (vol. 3:207).

155 loan arrangement: Casson, "New Light on Maritime Loans"; Young, *Rome's Eastern Trade*, 55–57.

155 "Aelia Isidora and Aelia Olympias": In Young, *Rome's Eastern Trade*, 58–59. For the text, translation, and discussion of the contract, see 55–57, and Casson, "New Light on Maritime Loans."

155 fifty million sesterces: Pliny, *Natural History*, 6.26.101 (vol. 2:417). On Romans' net worth, see Duncan-Jones, *Economy of the Roman Empire*, 1–32, 146. Some slaves could fetch vastly more than the average, the highest known price being 700,000 sesterces paid for a *grammaticus* (professor of literature).

156 "vast mansions": Tacitus, *Annals*, 3.53 (p. 141).

156   Chola town of Arikamedu: Ray, "Resurvey of 'Roman' Contacts," 100–103.

156   hoards of silver *denarii*: Ray, "Yavana Presence," 98–100.

157   "Noble daughter": Ilanko Atikal, *Tale of an Anklet*, 2.94 (p. 32). *Isaiah*: see above, chap. 4.

157   "the city/that prospered": Ilanko Atikal, *Tale of an Anklet*, 6.148–54 (p. 62).

157   "Swift, prancing steeds": Uruthirankannanar, *Pattinappalai*, 213, 246–53 (pp. 39, 41).

158   "In the past": Shattan, *Manimekhalaï*, §16 (p. 66).

158   "from the remotest countries": Cosmas, *Christian Topography*, 365–66. Invaluable as he is for his account of Indian Ocean trade, Cosmas offers up bizarre proofs (pp. 132, 252) that the world is not a sphere, as pagan philosophers had demonstrated and many Christians believed, but flat. These were never accepted as mainstream, and medieval people who thought about it at all generally believed the world was round. Nineteenth-century Darwinists promoted the notion that they thought otherwise to demonstrate the Christian Church's antagonism to science; but the concept of the flat earth had no influence on the course of navigation, exploration, or any other aspect of maritime endeavor. See Jeffrey Burton Russell, *Inventing the Flat Earth: Columbus and Modern Historians* (New York: Praeger, 1991).

159   Rev-Ardashir (Rishahr): Whitehouse, "Sasanian Maritime Activity," 342–43.

159   al-Bahrayn: This spelling is used of "the coastal region from Kazima in Kuwait through the Hasa province [of Saudi Arabia] and ending somewhat vaguely towards Qatar," to distinguish it from the island of Bahrain, which early Arabic writers called Awal. See Wilkinson, "Sketch of the Historical Geography of the Trucial Oman," 347n1.

159   wooing of a Sri Lankan princess: Weerakkody, "Sri Lanka Through Greek and Roman Eyes," 168.

159   "the greater": Cosmas, *Christian Topography*, 368–70.

159   "black Byzantines": Wink, *Al-Hind*, 1:47.

160   Byzantine fleet from Clysma: Christides, "Two Parallel Naval Guides," 58.

160   "always locate themselves": Procopius, *Persian War*, 1.20.1–2 (vol. 1:193).

161   "in a hundred-oared ship": Rig Veda, 1.116.5 (p. 287).

161   "a boat with strong planks": In Levi, "Manimekhala," 601.

161   "we embarked 200 passengers": Villiers, *Monsoon Seas*, 82–83. Villiers does not give the linear dimensions of his vessel, but he describes a 42-meter *boom* he saw in Zanzibar as "very large."

162   "the wretched quality": In Ray, "Resurvey of 'Roman' Contacts," 100.

162   common ancestor: Johnstone, *Sea-craft of Prehistory*, 214–15; McGrail, *Boats of the World*, 292, 326.

162   watercraft in the *Periplus*: Casson, *Periplus—sewn boats*: 15–16; *rafts*: §7, 27; *dugout canoes*: §15; *sangara* and *kolandiophonta*: §60; and *trappaga* and *kotymba*: §44.

162   *trapyaka*: In Chakravarti, "Early Medieval Bengal and the Trade in Horses," 206. *kolandiophonta*: Deloche, "Iconographic Evidence," 208–9, 222; Islam and Miah, "Trade and Commerce" (*trapyaga*); Manguin, "Southeast Asian Shipping," 190 (*Kolandiophonta*); Mariners' Museum, *Aak to Zumbra*, 330–31 (*kotia*), 508 (*sangara*); Ray, "Early Coastal Trade in the Bay of Bengal," 360ff., and *Monastery and Guild*, 117–19 (*kolandiophonta*, *kottimba*, and *sangara*).

163   "one boards": In Wolters, *Early Indonesian Commerce*, 43. For voyage time, see Casson, *Periplus*, 289–90.

163   wall painting at Ajanta: For a summary of the meager pictorial evidence of Indian ships in this period and later, see Deloche, "Iconographic Evidence."

163   "Her white sails outspread": Aryasura, *Once the Buddha Was a Monkey*, 102.

163   Mediterranean influence: Young, *Rome's Eastern Trade*, 63–64.

164   a first migration: Blench, "Ethnographic Evidence," 418, 432–33.

164   ethnobotany, ethnomusicology: Ibid., 420–30; Hornell, "Indonesian Influence," 305–6, 318–19, 327–28.

165   "a relic of an Indonesian type": Hornell, "Indonesian Influence," 319, 321.

165   "The only cargo-carrying vessel": Hornell, "Boat Oculi Survivals," 343. The oldest extant rendering of an *oculus* is on a rendering of seagoing ships from Sahure's temple at Abusir, Egypt; Wachsmann, *Seagoing Ships*, 14.

7. Continent and Archipelagoes in the East

168   "take advantage": *Collected Works of Liao Gang* (12th century), in Shiba and Elvin, *Commerce and Society in Sung China*, 9.

169   Asian Mediterranean: For a discussion, see Sutherland, "Southeast Asian History."

170   more than twenty-six thousand: The main groups are: Indonesia, 18,108 islands 17BBC report, February 2003); the Philippines, 7,107 islands; and Malaysia, about 1,000 islands.

170   Austronesian languages: Jacq-Hergoualc'h, *The Malay Peninsula*, 24.

170   languages are spoken: Bellwood, "Southeast Asia Before History," 106–15.

170   "Customs are not uniform": *Sanguo Zhi* (Records of the Three Kingdoms), 53.8b, in Taylor, *Birth of Vietnam*, 75–76.

171   a local tradition: Taylor, *Birth of Vietnam*, 1.

171   cast bronze drums: Bellwood, *Prehistory of the Indo-Malaysian Archipelago*, 269–71.

171   Sa Huyhn simply chose not to trade: Bellwood, "Southeast Asia Before History," 129–31.

172   "tribute" was an elaborate fiction: Bielenstein, *Diplomacy and Trade*, 675.

172   "The gentleman is conversant": *Analects of Confucius*, 4.16, 19 (pp. 69–70).

172   "an enlightened ruler": *Han Shu*, 24a:10b-12a, in Ban, *Food and Money*, 161–62.

173   naval or amphibious operations: Deng, *Chinese Maritime Activities*, 9.

173   "As the emperor considered": *Shiji* (Records of the Grand Historian), 6, 18a, in Needham et al., *Science and Civilisation*, vol. 4, pt. 3:551–52.

174   the main rivers: Needham et al., *Science and Civilisation*, vol. 4, pt. 3:220–22; Van Slyke, *Yangtze*, 13, 37.

175   "a force of men": Sima Qian, *Records of the Grand Historian*, 2:232.

175   "a chain of communication": Needham et al., *Science and Civilisation*, vol. 4, pt. 3:306.

175   "hanged themselves": Sima Qian, *Records of the Grand Historian*, 2:201.

175   "The cruelty": Zhou Qufei, *Information on What Is Beyond the Passes*, in Needham et al., *Science and Civilisation*, vol. 4, pt. 3:304.

176   "used boats": *Wu Yue Chun Qiu* (Annals of Wu and Yue), chap. 6, in Wang, *Nanhai Trade*, 2.

177   "a pair of white jades": *Han Shu*, 95, 9b, in Wang, *Nanhai Trade*, 11.

177   "the center for trade": *Shi Ji*, 129:11b, in Ban, *Food and Money*, 446.

177   "as well as 100,000 sailors": Sima Qian, *Records of the Grand Historian*, 2:215.

177   Jiaozhi, Jiuzhen, and Rinan: Taylor, *Birth of Vietnam*, 70. In Vietnamese, Jiaozhi is called Giao-chi; Jiuzhen is Cuu-chan; and Rinan is Nhat-nam. Cochin China derives from the Portuguese corruption of Cuu chan as Cochin.

177 "lustrous pearls": *Ch'ien Han Shu* (History of the Former Han), 28.2, in Wheatley, *Golden Khersonese*, 8–9.

178 sisters Trung: Taylor, *Birth of Vietnam*, 37–41.

178 Jiaozhi remained: Wang, *Nanhai Trade*, 24; Taylor, *Birth of Vietnam*, 71–72.

178 Funan: Hall, *Maritime Trade*, 21–22, 48–77; Wheatley, *Golden Khersonese*, xix. Funan is the Chinese rendering of the Khmer *bnam*, "mountain," now pronounced *phnom*, as in Phnom Penh.

179 "attacked and conquered": In Hall, *Maritime Trade*, 64.

179 "live in walled cities": In ibid., 48.

179 A lost work: Needham et al., *Science and Civilisation*, vol. 4, pt. 3:449–50.

180 "The Sea Route to Da Qin": Yu Huan, *Peoples of the West*, online.

180 "all the men": Hill, *Western Regions*, online.

180 "traffic by sea": *Han Annals*, in Wheeler, *Rome Beyond the Imperial Frontiers*, 174. See also Wang, *Nanhai Trade*, 25.

181 battle of the Red Cliffs: Crespigny, *Generals of the South*, 267–75.

181 horse pastures: Elvin, *Pattern of the Chinese Past*, 135–36; Chin, "Ports, Merchants, Chieftains and Eunuchs," 222.

182 "where only the poor": *Jin Shu* [Jin History], 90, in Wang, *Nanhai Trade*, 38.

182 a million northerners: Zheng, *China on the Sea*, 26.

182 for the first time: Ibid., 30.

182 "with his ships": *Jin Shu* [Jin History], 97, 9a, in Wang, *Nanhai Trade*, 35.

182 "The governor": *Nan Ch'i Shu* [History of the Southern Qi Dynasty], 32, 1a-1b, in Wang, *Nanhai Trade*, 44.

183 looting the capital's: Wang, *Nanhai Trade*, 49; Taylor, *Birth of Vietnam*, 117.

183 trade missions: Wang, *Nanhai Trade*, 117–21.

184 "in case of accidents": In Wheatley, *Golden Khersonese*, 38–39; Faxian [Fa-hian], *Travels of Fa-Hian*, lxxix–lxxxiii. See Manguin, "Archaeology of Early Maritime Polities," 238.

185 Kang Senghui: Grenet, "Les marchands sogdiens," 66; Taylor, *Birth of Vietnam*, 80.

185 Missions from Sri Lanka: Wang, *Nanhai Trade*, 38.

185 "valuable products": *Song Shu* (History of the Song), 97, 12b-13a, in Wang, *Nanhai Trade*, 51.

185 "would become rich": *Liang Shu* (History of the Liang), 54, 16b-17a, in Hall, "Local and International Trade," 222.

186 Buddhism received: Wright, *Sui Dynasty*, 126–38.

186 campaign along the Yangzi: Graff, *Medieval Chinese Warfare*, 129–35.

187 extensive network of canals: Needham et al., *Science and Civilisation*, vol. 4, pt. 3:269–70, 307–8.

187 "dragon boats, phoenix vessels": *Sui Shu*, 24.686, in Wright, *Sui Dynasty*, 180.

187 "The only reason": Lu You, in Chang and Smythe, *South China in the Twelfth Century*, 48.

187 "the barbarians": *Jiu Tang Shu* (Old Tang History), 41.43a, in Taylor, *Birth of Vietnam*, 167.

188 bronze- and ironworking technologies: The Chinese Bronze and Iron Ages began around 1750 and 770 BCE, respectively; for Korea the corresponding dates are 1100 and 400 BCE.

188 "the mountainous islands": *Wei Zhi* (History of Wei), in Lu, *Japan*, 11–12.

189 replacement ships: *Nihongi*, "Ojin," 10.18 (300 CE) (vol. 1:268–69).

189 Yamato invasion: Brown, "Yamato Kingdom," 111–12.

189 Sui Yangdi launched a second invasion: Deng, *Maritime Sector*, 11, 22.

190 lashings and mortise-and-tenon joinery: Bellwood and Cameron, "Ancient Boats," 11–19.

190 Many Dong-Son drums: Needham et al., *Science and Civilisation*, vol. 4, pt. 3:445–47.

190 bronze ship model: Spennemann, "On the Bronze Age Ship Model from Flores."

191 "In the kingdom of Fu-nan": *Shui Ching Chu* (Commentary on the Waterways Classic), 1.9a, in Needham et al., *Science and Civilisation*, vol. 4, pt. 3:450.

192 "the very big *kolandiophonta*": Casson, *Periplus* 60, 230.

192 "The people of foreign parts": Wan Chen, *Strange Things of the South*, in Manguin, "Southeast Asian Ship," 275. Needham et al., *Science and Civilisation*, vol. 4, pt. 3:600–601, feel this may describe vessels from Vietnam or even Guangdong Province; Ray, "Early Coastal Trade in the Bay of Bengal," 360ff.

192 "lashed-lug and stitched-plank": Manguin, "Southeast Asian Shipping," 183–85.

192 Sewn-plank fastening: McGrail, *Boats of the World*, 354.

193 the Chinese approach: Ibid., 367, 370–77.

193 centerline or axial rudder: Needham et al., *Science and Civilisation*, vol. 4, pt. 3:640–51, plate 975; McGrail, *Boats of the World*, 380.

193 layers of planking: McGrail, *Boats of the World*, 365–70, 372, 375.

193 bulkheads gave hulls: Ibid., 366–67; Needham et al., *Science and Civilisation*, vol. 4, pt. 3:420–22; Manguin, "Trading Ships," 268.

194 free-flooding compartments: Needham et al., *Science and Civilisation*, vol. 4, pt. 3:422.

194 "at a moderate speed": Worcester, *Junks and Sampans of the Yangtze*, 45.

194 *yulohs*: Ibid., 44–50.

194 Towing: Ibid., 50–56; Van Slyke, *Yangtze*, 119–26.

195 The primary materials: Needham et al., *Science and Civilisation*, vol. 4, pt. 3:441–48, 595–97; Van Slyke, *Yangtze*, 120–21; and Deng, *Chinese Maritime Activities*, 23–26, 32–33.

196 office of maritime administration (*Seonbuseo*): Kim, "Outline of Korean Shipbuilding History," 5.

196 Japanese cedar and camphorwood: *Nihongi*, 1.58 (vol. 1:58); *rugged terrain*: 5.16 (1:161); *gifts of salt*: 10.18 (1:268–69); *"enrolled among the number"*: 11.31 (1:297).

8. The Christian and Muslim Mediterranean

199 What prompted archaeologists: Bass et al., *Serçe Limani*, 1:52.

199 Yassi Ada B: Bass and van Doorninck, "Fourth-Century Shipwreck at Yassi Ada"; van Doorninck, "4th-Century Wreck at Yassi Ada"; McGrail, *Boats of the World*, 159.

199 Yassi Ada A: Bass, "A Byzantine Trading Venture"; Bass and van Doorninck, *Yassi Ada*; McGrail, *Boats of the World*, 159.

200 The Serçe Limani ship: Bass and van Doorninck, "11th-century Shipwreck"; Steffy, "Reconstruction of the 11th Century Serçe Liman Vessel."

200 saws rather than axes: "Never, in a long career of examining wooden hull remains, have I seen so many saw marks and so few signs of axes and adzes on the surfaces of a hull" (J. Richard Steffy, in Bass et al., *Serçe Limani*, 1:153.)

200 When, where, and why: Pryor and Jeffreys, *Age of the Dromon*, 145–52; Unger, *Ship in the Medieval Economy*, 37–42.

201 thirty to sixty tons burden: Pryor, *Geography, Technology and War*, 26; McCormick, *Origins of the European Economy*, 95.

201 suited to the times: Bass et al., *Serçe Limani*, 1:185.

201   pictorial evidence: Castro et al., "Quantitative Look," 348, 350.

202   associated finds: Bass et al., *Serçe Limani*, vol. 1.

202   Hellenized Bulgarians: Ibid., 1:4, 425–26, 488.

202   glass weight: Ibid., 1:8n5.

203   Pax Romana: Paine, "A *Pax* upon You," 92–93.

203   battle of the Hellespont: Zosimus, *New History*, 2.23–24 (pp. 34–35).

203   "the quiet shelter": Procopius, *Buildings*, 1.5.2–13 (vol. 7:57–61).

204   Gaeseric led: Procopius, *Vandalic Wars*, 3.6.17–24 (vol. 2:59–63).

206   attack Cyprus: Al-Baladhuri, *Origins of the Islamic State*, 1:236–37.

206   battle of the Masts: Cosentino, "Constans II and the Byzantine Navy," 586–93; Christides, "Milaha"; and Stratos, "Naval Engagement at Phoenix."

206   siege of Constantinople: Ostrogorsky, *History of the Byzantine State*, 124.

206   "When the barbarians": Leo VI, *Taktika*, in Jenkins, "Cyprus Between Byzantium and Islam," 1012–13; Hill, *History of Cyprus*, 1:290, which quotes Qudama ibn Ja'far al-Katib al-Baghdadi (ca. 873–948).

206   Cypriot waters: Jenkins, "Cyprus Between Byzantium and Islam," 1008–9; Pryor and Jeffreys, *Age of the Dromon*, 61–62.

207   Tunis, an almost impregnable site: Taha, *Muslim Conquest and Settlement*, 71–72; Fahmy, *Muslim Naval Organisation*, 69–71.

207   strung a chain: Pryor and Jeffreys, *Age of the Dromon*, 31.

207   Seville: Taha, *Muslim Conquest and Settlement*, 100.

209   The Franks' interest: Haywood, *Dark Age Naval Power*, 152–63; McCormick, *Origins of the European Economy*, 527–28, 641–44.

209   agreement with Muslim ambassadors: Aziz Ahmad, *History of Islamic Sicily*, 5; McCormick, *Origins of the European Economy*, 900.

209   The Aghlabids began: Aziz Ahmad, *History of Islamic Sicily*, 5–11; Ostrogorsky, *History of the Byzantine State*, 208; and McCormick, *Origins of the European Economy*, 906–7.

210   "renowned across nearly the whole world": William of Puglia, *Gesta Roberti Wiscardi* [Guiscard], in Citarella, "The Relations of Amalfi with the Arab World," 299.

210   "the most prosperous town": Ibn Hawqal, *The Book of Routes and Kingdoms*, in Citarella, "The Relations of Amalfi with the Arab World," 299.

210   emergence of the Fatimids: Hitti, *History of the Arabs*, 618–19.

211   "people, called Andalusians": Severus ibn al-Muqaffa, in Christides, *Conquest of Crete*, 83.

211   Taxation was moderate: Christides, *Conquest of Crete*, 107.

212   Leo of Tripoli's: Kaminiates, *Capture of Thessalonica*, 70 (p. 115); Christides, *Conquest of Crete*, 6, 40, 167–68; and Makrypoulias, "Byzantine Expeditions."

212   The Kalbids raided al-Andalus: Hitti, *History of the Arabs*, 521.

213   river and lake operations: Cosentino, "Constans II and the Byzantine Navy," 578–79, 582–83.

213   ships were considerably smaller: Ibid., 581; Pryor and Jeffreys, *Age of the Dromon*, 133.

213   *dromon*: Warships were known by various names, including *pamphylion*, *chelandion*, and the smaller *karabion*, but how they differed is hard to determine. Pryor, "From Dromon to Galea," 94–97; Pryor and Jeffreys, *Age of the Dromon*, 166–70, 260–64; Fahmy, *Muslim Naval Organisation*, 126; and Agius, *Classic Ships of Islam*, 273, 334–48.

214   fitted with a spur: Pryor and Jeffreys, *Age of the Dromon*, 143–44, 203–10; Cosentino, "Constans II and the Byzantine Navy," 583.

214 to carry horses: Pryor and Jeffreys, *Age of the Dromon*, 307–9, 320–25.

214 permanent regiments: Ahrweiler, *Byzance et la mer*, 19–22.

214 *karabisianoi*: Pryor and Jeffreys, *Age of the Dromon*, pp. xlii, 32; Cosentino, "Constans II and the Byzantine Navy," 602. The word *karab*, "war galley," originated in Muslim Egypt and was adopted by the Byzantines.

214 naval themes: Pryor and Jeffreys, *Age of the Dromon*, 32, 46–47, 88.

215 ports of different sizes: Ahrweiler, *Byzance et la mer*, 422–25; *shipyards*: 435–36.

215 conscription: Haldon, "Military Service, Military Lands, and the Status of Soldiers," 27–28, 53, 65–66.

215 "God made me an emperor": In Lopez, *Commercial Revolution*, 66. See McCormick, *Origins of the European Economy*, 14.

215 imperial precedence: Pryor and Jeffreys, *Age of the Dromon*, 390–91.

216 "Such Russes": Cross and Sherbowitz-Wetzor, *Russian Primary Chronicle*, Year 6415 (907 CE), 65.

216 "At worst, Islam was hostile": Planhol, *Islam et la mer*, 42.

216 "'The Sea is a great creature'": Ibn Khaldun, *Muqaddimah*, 2.33 (vol. 2:39).

216 "It is God": Quran 45:12.

217 *dar al-sina'ca*: McCormick, *Origins of the European Economy*, 238–39, 526–28.

217 Muslims built others: Fahmy, *Muslim Naval Organisation*, 23–50.

217 acacia plantations: Lombard, "Arsenaux et bois de marine," 131.

217 an arsenal at Akka: Fahmy, *Muslim Naval Organisation*, 51–63.

217 sources of support: Picard, "*Bahriyyun*, émirs et califes," 419–20, 425, 433–34, 443–44; Fahmy, *Muslim Naval Organisation*, 88, 95–106; and Christides, *Conquest of Crete*, 51.

217 *Muhajirun*: Fahmy, *Muslim Naval Organisation*, 105.

217 "fulfill their expedition": In ibid., 102–3.

218 three-part scale: Christides, "Milaha."

218 "from this time": In Bury, *History of the Eastern Roman Empire*, 293.

218 "men of the sea": Ibn al-Quttiya, *History of the Conquest of Spain*, in Picard, "*Bahriyyun*, émirs et califes," 428.

218 impressment: Bramoullé, "Recruiting Crews in the Fatimid Navy," 5, 9, 11–14.

218 "were at the same time": Procopius, *Vandalic Wars*, 3.11.15 (vol. 2:105–7).

218 "He should check": In Christides, "Two Parallel Naval Guides," 56.

218 had no other function: Christides, *Conquest of Crete*, 53–56.

219 "Moors": Picard, "*Bahriyyun*, émirs et califes," 429–31, 437–38.

219 arsenals at Seville: Ibid., 429.

219 unless the outcome: Christides, *Conquest of Crete*, 60.

219 surviving manuals: Pryor and Jeffreys, *Age of the Dromon*, 175–88, and their translations of: *The Naval Battles of Syrianos Magistros*, 455–81; *The Naval Warfare of the Emperor Leo [VI]*, 483–519; the *Naval Warfare* commissioned by Basil, 521–45; Nikephoros Ouranos, *On Fighting at Sea*, 571–605; and Muhammad Ibn Mankali, "Remarks on Sea Warfare," 645–66. See Christides, "Two Parallel Naval Guides."

219 long-range weapons: Pryor and Jeffreys, *Age of the Dromon*, 379–83.

219 "manufactured a naval fire": Theophanes, *Chronicle*, 493–94. As heirs to the Roman Empire, the Byzantines called themselves Romans and the weapon "Roman fire," as well as "prepared," "artificial," and "liquid" fire. "Greek fire" is a twelfth-century coinage used by crusaders for a variety of incendiary weapons.

219 "The fire to be hurled": Anna Comnena, *Alexiad*, 11 (p. 360).

220 "anathematized": Constantine Porphyrogenitus, *De Administrando Imperio*, 13.85–90 (pp. 69–71).

220 available to Muslim fleets: Christides, *Conquest of Crete*, 63.

220 "Every ship": Al-Muqaddasi, *Best Divisions*, 11. See Haldane, "Fire-Ship of Al-Salih Ayyub," 139.

220 "something which was never": *Biography of the Patriarch Michael*, in Kubiak, "Byzantine Attack on Damietta," 47.

220 fireproof clothing: Christides, "Fireproofing of War Machines," 13–14.

220 protective chain mail: Pryor and Jeffreys, *Age of the Dromon*, 381.

220 naval stores: Ahrweiler, *Byzance et la mer*, 427.

220 supplies of wood: Pryor, *Geography, Technology and War*, 7; Lombard, "Arsenaux et bois de marine," 132, 136–37.

221 *annona*: McCormick, *Origins of the European Economy*, 87, 104–5, 108–10; *population of Rome*: 66.

221 Jeddah, established in 646: Located 70 kilometers from Mecca and 420 kilometers from Medina, Jeddah replaced the older port of al-Shu'ayba.

221 Canal of the Commander of the Faithful: Fahmy, *Muslim Naval Organisation*, 24–25; Fahmy, *Muslim Sea-power in the Eastern Mediterranean*, 23–24, 27.

221 caused the population to fall: Hourani, *Arab Seafaring*, 60.

221 transalpine trade: McCormick, *Origins of the European Economy*, 79.

222 slave and lumber trades: Ibid., 729–32, 761–77; Lombard, "Arsenaux et bois de marine," 133–37.

222 "marmalades, concentrated juices": Khalilieh, *Admiralty and Maritime Laws*, 300, 314.

222 "Women on board": Mawardi, *Al-Ahkam al-Sultaniyya* (The ordinances of government), in Khalilieh, *Admiralty and Maritime Laws*, 77.

222 "If thou sailest": Al-Baladhuri, *Origins of the Islamic State*, 1:235; Fahmy, *Muslim Naval Organisation*, 105.

223 "[T]he barbarians": Kaminiates, *Capture of Thessalonica*, 66–67.

223 to end the traffic: McCormick, *Origins of the European Economy*, 765–66.

223 interest rates: Laiou, "Byzantine Traders and Seafarers," 80; Runciman, "Byzantine Trade and Industry," 143–45.

224 Rhodian Sea Law: Ashburner, *The Rhodian Sea-Law*.

224 *Treatise Concerning the Leasing of Ships*: Khalilieh, *Admiralty and Maritime Laws*, 21–22. The author is Muhammad ibn Umar al-Kinani al-Andalusi al-Iskandarini (d. 923).

224 "Whoever hires": *Treatise Concerning the Leasing of Ships*, in ibid., 274.

225 "company": Jackson, "From Profit-Sailing to Wage-Sailing," 605–28; Pérez-Mallaína, *Spain's Men of the Sea*, 195.

225 load lines: Khalilieh, *Admiralty and Maritime Laws*, 37.

225 freight charges: Ibid., 126–28, 148.

225 lending money at interest: Goitein, *Mediterranean Society*, 1:255; Lopez, *Commercial Revolution*, 73.

225 extended a sea loan: Pryor, "Origins of the Commenda Contract," 22–23.

225 the pope condemned: Roover, "Early Examples of Marine Insurance," 175.

225 "capital, labor": Pryor, "Origins of the Commenda Contract," 19.

225 *societas maris*: Byrne, "Commercial Contracts of the Genoese," 135–49.

225 "a semi loan": *Babylonian Talmud*, in Pryor, "Origins of the Commenda Contract," 26.

225 *qirad:* Pryor, "Origins of the Commenda Contract," 29–36.
226 "innovation of highest importance": Lopez, *Commercial Revolution,* 76.
226 "the lynch-pin": Pryor, "Mediterranean Commerce in the Middle Ages," 133.
226 "the ship . . . is broken up": Statutes of Marseille, in ibid., 147.
226 "partnerships according to Muslim law": In Goitein and Friedman, *"India Book,"* 12.
227 "if goods are thrown overboard": Paulus, *Digest XIV,* in Ashburner, *Rhodian Sea-Law,* pp. cclii, 116–17. On jettison, see Khalilieh, *Admiralty and Maritime Laws,* 150–94, and *Islamic Maritime Law,* 87–105.
227 *Libro del Consulado del Mar:* Constable, "Problem of Jettison," 215.
227 "if any one": Ashburner, *Rhodian Sea Law,* chap. 9 (p. 87). According to Ashburner, "What the [*mina*] is equivalent to in this place . . . is impossible to say" (p. 90).
227 "chosen by lot": Qadi Iyad, *Madhahib al-Hukkam,* 235, in Khalilieh, *Islamic Maritime Law,* 97.
227 human jettison: Constable, "Problem of Jettison," 208–11.

9. Northern Europe Through the Viking Age

229 paying duties: Middleton, "Early Medieval Port Customs," 320–24.
230 Ohthere: Storli, "Ohthere and His World."
230 "to investigate how far": Bately, "Text and Translation," 44–45.
230 Kaupang: Skre, *"Sciringes healh,"* 150.
231 Wulfstan: Jesch, "Who Was Wulfstan," 29–31.
231 York: Lapidge, *Blackwell Encyclopaedia of Anglo-Saxon England,* 497–99.
232 "for I cannot accept": Herodotus, *Histories,* 3.115 (p. 198).
232 The tin of Cornwall: Cunliffe, *Facing the Ocean,* 304.
233 Vix krater: Cunliffe, *Extraordinary Voyage,* 16; Boardman, *Greeks Overseas,* 221–23.
233 Aude-Garonne-Gironde corridor: Cunliffe, *Extraordinary Voyage,* 55. Strabo describes this route: "from Narbo[nne] traffic goes inland for a short distance by the Atax [Aude] River, and then a greater distance by land to the Garumna [Garonne] River. . . . And the Garumna, too, flows to the ocean." *Geography,* 4.1.14 (vol. 2:211). See Cunliffe, *Facing the Ocean,* 331–32.
234 between 6,860 and 7,150 kilometers: Cunliffe, *Extraordinary Voyage,* 97; *latitudes:* 61, 98–100, 132.
235 The *Classis Germanica:* Mason, *Roman Britain and the Roman Navy,* 93, 105–6; Starr, *Roman Imperial Navy,* 124–66.
235 lines of communication: Milne, "Maritime Traffic," 82.
235 "all the bireme": Tacitus, *Histories,* 4.12 (p. 212), 5.23–24 (p. 285). See Haywood, *Dark Age Naval Power,* 25, 35–39.
235 Frankish tribes: Haywood, *Dark Age Naval Power,* 30–31.
235 "some of them revolted": Zosimus, *New History,* 1.71.2 (p. 22). See Haywood, *Dark Age Naval Power,* 41, 48–49.
236 burning of the *Classis Germanica:* Haywood, *Dark Age Naval Power,* 60.
236 "sent letters to the cities": Zosimus, *New History,* 6.10.2 (p. 130).
236 "sent back news": Bede, *History,* 1.15 (p. 56).
236 barge excavated at Blackfriars: Marsden, *A Ship of the Roman Period.*
236 wreck from St. Peter Port: Rule and Monaghan, *Gallo-Roman Trading Vessel.*
237 ship burial at Sutton Hoo: Paine, *Ships of the World,* s.v. Sutton Hoo, citing Angela Care Evans, *The Sutton Hoo Ship Burial* (London: British Museum, 1986).

237   Lacus Flevo: Kirby and Hinkkanen, *The Baltic and the North Seas*, 8.

237   entrepôt at Ribe: Lebecq, "Northern Seas," 649, 652, 654; Skovgaard-Petersen, "Making of the Danish Kingdom," 172.

237   Skagerrak and Kattegat: Crumlin-Pedersen, "Boats and Ships of the Baltic Sea," 245–47.

238   Saxon and Danish raids: Haywood, *Dark Age Naval Power*, 89.

238   Chlocilaicus (Hygelac): Ibid., 114–26; *Beowulf*, ll. 1205–14, 2355–66, 2498–509, and 2912–21.

238   The Frisians': Lebecq, *Marchands et navigateurs frisons*, 105–9.

239   *Fossa Carolina:* Leitholdt et al., "Fossa Carolina." For another interpretation of the canal's purpose, see Squatriti, "Digging Ditches in Early Medieval Europe."

239   Viken: Sawyer, "Viking Expansion," 108.

239   "We and our fathers": Alcuin of York, *Letter*, 12 (p. 18).

240   southwesterly winds: Carver, "Pre-Viking Traffic," 122.

240   sailing season: See Larson, *King's Mirror* (13th century), 158, 161.

240   "The wind is fierce to-night": In Ó Corráin, "Vikings in Ireland and Scotland," 7.

241   "a Christian people": Rimbert, *Life of Anskar*, 7 (p. 38).

241   "was especially suitable": Ibid., 24 (p. 84).

241   Noirmoutier: Jones, *History of the Vikings*, 211.

241   expeditions against al-Andalus: El-Hajji, "Andalusian Diplomatic Relations," 70–81.

242   Danish prince Björn Ironside: This raid may have attacked the Italian port of Luni, but the details are confusing.

243   "bridge of ships": *Cath Maige Tuired* (The Battle of Mag Tuired), in Ó Corráin, "Vikings in Ireland and Scotland," 14.

243   *longphorts:* A coinage of medieval Irish annalists, *longphort* comes from the Latin (*navis*) *longa*, meaning longship, and *portus*, meaning landing place; Sheehan, "The Longphort in Viking Age Ireland," 282–83.

243   "king of the Norwegian Vikings": *Annals of Ulster*, in Ó Corráin, "Vikings in Ireland and Scotland," 37.

243   "there were men": Bessason, *Book of Settlements*, §1 (p. 114).

244   The pace of colonization: Magnússon, *Northern Sphinx*, 10.

244   Birka: Ambrosiani, "Prehistory of Towns in Sweden," 64–66.

244   Helgö: Holmqvist, "Helgö."

244   west of the Vistula: Jöns, "Ports and *Emporia* of the Southern Coast"; Gimbutas, *The Balts*, 143.

245   Staraya Ladoga: Jones, *History of the Vikings*, 250. The town is called Staraya (Old) Ladoga to distinguish it from Novaya Ladoga, founded nearer the lake by Peter the Great in 1703.

245   Novgorod: Birnbaum, *Lord Novgorod the Great*.

245   "They said to themselves": Cross and Sherbowitz-Wetzor, *Russian Primary Chronicle*, Year 6368–6370 (860–862 CE), 59–69. Varangian may come from an Old Norse word for "confederates." The Greek name was *barangoi*, the Arabic *varank*: Jones, *History of the Vikings*, 247. For a discussion of the "stranger as king," see Fernández-Armesto, "Stranger-Effect in Early Modern Asia," 181–85, 188–92.

245   "Whosoever come": Cross and Sherbowitz-Wetzor, *Russian Primary Chronicle*, Year 6412–6415 (904–907), 64–65.

246   "there came": Al-Masudi, in Dunlop, *History of the Jewish Khazars*, 209–10.

246   island of Rügen: Jöns, "Ports and *Emporia* of the Southern Coast," 173.

246   "quantities of such spices": In Brutzkus, "Trade with Eastern Europe, 800–1200," 33.

The account of ben Jacob (in Arabic, Ibrahim ibn Yaqub al-Tartushi) is preserved in a thirteenth-century cosmography by Zakariya al-Qazwini.

247 Coastal navigation: Marcus, *Conquest of the North Atlantic,* 114–16.

247 "sunstone": Seaver, *Frozen Echo,* 16–18.

247 "well wooded and with low hills": *Greenland Saga,* 2, in Magnusson and Pálsson, *Vinland Sagas,* 52–54.

248 Greenlanders' numbers too few: Wallace, "L'Anse aux Meadows and Vinland," 233.

248 year-round settlement: Ibid., 224; *occupied until about 1030*: 228. The name is a corruption of L'Anse au Méduse, Bay of the Jellyfish, as seventeenth-century French fishermen called the area.

248 until about 1030: Ibid., 226, 230; Seaver, *Frozen Echo,* 23–24.

248 "Vinland because vines": Adam of Bremen, *History of the Archbishops,* § xxxix (38) (p. 219).

248 "There came also a ship": *Skálholtsannáll hinn forni,* in Magnusson, *Vikings,* 173–74.

249 Norse Greenland seems: McGhee, "Epilogue," 243.

249 English cod fishermen: Seaver, *Frozen Echo,* 181.

249 Anglo-Saxon armies sailed north: Rodger, *Safeguard of the Sea,* 18–19.

249 "since Angles and Saxons": Swanton, *Anglo-Saxon Chronicles,* Year 937 (pp. 109–10).

249 Danegeld: Magnusson, *Vikings,* 186–88.

249 Duchy of Normandy: Flodoard of Reims, *Annals,* pp. xx–xxii.

250 Saint Patrick was enslaved: De Paor, *Patrick,* 22–26, 221, 227.

250 Northumbrian who was taken: Bede, *History,* 4.23 (pp. 244–45).

250 "a precious garment": Oddr, *Saga of Olaf Tryggvason,* 7 (pp. 44–45).

250 "He is captured": Warner of Rouen, *Moriuht,* 65–76 (p. 77); *"full to bursting"*: 271–72 (p. 91); and *"a quarter"*: 279 (p. 95).

251 massacre all the Danes: Magnusson, *Vikings,* 188.

251 "Leapt from the bloodied gunwales": Snorri Sturluson, *King Harald's Saga,* §63 (p. 114).

252 250 or more ships: De Vries, *Norwegian Invasion,* 241–42.

252 "travelled into England": Swanton, *Anglo-Saxon Chronicles,* Year 1085 (pp. 215–16).

252 cohorts of a hundred men: Tacitus, *Germania,* §6, 12 (pp. 106, 111).

252 *Census of the Men of Alba*: Haywood, *Dark Age Naval Power,* 91; Rodger, *Safeguard of the Sea,* 5.

253 levies of ships and men: Rodger, *Safeguard of the Sea,* 19–20; Hollister, *Anglo-Saxon Military Institutions,* 10–11, 38–39, 85, 115; and Jones, *History of the Vikings,* 93.

253 "No man younger": Oddr, *Saga of Olaf Tryggvason,* 53 (p. 104).

253 "Here William orders": Bayeux Tapestry. There is no text for the shipbuilding scene.

253 "gathered a greater ship-army": Swanton, *Anglo-Saxon Chronicles,* Year 1066 (pp. 194–96).

254 battle of Svold: Oddr, *Saga of Olaf Tryggvason,* 67–75 (pp. 118–34); *"much longer and higher"*: 70 (p. 124); *"extensively reinforced"*: 72 (p. 126); and *"posted small boats"*: 74 (p. 132).

254 line of development: Christensen, "Proto-Viking, Viking and Norse Craft," 72–75.

255 seventy miles per day: Carver, "Pre-Viking Traffic," 121; Haywood, *Dark Age Naval Power,* 107. A six-day (144-hour) passage from Shetland to Iceland yields a speed of 2.9 knots.

255 Broighter "boat": Cunliffe, *Extraordinary Voyage,* 103–5.

255 rig their hide boats: McGrail, "Boats and Boatmanship," 46; Cunliffe, *Extraordinary Voyage,* 119.

255   "The Gauls' own ships": Caesar, *Conquest of Gaul*, 3.1 (p. 98).

255   "Perfectly equipped": Ibid., 3.1 (p. 99).

256   "To enable them to be loaded": Ibid., 5.2 (pp. 128–29).

256   Roman-era vessels: Höckmann, "Late Roman Rhine Vessels"; Höckmann, "Late Roman River Craft"; and Haywood, *Dark Age Naval Power*, 70–75.

256   "frame-based" shipbuilding: McGrail, "Romano-Celtic Boats and Ships," 141.

257   "The shape of their ships": Tacitus, *Germania*, 44 (p. 138).

257   migration under oars alone: Haywood, *Dark Age Naval Power*, 108–9.

257   Sutton Hoo ship: Paine, *Ships of the World*, s.v. *Sutton Hoo*, citing Angela Care Evans, *The Sutton Hoo Ship Burial* (London: British Museum Press, 1986), and Edwin Gifford and Joyce Gifford, "The Sailing Performance of Anglo-Saxon Ships as Derived from the Building and Trials of Half-Scale Models of the Sutton Hoo and Graveney Ship Finds," *Mariner's Mirror* 82 (1996): 131–53.

257   more than twenty ships: Crumlin-Pedersen, "Boats and Ships of the Baltic Sea," 235–42. In October 2011, archaeologists announced the find of a Viking burial with a five-meter-long vessel on the Ardnamurchan peninsula in western Scotland.

258   warhorses in ships: Bachrach, "On the Origins of William the Conqueror's Horse Transports."

258   aesthetically dramatic: Sjövold, *Oseberg Find*; Brøgger and Sheltig, *Viking Ships*; and Christensen, "Proto-Viking, Viking and Norse Craft."

258   ships scuttled off Skuldelev: Crumlin-Pedersen, "Skuldelev Ships"; Olsen and Crumlin-Pedersen, *Five Viking Ships from Roskilde Fjord*.

260   "seventy-four ells": Oddr, *Saga of Olaf Tryggvason*, 53 (p. 103). In early Iceland, an ell was about 49 centimeters, but it later measured 54–57 cm. See Dennis, *Laws of Early Iceland*, 244.

260   "had the ship painted": Oddr, *Saga of Olaf Tryggvason*, 53 (p. 103).

260   "On one side lions": Campbell, *Encomium Emmae Reginae*, §4, 13.

260   "such tackle as is needed": Constantine Porphyrogenitus, *De Administrando Imperio*, 9 (p. 61).

261   wine, that of Burgundy and the Seine: Wickham, *Inheritance of Rome*, 547.

10. The Silk Road of the Seas

264   "the king of the island of Rubies": Al-Baladhuri, *Origins of the Islamic State*, 2:215–17. See Hitti, *History of the Arabs*, 207–8. "Barks" is a translation of *barija*, a generic term for pirate ship. See Agius, *Classic Ships of Islam*, 328–30.

264   "ships laden with men": Al-Baladhuri, *Origins of the Islamic State*, 2:217.

265   "a water-front for the world": Al-Yaqubi, in Hourani, *Arab Seafaring*, 64.

265   "in a place between rivers": Al-Muqaddasi, *Best Divisions*, 100.

265   "This is the Tigris": Al-Yaqubi, in Hourani, *Arab Seafaring*, 64.

265   "the frontier of India": Wink, *Al-Hind*, 1:53.

266   Basra attracted shipping: Hitti, *History of the Arabs*, 241.

266   "Siraf nearly equaled Shiraz": Al-Istakhri, in Hadi Hasan, *History of Persian Navigation*, 115n3.

266   Zanj unrest: Al-Tabari, *History of al-Tabari*; Wink, *Al-Hind*, 1:30–31; and Wilkinson, "Suhar," 893.

267   Siraf was wracked: Wink, *Al-Hind*, 1:58.

267   "all the merchandise": Ibn Khurdadhbih, *Book of Roads and Provinces*, in Wink, *Al-Hind*, 1:29.

268   port of Aydhab: Peacock and Peacock, "Enigma of 'Aydhab"; Brett, *Rise of the Fatimids*, 273; and Nasir-i Khusraw, *Book of Travels*, 85–87.

268   Omani traders: Risso, *Merchants and Faith*, 14; Wilkinson, "Oman and East Africa," 278.

268   impressive size: Blench, "Ethnographic Evidence," 439–41.

269   Swahili culture: Spear, "Early Swahili History," 271–75.

269   Shanga: Ibid., 261–63. A Friday mosque (*jama'a*) is a city's main mosque, as distinct from a smaller, local mosque (*masjid*).

269   town of Kilwa: Chittick, *Kilwa*, 13–17 and passim.

269   "welcomed hospitably": Al-Idrisi, *The Delight of Him*, in di Meglio, "Arab Trade," 113. Some feel trade between Southeast Asia and Africa is "rather improbable," notably Chittick, "East African Trade with the Orient," 103.

270   Chinese ceramics: Rougeulle, "Medieval Trade," 159.

270   2.5 million black Africans: Davis, *Slavery and Human Progress*, 42–46.

270   "a trade that was excellent": Buzurg ibn Shahriyar, *Book of the Wonders of India*, 32 (pp. 31–36).

271   stories take place: Ibid., xvii–xviii.

272   "escaped the customs": Ibid., 83 (p. 76).

272   "the port to al-Bahrain": Al-Baladhuri, *Origins of the Islamic State*, 2:53. See Wink, *Al-Hind*, 1:97.

272   "fixed the date": Yijing, *Record of the Buddhist Religion*, xxviii.

272   Vajrabodhi sailed: Chou, "Tantrism in China," 274–75; Sen, *Buddhism, Diplomacy and Trade*, 26–27.

272   "The inhabitants being": Huichao [Hwi Cao], in Hadi Hasan, *History of Persian Navigation*, 103–4.

273   "the goods are carried": Sulayman, *Account of China and India*, 13 (p. 38).

273   "Chinese boats": Hourani, *Arab Seafaring*, 75.

273   kingdom of "Zabaj": Arabic accounts refer to Kalah and al-Zabaj over many centuries. Kalah referred to Takuapa, on the west coast of the Malay Peninsula, until the eleventh century, after which it was used of Kedah, to the south. Al-Zabaj probably refers to Java until 860, when a younger member of the Sailendra Dynasty of Java established himself on the throne of the Srivijaya kingdom at Palembang, Sumatra. The Sailendras of Java were out of power by the tenth century, and subsequent references to al-Zabaj probably indicate Sumatra. See Hall, *Maritime Trade*, 200; and Tibbetts, *Study of the Arabic Texts*, 107, 118–28.

273   Major changes: Wink, *Al-Hind*, 1:225, 230, 256.

273   "lord of both": Keay, *India*, 170. On medieval India, see Keay, *India*, 160–74; and Thapar, *Early India*, 328–30.

274   the Palas exerted: Wink, *Al-Hind*, 1:270.

274   ports in Gujarat and Konkan: Ibid., 1:304–6.

275   Saymur had a population: Ahmad, "Travels of . . . al-Mas'udi," 511; Wink, *Al-Hind*, 1:68–72, 76.

275   "one whose wealth": Chakravarti, "Nakhudas and Nauvittakas," 37, 39–40.

275   Mappila: Wink, *Al-Hind*, 1:72. On "temporary marriage," see Shahla Haeri, *Law of Desire: Temporary Marriage in Iran* (London: Tauris, 1989).

275   "to be admitted": Lord, *Display of Two Forraigne Sects*, 3 (with modernized spelling).

276   Chola Kingdom of Tamil Nadu, "Naval Expeditions of the Cholas," 2.

276   merchant guilds: Mukund, *Trading World of the Tamil Merchant*, 25–41; Guy, "Tamil Merchant Guilds," 295–302; Clark, "Muslims and Hindus in Quanzhou," 63–65; and Wade, "Early Age of Commerce," 236–37.

276   strategic patronage of Buddhism: Spencer, *Politics of Expansion*, 144–45.

276   Southeast Asian rulers: Sen, *Buddhism, Diplomacy and Trade*, 220.

276   "There are certain Indians": Abu Zayd, *Concerning the Voyage*, 98–99.

277   *banias*: Wink, *Al-Hind*, 1:75.

277   Indian sources: Jacq-Hergoualc'h, *The Malay Peninsula*, 270.

277   "There are, among the Indians": Abu Zayd, *Concerning the Voyage*, 89.

277   "I am taken with a desire": Ibid., 64–68.

278   "most likely to rebel": *Telaga Batu* inscription, in Casparis, *Selected Inscriptions*, 37, 39. See Hall, *Maritime Trade*, 98–99; and Hall, "Economic History of Early Southeast Asia," 201.

278   thirty-seven monks: Jacq-Hergoualc'h, *The Malay Peninsula*, 194.

278   "the pair of sails": Yijing, *Record of the Buddhist Religion*, xxx.

279   "a recess of the sea": Xuanzang, *Si-Yu-Ki: Buddhist Records of the Western World*, 2:200–201. A Chinese Buddhist pilgrim and translator, Xuanzang spent seventeen years (630–647) in India, to and from which he traveled overland.

279   on the Malay Peninsula; Jacq-Hergoualc'h, *The Malay Peninsula*, 107–16; 161–66; 339–40, 350, 399–402.

279   Yet it is the west coast: Ibid., 337, 347.

279   Kedu plain: Hall, "Economic History of Early Southeast Asia," 202–4.

280   moved eastward: Hall, *Maritime Trade*, 110–13, 120–27.

280   presence of foreigners: Wade, "Early Age of Commerce," 251.

280   East Java: Hall, "Economic History of Early Southeast Asia," 208–15.

280   "Of all the wealthy foreign lands": Chou K'u-fei [Zhou Qufei], *Ling-wai-tai-ta* (1178), in Zhao Rugua, *On the Chinese and Arab Trade*, 23. See Hall, *Maritime Trade*, 195.

281   "nutmegs must be able": In Hall, "Economic History of Early Southeast Asia," 209. See Boomgaard, *Southeast Asia*, 182. "Clove" comes from the Latin *clavis*, meaning nail, from the shape of the dried bud.

281   "the like of which": Sulayman, *Account of India and China*, 28 (p. 44).

281   "dispatched many ships": In Spencer, *Politics of Expansion*, 138–39. The ports are identified in Christie, "Medieval Tamil-Language Inscriptions," 254n56. On motives, see Kulke, "Naval Expeditions of the Cholas," 1–2.

282   "oblations to the sea": In Chandra, *Trade and Trade Routes in Ancient India*, 214–21.

283   trade missions from Srivijaya: Wade, "Early Age of Commerce," 227.

283   attacks did loosen: Kulke, "Naval Expeditions of the Cholas," 10; Lieberman, *Strange Parallels*, 2:776; and Zhao Rugua, *On the Chinese and Arab Trade*, 23.

283   Buddhist monks from Pagan: Hall, *Maritime Trade*, 199; Aung-Thwin, *Mists of Ramañña*, 257–58, 300–306.

283   Our assumptions: McGrail, *Boats of the World*, 272: "The Indian sewn-plank boat can be traced back only to the early sixteenth century. Since sewn boats were used in east Africa, Arabia, and south-east Asia in the late first millennium BC/early first millennium AD, it is reasonable to suggest that there may have been similar early use in India: the evidence, however, is lacking." See also Tomalin et al., "Thaikkal-Kadakkarappally Boat," 257.

283   "stairways for loading": Li Zhao, *Tang Guo Shi Bu* (Supplemental History of the Tang State), in Gunawardana, "Changing Patterns of Navigation," 65.

283   The Belitung ship: Flecker, "A Ninth-Century AD Arab or Indian Shipwreck in

Indonesia." On sewn planks, see above, chap. 6. On the woods used, see Flecker, "A Ninth-Century AD Arab or Indian Shipwreck in Indonesia: Addendum."

284   "There are people, at Oman": Abu Zayd, *Concerning the Voyage*, 89.

284   "This oil": Ibid., 95, reading "preserving" for the translator's "caulking."

284   *nura:* Margariti, *Aden*, 56–57, 161.

284   "iron should not": In Chaudhuri, "Ship-Building in the *Yuktikalpataru*," 140.

284   "no iron [should be] used": Mookerji, *Indian Shipping*, 21. See Tomalin et al., "Thaikkal-Kadakkarappally Boat," 257–58.

284   "special vessels": In Chaudhuri, "Ship-Building in the *Yuktikalpataru*," 140–41.

284   the importance of iron: McPherson, *Indian Ocean*, 115–18.

285   Thaikkal-Kadakkarappally boat: Tomalin et al., "Thaikkal-Kadakkarappally Boat," 259–62.

285   "If a rock": Al-Muqaddasi, *Best Divisions*, 11. See Agius, *Classic Ships of Islam*, 204–5, and, on the *busi*, 282–83; and Mott, *Development of the Rudder*, 121.

285   hero stones: Tripati, "Ships on Hero Stones from the West Coast of India"; Mott, *Development of the Rudder*, 106–19. The hero stone inscriptions are illegible and nothing is known of the actions depicted.

285   "the largest and most elaborate": Miksic, *Borobudur*, 18, 40.

286   five ships: Together with archaeological and modern ethnographic evidence, the carvings of the outrigger ships were a source for the design and construction of a vessel that sailed from Java to Ghana via the Seychelles, northern Madagascar, and Cape Town, between August 2003 and February 2004, with a total of 151 days at sea.

287   obstacles against enemy boarders: Burningham, "Borobudur Ship," and personal communication.

288   "They say that once": Nasir-i Khusraw, *Book of Travels*, 121.

288   "In this sea": Al-Istakhri, *al-Aqalim*, in Naji, "Trade Relations," 432. Jannaba was a port on the coast of Fars north of Bandar Rig (29°28'N, 50°37'E). According to the twelfth-century Persian geographer Ibn al-Balkhi's *Description of the Province of Fars*, "in Persian they call it Ganfah, which signifies 'Stinking Water.' Now, a city that has 'Stinking Water' for its name must be described as of an evil stinking character, and therefore there is no occasion to speak of its condition."

288   "At dawn": Nasir-i Khusraw, *Book of Travels*, 122–23.

289   "Upon the whole coast": Abu Zayd, *Concerning the Voyage*, 93.

289   "after studying": In Chandra, *Trade and Trade Routes in Ancient India*, 217, 221.

289   "shipmasters, cargo masters": Al-Muqaddasi, *Best Divisions*, 9.

289   Ahmad ibn Majid: Tibbetts, *Arab Navigation*, 7–9. For a concise overview of Arabic navigation and navigation guides in this period, see Agius, *Classic Ships of Islam*, 187–202.

289   "the risings and settings": Ahmad ibn Majid, in Tibbetts, *Arab Navigation*, 77.

11. China Looks Seaward

292   Tang cargo: Flecker, "A Ninth-Century AD Arab or Indian Shipwreck in Indonesia"; Zheng, *China on the Sea*, 1, 6, 33; and Worrall, "China Made."

294   five canals: Xiong, *Sui Tang Chang'an*, 205–7.

294   Tang Gaozong, attacked Goguryeo: Twitchett and Wechsler, "Kao-tsung and the Empress Wu," 282–85; Lee, *Korea and East Asia*, 17, 66–68; and Graff, *Medieval Chinese Warfare*, 198–200.

295 "King Pungjang": *Nihongi*, "Tenchi," 27.7–8 (663 CE) vol. 2:280. See Mitsusada and Brown, "Century of Reform," 207.

295 state of Balhae: Twitchett, "Hsüan-tsung," 430; Lee, *New History of Korea*, 71–73.

295 droughts and famines: Twitchett and Wechsler, "Kao-tsung and the Empress Wu," 277–79.

296 renewal of the canal system: Twitchett, *Financial Administration Under the T'ang*, 87–89; Pulleyblank, *Background of the Rebellion of An Lu-shan*, 34–35, 183–87.

296 China was also resurgent: Grousset, *Empire of the Steppes*, 114–20; Twitchett, "Hsüan-tsung," 444.

296 occupied the strategic region: Taylor, *Birth of Vietnam*, 195.

296 attack on the Khitan: Pulleyblank, *Background of the Rebellion of An Lu-shan*, 97–99.

296 Hebei and Henan: Dalby, "Court Politics in Late T'ang Times," 562; Twitchett, "Hsüan-tsung," 457.

297 "destroy the warehouses": Clark, "Frontier Discourse and China's Maritime Frontier," 27.

297 number of ships: Wang, *Nanhai Trade*, 76.

297 permanently weakened: Peterson, "Court and Province," 484–86.

297 illegal ordinations: Wechsler, "T'ai-tsung the Consolidator," 218.

299 The Koreans in China: Reischauer, *Ennin's Travels*, 281–87. Although traders from Silla dominated the trade, the port of Tengzhou on the north coast of the Shandong Peninsula had separate inns to serve travelers arriving by sea from Balhae and Silla, and Ennin noted the arrival of a ship from Balhae on the Shandong Peninsula in 839 (p. 141). See Lee, *New History of Korea*, 94–95.

299 Jang Bogo: The details of his life story are not very clear, and there is disagreement over how and when he was killed, the date for which falls between 841 and 846. For Ennin's letter of thanks for the offer of passage to Yangzhou, *Ennin's Diary* 840-2-17 (pp. 166–67 and p. 100n438); Reischauer, *Ennin's Travels*, 287; Lee, *New History of Korea*, 95–97; and Henthorn, *History of Korea*, 79–81.

299 Wang Geon: Lee, *New History of Korea*, 91, 95–96, 100–103, where the names are given as Chakchegon and Wang Kon.

300 "There are several hundred Chinese": In Shiba and Elvin, *Commerce and Society in Sung China*, 187.

300 via Chinese ports: Henthorn, *History of Korea*, 100.

300 pirates in gangs: Peterson, "Court and Province," 555; Somers, "End of the T'ang," 684–85, 689–91.

300 "that the markets": Ouyang Xiu, *Biography of Huang Chao*, 3a (p. 18).

301 120,000 Muslim, Jewish, Christian, and Persian merchants: Abu Zayd, 41–42. See Clark, "Muslims and Hindus in Quanzhou," 55.

301 "Communication with the southeast": Wei Zhuang, "Lament of the Lady of Qin," ll. 127–31.

301 "tyrannizing those of the merchants": Abu Zayd, *Concerning the Voyage*, in Levy, *Biography of Huang Ch'ao*, 117, 119–20. See Wang, *Nanhai Trade*, 78–79.

302 Five Dynasties and Ten Kingdoms: Mote, *Imperial China*, 8–14.

302 importance of urbanization: Ibid., 164–65.

302 The Song purchased peace: Ibid., 116, 369.

302 forcibly relocated from Chang'an: Benn, *China's Golden Age*, 46.

303 "Giao [Jiaozhou] is a large frontier region": In Taylor, *Birth of Vietnam*, 183.

303 "tried to cheat them": [*Xin*] *Tang Shu*, 4.1b, in Wang, *Nanhai Trade*, 73.

303 "ferocious, pitiless": In Hall, *Maritime Trade*, 179. This raid of 774 was followed

by another in 787. Phan Rang is 150 miles northeast of the Mekong delta and Nha Trang 50 miles beyond Phan Rang.

304 "The merchants of distant kingdoms": Sima Guang, *Zi Zhi Tong Jian* [Mirror of History], 234, vol. 12:596, in Taylor, *Birth of Vietnam*, 208.

304 the armies of Nanzhao: Taylor, *Birth of Vietnam*, 245.

304 "You must give up hope": In Li, "View from the Sea," 84n2.

305 "Banish distress": Le Tac, *Annam Chi Luoc* 104, in Taylor, *Birth of Vietnam*, 252.

305 "How can a great man": In Taylor, *Birth of Vietnam*, 280.

305 "merchant boats": In ibid., 287.

305 not bothered to name: Whitmore, "Rise of the Coast," 105.

305 Van Don became: Ibid., 109–10.

306 "fish and vegetables mostly uncooked": Yijing, *Record of the Buddhist Religion*. On Tang cookery generally, see Schafer, *Golden Peaches of Samarkand*, 139–54.

306 "His Majesty": In Kuwabara, "On P'u Shou-keng," 6.

306 China's bulkiest imports: Schafer, *Golden Peaches of Samarkand; birds:* 100–102; *cuisine:* 140; *elephants:* 81–84; *incense,* 157–62; *musicians:* 56; and *sandalwood and rosewood:* 134–38.

307 easing of official attitudes: Shiba and Elvin, *Commerce and Society in Sung China*, 127–29.

307 "memorial-presenting courts": Lien-sheng, *Money and Credit in China*, 51–56.

307 office of maritime affairs—*shibosi*: So, *Prosperity, Region and Institutions*, 36. *Shibosi (shih-po-ssu)* is also translated as "bureau of the maritime trade superintendent" (Chin, "Ports, Merchants, Chieftains and Eunuchs," 236), "superintendent of the trading ships" (Kuwabara, "On P'u Shou-keng"), "superintendent of the shipping trade" (Wang, *Nanhai Trade*, 94), "trade superintendency" (Clark, *Community, Trade and Networks*, 169), and "maritime trade bureau" (Zheng, *China on the Sea*, 32).

307 "argosies of the Brahmans": In Schafer, *Golden Peaches of Samarkand*, 15. Posthumously known as "The Great Teacher Who Crossed the Sea," Jianzhen was on his fifth of sixth attempts to reach Japan, where he died in 763.

307 variety of responsibilities: So, *Prosperity, Region and Institutions*, 42–49.

308 Kyushu Headquarters (*Dazaifu*): Verschuer, *Across the Perilous Sea*, 34–35.

308 lack of trade missions: Bielenstein, *Diplomacy and Trade*, 106, 124, 138, 144; Verschuer, *Across the Perilous Sea*, 34.

309 "Typhoons for winds": Han Yu, in Schafer, *Vermilion Bird*, 128.

309 "Whenever the barbarian": *Wuguo Gushi*, 2.10a, in So, *Prosperity, Region and Institutions*, 25.

309 "the port was clogged": In Clark, "Muslims and Hindus in Quanzhou," 60.

309 10 percent: Clark, "Muslims and Hindus in Quanzhou," 58.

309 fourth *shibosi*: Kuwabara, "On P'u Shou-keng," 2–3, 19–20; So, *Prosperity, Region and Institutions*, 48–49.

309 trade with the south: Wang, *Nanhai Trade*, 79–81.

309 as far as Java: Clark, *Community, Trade and Networks*, 124.

309 Hokkiens: Chang, "Formation of a Maritime Convention," 148–50; Gladney, *Muslim Chinese*, 262.

310 "Great ships in thousands": Cui Rong, in Shiba and Elvin, *Commerce and Society in Sung China*, 4.

310 ten shipyards: Benn, *China's Golden Age*, 185.

310 "There is a saying": Li Chao [Li Zhao], quoted in *Tangguo Shibu* (Supplementary

Information on the Tang Dynasty), in Shiba and Elvin, *Commerce and Society in Sung China*, 5.

310 "floating boat people": Clark, "Frontier Discourse and China's Maritime Frontier," 17–18.

310 "in some shape or form": Worcester, *The Junkman Smiles*, 10.

310 "Two water buffalo": *Ennin's Diary*, 838–7–21 (pp. 19–20).

311 haulers with local knowledge: Shiba and Elvin, *Commerce and Society in Sung China*, 5.

311 introduction of iron fastenings: Manguin, "Southeast Asian Ship," 272.

311 "sand ships" (*shachuan*): McGrail, *Boats of the World*, 348.

311 Ships typically had no cabins: Wang, *Nanhai Trade*, 100.

311 "With the fibrous bark": In Manguin, "Trading Ships," 275.

311 lashings and dowels: Manguin, "Trading Ships," 268–69.

312 Sewn-plank fastening: McGrail, *Boats of the World*, 354.

312 "fore-and-aft sails": Ibid., 159, 309, 357.

314 built a fleet: Taylor, *Birth of Vietnam*, 226, 231.

314 "The Japanese warships": *Nihongi*, "Tenchi," 27.7–8 (683 CE), vol. 2:280. See also Mitsusada and Brown, "Century of Reform," 207.

315 fifty Jurchen ships: Verschuer, *Across the Perilous Sea*, 41. See Lee, *New History of Korea*, 517.

12. The Medieval Mediterranean and Europe

317 island parishes: Lane, *Venice*, 11.

317 river trades: Ibid., 7–8.

318 "We wed thee, Adriatic": Senior, "*Bucentaur*," 135.

318 sailed together: Spufford, *Power and Profit*, 400.

318 about three hundred ships: Pryor, "Venetian Fleet for the Fourth Crusade," 115.

318 "As in the Venetians' arsenal": Dante, *Inferno*, Canto 21, ll. 7–15 (p. 319).

319 the state required: Lane, *Venice*, 13–14, 48–51.

319 in 1085 Guiscard crossed: Frankopan, "Byzantine Trade Privileges," 143.

319 "with promises and bribes": Anna Comnena, *Alexiad*, 4.2 (p. 137).

319 chrysobull (imperial decree): Frankopan, "Byzantine Trade Privileges," 152–53; Frankopan prefers a date of 1092.

320 "from the ancient quay": Anna Comnena, *Alexiad*, 6.5 (p. 191). The Venetian quarter was on the Golden Horn just west of the Neorion, between the Gate of the Perama (the quay of the Hebrews) and the Gate of the Drungarios (the Vigla).

320 had to pay tariffs: Lane, "Economic Meaning of War and Protection," 387.

320 Genoa lies: Epstein, *Genoa and the Genoese*, 11–14.

320 Italians traded: Cowdrey, "Mahdia Campaign," 8–10; Abulafia, "Trade and Crusade," 6.

321 religious overtones: Cowdrey, "Mahdia Campaign," 6.

321 "for the salvation": Urban II, in Riley-Smith, *Crusades*, 12–13.

321 "In the name of God": In Pryor, "Venetian Fleet for the Fourth Crusade," 121.

321 the Fatimid fleet: Hamblin, "Fatimid Navy," 77–78.

322 Alfonso VI: Reilly, *Medieval Spains*, 92–93.

322 Almoravids: Lewis, "Northern European Sea Power," 141–43.

323 "who organized their fleet": Ibn Khaldun, *Muqaddimah*, 2:43; Lewis, "Northern European Sea Power," 150.

323 Norman Sicily: Matthew, *Norman Kingdom of Sicily*, 72–75.

323 the Genoese negotiated: Williams, "Making of a Crusade."

323   After taking Almería: Epstein, *Genoa and the Genoese*, 49–52.

324   "the attacks and damages": *Annali Genovesi*, 30, in Williams, "Making of a Crusade," 44.

324   gold caravans: Lewis, "Northern European Sea Power," 147.

324   165 ships: David, *The Conquest of Lisbon*, 53.

324   "the richest in trade": Ibid., 91.

324   "It became clear": Al-Kitab Imad ad-Din al-Isfahani, in Ayalon, "Mamluks and Naval Power," 4.

325   sixty thousand dead: Choniates, *O City of Byzantium*, 250–51. Choniates reports that four thousand survivors were sold as slaves. See William of Tyre, *History of Deeds Done Beyond the Sea*, 22.12–13 (pp. 464–67).

325   by way of Alexandria: Riley-Smith, *Crusades*, 151.

325   "because they could better": Villehardouin, *Conquest of Constantinople*, in Pryor, "Venetian Fleet for the Fourth Crusade," 114.

325   eighty-five thousand marks: Lane, *Venice*, 37.

325   "200,000 silver marks": Villehardouin, *Conquest of Constantinople*, 50.

326   "so much, indeed": Ibid., 92.

326   "lord of a quarter": In Ostrogorsky, *History of the Byzantine State*, 376.

326   minting gold coins: Lopez, "Back to Gold," 219–20, 229–30.

327   target for pirates: Charanis, "Piracy in the Aegean," 135–36.

327   "a man of inestimable worth": Boccaccio, *Decameron*, Day 5, Story 6 (p. 447).

327   "footsoldiers skilled": Ramon Llull, *Liber de Fine*, in Pryor, "Naval Battles of Roger of Lauria," 199. See Mott, *Sea Power*, 151–75; Lane, "Crossbow in the Nautical Revolution"; and Pryor, "From Dromon to Galea," 111.

327   compulsory service: Mott, *Sea Power*, 175–77.

328   employed as shipwrights: Lopez, "Majorcans and Genoese," 1164.

328   "ships come up": *Primera Crónica General de España*, in Constable, *Trade and Traders*, 244.

329   *Ilkhans of Persia*: 169n18; *Ugolino and Vadino Vivaldi*: Lopez, "European Merchants in the Medieval Indies," 169–70.

329   raze virtually every port: Ayalon, "Mamluks and Naval Power," 8–12.

329   caravan routes: Pryor, "Maritime Republics," 440.

330   "wonderful harbor": Ibn Battuta, *Travels*, 2:471.

330   "A plague attacked": Nicephorus Gregoras, *Ecclesiasticae Historiae*, in Herlihy, *Black Death*, 24.

331   city of Lübeck: Gläser, "Development of the Harbours," 79–81.

331   "during all the campaigns": Helmhold von Bosau, *Chronicle of the Slavs*, in Schildhauer, *Hansa*, 19.

332   city of Riga: Henricus Lettus, *Chronicle of Henry of Livonia*; Riley-Smith, *Crusades*, 131.

332   "Our two towns": In Lopez, *Commercial Revolution*, 117.

332   "across sand and sea": In Ellmers, "Cog as Cargo Carrier," 38.

332   Lübeck city seal: Ellmers, "Cog as Cargo Carrier," 37–38.

332   established *kontors*: Dollinger, *German Hansa*, 27–50.

333   "a community of German merchants": Ibid., 62–64.

333   primary arteries of trade: Thompson, "Early Trade Relations," 551.

334   alliance with Henry: Oakley, *Short History of Denmark*, 55.

334   "The east side of Zealand": Saxo Grammaticus, *Gesta Danorum*, Preface, in Gade, *Hanseatic Control of Norwegian Commerce*, 17. Sjælland is the largest island in Denmark.

334   tensions led to war: Sicking, "Amphibious Warfare in the Baltic," 76–81.

334   Treaty of Stralsund: Bjork, "Peace of Stralsund, 1370."

334   "God's friends": In ibid., 60. See Dollinger, *German Hansa*, 79–82.

335   Kalmar Union: Oakley, *Short History of Denmark*, 78–80, 87.

335   Hanse was likewise undermined: Dollinger, *German Hansa*, 81–82.

335   Zwin River: De Witte, "Maritime Topography of Medieval Bruges," 141–43.

335   could be found in Bruges: Spufford, *Power and Profit*, 113, 232, 266, 278, 319–20, 330.

336   trade of England: Friel, *Maritime History of Britain and Ireland*, 62–66.

336   When Henry II ascended: Ibid., 49.

336   rich vineyards: James, *Studies in the Medieval Wine Trade*, 9–10, 35.

336   the tun: Friel, *Maritime History of Britain and Ireland*, 64. For a history of tonnage measurement, see Lyman, "Register Tonnage."

336   Hundred Years' War: Friel, *The Good Ship*, 139.

336   Clos des Galées: Rose, *Medieval Naval Warfare*, 61–62.

337   Cinque Ports: Sylvester, "Communal Piracy," 170–73; Rodger, "Naval Service of the Cinque Ports," 646–47.

337   payment of a modest sum: Sherborne, "Hundred Years' War," 164ff.

338   letters of marque: Rodger, *Safeguard of the Sea*, 128; Petrie, *Prize Game*, 2–3; and Spufford, *Power and Profit*, 221–22.

338   Roger of Lauria issued: Mott, *Sea Power*, 124–32.

338   "Commission to William Prince": *Calendar of the Patent Rolls . . . Henry IV*, April 23, 1400 (vol. 1:271).

339   centerline rudder: Mott, *Development of the Rudder*, 106–19.

339   A survey of sealings: Friel, *The Good Ship*, 79.

339   Bremen cog: Paine, *Ships of the World*, s.v. Bremen Cog, citing Gardiner and Unger, *Cogs, Caravels and Galleons*, and Werner Lahn, *Die Kogge von Bremen—The Hanse Cog of Bremen* (Hamburg: Deutsches Schiffahrtsmuseum, 1992).

340   "At this time": Giovanni Villani, *Florentine Chronicle*, in Mott, *Development of the Rudder*, 138–40. See Ellmers, "Cog as Cargo Carrier," 39.

340   *Roccaforte*: Lane, *Venice*, 46; Spufford, *Power and Profit*, 398.

340   "that if they": Martino da Canale, *Cronaca veneta*, in Lane, *Venetian Ships and Shipbuilders*, 5. See Dotson, "Fleet Operations," 168–75.

340   specifications for war galleys: Pryor, "From Dromon to Galea," 110–11.

341   *alla sensile*: Bondioli et al., "Oar Mechanics," 173–83.

341   "great galley": Lane, *Venetian Ships and Shipbuilders*, 16–29; Casson, "Merchant Galleys," 123–26.

341   northern ships were still built: "The French royal dockyard at Rouen, the Clos des Galées . . . was the only place in northern Europe at which skeleton built craft were based" (Friel, *The Good Ship*, 172).

341   2,783 cloths: Holmes, "The 'Libel of English Policy,'" 199–200.

342   transport costs: Spufford, *Power and Profit*, 399–404.

342   Statutes of Marseille: The rule specified 2.5 *palmorum* by 6.5 to 7 *palmorum*, or 24.75 inches by 64.35 to 69.3 inches—about 11 square feet. Berlow, "Sailing of the *St. Esprit*," 350n1.

342   "The berths of the pilgrims": *The Book of Wanderings of Brother Felix Fabri in Palestine and Arabia*, in Lane, *Venetian Ships and Shipbuilders*, 21; Casson, "Merchant Galleys," 125.

343   cooperation between merchants: Constable, *Trade and Traders*, 68–70; Goitein, *Mediterranean Society*, 1:72; and Goitein and Friedman, "India Book," 25, 133–34.

343 representative of merchants: Goitein, *Mediterranean Society*, 1:186–92.
343 *fonduks:* Ibid., 1:349–50; Constable, *Trade and Traders*, 119–21.
343 required to pay duties: Khalilieh, *Islamic Maritime Law*, 82–83.
343 Armed with an *aman:* Wansbrough, "Safe-Conduct," esp. 32–34; Khalilieh, *Islamic Maritime Law*, 125.
343 Christian merchant ships were found in Alexandria: Ehrenkreutz, "Place of Saladin," 110.
344 discouraged trade: Khalilieh, *Islamic Maritime Law*, 126–27.
344 "The day they entered": Beha ed-Din, *Life of Saladin*, in Reinert, "Muslim Presence in Constantinople," 141.
344 "of God, of the sea": Roover, "Early Examples of Marine Insurance," 188–89.
344 premiums varied: Ibid., 190.
345 Russian furs at Bruges: Spufford, *Power and Profit*, 336.

13. The Golden Age of Maritime Asia

347 "the profit derived": Kuwabara, "On P'u Shou-keng," 24n22.
348 well-connected foreigners: Chang, "Formation of a Maritime Convention," 147–49.
348 Western mariners still: Ibid., 151.
348 "two types of foreigners": In Guy, "Tamil Merchant Guilds," 297.
348 direct trade: Zhao Rugua, *On the Chinese and Arab Trade*, 88–93.
348 "ordered the officers-in-charge": Guy, "Expansion of China's Trade," 14.
349 specify which types: Zhao Rugua, *On the Chinese and Arab Trade*, 259, s.v. "Porcelain."
349 Eager to support: Peterson, "Old Illusions and New Realities," 218–31.
349 "thunder-crash bombs": Needham et al., *Science and Civilisation*, vol. 5, pt. 7:163, 170–79.
350 more than nineteen thousand ships were registered: Lo, "Chinese Shipping," 171.
350 "Tens of thousand": In Deng, *Chinese Maritime Activities*, 83.
350 cost of building ships: Deng, *Chinese Maritime Activities*, 161.
350 transporting grain: Lo, "Controversy over Grain Conveyance"; Sung and Schurmann, *Economic Structure*, 108–30.
351 Huitong Canal: Lo, "Controversy over Grain Conveyance," 285; Needham et al., *3 and Civilisation*, vol. 4, pt. 3:306–20.
351 advances in navigational practice: Lo, "Chinese Shipping," 171.
351 "The ship's pilots": Zhu Yu, *Pinzhou Table Talk*, in Needham, *Science and Civilisation*, vol. 4, pt. 1:279.
352 compass was used: Needham et al., *Science and Civilisation*, vol. 4, pt. 1:279–92; Lane, "Economic Meaning of the Invention of the Compass." For references in Persian and Arabic sources, see Tibbetts, *Arab Navigation*, 290; Needham et al., *Science and Civilisation*, vol. 4, pt. 1:245–51.
352 "During the night": In Needham et al., *Science and Civilisation*, vol. 4, pt. 1:280.
352 world's first printed map: Needham et al., *Science and Civilisation*, 3:549 and fig. 227.
352 "seaway compass charts": Deng, *Chinese Maritime Activities*, 55.
352 ports with a *shibosi:* Sung and Schurmann, *Economic Structure*, 223–25.
352 ban on private overseas trade: Ibid., 224–25.
352 "in many cases": In ibid., 226.
352 "No gold, silver, copper": *Yuan Shih*, 25b1, in Sung and Schurmann, *Economic Structure*, 232.

352   "The splendid city of Zaiton": Polo, *Travels*, 237. Zaitun, "olive town," was the Persian and Arabic name for Quanzhou, possibly because of its similarity to the Chinese *citong*, a tree valued in shipbuilding for the preservative quality of the tung oil pressed from its nut and widely planted in Quanzhou in the tenth century. See Schottenhammer, "Transfer of Xiangyao from Iran and Arabia to China," 144–45.

353   Korea's withdrawal: Verschuer, *Across the Perilous Sea*, 47.

353   "The Genji had more": *Tales of the Heike*, 11.7 (p. 134).

353   "took him in her arms": Ibid., 11.9 (pp. 142–43). The Ryukyu chain stretches about 570 miles between northern Taiwan and southern Kyushu Island. Okinawa is halfway along the chain, about 425 miles east of Fuzhou.

353   fled overseas: Sakamaki, "Heike," 115–22.

354   "Lined up stern to bow": *Kaiqing siming xuzhi*, book 8, in Verschuer, *Across the Perilous Sea*, 77.

354   commercial revival: Verschuer, *Across the Perilous Sea*, 10, 33–47, 79–80, 151–52; Souyri, *World Turned Upside Down*, 2–5, 154–55, 158–60.

354   Against the advice: Lee, *New History of Korea*, 147–52.

354   Mongol invasion included: Conlan, *In Little Need of Divine Intervention*, 255–64; Rossabi, *Khubilai Khan*, 99–102.

354   erecting a coastal wall: Conlan, *In Little Need of Divine Intervention*, 214–15, 234–39.

355   *kamikaze*: Ibid., 254–55.

355   "a few large Chinese-type vessels": *Tales of the Heike*, 11.7 (p. 134).

355   scrolls of Takezaki: Conlan, *In Little Need of Divine Intervention*, 1–17.

355   size of the vessels: Souyri, *World Turned Upside Down*, 150–51.

356   exposed to attack: Hall, *Maritime Trade*, 210–12.

356   "The treasure in the island": Polo, *Travels*, 251.

356   disfigured and tattooed: Rockhill, "Notes," 15 (1914): 442, 444–47; Hall, *Maritime Trade*, 212; and Rossabi, *Khubilai Khan*, 219.

356   "People in vast numbers": *Hikayat Raja-Raja Pasai*, 161, in Reid, "Rise and Fall," 62.

357   introduced copper *cash*: Reid, *Expansion and Crisis*, 95–96; Wicks, *Money, Markets, and Trade*, 291.

357   kingdom of Ayutthaya: Taylor, "Early Kingdoms," 168–73; Reid, *Expansion and Crisis*, 205; and Lieberman, *Strange Parallels*, 1:245.

357   Marco Polo's account: Polo, *Travels*, 241–312.

358   geographic and economic knowledge: Deng, *Chinese Maritime Activities*, 57–58.

358   Zhao Rugua: See Hirth and Rockhill's introduction to Zhao Rugua, *On the Chinese and Arab Trade*, 36–38.

358   "several of the countries of the Dashi": Zhao Rugua, *On the Chinese and Arab Trade*, 227; *rattan mats*: 220; and *cotton*: 217–20; Rockhill, "Notes," pt. 1:419.

359   "when we conversed": Ibn Battuta, *Travels*, 4:899. Ibn Battuta's description of Southeast Asia and of his trip from Guangzhou to Hangzhou is so confused that some doubt he ever got that far. Similar questions have also been raised about the accuracy of Marco Polo's writing. See, for example, Ross E. Dunn, *The Adventures of Ibn Battua, a Muslim Traveler in the 14th Century* (Berkeley: University of California Press, 1986), 252–53, and Frances Wood, *Did Marco Polo Go to China?* (Boulder: Westview, 1996).

359   Cairo Geniza: Goitein, *Mediterranean Society*, 1:1–23; Goitein and Friedman, "India Book," 3–6.

360   Abraham ben Yiju: Goitein and Friedman, "India Book," 52–58, 69–70.

360   Madmun ben Hasan-Japheth: Ibid., 37–47.

360   "two [sets] of fine": Ibid., 313–17.
361   "partnerships according to Muslim law": Ibid., 12.
361   *karim*, "a convoy or group": Goitein, "Beginnings," 353, 360. See Goitein and Fried-man, *"India Book,"* 483n28; Margariti, Aden, 152–53. But see also the note on the "dock of Akkad," above p. 606.
361   "the lords of the seas and deserts": In Goitein and Friedman, *"India Book,"* 38.
362   Reynald de Châtillon: Ibn Jubayr, *Travels*, 52; Ehrenkreutz, "Place of Saladin," 109–10.
362   Aden did not begin: Margariti, *Aden*, 43; *duties:* 94.
362   "all sorts of silk": Benjamin of Tudela, *Itinerary*, 119.
362   "We faced each other": *Goitein*, "Two Eyewitness Reports," 256; Goitein and Fried-man, *"India Book,"* 342, 337–47.
363   "told me that": In Stern, "Ramisht of Siraf," 10.
364   twenty-four dinars a year: Goitein, *Mediterranean Society*, 1:359.
364   The freedman of a governor: Goitein, "Two Eyewitness Reports," 247.
364   the caprice of political rulers: Goitein, "Beginnings," 351; Serjeant, "Yemeni Mer-chants," 69; and Goitein and Friedman, *"India Book,"* 260n6.
364   "dispensed unaccustomed justice": In Serjeant, "Yemeni Merchants," 70.
364   pilgrimage by sea: Chakravarti, "Nakhudas and Nauvittakas," 42–43.
365   "The reason why": Al-Biruni, in ibid., 52.
365   Jain merchants and Siddharaja: Wink, *Al-Hind*, 2:273–75.
365   "great and respected chief": In Chakravarti, "Nakhudas and Nauvittakas," 53–55.
365   supplier of pepper: Hall, *Maritime Trade*, 225.
365   "moment of incandescence": Johns, "Islam in Southeast Asia," 39.
365   the religion flowed easily: Hall, "Upstream and Downstream Unification," 202–3.
366   emergent state of Ayutthaya: Hall, *Maritime Trade*, 226.
366   new port of Melaka: Taylor, "Early Kingdoms," 175–76; Hall, *Maritime Trade*, 227–28.
366   The commercial character of Melaka: Subrahmanyam, "Of Imarat and Tijarat," 756–57.
366   Melaka maritime code: Winstedt and Josselin De Jong, "Maritime Laws of Malacca," 27; Reid, *Expansion and Crisis*, 110; and Hall, "Economic History of Early Southeast Asia," 190–91.
366   women in trade: Reid, *The Lands Below the Winds*, 146–53, 163–65; Reid, *Expansion and Crisis*, 49, 91–93, 124.
367   Ming Taizu, as he is known, installed: Fairbank, Reischauer, and Craig, *East Asia*, 180–82.
367   "not even a little plank": In Blussé, *Visible Cities*, 15.
367   Neo-Confucian cast: Wang, "'Public' and 'Private' Overseas Trade," 138–39.
367   "To repel them at sea": Lo, "Decline of Early Ming Navy," 149–50, 157–63.
367   Chengzu's motives: Dreyer, *Zheng He*, 33–34.
368   "the great country": Ma Huan, *Overall Survey*, 137.
368   Ma Huan, visited Mecca: Ibid., 173–78; Dreyer, *Zheng He*, 158.
368   "the arrival of the vessels": *Chronicle of the Rasulid Dynasty*, in Serjeant, "Yemeni Mer-chants," 74–75. The *mithqal* was a gold dinar with a standard weight of 4.231 grams. Storax is an aromatic resin used as incense.
369   "had an audience": *Ibn al-Dayba, Bughyat al-mustafid fi tarikh Madinat Zabid*, in Ser-jeant, "Yemeni Merchants," 75.
369   generally pacific nature: Dreyer, *Zheng He*, 28–30.
369   a Chinese renegade: Ibid., 55–60, 66–73, 79–81.

369 Domestically, the empire endured: Lo, "Termination of the Ming Naval Expeditions," 129–31; Lo, "Decline of Early Ming Navy," 163.

370 "deceitful exaggerations": Gu Qiyuan, *Kezuo Zhuiyu*, in Duyvendak, "True Dates," 395–96. See Dreyer, *Zheng He*, 173–75.

370 "from Guangdong [Province] and Zhangzhou": Ma Huan, *Overall Survey*, 93. See Reid, *Expansion and Crisis*, 204–7; Wang, "Merchants Without Empires," 404–5.

371 Sam Poh Kong Temple: Needham et al., *Science and Civilisation*, vol. 4, pt. 3:494.

371 "cowrie shells and *qanbar*": Ibn Battuta, *Travels*, 4:827.

371 "in the mountains": Zhao Rugua, *On the Chinese and Arab Trade*, 133.

372 "ten thousand horses": Wassaf Abdu-llah, *Tazjiyatu-l Amsar Wa Tajriyatu-l Asar* (A Ramble Through the Regions and the Passing of Ages), 33.

372 "the merchants of Hormuz and Kais": Polo, *Travels*, 264.

372 "We had two tarides": Ibn Battuta, *Travels*, 4:820. In place of "tartan" in the original translation, I have used "*taride*." But note Agius, *Classic Ships of Islam*, 342: "I am not sure how accurate Ibn Battuta is in recording the name for this ship-type in the Indian Ocean context. No doubt the *tarida* he witnessed must have looked identical in structure to the Mediterranean one."

372 "they build ships": Wang Ta-yuan, *Tao-I Chih lio* [Wang Dayuan, *Daoyi Zhilue*], in Rockhill, "Notes" (1915), 623–24. See Chakravarti, "Overseas Trade in Horses," 351–52; and Deng, *Maritime Sector*, 112–13.

373 no more than forty horses: Agius, *Classic Ships of Islam*, 340–41. Horses require between 18 and 45 liters of water per day, depending on the conditions. Pryor estimates that a horse being carried in the Mediterranean during the summer would need about 36 liters, or 1.1 metric tons, for 30 days. Pryor and Jeffreys, *Age of the Dromon*, 327–29; air circulation: 330–31.

373 from Oman to the Malabar coast: Sulayman, *Account of China and India*, 14 (p. 38).

373 "endures all the strain": *Three Voyages of Vasco da Gama* (1869), 239–40, in Agius, *Classic Ships of Islam*, 163–64. On the advantages of sewn-plank construction, see chap. 2 and note on "The inherent flexibility," p. 604 above.

373 "carry a much bigger cargo": Polo, *Travels*, 242.

373 Quanzhou wreck: Green, "Song Dynasty Shipwreck"; Keith and Buys, "New Light on Ship Construction;" Li Guo-Qing, "Use of *Chu-Nam*"; and Merwin, "Excavation of a Sung Dynasty Seagoing Vessel."

373 Sinan (Shinan) wreck: Green and Kim, "Shinan and Wando Sites"; Kim and Keith, "14th-Century Cargo."

374 "The Chinese vessels": Ibn Battuta, *Travels*, 4:813. Chinese texts first discuss the flamethrower, or a device for "dispersing fierce incendiary oil," in the Song Dynasty.

374 60 meters: Sleeswyk, "*Liao* and Displacement," 12. The Chinese were apparently not alone in building such monumental ships, and the French traveler Augustin de Beaulieu described how "in 1629 the Acehnese built a grandiose galley about a hundred metres long." See Reid, *Expansion and Crisis*, 42, citing *Mémoires d'un voyage aux Indes orientales, 1619–1622: un marchand normand à Sumatra*. The Chinese use of multiple planking—in effect creating a laminated hull—would have made a significant difference in the longitudinal strength, and therefore length, of the hull.

374 Less contested: Ma Huan, *Overall Survey*, 10; Dreyer, *Zheng He*, 104–5. Zheng He organized but did not accompany the second expedition.

14. The World Encompassed

377   Some of the islands: Abulafia, "Neolithic Meets Medieval," 255, 259.

377   evidence of human habitation: Pliny, *Natural History*, 6.37.202–5 (vol. 2:489–91).

377   Almoravid expedition: Picard, *L'Océan Atlantique Musulman*, 34.

378   ousted by Castilian rivals: Fernández-Armesto, "Medieval Atlantic Exploration," 46–51.

378   prevailing northeast winds: Fernández-Armesto, *Before Columbus*, 153.

378   Isola de Legname: Verlinden, "European Participation," 73; the map is by Nicolo de Pasqualin. According to Cadamosto, the first settlers cleared the land on Madeira by burning the trees. "So great was the first conflagration, that this [governor] Zuancon-zales . . . was forced, with all the men, women, and children, to flee its fury and take refuge in the sea, where they remained, up to their necks in water, and without food or drink, for two days and two nights" (Crone, *Voyages of Cadamosto*, 9).

378   Genoese mariners: Epstein, *Genoa and the Genoese*, 202; Fernández-Armesto, "Spanish Atlantic Voyages and Conquests," 138.

378   Pessagno and his heirs: Verlinden, "European Participation," 71–73.

378   Catalan Atlas: Woodward, "Medieval Mappaemundi," 315. See Fernández-Armesto, *Before Columbus*, 156–57.

379   "As for his skill": Chaucer, *Canterbury Tales*, "Prologue," ll. 401–10 (p. 30).

379   first printed sailing directions: Jonkers, "Sailing Directions," 460.

380   *Lo Compasso da Navigare:* Campbell, "Portolan Charts," 382.

380   northern European instructions: Unger, *Ship in the Medieval Economy*, 175.

380   "An [when] ye come": In Taylor, *Haven-Finding Art*, 135; "2 parts over the sea" means two-thirds of the way.

381   "If it should happen": Jados, *Consulate of the Sea*, §251 (p. 157). See *The Customs of the Sea*, in Twiss, *Black Book*, 3:433–34.

381   "if a ship is lost": *Black Book*, in Twiss, *Black Book*, 1:129. The *Black Book* is believed to have been compiled between the reigns of Edward III (1327–77) and Henry VI (1422–61).

381   dead reckoning: This expression, as written, dates from the seventeenth century; the idea that it comes from "deduced reckoning" is a mid-twentieth-century fiction.

382   "[S]ailors, as they sail over the sea": Neckham, *De Naturis Rerum*, book 2, chap. 98, in C.N.B., "Alexander on the Compass Needle," 64.

382   "When clouds prevent sailors": Vincent of Beauvais, in Taylor, *Haven-Finding Art*, 94.

383   "half winds": Taylor, *Haven-Finding Art*, 100, 111.

383   portolan, or sea chart: Campbell, "Portolan Charts."

383   mariner's astrolabe: Paselk, "Navigational Instruments."

384   A Genoese contract: Friel, "Carrack," 78.

384   "ships"—*naves:* Ibid., 79.

384   caravel: Elbl, "Caravel"; Phillips, "Iberian Ships," 220–28.

384   *qarib:* Agius, *Classic Ships of Islam*, 271–74. Ibn Battuta uses *qarib* as a generic term for fishing and pearling boats in the Persian Gulf.

385   "the Navigator": Russell, *Prince Henry*, 8–9.

385   capture of Ceuta: Ibid., 31–34.

385   exploitation of the Madeira Islands: Ibid., 88–99.

386   Cape Bojador—the Bulging Cape: "A wise pilot will . . . pass Bojador eight leagues

out at sea. . . . Because Cape Bojador is most dangerous, as a reef of rock juts out in the sea more than four or five leagues, several ships have already been lost. This cape is very low and covered with sand . . . in ten fathoms you cannot see the land because it is so low." Duarte Pacheco Pereira, *Esmeralda de situ orbis: (1506–1508)*, in Diffie and Winius, *Foundations*, 69.

386   "Portuguese caravels are coming": In Crone, *Voyages of Cadamosto*, 17–18.

386   the Southern Cross: Cadamosto's reference to six stars probably refers to the four main stars in Crux and two from the constellation Centaur.

387   Cape Verde Islands: Diffie and Winius, *Foundations*, 103–7; Crone, *Voyages of Cadamosto*, xxxvi–xlii. *Distance covered:* Russell, *Prince Henry*, 342.

387   inability to communicate: Ibid., 314.

387   no one considered: Winius, "Enterprise Focused on India," 90–92.

387   These brutal campaigns: Diffie and Winius, *Foundations*, 110, 144–45, 213–14.

388   contemporary legal interpretation: Perruso, "Development of the Doctrine of *Res Communes*," 74–85.

388   "justly and lawfully": *Romanus Pontifex*, in Davenport, *European Treaties*, 23.

388   "equipped or provisioned": Treaty of Alcáçovas, in Davenport, *European Treaties*, 44.

389   circumnavigating Africa: Verlinden, "Big Leap Under Dom João II," 70.

389   "which enters the sea": Barros, *Asia*, dec. 1, book 3, chap. 3, in Diffie and Winius, *Foundations*, 155.

389   "the Guinea Sea": Barros, *Asia*, dec. 1, book 3, chap. 5, in Diffie and Winius, *Foundations*, 164.

390   Domestic problems: Subrahmanyam, *Career and Legend*, 43–57.

390   "that he would sail": Las Casas, *Las Casas on Columbus*, 43. On the direction of Columbus's voyages, see Wey Gómez, *The Tropics of Empire*, 37–45.

390   he failed: Fernández-Armesto, *Columbus*, 192.

390   Columbus served his apprenticeship: Phillips and Phillips, *Worlds of Christopher Columbus*, 87–99; Fernández-Armesto, *Columbus*, 18–19.

391   "the world was buzzing": Las Casas, *Las Casas on Columbus*, 31.

391   northern voyages took him: Fernández-Armesto, *Columbus*, 6, 18.

391   especially its great size: Fernández-Armesto, "Medieval Atlantic Exploration," 65.

391   Shortly before the start: Phillips and Phillips, *Worlds of Christopher Columbus*, 140. The Sargasso Sea is a large area of the Atlantic Ocean bounded by a number of currents but within which there is virtually no current and often no wind. Passage through it is further complicated by the presence of masses of sargassum weed. It lies roughly between 20°–35°N and 30°–70°W.

392   "Men of Cathay": In ibid., 105.

392   "On the island of Flores": Colón, *Life of the Admiral Christopher Columbus*, 24. Cape Verga is on the coast of Africa, 10°N.

393   "the perimeter of the earth": Phillips and Phillips, *Worlds of Christopher Columbus*, 110.

393   excessive compensation: Nader, *Rights of Discovery*, 63–64.

393   normally earned: Phillips and Phillips, *Worlds of Christopher Columbus*, 143.

393   Luis de Santángel: Ibid., 132.

394   "a central figure": Fernández-Armesto, *Amerigo*, 52.

394   the caravels *Niña* and *Pinta*: Experts' conjectures on the linear measurements of Columbus's ships differ widely. The minimum dimensions proposed are: *Niña*, 15m by 5m; *Pinta*, 17m by 5m; and *Santa María*, 18m by 6m. See Elbl, "Caravel"; Pastor, *Ships of Christopher Columbus*; and Phillips, "Iberian Ships."

395   Taino island of Guanahaní: The exact location of Columbus's first landing is based on educated guesswork. Prevailing opinion favors San Salvador; other claimants—all in the Bahamas and within 250 nautical miles of each other—are the Caicos Islands, Semana Cay, and Cat Island. The English called San Salvador Watlings Island until the island's strong claim to an historical pedigree was established.

395   "which I believe": In Phillips and Phillips, *Worlds of Christopher Columbus*, 163.

395   "I am not taking much pains": In ibid., 163.

396   "hearing the news": Barros, *Asia*, dec. 1, book 3, chap. 11, in Diffie and Winius, *Foundations*, 171.

397   a hundred leagues west: *Inter Caetera*, in Davenport, *European Treaties*, 74n18, 76. On the broader implications of dividing the ocean, see Mancke, "Early Modern Expansion." On dates of the bulls, see Linden, "Alexander VI," 3–8.

397   "found or to be found": "The Bull *Dudum Siquidem*," in Davenport, *European Treaties*, 82.

397   stealing gold and women: Phillips and Phillips, *Worlds of Christopher Columbus*, 199; Fernández-Armesto, *Columbus*, 104.

398   "earthly paradise": Columbus, "Letter of Columbus to Their Majesties," in Jane, *Select Documents*, 2:34. The rivers in Genesis 2.11–14 are the Pison (thought to be the Ganga or Indus), Gihon (Nile), Hiddekel (Tigris), and Euphrates.

398   in chains: Fernández-Armesto, *Columbus*, 153.

398   the last two years of his life: Ibid., 177–84.

398   his writings implausibly suggest: Fernández-Armesto, *Amerigo*, 67.

398   Martin Waldseemüller: Ibid., 185–91; Meurer, "Cartography in the German Lands," 1204–7.

399   "named Vasco da Gama": Barros, *Asia*, dec. 1, book 4, chap. 1, in Subrahmanyam, *Career and Legend*, 54.

399   "a youth who": In Subrahmanyam, *Career and Legend*, 93.

399   hired a pilot: This was long believed to be the navigator Ibn Majid, but this has been proved false. See Winius, "Enterprise Focused on India," 115.

400   second-rate offerings: Subrahmanyam, *Career and Legend*, 136, 142.

400   "Lord of the Conquest": In Radulet, "Vasco da Gama," 137.

400   Pedro Álvares Cabral: Subrahmanyam, *Career and Legend*, 174–84; Greenlee, *Voyage of Pedro Alvares Cabral*.

400   Cabral bombarded the city: Winius, "*Estado da India* on the Subcontinent," 193.

401   São Thomé de Meliapur: Winius, "Portugal's Shadow Empire," 248.

401   Francisco Serrão: Barbosa, Magalhães, and Dames, *The Book of Duarte Barbosa*, 200.

401   "Please God the Almighty": Sebastian Alvarez to Dom Manuel, in Stanley, *First Voyage Round the World*, pp. xliv–xlv. Credited with discovering Newfoundland for Portugal, the brothers Gaspar and Miguel Corte-Reals were lost at sea in 1501 and 1502, respectively.

402   "We ate biscuit": Pigafetta, *Magellan's Voyage Around the World*, 1:83–85.

403   "a true Portuguese": Camoens, *Lusiads*, book 10 (p. 246).

404   Portuguese and Spanish experts: Bourne, "Demarcation Line of Pope Alexander VI," 209.

404   "discovery, conquest and colonization": In Schurz, *Manila Galleon*, 21.

404   "to establish a route": In Schurz, *Manila Galleon*, 21.

404   "With this the foundation": Martin de Zuñiga, in Schurz, *Manila Galleon*, 27. See Spate, *Spanish Lake*, 161.

405   agreed to annul the boundaries: Davenport, *European Treaties*, 170–71.

15. The Birth of Global Trade

406   "they crawled like lice": Blussé and Fernández-Armesto, *Shifting Communities and Identity Formation*, 2.

407   "make a royal model map": In Fernández-Armesto, *Amerigo*, 180.

407   Jews and unconverted Muslims: Elliott, *Empires of the Atlantic World*, 51.

408   The New Spain fleet: Phillips, *Six Galleons*, 11–13; Pérez-Mallaína, *Spain's Men of the Sea*, 9–11.

409   "neither house, hut": Hernando de Castro, writing from Santiago de Cuba to his partner in Seville, in Lockhart and Otte, *Letters and People of the Spanish Indies*, 26.

409   four hundred Spanish households: Pérez-Mallaína, *Spain's Men of the Sea*, 13.

409   "These two towns": Juan Cristóbal Calvete des Estrella, in Cook, *Born to Die*, 105–6.

409   Buenos Aires: Rocca, "Buenos Aires," 323–24.

409   Realejo (Corinto, Nicaragua): Radell and Parsons, "Realejo."

410   five or six months: Spate, *Spanish Lake*, 106.

410   "Put all the Guinea countries": In Thomas, *Slave Trade*, 110. "The *peça* [piece] *de Indias* was a prime young male slave; all other slaves of both sexes counted less than a *peça*. This term might, therefore, include two or even three individuals" (Boxer, *Portuguese Seaborne Empire*, 100).

411   fifty thousand more Africans: Thomas, *Slave Trade*, 134; Boxer, *Portuguese Seaborne Empire*, 104.

411   number of ships: Boxer, *Portuguese Seaborne Empire*, 104.

411   diplomacy and aggression: Russell-Wood, *World on the Move*, 15, 21–22.

412   "the more fortresses": In Earle and Villiers, *Albuquerque*, 10.

412   Afonso de Albuquerque: Ibid., 1–3.

413   "I have taken Goa": In ibid., 16, 201. See Albuquerque, *Commentaries*, 3.258; and Diffie and Winius, *Foundations*, 250–51.

413   "And this is the result": Albuquerque, *Commentaries*, 3:260.

413   "often used to say": Ibid., 3:264.

413   "Then I burned the city": In Earle and Villiers, *Albuquerque*, 17.

413   "I am very sure": In ibid., 81.

413   "Whoever is lord of Malacca": Pires, *Suma Oriental*, 2:287.

413   sailed for the Spice Islands: Diffie and Winius, *Foundations*, 296–300.

414   spice cargoes at Alexandria: Lane, "Venetian Shipping," 11.

414   seized Gallipoli: Imber, *Ottoman Empire*, 287–92.

414   "the Sultan gave orders": In Kortepeter, "Ottoman Imperial Policy," 89.

414   "won the key": Sultan Bayezid II, in Kortepeter, "Ottoman Imperial Policy," 92.

415   destroyed an Ottoman fleet: Brummett, *Ottoman Seapower*, 69, 116–17.

415   "Urge the Mamluk sultan": In ibid., 43.

415   "if you desire": Albuquerque, *Commentaries*, 2:111–18, in Brummett, *Ottoman Seapower*, 45.

415   "new charts": In Casale, *Ottoman Age of Exploration*, 25.

415   "freedom for the Muslims of India": In Casale, *Ottoman Age of Exploration*, 68.

416   Sefer Reis: Casale, *Ottoman Age of Exploration*, 100–101, 110–14.

416   "the volume of spices": Da Silva, *Corpo Diplomático Portuguez*, 9:136, in Casale, *Ottoman Age of Exploration*, 115.

416   "in Sind, Cambay, Dabul": Diogo do Couto, *Década*, 8a, in Casale, "Ottoman Administration," 180.

417 spices continued to reach Alexandria: Braudel, *Mediterranean*, 1:550.

417 "When anger is felt": In Casale, "Ottoman Administration," 185–86.

417 different approaches: Casale, *Ottoman Age of Exploration*, 143–45.

417 dig canals: Ibid., 135–37.

417 "His Majesty's Servant Lutfi": Ibid., 123–29.

418 "500 Turks": Ibid., 133.

418 twenty thousand Zimba: Ibid., 174–76.

418 Indian merchants: These were known by a variety of names depending on their religion and place of origin. Hindus included *banias* from Gujarat, Chetties and Kelings (Tamil Nadu), and Oriyas (Orissa); Chulias were Tamil Muslims. See McPherson, *Indian Ocean*, 155; Prakash, "Indian Maritime Merchant, 1500–1800," 436, 440–41.

418 manned by Asians: Boxer, *Portuguese Seaborne Empire*, 57.

418 "without any doubt": Gemelli Careri (1584), in ibid., 205.

418 "some dying there": Linschoten, *Voyage*, 2:230.

418 marry natives: Mathew, *Portuguese Trade with India in the Sixteenth Century*, 215–16.

419 Surat: Subrahmanyam, "Note on the Rise of Surat," 32; Prakash, "Indian Maritime Merchant, 1500–1800," 444, 448, 451; and Chaudhuri, "Surat Revisited," 18.

419 "When they are still": Inspector Hendrik Adriaan van Reede tot Drakenstein to the Dutch factors, Feb. 21, 1687; in Prakash, "Indian Maritime Merchant, 1500–1800," 435.

419 into Mughal coins: Prakash, "Indian Maritime Merchant, 1500–1800," 442.

419 Mocha: Ibid., 444–46.

420 "King Manuel of Portugal": In Earle and Villiers, *Albuquerque*, 79.

420 guns and mercenaries: Glete, *Warfare at Sea*, 72.

420 about 5 percent: Prakash, "Asian Merchants and the Portuguese Trade in Asia," 133. There was a range of about 3.5 to 8 percent depending on the port and whether the tax was levied on exports or imports. See Diffie and Winius, *Foundations*, 321.

420 Nor did possession: Mathew, *Portuguese Trade with India in the Sixteenth Century*, 210.

420 banning all maritime trade: Wills, "Relations with Maritime Europeans," 339–40.

421 *wokou*, "Japanese pirates": So, *Japanese Piracy*, 1. The Japanese word is *wako*.

421 "the Portuguese sailed": Zhu Wan memorial of Feb. 5, 1548, in So, *Japanese Piracy*, 55.

421 clocks and other mechanical devices: Zheng, *China on the Sea*, 141–47.

421 served as middlemen: So, *Japanese Piracy*, 69.

421 harquebus: Brown, "Impact of Firearms on Japanese Warfare," 236–39.

421 three hundred thousand Japanese Christians: Sansom, *History of Japan, 1334–1615*, 372; Massarella, "Jesuits and Japan."

421 Christianity was outlawed: Sansom, *History of Japan, 1615–1867*, 39–45.

422 Japan remained off-limits: Sansom, *History of Japan, 1334–1615*, 176; Elisonas, "Inseparable Trinity," 262–63.

422 Hideyoshi also: Elisonas, "Inseparable Trinity," 265–70.

422 "sea captains and fishermen": In ibid., 264.

422 "On its upper deck": Yi Pun, "Biography of Yi Sun-sin," in Yi Sun-sin, *Imjin Changch'o*, 210.

423 battle of Myeongryang: Elisonas, "Inseparable Trinity," 287.

423 "a fitting end": Ballard, *Influence of the Sea*, 66.

424 reported at Jeddah: Lane, "Mediterranean Spice Trade," 30–31.

424 per capita consumption: Wake, "Changing Pattern," 392–95.

424 Malabar pepper crop: Mathew, *Portuguese Trade with India in the Sixteenth Century*, 213.

424   "responsible for more espionage": Braudel, *Mediterranean*, 1:572.

424   grain ships: Brummett, *Ottoman Seapower*, 135.

424   an elaborate black market: Braudel, *Mediterranean*, 1:591–94; Imber, *Ottoman Empire*, 300.

424   growth of Mediterranean trade: Braudel, *Mediterranean*, 1:616, 622.

425   "capitulations": Inalcik, "Ottoman State," 188–95, 188, 374.

425   protection of the French flag: Faroqhi, *Ottoman Empire and the World Around It*, 60–61, 144–47.

425   large, heavily armed ships: Andrews, *Trade, Plunder and Settlement*, 99.

425   ignoring papal interdicts: Inalcik, "Ottoman State," 370, 374, 380.

425   burden of reprisals: Wood, *History of the Levant Company*, 25–26, 30–31.

425   The Dutch followed: Braudel, *Mediterranean*, 1:599–602; Inalcik, "Ottoman State," 375–76.

426   most easily done at Antwerp: Paviot, "Trade Between Portugal and the Southern Netherlands," 26; Wee, "Structural Changes," 28–29; and Braudel, *Civilization and Capitalism*, 3:144–46.

426   "a heavy yearly expenditure": In Boxer, *Dutch Seaborne Empire*, 6.

426   a majority of ships: Palmer, *The Baltic*, 64; Barbour, "Dutch and English Merchant Shipping," 267.

426   virtually all its naval stores: Barbour, "Dutch and English Merchant Shipping," 272.

427   sixty-four shares: Israel, *Dutch Primacy*, 21. A memorandum of the English General Shipowners Society dated Dec. 11, 1823, explains the rationale for dividing a ship evenly—"upon the binary principle of halving the ship, and proportions under each, down to a sixty-fourth part"—that is, 1, 2, 4, 8, 16, 32, and 64 shares. Lloyd's Register, "Infosheet No. 25: 64 Shares," online at LR.org.

427   *fluit*: Unger, "*Fluit*," 115–23.

427   Antwerp was an early casualty: Wee, "Structural Changes," 30.

427   encroaching on the English and Hanse trade: Israel, *Dutch Primacy*, 46–48.

427   "robbed homewards by Flemings": Purchas, *Hakluytus Posthumus*, 12:50.

427   "the Russian Mesopotamia": Kerner, *Urge to the Sea*, 35.

428   "northwards, north-eastwards": In Willan, *Early History of the Russia Company*, 6.

428   more diverse selection: Israel, *Dutch Primacy*, 44.

428   port at Archangel: Kerner, *Urge to the Sea*, 179.

428   Muscovy turned to the east: Ibid., 41–43.

428   "being famed for attacking ships": *Remezov Chronicle*, 3, in Armstrong, *Yermak's Campaign in Siberia*, 91.

429   via river and portage: Armstrong, *Yermak's Campaign in Siberia*, 18–19; Hellie, *Economy and Material Culture of Russia*, 479–81.

429   "no kind of dues": Charter from Tsar Ivan Vasil'yevich to Grigorey Stroganov, Apr. 4, 1558, in Armstrong, *Yermak's Campaign in Siberia*, 281. See Kerner, *Urge to the Sea*, 73.

429   "a Countrey that hath": Raleigh, *Discoverie of . . . Guiana* (1596), 96.

429   staked competing claims: Simsarian, "The Acquisition of Legal Title to Terra Nullius," 111, 121–28.

430   "For those who used the sea lines": Glete, *Warfare at Sea*, 60.

430   monopolize the use of violence: Rodger, "New Atlantic," 233–36.

431   "very well treated": Antonio Barbarigo, in Capponi, *Victory of the West*, 199.

431   slaves and convicts: Capponi, *Victory of the West*, 196–98; Imber, *Ottoman Empire*, 302–7.

431   a new style of rowing: Capponi, *Victory of the West*, 194–99. *A scaloccio* is of uncertain derivation, possibly related to the Italian *scala*, meaning ladder.

431   access to bases: Domingues, "State of Portuguese Naval Forces," 191–92.

431   Portuguese ship types: Ibid., 195. See Elbl, "Caravel," 97–87; and Phillips, "Galleon," 100–102.

432   "the first ocean-going sailing ship": Domingues, "Portuguese Naval Forces in the Sixteenth Century," 195. See also Elbl, "Caravel," 97–87; Phillips, "Galleon," 100–102.

432   first printed shipbuilding manual: Diego García de Palacio's *Instrucion nauthica, para el buen uso y regimiento de las naos su traça, y govierno conforme à la altura de México* (Nautical instruction, for the good use and management of ships, their design, and conduct in accordance with the latitude of Mexico), published in Mexico City. See Ferreiro, *Ships and Science*, 47.

432   trend toward gigantism: The Danish *Engelen* and *Maria* displaced about 1,500–2,000 tons, the *Grand François* proved too big to sail, and *The Historie and Chronicles of Scotland* describes James IV's *Michael* as "the greatest scheip and maist [most] of strength that ewer saillit Ingland or France" (Macdougall, "'Greatest Scheip That Ewer Saillit'").

432   English naval establishment: Rodger, *Safeguard of the Sea*, 221–37.

432   Sound tolls: Glete, *Warfare at Sea*, 114–15.

433   favor shown the Dutch: Brand, "Habsburg Diplomacy During the Holland-Wend War," 122–23.

433   formation of a Swedish navy: Glete, "Naval Power and Control of the Sea," 220–23.

433   galleass: Capponi, *Victory of the West*, 191–92; Guilmartin, *Gunpowder and Galleys*, 246; and Martin and Parker, *Spanish Armada*, 271–73.

433   excellent gun platform: Rodger, "Guns and Sails," 82–85; Guilmartin, *Gunpowder and Galleys*, 107–9.

434   "crudely": Rodger, "Development of Broadside Gunnery," 306.

434   Scandinavian Seven Years' War: Glete, "Naval Power and Control of the Sea," 217–32; Glete, *Warfare at Sea*, 116–24.

434   one shot per hour: Rodger, *Command of the Ocean*, 17.

435   Curzolari Islands: Capponi, *Victory of the West*, 253–57.

435   "You have shaved": In Parker, "Lepanto," 263. See Capponi, *Victory of the West*, 296–313; and Lane, *Venice*, 374.

436   battle off the island of São Miguel: Glete, *Warfare at Sea*, 155–56; Padfield, *Tide of Empires*, 129–30. The battle is also called also Punta Delgada and, mistakenly, Terceira.

437   "convenient and fit harbor": Drake, *World Encompassed*, 64.

437   "ordered the ship itself": Letter from Bernardino de Mendoza, Spanish ambassador at London, to Philip II, Jan. 9, 1581, in Sugden, *Sir Francis Drake*, 150.

437   "piratically taken": In Sugden, *Sir Francis Drake*, 145.

438   this formidable assemblage: Rodger, *Safeguard of the Sea*, 259, 269.

438   "But unless God helps us": Anonymous officer to a papal diplomat, in ibid., 259.

439   "irretrievable miscarriage": Corbett, *Successors of Drake*, vi; Thompson, *War and Government*, 185–97.

16. State and Sea in the Age of European Expansion

440   "ledger and sword": This is the title of Beckles Willson's two-volume *Ledger and Sword; or, The Honorable Company of Merchants of England Trading to the East Indies (1599–1874)* (London: Longmans, Green, 1903).

440   merchant ships captured: Davis, *Rise of the English Shipping Industry*, 51.

441   Philip III banned: Israel, *Dutch Primacy*, 56–73.

441   routine destruction of logbooks: This may be one reason that no indigenous maps of Southeast Asia have survived, although their existence is known from accounts by European travelers and geographers, including Ludovico de Varthema, a Bolognese merchant who reached Southeast Asia shortly before the arrival of the Portuguese, and the Venetian diplomat Giovanni Ramusio, as well as from a letter by Afonso de Albuquerque to Manuel. See Gelpke, "Afonso de Albuquerque's Map," 76–77.

442   "Goa, and the Indies": Linschoten, *Voyage*, 1:42.

442   sixty-five ships: Gaastra, *Dutch East India Company*, 17.

442   commercial treaties: Parry, *Establishment of the European Hegemony*, 88.

442   "established . . . solely": In Steensgaard, *Asian Trade Revolution*, 132. Earlier companies may have sought to trade in peace, but they did not sail unarmed. The states of Holland and Zeeland had furnished ships' guns, small arms, and other weaponry gratis. See Israel, *Dutch Primacy*, 67.

442   "The great East India Company": In Steensgaard, *Asian Trade Revolution*, 128n41.

443   "a great town": In Blussé, "Brief Encounter at Macao," 651–52.

444   capture of the *Santa Catarina*: Ittersum, "Hugo Grotius in Context," 518.

444   "it is lawful": Grotius, *The Free Sea*, chap. 1 (p. 10). Grotius refined his defense of Van Heemskerck in *De Jure Belli ac Pacis* (On the Law of War and Peace, 1625).

446   "known continents": In Knecht, *Renaissance Warrior and Patron*, 375.

446   "that he did not send": Cardinal of Toledo to the Emperor, Jan. 27, 1541, in Biggar, *Collection of Documents*, 190.

446   "the sea & trade": Hakluyt, "Whither an Englishman May Trade into the West Indies with Certain Answers to the Popes Bull," in Armitage, *Ideological Origins of the British Empire*, 108. Hakluyt's chief work is *The Principal Navigations, Voiages, Traffiqves and Discoueries of the English Nation* (1598–1600). Following his death, Samuel Purchas enlarged upon this influential work with publication of *Haklvytvs posthumus; or, Pvrchas his Pilgrimes . . .* (1625). Hakluyt's last publication was an English translation of Grotius's *Mare Liberum*.

446   *Of the Dominion, or, Ownership of the Sea*: Armitage, *Ideological Origins of the British Empire*, 108–9; Berkowitz, *John Selden's Formative Years*, 52.

446   "Customs of so many Nations": Selden, *Of the Dominion*, 44, in Thornton, "John Selden's Response," 112.

447   "sea-territory of the British Empire": Selden, *Of the Dominion*, 459, in Thornton, "John Selden's Response," 121–22.

447   preserve their own monopoly: Knaap and Sutherland, *Monsoon Traders*, 20–22.

447   a fixed share: Marshall, "English in Asia," 271.

447   Spanish colony at Manila: Israel, *Dutch Primacy*, 172–73.

447   Batavia was a city: Blussé, *Visible Cities*, 37–40.

448   "The Chinese are the only bees": In Andrade, "Rise and Fall of Dutch Taiwan," 431, 441; Ts'ao, "Taiwan as an Entrepot," 96–100; Blussé, "Brief Encounter at Macao," 663; and Reed, "Colonial Origins of Manila and Batavia."

448   Zheng Chenggong: Struve, "Southern Ming," 666–67, 710–25; Wills, "Maritime China," 215, 226–28.

449   the Manchus ordered: Antony, *Like Froth Floating on the Sea*, 35–36.

449   lifted the prohibition: Ts'ao, "Taiwan as an Entrepot," 103.

449   government-issued vermilion seals: Blussé, *Visible Cities*, 20–21.

449   "four gates": Tsuruta, "Establishment and Characteristics," 30–31; Shapinsky, "Polyvocal Portolans," 19.

449   The Dutch hoped to trade: Blussé, "Divesting a Myth," 396.

450   "Company officials": F. Valentijn, *Van Oud en Nieuw Oost-Indiën* (Dordrecht, 1724–26), vol. 5b, p. 165, in Blussé, *Visible Cities*, 21.

450   tear down their warehouse: Blussé, *Visible Cities*, 22.

450   Japanese silver: Arasaratnam, *Maritime India*, 79.

450   East India Company alone shipped: Marshall, "English in Asia," 269.

451   "Bring us textiles": Van Heemskerck to the Directors of the United Amsterdam Company, Aug. 27, 1603, in Ittersum, "Hugo Grotius in Context," 534.

451   Gujarati merchants: Arasaratnam, *Maritime India*, 58.

451   corridors of political power: Steensgaard, *Asian Trade Revolution*, 120.

451   low-value, high-volume goods: Marshall, "English in Asia," 274–75.

452   negotiating with the English and Dutch: Arasaratnam, *Maritime India*, 61–64; Furber, *Rival Empires of Trade*, 40.

452   deeply invested: Arasaratnam, *Maritime India*, 76.

452   building merchant ships: Barendse, "Shipbuilding in Seventeenth-Century Western India," 179; Qaisar, "Shipbuilding in the Mughal Empire."

452   Shah Jahan: Prakash, "Indian Maritime Merchant, 1500–1800," 446.

452   rupees: Haider, "Structure and Movement of Wages," 305.

452   Bengal merchants preferred: Arasaratnam, "India and the Indian Ocean," 121.

453   Siddis of Janjira: Ali, *African Dispersal in the Deccan*, 157–92.

453   a coherent naval strategy: Kulkarni, "Marathas and the Sea," 210; this is known from Ramchandra Pant Amatya's *Adnyapatra* (royal edict), written before 1717, but after Shivaji's death.

453   the port was riven: Das Gupta, "Maritime Merchant of India," 99.

453   Mulla Abdul Ghafur: Ibid., 94–100.

453   Henry Avery: Ritchie, *Captain Kidd*, 85–89; Das Gupta, *Indian Merchants*, 98–99.

454   not all English were pirates: Furber, *Rival Empires of Trade*, 40.

454   The Omani reconquest: Ames, "Straits of Hurmuz Fleets"; Bathurst, "Maritime Trade and Imamate Government," 96–103.

455   "by which happy result": Ioannes De Laet, *Historie ofte Iaerlijke Verhael van de verrichtinghen der Geoctroyeerde West-Indische Compagnie* (History, or the True Story of the Operations of the Honorable West India Company), 2:4–5, in Goslinga, *Dutch in the Caribbean*, 168.

455   "for his lack of care": In Phillips, *Six Galleons*, 5.

455   Heyn predeceased him: Stradling, *Armada of Flanders*, 78–79.

455   sugar was more valuable: Padfield, *Tide of Empires*, 162.

455   Curaçao: Klooster, *Illicit Riches*, 41, 64, 73–74.

456   Port Royal became: Lane, *Pillaging the Empire*, 103–9, 169.

456   "No private offense": Treaty of Madrid, §14, in Davenport, *European Treaties*, 2:195–96.

456   Treaty of Whitehall: Lane, *Pillaging the Empire*, 125–27; Davenport, *European Treaties*, 2:321–22, 363.

457   "to seeke out": In Morison, *European Discovery of America*, 159.

457   "that the sea is covered": Raimondo di Soncino, Dec. 18, 1497, in Hoffman, *Cabot to Cartier*, 11.

457   Dried, salted, or pickled fish: Fagan, *Fish on Friday*, 54–55. See Unger, "Netherlands Herring Fishery," "Dutch Herring, Technology, and International Trade"; and Kowaleski, "Commercialization of the Sea Fisheries."

458   fishing ships at St. John's: Morison, *European Discovery of America*, 235.

458   Port Royal (now Annapolis Royal): Morison, *Samuel de Champlain*, 71–77.

458   Company of New France: Successor to the Compagnie des Marchands and Compagnie de Montmorency, the Company of New France was formally known as the Compagnie des Cent-Associés (Company of One Hundred Associates).

458   "the land of Louisiana": In Murat, *Colbert*, 240. La Salle named the Illinois River for Colbert's son and successor as minister of the marine, Seignelay.

459   A northbound flatboat: Surrey, *Commerce of Louisiana*, 58–74.

459   "Also we might inhabite": Gilbert, *Discourse of a Discouerie for a New Passage to Cataia*, in Quinn, *Voyages and Colonising Enterprises*, 1:160–61.

459   "no mynes discouered": "Davies Journal of the 1607 North Virginia Voyage," in Quinn and Quinn, *English New England Voyages*, 415.

459   indent themselves: Bergquist, "Paradox of American Development," 158–59.

460   The first slaves were landed: Heywood and Thornton, *Central Africans, Atlantic Creoles*, 27–28.

460   "To think of discovering": In Johnson, *Charting the Sea of Darkness*, 87.

460   "And of all the foure parts": Smith, *Description of New England*, 6.

460   Tisquantum (or Squanto): Humins, "Squanto and Massasoit," 58–59.

461   Great Migration: Horn and Morgan, "Settlers and Slaves," 24; Games, "Migration," 38–42.

461   astonishing safety record: Cressy, "Vast and Furious Ocean," 516. The one loss Cressy notes, the *Angel Gabriel*, was lost in a hurricane in 1635 while at anchor off Pemaquid, Maine, after completing her passage. See Riess, *Angel Gabriel*, 44–46.

461   "set our people on work": Winthrop, *Journal of John Winthrop*, June–August 1641, 353.

461   cost of transporting: Rodger, *Command of the Ocean*, 192.

461   "containing important inducements": M. Edward Hayes, "A Treatise, conteining important inducements for the planting in these parts, and finding a passage that way to the South sea and China" (1602), in Quinn and Quinn, *English New England Voyages*, 176.

462   "There is also the very good news": Pepys, *Diary*, Dec. 3, 1666 (vol. 7:397). On comparison with oil, see Albion, *Forests and Sea Power*, xi, 164. Albion was writing in 1926, when oil consumption was a fraction of what it is nine decades later.

462   from the Carolinas: Malone, *Pine Trees and Politics*, 24, 33–36.

462   place of refuge: Lane, *Pillaging the Empire*, 168.

462   new merchant centers: Morison et al., *Concise History of the American Republic*, 34–35.

463   Count-Duke Olivares: Stradling, *Armada of Flanders*, 60–62.

463   frigates stationed at Dunkirk: Glete, *Navies and Nations*, 1:61; Thrush, "In Pursuit of the Frigate."

463   "from now on": In Stradling, *Armada of Flanders*, 54; also 46–47, 58, 75.

464   Admiralty of the North: Almirantazgo de los Países Septentrionales, in Stradling, *Armada of Flanders*, 42; James, "Development of French Naval Policy," 386.

464   sweeping protectionist measures: O'Connell, *Richelieu*, 145.

464   La Rochelle fell: Burckhardt, *Richelieu*, 1:244–79.

464   France had no national navy: Ibid., 2:41; James, "Development of French Naval Policy," 387–88.

464   "true citadels of the sea": Burckhardt, *Richelieu*, 2:29–30.

464   battle of Guetaría: Stradling, *Armada of Flanders*, 104–8; Glete, *Warfare at Sea*, 181–82.

465   "the ignominy of seeing our king": Burckhardt, *Richelieu*, 2:32.

465   "Such a rotten, miserable fleet": J. Ashburnham to E. Nicholas, Oct. 26, 1627, in Rodger, *Safeguard of the Sea*, 363.

466 "ship money": Sharpe, *Personal Rule of Charles I*, 554–55; Cust, *Charles I*, 191; and Rodger, *Safeguard of the Sea*, 381–82.
466 "his princely resolution": Pett, *Autobiography*, 156.
466 "the art or wit of man": In Heywood, *His Majesty's Royal Ship*, xiv.
466 "Decorements whiche beautify": Ibid., xxx.
467 battle of the Downs: Rodger, *Safeguard of the Sea*, 413.
467 the organization of which: Bruijn, *Dutch Navy*, 5–11, 145–46.
467 "only in such [ships]": In Aughterson, *The English Renaissance*, 554.
468 "In the *Prow*": Evelyn, *Diary*, Apr. 1, 1655 (vol. 3:149–50).
468 line of battle: Rodger, *Command of the Ocean*, 17; *Anglo-Dutch War*: ibid., 14–18.
468 "the greatest [admiral]": In Rodger, *Command of the Ocean*, 85.
469 "the Dutch did take her": Pepys, *Diary*, June 22, 1667 (vol. 8:283).
469 "A very good town": Charles to Henriette Anne, in Fraser, *Royal Charles*, 232.
469 "In this city of Amsterdam": In Hart, "Intercity Rivalries," 196.
469 the French doubled customs tariffs: Murat, *Colbert*, 148.
469 program of internal improvements: Ibid., 159–60.
470 subsidized Charles II: Ibid., 208.
470 merchants of neutral England: Rodger, *Command of the Ocean*, 86.
470 "the final administrative recognition": Ibid., 220.
470 ship of the line: Lavery, *The Ship of the Line*.
471 guns were fired: Rodger, *Command of the Ocean*, 74, 540.
471 *Fighting Instructions*: Benjamin and Tifrea, "Learning by Dying," 987.

17. Northern Europe Ascendant

474 an apparently straightforward mission: Walter, *Voyage Round the World*.
474 "soldiers, who from their age": Anson, *Voyage Round the World*, 23.
474 "muster no more than two": Ibid., 102.
474 Despite the loss: Williams, *Prize of All the Oceans*, 202.
474 entitled to a share: Ibid., 217–18. For a fuller account of the prize system, see Petrie, *Prize Game*.
475 "It is an observation": Lind, *An Essay on the Most Effectual Means of Preserving the Health of Seamen* (1779), in Rodger, *Command of the Ocean*, 281; Baugh, *The Global Seven Years War*, 429–31.
475 Quiberon Bay: Baugh, *The Global Seven Years War*, 436–43.
475 ship fever: Duffy, "Passage to the Colonies," 23.
476 forced to subsist: Lloyd, "Victualling of the Fleet," 10.
476 "I began to allow": In Strachan, *East India Company Journals*, Apr. 7, 1614 (p. 69).
476 James Lind: Rodger, *Command of the Ocean*, 307–8; Bartholomew, "James Lind and Scurvy"; and Duffy, "Passage to the Colonies," 31, 38.
476 "The water and the wine": In Boxer, *Dutch Seaborne Empire*, 74.
476 normally needs: Pérez-Mallaína, *Spain's Men of the Sea*, 144.
476 Parliament awarded: Gratzer, *Terrors of the Table*, 24.
477 one gallon of beer per day: Lloyd, "Victualling of the Fleet," 10.
477 "we dranke the last Beere": In Sail Training Assoc. of Western Australia, *Duyfken 1606*.
477 "every day mixed": Pack, *Nelson's Blood*, 22–23.
478 "Slavery itself": Fox to the House of Commons, June 10, 1806, in Thomas, *Slave Trade*, 493.

478 fifteen autobiographical accounts: Handler, "Survivors of the Middle Passage," 25–30.

478 Olauduh Equiano: Ibid., 50–51n10. Equiano was employed for several years by Charles Irving and helped in his experiments with distilling water.

478 "During the voyages I made": Falconbridge, *Account of the Slave Trade*, 24–25.

480 space allotted to each slave: Garland and Klein, "Allotment of Space," 240–41.

480 opposition from traders: LoGerfo, "Sir William Dolben," 450.

480 "to harden the feelings": Falconbridge, *Account of the Slave Trade*, 46.

481 "The ship voyage": Christopher Sauer, letter of Aug. 1, 1725, in Wokeck, *Trade in Strangers*, 132.

481 "the sad and miserable condition": Mittelberger, *Journey to Pennsylvania*, 12.

481 2.7 million were Europeans: Horn and Morgan, "Settlers and Slaves," 20.

483 "better acquainted": Narborough's journal, in Rodger, *Command of the Ocean*, 82.

483 inadequate for a prolonged naval war: Pilgrim, "Colbert-Seignelay Naval Reforms."

483 "inferior sailors": Falconer, *Universal Dictionary of the Marine*, s.v. "ordinary."

483 "The fighting part": Russell, National Maritime Museum mss., SOU/13, in Aubrey, *Defeat of James Stuart's Armada*, 84.

483 naval bases, shipyards, and port facilities: Glete, *Navies and Nations*, 187–88; Murat, *Colbert*, 237; Rodger, *Command of the Ocean*, 105–6; and Kennedy, *Rise and Fall of British Naval Mastery*, 65–66.

483 Bank of England: Brewer, *Sinews of Power*, 42, 133 ("Dutch finance"); Padfield, *Maritime Supremacy*, 194–96; and Rodger, *Command of the Ocean*, 198–99.

484 most powerful navy in the world: Rodger, *Command of the Ocean*, 234; Harding, *The Emergence of Britain's Naval Supremacy*, 39–46.

485 capture of Portobelo: Harding, *The Emergence of Britain's Naval Supremacy*, 68.

485 hard-won lessons: Ibid., 341–48.

485 fought in the Indian Ocean: Baugh, *The Global Seven Years War*, 462–83; *Louisbourg*: 338–48; *all Canada*: 404–20, 483–92.

485 "If we lose our sugar islands": George III to Sandwich, Sept. 13, 1779, in Padfield, *Maritime Supremacy*, 250.

485 merchants and cod fishermen: Magra, *The Fisherman's Cause*, 130–32.

486 American shipwrights launched: Davis, *Rise of the English Shipping Industry*, 67–68.

486 enumerated goods: Nester, *Great Frontier War*, 76.

486 "I tell the Noble Lord": William Dowdeswell, in Labaree, *Boston Tea Party*, 71.

487 Intolerable (or Coercive) Acts: Leamon, *Revolution Downeast*, 50–51.

487 "carrying on any Fishery": In Magra, *The Fisherman's Cause*, 149.

487 expedition to Penobscot Bay: Leamon, *Revolution Downeast*, 107–19.

487 British privateers: Klooster, *Illicit Riches*, 96.

487 driving down Lake Champlain: Hagan, *This People's Navy*, 6–9.

488 the rebels might win: Dull, *The French Navy and American Independence*, 89–91.

488 battle of the Virginia Capes: Ibid., 239–49.

488 Cape Colony: The VOC had established a provisioning station for their ships at Cape Town, South Africa, at the start of the First Anglo-Dutch War in the seventeenth century. The initial inhabitants were VOC employees, whose numbers were augmented by Malagasy slaves and Dutch and French Huguenot settlers. Thompson, *History of South Africa*, 31–45.

488 "The good Dutchmen": In Mahan, *Influence of Sea Power*, 465.

489 The French Revolutionary and Napoleonic Wars: Rodger, *Command of the Ocean*, 427–30, 436.

489 "Exceeding hard Gales": Knight, *The Pursuit of Victory*, 272.

489 "Was I to die": Nelson to Earl Spencer, first lord of the admiralty, in Coleman, *The Nelson Touch*, 154.

489 Aboukir: Knight, *The Pursuit of Victory*, 288–98; Coleman, *The Nelson Touch*, 156–60.

490 attack on Copenhagen: Knight, *The Pursuit of Victory*, 371–84; Coleman, *The Nelson Touch*, 251–58. The story that the one-eyed Nelson ignored Parker's signal with the remark "I have a right to be blind sometimes" is apocryphal.

490 to keep the British from massing: Knight, *The Pursuit of Victory*, 480.

490 signal flags: Schom, *Trafalgar*, 311; Knight, *The Pursuit of Victory*, 511.

490 "The whole impression": In Schom, *Trafalgar*, 292; Knight, *The Pursuit of Victory*, 505–8.

491 "England expects": In Knight, *The Pursuit of Victory*, 514; Schom, *Trafalgar*, 320.

491 combined casualties: Rodger, *Wooden World*, 56–59; Knight, *The Pursuit of Victory*, 521.

491 "for failing to do": In Rodger, *Command of the Ocean*, 267; Baugh, *The Global Seven Years War*, 229–35. Byng's politically motivated execution made an inviting target for Voltaire, who in *Candide* explains that in England, "it is a good thing to kill an admiral from time to time to encourage the others."

492 stronghold of Azov: Phillips, *Founding of Russia's Navy*, 37–44.

492 yearlong tour: Ryan, "Peter the Great and English Maritime Technology," 138–39; Hughes, *Peter the Great*, 44–48, 52, 65–66, 75.

492 Naval Statute of 1720: Hughes, *Peter the Great*, 141.

492 where Peter founded St. Petersburg: Israel, *Dutch Primacy*, 43.

492 battle of Hangö: Phillips, *Founding of Russia's Navy*, 123–24, 200; Woodward, *Russians at Sea*, 22–25. The galleys, called *skampavei*, were eighteen meters long.

492 "This savage, cruel, and barbarous people": Count Gyllenborg, in Warner, "British Merchants and Russian Men of War," 109.

492 "seducing artificers": An Act to Prevent the Inconveniencies Arising from Seducing Artificers in the Manufactures of Great Britain into Foreign Parts, 1718, 5 Geo. 1, c. 26.

492 Treaty of Nystad: Hughes, *Peter the Great*, 158–59.

493 Bay of Chesma: Madariaga, *Catherine the Great*, 45.

493 commerce was disrupted: King, *Black Sea*, 156.

493 Treaty of Adrianople (Edirne): Esmer, "Straits," 292; King, *Black Sea*, 162.

494 *diwan* (treasurer): Ray, "Indian Society and British Supremacy," 511.

494 imports to Europe: Habib, "Eighteenth Century in Indian Economic History," 227.

494 exports from Bengal: Prakash, "Trade and Politics," 228, 248.

494 Chinese tea: Zhuang, "Impact of the International Tea Trade," 196–97.

494 between 79 and 127 percent: Keay, *Honourable Company*, 391.

495 Canton system: Hsü, *Rise of Modern China*, 150–54.

496 "merchants without empire": Wang, "Merchants Without Empire."

496 "the commerce between China and Borneo": Forrest, *Voyage to New Guinea*, 381.

496 a thousand seagoing junks: Marshall, "Introduction," 25.

496 Chinese settlers: Blussé, "Chinese Century," 113–29.

496 Stamford Raffles: Lee, *Singapore*, 5–8.

497 pepper from Sumatra: Morison, *Maritime History of Massachusetts*, 91.

497 the Dutch hired ships: Blussé, *Visible Cities*, 92.

498 Semyon Dezhnev: Haycox, *Alaska*, 44–46; Frost, *Bering*, 50–51.

498 fur rush: Miller, "Maritime Fur Trade Rivalry," 395, 401. The monopoly was for the region north of 55°N.

498   "to discover the partly known": In Paine, *Ships of the World*, s.v. *Heemskerck*, citing
      J. E. Heeres, ed., *Abel Janszoon Tasman's Journal* (Amsterdam, 1898) and Andrew
      Sharp, *The Voyages of Abel Janszoon Tasman* (Oxford: Clarendon Press, 1968).

499   "the advancement": Instructions of June 17, 1764, in Hawkesworth, *An Account of the
      Voyages*, 1:7.

499   "Land or Islands": *Byron's Journal of His Circumnavigation*, lix, note 1.

499   "examine the soils": *Memoir from the King to Serve as Instructions to Mr de Bougainville*,
      in Bougainville, *Pacific Journal*, xlv.

499   "the state of natural man": Philibert Commerson, "Post-Scriptum sur l'île de la
      Nouvelle-Cythère," in Bougainville, *Pacific Journal*, lvi.

499   "noble savage": Smith, *European Vision and the South Pacific*, 41–51.

499   "the improvement of astronomy": Feb. 15, 1768, Memorials of the Royal Society, in
      Cook, *Journals*, vol. 1, *Voyage of the Endeavour*, 604.

500   "No people ever went to sea": John Ellis to Linnaeus, in O'Brian, *Joseph Banks*, 65;
      specimens: 169–71.

500   "the great quantity of New Plants": Cook, May 6, 1770, *Journals*, vol. 1, *Voyage of the
      Endeavour*, 247.

500   heavily silted river: Blussé, *Visible Cities*, 43.

500   Cook's strict regimen: Beaglehole, *Exploration of the Pacific*, 284.

501   European interest in the Pacific Northwest: Olsen, *Through Spanish Eyes*, 6–10;
      Miller, "Maritime Fur Trade Rivalry," 396–97.

501   "In justice to Behrings Memory": Sept. 4, 1778, *Voyage of the Resolution and Discovery*,
      433.

501   "an asylum": Matra, "A Proposal for Establishing a Settlement in New South Wales,"
      in Hoffman, "Australia's Debt," 151.

501   well positioned to threaten: Frost, "James Mario Matra."

502   "We got into Port Jackson": Phillip to Lord Sydney, May 15, 1788, in Hoffman,
      "Australia's Debt," 156.

503   thirty-five or forty days: Walton, "Sources of Productivity Change," 73. There were
      exceptions. In his pursuit of Villeneuve, Nelson's fleet of thirteen ships maintained
      an average speed of almost six knots over fifteen days; Knight, *The Pursuit of Victory*,
      489.

503   Mathematicians, physicists, and others: Ferreiro, *Ships and Science*, 96, 282.

503   "Virginia-built": Chapelle, *History of American Sailing Ships*, 222.

503   extra crew: Walton, "Sources of Productivity Change," 69–70; *Jamaica ships:* 71–72;
      turnaround times: 76–77; *insurance:* 71. See Shepherd and Walton, *Shipping, Maritime
      Trade and the Economic Development*, 49–72.

504   "for such Person": Taylor, *Haven-Finding Art*, 253.

504   financial incentive: Turner, "In the Wake of the Act," 122.

504   lunar distances: Howse, "The Lunar-Distance Method of Measuring Longitude,"
      150–61.

505   John Harrison: King, "'John Harrison, Clockmaker at Barrow,'" 168–87; Andrewes,
      "Even Newton Could Be Wrong," 190–233.

505   he completed work on H4: Randall, "The Timekeeper That Won the Longitude
      Prize," 236–54.

505   "Mr Kendal's Watch": Cook to the Admiralty Secretary, Mar. 22, 1775, in *Journals*,
      vol. 2, *Voyage of the Resolution and Adventure*, 50.

505   Gerard Mercator: Koeman et al., "Commercial Cartography and Map Production in
      the Low Countries," 1323–28.

505 Edward Wright: Tyacke, "Chartmaking in England," 1743–45.

505 Lucas Janszoon Waghenaer: Schilder and van Egmond, "Maritime Cartography in the Low Countries," 1393–97.

506 Willem Blaeu: Ibid., 1398–1401, 1422–26.

506 Alexander Dalrymple: Ritchie, *Admiralty Chart*, 18–19.

506 Joseph F. W. Des Barres: Morgan, "Des Barres."

18. "Annihilation of Space and Time"

509 "attempt to facilitate": Fitch to Congress, Aug. 19, 1785, in Flexner, *Steamboats Come True*, 79.

509 "water craft, which might be urged": New Jersey state legislature, Mar. 18, 1786, in Flexner, *Steamboats Come True*, 94.

510 "The Mississippi, as I before wrote you": Fulton to Joel Barlow, Apr. 19, 1812, in Sutcliffe, *Robert Fulton and the* Clermont, 221.

510 sternwheels were not widely adopted: Hunter, *Steamboats on the Western Rivers*, 167–75.

510 in 1840 New Orleans: Carter, *Lower Mississippi*, 221.

510 average time: Mak and Walton, "Steamboats and the Great Productivity Surge," 630; Hunter, *Steamboats on the Western Rivers*, 22–25.

510 "great raft": Hunter, *Steamboats on the Western Rivers*, 196–99.

511 "At this point commences": Morris to John Parish, Dec. 20, 1800, in Rubin, "Innovating Public Improvement," 26–27.

511 The time needed: Bernstein, *Wedding of the Waters*, 327.

511 New York became the primary port: Page, "Transportation of Immigrants," 736.

511 Canada embarked: Desloges and Gelly, *Lachine Canal*, 21.

511 floating population: MacLeod, "Social Policy and the 'Floating Population,'" 105.

512 Johann Gottfried Tulla's: Blackbourn, *Conquest of Nature*, 97–119.

512 "directed into a single bed": In ibid., 91.

512 "It is our intention": Jeremiah Thompson et al. to Cropper Benson & Co., and Rathbone Hodgson & Co., in Albion, "Planning the Black Ball Line," 107.

512 averaged about twenty-five days: Butler, *Sailing on Friday*, 36.

513 "Arrival of the *Sirius* Steamer": *New York Herald*, in Penrose, *1838 April Fourth 1938*, 18.

513 *Sirius* and *Great Western*: Sheppard, "*Sirius*"; Griffiths, *Brunel's* Great Western, 32–44.

513 government subsidies: Bacon, *Manual of Ship Subsidies*, 17–18.

514 "Our cabin is something": Dickens to Frederick Dickens, Jan. 3, 1842, in *Letters*, 3:7.

514 "I suggest cost not be considered": James Ashton Bayard (Delaware), in Butler, *Atlantic Kingdom*, 101.

514 congressional subsidy: Bacon, *Manual of Ship Subsidies*, 75–77.

514 "under the inspection": In Morison, "*Old Bruin*," 256.

515 "extravagantly showy": Ibid., 259.

515 "an air of almost Oriental magnificence": Abbott, "Ocean Life," 62.

515 "*to take a whole state-room*": In Brinnin, *The Sway of the Grand Saloon*, 172.

515 The loss of the *Arctic*: *New York Daily Times*, Oct. 13, 1854, p. 4.

515 "Ocean tragedies": In Brown, *Women and Children Last*, 10.

516 "One in view of their conduct": *New York Daily Times*, Oct. 13, 1854, 4.

516　"Of the flower": Whitman, *Leaves of Grass*, 345.

516　"If [the Collins Line] had spent": William T. S. Barry (Mississippi), in Brown, *Women and Children Last*, 181.

516　"the well known practice": Franklin to Julien-David Le Roy, "Maritime Observations," August 1785, in *Writings*, 381. See Chaplin, *First Scientific American*, 317–18.

517　"Life-boats and life-preservers": Maury, *Steam-Lanes Across the Atlantic*, 5.

517　Maury recommended: Ibid., 6.

517　"to decide the momentous question": *New York Herald*, editorial, Oct. 26, 1889, in Williams, *Matthew Fontaine Maury*, 267.

518　Sloo Line: Bacon, *Manual of Ship Subsidies*, 71–72.

518　more than 750 sailing ships: Schultz, *Forty-niners 'Round the Horn*, 264n3.

518　more than thirteen thousand miles: Ibid., 10.

520　"the *Gulph Stream*": Chaplin, *First Scientific American*, 196–200, 289–91, 304–5, 310–11.

520　transmissibility of reliable information: Huler, *Defining the Wind*, 109–10.

520　"the very useful work": Dalrymple (1779), in ibid., 104–5.

520　"to generalize the experience": Maury to John Quincy Adams, Nov. 14, 1847, in Williams, *Matthew Fontaine Maury*, 178.

520　ten million dollars per year: Williams, *Matthew Fontaine Maury*, 190–92.

520　"the search for speed": The phrase is from Howard I. Chapelle, *The Search for Speed Under Sail, 1700–1855* (New York: Norton, 1967).

521　"This magnificent ship": Duncan McLean, "The New Clipper Ship *Stag Hound*, of Boston," *Boston Atlas*, Dec. 21, 1850, in Howe and Matthews, *American Clipper Ships*, 2:619.

521　medium clipper or Down Easter: Paine, *Down East*, 76–78.

522　"the most unsightly": Graham, "Ascendancy of the Sailing Ship, 1850–1855," 78.

522　twice the capacity: Ibid., 81.

522　economic advantages: Kaukiainen, "Aspects of Competition Between Steam and Sail," 114–15.

523　about three hundred junks: Viraphol, *Tribute and Profit*, 180.

523　10 percent of the British government's total revenue: Keay, *Honourable Company*, 452.

523　laws proscribing opium: Hsü, *Rise of Modern China*, 168–73.

523　Treaty of Nanking: Ibid., 184–91.

524　westerners next looked to Japan: Sansom, *History of Japan, 1615–1867*, 232.

524　Vasilii M. Golovnin: Golovnin, *Memoirs of a Captivity in Japan*.

524　Treaty of Kanagawa: Lee, *New History of Korea*, 281–82, 288–89.

524　"Knowledge shall be sought": In Tsunoda et al., *Sources of Japanese Tradition*, 2:137.

524　Peninisular and Orient Line established: Fox, *Britain and Japan*, 317.

524　The western expatriate community: Barr, *Deer Cry Pavilion*, 101; Murphey, *Outsiders*, 107.

525　Suez Canal: Schonfield, *Suez Canal in Peace and War*, 41.

525　"cut by French energy": In Fletcher, "Suez Canal and World Shipping," 564.

525　"all for the advantage": Herodotus, *Histories*, 2.159 (p. 145).

525　"the Suez Maritime Canal": Convention Respecting the Free Navigation of the Suez Maritime Canal, Article 1.

526　"'Steamers may occupy'": In Jones, *Pioneer Shipowners*, 119. See Smith et al., "Imitations of God's Own Works," 405.

526　reduced coal consumption: Smith et al., "Imitations of God's Own Works," 406, 415.

526 without the efficiencies: Fletcher, "Suez Canal and World Shipping," 560.

527 "Increased speed": In Paine, *Ships of the World*, s.v. *Turbinia*, citing Alex Richardson, *The Evolution of the Parsons Steam Turbine* (London: Engineering, 1911).

527 submarine cables: Clarke, *Voice Across the Sea*, 69–89, 96.

527 *Great Eastern:* Dugan, *Great Iron Ship*.

528 British merchant marine comprised: Roland, Bolster, and Keyssar, *Way of the Ship*, 419.

528 value of international trade: Røksund, *Jeune Ecole*, 9.

528 "Mexicans descend": Míguez, "Introduction," xxii. See also Moya, "Spanish Emigration," 10, 14.

528 Cuba's population: Moya, "Spanish Emigration," 15–17.

528 165,000 laborers to Brazil: Masterson and Funada, "Japanese in Peru and Brazil," 123–25.

528 1.3 million Irish emigrated: Hale, *Letters on Irish Immigration*, 23, 59.

528 more than 20 percent of all passengers died: Page, "Transportation of Immigrants," 739.

529 "We passed through the steerage": "Communication from John H. Griscom, M.D., of New York," in U.S. Senate, *Report . . . on the Sickness and Mortality on Board Emigrant Ships*, 54.

529 "2½ [pounds] of bread": New Passenger Act, 1849, 12 & 13 Vict., c. 33. On the space allowance, note that Byzantine regulations required 1.1 square meters per passenger; the Statues of Marseille, less than 1 square meter; and slave ships, 0.68 meter.

529 figures were halved again: Page, "Transportation of Immigrants," 740–42.

529 utensils and bedding: Ibid., 738.

529 "very injurious": In Charlwood, *Long Farewell*, 122, quoting New South Wales, Legislative Council, *Report from the Select Committee of the Legislative Council to Inquire into the Present System of German Immigration into this Colony*, Sydney, Aug. 11, 1858.

530 coolie trade: Yun and Laremont, "Chinese Coolies and African Slaves," 102–3, 110–11.

530 "almost as heart-rending": Douglass, *The New National Era*, Aug. 17, 1871.

531 "one vessel lost every eleven hours": "Why Are So Many Ships Lost?" *New York Daily Times*, May 23, 1854.

531 could be jailed: Jones, *Plimsoll Sensation*, 12–13.

531 hideous loss of life: National Maritime Museum learning team, "Ships, Seafarers and Life at Sea—Load Lines."

531 "Lloyd's rule": Jones, *Plimsoll Sensation*, 266.

532 without regard to the safety: Ibid., 14.

532 "They do not want": Lord Eslington, Feb. 2, 1876, in ibid., 232.

532 "Accidents, too": In Maxtone-Graham, *Only Way to Cross*, 2.

533 Hapag the largest shipping line: Bonsor, *North Atlantic Seaway*, 1:368, 378.

534 *Kaiser Wilhelm der Grosse:* Ibid., 1:354.

534 International Mercantile Marine: Navin and Sears, "A Study in Merger."

535 "unimprovable": *"nicht verbesserungsfählig":* in Maxtone-Graham, *Only Way to Cross*, 273; *"unmistakably and distressingly pear-shaped":* ibid. See also Maxtone-Graham, *"Normandie."*

536 "Doodle *San* will leave Japan": Edwards, *The Globe-Trotter at Kamakura*, in Barr, *Deer Cry Pavilion*, 171. *Joto* means "the best."

536 "a yacht in every sense": Williams, "Extent of Transport Services' Integration," 138.

536 between fourteen and twenty million passengers: *Cruise Baltic Status Report*, 9.

537 "designed especially to secure": "Steam Excursion Boats," 2; *"the only airings":* ibid.

538   horrific accidents: Kemp, "The COLREGS and the *Princess Alice*"; O'Donnell, *Ship Ablaze;* and Hilton, Eastland: *Legacy of the* Titanic.

538   Cruising and racing: Paine, *Ships of the World,* s.v. *Mary, Meteor,* and *Shamrock V;* Ross, "Where Are They Now? The Kaiser's Yacht."

538   "the most difficult": Brett, *Notes on Yachts,* 1–2.

540   "the greatest piece": "International Geographical Congress of 1895," 292.

540   screw corvette *Challenger:* Buchanan et al., *Report of the . . . Exploring Voyage of the H.M.S.* Challenger.

541   whales: Sperm whales and others of the suborder *Odontoceti* have teeth; baleen whales are in the taxonomical suborder *Mysticeti.*

541   Thomas Roys's: Bockstoce, "From Davis Strait to Bering Strait," 529–30.

541   "desiring to secure the prosperity": International Whaling Commission, "Whale Sanctuaries."

543   tanker *Zoroaster:* Frear, "History of Tankers," 135; Watson, "Bulk Cargo Carriers," 63.

543   "910,221 gallons": *New York Maritime Register,* Aug. 11, 1886, 3.

543   *Fliegauf:* Frear, "History of Tankers," 136.

543   eighty million tons of marine coal: Fletcher, "From Coal to Oil," 2–3.

543   diesel-powered motorships: Ibid., 10–11.

19. Naval Power in Steam and Steel

546   "castles of steel": Churchill, *World Crisis,* 1:212.

546   lost in action: Hepper, *British Warship Losses,* 211–13; Brown, *Warship Losses,* 229, 236.

547   cost 40 percent more: Brodie, *Sea Power in the Machine Age,* 118n27.

547   retrofit sailing ships with engines: Lambert, *Battleships in Transition,* 38–40, 58–59, 111.

547   *Nemesis:* Brown, "*Nemesis,*" 283–85; Guadeloupe: Brown, "Paddle Frigate *Guadeloupe,*" 221–22.

548   "ancient rule of the Sultan": Esmer, "Straits," 293.

548   floating batteries: Lambert, *Battleships in Transition,* 51; Lambert, Warrior, 11.

548   "perpetually interdicted": In Esmer, "Straits," 293.

549   "She looks like a black snake": This phrase has been attributed variously to Lord Palmerston, Napoleon III, and the French naval attaché, among others. HMS *Warrior* is today a museum ship in Portsmouth, England.

549   United States merchant marine: Roland, Bolster, and Keyssar, *Way of the Ship,* 419.

550   "If any person": In Gordan, "Trial of the Officers."

550   "Anybody dealing with a man": In ibid. See Lowe, "Confederate Naval Strategy."

550   "1. Privateering is, and remains abolished": Declaration of Paris, Apr. 16, 1856, in Lambert, *Crimean War,* 333.

551   Lincoln declared a blockade: Symonds, *Lincoln and His Admirals,* 39–49, 59–62.

551   blockade-runners: Wise, *Lifeline of the Confederacy,* 221.

551   country's largest export ports: Surdam, *Northern Naval Superiority,* 11.

551   commerce raiders: Gibson and Donovan, *Abandoned Ocean,* 66–78; Dalzell, *Flight from the Flag,* 238–40, 246.

552   "I regard the possession": Mallory to chairman of the House Committee on Naval Affairs, in Still, *Iron Afloat,* 10.

552   John Ericsson's *Monitor:* Symonds, *Lincoln and His Generals,* 132–42.

553   "enveloping them all": Scott to Lincoln, May 2, 1861, U.S. War Department, *War of the Rebellion*, ser. 1, vol. 51/1, p. 339.

554   "can be elevated": Mahan, *Influence of Sea Power*, 2.

554   "It is not the taking": Ibid., 138.

554   "unsettled political conditions": Mahan, "United States Looking Outward," 818, 820.

555   "strategy of the weak": Røksund, *Jeune Ecole*.

555   total war: Ibid., 24–51, 98–100.

555   Advocates of the Jeune Ecole: Ibid., 60–62.

555   "out of our ports": Mahan, *Influence of Sea Power*, 87.

555   Maritime Customs Service: Hsü, *Rise of Modern China*, 271–74.

556   "self-strengthening movement": Ibid., 278–91; Paine, *Sino-Japanese War*, 32.

556   briefly occupying Taiwan: Hsü, *Rise of Modern China*, 314–17.

557   remove Chinese influence: Paine, *Sino-Japanese War*, 32–34, 38, 52.

557   Japanese cruisers sank: Ibid., 132–33; *Japanese troops*, 157.

557   Yalu River: Paine, *Sino-Japanese War*, 179–85.

557   Russian diplomatic successes: Ibid., 69–71.

557   "The hostile actions": Sergei Iul'evich Witte, Apr. 11, 1895, in Paine, *Sino-Japanese War*, 104.

557   "Russia does hope": Nishi Tokujiro, May 8, 1905, in Paine, *Sino-Japanese War*, 321.

557   cede the Liaodong Peninsula: Paine, *Sino-Japanese War*, 308.

558   Trans-Siberian Railway: Ibid., 68; Work on the railway began in 1891.

558   "interested in a peculiar degree": Anglo-Japanese Alliance, 1902, Article 1.

558   attack against Port Arthur: Evans and Peattie, *Kaigun*, 97.

558   coaling facilities: Warner and Warner, *Tide at Sunrise*, 403–4, 415–25; Cecil, "Coal for the Fleet That Had to Die."

558   battle of Tsushima: Warner and Warner, *Tide at Sunrise*, 481–520; Evans and Peattie, *Kaigun*, 116–24.

559   Treaty of Portsmouth: Warner and Warner, *Tide at Sunrise*, 530–74.

559   "public opinion": In Rickover, *How the Battleship* Maine *Was Destroyed*, 127–28.

559   "we have much more likelihood": Mahan to Roosevelt, May 1 and 6, 1897, in Spector, "Triumph of Professional Ideology," 179.

559   The gunnery was appalling: Beach, *United States Navy*, 394.

560   "The fashion in building ships": Gladstone (1882), in Angevine, "Rise and Fall of the Office of Naval Intelligence," 296.

560   "a definite standard": Lord Charles Beresford, in Sondhaus, *Naval Warfare*, 161.

560   Alfred von Tirpitz: Kelly, *Tirpitz*.

561   "for Germany": In Craig, *Germany*, 309.

561   "risk fleet": Kelly, *Tirpitz*, 185–86, 195–202; Halpern, *Naval History of World War I*, 2–4; and Kennedy, "Development of German Naval Operations Plans," 176–77.

562   German Navy League: Kelly, *Tirpitz*, 166–69; Halpern, *Naval History of World War I*, 3.

562   German general staff: Kennedy, "Development of German Naval Operations Plans," 175. See also Kelly, *Tirpitz*, 266.

562   "Germany's accelerated [shipbuilding] program": Naval War College report (1904), in Hagan, *This People's Navy*, 237.

562   Panama Canal: Ameringer, "Panama Canal Lobby."

563   battle of Jutland: Halpern, *Naval History of World War I*, 310–29; Kelly, *Tirpitz*, 412–15.

563   surface raiders: Halpern, *Naval History of World War I*, 70–83, 370–75.

564   "locomotive torpedo": Fryer and Brown, "Robert Whitehead"; Briggs, "Innovation and the Mid-Victorian Royal Navy," 447–55.

564   Thorsten Nordenfelt: Maber, "Nordenfelt Submarines."

564   "we are going to recommence": In Røksund, *Jeune Ecole*, 193.

565   "The forerunner of all modern submarines": Compton-Hall, *Submarine Boats*, 96–97.

565   "I went down in it": Roosevelt to Brander Matthews, July 20, 1907, in Roosevelt, *Works*, 23.514.

565   "In view of ": Tirpitz memorandum, Jan. 24, 1915, in Halpern, *Naval History of World War I*, 47.

565   merchant ship losses: Davis and Engerman, *Naval Blockades in Peace and War*, 169.

566   "A blockade must not extend": Declaration Concerning the Laws of Naval War (1909), Articles 1–2.

566   pinned down at Gallipoli: Halpern, *Naval History of World War I*, 117. The first sea lord was, and remains, the chief of naval operations; the first lord of the admiralty was a cabinet post.

567   "we can not send": in Halpern, *Naval History of World War I*, 359.

567   "an entire success": Naval Staff, *Home Waters—Part VIII*, in Halpern, *Naval History of World War I*, 361.

567   four hundred submarine chasers: Hagan, *This People's Navy*, 255.

567   "to the lowest point": Wilson, "Fourteen Points," para. 2 and 4.

568   mutually suspicious: Hagan, *This People's Navy*, 238–39; Evans and Peattie, *Kaigun*, 151, 187–89; and Miller, *War Plan Orange*, 76.

569   "Japan has no rival": Baker, *Woodrow Wilson and World Settlement*, 3:301.

569   ratio of capital ship tonnage: Ibid., 3:203.

569   "wise administration": Capt. William V. Pratt, memorandum for Charles Evans Hughes, Aug. 8, 1921, in Hagan, *This People's Navy*, 264.

569   "Not only should these submarines": Benson to Wilson, Mar. 14, 1919, in Baker, *Woodrow Wilson and World Settlement*, 197.

570   "steam navies": Mahan, *Influence of Sea Power*, 2.

570   "The minds of the men": Beach, *United States Navy*, 443.

571   "I'm afraid": In Agawa, *Reluctant Admiral*, 93; "*the world's three great follies*": ibid. See also Yoshida, *Requiem for Battleship* Yamato, 77.

571   "incendiary shotgun" projectiles: Skulski, *Battleship* Yamato, 18–19.

571   nearly three hundred carrier planes: Spector, *Eagle Against the Sun*, 538.

571   Close study of the Taranto action: Evans and Peattie, *Kaigun*, 475.

571   "damage Major Fleet Units": Report of Joint Planning Committee, Apr. 21, 1939, in Major, "Navy Plans for War," 245.

572   Pearl Harbor: Murfett, *Naval Warfare*, 135–40.

573   over two thousand Allied and neutral ships: For a comparison of figures arrived at by five different authorities, see American Merchant Marine at War, "Battle of the Atlantic Statistics."

573   twenty-two seagoing U-boats: Murfett, *Naval Warfare*, 34; Terraine, *Business in Great Waters*, 218.

573   unreliability of German torpedoes: Murfett, *Naval Warfare*, 53; Terraine, *Business in Great Waters*, 231–41.

573   submarine operations to Brest: Terraine, *Business in Great Waters*, 244–57, 354; Murfett, *Naval Warfare*, 86–87, 97n82.

573   more than a thousand ships: Terraine, *Business in Great Waters*, 767–69.

574   "Happy Time": Ibid., 410; Lane, *Ships for Victory*, 138.

574   "any country whose defense": Lend-Lease Act, 3(1).

574   "Execute unrestricted": In Spector, *Eagle Against the Sun*, 480.

574   "a warship": Treaty for the Limitation and Reduction of Naval Armament, 1930, pt. 4, art. 22.

574   "violating long-established": Roosevelt, Fireside Chat 18 (Sept. 11, 1941), in Smith, *Voyages*, 2:242.

575   failure of American torpedoes: Spector, *Eagle Against the Sun*, 484–85.

575   commerce warfare doctrine: U.S. War Dept., *United States Strategic Bombing Survey*, 12.

575   slow to respond: Morison, *Two-Ocean War*, 496–97.

575   thirteen hundred Japanese merchant ships lost: Spector, *Eagle Against the Sun*, 487; *United States Strategic Bombing Survey*, 11.

575   "All attempts": In Miller, *War at Sea*, 320; Murfett, *Naval Warfare*, 226–27.

575   "On general principles": International Military Tribunal, *Trial of the Major War Criminals*, 17:380.

576   landing craft: Spector, *Eagle Against the Sun*, 232–33.

576   "did more to win the war": In Smith and Finch, *Coral and Brass*, 72.

576   "the man who won the war": In Ambrose, *D-Day*, 45.

576   more than thirty types: Leighton and Coakley, *Global Logistics and Strategy*, 2:826–28.

577   "The only thing": Churchill, *Second World War*, 2:529.

578   first of four acts: Hagan, *This People's Navy*, 284–90; Lane, *Ships for Victory*, 36–37.

578   Liberty ships: Lane, *Ships for Victory*, 55, 68. Prewar standardized ship types included the C-1, C-2, and C-3 dry cargo ships and T-1, T-2, and T-3 tankers.

578   figures were increased: Lane, *Ships for Victory*, 144, 202.

579   sailing under the Soviet flag: Leighton and Coakley, *Global Logistics and Strategy*, 1:113–14, 541, 564; 2:683, 731. A total of 1,332 ships sailed for the Soviet Far East, most of them to Vladivostok; 538 to north Russia; 541 to the Persian Gulf; 120 to the Soviet Arctic (via the Bering Strait); and, from January 1945, 76 to the Black Sea.

579   "The former rights of Russia": Protocol of Proceedings of Crimea Conference, Agreement Regarding Japan, para. 2; Heinzig, *Soviet Union and Communist China*, 65, 203–5.

579   divide the peninsula: Hastings, *Korean War*, 15–16.

580   landed thirteen thousand troops at Incheon: Ibid., 116–33.

580   "an amphibious invasion in reverse": "One for the Book: An Invasion in Reverse," *Life*, Jan. 8, 1951, p. 18.

580   "what created": Bruce Cumings, in Hastings, *Korean War*, 15.

20. The Maritime World Since the 1950s

582   "The world maritime industry": Gibson and Donovan, *Abandoned Ocean*, 239.

583   1.2 million seafarers: Round Table of International Shipping Associations, http://www.marisec.org/shippingfacts/worldtrade/world-seafarers.php.

583   the freighter *Warrior*: Levinson, *The Box*, 32–34.

584   *Ideal-X*: Ibid.; Broeze, *Globalization of the Oceans*, 32–33.

584   Belgian researchers: Broeze, *Globalization of the Oceans*, 19.

585   "McLean understood": Levinson, *The Box*, 53.

586   computer-generated loading plans: Ibid., 6, 247.

586   container ports: Broeze, *Globalization of the Oceans*, 20–21, 172–74.

586   freight forwarding, customs clearance, and insurance: Ibid., 23–25.

587   Singapore handled: UNCTAD, *Review of Maritime Transport*, 95.

587   busiest long-distance routes: Ibid., 85.

587   oil tankers began to outgrow: Stopford, *Maritime Economics*, 22. Launched as *Sea-wise Giant* in 1979, the ship was renamed *Jahre Viking* (1991–2004) and *Knock Nevis* (2004–2009). She was scrapped in 2010.

587   Louisiana Offshore Oil Port: Louisiana Department of Transportation, LOOP Program.

588   brig *Osceola*: Havighurst, *Long Ships Passing*, 81.

588   refrigerated ships: Greenway, "Cargo Ships," 43–50.

588   *Miranda Guinness:* Yenne, *Guinness*, 167.

588   people employed: Broeze, *Globalization of the Oceans*, 231–38; National Research Council, *Crew Size and Maritime Safety*, 1–12.

590   the right to grant nationality: Carlisle, *Sovereignty for Sale*, 154.

590   "The chief advantage": *New York Herald*, Oct. 1, 1922, in ibid., 10–11.

590   "German stewards": *New York Times*, Dec. 6, 1922, in Carlisle, *Sovereignty for Sale*, 17.

590   political instability in Panama: Carlisle, *Sovereignty for Sale*, 111–14.

591   Liberian-flagged ships: Ibid., 115–33.

591   "legal restraints": Ibid., 152.

591   global labor market: Dimitrova, *Seafarers' Rights*, 28, 128.

591   conditions are often substandard: Ibid., 27–46.

591   *Torrey Canyon:* Chelminski, *Superwreck;* Cowan, *Oil and Water*.

592   *Amoco Cadiz:* Petrow, *In the Wake of the* Torrey Canyon.

592   a raft of conventions: International Maritime Organization, "List of IMO Conventions."

592   Safety of Life at Sea (SOLAS) conventions: International Maritime Organization, *SOLAS 1974: Brief History*.

592   odds of dying: IMO, *International Shipping and World Trade*, 20.

593   "It's no fish ye're buying": Scott, *The Antiquary*, 1:252.

593   The principal tools: Smith, "Fishing Vessels"; Grescoe, *Bottomfeeder*, 199.

593   "Up to the time": In Donnellan, *The Shoals of Herring*, adapted by Philip Donnellan from the radio ballad "Singing the Fishing," by Ewan McColl, Peggy Seeger, and Charles Parker. Birmingham BBC Colour, 1972. Available at http://www.youtube.com/user/RadioBalladsFilms.

594   likened to clear-cutting: Grescoe, *Bottomfeeder*, 27.

594   expansion of the fisheries: FAO, *The State of World Fisheries*, 4, 12.

594   illegal, unreported, and unregulated: Ibid., 79–83.

594   The Agreement on Conservation and Management: United Nations, "Agreement . . . Relating to the Conservation and Management of Straddling Fish Stocks and Highly Migratory Fish Stocks."

594   exclusive economic zone (EEZ): Under the Law of the Sea, the EEZ is an area of the sea over which "a coastal State has sovereign rights (a) for the purpose of exploring and exploiting, conserving and managing the natural resources, whether living or non-living, of the waters superjacent to the seabed and of the seabed and its subsoil, and with regard to other activities for the economic exploitation and exploration of the zone, such as the production of energy from the water, currents and winds; (b) jurisdiction . . . with regard to: (i) the establishment and use of artificial islands, installations and structures; (ii) marine scientific research; (iii) the protection and preservation of the marine environment." All states have "the freedoms . . . associated with the operation of ships, aircraft and submarine cables and pipelines" in an EEZ. See United Nations, Law of the Sea, Part V, "Exclusive Economic Zone."

594 fundamentally democratic: Paine, *Down East*, 121; Kalland, *Fishing Villages in Tokugawa Japan*, 141–45.

595 Canadian cod fishery: Paine, *Down East*, 132–33.

595 local fishermen began seizing: Hansen, "Piracy in the Greater Gulf of Aden," 8–13; Weir, "Fish, Family, and Profit," 16–21.

596 USS *Triton*: Beach, *Around the World Submerged*. In 2007–2008, Francis Joyon completed a solo circumnavigation under sail in the thirty-meter trimaran *Idec II* in fifty-seven days—four days less than the *Triton*.

596 icebreaker *Lenin*: Paine, "*Lenin*," in Hattendorf, ed., *Oxford Encyclopedia of Maritime History*, 2:354–55.

598 "As we combine": Mullen, "Remarks."

598 "global system": U.S. Navy et al., "A Cooperative Strategy."

598 "challenges are too diverse": Mullen, "Remarks." See Ratcliff, "Building Partners' Capacity," 49–50.

599 over eight billion tons: UNCTAD, *Review of Maritime Transport*, 6.

599 "Sailing is a noble thing": Pachymeres, *Historia*, in Browning, "The City and the Sea," 110.

Bibliography

Abbreviations

IJNA   *International Journal of Nautical Archaeology*
JAOS   *Journal of the American Oriental Society*
JESHO *Journal of the Economic and Social History of the Orient*
JSEAS *Journal of Southeast Asian Studies*

Abbott, John S. C. "Ocean Life." *Harper's New Monthly Magazine* 5:25 (1852): 61–66.
Abu Zayd Hasan ibn Yazid al-Sirafi. *Concerning the Voyage to the Indies and China*. In *Ancient Accounts of India and China by Two Mohammedan Travellers, Who Went to Those Parts in the 9th Century*. Trans. Eusebius Renaudot. 1733. Reprint, New Delhi: Asian Education Services, 1995.
Abulafia, David. "Neolithic Meets Medieval: First Encounters in the Canary Islands." In *Medieval Frontiers: Concepts and Practices*, ed. by David Abulafia, 173–94. Burlington, VT: Ashgate, 2002.
———. "Trade and Crusade, 1050–1250." In *Mediterranean Encounters, Economic, Religious, Political, 1100–1550*. Aldershot, UK: Ashgate, 2000.
Adam of Bremen. *History of the Archbishops of Hamburg-Bremen*. Trans. Francis J. Tschau. New York: Columbia Univ. Press, 1959.
Adney, Tappan, and Howard Chapelle. *The Bark Canoes and Skin Boats of North America*. Washington: Smithsonian, 1964.
Aeschylus. *Lyrical Dramas*. London: Dent, 1940.
Agatharchides of Cnidus. *On the Erythraean Sea*. Trans. Stanley M. Burstein. London: Hakluyt, 1989.
Agawa, Hiroyuki. *The Reluctant Admiral: Yamamoto and the Imperial Navy*. New York: Kodansha, 1979.
Agius, Dionisius A. *Classic Ships of Islam: From Mesopotamia to the Indian Ocean*. Leiden: Brill, 2008.
Ahmad, S. Maqbul. "Travels of Abu 'l Hasan 'Ali b. al Husayn al Mas'udi." *Islamic Culture* 28 (1954): 509–24.
Ahrweiler, Helene. *Byzance et la mer*. Paris: Presses Universitaire de France, 1966.
Albion, Robert G. *Forests and Sea Power: The Timber Problem of the Royal Navy, 1652–1862*. 1926. Reprint, Annapolis: Naval Institute, 2000.
———. "Planning the Black Ball Line, 1817." *Business History Review* 41:1 (1967): 104–7.
Albuquerque, Afonso de. *The Commentaries of the Great Afonso Dalboquerque, Second Viceroy of India*. Trans. Walter de Gray Birch. 4 vols. London: Hakluyt, 1880.
Alcuin of York. *Alcuin of York, c. A.D. 732 to 804: His Life and Letters*. York: Sessions, 1974.

Ali, Shanti Sadiq. *The African Dispersal in the Deccan: From Medieval to Modern Times*. New Delhi: Orient Longman, 1996.

Allaire, Louis. "Archaeology of the Caribbean Region." In *The Cambridge History of the Native Peoples of America*. Vol. 3, *South America*, ed. by Frank Salomon and Stuart B. Schwartz, 668–733. Cambridge: Cambridge Univ. Press, 1999.

Ambrose, Stephen E. *D-Day, June 6, 1944: The Climactic Battle of World War II*. New York: Simon & Schuster, 1994.

Ambrosiani, Björn. "The Prehistory of Towns in Sweden." In *The Rebirth of Towns in the West AD, 700–1050*, ed. by Richard Hodges and Brian Hobley, 63–68. Oxford: Council for British Archaeology, 1988.

American Merchant Marine at War. "Battle of the Atlantic Statistics." http://www.usmm .org/battleatlantic.html.

Ameringer, Charles D. "The Panama Canal Lobby of Philippe Bunau-Varilla and William Nelson Cromwell." *American Historical Review* 68:2 (1963): 346–63.

Ames, Glenn J. "The Straits of Hurmuz Fleets: Omani-Portuguese Naval Rivalry and Encounters, ca. 1660–1680." *Mariner's Mirror* 83:4 (Nov. 1997): 398–409.

Ames, Kenneth M. "Going by Boat: The Forager-Collector Continuum at Sea." In *Beyond Foraging and Collecting: Evolution and Change in Hunter-Gatherer Settlement Systems*, ed. by Ben Fitzhugh and Junko Habu, 19–52. New York: Kluwer Academic/Plenum, 2002.

Anawalt, Patricia Reiff. "Ancient Cultural Contacts Between Ecuador, West Mexico and the American Southwest: Clothing Similarities." *Latin American Antiquity* 3:2 (June 1992): 114–29.

Andrade, Tonio. "Rise and Fall of Dutch Taiwan." *Journal of World History* 17:4 (2006): 429–50.

Andrewes, William J. H. "Even Newton Could Be Wrong: The Story of Harrison's First Three Sea Clocks." In *The Quest for Longitude*, ed. by Andrewes, 190–233.

Andrewes, William J. H., ed. *The Quest for Longitude: The Proceedings of the Longitude Symposium, Harvard University, Cambridge, Massachusetts, November 4–6, 1993*. Cambridge: Collection of Historical Scientific Instruments, Harvard University, 1996.

Andrews, Kenneth R. *Trade, Plunder and Settlement: Maritime Enterprise and the Genesis of the British Empire, 1480–1630*. Cambridge: Cambridge Univ. Press, 1985.

Angevine, Robert G. "The Rise and Fall of the Office of Naval Intelligence, 1882–1892: A Technological Perspective." *Journal of Military History* 62 (1998): 291–313.

Anglo-Japanese Alliance. Jan. 30, 1902. http://www.jacar.go.jp/nichiro/uk-japan.htm.

Anna Comnena. *The Alexiad*. Trans. E. R. A. Sewter. Harmondsworth: Penguin, 1969.

Anson, George. *A Voyage Round the World in the Years MDCCXL, I, II, III, IV*, ed. by Glyndwr Williams. London: Oxford Univ. Press, 1974.

Antony, Robert J. *Like Froth Floating on the Sea: The World of Pirates and Seafarers in Late Imperial South China*. Berkeley: Institute of East Asian Studies, 2003.

Appian. *Roman History*. Trans. Horace White. 4 vols. Cambridge: Harvard Univ. Press, 1913.

Arasaratnam, Sinappah. "India and the Indian Ocean in the Seventeenth Century." In *India and the Indian Ocean, 1500–1800*, ed. by Ashin Das Gupta and M. N. Pearson, 95–130. Calcutta: Oxford Univ. Press, 1987.

———. *Maritime India in the Seventeenth Century*. New Delhi: Oxford Univ. Press, 1994.

Aristophanes. *Lysistrata and Other Plays*. New York: Penguin, 2002.

Aristotle. *The Complete Works of Aristotle*. Trans. Jonathan Barnes. 2 vols. Princeton: Princeton Univ. Press, 1984.

Armitage, David. *The Ideological Origins of the British Empire*. Cambridge: Cambridge Univ. Press, 2000.

Armstrong, Terence. *Yermak's Campaign in Siberia: A Selection of Documents*. London: Hakluyt, 1975.

Arnold, Jeanne E., and Julienne Bernard. "Negotiating the Coasts: Status and the Evolution of Boat Technology in California." *World Archaeology* 37:1 (March 2005): 109–31.

Arrian. *Anabasis of Alexander; Indica*. Trans. E. Iliff Robson. 2 vols. New York: Putnam's, 1929–33.

Aryasura, and Peter Khoroche. *Once the Buddha Was a Monkey: Arya Sura's Jatakamala*. Chicago: Univ. of Chicago Press, 1989.

Ashburner, Walter. *The Rhodian Sea-Law*. 1909. Reprint, Aalen, Germany: Scientia Verlag, 1976.

Athenaeus. *The Deipnosophists*. Trans. C. B. Gulick. 7 vols. Cambridge: Putnam's Sons, 1927–41.

Aubet, Maria Eugenia. *The Phoenicians and the West: Politics, Colonies and Trade*. New York: Cambridge Univ. Press, 1996.

Aubrey, Philip. *Defeat of James Stuart's Armada*. Totowa, NJ: Rowman & Littlefield, 1979.

Aughterson, Kate, ed. *The English Renaissance: An Anthology of Sources and Documents*. New York: Routledge, 2002.

Aung-Thwin, Michael. *The Mists of Ramañña: The Legend That Was Lower Burma*. Honolulu: Univ. of Hawai'i Press, 2005.

Austin, M. M., and P. Vidal-Naquet. *Economic and Social History of Ancient Greece: An Introduction*. 2nd ed. Berkeley: Univ. of California Press, 1973.

Avienus, Rufus Festus. *Ora Maritima; or, Description of the Seacoast from Brittany Round to Massilia*. Trans. J. P. Murphy. Chicago: Ares, 1977.

Ayalon, D. "The Mamluks and Naval Power: A Phase of the Struggle Between Islam and Christian Europe." *Proceedings of the Israel Academy of Sciences and Humanities* 1 (1965): 1–12.

Aziz Ahmad. *A History of Islamic Sicily*. Edinburgh: Edinburgh Univ. Press, 1975.

Bachrach, Bernard S. "On the Origins of William the Conqueror's Horse Transports." *Technology and Culture* 26:3 (1985): 505–31.

Bacon, Edwin M. *Manual of Ship Subsidies: An Historical Summary of the Systems of All Nations*. Chicago: McClurg, 1911.

Baker, Ray Stannard. *Woodrow Wilson and World Settlement, Written from His Unpublished and Personal Material*. Vol. 3, *Original Documents of the Peace Conference*. Garden City: Doubleday, Page, 1922.

Baladhuri, Ahmad ibn Yahya al-. *The Origins of the Islamic State*. Trans. Philip Khuri Hitti. 1916. Reprint, Piscataway: Gorgias, 2002.

Ballard, G. A. *The Influence of the Sea on the Political History of Japan*. New York: Dutton, 1921.

Ban, Gu. *Food and Money in Ancient China: The Earliest Economic History of China to A.D. 25*. Trans. Nancy Lee Swann. 1950. Reprint, New York: Octagon, 1974.

Barbosa, Duarte, Fernão de Magalhães, and Mansel Longworth Dames. *The Book of Duarte Barbosa: An Account of the Countries Bordering on the Indian Ocean and Their Inhabitants*. London: Hakluyt, 1918.

Barbour, Violet. *Capitalism in Amsterdam in the 17th Century*. Ann Arbor: Univ. of Michigan Press, 1963.

———. "Dutch and English Merchant Shipping in the Seventeenth Century." *Economic History Review* 2:2 (1930): 261–90.

Barendse, René. "Shipbuilding in Seventeenth-Century Western India." *Itinerario* 19:3 (1995): 175–95.

Barr, Pat. *The Deer Cry Pavilion; A Story of Westerners in Japan, 1868–1905*. New York: Harcourt, Brace & World, 1969.

Bartholomew, Michael. "James Lind and Scurvy: A Revaluation." *Journal for Maritime Research*, Jan. 2002. http://www.jmr.nmm.ac.uk/server/show/conJmrArticle.3.

Bass, George F. "Bronze Age Shipwreck at Ulu Burun (Kaş): 1984 Campaign." *American Journal of Archaeology* 90 (1986): 269–96.

———. "A Byzantine Trading Venture." *Scientific American* 224.2 (1971): 23–33.

———. *Cape Gelidonya: A Bronze Age Shipwreck*. Philadelphia: American Philosophical Society, 1967.

———. "Return to Cape Gelidonya." *INA Newsletter* 15 (1988): 2–5.

Bass, George F., and Frederick H. Van Doorninck, Jr. "An 11th-Century Shipwreck at Serçe Limani, Turkey." *IJNA* 7 (1978): 119–32.

———. "A Fourth-Century Shipwreck at Yassi Ada." *American Journal of Archaeology* 75 (1971): 27–37.

———. *Yassi Ada*. Vol. 1, *A Seventh-Century Byzantine Shipwreck*. College Station, TX: IJNA, 1982.

Bass, George F., et al. *Cape Gelidonya: A Bronze Age Shipwreck*. TAPA New Series 57:8, 1967.

———. *Serçe Limani: An Eleventh-Century Shipwreck*. Vol. 1, *The Ship and Its Anchorage, Crew, and Passengers*. College Station: Texas A&M Univ. Press, 2004.

Bately, Janet. "Text and Translation." In *Ohthere's Voyages*, ed. by Bately and Englert, 40–50.

Bately, Janet, and Anton Englert, eds. *Ohthere's Voyages: A Late 9th-Century Account of Voyages Along the Coasts of Norway and Denmark and Its Cultural Context*. Roskilde: Viking Ship Museum, 2007.

Bathurst, R. D. "Maritime Trade and Imamate Government: Two Principal Themes in the History of Oman." In *The Arabian Peninsula: Society and Politics*, ed. by Derek Hopwood, 89–106. London: George Allen & Unwin, 1972.

Baugh, Daniel. *The Global Seven Years War, 1754–1763: Britain and France in a Great Power Contest*. London: Pearson, 2011.

Beach, Edward L. *Around the World Submerged*. New York: Holt, 1962.

———. *The United States Navy: 200 Years*. New York: Holt, 1986.

Beaglehole, J. C. *The Exploration of the Pacific*. 3rd ed. Stanford: Stanford Univ. Press, 1966.

Bede. *A History of the English Church and People*. Trans. Leo Sherley-Price. New York: Penguin, 1968.

Bellwood, Peter S. *Prehistory of the Indo-Malaysian Archipelago*. Honolulu: Univ. of Hawai'i Press, 1997.

———. "Southeast Asia Before History." In *The Cambridge History of Southeast Asia*, ed. by Tarling, 1.1:55–136.

Bellwood, Peter, and Judith Cameron. "Ancient Boats, Boat Timbers, and Locked Mortise-and-Tenon Joints from Bronze/Iron-Age Northern Vietnam." *IJNA* 36:1 (2007): 2–20.

Benjamin, Daniel K., and Anca Tifrea. "Learning by Dying: Combat Performance in the Age of Sail." *Journal of Economic History* 67:4 (2007): 968–1000.

Benjamin of Tudela. *The Itinerary of Benjamin of Tudela: Travels in the Middle Ages*. Introduction by Michael A. Signer, M. N. Adler, and A. Asher. Malibu, CA: J. Simon, 1983.

Benn, Charles. *China's Golden Age: Everyday Life in the Tang Dynasty*. New York: Oxford Univ. Press, 2002.

Bergquist, Charles W. "The Paradox of American Development." In *Labor and the Course of American Democracy: U.S. History in Latin American Perspective*. New York: Verso, 1996.

Berkowitz, David Sandler. *John Selden's Formative Years: Politics and Society in Early Seventeenth-Century England*. Washington: Folger Shakespeare Library, 1988.

Berlow, Rosalind Kent. "The Sailing of the *Saint Esprit*." *The Journal of Economic History* 39:2 (1979): 345–62.

Bernstein, Peter L. *Wedding of the Waters: The Erie Canal and the Making of a Great Nation*. New York: Norton, 2005.

Bessason, Haraldur, Paul Edwards, and Hermann Pálsson. *The Book of Settlements*. Winnipeg: Univ. of Manitoba Press, 1972.

Bielenstein, Hans. *Diplomacy and Trade in the Chinese World, 589–1276*. Leiden: Brill, 2005.

Biggar, Henry Percival, compiler. *A Collection of Documents Relating to Jacques Cartier and the Sieur de Roberval*. Ottawa: Public Archives of Canada, 1930.

Birnbaum, Henrik. *Lord Novgorod the Great: Essays in the History and Culture of a Medieval City-State*. Columbus: Slavica, 1981.

Bittlestone, Robert, with James Diggle and John Underhill. *Odysseus Unbound: The Search for Homer's Ithaca*. Cambridge: Cambridge Univ. Press, 2005.

Bjork, David K. "The Peace of Stralsund, 1370." *Speculum* 7 (1932): 447–76.

———. "Piracy in the Baltic, 1375–1398." *Speculum* 18:1 (1943): 39–68.

Blackbourn, David. *The Conquest of Nature: Water, Landscape, and the Making of Modern Germany*. New York: Norton, 2006.

Blench, Roger. "The Ethnographic Evidence for Long-Distance Contacts Between Oceania and East Africa." In *The Indian Ocean in Antiquity*, ed. by Reade, 417–38.

Blussé, Leonard. "Brief Encounter at Macao." *Modern Asian Studies* 22:3 (1988): 647–64.

———. "Chinese Century: The Eighteenth Century in the China Sea Region." *Archipel* 58 (1999): 107–29.

———. "Divesting a Myth: Seventeenth Century Dutch-Portuguese Rivalry in the Far East." In *Vasco da Gama and the Linking of Europe and Asia*, ed. by Anthony Disney and Emily Booth, 387–402. New Delhi: Oxford Univ. Press, 2000.

———. *Visible Cities: Canton, Nagasaki, and Batavia and the Coming of the Americans*. Cambridge: Harvard Univ. Press, 2008.

Blussé, Leonard, and Felipe Fernández-Armesto, eds. *Shifting Communities and Identity Formation in Early Modern Asia*. Leiden: CNWS, 2003.

Blussé, Leonard, and Femme Gaastra, eds. *On the Eighteenth Century as a Category of Asian History: Van Leur in Retrospect*. Aldershot, UK: Ashgate, 1992.

Boardman, John. *The Greeks Overseas: Their Early Colonies and Trade*. 4th ed. London: Thames & Hudson, 1999.

Boccaccio, Giovanni. *Decameron*. Trans. G. H. McWilliam. Harmondsworth: Penguin, 1972.

Bockstoce, John R. "From Davis Strait to Bering Strait: The Arrival of the Commercial Whaling Fleet in North America's Western Arctic." *Arctic* 37:4 (1984): 528–32.

Bondioli, Mauro, René Burlet, and André Zysberg. "Oar Mechanics and Oar Power in Medieval and Later Galleys." In *The Age of the Galley*, ed. by Gardiner and Morrison, 172–205.

Bonsor, N. R. P. *North Atlantic Seaway*. 5 vols. Jersey: Brookside, 1980.

Boomgaard, Peter. *Southeast Asia: An Environmental History*. Santa Barbara: ABC-CLIO, 2006.

Bougainville, Louis-Antoine de. *Pacific Journal of Louis-Antoine de Bougainville, 1767–68*. Ed. by John Dunmore. London: Hakluyt, 2002.

Bourne, Edward Gaylord. "The Demarcation Line of Pope Alexander VI." In *Essays in Historical Criticism*. 1901. Reprint, Freeport, NY: Books for Libraries Press, 1967.

Boxer, C. R. *The Dutch Seaborne Empire, 1600–1800*. New York: Penguin, 1965.

———. *The Portuguese Seaborne Empire, 1415–1825*. New York: Knopf, 1969.

Bramoullé, David. "Recruiting Crews in the Fatimid Navy (909–1171)." *Medieval Encounters* 13 (2007): 4–31.

Brand, Hanno. "Habsburg Diplomacy During the Holland-Wend War." In *Trade, Diplomacy and Cultural Exchange: Continuity and Change in the North Sea Area and the Baltic, c. 1350–1750*, ed. by Hanno Brand, 113–35. Hilversum: Uitgeverij Verloren, 2006.

Braudel, Fernand. *Civilization and Capitalism, 15th–18th Century*. Vol. 3, *The Perspective of the World*. New York: Harper & Row, 1985.

———. *The Mediterranean in the Age of Philip II*. 1949. Trans. Siân Reynolds. 2 vols. New York: Harper & Row, 1973.

Breasted, James Henry. *Ancient Records of Egypt: Historical Documents from the Earliest Times to the Persian Conquest*. New York: Russell & Russell, 1962.

Brendel, Otto J. *Etruscan Art*. Harmondsworth: Penguin, 1978.

Brett, Edwin. *Notes on Yachts*. London: Low, Son & Marston, 1869.

Brett, Michael. *The Rise of the Fatimids: The World of the Mediterranean and the Middle East in the Fourth Century of the Hijra, Tenth Century CE*. Leiden: Brill, 2001.

Brewer, John. *Sinews of Power: War, Money, and the English State, 1688–1783*. New York: Knopf, 1989.

Briggs, M. "Innovation and the Mid-Victorian Royal Navy: The Case of the Whitehead Torpedo." *Mariner's Mirror* 88 (2002): 447–55.

Brinnin, John Malcolm. *The Sway of the Grand Saloon: A Social History of the North Atlantic*. New York: Delacorte, 1971.

Briscoe, John. "The Second Punic War." In *The Cambridge Ancient History*. Vol. 8, *Rome and the Mediterranean to 133 B.C.*, ed. by A. E. Astin et al., 44–88. 2nd ed. Cambridge: Cambridge Univ. Press, 1989.

Brodie, Bernard. *Sea Power in the Machine Age*. Princeton: Princeton Univ. Press, 1941.

Broeze, Frank. *The Globalisation of the Oceans: Containerisation from the 1950s to the Present*. St. John's, NL: International Maritime Economic History Assoc., 2002.

Brøgger, A. W., and Haakon Shetelig. *The Viking Ships: Their Ancestry and Evolution*. Trans. Katherine John. Los Angeles: Mogensen, 1953.

Brown, Alexander Crosby. *Women and Children Last: The Loss of the Steamship Arctic*. New York: Putnam, 1961.

Brown, D. K. "*Nemesis:* The First Iron Warship." *Warship* 2:8 (1978): 283–85.

———. "The Paddle Frigate *Guadeloupe*." *Mariner's Mirror* 58 (1972): 221–22.

Brown, David. *Warship Losses of World War II*. Rev. ed. Annapolis: Naval Institute, 1990.

Brown, Delmer M., ed. *The Cambridge History of Japan*. Vol. 1, *Ancient Japan*. Cambridge: Cambridge Univ. Press, 1993.

———. "The Impact of Firearms on Japanese Warfare, 1543–98." *Far Eastern Quarterly* 7:3 (1948): 236–53.

———. "The Yamato Kingdom." In *The Cambridge History of Japan*, ed. by Brown, 1:108–62.

Browning, Robert. "The City and the Sea." In *The Greeks and the Sea*, ed. by Speros Vryonis, 97–110. New Rochelle: Caratzas, 1993.

Bruijn, Jaap R. *The Dutch Navy of the Seventeenth and Eighteenth Centuries*. Columbia: Univ. of South Carolina Press, 1993.

Brummett, Palmira. *Ottoman Seapower and Levantine Diplomacy in the Age of Discovery*. Albany: State Univ. Press of New York, 1994.

Brutzkus, J. "Trade with Eastern Europe, 800–1200." *Economic History Review* 13:1/2 (1943): 31–41.

Buchanan, J. Y., H. N. Mosley, J. Murray, and T. H. Tizard. *The Report of the Scientific Results of the Exploring Voyage of the H.M.S.* Challenger *During the Years 1873–1876.* Vol. 1, *Narrative of the Voyage.* London: 1885–95.

Buck, Peter (Te Rangi Hiroa). *The Coming of the Maori.* Wellington: Whitcombe & Tombs, 1950.

Burckhardt, Carl J. *Richelieu and His Age.* 3 vols. New York: Harcourt Brace and World, 1940.

Burningham, Nick. "The Borobudur Ship—Design Outline." www.borobudurshipexpedition .com/design-outline.htm (June 26, 2006).

Bury, J. B. *A History of the Eastern Roman Empire from the Fall of Irene to the Accession of Basil I.* 1912. Reprint, New York: Russell & Russell, 1965.

Butler, John A. *Atlantic Kingdom: America's Contest with Cunard in the Age of Sail and Steam.* Dulles: Brassey's, 2001.

———. *Sailing on Friday: The Perilous Voyage of America's Merchant Marine.* Dulles: Brassey's, 2000.

Buzurg ibn Shahriyar of Ramhormuz. *The Book of the Wonders of India: Mainland, Sea and Islands.* Trans. G. S. P. Freeman-Grenville. London: East-West, 1981.

Byrne, Eugene H. "Commercial Contracts of the Genoese in the Syrian Trade of the Twelfth Century." *Quarterly Journal of Economics* 31:1 (1916): 128–70.

Byron, John. *Byron's Journal of His Circumnavigation, 1764–1766.* Ed. Robert E. Gallagher. Cambridge: Hakluyt, 1946.

C.N.B. "Alexander on the Compass Needle." *Geographical Journal* 104:1 (1944): 63–65.

Caesar, Julius. *The Conquest of Gaul.* Trans. S. A. Handford. New York: Penguin, 1981.

Calendar of the Patent Rolls Preserved in the Public Record Office. Henry IV. A.D. *1399–[1413].* London: HMSO, 1903–9.

Callaghan, Richard T. "Prehistoric Trade Between Ecuador and West Mexico: A Computer Simulation of Coastal Voyages." *Antiquity* 77:298 (2003): 796–804.

Camoens, Luis Vaz de. *The Lusiads.* Trans. William C. Atkinson. 1952. Reprint, Harmondsworth: Penguin, 1973.

Campbell, Alistair, ed. *Encomium Emmae Reginae.* New York: Cambridge Univ. Press, 1998.

Campbell, Tony. "Portolan Charts from the Late Thirteenth Century to 1500." In *The History of Cartography.* Vol. 1, *Cartography in Prehistoric, Ancient, and Medieval Europe and the Mediterranean,* ed. by J. B. Harley and David Woodward, 371–463. Chicago: Univ. of Chicago Press, 1987.

Capponi, Niccolo. *Victory of the West: The Great Christian-Muslim Clash at the Battle of Lepanto.* New York: Da Capo, 2007.

Carlisle, Rodney. *Sovereignty for Sale: The Origins and Evolution of the Panamanian and Liberian Flags of Convenience.* Annapolis: Naval Institute, 1981.

Carter, Hodding. *Lower Mississippi.* The Rivers of America. New York: Farrar & Rinehart, 1942.

Carter, Robert. "Boat-Related Finds." In *Maritime Interactions in the Arabian Neolithic: Evidence from H3, As-Sabiyah, an Ubaid-related Site in Kuwait,* ed. by Robert Carter and Harriet Crawford, 89–104. Leiden: Brill, 2010.

Carvajal, Gaspar de. *The Discovery of the Amazon According to the Account of Friar Gaspar de Carvajal and Other Documents.* Trans. Bertram T. Lee. New York: American Geographical Society, 1934.

Carver, M. O. H. "Pre-Viking Traffic in the North Sea." In *Maritime Celts, Frisians and Saxons,* ed. by McGrail, 117–25.

Casale, Giancarlo. "The Ottoman Administration of the Spice Trade in the Sixteenth-Century Red Sea and Persian Gulf." *JESHO* 49:2 (2006): 170–98.

———. *The Ottoman Age of Exploration.* New York: Oxford Univ. Press, 2010.

Casparis, J. G. de. *Selected Inscriptions from the 7th to the 9th Century A.D. Prasasti Indonesia 2.* Bandung, Indonesia: Masa Baru, 1956.

Casson, Lionel. *The Ancient Mariners: Seafarers and Sea Fighters of the Mediterranean in Ancient Times.* 2nd ed. Baltimore: Johns Hopkins Univ. Press, 1991.

———. *Everyday Life in Ancient Egypt.* Baltimore: Johns Hopkins Univ. Press, 2001.

———. "The Grain Trade of the Hellenistic World." In *Ancient Trade and Society*, 70–95. Detroit: Wayne State Univ. Press, 1984.

———. "The *Isis* and Her Voyage." *Transactions of the American Philological Association* 81 (1950): 43–56.

———. "Merchant Galleys." In *The Age of the Galley*, ed. by Gardiner and Morrison, 117–26.

———. "New Light on Maritime Loans: P. Vindob. G 19792 (=SB VI 9571)." In *Studies in Roman Law in Memory of A. Arthur Schiller*, ed. by Roger S. Bagnall, A. Arthur Schiller, and William Vernon Harris, 11–17. Leiden: Brill, 1986.

———, trans. *The Periplus Maris Erythraei.* Princeton: Princeton Univ. Press, 1989.

———. *Ships and Seamanship in the Ancient World.* Baltimore: Johns Hopkins Univ. Press, 1995.

Castro, Filipe, N. Fonseca, T. Vacas, and F. Ciciliot. "A Quantitative Look at Mediterranean Lateen- and Square-Rigged Ships (Part 1)." *IJNA* 37:2 (2008): 347–59.

Cecil, Lamar J. R. "Coal for the Fleet That Had to Die." *American Historical Review* 69:4 (1964): 990–1005.

Chakravarti, Ranabir. "Early Medieval Bengal and the Trade in Horses: A Note." *JESHO* 42:2 (1999): 194–211.

———. "Nakhudas and Navittakas: Shipowning Merchants in the West Coast of India (c. AD 1000–1500)." *JESHO* 43:1 (2000): 35–64.

———. "Overseas Trade in Horses in Early Medieval India: Shipping and Piracy." In *Praciprabha: Perspective in Indology*, ed. by D. C. Bhattacharyya and Devendra Handa. New Delhi: Harman, 1989.

Chandra, Moti. *Trade and Trade Routes in Ancient India.* New Delhi: Abhinav, 1977.

Chang, Chun-shu, and Joan Smythe. *South China in the Twelfth Century: A Translation of Lu Yu's Travel Diaries, July 3–December 6, 1170.* Hong Kong: Chinese Univ. Press, 1981.

Chang Pin-Tsun. "The Formation of a Maritime Convention in Minnan (Southern Fujian), c. 900–1200." In *From the Mediterranean to the China Sea: Miscellaneous Notes*, ed. by Claude Guillot, Denys Lombard, and Roderich Ptak, 143–55. Wiesbaden: Harrassowitz, 1998.

Chapelle, Howard I. "Arctic Skin Boats." In *The Bark Canoes and Skin Boats of North America*, by Tappan Adney and Howard Chapelle, 174–211. Washington: Smithsonian, 1964.

———. *The History of American Sailing Ships.* 1935. Reprint, New York: Bonanza, 1982.

Chaplin, Joyce E. *The First Scientific American: Benjamin Franklin and the Pursuit of Genius.* New York: Basic Books, 2006.

Chapman, Anne C. "Port of Trade Enclaves in Aztec and Maya Civilization." In *Trade and Market in the Early Empires: Economies in History and Theory*, ed. by Karl Polanyi et al., 114–53. Glencoe, IL: Free Press, 1957.

Charanis, Peter. "Piracy in the Aegean During the Reign of Michael VIII Palaeologus." In *Social, Economic and Political Life in the Byzantine Empire: Collected Studies*, ed. by Peter Charanis. London: Variorum, 1973.

Charlwood, D. E. *The Long Farewell: The Perilous Voyages of Settlers Under Sail in the Great Migration to Australia.* Victoria: Penguin, 1983.

Chau Ju-kua. *Chau Ju-kua: His Work on the Chinese and Arab Trade in the Twelfth and Thir-*

teenth Centuries Entitled Chu-fan-chi. Ed. by Friedrich Hirth and W. W. Rockhill. 1911. Reprint, Amsterdam: Oriental Press, 1966.

Chaucer, Geoffrey. *Canterbury Tales*. Trans. Nevill Coghill. New York: Penguin, 1975.

Chaudhuri, K. N. "Surat Revisited: A Tribute to Ashin Das Gupta." *JESHO* 43:1 (2000): 18–22.

Chaudhuri, Mamata. "Ship-Building in the *Yuktikalpataru* and *Samarangana Sutradara*." *Indian Journal of History of Science* 1:2 (1976): 137–47.

Chelminski, Rudolph. *Superwreck: Amoco Cadiz—The Shipwreck That Had to Happen*. New York: Morrow, 1987.

Chin, James K. "Ports, Merchants, Chieftains and Eunuchs: Reading Maritime Commerce of Early Guangdong." In *Guangdong: Archaeology and Early Texts*, ed. by Shing Muller, Thomas O. Höllmann, and Putao Gui, 217–39. Wiesbaden: Harrassowitz, 2004.

Chittick, Neville. "East African Trade with the Orient." In *Islam and the Trade of Asia*, ed. by D. S. Richards, 97–104. Oxford: Bruno Cassirer, 1970.

———. *Kilwa: An Islamic Trading City on the East African Coast*. Vol. 1, *History and Archaeology*. Nairobi: British Institute in Eastern Africa, 1974.

Choniates, Nicetas. *O City of Byzantium: Annals of Nicetas Choniates*. Trans. Harry J. Magoulias. Detroit: Wayne State Univ. Press, 1984.

Chou Yi-liang, "Tantrism in China." *Harvard Journal of Asiatic Studies* 8:3/4 (Mar. 1945): 241–332.

Christensen, Arne Emil. "Proto-Viking, Viking and Norse Craft." In *The Earliest Ships: The Evolution of Boats into Ships*, ed. by Robert Gardiner and A. E. Christensen, 72–88. Annapolis: Naval Institute, 1996.

Christides, Vassilios. *The Conquest of Crete by the Arabs (ca. 824): A Turning Point in the Struggle Between Byzantium and Islam*. Athens: Akademia Athenon, 1984.

———. "Fireproofing of War Machines, Ships and Garments." In *Sailing Ships of the Mediterranean Sea and the Arabian Gulf*, ed. by Christos G. Makrypoulias, 1.11–17. *Graeco-Arabica*, Supplement 1. Athens: Kuwait F.A.S., 1998.

———. "Milaha." In *Encyclopaedia of Islam, New Edition*, ed. by C. E. Bosworth, E. van Dozel, W. P. Heindrichs, and Ch. Pellat, 7:40–76. Leiden: Brill, 1993.

———. "Two Parallel Naval Guides of the Tenth Century: Qudama's Document and Leo VI's *Naumachia*: A Study on Byzantine and Moslem Naval Preparedness." *Graeco-Arabica* 1 (1982): 51–103.

Christie, Jan Wisseman. "The Medieval Tamil-Language Inscriptions in Southeast Asia and China." *JSEAS* 29:2 (1998): 239–68.

Churchill, Winston. *The Second World War*. 6 vols. Boston: Houghton Mifflin, 1948.

———. *The World Crisis*. 4 vols. New York: Scribner, 1923.

Cicero. *Letters to Atticus*. Trans. E. O. Winstedt (Vol. 1). New York: Macmillan, 1912.

———. *Pro Lege Manilia, etc.* Trans. H. Grose Hodge (Vol. 9). Cambridge: Harvard Univ. Press, 1929.

Citarella, Armand O. "The Relations of Amalfi with the Arab World Before the Crusades." *Speculum* 42 (1967): 299–312.

Clark, Hugh R. *Community, Trade and Networks: Southern Fujian from the 3rd to the 13th Centuries*. Cambridge: Cambridge Univ. Press, 1991.

———. "Frontier Discourse and China's Maritime Frontier: China's Frontiers and the Encounter with the Sea Through Early Imperial History." *Journal of World History* 20:1 (2009): 1–33.

———. "Muslims and Hindus in the Culture and Morphology of Quanzhou from the Tenth to the Thirteenth Century." *Journal of World History* 6:1 (1995) 49–74.

Clarke, Arthur C. *Voice Across the Sea.* New York: Harper, 1958.

Cleuziou, Serge, and Maurizio Tosi. "Black Boats of Magan: Some Thoughts on Bronze Age Water Transport in Oman and Beyond from the Impressed Bitumen Slabs of Ra's al-Junayz." In *South Asian Archaeology 1993,* ed. by A. Parpola and P. Koskikallio, 745–61. Helsinki: AASF Ser. B 271, 1993.

Coe, Michael D. "Archaeological Linkages with North and South America at La Victoria, Guatemala." *American Anthropologist,* n.s., 62 (1960): 363–93.

Coke, Edward, Sir. *The Third Part of the Institutes of the Laws of England: Concerning High Treason, and Other Pleas of the Crown.* London, 1797. Eighteenth Century Collections Online, Gale Group.

Coleman, Terry. *The Nelson Touch: The Life and Legend of Horatio Nelson.* New York: Oxford Univ. Press, 2002.

Colón, Fernando. *The Life of the Admiral Christopher Columbus by His Son Ferdinand.* Trans. Benjamin Keen. New Brunswick: Rutgers Univ. Press, 1959.

Compton-Hall, Richard. *Submarine Boats: The Beginnings of Underwater Warfare.* London: Conway Maritime, 1983.

Confucius. *The Analects of Confucius (Lun Yu).* Trans. Chichuang Huang. New York: Oxford Univ. Press, 1999.

Conlan, Thomas D., trans. *In Little Need of Divine Intervention: Takezaki Suenaga's Scrolls of the Mongol Invasions of Japan.* Ithaca: Cornell East Asia Series, 2001.

Constable, Olivia Remie. "The Problem of Jettison in Medieval Mediterranean Maritime Law." *Journal of Medieval History* 20 (1994): 207–20.

———. *Trade and Traders in Muslim Spain: The Commercial Realignment of the Iberian Peninsula, 900–1500.* Cambridge: Cambridge Univ. Press, 1994.

Constantine VII Porphyrogenitus. *De administrando imperio.* Trans. R. J. H. Jenkins. Washington: Dumbarton Oaks Center for Byzantine Studies, 1985.

Cook, James. *The Journals of Captain James Cook on His Voyages of Discovery,* ed. by J. C. Beaglehole and R. A. Skelton. 4 vols. Cambridge: Hakluyt, 1955–74.

Cook, Noble David. *Born to Die: Disease and New World Conquest, 1492–1650.* Cambridge: Cambridge Univ. Press, 1998.

Corbett, Julian S. *The Successors of Drake.* London: Longmans, Green, 1916.

Cosentino, Salvatore. "Constans II and the Byzantine Navy." *Byzantinische Zeitschrift* 100:2 (2007): 577–603.

Cosmas Indicopleustes. *The Christian Topography of Cosmas, an Egyptian Monk.* Trans. J. W. McCrindle. London: Hakluyt, 1897.

Cowan, Edward. *Oil and Water: The* Torrey Canyon *Disaster.* Philadelphia: Lippincott, 1968.

Cowdrey, H. E. J. "The Mahdia Campaign of 1087." *English Historical Review* 92 (1977): 1–29.

Cowell, Edward B., trans. *The Jataka; or, Stories of the Buddha's Former Births.* 1895–1907. Reprint, London: Routledge & Kegan Paul, 1973.

Craig, Gordon A. *Germany, 1866–1945.* New York: Oxford Univ. Press, 1978.

Crespigny, Rafe de. *Generals of the South: The Foundation and Early History of the Three Kingdoms State of Wu.* Canberra: Australian National Univ., Faculty of Asian Studies, 1990.

Cressy, David. "The Vast and Furious Ocean: The Passage to Puritan New England." *New England Quarterly* 57:4 (1984): 511–32.

Crone, G. R., trans. *The Voyages of Cadamosto and Other Documents on Western Africa in the Second Half of the Fifteenth Century.* London: Hakluyt, 1937.

Crone, Patricia. *Meccan Trade and the Rise of Islam.* Princeton: Princeton Univ. Press, 1987.

Cross, Samuel Hazzard, and Olgerd P. Sherbowitz-Wetzor, trans. *Russian Primary Chronicle: Laurentian Text.* Cambridge: Mediaeval Academy of America, 1953.

Cruise Baltic. *Cruise Baltic Status Report*. 2007. http://www.cruisebaltic.com/media (636,1033)/Cruise_Baltic_status_report_Jan_07.pdf.

Crumlin-Pedersen, Ole. "Boats and Ships of the Baltic Sea in the 9th and 10th Centuries: The Archaeological and Iconographic Evidence." In *Wulfstan's Voyage*, ed. by Englert and Trakadas, 235–56.

———. "The Skuldelev Ships." *Acta Archaeologica* 38 (1967): 73–174.

Culavamsa: Being the More Recent Part of the Mahavamsa. Trans. C. Mabel Rickmers. London: Pali Text Society, 1973.

Cunliffe, Barry W. *The Extraordinary Voyage of Pytheas the Greek*. New York: Walker, 2002.

———. *Facing the Ocean: The Atlantic and Its People 8000 BC–AD 1500*. New York: Oxford Univ. Press, 2001.

Cust, Richard. *Charles I: A Political Life*. New York: Pearson/Longman, 2005.

Dalby, Michael T. "Court Politics in Late T'ang Times." In *The Cambridge History of China*. Vol. 3, *Sui and T'ang China, 589–906*, ed. by Denis Twitchett, 561–681. Cambridge: Cambridge Univ. Press, 1979.

Dalley, Stephanie, trans. *Myths from Mesopotamia: Creation, the Flood, Gilgamesh, and Others*. Oxford: Oxford Univ. Press, 1989.

Dalzell, George W. *Flight from the Flag: The Continuing Effect of the Civil War upon the American Carrying Trade*. Chapel Hill: Univ. of North Carolina Press, 1940.

Dante Alighieri. *The Divine Comedy of Dante Alighieri*. Vol. 1, *Inferno*. Trans. Robert M. Durling. New York: Oxford University Press, 1996.

D'Arms, John H. *Romans on the Bay of Naples: A Social and Cultural Study of the Villas and Their Owners from 150 B.C. to A.D. 400*. Cambridge: Harvard Univ. Press, 1970.

Das Gupta, Ashin. *Indian Merchants and the Decline of Surat: c. 1700–1750*. New Delhi: Manohar, 1994.

———. "The Maritime Merchant of India, c. 1500–1800." In *The World of the Indian Ocean Merchant, 1500–1800: Collected Essays of Ashin Das Gupta*, 88–101. Compiled by Uma Das Gupta. New Delhi: Oxford Univ. Press, 2001.

Davenport, Frances Gardiner, ed. *European Treaties Bearing on the History of the United States and Its Dependencies to 1648*. Washington: Carnegie Institution of Washington, 1917.

David, Charles Wendell, trans. *The Conquest of Lisbon*. 1936. Reprint, New York: Columbia University Press, 2001.

Davis, David Brion. *Slavery and Human Progress*. New York: Oxford University Press, 1984.

Davis, Lance Edwin, and Stanley L. Engerman. *Naval Blockades in Peace and War: An Economic History Since 1750*. Cambridge: Cambridge Univ. Press, 2006.

Davis, Ralph. *The Rise of the English Shipping Industry in the Seventeenth and Eighteenth Centuries*. London: Macmillan, 1962.

De Paor, Máire. *Patrick, the Pilgrim Apostle of Ireland*. New York: Regan, 2002.

De Vries, Kelly. *The Norwegian Invasion of England in 1066*. Woodbridge, UK: Boydell, 1999.

De Witte, Hubert. "The Maritime Topography of Medieval Bruges." In *Maritime Topography and the Medieval Town: Papers from the 5th International Conference on Waterfront Archaeology in Copenhagen, 14–16 May 1998*, ed. by Jan Bill and Berthe L. Clausen. Copenhagen: Nationalmuseet, 1999.

Declaration Concerning the Laws of Naval War, 208 Consol. T.S. 338 (1909). Univ. of Minnesota, Human Rights Library Online. http://www1.umn.edu/humanrts/instree/1909b.htm.

Deloche, Jean. "Geographical Considerations in the Localization of Ancient Sea-Ports of India." In *Trade in Early India*, ed. by Ranabir Chakravarti, 312–25. New Delhi: Oxford Univ. Press, 2001.

———. "Iconographic Evidence on the Development of Boat and Ship Structures in India (2nd C. B.C.–15TH C. A.D.)" In *Tradition and Archaeology: Early Maritime Contacts in the Indian Ocean*, ed. by Himanshu Prabha Ray and Jean-François Salles, 199–224. New Delhi: Manohar, 1999.

Demosthenes. *Against Meidias, Etc.* Trans. J. H. Vince. Cambridge: Harvard Univ. Press, 1935.

Deng, Gang. *Chinese Maritime Activities and Socioeconomic Development, c. 2100 B.C.–1900 A.D.* Westport: Greenwood, 1997.

———. *Maritime Sector, Institutions, and Sea Power of Premodern China.* Westport: Greenwood, 1999.

Dennis, Andrew, Peter Foote, and Richard Perkins, trans. *Laws of Early Iceland—Grágás: The Codex Regius of Grágás with Material from Other Manuscripts.* Winnipeg: Univ. of Manitoba Press, 1980.

Desloges, Yvon, and Alain Gelly. *The Lachine Canal: Riding the Waves of Industrial and Urban Development, 1860–1950.* Sillery: Septentrion, 2002.

DeVoto, Bernard, ed. *The Journals of Lewis and Clark.* Boston: Houghton Mifflin, 1997.

Di Meglio, R. R. "Arab Trade with Indonesia and the Malay Peninsula from the 8th to the 16th Century." In *Islam and the Trade of Asia*, ed. by D. S. Richards, 105–36. Oxford: Bruno Cassirer, 1970.

Dickens, Charles. *The Letters of Charles Dickens.* Ed. by Madeline House and Graham Storey. Oxford: Clarendon Press, 1965.

Diffie, Bailey W., and George D. Winius. *Foundations of the Portuguese Empire, 1415–1580.* Oxford: Oxford Univ. Press, 1977.

Dimitrova, Desislava Nikolaeva. *Seafarers' Rights in the Globalized Maritime Industry.* Alphen aan den Rijn: Kluwer Law International, 2010.

Dio Chrysostom. *Discourses.* 5 vols. Cambridge: Harvard Univ. Press, 1932–51.

Diodorus Siculus. *Library of History.* Trans. C. H. Oldfather. 12 vols. Cambridge: Harvard Univ. Press, 1933–67.

Dollinger, Philippe. *The German Hansa.* Trans. D. S. Ault and S. H. Steinberg. Stanford: Stanford Univ. Press, 1970.

Domingues, Francisco Contente. "The State of Portuguese Naval Forces in the Sixteenth Century." In *War at Sea in the Middle Ages and Renaissance*, ed. by John B. Hattendorf and Richard W. Unger, 187–98. Rochester, NY: Boydell, 2003.

Donnellan, Philip. *The Shoals of Herring.* Adapted by Philip Donnellan from the radio ballad "Singing the Fishing," by Ewan McColl, Peggy Seeger, and Charles Parker. Birmingham: BBC Colour, 1972.

Dotson, John E. "Fleet Operations in the First Genoese-Venetian War, 1264–1266." *Viator* 30 (1999): 165–80.

Douglass, Frederick. *The New National Era*, Aug. 17, 1871.

Doumas, Christos. *Wall-Paintings of Thera.* Athens: Thera Foundation, 1992.

Drake, Francis, and Francis Fletcher. *The World Encompassed.* 1628. Reprint, Ann Arbor: University Microfilms, 1966.

Dreyer, Edward L. *Zheng He: China and the Oceans in the Early Ming, 1405–1433.* New York: Pearson-Longman, 2007.

Duffy, John. "The Passage to the Colonies." *Mississippi Valley Historical Review* 38:1 (1951): 21–38.

Dugan, James. *The Great Iron Ship.* New York: Harper, 1953.

Duncan-Jones, Richard. *Economy of the Roman Empire.* Cambridge: Cambridge Univ. Press, 1974.

Dunlop, D. M. *The History of the Jewish Khazars*. Princeton: Princeton Univ. Press, 1954.

Duyvendak, J. J. L. "The True Dates of the Chinese Maritime Expeditions in the Early Fifteenth Century." *T'oung Pao* 34 (1938): 341–412.

Earle, T. F., and John Villiers, eds. and trans. *Albuquerque: Caesar of the East—Selected Texts by Afonso de Albuquerque and His Son*. Warminster, UK: Aris & Phillips, 1990.

Edwards, Clinton R. *Aboriginal Watercraft on the Pacific Coast of South America*. Berkeley: Univ. of California Press, 1965.

Ehrenkreutz, A. S. "The Place of Saladin in the Naval History of the Mediterranean Sea in the Middle Ages." *JAOS* 72:2 (1955): 100–116.

Elbl, Martin. "The Caravel." In *Cogs, Caravels and Galleons*, ed. by Gardiner and Unger, 91–98.

El-Hajji, A. A. "The Andalusian Diplomatic Relations with the Vikings During the Umayyad Period." *Hesperis Tamuda* 8 (1967): 67–110.

Elisonas, Jurgis. "The Inseparable Trinity: Japan's Relations with China and Korea." In *The Cambridge History of Japan*. Vol. 4, *Early Modern Japan*, ed. by John Whitney Hall, 235–300. Cambridge: Cambridge Univ. Press, 1991.

Elliott, J. H. *Empires of the Atlantic World: Britain and Spain in America, 1492–1830*. New Haven: Yale Univ. Press, 2006.

Ellmers, Detlev. "The Beginning of Boatbuilding in Central Europe." In *The Earliest Ships: The Evolution of Boats into Ships*, ed. by Robert Gardiner, 11–23. London: Conway Maritime, 1996.

———. "The Cog as Cargo Carrier." In *Cogs, Caravels and Galleons*, ed. by Gardiner and Unger, 29–46.

El-Sayed, Sayed Z. "Queen Hatshepsut's Expedition to the Land of Punt: The First Oceanographic Cruise?" *Quarterdeck* 3:1 (Spring 1995). www-ocean.tamu.edu/Quarterdeck/QD3.1/Elsayed/elsayed-hatshepsut.html.

Elvin, Mark. *The Pattern of the Chinese Past*. Stanford: Stanford Univ. Press, 1973.

Englert, Anton, and Athena Trakadas, eds. *Wulfstan's Voyage: The Baltic Sea Region in the Early Viking Age as Seen from Shipboard*. Roskilde, Denmark: Viking Ship Museum, 2009.

Ennin. *Ennin's Diary: The Record of a Pilgrimage to China in Search of the Law*. New York: Ronald, 1955.

Epstein, Jeremiah F. "Sails in Aboriginal Mesoamerica: Reevaluating Thompson's Argument." *American Anthropologist* 92:1 (1990): 187–92.

Epstein, Steven A. *Genoa and the Genoese, 958–1528*. Chapel Hill: Univ. of North Carolina Press, 1996.

Erlandson, Jon M., et al. "The Kelp Highway Hypothesis." *Journal of Island and Coastal Archaeology* 2 (2007): 161–74.

Errington, R. M. "Rome Against Philip and Antiochus." In *The Cambridge Ancient History*. Vol. 8, *Rome and the Mediterranean to 133 B.C.,* ed. by A. E. Astin et al., 244–89. 2nd ed. Cambridge: Cambridge Univ. Press, 1989.

Esmer, Ahmed Sükrü. "The Straits: Crux of World Politics." *Foreign Affairs* 25 (1947): 290–302.

Evans, David C., and Mark R. Peattie. *Kaigun: Strategy, Tactics, and Technology in the Imperial Japanese Navy, 1887–1941*. Annapolis: Naval Institute, 1997.

Evelyn, John. *The Diary of John Evelyn; Now First Printed in Full from the Manuscripts Belonging to Mr. John Evelyn*. Ed. by E. S. de Beer. Oxford: Clarendon Press, 1955.

Evelyn-White, H. G., trans. *Hesiod, the Homeric Hymns and Homerica*. London: Heinemann, 1914.

Fagan, Brian. *Fish on Friday: Feasting, Fasting and the Discovery of the New World*. New York: Basic Books, 2006.

Fahmy, Aly Mohamed. *Muslim Naval Organization in the Eastern Mediterranean from the Seventh to the Tenth Century A.D.* 2nd ed. Cairo: National Publication & Printing House, 1966.

———. *Muslim Sea-Power in the Eastern Mediterranean: From the Seventh to the Tenth Century A.D.* London: Luzac, 1950.

Fairbank, John King, Edwin O. Reischauer, and Albert M. Craig. *East Asia: Tradition and Transformation*. Boston: Houghton Mifflin, 1973.

Falconbridge, Alexander. *An Account of the Slave Trade on the Coast of Africa*. London, 1788.

Falconer, William. *An Universal Dictionary of the Marine*. London, 1780.

FAO Fisheries and Aquaculture Department. *The State of World Fisheries and Aquaculture, 2010*. Rome: Food & Agriculture Organization of the UN, 2010.

Faroqhi, Suraiya. *Ottoman Empire and the World Around It*. London: Tauris, 2005.

Faxian. *The Travels of Fa-hian*. In Xuanzang, *Si-yu-ki*.

Fernández-Armesto, Felipe. *Amerigo: The Man Who Gave His Name to America*. London: Weidenfeld & Nicolson, 2006.

———. *Before Columbus: Exploration and Colonization from the Mediterranean to the Atlantic, 1229–1492*. Philadelphia: Univ. of Pennsylvania Press, 1987.

———. *Columbus*. New York: Oxford Univ. Press, 1991.

———. "Medieval Atlantic Exploration: The Evidence of the Maps." In *Portugal, the Pathfinder*, ed. by Winius, 40–70.

———. "Spanish Atlantic Voyages and Conquests Before Columbus." In *Maritime History*. Vol. 1, *The Age of Discovery*, ed. by John B. Hattendorf, 137–47. Malabar, FL: Krieger, 1996.

———. "The Stranger-Effect in Early Modern Asia." In *Shifting Communities and Identity Formation in Early Modern Asia*, ed. by Blussé and Fernández-Armesto, 181–202.

Ferreiro, Larrie D. *Ships and Science: The Birth of Naval Architecture in the Scientific Revolution, 1600–1800*. Cambridge: MIT Press, 2007.

Ferry, David, trans. *Gilgamesh: A New Rendering in English Verse*. New York: Farrar, Straus & Giroux, 1993.

Fisher, Robin. "The Northwest from the Beginning of Trade with the Europeans to the 1880s." In *The Cambridge History of the Native Peoples of the Americas*. Vol. 1, *North America*, ed. by Bruce G. Trigger and Wilcomb E. Washburn, 117–82. Cambridge: Cambridge Univ. Press, 1996.

Fladmark, Knut. "Routes: Alternate Migration Corridors for Early Man in North America." *American Antiquity* 44:1 (1979): 55–69.

Flecker, Michael. "A Ninth-Century AD Arab or Indian Shipwreck in Indonesia: First Evidence for Direct Trade with China." *World Archaeology* 32:3 (2001): 335–54.

———. "A Ninth-Century AD Arab or Indian Shipwreck in Indonesia: Addendum." *IJNA* 37:2 (2008): 384–86.

Fletcher, M. E. "From Coal to Oil in British Shipping." *Journal of Transport History* 3 (1975): 1–19.

———. "The Suez Canal and World Shipping, 1869–1914." *Journal of Economic History* 18:4 (1958): 556–73.

Flexner, James T. *Steamboats Come True: American Inventors in Action*. New York: Viking, 1964.

Flodoard of Reims. *The Annals of Flodoard of Reims, 919–966*. Trans. Steven Fanning and Bernard S. Bachrach. Peterborough, ON: Broadview, 2004.

Florus, Lucius Annaeus. *Epitome of Roman History*. 1929. Reprint, Cambridge: Harvard Univ. Press, 1960.

Forrest, Thomas. *A Voyage to New Guinea and the Moluccas, 1774–1776*. Kuala Lumpur: Oxford Univ. Press, 1969.

Fox, Grace Estelle. *Britain and Japan, 1858–1883*. Oxford: Clarendon Press, 1969.

Franke, P. R. "Pyrrhus." In *The Cambridge Ancient History*. Vol. 7, pt. 2, *The Rise of Rome to 220 B.C.*, ed. by F. W. Walbank et al., 456–85. 2nd ed. Cambridge: Cambridge Univ. Press, 1989.

Franklin, Benjamin. *The Writings of Benjamin Franklin: 1783–1788*. Ed. Albert Henry Smyth. New York: Macmillan, 1906.

Frankopan, Peter. "Byzantine Trade Privileges to Venice in the Eleventh Century: The Chrysobull of 1092." *Journal of Medieval History* 20 (2004): 135–60.

Fraser, Antonia. *Royal Charles: Charles II and the Restoration*. New York: Simon & Schuster, 1979.

Fraser, P. M. *Ptolemaic Alexandria*. Oxford: Clarendon Press, 1972.

Frear, Hugo P. "History of Tankers." *New York Maritime Register* (1886): 135–44.

Friel, Ian. "The Carrack." In *Cogs, Caravels and Galleons*, ed. by Gardiner and Unger, 77–90.

———. *The Good Ship: Ships, Shipbuilding and Technology in England, 1200–1520*. Baltimore: Johns Hopkins Univ. Press, 1995.

———. *Maritime History of Britain and Ireland, c. 400–2001*. London: British Museum, 2003.

Frost, Alan. "James Mario Matra: Voyager with Cook." *Commonplace* 5:2 (2005), www .common-place.org.

Frost, Honor, et al. *Lilybaeum (Marsala): The Punic Ship, Final Excavation Report*. Rome: Notizie deglie scavi di antichità, 1976.

———. "The Marsala Punic Ship: An Obituary." *Mariner's Mirror* 83:2 (1997): 207–11.

Frost, O. W. *Bering: The Russian Discovery of America*. New Haven: Yale Univ. Press, 2003.

Fryer, S. E., and David K. Brown. "Whitehead, Robert," *Oxford Dictionary of National Biography*, ed. by H. C. G. Matthew and Brian Harrison. 58.670–71. 2nd ed. Oxford: Oxford Univ. Press, 2004.

Gaastra, Femme. *The Dutch East India Company: Expansion and Decline*. Zutphen, Netherlands: Walburg Pers, 2003.

Gabrielsen, Vincent. *The Naval Aristocracy of Hellenistic Rhodes*. Aarhus, Denmark: Aarhus Univ. Press, 1997.

Gadd, C. J. "The Dynasty of Agade and the Gutian Invasion." In *The Cambridge Ancient History*. Vol. 1, pt. 2, *Early History of the Middle East*, ed. by I. E. S. Edwards et al., 417–57. 3rd ed. Cambridge: Cambridge Univ. Press, 1971.

Gade, John Allyne. *The Hanseatic Control of Norwegian Commerce During the Late Middle Ages*. Leiden: Brill, 1951.

Games, Alison. "Migration." In *The British Atlantic World, 1500–1800*, ed. by David Armitage and Michael J. Braddick, 31–50. London: Palgrave Macmillan, 2002.

Gardiner, Robert, and Alastair Couper, eds. *The Shipping Revolution: The Modern Merchant Ship*. London: Conway Maritime, 1992.

Gardiner, Robert, and Ambrose Greenway, eds. *The Golden Age of Shipping: The Classic Merchant Ship, 1900–1960*. Annapolis: Naval Institute, 1994.

Gardiner, Robert, and John Morrison, eds. *The Age of the Galley: Mediterranean Oared Vessels Since Pre-Classical Times*. Annapolis: Naval Institute, 1995.

Gardiner, Robert, and Richard W. Unger, eds. *Cogs, Caravels and Galleons: The Sailing Ship, 1000–1650*. Annapolis: Naval Institute, 1994.

Garland, Charles, and Herbert S. Klein. "The Allotment of Space for Slaves Aboard Eighteenth-Century British Slave Ships." *William and Mary Quarterly*, 3rd Ser., 42:2 (1985): 238–48.

Gellius, Aulus. *Attic Nights.* Trans. John C. Rolfe. Cambridge: Harvard Univ. Press, 1927.

Gelpke, J. Sollewijn. "Afonso de Albuquerque's Pre-Portuguese Javanese Map, Partially Reconstructed from Francisco Rodrigues' Book." *Bijdragen tot de Taal-, Land- en Volkenkunde* 151 (1995): 76–99.

Genz, Joseph H. "Oceania: Polynesian and Micronesian Navigation." In *The Oxford Encyclopedia of Maritime History*, ed. by Hattendorf, 3:144–54.

Ghosh, A., ed. *An Encyclopedia of Indian Archaeology.* Vol. 2, *A Gazetteer of Explored and Excavated Sites in India.* Leiden: Brill, 1990.

Gibson, Andrew, and Arthur Donovan. *The Abandoned Ocean: A History of United States Maritime Policy.* Columbia: Univ. of South Carolina Press, 2000.

Gimbutas, Marija Alseikaite. *The Balts.* New York: Praeger, 1963.

Gladney, Dru C. *Muslim Chinese: Ethnic Nationalism in the People's Republic.* Cambridge: Harvard Univ. Press, 1996.

Gläser, Manfred, "The Development of the Harbours and Market Places of Lübeck." In *Maritime Topography and the Medieval Town*, ed. by Jan Bill and Birthe L. Clausen, 79–86. Copenhagen: National Museum, 1999.

Glete, Jan. "Naval Power and Control of the Sea in the Baltic in the Sixteenth Century." In *War at Sea in the Middle Ages and Renaissance*, ed. by John B. Hattendorf and Richard W. Unger, 217–32. Rochester, NY: Boydell, 2003.

———. *Navies and Nations: Warships, Navies, and State Building in Europe and America, 1500–1860.* Acta Universitatis Stockholmiensis. Stockholm Studies in History, 48. Stockholm: Almqvist & Wiksell International, 1993.

———. *Warfare at Sea, 1500–1650: Maritime Conflict and the Transformation of Europe.* London: UCL, 2000.

Goitein, S. D. "The Beginnings of the Karim Merchants and the Nature of Their Organization." In *Studies in Islamic History and Institutions*, 351–60. Leiden: Brill, 1966.

———. *A Mediterranean Society: The Jewish Communities of the Arab World as Portrayed in the Documents of the Cairo Geniza.* 6 vols. 1967. Reprint, Berkeley: Univ. of California Press, 1999.

———. "Two Eyewitness Reports on an Expedition of the King of Kish (Qais) Against Aden." *Bulletin of the School of Oriental and African Studies* 16 (1954): 247–57.

Goitein, S. D., and Mordechai A. Friedman. *India Traders of the Middle Ages: Documents from the Cairo Geniza, "India Book."* Leiden: Brill, 2008.

Goldsworthy, Adrian. *The Punic Wars.* London: Cassell, 2000.

Golovnin, V. M. *Memoirs of a Captivity in Japan During the Years 1811, 1812, and 1813; with Observations on the Country and the People.* 3 vols. London: Henry Colburn, 1824.

Gordan, John D., III. "The Trial of the Officers and Crew of the Schooner *Savannah*." *Supreme Court Historical Society 1983 Yearbook.* http://www.supremecourthistory.org.

Goslinga, Cornelis Ch. *The Dutch in the Caribbean and on the Wild Coast, 1580–1680.* Gainesville: Univ. of Florida Press, 1971.

Graff, David A. *Medieval Chinese Warfare, 300–900.* London: Routledge, 2002.

Graham, Gerald S. "Ascendancy of the Sailing Ship, 1850–1855." *Economic History Review*, n.s., 9:1 (1956): 74–88.

Gratzer, W. B. *Terrors of the Table: The Curious History of Nutrition.* New York: Oxford Univ. Press, 2005.

Green, J. N. "The Song Dynasty Shipwreck at Quanzhou, Fujian Province, People's Republic of China." *IJNA* 12 (1983): 253–61.

Green, J. N., and Zae Geun Kim. "The Shinan and Wando Sites, Korea: Further Information." *IJNA* 18 (1989): 33–41.

Green, Peter. *The Greco-Persian Wars.* Berkeley: Univ. of California Press, 1996.

Greenlee, William Brooks, ed. *The Voyage of Pedro Alvares Cabral to Brazil and India, from Contemporary Documents and Narratives.* London: Hakluyt, 1938.

Greenway, Ambrose. "Cargo Ships." In *The Golden Age of Shipping,* ed. by Gardiner and Greenway, 38–50.

Grenet, Frantz. "Les marchands sogdiens dans les mers du Sud à l'époque préislamique." *Cahiers d'Asie centrale* 1/2 (1996): 65–84.

Grescoe, Taras. *Bottomfeeder: How to Eat Ethically in a World of Vanishing Seafood.* New York: Bloomsbury, 2008.

Griffiths, Denis. *Brunel's* Great Western. Wellingborough: Patrick Stephens, 1985.

Grotius, Hugo. *The Free Sea.* Trans. Richard Hakluyt; ed. by David Armitage. Indianapolis: Liberty Fund, 2004.

Grousset, René. *The Empire of the Steppes: A History of Central Asia.* New Brunswick: Rutgers Univ. Press, 1970.

Guilmartin, J. F. *Gunpowder and Galleys: Changing Technology and Mediterranean Warfare at Sea in the Sixteenth Century.* Cambridge: Cambridge Univ. Press, 1975.

Gunawardana, R. A. L. H. "Changing Patterns of Navigation in the Indian Ocean and Their Impact on Pre-Colonial Sri Lanka." In *The Indian Ocean: Explorations in History, Commerce and Politics,* ed. by Satish Chandra, 54–89. New Delhi: Sage, 1987.

Guy, John S. "The Expansion of China's Trade with South-East Asia." In *Oriental Trade Ceramics in South-East Asia, Ninth to Sixteenth Century,* 13–22. New York: Oxford Univ. Press, 1986.

———. "Tamil Merchant Guilds and the Quanzhou Trade." In *The Emporium of the World: Maritime Quanzhou, 1000–1400,* ed. by Angela Schottenhammer, 283–306. Leiden: Brill, 2000.

Habachi, Labib. "Two Graffiti at Sehel from the Reign of Queen Hatshepsut." *Journal of Near Eastern Studies* 16 (1957): 88–104.

Habib, Irfan. "The Eighteenth Century in Indian Economic History." In *On the Eighteenth Century as a Category of Asian History,* ed. by Blussé and Gaastra, 217–36.

Habicht, C. "The Seleucids and Their Rivals." In *The Cambridge Ancient History.* Vol. 8, *Rome and the Mediterranean to 133 B.C.,* ed. by A. E. Astin et al., 324–87. 2nd ed. Cambridge: Cambridge Univ. Press, 1989.

Haddon, Alfred C., and James Hornell. *Canoes of Oceania.* 2 vols. 1936–38. Reprint, Honolulu: Bishop Museum, 1975.

Hadi Hasan, A. *A History of Persian Navigation.* London: Methuen, 1928.

Hagan, Kenneth J. *This People's Navy: The Making of American Sea Power.* New York: Free Press, 1991.

Hagy, James W. "800 Years of Etruscan Ships." *IJNA* 15:3 (1986): 221–50.

Haider, Najaf. "Structure and Movement of Wages in the Mughal Empire, 1500–1700." In *Wages and Currency: Global Comparisons from Antiquity to the Twentieth Century,* ed. Jan Lucassen, 293–321. Bern: Lang, 2007.

Haldane, Douglas. "The Fire-Ship of Al-Salih Ayyub and Muslim Use of 'Greek Fire.'" In *The Circle of War in the Middle Ages: Essays on Medieval Military and Naval History,* ed. by Donald J. Kagay and L. J. Andrew Villalon, 137–44. Woodbridge, UK: Boydell, 1999.

Haldon, John. "Military Service, Military Lands, and the Status of Soldiers." *Dumbarton Oaks Papers* 47 (1993): 1–67.

Hale, Edward Everett. *Letters on Irish Emigration.* Boston: Phillips, Sampson, 1852.

Hall, Kenneth R. "Economic History of Early Southeast Asia." In *The Cambridge History of Southeast Asia*, ed. by Tarling, 1.1:183–275.

———. "Local and International Trade and Traders in the Straits of Melaka Region: 600–1500." *JESHO* 47:2 (2004): 213–60.

———. *Maritime Trade and State Development in Early Southeast Asia*. Honolulu: Univ. of Hawai'i Press, 1985.

———. "The Upstream and Downstream Unification in Southeast Asia's First Islamic Polity: Changing Sense of Community in the Fifteenth Century *Hikayat Raja-Raja Pasai* Court Chronicle." *Journal of Southeast Asian Studies* 44 (2001): 198–229.

Halpern, Paul G. *A Naval History of World War I*. Annapolis: Naval Institute, 1994.

Hamblin, William James. "The Fatimid Navy During the Early Crusades: 1099–1124." *American Neptune* 46 (1986): 77–83.

"The Hamburg-American Yacht *Prinzessin Victoria Luise*." *Scientific American* 84:6 (Feb. 9, 1901): 86.

Handler, J. S. "Survivors of the Middle Passage: Life Histories of Enslaved Africans in British America." *Slavery & Abolition* 23:1 (2002): 25–56.

Hansen, Stig Jarle. *Piracy in the Greater Gulf of Aden: Myths, Misconceptions and Remedies*. Oslo: Norwegian Institute for Urban and Regional Research, 2009.

Harding, Richard. "Organizational Life Cycles, the SNR and Maritime History." *Mariner's Mirror* 97:2 (2011): 5–20.

Hart, Marjolein 't. "Intercity Rivalries and the Making of the Dutch State." In *Cities and the Rise of States in Europe, A.D. 1000 to 1800*, ed. by Charles Tilly and Wim P. Blockmans, 196–217. Boulder: Westview, 1994.

Hastings, Max. *The Korean War*. London: Pan, 1988.

Hattendorf, John B., ed. *The Oxford Encyclopedia of Maritime History*. 4 vols. New York: Oxford Univ. Press, 2007.

Havighurst, Walter. *The Long Ships Passing: The Story of the Great Lakes*. Reprint, Minneapolis: Univ. of Wisconsin Press, 2002.

Hawkesworth, John. *An Account of the Voyages Undertaken by the Order of His Present Majesty for Making Discoveries in the Southern Hemisphere*. 4 vols. 3rd ed. London, 1785.

Haycox, Stephen W. *Alaska: An American Colony*. Seattle: Univ. of Washington Press, 2002.

Haywood, John. *Dark Age Naval Power: A Reassessment of Frankish and Anglo-Saxon Seafaring Activity*. Rev. ed. Norfolk: Anglo-Saxon, 1999.

Heinzig, Dieter. *The Soviet Union and Communist China, 1945–1950: The Arduous Road to the Alliance*. Armonk, NY: M. E. Sharpe, 2003.

Hellie, Richard. *The Economy and Material Culture of Russia, 1600–1725*. 2nd ed. Chicago: Univ. of Chicago Press, 1999.

Henricus Lettus. *The Chronicle of Henry of Livonia*. Trans. James A. Brundage. 1961. Reprint, New York: Columbia Univ. Press, 2003.

Henthorn, William E. *A History of Korea*. New York: Free Press, 1971.

Hepper, David J. *British Warship Losses in the Age of Sail, 1650–1859*. Rotherfield, UK: Jean Boudriot, 1994.

Herlihy, David. *The Black Death and the Transformation of the West*. Ed. by Samuel K. Cohn, Jr. Cambridge: Harvard Univ. Press, 1997.

Herodotus. *The Histories*. Trans. Aubrey de Sélincourt. 1954. New ed., New York: Penguin, 1996.

Heywood, Linda M., and John K. Thornton. *Central Africans, Atlantic Creoles, and the Foundation of the Americas, 1585–1660*. New York: Cambridge Univ. Press, 2007.

Heywood, Thomas. *His Majesty's Royal Ship: A Critical Edition of Thomas Heywood's A True*

Description of His Majesties Royall Ship, ed. by Alan R. Young. New York: AMS Press, 1990.

Hill, George. *History of Cyprus*. Cambridge: Cambridge Univ. Press, 1940.

Hill, John E., trans. *The Western Regions According to the Hou Hanshu: The Xiyu Juan*. From *Hou Hanshu* 88. 2nd ed. 2003. http://depts.washington.edu/uwch/silkroad/texts/hhshu/hou_han_shu.html.

Hilton, George W. Eastland: *Legacy of the* Titanic. Stanford: Stanford University Press, 1995.

Hirth and Rockhill, see Chau Ju-kua.

Hitti, Philip K. *History of the Arabs from the Earliest Times to the Present*. 10th ed. New York: St. Martin's, 1970.

Hocker, F. "Lead Hull Sheathing in Antiquity." *Tropis* 3 (1995): 197–206.

Höckmann, Olaf. "Late Roman Rhine Vessels from Mainz, Germany." *IJNA* 22 (1993): 125–35.

———. "Late Roman River Craft from Mainz, Germany." In *Local Boats, Fourth International Symposium on Boat and Ship Archaeology, Porto 1985*, ed. by O. L. Filgueiras, 23–34. Oxford: British Archaeological Reports, 1988.

Hoffman, Bernard G. *Cabot to Cartier*. Toronto: Univ. of Toronto Press, 1961.

Hoffman, Philip G. "Australia's Debt to the American Revolution." *Historian* 17:2 (1954): 143–56.

Hollister, C. Warren. *Anglo-Saxon Military Institutions on the Eve of the Norman Conquest*. Oxford: Clarendon Press, 1962.

Holmes, G. A. "The 'Libel of English Policy.'" *English Historical Review* 76:299 (1961): 193–216.

Holmqvist, Wilhelm. "Helgö, an Early Trading Settlement in Central Sweden." In *Recent Archaeological Excavations in Europe*, ed. by Rupert Bruce-Mitford, 111–32. London: Routledge, 1975.

Homer. *The Iliad*. Trans. Robert Fagles. New York: Penguin, 1990.

———. *The Odyssey*. Trans. Robert Fagles. New York: Penguin, 1996.

Horn, James, and Philip D. Morgan. "Settlers and Slaves: European and African Migration to Early Modern British America." In *The Creation of the British Atlantic World*, ed. by Elizabeth Mancke and Carole Shammas, 19–44. Baltimore: Johns Hopkins Univ. Press, 2005.

Hornell, James. "Boat Oculi Survivals: Additional Records." *Journal of the Royal Anthropological Institute of Great Britain and Ireland* 68 (1938): 339–48.

———. "Indonesian Influence on East African Culture." *Journal of the Royal Anthropological Institute of Great Britain and Ireland* 64 (1934): 305–32.

———. "The Role of Birds in Early Navigation." *Antiquity* 20 (1946): 142–49.

———. *Water Transport Origins and Early Revolution*. Cambridge: Cambridge Univ. Press, 1946.

Hornung, Erik. *History of Ancient Egypt: An Introduction*. Trans. David Lorton. Ithaca: Cornell Univ. Press, 1999.

Horridge, Adrian. "The Story of Pacific Canoes and Their Rigs." In *From Buckfast to Borneo: Essays Presented to Father Robert Nicholl on the 85th Anniversary of His Birth, 27 March 1995*, ed. by Victor T. King and A. V. M. Horton, 541–58. Hull: Centre for South-East Asian Studies, 1995.

Hourani, George F. *Arab Seafaring in the Indian Ocean in Ancient and Early Medieval Times*. Revd. by John Carswell. Princeton: Princeton Univ. Press, 1995.

Howe, Octavius T., and Frederick C. Matthews. *American Clipper Ships, 1833–1858*. 2 vols. Salem: Marine Research Society, 1927.

Howse, Derek. "The Lunar-Distance Method of Measuring Longitude." In *The Quest for Longitude*, ed. by Andrewes, 150–61.

Hsü, Immanuel C. Y. *The Rise of Modern China*. 4th ed. Oxford: Oxford Univ. Press, 1990.

Hudson, Travis, Janice Timbrook, and Melissa Rempe. *Tomol: Chumash Watercraft as Described in the Ethnographic Notes of John P. Harrington*. Socorro, NM: Ballena, 1978.

Hughes, Lindsey. *Peter the Great: A Biography*. New Haven: Yale Univ. Press, 2002.

Huler, Scott. *Defining the Wind*. New York: Three Rivers, 2004.

Humins, John H. "Squanto and Massasoit: A Struggle for Power." *New England Quarterly* 60:1 (1987): 54–70.

Hunter, Louis C. *Steamboats on the Western Rivers: An Economic and Technological History*. Cambridge: Harvard Univ. Press, 1949.

Hydrographer of the Navy. *Ocean Passages for the World*. 2nd ed. London: Hydrographic Department, Admiralty, 1950.

Ibn Battuta. *The Travels of Ibn Battuta, A.D. 1325–1354*. Trans. H. A. R. Gibb. 5 vols. London: Hakluyt, 1958–2000.

Ibn Jubayr. *The Travels of Ibn Jubayr*. Trans. R. J. C. Broadhurst. London: Jonathan Cape, 1952.

Ibn Khaldun. *The Muqaddimah: An Introduction to History*. Trans. Franz Rosenthal. 3 vols. New York: Pantheon, 1958.

Ilanko Atikal. *The Tale of an Anklet: An Epic of South India. The* Cilappatikaram *of Ilanko Atikal*. Trans. R. Parthasarathy. New York: Columbia Univ. Press, 1993.

Imber, Colin. *The Ottoman Empire, 1300–1650: The Structure of Power*. New York: Palgrave Macmillan, 2002.

Inalcik, Halil. "The Ottoman State: Economy and Society, 1300–1600." In *An Economic and Social History of the Ottoman Empire, 1300–1914*, ed. by Halil Inalcik with Donald Quataert, 1:9–410. Cambridge: Cambridge Univ. Press, 1994.

"The International Geographical Congress of 1895." *Geographical Journal*, 8 (1896): 290–94.

International Maritime Organization. *International Shipping and World Trade: Facts and Figures*. London: IMO Maritime Knowledge Centre, 2009.

———. "List of IMO Conventions." http://www.imo.org/About/Conventions/ListOf Conventions/Pages/Default.aspx.

———. International Maritime Organization. *SOLAS 1974: Brief History—List of Amendments to Date and Where to Find Them*. http://www.imo.org/KnowledgeCentre/References AndArchives/HistoryofSOLAS.

International Military Tribunal. *Trial of the Major War Criminals Before the International Military Tribunal, Nuremberg*. Vol. 17, *Proceedings, 25 June 1946–8 July 1946*. Nuremberg: n.p., 1948.

International Whaling Commission. "Whale Sanctuaries." http://iwcoffice.org/conserva tion/sanctuaries.htm.

Irwin, Geoffrey. *The Prehistoric Exploration and Colonisation of the Pacific*. Cambridge: Cambridge Univ. Press, 1992.

Islam, Sirajul, and Sajahan Miah, eds. "Trade and Commerce." http://banglapedia.search .com.bd/HT/T_0204.htm.

Israel, Jonathan Irvine. *Dutch Primacy in World Trade, 1585–1740*. Oxford: Clarendon Press, 1989.

Isserlin, B. S. J., et al. "The Canal of Xerxes: Investigations in 1993–4." *Annual of the British School at Athens* 91 (1996): 329–40.

Ittersum, Martine Julia van. "Hugo Grotius in Context: Van Heemskerck's Capture of the

Santa Catarina and Its Justification in *De Jure Praedae* (1604–1606)." *Asian Journal of Social Science* 31 (2003): 511–48.

Jackson, Richard P. "From Profit-Sailing to Wage-Sailing: Mediterranean Owner-Captains and Their Crews During the Medieval Commercial Revolution." *Journal of European Economic History* 18:3 (1989): 605–28.

Jacq-Hergoualc'h, Michel. *The Malay Peninsula Crossroads of the Maritime Silk Road (100 BC–1300 AD)*. Leiden: Brill, 2002.

Jados, Stanley S. *Consulate of the Sea and Related Documents*. University: Univ. of Alabama Press, 1975.

James, Alan. "The Development of French Naval Policy: Richelieu's Early Aims and Ambitions." *French History* 12:4 (1998): 384–402.

James, Margery Kirkbride, ed. by Elspeth M. Veale. *Studies in the Medieval Wine Trade*. Oxford: Clarendon Press, 1971.

Jane, Cecil, ed. *Select Documents Illustrating the Four Voyages of Columbus*. 2 vols. London: Hakluyt, 1930–33.

Jay, Peter. *The Greek Anthology and Other Ancient Epigrams*. Harmondsworth: Penguin, 1981.

Jenkins, Nancy. *The Boat Beneath the Pyramid: King Cheops' Royal Ship*. New York: Holt, Rinehart & Winston, 1980.

Jenkins, R. J. H. "Cyprus Between Byzantium and Islam, A.D. 688–965." In *Studies Presented to D. M. Robinson*, ed. by G. E. Mylonas, 2:1006–1014. St. Louis: Washington Univ. Press, 1953.

Jesch, Judith. "Who Was Wulfstan." In *Wulfstan's Voyage*, ed. by Englert and Trakadas, 29–36.

Johns, Anthony H. "Islam in Southeast Asia: Reflections and New Directions." *Indonesia* 19 (1975): 33–55.

Johnson, Donald S. *Charting the Sea of Darkness: The Four Voyages of Henry Hudson*. New York: McGraw Hill, 1993.

Johnstone, Paul. *The Sea-craft of Prehistory*. London: Routledge & Kegan Paul, 1980.

Jones, Clement. *Pioneer Shipowners*. Liverpool: Journal of Commerce and Shipping Telegraph, 1935.

Jones, Gwyn. *A History of the Vikings*. New York: Oxford Univ. Press, 1968.

Jones, Nicolette. *The Plimsoll Sensation: The Great Campaign to Save Lives at Sea*. London: Abacus, 2007.

Jonkers, A. R. T. "Sailing Directions." In *The Oxford Encyclopedia of Maritime History*, ed. by Hattendorf, 3:457–63.

Jöns, Hauke. "Ports and *Emporia* of the Southern Coast: From Hedeby to Usedom and Wolin." In *Wulfstan's Voyage*, ed. by Englert and Trakadas, 160–81.

Juvenal. *The Sixteen Satires*. Trans. Peter Green. Harmondsworth: Penguin, 1967.

Kalland, Arne. *Fishing Villages in Tokugawa Japan*. Honolulu: Univ. of Hawai'i Press, 1995.

Kaminiates, John. *The Capture of Thessaloniki*. Trans. D. Frendo, A. Fotiou and G. Böhlig. Perth: Australian Assoc. for Byzantine Studies, 2000.

Kaukiainen, Yrjö. "Coal and Canvas: Aspects of the Competition Between Steam and Sail, c. 1870–1914." In *Sail and Steam: Selected Maritime Writings of Yrjö Kaukiainen*. Compiled by Lars U. Scholl and Merja-Liisa Hinkkanen, 113–28. St. John's, NL: International Maritime Economic History Assoc., 2004.

Kautilya, and R. P. Kangle, trans. *The Kautiliya Arthasastra*, pt. 2. 2nd ed. Bombay: Univ. of Bombay, 1972.

Keay, John. *The Honourable Company: A History of the English East India Company*. London: HarperCollins, 1995.

———. *India: A History.* New York: Grove, 2000.

Keith, Donald H., and Christian J. Buys. "New Light on Medieval Chinese Seagoing Ship Construction." *IJNA* 10 (1981): 119–32.

Kelly, Patrick J. *Tirpitz and the Imperial German Navy.* Bloomington: Indiana Univ. Press, 2011.

Kemp, John. "The COLREGS and the *Princess Alice.*" *Journal of Navigation* 61 (2008): 271–81.

Kennedy, Paul M. "The Development of German Naval Operations Plans Against England, 1896–1914." In *The War Plans of the Great Powers, 1880–1914*, ed. by Paul M. Kennedy, 171–98. London: Unwin Hyman, 1979.

———. *The Rise and Fall of British Naval Mastery.* London: Ashfield, 1987.

Kerner, Robert J. *The Urge to the Sea: The Course of Russian History—The Role of Rivers, Portages, Ostrogs, Monasteries and Furs.* Berkeley: Univ. of California Press, 1942.

Khalilieh, Hassan S. *Admiralty and Maritime Laws in the Mediterranean Sea (ca. 800–1050): The Kitab Akriyat Al-Sufun Vis-à-Vis the Nomos Rhodion Nautikos.* Leiden: Brill, 2006.

———. *Islamic Maritime Law: An Introduction.* Leiden: Brill, 1998.

Kim, H. Edward, and Donald H. Keith. "A 14th-Century Cargo Makes Port at Last." *National Geographic* 156:2 (Aug. 1979): 230–43.

Kim, Zae-Geun. "An Outline of Korean Shipbuilding History." *Korea Journal* 29:10 (Oct. 1989): 4–17.

King, Andrew L. "'John Harrison, Clockmaker at Barrow; Near Barton upon Humber; Lincolnshire': The Wooden Clocks, 1713–1730." In *The Quest for Longitude*, ed. by Andrewes, 168–87.

King, Charles. *The Black Sea: A History.* New York: Oxford Univ. Press, 2004.

Kirby, David, and Merja-Liisa Hinkkanen. *The Baltic and North Seas.* London: Routledge, 2000.

Kirch, Patrick Vinton. *On the Road of the Winds: An Archaeological History of the Pacific Islands Before European Contact.* Berkeley: Univ. of California Press, 2000.

Klooster, Wim. *Illicit Riches.* Leiden: KITLV, 1998.

Knaap, Gerrit J., and Heather Sutherland. *Monsoon Traders.* Leiden: KITLV, 2004.

Knecht, Robert Jean. *Renaissance Warrior and Patron: The Reign of Francis I.* Cambridge: Cambridge Univ. Press, 1994.

Knight, Roger. *The Pursuit of Victory: The Life and Achievement of Horatio Nelson.* New York: Basic Books, 2005.

Koeman, Cornelis, Günter Schilder, Marco van Egmond, et al., "Commercial Cartography and Map Production in the Low Countries, 1500–ca. 1672." In *The History of Cartography.* Vol. 3, *Cartography in the Renaissance*, ed. by David Woodward, 1296–383. Chicago: University of Chicago Press, 2007.

Kortepeter, Carl M. "Ottoman Imperial Policy and the Economy of the Black Sea Region in the Sixteenth Century." *JAOS* 86:2 (1966): 86–113.

Kowaleski, Maryann. "Commercialization of the Sea Fisheries in Medieval England and Wales." *International Journal of Maritime History* 15:2 (2005): 177–231.

Kramer, Samuel Noah, and John R. Maier. *Myths of Enki, the Crafty God.* New York: Oxford Univ. Press, 1989.

Kubiak, Wladyslaw B. "The Byzantine Attack on Damietta in 853 and the Egyptian Navy in the 9th Century." *Byzantion* 40 (1970): 45–66.

Kuhrt, Amélie. *The Ancient Near East.* 2 vols. New York: Routledge, 1997.

Kulkarni, A. R. "Marathas and the Sea." In *Maritime Heritage of India*, ed. by K. S. Behera, 206–13. New Delhi: Aryan Books, 1999.

Kulke, Hermann. "The Naval Expeditions of the Cholas." In *Nagapattinam to Suvarnadvipa*, ed. by Kulke, Kesavapany, and Sakhuja, 1–19.

Kulke, Hermann, K. Kesavapany, and Vijay Sakhuja, eds. *Nagapattinam to Suvarnadvipa: Reflections on the Chola Naval Expeditions to Southeast Asia*. Singapore: ISEAS, 2009.

Kuwabara, Jitsuzo. "On P'u Shou-keng, a Man of the Western Regions, Who Was Superintendent of the Trading Ships Office in Ch'uan-chou Towards the End of the Sung Dynasty." *Memoirs of the Research Department of the Toyo Bunko* 2 (1928): 1–79.

Labaree, Benjamin Woods. *The Boston Tea Party*. New York: Oxford Univ. Press, 1964.

Laiou, Angeliki E. "Byzantine Traders and Seafarers." In *The Greeks and the Sea*, ed. by Spyros Vryonis, Jr., 79–96. New Rochelle: Caratzas, 1992.

Lambert, Andrew. *Battleships in Transition: The Creation of the Steam Battlefleet, 1815–1860*. London: Conway Maritime, 1984.

———. *The Crimean War: British Grand Strategy Against Russia, 1853–56*. Manchester, UK: Manchester Univ. Press, 1990.

———. *Warrior: Restoring the World's First Ironclad*. London: Conway Maritime, 1987.

Landström, Björn. *Ships of the Pharaohs: 4,000 Years of Egyptian Shipbuilding*. New York: Doubleday, 1970.

Lane, Frederic C. "The Crossbow in the Nautical Revolution of the Middle Ages." In *Economy, Society, and Government in Medieval Italy: Essays in Memory of Robert L. Reynolds*, ed. by David Herlihy, Robert S. Lopez, and Vsevolod Slessarev, 35–41. Kent: Kent State Univ. Press, 1969.

———. "The Economic Meaning of the Invention of the Compass." *American Historical Review* 68:3 (1963): 605–17.

———. "The Economic Meaning of War and Protection." In *Venice and History: The Collected Papers of Frederic C. Lane*, ed. by Fernand Braudel et al., 383–98. Baltimore: Johns Hopkins Univ. Press, 1966.

———. "The Mediterranean Spice Trade: Its Revival in the Sixteenth Century." In *Venice and History: The Collected Papers of Frederic C. Lane*, 25–35. Baltimore: Johns Hopkins Univ. Press, 1966.

———. *Ships for Victory: A History of Shipbuilding Under the United States Maritime Commission in World War II*. Baltimore: Johns Hopkins Univ. Press, 1951.

———. "Venetian Shipping During the Commercial Revolution." *American Historical Review* 38:2 (1933): 219–39.

———. *Venetian Ships and Shipbuilders of the Renaissance*. 1934. Reprint, Baltimore: Johns Hopkins Univ. Press, 1992.

———. *Venice: A Maritime Republic*. Baltimore: Johns Hopkins Univ. Press, 1973.

Lane, Kris E. *Pillaging the Empire: Piracy in the Americas, 1500–1750*. Armonk, NY: M. E. Sharpe, 1998.

Lapidge, Michael, ed. *Blackwell Encyclopaedia of Anglo-Saxon England*. Oxford: Blackwell, 1999.

Larson, Laurence Marcellus, trans. *The King's Mirror*. New York: American-Scandinavian Foundation, 1917.

Las Casas, Bartolomé de. *Las Casas on Columbus: Background and the Second and Fourth Voyages*. Trans. Nigel Griffin. Repertorium Columbianum 7. Turnhout, Belgium: Brepols, 1999.

Lavery, Brian. *The Ship of the Line: The Development of the Battlefleet, 1650–1850*. London: Conway Maritime, 2003.

Lazenby, J. F. "Diekplous." *Greece and Rome*, 2nd ser., 34:2 (1987): 169–77.

Leamon, James S. *Revolution Downeast: The War for American Independence in Maine*. Amherst: Univ. of Massachusetts Press, 1993.

Lebecq, Stéphane. *Marchands et navigateurs frisons du haut Moyen Age*. Lille, France: Presses universitaires de Lille, 1983.

———. "The Northern Seas (Fifth to Eighth Centuries)." In *The New Cambridge Medieval History*. Vol. 1, *c. 500–c. 700*, ed. by Paul Fouracre, 639–60. Cambridge: Cambridge Univ. Press, 1995.

Lee, Edwin. *Singapore: The Unexpected Nation*. Singapore: Institute of Southeast Asian Studies, 2008.

Lee, Kenneth B. *Korea and East Asia: The Story of a Phoenix*. Westport: Praeger, 1997.

Lee, Ki-baek. *A New History of Korea*. Trans. Edward W. Wagner. Cambridge: Harvard-Yenching Institute, 1984.

Leighton, Richard M., and Robert W. Coakley. *Global Logistics and Strategy*. 2 vols. 1955. Reprint, Washington: Center of Military History, 1995.

Leitholdt, Eva, Christoph Zielhofer, Stefanie Berg-Hobohm, et al. "*Fossa Carolina:* The First Attempt to Bridge the Central European Watershed—A Review, New Findings, and Geoarchaeological Challenges." *Geoarchaeology* 27:1 (2012): 88–104.

Lend-Lease Act. Public Law 77–11, 77th Cong., 1st sess. (Mar. 11, 1941).

Leshnik, Lawrence S. "The Harappan 'Port' at Lothal: Another View." In *Ancient Cities of the Indus*, ed. by Gregory L. Possehl, 203–11. Durham: Carolina Academic Press, 1979.

Levi, Sylvain. "Manimekhala, a Divinity of the Sea." *Indian Historical Quarterly* 6:4 (1930): 597–614.

Levinson, Marc. *The Box: How the Shipping Container Made the World Smaller and the World Economy Bigger*. Princeton: Princeton University Press, 2006.

Levy, Howard S. *Biography of Huang Ch'ao*. Trans. Howard S. Levy. Berkeley: Univ. of California Press, 1955.

Lewis, Archibald R. "Northern European Sea Power and the Straits of Gibraltar, 1031–1350 A.D." In *Order and Innovation in the Middle Ages: Essays in Honor of Joseph R. Strayer*, ed. by William C. Jordan, Bruce McNab, and Teofilo F. Ruiz, 139–64. Princeton: Princeton Univ. Press, 1976.

Lewis, David. *We, the Navigators: The Ancient Art of Landfinding in the Pacific*. 2nd ed. Honolulu: Univ. of Hawai'i Press, 1994.

Li Guo-Qing. "Archaeological Evidence for the Use of '*Chu-nam*' on the 13th Century Quanzhou Ship, Fujian Province, China." *IJNA* 18:4 (1989): 277–83.

Li Tana. "A View from the Sea: Perspectives on the Northern and Central Vietnamese Coast." *JSEAS* 37:1 (2006): 83–102.

Lieberman, Victor. *Strange Parallels: Southeast Asia in Global Context, c. 800–1830*. 2 vols. Cambridge: Cambridge Univ. Press, 2003–9.

Lien-sheng Yang. *Money and Credit in China: A Short History*. Cambridge: Harvard Univ. Press, 1952.

Linden, H. Vander. "Alexander VI and the Demarcation of the Maritime and Colonial Domains of Spain and Portugal, 1493–1494." *American Historical Review* 22:1 (1916): 1–20.

Linschoten, Jan Huygen van. *The Voyage of John Huyghen van Linschoten to the East Indies*, ed. by Arthur Coke Burnell and P. A. Tiele. 2 vols. London: Hakluyt, 1885.

Lipke, Paul. *The Royal Ship of Cheops: A Retrospective Account of the Discovery, Restoration and Reconstruction. Based on Interviews with Hag Ahmed Youssef Moustafa*. Oxford: British Archaeological Reports, 1984.

Liritzis, Veronica McGeehan. "Seafaring, Craft and Cultural Contact in the Aegean During the 3rd Millennium BC." *IJNA* 17:3 (1988): 237–56.

Livy. *Rome and Italy: Books 6 to 10.* Trans. Betty Radice. New York: Penguin, 1982.

———. *Rome and the Mediterranean: Books 31–45.* Trans. Henry Bettenson. New York: Penguin, 1976.

Lloyd, Alan B. "Necho and the Red Sea: Some Considerations." *Journal of Egyptian Archaeology* 63 (1977): 142–55.

Lloyd, Christopher. "Victualling of the Fleet in the Eighteenth and Nineteenth Centuries." In *Starving Sailors: The Influence of Nutrition upon Naval and Maritime History*, ed. by J. Watt, E. J. Freeman, and W. F. Bynum, 9–15. London: National Maritime Museum, 1981.

Lo Jung-Pang. "Chinese Shipping and East-West Trade from the Tenth to the Fourteenth Century." In *Sociétés et compagnies de commerce en Orient et dans l'océan Indien: actes du huitième colloque international d'histoire maritime (Beyrouth, 5–10 septembre 1966)*, ed. by Michel Mollat, 167–75. Paris: S.E.V.P.E.N., 1970.

———. "Controversy over Grain Conveyance During the Reign of Qubilai Qaqn, 1260–94." *Far Eastern Quarterly* 13:3 (1954): 262–85.

———. "The Decline of the Early Ming Navy." *Oriens Extremus.* 5 (1958): 149–68.

———. "The Termination of the Early Ming Naval Expeditions." In *Papers in Honour of Professor Woodbridge Bingham, a Festschrift for His Seventy-Fifth Birthday*, ed. by James B. Parson. San Francisco: Chinese Materials Center, 1976.

Lockhart, James, and Enrique Otte. *Letters and People of the Spanish Indies, Sixteenth Century.* Cambridge: Cambridge Univ. Press, 1976.

LoGerfo, James W. "Sir William Dolben and 'The Cause of Humanity': The Passage of the Slave Trade Regulation Act of 1788." *Eighteenth-Century Studies* 6:4 (1973): 431–51.

Lombard, Maurice. "Arsenaux et bois de marine dans la Méditerranée musulmane (VIIe-XIe siècle)." In *Le navire et l'économie maritime du Moyen-Age au XVIIIe siècle principalement en Méditerranée*, ed. by M. Mollat, 53–106. Paris: S.E.V.P.E.N., 1958.

Longnaker, J. L. "History of Insurance Law." *Insurance Law Journal* 477 (1962): 644–46.

Lopez, Robert S. "Back to Gold, 1252." *Economic History Review*, n.s., 9:2 (1956): 219–40.

———. *The Commercial Revolution of the Middle Ages, 950–1350.* Cambridge: Cambridge Univ. Press, 1976.

———. "European Merchants in the Medieval Indies: The Evidence of Commercial Documents." *Journal of Economic History* 3:2 (1943): 164–84.

———. "Majorcans and Genoese on the North Sea Route in the 13th Century." *Revue belge de philologie et d'histoire* 29 (1951): 1163–79.

Lord, Henry. *A Display of Two Forraigne Sects in the East Indies: Vizt: The Sect of the Banians the Ancient Natiues of India and the Sect of the Persees the Ancient Inhabitants of Persia.* London: Francis Constable, 1630.

Louisiana Department of Transportation and Development. LOOP Program. http://www.dotd.louisiana.gov/programs_grants/loop/.

Lowe, William C. "Confederate Naval Strategy: Letters of Marque." http://ehistory.osu.edu/uscw/features/articles/0005/privateers.cfm.

Lu, David J. *Japan: A Documentary History.* Armonk, NY: M. E. Sharpe, 1997.

Lucian. "The Ship or the Wishes." In *Lucian.* Trans. K. Kilburn (Vol. 6). Cambridge: Harvard Univ. Press, 1959.

Lyman, John. "Register Tonnage and Its Measurement." 2 parts. *American Neptune* 5 (1945): 223–34, 311–25.

Ma Huan. *Ying-yai Sheng-lan: The Overall Survey of the Ocean's Shores [1433]*. Trans. J. V. G. Mills. 1970. Reprint, Bangkok: White Lotus, 1997.

Maber, John M. "Nordenfelt Submarines." *Warship* 8 (1984): 218–25.

Macdougall, Norman. "'The Greattest Scheip That Ewer Saillit in Ingland or France." In *Scotland and War, AD 79–1918*, 36–60. Savage, MD: Barnes & Noble, 1991.

MacLeod, Roy M. "Social Policy and the 'Floating Population': The Administration of the Canal Boats Acts, 1877–1899." *Past and Present* 35 (1966): 101–32.

Madariaga, Isabel de. *Catherine the Great: A Short History*. New Haven: Yale Univ. Press, 1990.

Magnusson, Magnus. *The Vikings*. Stroud, UK: Tempus, 2000.

Magnusson, Magnus, and Hermann Pálsson, trans. *The Vinland Sagas: The Norse Discovery of America (Graenlendinga Saga and Eirik's Saga)*. Baltimore: Penguin, 1965.

Magnússon, Sigurdur A. *Northern Sphinx: Iceland and the Icelanders from the Settlement to the Present*. Reykjavik: English Bookshop, 1977.

Magra, Christopher. *The Fisherman's Cause: Atlantic Commerce and Maritime Dimensions of the American Revolution*. New York: Cambridge Univ. Press, 2009.

Mahan, Alfred Thayer. *The Influence of Sea Power upon History, 1600–1783*. 5th ed. 1894. Reprint, New York: Dover, 1987.

———. "The United States Looking Outward." *Atlantic Monthly* 66 (Dec. 1809): 816–24. http://www.theatlantic.com/doc/189012/mahan-outward.

Major, John. "The Navy Plans for War." In *In Peace and War: Interpretations of American Naval History, 1775–1984*, ed. by Kenneth J. Hagan, 237–62. 2nd ed. Westport: Greenwood, 1984.

Mak, James, and Gary M. Walton. "Steamboats and the Great Productivity Surge in River Transportation." *Journal of Economic History* 32:3 (1972): 619–40.

Makrypoulias, Christos G. "Byzantine Expeditions Against the Emirate of Crete, c. 825–949." *Graeco-Arabica* 7–8 (2000): 347–62.

Malone, Joseph J. *Pine Trees and Politics: The Naval Stores and Forest Policy in Colonial New England, 1691–1775*. Seattle: Univ. of Washington Press, 1964.

Mancke, Elizabeth. "Early Modern Expansion and the Politicization of Oceanic Space." *Geographical Review* 89:2 (1999): 225–36.

Manguin, Pierre-Yves. "The Archaeology of Early Maritime Polities of Southeast Asia." In *Southeast Asia from Prehistory to History*, ed. by Ian C. Glover and Peter Bellwood, 282–313. London: RoutledgeCurzon, 2004.

———. "The Southeast Asian Ship: An Historical Approach." *JSEAS* 11:2 (1980): 266–76.

———. "Southeast Asian Shipping in the Indian Ocean During the First Millennium A.D." In *Tradition and Archaeology: Early Maritime Contacts in the Indian Ocean*, ed. by Himanshu Prabha Ray and Jean-François Salles, 181–97. New Delhi: Manohar, 1999.

———. "Trading Ships of the South China Sea." *JESHO* 36:3 (1993): 253–80.

Mann, Charles C. *1491: New Revelations of the Americas Before Columbus*. New York: Knopf, 2005.

Manning, Patrick. *Navigating World History (Historians Create a Global Past)*. New York: Palgrave Macmillan, 2003.

Manu. *The Laws of Manu*. Trans. Wendy Doniger and Brian K. Smith. Harmondsworth: Penguin, 1991.

Marcus, G. J. *The Conquest of the North Atlantic*. Woodbridge, UK: Boydell, 1980.

Margariti, Roxani Eleni. *Aden and the Indian Ocean Trade: 150 Years in the Life of a Medieval Arabian Port*. Chapel Hill: Univ. of North Carolina Press, 2007.

Mariners' Museum. *Aak to Zumbra: A Dictionary of the World's Watercraft*, ed. by Beverly

McMillan, Susannah Livingston, and Susan Beaven Rutter. Newport News, VA: Mariners' Museum, 2000.

Marsden, Peter. *A Ship of the Roman Period: From Blackfriars, in the City of London.* London: Guildhall Museum, 1967.

Marshall, P. J. "The English in Asia to 1700." In *The Oxford History of the British Empire.* Vol. 1, *The Origins of Empire,* ed. by Nicholas Canny, 264–85. Oxford: Oxford Univ. Press, 1998.

———. "Introduction." In *Oxford History of the British Empire.* Vol. 2, *The Eighteenth Century,* 1–27. Oxford: Oxford Univ. Press, 1998.

Martin, Colin, and Geoffrey Parker. *The Spanish Armada.* Manchester, UK: Manchester Univ. Press, 1999.

Mason, David J. P. *Roman Britain and the Roman Navy.* Stroud, UK: Tempus, 2003.

Massarella, Derek. "The Jesuits and Japan." In *Vasco da Gama and the Linking of Europe and Asia,* ed. by Anthony Disney and Emily Booth, 233–47. New Delhi: Oxford Univ. Press, 2000.

Masterson, Daniel M., and Sayaka Funada. "The Japanese in Peru and Brazil: A Comparative Perspective." In *Mass Migration to Modern Latin America,* ed. by Samuel L. Bailey and Eduardo José Míguez, 113–36. Wilmington: Scholarly Resources, 2003.

Mathew, Kuzhippalli Skaria. *Portuguese Trade with India in the Sixteenth Century.* New Delhi: Manohar, 1983.

Matthew, Donald. *The Norman Kingdom of Sicily.* Cambridge: Cambridge Univ. Press, 1992.

Maury, Matthew Fontaine. *Steam-lanes Across the Atlantic.* Washington, D.C., 1872.

Maxtone-Graham, John. *Normandie: France's Legendary Art Deco Ocean Liner.* New York: Norton, 2007.

———. *The Only Way to Cross.* New York: Macmillan, 1972.

McCormick, Michael. *Origins of the European Economy: Communications and Commerce,* AD *300–900.* Cambridge: Cambridge Univ. Press, 2001.

McGhee, Robert. "Epilogue: Was There Continuity from Norse to Post-Medieval Explorations of the New World?" In *Contact, Continuity, and Collapse: The Norse Colonization of the North Atlantic,* ed. by James H. Barett, 239–48. Turnhout: Brepols, 2003.

McGrail, Sean. "Boats and Boatmanship in the Southern North Sea and Channel." In *Maritime Celts, Frisians and Saxons,* ed. by Seán McGrail, 32–48. London: Council for British Archaeology, 1990.

———. *Boats of the World from the Stone Age to Medieval Times.* Oxford: Oxford Univ. Press, 2001.

———. "Romano-Celtic Boats and Ships: Characteristic Features." *IJNA* 24:2 (1995): 139–45.

McGregor, Malcolm F. *The Athenians and Their Empire.* Vancouver: Univ. of British Columbia Press, 1987.

McPhee, John A. *The Survival of the Bark Canoe.* New York: Farrar, Straus & Giroux, 1975.

McPherson, Kenneth. *The Indian Ocean: A History of People and the Sea.* New Delhi: Oxford Univ. Press, 1993.

Meiggs, Russell. *Trees and Timber in the Ancient Mediterranean World.* Oxford: Clarendon Press, 1982.

Merwin, Douglas. "Selections from *Wen-wu* on the Excavation of a Sung Dynasty Seagoing Vessel in Ch'üan-chou." *Chinese Sociology and Anthropology* 9 (Spring 1977): 3–106.

Meurer, Peter H. "Cartography in the German Lands, 1450–1650." In *The History of Cartography.* Vol. 3, *Cartography in the Renaissance,* ed. by David Woodward, 1172–245. Chicago: University of Chicago Press, 2007.

Middleton, Neil. "Early Medieval Port Customs, Tolls and Controls on Foreign Trade." *Early Medieval Europe* 13:4 (2005): 313–58.

Míguez, Eduardo José. "Introduction: Foreign Mass Migration to Latin America in the Nineteenth and Twentieth Centuries." In *Mass Migration to Modern Latin America*, ed. by Samuel L. Bailey and Eduardo José Míguez, xiii–xxv. Wilmington: Scholarly Resources, 2003.

Miksic, John N. *Borobudur: Golden Tales of the Buddha*. Singapore: Periplus, 1990.

Miller, David E. "Maritime Fur Trade Rivalry in the Pacific Northwest." *Historian* (1959): 392–408.

Miller, Edward S. *War Plan Orange: The U.S. Strategy to Defeat Japan, 1897–1945*. Annapolis: Naval Institute, 2007.

Miller, Nathan. *War at Sea: A Naval History of World War II*. New York: Oxford University Press, 1996.

Millett, Paul. "Maritime Loans and the Structure of Credit in Fourth-Century Athens." In *Trade in the Ancient Economy*, ed. by Peter Garnsey, Keith Hopkins, and C. R. Whittaker, 36–52. Berkeley: Univ. of California Press, 1983.

Milne, Gustav. "Maritime Traffic Between the Rhine and Roman Britain: A Preliminary Note." In *Maritime Celts, Frisians and Saxons*, ed. by McGrail, 82–85.

Mitsusada, Inoue, with Delmer M. Brown. "The Century of Reform." In *The Cambridge History of Japan*, ed. by Brown, 1:163–220.

Mittelberger, Gottlieb. *Journey to Pennsylvania*. Cambridge: Belknap, 1960.

Montet, Pierre. *Everyday Life in Egypt in the Days of Ramesses the Great*. Trans. A. R. Maxwell-Hyslop and Margaret S. Drower. 1958. Reprint, Westport: Greenwood, 1974.

Mookerji, Radhakumud. *Indian Shipping: A History of the Sea-Borne Trade and Maritime Activity of the Indian from the Earliest Times*. London: Longmans, Green, 1912.

Morgan, Robert J. "Des Barres, Joseph Frederick Wallet." *Dictionary of Canadian Biography Online*. www.biographi.ca/009004-119.01-e.php?BioId=36955.

Morison, Samuel Eliot. *The European Discovery of America: The Northern Voyages, A.D. 500–1600*. New York: Oxford Univ. Press, 1971.

———. *Maritime History of Massachusetts, 1783–1860*. Boston: Houghton Mifflin, 1941.

———. *"Old Bruin," Commodore Matthew C. Perry, 1794–1858*. Boston: Little, Brown, 1967.

———. *Samuel de Champlain: Father of New France*. Boston: Houghton Mifflin, 1972.

———. *The Two-Ocean War: A Short History of the United States Navy in the Second World War*. Boston: Little, Brown, 1963.

Morison, Samuel Eliot, Henry Steele Commager, and William Leuchtenberg. *A Concise History of the American Republic*. New York: Oxford Univ. Press, 1979.

Morrison, J. S., and J. F. Coates. *The Athenian Trireme: The History and Reconstruction of an Ancient Greek Warship*. New York: Cambridge Univ. Press, 1986.

Moseley, Michael Edward. *The Incas and Their Ancestors: The Archaeology of Peru*. London: Thames & Hudson, 1992.

———. *The Maritime Foundations of Andean Civilization*. Menlo Park, CA: Cummings, 1975.

Mote, F. W. *Imperial China: 900–1800*. Cambridge: Harvard Univ. Press, 1999.

Mott, Lawrence V. *The Development of the Rudder: A Technological Tale*. College Station: Texas A&M Univ. Press, 1997.

———. *Sea Power in the Medieval Mediterranean: The Catalan-Aragonese Fleet in the War of the Sicilian Vespers*. Gainesville: Univ. Press of Florida, 2003.

Moya, José C. "Spanish Emigration to Cuba and Argentina." In *Mass Migration to Modern*

Latin America, ed. by Samuel L. Bailey and Eduardo José Míguez, 9–28. Wilmington: Scholarly Resources, 2003.

Mukund, Kanakalatha. *Trading World of the Tamil Merchant: Evolution of Merchant Capitalism in the Coromandel*. Chennai, India: Orient Longman, 1999.

Mullen, Michael. "Remarks as Delivered for the 17th International Seapower Symposium, Naval War College, Newport, RI, September 21, 2005." http://www.navy.mil/navy data/cno/mullen/speeches/mullen050921.txt.

Müller, F. Max, ed. *Sacred Books of the East*. 50 vols. Oxford: Clarendon Press, 1879–1910.

Muqaddasi, Muhammad ibn Ahmad al-. *The Best Divisions for Knowledge of the Regions: A Translation of Ahsan al-Taqasim fi Marifat al-Aqalim*. Trans. Basil Anthony Collins. Reading, UK: Centre for Muslim Contribution to Civilisation/Garnet, 1994.

Murat, Inès. *Colbert*. Charlottesville: Univ. Press of Virginia, 1984.

Murfett, Malcolm. *Naval Warfare, 1919–1945: An Operational History of the Volatile War at Sea*. London: Routledge, 2009.

Murphey, Rhoads. *The Outsiders: The Western Experience in India and China*. Ann Arbor: Univ. of Michigan Press, 1977.

Murray, Oswyn. *Early Greece*. 2nd ed. Cambridge: Harvard Univ. Press, 1993.

Nader, Helen. *Rights of Discovery: Christopher Columbus's Final Appeal to King Fernando. Facsimile, Transcription, Translation and Critical Edition of the John Carter Brown Library's Spanish Codex I*. Providence: John Carter Brown Library, 1992.

Naji, Abdel Jabbar. "Trade Relations Between Bahrain and Iraq in the Middle Ages: A Commercial and Political Outline." In *Bahrain Through the Ages: The History*, ed. by Abdullah bin Khalid al-Khalifa and Michael Rice, 423–44. London: Kegan Paul, 1991.

Nasir-i Khusraw. *Book of Travels [Safarnama]*. Trans. Wheeler M. Thackston. Costa Mesa, CA: Mazda, 2001.

National Maritime Museum learning team. "Ships, Seafarers and Life at Sea." http://www.nmm.ac.uk/explore/sea-and-ships/facts/ships-and-seafarers/load-lines.

National Research Council. *Crew Size and Maritime Safety*. Washington: National Academy, 1990. http://www.nap.edu/openbook.php?record_id=1620&page=R1.

Navin, Thomas R., and Marian V. Sears. "A Study in Merger: Formation of the International Mercantile Marine." *Business History Review* 28:4 (1954): 291–328.

Needham, Joseph, with Wang Ling. *Science and Civilisation in China*. Vol. 3, *Mathematics and the Sciences of the Heavens and Earth*. Cambridge: Cambridge Univ. Press, 1959.

Needham, Joseph, with Wang Ling and Kenneth Robinson. *Science and Civilisation in China*. Vol. 4, *Physics and Physical Technology*. Pt. 1, *Physics*. Cambridge: Cambridge Univ. Press, 1962.

Needham, Joseph, with Wang Ling and Lu Gwei-djen. *Science and Civilisation in China*. Vol. 4, *Physics and Physical Technology*. Pt. 3, *Civil Engineering and Nautics*. Cambridge: Cambridge Univ. Press, 1971.

Needham, Joseph, Ping-Yü Ho, Gwei-djen Lu, and Ling Wang. *Science and Civilisation in China*. Vol. 5, *Chemistry and Chemical Technology*. Pt. 7, *Military Technology: The Gunpowder Epic*. Cambridge: Cambridge Univ. Press, 1986.

Nester, William R. *The Great Frontier War: Britain, France, and the Imperial Struggle for North America, 1607–1755*. Westport: Greenwood, 2000.

New York Maritime Register.

Nihongi: Chronicles of Japan from the Earliest Times to A.D. 697. Trans. W. G. Aston. 1924. Reprint, Rutland, VT: Tuttle, 1972.

Oakley, Stewart. *A Short History of Denmark*. New York: Praeger, 1972.

O'Brian, Patrick. *Joseph Banks: A Life*. Boston: Godine, 1993.

O'Connell, D. P. *Richelieu*. Cleveland: World, 1968.

O'Connor, David. "Boat Graves and Pyramid Origins: New Discoveries at Abydos." *Expedition* 33:3 (1991) 5–17.

Ó Corráin, Donnchadh. "Vikings in Ireland and Scotland in the Ninth Century." *Peritia* 12 (1998): 296–339.

Oddr Snorrason, and Theodore Murdock Andersson. *The Saga of Olaf Tryggvason*. Ithaca: Cornell Univ. Press, 2003.

O'Donnell, Ed. *Ship Ablaze: The Tragedy of the Steamboat* General Slocum. New York: Broadway, 2003.

Oleson, John Peter. "The Technology of Roman Harbors." *IJNA* 17:2 (1988): 147–57.

Olsen, Olaf, and Ole Crumlin-Pedersen. *Five Viking Ships from Roskilde Fjord*. Copenhagen: National Museum, 1978.

Olsen, Wallace M. *Through Spanish Eyes: The Spanish Voyages to Alaska, 1774–1792*. Auke Bay, AK: Heritage Research, 2002.

Oppenheim, A. Leo. "The Seafaring Merchants of Ur." In *Ancient Cities of the Indus*, ed. by Gregory L. Possehl, 155–63. Durham: Carolina Academic Press, 1979.

Ostrogorsky, George. *History of the Byzantine State*. New Brunswick: Rutgers Univ. Press, 1957.

Ouyang Xiu. *Biography of Huang Chao*. Trans. Howard S. Levy. Berkeley: Univ. of California Press, 1955.

Pack, James. *Nelson's Blood: The Story of Naval Rum*. Stroud, UK: Sutton, 1995.

Padfield, Peter. *Maritime Supremacy*. Woodstock, NY: Overlook, 2000.

———. *Tide of Empires: Decisive Naval Campaigns in the Rise of the West*. Vol. 1, *1481–1654*. London: Routledge & Kegan Paul, 1979.

Page, Thomas W. "The Transportation of Immigrants and Reception Arrangements in the Nineteenth Century." *Journal of Political Economy* 19:9 (1911): 732–49.

Paine, Lincoln P. *Down East: A Maritime History of Maine*. Gardiner, ME: Tilbury House, 2000.

———. "A *Pax* upon You: Preludes and Perils of American Imperialism." *Clio's Psyche* 10:3 (Dec. 2003): 91–97.

———. *Ships of the World: An Historical Encyclopedia*. Boston: Houghton Mifflin, 1997.

Paine, S. C. M. *The Sino-Japanese War of 1894–1895: Perceptions, Power, and Primacy*. New York: Cambridge Univ. Press, 2003.

Palmer, Alan. *The Baltic: A New History of the Region and Its People*. New York: Overlook, 2005.

Parker, Geoffrey. "Lepanto." In *The Reader's Companion to Military History*, ed. by Robert Cowley and Geoffrey Parker. Boston: Houghton Mifflin, 1996.

Parry, J. H. *The Establishment of the European Hegemony, 1415–1715: Trade and Exploration in the Age of the Renaissance*. New York: Harper & Row, 1961.

Paselk, Richard A. "Navigational Instruments: Measurement of Altitude." In *The Oxford Encyclopedia of Maritime History*, ed. by Hattendorf, 3:29–42.

Pastor, Xavier. *The Ships of Christopher Columbus:* Santa María, Niña, Pinta. Annapolis: Naval Institute, 1992.

Patai, Raphael. *The Children of Noah: Jewish Seafaring in Ancient Times*. Princeton: Princeton Univ. Press, 1998.

Pausanias. *Description of Greece*. Trans. W. H. S. Jones. 5 vols. Cambridge: Harvard Univ. Press, 1918–71.

Paviot, Jacques. "Trade Between Portugal and the Southern Netherlands in the 16th Century." In *Rivalry and Conflict: European Traders and Asian Trading Networks in the 16th and 17th Centuries*, ed. by Ernst van Veen and Leonard Blussé, 24–34. Leiden: CNWS, 2005.

Peacock, David, and Lucy Blue, eds. *Myos Hormos-Quseir al-Qadim: Roman and Islamic Ports on the Red Sea*. Vol. 1, *Survey and Excavations, 1999–2003*. Oxford: Oxbow, 2006.

Peacock, David, and Andrew Peacock. "The Enigma of 'Aydhab: A Medieval Islamic Port on the Red Sea Coast." *IJNA* 37:1 (2008): 32–48.

Pearson, Michael N. *The Indian Ocean*. London: Routledge, 2003.

———. "Introduction." In *India and the Indian Ocean, 1500–1800*, ed. by Ashin Das Gupta and M. N. Pearson, 1–24. Calcutta: Oxford Univ. Press, 1987.

Pennell, C. R., ed. *Bandits at Sea: A Pirates Reader*. New York: New York Univ. Press, 2001.

Penrose, Charles. *1838 April Fourth 1938: A Century of Atlantic Steam Navigation*. Princeton: Newcomen Society, 1938.

Pepys, Samuel. *The Diary of Samuel Pepys: A New and Complete Transcription*, ed. by Robert Latham and William Matthews. 11 vols. Berkeley: Univ. of California Press, 1970–83.

Pérez-Mallaína, Pablo E. *Spain's Men of the Sea: Daily Life on the Indies Fleets in the Sixteenth Century*. Trans. Carla Rahn Phillips. Baltimore: Johns Hopkins Univ. Press, 1998.

Perruso, Richard. "The Development of the Doctrine of *Res Communes* in Medieval and Early Modern Europe." *Tijdschrift voor Rechstgeschiedenis* 70 (2002): 69–93.

Peterson, C. A. "Court and Province in Mid- and Late T'ang." In *The Cambridge History of China*. Vol. 3, *Sui and T'ang China, 589–906*, ed. by Denis Twitchett, 464–560. Cambridge: Cambridge Univ. Press, 1979.

———. "Old Illusions and New Realities: Sung Foreign Policy, 1217–1234." In *China Among Equals: The Middle Kingdom and Its Neighbors, 10th-14th Centuries*, ed. by Morris Rossabi, 204–39. Berkeley: Univ. of California Press, 1983.

Petrie, Donald A. *The Prize Game: Lawful Looting on the High Seas in the Days of Fighting Sail*. Annapolis: Naval Institute, 1999.

Petrow, Richard. *In the Wake of Torrey Canyon*. New York: David McKay, 1968.

Pett, Phineas. *The Autobiography of Phineas Pett*, ed. by W. G. Perrin. London: Navy Records Society, 1918.

Phillips, Carla Rahn. "The Galleon." In *Cogs, Caravels and Galleons*, ed. by Gardiner and Unger, 98–114.

———. "Iberian Ships and Shipbuilding in the Age of Discovery." In *Maritime History*. Vol. 1, *The Age of Discovery*, ed. by John B. Hattendorf, 215–38. Malabar, FL: Krieger, 1996.

———. *Six Galleons for the King of Spain: Imperial Defense in the Early Seventeenth Century*. Baltimore: Johns Hopkins Univ. Press, 1986.

Phillips, E. J. *The Founding of Russia's Navy: Peter the Great and the Azov Fleet, 1688–1714*. Westport: Greenwood, 1993.

Phillips, William D., Jr., and Carla Rahn Phillips. *The Worlds of Christopher Columbus*. Cambridge: Cambridge Univ. Press, 1992.

Picard, Christophe. "*Bahriyyun*, émirs et califes: l'origine des équipages des flottes musulmanes en Méditerranée occidentale (VIIIe-Xe siècle)." *Medieval Encounters* 13 (2007): 413–51.

———. *L'Océan Atlantique Musulman de la conquête arabe à l'époque almohade: Navigation et mise en valeur des côtes d'al-Andalus et du Maghreb occidental (Portugal-Espagne-Maroc)*. Paris: Maisonneuve & Larose/Editions UNESCO, 1997.

Pierce, Richard. "After 5,000 Year Voyage, World's Oldest Built Boats Deliver: Archeologists' First Look Confirms Existence of Earliest Royal Boats at Abydos." www.abc.se/~m10354/mar/abydos.htm.

Pigafetta, Antonio, and James Alexander Robertson. *Magellan's Voyage Around the World.* Cleveland: Clark, 1906.

Pilgrim, Donald. "The Colbert-Seignelay Naval Reforms and the Beginnings of the War of the League of Augsburg." *French Historical Studies* 9:2 (1975): 235–62.

Pires, Tomé. *The Suma Oriental of Tomé Pires: An Account of the East, from the Red Sea to Japan, Written in Malacca and India in 1512–1515.* Trans. Armando Cortesão. 2 vols. London: Hakluyt, 1944.

"Pius Mau Piailug, Master Navigator, Died on July 12th, Aged 78." *The Economist* (July 24, 2010): 84.

Planhol, Xavier de. *L'Islam et la mer: La mosquée et le matelot VIIe-XXe siècle.* Paris: Perrin, 2000.

Plato. *The Collected Dialogues of Plato.* Ed. by Edith Hamilton and Huntington Cairns, 1225–513. New York: Pantheon, 1961.

Pliny the Elder. *Natural History.* Trans. H. Rackham. 10 vols. Cambridge: Harvard Univ. Press, 1938–63.

Plutarch. *Plutarch's Lives.* Trans. P. Bernadotte. 11 vols. Cambridge: Harvard Univ. Press, 1967.

Polanyi, Karl. "Ports of Trade in Early Societies." *Journal of Economic History* 23:1 (1963): 30–45.

Polo, Marco. *The Travels.* Trans. Ronald Latham. New York: Penguin, 1958.

Polybius. *The Histories.* Trans. W. R. Paton. 6 vols. Cambridge: Harvard Univ. Press, 1975.

———. *The Rise of the Roman Empire.* Trans. Ian Scott-Kilvert. New York: Penguin, 1980.

Polynesian Voyaging Society. http://pvs.kcc.hawaii.edu/index.html.

Potts, D. T. *Arabian Gulf in Antiquity.* 2 vols. New York: Oxford Univ. Press, 1991.

———. *Mesopotamian Civilization: The Material Foundations.* Ithaca: Cornell Univ. Press, 1997.

———. "The Parthian Presence in the Arabian Gulf." In *The Indian Ocean in Antiquity*, ed. by Reade, 269–85.

Powell, Barry B. *Homer.* Malden: Blackwell, 2004.

Prakash, Om. "Asian Merchants and the Portuguese Trade in Asia." In *Rivalry and Conflict: European Traders and Asian Trading Networks in the 16th and 17th Centuries*, ed. by Ernst van Veen and Leonard Blussé, 131–41. Leiden: CNWS, 2005.

———. "The Indian Maritime Merchant, 1500–1800." *JESHO* 47:3 (2004): 436–57.

———. "Trade and Politics in Eighteenth-Century Bengal." In *On the Eighteenth Century as a Category of Asian History*, ed. by Blussé and Gaastra, 237–60.

Pritchard, James B. *The Ancient Near East.* Vol. 1, *An Anthology of Text and Pictures.* Princeton: Princeton Univ. Press, 1958.

Procopius. *History of the Wars; The Secret History; Buildings.* Trans. H. B. Dewing. 7 vols. Cambridge: Harvard Univ. Press, 1924–40.

Protocol of Proceedings of Crimea Conference, Agreement Regarding Japan, February 1945. Avalon Project, Yale Law School. http://avalon.law.yale.edu/wwii/yalta.asp.

Pryor, John H. "From Dromon to Galea: Mediterranean Bireme Galleys, AD 500–1300." In *The Age of the Galley*, ed. by Gardiner and Morrison, 101–16.

———. *Geography, Technology and War: Studies in the Maritime History of the Mediterranean, 649–1571.* Cambridge: Cambridge Univ. Press, 1988.

———. "The Maritime Republics." In *The New Cambridge Medieval History: c. 1198–c. 1300*, ed. by David Abulafia and Rosamond McKitterick, 5:419–57. New York: Oxford Univ. Press, 1999.

———. "Mediterranean Commerce in the Middle Ages: A Voyage Under Contract of Commenda." *Viator* 14 (1983): 133–94.

———. "The Naval Battles of Roger of Lauria." *Journal of Medieval History* 9 (1983): 179–216.

———. "The Origins of the Commenda Contract." *Speculum* 52:1 (1977): 5–37.

———. "The Venetian Fleet for the Fourth Crusade and the Diversion of the Crusade to Constantinople." In *The Experience of Crusading*. Vol. 1, *Western Approaches*, ed. by M. Bull and N. Housley, 103–23. Cambridge: Cambridge Univ. Press, 2003.

Pryor, John H., and Elizabeth M. Jeffreys, with Ahmad Shboul. *The Age of the Dromon: The Byzantine Navy, ca 500–1204.* Leiden: Brill, 2006.

Pulleyblank, Edwin G. *The Background of the Rebellion of An Lu-shan.* London: Oxford Univ. Press, 1955.

Purchas, Samuel. *Hakluytus Posthumus; or, Purchas His Pilgrimes.* 20 vols. 1625. Reprint, Glasgow: James MacLehose & Sons, 1905–7.

Qaisar, A. Jan. "Shipbuilding in the Mughal Empire During the Seventeenth Century." *Indian Economic and Social History Review* 5 (1968): 149–70.

Quinn, David B., ed. *The Voyages and Colonising Enterprises of Sir Humphrey Gilbert.* London: Hakluyt, 1940.

Quinn, David B., and Alison M. Quinn. *The English New England Voyages, 1602–1608.* London: Hakluyt, 1983.

Radell, David R., and James J. Parsons, "Realejo: A Forgotten Colonial Port and Shipbuilding Center in Nicaragua." *Hispanic American Historical Review* 51:2 (1971): 295–312.

Radulet, Carmen. "Vasco da Gama and His Successors." In *Portugal, the Pathfinder,* ed. by Winius, 133–43.

Randall, Anthony G. "The Timekeeper That Won the Longitude Prize." In *The Quest for Longitude,* ed. by Andrewes, 236–54.

Ratcliff, Ronald E. "Building Partners' Capacity: The Thousand-Ship Navy." *Naval War College Review* 60:4 (2007): 45–58.

Ray, Himanshu Prabha. "Early Coastal Trade in the Bay of Bengal." In *The Indian Ocean in Antiquity,* ed. by Reade, 351–64.

———. *Monastery and Guild: Commerce Under the Satavahanas.* New Delhi: Oxford Univ. Press, 1986.

———. "A Resurvey of Roman Contacts with the East." In *Athens, Aden, Arikamedu: Essays on the Interrelations Between India, Arabia, and the Eastern Mediterranean,* ed. by Marie-Françoise Boussac and Jean-François Salles, 97–114. New Delhi: Manohar, 1995.

———. "The Yavana Presence in Ancient India." In *Athens, Aden, Arikamedu: Essays on the Interrelations Between India, Arabia, and the Eastern Mediterranean,* ed. by Marie-Françoise Boussac and Jean-François Salles, 76–82. New Delhi: Manohar, 1995.

Ray, Rajat Kanta. "Indian Society and British Supremacy." In *The Oxford History of the British Empire.* Vol. 2, *The Eighteenth Century,* 508–29. Oxford: Oxford Univ. Press, 1998.

Reade, Julian, ed. *The Indian Ocean in Antiquity.* London: Kegan Paul, 1996.

Redford, Donald B. *Egypt, Canaan, and Israel in Ancient Times.* Princeton: Princeton Univ. Press, 1992.

Redmount, Carol. "The Wadi Tumilat and the Canal of the Pharaohs." *Journal of Near Eastern Studies* 54 (1994): 127–35.

Reed, C. M. *Maritime Traders in the Ancient Greek World.* Cambridge: Cambridge Univ. Press, 2004.

Reed, Robert R. "The Colonial Origins of Manila and Batavia: Desultory Notes on Nascent Metropolitan Primacy and Urban Systems in Southeast Asia." *Asian Studies* (Quezon City) 5 (1967): 543–62.

Reid, Anthony. "The Rise and Fall of Sino-Javanese Shipping." In *Charting the Shape of Early Modern Southeast Asia,* 56–84. Chiang Mai, Thailand: Silkworm Books, 1999.

———. *Southeast Asia in the Age of Commerce, 1450–1680: Expansion and Crisis*. New Haven: Yale Univ. Press, 1993.

Reilly, Bernard F. *The Medieval Spains*. Cambridge: Cambridge Univ. Press, 1993.

Reinert, Stephen W. "The Muslim Presence in Constantinople, 9th–15th Centuries: Some Preliminary Observations." In *Studies on the Internal Diaspora of the Byzantine Empire*, ed. by Hélène Ahrweiler and Angeliki E. Laiou, 125–150. Washington: Dumbarton Oaks Research Library and Collection, 1998.

Reischauer, Edwin O. *Ennin's Travels in T'ang China*. New York: Ronald, 1955.

Rgveda Samhita, vol. 1. Trans. H. H. Wilson and Bhasya of Sayanacarya. New Delhi: Parimal, 1997.

Rickover, Hyman George. *How the Battleship* Maine *Was Destroyed*. Washington: Naval History Division, Dept. of the Navy, 1976.

Riess, Warren C. Angel Gabriel: *The Elusive English Galleon*. Bristol: 1797 House, 2001.

Riley-Smith, Jonathan. *The Crusades: A History*. 2nd ed. New Haven: Yale Univ. Press, 2005.

Rimbert. *Anskar, the Apostle of the North*. Trans. Charles H. Robinson. London: Society for the Propagation of the Gospel in Foreign Parts, 1921.

Risso, Patricia. *Merchants and Faith: Muslim Commerce and Culture in the Indian Ocean*. Boulder: Westview, 1995.

Ritchie, G. S. *The Admiralty Chart: British Naval Hydrography in the Nineteenth Century*. London: Hollis & Carter, 1967.

Ritchie, Robert C. *Captain Kidd and the War Against the Pirates*. Cambridge: Harvard Univ. Press, 1986.

Roberts, J. M. *History of the World*. New York: Knopf, 1976.

Rocca, Edgardo José. "Buenos Aires." In *The Oxford Encyclopedia of Maritime History*, ed. by Hattendorf, 1:323–24.

Rockhill, W. W. "Notes on the Relations and Trade of China with the Eastern Archipelago and the Coast of the Indian Ocean During the Fourteenth Century." *Toung Pao* 15 (1914): 419–47.

Rodger, N. A. M. *The Command of the Ocean: A Naval History of Britain, 1649–1815*. New York: Norton, 2005.

———. "Considerations on Writing a General Naval History." In *Doing Naval History: Essays Toward Improvement*, ed. by John B. Hattendorf, 117–28. Newport: Naval War College Press, 1995.

———. "The Development of Broadside Gunnery." *Mariner's Mirror* 82 (1996): 310–24.

———. "Guns and Sails in English Colonization." In *The Oxford History of the British Empire*. Vol. 1, *The Origins of Empire*, ed. by Nicholas Canny, 79–88. Oxford: Oxford Univ. Press, 1998.

———. "The Naval Service of the Cinque Ports." *English Historical Review* 111:442 (1996): 636–51.

———. "The New Atlantic: Naval Warfare in the Sixteenth Century." In *War at Sea in the Middle Ages and Renaissance*, ed. by John B. Hattendorf and Richard W. Unger, 233–48. Rochester, NY: Boydell, 2003.

———. *The Safeguard of the Sea: A Naval History of Britain, 660–1649*. New York: Norton, 1998.

———. *The Wooden World: An Anatomy of the Georgian Navy*. New York: Norton, 1996.

Røksund, Arne. *The Jeune Ecole: The Strategy of the Weak*. Leiden: Brill, 2007.

Roland, Alex, W. Jeffrey Bolster, and Alexander Keyssar. *The Way of the Ship: America's Maritime History Reenvisioned, 1600–2000*. New York: Wiley, 2008.

Roosevelt, Theodore. *The Works of Theodore Roosevelt.* New York: Scribner's, 1923.

Roover, Florence Edler de. "Early Examples of Marine Insurance." *Journal of Economic History* 5:2 (1945): 172–200.

Rose, Susan. *Medieval Naval Warfare, 1000–1500.* London: Routledge, 2002.

Ross, Lillian. "Where Are They Now? The Kaiser's Yacht." *The New Yorker* (June 22, 1946): 66–80.

Rossabi, Morris. *Khubilai Khan: His Life and Times.* Berkeley: Univ. of California Press, 1988.

Rougeulle, Axelle. "Medieval Trade Networks in the Western Indian Ocean (8th–14th Centuries): Some Reflections from the Distribution Patterns of Chinese Imports in the Islamic World." In *Tradition and Archaeology: Early Maritime Contacts in the Indian Ocean,* ed. by Himanshu Prabha Ray and Jean-François Salles, 159–80. New Delhi: Manohar, 1999.

Rubin, Julius, "An Innovating Public Improvement: The Erie Canal." In *Canals and American Economic Development,* ed. by Carter Goodrich, 15–66. New York: Columbia Univ. Press, 1961.

Rule, Margaret, and Jason Monaghan. *A Gallo-Roman Trading Vessel from Guernsey: The Excavation and Recovery of a Third Century Shipwreck.* Candie Gardens: Guernsey Museums & Galleries, 1993.

Runciman, Steven. "Byzantine Trade and Industry." In *The Cambridge Economic History of Europe.* Vol. 2, *Trade and Industry in the Middle Ages,* ed. by M. M. Postan, 132–67. Cambridge: Cambridge Univ. Press, 1987.

Russell, P. E. *Prince Henry "the Navigator."* New Haven: Yale Univ. Press, 2001.

Russell-Wood, A. J. R. *World on the Move: The Portuguese in Africa, Asia, and America, 1415–1808.* New York: St. Martin's, 1992.

Ryan, W. F. "Peter the Great and English Maritime Technology." In *Peter the Great and the West: New Perspectives,* ed. by Lindsey Hughes, 130–58. Basingstoke, UK: Palgrave Macmillan, 2000.

Sail Training Assoc. of Western Australia website. *Duyfken* 1606 Replica Foundation. http://www.stawa.org.au/linksmain.html.

Sakamaki, Shunzo. "The Heike: From Defeat at Dannoura to a Golden Age in Ryukyu?" *Journal of Asian Studies* 27:1 (1967): 115–22.

Salles, Jean-François. "Achaemenid and Hellenistic Trade in the Indian Ocean." In *The Indian Ocean in Antiquity,* ed. by Reade, 251–67.

Salmon, E. T. "The Coloniae Maritimae." *Athenaeum* 41 (1963): 3–38.

Salomon, Richard. "On the Origin of the Early Indian Scripts: A Review Article." *JAOS* 115:2 (1995): 271–79.

Sandars, N. K. *The Sea Peoples: Warriors of the Ancient Mediterranean, 1250–1150 B.C.* London: Thames & Hudson, 1978.

Sansom, George B. *A History of Japan.* 3 vols. Berkeley: Univ. of California Press, 1958–63.

Sawyer, Peter. "The Viking Expansion." In *The Cambridge History of Scandinavia.* Vol. 1, *Prehistory to 1520,* ed. by Knut Helle, 104–20. Cambridge: Cambridge Univ. Press, 2003.

Schafer, Edward H. *The Golden Peaches of Samarkand: A Study of T'ang Exotics.* Berkeley: Univ. of California Press, 1963.

———. *The Vermilion Bird: T'ang Images of the South.* Berkeley: Univ. of California Press, 1967.

Schilder, Günter, and Marco van Egmond. "Maritime Cartography in the Low Countries During the Renaissance." In *The History of Cartography.* Vol. 3, *Cartography in the*

Renaissance, ed. by David Woodward, 1384–432. Chicago: Univ. of Chicago Press, 2007.

Schildhauer, Johannes. *The Hansa: History and Culture*. Leipzig: Edition Leipzig, 1985.

Schom, Alan. *Trafalgar: Countdown to Battle, 1803–1805*. New York: Oxford Univ. Press, 1990.

Schonfield, Hugh J. *The Suez Canal in Peace and War, 1869–1969*. Coral Gables: Univ. of Miami Press, 1969.

Schottenhammer, Angela. "Transfer of *Xiangyao* from Iran and Arabia to China—A Reinvestigation of Entries in the *Youyang zazu* (863)." In *Aspects of the Maritime Silk Road: From the Persian Gulf to the East China Sea*, ed. by Ralph Kauz, 117–49. Wiesbaden: Harrassowitz Verlag, 2010.

Schultz, Charles R. *Forty-niners 'Round the Horn*. Columbia: Univ. of South Carolina Press, 1999.

Schurz, William Lytle. *The Manila Galleon*. 1939. Reprint, Manila: Historical Conservation Society, 1985.

Scott, Walter. *The Antiquary*. 3 vols. London: 1816.

Scrinari, V. Santa Maria, and Giuseppina Lauro. *Ancient Ostia: Past and Present*. Rome: Vision, 1981.

Seaver, Kirsten A. *The Frozen Echo: Greenland and the Exploration of North America, ca. A.D. 1000–1500*. Stanford: Stanford Univ. Press, 1996.

Sedov, A. V. "Qana' (Yemen) and the Indian Ocean: The Archaeological Evidence." In *Tradition and Archaeology: Early Maritime Contacts in the Indian Ocean*, ed. by Himanshu Prabha Ray and Jean-François Salles, 11–35. New Delhi: Manohar, 1999.

Selden, John. *Of the Dominion; or, Ownership of the Sea*. New York: Arno, 1972.

Sen, Tansen. *Buddhism, Diplomacy, and Trade: The Realignment of Sino-Indian Relations, 600–1400*. Honolulu: Assoc. for Asian Studies and Univ. of Hawai'i Press, 2003.

Seneca. *Natural Questions*. Trans. Thomas H. Corcoran. 2 vols. Cambridge: Harvard Univ. Press, 1972.

Senior, William. "The *Bucentaur*." *Mariner's Mirror* 15 (1929): 131–38.

Serjeant, R. B. "Yemeni Merchants and Trade in Yemen, 13th–16th Centuries." In *Society and Trade in South Arabia*, ed. by G. Rex Smith, 1.61–82. Brookfield, VT: Ashfield, 1996.

Severin, Timothy. *The Sinbad Voyage*. London: Hutchinson, 1982.

Shapinsky, Peter D. "Polyvocal Portolans: Nautical Charts and Hybrid Maritime Cultures in Early Modern East Asia." *Early Modern Japan* 14 (2006): 4–26.

Sharma, R. S. "Usury in Early Medieval Times." In *Trade in Early India*, ed. by Ranabir Chakravarti, 370–95. New Delhi: Oxford Univ. Press, 2001.

Sharpe, Kevin. *The Personal Rule of Charles I*. New Haven: Yale Univ. Press, 1992.

Shattan, Merchant-Prince. *Manimekhalaï (The Dancer with the Magic Bowl)*. Trans. Alain Danielou. New York: New Directions, 1989.

Sheehan, John. "The Longphort in Viking Age Ireland." *Acta Archaeologica* 79 (2008): 282–95.

Shepherd, James F., and Gary M. Walton. *Shipping, Maritime Trade and the Economic Development of Colonial North America*. Cambridge: Cambridge Univ. Press, 1972.

Sheppard, Thomas. "The *Sirius*, the First Steamer to Cross the Atlantic." *Mariner's Mirror* 23 (1937): 84–94.

Sherborne, J. W. "The Hundred Years' War—The English Navy: Shipping and Manpower 1369–89." *Past and Present* 37 (1967): 163–75.

Sherratt, S., ed. *The Wall Paintings of Thera: Proceedings of the First International Symposium*. 2 vols. Athens: Thera Foundation, 2000.

Shiba, Yoshinobu, and Mark Elvin. *Commerce and Society in Sung China.* Ann Arbor: Center for Chinese Studies, Univ. of Michigan, 1970.

Shimada, Izumi. "Evolution of Andean Diversity: Regional Formations (500 B.C.E.–C.E. 600)." In *The Cambridge History of the Native People of the Americas.* Vol. 3, *South America,* pt. 1, ed. by Frank Salomon and Stuart B. Schwartz, 350–517. Cambridge: Cambridge Univ. Press, 1999.

Sicking, Louis. "Amphibious Warfare in the Baltic: Holland, the Hansa and the Habsburgs (Fourteenth–Sixteenth Centuries)." In *Amphibious Warfare, 1000–1700: Commerce, State Formation and European Expansion,* ed. by Mark Charles Fissel and D. J. B. Trim, 69–101. Leiden: Brill, 2006.

Sidebotham, Steven E. "Ports of the Red Sea and the Arabia–India Trade." In *Rome and India: The Ancient Sea Trade,* ed. by Vimala Begley and Richard Daniel De Puma, 12–38. Madison: Univ. of Wisconsin Press, 1991.

Sima Qian. *Records of the Grand Historian of China.* Trans. Burton Watson. 2 vols. New York: Columbia Univ. Press, 1961.

Simpson, William Kelly, ed. *The Literature of Ancient Egypt: An Anthology of Stories, Instructions and Poetry.* Trans. R. O. Faulkner et al. New Haven: Yale Univ. Press, 1972.

Simsarian, James. "The Acquisition of Legal Title to Terra Nullius." *Political Science Quarterly* 53:1 (1938): 111–28.

Sjövold, Thorleif. *The Oseberg Find and the Other Viking Ship Finds.* Oslo: Universitets Oldsaksamling, 1966.

Skovgaard-Petersen, Inge. "Early Political Organisation: The Making of the Danish Kingdom." In *The Cambridge History of Scandinavia.* Vol. 1, *Prehistory to 1520,* ed. by Knut Helle, 168–83. Cambridge: Cambridge Univ. Press, 2003.

Skre, Dagfinn. "The *Sciringes healh* of Ohthere's Time." In *Ohthere's Voyages,* ed. by Bately and Englert, 150–56.

Skulski, Janusz. *The Battleship* Yamato. Annapolis: Naval Institute, 1989.

Sleeswyck, André Wegener. "The *Liao* and the Displacement of Ships in the Ming Navy." *Mariner's Mirror* 82:1 (Feb. 1996): 3–13.

Smith, Bernard. *European Vision and the South Pacific.* New Haven: Yale University Press, 1985.

Smith, Crosbie, Ian Higginson, and Phillip Wolstenholme. "'Imitations of God's Own Works': Making Trustworthy the Ocean Steamship." *History of Science* 41 (2003): 379–426.

Smith, Hance. "Fishing Vessels." In *The Shipping Revolution,* ed. by Gardiner and Couper, 167–76.

Smith, Holland M., and Percy Finch. *Coral and Brass.* New York: Charles Scribner's Sons, 1949.

Smith, John. *A Description of New England.* London, 1616.

Smith, Joshua M. *Voyages: Documents in American Maritime History.* 2 vols. Gainesville: Univ. Press of Florida, 2009.

Snorri Sturluson. *King Harald's Saga.* Trans. Magnus Magnusson and Hermann Pálsson. New York: Penguin, 1966.

Snow, Dean R. "The First Americans and the Differentiation of Hunter-Gatherer Culture." In *The Cambridge History of the Native Peoples of the New World,* ed. by B. G. Trigger and W. Washburn, chap. 4. Cambridge: Cambridge Univ. Press, 1996.

So, Billy K. L. *Prosperity, Region and Institutions in Maritime China: The South Fukien Pattern, 946–1368.* Cambridge: Harvard Univ. Asia Center, 2000.

So, Kwan Wai. *Japanese Piracy in Ming China During the Sixteenth Century.* East Lansing: Michigan State Univ. Press, 1975.

Somers, Robert M. "The End of the T'ang." In *The Cambridge History of China*. Vol. 3, *Sui and T'ang China, 589–906*, ed. by Denis Twitchett, 682–790. Cambridge: Cambridge Univ. Press, 1979.

Somerville, Boyle G., and A. F. B. Woodhouse. *Ocean Passages for the World: Winds and Currents*. London: The Admiralty, 1950.

Sondhaus, Lawrence. *Naval Warfare, 1815–1914*. London: Routledge, 2001.

Southworth, William A. "The Coastal States of Champa." In *Southeast Asia from Prehistory to History*, ed. by Ian Glover and Peter Bellwood, 209–33. London: RoutledgeCurzon, 2004.

Souyri, Pierre François. *The World Turned Upside Down: Medieval Japanese Society*. Trans. Kathe Roth. New York: Columbia Univ. Press, 2001.

Souza, Philip de. *Piracy in the Graeco-Roman World*. Cambridge: Cambridge Univ. Press, 1999.

Spate, O. H. K. *The Spanish Lake*. 2nd ed. Canberra: Australian National Univ. Press, 2007.

Spear, Thomas. "Early Swahili History Reconsidered." *International Journal of African Historical Studies* 33:2 (2000): 257–90.

Spector, Ronald H. *Eagle Against the Sun: The American War with Japan*. New York: Free Press, 1985.

———. "The Triumph of Professional Ideology: The U.S. Navy in the 1890s." In *In Peace and War: Interpretations of American Naval History, 1775–1984*, ed. by Kenneth J. Hagan, 174–85. Westport: Greenwood, 1984.

Spencer, George W. *The Politics of Expansion: The Chola Conquest of Sri Lanka and Sri Vijaya*. Madras, India: New Era, 1983.

Spennemann, Dirk R. "On the Bronze Age Ship Model from Flores, Indonesia." *IJNA* 14.3 (1985): 237–41.

Spufford, Peter. *Power and Profit: The Merchant in Medieval Europe*. London: Thames & Hudson, 2002.

Squatriti, Paolo. "Digging Ditches in Early Medieval Europe." *Past and Present* 176 (2002): 11–65.

Stanish, Charles. "The Origin of State Societies in South America." *Annual Review of Anthropology* 30 (2001): 41–64.

Starr, Chester G. *The Roman Imperial Navy: 31 B.C.–A.D. 324*. 3rd ed. 1941. Reprint, Chicago: Ares, 1993.

"Steam Excursion Boats." *New York Times*. Mar. 21, 1880.

Steensgaard, Niels. *The Asian Trade Revolution of the Seventeenth Century: The East India Companies and the Decline of the Caravan Trade*. Chicago: Univ. of Chicago Press, 1974.

Steffy, J. Richard. "The Reconstruction of the 11th Century Serçe Liman Vessel. A Preliminary Report." *IJNA* 11 (1982): 13–34.

Stern, S. M. "Ramisht of Siraf: A Merchant Millionaire of the Twelfth Century." *Journal of the Royal Asiatic Society of Great Britain and Ireland*, 2nd ser. 99:1 (1967): 10–14.

Still, William N. *Iron Afloat: The Story of the Confederate Ironclads*. Columbia: Univ. of South Carolina Press, 1988.

Stopford, Martin. *Maritime Economics*. 2nd ed. New York: Routledge, 2003.

Storli, Inger. "Ohthere and His World." In *Ohthere's Voyages*, ed. by Bately and Englert, 76–99.

Strabo. *The Geography of Strabo*. Trans. Horace Leonard Jones and J. R. Sitlington Sterrett. London: Heinemann, 1917–32.

Strachan, Michael, compiler. *The East India Company Journals of Captain William Keeling and Master Thomas Bonner, 1615–1617*, ed. by Michael Strachan and Boies Penrose. Minneapolis: Univ. of Minnesota Press, 1971.

Stradling, R. A. *The Armada of Flanders: Spanish Maritime Policy and European War, 1568–1668*. Cambridge: Cambridge Univ. Press, 1992.

Stratos, Andreas N. "The Naval Engagement at Phoenix." 1980. In *Studies in 7th-Century Byzantine Political History*, 230–47. London: Variorum, 1983.

Strauss, Barry. *Battle of Salamis: The Naval Encounter That Saved Greece—and Western Civilization*. New York: Simon & Schuster, 2004.

Struve, Lynn A. "The Southern Ming, 1644–1662." In *The Cambridge History of China*. Vol. 7, *The Ming Dynasty, 1368–1644*, pt. 1, ed. by Frederick W. Mote and Denis Twitchett, 641–725. Cambridge: Cambridge Univ. Press, 1988.

Subrahmanyam, Sanjay. *The Career and Legend of Vasco da Gama*. Cambridge: Cambridge Univ. Press, 1997.

———. "A Note on the Rise of Surat in the Sixteenth Century." *JESHO* 43:1 (2000): 23–33.

———. "Of Imarat and Tijarat: Asian Merchants and State Power in the Western Indian Ocean, 1400 to 1750." *Comparative Studies in Society and History* 37:4. (1995): 750–80.

Suetonius. *The Twelve Caesars*. Trans. Robert Graves. Harmondsworth: Penguin, 1957.

Sugden, John. *Sir Francis Drake*. New York: Simon & Schuster, 1990.

Sulayman al-Tajir. *Account of India and China*. In *Arabic Classical Accounts of India and China*. Trans. S. Maqbul Ahmad. Shimla: Indian Institute of Advanced Study, 1989.

Sung, Lien, and Franz Schurmann. *Economic Structure of the Yüan Dynasty*. Cambridge: Harvard Univ. Press, 1956.

Surdam, David G. *Northern Naval Superiority and the Economics of the American Civil War*. Columbia: Univ. of South Carolina Press, 2001.

Surrey, Nancy Maria Miller. *The Commerce of Louisiana During the French Régime, 1699–1763*. New York: Columbia Univ. Press, 1916.

Sutcliffe, Alice Crary. *Robert Fulton and the* Clermont. New York: Century, 1909.

Sutherland, Heather. "Southeast Asian History and the Mediterranean Analogy." *JSEAS* 34:1 (2003): 1–20.

Swanton, Michael James, trans. *The Anglo-Saxon Chronicles*. London: Phoenix, 2001.

Sylvester, David G. "Communal Piracy in Medieval England's Cinque Ports." In *Noble Ideals and Bloody Realities: Warfare in the Middle Ages*, ed. by Niall Christie and Maya Yazigi, 164–76. Leiden: Brill, 2006.

Symonds, Craig L. *Lincoln and His Admirals: Abraham Lincoln, the U.S. Navy and the Civil War*. New York: Oxford Univ. Press, 2008.

Tabari, al-. *The History of al-Tabari*. Vol. 36, *The Revolt of the Zanj*, A.D. 869–879/A.H. 255–265. Trans. David Waines. Albany: State Univ. of New York Press, 1992.

Tacitus. *The Agricola and the Germania*. Trans. H. Mattingly and S. A. Handford. Baltimore: Penguin, 1970.

———. *Annals of Imperial Rome*. Trans. Michael Grant. Rev. ed. New York: Penguin, 1956.

———. *The Histories*. Trans. Kenneth Wellesley. New York: Penguin, 1972.

Taha, Abd al-Wahid Dhannun. *The Muslim Conquest and Settlement of North Africa and Spain*. New York: Routledge, 1989.

The Tales of the Heike. Trans. Burton Watson, ed. by Haruo Shirane. New York: Columbia Univ. Press, 2006.

Tandy, David W. *Warriors into Traders: The Power of the Market in Early Greece*. Berkeley: Univ. of California Press, 1997.

Tarling, Nicholas, ed. *The Cambridge History of Southeast Asia*. Vol. 1, pt. 1, *From Early Times to c. 1500*. Cambridge: Cambridge Univ. Press, 1999.

Taylor, E. G. R. *The Haven-Finding Art: A History of Navigation from Odysseus to Captain Cook*. New York: Abelard-Schuman, 1957.

Taylor, Keith W. *The Birth of Vietnam*. Berkeley: Univ. of California Press, 1983.

———. "The Early Kingdoms." In *The Cambridge History of Southeast Asia*, ed. by Tarling, 1.1:137–82.

Tchernia, André. "Italian Wine in Gaul at the End of the Republic." In *Trade in the Ancient Economy*, ed. by Peter Garnsey, Keith Hopkins, and C. R. Whittaker, 87–104. Berkeley: Univ. of California Press, 1983.

Temin, Peter. "The Economy of the Early Roman Empire." *Journal of Economic Perspectives* 20:1 (2006): 133–51.

Terraine, John. *Business in Great Waters: The U-Boat Wars, 1916–1945*. London: Leo Cooper, 1989.

Thapar, Romila. *Early India: From the Origins to AD 1300*. Berkeley: Univ. of California Press, 2002.

Theophanes, the Confessor. *The Chronicle of Theophanes Confessor: Byzantine and Near Eastern History, AD 284–813*. Trans. Cyril Mango and Roger Scott. New York: Oxford Univ. Press, 1997.

Thiel, Johannes Hendrik. *A History of Roman Sea-power Before the Second Punic War*. Amsterdam: North-Holland, 1954.

Thomas, Hugh. *Slave Trade: The Story of the Atlantic Slave Trade, 1440–1870*. New York: Simon & Schuster, 1997.

Thompson, I. A. A. *War and Government in Habsburg Spain, 1560–1620*. London: Athlone, 1976.

Thompson, James Westfall. "Early Trade Relations Between the Germans and the Slavs." *Journal of Political Economy* 30:4 (1922): 543–58.

Thompson, Leonard Monteath. *A History of South Africa*. New Haven: Yale Univ. Press, 1990.

Thornton, Helen. "John Selden's Response to Hugo Grotius." *International Journal of Maritime History* 18:2 (2006): 105–28.

Throckmorton, Peter, ed. *The Sea Remembers: Shipwrecks and Archaeology*. New York: Smithmark, 1991.

Thrush, Andrew. "In Pursuit of the Frigate, 1603–40." *Historical Research* 64 (1991): 29–45.

Thucydides. *The Peloponnesian War*. Trans. Rex Warner. New York: Penguin, 1954.

Tibbetts, G. R. *Arab Navigation in the Indian Ocean Before the Coming of the Portuguese*. London: Royal Asiatic Society of Great Britain and Ireland, 1971.

———. *Study of the Arabic Texts Containing Material on South-East Asia*. Leiden: Brill, 1979.

Tomalin, Victoria, V. Selvakumar, M. V. Nair, and P. K. Gopi. "The Thaikkal-Kadakkarappally Boat: An Archaeological Example of Medieval Shipbuilding in the Western Indian Ocean." *IJNA* 33:2 (2004): 253–63.

Toynbee, Arnold J. *Constantine Porphyrogenitus and His World*. London: Oxford Univ. Press, 1973.

———. "My View of History." In *Civilization on Trial*. New York: Oxford Univ. Press, 1948.

Treaty for the Limitation and Reduction of Naval Armament, 1930. U.S. Treaty Series, No. 830, pt. 4, art. 22.

Tripati, Sila. *Maritime Archaeology: Historical Descriptions of the Seafarings of the Kalingas*. New Delhi: Kaveri, 2000.

———. "Ships on Hero Stones from the West Coast of India." *IJNA* 35:1 (2006): 88–96.

Ts'ao Yung-Ho. "Taiwan as an Entrepot in East Asia in the Seventeenth Century." *Itinerario* 21:3 (1997): 94–114.

Tsetskhladze, Gocha R. "Did the Greeks Go to Cholcis for Metals?" *Oxford Journal of Archaeology* 14 (1995): 307–31.

———. "Greek Penetration of the Black Sea." In *The Archaeology of Greek Colonisation: Essays Dedicated to John Boardman*, ed. by Gocha R. Tsteskhladze and F. de Angelis, 111–35. Oxford: Oxford Univ. Community for Archaeology, 1994.

———. "Trade on the Black Sea in the Archaic and Classical Periods." In *Trade, Traders and the Ancient City*, ed. by H. Parkins and C. Smith, 52–74. New York: Routledge, 1998.

Tsunoda, Ryusaku. *Sources of Japanese Tradition*. New York: Columbia Univ. Press, 1964.

Tsuruta, Kei. "The Establishment and Characteristics of the 'Tsushima Gate.'" *Acta Asiatica* 67 (1994): 30–48.

Turner, A. J. "In the Wake of the Act, but Mainly Before." In Andrews, ed., *The Quest for Longitude*, 115–31.

Twiss, Sir Travers, ed. *Monumenta Juridica: The Black Book of the Admiralty*. London, 1871–76.

Twitchett, Denis. *Financial Administration Under the T'ang*. 2nd ed. Cambridge: Cambridge Univ. Press, 1970.

———. "Hsüan-tsung (reign 712–56)." In *The Cambridge History of China*. Vol. 3, *Sui and T'ang China, 589–906*, Part I, ed. by Denis Twitchett, 333–463. Cambridge: Cambridge Univ. Press, 1979.

Twitchett, Denis, and Howard J. Wechsler. "Kao-tsung (reign 649–83) and the Empress Wu: The Inheritor and the Usurper." In *The Cambridge History of China*. Vol. 3, *Sui and T'ang China, 589–906*, Part I, ed. by Denis Twitchett, 242–89. Cambridge: Cambridge Univ. Press, 1979.

Tyacke, Sarah. "Chartmaking in England and Its Context, 1500–1660." In *The History of Cartography*. Vol. 3, *Cartography in the Renaissance*, ed. by David Woodward, 1722–53. Chicago: University of Chicago Press, 2007.

Unger, Richard W. "Dutch Herring, Technology, and International Trade in the Seventeenth Century." In *Ships and Shipping in the North Sea and Atlantic, 1400–1800*, 18:253–79. Aldershot, UK: Ashgate, 1997.

———. "The *Fluit*: Specialist Cargo Vessels, 1500–1650." In *Cogs, Caravels and Galleons*, ed. by Gardiner and Unger, 115–30.

———. "The Netherlands Herring Fishery in the Late Middle Ages: The False Legend of Willem Beukels of Biervliet." In *Ships and Shipping in the North Sea and Atlantic, 1400–1800*, 17:335–56. Aldershot, UK: Ashgate: Variorum, 1997.

———. *The Ship in the Medieval Economy, 600–1600*. London: Croom Helm, 1980.

United Nations. "Agreement for the Implementation of the Provisions of the United Nations Convention on the Law of the Sea of 10 December 1982 Relating to the Conservation and Management of Straddling Fish Stocks and Highly Migratory Fish Stocks." http://www.un.org/depts/los/fish_stocks_conference/fish_stocks_conference .htm.

United Nations. Law of the Sea, Part V, "Exclusive Economic Zone." http://www.un.org /Depts/los/convention_agreements/texts/unclos/part5.htm.

United Nations Conference on Trade and Development. *Review of Maritime Transport, 2009*. New York: United Nations, 2009. http://www.unctad.org/en/docs/rmt2009 _en.pdf.

U.S. Navy, U.S. Coast Guard, and U.S. Marine Corps. "A Cooperative Strategy for 21st Century Seapower." http://www.navy.mil/maritime/Maritimestrategy.pdf.

U.S. Senate. *Report of the Select Committee of the Senate of the United States on the Sickness and Mortality on Board Emigrant Ships: August 2, 1854*. Washington: 1854.

U.S. War Dept. *United States Strategic Bombing Survey Summary Report (Pacific War)*. Washington: 1946.

———. *The War of the Rebellion: A Compilation of the Official Records of the Union and Confederate Armies*. Washington: 1880.

Uruthirankannanar. *Pattinappalai*. In *Pattupattu: Ten Tamil Idylls*. Trans. J. V. Chelliah. Thanjavur: Tamil Univ. Press, 1985.

Van de Mieroop, Marc. *The Ancient Mesopotamian City*. Oxford: Clarendon Press, 1999.

Van Doorninck, Frederick H., Jr. "The 4th-Century Wreck at Yassi Ada: An Interim Report on the Hull." *IJNA* 5 (1976): 115–31.

Van Slyke, Lyman P. *Yangtze: Nature, History and the River*. Stanford: Stanford Alumni Assoc., 1988.

Verlinden, Charles. "The Big Leap Under Dom João II: From the Atlantic to the Indian Ocean." In *Maritime History*. Vol. 1, *The Age of Discovery*, ed. by John B. Hattendorf. Malabar, FL: Krieger, 1996.

———. "European Participation in the Portuguese Era of Discovery." In *Portugal, the Pathfinder*, ed. by Winius, 71–88.

Verschuer, Charlotte von. *Across the Perilous Sea: Japanese Trade with China and Korea from the Seventh to the Sixteenth Centuries*. Trans. Kristen Lee Hunter. Ithaca: Cornell East Asia Series, 2006.

Villehardouin. *Conquest of Constantinople*. In Joinville and Villehardouin. *Chronicles of the Crusades*. Trans. Margaret R. B. Shaw. Harmondsworth: Penguin, 1963.

Villiers, Alan. *The Monsoon Seas: The Story of the Indian Ocean*. New York: McGraw-Hill, 1952.

Viraphol, Sarasin. *Tribute and Profit: Sino-Siamese Trade, 1652–1853*. Cambridge: Council on East Asian Studies, Harvard Univ., 1977.

Vitruvius. *De Architectura*. Trans. Frank Granger. 2 vols. Cambridge: Harvard Univ. Press, 1962.

Vosmer, Tom. "Building the Reed-Boat Prototype: Problems, Solutions, and Implications for the Organization and Structure of Third-Millennium Shipbuilding." *Proceedings of the Seminar for Arabian Studies* 31 (2001): 235–39.

———. "The Magan Boat Project: A Process of Discovery, a Discovery of Process." *Proceedings of the Seminar for Arabian Studies* 33 (2003): 49–58.

———. "Ships in the Ancient Arabian Sea: The Development of a Hypothetical Reed Boat Model." *Proceedings of the Seminar for Arabian Studies* 30 (2000): 235–42.

Wachsmann, Shelley. *Seagoing Ships and Seamanship in the Bronze Age Levant*. College Station: Texas A&M Univ. Press, 1998.

Wade, Geoff. "An Early Age of Commerce in Southeast Asia, 900–1300." *JSEAS* 40:2 (2009): 221–65.

Wake, C. H. H. "The Changing Pattern of Europe's Pepper and Spice Imports, ca. 1400–1700." *Journal of European Economic History* 8 (1979): 361–404.

Walker, Ranginui. *Ka Whawhai Tonu Matou: Struggle Without End*. Auckland: Penguin, 2004.

Wallace, Birgitta Linderoth. "L'Anse aux Meadows and Vinland." In *Contact, Continuity and Collapse: The Norse Colonization of the North Atlantic*, ed. by James H. Barrett, 207–33. Turnhout, Belgium: Brepols, 2003.

Wallinga, H. T. *The Boarding-Bridge of the Romans: Its Construction and Its Function in the Naval Tactics of the First Punic War*. Groningen, Netherlands: Wolters, 1956.

———. "The Trireme and History." *Mnemosyne* 43 (1990): 132–49.

Walton, Gary M. "Sources of Productivity Change in American Colonial Shipping, 1675–1775." *Economic History Review*, New Series, 20:1 (1967): 67–78.

Wang Gungwu. "Merchants Without Empire: The Hokkien Sojourning Communities." In *The Rise of Merchant Empires: Long-Distance Trade in the Early Modern World, 1350–1750*, ed. James D. Tracy, 400–21. Cambridge: Cambridge Univ. Press, 1990.

———. *The Nanhai Trade: The Early History of Chinese Trade in the South China Sea*. 2nd ed. Singapore: Times Academic Press, 1998.

———. "'Public' and 'Private' Overseas Trade in Chinese History." 1970. Reprinted in *China and the Chinese Overseas*, 129–43. Singapore: Eastern Universities Press, 2003.

Wansbrough, John. "The Safe-Conduct in Muslim Chancery Practice." *Bulletin of the School of Oriental and African Studies* 34:1 (1971): 20–35.

Ward, Cheryl A. *Sacred and Secular: Ancient Egyptian Ships and Boats*. Boston: Archaeological Institute of America, 2000.

———. "World's Oldest Planked Boats: Abydos Hull Construction." In *Boats, Ships and Shipyards: Proceedings of the Ninth International Symposium on Boat and Ship Archaeology, Venice 2000*, ed. by C. Beltrame, 19–23. Oxford: Oxbow, 2003.

Warner, Denis Ashton, and Peggy Warner. *The Tide at Sunrise: A History of the Russo-Japanese War, 1904–1905*. New York: Charterhouse, 1974.

Warner, Richard. "British Merchants and Russian Men-of-War: The Rise of the Russian Baltic Fleet." In *Peter the Great and the West: New Perspectives*, ed. by Lindsey Hughes, 105–17. Basingstoke, UK: Palgrave Macmillan, 2001.

Warner of Rouen. *Moriuht*. Ed. by Christopher J. McDonough. Toronto: Pontifical Institute of Medieval Studies, 1995.

Watson, P. B. "Bulk Cargo Carriers." In *The Golden Age of Shipping*, ed. by Gardiner and Greenway, 61–80.

Wechsler, Howard J. "T'ai-tsung (Reign 626–49) the Consolidator." In *The Cambridge History of China*. Vol. 3, *Sui and T'ang China, 589–906*, pt. 1, ed. by Denis Twitchett, 188–241. Cambridge: Cambridge Univ. Press, 1979.

Wee, Herman van der. "Structural Changes in European Long-Distance Trade, and Particularly the Re-Export Trade from South to North, 1350–1750." In *The Rise of Merchant Empires*, ed. by James Tracy, 14–33. Cambridge: Cambridge Univ. Press, 1990.

Weerakkody, D. P. M. "Sri Lanka Through Greek and Roman Eyes." In *Sri Lanka and the Silk Road of the Sea*, 163–72. Colombo: Sri Lanka National Commission for UNESCO, 1990.

———. *Taprobanê: Ancient Sri Lanka as Known to Greeks and Romans*. Turnhout, Belgium: Brepols, 1997.

Wehausen, J. V., A. Mansour, and F. Stross. "The Colossi of Memnon and Egyptian Barges." *IJNA* 17 (1988): 295–310.

Wei Zhuang [Chuang]. "The Lament of the Lady of Ch'in." In *Sunflower Splendor: Three Thousand Years of Chinese Poetry*, ed. by Wu-chi Liu and Irving Yucheng Lo, 267–81. Garden City: Anchor, 1975.

Weir, Gary E. "Fish, Family, and Profit: Piracy and the Horn of Africa." *Naval War College Review* 62:3 (2009): 15–30.

Welch, Kathryn. "Sextus Pompeius and the *Res Publica*." In *Sextus Pompeius*, ed. by Anton Powell and Kathryn Welch, 31–64. Swansea: Classical Press of Wales, 2002.

Wendrich, W. Z., R. S. Tomber, S. E. Sidebotham, et al. "Berenike Crossroads: The Integration of Information." *JESHO* 46:1 (2003): 46–88.

Werner, Walter. "The Largest Ship Trackway in Ancient Times: The Diolkos of the Isthmus of Corinth, Greece, and Early Attempts to Build a Canal." *IJNA* 26:2 (1997): 98–119.

West, M. L. *The East Face of Helicon: West Asiatic Elements in Greek Poetry and Myth*. Oxford: Clarendon Press, 1997.

Wey Gómez, Nicolás. *The Tropics of Empire: Why Columbus Sailed South to the Indies*. Cambridge: MIT Press, 2008.

Wheatley, Paul. *The Golden Khersonese: Studies in the Historical Geography of the Malay Peninsula Before* A.D. *1500*. Kuala Lumpur: Univ. of Malaya Press, 1961.

Wheeler, Mortimer. *Rome Beyond the Imperial Frontiers*. Harmondsworth: Penguin, 1954.

Wheeler, Ryan J., et al. "Archaic Period Canoes from Newnans Lake, Florida." *American Antiquity* 68:3 (2003): 533–51.

Whitehead, Ian. "The Periplous." *Greece and Rome* 34:2 (1987): 78–85.

Whitehouse, David. "Sasanian Maritime Activity." In *The Indian Ocean in Antiquity*, ed. by Reade, 339–49.

Whitman, Walt. *Leaves of Grass*. Philadelphia: David McKay, 1891.

Whitmore, John K. "The Rise of the Coast: Trade, State and Culture in Early Dai Viet." *JSEAS* 37:1 (2006): 103–22.

Wickham, Chris. *The Inheritance of Rome: A History of Europe from 400 to 1000*. New York: Viking, 2009.

Wicks, Robert S. *Money, Markets, and Trade in Early Southeast Asia: The Development of Indigenous Monetary Systems to* AD *1400*. Ithaca: Southeast Asia Program, 1992.

Wiener, M. H. "Isles of Crete? The Minoan Thalassocracy Revisited." In *Thera and the Aegean World*. Vol. 1, *Archaeology*, ed. by D. A. Hardy, 128–61. London: Thera Foundation, 1990.

Wilkinson, J. C. "Oman and East Africa: New Light on Early Kilwan History from the Omani Sources." *International Journal of African Historical Studies* 14:2 (1981): 272–305.

———. "A Sketch of the Historical Geography of Trucial Oman Down to the Beginning of the Sixteenth Century." *Geographical Journal* 130 (1964): 337–49.

———. "Suhar (Sohar) in the Early Islamic Period: The Written Evidence." In *South Asian Archaeology 1977*, ed. by Maurizio Taddei, 888–907 (1–21). Naples: Istituto Universitario Orientale, 1979.

Wilkinson, Toby A. H. *Early Dynastic Egypt*. London: Routledge, 1999.

Willan, Thomas Stuart. *The Early History of the Russia Company, 1553–1603*. Manchester, UK: Manchester Univ. Press, 1956.

William of Tyre. *A History of Deeds Done Beyond the Sea*. Trans. Emily Atwater Babcock and A. C. Krey. 2 vols. 1941. Reprint, New York: Farrar, Straus & Giroux, 1976.

Williams, David M. "The Extent of Transport Services' Integration: SS *Ceylon* and the First 'Round the World' Cruise, 1881–1882." *International Journal of Maritime History* 14:2 (2003): 135–46.

Williams, Frances Leigh. *Matthew Fontaine Maury: Scientist of the Sea*. New Brunswick: Rutgers Univ. Press, 1963.

Williams, Glyn. *The Prize of All the Oceans: The Dramatic Story of Commodore Anson's Voyage Round the World and How He Seized the Spanish Treasure Galleon*. New York: Viking, 1999.

Williams, John Bryan. "The Making of a Crusade: The Genoese Anti-Muslim Attacks in Spain, 1146–48." *Journal of Medieval History* 23:1 (1997): 29–53.

Wills, John E., Jr. "Maritime China." In *From Ming to Ching: Conquest, Region, and Continuity in Seventeenth-Century China*, ed. by Jonathan D. Spence and John E. Wills, Jr., 201–38. New Haven: Yale Univ. Press, 1979.

———. "Relations with Maritime Europeans, 1514–1662." In *The Cambridge History of China*. Vol. 8, *The Ming Dynasty, 1368–1644*, pt. 2., ed. by John King Fairbank, Denis C. Twitchett, and Frederick W. Mote, 333–75. Cambridge: Cambridge Univ. Press, 1998.

Wilson, Woodrow. "President Woodrow Wilson's Fourteen Points, 8 January, 1918." Avalon Project, Yale Law School. http://avalon.law.yale.edu/20th_century/wilson14.asp.

Winius, George D. "The Enterprise Focused on India: The Work of D. João II." In *Portugal, the Pathfinder*, ed. by Winius, 89–120.

———. "The *Estado da India* on the Subcontinent: Portuguese as Players on a South Asian Stage." In *Portugal, the Pathfinder*, ed. by Winius, 191–212.

———. "Portugal's Shadow Empire in the Bay of Bengal." In *Portugal, the Pathfinder*, ed. by Winius, 247–68.

———, ed. *Portugal, the Pathfinder: Journeys from the Medieval Toward the Modern World, 1300–ca. 1600*. Madison: Hispanic Seminary of Medieval Studies, 1995.

Wink, André. *Al-Hind: The Making of the Indo-Islamic World*. 3 vols. Leiden: Brill, 1996–2002.

Winstedt, Richard, and P. E. De Josselin de Jong. "The Maritime Laws of Malacca." *Journal of the Malayan Branch of the Royal Asiatic Society* 29:3 (1956): 22–59.

Winthrop, John. *The Journal of John Winthrop, 1630–1649*, ed. by Richard S. Dunn, James Savage, and Laetitia Yeandle. Cambridge: Harvard Univ. Press, 1996.

Wise, Stephen R. *Lifeline of the Confederacy: Blockade Running During the Civil War*. Columbia: Univ. of South Carolina Press, 1988.

Wokeck, Marianne Sophia. *Trade in Strangers: The Beginnings of Mass Migration to North America*. University Park: Pennsylvania State Univ. Press, 1999.

Wolters, O. W. *Early Indonesian Commerce: A Study of the Origins of Srivijaya*. Ithaca: Cornell Univ. Press, 1967.

Wood, Alfred Cecil. *A History of the Levant Company*. New York: Barnes & Noble, 1964.

Woodward, David. "Medieval Mappaemundi." In *The History of Cartography*. Vol. 1, *Cartography in Prehistoric, Ancient, and Medieval Europe and the Mediterranean*, ed. by J. B. Harley and David Woodward, 286–370. Chicago: Univ. of Chicago Press, 1987.

Woodward, David, ed. *The History of Cartography*. Vol. 3, *Cartography in the Renaissance*. Chicago: University of Chicago Press, 2007.

Woodward, David. *The Russians at Sea: A History of the Russian Navy*. New York: Praeger, 1966.

Worcester, G. R. G. *The Junkman Smiles*. London: Chatto & Windus, 1959.

———. *The Junks and Sampans of the Yangtze*. Annapolis: Naval Institute, 1971.

Worrall, Simon. "China Made: A 1,200-Year-Old Shipwreck Opens a Window on the Ancient Global Trade." *National Geographic* 215:6 (2009): 112–22.

Wright, Arthur F. *The Sui Dynasty*. New York: Knopf, 1978.

Xenophon. *A History of My Times*. Trans. Rex Warner. New York: Penguin, 1979.

Xuanzang. *Si-yu-ki: Buddhist Records of the Western World*. Trans. Samuel Beal. 1884. Reprint, New Delhi: Oriental Books, 1969.

Yenne, Bill. *Guinness: The 250-Year Quest for the Perfect Pint*. New York: Wiley, 2007.

Yijing [I-Tsing]. *A Record of the Buddhist Religion as Practised in India and the Malay Archipelago (A.D. 671–695)*. Trans. Junjiro Takakusu. 1896. Reprint, New Delhi: Munshiram Manoharlal, 1966.

Yi Sun-sin. *Imjin Changch'o: Admiral Yi Sun-Sin's Memorials to Court*. Trans. Tae-hung Ha and Sohn Pow-key. Seoul: Yonsei Univ. Press, 1981.

Yoshida, Mitsuru. *Requiem for Battleship* Yamato. Trans. Richard H. Minear. Seattle: Univ. of Washington Press, 1985.

Young, Gary K. *Rome's Eastern Trade: International Commerce and Imperial Policy, 31 BC–AD 305*. New York: Routledge, 2001.

Yu Huan. *The Peoples of the West: From the* Weilue, *a Third Century Chinese Account Composed between 239 and 265 CE*. Draft English translation by John E. Hill, Sept. 2004. http://depts.washington.edu/uwch/silkroad/texts/weilue/weilue.html.

Yun, Lisa, and Ricardo René Laremont. "Chinese Coolies and African Slaves in Cuba, 1847–74." *Journal of Asian-American Studies* 4:2 (2001): 99–122.

Zeidler, James A. "Maritime Exchange in the Early Formative Period of Coastal Ecuador: Geopolitical Origins, Uneven Development." *Research in Economic Anthropology* 13 (1991): 247–68.

Zhao Rugua. See Chau Ju-kua.

Zheng, Yangwen. *China on the Sea: How the Maritime World Shaped Modern China*. Leiden: Brill, 2012.

Zhuang Guotu. "The Impact of the International Tea Trade on the Social Economy of Northwest Fujian in the Eighteenth Century." In *On the Eighteenth Century as a Category of Asian History*, ed. by Blussé and Gaastra, 193–216.

Zosimus. *New History*. Trans. Ronald T. Ridley. Canberra: Australian Assoc. for Byzantine Studies, 1982.

Zurara, Gomes Eanes de. *The Chronicle of the Discovery and Conquest of Guinea*. Trans. C. Raymond Beazley and Edgar Prestage. 2 vols. London: Hakluyt, 1896–99.

Index

Page numbers in *italics* refer to illustration captions.

A NOTE ABOUT THE AUTHOR

Lincoln Paine is the author of four books and more than fifty articles, reviews, and lectures on various aspects of maritime history. He lives in Portland, Maine, with his wife, Allison.

A NOTE ON THE TYPE

This book was set in Janson, an excellent example of the influential and sturdy Dutch types that prevailed in England up to the time William Caslon (1692–1766) developed his own incomparable designs from them.

Composed by North Market Street Graphics,
Lancaster, Pennsylvania
Printed and bound by Berryville Graphics, Berryville, Virginia
Cartography by Rosemary Mosher
Designed by Peter A. Andersen